Oxford Socio-Legal Studies

English Lawyers between Market and State

OXFORD SOCIO-LEGAL STUDIES

General Editor: Keith Hawkins, Reader in Law and Society, and Fellow and Tutor in Law of Oriel College, Oxford.

Editorial Board: John Baldwin, Director of the Institute of Judicial Administration, University of Birmingham; William L. F. Felstiner, Professor, Law and Society Program, University of California, Santa Barbara; Denis Galligan, Professor of Socio-Legal Studies and Director of the Centre for Socio-Legal Studies, Oxford; Sally Lloyd-Bostock, Professor of Law and Psychology, University of Birmingham; Doreen McBarnet, Senior Research Fellow, Centre for Socio-Legal Studies, Oxford; Simon Roberts, Professor of Law, London School of Economics and Political Science.

International Advisory Board: John Braithwaite (Australian National University); Robert Cooter (University of California-Berkeley); Bryant Garth (American Bar Foundation); Volkmar Gessner (University of Bremen); Vittorio Olgiati (University of Milan); Martin Partington (University of Bristol).

Oxford Socio-Legal Studies is a series of books exploring the role of law in society for both an academic and a wider readership. The series publishes theoretical and empirically informed work, from the United Kingdom and elsewhere, by social scientists and lawyers which advances understanding of the social reality of law and legal processes.

ENGLISH LAWYERS BETWEEN MARKET AND STATE

The Politics of Professionalism

RICHARD L. ABEL

OXFORD
UNIVERSITY PRESS

OXFORD
UNIVERSITY PRESS

Great Clarendon Street, Oxford OX2 6DP

Oxford University Press is a department of the University of Oxford.
It furthers the University's objective of excellence in research, scholarship,
and education by publishing worldwide in

Oxford New York

Auckland Bangkok Buenos Aires Cape Town Chennai
Dar es Salaam Delhi Hong Kong Istanbul Karachi Kolkata
Kuala Lumpur Madrid Melbourne Mexico City Mumbai Nairobi
São Paulo Shanghai Taipei Tokyo Toronto

Oxford is a registered trade mark of Oxford University Press
in the UK and in certain other countries

Published in the United States
by Oxford University Press Inc., New York

British Library Cataloguing in Publication Data
Data available

Library of Congress Cataloging in Publication Data
Data available

ISBN 0-19-826033-4

1 3 5 7 9 10 8 6 4 2

Typeset by Newgen Imaging Systems (P) Ltd., Chennai, India
Printed in Great Britain
on acid-free paper by
T. J. International Ltd. Padstow, Cornwall

To the public interest students at UCLA School of Law
and Daniel Abel Fernandez—
my hopes for the future

Foreword

When Professor Abel invited me to write a foreword to this book, I pointed to the obvious fact that I am not completely objective in my views on the matters with which it deals. But as one who had taken a very active part in the subject matter, I said I would accept the honour that he had offered and attempt to write a foreword.

I have concluded that my views on the matters dealt with as they unfolded are sufficiently disclosed in the text that my foreword should explain the background from my point of view to the events described rather than offer any comment on the text. Professor Abel has given the various participants fairly full citation in their own words of their views and it would be invidious for me to comment now on any of these. However, I hope that the background which I shall now describe may help to whet the reader's appetite for what is to follow and give some understanding of the motivation for my part in these events.

Up until 1979 I was in private practice as an Advocate at the Scottish Bar. In 1979 I joined the Government as Lord Advocate for Scotland on Mrs Thatcher's invitation. In 1984 I became a judge of the Supreme Courts of Scotland and 1985 a Lord of Appeal in Ordinary, that is to say, a Judge in the House of Lords and the Privy Council.

During my time in Scotland I had on a number of occasions been called on to work with members of the legal profession, barristers and solicitors. I had taken part as a leader in a number of English appeals to the House of Lords. Because the Scots Bar is much smaller than the Bar of England and Wales there is much less specialization in Scotland, and over my time in practice I had been instructed in at least one important case in each of the principal specialities in England. This was forcibly brought home to me when I appeared in an English action for damages for personal injuries which raised the issue of *forum non conveniens*. The leader for the respondents in the appeal was Mr John Wilmer QC, a distinguished Shipping and Commercial Lawyer. Whenever he rose to open his reply, Lord Diplock, who was presiding asked 'when did you last appear in a personal injuries action, Mr Wilmer?' to which the reply was: 'some considerable time ago'.

During my time as the Lord of Appeal in Ordinary I had the privilege of hearing a number of appeals from England and Wales as well as from Scotland and other jurisdictions. These contacts gave me some understanding of the way in which law was practised in England.

I had, as Dean of Faculty of Advocates (the elected leader of the Scottish Bar), given a considerable amount of evidence about professional practice in Scotland to the Royal Commission on Legal Services in Scotland presided over by Lord Hughes, so my views on quite a range of issues relating to legal practice had been canvassed publicly and recorded.

For a considerable time before I became Lord Chancellor in October 1987 there had been a struggle between the Law Society and the Bar Council over rights of audience in the courts and over the appointment of solicitors as judges in the High Court. Some had proposed fusion, and solicitors' conveyancing monopoly had also been questioned. Indeed, before I became Lord Chancellor, Parliament established the profession of licenced conveyancers, creating an inroad into the conveyancing work of solicitors.

After I became Lord Chancellor I was asked by Nigel Lawson (then Chancellor of the Exchequer), to prepare a paper on these and related matters for the Cabinet Committee sub-committee over which Nigel Lawson presided.

At that time a committee chaired by Lady Marre, set up jointly by the Bar Council and the Law Society but also containing independent members, was considering the question of rights of audience in the higher courts. In the paper for which I had been asked I gave my views on these matters and other aspects of legal services in the light of my previous experience and the way in which the issues had been canvassed before the Scottish Royal Commission to which I have already referred and the Royal Commission for England and Wales, which had been chaired by Lord Benson. I was clear that if the professions in England were prepared to move forward in agreement the Government should not intervene but leave matters to develop.

After I became Lord Chancellor a committee which had been set up by my predecessor, Lord Hailsham of St Marylebone, to review civil justice in England reported with a considerable number of recommendations for reform, which appeared generally acceptable and would require legislation to be brought into effect.

I was particularly anxious that any further reforms to courts and legal services should come into operation gradually but that the framework under which change might take place should be considered so that everyone concerned should appreciate what was envisaged and that only reforms justified on a sound basis of principle should be proposed by the Government if it should prove necessary for the Government to intervene and introduce legislation in relation to legal services.

Sadly, when the Marre Committee did report its recommendations were not accepted by the Bar Council, so that the wise foresight of the then Chairman of the Bar, now Lord Alexander of Weedon, in agreeing to set up the Marre Committee failed to produce an agreed way forward. Only when this happened did the Government issue the Green Papers.

This introduced the main matters with which this book is concerned, but I would think it appropriate to emphasize that reform of the Civil

Justice System was already in contemplation for some time before I became Lord Chancellor. What emerged after the Green Papers is recorded in a very fair and interesting way by Professor Abel. Anyone interested in the pitfalls of reform of the Courts and Legal Services in the United Kingdom will find here a mine of information in which those taking part are allowed to speak for themselves and such judgements as Professor Abel makes are clearly distinguished and can be considered on their merits by the reader on the basis of the full information which he has provided.

For me, it was fascinating to read this account of the events of that period. I am comforted by the fact that as I conclude this foreword the Bar of England and Wales as well as the solicitors' profession seem to be flourishing and in good heart.

Lord Mackay of Clashfern

General Editor's Introduction

The last two decades have seen turbulent times for the legal profession in this country, a profession caught up in the wider social and political changes that have taken place. Barristers and solicitors have found themselves at the centre of a series of struggles for the control of legal services and their provision. Competing forces created a series of tensions. Most notably, there had been an increased demand from the public for a variety of legal services, while at the same time the cost of providing those services had grown. The heavier burden on the Treasury, which prompted a determination in successive governments to cut lawyers' costs and costs to the taxpayer, also co-existed with a desire to extend the reach of legal services to a wider section of the community.

Professor Abel analyses these changes in this book, which explores in remarkable detail how a profession adapts to dramatic shifts in its environment. Richard Abel, a distinguished American socio-legal scholar, is ideally suited to this task. He possesses a formidable knowledge of legal professions, both in Britain and abroad, and his understanding of the events, institutions, and personalities that were central to the developments in this country is remarkable. Professor Abel presents us with an account of the legal profession and its response to powerful external forces for change, an account that is both provocative and stimulating. But the book is more than that, for it also tells a story of social and political life in Britain since Thatcher.

Keith Hawkins

Preface

This book tells the story of the English legal profession in the 1990s, the most tumultuous decade in centuries. Why should anyone care? Lawyers' concerns were obvious: the scrutiny launched by the Green Papers threatened their income, status, and autonomy, questioned the value of their work, and unsettled the very meaning of their professional identity. It was exciting, if often unpleasant, to be at the vortex of controversy, in the headlines, on the evening news. The Government's motives were less clear—perhaps a mix of ideological consistency (seeing the Bar Council and Law Society as just very powerful trade unions), cost control (of the legal aid budget), and populism (some voters disliked lawyers even more than Thatcher). Clients wanted cheaper services, better quality, greater attentiveness, and responsiveness to complaints. Some of the public undoubtedly exulted to see lawyers brought low, resenting their wealth, status, and power, convinced they obstructed rather than promoted justice. The media played to this gallery in the belief that lawyer-bashing made good copy. (Journalists and lawyers are often rivals for the mantle of protector of the public interest.) Competitors coveted the lawyers' market, seeking entry and an even playing field. But did this drama have any greater significance? Absolutely. Lawyers are a pivotal institution of civil society: mediating between citizens and state, workers and capital; allowing government to function (since it can act only through law); redressing civil wrongs; creating, dissolving, and managing families and their property; making the economy work (constituting its actors, defining their rights and obligations, facilitating transactions among them); and articulating essential concepts of justice and power. These roles are powerfully shaped by how many lawyers there are, who they are, how they practise, how they are paid, and how they regulate and govern themselves.

If that motivates the book, why did *I* write it? I did not always want to be a lawyer. The mysteries of cosmology, the fun of tackling problems with correct solutions, and the challenge of sputnik led me to read physics at university. But I quickly realized I was unlikely to do original science. And America in the late 1950s was gradually awakening from its stupor of post-war triumphalism, blinkered anti-communism, suffocating social conformity, and complacent prosperity. It rediscovered poverty. The civil rights movement exposed domestic racism; liberation movements created newly independent African nations. Above-ground nuclear testing polluted the atmosphere; reliance on nuclear deterrence required acceptance of Herman Kahn's unthinkable MAD (mutual assured destruction). Anyone who read Nevil Shute's *On the Beach* at that time will remember the apocalyptic dread.

Law's attraction for me has always been its promise of justice, which I followed to diverse destinations: civil rights in Washington, D.C., and Jackson, Mississippi; newly independent Kenya's attempt to remake its legal system; legal aid practice in New Haven, Conn.; helping to found critical legal studies; writing critiques of informal justice, torts, and legal aid and books on the struggle against apartheid and the role of speech in constructing respect; nurturing and training public interest lawyers. When I began teaching about the American legal profession in 1974 I kept rediscovering the chasm between its exalted ideals and selfish practices. Soon thereafter I read Magali Sarfatti Larson's *The Rise of Professionalism: A Sociological Analysis*, one of those rare books that made me see the world differently. My review in the (then) *British Journal of Law and Society* prompted Phil Thomas's invitation to a Cardiff conference on the Royal Commission on Legal Services' *Report*. I devoured its 1,600 pages and was hooked. For an American lawyer, the peculiarities of the English were irresistible (I know that the view from the other side of the Atlantic is often just as bemused). To paraphrase Churchill, American and English lawyers are two professions joined by their different customs. I hoped my outsider's eye would discern features hidden in plain sight by protective colouration, too obvious to register on their own practitioners (though my vision is inevitably distorted by my American lenses). Joining Philip Lewis in directing a project on the comparative sociology of lawyers, I contributed chapters on England and America, both of which grew into books.

When *The Legal Profession in England and Wales* was published in 1988 I thought I was finished with the subject. But two events promptly drew me back. First, the 1989 Green Papers proposed to reform many practices I had severely criticized, and I wanted to see what happened. Secondly, almost immediately after my book appeared, large envelopes began arriving from England, often several a week, full of newspaper clippings about the growing controversy. These have continued unabated for fourteen years, offering me a comprehensive picture of how the English press (popular and professional) has depicted lawyers. I am deeply indebted to Edward Arnold for these data, without which this book would have been impossible.

Those are some of the reasons why *I* wrote *a* book. Why *this* book? England has several attractions for sociologists of lawyers. Relations between state and profession are much easier to comprehend and theorize within its unitary polity (not withstanding the recent devolution) than across America's more than fifty jurisdictions. Decades ago American courts held that most of the profession's restrictive practices violated the Constitution and anti-trust laws. But English institutions and practices dating back a century or more had survived largely intact. The Green Papers exposed fault lines, both within the professions and in the fabric joining them to state, society, and economy, revealing its tectonic plates.

They punctuated the social equilibrium (to adapt Stephen Jay Gould's evolutionary metaphor). The contest forced each participant to offer justifications for either change or the previously unquestioned status quo. Like all politics, it forged unpredictable and surprising alliances.

History has no beginning or end. The 1989 Green Papers are a natural curtain raiser, introducing tensions, unsettling understandings (although I felt it essential to locate them in British politics starting with Thatcher). Contemporary history has no natural endpoint, but neither can it aspire to be current events since books are instantly dated. I have used the 1999 Access to Justice Act as a bookmark, treating it more as the culmination of the Green Papers than the inception of radically different innovations. The inevitable arbitrariness of these termini is less troubling because my goal is to understand an ongoing process, not a momentary outcome.

In explaining *why*, *where*, and *when*, I have also suggested *what* I am investigating. My quarry is the politics of professionalism, conceived as a process, not a set of traits or a static achievement to be won once and for all (or lost irrevocably and mourned). Critics have misunderstood my earlier writings as describing, predicting, even welcoming the decline of the legal profession. But my 1985 Chorley Lecture spoke of 'The Decline of Professional*ism*' (inspired by Larson's book) not the *profession*. I was not addressing lawyers' numbers, income, respect, quality, or integrity. Professionalism is a relationship among producers, consumers, and the state, whose distinctive features are highlighted by juxtaposition against the institutional alternatives for producing and distributing expert services: markets and bureaucracies. English barristers and solicitors created their divided, symbiotic professions and successfully defended them until the end of the twentieth century. My focus is the dynamics of the continuing contest after the Green Papers had destabilized those tacit understandings.

The principal players in this drama are the producers (solicitors and barristers, both internally divided), consumers (individual and corporate), third-party payers (government, insurers), state (executive, legislature, judiciary), employers (Crown Prosecution Service and other government departments, companies), competitors (accountants, claims agents), media, and academic commentators (lawyers and social scientists). I am interested in the resources each brings to the battle: money, status, power, but most of all rhetoric. Therefore I focus on collective action in public arenas (rather than how individual lawyers, firms, or chambers make a living). Politics is always persuasion (if it is also more); the politics of legal professionalism is especially normative because law is the highest norm in secular democracies. Since language lies at the core of my enquiry I quote speakers extensively, not for the truth of what they say but for the fact that they say it, the reasons they give in defending the status quo or advocating change, what they feel the need to justify, attack, or rebut, and how they do so. My primary sources are public statements in the media (popular and professional), especially by elected politicians and civil servants, leaders and professional spokespersons (sometimes self-appointed), interviews, Parliamentary debates, government position papers, and the professions' responses, as well as empirical research by the Law Society's Research and Policy Planning Unit and academic lawyers and social scientists.

Finally, *how* will be readily apparent. I have written narrative history because it illuminates the ineluctable specificity of politics, which can be understood only in relation to the past—and because it is a *story*, with colourful protagonists, drama and bathos, punctilious propriety and vulgar farce. After grounding it in British politics and setting the stage with the clashes over the Green and White Papers and Courts and Legal Services Bill, I have unravelled seven distinct strands of the struggle: how many and who become lawyers, barristers' and solicitors' restrictive practices, state funding, self-regulation, and governance. This narrative strategy favours continuity of story-line within each sub-plot over linkages among them (which the concluding chapter attempts to make). I begin each of those seven stories with a theoretical framework and brief pre-history; but thereafter I let the facts speak for themselves so readers can hear the distinctive voices and construct their own interpretations of meaning and motive, before I offer mine in the chapter conclusions. Still, the selection, arrangement, emphasis, and characterization inevitably reflect my theoretical approach and political biases. I have not concealed these, but neither have I stressed them, believing that an American legal academic's judgements are no stronger than the evidence on which they rest.

I am grateful to many people and institutions for sending me material, submitting to interviews, reading and commenting on drafts, or including me in discussions: the American Bar Foundation, Sally Attwood, the Bar Council, Benoit Bastard, Frank Belloni, Geoffrey Bindman, Charles Blake, Andrew Boon, Campaign for a National Legal Service, Gerry Chambers, Vicki Chapman, Christa Christensen, Bill Cole, Fiona Cownie, Kim Economides, Donald Fleming, John Flood, Hazel Genn, Tony Girling, Cyril Glasser, Peter Goldsmith, Peter Graham-Harris, Edwin Greenebaum, Heather Hallett, John Hayes, Anthony Holland, John Jenkins, the Law Society and its Research and Policy Planning Unit, the Legal Action Group, the Legal Aid Board (now the Legal Services Commission), the Legal Services Ombudsman, Philip Lewis, Richard Lomax, the London School of Economics Law Department, the Lord Chancellor's Advisory Committee on Legal Education and Conduct, the Lord Chancellor's Department, Mavis Maclean, Michael McConville, Walter Merricks, Carl Mesmery, Austin Mitchell, Richard Moorhead, Aoife O'Grady, Alan Paterson, Pascoe Pleasence, Simon Roberts, Robert Seabrook, Joanna Shapland, Mark Sheldon, Avrom Sherr, Judith Sidaway, Roger Smith, Hilary Sommerlad, Robert Stevens, David Sugarman, Charles Taylor, Philip

Thomas, William Twining, Sarah Tyerman, the University of Sheffield Institute for the Study of the Legal Profession, the University of Westminster Law Department, Julian Webb, Carole Willis, the Working Group for Comparative Study of Legal Professions of the ISA Research Committee on Sociology of Law, and Michael Zander. I also have major debts to UCLA: my secretary, Margaret Kiever; the UCLA Law Library (especially Adrian Adan and Laura Cadra); and financial support from the Academic Senate Council on Research and the Law School Dean's Fund.

Richard L. Abel

Contents

Dramatis Personae, Acronyms and Glossary

AA: Arthur Andersen

AAC: Law Society's appeals and adjudication committee

ABA: American Bar Association

Abbey: Abbey Legal Protection Ltd

Abraham, Ann: NACAB chief executive 1991–7; LSO 1997–2002

Ackner, Lord: Conservative; called in 1945, QC 1961; BC 1957–61, 1963–70, Treasurer 1964–6, vice-chair 1966–8, chair 1968–70; High Court Judge 1971–80, Lord Justice of Appeal 1980–6, Lord of Appeal in Ordinary 1986–92

ACLF: Association of Christian Law Firms

Adam Smith Institute: free market think tank

Addison, Neil: CPS barrister (eight years), elected BC representative of employed barristers 1994

ADR: alternative dispute resolution

AGM: annual general meeting

AJA: Access to Justice Act 1999

Alagappa, Alex: BLA committee member

Alexander of Weedon, QC, Lord: BC chair 1986; MMC chair; Westminster Bank chair

Allen of Abbeydale, Lord: crossbencher, senior civil servant, non-lawyer

AL: Accident Line (Abbey plan)

Andrew, Angus: LS Council 1996–2000

APIL: Association of Personal Injury Lawyers

Appleby, John: LS courts and legal services committee chair; LS indemnity insurance review group chair

Archer of Sandwell, Lord: Labour; called in 1952, QC 1974; Solicitor-General 1974–9

ASA: Advice Services Alliance

Aucott, John: Edge & Ellison senior partner; LS Council member; VP candidate 1995–6; LS remuneration and practice committee chair

AVMA: Action for Victims of Medical Accidents

AWB: Association of Women Barristers

AWS: Association of Women Solicitors

BACFI: Bar Association for Commerce, Finance and Industry (privately employed barristers)

Bach, Lord: Minister of State for Defence Procurement, Labour; called 1972

Bahl, Kamlesh: former EOC chair; LS Council member, DVP 1998–9, VP 1999–2000

Baker, Simon: Law Society training committee chair

Baldry, Tony: Conservative; called in 1975; member AJB committee E

Barnes, Michael: Legal Services Ombudsman (LSO) (to 1997)

Barrow, Dame Jocelyn: Broadcasting Standards Council chair

BC: Bar Council (properly the General Council of the Bar and the Inns of Court)

BC GMC: Bar Council General Management Committee

Benn, Tony: Labour MP from 1950; minister in Wilson Government

Benson, Lord: Royal Commission on Legal Services chair; Coopers & Lybrand partner

Berenson, Richard: President of Conquest Legal Marketing

Bermingham, Gerald: Labour MP; solicitor turned barrister

Best, Stanley: BLA founder and chair

Betts, Jane: LS Secretary-General 1996–2000

Bindman, Geoffrey: founder and senior partner of Bindman & Partners; Society of Labour Lawyers chair 1999–2001

Bingham of Cornhill, Lord: called in 1959, QC 1972; High Court Judge 1980–6, Lord Justice of Appeal 1986–92, Master of the Rolls 1992–6, LCJ 1996–2000; Senior Lord of Appeal in Ordinary 2000–

Birnberg, Benedict: solicitor critic of the profession and legal aid scheme, founded Action for Justice 1994

BLA: British Legal Association, founded in 1964 as LS critic

BLAGG: Bar Lesbian and Gay Group

Blair, Tony: Labour Prime Minister 1997–

Bledisloe, Viscount: called in 1959, QC 1978

Blom-Cooper, Sir Louis: called in 1952, QC 1970; 'Justinian' columnist in *Financial Times*

BMA: British Medical Association (interest group)

Boardman, Lord: Conservative; solicitor since 1947; director and chair of many companies and banks

Boateng, Paul: Labour MP 1987–, shadow LCD spokesperson 1992–7

Bogan, Anthony: established London Solicitors Property Centre (SPyC); LS Council 1995–9, VP candidate 2000–1; BLA vice-chair; founded Solicitors Association (SA) 1996

Boléat, Mark: Building Societies Association Director General 1986–93; CML Director General 1989–93

Booth, Cherie: prominent QC specializing in employment and discrimination law; wife of Tony Blair

Borrie, Sir Gordon: called in 1952, QC; legal academic 1957–76; DGFT 1976–92

Bowley, Martin, QC: BLAGG chair; BC Treasurer 1992–

Boxer, Clive: partner in City insurance defence firm Davies Arnold Cooper

Brennan, Dan: personal injury specialist; QC; BC chair 1999; life peer 2000

Bridge of Harwich, Lord: crossbencher; called in 1947; High Court Judge 1968–75; Lord Justice of Appeal 1975–80; Lord of Appeal in Ordinary 1980–92

Brown, Gordon: Labour Chancellor of the Exchequer 1997–

Brown, Sir Stephen: President of the Family Division (retired 1999)

Browne-Wilkinson, Lord: High Court Judge 1977–83; Lord Justice of Appeal 1983–5; Vice-Chancellor 1985–91; Lord of Appeal in Ordinary 1991–2000

Bruce, Ian: Conservative MP, non-lawyer

Buggins' turn: earning entitlement to office through seniority

Burnett, John: Liberal Democrat MP, partner in Devon solicitors' firm, member AJB standing committee E

BVC: Bar Vocational Course

Byers, Stephen: Labour MP since 1992, law lecturer

CA: Consumers' Association

CAB: Citizens Advice Bureau

Calvert-Smith, QC, Sir David: DPP 1998–

Campaign: Campaign for the Bar, founded 1982

Campbell of Alloway, Lord: Conservative; called in 1939, QC 1965

Carbury, Sir Bryan: Director General of Fair Trading (after Borrie)

Carlile, Alex: Liberal Democrat MP; secretary of the Parliamentary All-Party Barristers' Group, now Lord Carlile of Berriew

CBA: Criminal Bar Association

CBI: Confederation of British Industries

CCBE: Council of the Bars and Law Societies of the European Community/*Commission Consultative des Barreaux Européen*

CD: Claims Direct

CDS: Criminal Defence Service

CFA: conditional fee agreement

Chancery Lane: Law Society headquarters

Chessels, Sir Tim: LAB chair (c. 1995)

CJD: Creutzfeld-Jakob Disease (mad cow)

C&L: Coopers & Lybrand (merged into PricewaterhouseCoopers (PwC)

CLAF: contingency legal aid fund

Clarke, QC, Kenneth: Conservative Chancellor of the Exchequer 1993–7

CLE: Council of Legal Education (of the Inns of Court)

Clinton-Davis, Lord: Labour; solicitor (admitted 1993) in working-class London neighbourhood; co-president of Society of Labour Lawyers

CLLS: City of London Law Society (created by the liveried City of London Solicitors Company 1969)

CLS: Community Legal Service

CLSA: Criminal Law Solicitors Association

CML: Council of Mortgage Lenders

CNL: Campaign for New Leadership (Girling 1996–7 campaign vehicle)

Coleraine, Lord: Conservative; solicitor

CPAG: Child Poverty Action Group

CPD: Continuing Professional Development

CPE: Common Professional Examination

CPS: Crown Prosecution Service

Cranston, Ross: called in 1976, QC 1998; Labour MP 1992–; Solicitor-General 1998–2001

Crawford, Lincoln: chair of the BC race relations committee

CRE: Commission for Racial Equality

Creswell, Peter: BC chair 1990, High Court Judge

Dalton, Michael: solicitor who sought judicial review of his SIF premium

Darvill, Keith: solicitor, AJB standing committee E

Day, Martyn: partner in Leigh, Day, leading personal injury firm, which brought and lost the tobacco case

Deacon, Angela: sole practitioner; SPG founder

Dean, Iris: sole practitioner and OSS critic

Denning, Lord: Law Lord; Master of the Rolls

de Wilde, Robin: founder of Campaign for the Bar

DGFT: Director General of Fair Trading

DHA: District Health Authority

Dismore, Andrew: Labour MP; solicitor, APIL member; made early-day motions on QCs, judicial appointments, member AJB standing committee E

Dobson, Frank: Labour Health Secretary 1997–9

Donaldson of Lymington, Lord: crossbencher; called in 1946, QC 1961; High Court Judge 1966–79; Lord Justice of Appeal 1979–82; Master of the Rolls 1982–92

DPP: Director of Public Prosecutions

DSS: duty solicitor schemes

DTI: Department of Trade and Industry

Dubow, Leslie: SPyG founder and leader 1983–98

DVP: Deputy Vice President (Law Society)

ECHR: European Convention on Human Rights

Edge, John: solicitor campaigner to raise conveyancing fees

EGM: extraordinary general meeting

Elly, Charles: Law Society President 1994–5

Elwyn-Jones, Lord: Labour Attorney-General 1966, Lord Chancellor 1974–9

Ely, Philip: partner, Southampton firm; Law Society President 1991–2

ENPBA: Employed and Non-Practising Bar Association

EOC: Equal Opportunities Commission

ERM: Exchange Rate Mechanism

ESPyC: Edinburgh Solicitors Property Centre

E&Y: Ernst & Young (global accounting firm)

Falconer of Thoroton, Lord: called in 1974, QC 1991; Labour Solicitor-General 1997–8; Minister of State, Cabinet Office 1998–2001

FDA: First Division Association (trade union of government lawyers)

Fennell, QC, Desmond: BC chair 1989

Fernandes, Maria: LS Council member for Ethnic Minorities (and wife of Keith Vaz)

Field, Frank: CPAG Director 1969–79; Labour MP since 1979; Minister for Welfare Reform 1997–8

FOIL: Forum of Insurance Lawyers

Fraser, John: solicitor, Labour MP

FSA: Financial Services Act or Authority

Garnier, Edward: called in 1976, QC 1995; Conservative MP 1992–, Parliamentary Private Secretary (PPS) to Law Officers 1995–7, Shadow to LCD 1997–9, Shadow Attorney-General 1999–

Garson, Michael: solicitor, Kagan Moss; estate agent

Gaskell, Sir Richard: LS President 1988–9

Gazumping: breaking a contract to sell property to one buyer in order to sell it at a higher price to another

Gifford, Lord: Labour; called in 1962, QC 1983; radical barrister

Girling, Tony: senior partner in Kent firm; LS DVP 1995–6; President 1996–7

GLS: Government Legal Service (all government lawyers outside the CPS)

GMC: General Medical Council (regulatory body)

Goff of Chieveley, Lord: called in 1951, QC 1967; High Court Judge 1975–82, Lord Justice of Appeal 1982–6, Lord of Appeal in Ordinary 1986–98

Goldsmith, Peter: called in 1972, QC 1987; BC chair 1995; life peer 1999

Goodhart, Lord: Liberal Democrat; called in 1957, QC 1979; shadow spokesperson for LCD

Goodman, Lord: Labour; solicitor

Grant, Sir Anthony: retired solicitor, Conservative MP

Grantchester, Lord: Labour; farmer

Gray, Peter: NPBA/ENPBA founder; medical doctor

Gray, Wendy: London sole practitioner; SIF critic and Millenium Group founder

Green, Allan: former Director of Public Prosecutions (DPP)

Green Form: legal advice scheme

Grieve, Dominic: Conservative MP; barrister; member of AJB standing committee E; Opposition spokesperson for Home Office

Griffiths, Lord: called 1949, QC 1964; High Court Judge 1971–80, Lord Justice of Appeal 1980–5, Lord of Appeal in Ordinary 1985–93; ACLEC chair 1991–3

Hacking, Lord: solicitor

Hailsham, Lord: Lord Chancellor 1970–4, 1979–87

Haldane Society of Socialist Lawyers

Halifax: one of the largest building societies (mortgage lenders)

Hall, Stuart: sociology professor, Open University

Hallett, QC, Heather: BC chair 1998; High Court Judge 1999–

Hambro: Hambro Countrywide plc (largest estate agency; now Countrywide Assured Group plc)

Harman, QC, Harriet: Solicitor, Labour; Secretary of State for Social Security 1997–8; Solicitor-General 2001–

Harmer, Caroline: APIL President

Havers, Lord: Conservative Solicitor-General 1970–4, Attorney-General 1979–87, Lord Chancellor June–October 1987

Hawkins, Nick: Conservative MP, spokesperson on legal affairs, former BACFI chair, member AJB standing committee E

Hayes, John: Law Society Secretary-General to 1996

Hayes, Josephine: called 1980; AWB chair

Heaps, Chris: LS adjudication and appeals committee chair

Hegarty, Richard: founding partner of Hegarty & Co. (1974); elected to LS Council 1989; PACS chair

Henderson of Brompton, Lord: crossbencher (from 1984)

Herbert, Peter: barrister, SBL chair

Hirst, Jonathan: called in 1975, QC 1990; BC chair 2000

HLPA: Housing Law Practitioners Association

Hodge, Henry: Camden Town legal aid firm partner; LS Council member, DVP 1994–5; Legal Aid Advisory Committee 1977–83; deputy chair LAB 1996–9; circuit judge; Chief Immigration Adjudicator

Holland, Tony: Law Society President 1990–1; Personal Investment Authority Principal Ombudsman 1997–

Hoon, Geoffrey: law lecturer 1976–82; privately practising barrister 1982–4; Labour MP 1992–7; Minister of State in the LCD 1997–9; Secretary of State for Defence since 2001

Hooson, Lord: Liberal Democrat; called in 1949; leader Wales and Chester Circuit 1971–4

Howe, QC, Sir Geoffrey: Conservative Chancellor of the Exchequer 1979–83; Foreign Secretary 1983–9; now Lord Howe of Aberavon

Howells, Michael: Law Society Treasurer 1995–96; Mears critic
HSSK: High Street Starter Kit (solicitor software package)
Hunt of Wirral, Lord: Conservative, solicitor
Hutchinson of Lullington, Lord: called in 1939, QC 1961; Liberal
    Democrat leader
IBA: International Bar Association
ICLS: Inns of Court School of Law
IEC: Interim Executive Committee of the Law Society
ILEX: Institute of Legal Executives
ILPA: Immigration Law Practitioners Association
ILS: Incorporated Law Society
IPS: inadequate professional service
IRA: Irish Republican Army
Irvine of Lairg, Lord: called in 1967, QC 1978; Labour Shadow Lord
    Chancellor 1992–7; Lord Chancellor 1997–2003; co-president, Society
    of Labour Lawyers
IVA: Individual Voluntary Arrangement (alternative to bankruptcy)
Jarndyce v Jarndyce: endless lawsuit in Dickens's *Bleak House*
Javaid, Makbool: SBL chair
Joseph, Keith: founder (with Thatcher) of the Centre for Policy Studies;
    Conservative Secretary of State for Industry 1979–81, Secretary of
    State for Education 1981–6
Joseph, Michael: solicitor critic of the profession
Justice: British section of the International Commission of Jurists
Keating, David: Hartlepool sole practitioner; international committee
    chair; candidate for Law Society DVP with Mears 1996–7,
    independent candidate 1998–9; candidate for VP with Mears 1997–8,
    candidate for President 1999–2000
Kennedy, Andrew: LS Council member and SIF chair
Kennedy of The Shaws, Baroness: Labour; called in 1972; QC 1991
Kidney, David: Labour MP; member of AJB standing committee E;
    non-practising solicitor
Kingsland, Lord: Conservative; called in 1972, QC 1988; Opposition
    leader 1997–; Shadow Lord Chancellor 2002
Kinnock, Neil: Labour Party leader 1983–92
Kirby, Carolyn: Law Society DVP 2000–1, VP 2001–2, President
    2002–3
KPMG: Klynveld Peat Marwick Goerdeler (following the 1987 merger of
    Peat Marwick and Klynveld Main Goerdeler)
LAB: Legal Aid Board
LAG: Legal Action Group
Lamont, Norman: Conservative Chief Secretary to the Treasury 1989–90,
    Chancellor of the Exchequer 1990–3

Lane, Lord: crossbencher; called in 1946, QC 1962; High Court Judge
    1966–74, Lord Justice of Appeal 1974–9, Lord of Appeal in Ordinary
    1979–80, Lord Chief Justice 1980–92

LAPG: Legal Aid Practitioners Group

Lawrence, QC, Sir Ivan: chair of the All-Party Parliamentary Barristers
    Group and Backbench Conservative Law Committee

Lawrence, Stephen: black youth murdered by white racists who escaped
    punishment

Lawson, Nigel: Conservative Secretary of State for Energy 1981–3;
    Chancellor of the Exchequer 1983–9, now Lord Lawson of Blaby

Lawton, Sir Frederick: retired Lord Justice of Appeal, former chair of the
    Lord Chancellor's Advisory Committee on Legal Education

LCCSA: London Criminal Courts Solicitors' Association

LCD: Lord Chancellor's Department

LCF: Law Centres Federation

LCJ: Lord Chief Justice

Leamington Spa: OSS headquarters

Levin, Bernard: *Times* columnist

Linton, Martin: Labour MP; member of Standing Committee
    E on the AJB

Lloyd of Berwick, Lord: called in 1955, QC 1967; High Court Judge
    1978–84, Lord Justice of Appeal 1984–93, Lord of Appeal in
    Ordinary 1993–8; Treasurer of Inner Temple 1999–

Lockley, Andrew: Law Society 1982–96, legal practice director 1987–95,
    corporate and regional affairs director 1995–6, consultant, Irwin
    Mitchell 1996–9

Lowe, Veronica: SCB Director to 1996

LPC: Legal Practice Course

LS: Law Society

LSCL: Law Society's College of Law

LSO: Legal Services Ombudsman

LSSC: Legal Services Complaints Commissioner

Lyell, Sir Nicholas: QC 1980; Conservative MP 1979–; Solicitor-General
    1987–92, Attorney-General 1992–7; Shadow Attorney-General
    1997–9

Lytton, Earl of: chartered surveyor

Mackay of Clashfern, Lord: called to Scots Bar in 1955, QC 1965; Vice
    Dean and Dean, Faculty of Advocates 1973–9; Lord Advocate
    1979–85; Lord of Appeal in Ordinary 1985–7; Lord Chancellor
    1987–97

Major, John: Chancellor of the Exchequer 1987–8, Chief Secretary
    1988–9, Prime Minister 1990–7

Malins, Humfrey: Conservative MP 1983–92, 1997–, solicitor

Mandelson, Peter: Labour MP 1992–; Minister without Portfolio in the
     Cabinet Office; Secretary of State for Trade and Industry
Mansfied, QC, Michael: radical silk
Marshall-Andrews, Robert: called in 1967, QC 1987; Labour MP 1997–
Matthews, Michael: Clifford Chance partner; Law Society DVP 1996–7,
     VP 1997–8, President 1998–9
Mayhew of Twysden, Lord: called in 1955, QC 1972; Solicitor-General
     1983–7; Attorney-General 1987–92
MBA: Master of Business Administration
McIntosh, David: partner at City insurance defence firm Davies Arnold
     Cooper; Law Society Council 1996–2000; VP candidate 1998–99; DVP
     2000, VP 2000–1, President 2001–2
MDP: multidisciplinary partnership
Mears, Martin: Great Yarmouth small firm partner; LS Council 1994–8,
     President 1995–6
Mencap: learning disability advocacy group
MEP: Member of the European Parliament
Merricks, Walter: Law Society Assistant Secretary-General (to 1996);
     Insurance Ombudsman 1996–2000; Financial Services Chief
     Ombudsman 2000–
Meston, Lord: barrister with legal aid practice
Middleton, Sir Peter: Permanent Secretary to the Treasury 1983–91;
     Chair of Barclay's Bank 1991–; author of the 1997 review of civil
     justice and legal aid
Millenium Group: small firms critical of SIF
Mills, Dame Barbara: DPP 1992–8
MIND: mental health advocacy group
Mishcon, Lord: Labour, solicitor
Mitchell, Austin: Labour MP and legal profession critic
MMC: Monopolies and Mergers Commission
MNP: multinational partnership
Moorhead, Richard: TSG President
Morris, John: shadow Attorney-General before 1997, Attorney-General
     1997–99, now Lord Morris
Mortimer, QC, Sir John: former barrister and Rumpole creator
Mullin, Chris: Labour MP 1992–, home affairs select committee chair
     1997–9, crusader against miscarriages of justice
Murdoch, Rupert: publisher of *The Times, Sunday Times, News of the World,*
     and *Sun*
Murray, Trevor: Essex sole practitioner; Law Society DVP candidate
     1999–2000
NACAB: National Association of Citizens Advice Bureaux
NACRO: National Association for the Care and Resettlement of Offenders

NAEA: National Association of Estate Agents

Napier, Michael: Irwin Mitchell partner (Sheffield); Law Society presidential candidate 1998–99; DVP 1999–2000; VP 2000; President, 2000–1; APIL President

Napley, Sir David: Law Society President

NASPyC: National Association of Solicitors Property Centres (renamed Solicitors Property Group)

NCC: National Consumer Council

NHS: National Health Service

November Group: City firms critical of SIF

NPBA: Non-Practising Bar Association

NSPyS: Newcastle Solicitors Property Shop

NVQ: National Vocational Qualification

OFT: Office of Fair Trading

Oliver of Aylmerton, Lord: crossbencher; called in 1948, QC 1965; High Court Judge 1974–80; Lord Justice of Appeal 1980–6; Lord of Appeal in Ordinary 1986–92

Onslow, Earl of: Conservative, farmer

Oppenheim-Barnes, Baroness: Conservative MP 1970–87; Minister for Consumer Affairs 1979–82; NCC chair 1987–9; life peer 1989–

Orchard, Stephen: LAB chief executive 1989–2000; LSC chief executive 2000–3

Owen, Robert: BC chair 1997

PACH: Pupil Application Clearing House

PACS: Law Society's Property and Commercial Services committee

Pannick, David: called in 1979, QC 1992; fellow of All Souls College, Oxford

Pannone, Rodger: Law Society President 1993–4; senior partner Manchester personal injury firm

PCC: Bar Council's Professional Conduct & Complaints committee

PD: public defender

Peach, Sir Leonard: former Commissioner for Public Appointments; conducted inquiry into silk and judicial appointments

Pembridge, Eileen: LS Council member 1990–, training committee member, presidential candidate 1995–6, family law specialist, medium-sized South London firm

Penry-Davey, QC, David: BC chair 1996; High Court Judge 1997–

Pharaoh, Paul: Law Society's appeals and adjudication committee chair

Phillips, Baroness: Labour, consumer advocate

Phillips of Sudbury, Lord: Liberal Democrat life peer 1998; founding chair of LAG, senior partner in smaller City solicitors' firm

Pitts, John: LAB chair

Portillo, Michael: Conservative MP 1984–97, 1999–, Chief Secretary to
    the Treasury; Secretary of State for Employment; Secretary of
    State for Defence; Shadow Chancellor of Exchequer 2000–1
PPD: Law Society's Professional Purposes Department (SCB precursor)
Prys-Davies, Lord: Labour, solicitor
PwC: PricewaterhouseCoopers
PSI: Policy Studies Institute
RADAR: Royal Association for Disability and Rehabilitation
Rawlinson of Ewell, Lord: called in 1946, QC 1959; BC chair 1975;
    Senate President 1986; Conservative backbencher 1955–64, whip,
    Attorney-General 1970–4; Solicitor-General
Rees-Mogg, Lord: crossbencher; *Times* editor 1967–81
Refuge: immigrant advocacy group
Regis: LS computer system
Renton, Lord: Conservative; called in 1933, QC 1954; Lincoln's Inn
    Treasurer 1979
Rippon, Lord: barrister, QC
Rosen, Arnold: SPG founding chair
Ross, Peter: Crown Prosecutor 1986–96; OSS director 1996–9; called in
    2000
Rossi, Sir Hugh: retired solicitor, Parliamentary All-Party Solicitors Group
    chair
Rowe, J J: BC chair 1993
RPPU: Law Society Research & Policy Planning Unit (renamed Strategic
    Research Unit)
SA: Solicitors Association (created by Bogan in 1996)
SAHCA: Solicitors' Association of Higher Court Advocates
Savage, David: partner in small Hampshire firm; DVP candidate with
    Mears 1997–8, independent candidate 2000–1
Sawyer, Lord: trade unionist, Labour Party General Secretary 1994–8
Sayer, Robert: partner in Sayer Moore & Co (Acton); Law Society VP
    1995–6, 1998–9, DVP 1997–8, President 1999–2000, vice-presidential
    candidate 1996–7, presidential candidate 2000–1
SBA: Specialist Bar Association
SBL: Society of Black Lawyers (established 1973)
Scargill, Arthur: National Union of Mineworkers President 1982–2002;
    left Labour Party to found Socialist Labour Party 1996
Scarman, Lord: retired Law Lord
SCB: Solicitors Complaints Bureau
SCF: Solicitors Compensation Fund
Scrivener, Anthony: called in 1961, QC 1975; Campaign for the Bar; BC
    chair 1991

Scott, Sir Richard: High Court Judge 1983–91, Lord Justice of
  Appeal 1991–4, Vice Chancellor 1994–2000; Lord of Appeal in
  Ordinary 2000–

SDT: Solicitors Disciplinary Tribunal

Seabrook, Robert: called in 1964, QC 1983; BC chair 1994

SEC: Securities and Exchange Commission (United States)

Senate: grouping of the four Inns of Court

SFLA: Solicitors Family Law Association

Sheldon, Mark: Law Society President 1992–3; Linklaters & Paines senior
  partner to 1993

Shephard, Nigel: SFLA chair

Sherr, Avrom: Woolf Professor of Legal Education, Institute for Advanced
  Legal Studies

Siddle, Hilary: partner in Lancaster firm; LS family law committee chair;
  DVP candidate 2000–1

SIF: Solicitors Indemnity Fund

Simon of Glaisdale, Lord: crossbencher; called in 1934, KC 1951; High
  Court Judge 1962–71, Lord of Appeal in Ordinary 1971–7

SMI: standard mortgage instructions

Smith, John: Labour Shadow Chancellor of the Exchequer under
  Kinnock, then party leader

Smith, Roger: LAG director, Law Society training director; director of
  Justice

Sogat: Society of Graphical and Allied Trades (merged with National
  Graphical Association 1991 to form Graphical, Paper and Media
  Union)

SPG: Sole Practitioners Group

Spiv: parasite, shirker

SPyC: Solicitors Property Centre

SPyCL: Solicitors Property Centres Ltd (created by Conquest Legal
  Marketing)

SPyG: Solicitors Property Group

Stanbrook, Ivor: Conservative MP, barrister

Stapely, Sue: solicitor, Law Society public relations director (until 1996);
  independent communications consultant

Steyn, Lord: called in 1973, QC 1979; High Court Judge 1985–91; Lord Justice
  of Appeal, 1992–5; Lord of Appeal in Ordinary, 1996–; ACLEC chair,
  1994–6.

Stinchcombe, Paul: member AJB standing committee E

Straw, Jack: called 1972; Labour Home Secretary 1997–2001; Secretary of
  State for Foreign and Commonwealth Affairs 2001–date

Streeter, Gary: Conservative MP 1992–; Parliamentary Under-Secretary of
  State in the LCD 1995–7

Sycamore, Phillip: partner in small Blackpool firm; LS VP 1996–7,
    President 1997–8
Taylor, John M.: solicitor, Conservative MP 1983–92; Parliamentary
    Under-Secretary of State in the LCD 1992–5, member of AJB
    standing committee E
Taylor, Lord: LCJ 1992–7
Tebbit, Norman: Conservative Secretary of State for Employment 1981–3;
    Secretary of State for Trade and Industry 1983–5; Party Chair 1985–6
Temple: Inner and Middle Temple are two of the four Inns of Court
Templeman, Lord: crossbencher; called in 1947, BC member, 1961–5,
    Senate President, 1974–6; member of Royal Commission on Legal
    Services; High Court Judge 1972–8, Lord Justice of Appeal, 1978–82,
    Lord of Appeal in Ordinary, 1982–94
Temple-Morris, Peter: called in 1962, solicitor 1989; Labour MP
    1974–2001; life peer 2001
TGWU: Transport and General Workers' Union
Thatcher, Margaret: Conservative Prime Minister 1979–90
Thomas, Gareth: barrister; Labour MP, member of AJB standing
    committee E
Thomas of Gresford, Lord: Liberal Democrat; solicitor 1961–6; called in
    1967, QC 1979, life peer 1996
Thornton, Anthony: BC professional standards committee chair; High
    Court Judge
Thornton, Baroness: Labour; Fabian Society General Secretary 1993–6
Thwaites, Ronald: called in 1970, QC 1987; CBA spokesperson
Todd, Mark: Labour MP; Minister of State, FCO and DTI; company
    managing director; member AJB standing committee E
Tordoff, Lord: Liberal Democrat; business executive
TSG: Trainee Solicitors' Group
TUC: Trade Unions Congress
UDI: unilateral declaration of independence (Rhodesia 1965)
UKIAS: United Kingdom Immigrants' Advisory Service
Vaz, Keith: solicitor turned barrister; Labour backbencher, Parliamentary
    Under-Secretary of State in the LCD (1999–2000); Minister for
    Europe (2000–1); husband of Maria Fernandes
Walker, Ian: partner in solicitors' firm Russell Jones & Walker; APIL
    President 1998–2000
Wallman, Russell: Law Society Director of Policy Development
Ward, David: Law Society President 1989–90
Ward, Susan: AWB chair, BACFI chair
Watson-Lee, Peter: partner in Dorset solicitors' firm; Law Society Council
    and family law committee; Mears supporter and 1996–7 campaign
    manager

Wheatley, Derek: BC Chair; BACFI vice-chair and chair

Whitehead, Dr Alan: Member AJB standing committee E

Wigoder, Lord: Liberal Democrat; called in 1946, QC 1966

Wilberforce, Lord: crossbencher; called in 1932, QC 1954; High Court Judge 1961–4; Lord of Appeal in Ordinary, 1964–82

Wilcox, Baroness: Conservative whip; NCC chair 1990–6; business executive

Williams of Mostyn, Lord: called in 1965, QC 1978; Leader of Wales and Chester Circuit 1987–9; BC 1986–92, chair 1992; Labour, Opposition legal affairs spokesperson in Lords 1992–7; Attorney-General 1999–2001; leader, Lords 2001–

Woolf, Lord: crossbencher; called in 1954; chair Lord Chancellor's Advisory Committee on Legal Education 1986–90; High Court Judge 1979–86, Lord of Appeal in Ordinary 1992–6, Master of the Rolls 1996–2000; Lord Chief Justice 2000–; author of 1996 report on civil justice

Young, John: City solicitors' firm partner; SIF chair; LS Council, VP 1994–5

Young of Graffham, Lord: solicitor (admitted 1956); Secretary of State at the Department of Trade and Industry 1987–9

YSG: Young Solicitors Group

Zander, Michael: honorary QC 1997; LSE law professor 1963–98, critic of the profession, member of the Runciman Royal Commission on Criminal Justice

1 Party Politics

> I knew from my father's accounts that the free market was like a vast sensitive nervous system, responding to events and signals all over the world to meet the ever-changing needs.... [Margaret Thatcher]

> [W]henever we have extended choice for the people, the Left have fought us all the way...choice has improved the standard of services for all. [John Major]

> [M]y socialism ... is social-ism.

> Our legal system is a nest of restrictive practices.

> [A] thriving competitive market is essential for individual choice. [Tony Blair]

> Labour will have no new money to throw at problems whose solution calls for structural change. [Lord Irvine]

The English legal profession experienced extraordinary turmoil in the 1990s. Rising numbers, insufficient apprenticeships and first positions, and stagnant or falling demand (especially for conveyancing) led to calls for restricting entry. The growing proportions of women and ethnic minorities increased pressure to reflect the demographics of the larger society at all levels of the professional hierarchy. To accommodate mothers (and fathers), the profession would have to restructure work radically. Intensifying competition among lawyers accelerated concentration, especially of solicitors' firms but also of barristers' chambers. Professional monopolies were challenged by outsiders: foreign lawyers (especially American) and other professionals (notably accountants, eager to form multidisciplinary partnerships) and other occupational categories (claims adjusters, immigration advisers). Third-party payers (primarily government through the legal aid scheme but also private legal expenses insurers) exercised increasing control over professional practice, especially pricing. Chronic tensions between protecting clients and defending lawyers were complicated by intraprofessional differences in the targets of disciplinary complaints and malpractice claims. Centrifugal forces made self-governance increasingly contentious and spawned rival associations.

But all these changes were gradual (if cumulative). The unprecedented rupture was Lord Mackay's 1989 Green Papers, leading to the Courts and Legal Services Act 1990, and Lord Irvine's effort to complete this transformation and radically restructure legal aid in the Access to Justice Act 1999. These dramatic political acts—characterized by most observers as radical, even revolutionary—pose two conundrums. First, why did the state, which had let lawyers govern themselves for centuries, decide to intervene? It had ignored decades of increasingly acerbic criticism by academics, practitioners, and politicians. The Royal Commission on Legal Services, created by the Labour Government in 1977, gave the profession a clean bill of health in 1979. Its Conservative successor took four years to respond and then accepted most of the bland recommendations. Why did it change its mind six years later? (Although Lord Mackay pointed to the Marre Committee's failure to get barristers and solicitors to agree on audience rights, that was hardly a sufficient reason.)

Secondly, both parties took paradoxical positions. Conservatives claim to defend tradition. Lawyers seem a natural constituency by virtue of their class origin and position, client interests, and congenial caution.[1] Because judges are chosen from barristers and senior judges from Queen's Counsel, the bench is even more strongly Conservative. Yet Lord Mackay used the Government's solid majority to enact reforms that infuriated bench and Bar and alienated many solicitors. The Opposition predictably assailed the Conservatives' blind faith in the market and neglect of a legal aid scheme Labour had founded and proudly defended for half a century. Once Labour regained power in 1997, however, it displayed even greater enthusiasm for laissez faire, substituted conditional fees for legal aid in most money claims, and capped the budget. This chapter mines the political history of the last quarter of a century for insights into the parties' motivations. But though the confrontations preoccupied lawyers, they did not even register on anyone else's political radar screen. Histories, biographies, and autobiographies of the period (with the exception of Nigel Lawson's) never mention them. Promises and practices affecting the economy, health care, education, and crime may influence elections; legal services are electorally insignificant. All I can do, therefore, is speculate on the implications of party platforms and policies for the positions governments took concerning lawyers.

A. Thatcher

All historians portray Margaret Thatcher's 1979 victory as a turning point in British politics. More than two million voters abandoned Labour, angered by inflation (which soared to 26 per cent), devaluation of the pound (by nearly 40 per cent), and especially Labour's chronic capitulation to the unions, whose increasingly frequent and disruptive industrial actions culminated in the 1978–9 winter of discontent. The Conservative manifesto promised to control inflation through monetarism and public spending cuts, privatize state industries, lower taxes, and subdue the unions. Thatcher offered a cure for the decline Britain had experienced since the war, as it lost its empire and was overshadowed militarily, geo-politically, and economically.[2]

Although Thatcher never articulated a systematic philosophy, she was supremely confident. As early as the 1968 party conference she warned the Conservative Political Centre about the:

dangers in consensus: it could be an attempt to satisfy people holding no particular views about anything. It seems more important to have a philosophy and policy

which because they are good appeal to sufficient people to secure a majority.... No great party can survive except on the basis of firm beliefs about what it wants to do.

In her autobiography she reported sharing the 'inner conviction' of the eighteenth century Prime Minister Chatham: 'I know that I can save this country and that no one else can'. She told her first Cabinet: 'It must be a conviction government. As Prime Minister I could not waste time having any internal arguments'. She rebuked a subordinate: 'Don't tell me what; tell me how. I know what'. Responding to criticism by her predecessor, Ted Heath, in 1981, she decried consensus as 'the process of abandoning all beliefs, principles, values and policies'. She boasted proudly: 'The lady's not for turning'.

She extolled individual responsibility, notoriously announcing: 'there is no such thing as society; there are only individuals, and families'. Society was 'you and me and our next-door neighbour and everyone we know in our town'. '[N]o government can do anything except through people, and people must look to themselves first. It's our duty to look after ourselves and then to look after our neighbour'. This was not selfishness. 'Does someone's natural desire to do well for himself, to build a better life for his family and provide opportunities for his children, does all this make him a materialist? Of course it doesn't. It makes him a decent human being, committed to his family and his community. ...'

'I came to office with one deliberate intent. To change Britain from a dependent to a self-reliant society—from a give-it-to-me to a do-it-yourself nation; to a get-up-and-go instead of a sit-back-and-wait-for-it Britain.' She detested both aristocratic contempt for trade and welfare dependency and found a religious mandate for personal striving. 'We are told we must work and use our talents to create wealth.' '[A]bundance rather than poverty has a legitimacy which derives from the very nature of Creation.' Like her good friend Ronald Reagan, she paradoxically proposed to use state power to shrink the state. 'Conservatives should aim to reduce the range of government decision-making and restore greater individual choice.' Growing up above her father's grocery shop, she imbibed an instinctive belief in the market, confirmed by her marriage to a successful businessman:

Before I read a line from the great liberal economists, I knew from my father's accounts that the free market was like a vast sensitive nervous system, responding to events and signals all over the world to meet the ever-changing needs.... Governments acted on a much smaller store of conscious information and, by contrast, were themselves 'blind forces' blundering about in the dark, and obstructing the operations of markets rather than improving them.

Those who inspired and implemented her decisions were equally emphatic. Keith Joseph (Secretary of State for Industry) maintained that 'industry is about competition—and risks'. A Conservative Government would 'aim to reduce the volume of new legislation as well as to remove current restrictions'. '[I]ll-considered rescue schemes' to save failing industries 'take money from the more efficient to give it to the less efficient'. Nigel Lawson, her first Chancellor, claimed: 'we were not seeking simply to remove various controls and impositions, but by doing so to change the entire culture of a nation from anti-profits, anti-business, government-dependent lassitude and defeatism, to a pro-profit, pro-business, robustly independent vigour and optimism'. Lord Young (Secretary of State at the DTI) decried the way in which the 'gentrification process' had sapped the energy unleashed by the industrial revolution, suggesting that ontogeny recapitulated phylogeny:

We are all born with enterprise. None of us would survive without enterprise. Every baby and toddler demonstrates every day… that early in life we all have an abundance of enterprise, initiative, the ability to spot an opportunity and take rapid advantage of it. So when we are young, we are all entrepreneurs. But along the way to adult life too many of us change.

He praised 'the success of American entrepreneurs that has been reflected in the standard of living of Americans generally' and warned that 'cut off from that competition, human nature tends to opt for the quieter life and inefficiency'. Commending the fall in the price of spectacles following the deregulation of opticians, he urged the dissolution of the British Medical Association and the Law Society.[3]

Thatcher championed not only entrepreneurship but also entrepreneurs, sharing their resentment of the establishment. 'They didn't speak with Oxford accents. They hadn't got what people called the "right connections".' Her Finchley constituency was strongly Jewish (though she lived in Kent and then Chelsea); when she was first elected in 1959 its golf club excluded Jews. She noted that 'in the thirty-three years I represented it, I never had a Jew come in poverty and desperation to one of my constituency surgeries. They had always been looked after by their own community' (which coincided with her definition of 'society'). 'There have always been Jewish members of my staff and indeed my Cabinet', including Keith Joseph, Nigel Lawson, David Young, Leon Brittan, Malcom Rifkind, and Michael Howard. 'In fact, I just wanted a Cabinet of clever, energetic people—and that frequently turned out to be the same thing.'[4]

Thatcher detested unions, not only for holding the nation hostage through strikes (more days were lost from 1970 to 1972 than in any year since the 1926 General Strike) but also for oppressing workers. She wanted to 'liberate' the 'rank-and-file unionists' from their 'union bosses' by 'breaking down the closed shop and ensuring genuine democracy within the unions; then they themselves would bring the extremists and union *apparatchiks* into line'. The problem 'was the whole socialist economic approach to which the union bosses were wedded, and in particular their preference for monopoly and protection'. 'Communism is a system which gives privileges to the few at the top, and none to the many. Capitalism and enterprise is a system that only works by spreading ever more widely to more and more of the population what used to be the privileges of the few.' The real conflict was between unions and workers, not capital and labour. 'Don't talk to me about "them" and "us" in a company. You're all "we" in a company. You survive as the company survives, prosper as the company prospers—everyone together.' Following Friedrich von Hayek, she maintained that 'the level of unemployment was related to the extent of trade union power. The unions had priced many of their members out of jobs by demanding excessive wages for insufficient output....' Brian Griffiths (head of the 10 Downing Street policy unit) said that by controlling entry, trade unions 'are able to raise their real wages but only at the expense of either trade-union members who are unemployed or other workers who receive lower wages'. In 1981 Thatcher replaced Jim Prior (a wet) as Secretary of State for Employment with Norman Tebbit, who told the unemployed to 'get on your bike' and look for work. He saw the closed shop as a 'form of conscription' with the 'power to put people out of work with no possibility of redress if they refused to obey orders'.[5]

Thatcher sought to undermine union power through the Employment Acts of 1980, 1982, and 1988, the Trade Unions Act of 1984, and the Wages Act of 1986, which effectively ended closed shops, banned flying pickets, sympathy strikes, and secondary boycotts, made unions liable for illegal activity, required secret ballots for union office, industrial action, and political contributions, allowed workers to sue unions, freed government from paying union wages, and lowered the minimum in the sweated trades and retail sector. She banned the trade union from the Government Communications Headquarters at Cheltenham. Partly as a result (but also because of economic change), trade union membership fell from 13.2 million in 1979 to 10.7 million in 1985. Union strength declined dramatically. Fewer than a million workers stayed at home in response to the TUC's 1980 'Day of Action'. Arthur Scargill called out his members in 1984–5 to halt pit closures, declaring: 'Where there are resources of coal...even if there is a loss on the production of that coal, then the coal should be produced'. Thatcher boasted that:

the strike's defeat established...that Britain could not be made ungovernable by the Fascist Left. Marxists wanted to defy the law of the land in order to defy the laws of economics. They failed, and in doing so demonstrated just how mutually dependent the free economy and a free society really are.

Rupert Murdoch crushed the NGA and SOGAT strikes in his new Wapping plant. The National Union of Seamen not only lost its strike against P&O for laying off European ferry workers in 1988 but also had its assets sequestered. Although 73 per cent of the population named union power as the most important issue facing the country in 1979, only 1 per cent did so by 1987.[6]

Thatcher maintained that 'privatization shifted the balance away from the less efficient state to more efficient private business' and 'state ownership effectively removes—or at least radically reduces—the threat of bankruptcy which is a discipline on privately owned firms'. But her motivation was as much ideological as economic. In 1982 a Conservative minister said 'we're bloody fed up with' the nationalized industries. 'They make huge losses, they have bolshie unions, they are feather-bedded. It seems almost impossible to do anything with them; therefore, the view has grown, get rid of them'. Privatization of British Steel, British Airlines, and British Telecom not only increased quality and reduced price but also generated income (£4.4 billion in 1986–7) to allow the Government to postpone tax increases and created five million new share owners, raising the proportion from 7 to 20 per cent of the population. (In 1987, 56 per cent of shareholders in the newly privatized industries voted Conservative and only 16 per cent Labour.) Thatcher called this 'the greatest shift of ownership and power away from the state to individuals and their families in any country outside the former communist bloc'. The Adam Smith Institute compared it to Henry VIII's dissolution of the monasteries.[7]

Thatcherites resented the tax and redistributive consequences of social services, and accused them of being inherently inefficient and inviting dependency. Sir Geoffrey Howe, her second Chancellor, found 'powerful reasons why we must be ready to consider how far private provision and individual choice can supplement, or in some cases possibly replace, the role of the Government in health, social security and education'. Thatcher assailed former Labour minister Douglas Jay for claiming that 'the gentleman in Whitehall really does know better what is good for the people than the people know themselves'. She condemned previous Tory governments for 'merely pitch[ing] camp in the long march to the left' but 'never tr[ying] seriously to reverse it'. Indeed, they 'boasted of spending more money than Labour' on welfare, 'not of restoring people to independence and self-reliance'. She sold off 1,375,000 council houses, coincidentally raising revenue and increasing home ownership, and transferred many rental properties to Housing Action Trusts and private landlords. (In 1987, 44 per cent of working-class homeowners voted Conservative and only 31 per cent Labour.) But though Thatcher reduced entitlement to social security and increased private pensions, health insurance, and especially housing, real spending on public services rose during her administration, both absolutely and as a proportion of GDP, largely because of rising unemployment.[8]

Although Thatcher was determined to control the budget of the NHS, 'a bottomless pit', whose staff were not 'cost conscious', real expenditures on health care increased 20 per cent from 1978–9 to 1985–6. The 1982 leak of a Cabinet document considering privatization of some medical services forced her to declare 'the NHS is safe with us' and boast in her 1983 election manifesto that 'we have more than matched our pledge to maintain spending on the NHS and secure proper value for money'. But Thatcher wanted 'to tackle restrictive practices and other inefficiencies in the medical profession, directing the system of merit awards more to merit and less to retirement bonuses, and we planned the general introduction of "medical audit" '. She was determined to break the 'locally monopolistic DHA'. (With typical immodesty, Nigel Lawson took credit for convincing Thatcher after the 1987 election to initiate the review of health care that led to the January 1989 White Paper *Working for Patients.*) The 'moves to self-governing hospitals and GPs' budgets, the buyer/provider distinction with the DHA as buyer, and money following the patient were the pillars on which the NHS could be transformed'. '[T]here was an outcry from the British Medical Association, health trade unions, and the Opposition, based squarely on a deliberate and self-interested distortion of what we were doing'. But 'the stridency of the BMA's campaigns against our reforms was leading to a backlash among moderate doctors'.[9]

Criticism and resistance only solidified Thatcher's certitude. The Government cut the universities' budget by 15 per cent over three years, shifted funding from capitation to centralized evaluations of teaching and research, and favoured science and engineering. Thatcher claimed that 'by exerting financial pressure...we had increased administrative efficiency and provoked overdue rationalization', making universities 'more entrepreneurial'. Student loans 'would make students more discriminating about the courses they chose', and tuition fees 'would lead in the same direction of greater sensitivity to the market. Limits placed on the security of tenure enjoyed by university staff also encouraged dons to pay closer attention to satisfying the teaching requirements made of them.' When Oxford voted by more than two to one to deny her the honourary degree it had awarded every previous Prime Minister (even though she was an alumna), because she had done 'deep and systematic damage' to higher education, she retorted that opposition to wealth creation 'nowhere is... more marked than in the cloister and common room'. Indeed, the Archbishop of Canterbury's 1985 Commission on Urban Priority Areas declared that 'the creation of wealth must go hand in hand with just distribution'. And four years later the Roman Catholic Archbishop and the Anglican Bishop of Liverpool declared that 'the deprivation of our neighbour is a matter of concern to our faith'. (During Thatcher's decade the after-tax incomes of the top 10 per cent increased by 65 per cent while those of the bottom 10 per cent fell by 14 per cent.) But when the Church of England rebuked her callousness, she dismissed the criticism of 'cuckoos' and urged Christian leaders to 'take a leaf' from the teaching of the Chief Rabbi, Sir Immanuel Jakobovits, whom she made a peer.[10]

Her hostility to the media and arts may have expressed partisanship as well as ideological opposition to monopoly and public services. She undermined the BBC in the name of giving 'viewers a far wider choice' and encouraging 'the widest competition among and opportunities for the independent producers'. She made the National Theatre, Royal Shakespeare Company, and Royal Opera House raise private funds and museums charge admission. The chattering classes responded with invective: a 'quite extraordinary lack of comprehension', without parallel 'even among the many philistines I have escorted around the museum' (Sir John Pope-Hennessy, Director of the Victoria and Albert Museum); 'well over 90 per cent of the people in the performing arts, education, and the creative world are against her' (Sir Peter Hall, Director of the National Theatre); 'loathsome, repulsive in almost every way' (Jonathan Miller). Harold Pinter and Lady Antonia Fraser organized an opposition that included Salman Rushdie, Ian McEwan, Germaine Greer, and Richard Rogers. David Hare and John Mortimer ridiculed her in plays and films. But some of the press became more Thatcherite than the Iron Lady. In 1985 *The Times* asked rhetorically 'whether the structures and institutions of British life have been so shaken by six years of Mrs Thatcher that they can no longer fall back into their old ways—or whether more shaking is needed' and answered emphatically: 'More shaking is still needed'.[11]

Some of her targets were perverse. Although Conservatives maintain that localism enhances autonomy, Thatcher waged war on local government, capping its spending and rates, partly because it was dominated by Labour (sometimes the Trotskyite Militant Tendency) and partly because she was at heart a centralizer. She even applied cost-cutting measures to that central Conservative symbol, the Crown, imposing block grants on the royal palaces, air squadron, and train, and forcing the sale of the royal yacht. Although she sought to increase parental choice in education and allow schools to opt out of local control and charge for extra services, she simultaneously imposed national standards, evaluations, and league tables and tied teacher salaries to performance.[12]

B. Major

Although Thatcher's growing unpopularity (aggravated by the poll tax debacle—another centralizing action) forced her to resign in 1990, John Major, her chosen successor, differed less in policy than personality and style— 'Thatcherism pursued by non-Thatcherite means'. He was a consensus politician, one of the best whips before joining the Cabinet, and much less doctrinaire. Norman Lamont, his first Chancellor, complained: 'there was no fixity of purpose. It was difficult to know where he stood on any of the big issues.' Major acknowledged 'I followed Keynesian policies. If I had not let government spending increase, unemployment would have been much higher.' Lamont commented: 'In the battle of ideas, the Conservative party stopped fighting and switched sides'. But Major did not see sides. 'There is no easy definition of a Conservative.' He sought to frame 'policies attuned to current practicalities, and not dictated by some abstract, frozen political ideology'. Unfortunately, that led the public to see him as indecisive (70 per cent), ineffective (71 per cent), and not really in charge or tough (81 per cent).[13]

Still, he did have strong convictions. He had had to leave school at sixteen in order to contribute an essential £5/week to the family income. An insider biography said he 'hated pretension and prejudice; knew from experience what life was like inside a struggling city heap, and wanted to widen the channels of opportunity which Thatcherism had opened for the toughest and most able'. 'You give each family the tools to make their own choices and find their own way forward. It is called opportunity.' They should be 'free' to choose private education 'without political hectoring'. Labour said: ' "We do not want you getting above yourself". It is towering humbug.' 'I do want children to get above themselves....' He wanted 'to build a dynamic, enterprise economy...in which small businesses are encouraged'. Welfare 'perpetuates the myth that the State can satisfy the dreams of its people'. This 'ignores the fact that people have a desire and a responsibility to provide for themselves and their families'. 'Opportunity and ownership belong together.' 'Some call this materialism.... That is patronising rubbish'. The 'case for a smaller government is as much a moral case as an economic one'.[14]

Major retained most of Thatcher's policies (as well as her last Lord Chancellor, Lord Mackay, the only Thatcher Cabinet member who stayed throughout his administration). Major emphasized choice in schools. Although he eliminated the division between polytechnics and universities and proposed to double enrolment in higher education, he offered no more money, forcing universities to seek private funding and students to borrow. By 1993–4, 20 per cent of students were considering dropping out because of financial hardship. Government cut maintenance grants by 10 per cent a year for three years starting in 1994. Major centralized quality control through the Teaching Quality Assessment and the Research Assessment Exercise.[15] While claiming to be more caring, he was determined to control welfare expenditure and could not 'stand the welfare cheats'. He wanted to build 'a system for a self-help society' and force recipients to find work or be cut off.[16] He further developed the internal market for health care. By 1997, 16,000 of the 30,000 GPs had become fundholders and 90 per cent of hospitals were trusts; 12 per cent of the population was covered by private health insurance.[17] He continued Thatcher's attack on

the unions, making strikes more difficult to authorize, allowing public services customers to challenge illegal strikes, requiring workers to agree to
dues deductions, and forcing unions to compete for members. 'The tide of
collectivism—the drift towards a world where the workforce was treated as
an undifferentiated mass with identical interests and objectives—was turned
back.'[18]

Major's central concern was the quality of public services (perhaps
because his family had depended on them when he was growing up). He
boasted of privatizing forty-six major activities and many smaller ones. 'You
know, whenever we have extended choice for the people, the Left have
fought us all the way . . . choice has improved the standard of services for
all.' When government deregulated the sale of spectacles 'the range of
glasses was widened and better value ensued'. When new air routes were
allocated prices dropped by 15 per cent. Competition drove down the cost
of telephone calls. '[W]here services do remain in public hands, we will not
hesitate to apply private sector skills to ensure that they are more efficient
and deliver the high quality that people deserve and demand.' The 1982
Financial Management Initiative had made government departments
responsible for managing their own budgets and measured output and
cost-effectiveness. In 1991 Major required all departments and agencies to
set targets for work to be market tested and subjected them to inspectorates
(which included lay members), and directed local government to put work
out for compulsory competitive tender. Central government began
contracting out civil service work: by the end of 1993 £850 million of the
£1.1 billion offered was won by outside providers, allegedly saving 20 per
cent, and another £830 million was put out for tender. Major's centrepiece
was the Citizen's Charter, one of the five great principles in his 1992
election manifesto. This promised improved quality, 'choice, wherever possible between competing providers', service standards and remedies, and
'value for money within the resources the nation can afford'.[19]

Major's campaign for a second term clarified the party line. His core
strategy was to portray Labour as fiscally irresponsible. When Neil Kinnock
published proposals for 'Opportunity Britain' in April 1991, the Conservatives promptly costed them at £35 billion and plastered the country
with posters declaring 'Labour's going for broke again'. Major told his
first party conference as Prime Minister the following October that Labour
'have eight new taxes lined up already'. When Conservative posters warned
that a Labour government would increase every household's taxes by
£1,250 the Tories took a 2 per cent lead in the polls. A day after publishing
his election manifesto, Major ridiculed 'John Smith's mockery of a budget'.
Labour was proposing 'the biggest increase in personal tax since the War . . .
worse even than Labour's notorious promise in the 1970s to squeeze
the taxpayers until the pips squeaked'. 'The combined rates of tax and

contributions would be 49 per cent and 59 per cent.' It would 'rip the very heart out of the housing market...for good'. 'No one at any stage in the history of Britain has launched such an onslaught on the security of hard-working, middle-income families'.

Remember Red Wednesday [1.4.1992] when shares in water, gas, telecom, and electricity plunged by £1,300 million, just because of the fear of a Labour government. If Labour were to win on Thursday, we would see a cut—almost overnight—in the value of homes, shares, pensions....

Labour said 'Trust us—we'll decide for you,—we'll provide for you', like 'some feudal lord discussing his serfs'. '[B]ack in the Seventies, we had a closed door society. If you could afford it, you had a choice. But if you couldn't afford it, the council, the union, or the State made your choices for you.' 'I want services that put customers first and respond to their needs.' 'Of course that is why Labour oppose us. It is inconvenient for some of their union friends.' 'Labour would let the trade unions loose once again.' Major claimed Kinnock had told trade unionists 'you'll be all right, boys'. 'The British people are not ready to see the TUC limousines lined up in Downing Street.' 'A Labour vote gives you a Striker's Charter.' Labour had waged 'a bitter rearguard battle against the Right to Buy' because its 'concern is for the welfare of housing departments rather than for the tenants they so often neglect'. It would 'turn backwards into what even the Labour Leader admits is still the world of Clause IV—the world of outdated class divisions, the world of high taxes, state regulation and control'.

Socialism is over. It belongs to the past. It failed—totally. And it deserved to. In Eastern Europe, in its most brutal form, it suppressed human rights and dignity. In Britain, whenever Labour formed a government, it ended in incompetence, frustration and chaos.

'Labour are like Sunday converts. They come to church on the Sabbath—but boil the missionaries the rest of the week.' John Smith had called stable prices an 'unnecessary virtue'; 'those are the words of a shallow "chancellor"'. Major boasted he had 'secured stable exchange rates in the ERM—and we will keep our position there'. Cutting taxes 'is the greatest thing any government could do for the people'. 'Low tax creates wealth. So we cut income tax. We cut it, and cut it, and cut it, and cut it. We cut it, and cut it, and cut it again.' 'Now we are starting on the next stage of our mission—towards a 20 pence basic rate for all.'[20]

Major won (though only a twenty-one-seat majority) because the Conservatives remained the natural party of government (in power for seventy-eight of the 125 years from 1867 to 1992), believed to be better at managing the economy. But that reputation was crumbling. Major was obsessed with inflation. As Chancellor in October 1989 he declared: 'if policy isn't hurting, it isn't working'. He cut inflation from 10.9 per cent in

October 1990 to 3 per cent at the end of 1992 by raising interest rates to 15 per cent, justifying the pain by reference to ERM membership and the need to maintain parity with the Deutschmark. But there were huge costs. Housing prices tumbled, owners with negative equity could not sell, more than 70,000 mortgages were foreclosed in 1991, high mortgage payments curtailed consumer spending, the economy contracted 2.5 per cent from 1990 to 1992, and unemployment reached 10.4 per cent in the north in 1993. Public spending rose from 39.7 per cent of GDP in 1989–90 to 45 per cent in 1993–4, transforming a 1.5 per cent government surplus in 1989 into a 6 per cent deficit in 1992–3. Chancellor Norman Lamont quickly regretted his claim at the October 1991 party conference to have seen 'the green shoots of economic spring'. Most dramatically, after a desperate attempt to stay in the ERM, which cost Britain £16 billion in its final day, Lamont precipitately withdrew on Black Wednesday in September 1992. And after a campaign based on the spectre of Labour taxation, he raised taxes on alcohol and tobacco, increased the National Insurance contribution, reduced deductions, and extended VAT to domestic fuel and power. Replacing him a few months later, Kenneth Clarke 'discovered' a £50 billion deficit and further restricted deductions and imposed new taxes on insurance premiums and air travel—the largest peacetime increase—and froze public sector spending and wages for three years. Polls confirmed that voters had lost confidence in the Conservatives' economic competence.[21]

Thatcher's and Major's policies contained other contradictions central to questions of this book. Their ideologically driven 'politics of power' undermined their electoral 'politics of support'. Economic liberalization benefits consumers (at least in the short run), but it inevitably fosters concentration, endangering and ultimately eliminating the small entrepreneurs who are a core Conservative constituency. Harold Macmillan's repeal of resale price maintenance allowed supermarkets and discount retailers to drive out small shops. Farmers resented the elimination of price supports. The BMA denounced the internal market's 'competition culture'. But Conservative governments seemed indifferent to concentration. The OFT steadily raised the threshold for mergers it would review, with the result that the proportion it examined fell from half in 1979 to 20 per cent in 1989. During that decade it referred only eighty-six of the 2,400 mergers (0.035 per cent) to the Monopolies and Mergers Commission, which approved most of them. Lord Young resigned as DTI Secretary of State in July 1989 when the brewers prevailed against his recommendation that tied houses be abolished.

Liberalization had other perverse consequences. The 'Big Bang' embodied in the Financial Services Act 1986 allowed greater competition among retail, deposit-taking banks, building societies specializing in mortgage lending, discount houses bidding for Treasury bills, merchant banks advising companies, stockbrokers, and insurance companies; but it also saw prices for small consumers increase and required more regulation, a demand intensified by the collapse of Barlow Clowes and Levitt. Although Thatcher railed against quangos, reducing them from 2,167 in 1979 to 1,539 in 1990, they increased to 2,134 by 1993, employing 1.5 million staff and spending £43 billion—a fifth of public expenditure and a larger share than in 1979. Efforts to create an internal market in the NHS saw administrative costs triple from £158.8 million in 1989–90 to £494.2 million three years later. Nor was this a true market: most purchasers could look to only one hospital provider. As a result, the health budget increased by 6.0 and 6.2 per cent in 1991–2 and 1992–3.[22]

If Government accepted and even encouraged concentration, it was increasingly suspicious of restrictive practices. As Minister without Portfolio, Lord Young issued a White Paper in 1985 criticizing anti-competitive self-regulation by the professions, including opticians and lawyers. In April 1987 DGFT Sir Gordon Borrie called the 1956 Restrictive Trade Practices Act ineffective. 'The obvious alternative is to prohibit agreements which restrict or prevent competition....' The following March he issued a Green Paper declaring that 'the promotion of competition...is at the root of the Government's economic philosophy' and 'since it is anti-competitive agreements which have to be suppressed, the law should be targeted on these at the outset', prohibiting price-fixing, collusive tendering, market sharing, restrictions on information, and refusal to supply or deal with suppliers. His July 1989 White Paper urged that a new restrictive practices tribunal be empowered to impose fines up to £250,000 or 10 per cent of turnover.[23]

Laissez faire not only accelerated concentration but also undermined tradition, which Conservatives were pledged to defend. A senior high Tory delineated 'the real line of cleavage' in the party 'between those who want to sell off every cathedral close to Tescos in the name of the free market, and those who want to preserve them in the name of being British....'[24] Lord Hailsham embodied this contradiction. He was the only member of Heath's cabinet whom Thatcher reappointed (as Lord Chancellor). He praised her for being 'the first leader of the Conservative Party to draw the correct lessons' from 'the ratchet effect of socialism', which inevitably tended toward 'an Eastern-type "people's democracy"'. '[T]he only way out of this dilemma was to roll back the frontiers of the socialist state during the periods of Conservative government' by 'turning the Conservative Party from its traditional conservatism into a party of change committed to a reversal of its natural role and to turning back the whole bias of society to something nearer the ideal of the liberals of the previous century'. Yet two years into Thatcher's administration Hailsham joined four other wets in deploring the rise in unemployment (provoking her to fire Gilmoure, Carlisle, and Soames and transfer Prior).

Looking back in 1990, Hailsham (one of the most vehement critics of the Green Papers and Courts and Legal Services Bill) expressed the concerns of 'a conservative with a small as well as a large "c"'. He had 'instinctively more sympathy with those who stress the need for continuity, durability and precision in a legal system than with the enthusiasts for legislation as the automatic response to the identification of any perceived need or social anomaly'. If change was unavoidable, the correct process was 'fairly clearly laid down'. '[Y]ou begin with preliminary identification of a problem. You then start work with questionnaires directed to interested persons or bodies.' He shared the conviction of all post-war Lord Chancellors that 'the most important function of their office' was not law reform but 'to maintain the independence, integrity and impartiality of the judiciary'. For this it was 'essential...to retain the confidence of the profession and the judiciary' and resist the 'elective dictatorship' of an 'inextricably intertwined' executive and legislature increasingly sensitive 'to passing waves of popular emotion'.

Hailsham was particularly protective of the professional classes, 'the Cinderellas of the modern economic scene...without a Prince Charming to protect them'. Their 'somewhat arcane ethical rules...can easily be misrepresented as restrictive practices', but 'for the most part' they 'are really imposed in the interest of professional integrity and consumer protection'. Given the 'inherent danger of corruption and dishonesty' in litigation, he felt 'we are insufficiently aware of the extent that our own professionals... show a shining example to the rest of the world', which 'is a direct product of the particular internal arrangements which excite most criticism....' Although the divided profession, 'like Topsy, has largely growed, I cannot myself see that any positive advantage to the public is likely to occur by attempting to blur the separation of functions between them'. (After Hailsham died in 2001, Lord Heseltine said 'Lady Thatcher was wary of him. He was one of the people she was not prepared to take on or counter'. Lawson, her Chancellor, also 'saw little point in opening up the issue [of reforming lawyers] while Quintin Hailsham was Lord Chancellor'.)[25]

C. Old Labour

If the Conservative programme contained contradictions undermining its electoral support, Labour's political problems were chronic and seemingly insoluble. It was deeply divided between an old left (riven by conflict between trade unionists and Militant Tendency) and a new left fragmented into social movements: anti-nuclear, environmental, feminist, anti-racist, gay and lesbian, single parents, tenants. Labour's 1974 election manifesto promised a 'fundamental and irreversible shift in the balance of power and wealth in favour of working people and their families', including further nationalization. The 1981 defection of four leaders to launch the Social Democratic Party threatened Labour with permanent minority status (while foreshadowing the political reorientation of New Labour). Yet its 1983 election manifesto remained steadfast: withdrawal from the EEC, unilateral disarmament, and the expansion of public ownership and spending. The result was disastrous: just 28 per cent of the electorate, down from 40 per cent in 1974, and its lowest proportion since 1918. A higher percentage of skilled workers voted Conservative (forty versus thirty-two), as did a significant percentage of trade unionists (thirty-two versus thirty-nine).[26]

Labour began to change its strategy when Thatcher sought an unprecedented third term in 1987. It portrayed her as uncaring, producing a television commercial of slum schools lacking adequate books, with the caption 'This is how Mrs Thatcher cares for your children's education', and noted that she and her ministers chose private schools and medicine for their families. The Iron Lady was unapologetic: 'I exercise my right as a free citizen to spend my own money in my own way, so that I can go on the day, at the time, to the doctor I choose and get out fast'. Another election film featured working-class men and women who were the first in their families to go to university. Kinnock identified Labour with such aspirations by talking of 'socialist individualism'. But Labour still lost, with just 31 per cent of the vote. The Conservatives were triumphant. Sir Geoffrey Howe, the Chancellor, claimed 'the establishment of a new national common ground of politics...there is no political, moral or intellectual challenge in sight....' Nigel Lawson declared that 'history will judge that intervention and planning were the aberration and that the market economy is the normal, healthy way of life'.[27]

The following year Labour published 'Democratic Socialist Aims and Values', reaffirming public ownership as the only way to protect 'each individual's right to control his or her own life, to have a say in the decisions by which he or she is affected, and to share fairly in the benefits to which... [he or she] contributes and is entitled', 'a basic protection against the concentration of social and economic power in the hands of a few'. It was 'immoral as well as irrational to distribute some goods and services according to the market principle'; these included health care, education, social services, housing, and transport. But Labour also launched a Policy Review, whose first paper began: 'Labour's aim is to develop a talent-based economy for the 1990s and beyond'. It sought greater flexibility in entry to and exit from the labour market. While endorsing universal benefits, it warned that Labour 'will not spend, nor will we promise to spend, more than Britain can afford'; any increase would have to reflect economic growth. Public ownership became a means, not an end, as the party hedged on renationalization; the state's role shrank to correcting market failure. Labour abandoned the Keynesian goal of full employment and looked to monetarism to control inflation. It repudiated unilateral disarmament. The independent Commission on Social Justice it initiated staked out an 'investors' future for Britain, between Thatcherite deregulators and radical levellers, which sought to equalize opportunity to promote efficiency at least as much as equity.[28]

Although Labour reached rough parity in the opinion polls with the Conservatives by mid-1988, Major won the 1992 election by playing on voters' fears of taxes and economic mismanagement. Following this fourth defeat, John Smith replaced Kinnock as leader. He had been on the right of the party, supporting Britain's entry to the ERM as shadow chancellor, and breaking with the big unions over a national minimum wage. But he was a cautious leader, telling the TUC 'Labour must not and will not sever its links with the trade union movement' and pledging full employment.[29]

D. Blair

Tony Blair's accession to the leadership following Smith's sudden death in 1994 rapidly accelerated the transformation. Blair had always been a centrist. As early as 1982 he declared that Labour needed to 'look for its political philosophy to something more sensitive, more visionary, in a word more modern, than Marxism'. Immediately after winning election to Parliament the following year he reiterated that 'the image of the Labour Party has got to be more dynamic, more modern. Over 50 per cent of the population are owner-occupiers—that means a change in attitude that we've got to catch up with.' After Labour's 1987 defeat he exhorted: 'to succeed we must have not just the appearance but the reality of being modern'. Becoming shadow energy secretary, he elevated consumer interests over the party's traditional constituencies: coal and nuclear power producers. As shadow employment secretary during Major's first term he opposed the closed shop (which he had endorsed five years earlier).[30]

Blair was also a pragmatist, more committed to wielding power than ideological purity. He observed in 1982 that the 'exercise of political judgement…means knowing when to fight and when to accept defeat. It acknowledges that not every compromise is a sell-out.' Four days after Smith's death he repeated: 'we should concede and move on—agree with the Conservatives where we could only lose, fight only where we could win'. During the next three years he elaborated this view:

There will, inevitably, be overlap between Left and Right in the politics of the twenty-first century. The era of the grand ideologies, all-encompassing, all-pervasive, total in their solutions, and often dangerous—is over.

Addressing the Newscorp Leadership Conference in Australia (successfully wooing Murdoch), he agreed the new right 'got certain things right—a greater emphasis on enterprise; rewarding not penalising success; breaking up some of the vested interests associated with state bureaucracy'. '[R]each-ing out' to a new electorate 'is not a jettisoning of principle'. 'To tie ourselves to the policy perspective of one era is to chain ourselves to history rather than to learn from it.' 'The process of what is called "modernisation" is in reality, therefore, the application of enduring, lasting principles for a new generation....' 'It is not destroying the Left's essential ideology: on the con-trary, it is retrieving it from an intellectual and political muddle.' A good example was Blair's neutralizing of Conservative claims to the law-and-order vote by coining the phrase: 'tough on crime, tough on the causes of crime'.[31]

Blair determinedly distanced himself from old Labour. He told the Confederation of British Industry he would 'get Labour out of outdated policy perspectives and the quasi-Marxist traditions of a small part of the party'. He repudiated the 'model of the corporate state popular a genera-tion ago. Today the role of government is not to command but to facilitate, and to do so in partnership with industry in limited but key areas.' In another speech he acknowledged that 'society changed. Alongside the vested interests of capital and wealth sat the vested interests of the state and the public sector—not always faithfully delivering what they were supposed to.'[32] Peter Mandelson and Roger Liddle, an important source of Blair's slogans and freer to send up trial balloons, explained that:

whereas the old left saw its job as to represent trade unions, pressure groups and the 'working class', and the right saw its role as to protect the rich together with powerful corporate interests, New Labour stands for the ordinary families who work hard and play by the rules.[33]

Blair's most dramatic rupture was revising Clause IV in his first year as leader. That foundation stone had committed the party since 1918 to 'com-mon ownership of production, distribution and exchange, and the best obtainable system of popular administration and control of each industry and service'. Blair substituted 'a dynamic economy, serving the public interest, in which the enterprise of the market and the rigour of competi-tion are joined with the forces of partnership and co-operation to produce the wealth the nation needs and the opportunity for all to work and pros-per, with a thriving private sector and high quality public services'. The National Executive Committee approved that by twenty-one votes to three and the membership by 85–15 per cent (though fewer than half voted). Instead of renationalizing 'natural' monopolies, Labour would foster competition and regulate where that was impossible.[34]

At the same time, Blair exaggerated his differences with a caricatured Thatcherism:

All around, people on this planet sing hymns of gratitude to the invisible hand of the market, as it brings equality and prosperity to all, as 'cascades of wealth' tumble down from generation to generation . . . it is the theatre of the politically absurd.

Individuals cannot buy 'rapid technological and economic change', 'a safe society', 'an option on whether we grow old'. Blair asserted his 'belief in society, working together, solidarity, cooperation, partnership'. 'This is my socialism . . . it is social-ism'. Government had to 'protect the ordinary against the abuse of power'. He denounced 'water, gas and electricity-company bosses, running monopoly services at our expense, awarding themselves massive salaries'. The Conservatives:

never wanted to bust the establishment, just buy their way into it. And the new establishment is not a meritocracy but a power elite of money-shifters, middle men and speculators—people whose self-interest will always come before the national or the public interest.

We still have hereditary peers voting on legislation in the House of Lords. Our legal system is a nest of restrictive practices. The old-boys network is much in evidence. The intake at Oxford and Cambridge from public schools has barely shifted in thirty years.

Mandelson and Liddle blamed Britain's decline on 'deep-seated institutional and interest-group resistance to modernisation throughout society—from the hold of vested interests over the education system to the grip of lawyers on the legal system'. 'Consistency of policy' had to prevail over 'interest-group claims . . . modernisation over privilege and out-of-date though sometimes cherished tradition'. Blair assured voters three days before the 1997 election: 'I am of the centre-left and I want the left to be part of this project. . . . I'm going to be a lot more radical in government than many people think.' At the party conference a year later he stressed Labour's differences from Conservatives: redistribution, social services, the minimum wage, and family tax credits.[35]

But focused on winning two terms (which Labour had never done), Blair was acutely aware of changes in the electorate. In the five years since the last defeat, the working class had declined from 36.9 to 34.1 per cent of the labour force, union membership from 29.5 to 27.3 per cent, and council tenants from 20.5 to 17 per cent. During the eighteen years of Conservative rule, the petty bourgeoisie had risen from 17.4 per cent of the electorate to 26.6 and the non-union salariat from 17.4 to 25.6. Blair recalled a voter who had switched from Labour to Conservative in 1992. 'His instincts were to get on in life. And he thought our instincts were to stop him.' At the same time, public opinion was moving toward Labour. Between 1979 and 1997 concern about union power declined (from 79 to 21 per cent), as did enthusiasm for tax cuts (from 34 to 7 per cent), while the desire for more public services grew (from 34 to 72 per cent). In the decade from 1987 to 1997 the belief that Labour looked after trade union interests fell from 67 to 31 per cent while the belief that Conservatives were the party of big business increased from 73 to 75 per cent.[36]

Determined not to repeat the mistakes of 1992, Blair assured the British American Chamber of Commerce a year before the election that Labour's aim was 'fair taxes, not high taxes...the days of reflex tax and spend politics are over'. He proposed to cut the lowest rate to fifteen or even ten pence and promised 'no return to...penal rates of high personal taxation' for the rich. He told voters the month before the election that Labour had 'put the final nail in the coffin of the old tax and spend agenda' by adopting the Conservatives' own spending ceilings and promising no tax increases for five years. Gordon Brown, who had been shadow Chancellor for five years, kept this promise. Partly for this reason, but also because Conservative tax increases and economic expansion swelled revenues and reduced social security payments, Brown was able to turn public sector net borrowing from 3.6 per cent in 1996–7 to a 2 per cent surplus in 1999–2000; spending for the first term was expected to average less than 40 per cent of GDP, compared with 44 per cent during the Conservatives' eighteen years. Brown initiated a three-year spending plan beginning in 1999, increasing health by £20 billion, education and science by £19 billion, housing by £4.4 billion, pensions by £2.5 billion, and transport by £1.7 billion. The 2000 Spending Review (presumably timed to influence the 2001 election) proposed another 1 per cent increase for both health care and education, funded in part by a 0.4 per cent reduction in social security.[37]

Because Labour's bond with the unions was the third strongest reason for voter aversion in 1992, Blair also distanced himself from them. Having won the party leadership with their support, he told the next TUC Congress: '[W]e will be the government and we will govern for the whole nation, not any vested interest within it'. A confidante explained that the unions 'are in continuing decline...have nowhere else to go but to Labour... [and] must not be brought into the central policy-making centres once Labour is in Government'. A few months later Blair told the 1996 party conference: 'there will be fairness not favours for employers and employees alike. The Labour government is not the political arm of anyone today other than the British people....' At the end of 1996 Brown told the CBI that Labour had 'no intention of importing any European-style legislation that would threaten jobs' (i.e. the Maastricht Treaty social chapter). The following March his foreword to the business manifesto promised Labour 'would not turn the clock back to the 1970s in industrial relations because we know that flexibility is vital for business to prosper'. 'It is business not government that creates lasting prosperity.' Just before the election Blair assured voters:

We will not be held to ransom by the unions....We will stand up to strikes. We will not cave in to unrealistic pay demands from anyone....Unions have no special role in our election campaign, just as they will get no special favours in a Labour Government.

When focus groups that night indicated that 'union domination is people's core fear of Labour', Blair reinforced his message the next day: 'Anyone who thinks Labour has made changes in the party to give it all away to the unions or anyone else does not know me'.

In power he warned the TUC that New Labour 'will keep the flexibility of the present labour market. It may make some shiver, but I tell you in the end it's warmer in the real world.' His 1998 book on the third way referred to unions only in connection with Old Left defence of 'producer interests' and 'armies of unionized male labour'. The *Fairness at Work* White Paper that year redirected attention from collective bargaining to state structuring of the work relationship, with an emphasis on individual rights. In his preface, Blair boasted the UK would still have 'the most lightly regulated labour market of any leading economy in the world'. Two years later he characterized trade unions as 'authors for individual empowerment...in increasing people's skills, in issues of pensions, helping with financial and legal problems'. TUC general secretary John Monks understandably felt 'that trade unions are, to coin a phrase "embarrassing elderly relatives" '.[38]

New Labour embraced the market almost as enthusiastically as did the Conservatives. As early as 1991 Blair pronounced 'a new economics of the public interest, which recognises that a thriving competitive market is essential for individual choice'. In a later speech he envisaged 'a new partnership between government and industry, workers and managers—not to abolish the market but to make it dynamic and work in the public interest'. His vision was intensely individualistic. Government should 'give people the education, skills, technical know-how to let their own enterprise and talent flourish in the new market place'. Mandelson and Liddle went further:

New Labour welcomes the rigour of competitive markets as the most efficient means of anticipating and supplying consumers' wants, offering choice and stimulating innovation. Competition is the only effective force that prevents capitalists opting for a quiet life and managers spending their afternoons on the golf course.

[New Labour recognized that] substantial personal incentives and rewards are necessary in order to encourage risk-taking and entrepreneurialism. Profit is not a dirty word—profits are accepted as the motor of private enterprise. Differences in income and personal spending power are the inevitable consequence of the existence of markets.[39]

But Labour also understood the need to regulate markets. Its 1996 manifesto declared that the economy would be 'run for the many and not for the few'. 'We will put the consumer first, so that companies make money by serving customers in a competitive market-place, not through regulatory protection.' It accused the Conservatives of protecting the monopolies of the privatized industries. Enthusing about the information highway (like his role model, Clinton), Blair declared that 'low barriers will mean new entrants and new services. As supply expands, prices will fall....' To encourage this 'Labour will promote universal access as soon as possible'. Its 1998 White Paper on competition policy sought to block anti-competitive agreements between companies and give the OFT greater enforcement power.[40]

If Labour was defensive about taxes and unions and a late and anomalous (if enthusiastic) convert to the market, it was the natural champion of social services. The electorate felt strongly that services had deteriorated under the Conservatives and disbelieved their promises to reform. But New Labour was bound by the constraints it had adopted to convince the electorate it was fiscally responsible. There would be 'no public-expenditure bonanza which permits greatly increased resources for public services'. Given the impossibility of providing universal high benefits on low taxes, New Labour advocated 'selective universalism'. At the same time, Blair deplored 'an education system where one part of the nation is taught apart from the other' and warned against the emergence of 'two classes of health service, two classes of state schools, two Britains—one on welfare; the other paying for it'.

Mandelson and Liddle maintained that:

> what is important is not just how much the public sector spends but how it is spent. Cutting waste and improving efficiency should be a priority, as should ensuring that public spending reaches the groups it is intended to benefit.

New Labour 'emphatically does not seek to provide centralised, "statist" solutions to every social and economic problem'. It preferred 'voluntary and community-based organisation'. The authors also called for 'a radical renegotiation of the relationship' with public sector professionals: 'independent outside inspection and tough, decisive action to remedy areas of service failure', extension of 'the principle of competency testing... particularly where standards of performance were perceived to be inadquate', and 'no job protection for professionals who consistently fail to deliver'. They hoped for 'the emergence of a new generation of "social entrepreneurs"—individuals motivated by the desire to serve the public, but keen to have the freedom to run their own show'.[41]

New Labour's concrete proposals for public services strikingly resembled the Conservatives'. At the 1994 launch of the final report of the Commission on Social Justice, Blair expressed interest in 'the recovery principle—i.e. that students themselves should, after they graduate and when they are in reasonably paid work, make a contribution to the system'. Two years later he advocated 'a fair balance in university funding between public subsidy and student contributions'. When the Dearing Committee (created by the Conservatives) recommended in July 1997 that students pay fees, Labour imposed a means-tested tuition and replaced maintenance grants with loans, tacitly abandoning its commitment to free higher education. It also continued Major's schools policies of parental choice, information, centralized standards, and accountability through league tables.[42]

Labour's 1992 election manifesto had promised to increase the child benefit and basic pension. The 1994 report of the Commission on Social Justice had embraced four principles: equal worth of all, rights to basic needs, redistribution of opportunity, and reduction of unjust inequalities. But Blair sounded even more neo-liberal on these benefits. Although 'our welfare state ... is one of our proudest creations ... it suffers from two major weaknesses: it does not alleviate poverty effectively and it does not properly assist the growth of independence'. Brown agreed that 'the welfare state must be about supporting people as they respond to these challenges—extending their choices and opportunities; acting as a trampoline rather than as a safety net'. Just months after the election, Harriet Harman announced that single parents would have their benefits reduced and be encouraged to work. Two years before being appointed Minister for Welfare Reform in 1997 Frank Field had denounced means tests, which 'penalise all those human attributes—such as hard work, work being adequately rewarded, savings, and honesty—which underpin a free, let alone a civilised society'. But now he succumbed to Treasury pressure to impose them. New Labour also abandoned the goal of universal adequate pensions, instead introducing tax incentives to encourage private supplementation. Sounding very much like Thatcher justifying her use of private health care, Mandelson and Liddle said 'this would give individuals freedom to choose when to retire and what type of provision they wish to make for the rest of their family'.[43]

Convinced that the electorate was angry at the deterioration of the NHS, Blair made (a caricature of) Conservative health policy a focus of his attacks. 'We created the NHS. We will save it.' '[A] market in health care does not work because health should be based on need not purchasing power. Those who enter the market with little or no money end up doing worse.' 'Health care is about team work, integration and sharing of information. How perverse then to have set up a market system which makes team work so difficult.' 'On-going treatment does not lend itself to the simple contract.' '[M]any of the transaction costs of the market are unnecessary.' 'The market is bad for patients and it [*sic*] worse for taxpayers.' 'Let the internal market that pits hospital against hospital cease.... Let the doctors do what the doctors should do: care for the sick, not be forced to make a business of them.' '[C]ompetition is not the best way of organising health services, which rely as they do on the creativity and dedication of all those in the service. Trust is a fragile thing. It takes years to build up; it can take seconds to destroy. Crude use of market mechanisms threatens to undermine that trust.' 'If doctors feel their clinical judgement is second-guessed by accountants then trust breaks down.' Blair promised 'an NHS rebuilt as a people's service, free of market dogma, but also free of the old and new bureaucratic constraints'.

But 'The New NHS—Modern, Dependable', promised in the 1997 White Paper, differed little from Major's. The majority of GPs who had become fundholders would join nurses and community health services in larger Primary Care Groups, which would enter long-term contracts with hospitals (now all trusts). Budgets would be capped (although Brown increased them). A National Institute for Clinical Excellence would develop standards for evidence-based medicine, and a Commission for Health Improvement would conduct annual appraisals of all clinicians.[44]

Although law had too little salience to warrant mention in the election manifesto, a 1996 book presented Labour's law reform proposals. In the foreword, Blair accused the Conservatives of shrinking legal aid coverage from 79 per cent of the population in 1979 to just 48 per cent. But instead of promising more money, he advocated ADR, elimination of 'restrictive practices in the profession', and a 'community legal service which will be more responsive to the needs of the consumer rather than the lawyer'.

Lord Irvine, the shadow Lord Chancellor (and one of Blair's closest advisers), reiterated the criticisms of eligibility. Because expenditures had stopped rising there was 'no current imperative for cost capping the legal aid budget' as proposed by Lord Mackay's Green Paper, which 'has the fingerprints of the Treasury all over it'. 'Capping signifies an abandonment of an entitlement basis for the grant of legal aid, based on merits. . . . It will in practice become a discretionary benefit, available at bureaucratic disposal. . . .' He was sceptical of conditional fees and thought the 100 per cent uplift too high. The denial of legal aid in tribunals 'cannot rationally be justified'. '[T]here is no greater unfairness than the legally unrepresented applicant against the legally represented employer in industrial tribunals.' But though he promised 'to restore legal aid to the status of a public social service which is so highly regarded for its economy and efficiency in securing access to justice that . . . it can compete for scarce resources with the most highly regarded services such as health', he also warned that 'Labour will have no new money to throw at problems whose solution calls for structural change'. Courts and lawyers should put 'their houses in order'. The community legal service would deploy 'a much greater proportion of publicly funded services through CABs, law centres and the advice agencies'. Ross Cranston (who became Blair's Solicitor-General) reaffirmed 'the plain economic fact . . . that no government, including a Labour government, can fund without limit a system which is largely driven, as is traditional legal aid, by market forces'.[45]

New Labour was treason to those on the left: 'the Thatcherisation of the Labour Party' for Tony Benn, fatalistic Thatcherism for Stuart Hall. Arthur Scargill observed in 1996: 'If the church to which you went decided to stop worshipping God and started worshipping the devil, you should have second thoughts'. A few months later Tony Callaghan declared that Labour's alliance with the trade unions 'is part of our heritage and it is instinctive in our party and movement that we should keep the link'. Two years later Roy Hattersley said: 'If Christians sat down to invent a new religion and decided that the Sermon on the Mount was incompatible with the global economy we would conclude that they had ceased to be Christians'. Just before the 1997 election Margaret Thatcher disloyally commented: Blair 'won't let Britain down'. Just after it William Rees-Mogg pronounced: 'Thatcherism is safe with New Labour: that is the core message'. A year later Lord Rothermere, owner of the *Daily Mail*, said: 'I joined New Labour because that was obviously the New Conservative party'.[46]

Mandelson and Liddle had claimed: 'New Labour dumps the ideological baggage of the past to offer new solutions based not on dogma but on a simple test: What will deliver results?' It certainly delivered. Its 1997 May Day victory broke multiple records: Labour's largest share of the vote (43.2 per cent) since 1966, its largest ever number of seats, largest majority (the largest of any party since the 1935 National government), largest percentage swing (double Thatcher's in 1979) and gain in seats. The Conservatives held fewer seats and received a smaller share of the vote than they had since the 1830s, none in Scotland or Wales, and only seventeen of the 172 urban seats. Labour defeated seven Conservative former cabinet members (including Michael Portillo and Norman Lamont). It won the suburbs and the South. The swing spanned all demographic categories, making this the least class-aligned election of modern times. Labour won 60 per cent of manual workers but also 40 per cent of professional and managerial workers. Women, who had favoured Conservatives by 15 per cent, now favoured Labour by 20. At the same time, the turnout (71.4 per cent) was the lowest since the War.

One reason for the sweep was the shift in media alignment. Conservative newspapers had three times the readership of the Labour press; but the gap narrowed after 1992 and reversed in 1995. The *Sun* blamed Major for Black Wednesday. All the tabloids featured the numerous Conservative sex and corruption scandals. Mandelson and Liddle courted Murdoch, and Blair met him in 1995. In the 1997 election six of the ten national dailies and five of the nine Sundays endorsed Labour. At the beginning of the campaign the *Sun* told its 10 million readers that Blair was 'a breath of fresh air'. On the last Sunday of the campaign the *News of the World*, another Murdoch paper, endorsed Blair. The *Independent* was anti-Conservative (if not pro-Labour); and *The Times* backed the Eurosceptics. Only the *Daily Telegraph* and the *Mail* stayed loyal to Major.

The Conservatives could not even capitalize on the facts that the economy was growing, inflation low, unemployment the lowest in Europe and decreasing, and the balance of payments almost equal; interest rates were low and housing prices rising; and spending on public services had increased. Major had fatally lost credibility by raising interest rates, deflating the economy, precipitately quitting the ERM, and raising taxes. He waged another negative campaign, with posters warning: 'Britain Is Booming—Don't Let Labour Blow It' and 'New Labour, New Danger'. This time, however, the electorate believed neither his record nor his promises.[47]

Four years later Labour lost only 2.4 per cent of the vote and just six seats; the Conservatives gained only 1.3 per cent and a single seat. Nearly five million fewer people bothered to vote, cutting the turnout to 59 per cent, the worst since 1918 (during the First World War). Foot and mouth disease overshadowed the NHS; unemployment and the economy were much less salient. The media overwhelmingly supported Blair; only the *Daily Mail, Daily Telegraph,* and *Sunday Times* backed the Conservatives. Class allegiances weakened further; there was no gender gap despite the much larger proportion of Labour MPs who were women; but younger voters strongly favoured Labour. Although voters expected Labour to increase taxes, they were prepared to pay more for better services. Almost half disbelieved Labour was still controlled by the unions. Blair had convinced voters Labour was New (a word he had used 107 times in the 'Road to the Manifesto' and thirty-seven times in his first speech to the 1995 party conference as leader).[48]

E. Politics and Lawyers

What does this highly selective political history reveal about the motivations of the Thatcher, Major, and Blair Governments? The first rupture, Lord Mackay's Green Papers, occurred in Thatcher's third term, when she may have been less concerned about political costs. It strongly expressed her style: confident, confrontational, provocative, a deliberate break with the past. It followed attacks on other state-supported institutions, including universities, media, and the arts.[49] Thatcher displayed the anger of an outsider: from lower-middle class origins in a party led by the privileged, a dissenter from an established church sometimes called the Tory party at prayer. (In these traits she resembled Richard Nixon; both provoked attack in order to feel beleaguered.) Although no feminist, she was still a woman in a man's world: at Oxford (especially reading chemistry), at the Bar, and in politics. Although she never wrote about it, her experience as a barrister (called nine years before entering Parliament) cannot have been happy (and her tax specialty further marginalized her). Although she did not choose the Finchley constituency, she strongly identified with its Jewish population, valued the Chief Rabbi's support, and surrounded herself with clever iconoclasts—who just happened to be Jews.

Once she decided to extend her spring cleaning to lawyers, she clearly had to replace Lord Hailsham (who was eager to retire). A passionate champion of the Bar, he approached all problems 'conservatively' by consulting existing institutions—a recipe for incrementalism. He believed the Lord Chancellor's paramount consideration should be to retain the confidence of the legal profession, whose restrictive practices ensured the integrity essential to consumers, and to protect the independence of the judiciary in the face of an 'electoral dictatorship' in which one party (only temporarily his own) dominated both executive and legislature. Yet Thatcher's selection of the equally establishment Lord Havers suggests that her third election victory had not yet committed her to an assault on lawyers. (During the 1989 Green Papers debate he said that when he had been appointed he was unpersuaded by arguments for extended audience rights.[50]) His replacement by Lord Mackay four months later set the stage for radical rethinking. Mackay had read and then taught maths at university, as Thatcher had read and worked in chemistry, before each turned to the Bar (which may have imbued both with faith in systematic theory). As a Scottish advocate, Mackay also was an outsider. As a Wee Free, he was a dissenter (and a sabbatarian, like Thatcher). Like Thatcher (and unlike Hailsham and Havers), he came from a modest background. Within a year he appeared to have formulated his basic position on reform of the legal profession.

Even if Thatcher displayed a consistent animus against tradition and the establishment, the legal profession was an unlikely object (which may explain why she waited ten years to confront it). She began with other targets. Like her friend Ronald Reagan and her protégé John Major, she mistrusted the state as inherently less efficient than business, always a source of constraint, never liberation. Because marriage to a successful businessman let her experience the market as a domain of choice she extolled the freedom to buy—private health care, for instance (oblivious to the fact that the market offered most people only the freedom that Anatole France parodied: to go without). She saw labour as a commodity like any other (exactly what Marx criticized in *Capital*). Doing to Marx what he claimed to have done to Hegel, she attacked communism for benefiting the few (*apparatchiki*) at the expense of the many and saw capitalism as the rising tide that lifts all members of an enterprise (disregarding that CEOs earn hundreds of times as much as workers). Indeed, both Thatcher and Major equated their defeats of Labour with the collapse of communism.

Thatcher was a true believer in the market (rare among economists other than her guru, von Hayek). It offered choice to consumers, ensuring efficient allocation of resources. Whereas the state made disastrous mistakes, the market decentralized decision-making, reducing the risk of error. The market's hand was not only invisible but also inexorable, a natural law (like those of chemistry). She even endowed it with moral force. Her Government's success in crushing the miners' strike (by widespread use, even abuse, of police power) demonstrated the inevitability of market forces (which would not tolerate unprofitable industries). She identified free societies with free markets (disregarding unfree laissez faire societies like Singapore and the freedoms of precapitalist societies, or even pre-Thatcher Britain). With the neophyte's oversimplification, she (and her acolytes) believed that the success of competition in reducing the price of spectacles, or even services like telephones and air travel (which were purchased repeatedly and whose quality could be evaluated cheaply, objectively, and in advance) could easily be extrapolated to radically different domains: education, health care, and ultimately law. Hence the attempt to replicate the 'choice' shoppers experience in supermarkets or department stores in the context of schools or medicine. Sometimes this was little more than rhetoric, as when primary care providers had only one choice of hospital or specialist doctor. It always ignored information asymmetries.

Health care offered the greatest challenge to the Conservative commitment to substitute market for state. Thatcher railed against the 'restrictive practices and other inefficiencies in the medical profession'. The British Medical Association was just another Labour-backed trade union, whose power she was determined to break. Convinced that it oppressed doctors (as all unions did their members), she (mistakenly) expected them to repudiate it for resisting her market reforms. Both Thatcher and Major pitted the mass of general practitioners against the consultant-dominated hospitals. But the health care reforms failed politically. Costs continued to rise. The ideal of entrepreneurship, which Conservatives extolled in private markets, created 'supplier-induced demand' for public services like health care. It also undermined the ideal of a professional dedicated to the client's interest and indifferent to personal gain. The public suspected the Conservatives of disloyalty to the NHS, by far the best-loved social service.

I can only speculate about the lessons Thatcher drew from this experience when she turned to lawyers. (Lord Mackay initiated the most dramatic changes in the profession during his three years as Thatcher's Lord Chancellor, although he served under Major for another seven. Indeed, Major's apparent lack of interest in lawyers may explain why the bench and Bar managed to obstruct the extension of audience rights.) Thatcher may (rightly) have thought that lawyers were much less popular than doctors and Labour would not support the Bar Council and Law Society (or would suffer politically for doing so). By making audience rights the most visible legal reform, Thatcher may have hoped (correctly) to split the mass of solicitors away from the much less numerous barristers (although the proposal of corporate conveyancing compromised this strategy). But whereas general medical practitioners merely rationed consultant and hospital services, solicitors (and employed barristers) were encouraged to displace barristers—a far more threatening proposition, which generated vigorous and temporarily successful opposition from bench and Bar.

The Conservatives' market reforms generated other problems. They glorified materialism and greatly exacerbated inequality. They accelerated the tendency toward concentration inherent in all capitalist economies. The Tory ideal is the small businessman (like Thatcher's grocer father). But the elimination of resale price agreements by the post-war Conservatives allowed supermarkets to drive many small grocers out of business (just as the City giants and regional consortia have overshadowed high-street solicitors' firms and hired the best law graduates, and barristers, although nominally sole practitioners, function within ever larger and more collectivized chambers). The privatization of nationalized industries created monopolies, distorting market forces and producing inefficient outcomes (while also giving the Bar ammunition for its critique of the 'nationalization' of the prosecutorial function in the CPS). The irreducible (and growing) asymmetries of information attending the proliferation and refinement of expert services and the difficulty of creating shadow markets for public services (like education, health, and legal aid) and of correcting the market imperfections generated by concentration and monopoly forced Conservative governments committed to shrinking the state instead to create and elaborate regulatory mechanisms: centralized standards, audit, and evaluation. Hence the marketization of the legal profession paradoxically required greater state involvement in the qualification and training of lawyers, recognition of specializations, levels of remuneration, regulation of misconduct, even self-governance.

The Conservatives were determined to control, even contract, the social service budget for reasons that were ideological as well as economic. They were hostile to welfare services, which they accused of fostering dependence on the state (while seeing nothing wrong in the way the market forced non-earners—women, children, the elderly—to depend on relatives). They perversely maligned the welfare state as a 'closed door society' (although it had opened the door to health care, education, housing, and subsistence for millions). They blamed it for limiting choice (obscuring the choice it had conferred on most for the first time). Inverting the course of history, they equated the welfare state's efforts to correct market imperfections with the feudal paternalism the market had supplanted. Thatcher repackaged selfishness as family responsibility. Conservatives opposed welfare's redistributive effects. Pensions should reflect lifetime earnings rather than guarantee an adequate income to all. Major, who had inherited nothing, perversely wanted to abolish the inheritance tax so that wealth would 'cascade down the generations'. He was even more insistent than Thatcher on cutting taxes and reducing inflation.

But the recession of the late 1980s and early 1990s (and the business downsizing that accompanied it) increased unemployment and hence social security payments while decreasing tax revenues. Because it would have been political suicide to cut the most popular and expensive social services—health and education—the Conservatives attacked the more marginal. Legal aid was an obvious target: most people used it rarely or never, the most visible beneficiaries were unpopular (criminal accused, immigrants), lawyers were associated with chicanery rather than justice (especially in criminal defence), and a few earned extraordinary incomes. If the impact on government spending was trivial, controlling legal aid expenditures at least justified cuts in more popular programmes.

Conservatives also were intensely hostile to unions for many reasons. The party extolled individualism and suspected collectivism, which could only inhibit freedom. Thatcher denied the very existence of society; her horizon was limited to families and neighbours. Conservatives blamed unions for ratcheting up wages and fuelling inflation. They accused unions of restrictive practices: entry controls, featherbedding. Unions sought to 'defy the laws of economics'. Conservatives rightly saw unions as both supporting Labour (politically and economically) and exercising disproportionate influence over its policies. Union limousines in Downing Street would dominate a Labour Government (while those of capitalists presumably exercised a benign effect on Conservative governments). The Conservatives charged Labour with favouring (organized) producers over (unorganized) consumers. Correctly perceiving that voters increasingly saw themselves more as consumers than producers, the Conservatives championed homeowners over coal miners, commuters over transport workers, patients over health care providers, and pupils and parents over teachers and educational administrators. In another post-Marxist inversion they defined consumers, not workers, as the universal class.

These were electorally popular positions in the aftermath of the 1978–9 winter of discontent. But the Conservatives went further. The real workplace conflict was not between labour and capital (which Thatcher misrepresented as equally interested in profitability) but between workers and union bosses. Workers were exploited not by capitalists but by union officials (who misused their dues). The most egregious violation of democracy occurred not in the capitalist enterprise (which totally disenfranchised workers) but in the union (which voted with insufficient frequency or transparency). Workers would repudiate unions if free to do so. Weakening the unions was one of Thatcher's primary goals during her first two terms.

Thus Thatcher's decision to attack lawyers' restrictive practices was at least consistent with her ten years in office. The profession, especially the Bar, represented the establishment, the forces of tradition. It obstructed entry and advancement (in ways she may have experienced) and artificially inflated prices. It limited consumer choice. Thatcher may well have seen both the Bar Council and the Law Society as little more than glorified trade unions, like the British Medical Association. She may have confronted them out of ideological consistency, as well as to forestall accusations of class bias. And though legal services were not a significant item of public expenditure, price reductions achieved by eliminating restrictive practices would lower the cost of both prosecution and legal aid. At a time when her voter appeal was waning, lawyers were a popular whipping-boy. The press, presumably intuiting public sentiment, cheered her assault.

If the question for Thatcher is why Conservatives turned against a natural constituency, the question for Blair is why Labour acquiesced in opposition and adopted similar policies in power. One response is to reject the question: since Labour was congenitally suspicious of lawyers (by reason of their class origins, privilege, innate conservatism, and defence of state and capital), it had no reason to demur when the Conservatives attacked them. Labour always presented itself as the party of modernity rather than tradition (which it blamed for Britain's economic decline), the champion of the general good over special interests (of which the professions were notorious examples).

But though Labour was predisposed to see lawyers as a problem, it might be expected to disagree with Conservatives about the solution. Nevertheless, eighteen years of Conservative rule had fundamentally changed the political terrain. Labour was not instinctively anti-state, like Thatcher; but it increasingly acknowledged that governmental solutions created new problems. Blair deplored the 'vested interests of the state and the public sector—not always faithfully delivering what they were supposed to' and called for 'breaking up some of the vested interests associated with state bureaucracy'. By revising Clause IV, he dramatically repudiated the statist solution of re-nationalization. This at least raised doubts about Labour's loyalty to the legal aid scheme. By extending Conservative policies that shifted the cost of social services from taxpayers to beneficiaries—in higher education and private pensions, for instance—Labour created precedents for its decision to transfer the cost of money actions from the legal aid scheme to the parties through conditional fees and legal expenses insurance.

Most surprising, perhaps, was Labour's embrace of laissez faire. After all, socialists saw the labour market as inherently exploitative, enriching capitalists by extracting surplus value from exploited workers. And Labour knew that the free market had catastrophically failed to deliver what Franklin Roosevelt (who founded the American welfare state) called 'the necessities of life' to 'one third of a nation ill-housed, ill-clad, ill-nourished'.[51] Indeed, Labour consistently attacked Conservative market-fetishism. Blair's examples of the public goods the market could not provide, however, were not those necessities but rather technological innovation and domestic and foreign security. Justice was strikingly absent. Although Blair played on voter loyalties to the NHS by attacking the Conservatives for creating an 'internal market', he left it largely unchanged. Blair shared the Conservative belief that a market whose imperfections had been corrected by judicious state intervention remained the best way to distribute most goods and services. (He was even less troubled than Conservatives that the necessary regulatory apparatus would expand rather than contract the state.) Thatcher was right: even Labour had to accept the 'natural law' of the market, in which removing restrictions on supply inevitably would lower price.

Labour preserved the Conservatives' emphasis on consumer choice of health care, housing, education (including university), even pensions, which laid the foundation for giving parties a similar 'choice' to litigate (by purchasing the insurance necessary in conditional fee cases) and select an adviser or representative (solicitor, barrister, or layperson, privately practising or employed). Believing that traditional Labour voters found the party hostile to individual initiative, Blair vied with the Conservatives in championing entrepreneurship, striving. Indeed, he converted Labour from a party of collective mobility to a party of individual success, epitomized by the right to accumulate and spend personal wealth. The party championed a future of 'investors' in individual human capital. Unions ceased to be vehicles of solidarity, institutions for group action, especially in the class struggle, and became mechanisms enabling workers to assert their individual legal rights. At the same time, Blair sought to associate Conservatives with old-boy networks, the establishment. It was a natural step to attacking the professions as bastions of privilege.

Labour had a more complex relationship with trade unions than did the Conservatives. On one hand, it could not simply wage war against them. Beyond the powerful historical and ideological links, Labour still depended heavily on union financial support. But Blair was determined not to lose anti-union voters because of the union connection; and a cynical Labour strategist correctly observed that trade unionists had nowhere to go (except apathy, which may have accounted for declining voter turnout). In any case, the connection between class and voting was steadily weakening. Labour had been a party of workers allied against capital; New Labour was a party of consumers (since everyone was a consumer) allied against producers (now maligned as special interests).[52] Blair's 'social-ism' had nothing to do with production, everything to do with consumption. (As shadow energy secretary he anticipated this switch by siding with those paying heating bills over coal miners.) Thus, just as Thatcher may have felt that consistency required her to attack professional cartels as well as trade unions, so Blair may have wanted to soften his coolness towards the unions by confronting restrictive practices in professions. Although (perhaps because) Blair, like Thatcher, had been a barrister, he was intensely suspicious of lawyers, assailing their 'grip . . . on the legal system' (as though that were surprising, or pernicious). Labour's 1996 manifesto 'Law Reform Now' promised to free law from lawyers so it could better serve consumers.

Labour was as determined as the Conservatives to rein in expenditure on social services—perhaps even more so because of its reputation as a tax-and-spend party. In order to win the 1997 election, Gordon Brown adopted the Conservative budget and promised not to increase taxes for five years. In pursuit of a second term, he raised spending on health and education, forcing cuts in other social services. New Labour clearly made an electoral calculation to expand 'universal' benefits (disproportionately consumed by the middle class) at the expense of means-tested services for the poor (welfare, legal aid). Blair sought to distinguish himself from the Conservatives by vigorously championing the NHS. 'Health should be based on need not purchasing power'; 'on-going treatment does not lend itself to the simple contract'; medical care requires 'creativity and dedication'. But Labour rejected the obvious parallels to legal services. Indeed, its 1996 manifesto adamantly declared there would be no additional money for them. Ross Cranston accused them of being 'largely driven...by market forces'—presumably another term for 'supplier-induced demand'. Labour's emphasis on prioritizing legal aid clients and substantive areas was consistent with its emphasis on social exclusion in welfare, education, and criminal justice. Labour also adopted the Conservative view that ending restrictive practices would significantly reduce costs to legal aid as well as private clients. And Labour jettisoned the scepticism about conditional fees it had expressed in opposition, promoting them as expressions of individual choice.

Labour's conversion to laissez faire offers some evidence for the hegemony of the market (as both ideology and practice) and the convergence between the two parties.[53] And its campaign to cap the legal aid budget and shift some of the cost to the litigants reflects both electoral strategy and its determination to direct limited social services to areas of greatest need. With this brief history of motivations, electoral strategies, and policies, we can turn to the way that parties, lawyers, clients, and the media played the politics of professionalism in the 1990s.

2   An Unlikely Revolutionary

> The Green Papers propose 'radical' reforms 'going to the very root of the question'. [Lord Mackay]
>
> They are 'one of the most sinister documents ever to emanate from Government'. 'Oppression does not stand on the doorstep with a tooth-brush moustache and a swastika armband. It creeps up insidiously....' [Lord Lane]
>
> They are a 'woefully uninformed...mass of claptrap and many platitudes'. [Lord Hutchinson]
>
> The Lord Chancellor has 'run at these things like a bull in a china shop'. [Lord Hailsham]
>
> 'Get your tanks off my lawn'. [Lord Donaldson]
>
> 'This dirigiste policy [is] more suited to a Marxist government....' [Lord Benson]

Toward the end of the 1980s the English legal profession could congratulate itself on having survived two decades of critical scrutiny virtually unchanged. Four books published in 1967–8—one by American legal academics, three by English academics with American experience—had ended a century of complacency.[1] A few years later two government reports urged elimination of some professional monopolies and radical reform of legal education.[2] Within ten years an English legal academic exposed *The Politics of the Judiciary*, a solicitor condemned the *Conveyancing Fraud*, a barrister put *The Bar on Trial*, and a lawyer and a sociologist unmasked the *Images of Law*.[3] Organizations like Justice, the Haldane Society, Society of Labour Lawyers, Consumers' Association (CA), National Consumer Council (NCC), and Legal Action Group (LAG) sought to translate criticism into reform. Other government critiques of restrictive practices culminated in Labour's creation of a Royal Commission on Legal Services.[4] In its wake, academics, journalists, and practising lawyers exposed anachronistic traditions and restrictive practices, the customs of barristers' clerks, and solicitor sexism.[5]

Despite the clamour, the Royal Commission gave the profession a clean bill of health, and the subsequent Conservative Government embraced its anodyne recommendations.[6] When Labour backbencher Austin Mitchell won a low lottery number for a first reading of the CA-drafted Home Buyers' Bill in 1983, which would have ended the solicitors' conveyancing monopoly, and a surprising affirmative vote following the Second Reading, the Government responded with the Administration of Justice Act 1985, creating a new occupation of licensed conveyancer, and the Building Societies Act 1986, which allowed lenders to convey, but only for non-borrowers. Mitchell's Legal Profession Reform Bill 1985 went nowhere. And when solicitors reacted to the minimal threat to conveyancing by seeking expanded audience rights, the Marre Committee endorsed the status quo.[7]

Yet warning signals remained. Thatcher began her third term by replacing Lord Hailsham, the twentieth century's longest serving Lord Chancellor and the Bar's staunch defender, with Lord Havers. Chancellor Nigel Lawson asked Havers to prepare a paper on reforming the legal profession for the competition policy sub-committee of the Cabinet's economic committee, which Lawson chaired. But the former Attorney-General's paper 'read as if it had been written entirely by his officials. It was a thoroughly complacent document, which concluded that there was no case for change of any kind.' When ill-health forced Havers to resign in four months, Thatcher appointed Lord Mackay. Lawson found his paper 'totally different from its predecessor... remarkably radical... [but] cautious and measured'. Mackay 'looked at the matter afresh, and thought through his position from first principles'. 'The subsequent Cabinet discussion was prolonged but, with Margaret's unqualified support, the proposals emerged unscathed.'[8]

Only a year after taking office, and three months after the Marre Committee reported, Lord Mackay asked the Bar's annual conference whether its 'sole preserve', including 'all work done in the Crown Court', was 'really appropriate for a specialist profession?' Such monopolies 'can only be justified by careful attention not to self-interest... but to the interests of the public'. His widely reported speech warned against 'ignor[ing] change'. Somewhat prematurely, the *Evening Standard* called for fusion. The 'two highly expensive closed shops... only double the cost and delay which are now endemic in law'. The *Guardian* lauded this new 'consumer's champion' for defying 'the religious fervour with which lawyers will protect their hallowed restrictive practices' and denounced 'the Spanish Customs of the profession'.[9]

The BC chair could only agree that 'the overriding consideration must be what is best for the public'. But three weeks later Law Society President Richard Gaskell told its annual conference he had felt 'for some time that what is required is a complete reorganisation of the profession so that everybody starts off as a solicitor and only goes on to consultant status as a barrister later'. Solicitors should immediately have Crown Court audience rights, not as 'a matter of status' but as 'a matter of justice for our clients; a matter of efficiency and value for money in the courts'. 'We face the competitive present and future with our own house largely in order. It is time the Bar did the same.' He broke a long tradition by not inviting the BC chair to open the second day of the conference.[10]

A. The Green Papers

Within a week Mackay promised three Green Papers in the new year examining 'the fundamental issues of what activities require the services of lawyers and on what basis such services ought ideally to be provided'. While not favouring 'change for change's sake', he reported public complaints 'about delays'. Gaskell said solicitors were 'happy to be the subject of modernisation'. Assistant Secretary-General Walter Merricks added: 'the legal profession richly deserves a kick in the pants'. The *Solicitors Journal* urged that 'the medicine...be swallowed as soon as possible'. But the Bar complained that Thatcher was pressuring Mackay to treat the professions as trade unions. Its chair denied that 'any of the rules of the Bar were restrictive practices against the interests of the public' and did 'not accept we are operating a monopoly'. The Bar 'is already about the most competitive business that there is'. John Mortimer (Rumpole's creater) had never heard of a 'bent barrister. But I have heard of bent solicitors.' Louis Blom-Cooper QC warned that fusion would lead to an 'inability to control the profession', as shown by the 'extremes of advice available' in the United States. BC chair-elect Desmond Fennell QC predicted the 'disaster' of large 'US-style' firms hiring all the advocates. Lord Denning said Mackay's 'trial balloon' was 'filled with hot air'. The 'appalling suggestion' of contingency fees would lead to 'an American nightmare' in which lawyers 'cook the witnesses' and fabricate 'excessive damages'. The Bar even enlisted Warren Burger, former U.S. Supreme Court Chief Justice, to display his Anglophilia: English litigation was much faster 'in large part because... three highly trained professionals conduct the affair'. Fusion in the United States 'gravely impairs the administration of justice'.[11]

Across the political spectrum the press cheered this 'radical' 'shake-up' of lawyers' 'closed shop'. Ending the Bar's monopoly, pronounced the *Evening Standard*, would 'do most to render the law and the courts accessible to ordinary people'. Although 'English lawyers still beat all records for resisting change', the *Economist* predicted barristers were 'likely to lose their battles'. The *Guardian* complained that the Royal Commission had been 'nobbled by the profession'. In the subsequent nine years the 'Old Boys' had protected lawyers, 'first through a Lord Chancellor who was burnt out (Hailsham) and then by a Lord Chancellor who had never been fired up (Havers)'. 'No public service at present is so laced up with shameless practices.' It endorsed fusion but preferred 'lawyer-free services'. Displaying uncharacteristic cross-party enthusiasm, a *Guardian* columnist lauded 'the general desire to curb the overweening power of producer interests' as 'the most important and durable sea-change of the Thatcher years'. The *Sunday Times* dismissed judicial support as 'collusion on a grand scale'. The *Independent* advised 'a sceptical frame of mind' towards 'lawyers' trade union...talk of fundamental rights and freedoms'. '[C]hoice and competition is the best way of ensuring that people who use the law will be in a position to weigh quality against cost.' But though the *Daily Telegraph* cautioned against lawyers' 'special pleading', it feared 'the spectre of a Britain as rampantly litigious as America, where every doctor is now obliged to take a course in law before picking up a scalpel'.[12]

The press anticipated the Green Papers as 'the most significant event for the legal profession' (*The Times*), 'the biggest shake-up' of the century (*The Guardian*). The *Daily Mail* called Mackay 'the most radical and reforming Lord Chancellor for centuries'. The *Economist* quoted John Evelyn's account of dining with the Lord Chancellor 300 years earlier:

> three Serjeants at Law told their stories, how long they had detained their clients in tedious process by tricks, as if so many highway thieves should have met and discovered purses they had taken. This made but a jest of: but God is not mocked.[13]

The Law Society president asked why 'an incompetent barrister should have the sole right to appear in any court, even the House of Lords, while a highly competent and experienced solicitor cannot do so'. The *Solicitors Journal* derided the Bar's 'grubby offices and chambers, delays, lack of communication, lack of expertise in cases undertaken, and the inability to give a straight answer or even to tell clients how much the exercise is likely to cost'. Sir David Napley, a former president, predicted 'a major tragedy if the powerful Bar lobby, which has always protected its interests, forced a stalemate again'. Fennell, now BC chair, responded in kind: to 'allow solicitors to have rights of audience would simply be to lower the standards of advocacy'. Their 'first access to the client' precluded 'an informed choice' of advocate. He quoted Thomas Erskine's defence of Thomas Paine: 'I will forever—at all hazards—assert the dignity, independence and integrity of the English Bar without which impartial justice, the most valuable part of the English constitution, can have no existence'. Fennell concluded: 'Imperil the Bar and you imperil the standard of justice, that hallmark of a free and civilised society'.[14]

A week before publication, Sir Robert Andrew's *Review of Government Legal Services* urged limited Crown Court audience rights to let the CPS attract and retain skilled lawyers. At a meeting of 250–300 heads of chambers to strategize a response to the impending Green Papers, the Criminal Bar Association opposed Sir Robert's proposal. The meeting warned that the services of the 'Robert Alexanders' would be lost if firms hired QCs. Lord Goodman, a solicitor, assailed 'the paranoia displayed . . . the cries of blue murder'. Did Fennell believe that 'the nation's essential liberties were dependent on the handful of barristers then in active practice'? Even Lord Donaldson, Master of the Rolls, called the Bar's monopoly of higher court appointments an 'indefensible . . . sacred cow'. Lord Denning agreed there were too few 'high-quality barristers' to staff the High Court and some 'high quality solicitors and professors of law who could fill some of these posts'. But Fennell was adamant that only barristers 'have had years of experience of the present process'.[15]

The Green Papers declared their 'overall objective' was 'to see that the public has the best possible access to legal services...of the right quality... by ensuring that...a market providing legal services operates freely and efficiently'. The Lord Chancellor should approve specialist education, training, and qualification requirements and promulgate professional codes of conduct with advice from a committee with a lay majority. '[T]he present distinctions in the treatment by the courts of the different branches of the profession would disappear.' All new lawyers would have limited audience rights (including in some Crown Court and High Court proceedings) before fully qualifying. CPS lawyers and even 'lay representatives' would gain some audience rights. All advocates could accept instructions from clients and become silks and judges. The Bar should improve access to pupillages and tenancies, allow practice without clerk or chambers, expand accommodation beyond the Inns, permit partnerships and employment, cease requiring circuit or specialist association membership, and allow barristers to attend on solicitors. Both branches should allow multidisciplinary and multinational partnerships (MDPs and MNPs). Lawyers could advertise. A Legal Services Ombudsman (LSO) would oversee discipline. Probate should be opened to non-solicitors and conveyancing to lenders (without subsidization). Lawyers could charge an uplift in speculative actions and possibly contingent fees.[16]

Indulging in uncharacteristic hyperbole, Lord Mackay called the Green Papers 'radical...going to the very root of the question'. The media agreed. *The Times* said the 'Big Bang for the Bar' presaged 'the most radical change to the legal profession in this century', which 'would sweep away restrictive practices and give clients the widest possible choice of cost-effective services'. The *Independent* welcomed competition in 'one of the last great closed shops'. The *Financial Times* called the changes 'revolutionary'. The *Evening Standard* said they would 'OPEN UP THE LAW TO THE PEOPLE', ending the 'entrenched privileges and hidebound customs of the legal system'.[17]

Columnists concurred. A.H. Hermann was delighted to see 'Britain's legal elite under sentence'. The 'club loyalty' between barristers and judges 'can be bad for the client'. Clare Dyer applauded that 'All become equal before the law'. Competition would force barristers 'to scrap outdated practices and adapt to a changing market place'. The *Sunday Telegraph* reported that 'many of the public, as well as MPs and lawyers, feel that the Bar deserves a sharp clout round the ears'. The *Observer* agreed that the 'squeals of anguish from barristers', who retained their 'archaic paraphernalia of wigs and gowns' and 'love of incomprehensible Latinisms', were 'received with quiet, if not smug, satisfaction by the rest of the community'. Susan Crosland ridiculed the 'closed shop of 5,500 barristers...in full cry, trying its histrionic best to hold on to privileges' and hoped home buyers would be offered 'a less expensive way to handle a simple clerical job'. Simon Jenkins called Mackay 'a saint...the first lord chancellor since Thomas More to merit canonisation'. Jenkins half expected Fennell to 'lapse into pure Scargillese and weep over the loss of "close-knit legal communities" huddled round the Temple pithead and of jobs "handed down from father to son"'.

[A]n ancient trade union at bay is never an edifying sight. Spurious appeals are made to a public interest which is crudely equated with union custom and practice.... Only the Bar Council and its monopolies stand between the poor barrister and Sodom and Gomorrah.

George Gale mocked the 'fuss and gnashing of furious teeth from the top barristers...a clique of highly privileged monopolists'. 'Never can more self-serving humbug have been uttered!' 'With hide-bound enemies [Hailsham and Rawlinson] and spluttering arguments like these, the proposals cannot possibly be all bad'. Indeed, they did not 'go half far enough. What we want is some kind of National Legal Service.'[18]

The leaders were equally caustic. The *Daily Mail* exulted that 'the last great restrictive practice in the land...is to be busted'. The Bar's 'Luddite fulminations' proved that the 'Scottish hammer' had 'hit the target'. The 'Scottish lion' was 'making the fur fly among the fat cats'. The *Independent* thought it a 'good sign' that 'those likely to be affected are protesting loudly' at the 'assault on one of the great bastions of middle-class privilege'. The *Guardian* applauded that 'concern for consumer interests has been given priority' over lawyers, long 'protected by their Old Boys'. The chambers system had 'restricted competition, shut out minorities and boosted fees'. The *Financial Times* predicted the Green Papers would transform the English profession 'from an international laggard to one of the most advanced systems'. The *Evening Standard* welcomed 'root-and-branch' reforms that would 'open the musty corridors of the law to the ordinary plaintiff who for centuries has stood outside the gates, cap in hand, waiting for judgement to be handed down from a high window'.[19]

But some expressed reservations even at this stage. The *Daily Telegraph* warned that 'big solicitors would be able to recommend their own advocate'. The contingency fee 'raises the spectre of a rash of vexatious litigation of the kind seen in the United States'. Its columnist added the reforms could 'push thousands of small practices out of business and give birth to super-firms'; and a lender 'could override the individual's interest for the benefit of itself'. *The Times* cautioned that 'part-time advocates' were less skilled and doubted that 'the competitive language borrowed from the Department of Trade and Industry has been accurately applied in its unaccustomed home'.[20]

The Bar's response was predictable. Fennell warned against 'an American style of justice with district attorneys'. 'The proposals for licensing advocates under government control' threatened 'everyone's constitutional right to have an advocate utterly independent of the state'. Five days after publication he sought £1 million for an advertising blitz, declaring the 'unanimous feeling we must stand firm and conduct a crusade throughout the country'. Sir Ivan Lawrence QC, chair of the All-Party Parliamentary Barristers Group and the Backbench Conservative Law Committee, foretold the end of 'the independent Bar', loss of the 'detachment and objectivity of the barrister', diminished 'availability of legal services', less 'personal and friendly' advice, and reduced competition. Lord Rawlinson (Conservative whip and former Attorney-General and Solicitor-General) resented having 'the creatures of Government assess my "specialist" qualifications for a "dog licence" to plead in the courts'.

Lord Hailsham attained new rhetorical heights. '[I]n the whole realm of human relations there is no field more vulnerable to corruption, dishonesty, chicanery and sheer quackery and charlatanism than contested litigation....' The existing 'high standard', attributable to 'fierce internal competition' within each branch, would deteriorate if you 'remove the incentives to honourable conduct imposed by delicately balanced, slowly evolved but brilliantly successful experience of centuries'. There was no 'question of restrictive practices ... there are already enough market forces built into the system to do whatever market forces are capable of doing'. Contingency fees were 'definitely sinister', 'inherently immoral'. The 'very seriously flawed' Green Papers were 'not particularly well timed, not particularly well thought out', and 'divisive of the two professions'. William Rees-Mogg extolled Hailsham as the embodiment of 'patriotism, religious faith, and the intellectual's pride in Britain's constitutional history'. The Green Papers would import a legal system 'like the one that exists in New York. It is hard to describe how much harm [that] does, and how little good.' It 'is regarded by some American economists as one of the reasons why American industry has ceased to be competitive with the Japanese.' In America 'power prevails, because power can afford the strongest law firms. Such a system is essentially monopolistic, and monopoly and justice always walk on different sides of the street.' He urged the Government to follow the 'good Conservative principle to bring decisions down to the level of the community which is affected', ending with the obligatory nod to Burke: 'I feel an insuperable reluctance in giving my hand to destroy any established institution of government upon a theory, however plausible it may be'. But an American found it 'insulting' to suggest that 'a divided profession is the only way to maintain ethical standards'. And the Scottish Law Society president, whose members appeared in 90 per cent of cases, refused to 'believe that English solicitors are in any way inferior'.[21]

Senior judges ominously sided with Hailsham. Lord Scarman (a retired Law Lord) warned that the Green Papers went 'dangerously near undermining the independence of the legal profession' and called on bench and Bar to 'resist any take-over of work by the Lord Chancellor'. Lord Roskill (another retired Law Lord) said fusion would create 'a terrible danger of an overall lowering of standards'. Lord Ackner (a sitting Law Lord) predicted the reforms 'would lead to the destruction of the Bar . . . substantially increase the cost of litigation and seriously diminish the administration of justice'. They 'raised serious constitutional questions about the interference of the executive, both directly, with the legal profession, and thus indirectly, with the judiciary'.[22]

Letters to the editor stoutly defended the status quo. A solicitor called the English legal system 'the envy of others', blessed with 'the world's best advocates and best judges . . . the best commercial lawyers . . . [and] a body of solicitors throughout the country who are dedicated to the interests of their clients'. Former prisoners displayed their expertise: 'During the life sentence that I served I met dozens of solicitors convicted of crimes but not one barrister'. No self-respecting criminal 'would dream of selecting and instructing a straight solicitor. Fixing is what he wants and gets—a wheeler-dealer, learned in the art of corruption'.[23]

The few dissenting barristers were outsiders. Calling the Bar 'the only job in the country where you need the permission of your competitors before you are allowed to be self-employed', Crown prosecutor Neil Addison said fusion had not 'harmed freedom' in the United States, Australia, or New Zealand. The 'constitutional arguments presented against Lord Mackay's proposals have, perhaps, been the most disgraceful aspect of a campaign characterized by ignorance and inaccuracy'. DPP Allan Green QC promptly directed staff not to 'comment publicly on matters of political controversy' and ordered Addison to withdraw letters and articles already submitted. The association of privately employed barristers (BACFI) thought it might endorse 'aspects of the Green Papers' and was 'troubled' by the Bar's obduracy. Prominent barristers acknowledged the public's conviction that 'restrictive practices' were 'a serious impediment to providing a quality service', resistance made them appear 'moribund and afraid', and apocalyptic prophecies might be self-fulfilling.[24]

By contrast, Gaskell was 'delighted at the truly radical proposals', which addressed 'long-standing problems of a profession operating within an outdated framework by going back to first principles'. The reforms augured 'a new era in which competence and merit . . . can lead to advancement and a more open choice for clients'. Merricks said 'the restrictive ring fence around advocacy sticks out like a sore thumb'. Solicitors' firms would welcome dissatisfied barristers. But Gaskell warned that conveyancing by 'market giants' could reduce 'public choice'. Lenders would 'subsidise their conveyancing fees until solicitors' firms are no longer there'. Scale charges had assured 'a decent living for most solicitors' and

'let them provide many clients with free legal services'. City firms, sole practitioners, and the Legal Aid Practitioners Group all predicted 'mass
closures of the network of 10,000 solicitors' offices around the country'.
Proposing to offer 'one-stop housing services', thereby 'introducing
greater competition and wider choice', building societies maintained that
'employed professionals are...more independently-minded than professionals in private practice'. The CA agreed the Green Papers were 'the sort
of shake-up of the legal world we have been calling for since the early 70s'.
The NCC wanted to give clients 'the widest possible choice of cost-effective
legal services'. But LAG worried that government might 'decide that
certain types of cases—say, those involving national security or allegations
against the police—should be handled in a particular way'.[25]

In the first of many futile efforts to neutralize such fear-mongering,
Lord Mackay insisted advocacy certificates 'would be issued and, where
appropriate, varied, suspended, or revoked' not by 'the Government or the
advisory committee' but by 'the Bar and the Law Society'. Thatcher praised
the Green Papers for 'tackl[ing] the problem in a bold and courageous
way'. (A silk sneered that her 'career at the bar was...too brief to give her
a proper understanding of the vital national interests she is now intending
to tear apart'.) Ivor Stanbrook (Conservative MP and barrister) said
Hailsham 'should have known better'. The Social Democratic spokesperson
on home affairs (also a barrister) called the Papers 'a breath of fresh air'.
But Peter Archer QC, a former Labour Solicitor-General, feared they
would reduce client choice.[26]

Three weeks later Fennell wrote to all barristers that the Heads of
Chambers meeting had expressed 'overwhelming opposition to fusion...
strong opposition to any extension of rights of audience', and 'a majority
against partnerships'. Despite hostile press coverage of the Bar's response,
he claimed it 'achieved what I wanted'. Henceforth it 'will be positive in
attitude and content'. He boasted of the 'deep chord we have struck with
many solicitors who are entirely dependent upon an independent Bar', as
shown by a £2,000 contribution from a 'modest sized firm in London'. But
after nearly a month, the advertising appeal had raised only £160,000.[27]

The next day, however, the Bar received embarrassing support from the
Lord Chief Justice. Laying a court foundation stone, Lord Lane placed the
Green Papers in a time capsule and hoped the burial was 'both symbolic
and prophetic'. They were 'one of the most sinister documents ever to
emanate from Government', threatening the independence of lawyers and
judges: 'the last bastion, the last protection, between the citizen on one
hand and tyranny on the other'. The *Daily Telegraph*, which had expressed
reservations about the Green Papers, regretted Lord Lane's lack of 'judi-
ciousness' and suggested that the Bar's hiring of 'the brothers Saatchi
smacks of...desperation'. Both actions revealed 'fevered anxiety to protect

musty vested interests'. Lord Denning, who had criticized the Green Papers, denied they 'threatened the independence of the Bar or of the judges' and termed the Lord Chief Justice's language 'most unfortunate'.[28]

In just over three weeks the BC produced its first response, calling for 'evolutionary change, not revolution'. It proposed to extend the cab-rank rule (on which the 'reputation of British Justice is founded') to legal aid briefs (in order to obstruct solicitors' audience rights). Contingent fees were 'a third-rate substitute' for legal aid. It feared government 'pressure' on 'barristers who defended clients accused of crimes or who conduct[ed] proceedings on behalf of clients affected by Governmental abuse of power'. Licensing advocates was 'constitutionally inappropriate, and would involve a reversion to the kinds of Government interference in the administration of justice which led to the 1688 Bill of Rights. . . .' American district attorneys were swayed by 'the need of the state to be seen to secure enough convictions and the desire . . . to secure promotion'. Seeking solicitors' support, it called lender conveyancing 'anti-competitive'.[29]

Defenders argued the Bar's case. Sir Ivan Lawrence QC insisted judicial opposition was unmotivated by any 'conceivable self-interest'. Declines in quality and standards would 'follow the abolition of the specialist Bar as they have followed the fusion of the profession in the United States'. Sir Stephen Brown, president of the Family Division, accused the media of making barristers 'hate targets' and fomenting antagonism between the branches and between judiciary and executive. The proposals created 'a most serious constitutional crisis', whose outcome affected 'the administration of the law on which our civilisation depends'. The BC Public Affairs Committee vice-chair asserted that 'the criminal process ought not to be subjected to the same market principles as govern the chocolate industry'. The Criminal Bar Association vice-chair sneered that the Papers exhibited 'all the profundity of sixth-form economic theory'. The Bar was already 'a model of the application of the forces of supply and demand'. Professionalism would 'be swept away to be replaced by the sleaze of Wall Street'. The Green Papers were 'an elaborate joke', said Julian Malins (a barrister), 'written by a man from Mars'; he doubted whether 'this Spivs' Charter will be good for the nation'. The Senior Treasury Counsel warned that 'sound judgment, fairness and balance . . . would disappear' when the 'independent Bar disappears from the prosecuting process' and 'independent advice' and 'independent advocates' vanish. (He owed his prestigious remunerative position to the Government and hoped it would lead to the bench.[30])

Such overreactions provoked the press to further ridicule. 'Faced with the sight of these legal lords a-leaping in alarm', said the *Financial Times*, 'the Man on the Clapham Omnibus (or the Man in the Threadneedle Street Taxi, for that matter) might take the cynical view that: "If that lot are against him, Mackay must have got it about right" '. The *Guardian* said the law was making itself 'a silly ass'.

> The most senior judges in the land are making fools of themselves. So are their co-defendants, the leaders of the Bar. Like many guilty people placed in the dock before them, they have resorted to bluster, exaggeration and invention to cover up their inadequate defence.... they fail to see that their cry 'The End Is Nigh' will cause cheers not consternation among the consumers who have been so badly served by the legal profession for so long.

George Gale lampooned 'Bar and Humbug'. 'Our lawyers are making themselves a laughing stock'. To 'defend privilege with such absurd and intemperate hyperbole' shows the Bar is 'very rattled'. Hiring Saatchi and Saatchi was 'a confession of weakness', provoking 'instant merriment and mockery' and showing 'the Bar has gone off its collective head'.[31]

But the judges just intensified their denunciations. Lord Ackner accused a government 'deluded by dogma' of 'embarking on the most radical changes in...any century...in a state of hopeless confusion'. It was 'hell bent on the destruction of the Bar, with consequent serious prejudice to the whole administration of justice' and wanted to subject the profession to 'the control of a quango controlled by the Lord Chancellor'. Lord Scarman maintained: 'you don't change an existing system that has served the nation well by abstract theorising and superficial analysis'. Lord Benson, whose 1979 Royal Commission report had affirmed the status quo, warned that 'the radical changes' would do 'irreparable harm'. He derided 'the political dogma that competition must be advantageous'; it was 'common sense' that lower quality was 'inevitable'. Fusion would restrict choice, reduce competition, and diminish specialization. As the 'cancer' of contingent fees spread, 'the lawyer and the plaintiff combine together as a team to scavenge what they can out of insurance companies'. The Bar Council and Law Society would become 'creatures of the Government to do its bidding' as it pursued 'dirigiste policies'.[32]

In a rare interview, Mackay assured John Mortimer that 'Rumpole will go from strength to strength'. The 'extension of freedom' had worked 'very well in New South Wales, where a young solicitor' won the *Spycatcher* case 'against a QC in a wig and gown'. That few Australian solicitors 'bother doing a great deal of advocacy' suggested the Bar was unduly alarmed. Because the Marre Committee showed the profession could not agree, 'someone had to step in and decide'. The Green Papers 'approached the subject in a rational way. From first principles.'[33]

The opposition's excesses offered an easy target. The *Economist* told the judges it was 'too late to harrumph'. The Bar had 'always thought Thatcherism was for everybody but barristers'. For decades it had 'arrogantly ignored the need to explain to the public why it had such privileges, why its members dressed so funnily, and why its pomposity knew no bounds'. Even conservative columnist Bernard Levin denounced the Bar's 'great lie' and its 'smear campaign' against Lord Mackay, whom the public viewed 'admiringly, even lovingly'. The profession's 'inward looking tendency' explained Lord Lane's 'screaming', Lord Ackner's 'shrieking', and Sir Stephen Brown's 'squealing'. How would readers 'like to be tried… by such a gibbering crew', who proclaimed 'What we have we hold'? The 'entire nation, from Ventnor to Stornoway, stood up and cheered' the Green Papers because:

for centuries, both the legal professions, but the Bar far more fanatically, rapaciously and successfully, have managed to keep a structure of monopoly and restrictive practices that have no parallel anywhere in our society—not even Sogat or the dockers' section of the TGWU.

The 'incessant public claims of the Bar's leaders' that 'everything most resented by the public—monstrous fees, restrictive jargon, the monopoly itself—were designed, and are maintained, solely in the interests of the nation in general and clients in particular' were deeply offensive. The only reform the Bar endorsed was expanding legal aid, 'in other words that we should pay more to enable them to carry on as before'. Solicitors had predicted 'the ruin of the entire profession and of the nation' when their conveyancing monopoly was broken, but he had 'seen no rain of solicitors throwing themselves out of high windows'.[34]

   At the first conference of the principal protagonists, Lord Mackay accused the Bar of 'perpetuating the myth of [its] imminent demise'. 'I had thought the Bar thrived through excellence and by providing members of the public with a much-needed service. I was obviously mistaken'. While claiming to be 'the most competitive profession', it 'sees itself unable to survive competition from outside its own ranks'. 'It seems to be very odd that restrictions are required to keep people inside a profession'. Fennell retorted that 'the political doctrine of market forces… had no relevance in the administration of justice', which 'is not a consumer durable' but 'the hallmark of a civilised democratic society'. Lord Hailsham predicted an 'elective dictatorship' in which judicial independence would go 'out of the window'. 'First principles' were just another name for dogma and 'a very bad place to start'. The Government's 'concession to populism' was 'an apple of discord' within the profession. Gaskell warned that lenders would 'stop house buyers consulting independent solicitors' and estate agents would 'use all the tricks of the trade' to sell ancillary services. The Building Societies Association denounced the 'monstrous' insinuation that employed solicitors were insufficiently independent. Even Sir Gordon Borrie QC, Director General of Fair Trading, showed more loyalty to his Bar brethren than his employer. The 'size and quality and range of skills' of the practising Bar would seriously decline, reducing competition and choice. It needed to prune 'the undergrowth of restrictive practices'; but 'a "Big Bang" approach could jeopardize the long term future of an independent Bar'.[35]

The press continued to cheer the 'bonny advocate' and ridicule his detractors. The *Daily Mail* 'relished...the spectacle of a discomfitted English Bar trying to sit on this unrepentant Scottish thistle'. Susan Crosland enjoyed seeing him 'deftly insert the needle in noisy legal eminences'. Neal Ascherson mocked the 'great squeaking...from the Temple about threats to the very Palladium or Ark of English liberty'. In 1381 Wat Tyler had led the peasants in burning the Temple and 'swat[ting] the lawyers as they scampered out of the smoke, their black gowns singeing... it beat real rat-hunting as a sport'. 'But now, of course, the lawyers of England are true friends of the people, their services open to all comers without thought of profit or fame.' The *Independent* felt 'logic is on the Lord Chancellor's side' and the Bar was reacting 'emotionally'. But four days later it asked: 'Has the Prime Minister gone mad?' She was spring-cleaning 'rooms which already look quite clean enough to their inhabitants'. 'The great danger...is that she will not know when to stop.'[36]

Press contumely drove leading barristers and judges to greater raptures of indignation. Lord Rawlinson called the proposal 'an extraordinarily ill-conceived, ill-thought-out, populist sort of venture...destroying something which works'. Lord Scarman assailed 'abstracted theorising which takes no account of what the English profesion not only can but does offer to the client'. Lord Devlin accused Government of seeking 'to break the Bar...by assuming control of the right of audience in the High Court'. That territory 'belongs' to the judges; the 'invasion threatens their independence'. By failing to take 'even soundings' and 'treating the judges as civil servants', Lord Mackay raised questions about whether he should 'continue to act as [their] head'. Lord Beloff (retired Oxford professor) and Michael Beloff QC (his son and chair of the Administrative Bar Association) declared (somewhat circularly) that the 'uniform hostility of senior judges' showed the proposals 'undermine the status of the judiciary'. The proposed quango would be 'composed of part-time "lay" (a euphemism for uninformed) figures, who are thus potentially pliable in the hands of civil servants', whose ideas about training 'seem to have been designed by individuals more used to devising qualifications for fitters' mates than for members of a learned profession'. Control over rights of audience and codes of conduct crossed 'a constitutional Rubicon'.[37]

A senior judge called for the resignation of the Attorney-General, who could not be the Government's chief legal spokesperson in the Commons and lead the Bar. (Sir Patrick Mayhew QC did allegedly threaten to resign if the Government extended solicitors' audience rights.) Noting that ten Lords had already registered for a preliminary debate, a senior Conservative peer declared defiantly: 'If they already have a draft bill, they may as well rip it up'. Lord Hailsham called the Green Papers 'obviously a major blunder. What one must aim at isn't to rub people's face [*sic*] in the dirt but to play it into the long grass and pretend it hasn't happened'. The day after *The Times* reported that Lord Mackay probably would introduce legislation without a White Paper, Lord Rawlinson said he would relinquish the Tory whip and (seconded by Lord Havers) urged the Attorney-General and Solicitor-General to resign. 'To think that a Conservative administration which is dedicated to conserve what is best should bring forward these proposals in this thoughtless way, without any consultation with the judges fills me with utter despair.' A day later he dismissed Mackay as the Government's 'office boy', 'an extremely nice man, a distinguished Scottish jurist, but... [with] no knowledge of English courts'. His predecessors would be 'turning in their graves'.[38]

Some media were openly contemptuous. The 'particularly nasty species of Tory backbencher whose principle [*sic*] motivation is terror at anything which might upset the established order', said the *Evening Standard*, 'defy common sense and the will of the people' and 'obstruct rather than serve the democratic process'. Lord Lane's characterization of the Green Papers was 'memorably ludicrous'. The 'cabal of senior lawyers', whose 'belligerent behaviour, more reminiscent of Arthur Scargill than of a Law Lord, might cut more ice if they had ever in the past shown interest in making the law more accessible to the man in the street'. The *Guardian* berated the 'rebellious judiciary' for 'vying with each other in the vividness with which they describe the ultimate apocalypse'. The judges 'have become accustomed to their feather beds'. 'If one thing binds stronger than the old school tie, it is a claret-stained Inns of Court tie.'[39]

But newspapers across the political spectrum began criticizing the proposals. Perversely asserting they failed 'to start with the interests of the consumer', the *Daily Telegraph* declared that the 'reforms as they stand do not deserve to become law'. Revealing its true colours, it urged Lord Mackay to provoke equal 'rending of raiment among the members of the Law Society' by authorizing institutional conveyancing and contingent fees. While reviling Lords Lane and Ackner as (respectively) 'temperate as an ayatollah' and 'fit to lead a book-burning on Lincoln's Inn Fields', *Guardian* columnist Hugo Young also condemned the Government for having 'consciously eschewed the processes of reason' by embracing 'late Thatcherism in all its gore and glory', the 'quite naked and unashamed' ideology that 'in every corner of human existence, only competition will produce the right result'. In *The Times*, Robin Oakley recommended 'slow speed ahead'. Given the 'Maoist ferment of constant change... the nation should be granted a little breather before the next burst of radicalism'.[40]

Government seemed unmoved. Two days after Mackay reiterated his determination to introduce legislation the Prime Minister called the reforms 'broadly speaking' correct. The Lord Chancellor defended them at a major conference by invoking the 1987 Conservative Manifesto: 'Competition forces the economy to respond to the needs of the consumer. It promotes efficiency, holds down cost, drives companies to innovate and ensures that customers get the best possible value for money'. The 1988 DTI Green Paper had urged that 'rules of professional bodies should be subject to the same tests . . . as other sectors of the economy'. The administration of justice was 'too important to be left entirely to the legal profession'. Judicial outrage was unconvincing after 150 years of Parliamentary regulation of audience rights. Opponents were abusing the shibboleth of 'independence', which Lord Devlin had defined as 'a mind which is open'. '[D]o you really believe . . . that the independence of the present holder of the office of Director of Public Prosecutions—a distinguished and most respected member of the Bar—is compromised in any way now that he is a member of the Civil Service?' 'Are the leaders of the Bar showing . . . independence of mind?' Dissenting barristers 'are being prevented from attending meetings of the specialist Bar associations'. The latest *Bar News* sought to ensure that 'everyone sings from the same hymnsheet'. The Bar had to stop 'living in an age of wish fulfillment'. It should 'explain exactly what sort of cab-rank rule it is talking about', given the numerous exceptions. (Two ex-barrister solicitors commented that 'cabs, like barristers, are seldom available when wanted, are often late even if booked in advance, and finally, when hailed and acknowledged . . . someone else often jumps in first'.[41])

Lord Ackner responded that since the 'proposals at the very least involve a substantial risk of the destruction of the Bar', Mackay 'just cannot proceed'. '[P]erhaps what the executive really wants' is to eliminate the 'small elite of practitioners' from which judges are chosen, 'for a strong and independent judiciary has often proved a deep thorn in its side'. Lord Alexander of Weedon QC (sounding more like a former BC chair than a Monopolies and Mergers Commission chair) dismissed the proposals as 'superficial' and 'unsupported by research and unaided by consultation'. There was 'an elementary conflict of interest in the state taking a power of control over the very profession which is there to help secure fearless and able help to those whom the State prosecutes'. Fennell strategically yielded to a black woman barrister, who told of judges stopping her from questioning police about racism and feared threats to her independence.[42]

Enjoying the senior branch's discomfiture, Law Society Vice-President David Ward observed 'there were only ten years left in the twentieth century and we do not wish the Bar to miss out altogether'. Sir David Napley accused the Bar of 'scaring people' with 'arrant nonsense'. Predictably, the presidents of the Association of Trial Lawyers of America and the American Bar Association defended contingent fees, while the American Tort

Reform Association president, an insurance defence solicitor, and a barrister were sceptical.[43]

The media awarded this round to Mackay. Two days after accusing the government of naked Thatcherism, Hugo Young called solicitors' audience rights 'a minimal piece of common-sense'. A Bar that 'for decades imposed such an array of restrictive practices cannot cavil too loudly if Parliament now imposes different rules'. The *Economist* dismissed the 'judicial huffing and puffing and you-may-thinking. A wise public may react as juries are apt to: with scorn.' The 'notion of courts as the judges' private demesne should be laughed out of Parliament as the seigneurial codswallop it is'. In the *Evening Standard*, Christopher Monckton delighted that lawyers were squealing 'louder and louder than all the other squealers put together ... the more they squeal the more we shall all revel in the sound of it'. An *Independent* column (by a judge's daughter!) claimed barristers were 'hated by lay people'. The pupillage system was 'a scandal', exhibiting 'all the worst aspects of trying to join a gentleman's club' by excluding 'blacks, Asians and insufficiently pretty women'. Even the *Daily Telegraph* said the Bar's response resembled 'the industrial methods formerly used by those such as dockers, miners and transport workers'. Although the *Financial Times* surprisingly sought a middle ground between 'allegiance to a privileged group' and 'a doctrinal belief that competition can heal all ills', it hoped a profession 'unprotected by monopoly' would be 'more interested in simplification of court procedures'.[44]

The Bar answered press criticism by raising its voice. Its £750,000 public relations campaign included leaflets declaring 'Justice in Danger', radio commercials threatening 'Americanisation', and a two-page *Times* advertisement warning that 'a defendant could be prosecuted by state prosecutors, tried by a Judge drawn from the ranks of state prosecutors, and represented by an advocate licensed by a body controlled by—you've guessed it—the state'. The DPP rebuked Fennell for the 'unfair and inaccurate' (and contradictory) charge that 'criminals [would] stand a better chance of getting off' if the CPS prosecuted. In Parliament, the Prime Minister called the Bar Council 'unprofessional' for denigrating other lawyers. Ivor Stanbrook MP deplored the Bar leaders' 'intemperate language' and urged that Government not surrender to the 'voices of reaction'. But the Council of Her Majesty's Circuit Judges confidentially wrote to its 400 members doubting 'the constitutional propriety of taking a learned profession concerned with the liberty of the subject under government control' and asking (rhetorically) if the proposals 'substantially diminish' the 'constitutional independence of the judiciary', effectively 'neuter' the profession, and give the LCD 'control of the whole legal profession'.[45]

On 7 April, fifty-six peers debated the Green Papers on television for nearly thirteen hours. Lord Mackay attributed the Government's policy change since accepting the Royal Commission Report in 1983 to the end of the solicitors' conveyancing monopoly, the 1988 DTI Green Paper proposing to subject professions to 'a general prohibition of agreements which have the effect of restricting or distorting competition', and the Marre Committee's 'complete impasse' after two years of deliberations 'because the Bar Council made clear' it 'would not agree to any extension of rights of audience'. The 'way out of this impasse was to go back to first principles'—that audience rights should be extended to everyone with 'the necessary level of competence' and 'governed by an appropriate code of conduct'. He reassured members that ACLEC 'will not issue or grant' advocacy certificates. 'There is no question whatsoever' of Government 'control directly or indirectly on which individuals should be entitled to practise'. The Green Papers' 'modest framework' had been unfairly attacked 'as state control of the legal profession'.[46]

This merely inflamed critics. Lord Lane accused the Lord Chancellor of seeking to 'disembowel' a system that 'deserves more respect'. Lord Hailsham was 'frankly appalled'; Lord Mackay had 'run at these things like a bull in a china shop'. Lord Rippon called the Green Paper 'one of the most sinister documents ever to emanate from Government'. Lord Alexander of Weedon denounced 'sweeping structural reform' as 'a divisive distraction'. 'Why should we recreate the profession from scratch as if this country were a newly discovered land or a legal greenfield site?' Lord Oliver of Aylmerton warned that these 'very radical measures' were 'irreversible'.[47] The Green Paper was a 'woefully uniformed' 'mass of claptrap and many platitudes', said Lord Hutchinson; it was 'misleading', 'suppresses known facts', and 'masks its true intentions'. The 'aim of this paper is to break the Bar and the criminal Bar in particular'. Lord Mackay had lost 'the respect and loyalty of the legal profession'.[48] Defending the Lord Chancellor, Lord Goodman (a solicitor) said 'the extravagance of the language reflects discredit on its users'; some comments 'have been wholly ridiculous'. Lord McGregor (a non-lawyer) was 'saddened by the recent ululations of some members of the Bar'. Even Viscount Bledisloe (a barrister) called the Bar Council reaction 'shrill and inept'.[49]

Peers vied in invoking the great evils of history. Lord Elwyn-Jones (the last Labour Lord Chancellor) 'well remember[ed] that in Nazi Europe and the Fascist countries before the war the authoritarian regimes' first victims were the independence of the judiciary and the independence of the legal profession'. Lord Lane pronounced: 'Oppression does not stand on the doorstep with a toothbrush moustache and a swastika armband. It creeps up insidiously; it creeps up step by step; and all of a sudden the unfortunate citizen realizes that it has gone.' Lord Donaldson denounced 'The New Despotism'. We 'have too often seen freedom disappear in other countries not only by coup d'état but by gradual erosion'. He quoted a

'distinguished former Prime Minister':'Get your tanks off my lawn'.
Lord Benson noted that in South Africa 'the only thin channel from that
government to justice was the independent Bar'. Lord Alexander added
that 'if the language of this Green Paper had emanated from the
Government of South Africa, there would have been howls of cynical
protest throughout the civilized world'. Lord Meston warned of the 'corruption and oppression in countries where the independence of the
lawyers has either been lost or has never been achieved'.[50]

Several saw constitutional threats. Lord Beloff thought it:

quite extraordinary that on the anniversary of ['the great events of 1689 when the
foundations of our constitutional liberties were affirmed'] proposals should be put
forward to reverse the main element in the Constitution; namely, the independence of the legal system from the executive branch. It is as though the French, who
this summer will celebrate the fall of the Bastille, should mark the occasion by
reintroducing lettres de cachet or the droit de seigneur.

Lord Rippon warned that 'frail democracy—it is a frail thing—depends on'
the 'independence of the legal profession'. With 'the Executive and
Parliament virtually combined our constitutional rights are a very fragile
matter'.[51] But Lord Henderson of Brompton deplored the 'extravagance
of...utterance'. '[W]henever I hear the word "constitution"...I reach for
my scepticism, especially when [it is] uttered by interested parties'. And
Lord Goodman thought it required 'a vigorous imagination' and 'an
exceptionally sensitive nose for smelling sulphur' to detect a 'threat to the
constitution'.[52]

Lord Hooson called the Lord Chancellor's power 'totally excessive' and
'dangerously authoritarian'. Lord Hutchinson saw 'an authoritarian streak'
in Lord Mackay's opening address. Lord Havers was 'unable to accept the
transfer of responsibility for control of the profession from two self-
regulating governing bodies to the office of the Lord Chancellor'. Lord
Beloff advanced the 'sinister' explanation that this was 'another attempt by
the Civil Service to establish its control over what has hitherto been an
independent and separate part of our national life'. Lord Benson agreed
that the Law Society and Bar Council 'will become creatures of the government to do their bidding'. 'This dirigiste policy more suited to a
Marxist government will involve a great host of government restrictions
and a large bureaucracy.' Lord Lane derided the 'so-called' Advisory
Committee as 'an ill-sorted conglomerate' with 'a majority of lay persons',
which 'threatens...to give civil servants control of...matters which up to
now have been the province of the judges'. Lord Oliver warned that the
'preponderance of lay representatives' may 'simply be the political
appointees of the government of the day'.[53]

Such critics insisted the proposals undermined the independence of the
judiciary (while rarely articulating the connection). Lord Lane portrayed

judicial review as 'the principal means available to the ordinary citizen of controlling' the executive, 'the one thing that will stop a bullying government in their tracks'. Lord Hailsham called the judiciary 'the guardian of the liberties of the people'. Lord Ackner (a Law Lord) agreed that 'a strong and independent judiciary, frequently exercising its power of judicial review, is often a most uncomfortable thorn in the flesh of the Executive'. 'From time to time the judiciary have maintained freedoms', replied Lord Goodman, but 'from time to time they have done the reverse'.[54]

Many more stressed the threat to the independence of lawyers (by which most meant the Bar, though several objected to corporate conveyancing).[55] In his maiden address, Lord Rees-Mogg called 'the independence of the Bar . . . one of the great glories of our nation'. Lord Rippon saw the Green Paper as 'a direct threat'. Lord Campbell (a barrister) feared that 'the independence, dignity and indeed the integrity of the Bar . . . are being called into question'. Lord Renton (another barrister) believed these traits were 'largely founded' on 'the collegiate life of the Inns of Court'. Lord Wigoder (a barrister) declared it:

of crucial importance to our society—that there should be a core of people able and willing to stand up for the ordinary citizen, for the little man, in his constant battles against the big battalions and the power, the size and the potential oppression than [*sic*] can be represented by the activities of government . . . the police, local authorities, nationalized industries, big business or the trade unions. . . .[56]

Lord Rawlinson denounced the 'certificate scheme' for advocates as a 'bureaucratic nightmare', which did not exist 'anywhere else in the world'. Lord Wilberforce (another barrister) called it 'a denial of professional values'. '[W]hat is there to prevent an ill-disposed government with an overwhelming majority in the other House, acting through a compliant Lord Chancellor', asked Lord Murray, 'from putting pressure on to a barrister defending a client accused of a crime against the government?' Lord Oliver decried the 'new structure of licensed advocates . . . untrammelled by any worthy tradition; freed from the collegiate restraints of close association', 'a new invented creature which I am tempted to say has this in common with the mule—that it will have neither pride of ancestry nor hope of posterity'.[57]

Opponents identified independence with the Bar's unique attributes. 'Of course', pronounced Lord Hooson, a sole practitioner was 'more independent than a partner'. To Lord Rawlinson, 'an independent Bar means a man practising on his own'. Partnerships, insisted Lord Goff of Chieveley (another barrister), would 'amount to a complete denial of an independent Bar'.[58] Few heeded Lord Gifford's protest that for fifteen years he had headed a chambers that shared fees with 'no loss of responsibility' or 'independence'.[59] Unaware of (or indifferent to) the insult to solicitors, judges and barristers called it axiomatic that extending audience rights 'would dilute the quality of the advocacy' (Lord Ackner), 'inevitably dilute standards' (Lord Alexander).[60] Speakers predicted the demise of the Bar, 'inevitably within one generation' (Lord Rawlinson), 'over the next 30 years' (Viscount Bledisloe). It 'would be so injured as to be incapable of continuing as a separate profession' (Lord Ackner). The proposals 'will inevitably lead to fusion' (Lord Benson).[61]

The Bar's defenders maintained that 'a system which has developed slowly and painstakingly over the centuries' (Lord Lane) had attained a perfection that could only be marred by change. The English legal profession was 'highly esteemed in much of the world' (Lord Saint Brides), 'the most upright and most independent...known to man' (Lord Hailsham), 'superior to all others' (Lord Rawlinson), 'the best in the world' (Lord Wilberforce). The Chief Justices of the United States, Australia, and New Zealand had told Lord Benson: 'Do not tamper with the present structure of the legal profession. It is the envy and admiration of everybody abroad.'[62] Lord Rees put 'the onus...upon those who introduce radical reforms of this kind to established institutions of this country'. Lord Longford claimed the Labour party also had 'always been aware of the greatness of the traditions'. And Lord Saint Brides quoted President Truman: 'If it ain't broke, don't fix it'. Lord Mishcon retorted with Sir Edward Coke: 'however so long traditions and procedures have gone on', if it 'lacks reason or...benefit for the public that we serve, then it hath no force...and should be capable of change'.[63]

Lord Hutchinson rejected criticism of Bar rules as 'wicked, restrictive practices'; they 'do not add one penny' to barristers' incomes but rather guarantee 'a genuine choice to the consumer'. Lord Ackner denied that 'rights of audience were a preserve and a restrictive practice imposed by the Bar for the Bar's benefit. It is a restriction imposed through the judiciary...for the benefit of the litigant....' Lord Oliver called the alleged restrictive practices 'merely the self-denying ordinances which are assumed by the Bar as the price of its monopoly'. Because 'the reaction is not just that of the Bar but also that of the highest judiciary in the land', Lord Meston insisted, it was 'not the product of self-interest' but of 'far deeper considerations'.[64] Lord Renton maintained the Bar was 'not opposed to change'; its 'stonewalling attitude...does not exist and, in my recollection, never has done so'. Lord Donaldson asserted that 'both branches on their own initiative have made tremendous improvements'. Lord Alexander agreed that 'in the last few years there have been striking changes'. Solicitors were sceptical. 'For too long', said Lord Hacking, the Bar had 'clung to restrictive practices'. Lord Goodman felt change 'proceeds at the pace of a rheumatic snail'. The Earl of Longford, an academic, could not 'believe that the members of the legal profession themselves would ever reform their own profession'.[65]

If the English profession was the embodiment of perfection, the American—which the proposals threatened to import—was evil incarnate. The Chief Justice of the U.S. Supreme Court had told Lord Templeman that 'we have a much better system' and 'would be mad if we were to tear it up'. In America, 'an attorney in the far west' (where I teach future lawyers!) 'can take a case to the Supreme Court and 'make a mess of it'. Lord Rawlinson called America 'the most litigious society there is, mostly due to its system of contingency fees'. Litigation cost most, took longer, and produced less satisfactory results. Lord Bridge of Harwich thought it ironic that just when Americans were 'seeking to emulate the ethos of a profession rooted in the traditions of the English Inns of Court...we are debating...a proposal which would relegate the Inns of Court to an insignificant status....' The Earl of Onslow declared the 'American system of criminal justice' full of 'delays and horrors'. In 'Texas at the moment the system of law has stopped' until President Bush appointed 'political lawyers'. 'In the United States Supreme Court the time that elapses between hearing and judgment is two years.' Lord Hooson warned against 'the American route': 'resort to law is expensive, uncertain and perilous. Personal and professional insurance premiums are enormous. Predatory lawyers are licensed to seek the maximum return for themselves and their clients from every human misfortune....' Lord Oliver asserted that 'the costs of conveyancing undertaken by lending institutions in the United States' were 5–7 per cent of the price. Lord Ackner maintained that American judges needed clerks to 'check the voluminous papers that are full of the irrelevancies which are the inevitable by-product of bad advocacy'.[66] Contingency fees were 'abhorrent' in 'any shape or form, however diluted' (judgements Lord Irvine would regret), 'inherently immoral and corrupting' (Lord Hailsham). Warning of 'spurious blackmailing actions', Lord Saint Brides blamed contingency fees for 'the astronomical cost of medical treatment in America' and claimed in Buffalo that 'no consultants were left who were willing any longer to practise obstetrics and gynaecology....'[67]

Critics assailed laissez faire. 'Decent practitioners', warned Lord Hooson, will 'have to compete with people of lower standards, who are prepared always to drag down the level'. Lord Irvine derided the 'absurd free market hype', which 'confuse[d] deregulation with securing consumer rights, access and quality of service'. 'Members of professions', pronounced Lord Hailsham, 'are not like the grocer's shop at the corner of a street in a town like Grantham' (an unkind slur on a Prime Minister he had served for eight years). Lord Wilberforce rejected the Green Papers for using 'the standard jargon: market prices, value for money, cost effective... the standard is to be one of short-term economic gain'. But 'professions cannot be added to cartels as another item to be dealt with in the same way'. 'One is concerned primarily not with economic considerations at all...'. Even Lord Benson attacked 'the political dogma of competition'. (Where would he be without it?[68]) Opponents denounced the 'claim to go back to first principles'. That 'might have been appropriate for a blueprint for a former colonial territory' (such as my own?), said Lord Hooson, but 'we have honourable, responsible, decent professional bodies in this country....' Lord Wilberforce declared that 'one starts from the fact that one already has a profession, an existing structure which in itself and by its nature is in the public interest'. 'First principles' were 'about the worst point from which to start', said Lord Hailsham, either 'unproven dogma' or 'platitude'. Lord Wigoder dismissed them as 'first prejudices', Lord Bridge as 'an ideological blueprint'. The Earl of Onslow warned against 'overpassionate love for the ideas of John Bright or Adam Smith'.[69] Lord Lane discerned the 'clear...influence' of DTI in such 'classic...jargon' as 'the widest possible choice of cost-effective services...the discipline of the market' and 'competition'. Lord Rawlinson used more vivid imagery: the 'voice may be the voice of Jacob who is the Lord Chancellor but the hand is that of Esau...the Department of Trade and Industry...with the Treasury behind it'.[70]

Lord Hutchinson asked: 'where is...the informed choice—for the accused? The choice is not like the choice of a tin of peas in a supermarket'. Lord Benson said the proposals would 'reduce the specialisms available and the freedom of choice open to the user' and 'often increase costs'. Lord Rees declared it 'incontrovertible' that 'the range of choice for the law client must be diminished'. Lord Goff did not believe competition 'would deal with such matters as cost and delay'. Lord Lane and Lord Campbell asserted the reforms would increase both. None was persuaded by Lord Goodman's argument that 'if you can employ one person instead of three, that seems a very good reason for believing that the cost will be a good deal cheaper'.[71] Many opponents argued that competition would increase concentration, reducing choice and increasing cost, as had allegedly happened after the Big Bang of the Financial Services Act 1986.[72] Corporate conveyancing would drive the high-street solicitor out of business or into employment with lenders. 'If one gets rid of the high street solicitor, one gets rid of the Bar', declaimed Lord Templeman, and 'everything is on the side of the big battalion and no one is on the side of the small citizen'.[73] Employment and partnership would reduce the 'availability of barristers to appear for people'. Viscount Dilhorne pronounced it 'common' for an American plaintiff to brief a firm 'in order to prevent the stars of that partnership from appearing'.[74]

Even if competition might benefit some private clients, the Green Papers did nothing to redress the plight of legal aid. Lord Elwyn-Jones called such disregard 'remarkable'. Eligibility had fallen from 70 to 50 per cent, and 'about 40 per cent of legal aid solicitors' firms are considering giving up the work'. Assailing the 'absurdly low qualifying limits', Lord Irvine accused the Government of seeking 'to restrict coverage to the minimum'. Lord Hutchinson denounced 'the overt hostility of the Lord Chancellor's Department to those who act for the most disadvantaged in society—those in receipt of legal aid'.[75]

Opponents accused the Government of populist politics and pandering to the press. Lord Irvine regretted that 'lawyers are so soft a target' that the 'simplistic populist line, was working a treat'. Lord Lane agreed that such 'populist proposals...inevitably will be applauded by the tabloid press'. Lord Hutchinson said the Green Papers had 'given the intellectual Murdoch mafia...a field day as they pop up from the squalor of their own profession...singing from their masters' hymn sheet of the great God of the morality of the market place'. Lord Rippon deplored that voters were 'being seduced by a modern Eve with the populist cry that lawyers are elitist and expensive....'[76] Critics reiterated lawyers' favourite objection—procedure. The three months consultation was 'wholly inadequate' (Lord Elwyn-Jones), 'an outrage' (Lord Hailsham), 'insulting' (Lord Rawlinson).[77] Lord Lane said it would 'have been courteous, or even helpful, if those responsible for drafting the paper...had seen fit to consult the judges upon the draft, at least, before proposing in "white" rather than "green" terms....' Lord Rawlinson 'cringed' at the conflict between the Lord Chief Justice and Lord Chancellor. But during the debate Lord Mackay had shown their correspondence to Lord Lane, who 'generous[ly] withdrew the word "discourteous" '.[78]

Although Lord Alexander insisted that 'all of us who speak in this debate, whether as lawyers or non-lawyers, speak and declare only one interest...the administration of justice', barristers (like himself) and judges (former barristers) spoke for the Bar and solicitors for solicitors.[79] Lay persons, although greatly outnumbered and (excessively) modest about their expertise and rhetorical prowess, strongly supported the proposals. As chair of the National Consumer Council, Baroness Oppenheim-Barnes felt 'instinctively' that it was 'a rather healthy sign from the point of view of the consumer' that the two branches had been 'both shaken and stirred by the Green Papers'. The 'law is not there for its prac-titioners' but 'for those who are forced to use it in order to try to obtain justice'. 'After 700 years we are...standing at the crossroads of legal reform'. Baroness Phillips was 'the first to congratulate...the Lord Chancellor on having the courage to attack this profession'. Lord Allen felt the proposals introduced 'a breath of fresh air' and had received 'a wide welcome outside the profession'. (He was promptly dismissed by Lord Wigoder as a Home Office mouthpiece.) Baroness Faithfull pronounced it 'axiomatic' that the litigant 'should be free to choose to be represented by a lawyer of his choice, be it solicitor or barrister'. Baroness Macleod of Borve quoted the 1987 Conservative manifesto. Lord Lloyd of Hampstead called the legal system 'extremely expensive and...not easily accessible to the ordinary man in the street'. Supermarkets put some corner shops out of business, said Lord Reay, but they 'brought great benefits to the public'. The Bar's advocacy resembled 'another expensive British product, also of legendary quality and also famous throughout the world—the Saville Row suit. But do we give Saville Row a monopoly on making suits?' Lord Trafford, a consultant doctor, maintained Lord Mackay had 'very considerable support in many other fields, and also from the general public at large'; the debate, 'dominated by members of the legal profession', was not 'really representative'. Lord Morris accused the Bar Council and Law Society of doing 'little' to 'put their own house in order'. There was 'no threat in the Green Papers to the independence of the Bar let alone its existence'. Lord Wilberforce claimed the Bar by its very nature was in the public interest, but 'I have always believed that the user of legal services must and should be the final arbiter of the quality and the value for money'.[80]

Lord Mackay concluded the debate by denying he had 'criticised the Bar or anyone else in respect of their responses to the Green Papers' or 'ever described the Bar's reaction as partaking of hysteria'. It was 'very important—not least from the point of view of young people who may be considering what they may do—to say as rapidly as possible what is the Government's intention'. Employed solicitors would have a primary duty to house buyers. The 'cab rank rule in that extended form would apply' because a right of audience entailed 'a corresponding obligation to give one's services'. The 'much larger branch of the legal profession', which permitted partnerships and employment and had direct access to clients, 'is also properly regarded as independent'.[81]

Newspapers delighted in the spectacle. The *Guardian* urged readers to contrast 'yesterday's Lordly rhetoric' with 'the simple, reasonable idea of abolishing the Bar's unloved restrictive practices'. The attack was 'all party and yet, with only a few exceptions, One Party. The party of Law Lords and ex-Lord Chancellors and Practising Pillars of the Bar'. The Lords were 'the Bar in Ermine', a 'manifestly stacked jury'. The *Observer* columnist accused the 'lawyers in the Lords' of 'judging in their own case'. There was an:

unbridgeable chasm...between those who believe that legal services (which are largely paid for out of the Exchequer) should be subjected to empirical tests of efficiency and accessibility, and those who believe that the present disposition of the English legal system was brought down from Sinai by the framers of the Revolution Settlement....

In the *Spectator* Noel Malcolm declared that the 'crudity and arrogance of the attacks...by one legal grandee after another...almost foaming at the mouth' demonstrated that 'the Lord Chancellor must be on to something after all'. The silks and judges displayed such 'snobbery and disdain... you could hardly expect them to criticise the present system'.[82]

Lord Lane worsened matters by convening a Judges' Council discussion of the Green Papers, effectively closing the courts for half a day. In a Commons debate about prisons, a Labour backbencher asked: 'When the law-breaking lords... decide to go on strike... will they be sent to a Category C prison or will it be something even harsher?' Newspaper articles headlined 'Rebel Judges Stop Courts' compared the job action with 'walkouts organised by unions' and called judges 'no better than the dockers'. A Conservative MP assailed the LCJ's 'outrageous' action. 'Beneath the wigs and gowns, we have seen the feet of clay!' 'The rule of law cannot—and must not—be subordinated to any group of workers' self-interested withdrawal of labour....' The Lord Chancellor ought to amend 'the judges' oath of office so that, like policemen, they undertake an absolute commitment not to withhold their labour for their own benefit' and introduce 'a judges' disciplinary code, similar to that imposed by Parliament on the police, whereby "discreditable conduct" by judges is an offence'. The *Daily Mail* headlined its report of the judges' meeting (rescheduled for a weekend) 'Abuse of privilege' and complained of the 'outrageous misuse of judicial power' to ban 'the Press and public and even threaten photographers with prosecution... police and uniformed attendants, paid for by the taxpayer, manned the gates and vetted those entering'.[83]

A week after the Lords debate Sir Frederick Lawton, a retired Lord Justice of Appeal who supported the reforms, noted that legal aid had let the Bar triple in thirty years and 'the less competent... get started'. If the proposals caused shrinkage, the Bar's 'standing with the public will be higher; and its members as prosperous as ever, maybe more so'. Lord Justice Bingham became the first sitting senior judge to side with the Lord Chancellor. Most people rightly saw the profession as 'riddled with anachronistic conventions and privileges'. Restrictions on audience rights were 'illogical and indefensible'. Venturing well beyond what her bare 8–7 majority had recommended, Lady Marre urged unrestricted audience rights. The public correctly perceived the 'hysterical' reaction of Bar and bench as 'political campaigning for the maintenance of restrictive practices'. Lord Hailsham promptly supplied more evidence. The Government 'have made asses of themselves'. Instead of 'thinking with its bottom and sitting on its head', it should 'start from scratch', display 'some degree of political sense and not go on running about like a bull in a china shop'.[84]

Although audience rights occupied centre stage, corporate conveyancing also was contentious. Building societies, like solicitors, sought to act for both parties. The National Association of Estate Agents proposed that members supervise the exchange of contracts, sweeping away 'the entrenched and antiquated conveyancing system'. But the Law Society decried the 'scandal' of 'hidden commissions', warning that the NAEA proposed code of conduct failed to eliminate the conflict of interest in selling mortgages and insurance. The NAEA president was 'speechless' and 'horrified'. The National Association of Solicitors Property Centres maligned estate agents as 'predators of the marketplace'. The Society of Licensed Conveyancers denounced the Green Papers as 'a charter for the benefit of money-lenders'.[85]

Critics on the left welcomed the attack on professional privilege, but most had reservations. The Social and Liberal Democratic Lawyers' Association feared an excuse to cut legal aid. The Law Centres Federation found the proposals 'largely irrelevant to the majority of poor and deprived people' and worried about the 'serious civil liberties implications'. LAG shared the concern 'for the independence of lawyers—particularly advocates known for defending politically unpopular cases' and correctly saw conditional fees as 'the thin end of the legal aid cuts wedge'. The LAPG warned that corporate conveyancing would have a 'profound effect on the viability of legal aid practices', which were 'least likely to be able to afford the capital burden' of conditional fees. Justice opposed almost everything, even the 'revolutionary change' of CPS audience rights. The Haldane Society condemned 'any proposals which deify the marketplace'. The NCC opposed expanding the Lord Chancellor's authority. Only the CA enthusiastically endorsed competition as 'one of the main means through which the interests of consumers are protected'.[86]

The Law Society response to the Green Papers deplored the 'end of the civilised world' approach of Bar and bench. 'Language of such colour, expressions so intemperate and an assertion of discourtesy...which then had to be withdrawn, has done the judiciary...no good whatever'. Solicitors had adapted to loss of the conveyancing monopoly and conceded their probate monopoly. Still, the Society opposed corporate conveyancing, MDPs, and the Lord Chancellor's advisory committee.[87]

The Bar's 275-page response mixed concessions with intransigence. '[V]iewing the legal profession as an economic activity' put 'money before duty to a client and before service to the public'. The Bar promised to ease entry, allow advertising, and 'remove or relax all restrictions contained in its rules in so far as they are not necessary for the maintenance of the quality and standards'. It opposed all partnerships. Solicitors' audience rights would increase legal aid costs. And CPS audience rights betrayed 'the Government's normal approach...to privatize whatever can sensibly be privatized'. The Bar courted solicitor support by declining direct access ('expensive for the public and damaging to the quality of advocacy') and opposing corporate conveyancing. It inveighed against Americanization: 'inexperienced advocates', 'cases take longer and are tried less efficiently', 'mega-firms', 'increased delays', 'increased costs', 'the money ethic superseding the ethic of professionalism', 'employed prosecutors whose primary interest is in their success rates'.[88]

Lord Mackay denounced critics 'so keen to find some concealed horrors that they are throwing down their own stones in order to look under them' for 'a sort of creeping state control'. '[W]e spent most of last year dealing with' legal aid. He seemed ready to concede that the advisory committee— target of 'a lot of representation'—should be independent and powerless. But he found 'it difficult to believe that increasing the supply of advocates will not in the long run have the usual economic effect of decreasing their price'. He cautioned 'those who practise advocacy' that it was 'not self-evident to all' that it should remain 'an exclusive specialism'.[89]

The press continued to accuse each branch of 'overwhelming concern... for the well-being of its own members'. The *Daily Telegraph* published a London Business School professor lauding the government for promoting competition by:

ending the Dock Labour Scheme, forcing universities to adapt to the needs of the economy and of their students, and asking the Monopolies and Mergers Commission to see whether the oil industry is indeed competitive.... So why would it not work for the professions as well?

Professional standards were ensured by 'precisely the same market forces which maintain the quality of baked beans and soap powder—the provider's concern with his own continued reputation'. If 'the separation of the two branches of the legal profession is really so clearly the most efficient way of doing things, why do we have to enforce it by law?' Retiring after seventeen years as *Financial Times* legal columnist, A.H. Hermann warned against entrusting reform of the Bar to judges. They 'all started as barristers, their names still figure at the top of the shields displayed by chambers, they preside, as benchers, at dinners of the Inns of Court'.

In much the same way as Mr Mikhail Gorbachev cannot open the resources of his country to its citizens without first breaking the monopoly of power held by the higher ranks of the Communist Party, UK law cannot be placed at the service of the people until the monopolies and restrictive practices of the legal profession have been broken.

But though the *Economist* thought it 'funny... that in vital respects the bar's interests and those of the public should coincide', it declared legal aid Mackay's 'weak spot' and conditional fees no solution. And the *Independent* considered 'it may be necessary... to prevent financial institutions from carrying out conveyancing for their own borrowers' in order to forestall concentration and 'to go on denying solicitors the right of audience in the higher courts'.[90]

Getting the last word, the senior judges rebuked the Lord Chancellor's 'very firm terms' and 'peremptorily short period for comments' (four months), which were 'not conducive to calm and rational discourse'. They then showed again who was the culprit. The 'objectionable and irresponsible' proposals raised a 'constitutional issue'. The advisory committee was 'a grave breach of the doctrine of separation of powers'. Giving solicitors audience rights would admit 'unsuitable persons' and impair the 'competence, integrity and trustworthiness of advocates'. Chicanery in America's fused profession compelled judges to employ law clerks. The Lord Chancellor should exercise his powers 'only with the concurrence of the judiciary'. The 410 (barrister) Circuit judges concurred that the 'revolutionary' proposals threatened the constitution.[91]

The Law Society deplored the 'common thread of unreality running through' the Bar's 'transparently obstructionist' response. Consumers resented being 'required to use two lawyers where one would do'. It was 'extraordinary' for the Bar to insinuate that solicitors would retain advocacy in-house to increase earnings and 'absurd' for judges to insist on separation of preparation and advocacy.[92]

The *Guardian* denounced the 'overblown rhetoric' and 'objectionable prejudice' of the judges, who 'have willfully misused their power in denying solicitors a right to be heard'. 'The courts ... belong to the people'. But though columnist Hugo Young resented the judges' '*hauteur*', he surpassed them in concocting imaginary threats, condemning 'the more insidious and irrelevant piece of free-market cant: the plan inspired by the Department of Trade to permit any untutored jackanapes from any profession, to hang out his shingle as a legal advocate'. Decrying 'the propensity of every minister in the Thatcher government to pack even the smallest quangoid sub-committee with its reliable placemen', he proclaimed the 'independence of the Bar ... worth fighting for'. Displaying bipartisan scepticism, *The Times* agreed the advisory committee was 'dangerous' and urged the Lord Chancellor to 'accommodate as far as possible those principles most dear to his brothers in the judiciary'.[93]

Criticism did not end with the consultation period. Lord Benson joined business executives in warning: 'The US experience demonstrates where the contingency-fee system can lead'. The (British) Adam Smith Institute and the equally laissez faire (American) Manhattan Institute for Policy Research held a conference on the awful 'Lessons from America', whose 'own legal experts readily admit justice comes a poor second to economics'. American lawyers exploit the legal system's 'instability to make quick profits'. The 'most successful lawyers are the slickest salesmen and sharpest entrepreneurs'. 'The American delegates were unanimous ... leave both branches intact.' America suffered 'a litigation explosion which is out of control'. 'Advertising would be another undesirable by-product of a US-style system ... billboards, neon lights and special offers, coupled with outlandish success claims'.[94]

Lord Hailsham sounded as though he were still Lord Chancellor. The Green Papers filled him 'with a mixed feeling of outrage and betrayal'. Outdoing Dr Pangloss, he pronounced that 'the organisation of the legal profession...has produced almost complete incorruptibility....Each [branch] monitors and guarantees the integrity and competence of the other'. '[P]rofessional organisations are not, in the ordinary sense, trade unions....' 'What has been built up over the years in the way of integrity and impartiality, mutual trust and avoidance of conflicts of interest, will be swept away in a wave of populist enthusiasm'. The Government had 'introduced proposals for the nationalisation of one of the oldest and most honourable of our learned professions'. It proposed to extend audience rights 'to Trade Union Officials, Officials of the British Legion'. Contingency fees would expose defendants 'to a whole world of frivolous, vindictive, or purely blackmailing claims'.[95]

B. The White Paper

As newspapers (accurately) reported the Lord Chancellor was softening, they rallied to his cause.[96] That Mayhew 'appears to have won the day', the *Lawyer* regretted, was no 'victory for reason'. Lauding the Green Papers as 'bold, rational and unequivocal', the *Guardian* called a judicial veto 'the reassertion of the most reactionary restrictive practices in the legal profession...as daft as letting offenders select the jury'. A *Daily Mail* columnist bemoaned that:

the self-perpetuating oligarchy of top judges will continue to rule the profession. Silks will continue to command fat fees, without, as often as not, doing anything very much to earn them....The Bar—that most privileged of all monopolies—is the victor; British justice is the vanquished.

Like Italian tanks, said the *Evening Standard*, the British government 'had more reverse gears than forward ones'. The *Financial Times* warned that 'the senior judges, all of whom were drawn from the ranks of the Bar, cannot be trusted to exercise such a veto impartially'. The *New Law Journal* called it 'totally uncharacteristic for this Government to abandon its publicly professed aim of sweeping away restrictive practices and bringing greater competition into the provision of legal services. Can the Ethiopian change his skin or the leopard his spots?'[97]

At the Cabinet's Economic (Competition Policy) sub-committee meeting in early July, Lord Young (DTI), Nigel Lawson (Exchequer), and Norman Lamont (Chief Secretary) opposed concessions, while Mayhew and the Solicitor-General favoured them. (Lawson later recalled that 'it was clear that the reforms would have to be modified if they were to reach the statute-book'.) A week later the Cabinet accepted the changes at the instance of Lord Mackay, backed by the Prime Minister. A week after that the DTI issued its White Paper on restrictive practices, directing thirty-two professional organizations to demonstrate the economic benefits for consumers of any agreement preventing, distorting, or restricting competition but excepting rules mandated by statute or subject to ministerial approval (most of those governing solicitors).[98]

The next day Lord Mackay published his White Paper. Although it declared that 'the legal profession exists for the benefit of its clients, and for the proper administration of justice', Government had significantly diluted the reforms. Expanded audience rights would require unanimous approval by the Lord Chancellor and four senior judges (who would have to give reasons for rejecting proposals and be subject to judicial review). Corporate conveyancers would have to offer clients a personal interview with a solicitor or licensed conveyancer and could not act for both parties. The Lord Chancellor's committee would be 'purely advisory' and 'wholly independent'. Professional codes of conduct approved by the Lord Chancellor and four senior judges would be exempt from challenge as restrictive practices. The Law Society and Bar Council would decide about partnerships (including MNPs and MDPs). Contingent fees would remain unlawful.[99]

Gaskell exulted prematurely: 'We saw a danger in the judges being offered control... but this is clearly not what is proposed'.[100] The Bar made the opposite mistake, denouncing the 'government-appointed quango' as 'an unacceptable interference with the independence of the judges'. Lord Donaldson, who would have a veto, rightly observed that Government had 'taken account of the judges' professional advice in quite large measure'. Mayhew extolled the 'skillful balance' he had engineered. The CA hailed the White Paper as a 'major victory' if 'not quite the revolution we had hoped it would be' (rather an understatement). But Labour backbenchers were scathing. The 'humiliating climbdown', said Austin Mitchell, sanctified government by and for barristers. Brian Sedgemore added: 'the Government has surrendered to a self-seeking bunch of judicial hooligans led by Lord Chief Justice Lane choking on his own hyperbolic verbosity'.[101]

Although the media had opposed compromise, they now called it 'balanced', 'canny', and (with unconscious irony) 'judicious'. The *Daily Telegraph* said the sensible 'climbdown' preserved the Bar. Its columnist declared it 'no business of a Tory government to have a public row with one of the main arms of the constitution'. *The Times* felt Mackay had given 'too little weight to existing professional institutions and practices' and 'wisely now builds far more on what is already there'. Reversing itself, the *Financial Times* declared: 'the administration of justice is not an activity which can be equated directly with the manufacture, say, of baked beans. Competition has a role to play, but it can never be the only consideration.'

But its columnist Robert Rice feared judicial review 'could quickly degenerate into farce'. A.H. Hermann agreed junior judges were unlikely to scrutinize their seniors' decisions rigorously. The *Independent* commented cynically: 'pause for laughter'. Exaggerating the victory 'against the combined forces of the senior judiciary and the barristers' mafia known as the Bar Council', the *Observer* lauded 'the most fundamental revolution of our legal system for more than a century'. A *Guardian* columnist agreed the proposals 'amount to a revolution in the holy of holies. The Bar has been routed.... The judges have been tied up in knots'. But its leader criticized Mackay for having ignored the old Scottish saying: 'Never try to cross a ravine in two strides'. Because 'the judges have consistently protected the Bar's interests', their veto was 'unnecessary, undesirable and nowhere justified in public argument'.[102]

The legal press reflected the divided profession. Given the Bar's 'sorry', 'arrogant', and 'clumsy' performance, the *Solicitors Journal* said it should 'make the first peace overtures'. The *New Law Journal* confidently predicted 'the Bar's monopoly of rights of audience will be broken in the next few years'. *Counsel* was equally apprehensive the White Paper would allow 'solicitors to impersonate barristers with impunity'. 'Nobody will thank [Parliament] if through a temporary hole in the political ozone layer our legal system is irreparably damaged'.[103]

The judges made no effort to hide their intentions. Lord Lane cancelled the formal opening of the legal year for the first time since the Middle Ages because Lord Mackay would have led the procession. Lord Donaldson told the Bar's annual conference he favoured limiting audience rights to full-time advocates practising alone and separating preparation and advocacy in cases involving crime, family, children, the disabled, and judicial review because lawyers doing both 'might run the risk of becoming Jack of both trades and master of neither'. The Law Society denounced such 'double manning' for perpetuating 'the absurdity that the one person who knows most about the case can't present it'. *The Times* rebuked Donaldson for 'not only throw[ing] into question current daily practice by solicitors' but also 'rob[bing] the client of one of the main benefits of the proposed reforms'. Repeating the Scargill analogy, the *Evening Standard* denounced the Master of the Rolls for reassuring 'his trade union' he would 'stymie this measure' and protect their 'closed shop'. Lord Mackay called it 'misleading and unfair' to see a veto threat in the speech.[104]

The branches jockeyed for advantage. Fennell argued that the judges, who 'administer the courts', should make the decisions and not 'be seen as a rubber stamp'. He opposed 'too much power being concentrated in the hands of the Lord Chancellor' and wanted the Lord Chief Justice to appoint the advisory committee. The Law Society responded that judges should have 'a voice, not a veto'. Its new strategy plan put 'less faith in maintenance of areas of work reserved' for solicitors and more in 'the breaking down of restrictions and the improvement of skills'. Vice President Tony Holland, whose committee produced it, called the loss of the conveyancing monopoly a 'salutary shake-up' and declared himself 'Mackay's greatest fan'. 'We have one of the most antiquated legal systems in the whole of Europe, if not the world.' But the report also wanted to subject all members of MNPs and MDPs and the 'rules relating to accountant's reports, compensation fund contributions, professional indemnity and the power of intervention' to 'a degree of control by the Law Society'.[105]

C. The Courts and Legal Services Act 1990

Giving the Courts and Legal Services Bill its first reading in the Lords on 6 December, Lord Mackay stressed moderation. 'Huge change in this area might not be right. Evolution may be a better way forward.' He wished to eliminate 'such current anomalies as solicitors being barred from representing defendants in the crown court, where the judge in the very same court may have trained as a solicitor'. Mayhew endorsed this 'wisely constructed framework'. Claiming the Bill as its 'real achievement', the Law Society hailed this 'modern statutory foundation for the legal profession of the future'. But the Bar still wanted it 'improved' so as not to 'upset the balance between the Government as Executive and those who administer justice'. Denying the Bill had 'solve[d] the problem at a stroke', Fennell belligerently declared 'the beginning of the hundred years war'. LAG Director Roger Smith sceptically predicted that the 'fudged compromise' was 'unlikely to result in a legal profession free of outdated restrictions'. 'Apart from a few specialist solicitor advocates, the conditions which the senior judiciary is likely to impose . . . will allow the barrister's monopoly to be maintained.'[106]

Media enthusiasm for the compromise had grown in the five months since the White Paper. *The Times* praised the Bar for alerting 'public opinion to the danger' of 'killing off the profession of barrister altogether'. It was 'in the public interest that there should be an independent Bar' even if this required 'continuance of restrictive practices and a limitation on the influence of market forces'. The *Guardian* called the 'slightly addled Lord Chancellor's egg' a 'success' by the 'one simple test . . . who gets the most out of the Bill: the lawyers or the consumer?' The *New Law Journal*, more cynically, analogized Lord Mackay to the Prince in Lampedusa's *The Leopard*, who 'made changes in order to maintain the status quo'.[107]

The Lords gave the Bill a Second Reading on 19 December, devoted six days to the Committee stage (16 January to 5 February 1990) and another three to the Report stage (20 February to 1 March), and gave it a third reading on 15 March.[108] Maintaining the White Paper's conciliatory approach, Lord Mackay said the Bill created 'a framework which will foster evolution', not 'a ready-made and immutable template', and preserved a 'vital role for the independent judiciary'.[109]

This failed to mollify critics. Lord Hutchinson derided the Lord Chancellor's 'remarkable' 'Lone Ranger performance', which had 'avoided discussion of…great issues of principle'. Lord Rawlinson called him 'a party politician'. No previous Lord Chancellor would 'have allowed there to be introduced into such matters the party political philosophy of the Administration to which they belonged'.[110] While 'reject[ing] with contempt' the suggestion that he was 'inspired by resentment' or intended a 'personal reflection', Lord Rawlinson moved amendments to eliminate the Lord Chancellor's power over conveyancing or to sit as a judge or appoint QCs or judges. 'Are we really going to accept that a Cabinet member should be involved in controlling the independent legal profession in such a matter as the sale of a house?' Lord Mackay's tenure had 'created a precedent…that no longer must the Lord Chancellor be an English Lawyer trained in the English courts'. He 'cannot, through no fault of his own, know the English profession'. Appointive power should be 'independent of the government of the day'. Lord Ackner agreed there was 'a far greater risk…of the Prime Minister of the day saying to his or her Lord Chancellor, "Is he one of us?"' '[P]olitical appointees as judges' was the 'most objectionable' of the 'many undesirable features of the American system for the administration of justice which this proposed legislation will undoubtedly impose on the United Kingdom'. (This motion was withdrawn, as were all others on which no action is noted.[111])

Lord Rippon thought the Bill 'bad in some respects' and 'dangerous in others'. Calling it an 'improvement' on the Green Papers 'is rather like saying that a man who was threatened with two black eyes should be pleased if he gets only one'.[112] Lord Ackner quoted 'Chief Justice [*sic*] Cardozo's' warning to 'safeguard the law against the assaults of opportunism, the expediency of the passing hour, the erosion of small encroachments, and the scorn and derision of those who have no patience with general principles'. 'The word "sinister"…would aptly describe legislation which essentially plays politics with the administration of justice.'[113] Lord Simon expressed 'almost unrelieved gloom and foreboding'.[114] Lord Oliver voiced the 'widely felt concern that our legal system…an essential foundation for any civilised state—was about to be subject to a hasty, ill-considered and therefore a most perilous experiment from which, once accomplished, there could be no retreat should it prove to be a disaster, as many predicted it would'.[115]

Although Lord Mackay was 'puzzled' by his critics' focus on legal aid, which the Legal Aid Act 1988 had 'decisive[ly] change[d]', Lord Alexander called the review of legal aid 'a much more important priority…than restructuring the legal profession', which 'will not enhance access to law'. The real 'scandal', agreed Lord Irvine, was 'inadequate provision of legal aid'.[116]

Critics renewed procedural objections. The Bill 'has been generated entirely inside the government machine', complained Lord Hailsham. '[A]bout two months were allowed for consultation' and 'both Houses of Parliament were denied the possibility of debate on the White Paper'. Lord Ackner said the Green Paper 'was produced in a rush in a matter of two or three months'. 'Why no prior consultation before embarking on what is proudly asserted to be the most radical changes in our legal system in centuries?' The Government had 'disregarded...almost every principle of methodology which law reform ought to attract'. Lord Beloff found 'no evidence of any particular grievance or public clamour' about lawyers. 'I cannot think of another Bill in the course of British history that has been rushed through unnecessarily in this way as though it were an emergency powers Bill with an enemy on our doorstep.'[117] Lord Simon protested that the Lord Chancellor's 'obduracy' had carried a Bill 'absolutely torn to shreds'. He objected to continual late sittings, putting 'on record the sense of outrage...at the way that the Bill is being driven through', 'hustled through' with 'breathless haste' and comment 'stifled or muffled'. He did 'not doubt that there is a silent and deaf majority faithfully assembled by the noble Lord, the Chief Whip, ready to vote down any attempt' to resist the Government.[118]

Opponents accused the Government of 'pandering to the populist appeal of the marketplace' (Lord Oliver), 'seeking to placate a populous clamour for reform' (Lord Benson), making a 'populist appeal' by 'attacking the so-called restrictive practices of lawyers' (Lord Ackner). Lord Irvine mocked 'the simplistic, populist line...inflict some popular pain on the lawyers and this will guarantee better access to legal services, lower costs and increase consumer choice. It is a false prospectus' (if one he embraced seven years later). Lord Rawlinson was 'saddened' by 'the abandonment of Tory principle and the putting of populist interests before the defence of excellence'. Lord Beloff asked: 'what is the passion which this Government have for getting away from the historic self-reliance and self-governance of our institutions and our professions in favour of what can only be called populism? That is to say, the constant pleas of the ignorant that ignorance is in some sense a virtue.'[119]

Conservatives extolled tradition and suspected change. Lord Rawlinson, who had served in three governments, invoked 'the Tory principles of Disraeli that the purpose of a Conservative administration should be to... maintain our institutions'. 'The word "development" is not one which is usually associated in the mind of the public....as being something which is totally desirable.' '[V]oluntarily to set aside those centuries of experience and the institutions which have grown out of them' seemed to Lord Beloff 'most extraordinary'. 'Novelty in itself' was 'not a virtue' for Lord Oliver. Lord Hailsham distinguished two kinds of human institutions: 'The American Constitution is an example of the contrived. Our own system is largely a matter of tradition...the test of what makes a traditional system good is whether it works.'[120]

Bench and Bar were strongly united in opposition (although barristers who had retired or been elevated to the bench loudly denied personal interest). Solicitors supported much of the Bill. Some, like Lord Mishcon and Lord Prys-Davies, were briefed by the Law Society; all resented the sneers of judges and barristers. Recalling 'the days when the Bar was recruited from the sons of gentry and attorneys from the middle classes', Lord Simon observed that 'wounding things have been said...which have remained'. Lord Hutchinson warned that the Bill exposed judges to being 'sued in their own courts for personal damages...by any little upstart solicitor'. Unlike an independent barrister, a solicitor would assure an accused: 'We know the local police. We can speak to our colleague about your plea, or of course we can speak to our colleague in the local Crown Prosecution Service'. Lord Benson had seen 'the unofficial list of lawyers who could not be trusted to conduct any litigation honestly'. Now 'that black-list will become a library'. Lord Grantchester warned that the 'standards of justice will tend to be under attack' if solicitors appear in higher courts because 'the members of those concerns [firms] will be concerned as much for their bonuses and profits as for other considerations'. Lord Hacking, a City solicitor, was 'thoroughly unconvinced' by Lord Hutchinson's 'hyperboles and apocryphal accounts of solicitors in the High Street'. 'I have been no less independent or honest because I am a partner in a large law firm with 75 partners or because I have big and powerful clients.'[121]

The few lay speakers were equally unpersuaded. Baroness Phillips accused judges of 'arrogance' in claiming to have 'a monopoly of words of wisdom'. Although Lord Hailsham had bridled at lawyers being called 'fat cats', it 'seems pretty expensive to talk to anyone in the law'. 'Anyone who has gone through the trauma of trying to buy a house is absolutely mystified by the number of professionals whom one must consult and pay.' Lawyers had 'too long tried to dazzle and impress their clients by their importance when there has been a complaint about their advice'. Lord Allen of Abbeydale offered 'warm support' for the Bill from 'the consumer's point of view'. He found it 'difficult to understand what there is so special about this country which makes it essential to preserve the split profession which exists hardly anywhere else'. Lord Lloyd saw no constitutional objections: 'it is after all, what occurs in almost every country'. The Earl of Shannon said conveyancing had 'been crying out for reform'. It 'should not be a legal service but a consumer product' because the 'actual legal input' was 'minimal' and the rest 'largely ritual paper-pushing which can be replaced today by computers'. Lord Morris declared that 'law is there for the people of this country' not 'for the benefit of those who practise it at any level'. For eight years Lord Hailsham had exposed 'the conservatism of his profession'; now 'the same gamekeeper...has turned poacher'.[122]

Lord Rawlinson continued to rail against executive power. The Lord Chancellor's office had worked because it was 'designed for a Minister beyond political ambition'. It:

must be axiomatic that it cannot be acceptable for the Minister...responsible for appointing the judges, to have in effect, the ultimate say through his appointees over who may appear in the courts to plead before those judges. Nowhere in the civilised world—certainly nowhere outside the fading Marxist societies—does a Minister have such powers.

...

I returned earlier this week from Poland where the people were celebrating the freedom of the judges from any restraint or control, that is, freedom of the Bar from government agencies and from supervision and direction. They were anxious to follow our practices. I told them that they should hurry because the shadow of authority, disguised in a British compromise, stalks our profession.[123]

The Earl of Selkirk concurred:

In Eastern Europe everyone is screaming out for democracy though they have not much idea what it is. But what have we got? We have government regulations by the pile. That is a strong example of how bureaucratic dictatorship is likely to be extended.[124]

Lord Hutchinson predicted the Bill 'will do injury to the civil liberties of the ordinary citizen'. The 'independence, availability and expertise' which have been 'the absolute essential protection of the citizen...against abuse of the executive power or that of the police...now all goes'. The Bill 'will achieve the Government's aim to clear the Crown Courts of the Bar....'[125] Peers decried the 'ludicrous...over-burden of administration' (Lord Benson), a 'bureaucratic machinery of a complexity and density which could have been devised only in the darkest caverns of the Civil Service' (Lord Hutchinson).[126]

ACLEC was a lightning rod. Lords Hailsham, Griffiths, Ackner, Murray, Alexander, Rawlinson, Beloff, Oliver, Rees, Campbell, and Donaldson and the Earl of Onslow assailed the lay majority. 'No one knows better the needs of lay people than the judges before whom such people appear' (Lord Murray). It was like replacing 'the General Medical Council by a lay-dominated body' (Lord Oliver). Lord Beloff invoked 'the catastrophe which has befallen the universities under the regime of the new funding council which has a heavy ignorant lay element'. ACLEC would contain 'a number of superannuated old ladies and gentlemen, who have nothing better to do' (this from Lord Hailsham!), the token director, trade unionist and retired civil servant 'totally ignorant of the law and totally unschoooled in the science of the law' (Lord Rawlinson), 'political appointees of the government of the day', giving the Civil Service 'control over what has hitherto been an independent and separate part of our national life' (Lord Ackner). Interest groups urged representation for consumers, commerce, and industry, a presiding and a circuit judge, a stipendiary magistrate, a legal executive, women, racial minorities, and 'disadvantaged members of the public'.[127] Lord Rawlinson moved to limit ACLEC to 'supervising the duties of proper professional bodies manned by independent persons of learning in the law'. He moved that it be appointed by the Lord Chief Justice. For it to be chosen by 'a Minister who will be a member of the Cabinet' was 'rather like the Chief Whip approving his supporters'. Lord Ackner moved that the appointment of judicial members be approved by the Lord Chief Justice so as to 'somewhat dilute' the 'epithet "Lord Chancellor's committee"'. Lord Ackner proposed striking out Lord Mackay's amendment to require ACLEC to 'have regard to the desirability of equality of opportunity'. Only Lord Mackay's amendment was agreed.[128]

Peers offered new diatribes against the market. Lord Hutchinson expressed solicitude for 'the small man', who 'will now be left to the tender grasping mercies of the market... represented by a cosy lot of generalist advocates or paralegals working by the book on a strictly commercial basis'. The 'catch phrase' of 'market forces', sneered Lord Rawlinson, must now apply 'to the behaviour of the surgeon in the operating theatre and certainly now to the pleader in the courts'. That 'philosophy... could never be appropriate in the administration of justice'. His American friends told him 'frankly that in the United States the law is no longer a profession but rather a business....' Others 'paid a ritual genuflexion to the interest of the customer'. 'But justice is not always in the interests of a customer, for example, the rapist, the fraudster, the renegade... want the avoidance of justice.' Lord Oliver accused the Government of promoting the 'optimism of the alchemist' that 'by commercialising the learned professions so that their exercise becomes merely a facet of business, one can somehow discover a crock of gold from which will flow cheap law'. Resisting subordination to the DGFT, Lord Renton asked how Lord Mackay would have felt as an advocate had he been told 'he was a trader'. Lord Beloff said the DGFT's role was to ensure 'that there is no hanky-panky with the market for crispies, pop-up toasters or video nasties'. What does he have 'to do with legal practice or appearances before the courts'? It was 'an insult to the profession'. The Government sometimes 'behave as though they were a wholly owned subsidiary of the Institute of Economic Affairs'.[129] Critics scorned the 'dogma' of the DTI (Lord Meston), that 'free competition through market discipline will ensure the most efficient and effective network of legal services at the most economical price' (Lord Ackner). Lord Irvine derided 'free-market hype' four times in one speech.[130] Lord Hailsham took the opposite tack, declaring it 'distinctly paradoxical that a government...devoted largely to the privatisation of industry, should publish a document' whose effect 'is the nationalisation of the legal profession and part of the judiciary'. Lord Hutchinson agreed that 'the creation of this huge nationalised monopoly [the CPS] protected from the forces of the market place, surely does not sit happily with the Government's supposed philosophy underlying this Bill'.[131]

Such denunciations alternated with market arguments that the Bill would hurt consumers. Lord Grantchester was 'unable to accept' that solicitors would be cheaper because 'the income of the average barrister is lower than that of the average solicitor partner'. Lord Renton agreed because the Bar was an 'overmanned' and 'very competitive profession'. (If solicitors were more expensive, retorted Lord Boyd-Carpenter, they would be 'driven out by competition'. If Lord Hailsham 'really believes that it is cheaper to employ two men than one I can only say that I am lost in admiration of his credulity'.[132]) Many plausibly predicted concentration but unjustifiably concluded it would reduce meaningful choice or competition.[133] 'If one applies market forces to the legal profession and the structure of the legal system', declared Lord Hooson, 'everybody undercuts everyone else and one ends up with lower standards'.[134] (In fact, consumers obtain more varied mixtures of price and quality.) Lord Benson complained that the Government sought 'to impose competition on a playing field that is as uneven as the Canadian Rockies'.[135]

Recognizing that all did not share their detestation of the market, opponents invoked the unsavoury prospect of Americanization. The English legal system, asserted Lord Beloff, 'has a much higher reputation than the system in the United States upon which our new-fangled legal system is to be based'. 'No one whom I have met from the United States', said Lord Hooson, 'pretends that the American system is cheaper, speedier, or held in more regard than ours—quite the contrary'. '[A]s the Cabinet desires', Lord Rawlinson deplored, the Bill 'will lead to the establishment of the American system where everyone sues everyone else and lawyers are very rich'. Lord Ackner warned 'we will in fact out-America America'.[136] The Bill would introduce 'the American legal factory system' (Lord Rawlinson) (although English lawyers were more concentrated than American), the 'unethical and abhorrent' 'American system of the state prosecution service' (Lord Campbell), fusion, which Americans were 'stuck with' but 'would like to get away from' (Lord Renton).[137]

Worst of all were conditional fees: 'the American practice where the lawyers descend like vultures upon the scene of every disaster, soliciting

clients' (Lord Rawlinson). They were 'inherently corrupting', said Lord
Hailsham, and created the 'temptation...to prolong the costs until the
same result is obtained two years later'. (They do the opposite; that is the
perverse incentive of the existing fee structure.) American civil juries
award 'against the unsuccessful defendant a sum approximately twice that
to which [the plaintiff] is entitled by way of compensation'. This was
'a straightforward moral issue...if there is one doctrine of the Christian
church which can be proved by experience it is the doctrine of original sin.
If we make it pay to be dishonest, people will become dishonest....' 'The
courts will be flooded with frivolous, vexatious and frankly blackmailing
cases....' It was 'a poor substitute for legal aid' (Lord Renton), a 'mockery
of the famous ideal that our courts of justice are open to all' (Lord
Mishcon), 'wholly contrary to the interests of the proper and efficient
administration of justice' (Lord Donaldson). But it was approved by 136 to
56.[138] During the third reading Lord Ackner moved to prohibit uplifts,
which 'many of us recognise...as being evil...inherently immoral'. Lord
Donaldson 'very much' supported the amendment, which 'would prevent
barristers and solicitors becoming involved in a market-place approach'.
After Lord Mackay reassured the Chamber that the 'uplift would be of
fairly modest proportions' and agreed it was not 'a realistic alternative to
legal aid', the amendment failed by 10 votes to 45.[139]

Opponents continued to worry about the independence of the judiciary
and the profession. Lord Hailsham objected that the Lord Chancellor 'in
his infinite wisdom will be able to publish the name of the judge who has
differed' with him and 'the reasons he has for differing'. 'If that is not
inconsistent with judicial independence, I could almost say that noble
Lords may call me a Dutchman.' Lord Ackner accused the Government of
having 'dangerously disregarded' the 'supreme truth' voiced by Lord
Simmonds (a previous Lord Chancellor) that 'the safeguard of liberty lies
in the independence of a judiciary which fears not nor favours the
Executive'.[140] Designated judges who 'dare[d]' to disagree with the Lord
Chancellor, warned Lord Hutchinson, 'can for the first time in the long
legal history of this country be sued in their own courts for personal damages'. Lord Hailsham concurred. Lord Alexander moved an amendment
to immunize them, which it would be 'an affront' not to pass. Lord Mackay
promised to deal with the matter. Lord Ackner renewed it during the
Report stage.[141]

Asking pointedly if 'the Government accept that the interests of justice
require an independent Bar', Lord Alexander moved an amendment to
add to the purpose clause 'in ways which uphold and advance the interests
of justice' so judges could 'take into account...the importance of maintaining a separate and independent Bar'. Lord Benson agreed that 'there
is nothing in this Bill to sustain a strong and independent Bar in the

future'.[142] Baroness Elles, a barrister, declared Britain would be the only EC member 'to place the control of the legal profession into the hands of the Executive'. Lord Beloff found 'the enforcement of executive control' 'sinister'. Lord Hooson expressed 'the great fear' that 'gradually the judiciary, the Bar, the Law Society and everything else, will come under the control of the administrative arm of the Lord Chancellor's Department'. The Bill's 'school-masterly and essentially authoritarian powers as regards the training and practice of the law', said Lord Rawlinson, were 'nothing but the triumph of the Executive; and perhaps of civil servants'. Britain would be 'the only country outside a few remaining communist dictatorships where so much regulatory power is given to a Minister over an independent legal profession'.[143] He and Lord Simon believed fusion inevitable.[144] To protect the Bar, Lord Renton moved an amendment to require the Lord Chancellor and designated judges to approve any Bar Council rule allowing partnerships and renewed it during the third reading.[145]

Judges and barristers resisted the extension of audience rights. Lord Rawlinson reasserted his 'belief that the rights of audience should be limited to those who are barristers'. He was 'not going to see this Bill passed without having my say and keeping up my opposition to the bitter end'. He moved eight amendments to retain 'the separate roles and duties of the separate branches of the profession'. Reiterating that 'the whole spirit of this Bill is to clear the criminal court of barristers', Lord Hutchinson moved an amendment to exclude CPS lawyers from the higher courts. Lord Hailsham said 'it would be a disaster if certain prosecutors came to be known, as...the district attorney of the United States system'. 'Polarisation inevitably leads to the concept of a public defender.' Lord Havers warned against 'too cosy an atmosphere between prosecuting counsel and the judges', which was Lord Campbell's experience at the Old Bailey. Lord Mackay bristled. He had been 'responsible for some five years for a state prosecution service when a great many jury trials were conducted in the sheriff court by those who were in the full-time service of the state'. 'I should regard it as a gross insult to a person of the standing of the Director of Public Prosecutions to say that merely because he holds an office or is employed he could not exhibit independence of mind.' The idea was 'absolute nonsense', 'absurd', 'indefensible'. Security of employment actually increased independence. Lord Hutchinson found the reply 'completely unconvincing'. He resented that 'every time a former barrister puts forward an amendment, it is suggested—as it was suggested this morning in the *Guardian*—that it is on behalf of one's own profession, on behalf of one's own interests'.

He renewed the amendment at the Report stage. Did Lord Mackay 'really mean to describe...Lord Benson...Lord Templeman,

Mr. Dahrendorf and their colleagues as talking "absolute nonsense" and their views as "indefensible"'? Was 'the present Attorney-General' talking 'nonsense'? Lord Mackay stood firm. It was 'nonsense', 'an absurd notion', 'utterly wrong'. Lord Mishcon thought it a 'Gilbert and Sullivan situation' to imagine three lay magistrates reproving 'aggressive and improper conduct of the case' while a Crown Court judge would be 'sitting absolutely silent'. Lord Hutchinson replied that 'salaried employees in the Crown Prosecution Service will have annual reports made upon their performance. Their promotion within the service will be considered.' Lord Irvine called 'the vulnerability of employees under a contract of employment...a matter of constitutional importance'. The motion failed by 49 votes to 143.[146]

The cab rank constituted an even more important line of defence. Lord Alexander moved an amendment to subject all higher court advocates to the rule, which 'has been the obligation of the Bar for centuries'. (He included legal aid work, which the Bar had just added.) It will 'secure representation for all clients, however unpopular their cause' and ensure 'that advocates who act in those cases do not themselves become victims'. Lord Hutchinson noted that a decade earlier Lord Mackay had called it 'an important constitutional guarantee'. Solicitors objected. Lord Boardman thought partnerships would create difficulties. Lord Byron (a barrister turned solicitor) reported 'a great deal of manipulation by barristers' clerks'. Lord Goodman thought it 'a disservice to replace a voluntary impulse of a kind that has never failed with a legal obligation'. It would be 'suspected in some quarters to be a disincentive to solicitors to become advocates'. Lord Mackay preferred to leave it to professional rules. The amendment failed by 79 to 90.[147] Lord Mishcon moved an amendment, whose principle the Consumers' Association favoured, obligating the Law Society to find any client a solicitor and exposing a member who rejected such a request to discipline. Lord Ackner did not consider this an alternative to the cab rank rule; Lords Hutchinson and Rawlinson concurred, offering only half-hearted support.[148]

Lord Alexander renewed his motion at the Report stage. The rule was a 'corollary' of the 'monopoly' of audience rights. This clause was not 'directed against solicitors' and 'transcend[ed] professional sectional interests'. He and others had 'consistently recognised that there should be extended rights of audience' and had 'sought to ensure that the strength of the solicitors' profession is not diminished by changes in the law with regard to conveyancing'. He recently read that two 'leading London legal aid firms have refused to take the case of a man accused of raping his girlfriend'. Lord Ackner criticized them for saying:

'We act only for the prosecution because if we did not we would offend our clients'—organisations mainly of ladies who are, as we all are for that matter, fiercely opposed to the crime of rape. Because of the harm it would do their practice, and for no other reason...they opted not to act for defendants.

This showed 'how undesirable it would be if they were entitled to advocacy in the higher courts'. Lord Hutchinson emphasized 'there is no question of barristers against solicitors....' 'This is the one amendment...which puts legal aid to the front.' Lord Irvine supported the amendment 'not from any partisan reason as a member of the Bar' but because of its 'major constitutional importance'. Lord Campbell did so because 'it affords fair terms of competition'.

Most solicitors demurred. Although the rule had never applied to them in lower courts, Lord Boardman knew of no complaint by clients unable to obtain representation. Consumer organizations were opposed. When Citizens' Advice Bureaux sought representation, said Baroness Phillips, 'the first inquiry is whether the client is legally aided'. Was the purpose 'to make unworkable solicitors rights of audience'? Lord Marshall of Leeds feared 'that the cumulative effect of such an amendment may be to frustrate the general aim of the Bill'. Lord Hacking felt it would be difficult 'to apply the cab rank rule...because we offer wider services to our clients, such as providing financial references', which presupposed 'trust between us and our clients'. 'Why cannot members of the Bar turn that rule to their advantage?' But Lord Mishcon, who had voted for the amendment the first time, declared that 'if one asks for a privilege...one accepts the burdens that have been borne by those who had that privilege in the past, and one accepts those burdens proudly'. (Outside the Chamber the *New Law Journal* dismissed the rule as 'a sham and a paper tiger' but regretted that 'only "politically acceptable" offences will be defended by certain firms and certain barristers'. A silk misused the statement by an American that though 'a notorious person was entitled to the services of a lawyer, "he is surely not entitled to the services of a good one" '. (The non-lawyer commentator was being ironic.) Lord Mackay reiterated that the need for exceptions 'demonstrates beyond all doubt that this is properly a matter for the rules' and not primary legislation. Lord Alexander resented Lord Hacking's suggestion 'that the Bar would prosper in certain circumstances'.

[W]ho gives a damn whether the Bar will prosper? Who gives a damn whether the measure is inconvenient to solicitors? ...We should all forget which side of the profession would benefit from this and decide the issue as one of principle.

He wondered:

whether the Government want, if by any chance there are some of their troops within this House who have been unavoidably prevented from hearing the debate, to take them into the Lobbies against us on what has been described on all sides not as a political issue but as an issue of conscience.

The amendment was adopted by 99 to 92.[149]

Judges and barristers made other attempts to defend the Bar's turf. Lord Donaldson repeated what he had told the last Bar Conference: 'the interests of justice may demand special requirements as, for example, that the preparation and presentation of the case be in separate and independent hands'. The charge that this was 'no more than a transparent bid to retain the barristers' monopoly by other means' was 'wholly unworthy' of solicitors. Lord Campbell agreed that separation was essential to prevent the 'blackmailing of juries'.[150] Lord Renton moved an amendment to prohibit contracts between barristers and lay clients, which Lord Hutchinson wanted applied to all advocates, or else there would be 'a totally unacceptable bumpy playing field'. Lord Mackay said the Bar Council retained the power to prohibit direct access. But Lord Mishcon feared the OFT could order direct access. The amendment was passed by 112 votes to 63.[151]

Solicitors were equally wary of corporate conveyancing. Lord Rippon called it 'thoroughly objectionable'. The multiple conflicts of interest could not be managed by Chinese Walls. 'The City...is full of Chinese Walls, some of them made of rice paper. Others have grapevines growing round them....' Lord Mishcon moved an amendment to require authorized practitioners to charge 'fair and reasonable prices'. '[L]arge financial institutions' with 'very substantial resources' would 'be able to destroy the very competition'. He moved an amendment requiring an authorized practitioner to have a solicitor or licensed conveyancer responsible for ensuring that the conveyance is carried out according to rules. The Law Society urged this 'not for its own good or for the good of its membership but because of its worries' about clients. Lord Prys-Davies moved an amendment to require that a solicitor or licensed conveyancer supervise all stages of a conveyance. Lord Tordoff moved an amendment making it a conflict of interest to act for more than one party to a transaction, fearing:

that a few large chains of financial services firms, estate agents, insurance agents and authorised practitioners will be created, backed by massive television and press advertising to promote the one-stop conveyancing shops to which people are urged to go. The effect on the high street solicitor could be disastrous.

Lord Hailsham declared that people 'often go to a quite small firm of family solicitors where they happen to know one or more of the partners', who might urge the client 'to borrow the money off your father-in-law'. Lord Tordoff added: 'the ordinary high street solicitor' treats clients 'in an avuncular way'. Lord Mackay replied that 'recent surveys carried out by the National Consumer Council indicate that many people who go to solicitors for their conveyancing neither ask for nor obtain independent financial advice'. There was 'no inevitable conflict of interest' in corporate conveyancing and 'a substantial body of evidence...that that is what people want'. But regulations would 'provide that the qualified person in charge of the transaction should have a personal interview with the client at the beginning of the transaction', and an employed solicitor's primary duty would be to the client. Lord Prys-Davies moved that this interview be free. Lord Mishcon moved an amendment to require institutional conveyancers to observe solicitors' rules of disclosure and accounting for commissions. When Lord Mackay proposed to leave this to the regulations, Lord Mishcon forced a division, which adopted the amendment by 31 votes to 30.[152]

The Earl of Lytton and Lord Mishcon both moved amendments to prevent tying-in services, which the Lord Chancellor promised to consider very carefully. In the stand part debate Baroness Gardner of Parkes, speaking for the Council of Mortgage Lenders and as vice-president of the Building Societies Association, said the entire clause was 'based on an incorrect supposition...that the mortgage-lending institutions have it within their power to force borrowers to use related services....' Nevertheless, the clause was agreed to.[153] During the Committee Stage Lord Prys-Davies moved an amendment to prohibit lenders from publicizing combined services without offering each component at its proportionate price and renewed it in the third reading debate. Lord Mackay replied it 'would not allow lenders to offer a package of services to a customer at a discount'.[154] In the Third Reading debate Lord Mishcon moved an amendment to require the Authorised Conveyancing Practitioners Board to maintain fair competition. '[M]any types of competition...in the market place among traders...should not exist between professional people carrying out responsible work'. Lord Mackay moved his own amendment empowering the Lord Chancellor to require charges 'consistent with the maintenance of fair competition', which was agreed. Lord Boardman moved an amendment imposing on authorized practitioners the solicitor's duty to a client. He wanted 'something like a health warning put on the building society or financial institution's name plate outside saying, "You will not get independent advice here, we shall keep to ourselves any side profits we make...."'[155]

The Earl of Shannon moved amendments to prevent the Law Society or Bar Council from prohibiting MDPs and requiring the DGFT to review such bans. Calling it 'unfair on the other professional bodies to imply that they are not capable of keeping a confidence or are not bound by rules and regulations as to their conduct', the Earl of Lytton (a chartered surveyor) moved an amendment to require any prohibition to be approved by the Lord Chancellor and Secretary of State. But judges and barristers opposed MDPs as leading to fusion. Baroness Elles warned that lawyers in MDPs might not be able to practise in the USA or EC. Lord Templeman said the amendments 'would have the effect of destroying the profession....All kinds of fringe people could become partners or directors of a company, so long as it had a token lawyer.' '[I]f there is no case for a separate profession, let us abolish every profession. Let everybody be able to do everything.' '[I]f you throw everybody into the melting-pot or if you take all your eggs, break them and make them into an omelette, the one bad one will affect the rest.'[156] Lord Mishcon then moved an amendment to prohibit the Law Society from allowing solicitors to enter MDPs with non-lawyers or non-lawyers to be shareholders in solicitors' firms, which was defeated by 23 to 38. During the Report stage he moved an amendment prohibiting the Law Society from authorizing MDPs unless the solicitor had primary obligations to the client and professional privilege was protected. This was defeated by 69 votes to 86.[157]

The Bill's provisions for non-lawyer practice provoked derision. Lord Hutchinson called it 'quite unacceptable for unqualified persons to deal with bail applications'. Lord Hacking reported: 'Law Society and Bar Council united; House to be divided'. But the clause was agreed to. In the Report stage Lord Hutchinson moved an amendment to eliminate such an 'incredible' practice. The Criminal Bar Association agreed. Lord Hacking renewed the motion in the Third Reading debate.[158]

Peers were even angrier at the power of the Lord Chancellor and design-ated judges to recognize bodies to qualify non-lawyers to practise and become eligible for the bench. Non-lawyers would 'parade as paralegals and claim skills in advocacy, as litigators, and in conveyancing', objected Lord Benson. 'The public will not be able to distinguish between lawyers and paralegals.' 'The judiciary will not know whom they can trust and whom they cannot trust.' The 'quality of the professions in this country will inevitably fall into the standards of a third world country'. The public would 'lose confidence in' a judiciary of 'enthusiastic but half-trained amateurs'. Lord Ackner and Lord Rawlinson each moved amendments at the Committee stage to exclude non-lawyers from the bench. Lord Ackner expostulated: 'Perhaps we are to have People's Courts!' Lord Rawlinson called it 'absolutely absurd': 'this country would be a laughing stock....' Lord Hutchinson agreed 'that the only word that is suitable is "grotesque"'. It was 'almost unbelievable' that candidates for the bench might include members of 'the Royal Institute of British Architects, the Scottish Citizen's Advice Bureau, the Orange Lodge, the Showman's Guild, and the Licensed Victuallers Association'. Codes of conduct would be 'policed by an unknown number of authorised bodies from whose ranks will spring a new race of paralegals....' Lord Ackner renewed his motion at the Report stage. The Lord Chancellor wanted 'approval to dilute the quality of the future judiciary'. Lord Goodman quoted Harvard Law School Dean Roscoe Pound on 'the harm which this de-professionalisation of the practice of law did' in America, adding that the UK was fortunate to 'have been spared such excesses of democratic zeal'. The Bill's 'fundamental aberration' would allow a patent agent or chartered accountant to become a High Court judge. The amendment failed by 14 votes to 35.[159] Lord Mishcon moved amendments at the Committee and Report stages to make solicitors and barristers of ten years' standing eligible for the bench (regardless of audience rights). Lord Ackner complained that solicitors' 'appetite is growing in the feeding'. Lord Hacking wanted eligibility extended to legal academics. Lord Ackner objected that 'experience in advocacy is the criterion for appointment to the Bench'. The Lord Chancellor agreed that solicitors with audience rights would be deemed to have had them from the date of admission.[160]

The day before the Bill was introduced the Law Society sought greater power to deal with complaints against solicitors. Nevertheless, Lord Coleraine (a solicitor) moved an amendment to prevent it from requiring solicitors to compensate clients for inadequate professional service. It was 'axiomatic that the disciplinary sanction should reflect the gravity of the wrong whereas compensation is to reflect the loss sustained'. The remedy 'opens the door to frivolous and mischievous applications about minimal complaints', fostering hope 'in every disgruntled client's breast of having his costs bill reduced when his solicitor does not reply to letters by return post'. Complaints had increased from 6,000 to 20,000 in the last five years and cost the Society £5 million a year, a 'substantial part' of its budget.[161] Consumer organizations pushed unsuccessfully to eliminate advocates' immunity from liability for negligence (rather than extend it to solicitors). Baroness Phillips declared that the rule 'exists for the benefit of the legal profession and results in a denial of justice to their clients'. Lord Allen echoed the identical words (suggesting they were reading from the same briefing paper).[162] Both branches supported amendments at the Report stage and Third Reading to eliminate the legal services ombudsman's power to order a practitioner who rejected an LSO recommendation to advertise that refusal. Lord Renton called the provision 'almost unbelievable and quite without precedent'. Lord Boardman warned of 'blackmail pressure'. Lord Donaldson thought this was 'wholly different' from an order directed to a building society or local authority. Lord Mishcon agreed: 'we are dealing with professional people'. But the amendment failed by 59 to 63.[163]

Attacks continued even after the Bill left the Lords. Lord Ackner called Part I 'unfinished, sent before its time into this breathing world, scarce half made up'. Part II ignored 'every principle of methodology which law reform ought to attract'. The 'integrity of our system of justice, which has been developed over the centuries', will be 'heavily undermined, and its quality seriously diminished'. Lord Simon called the provisions 'mere extrusions from departmental entrails. In stud-book terms, they were by the Department of Trade and Industry out of the Lord Chancellor's Department'. Government had 'implacably' used its 'pay vote' of ministers to produce a majority. The 'timetable of inordinate haste, effectively inhibit[ed] proper debate'.[164]

The Bar Council sought to appear magnanimous in victory. Vice-chair Scrivener courted the BLA by opposing corporate conveyancing

and MDPs and supporting solicitor judges. The wide dispersal of high-
street firms 'is a fundamental characteristic of our profession admired by
foreign lawyers and worth fighting for'. Small firms can face 'Goliaths'
because 'they have access to the same advocates'. Declaring the two
branches equal, he claimed to have learned from the experience 'to do
what is right for the profession as a whole'. The Law Society thought this a
bit rich. Bar opposition to one lawyer preparing and arguing a case was 'no
more than a transparent bid to retain the barristers' monopoly by other
means'.[165]

The Times lauded the 'doughty' Lord Chancellor for seeing off 'vested
interests'. 'The louder the lawyers howled, the more insistently the public
called for reform'. He had become 'a popular hero'. 'Apart from a few
lawyers' who should 'come out of their corsets . . . we are all free marketeers
now'. 'The derestriction of legal services will increase competition, efficiency and client choice . . . with the dismantling of some of the traditional,
irrational and protectionist demarcations between solicitors and barristers,
and indeed between lawyers and other professions.' The *Guardian* warned
against 'the unholy alliance of barrister MPs' who would try to torpedo 'the
Government's move to end the elaborate and expensive restrictive practices of the Bar' for 'the good of society'.

[F]ew bastions of privilege have relinquished power voluntarily. When the bastion
lives in cloisters, refuses to meet its clients anywhere else and still dresses up in old-
fashioned clothes, voluntary abdication is even less likely.

It also castigated Labour and Liberal Democrats for having 'meekly lined
up behind the forces of reaction' like 'dinosaurs,' embracing a 'Bar
Council-backed amendment designed to completely enfeeble the new
right of audience for solicitors'.[166]

The Commons held a Second Reading debate on 18 April, sent the Bill
to a Standing Committee, and debated its amendments on 25 July.[167]
Anticipating the Opposition strategy, Sir Patrick Mayhew, the Attorney-
General, noted that civil legal aid certificates had increased from 190,000
to 259,000 during the Conservatives' ten years in office, the Lord
Chancellor had extended coverage to five million children a year ago, and
a 'full review' of eligibility was under way. It was 'idle' to criticize the Bill for
disregarding legal aid and not 'awfully respectable' to vote against it on
that ground.[168] But John Morris, shadow Attorney-General, moved that the
House decline a Second Reading because the Bill failed to provide sufficient financing for the courts, make financing accountable to Commons,
deal with legal aid eligibility, ensure 'wider opportunities for legal representation', or 'modernise the system of selection and appointment of
the judiciary'. Legal aid was being allowed 'to wither on the vine'. Keith Vaz
(a Labour backbencher) denounced 'justice-capping'. 'Justice must never

be seen to be cost-effective....' Morris called the writer of the Green and
White Papers the 'handmaiden of the Department of Trade and Industry.
They reek of the furnaces of that Department.' He questioned 'whether the
philosophy of market forces is appropriate for achieving the best for the consumer in an area where so much is taken on trust, and where integrity and
independence are so vital'. Sounding much like a Conservative peer (or perhaps
just a QC), he declared that the legal profession 'must be independent and
fearless. The judiciary, drawn from that profession...must of necessity be
independent.' The motion failed by 101 votes to 203.[169]

Not all Labour backbenchers followed the party line. Austin Mitchell
congratulated the Lord Chancellor for breaking the 'logjam' with 'ingen-
ious solutions'. Chris Mullin called the Bill 'a long overdue shake-up of a
profession which...has managed to combine appalling levels of service,
outrageous fees and a degree of self-satisfaction unmatched by any other
profession'. 'I am a socialist, but I must say that if ever a profession urgently
needed a dose of market forces, it must be the legal profession.' Ian Bruce
could 'think of no less efficient, less effective or slower profession'. It
needed 'a thorough shake-up'. 'The more that we can do to open up the
profession and introduce competition the better.' Vaz paid 'tribute to the
radical nature of the Lord Chancellor's proposals'.[170]

As in the Lords, lawyers were sceptical about consumerism. 'The interests
of an unmeritorious plaintiff or a guilty defendant consist of winning the case
at all costs', said Peter Archer (a barrister for thirty-seven years). Because 'the
interests of justice require that the consumer's choice does not extend to
those prepared to bend the rules in order to win' he opposed non-lawyer
practitioners or judges.[171] A former solicitor declared: 'cheapness is not
always best. The old phrase "cheap and nasty" is as applicable today as when I
learned it from my grandmother'.[172] Others rejected laissez faire: 'the market
place is not everything, and professional standards are something' (Peter
Temple-Morris); 'too many partnerships look not so much to the service for
their clients, but to the service for their fleet of BMWs' (Humphry Malins);
'the Government...are beginning to walk a dangerous road by allowing
commercialism to override professionalism' (Gerald Bermingham); 'we have
likened the profession's activities to selling bananas and second-hand motor
cars. They certainly are not' (Sir Anthony Grant); 'there must be an ethical
commitment to an ideal of truth, trust and fairness...one simply cannot have
purely competitive, market, money-making considerations as the only basis
for this legislation' (John Fraser).[173] Many assailed 'the contingency free [*sic*]
racket that prevails in the United States. Far too many litigants are dragged
into all the traumas of court by over-exuberant Perry Masons or people like
him.' 'What we really need is not more but less litigation.'[174]

Barristers predictably favoured the cab-rank rule, opposed partnerships
and litigator-advocates, and predicted 'the beginning of the end of the

independent Bar'. It was 'difficult to think of any major improvements in our legal system that the British people feel is [*sic*] necessary which the Bill will achieve....' The secretary of the Parliamentary All-Party Barristers Group called the Bar 'the ideal profession' in DTI terms, 'entirely market-oriented', 'extremely egalitarian'. Other barristers agreed it was 'fiercely competitive', 'the most competitive' profession. 'Solicitors cost much more than barristers.'[175]

Solicitors supported much of the Bill. Sir Hugh Rossi welcomed 'the Lord Chancellor's brave attempt in the Green Paper to set out a framework for reform'. Deploring the 'judicial apoplexy' in the Lords, Peter Temple-Morris insisted the Bill was not an 'extreme measure'.[176] Vaz (a former law centre solicitor becoming a barrister) moved an amendment to 'remove the spectre of solicitors' rights of audience in the High Court being blocked by judges unreasonably requiring the society to adopt rules that ape the practices of the Bar—"ape" being an appropriate word—such as separating preparation from advocacy....' It failed when the Government resisted.[177]

Outside Parliament the branches continued fighting over the cab-rank rule. BC chair Peter Cresswell insisted it was 'intended to benefit the man or woman in the street, not the lawyer'. Scrivener claimed it was absolutely binding and the only alternative to the American public defender system, where 'the young lawyer cuts his teeth on murders and all types of serious crime. He does this until he can afford to shake it off and join the older and the more experienced doing only the well paid cases.' Sir David Napley mocked the Bar's idealization of the rule as 'the acme of virtue'; because exceptions had proliferated 'ad infinitum' it 'would not make the slightest difference'. The *Solicitors Journal* agreed it was 'one of the great illusions of legal life'. Geoffrey Bindman (whose firm was one of the two declining to represent defendants) called it a 'delusion' and a 'sham', 'just another ploy in the devious rearguard action by the Bar to maintain its long-standing privileges'. The Law Society opposed its extension 'at a time when solicitors who are doing legal aid work are finding it hard to make ends meet and when the remuneration offered by the government fails to keep pace with increasing costs'. The Society reluctantly accepted the rule only because it allowed an advocate to decline a case when 'the fees for legal aid are inadequate'. The chair of the working party that drafted the BC code admitted 'there was no way, with the attitude to legal aid funding, that we felt it was sensible to make barristers vulnerable to Government saying "you have got to take legal aid work whatever we pay you"'. Within a month, however, the Bar Council had declared that 'any instructions or brief in a legal aid matter shall...be deemed at a proper fee'. Cresswell called this 'vital to ensure that all advocates are available to everyone'. (Later that year, however, a murder defendant's brief was returned by the first QC less than a month before trial, by a second from the same chambers less than two weeks before trial, and then rejected by 108 more![178])

Mayhew told the Commons that the Government had accepted the cab-rank rule and would introduce its own amendment, which allowed an advocate to refuse a legally-aided case where 'the fee is not a suitable one for him in all the circumstances'. Morris hedged. 'It would be a sad day if the finest advocacy were not available for odious cases to ensure that in the dispensation of justice every argument had been advanced in the exercise of every man's right under Magna Carta.' It was 'part of the price that the Bar...has paid for its monopoly'. But he 'would have no truck with it' if it 'was expected to, and would, undermine the widening of advocacy rights'. Mitchell accused the Bar of trying 'to restrict competition from solicitors'. Mayhew retorted: 'The rule matters not one iota to the profession. It is a burden on the profession....' Sir Hugh Rossi, chair of the Parliamentary All-Party Solicitors Group, assailed this 'wrecking amendment', 'the latest... manifestation of the campaign by those opposed to reform'. During twenty-five years in practice he had 'great difficulty...securing the man I wanted'. The rule would undermine 'the sensitive relationship between solicitor and client', such as 'a relationship of trust with rape crisis centres'. Temple-Morris called the rule 'hypocritical'. 'I have never yet encountered a clerk who was not good enough at least to protect in general the careers of those for whom he was responsible'. But a provincial solicitor for twenty years thought the rule, which the Bar applied 'pretty well', should be extended to solicitor advocates.[179] The Government amendment was agreed.[180]

Morris appeared to oppose CPS audience rights, which he saw as Treasury cost-cutting. He quoted a QC on the 'fundamental importance— the guarantee of an independent element in the State machinery of justice' and worried about 'the effect on the junior criminal Bar'.[181] Morris also expressed 'anxiety about institutions undertaking conveyancing work'. It would be 'a grave disadvantage to the public' if the high-street solicitor's 'role was made more difficult or if services were made less comprehensive'. (When the Government rejected corporate conveyancing in Scotland to protect rural solicitors, the Law Society noted 'these dangers do not cease at the border'.) Because solicitors were 'subsidized by' conveyancing, a barrister predicted that 'large numbers of small firms...are likely to go to the wall' without it. Solicitors agreed that conveyancing was an essential subsidy. A layman reported he had bought five houses 'but no solicitor ever gave me financial advice'. 'All the humbug about solicitors protecting people is so much hot air', 'absolute bunkum'.[182] The Government moved an amendment about tying-in with respect to mortgages, which passed over lender and insurer objections.[183] A solicitor's amendment requiring lenders to use objective criteria in instructing conveyancers was opposed by the Government and failed.[184]

Some members sought (unsuccessfully) to eliminate advocates' immunity. The Attorney-General resisted, fearing 'a retrying of the whole issue'. But Vaz called immunity 'ludicrous'. Two non-lawyers welcomed the LSO. One, pursuing a constituent's case for two years, was told by the Law Society within thirty seconds 'there was nothing that could be done about it'. Another said any member 'who has dealt with a case against a firm of solicitors or a barrister knows of the appalling difficulties presented. . . .' A third called 'the difficulties of complaining about barristers . . . legion'. 'The Law Society has probably been the body most effective at protecting its members rather than the general public when complaints are made.'[185]

Chris Mullin, a tireless campaigner against miscarriages of justice, used the debate to excoriate the judiciary, moving an amendment to create an Independent Review Body to advise the Lord Chief Justice on criminal appeals. Despite Labour backing, the clause was rejected by 37 votes to 96.[186] John Fraser moved amendments to create a Department of Legal Administration and a Judicial Appointments Commission to 'bring the administration of the law . . . into the political arena' and 'take the appointment of the judiciary out'. He received support from Morris, Mitchell, Mullin, Temple-Morris, and Vaz, who offered damning evidence of class, gender, and racial unrepresentativeness. The Attorney-General retorted: 'Those of us who know the people who became judges in the time that we have been in the profession know that is [*sic*] absurd to say that there is some sort of bias towards a social background of one kind or other'. A judicial appointments commission would permit 'unacceptable interference by the Government in the affairs of the independent and self-governing professions'. The question was negatived without a division.[187]

Both branches (supported by the CA) opposed government power to decide whether a solicitor or barrister would represent a defendant. When they accused the Government of a ' "hidden agenda" for cuts in legal aid', Mayhew retorted: 'After all, this is taxpayers' money'. Lord Mackay concurred: 'surely the public, who pay for it, have to be assured it is obtaining the best value' by 'doing away with any unnecessary restrictions on the functions of the many professional strands'. Although Government capitulated, it reported that a two-year campaign to reduce double-manning had persuaded QCs to appear without juniors in only eight of 1,700 suitable cases and barristers without solicitors almost as rarely. The Bar lamely suggested 'educating the profession'. Lord Hailsham pronounced: 'You simply cannot do a case which will take more than a day or so without having two hands to the pump', adding with a condescension so ingrained as to be unconscious: 'you need a solicitor to hold the papers and collect the material'. Calling Hailsham 'the lapdog of the profession', the *Guardian* declared it 'high time that the legal gravy train was taken out of service'.

Abolishing silk was 'long overdue'. *The Times* claimed that one of the profession's 'most glaringly corrupt practices—over-manning in court—is still as bad as ever'.

[H]aving a junior to assist is not so much an aid to good presentation in court as a status symbol, a badge of seniority, for which the client...has to pay through the nose. It is also a crude method of milking the legal aid taxpayer for the benefit of a restrictive practice; the sort of behaviour which lawyers would excoriate in a trade union.

The BC treasurer resented the charge, brazenly maintaining 'the Bar has been in the forefront of change'. Each practice was essential 'to avoid criminal legal aid becoming a second-class service'. Agreeing that 'the interests of the defendant must be paramount', the LS criminal law committee chair denied that 'solicitors still regularly attend when they are not needed'. But the CA urged courts to be 'tougher': 'unless the lawyers are squalling, nothing is really happening'.[188]

The Commons standing committee discussed the Bill for ten days. It rejected motions to add a presiding judge to ACLEC (Ivan Lawrence), to limit the designated judges' veto to a majority rather than an individual (John Fraser), to give authorized practitioners the same fiduciary responsibilities to clients as lawyers and to require such practitioners to give written notice of commissions (Fraser). Fraser withdrew amendments to require authorized practitioners to provide more than one quotation for a loan and disclose the relative advantages of in-house and outside services.

Nine barristers (seven silks) and four solicitors faced just six non-lawyers. Austin Mitchell (added in response to a *Guardian* leader written at the instance of the Law Society and CA) called for an end to the 'medieval lunacy' of Bar dinners: 'acculturisation through which the great can sit in on the peasants', 'ancestor worship of the worst sort: perhaps even ancestor eating'. The barrister members dismissed this 'sanctimonious twaddle' as a 'cascade of unadulterated drivel', 'a great deal of rubbish'. Dining 'makes an outstanding contribution to the quality of the Bar and by doing so protects the consumer'. (The BC and Inns cut dinners from twenty-four to eighteen two years later and considered abolishing them four years after that.) Finding no allies, Mitchell condemned the other Opposition members as 'instinctively conservative in legal matters'. 'Labour's craving for respectability is advanced by slapping down my dangerous radicalism': abolishing the cab–rank rule and silk, making barristers liable for negligence, paying pupils, retiring elderly judges, and creating a public defender. He claimed that: the Liberal Democrat spokesman on legal affairs (a barrister) argued 'eloquently that disaster and social revolution must follow any reduction in the perks of the bar', the Attorney-General's 'instinctive prejudices as head of the Bar go against his brief', and Conservative backbencher Sir Ivan Lawrence QC 'speaks for the Bar'. Mitchell depended on the Haldane Society (which did not attend), the NCC and LAG (which could not provide a 'continuous tutorial presence'), and the CA. He was a 'lightning conductor...attracting the bolts while [the Government] smuggle the Lord Chancellor's sensible reforms through far more unscathed than they were in the Lords, and even repair some of the damage done to them there'. The Law Society failed to secure an amendment limiting the four senior judges to consultation.[189]

When the Lords considered the Commons amendments on 24 and 26 October, Lord Mackay called the Government's formulation of the cab-rank rule 'a principle of non-discrimination'; but 'an advocate has always been able to stipulate a proper fee'. The 'best mechanism for determining the correct level of payment for any practitioner is the way in which the market operates....' The QC who had just revised the Bar Council's rule had warned that if a barrister were not 'entitled to refuse work if it is not properly paid' the Government could 'hold a pistol to our heads'. Lord Campbell moved an amendment that legal aid would constitute a proper fee in order 'to ensure parity of treatment between the two branches of the profession'. Lord Hutchinson worried that the Government's exception 'appears to drive a coach and horses through the great principle...legal aid cases will only be taken by those at the bottom of the pile of advocates'. But Lord Campbell withdrew his amendment, and Lord Mackay's was agreed.[190]

After more than 110 hours of debate over fifteen days (thirteen lasting past 10 pm, seven past midnight, and one until 2.50 am), occupying more than 1,600 columns of Hansard, the Bill received the Royal Assent on 1 November, largely unchanged.[191]

The Law Society rightly feared that 'after all the rhetoric of the last two years the bill will settle very little. Progress on rights of audience could yet be frustrated by the judiciary's reluctance to see the Bar monopoly weakened.' Roger Smith noted that the Green Paper proposed to subject the profession's restrictive practices 'to the same tests administered by a new competition authority as other sectors of the economy'. Now, however, they only had to be 'appropriate' to the 'proper and efficient administration of justice'. 'This is the legal equivalent to being "as long as a piece of string".' Marcel Berlins reported that a silk called it 'very simple. We won', observing: 'the senior judiciary and the Bar can scarcely talk about the imminent legislation without smirking. A potentially radical reform has been reduced to a benign tinkering....' Robert Rice agreed the 'Big Bang for lawyers' had turned into 'little more than a damp squib'. Exultant that the Bar had demonstrated its 'fighting weight' and 'ability to wrestle with government and legislature', the *Financial Times*'s 'Justinian' (Louis Blom-Cooper QC) declared it 'the clear winner'. Cresswell expressed satisfaction that 'repeated attempts by the Law Society and others to undermine the position of the four senior judges in the new machinery have been defeated'.[192]

Both sides departed the fray greatly overestimating what had happened. At the Law Society annual conference President Tony Holland called the Bill 'a notable success'. 'The days of cosy agreements to decide on the division of functions...are over'. 'There is, from here on, no distinction between the work that can properly be described as the function of a barrister as opposed to that of a solicitor.' Secretary-General John Hayes urged that a single body represent all legal practitioners within a few years. But though Holland was 'confident solicitors can take on any competition', the *New Law Journal* warned that when the property market revived 'there circling like buzzards over the remnants of the wagon train, will be the institutions'.[193]

The Bar was conciliatory but confident. Where his predecessor had declared a 'hundred years war', Cresswell vowed that 'the two branches... must never again air their differences in public'. 'If a united position is taken...we are an extremely powerful force—we can influence government policy.' 'We must not allow the practice of law to pass into the hands of accountants.' He hoped the Act 'will remove any differences that have obtained in the past' but reiterated his 'determination to develop strategies to ensure that the continued existence of the independent Bar is never threatened again'. There was 'a clear distinction between preparation and presentation in serious cases'. And though Scrivener, his successor, disavowed 'restraint of trade or protectionism of any kind', he was 'prepared to fight for...principles', such as the cab-rank rule, self-employment, and the requirement that solicitor advocates have the 'same training' as barristers.[194]

But Lord Ackner reiterated a 'settled hopeless expectation' that the Act 'will heavily undermine the integrity of our system of justice'. The Advisory Committee 'is going effectively to dictate, not just the framework and detail of the education, training standards and discipline of those who provide legal services in our courts, but the very way in which the services are to operate'. He agreed with Lord Hailsham that it 'is too terrifying to imagine' lawyers 'governed by such a ludicrous body'. '[W]hat the Government are seeking to achieve by this legislation is...increased control of the independent legal profession and, ultimately, the judiciary.'[195]

D. A Revolution?

Lord Mackay's Green Papers profoundly altered the terms of engagement among the legal professions, state, market, and media in terms of rhetoric, resources and alignments. Before Mackay professional behaviour was presumptively proper. After his intervention it was suspect as 'shameless' restrictive practices, 'Spanish customs' inflating costs and compounding delays. The Law Society and Bar Council had been respected as selfless guarantors of professional integrity; now they were anathematized as trade unions defending closed shops.

The Government's motivation and timing are puzzling. Lord Mackay invoked the 1987 Conservative Election Manifesto (on which Thatcher won an unprecedented third term), the DTI 1988 Green Paper on Restrictive Trade Practices, and the Marre Committee's 'failure'. But the Green Paper never became legislation; and the Marre Committee's endorsement of the status quo differed little from that of the 1979 Royal Commission, which the Government had accepted five years before. Whatever the reasons for the reversal, it hit the media jackpot. Even before Lord Mackay spelled out his ideas, the press were ready to 'kill all the lawyers'. As Wat Tyler's assault on the Temple 600 years earlier had shown, lawyer bashing 'beat real rat-hunting as a sport'. Articles and leaders cheered the Green Papers as a 'radical', 'revolutionary', 'Big Bang', and 'shake-up' of the 'entrenched privileges', 'hidebound customs', 'musty corridors', 'outdated practices', 'monstrous fees', 'club loyalty', 'archaic paraphernalia of wigs and gowns', and 'love of incomprehensible Latinisms' of the 'legal elite', one of the 'last great closed shops'. Lawyers were 'highwaymen' and 'top barristers' a 'clique of highly privileged monopolists', who 'dressed funnily' and whose 'pomposity knew no bounds'. One critic replaced the metaphor of the medieval guild with that of the Communist Party of the Soviet Union. Law was more 'laced up with shameless practices' than any other public service. Lawyers had 'beat all records for resisting change' 'fanatically, rapaciously and successfully'; they had 'nobbled' the Royal Commission and were protected by the 'Old Boys'. The Bar deserved a 'sharp clout around the ears'. Observers welcomed its 'squeals of anguish' and ridiculed its 'luddite fulminations'.

The intemperate reactions of the profession and its champions further fuelled such criticisms. They were unapologetically complacent. The English legal profession was 'highly esteemed in much of the world', the 'most upright and most independent...known to man', 'superior to all others', the 'best in the world'. There was 'no evidence of any particular grievance'; it was 'difficult to think of any major improvements...that the British people feel is [*sic*] necessary'. After warning against 'elective dictatorship' and 'nationalisation', Lord Hailsham accused the Government of 'running about like a bull in a china shop'. The Lord Chief Justice called the Green Papers 'one of the most sinister documents ever to emanate from Government'. They portended an 'oppression' he associated with 'a toothbrush moustache and a swastika on the armband'. Others compared the threat to Nazi Europe, Fascism, South Africa, *ancien régime* France, and the dirigiste policies of the few remaining (but fortunately fading) communist dictatorships. Lord Mackay sought to 'disembowel' the Bar (Lord Lane); he was 'hell bent on the destruction of the Bar', the 'elimination' of elite practitioners (Lord Ackner). The Green Papers were a 'misleading' 'mass of claptrap', which suppress[ed] known facts' (Lord Hutchinson). The independence of lawyers and judges was the 'last bastion' between citizens and 'tyranny' (Lord Lane), essential to 'civilisation' (Sir Stephen Brown), antithetical to 'communism' (Lord Rawlinson). 'Licensing' advocates would betray the Glorious Revolution (Lord Beloff). The Green Papers were a 'Spivs' charter', an 'elaborate joke' by a 'man from Mars' (Julian Malins). Lord Rawlinson demeaned Lord Mackay as a 'Lone Ranger', a Government 'office boy' with 'no knowledge of English courts', who had lost 'the respect and loyalty of the legal profession'. Rawlinson patronized his former boss (Thatcher) as an ex-barrister whose career was 'too brief to give her a proper understanding of the vital national interests she is now intending to tear apart'. His biblical reference was equally unflattering: the Green Papers might speak with 'the voice of Jacob who is the Lord Chancellor', but they revealed 'the hand...of Esau... the Department of Trade and Industry'. An MP said the Green Papers 'reek[ed] of the furnaces of the Department' of Trade and Industry, and their author was 'the handmaiden of the DTI'. Government acted like a 'wholly owned subsidiary of the Institute of Economic Affairs'. Lord Simon was even more insulting: the Bill's proposals were 'mere extrusions from departmental entrails'—i.e., excrement; 'in stud-book terms' they were 'by the Department of Trade and Industry out of the Lord Chancellor's Department'—i.e., DTI had mounted the LCD.

This produced the predictable media response. Lord Lane was an 'ayatollah' and Lord Ackner 'fit to lead a book-burning on Lincoln's Inn Field'. Newspapers assailed the 'screaming', 'shrieking', 'squealing,' 'gibbering crew'. A Labour backbencher derided Lord Lane 'choking on his own hyperbolic verbosity' and denounced the rest of the 'self-seeking bunch of judicial hooligans'. Nobody thought it odd to hear judges rail against a state from which they derived their own power. When a Conservative MP declared that the Law Lords 'have no career structure to maintain' and 'no financial interest in opposing' audience rights, Labour laughed loudly. Far from being respected for its disinterested expertise, the bench was discredited by its partisan advocacy. And the Bar's boastful expenditure of £1 million on a Saatchi and Saatchi advertising campaign appeared to be an act of desperation. Claims to be championing the public interest rang hollow, given the Bar's historical defence of its own interest. Media critics dismissed the law as a silly ass, a laughing stock, while extolling the Lord Chancellor as a 'saint', a 'Scottish hammer' or 'lion', an 'unrepentant Scottish thistle', a 'bonny advocate', a 'popular hero' whom the public 'loved'.

The Government sought to apply market discipline to this last enclave of protectionism. Lord Mackay repeatedly invoked 'first principles'. Suggesting the neo-classical model's appeal to a former mathematician, he 'found it difficult to believe that increasing the supply of advocates will not in the long run have the usual economic effect of decreasing their price'. Traditional adversaries accepted this view. Asserting the proposals would 'increase competition, efficiency and client choice', *The Times* declared 'we are all free marketeers now'. The *Guardian* assailed the 'elaborate and restrictive practices of the Bar', a 'bastion of privilege', which lives in a 'cloister', 'dresses up in old-fashioned clothes' and enlists an 'unholy alliance of barrister MPs' in the 'forces of reaction'. Even the *Daily Telegraph*, the Bar's best friend, published an economist proclaiming no difference between professions and those selling 'baked beans and soap powder'.

Hoping (successfully) to focus attention on the Bar, the Law Society eagerly adopted the Government's buzz words: efficiency, value for money, competition, modernization. It claimed to be well rid of the conveyancing monopoly (although it had fiercely resisted the loss three years earlier and now backed numerous amendments to make it more difficult for corporate conveyancers to compete). Gaskell expressed delight that the Government was returning to 'first principles' and retiring an 'outdated framework'. Solicitors wanted to reduce cost and delay and let 'competence and merit' prevail without a 'restrictive ring fence around advocacy'. The Bar had little choice but to fight on those terms. The 'stonewalling attitude' of which it was unfairly accused never existed. It had made 'tremendous improvement[s]', 'striking changes'. It did 'not accept we are operating a monopoly' and denied barristers had 'any restrictive practices against the interests of the public'; indeed, they already were 'fiercely competitive', the 'most competitive' profession, 'extremely egalitarian', the 'ideal profession' in DTI terms. At the same time, the Bar argued (implausibly) that the reforms would reduce competition and (inconsistently) that 'cheap' was not always 'best' but often 'nasty'. Lord Mackay promptly challenged the Bar to make good its boast that it 'thrived through excellence and by providing members of the public with a much-needed service'. The profession's defences only intensified the resentments and suspicions of laypeople, especially MPs. Judges displayed 'arrogance' by claiming a 'monopoly of words of wisdom'. Lawyers offered 'appalling levels of service', charged 'outrageous fees', sought to 'dazzle and impress clients', and exhibited 'a degree of self-satisfaction unmatched by any other profession'. They needed a 'dose of market forces', a 'thorough shake-up'.

A few opponents disparaged 'first principles' as a 'very bad place to start', 'unproven dogma', 'abstracted theorising', 'platitude', 'first prejudices', 'ideological blueprints', 'overpassionate love for the ideas of John Bright or Adam Smith'. Lord Lane derided 'classic Department of Trade

and Industry jargon'. '[S]tandards of integrity and a concept of freedom...
go far beyond the ideas of the market place...where the prime consideration is "what is the best buy?"' Lord Irvine assailed 'absurd free market
hype'. Others denied professions were cartels; 'one is concerned primarily
not with economic considerations at all'. Critics expressed concern for the
'small man...left to the tender grasping mercies of the market' and
deplored 'paralegals working by the book on a strictly commercial basis',
prepared 'to bend the rules in order to win', or the application of market
principles to the 'surgeon in the operating theatre'. Law was 'not like the
choice of a tin of peas in a supermarket' or 'the grocer's shop at the corner
of a street in a town like Grantham', or 'selling bananas and second-hand
motor cars'. DGFT oversight was an 'insult to the profession'. A *Guardian*
columnist mocked the 'naked and unashamed' ideology of 'late
Thatcherism in all its gore and glory'. A barrister disparaged 'sixth-form
economic theory'. Even a true believer like the *Financial Times* denied that
'the administration of justice...can be equated directly with the manufacture, say, of baked beans'. A barrister complained that 'the criminal process
ought not to be subjected to the same market principles as govern the
chocolate industry' and warned that 'professionalism' would be swept away
by the 'sleaze of Wall Street'. The BC chair asserted that 'the political doctrine of market forces...had no relevance in the administration of justice',
which 'is not a consumer durable'. Lord Hailsham objected that the Bar
was a professional association, not a trade union. A barrister resented being
treated like a 'fitter's mate'. Would Lord Mackay have appreciated his practice of advocacy being viewed as a 'trade'? Opponents even attacked a
laissez faire reform as dirigiste because it was state initiated (ignoring that
the state had to act because the profession had used state power to create
and preserve restrictive practices). Some openly defended the conveyancing monopoly as a necessary subsidy for high-street solicitors, who in turn
were essential to the Bar's survival. Ralf Dahrendorf declared that 'liberty
hinges neither on government nor on the market, but on the creative
chaos of intermediate institutions...which protect people from the iron
grip of government as well as the temptations of greed'.[196]

But the Government was quite successful in keeping debate on its
terrain. It publicized silks' continued insistence on being accompanied by
a junior despite the abolition of the two-counsel rule more than a decade
earlier. Lord Hailsham proclaimed the impossibility of doing a case lasting
more than a day 'without having two hands to the pump'. The media
constantly equated the Bar Council (and to a lesser degree the Law
Society) with trade unions, intensifying the opprobrium with references to
Arthur Scargill and the intransigence of miners, dockers, and transport
workers. When the Lord Chief Justice called a half-day meeting of judges

during working hours, Labour and the media denounced the illegal job action and demanded criminal penalties.

Lawyers offered market justifications for their practices. The Bar argued that large firms would hire the best barristers (ignoring that they already largely monopolized them and few private clients could afford QCs). It claimed client choice would be curtailed by solicitors flouting the cab-rank rule (although solicitor advocates could only increase client choice). The Bar compared barristers to consultant doctors and solicitors to GPs (but neophyte barristers had less training than solicitors, and many experienced barristers were less specialized). The Bar defended the indefensible: Inns dinners as essential training, its monopoly of higher court appointments (which even Lords Donaldson and Denning criticized). Although solicitors presented themselves as 'modernizers', laissez faire converts, they firmly resisted corporate conveyancing and MDPs ('fringe people', 'bad eggs'), advancing the same arguments against concentration that the Bar did in defence of its exclusive audience rights, while simultaneously seeking to offer mortgage lending, estate agency, insurance, and other financial services. The claim that the 'client is often simply not sufficiently informed to make a sensible choice' was unconvincing coming from the Linklaters senior partner.[197]

Lawyers, especially barristers and judges, repeatedly evoked the spectre of Americanization (meaning vulgarity). England was no 'newly discovered land', 'former colonial territory', 'legal greenfield site' to be redesigned 'from scratch', subjected to the 'sweeping structural reform' of a 'contrived' constitution. Joining many others in opposing non-lawyer practitioners and judges (whom Lord Oliver called 'mules' without ancestry or posterity), Lord Goodman warned against American 'de-professionalization' (all American judges are lawyers, unlike English magistrates). 'People's Courts' staffed by a 'new race of paralegals'—members of the Orange Lodge, Showman's Guild, or Licensed Victuallers Association—were 'grotesque', 'almost unbelievable', 'absolutely absurd'; standards would fall to those of a 'third world country' and make England a 'laughing stock'. Sir Ivan Lawrence QC declared that fusion had lowered quality and standards in the USA. (It occurred two centuries ago, and we know nothing about its effect.) The Bar claimed American lawyers lacked integrity, giving clients whatever advice they wanted; it even enlisted a former U.S. Supreme Court Chief Justice to denounce his brethren. Americans were adopting the Inns (they are not) and wished to end fusion (they do not). American justice was slower: two years from Supreme Court hearing to judgement (all Supreme Court cases are decided in the term they are argued). Texas criminal justice halted until President Bush made political appointments to the bench (almost all criminal cases are heard by state courts, over which the President has no authority). The senior judges pronounced that the low quality of advocacy forced American judges to use clerks. (Clerkships are an elite post-graduate training, which England has recently adopted.) William Rees-Mogg called American lawyering 'essentially monopolistic' (although City firms soon grew larger than their Wall Street competitors) and the reason 'why American industry has ceased to be competitive with the Japanese'. (Some attributed American economic growth and Japanese stagnation in the 1990s to America's abundance of lawyers and Japan's paucity.) American juries award plaintiffs twice their compensatory damages (they do not). American mortgage lenders charge 5–7 per cent for conveyancing (they do not). American criminal lawyers were said to be both excessively vigorous prosecutors and insufficiently zealous defenders. They had no cab-rank rule. (But prosecutors and public defenders have to take every case.) A 'young lawyer cuts his teeth on murders and all types of serious crime'. (They start with misdemeanours.) And Americans were associated with litigiousness, ambulance chasing, Bhopal: 'everyone sues everyone else and the lawyers are very rich'. Litigants were 'dragged into all the traumas of court by over-exuberant Perry Masons'. Lord Hailsham blamed the numerous 'frivolous, vindictive or purely blackmailing claims' on contingent fees, which were 'abhorrent', 'inherently immoral and corrupting', 'definitely sinister'. Lord Denning warned against an 'American nightmare' in which lawyers 'cook witnesses' and fabricate 'excessive damages'. Lord Rawlinson said American lawyers 'descend like vultures upon the scene of every disaster, soliciting clients'.

The profession's trump card was independence. Barristers cited Erskine's defence of Paine and Lord Brougham's of Queen Caroline (as though these were daily fare). The Bar stood up for 'the little man...the ordinary citizen, in his constant battles against the big battalions'; it protected 'civil liberties' against 'abuse of the executive power'. Judicial review was a 'thorn in the flesh of the Executive', the 'bullying government'. The reforms would allow Government 'creatures' to grant or deny 'dog licences' to advocates, 'putting pressure on to a barrister defending a client accused of a crime', threatening the Bar's independence, crossing a 'constitutional Rubicon' by endangering the independence of the judiciary, and subverting 'free and civilised society'. 'Oppression' would 'cre[ep] up insidiously, step by step, until all of a sudden, the unfortunate citizens realized freedom had gone'. The Bill conferred on the executive powers that were 'totally excessive', 'dangerously authoritarian'. The judiciary and Bar kept repeating this big lie; even LAG worried the Lord Chancellor might curtail advocacy on behalf of politically unpopular clients. Opponents managed to divert attention to peripheral issues. ACLEC became a statist emblem, the dreaded quango run by despised civil servants, an 'ill-sorted conglomerate' packed with 'political appointees of the government of the day', whose lay majority (as outlandish as a General

Medical Council of non-doctors) would be 'superannuated old ladies and gentlemen', 'totally ignorant of the law and totally unschooled in the science of the law'. To the end Lord Ackner evoked the 'terrifying' prospect that this 'ludicrous body' would 'dictate' the 'very way in which the [legal] services are to operate'. The Bar also fetishized the cab-rank rule to resist solicitor advocates, extending it to legal aid (thereby undermining any traditional warrant). The rule undergirded the 'reputation of British justice'; Lord Mackay had called it an 'important constitutional guarantee' a decade earlier. Lord Irvine agreed it was of 'major constitutional importance'. Lord Hooson extolled it as 'one of the great guarantees of liberty'. But those outside the Bar denounced it as 'hypocritical', 'easily avoided', a 'wrecking amendment'. Indeed, Lord Campbell openly admitted wanting 'to create parity of treatment between the branches'.

Lord Hailsham accused his successor of fomenting conflict between the branches; senior judges and barristers concurred. Whether or not Mackay was this Machiavellian, he clearly intensified deep-rooted antagonisms. Solicitors demanded to be treated as equals: competing on an even playing field, ending the Bar's insufferable condescension, securing appointment to the highest courts. The Law Society Secretary-General even proposed that a single body (presumably his) regulate all lawyers. The Bar responded with its habitual hauteur. 'Little upstart solicitors' would have the gall to sue judges. Solicitors were 'cosy with police' and would 'dilute the quality of advocacy'. John Mortimer declared that only solicitors were 'bent', never barristers. Lord Hailsham warned against 'corruption, dishonesty, chicanery and sheer quackery', from which barristers were immunized by 'the incentives to honourable conduct imposed by delicately balanced, slowly evolved but brilliantly successful experience of centuries'. Solicitors were only good enough 'to hold the papers and collect the material' for barristers. The senior judges impugned the 'competence, integrity and trustworthiness' of solicitors, who were 'unsuitable' to be advocates. That 'solicitors pick and choose', said Lord Ackner, shows 'how undesirable it would be if they were entitled to advocacy in the higher courts'. Resisting audience rights for employed lawyers, Lord Hutchinson accused the Government of seeking to 'clear the criminal court of barristers'. Lord Alexander moved to amend the purpose clause so that judges could take account of the 'importance of maintaining a separate and independent Bar'. Lord Rawlinson moved eight amendments to protect the Bar, vowing a fight 'to the bitter end'. The BC chair declared a 'hundred years war' in 'defence of excellence'. It is hardly surprising that the LS Assistant Secretary-General said the profession (by which he meant the Bar) 'richly deserves a kick in the pants', or that the Society snubbed the Bar by not inviting its chair to address the annual conference. The Bar also angered employed barristers by resisting their audience rights on the ground of insufficient independence.

   The politics of professionalism made unusually strange bedfellows—and adversaries. The oddest, of course, was a Conservative Government attacking lawyers, especially the Bar. (Anti-Thatcher Conservatives accused the Government of indulging in populist politics, pandering to the 'tabloid press', the 'intellectual Murdoch mafia', making 'ignorance' a virtue, failing to defend 'excellence'.) This created a dilemma for those to its left: Labour, newspapers like the *Guardian,* and organizations like LAG. These long-standing critics of the profession were reluctant to let the Government play their populist card and ideologically hostile to laissez faire (although the 'socialist' Chris Mullin had to agree that if 'ever a profession needed a dose of market forces, it must be the legal profession'). Furthermore, the reforms did little or nothing to increase legal aid, the critics' preferred instrument for equalizing justice. (Labour made this the basis for its futile motion to deny the Bill a Second Reading in the Commons.) Consequently, some left critics took a position as paradoxical as the Government's: the state (whose power they usually sought to enlarge) threatened the independence (in which they did not believe) of the Bar and bench (their traditional whipping boys). Only Austin Mitchell surpassed Lord Mackay in enthusiasm for the market and detestation of tradition, helping the bill through the Select Committee by acting as a radical foil. The other end of the political spectrum—represented by the (British) Adam Smith Institute and (American) Manhattan Institute—blithely shed their laissez faire principles to advocate on behalf of corporate donors against contingent fees. Both Sir Gordon Borrie, Director-General of Fair Trading, and Lord Alexander of Weedon, chair of the Monopolies and Mergers Commission, displayed greater loyalty to their brethren at the Bar than to their official charge to correct market imperfections. The Green Papers and the Courts and Legal Services Act 1990 may have been a last gasp of Thatcherite laissez faire, but they effectively paralysed critics, who could neither reject the (now hegemonic) ideology nor define independent positions within it.

   All the protagonists exaggerated the proposals' import. Lord Mackay, uncharacteristically, called them radical. Escalating the rhetoric, the press said they were the biggest shake-up of the century. And Bar and bench offered eschatological prophecies of the end of civilization. Yet the reforms with the greatest potential significance were severely (and it turned out fatally) compromised. The four senior judges retained individual vetoes over audience rights, and the requirement of an interview with an independent solicitor made corporate conveyancing unprofitable (especially during the recession just beginning). Given the deep division between solicitors and barristers, the lack of a compelling anti-market ideology, the counter-productive resistance by bench and Bar, the Opposition's weakness, the media's fervid and unanimous support, and strong popular resentment of lawyers, why did the Government retreat? Was it resistance by Conservative and other peers, especially present and former Law Lords, silks, and barristers? The resignation by Lord Rawlinson and threat by the Attorney-General? Were the Green Papers trial balloons, designed to allow Mackay room for manoeuvre? The White Paper was sufficiently ambiguous for observers to be uncertain who had won. The media rediscovered the virtues of tradition, swallowed the Bar's doomsday predictions, questioned the value of competition, and accepted the inevitability of restrictive practices. British caution triumphed. Lord Mackay returned to the fold, embracing the Bar's call for evolution rather than revolution, denying that the Courts and Legal Services Bill sought 'huge change'.

And yet the Green Papers transformed the politics of professionalism in ways that are still unfolding. The rest of the decade reveals those directions.

3 Halting the Tide

> [I am] not convinced of the desirability of a totally demand-led vocational training system. [Desmond Fennell QC, BC chair]
>
> [A]t a time of diminishing demand for legal services we are being engulfed by a tidal wave of applications. [Anthony Thornton QC, BC professional standards committee chair]
>
> The number of LPC places has 'unfortunately created a situation in which there is a vast oversupply in the market'. [TSG publicity officer]
>
> [The Law Society should reduce LPC] places to a level that replaced those leaving the profession but did not increase 'stock'...around 1000. [It is] the same old story, bums on seats, money, money, money. [Robert Sayer, LS VP]

All producers seek protection from the competition that is the defining characteristic of market economies.[1] The first line of defence is control over entry. Strategies are legion: geographic monopolies over raw materials defended by force (Zanzibari cloves, Chinese silk), powerful cartels created by contract (diamonds, oil), tariff barriers, secrecy, and laws and treaties defining intellectual property (increasingly important in our information economy). Those who sell their labour (rather than raw materials or processed goods) employ a distinct repertoire of controls. Some societies limit tasks to kinship groups: blacksmiths' clans in precolonial Africa, the Jewish priesthood of the Cohanim, the Indian caste system. Everywhere the division of labour is gendered. As such ascribed restrictions lose their force, workers associate with others (in guilds or trade unions) or appeal to employer paternalism (civil service, academic tenure, lifetime employment in large private enterprises).

Professions justify entry controls as essential to protect consumers rendered incapable of judging quality or integrity by the very increase in technical expertise they seek to purchase. Professions construct warrants of knowledge and character embodied in apprenticeship, formal education, and examinations. These can become either credentials (allowing consumers to trade quality for price) or state-mandated floors. Professionalization is the process of moving from the former to the latter; psychotherapists and investment advisers exemplify incompletely professionalized occupations.

English lawyers are a classic example of a successful professionalization project.[2] By the beginning of the nineteenth century the Bar had long enjoyed professional status. The Benchers of each Inn had complete discretion to admit students, who had to state their 'condition in life' and furnish two barrister references. Partly because university non-matriculates had to pass an examination in history and Latin or Greek and non-graduates had to dine in hall nearly three times as often, half of all barristers had university degrees (though not in law), three-quarters by the twentieth century. Pupillage of one to two years (in London) was strongly encouraged (though widely acknowledged as worthless). Barristers generally opened their own chambers, had to practise alone, and were barred from most non-legal work. A contemporary estimated that a barrister would pay fees of £300 and require £250 annually for up to ten years before attaining economic self-sufficiency. At the same time, the Bar was singularly uninterested in technical expertise. Graduates sat the legal examination (imposed only in 1872) a few months after leaving university, and 80–90 per cent passed. The Inns had long abandoned any pretence at teaching; even when they established the Council of Legal Education in the mid-twentieth century, most students preferred private crammers.

Solicitors entered the nineteenth century with none of these perquisites. Various courts, not the profession, set entry criteria. Almost no solicitors attended university (still less than a fifth by the twentieth century). Although the cost of entering articles was about £300, clerks could minimize expenses for the mandatory five years by living at home (throughout England) and expect to be paid after qualifying. Partly in response to an apparent doubling in the number of solicitors in the first third of the nineteenth century, the new Incorporated Law Society imposed a professional examination in 1836; new practising certificates dropped by almost a quarter over the next fifteen years, and the number of solicitors stabilized for four decades. The Society added a second examination in 1862 and a third in 1906; steadily declining pass rates—approaching 50 per cent each by the beginning of World War II—made the cumulative barriers substantial. Although most solicitors relied on private crammers, the Society mandated a year of lectures and subsidized such instruction at the College of Law and provincial universities.

Although solicitors stressed technical expertise acquired through formal instruction and tested by examination, while barristers emphasized character certified by background and socialization, both seem to have controlled numbers. It took the entire nineteenth century for the practising Bar to double, and it did not recover from the 25 per cent loss suffered during World War I until well after World War II. After the Law Society required the first professional examination in 1836, the number of solicitors stagnated for three decades, grew slowly for two, and froze for three. Because the solicitors' branch also lost more than 10 per cent during World War I, its size after World War II was almost exactly what it had been nearly sixty years earlier.

The post-war era initiated a major transformation. The Bar mandated a university degree, and then a lower second, and required those who had read another subject to study law for a year and pass an examination. It lowered entry fees but required pupillage and prohibited pupils from taking briefs during their first six months. Substantial proportions of pupils—some years as many as half—could not find tenancies. At the same time, the growth of legal aid drastically reduced attrition among those beginning practice. Although solicitors were not required to have university degrees, 90 per cent obtained them, most in law. Partly for this reason, final examination pass rates rose to resemble those among barristers (and law graduates were exempt from other exams). Solicitors stopped charging clerks for articles (whose length declined from five years to two) and began paying them. Tertiary education exploded: women entered in significant numbers for the first time, becoming half of law students by the mid-1980s; new universities and polytechnics proliferated; and the number of law graduates rose more than tenfold, from 1,500 in 1938–9 to nearly 16,000 in 1980–1.

The consequence was an enormous increase in those seeking to become lawyers (by reading law or some other subject and then doing the CPE), who then confronted the profession's remaining barriers of apprenticeship and first positions. After the surge of World War II veterans abated, production declined until the mid-1960s (demonstrating the strength of surviving entry controls). But then a profession whose size had remained frozen in the face of the extraordinary economic growth and technological change of the first six decades of the twentieth century thawed rapidly. Starts at the Bar tripled in two decades and the number of private practitioners nearly doubled; admissions of solicitors grew nearly fivefold, increasing the number on the Roll by 139 per cent.

In the late 1980s, however, the profession was concerned about a 'recruitment crisis', not overcrowding.[3] This was particularly true among solicitors, as the housing market overheated and corporate mergers multiplied. Once women were half of law undergraduates, the total number stopped growing (and actually declined as government reduced funding).[4] Furthermore, women solicitors were much more likely than men to interrupt their careers for childrearing and return part time, if at all.[5] The Law Society's College of Law increased places on the solicitors' final examination course by opening an additional branch at York and expanding existing facilities.[6] The Marre Committee recommended that local authorities fully support both the CPE course (for non-law graduates) and the vocational stage for both branches.[7] Since the Bar depended more on litigation (which fluctuated less dramatically), did not rely on employees, and remained predominately male (two-thirds of entrants), it was less concerned about a shortfall in supply. Nevertheless, both the Lord Chancellor and the BC chair urged that pupillages be guaranteed to all and chambers ensure a living income for the second six months.[8]

A. Raising the Bar

The Bar continued to ease entry until 1990. CLE chair Mr Justice Hoffmann said it replaced the highly unpopular Bar Final course with the more palatable Bar Vocational Course both 'to persuade Lady Marre's committee that the Bar is a specialist profession requiring certain specialist skills' and 'for political reasons to get into a good position at the time of the green paper'.[9] Concurring with Marre, the Bar Council approved a Young Barristers Committee resolution that all pupils be 'adequately remunerated'. By the end of 1989 a working party chaired by Mr Justice Hoffmann and Mr Justice Phillips proposed that each of the 450 chambers pay £6,000 twelve-month pupillages (out of the 560 offered that year). Claiming that barristers had been 'the only profession which in effect said to everyone on a free market basis you can all come to the Bar', BC chair Desmond Fennell QC said 'that is no longer appropriate in a changed climate'. A small profession cannot:

undertake to finance anybody who wants to come to the Bar. What we can do is say we have a professional obligation to help the young coming in and then, like any medical school, take those of the highest quality and make it attractive to them.

This statement is doubly extraordinary. First, Fennell claims that the Bar uniquely embodied laissez faire and never erected entry barriers. Secondly, he disguises a restriction on the number of pupillages as a promise to pay them and a meritocratic warrant. In the event, only two-thirds of chambers complied, funding just 400 first-six-month pupillages.[10]

Tenancies remained the real obstacle. The BC rejected Phillips' recommendation of a guaranteed minimum income. With great fanfare it launched the Bar Practising Library, modelled on the system in Scotland and Northern Ireland, where all barristers are served by a pool of clerks and secretaries. But though the BC secretary insisted this would not be a 'second-best' arrangement, only three barristers signed up for the fifty places, and the Council pulled the plug after spending £350,000 in five months. Still, some pressure was relieved by the dozen sets that had moved outside the Inns and the forty barristers who took advantage of the 1990 decision allowing practice from home.[11]

By 1990, however, pressure was building to restrict entry. The Young Barristers Committee chair urged that BVC places be limited to the number of pupillages. A year later the BC Entry and Training Working Party questioned the Bar's 'Open Door Policy'. Echoing Fennell, it 'was not convinced of the desirability of a totally demand-led vocational training system'. Production should be 'led by the numerical requirement for trained barristers'. 'Superfluous numbers who would drift into other walks of life, and persons wishing merely to gain paper qualifications or find a way into employment as lawyers, do not in our view justify the expenditure of scarce training resources'. It rejected replacing pupillage with additional academic education, which 'would preserve an open profession where the fittest survived', and instead proposed deferring Call until after pupillage. But because even this would not 'solve the problem of over-demand', it urged cutting BVC places from 900 in 1990 to 750 in 1991 (out of 1,200 applicants).

When enrolment instead grew to 1,100 in 1992 the BC embraced the Phillips proposal and sought ACLEC approval to choose 750 from the 2,000 applicants through interviews and a test of critical reasoning and comprehension. The BC declared: 'physically and financially we can't accommodate the number of people who want to get on the course'. Anthony Thornton QC, chair of the BC professional standards committee, explained: 'at a time of diminishing demand for legal services we are being engulfed by a tidal wave of applications'. He promised that 'the new system will ensure equality of opportunity for all qualified students, regardless of background, race or gender'. Condemning this 'significantly anti-competitive' measure for underestimating 'the ability of individuals to decide for themselves', the DGFT urged the Lord Chancellor to raise the quota and limit its duration. But the Lord Chancellor and designated judges approved the Bar's request as of 1994. Although Phillips proposed to increase BVC places by allowing universities to offer the course (as they did the solicitors' course) and permit those unable to obtain pupillages to appear in the lower courts (like solicitors), a meeting of heads of chambers overwhelmingly refused, endorsing the BC plan to limit BVC places.

The Bar announced that Peter Goldsmith QC would conduct 'a no-nonsense and realistic assessment of what the environment will be by the turn of the century' in order to assess demand. Urging the BC to 'find a more realistic method of entry' instead of 'setting up people to fail', Council member Nadine Radford proposed a three-month pupillage before the vocational course to determine competence. 'This profession has no room for unremedial [*sic*] incompetence'. Richard Southwell QC (an unsuccessful candidate for BC chair) deplored that 'the number of students wanting to enter the profession has increased beyond all sensible limits'. 'All learned professions have to select... the medical and veterinary professions being obvious examples.' To allow those without pupillages to practise in lower courts 'would do irreparable damage to the Bar'.[12]

At the end of 1993 Goldsmith declared the young Bar in crisis. While the Bar had grown 23 per cent in four years, magistrates' court work had declined 5 per cent in two and the CPS had halved the proportion of such cases in which it briefed barristers, planned to halve it again, and had cut Crown Court briefs by 10 per cent. Pupils had an average debt of £6,250. (A 1996 study found that more than three-quarters of BVC graduates were in debt, averaging £9,000.) Respondents to an academic study 'appeared to have enough work', despite a slight decrease among younger barristers, but 20 per cent of new tenants experienced financial difficulties. Incoming BC chair Robert Seabrook QC, who had commissioned Goldsmith's report, called education and training 'the most pressing and difficult immediate problem' and reiterated the Bar's 'strong public interest argument against training unlimited numbers'. Sir Frederick Lawton nostalgically urged the Inns to 'turn themselves into the legal equivalents of the medical Royal Colleges, setting standards for admission'. A barrister was much blunter: 'We already have too many lawyers. A society which has a large number of lawyers is unhealthy—just look at California. . . . So when is the BC going to sort out the CLE?'[13]

In 1994 the ICLS used a test of critical reasoning and comprehension—eighty multiple-choice questions in forty minutes—and a questionnaire to select 882 out of 2,350 applicants (at a cost of £250,000). Despite Thornton's promise of 'equality of opportunity', ethnic minorities were 21 per cent of applicants but only 10 per cent of admittees and women 40 and 34 per cent. Appeals to the CLE were filed by about 500 rejectees, including sixty recipients of Inns of Court scholarships and all seven CPS scholarship winners. Four obtained leave to apply for judicial review of the CLE's disregard of university performance in favour of A-levels. Although its chair insisted 'we have devised the best system we could', it promptly gave another 250 places to all firsts and those upper seconds rejected because of their A-levels or applications. Seabrook called this 'a fair and equitable solution', but *The Times* dismissed the process as 'ridiculous . . . not far short of irrational'. 'The fiasco has strengthened the hand of those who argue for an end to the Bar school's pedagogical monopoly' and 'should make common education for putative barristers and solicitors irresistible'.[14]

Days later the BC allowed universities to offer the BVC and agreed in principle to the 'introduction of an element of common vocational training'. But it vowed to 'maintain control over the numbers of people trying to enter the profession. Institutions seeking validation will have to go through a strict qualifying process'. '[T]here must be a very clear health warning to remind students that an expensive Bar qualification will not be a passport to chambers.' Lawton reiterated that 'some action will have to be taken, and soon, to reduce the overproduction of lawyers', noting that only 505 of the 1,031 admitted to the ICSL in 1993 found tenancies.

Although the ICSL immediately expanded to 1,200 places, Peter Goldsmith, now BC chair, assured barristers that 'only a limited number of institutions will be allowed to teach the BVC' in the 'interests of maintaining high levels of quality and in the interest of students who otherwise may suffer the expense and disappointment of not being able to go on to the next stage of training'. The ICSL Students' Association president agreed that 'if you cannot get into a career at the end' of the BVC 'there is not a lot of point to it'.[15]

In July 1996 the Bar Council chose six institutions to offer the BVC, increasing places to 1,430. Because four were outside London, some students would have to travel up to 10,000 miles to eat the eighteen compulsory

Inns dinners (reduced from twenty-four three years earlier). A working party of the BC and Inns urged a further reduction to twelve and inclusion of an educational element or opportunity to meet a barrister. But the Inns recommended replacing dining with a variety of educational activities, thereby 'returning to the original idea'. When Martin Bowley QC mocked them as 'legal theme parks' ruled by 'self-perpetuating geriatric oligarchies', Goldsmith retorted they provided 'a framework within which professional conduct and ethical standards can be maintained'.[16]

Outsiders broached more radical reforms. In March 1994 ACLEC chair Lord Justice Steyn said it was seriously considering that all lawyers begin as solicitors, following common vocational training; those seeking to become advocates would enter pupillages only after six to twelve months (as in Scotland). Declaring that the proposals made 'a great deal of sense', Law Society President Rodger Pannone reassured the Bar that a 'distinct corps of higher court advocates' persisted in New Zealand and some Australian states without formal divisions. *The Times* declared that 'the divided profession is living on borrowed time—with only the conservativism of the Bar as its scaffolding'. Division was 'more expensive' and 'a waste of public money'. The 'politics of Fortress Bar has ensured that reform is only possible by circumnavigation'. A month later Seabrook issued the Bar's own consultation paper, acknowledging that 'retention of the present system is not an option'. Common training would 'enable a greater understanding to develop between students on both sides of the profession, allow further deferment of choice on which profession to go for and go some way to break down the historical differences between the two professions'.[17]

Pupillage also was under attack. The *Lawyer* called it often 'virtually worthless'. BVC students made an average of forty applications—a quarter of them more than eighty—yet 22 per cent received no offers. After a group of eleven common law sets organized a clearing-house for selecting pupils, a BC committee chaired by Michael Beloff QC proposed a voluntary scheme for a single form, limit on number of applications, uniform timetable, and pool system after the first round. The Council unanimously approved the Pupil Application Clearing House (PACH), which chair Goldsmith promised 'will put an end to the chaotic selection procedures...and help the Bar choose on merit alone, the best and brightest to be barristers of the 21st century'. Others praised its 'justice and convenience', calling it 'fairer and more efficient'. But though 80 per cent of sets joined the first year, it was a (predictable) disaster. All 850 offers went to just 365 students (some amassing seventeen), leaving the other 1,400 aspirants without any prospects. Angry students vowed to boycott the process and create their own. The Bar blamed competition by the 800 BVC graduates from previous years with the 1,000 from this year. But two years later 596 initial offers went to 335 students, forcing the other 1,646 to go through additional rounds.

To alleviate this, Beloff recommended that chambers be required to participate.[18]

ACLEC's June 1995 consultation paper and April 1996 report declared that 'a common educational foundation...needs to become an essential element in the professional formation of all lawyers'. Because universities would offer this vocational course, 'professional bodies will be freed from the pressure to limit numbers....' The Bar insisted 'the scope for commonality in legal training will always be limited because the skills of a top class court advocate are different from those of a good solicitor'. Although the Law Society favoured 'the natural emergence of common and complementary training', it also wanted to control the vocational course. And though Seabrook had seemed open to common training in 1994, the 1999 report by a Bar Council committee chaired by Sir John Collyear rejected it. The 'profession of specialist advocates...should resist becoming a profession of general legal practitioners'. Instead, the Bar proposed to facilitate transfer by solicitors and qualification by employed barristers.[19]

Outsiders continued to complain about overcrowding. When the Non-Practising Bar Association asked in May 1997 'are we training the correct number of barristers?' the Bar Council replied disingenuously that the DGFT had 'advised the Lord Chancellor that the number of people taking up legal training should be determined by natural competition, rather than by constraints set up by professional bodies'. Calling ACLEC 'the main culprit', the NPBA urged members to tell the Committee 'how much money it has cost you [to qualify], and ask them for a refund'. At the Bar AGM that June, the NPBA successfully moved that the BC publish 'wastage' rates among young barristers. BC chair Robert Owen QC conceded the figures were 'worrying'. 'Less than 3% of those qualifying with a law degree or the Common Professional Examination will go on to obtain a tenancy'. (Of course, only a small proportion wanted one.) The NPBA deplored the 'population explosion' and urged that the Bar either guarantee pupillage to every BVC graduate or limit places to the number of pupillages. Insisting that 'the number of new tenancies is essentially dictated by market forces', Martin Bowley QC declared 'the blunt fact...that we are simply putting too many people through Bar School'. 'In medicine the Government decides how many doctors the country requires and funds the education of that number and no more. Surely the Bar, which largely funds education out of its own pocket is entitled to do no less.' A contemporaneous academic study, however, found junior barristers 'reasonably busy' and their work 'more evenly distributed' than in 1993; indeed, three-quarters sometimes had too much.[20]

Despite its obeisance to market forces and the DGFT, the BC had voted 30–19 in 1995 to 'solve' the problem of too many BVC graduates chasing too few pupillages by delaying Call until after the first six months. But while this proposal was awaiting ACLEC approval, the Bar obtained an opinion by Michael Beloff QC that it would be racially discriminatory. The Society of Black Lawyers complained it 'would have driven a coach and horses through the Bar's anti-discrimination policy'. AWB chair Barbara Hewson warned it 'would drastically reduce the number of ethnic minorities and employed barristers coming to the Bar'. The Bar postponed implementation until 1999, at which time it considered replacing the first six-month pupillage with a practical training period within the BVC, followed by Call and a longer second pupillage. Nigel Bastin, BC head of education and training, invoked the 'general agreement' that the number of BVC places (1,500) was 'too high. It relates more to demand from people who want to come to the Bar than reflecting the numbers which the profession can absorb.' BACFI saw 'no good reason for these rules. All who pass their academic exams should be assured of the chance of completing their training'. But the BC continued to claim the proposal linked '*the numbers training for the Bar... to the demands of the market for barristers*'. Its annual target of 1,000 (compared with the 2,672 BVC applicants in 1998) 'will be governed by market demand'.[21]

The Bar sought to condition financial support for training on control over numbers. A working party chaired by Goldsmith recommended that the Bar provide £2 million annually for 500 BVC students (no longer supported by local authorities) and chambers pay 500 pupils £10,000 a year. A 'return to the days when the Bar was a preserve of the privileged and the monied... could threaten the very existence of the Bar'. But it refused to support all BVC students because the number 'is much greater than the demand for new members of the Profession'. It proposed that chambers select pupils before they started the BVC, expecting 'that some, perhaps a large number, who at the moment take the Bar Vocational Course in the hope of obtaining a pupillage would not do so'. 'In our opinion, that would be no bad thing....' An Inns of Court working party chaired by Lord Justice Tuckey suggested that all barristers contribute £100 annually for students and pupils. The Lord Chancellor told the 1999 Bar conference it was 'crucially important that the Bar is, and is seen to be, a profession open to all the talents. The public will not tolerate a situation of privilege and exclusivity.' The Bar should use its new power under the Access to Justice Act 1999 (see Chapter 10) to compel members to fund the vocational year and pupillage.

While the Bar temporized, it received an opinion in 1999 that pupils over 26 had to be paid the national minimum wage of £3.60 an hour. It encouraged a friendly test case by a 30-year-old woman who had been paid nothing during her first six months and was grossing only £720 a month during her second. The previous year 40 per cent of pupils were paid less than £6,000 for the first six months (32 per cent nothing). When the High

Court upheld the claim, BC chair Dan Brennan QC said the Bar could afford the cost of £120 a pupil a week but might offer fewer pupillages to those over 26. Lord Irvine warned he would 'take a keen interest in how a self-regulated legal profession controls its own size by determining how many pupillages or traineeship contracts it chooses to offer'. Noting that there were ten times as many law students as BVC places, Brennan retorted 'there will always be far more students than we can absorb'. The case was reversed on appeal.[22]

B. Solicitors Shutting the Barn Door

The Law Society entered the 1990s even more preoccupied than the Bar with the 'recruitment crisis'. It increased the 800 CPE places by thirty (hardly appeasing the 3,200 applicants) and proposed replacing the finals course with a shorter skills-oriented Legal Practice Course (LPC) in emulation of the BVC. But when it suggested allowing the nine instructional institutions to write their own exams, the College of Law cautioned the Society against relinquishing control over entry, and the *New Law Journal* warned of the 'vested interest for Universities and Polytechnics to see their candidates pass the examinations'. Nevertheless, the College of Law added 360 evening places and authorized Birkbeck College to offer another 460 full-time places (in the face of 8,000 applicants for what had been 4,000 places).[23]

Even before these measures could take effect, the recession sharply reduced demand. The number and value of residential conveyances (which still accounted for a fifth of solicitors' aggregate gross fees and much more for smaller firms) fell by half between 1988 and 1992. In the first half of 1991 mergers and acquisition work by the top ten firms was £1 billion less than such work by Freshfields alone a year earlier. A leading recruitment firm said 'newly qualified solicitors have been faced with a virtual shutdown of the job market among big commercial firms'. Clifford Chance received 1,500 applications for 100 places in 1989; 2,000 applied for 200 places the CPS had been unable to fill. The 5,420 attending the 1991 London law fair found that firms had cancelled twenty of the forty provisional bookings. Firms began to rescind or postpone traineeship offers. Calls to the Young Solicitors Group helpline increased sixfold in its first year. City firms began to lay off assistants and even partners. *The Solicitors Journal* declared that 'if demand does not increase the profession will have to limit the supply of lawyers'. But *The Times* warned that 'public good will was exhausted' by the profession's opposition to the Green Papers. 'There is no shortage of work for solicitors, merely of solicitors ready to get out of their Rolls-Royce, on to their bikes and retrain for it'.[24]

1992 was the 'worst year for graduate recruitment since the 1930s'. Partner profits were down 20 per cent in London and more than 50 per cent outside (where a third of firms actually lost money). The 5,000 applicants at the London job fair besieged the forty-five exhibitors (down from seventy in 1991). Herbert Smith received more than 2,500 traineeship applications, Macfarlanes 2,300; the Law Society's recruitment service could offer its 1,800 student subscribers only eight traineeships. City firms laid off more fee earners and partners. Law Society President Mark Sheldon cautioned the TSG 'that the profession will not be able to absorb the number of trainees coming in at the bottom' but opposed manpower planning: 'We would almost certainly get it wrong'.[25]

Cost restricted entry but intensified class bias in selection and career path. Local authority grants fell from 65 per cent of College of Law fees in 1990 to 9 per cent in 1993. Nearly three-fifths of the 100 admittees who failed to matriculate at the 1991 course gave financial reasons, as did 90 per cent of the 200 in 1992. At the same time, the 20 per cent of matriculates with City traineeships received bursaries of up to £5,000. Warnings that the poor, and especially ethnic minorities, would be unable to qualify were expressed by the TSG, *Solicitors Journal, New Law Journal,* CA, LS President, former BC chair, and Labour spokesperson on legal affairs. But the Minister for Further and Higher Education retorted: 'At a time of effective professional unemployment among lawyers, doesn't the case for extending mandatory grants ... effectively fall down?'[26]

The recession generated pressure to abolish minimum trainee salaries. In Newcastle, 75 per cent of a small sample of trainees expressed willingness to accept less, half the firms without trainees blamed this on the minimum, and almost all with trainees said they would hire more but for the minimum. Several local law societies concurred. But the TSG chair defended minima as necessary to maintain quality and prevent 'exploitation'. Still, the YSG decided against seeking an increase in 1993. And the Law Society training committee retained minimum salaries without an increase by a single vote. Although a slight majority of the firms and local law societies responding to the Society's consultation favoured abolition, the Council approved the committee decision. Nevertheless, some students were paying premiums for traineeships, and assistants were accepting worse terms than trainees.[27]

The recession deepened in 1993. The 4,000 attending the London law fair found only nine employers, and just one firm, offering a few vacation places. Firms responded to lower turnover with increased layoffs. But there were signs of a rebound in 1994. Firms raised fees and began hiring and promoting again. Recruiters offered more jobs—sometimes exceeding the number of applicants. The recovery strengthened in the next two years, especially at larger firms, as mergers and acquisitions work increased 50 per cent. City firms had to 'scour the Commonwealth' to fill positions. By 1998 property values had regained their 1989 levels.[28]

The profession responded to these fluctuations erratically. As the recession deepened in 1992 the College of Law accepted a record 4,200 students. The *Solicitors Journal* doubted it was 'wise, or responsible for the college to give some 5,000 trainees the hope of qualifying as a solicitor when up to 30% of them may not get articles'. The following year 8,900 applied for the 5,300 places on the first LPC and 9,000 for the 6,000 places a year later (including the first part-time course at the private Nottingham Law School). Despite these imbalances, 96 per cent of the persistent ultimately secured places. The pass rate increased from 80 per cent for the last LS Final to 85 per cent for the first LPC, and the 10 per cent failing a single paper could resit it.

The real bottleneck was not the course or examination but traineeships. Just 3,000 articles were registered in 1992–3; nearly 1,000 who passed their Finals failed to obtain articles within two years; the Law Society scrapped its list of 1,600 candidates because too few firms were interested. Among LPC course dropouts, 43 per cent attributed their decisions to lack of a training contract in 1994 (up from 22 per cent two years earlier). LPC students in 1993–4 made an average of fifty applications for a traineeship—a quarter of them more than 120; nearly two years later 32 per cent had found none.

LAG director Roger Smith favoured abolishing the requirement, allowing the thousands without articles to become 'non-practising solicitors, in much the same way as there are currently non-practising barristers'. Former Law Society President Tony Holland told the 1993 annual conference that articles were 'outmoded'. The chair of the Society's training committee urged that articles be shortened from two years to one (to resemble pupillage). But the *Solicitors Journal* warned this 'may just move the problem further down the line', creating 'even greater unemployment of newly qualified solicitors'. It had 'been saying for the past two years that an expansion of training places is unjustified and should be halted....' (A year later, however, it called articles 'an extraordinarily odd form of training...toward the end of the 20th century, depending...upon the performance of what, at best, may be gifted amateurs rather than professional teachers and, at worst, something quite inappropriate to the training of a professional person'.) The *New Law Journal* warned against the 'expansionist dynamic' of entrusting the LPC to 'universities with agendas and balance sheets of their own'. Even if the LPC's higher skills component might justify halving the length of traineeships, allowing the number to be doubled, 'the legal profession will be hard put to expand at the rate that it did during the 1980s'.

Anticipating the Bar, the TSG chair urged that only those with traineeships be admitted to the LPC. The TSG publicity officer deplored that the number of LPC places had 'unfortunately created a situation where there is a vast oversupply in the market'. The Law Society professional standards director replied that it was not 'our job to tell people that they can not become qualified and have their chance at making a career in the law'. Members of the African, Caribbean, and Asian Lawyers Group who had passed their Finals but not found traineeships asked why the Law Society approved twenty-five institutions to offer the LPC when there were 2,500 in their predicament. The Society's training committee proposed to inform LPC students about the grim employment situation but opposed any 'moratorium on the acceptance of applications for authorisation' to offer the course. Instead it suggested allowing CABx, law libraries, and university law departments to offer traineeships. LS President Charles Elly told the 1994 conference that the solution 'will only be found when this recession has clearly ended and business starts recruiting graduates in increasing numbers'. When the Liverpool University senior careers adviser observed that 'other professions can control their training process' and asked 'why can't the Law Society?', the latter declared: 'we have no legal powers'.[29]

Nigel Savage, dean of Nottingham Law School (the only private LPC provider), urged the OFT to investigate Law Society officials serving as governors of the College of Law (which licensed the twenty-seven other course providers) and 'the relationship between the college and an elite group of university law schools...which appears to guarantee places to students on the college in return for a promise by the university not to run an LPC'. Although the Society claimed to have delegated all authority to the LPC board and the College denied any 'commercial advantage...from the relationship', the Society stopped appointing College governors. (Two years earlier Finals course providers complained that the College was negotiating to allow nineteen universities to grant a four-year law degree incorporating the LPC if they agreed not to offer a competing course for five years.[30])

Despite these pressures, the Society's training committee very narrowly defeated a proposal to match LPC places with the number of articles because 'no estimate of future demand can be infallible' and it did not wish to 'intervene in the working of the market'. (Observers said the committee would have approved the cap had voting excluded those with a conflict of interest: two governors and the management board chair of the College of Law.) It urged 'sensible restraint' on course providers but felt powerless to impose a moratorium, a 'blunt instrument', which 'could hamper institutions in tailoring their provision more closely to demand'. But if competition among LPC providers 'produced a growth in numbers of places that bore no resemblance to any likely growth in the number of training contracts, that would be a matter the Law Society could not ignore'. Simon Baker, the incoming chair, also wanted course places 'geared to a wider view of the market for legal services' so as to avoid 'too much...wasted effort and disappointment'. He urged everybody to 'take an utterly realistic view of the employment prospects within the legal profession'. A week later the training committee vice-chair told LPC graduates that 'the solicitors' profession cannot grow at the rate necessary to employ all those who aspire to join our ranks' and urged them to find 'other suitable opportunities'.

Calling students 'desperate', the TSG urged the Society to 'do all it can to ensure that no more places are accredited' and expressed 'considerable resentment at the Law Society's failure to seize the initiative'. Accusing the profession of 'practising a form of con-trick on the guileless young', the *New Law Journal* asked: was it 'fair to allow thousands of young people to go through extensive rigorous and costly examinations ending with substantial debts, only to find there is really no place for them in which to exercise their skills?' Nevertheless, the College of Law added 192 places in London. 'We are in a commercial environment. We cannot run at a loss or put staff out of work.... The Law Society cannot reduce the number of places available.' Because restricting places to those with training contracts would 'limit the opportunity...for those from less advantaged backgrounds', it challenged 'those who criticise the LPC [to explain] how students should be cut down at selection'. The Society's legal education director declared: 'people want to have a chance to do it and at the end of the day it's somewhat unfair of them to complain'. But Baker denounced the expansion as 'irresponsible'. Although 'this is said to be the operation of the market... this market trades in the unrealistic expectations of young people and their constant disappointment'. Savage called it tantamount to 'putting another 200 kids straight on the dole'.[31]

Although the Society had retained minimum traineeship salaries in 1993, the then training committee chair Roger Jones and members Henry Hodge and John Young again urged abolition in 1995. The TSG warned this would exclude 'significant sections of society (especially ethnic minorities)...from the profession'; 85–90 per cent of the African, Caribbean, and Asian Lawyers Group agreed. But the Society of Nigerian Lawyers called the minimum 'a classic example of a restraint of trade which is open to legal challenge...supported only by a few privileged white trainees'. It is 'prejudicial, unfair and works to the disadvantage of ethnic minority trainees.' The committee voted 10–4 with four abstentions for retention. Member Eileen Pembridge said 'trainees should not just be let into the profession as cheap labour'. But Martin Mears, a new Council member, was characteristically blunt: 'the only valid argument in favour of the minimum salary is that it would reduce the number of entrants into the profession'. A year later Baker, now chair, predicted abolition by 1997. Indeed, the Society obtained counsel's opinion in October 1996 that the minimum lacked legal force, though the problem could be remedied. The new TSG chair declared abolition would be 'a real tragedy'.[32]

Just as the Bar responded to the disparity between BVC graduates and pupillages by contemplating a lower-tier advocate, so the Law Society and the Institute of Legal Executives (ILEX) applied to the Department of Employment to develop a national vocational qualification for paralegals; half of all firms already employed an estimated 24,000. The LS director of professional standards hoped this would dispose of some of the 11,000 annual law graduates. 'You have all these people swilling around with law degrees and they need a qualification.' The LS training contracts casework committee again considered authorizing traineeships at CABx.[33]

Solicitors suffering from recession, inefficiency, and competition blamed 'overproduction'. At the first of a series of Law Society roadshows in Exeter in January 1995, a solicitor demanded: 'What was the Society doing about the over-population of the profession?' Later that year Martin Mears and Robert Sayer exploited the issue in their victorious campaigns for president and vice-president. Sayer's position paper, 'Too many lawyers', called for reducing 'course places to a level that replaced those leaving the profession but did not increase "stock"...around 1000' course places. He blamed solicitors who 'borrowed' client money on excess supply. 'Expecting those already in the profession to leave is unrealistic. We must look instead at reducing the inflow of new entrants. This can be seen as an opportunity to raise their standard.'

The TSG called Sayer's proposal 'a recipe for disaster and decline, a seriously bad idea'. Chair Richard Moorhead was 'opposed to limiting entry via the number of training contracts but not to limiting the number of places on the LPCs at a sensible level'. 'A reduction of over 75% would be extraordinary and suggest keeping fees high for the old fat cat lawyers.' Angry at being excluded from Mears's working party on overcapacity, he hoped 'that a President who stood upon his desire for democracy within the Law Society would not turn his back on such a large portion of its membership'. Mears accused Moorhead of 'gross discourtesy' and attempting 'to hold a gun to my head'. Some trainees 'delude themselves. If you're admitted to an LPC course with a poor degree your chances of finding a training contract are virtually nil.' Given the 'consensus' that the profession was 'overcrowded', there was:

a simple choice between allowing 'market forces' to take their course or doing something. The consequence of doing nothing is that in the short and medium term at any rate, solicitors' incomes will fall, the pressures on high street practices will increase and the weakest will go to the wall. That is not a situation which I believe our professional body should accept.

'Let someone explain to me why it's in the public interest that only half the LPC graduates find training contracts.' If the OFT objected, the Society would show 'that it is in the public interest that a nation's legal profession should enjoy a reasonable level of security and prosperity'. When the College of Law proposed to ACLEC that everyone passing the LPC be able to call themselves attorneys, Sayer denounced it as 'the same old story, bums on seats, money, money, money'.[34]

At the working party's first meeting Sayer suggested that LPC applicants take personality or psychometric tests like those used by the Civil Service, Army, banks, and (he claimed) the French and Irish legal professions. 'Are the people who are coming in the right kind of people ... ? A lot of people are not temperamentally suited to becoming solicitors and you can see their frustration.' The College of Law principal agreed that 'if we could find a way of determining [honesty] it would save the compensation fund a lot of money'. Moorhead called it 'unacceptable' for the Law Society 'to decide how many trainees and what type of trainee should be coming into the profession' and repeated his complaint about exclusion. 'Is it possible that Mr Mears is afraid of what the TSG has to say?' But his successor 'absolutely applaud[ed] Mr Mears' recognition that entry to the profession is a vital issue which people have tried to brush under the carpet for too long'. And YSG chair Lucy Winskell, newly appointed to the working party, urged it to send a clear 'warning ... that this is a very overcrowded profession'.[35]

Mears, however, encountered opposition within the Society. Training committee chair Baker declared that:

what is happening to solicitors is happening everywhere. It is not happening because of some conspiracy by Mrs Thatcher. It is happening because the world is changing. ... If we look to defend monopolies or reserved areas we are bound to be disappointed because we would be shouting in the face of all the laws of economics.

Declining to join the working party, he challenged Mears to:

meet again in the year 2000 at the solicitors annual conference and compare notes between those solicitors who followed an agenda of protectionism and those who followed the training committee's agenda of competitiveness. ... Show me anywhere else in the history of business where that kind of crude cap has ever brought prosperity.[36]

Mears dismissed as 'negative and pessimistic' and 'irrelevant' a QC's opinion to the working party that the Society could not proportion entry to demand, require a specific class of university degree or condition LPC places on traineeships. Declaring 'the standards of a small minority' of solicitors too low, Mears urged the Society to examine logical skills, literacy, and communication abilities in screening LPC applicants. There 'might be the desirable side effect of a reduction in numbers'. Sayer promptly inflated the claim: 'a substantial number of recruits are not excellent. There are plenty of examples of illiterate letters from people who have passed the LPC and have got fairly good degrees.' But Baker, who resented Mears's invasion of his turf, praised the QC's opinion as 'authoritative and lucid'. The College of Law board of management chair warned that such tests would be expensive, create work for crammers, and might be discriminatory. The TSG chair said 'if there's a problem with the quality of entrants, it's the first we've heard about it'.[37]

As the rhetoric escalated, however, the problem eased. LPC applications fell by 887 in 1995–6 (leaving 852 places unfilled) and another 1,364 the next year. Pass rates declined from 82 to 70 per cent between 1994 and 1995, and the number of training contracts increased slightly. CPE applications halved in 1996. Baker felt that 'the serious over-supply of applicants to the profession seems to be correcting itself'. But Mears accused the Law Society annual report of 'complacency'. 'The market will even out the numbers eventually but meanwhile there have been too many dead bodies... about 12,000 graduates currently without jobs as solicitors.' Baker retorted: 'No one can be guaranteed a place or job for life'.[38]

At the TSG conference a month later members denounced the training contract shortage. Urging them to work as paralegals, Baker dismissed Mears's agenda as 'out of touch with the great changes going on in the world around us'. 'The regulations are not there to protect existing solicitors.' LAG director Roger Smith said Mears 'has picked the wrong fight at the wrong time on the wrong issues'. Mears retorted: 'The fight I have picked is on the profession's issues and the profession's agenda. But in a Council dominated by people like Mr Baker, I'm bound to fail.' Faced with such opposition, he dissolved the working party but vowed to continue his crusade.[39]

Although training contracts increased by 323 in 1997 and LPC applicants declined by 811 in 1998, leaving 1,774 places unfilled, the training committee froze LPC places from 1997 to 2000. Furious at having its planned expansion blocked, the Oxford Institute of Legal Practice took counsel's advice. '[T]he situation Simon Baker seems to think acceptable is that of an institution such as mine having to buy quotas from other institutions. It's preposterous.' Bristol University complained that 'the Law Society set up the system... on the basis that the market would deal with excess capacity. We never expected that the rules would be changed at five minutes notice.' Nigel Savage, now College of Law CEO, said 'I don't like any professional body interfering in the market. The Law Society is behaving like a trade union, not an informed and reasonable regulator.' But Baker declared that any legal challenge 'will be resisted with the utmost determination. ... There has been a consistent pattern of a fall in demand for LPC places. ... If we continue to increase places providers will be put at risk.' The TSG concurred, expressing 'concern that the number of places sent out a false message to students'. Mears declared that the 'lack of demand for places or otherwise is surely a problem for the course providers and not the Training Committee'.

Nine months later, when LPC enrolment had fallen by another 314 (after dropping by 140 the previous year) and training contracts increased by 442, reducing the disparity to about 400, the Society lifted the freeze. The following year the ICLS sought to offer an LPC course for 100 students from September 2000. 'If the LPC providers are going to teach the bar course, then obviously it helps for us to do this.' Over the Society's opposition, eight City firms (which hired 900 trainees annually) jointly devised a new LPC emphasizing corporate practice and sought existing providers to teach it. The other 132 firms in the Legal Education and Training Group worried that the existing LPC would be deemed inferior.[40]

Just as the Society froze LPC places when nearly 2,000 went unfilled, so it questioned minimum trainee salaries for the third time in four years as demand was rising. The consultation found 70 per cent of respondents opposed the minimum. But though Baker boasted of the highest response ever, the TSG objected that less than 20 per cent of firms replied and the methodology was 'deeply flawed'. Its own survey of LPC students and trainees found that 85 per cent wanted to retain the minimum, which was more likely to be paid to women and minorities. At the TSG annual conference, ex-chair Moorhead complained of a 'stitch up', and the current chair was 'amazed and disappointed' that Baker refused to address the audience, which vilified him. Despite LS President Tony Girling's opposition, the training committee recommended retention, which a large majority of the Council approved for two years.

Ex-president Mears admitted that 'seven years ago when I was a Thatcherite, I opposed minimum salaries. Those days are gone. What sort of training can firms give if they can't afford to pay the minimum salary? ... [Y]ou create a proletariat of trainee solicitors and assistant solicitors.' Mears's ally Peter Watson-Lee declared 'there are far too many students chasing too few training places. If you abolish minimum salaries altogether, solicitors might start taking on trainee solicitors in their droves as cheap labour. All restriction on entering the profession would then disappear.' Sayer thought it 'obvious we should have one' so as not to 'flood the profession with yet more people. We don't need volume, but people of the highest quality'. Council member Kamlesh Bahl agreed: 'Most employers value women less than men. Only where there is a minimum wage is there no gap in salaries'. Council member Trevor Murray, however, did not understand why the Council was 'more frightened of the TSG than of the 67 per cent of the profession'. Two years later, in response to the High Court's application of the minimum wage to Bar pupils, the training committee urged observing it, restricting exceptions to its own minimum, and declaring a higher aspirational target.[41]

If Mears had converted to protectionism, the Society claimed to have embraced laissez faire, now that the imbalance between supply and demand had corrected itself. Noting that 4,460 students passed the July 1998 LPC and 4,826 new traineeships were registered in 1997–8, the chair of the training contract review group boasted of solicitors' superiority to doctors, 'always held up as a marvellous example of regulating entrance to a profession. They have artificially restricted the market, and now they have created the mayhem of a shortage of junior hospital doctors.' Roger Smith, now the Society's training director, declared:

We don't control this market. We are not restricting entry to the profession in any way. ...We will approve any provider who meets the criteria of LPC places. ...We can't control the number of training contracts...this is a modern economy. ...we'll give you all the information we can about how the market is going to operate... then you make an informed choice.[42]

C. The Imperative and Impossibility of Controlling Supply

Some critics have rejected my (unoriginal) argument that the English legal profession, like all professions, has tried to control supply by limiting entry.[43] Yet the central actors in the 1990s openly proclaimed that goal: the NPBA ('population explosion'), Desmond Fennell QC (to say 'you can all come to the Bar...is no longer appropriate in a changed climate'), Martin Bowley QC ('we are simply putting too many people through Bar School'), Anthony Thornton QC ('we are being engulfed by a tidal wave of applications'), Nigel Bastin (BVC places should reflect 'the numbers which the profession can absorb'), Robert Seabrook QC ('strong public interest argument against training unlimited numbers'), and Richard Southwell QC ('the number of students wanting to enter the profession has increased beyond all sensible limits') among barristers, and Martin Mears ('consensus' that the profession was 'overcrowded') and Robert Sayer (a position paper entitled *Too Many Lawyers*) among solicitors. Local law societies and professional journals generally agreed.

The Bar rejected 'a totally demand-led vocational training system' in favour of one 'led by the numerical requirement for trained barristers' (which it claimed to know). Leading barristers envied medicine's apparent ability to control entry (disregarding that government was doing so, not the profession, and doctors were NHS employees). The training committee said 'the Law Society could not ignore...a growth in the number of [LPC] places that bore no resemblance to any likely growth in the number of training contracts'. The fall of the LPC pass rate from 82 to 70 per cent from 1994 to 1995 seems no more accidental than the Law Society's manipulation of pass rates throughout the preceding 160 years.[44]

Protectionists exaggerated the problem. BC chair Robert Owen QC found it 'worrying' that 'less than 3% of those qualifying with a law degree or the Common Professional Examination will be able to go on to obtain a tenancy'. Mears warned of the 'dead bodies' among 'the 12,000 graduates currently without jobs as solicitors'. Individuals changed their views with their institutional positions: Nigel Savage from free marketeer as private law school head to protectionist as College of Law director, Simon Baker from critic of Mears's proposal to protect solicitors from competition to defender of his own to protect LPC providers, Roger Smith from urging abolition of articles as LAG director to proclaiming the Law Society was 'not restricting entry to the profession in any way' as its training director.

The salience of protectionism is also evidenced by the number, visibility, and vehemence of its critics: not only the DGFT but also ACLEC and Lord Mackay. Asked by the NPBA if the Bar was 'training the correct number of barristers', the Bar Council replied that the DGFT had told the Lord Chancellor that 'the number of people taking up legal training should be determined by natural competition'. LS President Sheldon insisted 'we would almost certainly get [manpower planning] wrong'. Elly, his successor, said, 'the solution will only be found when this recession has clearly ended'. Baker refused 'to defend monopolies or reserved areas…because we would be shouting in the face of all the laws of economics'. Savage accused the Society of 'behaving like a trade union' by 'interfering in the market'. The chair of the Society's trainee contract review committee boasted of solicitors' superiority to doctors, who had 'created the mayhem of a shortage of junior hospital doctors' by 'artificially restrict[ing] the market'. The mass media unanimously cheered government attacks on entry barriers.

Even those who knew better felt compelled to speak the language of laissez faire. Fennell claimed his was 'the only profession which in effect said to everyone on a free market basis you can all come to the Bar'. Bastin entitled his defence of protectionism 'survival of the fittest'. Bowley maintained that the number of tenancies was 'dictated by market forces'. Mears justified his proposal to test LPC applicants as necessary to raise standards, while acknowledging there 'might be the desirable side effect of a reduction in numbers'.

If professions must seek to control supply, however, they are doomed to failure. Whipsawed by sharply fluctuating demand but immobilized by entry barriers it had labouriously constructed and vigorously defended, the legal profession displayed the inertia of a supertanker, consistently under- and over-shooting targets.[45] (Labour is always the most sluggish factor of production, and professional labour displays unusual friction.) Both branches were still responding to the 'recruitment crisis' when most other businesses had discerned the recession. The Law Society froze LPC places and questioned minimum traineeship salaries for the third time just when economic recovery was rapidly increasing demand for solicitors. Students who had to commit to a legal career three to six years before qualifying were unwilling to lose sunk costs or, like gamblers, indifferent to statistics. Few could accept the downward mobility inherent in Baker's realistic advice to become paralegals.

Each constituency pursued self-interest. Solicitors urged common training, invoking the Bar's claim of specialist expertise to propose that all advocates gain further experience and education and demonstrate competence through examination (like medical consultants, the Bar's favourite analogy). Employed barristers wanted to eliminate the pupillage barrier. The Bar preferred to ease transfer by solicitors and pupillage for employed barristers so it could continue to control entry. City firms were concerned with legitimating the profession, high-street firms with economic survival. Aspirants to both branches were torn between easing their own entry and obstructing competitors in later cohorts. The TSG accused Sayer's drastic proposal to cut entry by 75 per cent of 'keeping fees high for old fat cat lawyers'. Educators (both universities and others offering vocational courses) wanted to maximize their own production and exclude newcomers.

At the same time, all disavowed self-interest. Both branches professed concern not to waste scarce resources—of candidates, educational institutions, and taxpayers—by training those the branches were determined to keep out. (They had never previously exhibited solicitude for the cost of surmounting the barriers they had erected.) The College of Law defended its expansion on the ground that 'in a commercial environment...we cannot run at a loss or put staff out of work'. Only Southwell, an unsuccessful candidate for BC chair, spoke of 'irreparable damage to the Bar'; and only Mears, who lost three bids for a second term as LS President, declared it was 'in the public interest that a nation's legal profession should enjoy a reasonable level of security and prosperity'.

A decade of criticism by academics, submissions to the Royal Commission, Austin Mitchell, the Marre Committee, and Lord Mackay's Green Papers made it increasingly difficult to defend entry barriers that had been unquestioned for centuries. The same charges of monopoly advanced against the profession were levelled at the College of Law and ICSL strangleholds on the vocational course. The Labour Party's 1995 'Access to justice' position paper declared that 'the chronic shortage of course and training places for the two branches of the legal profession has brought both the Inns of Court School of Law...and the College of Law...into disregard'.[46] The dramatic growth in numbers seeking admission forced the rationalization of selection processes, replacing personal contacts with objective, quantitative criteria. The confrontation between protectionism and laissez faire played out differently at each hurdle. Their defensibility varied with the degree to which they were visible or hidden, collective or individual, deliberate or 'natural', with the Inns' control over the number of tenancies at one end and market demand for assistant solicitors at the other. A traditional barrier like Inns dinners fell when the ICSL could no longer defend its BVC monopoly; but it was already tainted through association with an anachronistic warrant of character rather than expertise (hence the abortive proposal to revive an 'educational' element alleged to be its 'original idea') and with a public school collegiality, based on male rites of passage, incompatible with the growing number of women. Although the branches exerted greater control through pupillages and traineeships, entrants who now were all university graduates objected to the waste and humiliation of apprenticeship (roundly criticized by every empirical study). The vocational courses were an uncomfortable hybrid between academic science and apprenticeship craft. When both branches lost their training monopolies, other providers (and those wishing to become providers) intensified pressure for entry. As the rise in the pass rate for the LS Finals in the 1980s demonstrates, examinations could not stem the flow (exactly why the Bar was reluctant to introduce them in the nineteenth century). Given sufficient incentives, aspirants will surmount any hurdle (as the tides of global labour migration demonstrate).

All efforts to raise the dikes failed. Selection procedures became more difficult to justify with increased investment in human capital (by aspirants, the profession, and the state). The multi-stage winnowing process in both branches, involving grossly redundant applications, wasted the time and money of both applicants and gatekeepers and inflicted heavy emotional costs. Because the Bar had remained more patently particularistic, it displayed special enthusiasm for meritocracy, boasting that the CLE's 'test of critical reasoning' would 'ensure equality of opportunity'. But the subordination of university degree results to A-levels (some taken years earlier) made a mockery of BVC selection procedures and even cost the ICSL its monopoly. (Goldsmith, however, reassured barristers that 'only a limited number of institutions' would be accredited.) And the PACH committed the typical meritocratic sin of over-rewarding the few at the expense of the many. Exposés of professional self-interest made it impossible for solicitors to adopt the minimum degree result the Bar had imposed in 1984. The Bar's argument against common vocational training—contrasting its 'top class' or 'specialist' advocates with merely 'good solicitors' and 'general legal practitioners'—dripped with condescension. All entry barriers were (rightly) suspected of reproducing ascriptive biases of class and race. Proposals to postpone Call until after pupillage or abolish minimum salaries were defeated by such charges. Sayer's psychometric tests foundered on the impossibility of predicting those 'not temperamentally suited' (as well as the anachronism of predicating entry on character).[47]

Both branches flirted with a *numerus clausus* on vocational course places, but their arguments were transparent rationalizations. Insufficient physical accommodation? Acquire more. Manpower planning? Impossible to predict demand. Unfairness to frustrated applicants? Adults are entitled to choose. Analogy to medicine? Government, not the medical profession, determined supply. The Bar pays the cost? More boast than fact. Threat of lower quality (Radford's 'unremedial incompetence', Sayer's 'not excellent' recruits)? No evidence. Too many lawyers? Who are they to say. The market controls? Let it do so. Indeed, the LS training committee declined to limit LPC places to traineeships because it did not want to 'intervene in the working of the market'.

The branches then sought to use their continuing control over apprenticeship to restrict vocational course places, either by making the former a prerequisite or by incorporating it into the latter. (The unavailability of traineeships may have dampened interest in the LPC because commercial firms paid its cost; the Bar hoped that moving pupillage offers to before the BVC would have a similar effect.) At the same time, the branches contemplated multiplying apprenticeships by shortening them or allowing additional placements. But this exposed the arbitrariness of the existing number, undermined the claim that apprenticeship provided essential training, and just moved the bottleneck to entry-level positions. (Each lowering of an upstream hurdle in response to criticism increases pressure on downstream hurdles by allowing aspirants to invest more and approach their goal of entry.)

Here the Bar was on shakier ground. Even if it no longer confined chambers to the Inns, the requirement of a tenancy excluded many aspirants, and the failure of the library system exposed the power of clerks. Solicitors could hide behind the market's invisible hand, which appeared to regulate the number of assistants. Solicitors also sought to imitate the Bar by creating a subordinated para-legal position for LPC graduates unable to obtain a traineeship (like employment for BVC graduates unable to obtain a pupillage), thereby offering an outlet for thwarted ambitions while eliminating any competitive threat (employed barristers lacked rights of audience; firms controlled employed paralegals).

All these efforts set educators against the profession. First the universities (and what had been polytechnics) opened the floodgates in the 1970s by dramatically increasing the number of law degrees and offering CPE courses. Then the universities breached both branches' monopoly over the vocational course. Lawyers assailed educators' self-interest—in Sayer's typically plain words it was 'the same old story, bums on seats, money, money, money'. Professional journals warned against entrusting the LPC to universities and polytechnics, which had a 'vested interest...to see their candidates pass the examinations'. Educators fought among themselves: the College of Law and the ICSL for each other's students, existing providers against newcomers, large commercial firms against the rest of the profession over the content and status of the vocational course. The market had conquered legal education and training, just as it had the profession.

The one entry barrier that continued to rise during this decade—consistent with market hegemony—was cost: tuition for university degrees, the CPE, and the vocational course; and subsistence during the three to six years before qualification. Simultaneously, government support declined—precipitately for the vocational course—forcing most students into debt, many heavily, and influencing career choices.[48] (That law is valued less than medicine allowed government to refuse to pay the cost of training.) Although the profession pontificated about its obligation to future cohorts, its limited contribution focused on the least needy: winners of merit scholarships, pupils and tenants in prosperous (commercial) sets, City trainees. Market barriers were less visible and easier to justify (seemingly impersonal and inevitable) but also reproduced class advantage.

If the profession did not control cost, it did determine income during apprenticeship and employment. Most firms and chambers naturally opposed minimum salaries. Entrants were divided. Those confident of positions favoured minima; those uncertain or unsuccessful would accept less. The African, Caribbean, and Asian Lawyers Group supported minima, but the Society of Nigerian Lawyers opposed them; Kamlesh Bahl was convinced they helped women. Both branches made no secret of their hope that minima would limit entry, while rationalizing them (unconvincingly) as necessary to maintain the quality of training or entrants. The Bar explicitly conditioned its willingness to fund pupillages and tenancies on control over their numbers (thereby replacing the discredited traditional warrant of ability to pay with a modern meritocratic warrant). At the same time, it lacked the collective authority to fulfil its commitments.

In the end, however, the profession was no more able to control the ebb and flow of supply than Canute to halt the tide. Its efforts to do so during this decade further delegitimated its claim to speak in the public interest rather than its own.

4   Reflecting Society

[The Bar has] the most progressive [racial] policy of any profession or industrial concern. [Anthony Scrivener QC, BC Chair]

To me there can be no more basic right than not to be persecuted.... [Rodger Pannone, LS President, supporting ban on sexual orientation discrimination]

[This] disgrace [must] represent the high water mark of progressive bigotry. [Martin Mears, LS Council member, opposing ban]

I don't believe there is any discrimination in the major City firms. [Linklater hiring partner] [I am] not sure how you can force someone to take on someone who is not quite the norm. [LS Council member]

[O]ne man's discrimination may be another man's sensible business choice. [LS Council member]

[N]othing would be worse for the reputation of the judiciary in this country than for me to lower the standards for appointment...simply to ensure a different racial or sexual mix. [Lord Mackay]

I do not think the judiciary should be representative of the public any more than a brain surgeon is representative. [Lord Taylor]

[T]his is a merits-based appointments system. I don't want gender balance, or political balance as an objective. [Lord Irvine]

Entry barriers affect who as well as how many join a profession. The belief that ascriptive characteristics (class, gender, race, sexual orientation, disability) should neither confer nor deny privilege, including professional membership or success, is gaining strength. But this must not blind us to the fact that until the late twentieth century social exclusivity defined professions. Indeed, they initially sought closure by prescribing who could enter, confident that this would adequately limit numbers. Identity was central to admission and preferment for two reasons. First, professionals were valued more for who they were than what they knew. Dependence on them to mediate with God (the priesthood) or the state (lawyers), wield force (the military), or confront the mysteries of life and death (doctors) required trust, which could be guaranteed only by character, believed to reflect breeding. Secondly, membership in a profession conferred high status in the great chain of being, which could be compromised by low birth or boorishness. Many have noted that all-male occupations lost status when they were feminized: school teaching and clerical work under capitalism, medicine under communism.

Professions have controlled background in various ways. The four traditional professions excluded women (and two still formally subordinate them). When Jacksonian America eliminated all other requirements for becoming a lawyer, states still admitted only white men.[1] Harlan Fiske Stone, later Chief Justice of the U.S. Supreme Court, warned against 'the influx to the bar of greater numbers of the unfit', who 'exhibit racial tendencies toward study by memorization' and display 'a mind almost Oriental in its fidelity to the minutiae of the subject without regard to any controlling rule or reason'.[2] Yale (like many American universities) limited Jewish enrolment until 1960; its law school dean did not want to base admission on college grades because immigrants' children performed so well, and he wanted them to complete more years of college.[3] American states require bar applicants to provide lawyer references and pass a 'character test'—which Pennsylvania explicitly used to reduce the number of immigrants.[4] Nazi Germany combined patriarchy and anti-Semitism with a protectionist response to the Depression by expelling the few women and the many Jewish lawyers (60 per cent of the Berlin Bar, perhaps 80 per cent in Vienna).[5]

Both branches of the English profession sought to elevate or preserve their status by exclusion. The costs of qualifying (both direct and opportunity) long exceeded the means of all but the wealthiest. The Inns still require all applicants to state their fathers' occupations; virtually none was a worker until the late 1970s, and workers' children remain severely underrepresented today.[6] Although Bar students from the 'new' Commonwealth greatly outnumbered domestic students in the decades after World War II, almost all returned home. The few racial minority students who stayed found it almost impossible to obtain a pupillage or tenancy or briefs from (white) solicitors. In 1983, 78 per cent of the 210 black barristers practised in just 5 per cent of the 286 set of chambers, while 83 per cent of chambers had none.[7] Both branches banned women until Parliament compelled admission in 1919. The same barriers that excluded racial minorities kept women to just 2 per cent of practising barristers as late as 1957. A smaller proportion of women than men called started practice, and a larger proportion left prematurely. Some Circuits overtly discriminated through the 1960s. All this may explain why 57 per cent of chambers still had no women and less than 12 per cent had more than one as late as 1984. Clerks (95 per cent men) openly disliked women tenants, whose lower earnings (depressed by clerks' own biases) reduced clerks' incomes. Women were underrepresented in more remunerative work and earned far less than men with comparable experience. They were only 2 per cent of QCs in 1985 and almost entirely unrepresented in Bar governance. Yet in 1983 the Senate of the Inns of Court and the Bar declared that 'discrimination against women… is a thing of the past…[and] has ceased to be a serious problem'.[8]

Although solicitors long acknowledged social inferiority to barristers (if resentfully), the costs of qualifying ensured that their own class origins would be equally narrow. Non-citizens were excluded until 1974 (as they were in the

United States until 1973). As late as 1982, consequently, there were no more than 200 racial minority articled clerks and solicitors, just 0.25 per cent of the profession. Although women were only 1.8 per cent of solicitors in 1957, they had become 10 per cent of new admissions in 1971 and nearly half of new articles by 1983. In the latter year, however, just 54 per cent of enrolled women 30–34 years old and 47 per cent of those 35–39 years old were in private practice (compared with 80 and 73 per cent of men). Partly for this reason women were less than 1 per cent of partners in the fifteen leading City firms in 1980 and just one of the seventy Law Society Council members.[9]

The 1979 Royal Commission optimistically declared that 'sex discrimination based on prejudice has diminished' and 'steady improvement is being made'. Fearing that:

an effect similar to that of discrimination arises from hesitancy in accepting women as members or partners in any numbers in case they are lost to the demands of the family or for fear (not always unjustified) that they may be less acceptable to clients than men,

the Commission recommended 'a guide, for circulation to heads of chambers and to firms, outlining their obligations as regards discrimination'. It had 'no doubt that the great majority of practising lawyers are against' race discrimination. '[G]hetto chambers' existed because it was 'not surprising' that 'a young barrister from an ethnic minority gravitates to chambers whose members are drawn exclusively from ethnic minorities', given the difficulty of finding a tenancy. Again it recommended that 'guidance in written form should be issued by the governing bodies of the profession to all firms and chambers' but opposed for now reserving places on those governing bodies. It understood 'the objections to reverse discrimination' and 'appreciate[d] the objections to compulsory measures'.[10] In 1988 the Secretary of State for Education urged the Polytechnics and Colleges Funding Council to make widening participation in higher education a priority.[11]

By the 1990s women were more than half of university law students and racial minorities 18 per cent. But if their numbers justified a claim to proportionate representation within the profession, they started with disadvantages. Both were more likely than men or whites to attend new universities. Though women had better law degrees and Law Society Finals results than men, minorities (other than Chinese) had substantially lower A-levels, and 30 per cent of blacks entered through access courses.[12]

A. Breaking into the Bar

The Bar took the Royal Commission's advice, prohibiting race and sex discrimination against pupils and tenants in 1984. Two years later it issued guidelines on those subjects and the distribution of work in chambers but, bowing to clerks, did not make them enforceable. Although it warned chambers in 1988 against requesting applicant photographs, it accepted that many sets required an upper second class degree, excluding most blacks. Some of the responsibility rested on (white) solicitors. In 1989 the *New Law Journal* deplored the way they 'regale each other with stories of faux pas committed, mainly by black barristers....' The Law Society's race relations committee urged the SCB to discipline discrimination against black barristers and endorsed contractual relations with barristers, which would subject briefing to the Race Relations Act 1976.[13] Research reconfirmed segregation of minorities (more than half in 5 per cent of sets, none in half the sets) and the under-representation of minority silks (one tenth the proportion of minority barristers). But the Bar would not go beyond exhortation. Indeed, the 1990 BC chair blamed solicitors for not briefing black barristers. The Council paired black sets with a civil and a criminal mainstream set, although one of the four minority silks found this 'patronizing'.[14]

1991 BC chair Anthony Scrivener QC initiated brief secondments of black barristers to mainstream chambers, co-opted the first black to the Council, and appointed blacks to all committees. He boasted that the Council's aspirational goal of 5 per cent minority tenants was 'the most progressive policy of any profession or industrial concern'. The CRE agreed it was 'exactly right', and an *Independent* columnist praised this 'most radical equal opportunities policy of any profession'. But the *Daily Telegraph* denounced the 'quota system', which 'may put the BC in a good light' but 'will do nothing in the longer run to enhance the dignity of black barristers'. Mr Justice Brooke, whose race relations committee had proposal the goal, was distressed that 'commentators confused this with positive discrimination' and a 'good deal of press coverage [drew] attention to the unattractive aspects of the American quota system'. Although the Bar appointed two equal opportunities officers, the Society of Black Lawyers attacked it for choosing whites.[15]

Claiming blacks were 20 per cent of ICSL applicants but only 9 per cent of admittees in 1992, the SBL accused the CLE of discriminating by reserving places for 'predominately white' CPE students. The Bar replied that 16 per cent of ICSL students were minority and promised to end the CPE preference in two years. A few months later the SBL accused the Bar and the CLE of 'ethnic cleansing', claiming that blacks resitting the Bar Finals in 1992 failed four times as often as whites (80 per cent versus 20 per cent) and blaming 98 per cent of black failures on audio-visual work alone, graded by 'discretion irrespective of merit'. SBL chair Peter Herbert called the CLE 'riddled with racism' and 'far worse that the [Law Society's] College of Law'. The CLE replied that the relative failure rates were 46 and 16 per cent and only 3 per cent of minority failures were attributable to audio-visual work alone. Nevertheless, some seventy CLE students formed Bar Vocational Students for Justice, and five were granted legal aid to challenge their failures. When the CRE announced an investigation, the CLE appropriated £200,000 for an inquiry by Dame Jocelyn Barrow, Broadcasting Standards Council chair. Although Barrow was black, the SBL boycotted her investigation as a 'white wash' because she had 'no legal qualifications, no knowledge of the Bar and has never conducted an enquiry of this nature'. It also denounced the delay by the CRE, which was waiting for Barrow.

Her interim report concluded that the different failure rates (28 versus 13 per cent graded race-blind, 16 versus 5 where race was indicated) 'cannot be explained by direct discrimination'. She attributed them to the fact that 52 per cent of minority students but only 28 per cent of white graduated from polytechnics. Concerned that minority students incurred heavier debts and had to work part time, she recommended need-based Inns scholarships and better study facilities and support services. The SBL called the report 'ambiguous', and the student plaintiffs criticized its focus on 'social welfare aspects' rather than 'the structure of the course itself'. The CLE allowed the eighteen repeaters who had failed the 1992 exam to resit. The five plaintiffs feared being 'victimized' by the examiners but reluctantly agreed. The CLE was 'delighted', and the SBL called it 'an historic victory'.

Barrow's final report said that academic performance did not explain why 71 per cent of whites but only 48 per cent of blacks found pupillages, an advantage reflected in subsequent exam pass rates. The Inns' emphasis on 'chapel, grace and drinks' alienated some minorities. Inadequately prepared students suffered a 'grave loss of confidence' during the course. She recommended allowing failing students to resit within six months, double marking, a student union, an equal opportunities officer, and an end to the CLE monopoly. The CLE allocated £500,000 to hire five staff and contract with the CRE to monitor the course. The SBL denounced the 'whitewash' for not finding 'evidence of direct or indirect discrimination'. Yet even before the report the gap in failure rates had shrunk to 20 versus 10 per cent and narrowed further over the next two years. When the comparison controlled for undergraduate institution, degree class, and tutorials attended, the difference was less than 2 per cent. An independent study confirmed that the correlation of race with success in obtaining BVC places, passing, and obtaining a pupillage became statistically insignificant when the comparison controlled for prior education.[16]

In the mid-1980s there were only four minorities and eleven women among the nearly 600 silks. Appointment of the first black woman in 1991 received broad and favourable press coverage. Later that year, however, the newly formed Association of Women Barristers persuaded the Bar AGM to vote 102–19 for an equal opportunities committee to investigate gender barriers. Three-fifths of women responding to a survey by the new committee and the LCD reported discrimination. They made 50 per cent more pupillage applications than men with equivalent credentials and underwent a third more interviews, at which they were asked about marriage and parenthood about twice as often. They were less likely to practise in the more remunerative areas, perhaps because nearly half the heads of chambers reported solicitors preferred men. Nevertheless, nearly two-thirds of heads also denied the need for change, and only 16 per cent of sets had a written equal opportunity policy.

In response, the BC published an *Equality Code of Practice*, recommending that chambers advertise pupillages and tenancies, interview in teams, distribute work fairly, offer maternity leave, and adopt a written complaints policy. Chair J J Rowe boasted:

the great majority of entrants to the Bar now are from grammar schools, comprehensive schools and non-Oxbridge universities, the percentage of ethnic minority at the Bar is greater than the percentage in the population at large; and 42 per cent of barristers called are women.

Yet among barristers who completed their academic education that year, complaints of discrimination or harassment were voiced by 40 per cent of women pupils, 33 per cent of minority, all African Caribbean, and half of those openly gay or lesbian. When the BC adopted the Code in 1995, chair Peter Goldsmith QC boasted it

had led the way among professions in not simply acknowledging but doing something practical about discrimination . . . [because] concern with fair treatment and respect for individual dignity is especially important in a profession whose own task is to uphold people's rights without fear or favour.

It had exceeded legal requirements because of its 'historic character as a profession where ability and integrity alone are what matter'.[17]

By contrast, three of the four Inns rejected the Code. A supporter said a poorly attended Gray's Inn AGM disparaged it as a 'piece of political correctness' and denounced her as 'a viper in the bosom of the Inn'. Warning that this rejection had 'compromised' the Bar's 'public standing', the next AGM called on the Inns to accept the Code. BC chair Robert Seabrook QC called the Inns' action 'unwise and mistaken', and *The Times* criticized them as 'old-fashioned', 'reactionary', 'impolitic', and 'unnecessary'. The *New Law Journal* declared that 'anyone who has ever been near the Temple . . . must have been aware of the potential for sexist and racist behaviour'. Nearly three years later the Bar AGM again criticized the Inns for stonewalling.[18]

In early 1995 the Bar decided its first case of sexual harassment, imposing a three-month suspension on the offender—a QC, Council member, and assistant recorder. Both the AWB and the *New Law Journal* called the penalty insufficient. A survey published that month found that although nearly three-quarters of women juniors had experienced discrimination and nearly two-fifths harassment, none had ever complained to the Bar. David Penry-Davey QC, 1995 BC vice-chair, told the AWB the Council would require chambers to appoint two senior members to resolve grievances, create a confidential hot line to the Sex Discrimination Committee, and ask sets to offer 'safe havens' for victims of discrimination or harassment. The *New Law Journal* was contemptuous of the last: 'surely every chambers should be a safe haven and sanctions should be taken against the Head of those Chambers which are found not to be'. At the second Woman Lawyer conference the following year the Institute of Barristers' Clerks chair denounced the 'myth' that clerks heeded solicitors' requests for male barristers but then admitted doing so himself, explaining that 'work over the last three or four years has not been as plentiful as it was'.[19]

As women and minority barristers increased in numbers and seniority, silk became a growing embarrassment. Lord Williams of Mostyn QC, 1992 BC chair, criticized the Lord Chancellor's reliance on 'secret files' and refusal to let him see those of disappointed candidates. *Counsel* questioned whether the appointment process was 'compatible with the Bar's cherished image of itself as an independent profession' and feared that 'originality is discouraged and orthodoxy rewarded'. It urged that 'senior members of the practising profession' advise the Prime Minister. The AWB agreed it was 'quite bizarre' that the state should 'decide who are the top barristers'. The *Lawyer* thought the Lord Chancellor's reliance on gossip might explain why women were 15 per cent of barristers but just 8 per cent of applicants. The *Daily Mail* accused the institution of reinforcing the Bar's 'upper class image'. A leading barristers' clerk said 'you just need to look at the addresses—it's incestuous...very political'. An anonymous barrister charged that judges blocked appointments capriciously—once because a judge and an applicant shared a mistress. It helped to be related to a judge or in a set one of whose members had become a judge. Outraged that 'barristers had been lied to', Robin de Wilde moved that the 1993 Bar AGM 'views with grave concern the present system of appointing silks'. Over the opposition of incoming chair Robert Seabrook QC, the meeting adopted the resolution by 82 votes to 36. Lord Mackay insisted the process recognized 'merit as advocates...judged by the judiciary and the professional community' and was 'essentially promotion to a function rank, rather than an honour'. But though Rowe and Seabrook praised the 'quite exceptional care, conscientiousness and integrity' of the process, they appointed a working party to investigate it.

When the 1994 silk list contained just nine women and one minority (little different from six and one the year before), the *Solicitors Journal* denounced the process as 'most unsatisfactory'. 'It will have taken place behind closed doors, in a dark room, doubtless with the curtains drawn and a guttering candle providing the sole illumination...the solicitor's [*sic*] branch of the profession wants no part of such an unattractive procedure'. SBL chair Makbool Javaid condemned the 'shadowy' system. The Society of Asian Lawyers declared it helped if 'you have friends in high places, are part of the "old boy network", happen to be in "influential" sets, and mix in the right company'.

Nevertheless, the working party praised the selection process for exhibiting 'the utmost care and impartiality'. Since the reason for under-representation of women and minorities was 'historical...the balance will redress itself over a period of time'. 'To seek to redress the balance artificially would devalue both the system and also the status of those women and members of ethnic minorities who are granted silk on merit.' AWB chair Susan Ward condemned the report as 'superficial and poorly researched' and the selection process as an 'old boy's network at its very worst. It may have been acceptable fifty years ago but it is totally unacceptable in the mid-1990s.' The earnings criterion was 'particularly discriminatory against women, who not only have to tailor their careers to fit in family commitments but also face discrimination in the types of work they get'.

Lord Mackay expressed willingness to delegate appointments to a committee 'if that is the profession's wish'. While denouncing 'positive discrimination' and 'quotas' a year later, he expressed concern for 'the special position of those who have come late to the profession or who have had a break in their career' and boasted that 21 per cent of women applicants obtained silk, compared with 14 per cent of men.

The 1996 list of sixty-six contained only four women (half the previous year), still just one minority, and no solicitors (who had just become eligible). In his first list of sixty, two years later, Lord Irvine appointed the highest numbers and proportions of women (ten) and minorities (four) and the third solicitor, 'hoping their success will encourage others from these groups to put themselves forward next year'. Lincoln Crawford, the (black) chair of the BC race relations committee, was sure 'this will go a long way to restore the confidence of visible minority lawyers who have virtually given up the idea of ever applying'. Indeed, minority applicants increased from eighteen to twenty-seven the following year (compared with eleven to fourteen during Mackay's tenure), and five succeeded, although women applicants and appointees remained constant. The AWB gave 'two cheers' for Irvine but continued to criticize 'secret soundings' and denied any 'need for government to give this kind of seal of approval'. In 1999 women (but not minorities) were still under-represented among applicants, but both groups were overrepresented among appointees.[20]

In spring 1994 some twenty ICSL students founded the Bar Lesbian and Gay Group, whose purpose was support, not lobbying. Three years later

Martin Bowley QC, its first president, claimed that despite the 600–900 lesbian and gay barristers (based on alleged proportions in the general population) students and pupils were 'still fearful of coming out in case it may adversely affect their career development'. BLAGG held its first major conference on gay and lesbian law reform in 1997.[21]

That year BC chair Robert Owen QC apologized to an interviewer that:

the majority of the Bar are white, male and middle-class, so it's inevitable that you'll get someone like me. But Heather Hallett QC is my vice-chairman and Lincoln Crawford is chairman of the Bar Council's race relations committee, so we are seeing the pattern start to break down. There is now an equal balance between men and women coming to the Bar and the ethnic minorities are also well-represented.

At the third Woman Lawyer conference a few months later he was 'determined to see the eradication of discrimination in all its forms. Discrimination is injustice; it is unfairness; it is simply wrong.' A contemporaneous survey still found significant gender differences in perceptions about sexual discrimination and harassment, although the gap and the proportions of women experiencing both were down from three years earlier.[22]

Later that year Cherie Booth QC told the first Minority Lawyers Conference (which she chaired): 'It is a tragedy that people from backgrounds such as my own are now finding it difficult to enter the profession'. But she had never encountered discrimination. 'I think it is perfectly possible for women to have children, maintain an active role with those children and still develop a practice to a degree which allows you to apply for silk and get it.' Heather Hallett QC hoped her election as 1998 BC chair 'sends out the message that the Bar is open to all—and that it is possible to be a working mother and get to the top'. But she also was 'desperately concerned that the likes of me could not enter the Bar through lack of funds'. Her successor, Dan Brennan QC, who had gone to grammar school in Bradford, where his father ran a pub, agreed 'it would be a tragedy if we went back to the middle-class Bar of the past'. Three years earlier, more than three-quarters of BVC graduates were in debt, averaging £9,000.[23]

A review of Bar policies directed by the BC GMC in response to the Stephen Lawrence Inquiry Report found 'stark differences' among PACH applicants, including biases for graduates of Oxbridge (and the old redbrick universities) and against minority students with upper seconds (though none was statistically significant). The Council unanimously adopted the recommendations that it, its staff and committees, and the benchers should reflect the Bar's racial composition, all barristers receive racial awareness training, chambers conduct ethnic monitoring, heads of chambers without minorities be reminded of the equality code, all pupillages be advertised on a website, employment tribunals hear complaints about chambers discrimination, and heads be responsible for preventing discrimination in the allocation of work. In response to the recommendation that more scholarships be need-based, the Inns replied that 'academic excellence remains, and must remain, the prime criteria [*sic*]'. They insisted that 'the two main criteria for selection as a Bencher are distinction at the Bar and evidence of active involvement in supporting the activities of the Bar Council, Circuits, SBAs or Inn'.[24]

B. Succeeding as a Solicitor

By 1986 more women than men passed the LS Finals, performing better on that examination (and at university).[25] The profession was therefore embarrassed that women were overrepresented in less prestigious and remunerative positions—for example, local government and suburban London practices—and underrepresented among partners (within their age cohorts).[26] The obvious reason was that women interrupted their careers to raise children. This also aggravated the 'recruitment crisis'. The 1988 report of the Law Society Working Party on Women's Careers proposed to solve both problems by exhorting women to 'THINK PART-TIME!' in order to facilitate the 'reconciliation of social responsibilities for children with the needs of a career'. It recommended applying the Sex Discrimination Act 1975 to job interviews for solicitors, making sex discrimination a disciplinary offence, reducing the cost of practising certificates for women raising children and automatically restoring those that had lapsed, offering tax relief for childcare costs, and expanding part-time work. The Society allowed part-time articles in 1990. Only 14 per cent of firms allowed part-time work, however, which may explain why three-quarters of all firms had no women equity partners in 1989 (thirteen years after women accounted for 20 per cent of new practising certificates, eight years after they accounted for 30 per cent); five years later women were 36 per cent of fee earners but still only 11 per cent of equity partners.[27]

Perhaps because the absence of minorities was more visible among solicitors, the Law Society established a race relations committee soon after the First National Conference on Minority Entry to the Legal Profession in 1985 and began to monitor access to traineeships, assistant solicitorships, and partnerships, ask about race on annual practising certificate applications, and investigate discrimination complaints. Two years later it appointed a minority careers officer. But in 1989 it deplored that 'things have not changed for the better'. Minorities were still just 1 per cent of solicitors, more than twice as likely to be sole practitioners and less than half as likely to be in firms with more than ten solicitors. In response to a 1990 study finding that minorities were only half as likely to have attended Oxbridge and made twice as many applications for articles but received proportionately fewer interviews, the *Solicitors Journal* urged large firms to recruit at polytechnics, ensure interviews did not discriminate, and introduce ethnic monitoring. A survey found, however, that only eight of some 600 firms, companies, and government agencies were willing to consider black trainees. A recruiting partner at one City firm said he wanted 'people who will feel comfortable with us and we with them'. Another pronounced that minorities 'don't seem to be able to satisfy the high education [*sic*] demands we have'. The British-born daughter of Sri Lankan immigrants won a £400 judgment against a London firm, which refused her a training interview but granted one a month later when she applied under an English pseudonym. The Law Society ethnic minorities career officer reported similar incidents.[28]

The College of Law's decision to select applicants on the basis of their degrees and prefer those with traineeships was criticized for discriminating against polytechnic graduates and hence minorities. (The CLE's 1994 cut in BVC places reduced the percentage of women from 46 to 34 and of minorities from 15 to 10.) The SBL accused the Society of suppressing an opinion by David Pannick QC that such preferences were illegal and asked the CRE to investigate. But the Law Society training committee 'was satisfied that no case of discrimination, direct or indirect, had been made out'.[29]

In 1992 the SBL called racism a 'serious problem'. Declaring that minorities were 16 per cent of Finals students, it urged the Law Society to adopt a 10 per cent target for Council and committee members and make firms do so for trainees, assistant solicitors, and partners. Although the secretary of the Society's race relations committee called these illegal quotas, the Council exhorted firms with more than ten fee earners to aim for 10 per cent of trainees and 5 per cent of fee earners. Freshfields' managing partner thought this 'on the high side' and 'quite difficult to achieve' in view of 'the need to maintain quality'. Linklaters' hiring partner announced 'there is no way that we or I suspect any of our rivals will change our basic requirements because of these targets'. 'I don't believe there is any discrimination in the major City firms.' Lovell White and Durant's deputy managing partner declared 'positive discrimination is not a good idea'. An anonymous solicitor bristled: 'It is not for the Law Society to tell any member firms who [*sic*] they should recruit in any field.... We are independent businesses and need freedom of choice in who [*sic*] we select.'[30]

Two years later another study found white applicants four times as likely to obtain LPC places (45 versus 12 per cent) and nearly seven times as likely to get traineeships (47 versus 7 per cent). Race correlated significantly with LPC places and very significantly with traineeships even when prior education was controlled. The figures were 'deeply disheartening' to Henry Hodge and gave Kamlesh Bahl 'a statistical face to the anecdotal evidence we had'. But the *New Law Journal* wondered if 'we want the equivalent of "busing" ' to achieve the Society's targets. It agreed with Council member John Franks that 'positive discrimination can be as debilitating as negative discrimination. We are talking about a class problem.' Rebuffing the CRE and SBL, the secretary to the Society's race relations committee said:

We won't be setting up a monitoring unit because we don't have the resources.... We are trying to get the balance right between the carrot and the stick. We don't want firms to feel they have got to employ token blacks or to become resentful of these policies.

Another Council member was 'not sure how you can force someone to take on someone who is not quite the norm'.[31]

When Tony Holland proposed a newspaper campaign to seek information from students unable to obtain traineeships, the trainee committee chair warned against unfavourable publicity. Noting that 'we are qualifying something like three times the number of solicitors required to replace natural wastage', a West London Council member said, 'one man's discrimination may be another man's sensible business choice'. The SBL cynically expected a Society leaflet offering guidance on avoiding discrimination to end up 'in the waste paper bin like most leaflets'. Confirming this, the twenty-five firms attending a City of London Law Society meeting with black lawyer groups 'denied there was discrimination operating' and rejected even modest proposals for a recruitment fair and summer work places. Maintaining that 'the articles system leads to indirect discrimination', the SBL was considering legal action.[32]

The Council rejected a proposal by the equal opportunities working party on discrimination to seek relevant information on the annual practising certificate renewal. Makbool Javaid called 'fine words...meaningless without an effective monitoring mechanism'. But Vice-President John Young termed the proposal 'too extreme'. 'You would lose everybody's support in what is a very sensitive area.' The Council would invite trainees to state their ethnicity and ask firms why they failed to meet the targets, but 'there will be no formal mechanism to ensure that the targets are actually reached'. Martin Mears, just elected president, attacked even these mild measures but conceded 'I can't change things overnight'. Young Women Lawyers noted 'with regret' Mears's opposition to anti-discrimination measures and his 'general belief that the Law Society should not be taking proactive steps in relation to the elimination of discrimination and harassment'. The CRE found 'worrying' the TSG publicity officer's advice that students 'neutralize' their traineeship applications and 'think long and hard' about disclosing 'involvement in your local synagogue'.[33]

The Law Society at least paid lip service to equal opportunity for women and ethnic minorities. But when *Outrage* declared that lesbians and gays 'shamefully are still often subjected to discrimination in the legal profession', the standards and guidance committee chair opposed excessively 'intrusive' rules concerning 'matters which are highly charged emotionally, involving people working in partnerships'. At the January 1993 conference of local law societies, the Bradford president denounced that 'stab in the back' to his gay and lesbian members; the rationalization had inflicted 'significant damage to the reputation of the profession as a fair and just profession'. A majority of the 120 responses to the Society's consultation favoured inclusion of sexual orientation.[34]

The LS strategy committee recommended employment targets for ethnic minorities and a ban on sexual orientation discrimination, with an exception for religious scruples. As Council members entered Chancery Lane to vote, fifty representatives of Stonewall and the SBL demonstrated. LS Vice-President Charles Elly asked: 'How can it be right to say that because a person is gay, I can't work with him?' The issues were 'central to everything that the Law Society stands for...freedom in employment, access to legal services and to justice'. Rodger Pannone broke the tradition of presidential silence because 'it is an issue on which I have strong views. To me there can be no more basic right than not to be persecuted.... Conscience or religion does not give anybody the right to deny or ignore those basic rights.' Some Council members disagreed. Roger Wilson invoked 'freedom of choice before the law, rather than this straitjacket'. Peter Verdin condemned 'an invidious philosophy that says to all of us what we must think'. People had every right to be bigoted. The LAPG chair worried that small practices found it 'increasingly difficult...to keep up with what's expected of them. This is just another thing we can...be disciplined for'. After passionate debate, the Council approved the ban without a religious exception (as well as the minority target).[35]

The forty-member Association of Christian Law Firms objected that 'a commitment not to discriminate on grounds of religious belief is an essential element in the mutual respect for individual conscience and privacy the members of an ethically founded and civilised society owe to each other'. 'The Law Society cannot go beyond what English law already says on discrimination.' 'You cannot be in a partnership with someone who has got a different ethos, whether political, religious or sexual.' Although ACLEC supported the new rule, it urged the Society to ban religious bias too. The strategy committee declined because 'the material aspects of discrimination against minority religions are covered under the heading of race'. Declaring 'the Law Society has no authority to impose its own ethical standards on us', the ACLF proposed to seek judicial review. The aptly-named Kenneth Byass declared that Christian firms could bar blasphemers or adulterers, and 'homosexuality may be just as odious to them....'[36]

As a new Council member a year later, Martin Mears moved to repeal the 'outrageous' protection because 'no right of conscientious objection is now recognised'. This 'disgrace' must 'represent the high water mark of progressive bigotry'. 'What...of a homosexual' whose ' "sexual orientation" was sado-masochistic and he was one of the proselytisers for that cause. Suppose a staff member turned up in cross dress...?' The Society had treated objections by the ACLF and the Lawyers Christian Fellowship 'with contempt'. 'If the anti-discrimination measure had been criticised, say, by the Association of Asian Lawyers on behalf of the Muslim community, would their scruples have been brushed aside so easily?' Gays 'demanded special legislation in their favour'. They were no

weak, oppressed minority...the evidence of their power and influence is all around us. ... Self-proclaimed sado-masochists...strut down Picadilly with banners, clad in leather and chains and escorted by the police. ... The Met announced that gays importuning in public lavatories can now expect a more 'user friendly service'.

There was no evidence 'that solicitors practise discrimination'. 'Gay propaganda needs grievances and the notion that homosexuals are a beleaguered and oppressed minority.' 'Militant gaydom' had migrated from the USA. When his motion was overwhelmingly rejected, Mears denounced his fellow Council members as 'so many sheep', who 'climb on to a worm-ridden bandwagon which is already so full that there is standing room only'. 'It is a simple fact that the majority of people outside liberal left circles do find homosexual practices objectionable.' The rule was 'another example of the political correctness that is so deeply entrenched at the Law Society'.[37]

Elected president three months later, Mears used his keynote speech to the annual conference to ask: should the CRE and EOC 'have their wings clipped? Is it not time to consider whether they have outlived their usefulness?' He denounced 'preposterous applications' to industrial tribunals, which 'have allowed themselves to be hijacked (all too willingly, I fear) by the discrimination industry'. EOC head Kamlesh Bahl retorted that 'fewer than 3% of cases registered in the industrial tribunals concern sex discrimination and less than one quarter of these go forward to a full hearing'. The high awards Mears cited 'distort the real picture...the average sex discrimination award is still below £3,000'. Anti-discrimination lawyers resented 'the way in which their area of practice has been held up to ridicule and contempt'. Young Women Lawyers denounced the 'complacency and ignorance' of Mears's 'outburst'. He called this 'contemptible'. Rather than suffering discrimination, 'many women solicitors...put their families before their careers'. The tribunals' 'worst excesses' were 'in the pregnant servicewomen cases'. He ridiculed a £21,500 award to a trainee pilot whose boss had 'hugged and kissed [her] at every opportunity' and 'wined and dined her' with ulterior motives.[38]

Among solicitors who completed their academic education in 1993, the significant gender differences in where and what they began to practise, which characterized earlier cohorts, had disappeared. But when Lovell White Durant boasted of being the first City firm to appoint a woman joint managing partner in 1995, women remained only 25 per cent of new partners at the 100 largest firms, although they were 40 per cent of third-year assistants and 44 per cent of ninth-year solicitors. (The gap had not narrowed four years later, when another five prominent firms had women managers.) Contemporaneously, the Policy Studies Institute reported that 94 per cent of minority law students expected to encounter bias, as did 80 per cent of women and half of those whose parents had not attended a selective school or were not professionals. The *Gazette* urged the profession 'to counter this damaging perception' by demonstrating 'wherever it can that it is open and fair-minded'. The Association of Women Solicitors warned against 'the profession becoming even less representative of its client base and society at large'. The report confirmed for the SBL 'what we've been saying for a long time'.

But Mears simply derided 'the deeply ingrained liberal attitudes of academe' and asked if it was 'the least bit probable that any such bias exists'. During the recession 'a small firm might not intend to offer training contracts at all but would make an exception for the son or daughter of one of its partners or valuable clients. To do so is not to "discriminate" against anyone.' No more than 'a very few' of his colleagues 'exercise any kind of discrimination, direct or indirect'. He also ridiculed the Bar's new equality code as 'Alice in Wonderland stuff...the very quintessence of political correctness'. Finding it 'quite extraordinary' that the code called recruitment purely on academic achievement 'indirectly discriminatory', he insisted 'there's no need to look at anything else'. Peter Goldsmith QC, the code's author, retorted: 'It is easy to ridicule, cheaply and out of context, the advice given in any guide like this'.[39]

A few months later the Council rejected a proposal by its equal opportunities committee to create a helpline for sexual harassment victims and instruct the SCB to accept a civil standard of proof. 'It has been three years since I was given an assurance this would be dealt with', objected Council member Eileen Pembridge. 'Some of you may be surprised to learn that women already have the vote.'

Immediately thereafter Mears told the second Woman Lawyer conference that only 'zealots', 'heresy hunters', and members of the 'discrimination industry' believed the 'nonsense' and 'fiction' that 'there is any kind of prejudice against women'. 'In nearly all the circles in which I mix, feminism is the orthodoxy.' Following Mears, BC chair David Penry-Davey QC departed from his text. 'I have spent 30 years at the Bar. Those who know me would not easily recognise the description of me as a trendy lefty or as politically correct. Martin, I profoundly believe you are wrong.'[40]

A 1996 report found that though women assistants earned 87.5 per cent as much as men, equity partners earned only 70.6 per cent; differences remained after controls for age, experience, and firm size. Tony Girling, Mears's successor, was 'ashamed' that 'some solicitors feel that they can get away with paying women less'. Kamlesh Bahl congratulated Girling and called for an annual comparison. The AWS chair welcomed this 'official recognition that discriminatory practice was a real issue for the profession'. The *Gazette* said 'such a disparity reflects very poorly on a profession that ought to be the staunchest observer of equal opportunities'.[41]

Bahl declared the 'urgent need to introduce flexible, family-friendly policies which recognise caring commitments so that legal firms can recoup the considerable investment they make in training staff'. The *New Law Journal* found 'more than sufficient evidence to show that [women] suffer from discrimination at all stages of their career' and deplored the absence of someone like Heather Hallett QC (then BC vice chair) in the Law Society. The *Solicitors Journal* agreed that 'discrimination, on whatever grounds, should have no place in our society' and urged it to comply with 'the spirit as well as the letter of the law'. At the third Woman Lawyer conference Girling called equal opportunities 'sound good business sense'. 'If there were muddled messages from the Law Society on this issue before, they are clear now.' Secretary-General Jane Betts called on 'women solicitors to breach the walls at Chancery Lane'. And Bahl stood for Deputy Vice President six months later, just as Hallett was elected the first woman BC chair.[42]

Publishing the EOC Code of Practice on Equal Pay, Bahl urged lawyers to 'take the lead in...implementing it in their own workplace'. A TSG survey found that women trainees were 50 per cent more likely to earn no more than the minimum and minorities twice as likely. Although the gender gap for assistants had shrunk (from £3,000 to £2,340), women equity partners now earned only 63 per cent as much as men (down from 71). Girling and Bahl wrote asking every firm to examine its pay scale. Condemning the 'staggering' differences, the *Gazette* said: 'In a profession which has at its root an overriding concern for justice, there is no room for inequality based on gender'.

Another study found trainee selection biased against women, minorities, the disabled, and those from lower class backgrounds or attending new universities and toward graduates of independent schools and Oxbridge. The SBL was 'dismayed at the lack of progress'. Young Women Lawyers called it 'depressing reading'. Phillip Sycamore, the new LS President, said 'we are keen to see the widest range of people in the profession and want to see the obstacles removed from the very brightest of the poor who wish to come into the profession'. 'Of all professionals', pronounced the *Gazette*, 'lawyers must be seen to stand on the highest moral ground regarding issues of discrimination'. A reanalysis of the trainee data found no statistically significant differences once the comparison controlled for prior education. A year later the gender difference among equity partners had halved (to £10,000); but though women assistants earned 92 per cent as much as men in 1999, women equity partners still earned just 69 per cent.[43]

If women hit a glass ceiling later in their careers, minorities encountered hurdles at the outset. Jerry Garvey, chair of the Society's race relations committee, saw opportunities for Asians in the City 'because of the growing potential these firms see in a tiger economy' but not for Afro-Caribbeans. The 1995 equal opportunities policy was backed by 'absolutely no rules of enforcement'. 'I could count the number of discrimination cases actually taken to a tribunal on one hand.' Minorities used to launch their own firms, noted Makbool Javaid, but 'with all the cutbacks in legal aid this is no longer an economically viable alternative'. The *New Law Journal* agreed that minorities entered the profession 'under a considerable handicap'. 'They will have, in general, found it impossible to obtain training contracts in major City firms and when they have actually obtained a contract they will have been marginalised in legal aid and poor law practices.' There was a 'considerable argument' that 'minorities should be attracted into the profession' and once 'so enticed...should be nurtured rather than change the rules so that it is effectively impossible for them to make a living'. Bahl told those attending the first Minority Lawyers Conference in 1997 that they did not receive their 'just rewards' and still tended to practise 'within their own communities'. 'What steps is the profession going to take to shatter the concrete ceiling and encourage individuals?' Addressing the Society's annual conference a month later, Sycamore warned that the end of discretionary grants for vocational courses ran

the risk of creating a profession—and a judiciary—drawn exclusively from one social class. Surely it is the best policy to get the social mix of the profession right at the outset, rather than being forced into remedial action at some later stage.

(Indeed, financial barriers continued to rise. The 1998 LPC cost more than twice as much as the 1992 Finals course; universities started charging tuition in 2000.[44])

The next trio of officers (with Bahl now Deputy Vice President) expressed satisfaction in early 1999 that 'the profession is beginning to reflect the shape of the community it serves as solicitors' but acknowledged that 'the Law Society still has much work to undo some of the obvious elements of discrimination'. Two months later, however, the 'Law 4 All' conference sponsored by the AWS, Group for Solicitors with Disabilities, TSG, and African, Caribbean & Asian Lawyers Group was cancelled when only fifty registered. The *Gazette* noted that the four groups' membership 'easily accounts for the majority, not the minority' of solicitors and exhorted: 'while the evolution of the profession into one that more greatly reflects society at large is long, it is worth the trouble'. NACRO observed that the Society's equality policies 'to a great extent remain on paper when it comes to distribution of work'. Although one in six new solicitors was from an ethnic minority, only 14 per cent of new ethnic minority solicitors obtained satisfactory employment, compared with 70 per cent of whites. Council member Maria Fernandes revived the call for ethnic monitoring by firms, decrying the lack of progress in the five years since the Society adopted its anti-discrimination rule. The proportions of women and minority trainees reporting harassment or discrimination had nearly doubled over two years earlier (to 20 and 16 per cent). Two City firms were accused, and a third dissolved after its chair was the focus of three claims.[45]

C. Joining the Judges

As early as 1972 Justice had recommended an advisory committee on judicial appointments. The Bar Council revived the idea in 1986, only to be summarily rebuffed by Lord Hailsham.[46] Calls for a more representative judiciary grew as its power expanded, compelling grudging acknowledgement of its inescapably political role.[47] Pressure was periodically intensified by egregious misbehaviour. Summing up an Old Bailey rape trial in 1990, Judge Raymond Dean instructed 'the gentlemen on the jury' that 'when a woman says no she doesn't always mean it. Men can't turn their emotions on and off like a tap like some women can.' They acquitted in less than an hour. Former Law Society President Sir David Napley called for a 'radical overhaul' of the 'old boys' network' of appointments. Two weeks later the Labour spokesperson for legal affairs urged a judicial appointments commission. A week after that a Labour MEP tabled a resolution in the European Parliament accusing the British system of 'administrative racism'. Eight years later Lord Irvine (now Lord Chancellor) accepted Mr Justice Harman's resignation from the High Court (only the second in the twentieth century) after *Legal Business* again named him the worst judge. He once told a witness who asked to be called Ms: 'I've always thought there were only three kinds of women: wives, whores and mistresses. Which are you?' At the annual CBA dinner the following year, Judge Graham Boal (its former vice chair) told a joke about a white heterosexual barrister who woke up in hospital after a serious accident with a lesbian's breasts, a homosexual's backside, and a large black penis. 'Not to worry', he was told, 'this is just the kind of barrister that is much wanted by the authorities who choose QCs and judges'. Some laughed, but others called 'shame'. After outcries by the Bar's sex discrimination, race relations, and human rights committees, Irvine rebuked Boal. A few months later the Judicial Studies Board distributed its first *Equal Treatment Benchbook*, and Irvine and the Lord Chief Justice promised guidelines on judicial behaviour toward litigants and witnesses. Irvine revealed that five judges recently had been reprimanded for racially offensive behaviour and two sent to racial awareness training.[48]

When Judge Mota Singh (the bench's only ethnic minority member) and NACRO criticized the judiciary's racial composition in 1989, Lord Mackay promised to appoint more minority magistrates, increasing their proportion from 1.9 per cent toward the population's 4.4 per cent. A survey that year found that women required an average of three more years to be appointed recorders, but if they went 'past the sell-by date of 46 years, they end up on the shelf and not the bench'. We have seen (Chapter 2) that Labour backbenchers used the debate over the Courts and Legal Services Bill to attack the judiciary as unrepresentative and argue (unsuccessfully) for a judicial appointments commission.[49]

Just before becoming Law Society President in 1990, Tony Holland objected that 'barristers needn't apply' to become judges 'while solicitors must'. The requirements of part-time appointments and Crown Court experience were 'absolutely ludicrous'. The LCD replied the number of women and minority judges would increase once solicitors obtained audience rights, but this 'will take time'. Holland retorted that the delay of 'at least 20 years' was 'too high a price to pay'. At the annual conference Holland deplored the 'judicial conservatism' of the 'monochrome male middle-aged judges'. The senior judges' opposition to the Green Papers heightened his concern about their control of appointments. It would be 2030 'before we can expect to see a judiciary equally balanced between men and women, and with an appropriate mix of ethnic minorities'. While rejecting 'quotas' or 'preferment', the *New Law Journal* condemned the 'tortuous' system's 'whiff of patronage' and the Bar's 'faster track'.

Sir Frederick Lawton (a former appeal court judge) said Holland's remarks 'could not have shown more clearly that he knows little, if anything, about judicial attitudes and why there are so few women and coloured judges'. 'There is no longer any prejudice against women barristers', and 'coloured barristers will soon be eligible for judicial appointments and will get them on their own merits'. Lord Mackay agreed that 'nothing would be worse for the reputation of the judiciary in this country than for me to lower the standards for appointment...simply to ensure a different racial or sexual mix'. He always appointed the 'best qualified' candidate. It was 'not a function of the professional judiciary to be representative of the population' and 'a simple fact that, at present, there are not enough women, or ethnic minority, candidates in the legal profession in the appropriate age groups who are suitable for appointment'.

Dismissing 'the same tired old excuse that has been trotted out over the last 25 years', the *New Law Journal* was sceptical that Lord Mackay 'would like to see more women and members from the ethnic minorities on the bench'. It was 'more worrying' that he found the present situation 'perfectly acceptable'. 'Small wonder that there are increasing numbers of our growing ethnic population who no longer have any faith in British justice.' His warning about 'lower[ing] the standards' was insulting. The *Lawyer* agreed that 'the existing undiluted judiciary, for all its pomp and self-congratulation does not dispense objective, unbiased justice'. The Lord Chancellor would raise 'standards through widening the pool of those eligible to be chosen'.

Anthony Scrivener QC, incoming BC chair, agreed there were 'a number of extremely able women advocates who would make ideal judges' and 'no good reason why a solicitor with proper training cannot be a good judge'. 'How on earth', he asked, does the Lord Chancellor 'know who is good and who is bad?' LAG (surprisingly) worried about 'the spectres of positive discrimination and the lowering of standards' but concurred that 'judges need to command respect from all who encounter them'.[50]

In February 1991 Geoffrey Bindman, relying on a report by the Society's equal opportunities committee (of which he was a member), suggested that judicial appointments might violate the Race Relations Act 1976 and the CRE code of practice. Lord Mackay demanded an assurance that the Society was not contemplating legal action before meeting the committee. He might make allowances for a married woman who had interrupted her career to have children, he said, but he sent the Society an opinion by David Pannick QC calling Bindman 'wrong in law and fact'. A month later two other Society committees concurred that the appointments process might discriminate. One chair denounced 'outmoded word-of-mouth recruitment' favouring 'candidates who fit the mould of those already in post' and producing an 'inward-looking' judiciary. He urged a 'strong lay element' in appointments 'to ensure that the magic circle is broken, rather than simply expanded'. The Society rejected Lord Mackay's offer to consult with local law societies and endorsed a judicial appointments commission, including academic lawyers and laypersons, and using tests and interviews, and contemplated a career judiciary. Scrivener 'agreed with at least 90 per cent' but opposed 'positive discrimination'. Calling the report 'a welcome break in the round of self-congratulation', the *Lawyer* said 'for too long the process of judicial appointments has been shrouded in unnecessary and unhealthy secrecy'.

A week after the Society's statement, the *Sunday Times* magazine cover story asked whether the judiciary was 'Old and Out of Touch', noting that 85 per cent of senior judges were Oxbridge and more than two-thirds public school. Perhaps in response, the Judicial Studies Board created an ethnic minorities advisory committee chaired by Mr Justice Brooke, who acknowledged 'a perception that the justice system does treat members of some racial minority communities unfairly'. Two months later the Society updated its report showing that women barristers required more years in practice before being appointed recorders. Holland called it a 'marvellous piece of work which shifts the burden of proof to the LCD'. Scrivener agreed the picture was 'pretty clear'. When Lord Mackay claimed that 'overall those women remaining in practice are fairly represented in judicial appointments', the report's author replied that more than half the men entering in the 1970s were circuit judges but only 17 per cent of the women, and accused the Lord Chancellor of having 'moved the goalpost' by limiting solicitor appointments to partners.

Holland called the Lord Chief Justice's plea for more High Court judges 'a wonderful opportunity for the Lord Chancellor to consider the appointment on merit of all well-qualified solicitor judges and well-qualified female judges' instead of 'scraping the barrel' of barristers. When Mackay announced that all applicants for the bench (and silk) would be invited to disclose ethnic origin, the SBL (which had sought this) now said the entire system 'has discrimination built in' and should be dismantled. But a month later the Lord Chancellor merely restated his earlier claim that it would take 'ten or 20 years' for the bench to 'look very different in terms of racial and sexual composition'.[51]

On his elevation to Lord Chief Justice in 1992, Lord Taylor rejected a judicial appointments commission, calling the American experience 'a terrible example of how it could go wrong'. It would be 'wrong artificially to achieve proportionate representation of women and ethnic minorities'. Appointees had to be 'the best candidates for the job'. He argued, strangely, that 'even with a judiciary of equal numbers male and female the judge in any given case can only be one or the other'. But he had 'no doubt' that 'the present imbalance...will be redressed in the next few years.... This is not just a pious hope. It will be monitored.'[52]

Accusing Taylor of 'dangerous compliancy [*sic*]' with the status quo, Labour MP Stephen Byers documented that judges appointed in the previous three years were as likely to have attended public school and Oxbridge as those appointed thirty to forty years earlier and called for a judicial appointments committee with a lay majority. Justice concurred, noting that smaller proportions of eligible women and ethnic minorities still were being appointed Assistant Recorders and Recorders. A survey found that two-thirds of the public felt 'judges are out of touch with everyday life and everyday people', four-fifths that there should be more women, and three-fifths that judges should 'reflect the ethnic mix'. The 1992 BC chair, Lord Williams of Mostyn QC, denounced judicial appointments as 'hidebound by an obsessive secrecy and a degree of amateurism which are simply unacceptable...the whole of the judiciary is damaged by the present system of appointment and training and the belief that the judges are out of touch and unaccountable'.[53]

Nearly five years after Lord Mackay agreed to appoint more solicitor circuit judges the number had increased from forty to just fifty-seven (out of 493). In 1993 he named the first solicitor to the High Court. At the same time, the LCD refused to consider GLS lawyers because of the 'latent danger to public confidence' in their 'independence'. The First Division Association assailed this for retarding representativeness and noted that private practitioners frequently declined the bench because they were earning too much: eight of thirty-five QCs who were offered High Court appointments and seventy-two barristers offered circuit positions.

Makbool Javaid declared the SBL would 'continue to have little confidence in the judiciary as long as it remains the exclusive domain of white, upper class, Oxbridge educated males'. The Law Society asked minority lawyer groups to suggest names for the LCD's 1,700 appointments and published criteria including empathy across lines of class, race, religion and gender. The AWS felt that Mackay seemed 'actively to want to encourage more women to apply for judicial appointments'. Soon thereafter he promised to advertise vacancies, appointing ten laypeople—including four women and two minorities—to join a senior judge and a civil servant in interviewing the first 250 candidates. But Susan Ward, the first employed barrister to head the AWB, objected that 'the current emphasis on advocacy and judicial recommendation means that judges come from a very select little group', which excluded 'many capable and talented women lawyers'. Lord Mackay continued to reject 'positive discrimination' and 'quotas', while boasting that the number of women recorders had increased from 10 to 16 per cent between 1992 and 1994. Change would occur 'naturally and properly'. However, a 1994 study found that 87 per cent of judges still were Oxbridge and the proportion of public school graduates was rising.[54]

A home affairs select committee inquiry elicited familiar positions. The Law Society called for objective tests and interviews, an independent commission, and more flexible part-time opportunities. A Hansard Society Commission had found serious under-representation of women, declaring that 'a judiciary without women is unbalanced'. Urging an end to the requirement of silk, the AWB criticized the Lord Chancellor for consulting 'a very select group who are predominantly men. It has become a self-perpetuating system and is indirectly unfair to women.' But Lord Taylor insisted there was 'no place for "affirmative action" involving the appointment of anyone other than the candidate most fitted for office'. He told the *Sunday Telegraph*: 'I do not think the judiciary should be representative of the public any more than a brain surgeon is representative'. Other judges declared experience as a higher court advocate and recorder indispensable. Committee chair Sir Ivan Lawrence QC expressed unease about solicitors. 'Fraud arises because solicitors are constantly dealing with the very lowest level. Barristers never operate on a private basis with clients and whether or not they may be tempted to dishonesty they are less likely to succumb.' 'How do you respond to allegations of large scale fraud? Are you going to make judges of people like that?' Law Society President Charles Elly, himself a recorder, retorted: 'There are fraudulent solicitors, barristers and even MPs, but nobody would draw the conclusion that a small number of dishonest solicitors should make it undesirable to make any solicitors judges'. Council member Henry Hodge, an assistant recorder, was less restrained: 'I do not think the committee has read all our papers. They have not got much idea what the issues are. Sir Ivan acted disgracefully. He was trying to promote the interests of the Bar at the expense of the public interest.' While acknowledging the under-representation of women and minorities, the committee found no need for major reform. The Bar Council was delighted, but the Law Society and AWS were critical. The new AWB chair declared that 'the chances of significant numbers of women becoming full-time High Court judges in the next few years are negligible. This is simply not acceptable....'[55]

A year later the same committee investigated Freemasonry among judges (as well as other criminal justice system officials) and urged compulsory disclosure; Lord Mackay was opposed to it. Labour (poised to win the imminent election) promised to compel it. The AWB supported this because the United Grand Lodge excluded women. Declaring it 'vital to maintain public confidence in the legal system', BC chair Robert Owen QC called the report 'a welcome and thoughtful contribution to the debate'. After Labour's victory, Home Secretary Jack Straw told the 1997 Bar Conference he might require disclosure. The AWB wanted Masons to resign. Although Lord Irvine supported disclosure, senior judges strongly resisted. Straw asked for voluntary disclosure, threatening legislation if it were refused. Lord Justice Millett, a Mason, called it 'a very silly proposal...an unwarranted interference in our private lives. ... You can't choose which judge will try your case, so what's the point?'

Chris Mullin, the new home affairs select committee chair (who sought information about Masonic involvement in the miscarriages of justice in the IRA Birmingham bombing convictions, which he had exposed), warned: 'We're up against some mighty vested interests here, and they might not recognise words like "voluntary"'. *The Times* promptly proved him right. Comparing the proposal to Japanese American internment during World War II, the paper called it 'intrusive, ill-judged, illogical and illiberal', discrimination 'against one of a hundred social bonds'. Supporters were

already claiming this move is a step toward ending the 'male, white, middle-class' composition of the judiciary. It is, sadly, a step towards the Balkanisation of the Bench...the politicisation of the judiciary.

Lord Bingham, the new Lord Chief Justice, could 'not recognise the possibility of the problem so far as judges are concerned. They take a judicial oath and take it very seriously.' Lord Saville of Newdigate (a law lord) saw 'no difference between asking that question and whether you are a trade unionist or, in Vichy France, whether you were Jewish'. 263 of the 5,290 judges and 1,208 of the 24,964 magistrates voluntarily identified themselves as Masons, but 281 and 3,456 respectively did not answer.[56]

The Labour Party had endorsed a judicial appointments commission in 1995. In its unofficial 1996 policy document, Lord Williams of Mostyn QC called for 'selection, promotion, training and monitoring' by 'a judicial college...free of political interference'. Women and ethnic minorities were 'grossly under-represented among the judiciary'. Although it would be 'a foolish parrot call to expect perfect representation', it was 'reasonable to require that the judiciary at least reflect the wider community that they serve'. Addressing the 1996 Bar Conference as Shadow Lord Chancellor less than six months before the election, Lord Irvine said the public should play a greater role in judicial appointments. Shortly after taking office he initiated consultations. The *New Law Journal* asked:

How much longer do we have to wait before the number of suitably qualified women or black lawyers reaches a total sufficient to change the overall profile of the judiciary? ... That self-regulation is dangerous is a concept which the new government has taken on board.... Now it must take a firm stand on self-selection in the judiciary.

But Irvine repudiated Labour's earlier commitment. Encouraging applications to supplement the traditional system of invitations, he told the first Minority Lawyers Conference: 'don't be shy, apply' but reasserted the 'firm principle' that all judicial appointments 'must be made on merit' and insisted the process was 'basically sound'. Confidential consultations were 'altogether more systematic and objective' than critics allowed.

Do you honestly believe that my Permanent Secretary turns up at a senior judge's door asking whether old Copperfield is a good chap or whether young Pickwick is a bit suspect because, rumour has it, he voted for the Green Party at the last election? No, our consultations are not like that.

(Ten years earlier Robert Stevens documented deliberate discrimination by the Lord Chancellor's Office.) Although Opposition leader William Hague flirted with American-style confirmation hearings, *The Times* warned that 'populist credentials' would be an 'entirely lamentable development'. 'Nor should there be an attempt to preordain legal opinion through the application of informal quotas—by age, ethnicity, or gender—in the appointment of the judiciary'.[57]

Irvine took every opportunity to urge minorities and women to apply, even accusing the latter of 'robbing' him of candidates. (He told the *Sun* in 1998: 'My mother was an unusually clever woman and was frustrated to be held back. I took the view that it was a gross injustice.') The *New Law Journal*, however, dismissed the first advertisement of judicial vacancies as 'so much pandering to popularity' and 'another example of a waste of good money'. Anyone 'who is remotely near an appointment knows perfectly well how to have his, or more rarely, her name put into the frame'. The *Solicitors Journal* welcomed the innovation but reiterated its call for a commission.[58]

Launching a £420,000 advertising campaign to seek magistrates, the LCD declared the Lord Chancellor to be 'keen that the bench should be balanced in terms of gender, ethnic origin, where people live, occupation and age'. But when a consultation revealed that only 45 per cent of magistrates favoured ending the 'political balance' test and just 13 per cent supported geo-demographic balance, he retained the status quo. He took satisfaction that in his first full year of appointments, 46 per cent were solicitors, 24 per cent women, and 5 per cent minorities (but downplayed the fact that women remained 11 per cent and minorities 1.7 per cent of the entire judiciary—and much less of the higher bench).[59]

Replacing two moderate law lords with two conservative commercial lawyers (one the highest ranking Freemason in the judiciary), Irvine conceded the Human Rights Act 1998 would increase scrutiny of such choices but insisted: 'I will always hold fast to the proposition that this is a merits-based appointments system. I don't want gender balance, or political balance as an objective.' The *Guardian* and the *Sun* criticized the process, but *The Times* praised him for having 'rightly rounded on his critics' and rejecting 'the evolution of an American-style Bench in which merit would be hostage to other, political, considerations'.

Irvine held out the possibility of a commission while insisting that 'one of the best parts of the [existing] system is the consultation that takes place over a very very wide range of people to assess the qualities of those who apply'. Claiming that 'the profile of women judges today reflects broadly speaking the profile of women entering the profession 20 years ago' (by which he meant the Bar!), he called his appointment of eight women among forty-eight circuit judges 'excellent, a high percentage, a higher percentage than the relevant proportion of the Bar'. 'It's a credit to women; it is also evidence that there is no discrimination in the system.' Several months later he made Dame Elizabeth Butler-Sloss (the only woman on the Court of Appeal) President of the Family Division and thus one of the four senior judges.[60]

At the second Minority Lawyers Conference in 1999 Irvine refused a request by its chair, Kamlesh Bahl (now LS DVP) that he promise to subject judicial appointments to anti-discrimination law, instead arranging for minority lawyers to shadow judges. LS Council member Maria Fernandes complained that 'the Lord Chancellor has said virtually nothing about ethnic minorities. He was almost flippant. There was nothing in it for us.' (Two months later Irvine made her husband, Keith Vaz, his under-secretary, one of the first ethnic minorities to hold a ministerial position.) Michael Mansfield QC accused Irvine of 'just playing around with cos-metics'. The SBL vice chair said Irvine was only 'scratching the surface. I would rather energies were spent on creating a judicial appointments commission.' The *Solicitors Journal* agreed he was 'merely tinkering with the system'. The 'process of widening the overall composition of the judiciary is painfully slow'.[61]

Three months later Labour's own research journal documented that after two years in office judges on the circuit bench and higher were as white, male, and public-school as ever. Of the eighty-five judges appointed since January 1997, 79 per cent had attended public school and 73 per cent Oxbridge (compared with 69 and 64 per cent of sitting judges); just 8 per cent were women and none minority. LAG director Vicki Chapman main-tained: 'Until there is a proper Judicial Appointments Commission, they will not be able to break the mould'. The *Solicitors Journal* complained that Labour had 'not done anything to redress the balance'. The system needed 'a complete overhaul'. An LSE law lecturer's book-length critique of the judiciary called for a commission. Two solicitors predicted pessimistically that 'by the time our children are middle-aged, they might see a few black and female judges'.[62]

The credibility of the Government's commitment to a more representa-tive bench was damaged by its record in employing lawyers. After eight race discrimination claims were filed against the CPS in 1998, David Calvert-Smith, the new DPP, admitted to minority lawyers that no senior staff had ever been disciplined for discrimination or harassment because 'the CPS is not the best paid organisation and we can ill afford to lose lawyers of real quality'. An Asian law centre solicitor called this equivalent to saying 'the CPS condones racism as long as you are a good lawyer'. Acknowledging that the Service's 'working practices are not friendly to ethnic minority women', Calvert-Smith promised 'positive action, but not positive discrimination'. Yet the CPS's first equality statement committed it to diversity 'not as an optional extra' but as 'an essential precondition of achieving success in our work and a reputation to match'. The SBL responded by announcing the formation of the National Association of Black and Asian Prosecutors (modelled on the U.S. Black Prosecutors Association) to address CPS racism, and the CRE launched a formal investigation. 'We have tried to work with [the CPS]...and come up with a plan that would change and drive things forward but we are not satisfied that there is a commitment and understanding at the top to drive that through'.[63]

Shortly after Labour's victory, the Treasury passed over three more experienced candidates for First Junior to choose Philip Sales, a 35-year-old member of Irvine's former chambers, who specialized in European public law. The position generated £100–200,000 annually in briefs and virtually ensured a judicial appointment. *The Times* reported 'consternation among the legal profession' and the *New Law Journal* 'a considerable number of legal eyebrows raised'. The chairs of the BC race relations and sex discrimination committees asked Attorney-General John Morris QC to disclose the process for appointing all standing counsel. AWB chair Josephine Hayes filed a sex discrimination complaint against Morris. Her solicitor said that 'unless the appointments are advertised and there is a transparent system of selection, no one can have any confidence that gender is not a criterion for selection'. Morris launched an inquiry chaired by the Solicitor-General and, amazingly, including both Sales and the newly-appointed chief Treasury Counsel for Chancery cases. The *Solicitors Journal* denounced these choices as 'politically inept, and symptomatic of the very ills that the review is designed to cure'. After the employment tribunal ordered Morris to disclose the 'secret soundings', he settled by paying £5,000 to a feminist organization chosen by Hayes. While denying discrimination, he acknowledged that the process had been 'far from perfect' and promised to make it 'transparent'.[64]

Less than three months after the Sales affair Jane Coker, a solicitor, challenged Irvine's appointment of Garry Hart as his adviser without advertising the position. Mocking the Lord Chancellor's encouragement of women and minorities, former SBL chair Peter Herbert said 'it seems to be more a case of "don't apply, sue"'. Coker was joined by Martha Osamor, a Nigerian-born law centre legal adviser. Their solicitor said 'women and black lawyers had sensed that something was really wrong and now they are delighted it has been expressed in legal terms'. When Irvine explained that he only considered those he knew well, Coker's counsel added: 'Our research suggests the Lord Chancellor has only known one black person for a long time'. He had gone to a Cambridge men's college, belonged to the all-male Garrick Club, and hired only whites and just one woman when he established his chambers in 1981. (Indeed, he had given a tenancy to Tony Blair but not Cherie Booth, both his pupils, in 1977 although Blair had a second class degree and a third on his Bar Finals while Booth had two firsts.) His chambers had few women tenants and no blacks as late as 1994. Irvine's counsel retorted that the Lord Chancellor had appointed a woman as his personal secretary and granted silk to ethnic minorities.

Calling the case mischievous and political, Irvine refused to dignify it by testifying.

The employment tribunal found for Coker (but against Osamor). 'Any minister who chooses to take advantage of the discretion given to him... needs to take account of the imbalance of gender or race that might exist from the circle from which he is minded to select a special adviser'. Coker's solicitor said this jeopardized all sixty-nine special advisers. The plaintiffs demanded Irvine's resignation because he had 'thrown abuse' at women and minorities. Instead he appealed. A Tory MP accused Tony Blair of 'breathtaking arrogance' for 'approving the appointment of [Hart] the godfather of his child as adviser to his biggest crony appointment, his former pupilmaster'.[65]

Launching a campaign against silk (discussed in Chapter 4), Labour backbencher Andrew Dismore tabled amendments to the Access to Justice Bill to create a judges' register of interests and a judicial appointments commission after more than 100 MPs had signed his early day motions to that effect. Paul Stinchcombe commented that he had come to Parliament on the Clapham omnibus: 'at least half the passengers were women' and 'between 30 per cent and 40 per cent of passengers were from ethnic minorities'. Keith Darvill said a commission 'would lead to a more inclusive society'. When John Taylor asked 'why the judiciary should be more representative of society than should airline pilots', Geoff Hoon declared it 'extremely important in a democratic and free society that people who make vital decisions, especially those that affect the liberty of the citizen, should broadly reflect the citizens on whom they sit in judgment'. Liam Fox, Opposition spokesperson on constitutional affairs, also endorsed a commission and Parliamentary confirmation hearings. A joint working party of the Law Society and Bar Council recommended opening the bench to GLS and CPS lawyers, 'positive action measures' for 'candidates from underrepresented groups', aptitude tests, references, and a multi-day assessment (for shortlisted candidates) and possibly an appeals process for those rejected.

Lord Irvine responded by asking Sir Leonard Peach (former commissioner for public appointments) to investigate the selection of both QCs and judges. LAG regretted that 'the Lord Chancellor has not moved straight to a consultation on an appointments commission'. BACFI complained that employed barristers lacked the criminal experience required for assistant recorders. Most dramatically, the Law Society announced a boycott of 'secret soundings' for judges (and silks). President Robert Sayer called the system 'more appropriate to the Nineteenth Century than the Twenty-first', a 'self-selecting, self-cloning, self-perpetuating cabal of middle-class white, male barristers' with 'all the elements of an old boys network'. 'More than 50% of the senior judicial appointments come from just seven sets of chambers'. 'We live in a multi-cultural, multi-racial, multifaceted society and yet we have a judiciary that is monochrome and one-dimensional.' Emphasizing the gross underrepresentation of women and minorities, the Society told Peach 'there must be a major drive for a judiciary that reflects all members of society'. Justice, the AWB, CRE, and EOC echoed those criticisms. Liberty demanded a commission 'to ensure that the system . . . is not in breach of the European Convention on Human Rights'. Declaring that the 'ill-judged system . . . discriminates not just against solicitors but against women and ethnic minorities as well', the *Gazette* called 'a completely transparent system . . . an essential prerequisite for redressing the balance'.

Although Irvine denounced the boycott as 'staggering' and 'contrary to the interests' of solicitors, it was joined by the AWS, YSG, Commerce and Industry Group, and African, Caribbean and Asian Lawyers Group. The *Solicitors Journal* praised the 'courageous and principled step'. 'Not only does the Bar have a near monopoly of higher judicial office, but those barristers are predominantly white, male, middle-aged, middle-class, and educated at public school and Oxbridge.' '[P]erpetuation of white, male, public-school dominance', said the *Financial Times*, was the 'inevitable result' of 'secret soundings'.

A straw poll found that a substantial majority of the 800 attending the annual Bar conference favoured changing the appointment of judges and silks, although the Bar Council insisted 'the vote was put in such an informal way you can't read too much into it'. Lord Steyn (a Lord of Appeal) supported a commission. But Irvine maintained that 'the beauty of this [existing] system . . . is that it is so wide-ranging across so many people that the risk of discrimination or prejudice on the part of a particular candidate is reduced'. The Lord Chief Justice declared himself 'an unashamed apologist of our existing judiciary, which I believe are as good as are to be found anywhere in the world'. Although the term 'secret soundings' had 'blackened it', the 'present system is extraordinarily thorough and comprehensive and extraordinarily successful'. No one 'has made a case that the wrong people are being appointed or that people who would make better judges are somehow being overlooked'. Lord Browne-Wilkinson warned: 'I myself would never have become a judge if there was any question that I would have to go through the kind of performance that Judge Bork or Clarence Thomas had to go through and a very large number of people of the kind who become judges in England and Wales would say the same'.

Peach did not disappoint, recommending that the Lord Chancellor continue to appoint judges, though QCs would no longer be preferred, rejected candidates and organizations could complain, and psychometric and competency tests would be piloted and the performance of new judges evaluated. The Bar Council naturally praised the 'searching and thoughtful' report. But the Law Society maintained the boycott, deploring the 'wasted opportunity for real reform'. An 'old boys' network which uses flawed criteria...will be replaced by an old boys' network which will use slightly better criteria'.

Press headlines agreed: '"Secret" selection of judges to stay' (*Financial Times*); 'Veil of secrecy to continue over appointment of judges' (*Daily Express*). A survey of lawyers found support for a commission to remedy the influence of patronage, the advantages of elite chambers, and the need to be 'known'; these sentiments were stronger among solicitors and women, and especially minorities. The Bar Council's own report on the failure to convict Stephen Lawrence's murderers called the judiciary 'unrepresentative' because they were 'almost exclusively drawn from the senior Bar'.[66]

D. From an Exclusive to a Representative Profession

The ideal that lawyers and their higher strata should reflect the demography of the larger society has triumphed so rapidly and completely it is hard to remember that for centuries—indeed, until little more than a decade ago—the profession vigorously and successfully insisted on exclusivity as a means of and justification for limiting its numbers and elevating and defending its social status. The Bar's claim to be the 'senior' branch rested on its members' superior class origins (as well as its longer pedigree and greater distance from clients).

Now those status symbols have become embarrassments. While insisting that 'it is not the function of the professional judiciary to be representative', Lord Mackay blamed unrepresentativeness on the 'simple fact' that there were too few 'suitable' women and minorities of the 'appropriate age groups', and confidently predicted 'the bench in ten or 20 years time should look very different in terms of racial and sexual composition'. Although denying that 'the judiciary should be representative of the public any more than a brain surgeon is representative' and decrying any effort 'artificially to achieve proportionate representation', Lord Taylor had 'no doubt...the present imbalance between male and female, white and black ...will be redressed in the next few years' and promised this 'will be monitored'. Lord Irvine insisted all his appointments were 'merit based' and rejected gender balance 'as an objective' but also bragged that his record of appointing women was 'excellent, a high percentage, a higher percentage than the relevant proportion of the Bar', inconsistently citing this as evidence of 'no discrimination'. Bar Council chair Robert Owen QC apologized for being white, male, and middle class, pointing eagerly to his successor, Heather Hallett QC, and race relations committee chair Lincoln Crawford. Both Hallett and her successor, Brennan, boasted of their modest origins. Law Society President Robert Sayer denounced the LCD's secret soundings for silk and judges as a 'self-selecting, self-cloning, self-perpetuating cabal of middle-class white, male barristers', 'more appropriate to the Nineteenth Century than the Twenty-first'.

Both branches protested their commitment to reflecting social diversity and proudly documented their progress. The Bar, whose superior status rested on ascriptive warrants, paradoxically exhibited greater energy and fewer reservations. Entry barriers (vocational course places, examinations, apprenticeships, and first positions) and rewards (silk, the bench, and partnership) were jeopardized by unrepresentativeness. But just as the imperative of technical competence chafed against the traditional warrant of character (legitimating ascriptive exclusivity), so it disputed the postmodern warrant of multiculturalism (legitimating representativeness). Thus, just when meritocracy appeared hegemonic it again encountered opposition based on personal identity (though now valuing disadvantage rather than privilege).

The profession responded differently to each demand for inclusion. Labour's creation of the post-war welfare state, especially the dramatic expansion of tertiary education, challenged class privilege. Lawyers felt similarly obligated to level the playing field, though not to ensure success (equal opportunity, not outcome). The entry of women (ultimately outnumbering men), however, may have narrowed class recruitment both because it doubled competition for entry and because women, confronting sex discrimination, may have come from higher social classes than men. The entry of minorities racialized class differences, making those more visible and underrepresentation harder to justify.

Perhaps because all men have mothers and most have sisters, wives, and daughters, the profession unconditionally condemned sex discrimination and harassment and celebrated the few women who reached the pinnacles of both branches and the judiciary. At the same time it accepted, even encouraged, women to 'choose' less remunerative and prestigious careers. The 1979 Royal Commission attributed the gender gap to firms' and chambers' concerns that women would be 'lost to the demands of the family'; a decade later the Law Society urged mothers (never fathers) to work part time; as late as 1995 Mears blamed women who 'put their families before their careers'.

Although lawyers were discomforted by ethnic minority underrepresentation, they continued to oppose 'American quotas', 'reverse' or 'positive discrimination', associating these (erroneously) with busing to promote school integration. Even LAG worried about 'the spectres of positive discrimination and the lowering of standards'. Perhaps because the Inns long had many students from the new Commonwealth and 'ghetto' chambers were so visible, the Bar took more vigorous corrective action. City firms, by contrast, continued to hire 'people who will feel comfortable with us and we with them'.

Law Society leaders declared it cannot 'be right to say that because a person is gay, I can't work with him' (Charles Elly) and 'there can be no more basic right than not to be persecuted' (Rodger Pannone). But Martin Mears pronounced the 'simple fact that the majority of people…find homosexual practices objectionable' (as though distaste justified discrimination), and other solicitors invoked religious dogmas long discredited by association with racism and sexism. One Council member declared people had every right to be bigoted.

Opposition to discrimination always begins with victims (who sometimes indulge in hyperbole, as when the SBL accused the CLE of 'ethnic cleansing'). Organizations and leaders of women, ethnic minorities, gays and lesbians, and the disabled campaigned for rules, enforcement, and results. They found allies among solicitors and employed barristers, who sought to strengthen their claim to silk and the bench by arguing they could make both more representative. Complainants were backed by government agencies (EOC, CRE) and most newspapers. Extrinsic events fuelled the struggle, such as the exposé of police and prosecutorial bungling of the racist murder of Stephen Lawrence, or Irvine's incredible hubris in making crony appointments: a former tenant of his chambers, and the godfather of Blair's children. Victims were far likelier to perceive discrimination than those whose privilege depended on it. Wooing the latter, Mears denied 'there is any kind of prejudice against women'. No more than 'a very few' of his colleagues 'exercise any kind of discrimination, direct or indirect'. Yet the most privileged often were sufficiently secure to champion the subordinated, as illustrated by the exchange between Mears and Penry-Davey.

Once equality has been embraced as a goal it is necessary to demonstrate inequality. Critics easily, and repeatedly, documented unrepresentativeness. But statistics can also demonstrate that unequal outcomes reflect achievement, not ascription, or even that the disadvantaged are overselected (for example, as a proportion of applicants for silk). Because lawyers feel a special obligation to embody ideals of justice, both branches consistently condemned discrimination. But though (or perhaps because) lawyers are experts in evasion, they preferred to exhort rather than command (for example, clerks' distribution of work in chambers, firms' minority hiring targets) and refused to create enforcement mechanisms or give them the necessary resources. The Bar offered 'safe havens' for victims of discrimination and harassment instead of punishing offenders. Rather than fight discrimination, the TSG urged members to 'neutralise' their traineeship applications by deleting 'involvement in your local synagogue'. While adopting targets for minority trainees in larger firms, the LS Council explicitly rejected any 'formal mechanism to ensure that the targets are actually reached'.

Although fears of retaliation and blacklisting deterred most complainants, a few began proceedings: against the CLE over examination failures, and law firms and government over employment. Even unsuccessful claims generated publicity and hence pressure for change. But many decisions were exempt from judicial review: chambers' about pupillages and tenancies, firms' about traineeships and partnerships, the Lord Chancellor about silk and the bench. Anger at such opaque and uncontrolled discretion is one reason the Law Society and others boycotted secret soundings. By exposing the inadequacies of self-regulation, these challenges intensified demands for external control: treating tenancy as employment (and chambers more like firms), making briefs contractual, subjecting lawyers to anti-discrimination law, and increasing transparency and lay participation in the appointment of QCs and judges.

Representativeness has a dual meaning. The obvious one is outsider access to positions of power, prestige, and pecuniary reward. More ambiguous is the possibility that new role occupants will perform differently. Such a claim has two disturbing implications. First, it implies the essentialist view that behaviour is a function of genetics (or at least an almost immutable socialization). Secondly, their identities become more salient if judges are seen as making rules rather than just applying them. It is no coincidence that decades of vocal criticism of an unrepresentative judiciary began to produce reform only when the Human Rights Act 1998 made it impossible to perpetuate the myth of mechanical jurisprudence. Advocates of representativeness highlighted judges' outrageous racist, sexist, and homophobic comments. Critics warned that ethnic minorities were alienated from a legal system in which they were overrepresented among criminal accused but virtually invisible in positions of power, as advocates and especially on the bench. They noted that government had long sought 'political balance' among magistrates (although Lord Irvine declined to substitute demographic balance). Although Lord Mackay did not relinquish control of judicial selection, he added lay interviewers, publicizing his choice of women and minorities. Perhaps to substantiate his claim that judicial appointments were apolitical, Lord Irvine replaced two moderate law lords with two conservatives.

The passion this issue generated surfaced in the reaction of those who obscenely analogized the government's request that Masons identify themselves to America's internment of Japanese-American citizens during World War II (*The Times*) and Vichy France's complicity in genocide (a law lord). Lord Browne-Wilkinson declared that he and most of his colleagues would never submit to the degradation ritual of the Senate confirmation hearings of Robert Bork and Clarence Thomas. Confusing that process with judicial appointments commissions, Lord Taylor called the latter 'a terrible example of how it could go wrong'. *The Times* warned against the 'politicisation of the judiciary', an 'American-style bench in which merit is hostage to other, political considerations'; confirmation hearings would privilege judges with 'populist credentials' and seek to 'preordain legal opinions' through gender and ethnicity 'quotas'.

Speakers who knew better insisted on the irrelevance of judicial demographics because litigants could not choose their judge (Lord Justice Millet), who had to be either a man or a woman (Lord Taylor) and took an oath of office (Lord Bingham). They extolled the 'beauty' of the 'systematic and objective' selection process, which consulted a 'very very wide range of people' (Lord Irvine) and was 'extraordinarily thorough and comprehensive and extraordinarily successful' (Lord Bingham); both Lord Chancellors maintained they simply appointed the 'best qualified' (as though there were a single unambiguous criterion). After all, said Lord Bingham, no one 'has made a case that the wrong people are being appointed or that people who would make better judges are somehow being overlooked'. Once in power, Labour promptly recanted its support for a judicial appointments commission. *The Times* (usually the profession's outspoken critic) warned that demands for representativeness were Balkanizing and politicizing the judiciary. These defenders were unable to see, or unwilling to concede, that the judiciary was inescapably political, society already balkanized, and autocratic secretive decisions undemocratic. Government was simply unwilling to relinquish control over a pivotal organ of state power.

The paradox of representativeness lies in the fact that the same academic institutions and meritocratic processes that make the profession ascriptively more inclusive (and justify the remaining entry barriers) also construct and legitimate internal differentiation. Just as the traditional ethos was equality within the profession, so the post-modern is hierarchy. The transformation from ascribed to achieved criteria and from apprenticeship and patronage to formal education and examination eased the entry of those previously excluded by reason of class, gender, and race. But the new signs of election—educational institutions attended and academic performance—both admit and sort. There is a certain false naiveté (like Peter Lorre's shock at finding gambling at Rick's Bar in 'Casablanca') when the media and other critics profess surprise and outrage that the professional apex—City partners, silks, and judges—is virtually monopolized by those who attended public school and Oxbridge (notorious for competitive admissions but also for being swayed by ascriptive criteria, as American universities are by 'legacy'). Families seek to transmit privilege to their children, increasingly by conferring human capital signalled by educational credentials (although the older currencies of land and capital remain significant).[67] Meritocracy makes such credentials the principal criteria and correlates of success at each step up the career ladder: vocational course place and examination result, traineeship and pupillage, assistant solicitorship and tenancy. (The preference for CPE graduates who have not studied law may be a vestige of class privilege, however, and no one has tested whether the ultimate accolades of partnership, silk, and the bench—and the quality of performance in those roles—are correlated with achievement in the academy or practice.)

Consequently, greater inclusiveness simply moves unrepresentativeness downstream. The ideal of equal opportunity confers the right to attempt the hurdles but also imposes a duty to accept the outcome. Criticizing the Bar's equality code for warning that 'recruitment purely on academic achievement' could be 'indirectly discriminatory', Mears insisted 'there's no need to look at anything else'. Women have climbed the ladder's lower rungs but encountered a glass ceiling created by gendered childrearing roles and socializing patterns; academic competition reproduces class inequality (via cultural and educational endowments); race not only correlates with class but also constructs additional obstacles (unusually acknowledged when Dame Jocelyn Barrow criticized the Inns' emphasis on 'chapel, grace and drinks'). This antagonism between meritocracy and representativeness is inescapable: when outcomes are insufficiently representative, meritocracy is questioned (CLE examination results, silk and judicial selection); when meritocracy is compromised to increase representativeness, critics complain of political correctness.

The fundamental flaw in the meritocratic ideal, of course, is that playing fields are never level. True equal opportunity would require radical redistribution of initial endowments, not just advantaging those with too little but also handicapping those with too much (family environment as well as formal education). No liberal society will do this: the private sphere is sacrosanct; expropriation is punishment; and privilege is not a crime. Neo-liberalism, indeed, accentuates the reproduction of inequality by shrinking the state and enlarging the market—in the educational domain like all others. Professions, in any case, lack such redistributive powers and feel little responsibility to compensate for antecedent inequalities they did not create.

The central dilemma of remediation, therefore, is reconciling meritocratic warrants with representative outcomes. The starting point, as always, is framing the problem. If it is 'direct' or intentional discrimination, the wrongdoers should be punished; but the profession's leaders deny this exists, and those members who privately confess bias rarely express it in public. Clerks blame solicitors for requesting white or male barristers, and solicitors blame their clients. If the problem is defined as the unreconstructed attitudes of 'old boys' networks', their gradual disappearance will eliminate it. Critics find it harder to challenge dispersed invisible private 'market' decisions by law firms and chambers than centralized highly visible public choices by the Lord Chancellor appointing silk and judges.

Most tenuous is the contention that unequal outcomes are the problem. Meritocracy's defenders offer two ripostes. First, unrepresentativeness reflects aspirant choices: minorities for 'ghetto chambers', women for raising children. As late as 1997 Kamlesh Bahl, a dedicated champion of women and minorities, advocated part-time work for lawyer mothers, disregarding the way this entrenches gender hierarchy. Offering herself as a role model, Heather Hallett QC hoped her election as 1998 BC chair 'sends out the message that the Bar is open to all—and that it is possible to be a working mother and get to the top'. Lord Irvine hectored ethnic minorities 'don't be shy, apply' and accused reticent women of 'robbing' him of appointments. The second response is the inadequacy of qualified candidates. Most blame this on the bad old days, when women and minorities did not seek or gain entry, and insist time will solve it. But some City firms continued to protest that even low minority targets threatened their 'high educational demands' and 'the need to maintain quality'.

If neither perpetrator nor victim is to blame, however, what is the appropriate response to 'indirect' or institutional discrimination? The problem with all remedies is that they question the meritocratic legitimacy of either the process that produced unrepresentativeness or the more representative outcome. While denouncing 'positive discrimination', Mackay acknowledged the need to accommodate women who combined careers with motherhood. That Mackay granted many more women silk than did Hailsham and Irvine many more ethnic minorities than did Mackay (without comparable changes in the eligible pool) suggests that at least one of each pair was compromising meritocracy. How could these Lord Chancellors reconcile the satisfaction they publicly took in these achievements with their repeated commitments to meritocracy? There is no principled way of balancing the two.

Even when justified by prior disadvantage, remedial action jeopardizes the merit claimed by the group assisted. Compensatory education is stigmatizing and pairing 'ghetto' and white chambers patronizing; affirmative action 'will not enhance the dignity of black barristers'. (These remedies also assume that minorities should assimilate to the dominant white culture.) Just documenting inequality implies that those who fail to enter or do as well are unworthy (one reason why ethnic monitoring was long suspected of expressing rather than correcting racism). Assertions that greater representativeness inevitably compromises merit are deeply insulting, as when Freshfields' managing partner said the target for minority trainees would be 'quite difficult to achieve' in view of 'the need to maintain quality', or Lord Mackay declined to 'lower standards for appointment...

simply to ensure a different racial or sexual mix', or Sir Ivan Lawrence QC associated solicitors with fraud and asked: 'are you going to make judges of people like that?'

How, then, does the profession reconcile representativeness with meritocracy? It is always easier to accommodate outsiders when demand exceeds supply. During the late 1980s 'recruitment crisis' firms created part-time positions to lure mothers back to practice. By contrast, the 1990s recession provoked a LS Council member to defend nepotism as one 'man's sensible business choice'. For a firm to offer a training contract to 'the son or daughter of one of its partners or valuable clients', said Mears a few years later, 'is not to "discriminate" against anyone'. Tokenism was a common response to pressure for representativeness. City firms appointed women managing partners (while continuing to give men partnerships at three times the rate of their women peers). Newspapers cheered the first black woman silk. The profession extolled Cherie Booth's achievements. The Lord Chancellor elevated Elizabeth Butler-Sloss to head the family division. Associations chose women and ethnic minorities as leaders: with great effect when Heather Hallett QC chaired the Bar Council, disastrously when Kamlesh Bahl's confident ascent to the Law Society presidency was aborted by charges of bullying (see Chapter 10). Tokens can relieve pressure for change by making success seem easy; Booth and Hallett both denied suffering discrimination or even having difficulty combining motherhood with brilliant careers. But tokens also are role models, raising expectations and allaying quality concerns; and most feel obligated to ease the path of others. Indeed, all remedial efforts—raising the academic performance of the disadvantaged, admitting and advancing the excluded, redressing discrimination and harassment—provoke calls to do more.

The paradigm shift from exclusivity to representativeness inevitably provoked resistance. Some reflected generational differences of culture and socialization, which should diminish with time. This may explain rejection of the Bar Council's equality code and need-based scholarships by the Inns, which are still governed gerontocratically by benchers. Most leaders (BC chairs and LS presidents) were ahead of their members. Rank-and-file solicitors objected to 'interference'; they were 'independent businesses and need freedom of choice'. People could not work in 'partnerships with someone who has got a different ethos'. Anti-discrimination rules were a 'straitjacket' that 'says to all of us what we must think'. Compelling judges to disclose Masonic membership was 'intrusive', an 'unwarranted interference in our private lives'. Even the LAPG worried that discrimination 'is just another thing we can … be disciplined for'. A Council member did not believe 'you can force someone to take on someone who is not quite the norm'. Linklaters' hiring partner denied 'there is any discrimination in the major City firms'.

This gap encouraged Martin Mears to appeal to white male anxieties about declining social status and material comfort. He began by attacking the newest and hence most vulnerable opponents of discrimination—gays and lesbians—playing on the (realistic) fear that greater acceptance of homosexuals would erode respect for conservative Christians' homophobia. Maximizing publicity through carefully calculated exaggeration, Mears inverted the roles of oppressor and victim through typical Orwellian double-speak. Christians, not homosexuals, were being 'treated with contempt'; prohibiting discrimination against homosexuals was 'special legislation', 'the high watermark of bigotry', which failed to recognize the 'right of conscientious objection'. Homosexuals pretended to be a 'beleaguered' 'weak, oppressed minority' in order to win sympathy but actually had the 'power and influence' to make the Metropolitan Police adopt 'a more "user friendly"' approach to 'gays importuning in public lavatories'. '[F]eminism is the orthodoxy' and 'any kind of prejudice against women' a 'nonsense and a fiction'. Insisting that sexual orientation was not an ascribed characteristic like race and gender but rather a lifestyle choice by 'self-proclaimed sado-masochists' who 'strut down Picadilly with banners, clad in leather and chains', Mears asked whether firms had to tolerate 'proselytisers' who 'turned up in cross dress'. (A member of the Association of Christian Law Firms equated homosexuals with blasphemers and adulterers.) Mears dismissed the entire 'discrimination industry' as nothing but 'zealots' and 'heresy hunters'.

But though Mears won the Law Society presidency three months after this diatribe, the backlash was brief. Tony Girling, an equality advocate, defeated Mears's bid for re-election; Kamlesh Bahl easily won the Deputy Vice Presidency two years later and then was unopposed for Vice President; three LS officers (headed by a Clifford Chance partner) declared that the profession must 'reflect the shape of the community it serves'; and Robert Sayer, as president, repudiated his former mentor, Mears, acknowledging that 'we live in a multi-cultural, multi-racial, multifaceted society'. A Law Society and Bar Council working group recommended 'positive action measures' to identify judicial 'candidates from under-represented groups'.

The inevitable outcome of pressures for and against representativeness is the classic compromise of symbolic action: proclamations of ideals without the political will or resources to achieve them. Education, grounded on faith in the perfectability of human nature through suasion, remains the liberal creed. Lawyers were told that non-discrimination is good for business (dangerously close to laissez faire apologists who deny the possibility of bias because it is inefficient). Representativeness would increase without effort as unregenerate elders left the profession and talented outsiders entered. At moments of crisis both the profession and the government resorted to that quintessentially British response, an inquiry by the great and the good. Professional associations and their leaders exhorted members to behave better but did little to ensure or even measure compliance. Both branches announced targets for minority apprenticeships and first positions but explicitly refused to monitor, much less enforce, them. Penalties for sexual harassment remained trivial. But symbolic politics postpones the need to deliver by making a promise that is costly to revoke and can always be invoked. If ideological transformation has anticipated behavioural change, it remains a constant goad to action.

5 Defending the Temple

[CPS audience rights are] extremely stupid and foolish [and there is] no question of the Bar Council ever agreeing. [Gareth Williams QC, BC chair]

[Opposition to that] foolish bogey...has nothing to do with the Bar monopoly, nothing to do with trade union practices. [Bar AGM]

[ACLEC] is to progress what the Iron Curtain was to freedom. [Tony Holland, former LS President]

[ACLEC's] handling of the Law Society's application is little short of a public scandal. [Charles Elly, LS President]

Barristers do not fear competition in advocacy. [Heather Hallett QC, BC chair]

[To] equate good standards with a restrictive practice...[is] to put a premium on mediocrity. [Dan Brennan QC, BC chair]

Control over how many and who become lawyers—the production of producers—is only a first step toward professionalization. The next is control of competition from outside and within the profession—production by producers—both to increase profits and to enhance status by presenting an image of disinterest. Some professions are unable to ban competitors: psychiatrists cannot stop psychologists, social workers, clergy, family and friends, self-help manuals, talk shows, and quacks from offering therapy; professors have no monopoly over education nor architects over home remodelling. A profession's success encourages challenges to its jurisdiction: pharmacists, nurses, and midwives to doctors; hygienists to dentists; claims adjusters to lawyers. Professions justify and defend their monopoly rents by pretending commercial indifference. The academic hood (derived from clerical garb) into which medieval university students dropped their 'donations' was conveniently located out of sight. In *The Mikado* the civil servant Pooh-Bah derided bribes as insults—and then told supplicants to insult him again. Barristers consign to clerks the degrading task of negotiating fees and decline to enter contracts with clients (although they angrily boycott solicitors who fail to ensure payment).

Just as barristers successfully controlled the number and identity of entrants, so they stifled competition.[1] The core of their monopoly—higher court audience rights—is highly visible and thus easily policed. Nineteenth-century judges excluded solicitors explicitly 'for the sake of members of the Bar' and because it would be 'unfair to the Bar'.[2] Solicitors made half-hearted challenges whenever conveyancing income declined, seeking fusion in 1919 and 1922, and Quarter Sessions audience rights between the wars, and again before the Royal Commissions on Assizes and Quarter Sessions in the 1960s and on Legal Services in the late 1970s. The Bar repelled these incursions, although the value of its monopoly eroded as government expanded the jurisdiction of lower courts, in which solicitors could appear. And government determination to reduce its costs led to threats that solicitors would gain Crown Court audience rights following the launch of the Crown Prosecution Service (over barrister protests) and the Legal Aid Scrutiny Report, both in 1986. When government declared its intention that year to allow licensed conveyancers to compete with solicitors (see Chapter 6), the Law Society responded within a month by requesting full audience rights. The Bar warned that these 'self-serving proposals' would 'destroy the Bar as we know it' and 'seriously weaken the whole administration of justice'. Lord Hailsham reassured barristers that the existing market divisions would remain. After Thatcher rejected the Society's proposal, a solicitor obtained the right to read an agreed statement settling a High Court libel action. Austin Mitchell, who had initiated the Parliamentary assault on the solicitors' conveyancing monopoly, now took their side by tabling a private member's bill to grant full audience rights. The Law Society's contentious business committee and the Young Solicitors Group seconded this.

The Bar restricted internal competition (and controlled entry) by requiring barristers to practise in chambers served by a clerk and approved by the Bar Committee in London and the Circuits outside. Independently practising barristers could not enter partnerships, be employed, or engage in other occupations. (Employed barristers had the same limited audience rights as solicitors.) Barristers could not seek business (delegating such dirty work to their clerks) or accept briefs directly from clients rather than through solicitors. They could not even accept a brief withdrawn from another barrister unless the solicitor gave adequate reasons. The cab-rank rule required barristers to accept any brief within their competence (if the client could pay their fee). The small number of clerks (about 200 in London until recently, and just handfuls in major provincial cities) encouraged informal understandings about fee levels. The full fee was due when a brief was delivered, even if the case settled quickly.

Circuits controlled admission to practise outside London, and members could belong to only one. Non-members had to charge clients substantially higher fees than members as well as kite briefs paid to members (both abolished in 1965) and pay five guineas a day place money.

Silks constituted an elite within an elite. Until 1961, applicants had to notify all circuiteers with greater seniority so they could apply first. Lord Chancellors repeatedly denied maintaining a quota, insisting they appointed all qualified applicants; but silks remained between 9 and 11 per cent of the Bar for the entire twentieth century, although the number of applicants (and hence the percentage which was successful) fluctuated widely. Silks had to charge significantly higher fees, decline preliminary work, and appear only with a junior, who had to be paid two-thirds of the silk's fee. Although the Bar abrogated the two-thirds rule under strong pressure in 1971 and the two-counsel rule at the DGFT's insistence in 1977, both practices persisted.

The 1979 Royal Commission rejected barrister partnerships (while approving practice from home), direct access (even by other professionals, such as accountants), or any expanded audience rights for solicitors or employed barristers. It endorsed silk, while opposing a quota on their appointments and the two-counsel rule. The Government accepted the recommendations. Mitchell's 1985 Legal Profession Reform Bill would have abolished silk but had no chance of passing.

Every non-barrister group addressing the Marre Committee—the Law Society, City of London Law Society, Young Solicitors Group, LAG, NCC, and DGFT—favoured full solicitor audience rights. The Bar Council and Criminal Bar Association naturally resisted, supported by the Lord Chancellor, Lord Hailsham. When the Committee, over the barrister members' vigorous dissent, recommended Crown Court audience rights for certified solicitors, the Bar reacted with predictable outrage. But the interest in the recommendation displayed by the new Lord Chancellor, Lord Mackay, presaged the Green Paper's radical proposal and the 1990 Act's limited reforms. The Bar initially responded to the Law Society's demand for audience rights by seeking direct access to clients, which the Society strongly resisted. But when the Society reversed its position, conceding direct access, the Bar restricted its request to specified professionals. The Marre Committee explained such seeming disinterest: direct access would make it impossible 'to maintain an effective two branch profession'.[3]

A. Rights of Audience

Just before the Green Paper Sir Robert Andrew reported that the Government Legal Service was chronically understaffed and unable to retain experienced lawyers and recommended limited Crown Court audience rights (as well as higher pay) for employed barristers and solicitors. Five months later the National Audit Office reiterated that criticism of the CPS. In response to Police Federation attacks on CPS competence, DPP Allan Green told a Parliamentary committee 'the boost in morale will be very substantial if those rights are ultimately extended'. In April 1990 a Home Affairs committee made a similar recommendation. The *New Law Journal* agreed such rights were necessary 'to keep advocates of ability who would otherwise sicken on an undiluted diet of magistrates' court work'.[4]

As City firms began training solicitors in advocacy, the previous BC chair warned: 'it's like a bicycle race—no one wants to start first, but as soon as someone does, everyone has to'. At least fifty solicitors already practised as freelance advocates. The Law Society estimated 6,700 might seek expanded rights. Its plan for *Succeeding in the 90s* proposed common entry followed by specialization, including advocacy.[5]

Soon after the passing of the 1990 Act the Society sought limited audience rights for all solicitors and full rights for those with three years' experience and twenty days of advocacy in contested proceedings, who took a thirty-hour course in procedure and evidence and passed a test. Objecting that such criteria would 'reduce standards to the detriment of clients', BC chair Anthony Scrivener QC called for a year of additional training and another of apprenticeship. He also denounced solicitors' failure to include legal aid cases in their modified cab-rank rule. The BC legal services committee chair warned that solicitor-advocates with 'first access to lay clients' would 'be able to "self-select", and to engage in anti-competitive "tying-in" of advocacy and litigation services'. Consultants Hodgart Temporal predicted that within two years half the practising Bar would join solicitors' firms. LS Vice-President Philip Ely called the response 'entirely predictable and consistent with the Bar's age-long protection of the barristers' monopoly'. The *New Law Journal* assailed the Bar's 'special pleading for maintenance of the status quo' and dismissed its claim to accept 'all legal aid work' as 'utter nonsense'.[6]

The CPS and GLS applied together, noting that employed barristers already appeared in magistrates' courts, which could hear 85 per cent of Crown Court cases. Both promised to limit advocacy: GLS to the audience rights it already enjoyed in civil cases, CPS to non-serious crimes and trials of less than four days. The Attorney-General, who had championed the Bar's resistance to audience rights for employed barristers until the Act was passed, now supported the application. So did the Law Society, which thought it 'certainly odd that the Bar doesn't treat all its members the same way'. An (anonymous) CPS lawyer accused the BC of 'denigrating the professional standards and sacrificing the career interests of a substantial number of barristers whom it neither represents nor cares about'.[7]

The Bar Council's 160-page response opposed both applications. 'Parliament did not intend that overnight there would be revolutionary changes' but only 'a step-by-step evolutionary approach'. The Society's 'momentous' proposals would have 'irreversible consequences', including 'the disappearance or severe reduction of the independent Bar'. By contrast with barristers' 'independence', it was a 'well-known fact of life that a firm of solicitors may sometimes rely so heavily upon the goodwill of a particular client that they find the financial pressure to give undue preference to that client's wishes difficult to bear'. There were 'fundamental constitutional objections to the employment of state prosecutors in serious cases' because it was 'much more difficult for an employed lawyer to view his employer's legal problems with [an] objective frame of mind'. Barristers 'who have tried, and failed, to succeed in independent practice tend to try employed work'. The application 'would confer upon many a prize which in straight competition they failed to win'. Pointing to 'recent publicity concerning complaints and disciplinary action against solicitors', the Council declared that 'the problems experienced by the Law Society in ensuring compliance with their existing rules of conduct are greater than those faced by the Bar'. In the USA and continental Europe 'it is all too common for lawyers inexperienced in advocacy to see individual cases as opportunities for self-promotion'. The Law Society ought to require a 'solicitor not to recommend himself or a member of his firm unless he can put forward positive reasons'. The BC wanted to impose the cab-rank rule on solicitors and prohibit firms from litigating and advocating in the same case. Because solicitors' overheads were higher, 'advocacy services as a whole would be less available to any but the richest litigants'. '[M]ore training should be required of solicitor advocates than of barristers' because the director of education at a City firm had observed 'how ill-trained some solicitors are when they first appear'. But the Council lowered its demands to three months of education and three of pupillage.[8]

Although ACLEC chair Lord Griffiths rejected 'entrenched attitudes' and the 'view that nobody should be given rights of audience unless they are sole-practitioners', ACLEC applied the brakes by announcing a public consultation with more than sixty organizations. Lord Taylor, the new Lord Chief Justice, openly opposed the application: 'This is highly skilled work, which is not to be dabbled in'. Training could not occur 'on a part-time basis'. The chair of the Institute of Barristers' Clerks warned that 'up to 1500 [barristers] may have to go'. When the consultation had dragged on for a year, LAG director Roger Smith worried it had become 'bogged down on the issue of the economic effect on the Bar', and the Consumers' Association was 'disappointed, dismayed, less than optimistic'.[9]

Their scepticism was warranted. ACLEC supported the Law Society's application with respect to independently practising solicitors but opposed the GLS/CPS application because a CPS 'virtual monopoly' would be 'the thin edge of the wedge'. Lord Griffiths warned that a 'monolithic state service' would polarize prosecution and defence. Judges invested 'great trust' in advocates' 'objectivity'; employed lawyers were too 'close to the ethic of the organisation'. In a bizarre mixture of metaphors he insisted a young barrister needed work on which to 'cut his teeth' but added: 'I wouldn't want to go and have my teeth taken out by a dental surgeon who only practises two or three times a year'.

A disgusted *Guardian* deplored that 'six years on, the Bar Wars continue. Desperate and defensive action by barristers' and 'clever political footwork' had preserved their monopoly. ACLEC's recommendation was 'preposterous', 'dotty'. *The Times* assailed the 'naked plea to protect the criminal Bar from competition'. The *Economist* said the surviving restrictive practices preserved barristers' 'snobbery' and solicitors' 'self-interest'. Philip Ely, now LS President, denied that ACLEC's reasoning could withstand 'serious analysis'. The imputation 'that employed solicitors may lack detachment or impartiality...is offensive'. A local government solicitor experienced it as 'a kick in the teeth'. The Times Newspapers company solicitor resented the 'insult' based on 'the extraordinary premise that lawyers in employment are more likely to be pressured and manipulated' than 'small firms of solicitors in private practice doing little or nothing other than looking after the interests of heavy-weight criminals in big fraud cases'. The LS Commerce and Industry Group chair claimed that 'employment protection laws' rendered his members' independence 'more firmly secured than that of our colleagues in private practice'.[10]

The Bar was equally distressed at the report's 'profound failures' to 'understand the public importance of the cab rank rules'; the advocacy course was just 'an extended weekend'. 'It is idle to speak of a free market or market forces. Sometimes all that the market wants or offers is a second rate service to those who cannot pay privately.' But Sir Gordon Borrie, the DGFT, who had opposed the Green Paper, now found the Bar's denial of audience rights to employed barristers anti-competitive to a 'significant extent'. BACFI promptly sought those rights, and the GLS/CPS renewed their application.[11]

Solicitors narrowly avoided a split. Those claiming to represent 100 freelance advocates urged the Law Society to abandon employed solicitors. But though the *New Law Journal* endorsed this 'practical solution', a week later it proclaimed: 'Either the Law Society is for all solicitors or for none....' Tony Holland, president when the application had been made, declared 'a solicitor is a solicitor is a solicitor'. The Society revised its practice rules to 'bolster the independence of in-house lawyers' and reapplied. Its Commerce and Industry Group asked twenty major companies to write to ACLEC, whose disdain 'makes us see red'. Barbara Mills, the new DPP, told the Group's annual conference: 'Whether is not on the table, the question is when'. The Rolls Royce general counsel (who represented privately employed solicitors on the Council) called ACLEC's decision 'extraordinarily offensive'.[12]

On becoming Master of the Rolls, Lord Justice Bingham endorsed solicitors' audience rights 'subject to suitable safeguards and rules'. But at his first press conference, the new Lord Chief Justice reiterated his opposition to CPS audience rights. It was no surprise, therefore, that Lord Mackay and the designated judges rejected immediate audience rights for employed lawyers. But finding no objection in principle, they gave the Bar five months to reconsider its denial. The Law Society boasted the question was 'no longer whether, but on what terms', and the GLS/CPS hoped 'this will begin the process of removing the restrictions'. But BC chair Gareth

Williams QC, who had pronounced CPS audience rights 'extremely stupid and foolish', declared there was 'no question of the Bar Council ever agreeing'. Peter Goldsmith QC, BC legal services committee chair, insisted it was not 'about a monopoly by the Bar but about independence'. The Bar AGM agreed that opposition to the 'foolish bogey' was not motivated by 'keeping our own patch' and 'has nothing to do with the Bar monopoly, nothing to do with trade union practices'.

The First Division Association secretary warned the Bar against 'going for double or bust—and it will be bust'. Derek Wheatley QC, BACFI vice-president, called the charge of insufficient independence 'outrageous'. 'For over 20 years I earned a living as a barrister. I could be trusted. They made me a recorder. Then overnight I could not appear in court.' A former BACFI president denounced the Bar's objection as 'arrogant and offensive'. ACLEC had displayed 'breathtaking illogicality'. 'It should be for those who seek to maintain the restrictive rule to justify it by examples of bad behaviour; but it has never been suggested that there are any. It should be for employers to decide which class of lawyer to employ....' The *New Law Journal* dismissed Williams's bluster as 'nonsense', the 'fire and brimstone of the Methodist preacher'. 'There have been whole sets of chambers who have, in effect, been permanent prosecutors. And what of Treasury Counsel?' The *Solicitors Journal* thought it 'difficult to argue that an independent barrister who is anxious to build up a practice prosecuting is any more of a safeguard than a conscientious CPS employee who has job security'.[13]

As the Bar's deadline approached it sought further delay until the Law Society's application was resolved. Robert Seabrook QC thought it 'quite possible' that the BC could challenge any CPS barrister who appeared in court, which would 'become very messy'. When the delay was granted, the BC asked the DGFT to recommend that solicitors appear only if their firms had not prepared the case.[14]

ACLEC rejected the Society's code for employed lawyers, proposing civil audience rights only if the head lawyer held no other role in the organization (excluding most local authority solicitors) and delaying criminal audience rights until the Royal Commission on Criminal Justice reported. The next day Norman Lamont, Chancellor of the Exchequer, expressed frustration to Lord Mackay 'that lawyers in the government legal services are no further forward in obtaining wider rights of audience some two years after the reformative legislation was passed'. The Law Society called ACLEC's objections 'shameful' and 'disgraceful', and past president Philip Ely denounced its process as 'stultifying and debilitating'. 'The Advisory Committee is to progress,' said Tony Holland, 'what the Iron Curtain was to freedom'. 'We demean ourselves by arguing with those who, I suspect, will never be on our side.' But a third past president, Sir David Napley, expressed his 'strongest possible' opposition to broad CPS rights: 'Look at what they have under such a system in the USA'. The two and a half year delay was 'partly the fault of the Council' for following a 'negligent' strategy. Employed solicitors, after all, were 'a relatively small section of the population'.[15]

In a contemporaneous public lecture, Lord Griffiths opposed any audience rights for employed solicitors because 'you don't want an orthopaedic surgeon doing the job of a neurosurgeon'. Two months later ACLEC unsurprisingly recommended against the Society's application. 'All the evidence the committee has received has advised us that it would not be a healthy development for this country to have a monolithic state prosecution service.'

Austin Mitchell called the recommendation 'a squalid attempt by the legal establishment to close the door on a more democratic and effective legal profession'. Barbara Mills complained that 'to suggest we can't exercise independent judgment in the Crown Court is not a nice thing to say about' the CPS. LS President Mark Sheldon accused ACLEC of relying on 'speculation about hypothetical problems rather than on the unchallenged evidence that employed solicitors have conducted cases for years in the lower courts without complaint'. He warned that the decision 'opened a potential new division between private practice and employed lawyers'. Indeed, a City insurance defence firm's senior partner called the Society's position 'crazy. We come across an opportunity for the vast majority of solicitors and the Law Society turns it down.' Even the NCC urged the Society to abandon employed lawyers. But Sheldon insisted that the single application 'represents not mere bravado, nor just a futile gesture of solidarity. It is fundamental to the integrated nature of our profession.' The *Lawyer* praised the Society for having 'rightly nailed its flag to the mast of a single solicitor's profession'.[16]

During the fifteen months it took the designated judges to decide several events raised hopes. The Royal Commission on Criminal Justice recommended that both branches receive advocacy training. An OFT report found that solicitor advocacy would have no competitive disadvantages. Lord Steyn replaced Lord Griffiths as ACLEC chair. After Crown prosecutor Neil Addison and an ally won the most votes in the first election for four employed barrister BC seats, Addison attacked the Council's accusation that getting 'our cheques once a month rather than case by case...makes us less trustworthy'. But an FDA survey found low morale among Crown prosecutors, one of whom disclosed that management set conviction targets.[17]

In December 1993 the designated judges granted the Society's application on behalf of independent practitioners and referred the issue of employed lawyers to ACLEC for the third time. Newspaper headlines proclaimed 'Barristers' monopoly is broken by Mackay' and 'Victory won by solicitors'. The London Criminal Courts Solicitors Association hoped 'the first freelance solicitor advocates appear in higher courts by Easter'. A Lovell White Durant senior litigation partner thought the firm might do up to half its High Court advocacy work in-house within ten years. McKenna & Co boasted its advocacy service was a third cheaper than the Bar's and available through conditional fees. Mills was still confident that CPS audience rights were 'only a matter of time', the GLS was 'hopeful', and the LS Commerce & Industry Group 'totally optimistic'. The LCD junior minister agreed rights were inevitable.[18]

Such triumphalism was premature. Although more than 1,000 people inquired about qualifying, many of the thirty-two admitted in February 1994 were former barristers or recorders, exempt from training and testing. The examination became a significant hurdle as pass rates on civil evidence and procedure fell from 60 per cent in June 1994 to 29 per cent in September 1995. Two-thirds of a sample of City firms wanted the barriers lowered, and the YSG chair thought the tests 'far too hard'. When the Law Society urged ACLEC to relax the requirements, BC vice-chair Robert Owen QC observed caustically: 'advocacy is best conducted by full-time advocates and these results seem to bear that out'.

The Bar was not yet raising a white flag. Chair Robert Seabrook QC wanted to incorporate solicitor advocates through 'virtually automatic transfer' in order to avoid 'fragmentation of professional regulation'. Sir Thomas Bingham, Master of the Rolls, concurred. BC vice-chair Peter Goldsmith QC said the Council would launch a major advertising campaign on behalf of barristers and urge that solicitors be required to inform clients in writing of their right to choose an advocate.

The burning question now became whether solicitor advocates could wear wigs. In 1990 a barrister had argued that 'this affectation of seventeenth century French fashion has had its day'. A year later the Lord Chief Justice worried that 'the wig makes us look antique and slightly ridiculous... thinking in an eighteenth century way'. *The Times* mocked 'barristers and judges resplendent in wigs and gowns' as 'crusty creatures... a Victorian relic'. Mills feared 'wigs, gowns and archaic language... led to a "them and us" feeling'. The 1992 BC chair Gareth Williams QC called wigs 'an irrelevance', which should 'be used for pantomimes at Christmas'. The Commercial Bar Association favoured change. The *New Law Journal* associated wigs with 'pomposity' and the *Solicitors Journal* with anachronistic 'wing collars'.

Counsel, however, used leading questions to elicit support from court users, asking rhetorically whether 'a powerful reminder of the 18th century... at this hour [is] such a bad thing'. Its real agenda was clear.

Maybe the Bar has nothing to fear from solicitors' rights of audience in the Crown Court after all, as long as we retain our current robes. 'I want to be represented by a proper barrister with a wig' appears to be the message of Crown Court defendants.

Wigs were 'a gift to cartoonists', conceded the Lord Chief Justice, but they also preserved 'the dignity of the court and you need to be able to identify who is the judge'.

Lord Mackay launched a consultation on this 'extremely important question', in which the Queen 'has an important interest'. Lord Donaldson, Master of the Rolls, felt wigs 'admirably' differentiated judges. Lord Campbell of Alloway thought them 'utterly essential to maintain the dignity and authority of solemn proceedings'. 'Pomposity' was simply 'a chronic occupational disease'. Lord Renton claimed they 'make the young look old and... the old look young' and put women 'on more equal terms'. Lord Morris disparaged 'populist and facile' attacks on 'formal dress'. After eighteen months of delibertion, Lord Mackay and Lord Taylor preserved the status quo, which had attracted 'strong support' among jurors, witnesses, the public, the profession, and the judiciary.

LS President Rodger Pannone then asked that solicitor advocates wear wigs. But though ACLEC agreed, the Lord Chancellor refused, 'confident that solicitors will be able to show that not wearing a wig does not imply in some way a second class advocate'. When Lord Taylor prohibited individual judges from letting solicitors wear wigs, Lord Mackay initiated a second consultation. Charles Elly, the new LS president, favoured 'modern court dress for all advocates'. But the BC was advised by counsel to commence proceedings against solicitors wearing wigs. The author, Robert Owen QC (BC chair two years later), found it 'difficult to see why [a client] should perceive his [solicitor] advocate as inferior simply because he is not wearing a wig, although there may be other valid reasons for such a view'.

The first solicitor advocate to appear in a Crown Court jury trial and in the Court of Appeal called the prohibition 'a kick in the teeth'. Another said police officers, social workers, and probation officers all asked if he 'was not yet "fully qualified"?' A third said criminal defendants wanted ' "a proper brief" and they associate the wearing of a wig, as do jurors and other court users, with a first division of advocates, and solicitors being "apprentices" '. A judge accused a gowned solicitor of 'stealing someone's clothes', adding ominously: 'you have been warned'. Barristers referred to each other as 'my Learned Friend' and solicitors as 'my Friend' or even 'my Friend the Solicitor'. Solicitor-advocates formed the Solicitors Association of Higher Court Advocates (SAHCA) partly to redress these grievances.[19]

In December 1994 ACLEC chair Lord Steyn declared that 'in the eyes of the court all advocates ought to be treated as equal'. But BC chair Robert Seabrook QC could not 'see why solicitors should pass themselves off as what we are'. Lord Mackay concluded that 'the case for change is not made out'. LS President Elly condemned the decision as an 'indefensible' perpetuation of 'petty distinctions' and 'out-dated prejudices'. The Criminal Law Solicitors Association denounced it as 'plainly wrong and quite illogical'. When legal executive advocates were allowed to dress in court like solicitors in 1998, the *Solicitors Journal* again urged barristers to doff their wigs. But BC chair Heather Hallett QC insisted on keeping them. And though Lord Irvine won a significant relaxation in his own dress as Lord Chancellor, he retained wigs for barristers. Andrew Dismore moved an amendment to the Access to Justice Bill to abolish wigs—a 'style of dress introduced to mourn the death of Charles II'—and adopt uniform attire for all advocates. Martin Linton, another Labour backbencher, commented: 'Whenever I feel a need to lose my respect for my opponents in the heat of debate, I do not…imagine them naked; I imagine them wearing wigs and it works an absolute dream'. 'Pupils at my old school still wear yellow stockings…because it was believed in Elizabethan times that that colour deterred lice.' Wigs were 'a form of clubmanship or one-upmanship'. But Government refused to support the motion.[20]

Solicitor advocates encountered other rebuffs. Barristers (but not solicitors) still dined with judges in the Inns. When a prosecutor suggested a defendant be represented by a solicitor in March 1995, the Crown Court judge objected: 'We don't need to stoop that low, do we?', apologising only when the CLSA chair (who happened to be present) complained about the 'gratuitously offensive remark'. But two months later a Family Division judge 'regretted' that a local council had been represented by its solicitor, who could not advise 'with the same detachment and strength'. As late as spring 1999 a solicitor advocate complained that Ian Kennedy J displayed 'ordinary cordiality' to the opposing barrister but repeatedly interrupted his own opening argument. Clients saw the judge 'constantly looking at the clock' and throwing 'down a file…before I had finished referring to it'. The solicitor contemplated abandoning advocacy because 'I have appeared six times this year in the High Court and each time it has been a nightmare'.

Only 400 solicitors had qualified by mid-1996, mainly because of the opportunity cost of attending the mandatory course. Even those hesitated to exercise their rights for fear that barristers would refuse briefs. SAHCA conceded that most solicitors still preferred barristers. Only six of forty-six City firms surveyed planned in-house advocacy units. Academic studies in Bristol and London confirmed that most privately practising solicitors encountered structural obstacles to doing advocacy: low case volume, high time costs and overheads, low profitability relative to other work, inconsistent client demands, and inconvenient court listing practices.[21]

Employed lawyers still had no audience rights. Soon after winning election to the BC, Neil Addison pushed the Council to seek them. But the BACFI chair (and fellow Council member) attacked Addison's 'extremely provocative, counterproductive and unhelpful speeches'. The CPS seriously undermined its claim that employees were independent by ordering Addison not to communicate with the media on CPS policy (see Chapter 2). Addison's motions at the 1994 and 1995 AGMs lost with worsening margins. Nevertheless, the BACFI Vice-President (now consultant to a City firm) denounced the earlier ACLEC recommendation as 'absolute rubbish', and the *New Law Journal* called doubts about independence 'arrant nonsense'. The BC's opposition was motivated by 'self-preservation. There is not sufficient work to go round the junior Bar.'

In June 1995, ACLEC (by a majority of one that included three barristers and two judges) again rejected audience rights for employed solicitors, who would be 'insufficiently protected against a range of pressures'. Threatened with losing jobs or promotions, employed lawyers 'may become prosecution-minded'. Civil litigation offered 'too much scope for conflicts arising from the policy functions, objectives and interests of the government department'. The minority objected that the majority had offered no empirical evidence. 'Indeed it is equally arguable that professional employees protected by the formal published code of the organisation which employs them are less open to pressure....' The minority questioned whether 'policy should be driven by the need to provide training for one particular part of the legal profession'. The Royal Commission on Criminal Justice had found 'inefficiencies' in the 'current division of responsibilities between the CPS and private counsel'. The 'existing artificial restrictions... can best be described as monopolistic'.

LS President Charles Elly was incensed.

The committee's handling of the Law Society's application is little short of a public scandal. Over more than four years it is a history of prevarication, evasion, flawed argument and delay. Their report rests entirely on unsubstantiated opinions... and makes no reference to the wide body of evidence which shows an imperceptible level of complaint.

Assistant Secretary-General Walter Merricks accused the committee of 'scraping the barrel' for justifications. 'The real issue is not this independent stuff.' Holland called ACLEC 'a monument to the determination of an alliance of the judiciary and the Bar to protect what can only be described as the Bar's vested interest in the status quo'. Nevertheless, the Society amended its proposal to limit employed solicitors to less serious cases.

The Bar Council was delighted. Chair Peter Goldsmith QC maintained that 'all the arguments have been fully canvassed and explored' during the 'long debate', which was not 'about maintaining some monopoly for the

Bar' but 'about ensuring in the more serious criminal cases that there are independent prosecutors...to act as an important check on the power of the State'.[22]

The CPS's chronic problems undermined its case for audience rights. In April 1996 the FDA (representing 1,300 of its 2,000 lawyers) declared prosecutors were 'no longer able to serve the interests of justice' and threatened a one-day strike. The survey it commissioned found extreme dissatisfaction: more than half wanted to leave, more than 90 per cent feared that disagreeing with supervisors could harm their careers, and only 11 per cent wanted expanded audience rights. The *Solicitors Journal* urged the CPS to become a 'purchasing agent' like the LAB (as the Centre for Policy Studies had recommended three years before). The Chief Constable of Kent wanted a return to police prosecutors.[23]

In February 1997 the designated judges granted employed solicitors rights only to enter guilty pleas and conduct preliminary hearings in criminal and civil cases. The Law Society was 'insulted' and deplored that 'public bodies will continue to spend millions of pounds of taxpayers' money instructing barristers'. The Bar Council was pleased by the acknowledgement that 'contested cases...should be conducted by independent advocates'. Chair Robert Owen QC called it an unsatisfactory compromise. Although it was 'unthinkable' that the employed Bar would eventually be placed in a 'less advantageous position', the issue had 'been considered at great length and in great depth' and 'has now finally been concluded'.[24]

Eight months after becoming Lord Chancellor, Lord Irvine told the Minority Lawyers Conference that the consultative process was too 'cumbersome' and a 'statutory quagmire'. The Law Society applauded; expanded audience rights would save prosecution costs and give clients a 'choice of advocate'. Although the Bar Council denied it was 'speaking as a vested interest', chair Heather Hallett QC said an 'independent advocate' was 'the safest way to assure that you don't have a miscarriage of justice'. But within weeks the National Audit Office reported that 'independent advocates' returned 70 per cent of CPS briefs. Deploring the last-minute substitution of 'white wigs and incompetents', the *New Law Journal* condemned 'the restrictive practice which prevents defendants and prosecutors alike from having the best person available to undertake essential advocacy'. The Commons Public Accounts Committee planned to investigate complaints of delay, cost overruns, and returned briefs. The June 1998 Glidewell Report confirmed that only 35 per cent of barristers originally instructed in London Crown Courts attended trial.[25]

In January 1998 two Labour backbenchers used a Parliamentary question to urge full audience rights in order to 'unify the legal profession and ensure that people don't have to pay two sets of fees'. LCD Parliamentary Secretary Geoff Hoon found it 'surprising' that employed barristers had not yet obtained them; 'current restrictions' were not 'in the public interest', and the procedure for reviewing them was 'complex, bureaucratic and slow'. The BC public affairs committee chair maintained unconvincingly that 'the Bar has always welcomed competition' but also suggested it was prepared to make strategic concessions: 'we have no objection to any practitioner—whether solicitor or barrister, employed or in private practice—acting as an advocate in the crown court'. The SAHCA chair was 'delighted that progress is being made towards a level playing-field'. The LS head of policy emphasized the need to 'get rid of the slur on' and end 'discrimination against CPS lawyers' and criticized the qualification requirements as 'grossly disparate ... prohibitively expensive and complex'. The *Solicitors Journal* reassured the Bar that 'only a few solicitors will choose to specialise in advocacy'.[26]

But though the Commons Public Accounts Committee reiterated criticisms of returned briefs, it also was sceptical about CPS competence. Chair David Davis deplored the 'unjustifiably high discontinuance rate' and the declining number of lawyers in post. Christopher Leslie wondered whether the CPS 'operate on a different planet' and told Mills: 'a lot of people regard your organisation as highly bureaucratic and absolutely subject to inertia and immovable'. Charles Wardle said the 'creaking system ... has not got better since 1990'.[27] The Crime and Disorder Bill extended solicitors' rights by moving pre-trial procedures in serious cases to magistrates' courts. LS President Phillip Sycamore applauded that this would 'save costs, ensure continuity of representation, speed up the criminal justice process and allow more flexible use of lawyers' skills'.[28]

At the end of March Hallett wrote to Irvine that the BC had approved employed barristers' audience rights. But the vast majority who had not completed pupillage in chambers within five years and the BVC within six would have to take the solicitors' exam. 'A free for all in the courts of this country would not be in anyone's interest.' The designated judges 'are obviously in the best position to assess impartially who is properly qualified to conduct cases before them'. Three months later Hallett protested this was 'not a trade union argument', claiming support by the 'Royal Commission and every other independent committee which has considered this question'. In 1985, she noted, the Attorney-General had 'warned of the inevitable Treasury pressure on the CPS to do more and more of its work in-house' and 'feared for the future of the independent Bar'. At the same time, the BC ordered barristers who requalified as solicitors to describe themselves as 'suspended from practice', only to bow to pressure and substitute the term 'non-practising barristers'.[29]

Reporting on the CPS in May, Sir Iain Glidewell and his colleagues found 'a great degree of dissatisfaction amongst the staff', partly because 'the CPS has more work to do and fewer experienced people to do it'.

The report urged the ending of 'constraints, both internally and externally imposed, particularly on the career options for CPS lawyers'. The 400 most qualified 'devote the majority of their time to management' and 'spend less than a third of their time on casework and advocacy'. Tensions 'between the police and the CPS...have not disappeared' because 'inappropriate downgrading [of charges] does occur' and there were too many acquittals.[30]

The following month Mr Justice Lightman used his Chancery Bar Association lecture to express 'anxiety' about 'the undue economic exploitation of the Bar's monopoly of advocacy in the High Court', which 'restricted' the market so that 'in a number of specialist fields, a limited number of chambers have...the field to themselves and charge accordingly'. Fee negotiation was 'scarcely feasible in a system in which a single clerk represents all the (potentially competitive) members of the same chambers, and the clerks to a number of chambers have a practice of coordinating their responses—i.e. fixing prices'. Because there was no 'equality of bargaining position' once 'counsel has acted for any period of time for a client in any litigation' there was need for 'some mechanism enabling fees to be reviewed after the event'. A clerk replied that 'barristers chasing a diminishing amount of work' were 'undercutting each other on price'.[31]

In response to the contemporaneous inquiry into legal aid payments to QCs in House of Lords appeals (see Chapter 8), the *Sunday Times* leaked the news that:

Britain's 'fat cat' lawyers are to lose their high court monopoly in far-reaching reforms that will cut legal costs for clients and taxpayers. Independent barristers who can command fees of more than £1,000 a day, will no longer have exclusive rights of audience in the higher courts.

The Law Society declared 'it will bring real competition and choice into advocacy in the higher courts'.[32]

The cab-rank rule came under attack when Lord Neill of Bladen QC, Lord Protector of High Standards, invoked it to justify defending Dame Shirley Porter against gerrymandering and vote-buying charges. Noting that conflict of interest rules take precedence, Paul Foot declared that 'everyone in the business knows the cab-rank principle is a myth'. A former barrister added that 'clerks get rid of unwelcome cases by quoting ludicrous fees' or telling the solicitor 'that the barrister was less likely to perform well than someone who had no such objections'.[33]

Addressing the SAHCA annual dinner, Lord Irvine declared that 'the government has a duty to benefit the consumer in legal services by breaking down unnecessary barriers to entry into the marketplace'. SAHCA praised this 'refreshing common-sense approach' and urged that the LPC and traineeship qualify for all advocacy. When the BC proposed that new entrants to both branches have limited audience rights, gaining more with experience, training, and qualification, SAHCA denounced this 'attempt to preserve the Bar's monopoly for another generation' while 'accepting that the writing is on the wall'.[34]

On 25 June Irvine published a consultation paper proposing that he be empowered to grant full audience rights to all solicitors and employed barristers, direct access to barristers, and the right to conduct litigation to barristers and legal executives; senior judges would advise him but have no veto. His 'one clear aim' was 'a modern and fair system which will promote quality and choice...while...providing value for money'. The proposal 'would increase competition and could force barristers to cut their fees'. 'Independence' was not threatened; if 'it is wrong in principle for someone to be prosecuted by an employed lawyer, how is it that we tolerate this practice in the magistrates' courts, where over 95 per cent of criminal cases are tried?' 'The perception has grown that the legal system is dominated by the interests of lawyers, rather than by the need to provide justice for the people.' The 'right to maintain properly high entry standards to a profession must not be allowed to impose restrictive practices for the benefit of those already established in the profession'. The 'Byzantine procedure' of the 1990 Act 'provided too much scope for deadlock, for delay, for constant replays of the same arguments' and ultimately 'produced a mouse of reform'. The LS application was 'the most striking example of delays and problems'. It took 'no less than six years to resolve, and was considered by ACLEC at least three times and by the Director General of Fair Trading, the Lord Chancellor and the designated judges twice'. ACLEC 'initially gave defective advice' and ultimately 'split down the middle'.

The Bar did not need 'the protection of restrictive practices in order to flourish'. In any case, 'it is not the role of the Government to safeguard the supply of work for barristers'. Litigants had been denied 'effective choice' and forced by 'out of date restrictive practices' to 'pay for two lawyers where one might suffice'. Given the importance of cases in which solicitors already appeared, 'it is difficult to see why they should be denied full rights of audience in the higher courts'. That 'an experienced barrister becomes unsuitable to appear in the higher courts the moment he becomes an employee... is not rationally defensible'. The 'financial independence' claimed by private practitioners 'may be less substantial than it appears' because specialists 'come to depend on regular instructions from particular firms of solicitors and even particular clients' and the CPS. 'Arguably as great a guarantee of independence is to be a salaried lawyer...enjoying a degree of job security and protection from unfair dismissal.' Extending audience rights to the CPS may 'make that career more attractive to able barristers'.

The press applauded loudly: 'Irvine puts end to Bar's courtroom dominance' (*Guardian*); 'Lord Irvine Says the Bar's Open' (*Independent*); 'Court shake-up to break barristers' monopoly' (*Independent*); 'Irvine wants no bar on seeking justice' (*Financial Times*); 'Cost of legal action may be slashed' (*Daily Telegraph*); 'Irvine to scrap Bar's court monopoly' (*The Times*). The *Independent* said 'barristers have never been so much on the defensive— and for their own cause'. The *Daily Telegraph* predicted the changes could cut costs 'drastically'. *The Times* praised Irvine for 'taking a battering ram to the Temple' and demonstrating a 'radicalism of which [Thatcher] might have been proud'. The *Financial Times* said Irvine was driving 'the final nail into the coffin of an independent Bar...modernising the justice system at breakneck speed' and abolishing ' "antiquated restrictions" that can force people to pay for two lawyers...where one would do'.

Insisting 'barristers do not fear competition in advocacy', Hallett now opposed 'any member of the Bar or solicitor having automatic rights of audience on qualifying'. Warning that the Law Society had relaxed its advocacy requirements and was urging further reductions, she declared:

it cannot be in the interests of justice to allow inappropriately qualified lawyers the right to present complex cases in court....What would be the reaction of the patient about to undergo heart surgery to learn that the GMC had been forced to reduce their entry requirements for surgeons to a degree in biology for fear of being described as unduly restrictive and anti competitive?

The Society's own adviser had called the examination 'a fair test on matters that advocates going into the higher courts really ought to know'. It was not 'sensible' to give the CPS additional tasks when it was facing reorganization in response to Glidewell. 'Anyone who has studied the American system would have concerns....' It was 'misleading' to claim the proposal 'neces- sarily means savings'. She warned the Bar's annual conference that City firms' advocacy departments 'threaten the very existence of the high street solicitor and the high standards of independence and integrity currently demanded of our lawyers'. She extolled advocates 'prosecuting one day, defending the next, acting for the injured plaintiff one week, the insurance company the next'. How long would there be 'an independent legal profession ready and willing to take on a case for the individual against the state or large organisations?' She deplored the 'chipping away at the edges of the system in the name of cost cutting and market forces which could prove disastrous for the country in the long term. Around the world, Law has become big business.' The BC professional standards committee vice chair pointed to the 'real risk that the independent Bar...will shrink to a rump that will never be replaced'.

Writing for the BC, Sydney Kentridge QC called Irvine's proposal a 'quiet constitutional revolution', which 'will obviously increase the power of the government to control the legal profession and...in the hands of another Lord Chancellor less committed to the independence of the Bar,

destroy it'. During 'the years of apartheid in South Africa' he had experienced 'frequent threats from the government to place the Bar under the
control of a central council with government nominated members'.

The Bar's response said Irvine's power grab raised a 'constitutional
issue', which the judges in 1989 had called 'a grave breach of the doctrine
of separation of powers'. It was only prepared to concede that a majority of
the designated judges (not each one) possess a veto. 'The high failure rate'
on the advocacy test demonstrated the need 'to tighten, rather than relax
standards'. It deplored the 'growing tendency of solicitors choosing themselves as advocates so as to maximise turnover and profits'. 'Indeed, some
firms of solicitors have made no secret of their determination to exclude
barristers from advocacy on behalf of their lay clients wherever and whenever possible....' It urged that 'tying in arrangements for advocacy should
be dealt with in the same way' as lender conveyancing—a criminal offence
under the 1990 Act. Taxing Masters 'should be required to disallow for [*sic*]
advocacy costs charged by solicitors, which exceed what would be charged
by barristers of the right seniority and experience'. 'Prosecution success
rates are a primary feature of all state prosecution systems.' Glidewell had
found that the CPS was neither 'successful' nor 'esteemed'. 'In the USA'
employed lawyers 'are known as "oncers"...and cause almost as many
problems for the courts as litigants in person'.

BACFI's representative on the BC drafting committee opposed a judicial
veto and resented the reply's 'very offensive tone towards employed and
non-practising barristers'. It sought an end to 'unjustifiable restrictions',
including those on CPS lawyers, in order to promote 'proper access to justice for all'. '[F]ull, free and open competition' had 'long been accepted
as fundamental to the existence of a thriving and healthy business community. It drives down prices and widens consumer choice.' BACFI wanted
to offer pupillage and conduct litigation.

Even private practitioners no longer were monolithic. David Pannick
QC thought it

high time for the Bar and the judiciary to recognise the necessity for, and the
inevitability of, reform of practices that confine access to the higher courts to a particular class of lawyers. The special pleading of judges and barristers has no persuasive
effect on lay people, save to reinforce their low opinion of the legal profession.

And Ronald Thwaites QC conceded that:

no one can deny that competition is good and that restrictive practices are bad:
monopoly situations inevitably produce many evils, including complacency, the
enemy of motivation, originality and efficiency. Judges and recorders frequently
complain about the poor advocacy of barristers...if the only way in which an
observer can distinguish between the courtroom advocacy of a barrister and that of
a solicitor is by noting that one of them is wearing a horsehair wig, the time cannot

be far off when we are consumed by fusion of the professions. No-one will lament our passing.

Supporting CPS audience rights, Attorney-General John Morris QC praised 'the Bar's recognition of the need for changes which serve the public interest rather than any sectional interests'.

Solicitors were triumphant. Russell Wallman said the Society was 'not actively seeking' fusion but would have 'no objection'. Newly qualified solicitors should gain audience rights by studying advocacy during the LPC. SAHCA declared that 'many clients resent their first choice of litigation lawyer having to explain the case again to a barrister...when all parties know that the solicitor could have done a better job at far less cost'. It predicted that all lawyers would start as solicitors, who 'will increasingly conduct advocacy in all cases on which they are instructed'. LAG called the proposals 'excellent—if long overdue—news for consumers'. The *Solicitors Journal* predicted that 'distinctions between the two sides of the profession will disappear'. Among the 151 respondents to a survey of *The Times* 500 companies and merchant banks, 73 per cent supported and only 6 per cent opposed full audience rights; all but one of the sixteen that had instructed solicitor advocates found their services at least as good as barristers'. Despite his criticisms of the CPS, Sir Iain Glidewell declared it 'absurd' that its barristers could not appear in the High Court and accused the BC of 'foot-dragging of the highest order...fighting a losing battle, and... [being] very foolish'.

Still, many worried about empowering the Lord Chancellor. The Law Society preferred the Master of the Rolls. APIL warned that 'granting a politician licence to interfere with rules honed independently over hundreds of years' would 'seriously threaten' the 'independence of the judiciary and of all advocates'. All ninety-eight High Court and thirty-six Court of Appeal judges objected. Lord Ackner called it 'quite monstrous' that Irvine had not consulted Sir Stephen Brown (a designated judge). The 'Lord Chancellor really wants to achieve...total control of the legal profession'.[35]

A month after Irvine's bombshell, Home Secretary Jack Straw announced a review of jury trials, which would consider shifting 22,000 cases a year to magistrates' courts, where solicitors had audience rights. Hallett complained that 'a cynic would begin to suspect that the timing of these consultation papers [in the summer] has become something of an art form as far as the Government is concerned'. In opposition eighteen months earlier, Straw had denounced such proposals as 'not only wrong, but short-sighted, and likely to prove ineffective'. Hallett felt 'as if I have changed my name to Alice and wandered through the looking glass'. The 'only suggested justification...must be the fact that jury trials cost more'.

Although *The Times* called jury trials 'one of the golden threads of British justice which, like the right to silence, has frayed and tangled rather in recent years', it attributed some of the resistance to 'the same reactionary chambers who have opposed other, worthwhile, reforms. The Bar Council, in the best trade union manner' was expressing the 'professional self-interest [that] animates those who see another source of income diminishing'. The BC public affairs committee chair protested: 'Surely the Bar can be acquitted of the baser motives which your leading article imputes'. Indeed, the change was opposed by the Law Society (whose members would benefit), LAG, Justice, and Liberty.[36]

The CPS's travails continued to weaken its case for audience rights. David Calvert-Smith, the new DPP, admitted there were 'tens' of employees 'beyond redemption'. Two surveys identified 200 recent cases in which prosecutors had withheld evidence. A judge ordered the CPS to explain concealment of a videotape proving the innocence of a teenager accused of rape; another condemned CPS failure to prosecute two deaths in police custody and acquittal in a third such case. A CPS employee sold the names of thirty-three informants to a notorious crime family for £1,000. Conviction rates fell slightly. The CPS inspectorate found serious weakness in the preparation of Crown Court cases (though it praised the 158 solicitor advocates with higher court audience rights). After two senior lawyers committed suicide, apparently from work stress, Calvert-Smith ordered an investigation (which the FDA had been seeking for two years); the 2,000 CPS lawyers handled 1.4 million cases annually. (At the same time, the reversal of Derek Bentley's 1953 conviction and the review of James Hanratty's 1962 conviction raised even more serious questions about the 'independent' prosecutors in those notorious executions.[37])

During the Second Reading of the Access to Justice Bill on 14 December, Lord Irvine argued for extending audience rights to employed lawyers, who are 'not on that account ethically deficient'. 'Judges are employed and salaried but their independence is unquestioned.' The Lord Chief Justice and the Master of the Rolls disavowed the concerns of other judges. Lord Falconer denied that DPPs 'lost their ability to be independent from the moment they came to be employed'. As Solicitor-General he found the CPS's 'standards of propriety and independence were extremely high'. But insisting that employed lawyers felt 'the pressures of preferment, of success rates, of performance related pay', Lord Hutchinson assailed the 'sinister figure of the salaried state defender, paid, selected and controlled by the state ... the dark night of dependence'. Lord Thomas had seen 'in Hong Kong how the system adopted by the Attorney-General's chambers can breed difficult prosecutors who will over-charge', and he reviled American public defenders as 'notorious for incompetence'. Based on 'direct experience of the public defender system in the United States',

Baroness Kennedy also voiced 'great alarm'. She had 'a young black lawyer [friend], working in Washington, who is handling cases which no lawyer of his age and experience should handle'. The horrifying levels of plea bargaining in the United States will almost certainly visit themselves upon our courts....'[38]

Assuming the 1999 BC chair, Dan Brennan QC declared that 'the Bar no longer has, nor seeks, a monopoly on rights of audience in the higher courts'. He 'accept[ed] that the Government is determined to make these changes' but insisted it should not 'have the sole power to determine who should prosecute, who should defend...who shall appear in court and how cases shall be paid for'. Irvine was 'creating a huge amount of executive power, with no apparent means of testing it by judicial review'. Brennan refused to 'equate good standards with a restrictive practice. That's to put a premium on mediocrity.' The leader of the North Eastern Circuit called for a 'level playing field' in which solicitors were 'compelled to offer the defendant a choice of a solicitor advocate or barrister', 'compelled to instruct the barrister whenever the barrister offers a cost advantage', and 'prohibited from taking any share of the advocacy fee' when the case is not conducted in-house. The 'young Criminal Bar is feeling the pinch...meanwhile the Government is allowing some firms of solicitors to get rich at their expense'.[39]

Warning that the BC was 'devoting massive resources to its efforts to reduce the ambit of many sections' of the Access to Justice Bill (embodying Irvine's proposals), BACFI urged members to tell their MPs that expanded audience rights will 'help to create jobs and reduce costs for industry'. It ridiculed the 'prophets of doom' who predict that the changes will 'bring civilisation to the brink of virtual collapse'. Calling the BC and LS 'trade unions, actively campaigning to protect what they see as the interests of sections of their membership', BACFI asked: 'How can the ordinary citizen know whose interests are being protected by the professional rules these bodies make?'[40]

During the Committee stage Peers relitigated the issue of executive power. Because of 'the shift in focus from the needs of providers of legal services towards the needs of users', Lord Irvine refused to specify the number of lawyers on the LSC but accepted an amendment to ensure consumer representation. Insisting that 'Parliament is Supreme', he refused to preserve a veto by even a majority of the designated judges. In 1990 'the opponents of change thought [the veto] would prove an effective means of preventing any significant liberalization of rights of audience', and 'their hopes were not disappointed'. Lord Kingsland lost a division by 89 to 109.[41]

Lord Ackner noted that only 28 per cent of solicitors passed the 'not unduly onerous' civil test in 1995. The chief examiner found 'the quality of answers on professional conduct and ethics...very disappointing'. Lord

Mackay was concerned the Law Society would 'propose changes to the requirements of its higher courts qualifications, in order to encourage more solicitors to take up rights of audience' and 'might reduce the standard marginally or more than marginally'. Lord Thomas moved to freeze existing audience rights. Because the CPS 'will be paid less than the independent barrister' the quality 'will be less'. Denouncing these 'special pleadings by the Bar', Irvine called Thomas 'a barrister first and a Liberal second, a card-carrying member of the barristers' party, QC section. Bright and Cobden must be turning in their graves.' Thomas resented that his 'integrity has been attacked'. The CPS 'is not up to the kick and rush in the higher courts and appeal courts'.

Ackner moved to limit employed lawyers to serving their employers and employers' clients. Lord Borrie resisted, briefed by BACFI, which 'feels that it is not really represented by the Bar Council'. Although Lord Irvine did not wish to 'enable an insurance company, bank or supermarket for that matter—or indeed, what might be called a Virgin law shop—to provide professional legal services to the public', Lord Hacking saw 'no valid argument' for such 'a restrictive practice which everywhere else in the Bill my noble and learned friend is opposing'. Lord Kingsland moved to prevent the CPS from prosecuting serious cases.

In the stand part debate on the clause (clause 31) extending audience rights to employed lawyers, Ackner reiterated that 'standards inevitably would have to come down'. The accusations of restrictive practices were 'wholly unjustified... redolent of one of the unfortunate features of excessive power; namely, arrogance'. He detected 'considerable Treasury input'. Lord Hutchinson of Lullington asked whether Irvine viewed two Royal Commissions and Lord Ackner as 'irrational'. He accused Irvine of 'lower[ing] the level of debate' and 'mislead[ing] Members of the Committee'. Having retired fifteen years ago, he did 'not come to this House to peddle trade union trivialities'. 'Many restrictive practices are absolutely essential in any profession to ensure suitable and appropriate expertise.' 'Every criminal advocate knows that in-house lawyers—that is lawyers from the DTI... Inland Revenue... Customs & Excise—are clearly and fiercely partisan.' Irvine's reference to salaried judges 'almost descended into farce'. Lord Wigoder had encountered 'prosecuting solicitors who, in total defiance of the evidence, asked me to press for a conviction'. If they 'had been given rights of audience in our senior courts, the result would have been a lowering of the general standards'. Baroness Thornton mocked 'talk about maintaining standards and the protection of independence... whenever there is a proposal to make a procedure more democratic'. Irvine regarded 'the proposition as exorbitant that only the Bar can bring integrity to the prosecution process'. But the clause was negatived by 88 to 77.[42]

In the Report Stage two weeks later Lord Ackner sought to repeat his triumph by eliminating the clause (clause 30) giving solicitor advocates higher court audience rights, which would 'enable the Law Society to reduce its standards substantially in order to encourage the reluctant to qualify'. Lord Irvine noted that 'the 80-odd Conservative hereditary Peers who went into the Lobbies' against the previous clause 'had not even listened to the debate'. When Lord Ackner noted that Lord Mackay had opposed Clause 31, Lord Irvine called this 'the first time in 12 years in this House that I have heard him praise my noble and learned predecessor'. He compared Lord Ackner to a 'latter day Laocoön, declaring to the Bar, "I am still your friend", and the Bar replying timorously, "But Desmond...I do not really want to be your friend on this" '. 'The current position is a relic of the time when solicitors were thought of as second class legal citizens....' The clause was agreed.[43]

BACFI was 'amazed and dismayed'. Its chair found it 'a deeply unpleasant experience to hear myself and thousands of other employed lawyers being described as people who could not be trusted'. The LCD condemned the 'blatant restrictive practice'. 'It is insulting to employed lawyers to suggest that only barristers in private practice can bring integrity to the prosecution of cases.' The *Gazette* warned that the 'old guard' was 'deeply opposed to the breaking of the Bar's monopoly'. 'It would be a pity', said the *Solicitors Journal*, if 'a last-ditch stand' on audience rights 'were to be one of the last actions of the unreformed House of Lords'.[44]

Brennan applauded. 'We have warned that the American experience of public defenders is chilling....' The Lords Select Committee on Delegated Legislation had been 'sharply critical of the wide-ranging powers that the Bill would hand to the Lord Chancellor', including 'the constitutionally unprecedented power...to change the rules of independent legal professions, a power repeatedly and unsuccessfully sought by the pre-democracy apartheid governments of South Africa'. At the same time, he wrote employed barristers a 'Dear Colleague' letter claiming the BC 'fully accepts' they 'should be entitled to exercise equivalent rights of audience to those of employed solicitors' and was 'committed to preserving a united profession'. BACFI reminded members that the BC had sought to impose requirements 'which we believed would be difficult...to comply with and which were unreasonable and unfair'.[45]

Former BACFI chair Derek Wheatley QC reminded members that the Bar had opposed Mackay's original proposals, 'anxious to protect the interests of barristers in private practice, uncaring of the interests of... employed barristers', whom it treated as 'second class citizen[s]'. The BC's 'persistent objection to change' was a 'misconceived' 'protectionist measure' 'in conflict with the concept of freedom of competition now universally regarded as a cornerstone of a thriving economy'. Irvine recently had written to him criticizing the BC for 'too often see[ing] its task as being simply to defend the interests of barristers in private practice' and expressing dismay at 'the belief in the inherent lack of integrity of the employed Bar'. Brennan responded by expressing 'great despondency' that 'the antipathy and acrimony of yesteryear seems ingrained'. But he also warned the BACFI AGM that American house counsel suffered employer pressures. Nevertheless, the BC's own committee, chaired by Sir John Collyear, could see 'no need nor justification for any further restriction or rule governing practice as an employed barrister which does not apply to all practising barristers'. Although the Act entrusted employed barristers' audience rights to the BC, Irvine told BACFI he was ' "minded" to refer this matter to the Legal Services Consultative Panel if the BC cannot be persuaded to review this in the meantime'.[46]

In the Commons standing committee Nick Hawkins, a former BACFI chair (and Conservative spokesman), said that the BC did not support the Lords amendment. Gareth Thomas, a privately practising barrister, regretted the Council's 'previously dogged and vehement opposition'. Edward Garnier QC was 'disappointed that those of us who have lived most of our adult professional lives in the independent Bar should...think it clever or convenient to deprecate the profession that has sustained us'. 'There is a danger that to allow every barrister and solicitor to appear in our higher courts will lead to a down turn in quality' and 'inhibit people from coming to the Bar at a young age'. LCD Minister of State Geoff Hoon denounced the 'worst kind of restrictive practice', which offers 'no shred of benefit to the public'. It was 'redolent of an era when solicitors, let alone employed lawyers, were thought to be not quite gentlemen, not quite the sort of people who could be trusted to know how things are done, or which knife to use'. Dominic Grieve predicted the 'fusion that the Minister desires will come in by the back door'. 'Standards must be maintained.' Hoon called these objections 'the authentic voice of Conservatism'. When 'any major change is promoted...the reaction of certain members of the Bar is always, "This is the end of the Bar as we know it" '. Garnier heard 'all the tricoteuses at the bottom of the guillotine; let them knit away...it is a far, far better thing that I do'. The clause was restored, and the Report Stage agreed.[47]

When the Bill returned to the Lords, Ackner made a last stand, denouncing the 'quite monstrous attack on the profession...which has not sought to support what I am putting forward...because it knew from past experience that the matter would be treated as a trade union dispute between the two branches of the profession, which it is not'. But he surrendered, and the Access to Justice Act 1999 granted solicitors (including CPS and LSC employees) plenary rights of audience and to conduct litigation (subject to LS conditions) and barristers employed by a solicitors' firm the right to serve its clients. Irvine declared: 'We have ended once and for all restrictive practices in rights of audience'. But Brennan reiterated that 'the Bar will fight against any "more liberal" [higher court audience rights] regime if that means lowering standards. The consumer mantra of choice should not be allowed to mask the arrival of incompetent advocates into the market place.'[48]

Perhaps suffering Napoleonic delusions induced by the Euro Disneyland venue, President Robert Sayer advocated fusion at the Law Society's annual conference. 'Within five years, let there be one legal profession.' 'As we enter the new millennium, let us think the unthinkable.' 'The Bar is an anachronism. We stand for 90 per cent of lawyers. Who is the tail and who is the dog?' Tony Girling (a predecessor) hastened to reassure barristers: 'There will always be a place for an independent Bar'. The City of London Law Society felt 'the public needs to have some idea of what skill level they're dealing with'. The British Legal Association feared fusion would force small firms either 'to abandon litigation or pass their clients to the larger firms maintaining an advocacy department'. ILEX wanted to maintain the division. APIL found the proposal 'preposterous...at the moment'. Asking whether Sayer's brains had 'atrophied at the anticipation of...Space Mountain', the *New Law Journal* found his timing 'unfortunate, if not crass. He has probably set the prospects of a unified profession back for some period.' Declaring that 'many solicitors find Mr Sayer's proposal equally objectionable', the *Solicitors Journal* saw no 'real prospect of the planned creation of a statutory, structured fused profession'.

Echoing the predictable media gibes, the Bar called it 'a Mickey Mouse policy dreamt up in Disneyland'. Former chair Robert Owen QC dismissed it as 'headline grabbing stuff but far removed from reality. The divided profession exists because it works.' Brennan was even more contemptuous. 'The Bar Council has too busy an agenda to waste time promoting ideas which are complete non-starters.' In his final statement he declared 'there is no question of the profession becoming fused...the vast majority of solicitors do not agree with fusion'. Only one solicitor had qualified for audience rights under the relaxed standard.

But Austin Mitchell proposed to put blue plaques 'on the Inns of Court (RIP). Near this spot, bewigged lawyers known as barristers once earned lavish livings, graciously allowing the many to feed the few.' And Sayer insisted fusion 'would almost certainly [produce] greater efficiency and lowered costs'.

[W]e should aim for a legal system freed from restrictive practices and old boys— and old girls—networks. The Bar believes in tradition. It dominates all the major judicial appointments and wields a political influence in government circles out of all proportion to its size. As a result we have a system which does not reflect the society most of us live in and is remote and out of touch. Society deserves a modern relevant legal system from top to bottom. Solicitors are already there.

(This conveniently ignored solicitors' vigorous opposition throughout the 1990s to requests for rights of audience and to conduct litigation by patent agents, licensed debt practitioners, quantity surveyors, construction consultants, and legal executives.[49])

B. Direct Access

Just as solicitors responded to erosion of their conveyancing monopoly by seeking audience rights, so barristers reacted to the latter challenge by increasing direct access. Immediately after the Green Papers the Bar expanded direct access by accountants and surveyors in non-contentious matters. A year later the professional standards committee chair urged barristers to market themselves to other professions so they 'didn't have to go through the expensive middle-man—the solicitor'. But the strategy group persuaded the BC that direct access to lay clients would 'undermine the whole nature of the Bar and what it had to offer'. In response to this liberalization the Official Referees' Bar Association negotiated direct access to architects and civil engineers, the Local Government and Planning Bar Association to surveyors and town planners, and the Revenue Bar Association to the Institute of Chartered Accountants. But when the BC added the Institute of Electrical Engineers, LS President Mark Sheldon warned the BC annual conference that 'the more you compete with solicitors, the more solicitors are likely to respond by decreasing their current level of dependence on the Bar'. 'There is no solicitor who will really want to refer work to a barrister who might pinch his clients.' Speaking as a Linklaters senior partner, however, Sheldon reassured barristers: 'When we need them, we love to have them on our side. But we would hate to have them on our overheads.' A year later the BC rejected three direct access proposals (although the reasons were peculiar to each case). Chair Rowe told the AGM that 'direct access to the lay client is a move along the road to fusion and I am implacably against it'. He also opposed the right to conduct litigation: 'The boast of the Bar is that it is cheap; it does not maintain extensive support systems'.[50]

In January 1994 Neil Addison, newly elected to the Bar Council, challenged it 'to think—something it hasn't done for 50 years' and proposed direct access together with other reforms adding up to fusion: 'the "F" word of the profession'. The *New Law Journal* was predictably cool. BC chair Robert Seabrook QC charged its Policy Unit to 'think the unthinkable' (an unfortunate, and presumably unconscious, reference to Herman Kahn's provocation that the USA should contemplate nuclear war). '[T]he strengths of the Bar', said the unit's chair, James Munby QC, 'arise predominantly…from the fact that it is a specialist consultancy profession; the fact that referrals must usually be made through an intermediary is a secondary characteristic'. He recommended reviving the pre-1955 rule allowing lay clients direct access in non-contentious matters. The present rules were 'not satisfactory', 'have no obvious underpinning, in the sense of an underlying principle', and could easily be evaded by 'a post-box/back-sheet solicitor' and 'nominal in-house lawyers'. LS President Rodger Pannone raised the spectre of fusion if barristers repudiated their 'unique feature'. They 'will become second class solicitors if they try to offer a one-stop shop'.

Although three-quarters of barristers responding to the consultation favoured the proposal, the Policy Unit disavowed it. '[T]he strength and independence of the Bar can only survive for so long as we are a clearly defined separate and identifiable profession. Barristers should do barristers' work; they should not do solicitors' work.' Seabrook attributed the Council's overwhelming rejection (49–3) to barristers' determination to 'devote much more time to the actual practice of advocacy rather than administrative and routine tasks'. Pannone applauded the 'sensible decision'. Two months later the Bar Standards Review Body agreed that the Bar should 'remain a referral profession'; otherwise 'the two branches of the legal profession would become fused'.

Criticizing the 'obduracy' of the 'old guard', the *New Law Journal* predicted that fusion 'will come . . . no matter how much effort is made to keep the tide from coming in'. The *Evening Standard* attacked the 'wasteful and restrictive' practices of 'this baroque system, which contributes so substantially to the law's delay, is bad for the law and bad for the public'. The former chair of the 600-member Chancery Bar Association was 'disappointed' at 'the loss of an opportunity to enable us to be more competitive and also to provide a better service to clients'. 'Now that solicitors can obtain rights of audience in all courts, there seems no reason for hanging on to the rule.' The AWB warned that 'the Bar now faces competition on a scale from which it was always sheltered before. Until they are prepared to modify their restrictive working practices, barristers in independent practice run the risk of becoming marginalised.'[51]

Addison called the decision 'a kick in the teeth for the young Bar'. Because the Council was 'run by people who lack imagination and are incapable of producing any real change', he appealed over their heads to the AGM. Seabrook urged a high turnout to prevent 'a well organised lobby or self-interested group carrying a resolution'. The *New Law Journal* criticized the resolution's 'flabby drafting'. Addison's inflammatory rhetoric may have hurt his cause. 'The Bar is in many ways the last refuge for believers in the Stalinist concept of the planned economy.' It will die 'if it insists on entering the 21st century with 18th century wigs and 19th century restrictive practices'. Vice chair Peter Goldsmith QC attacked Addison's 'defeatist message' and urged the Bar not to 'rush to mimic solicitors'. Seabrook minimized solicitors' competitive threat: only 150 had acquired audience rights, and just 140 others were seeking them. Addison retorted provocatively: 'The Luftwaffe started off with only one bomber.' The resolution was lost by just five votes (69–77) and the request for a postal ballot by one.[52]

Perhaps in response, the Law Society advised solicitors to charge for advocacy referrals, including those to barristers. Having obtained counsel's opinion that this was unlawful, the BC considered complaining to the OFT and ACLEC. Seabrook declared that 'a most unsavoury market in advocacy services where people buy and sell briefs... can't possibly be in the public interest'. Within days, LS President Charles Elly denied the Society had any 'devilish plans to create in the advocacy market a structure of referral fees'.[53]

Addison's ally Rachel Brand resubmitted the resolution in 1995, calling herself a 'realist', not a 'crazed fusionist, nor merchant of doom, nor defeatist'. 'There is a public perception that the one-stop shop is more efficient....' Nearly 500 solicitor advocates soon would be qualified: 'Will the Bar wait until there are 2000 before amending its rules?' Goldsmith, now chair, warned: 'if we allow this package to be adopted then in ten years' time there will be no separate profession and no Bar Council'. 'We have not been fighting outside forces for six years to have the Bar destroy itself from within'. This time the proposal was lost overwhelmingly (58–179).[54]

The 1996 BC chair David Penry-Davey QC reaffirmed his opposition. There was 'an element of myth about the one-stop shopping for legal services'. Still, the Council approved the recommendation by Hilary Heilbron's strategy and policy committee of direct access by CABx in cases worth less than £10,000, which would make

access to justice more widely available at less cost, without at the same time undermining the essential referral nature of the profession. It would also provide a source of new work for the young Bar.... It introduces a level playing field to compete for this potentially large source of work.

This 'permissive measure' was designed not to 'ruffle people's feathers' or appear 'predatory' but rather to respond to 'compelling political realities' and 'adopt and capitalize on new opportunities'. An LAPG spokesman said: 'Half of me thinks "right, let them try". The other half of me thinks "Oh my god".' LS President Martin Mears called the proposal 'mad'.[55]

At the end of 1997 the Bar launched a pilot scheme offering direct access to eighteen chambers by Shelter, the Housing Action Centre, and five other advice agencies. Heilbron boasted 'the client and agency will have a much wider choice of lawyer and greater flexibility in how to handle a case. Costs will be reduced' and legal aid resources 'more effectively targeted... enabl[ing] those above the legal aid threshold, "middle-income Britain", to acquire the services of a lawyer at a price they can afford'. Lord Irvine was 'delighted'.

People, understandably, wonder whether it is really always necessary to instruct a solicitor when they want advice from a barrister and whether this is just another way of ensuring that, whatever else happens, that lawyers continue to make money.

He urged the Council to 'consider what other areas can be opened up to direct referral'. *The Times* praised the Bar for 'dismantl[ing] one of the last restrictive practices of the legal profession'. Although the LS head of legal aid policy expressed 'doubts' that agencies were 'competent to diagnose legal problems' and 'interest' that 'the Bar is so keen to compete with solicitors', the Society could not see 'any problem. After all, we are pressing to break down the Bar's monopoly of advocacy in the Crown Court so we cannot really object to this'.[56]

In the wake of Irvine's June 1998 consultation paper, the BC contracts working group urged that extending direct access to public employees and members of organizations like building societies and trade unions would achieve 'increased client choice', 'improved access to specialists', 'more cost-effective legal services', and 'maintenance of the Bar's competitive edge'. The Law Society denied any 'fear' but insisted that barristers 'provide the same level of consumer protection as solicitors if they are to be the first port of call'. Brennan favoured 'direct licensed access' (DLA) for trade unions, insurance companies, and health authorities. A barrister suggested that those instructing barristers take a one-week course. It 'might be opportune for the Bar in 1999 to adopt a twin track policy, i.e. to cede gracefully monopoly rights [of] audience with one hand while introducing DLA with the other'. Meanwhile the BC approved direct access by the Notaries Society and the Institute of Indirect Taxation.[57]

The Bar's response to the consultation paper proposed ' "direct lay access" in some non-contentious work, where the interposition of a solicitor or other professional may not be necessary, and may materially add to the lay client's expense'. There might be 'considerable advantages in having the advocate choose the person who is to prepare the case and conduct the litigation ... rather than the other way round'. It was essential 'to subject the nearly monopolistic rights of solicitors to conduct litigation to a due measure of competition' because 'the costs charged by solicitors for conducting litigation much exceed barristers' fees for advocacy'. Litigation 'could be valuable for the employed Bar' and should be authorized for CABx and other advice agencies. Courses could easily provide the necessary training.[58]

The BC launched BarDirect in July 1999, offering access to members of the Insolvency Practitioners Association, two probation services, the North Yorkshire Police, the Association of University Teachers, the Medical Protection Society, and the British Psychological Society. This 'recognises that there are significant areas of work in which the traditional two layered legal system ... may unnecessarily increase the costs'. When the LCD announced the Community Legal Service (see Chapter 8), the BC promised to 'play its full part' through BarDirect. The LAB contracted directly with two chambers for legal advice and representation, provoking the Law Society to complain that 'a number of good firms have applied'.[59]

C. Practising Arrangements

The BC responded to the Green Papers by creating a committee to 'remove all unnecessary restrictions on practice'. On its recommendation, the Council allowed barristers to visit solicitors' offices, practise anywhere after three years, and appear without a solicitor, made circuit or specialist association membership voluntary, and abolished dress rules. But the committee rejected BACFI's proposal that employed barristers be able to advise an employer's clients, declaring: 'any profession has the right to regulate its own profession in its own as well as in the public interest'. Indeed, the Council threatened to disbar four barristers (including the prominent tax specialist Reg Nock) who advised their accounting firms' clients. A dozen barristers considered appeals to the Lord Chancellor, DGFT, and European Court of Human Rights. The rule's arbitrariness was highlighted by Stanbrook & Hooper, whose thirty-seven barristers could be partners and serve clients directly in their six foreign offices but not in London. The Council compromised by allowing 'non-practising barristers' to advise an employer's clients if they relinquished their right to brief barristers or appear in court.[60]

Addison's 1994 BC AGM resolutions would have permitted partnerships and employment and had all lawyers start as solicitors before specializing (in advocacy, among other things). The *New Law Journal* endorsed both ideas. ACLEC's 1995 consultation paper embraced common vocational training, which LS President Rodger Pannone thought 'makes a great deal of sense'. But BC chair Robert Seabrook QC wanted 'full and open debate', James Munby's Policy Unit was opposed, and BC Treasurer Martin Bowley QC sneered: 'If you want one-stop shopping, go to Marks & Spencer, where you get good value for money, but not the best'. *The Times* had expected the Green Papers' 'most significant casualty would have been the professional distinction between barristers and solicitors'. Five years later 'the belief that the divided profession is living on borrowed time—with only the conservativism of the Bar as its scaffolding—has gathered ground'. '[T]he politics of Fortress Bar has ensured that reform is only possible by circumnavigation.' Declaring the divided profession 'to put it bluntly, more expensive', it deplored the 'waste of public money'.

Sir Frederick Lawton, a retired Lord Justice of Appeal and former chair of the Lord Chancellor's Advisory Committee on Legal Education, proposed common training and seven to ten years' experience prior to specialization in advocacy. The 60,000-member Federation of Small Businesses urged Lord Mackay to encourage fusion. 'We can't afford this eighteenth century legal system. If the Bar won't reform its code of conduct then it should be excluded from the legal aid scheme.' LS President Charles Elly agreed with Lawton. But Addison's proposals lost by increasing margins in 1994 and 1995.[61]

In March 1995, however, the Labour Party's National Policy Forum approved *Access to Justice: Labour's proposals for regenerating the justice system*, which questioned 'the whole structure of the legal profession and whether there is a need any more for a distinction between barristers and solicitors'. While rejecting fusion, it endorsed barrister partnerships and direct access and promised to refer 'every aspect of the operations of the legal profession' to the MMC. Author Paul Boateng said the party was 'committed to reform and will not hesitate to legislate'. He told the Society of Labour Lawyers the party would treat both professional organizations 'just like any other trade union'. The Law Society endorsed 'Labour's holistic approach', but the Bar Council invoked 'the public interest in favour of an independent Bar', which 'did not emerge by accident or as a result of restrictive practice'.[62]

In April 1996 ACLEC recommended common professional legal studies. Lord Mackay expressed reservations; he had 'never favoured fusion' but only 'flexibility around the edges'. When Sir Thomas Bingham became Lord Chief Justice two months later he observed that 'a large body of responsible middle-of-the-road opinion...regards the legal profession as riddled with anachronistic conventions and privileges'. A year later, however, chair Robert Owen QC reassured the Bar AGM that 'fusion is no longer an issue...the vast majority of solicitors do not want it'. Indeed, information technology might render 'much of the traditional function of the lawyer, particularly the solicitor...redundant'.[63]

If the Bar successfully repelled the solicitors' challenge, it continued to suffer internal dissension. In 1997 the Council adopted a recommendation by its working party on the employed Bar requiring non-practising barristers to use that stigmatizing title and prohibiting them from appearing in any court or tribunal, giving legal advice (even on a *pro bono* basis) without being insured (which the Bar Mutual Indemnity Fund refused to do), or drafting any formal legal document. The AGM overwhelmingly defeated a motion to overturn the ban. Dr Peter Gray, the mover (and founder of the Employed and Non-Practising Bar Association), urged non-practising barristers to support the Lord Chancellor's proposals to cut legal aid costs by diverting money to law centres and alternative dispute resolution. ACLEC warned the BC ban would deny 'advocacy rights enjoyed by ordinary citizens'. Although the LCD required the BC to seek ACLEC approval, the BC defiantly adopted the ban, then claimed existing rules had the same effect, and finally submitted it to ACLEC, which found that the ban 'runs counter to the statutory objectives'. Although the 1998 AGM defeated ENPBA's resolution to overturn the ban (by 30–43), it told members 'you are not obliged to comply with it'. The BC Professional Conduct Committee continued to maintain 'it would take action against non-practising barristers who had exercised rights of audience without a waiver'.[64]

D. Silk and the Bench

The previous chapter presented mounting criticism of the unrepresentativeness of silks and judges. The selection process was particularly vulnerable: an anonymous barrister denounced 'favouritism and the misuse of privilege'; the 1995 Bar AGM (by 82 votes to 36) expressed 'grave concern'; and LS President Rodger Pannone declared that 'current practice owes nothing to the principles of defining quality'. A BC Working Party declared 'some outward indication of an individual's achievement and career progression' was 'an almost universal aspect' of 'professional work'. Silk had 'supreme importance' as 'a means of identification...of those practitioners of outstanding ability'. Without 'an objective indicator of ability, the perception of who comprised the front rank might owe more to a person's public relations skills or extrovert character....' 'There is a real desire among silks to live up to their silk gowns and to lead by example.' It 'carries a responsibility to take on certain matters of public service....' The criticism that silk 'increases the level of fees and therefore costs' was not 'justifiable' because 'it is a commercial truth that the members of the perceived front rank of any profession are always able to command higher fees....' Judges, Council officials, circuit leaders, and specialist bar association chairs 'are asked to give their perception of the need for new silks in their fields'; but this 'does not itself govern the number of successful applications'. '[A]lthough there has been no policy to restrict the number of appointed silks to a particular percentage, in fact the practice of successive Lord Chancellors has meant that silks have for some years represented about 10% of the Bar as a whole.' The Working Party opposed selection by the Bar because of the 'enormous' cost (£200,000) and the risk of creating 'a public perception of the Bar...[as] a cosy professional clique handing out recognition—and a concomitant excuse for increasing fees—to each other'. Employed barristers should remain ineligible because silk was 'essentially a functioning rank'. So should a solicitor-advocate who 'provides advocacy services only to the firm which employs him or of which he is a partner'.

Once solicitors gained full audience rights, however, they were furious when Lord Mackay invited only 'barristers in private practice' to apply for the 1994 silk list. Although he corrected this the next year, the LCD considered only those with five years' experience. The Law Society questioned 'the present practice of taking the opinion of judges and senior barristers rather than users of legal services'. The *Solicitors Journal* criticized this 'strange system' and urged 'a more open and objective competition'. Calling the rejection of all five solicitor candidates 'disappointing', the *Gazette* declared: 'In the interests of achieving greater consumer choice—the principal aim behind the award of extended advocacy rights to solicitors—the system of selecting QCs must be overhauled'.[65]

LS President Tony Girling was 'delighted' by the appointment of the first two solicitor QCs a year later but retained 'serious doubts about whether the silk system is of continuing relevance in a modern justice system'. It should not be a requirement for solicitor appointment to the higher courts. SAHCA defended the distinction but criticized the selection process. Later that year Lord Irvine made both solicitor silks deputy High Court judges, seeking to 'open up the ranks of the higher judiciary'.[66]

At the beginning of 1998 the Adam Smith Institute published a call for abolition by Peter Reeves (a solicitor who, twelve years earlier, had prematurely advocated fusion).

The profession in effect sets up a price ring which raises legal costs.... [W]ithout the title of 'silk', reputations would be gained or lost by performance, and a free market in advocacy would generally prevail, with all barristers and solicitors competing equally. This would control costs, and save the taxpayer money in legal aid cases.

Condemning QCs' 'excessive' legal aid fees, the Law Society called for 'a proper analysis, including an economic one, of the whole system'. The Bar public affairs committee chair (naturally a QC) retorted that silk 'is a recognition of performance and ability in exactly the same way as the appointment of a hospital consultant'. The Attorney-General and Solicitor-General (always QCs) praised the 'widespread consultation'. But when that year's list included just one solicitor, the Law Society again attacked silks' 'unjustified level of fees' and questioned 'whether the QC system should continue to exist in its current form'. Employed barristers also complained about extreme underrepresentation.[67]

In his Chancery Bar Association lecture several months later Mr Justice Lightman attacked silk as not 'necessary or even valuable', a 'licence to print money...the occasion and pretext for a mark-up in fees'. He condemned 'extravagant fees': briefs of £350,000 or more and refreshers of £2,000 a day or more, far 'beyond the range reasonably affordable by ordinary litigants'. Silks and juniors received dramatically different amounts 'out of public funds' for 'the same work'. The numerical quotas also 'support the fee levels'. 'One distinguished silk recently expressed a sense of grievance at a newspaper article which attributed to him an income of

£1 million a year. "How can you say that? I earn more than twice that figure".' The 'privilege of sitting in court in the row in front of juniors...is calculated to give litigants the impression that silks are closer to the "ear" of the judge and are treated by him or her with greater respect'. Silk was 'a form of patronage which can make or break careers'.

The Bar discounted such criticism by a Chancery judge whose 'experience is based on a very small area of legal work involving major plcs and banks' and had himself enjoyed the benefits of silk. David Pannick QC said QC earnings were 'modest' by the standards of 'any Premier League footballer, rock musician, or director of a successful business'. It was 'curious' that instant fortune was acceptable through the lottery but it was 'shameful to be well remunerated for the hard work and effort necessary to reach, and remain at, the head of a demanding profession'. This 'highly competitive market' allowed no 'undue economic exploitation'.[68]

Six months after Lightman's blast, Labour backbencher Andrew Dismore tabled an early-day motion to abolish silk, enlisting eighty-two MPs in three weeks. If it was a kite mark, as the Bar claimed, 'there must be proper mechanisms for monitoring it'. 'Once appointed, [silks] can go on until they are 90.' The annual selection cost taxpayers £60–80,000. (The Bar promptly offered to pay.) When Sir John Lea pointed to the 'far greater need for a system to keep MPs up to scratch', especially those who 'could not make the grade as lawyers', Dismore (a solicitor) retorted that MPs were 'elected through an open, competitive procedure', while 'QCs are appointed from second-hand information based on secret references'. Alan Mackinnon rejoined that QCs were subject to the 'simplest' test, failure to get instructions, whereas a 'sitting MP in a safe seat seems far more secure'. Silk was attacked as a 'self-serving designation' by solicitor Benedict Birnberg and a 'market-rigging exercise' by LAG. As the 1999 selection approached, Dismore reiterated his criticism that 'double manning, theoretically abolished years ago, remains rife'. Fees 'would make a premier footballer blush'. Why did the Queen appoint counsel but not 'accountants or plumbers'? Many silks earned more from public funds than judges. 'And, unlike doctors, if they botch a case, they are largely immune to being sued.' If silk were retained, the 'old boy network' should be replaced by the UK Accreditation System.

Appointing just one solicitor (who had been a barrister for seventeen years) from the eight applicants, Irvine defended silk as 'a kite mark of quality', declaring that 'every profession has a major professional staging point' and the selection process was thorough, scrupulous, impartial, sound, efficient, and fair.

During Commons consideration of the Access to Justice Bill the Government accepted Dismore's proposal to make applicants pay for the selection process (estimated at £120,000/year). Dismore also moved to abolish QCs or alternatively publish applicants' names, consider past and require future *pro bono* service, and appoint to a five-year renewable term. The average income of the most recent appointees was £250,000, and one earned £550,000. Dismore objected to the fact that QCs sat in the front row, got to use a lectern, and wore different dress. 'The QC system has more in common with the application procedure to join a gentleman's club in Piccadilly or the Marylebone cricket club [*sic*]....' Dismore also moved amendments to require leave of court for a QC or two counsel, based on a finding that it 'does not constitute substantial unfairness to any other party'. LCD Minister of State Geoff Hoon retorted that Dismore had 'not so far proposed that the number of litigators should be similarly limited', and the Woolf reforms gave judges 'considerable powers to pre- scribe the nature of the use of advocates'. Hoon expressed 'considerable sympathy' for Dismore's motion that costs disregard silk, but 'there already exist sufficient powers to cure the problem'.[69]

Although Gareth Williams QC had equated the system with 'the Franz Kafka school of business management' when he was BC chair in 1992, David Pannick QC now claimed 'decisions are no longer made by refer- ence to irrelevant factors' and higher fees were inevitable 'in a market economy' where the 'best barristers will be in greater demand'. The *New Law Journal* condemned 'this annual self-congratulation', which rewarded 'faces [that] have fitted socially', and proposed the 'almost faultless idea' that all barristers of twelve years' Call without a major blot on their repu- tations should become QCs.[70]

Encouraged by the publicity his first attack had attracted, Dismore tabled another early-day motion, signed by more than 100 MPs, calling for a Judicial Appointments Commission. The Opposition spokesperson on constitutional affairs concurred, urging American-style hearings before a committee of both Houses. Launching her timely book on *The New Judiciary*, LSE law lecturer Kate Malleson endorsed a commission. The *Solicitors Journal* denounced mere 'tinkering with the system, when what is needed is a complete overhaul'. 'The Lord Chancellor might even be required to share the ultimate decision with the President of the Law Society and a distinguished layperson'. Shortly after the *Guardian* deleted QC from names (only to reverse itself two weeks later), Lord Irvine appointed Sir Leonard Peach to review the appointment of QCs and judges.[71]

But two months later, unwilling to await his report, the Law Society announced its boycott of 'secret soundings'. The Lord Chancellor 'regu- larly fails to acknowledge that solicitors can be appointed'. Silk constructed 'an artificial market for experienced advocates with the intention of creat- ing scarcity and raising fees' and should be abolished. The *Gazette* endorsed abolition of the 'elitist club patting its members on the back and reaping financial reward in the bargain'. At 'the dawn of the 21st century, a system which effectively manipulates the market for professional services cannot be justified'. After the Woolf reforms 'the natural stamping ground for experienced lawyers with case management skills' was not the Bar but the 'far richer recruitment seam' of solicitors.

'Old traditions die hard', said the *Financial Times*, 'and nowhere more so than in the sheltered world of the legal profession'. Created in the sixteenth century, silk was 'looking outdated'. Irvine 'should be asking the more radical question of whether QCs are needed at all'. The 'rigid two-tier system . . . distorts the market for experienced lawyers, artificially inflating the price of those who have crossed the barrier. . . .' 'If QCs did not exist, would we choose to invent them?' asked the *Independent*. 'It seems unlikely'. Writing in the *Express*, solicitor Anthony Julius criticized Irvine's 'commitment to legal reform' as 'always second to his commitment to retain his own power of patronage'. 'Like the nobility of Imperial Russia, each rank has distinct powers and privileges', which 'adds to the expense'.

The Law Society invoked the guidelines of the Commission for Public Appointments, 'which require transparency, accountability, equality and openness'. It complained to the Peach Commission that the proportion of solicitor circuit judges actually declined from 1995 to 1999 and the proportion of solicitor recorders and High Court judges remained a woeful 10 and 1 per cent. The Lord Chancellor invited only barristers to apply for district judgeships and QCs to nominate members of their chambers for silk. At a Law Society debate Michael Mansfield QC thought silk belonged on jockeys and compared secret soundings to McCarthyism. Dismore agreed they 'plumb the depths of private prejudice'. Martin Mears objected to favouritism of barristers. 'There can hardly be a practising litigation solicitor who has not . . . instructed a QC who turned out to be an expensive and mediocre windbag.' Lord Steyn of Swafield, a Lord of Appeal, thought there was a 'powerful argument' that the BC should select QCs and supported a judicial appointments commission. Channel Four broadcaster Jon Snow called the process 'offensive nonsense' fuelling a 'public perception of elitism'.

BC chair Dan Brennan QC asked whether this was 'the beginning of a campaign for mediocrity and the abandonment of valuable traditions'. 'There is no other country in the world that doesn't somehow mark excellence in the legal profession.' The Council called silk 'synonymous with independence and investigative skill', although a straw poll at the annual conference found that a substantial majority wanted to change the process of appointing QCs and judges.

But the LCD assured the Bar the Government had 'no intention' of abolishing silk. And though Irvine agreed that the Bar's 'greatest future challenge' was the 'charge of exclusivity', he praised the 'beauty' and 'thoroughness' of the judicial selection system. Sir Leonard followed the Lord Chancellor's cues. Silk would remain, though applicants would be chosen for competence as advocates and have no advantage in judicial appointments. A commission would monitor 'procedures and act as an ombudsman for disappointed candidates'. Deploring this 'wasted opportunity for real reform', the Law Society extended its boycott.[72]

E. Razing the Temple?

The struggles over rights of audience and to conduct litigation, direct access, practising arrangements, silk, and the bench were classic turf battles—what Abbott calls competition over jurisdiction.[73] Just as solicitors reacted to the erosion of their conveyancing monopoly (discussed in the next chapter) by displaying interest in advocacy, so barristers responded to that threat by invading the solicitors' domain—access to clients. The AWB and Chancery Bar Association made such tit-for-tat explicit. The Bar Council promoted direct access as allowing barristers to choose solicitor-litigators rather than solicitors to choose barrister-advocates.[74] Even after the Bar lost its monopoly it sought to elevate barriers for solicitor-advocates (just as both branches had done for entry): formal education, apprenticeship, experience, and examinations. Solicitors replied that barristers should meet the same criteria for advocacy and jump additional hurdles before dealing with lay clients. Angered by effective exclusion from silk, the Law Society boycotted 'secret soundings'. Many of these controversies also implicated status, which was associated with distance from clients, who attended on whom, higher court advocacy, eligibility for the bench, and of course modes of dress (wigs, silk gowns), address ('non-practising barrister', QC, 'my learned friend'), precedence (first, second, or third row in the courtroom), and clubability (exclusion from robing rooms, Inns dining).

The Bar displayed the same intransigence it had shown toward the Green Papers. Far from thinking the unthinkable (as Seabrook charged Munby), it defended the indefensible. It shamelessly advanced transparent rationalizations: the grant of silk enhanced quality and encouraged public service; that QCs were always 10 per cent of privately practising barristers was mere coincidence. Robert Owen sneered that there might be 'valid reasons' for belief in the inferiority of solicitors, whose low pass rates in the examination for audience rights showed that 'advocacy is best conducted by full-time advocates'. Martin Bowley invidiously compared solicitor advocates to Marks & Spencer, whose goods were cheap but 'not the best'.[75] (Were there overtones of anti-Semitism?) The Bar cheered victories certain to be reversed, like the House of Lords amendment denying audience rights to employed lawyers. It constantly declared the war won—and over.

It even sought to turn back the clock: elimination of all state prosecutors, imposition of the cab-rank rule on litigators, prohibition on advocacy by a solicitor whose firm had litigated the case, disbarment of barristers who advised their employers' clients. The restrictive practices it 'voluntarily' relinquished (under imminent threat) involved either intraprofessional competition (advertising, practising arrangements, circuit and specialist association membership) or trade-offs of status for income (visiting solicitors' offices, appearing without solicitors).

This adamantine resistance infuriated critics. Government had shown its determination to save money as early as 1986 through the legal aid scrutiny and creation of the CPS. As Chancellor, Lamont expressed impatience at the glacial progress toward audience rights for employed lawyers. Both Conservative and Labour Governments saw the Bar as a politically useful whipping boy. Labour backbenchers Austin Mitchell and Andrew Dismore pushed the Government to do more. ACLEC split along the same lines as the Marre Committee: barristers and judges against the rest. (Judges had seriously compromised their claimed impartiality by intemperately attacking the Green Papers and Lord Mackay.) Media criticism became unanimous and even more acerbic. The Bar lost powerful allies: the Attorney-General (who had to implement the Conservative Government's policy); the DGFT (another silk). Left and right converged when the Adam Smith Institute published Peter Reeves's assault on silk (sounding strangely like Paul Boateng). Even senior judges were divided (if the bench remained united against Irvine's power grab). By the end of the decade influential voices like Thwaites, Pannick, and Collyear acknowledged the inevitability of change.

The Bar's strategy backfired badly. Although few solicitors actually wanted to exercise audience rights, opposition provoked the Law Society to push harder. Solicitors and employed barristers smarted from accusations of incompetence, failure in private practice, insufficient independence, and unethical behaviour, and resented exclusion from silk and the bench. The Law Society felt abused and ignored by ACLEC, the designated judges, and the Lord Chancellor (in grants of silk and judicial appointments). Society officials called ACLEC's behaviour a 'scandal', accused it of 'prevarication' and 'evasion', and assailed the process as 'stultifying and debilitating': 'we demean ourselves by arguing with' such a 'disaster'.

Just as the Conservative Government pitted the branches against each other in 1989, so the Labour Government exploited divisions within the Bar in 1998. Although barristers are more cohesive than solicitors because they are fewer and more localized and homogeneous (by origin and function), the battle over audience rights severely tested their unity. Because barristers depend far more than solicitors on advocacy and about half are employed (compared with less than a sixth of solicitors), employed lawyers' audience rights posed a much more serious economic threat to the Bar. Some employed barristers harboured grievances about their treatment by chambers and clerks. All felt neglected and disrespected by the Bar Council, which compounded the insult by vigorously opposing their audience rights (while the Law Society proclaimed the unity of solicitors). But the Bar Council (unlike the Law Society) effectively disenfranchised employed lawyers (see Chapter 10). Furthermore, employed barristers were divided and marginalized. BACFI repudiated Addison (the Crown Prosecutor champion) and was highly suspicious of the maverick ENPBA (which had few members). And neither non-practising nor employed barristers had nearly as much economic interest in higher court audience rights as high-street solicitors had in conveyancing. But once employed solicitors gained audience rights, the Bar felt obliged to seek them for employed barristers (partly for status reasons). At the same time, it seemed prepared to sacrifice automatic audience rights for newly qualified barristers in order to justify high barriers against solicitor advocates. Direct access also pitted specialist bar associations (which sought it) against a Bar Council (which feared it was a step toward fusion), and younger barristers eager for clients against older barristers who enjoyed established referral relationships with solicitors' firms.

If the outcome of the decade-long 'Bar Wars' is partly attributable to the electoral strength of both Conservative and Labour Governments and eroding judicial support, it also is related to changes in the power of rhetoric. Reformers were armed with irrefutable logic. Solicitors already appeared in magistrates' courts, which could hear the vast bulk of criminal cases. Government could expand audience rights by modifying jurisdictions (although curtailing jury trials gave the Bar disinterested allies: the Law Society, LAG, and Justice). Barristers gained and lost such rights instantaneously as they moved between employment and private practice. Privately practising barristers were free from many restrictions when dealing with foreign clients. James Munby was prepared to let the Bar's survival depend on its claims of specialist expertise.

More important than logic (since restrictive practices are never logical) was the emerging hegemony of laissez faire. The Law Society could invoke the powerful trope of consumer choice (although this strengthened the argument for corporate conveyancing and multidisciplinary partnerships: see Chapter 6; and solicitors could not decide whether they wanted to abolish silk or share in the spoils). The Society even flirted with charging for referrals to advocates. Holland analogized ACLEC's protection of the Bar to the Iron Curtain; Addison accused the Bar of Stalinism. Adopting many of the Society's criticisms, the Government claimed to speak on behalf of consumers (although its interests were hardly identical). Mr Justice Lightman was sharply critical of the oligopoly of specialist sets and clerks' market power and collusion. BACFI now made common cause with the CPS to end 'unjustified restrictions' on employed lawyers in order to promote 'access to justice' (although none of these employed lawyers represented individuals). Reformers appealed to the common sense contention that one lawyer was cheaper than two to justify solicitors' audience rights and direct access to barristers. These arguments carried particular force when taxpayers were footing the bill (especially for high-priced QCs, who cost the government more than judges). Market enthusiasts even maintained (dubiously) that competition enhanced quality (ignoring the informational asymmetries that create professions).

The Bar contested market rhetoric. 'It is idle to speak of a free market or market forces. Sometimes all that the market wants or offers is a second rate service to those who cannot pay privately.' Seabrook declared that 'a most unsavoury market in advocacy services where people buy and sell briefs... can't possibly be in the public interest'. Hallett criticized the Government for trying to save money and warned against a 'free for all in the courts'. The Bar defended silk with arguments that had been discredited for professional privileges generally: QCs displayed 'a real desire... to live up to their silk gowns and to lead by example' and 'take on certain matters of public service'. The BC even claimed the 'right to regulate its own profession in its own... interest'.

Unable to avoid engaging adversaries on this terrain, the Bar maintained it was cheaper (but then it had nothing to fear), called itself the most competitive profession (internally!), protested it neither enjoyed nor sought a monopoly, and denied it was a trade union protecting its turf (although clerks candidly mourned the loss of business). Direct access reduced double-manning and hence cost and increased client choice. (A one-week course conferred the necessary skills, although the Bar derided solicitors' much more demanding advocacy training.) The Bar claimed (falsely) that every country marks 'excellence in the legal profession'; Lord Irvine agreed: 'every profession has a major professional staging point'. Silk was simply a reward for 'hard work and effort', recognition of having reached the 'head of a demanding profession'; it offered the best information about quality, which 'inevitably' cost more 'in a market economy' where the 'best barristers will be in greater demand'. David Pannick QC misleadingly compared silks with athletes, entertainers, and entrepreneurs (none of whom depends on state certification). Such defences opened silk to criticism that it constructed a 'rigged', 'artificial', 'distorted', 'manipulated' market by 'intention[ally]... creating scarcity', conferring a 'licence to print money' and 'inflating the price' in order to 'reap financial reward'. And they intensified pressure to make selection more meritocratic, transparent, and continuous, create finer gradations, and eliminate the 10 per cent quota. The Bar denounced the CPS as a monopoly, making the DPP promise to limit the proportions and kinds of cases handled in-house (but why should the state be denied a choice of advocates?). The Bar accused solicitors of monopolizing litigation while warning high-street firms that the City would lock up the best barristers (presumably to satisfy a demand for in-house advocacy). The Bar even argued (in defiance of economic logic) that competition would increase prices because of solicitors' higher overheads. But BACFI, whose members were immersed in commerce, more credibly invoked 'full, free and open competition' as 'fundamental to the existence of a healthy business community'.

At the same time, the Bar insisted on the state's indispensable role in correcting market failures. Barristers resisted audience rights by borrowing solicitors' arguments against lenders and estate agents tying in conveyancing to urge rules against litigators tying in advocacy (as SAHCA openly planned to do). But its own proposals that litigators inform clients of their choices or even abstain from advocacy exposed the arbitrariness and potential inefficiency of state intervention. The Bar denied the market's ability to provide trustworthy information about quality: without 'an objective indicator of ability, the perception of who comprised the front rank might owe more to a person's public relations skills or extrovert character'.

Acknowledging the weakness of its market arguments, the Bar turned to others. Brennan invoked 'valuable traditions' (to justify silk); but critics noted that another 'tradition'—solicitor referral in non-contentious matters—was mandated only in 1955. Few outsiders still wanted to protect beginning barristers from competition (though government did argue that full audience rights were essential for the CPS to recruit and retain lawyers). Although the Bar rallied its own troops (and some judges) with the spectre of fusion, others simply cheered (even *The Times*). Both the Law Society and ACLEC favoured common entry followed by specialization— little different from the 1971 Ormrod report or Sayer's 1999 bombshell.[76] (But Sayer was characteristically inept, deriding the Bar as 'anachronistic' and arguing that the solicitor dog should wag a barrister tail.)

The Bar's resistance weakened the claim that its privileges reflected unique competence. It repeatedly drew misleading analogies to medical specialization (dental, orthopaedic and neurosurgeon, hospital consultant); but all doctors train together before some acquire formal specialist credentials. Furthermore, this argument could not be used against audience rights for the CPS (or proposed public defenders), who were accused of specializing too much. The Bar could, and did, inveigh against the CPS's numerous failings: understaffing, turnover, high caseloads, poor quality (perhaps worsened by bureaucratic incentives), failures to prosecute or convict, low morale, and disrespect for management. The Service was further embarrassed by the forced resignations of DPPs Green and Mills, the muzzling of Addison, and a constant stream of criticism from Parliament, government commissions, the media, the FDA, and conservative think-tanks. But this did little to advance the Bar's cause since the Service's problems were attributable to the Government's reason for wanting to replace private practitioners with salaried employees—cost control. And private practitioners also were vulnerable to quality criticisms: late returns of briefs, the substitution of less competent counsel, and notorious miscarriages of justice.

The Bar invoked the cab-rank rule, which had done good service in blunting the Green Papers; but more commentators, now including some barristers, conceded the ease of evasion and the temptations of private practitioners (notably Treasury Counsel) towards partisan loyalty. The Bar's trump card, however, was 'independence'—a protean concept it also invoked to oppose partnership and employment (while conveniently ignoring the threat of direct access to independence). The argument (never clearly stated) apparently was that advocates must preserve distance from their clients in order to meet conflicting obligations to adversaries and the legal system. Silk was 'synonymous with independence'. House counsel were too close to their employers and Crown Prosecutors to the state. (Few drew the logical inference that only private practitioners should prosecute.) Public defenders, by contrast, were insufficiently loyal to clients. That inconsistency exposed the fundamental ambiguity of the proper degree of independence. Furthermore, the Bar offered no evidence that employment fatally compromised independence. Job security might actually enhance it; and many private practitioners depended heavily on particular solicitors' firms or the CPS.

The Bar upped the ante by insisting that its privileges were not mere 'historical accidents' but had acquired constitutional stature. Just as ACLEC became the lightning rod in 1989, so Lord Irvine's arrogation of the power to make and change professional rules outraged Bar and bench in 1998. (He already had gained notoriety by lavishly redecorating his apartment and making crony appointments.) The hyperbolic innuendos about fascist and communist totalitarianism a decade earlier reappeared in Sydney Kentridge's equally irrelevant invocation of his experience under apartheid. The Bar took every opportunity to associate proposed reforms with alleged American atrocities: excessive zeal by state prosecutors, neglect and incompetence by public defenders, bumbling by house counsel 'oncers' (a phrase unknown in the United States). These distractions may have helped keep the judges on side, but they won no points with others.

The buzz words suffusing this controversy express a dramatic and rapid shift in fundamental values. Competition, the market, choice, consumers, efficiency, and value for money were good. The closed shop, restrictive practices, monopoly, the monolithic state, strangleholds, entry barriers, price rings, curbs, double manning, and market rigging were bad. Change (especially radical, even at breakneck speed), originality, flexibility, shake-ups, relevance, and modern were good. Reformers were lauded for taking a battering ram to the Temple or a broom to the stables, hammering a nail in the coffin, or opening the windows to let in a long overdue breath of fresh air. Tradition, conservatism, rigidity, delay, complacency, pomposity, snobbery, a sheltered world, the status quo, relics, and inertia were bad; so was anything anachronistic, antiquated, archaic, outdated, crusty or irrel-evant. The twenty-first century was in, the wigs and wing collars of the seventeenth, eighteenth, and nineteenth were out. The public interest was good; fat cats, special pleading, and interest groups bad; so were selfish, vested, entrenched, special, and sectional interests. Openness, objectivity, transparency, and accountability were good; old-boy networks, the nod and wink, McCarthyism, secrecy, and patronage were bad.

Despite a decade of resolute resistance, most of the Bar's restrictive practices were abolished. Solicitors and employed barristers gained full audience rights. Although privately practising barristers could not enter partnership or employment, employed barristers could retain audience rights and advise their firms' clients. Private practitioners could offer direct access to more clients. Although the selection of QCs and judges remained virtually unchanged, political pressures and barristers' reluctance to accept judicial appointments will swell the number of solicitor judges. Because restrictive practices are unavoidably arbitrary, successful challenges to one threaten the entire edifice.

Both opponents and advocates sought rhetorical advantage either by depicting these changes as apocalyptic (the 'disappearance...of the inde-pendent Bar') or declaring premature victory. Irvine boasted the 1999 Act 'ended once and for all restrictive practices in rights of audience'. Sayer wanted to take over the Bar; Owen expected technology to make solicitors obsolete. Yet social institutions and habitual behaviours change slowly.[77] Barristers used their economic leverage to preserve the status quo, threat-ening to refuse briefs from solicitors who engaged in advocacy (just as soli-citors threatened not to brief barristers who accepted direct access). Judges favoured barristers over solicitor-advocates. QCs appeared with juniors decades after repeal of the two-counsel rule. Few lawyers seized the new opportunities. The Bar chose not to apply to conduct litigation. It was cautious about allowing direct access, and most barristers were reluctant to offer it (because it required changing practice arrangements and endan-gered the Bar's claim to superior status). Although some City firms sought a competitive edge by publicizing their advocacy competence, most soli-citors were uninterested: they had enough better-paying work (though this may change), feared judicial prejudice and barrister condescension, and would have to modify staffing patterns and client interaction. Both high-street and City firms wanted continued access to the Bar. *Plus ça change....*

6   Controlling Competition

[H]aving got them into the office [solicitors] may either recommend their own property selling service or a pet estate agent, perhaps not you. [National Association of Estate Agents]

Either we do it; or the estate agents do it.... Clients are stitched up by agents time after time and solicitors are powerless to do anything about it because they are under the agents' thumb. [Robert Sayer, LS Vice President]

[Buyers should start house hunting with a solicitor, who] will be able to negotiate lower selling fees with estate agents. Let's see how estate agents like having *their* fees dictated by others! [John Edge, solicitor champion]

Panels are not primarily about increasing the amount of work done by the profession as a whole [but about] taking the work away from some of those who do it now (the generalists) and giving it to others (the specialists). [Peter Watson-Lee, LS Council member]

[At a time of] greater focus on quality by consumers [the Law Society] should be jumping on the bandwagon with more specialist panels. [Its capitulation to] pressure from some quarters to spread the work around [was] yet another instance where the Society's duty to the public and its trade union role work against each other. [National Consumer Council]

Although conveyancing does not define solicitors as advocacy does the Bar, it did produce about half their income for much of the twentieth century.[1] Solicitors became conveyancers almost by accident. After successfully challenging the Scriveners' Company's monopoly in the City of London in 1760, solicitors still shared the market with them, licensed conveyancers, barristers, and laypeople. When Prime Minister Pitt sought to raise the stamp duty on practising certificates and articles in 1804 to pay for the Napoleonic Wars, solicitors demanded and readily obtained a monopoly over conveyancing (though the Bar Council did not unambiguously concede for another 100 years). The Society repelled a Bar Council foray on behalf of employed barristers in 1949. Solicitors also contained efforts by the National House Owners' Service to encourage DIY conveyancing. To preserve its members' role in conveyancing, the Society delayed land registration for many years, with the result that little more than a third of homes were registered as late as 1984. That Michael Joseph sold 44,000 copies of his virulent attack on conveyancing (self-published in 1976) indicates the level of public dissatisfaction. Nevertheless, the 1979 Royal Commission unconditionally endorsed the monopoly, urging that the newly appointed provincial notaries lose the power to convey and penalties for unauthorized practice be increased.

The Government's 1983 response was uncharacteristically non-committal, perhaps because Austin Mitchell, a new Labour MP, had won the lottery and introduced a private member's bill in July to abolish the monopoly.[2] In November the DGFT urged reducing house-buying costs by combining the functions of several occupations. Two weeks later the Government eliminated the opticians' monopoly over the sale of spectacles. Although Mitchell's bill won a 96–76 vote on the Second Reading, he knew it could not pass without Conservative support and withdrew it in February 1984 on the Government's promise to introduce its own. Solicitors and their potential competitors fought in the media for the next two years. Each side commissioned survey research: the Society's showed that the public wanted privately practising solicitors to convey their houses but was dissatisfied about cost and speed; the Halifax Building Society's showed borrowers wanted it to be able to convey.

A few estate agents tried to enter this market (partly responding to solicitors' threats to theirs), offering free conveyancing to vendors listing with them and cut-price conveyancing to purchasers. The Society backed legal proceedings against the estate agents and considered disciplining their solicitors. Woolworths and Debenhams put estate agents in their stores, offering fixed price conveyancing, though Woolworths abandoned the experiment after a few months. In the late 1980s large insurers rapidly acquired estate agencies, some of which responded by expanding their own chains.[3] An insurance broker proposed to offer conveyancing. Chartered surveyors asserted their right to enter partnerships with or employ solicitors to do conveyancing. And the Administration of Justice Act 1985 revived the occupation of licensed conveyancers (although these could not offer other services in land transactions).

Although solicitors insisted that conveyancing required legal training, most firms relied heavily on legal executives and other unadmitted staff; and the forty Halifax employees checking conveyances by independent solicitors found frequent errors. The Society warned against the anti-competitive threat of highly concentrated mortgage lenders (five owned 55 per cent of all assets, sixteen owned 84 per cent). But solicitors refrained from price competition, declined to offer advance estimates, and charged widely divergent fees. Solicitors pointed to the potential conflict of interest between eager lenders and purchasers needing independent advice. But most first buyers obtained mortgages before consulting solicitors, who had their own conflict in the interest they earned on trust accounts (the purchaser's 10 per cent deposit) as well as conveyancing profits.

Solicitors acted as well as argued. They proposed forming their own building society but failed to raise the capital. Emulating Scots solicitors, they established property centres (SPyCs), in Berwick-on-Tweed in 1984 and then in four other towns. Although estate agents responded by boycotting participating solicitors, the National Association of Solicitors Property Centres (NASPyC) claimed to have captured 25–40 per cent of those markets, and most local law societies endorsed the idea. But though more than 1,000 firms quickly joined NASPyC, membership dropped to 270 within three years, only half of which actually offered property (few very successfully). The Society challenged individual solicitors seeking to offer one-stop services at the same time that its own Remuneration and Practice Development Committee embraced this idea.[4] Firms also collaborated to advertise their services at fixed competitive prices, allocating members exclusive territorial jurisdiction. As early as 1984 solicitors began advertising low fixed fees for conveyancing. Although the Law Society took comfort in the fact that the Government substitute for Mitchell's Bill, the Building Societies Act 1986, allowed lenders to convey only for non-borrowers (an empty concession), a local law society urged members to boycott lenders that did any conveyances.

The licensed conveyancers created by the 1985 Act posed no threat; by the end of 1987 fewer than 200 had qualified (mostly solicitors or their employees). Nevertheless, two studies found that limited advertising (discussed below) and fear of corporate conveyancing cut prices about 25 per cent from 1983 to 1985 (strong evidence of the efficacy of restrictive practices). Solicitors complained that 'competition in this field is suicidal' and 'people are quoting daft prices'. But the effects remained local: quotations for the identical transaction varied two- or three-fold around the country. And Michael Joseph still claimed firms billed £200 an hour for unqualified employees. Nevertheless, the Marre Committee also opposed corporate conveyancing.[5]

The Society vigorously patrolled its other jurisdictional boundaries, which were less well defined and harder to defend than the Bar's. It brought prosecutions for unauthorized practice against law stationers preparing probate documents, laypeople drafting contracts, collection agencies assisting creditors, patent agents, even laypeople acting gratis for the poor. To control the use of unadmitted personnel it required solicitors to practise in the same office as their clerks. The Government rejected the Royal Commission recommendation that trust companies probate wills. The Attorney-General appeared to disagree in 1985, but the Administration of Justice Act that year preserved the monopoly, and Austin Mitchell's Freedom of Probate Bill died for lack of government support. The Royal Commission recommended that estate agents' agreement not to draft sales contracts become law. But the Society failed to prevent trade unions from negotiating injury claims for members in industrial tribunals or courts.

Solicitors sought to dampen internal competition as well. The OFT recommended repeal of the ban on MDPs, but the national and local societies were strongly opposed. Although nineteenth-century solicitors openly advertised for business, the Society now prohibited 'touting' (which included undercutting fees), fee-paying work for clients given free advice, employed solicitors privately serving their employers' clients, and trade unions recommending their solicitors to members for personal matters. Although the Society opposed proposals by the MMC and Royal Commission to allow some advertising, it abruptly reversed course in response to the threat to the conveyancing monopoly. At first it strongly favoured collective promotion. Opposition to individual advertising by smaller firms (led by the BLA) forced the Society to submit the issue to a postal ballot in 1984, which narrowly approved limited liberalization but rejected major reform by more than three to one.

Solicitors early succeeded in suppressing price competition. By the eighteenth century courts set fees for most contentious matters; toward the end of the nineteenth the Society made conveyancing fees a function of property values rather than document length, instantly multiplying profits from large transactions two- or three-fold. (Numerous empirical studies showed that time expenditure did not vary linearly with property value.) Solicitors managed to raise fees another 50 per cent by 1944. Although scale fees initially were justified as maxima protecting clients from unscrupulous solicitors, by 1936 the Council prohibited conveyances for less than the scale fees set by local law societies (which policed them and, by 1964, had made maxima minima). Under pressure, the Society abolished scale fees in 1972 but substituted eight criteria, ensuring similar results. In 1953 the Society also replaced its schedule for other non-contentious work with a set of seven factors (though in 1959 it recommended proportioning probate fees to estate value).

A. Conveyancing

Repelling Boarders

When the Green Paper proposed corporate conveyancing, solicitors confronted the disadvantage that buyers found a property (through estate agents), sought financial and insurance advice (primarily from lenders and financial advisers), and shopped for a mortgage (from lenders) before consulting a solicitor. They either had to block the reform or leapfrog their competitors. The 345 firms in the Solicitors Property Group (SPyG, successor to NASPyC), whose membership was up 20 per cent from the previous year, threatened to withdraw all deposits from lenders engaging in conveyancing. Members were 'competing for professional work as now but not advertising against each other—only advertising en bloc against estate agents en bloc'. Efforts to engage in lending failed again. The 500 firms that joined Solicitors Financial and Property Services Co., launched and guaranteed by the Law Society in 1988, soon fell to 300, and by 1991 the Society was left with a debt of almost £300,000.[6]

Solicitors also assailed estate agents (two-thirds now owned by lenders) for steering buyers to insurance companies offering 'substantial hidden commissions'. The Consumers' Association reported agents persuading sellers to accept low offers in order to sell insurance to buyers and promoting excessive mortgages and unnecessary insurance. The (competing) Institute of Insurance Brokers claimed that buyers were wasting £680 million a year by trading in existing policies. The Halifax Building Society retorted that nearly 30 per cent of buyers complained about their solicitors; the CA replied that half were dissatisfied with their estate agents. The DGFT proposed regulating financial advice given by estate agents, but the Law Society demanded a total ban. The Government rejected a recommendation by the National Association of Estate Agents (NAEA) and the Royal Institution of Chartered Surveyors that agents be required to pass a test because it 'provides a barrier against entry'; instead, the Government promulgated rules against fraud and overreaching. Condemning the DTI consultation on tying-in as 'half-hearted', the Law Society accused the Government of having 'shamefully abandoned the interests of consumers and given in to pressures from commercial lending institutions'.[7]

Launching its new conveyancing protocol in 1990, the Society boasted that TransAction would allow solicitors to 'see off' the competition and, within a decade, routinely offer estate agency and financial services. NAEA responded by urging members to conduct title searches for sellers, accusing solicitors of promoting vendor searches as an 'excuse for getting the intending seller to go to the solicitor first.'

The effect will be more sinister—having got them into the office they may either recommend their own property selling service or a pet estate agent, perhaps not you. If they succeed in brainwashing intending sellers to go to them before us they may also see the advantage of opening their own property sales department. . . .

Indeed, the SPyG did urge members to encourage clients to list properties through solicitor estate agents and sought authority to advise purchasers about mortgages (like estate agents), act for both parties (like licensed conveyancers), and offer discount packages of estate agency and conveyancing services. Its chair, Leslie Dubow, denounced the NAEA response as 'very much against the public interest'. A few weeks later the NAEA president bragged that he had 'not seen sight nor sound' of TransAction. The Law Society spent £60,000 for a cinema commercial featuring 'Brookside' television soap opera stars urging viewers to 'Make the right move—see a solicitor first'. In Scotland, whose solicitors had captured 37 per cent of the house-selling market by 1996 (more than 70 per cent in major cities), NAEA persuaded the DGFT to refer to the MMC its complaint that solicitors property centres refused to accept estate agent listings, some even excluding solicitors who listed properties jointly with estate agents. The

MMC found a monopoly but declined to declare it against the public interest.

English solicitors, however, were unable to replicate the Scots success. Dubow complained that half the solicitors in two towns 'went off to estate agents, made themselves out to be good guys and got all the instructions'. Five of the six centres failed, partly because the Society prohibited solicitors from offering conveyancing or financial services to buyers to ensure that 'the buyer receives independent financial advice from his own solicitor or elsewhere'. Yet an NCC survey found that only 16 per cent of clients asked solicitors for such advice. As the recession eased, LS President Tony Girling hoped buyers 'will have less strong ties of loyalty with estate agents, so the opportunity to seek to be the first point of call for the house-buying public is there'.[8]

Solicitors continued to resist corporate conveyancing. The *Solicitors Journal* criticized the LCD for failing 'to prevent financial institutions using conveyancing as a loss leader'. LS Council member Tony Girling warned against 'free' conveyancing tied to endowment mortgages; the latter had increased from 54 per cent of conveyances in 1983 to 90 per cent in 1991, generating commissions accounting for 20–30 per cent of lenders' pre-tax profits. The SJ also complained that the 1990 Act's requirement of a solicitor interview (which obstructed corporate conveyancing) 'has been watered down and the client faced with paying an extra charge may dispense with the interview and the advice he needs'. The Leeds Permanent Building Society, by contrast, resented that 'plans to do conveyancing have been tripped up because [lenders] are unable to offer a centralised service'.[9]

But it was the recession, not legal obstacles, that discouraged corporate conveyancing. Freehold residential sales fell by half between 1988 and 1992. In February that year the Nationwide, Leeds Permanent, Halifax, and Alliance and Leicester Building Societies all denied any interest. The Authorised Conveyancing Practitioners Board called this 'the worst possible time to expect building societies to sign up for something like this'. Lord Mackay claimed to have encountered insuperable 'difficulty in fixing a reasonably workable clause that would produce any kind of parity across the different enterprises involved'. The Council of Mortgage Lenders (CML) was 'disappointed' that 'the Lord Chancellor has decided not to implement what is clearly the will of Parliament'. Mitchell accused Mackay of using a 'crude political trick' to give 'solicitors the chance to increase conveyancing charges without a threat from the institutions because he can't get the cash from cabinet for legal aid'. The *Solicitors Journal* thought the Society 'wise' to take 'a low profile in welcoming this major victory for its lobbying efforts'.[10]

Because neither was able to go it alone, lenders and solicitors vied for control. The Bradford & Bingley (the eighth largest building society) required solicitors to offer agreed prices, twenty-four-hour response, and three meetings with clients. It was 'not interested in having any one-man bands on the panel'. Although the Law Society acquiesced, sole practitioner Arnold Rosen assailed both lender discrimination and the Society's acceptance, which 'engendered the feeling that it sees the sole practitioner as expendable'. Some forty firms formed the National Conveyancing Network to negotiate collectively with the twenty largest lenders, only two of which demanded exclusivity. Soon more than 1,000 firms had joined. Conquest Legal Marketing launched a competitor, starting with thirty firms. The SPyG, whose membership had fallen to 250 because of the recession, also negotiated with financial institutions for referrals.[11]

The Sole Practitioners Group (SPG) asked the Law Society to stop banking with Barclays while it continued 'to discriminate against one-man bands'. Noting that the Monopolies Commission had investigated building society discrimination against solo chartered surveyers, the Society asked the OFT to review the 'restriction on the choice of a solicitor'. The Skipton (the fourteenth largest building society) stopped instructing all but forty sole practitioners personally recommended by local managers. It had 'increasingly suffered as a result of both fraud and negligence by solicitors, in particular sole practitioners', and condemned the Society for 'trying to minimise the payments from the compensation fund'. SPG members were 'hurt and angry', but the Skipton dismissed them as 'emotive and hysterical', claiming the twenty largest lenders all were 'considering their stance regarding sole practitioners' and already imposed limitations. The CML declared the end of open panels. In 1999 the fourth largest chain of estate agents cut its conveyancing panel from 1,000 firms to fewer than ten, which would work to 'common standards', possibly at fixed prices.[12]

Nearly eight years after the Green Papers, Hambro Countrywide PLC, the largest estate agency, selling nearly 7 per cent of residential property, contracted to offer licensed conveyancers to buyer or seller. The SPyG feared this would 'put the livelihood of solicitors undertaking residential conveyancing at risk'. Dubow accused the Law Society's 'very restrictive' practice rules of putting solicitors at 'a very considerable disadvantage'. 'Whilst [the Society] worry about the high moral ground conveyancers are worried about whether they will have a crust to eat next year'. The *Solicitors Journal* agreed it was 'time for the Law Society to encourage solicitors to become involved in the property selling process... if the estate agents, mortgage brokers and licensed conveyancers are not to take away altogether the solicitors' role as conveyancer for residential property'.

Richard Hegarty, chair of the Society's Property and Commercial Services (PACS) committee, said Hambro had promised not to act for both sides, which the Standard Mortgage Instructions (SMI) agreed between the Society and major lenders also prohibited. But Hambro negotiated exclusive referrals of the other party to three large regional firms (Shoosmiths &

Harrison, Eversheds, and EDC Lord & Co), which would requalify their solicitors as conveyancers, locate them in Hambro offices in Northamptonshire, Manchester, Bristol, Surrey, and Essex, open twelve hours a day seven days a week, and charge £350. Declaring that 'the volumes of work are dictated not by how many people come through the door but by how many transactions we can process', it quickly opened in Northampton, bought Lord's Surrey and Essex offices, and added offices in Cardiff and Manchester; in 1998 it conveyed 22,000 freehold properties and was contemplating offices in Southampton and Bristol.

Hegarty bravely maintained that this was 'something solicitors have been allowed to do for years', but the *Gazette* discerned 'a significant shift in the market in favour of the big, customer-friendly supplier'. Complaining that the Society had rejected his similar proposal seven years earlier, Dubow warned that 'once one estate agency group provides a conveyancing service, others are bound to follow'. His SPyG urged the Society to amend Rule 6 to allow solicitors to act for both sides and offer buyers financial services. The Society's 1997 conference heard that the Halifax, Woolwich, and Barclays were considering following Hambro. The Woolwich had already created HomeSmart to end gazumping by buying and selling homes as a principal. The Halifax (the largest building society) joined with First American Title Insurance and Marsons (a solicitors' firm handling 3,000 conveyances a month), intially offering title insurance in Kent but hoping to expand nationwide and add conveyancing. A Somerset firm also used First American's software to expedite conveyancing.

When corporate conveyancing first threatened in 1990, the Society contemplated an outright ban on solicitors acting for both parties in order to oppose licensed conveyancers doing so without displaying 'naked self-interest'. But the change was blocked by local law societies, whose members feared losing half the transaction and an ongoing client. Six years later, when corporate conveyancing seemed imminent, the Society obtained the Master of the Rolls' permission to allow solicitors to convey for sellers served by a hived-off estate agency and buyers to whom they had given financial advice. Two-thirds of the 800 responding to the Society's consultation agreed. Warning that solicitors' share of the conveyancing market might drop from 96 per cent to 10–15, Hegarty said 'anything that reduces regulation in this area must be good'. Dubow called it 'a window of opportunity'. Robert Sayer declared:

Either we do it; or the estate agents do it. We should trust solicitors to be honest; they are, by and large. Clients are stitched up by agents time after time and solicitors are powerless to do anything about it because they are under the agents' thumb.

Conflict of interest concerns were 'complete nonsense'. Council member Anthony Bogan hoped estate agents would be 'worried' by this 'truly watershed decision'.

Instead, the Society launched another consultation. Calling for an end to such 'pusillanimous dithering', the *New Law Journal* urged that 'what the profession should do to repel boarders should be discussed openly'. Dubow warned that 'if other financial institutions follow the lead of Hambro Countrywide there will be precious little conveyancing left for our profession...what is at stake is the very existence of high street practice'. The Council ultimately modified Rule 6 to allow Solicitors Estate Agencies Ltd (Seals), formed by at least four firms and operating from separate premises, to convey and offer financial and mortgage advice to both sides.

This revived interest in property centres. The SPyG boldly proposed opening one in Woking, Hambro's first site. At a February 1997 meeting of Surrey solicitors organized by solicitor-estate agent Michael Garson, Sayer pronounced: 'Either we do this or we give up conveyancing'. Bogan, the local Council member, distributed plans to the 100 participants and subsequently offered shares in the scheme to the 12,700 solicitors who had supported John Edge's 1996 conveyancing fee initiative (see below), hoping to raise £200,000. The next month the Surrey Law Society and SPyG proposed to establish a company for this purpose, directed by Sayer, Bogan, Dubow, Garson, and Edge. A month after that Conquest Legal Marketing launched Solicitors Property Centres Ltd (SPyCL), boasting it would open twelve within a year and up to 150 in two. Its survey of 250 firms found that 92 per cent believed SPyCs were necessary for 'gaining market control at source' and 'obtaining new conveyancing referrals'. Although Conquest's president, Richard Berenson, offered to liaise with the SPyG, since 'it would be foolish to present two national networks to the profession at the same time', Bogan refused because his group was non-profit and owned exclusively by solicitors. Dubow accused Berenson of 'trying to muscle in on something we've been doing for the past twelve years'. 'He's talking about working with estate agents, while we see ourselves as operating entirely for the benefit of solicitors....' PACS supported the SPyG initiative, and Hegarty said Conquest's plan violated Society rules. But when past LS president Rodger Pannone became SPCL chair, Bogan agreed to merge the SPyG initiative with it. One of three government ministers reviewing house selling told Pannone he was 'clearly in favour of the one-stop operation'. So was the CA. The Society's own survey found that consumer focus groups had 'overwhelmingly negative' views of the house transfer process. The Adam Smith Institute warned that 'this Government may be more inclined to...take lawyers by the scruff of the neck and say you will have to change your ways'.

Within four months SPyCL had convinced 500 firms to pay a £750 enrolment fee, and twenty were inquiring daily. Berenson repeatedly missed his targets but just set new ones: twelve within a year became just one, but 'then there will be a great wave of centres forming throughout next year'—five by January 1998 and 1,700 firms enrolled by the middle of that year. In February Bogan admitted the first five would not open until at least June but claimed that enough solicitors had registered to warrant another forty centres, which 'will follow much quicker than they would have done had we launched in January'. The first centre, in Shepherd's Bush, did not open until March 1999. The next, planned in Preston, was aborted when the fifteen firms withdrew and threatened to create their own rival, attacking SPyCL's contract with Berenson's for-profit business and the £750 enrolment fee. Solicitors in Swansea, the third site, threatened to follow suit, persuading SPyCL to sever its ties with Berenson (who kept £500,000 in enrolment fees). Dubow's SPyG then launched a competitor under Garson: 'solicitors' group practices rather than estate agencies owned by solicitors'.

The Law Society became the third player when it allocated £80,000 to design a model SPyC under the aegis of one of its officers, Bogan, and Hegarty. In August 1997 it boldly announced a chain of 200 SPyCs—one in every high street—employing independent financial advisers to arrange mortgages. NAEA objected that 'the playing field is not level and our members will obviously not welcome this'. But a year later a Society-commissioned study found insufficient solicitor interest to capture even a small part of the house-selling market.

Finally, Scottish solicitors sought to replicate their success south of the border. The Edinburgh Solicitors Property Centre (ESPyC) conceded that 'market forces' had convinced the public that conveyancing was 'something that anybody can do, with no particular skills needed'. Acknowledging that the profession would never 'again be able to persuade people that conveyancing is a function that they should be prepared to pay even a reasonable fee for', it viewed property selling as 'a way of introducing new clients to the firm, and then cross-selling other services to them, particularly in the financial services field'. With the caution of experience (and perhaps culture) it proposed to open a London centre if 350 firms signed up. The *Gazette* called this 'a chance too good to squander'. But the failure to reach that target led ESPyC to refocus on the north-east, where it told a meeting of 170 firms it would open if 100 enrolled. When sixty did so, it launched the Newcastle Solicitors Property Shop in January 1999 with twenty-nine firms. Although local estate agents withdrew their boycott threat when warned it was anti-competitive, a Newcastle solicitor observed that such 'instructions have dried up'. One estate agent wrote to every home displaying a NSPyS sign saying that solicitors could not sell property. Still, NSPyS sold £3.5 million worth of property in its first two months and £12 million in ten. It was talking with solicitors in Liverpool, Leeds, the Lake District, Manchester, Bradford, and York and was willing to co-operate with the SPCL and the Preston dissidents.[13]

Disciplining the Crew

If external threats tended to unite solicitors, internal competition divided them. As Law Society President in 1990, Tony Holland declared 'little or no respect for those solicitors who insist on offering cut-price conveyancing of a mediocre quality', 'secretarial conveyancing' under 'the trademark, if you like, of solicitors'. Three years later he launched a 'crusade' against them. The Society should warn the public 'it is unlikely that a solicitor can carry out this work adequately at a fee for less than' £200. But the chair of the Society's cost of default working party noted that the OFT 'just wouldn't let us' set a minimum fee. He even questioned the warning: 'a sole practitioner doing it on the kitchen table could possibly do it'. The Council rejected Holland's proposal to deny or reduce lenders' compensation claims against firms charging inadequate fees.

At the 1993 AGM solicitors called for a return to scale fees or the denial of indemnity cover to those charging less. While conceding the inevitability of 'loss leaders', the PACS chair warned that the 'crisis' of cut-price conveyancing would cause a 'slow slide into bankruptcy'. Yet a study found no relationship between prices and SCB complaints or SIF claims. And the OFT threatened to 'examine carefully the impact of any minimum conveyancing fee or any recommended fee scale'. Its Director-General, Sir Bryan Carsberg, cautioned the Society's annual conference against 'pricing cartels'. He told North Devon solicitors that openly circulating an agreed scale was 'not an acceptable remedy'. He accepted their 'voluntary assurance' of discontinuance but warned that 'this may not be the case with any future attempts to fix fees'. The Society responded by issuing 'guidelines' and urging solicitors to report suspect pricing practices. The *Gazette* retailed horror stories of 'cutting corners, secretarial conveyancing', insisting that professional advice was 'a genuine hand-holding exercise'. But the *Solicitors Journal* conceded that much conveyancing 'now relies on knowing which form to fill in'. Indeed, the Society told members 'there are many parts of a conveyancing transaction which can properly be delegated to fully trained and supervised non-solicitor staff'. Nor did solicitor control guarantee quality: the Land Registry was 'pointing out errors or deficiencies in solicitors' applications'.[14]

In March 1994 a Society working party reluctantly concluded that 'compulsory and recommended fee scales would be unworkable and ineffective'. Instead it proposed separate solicitors for buyer and lender (in response to lender conveyancing) and a kite mark to fight price cutting, 'which put the quality of service at risk'. But it inconsistently urged solicitors to see conveyancing as an 'opportunity for cross-selling other services, including will-making and financial advice'. Describing the loan market as 'a vicious, highly competitive, plundering jungle', in which 'the borrower is the prey', the *Solicitors Journal* lauded the report as 'the single most important document that has come out of Chancery Lane on an issue so fundamental to the survival of the majority of the profession'. It 'inevitably... will mean more paid work for the profession'. (Conveyancing had declined from 50 per cent of solicitors' gross income in 1965–6 to 21 in 1989 and 10 in 1993—34–36 per cent even in firms with fewer than five partners.)

The Society's director of legal practice claimed the proposal responded to 'an inherent conflict of interest' in joint representation. But the CML dismissed this as merely 'theoretical' and feared increased cost and delay. Echoing the *Solicitors Journal*, the Halifax called the proposal 'just an attempt... to generate more work'. Even the SPyG had 'grave reservations', preferring a 'recommended' fee scale and discipline of those who 'woefully undercut it'. It wanted lenders to maintain open panels and pay a separate fee for conveyancing while limiting solicitors' liability to a guarantee of good title. Displaying unwarranted bravado, it was eager to 'take the institutions on—head on if necessary'. But the LS working party chair saw 'absolutely no prospect' of this alternative. Lenders were 'thoroughly fed up with the cavalier way in which they see the profession is treating them' and would set their own standards.

In Birmingham, 100 conveyancing solicitors opposed the Society's plan, preferring to expose those who took short cuts. Finding it 'very difficult to recall any actual conflicts of interest' between lenders and borrowers, Bristol solicitors declared that the proposal's 'underlying reason' was 'the desire to increase the fees'. The Society's consultation found that 72 per cent of firms and 75 per cent of local law societies opposed separate representation, as did most lenders, the CA and NCC, and the DGFT. Solicitors feared lenders would retaliate by eliminating more from conveyancing panels, eventually bringing such work in house, and exhorting buyers to do their own conveyancing. Robert Sayer (a new Council member) warned it would 'put the final nail in our coffins'. A majority of firms favoured a quality mark, however, and 80 per cent of the sixty lenders responding (out of 152) would consider limiting panels to those certified. The National Conveyancing Network and Conquest were enthusiastic, and Network 2000 said 'firms like our [fifty] members, who set themselves high standards, are tired of footing the compensation fund bill which has been caused by those who pay little or no regard to standards of probity, service and quality'.

When the Society disregarded both internal opposition and external criticism by proceeding with separate representation, the OFT threatened a referral to the MMC. Assailing this 'public relations disaster', the *Solicitors Journal* pronounced that 'asking clients to pay twice as much for a conveyance was a no-hoper'. The SPyG called the decision 'quite incomprehensible', 'highly divisive', and certain to 'attract a lot of damaging and adverse publicity'. 'I can see the headlines now: "Solicitors rip off the public".'

Sayer predicted that solicitors would 'be forced to do more work for no extra money'. The Society should 'adopt a modern, commercial attitude and put our interests first and stop imposing unnecessary restraints on the way we conduct our business'.

After nearly five hours of debate the Council decided on further consultation but declared that 'unrestricted joint representation of borrower and lender may in some circumstances no longer be an option'. Within weeks the CML rejected the proposed compromise that solicitors limit unpaid services to lenders. It was 'objectionable in principle' to treat the lender as 'a second class citizen' and would bring in separate representation 'through the back door'. The working party chair retorted: 'we are undertaking for nothing the work that other people should be doing'. But the Society abandoned separate representation in favour of a limited retainer for lenders, who threatened to instruct their own solicitors if it proved unsatisfactory.[15]

The Society renewed the battle a year later. After long, difficult negotiations it tentatively agreed with the CML on standard mortgage instructions requiring that lenders exhort borrowers to pay solicitors for mortgage work at an 'indicative range of fees'. The OFT insisted these be negotiated in each instance. The LS Council then narrowly voted to revise Rule 6 to allow solicitors to limit lender representation to title issues. Nearly four-fifths of the more than 2,000 responses to its consultation favoured the change. PACS, however, supported it by just one vote; the standards and guidance committee was concerned; and both SIF and SCF worried about increased fraud, negligence, and conflict of interest. Tony Girling, immediate past LS president, objected: 'I thought we had shed the nanny's clothes'. 'Let's not put the nanny's uniform on again.' The CML responded by approaching the government about activating the dormant authorized conveyancing practitioners' scheme, adopting SMI unilaterally, and contracting with firms doing bulk conveyancing. In 1999 the Society and CML finally agreed on a revised Rule 6, lender's handbook, and SMI.[16]

More than half those responding to the second consultation opposed even the kite mark. Mark Sheldon thought standards superfluous for 'such a basic activity'. Another Council member feared they would shave 'already wafer thin' profit margins. When the Council made the kite mark optional, the SPyG chair accused it of treating solicitors like 'silly little children to be told by "Mummy Law Society" what is best for them'. The *Solicitors Journal* felt the controversy reflected 'the amount of heat rather than light surrounding the profession just now'. At the same time, Conquest and Network 2000 announced a proprietary conveyancing standard.[17]

Many solicitors were unreconciled to price competition. Tony Holland complained that buyers at firms charging £99 plus VAT were 'given too little advice' and saw a solicitor 'rarely, if ever'. Fees for conveying more expensive properties fell by 10 per cent in 1993; in the first six months of 1994 70 per cent of buyers paid less than £300 plus VAT. The Council responded by amending Rule 13 to require that every office be supervised by a solicitor with three years' experience, who had completed further training. Sayer blamed the fact 'that we currently have the lowest charges in the western world' on 'an appalling error of judgment in the mid-1980s when we were first allowed to advertise', which 'condemned us all to an unnecessary price war'. His firm resisted by charging hourly rates. Many of the 500 responses he received in the following two weeks 'expressed a deep bitterness towards those firms which are charging fees so low as not even to pretend to cover true costs'. This 'groundswell of anger... if properly focused could be the salvation of all'.

At a Law Society meeting in Oxfordshire two months later a solicitor claimed that the OFT had condoned the Royal Institute of British Architects' indicative fee scale. But the Society noted that the DGFT had found 'that fee competition in the [architecture] market is strong and that publication of the scales is unlikely to have a significant effect'. Still, the 200 participants called for a return to scale fees, discipline of those working at a loss, and denial of indemnity cover for work charged below an hourly rate. The Society floated the possibility of recommending minimum fees.[18]

Celebrating the upset victory of Martin Mears and Robert Sayer as 1995–6 LS President and Vice-President, dissident John Edge hoped they would

remind committee [*vide* Council] members that they exist to preserve, protect and promote the interests of individual solicitors and the profession as a whole. If the Law Society is not prepared to carry out this function then I would like to see all conveyancing solicitors resign en masse from the Society with a view to forming our own 'trade union' to fight for and protect our interests.

Claiming that 2,200 solicitors supported him (and 200 were enlisting daily), Edge proposed a fee schedule and 'demand[ed] that the society finds some way of enforcing it. I am sick and tired of being told that it cannot be done'. The Society should persuade buyers to start house-hunting with a solicitor, who 'will be able to negotiate lower selling fees with estate agents. Let's see how estate agents like having *their* fees dictated by others!' 'I personally find it offensive, depressing, and degrading that 25 years hard work as a solicitor should result in meagre financial reward'. When Edge and Bogan submitted 7,000 letters of support, Sayer declared that 'bringing conveyancing income back to a fairer level is one of my main objectives'. Mears 'applaud[ed] Mr Edge's energy and initiative' and pledged to give him 'all the support I can'.

Although 'suspending solicitors for breaching price guidelines' struck the *New Law Journal* as 'a bit harsh', it was 'worth exploring'. The OFT might not 'automatically' veto a proposal to fine solicitors 'the difference between the price charged and the guideline price'. There was

an argument for saying that ensuring a reasonable return for conveyancing work through guideline fees would be in the public interest if it reduced the temptation for solicitors to cut corners and produced a consequent fall in the incidence of solicitor negligence and dishonesty.

But the *Solicitors Journal* warned that minimum fees 'will stimulate competition from licensed conveyancers'. A high-street solicitor ridiculed those who denied any 'link between cheap conveyancing and negligent conveyancing. The same was said for many years about smoking and lung cancer.' Bogan argued that the fact that solicitors' 'regulatory structure distorts the market' justified other restrictive practices. In any case, 'could 8,500 solicitors all be wrong?' The SPG urged members to support Edge's initiative, emulating estate agents who 'have restored their commission charges to a sensible level' and chartered surveyors who 'have recommended fees for various types of house surveys'.[19]

Retreating from his own bluster, Edge urged SIF to exclude solicitors charging less than specified fees. Sayer concurred, maintaining that two firms were going bankrupt a week. The *Gazette* reported its postbag 'bulging with anguished correspondence' but worried about the profession's image. 'A public with a sour taste in its mouth will not be receptive to approaches from those solicitors who hope to break into the important field of financial advice.' Although 'the campaign has only just begun, they have been cast as money-grabbing protectionists'. Indeed, *The Times* dismissed the equation of cheapness with shoddiness as 'specious, protectionist and ill-judged'.

When 10,000 had endorsed his proposal, Edge urged the Society to agree scale fees for lenders with the CML. The grassroots response was 'a true "snap shot" of the way the profession is feeling, not only about the conveyancing issue but about its attitude to the Law Society Council members and the professional body generally'. Edge and Bogan obtained a solicitor's opinion that scale fees enforced by either a practice rule or the denial of indemnity would not be illegal *per se*. A reference to the MMC would at least win two years, during which time the property market might recover. At the Society's annual conference a few weeks later the Cheltenham & Gloucester Building Society legal controller warned that panels might exclude smaller firms and lenders move conveyancing in-house. But Sayer supported the proposal as 'a way of bringing the matter to a head with lenders'. And Edge was 'not impressed by the bullying threats'; it was 'both absurd and obscene that lenders cynically expect solicitors to collect the lenders' legal fees from buyers, knowing full well that the present market will not support such fees.' Indeed, estate agents were conditioning referrals to solicitors on low conveyancing fees or illegal kickbacks.[20]

Sayer claimed to have demonstrated the 'obvious and direct' relationship between price competition and SIF exposure: £4.9 million in claims between 1989 and 1995 against forty cut-price firms compared with £430,000 against a 'control group' of twenty-five 'ordinary' firms. (He ignored the wide variation in claims incidence within both groups and did not test statistical significance.) 'It cost £1 million more to insure the cut-price firms than the amount of premiums they contributed. If every firm had the same claims record as these cut-price firms, the SIF would no longer exist.' The PACS committee chair had 'been desperately trying to find a link' and 'thought there was one', but SIF data offered 'very weak' evidence. SIF chair and Council member Andrew Kennedy was unconvinced. Conveyancing claims were the same (absolutely and proportionally) as they had been three years earlier, in the depths of the recession. The 'conveyancing fee issue is not an indemnity matter'. Edge's proposals 'hit the innocent as well as those who may not be innocent'. When SIF objected that 'the sample was not big enough to prove a pattern', Sayer asked 'why did they not increase its size?' Mears maintained he and the Council were 'doing everything possible to restore an enforceable fee scale' and seeking the Master of the Rolls' consent.

Bogan decried 'the appalling picture in our high streets today: the loss of nearly 4000 firms since 1989 with an average voluntary closure of about four each week. It is estimated that more than 1000 solicitors are the subject of IVAs and each week another is made bankrupt.' (The number of firms actually declined only 1,200 during this period, mostly through concentration: 2,700 fewer sole practitioners but 300 more firms with two to four partners and 600 more with five to ten.) Noting that 12,700 solicitors now supported Edge's proposal and dismissing the 'minority' who advocated 'unfettered competition', Bogan invoked (anachronistic) precedents: a 1968 decision pronouncing that 'the professional man must submit to some restraints of trade' and refuse 'by undercutting or otherwise to snatch work from another practitioner'; a 1973 MMC report accepting price regulation if 'it were shown that the profession would otherwise be exposed to exceptional danger of a fall in incomes and that this would result in a serious deterioration of the quality or quantity of service offered'; and Lord Diplock's assertion that 'on any long term view it was unlikely that the interests of solicitors would conflict with those of the public'. 'Perhaps on this occasion', said Bogan, the Society 'needs to behave as a trade union and protect its members'. The Croydon and Shropshire law societies voted overwhelmingly for scale fees.[21]

In December 1995 Sayer urged the Council to condition SIF coverage on a fee of £250 plus 0.5 per cent of the sale price. Mears called this 'one of the most important motions ever', capable of transforming 'the financial health and morale of high street solicitors'. But though the relationship between price, quality, and indemnity claims was 'inherently probable', critics' 'contributions to the debate have been entirely destructive and negative' and 'reactionary elements on the Council and in the bureaucracy' were 'doing their utmost to dispute the means'. The Council voted by 39 to 25 to discuss the issue (although some had not seen the Master of the Rolls' cautionary note). Sayer denounced firms that 'are getting business by not doing work properly'. Some secretaries learned conveyancing in just fifteen hours. Sayer insisted on the 'very strong link' between prices and claims, attributing SIF scepticism and opposition to fear that the proposal was 'the thin edge of the wedge' and could lead to 'splitting up the SIF' (see Chapter 9). Nevertheless, he accepted a compromise incorporating quality standards.

Henry Hodge supported the compromise but tabled an amendment against 'forcing up conveyancing fees'. 'We can't change the world and recre- ate scale fees…it's cynical and cruel raising the hopes of the profession.…' Also opposing a 'quick fix', Eileen Pembridge exhorted: 'Conveyancers, improve your standards'. The head of the Serious Fraud Office warned of 'the liability of Council members if we are inducing solicitors to enter into an unlawful contract'.

While the Council dithered, Edge raised £19,000 from 1,000 solicitors in less than a month to pay Michael Beloff QC for an opinion on the scheme's legality. David Pannick QC advised the Society that use of discipline or SIF rules to enforce minimum fees would be illegal, but low-cost conveyancers might be required to purchase insurance on the market if there were suf- ficient evidence that they generated more claims. David Vaughan QC advised the Society that all the proposals would provoke a referral to the MMC. Indeed, the new DGFT told Mears that 'setting minimum prices' was not 'a suitable way to protect consumers against negligence in the provi- sion of conveyancing'. 'Any mechanism designed to raise and maintain the level of fees' would require 'very good reasons'. He sent a copy to the Master of the Rolls, who would have to approve any rule change.

The insistence by PACS committee chair Richard Hegarty on 'incontro- vertible evidence' of the alleged relationship between prices and claims infuriated Sayer. He determined to write a separate paper because 'there are four lines on the advantages of my scheme and half a page on why it's no good'. Based on an opinion from Gerald Barling QC that an adverse MMC ruling was not a 'foregone conclusion' because there were 'likely to be cogent public interest arguments both for and against the changes', Edge again urged the Council to publish a 'fair and reasonable' fee and deny price cutters indemnity coverage. Although SIF's scepticism was sec- onded by actuaries appointed by the Law Society, specialist brokers chosen by its indemnity working party, and a leading professional indemnity under- writer, Mears was unmoved, insisting that the original sample of sixty-five firms was sufficiently large and its results 'more than confirm what common sense would tell one to expect, i.e., cut-price conveyancing = indemnity claims'.

In March 1996 the Council dropped the idea of barring low-cost conveyancers from SIF because they could not buy private insurance but considered charging premiums by the conveyance. Mears conceded 'I'm not the dictator of the Law Society'. But Edge dismissed this as 'only tinkering with the problem'. Making it clear that his real animus was price competition, he complained that 'some firms will simply fail to charge the indemnity fee at all to retain a market advantage'.[22]

Dispelling any uncertainty about the government's attitude, the OFT investigated price fixing by Burnley and Pendle solicitors and estate agents and then asked all 125 local law societies if they had a similar 'arrangement which sets out the minimum costs for conveyancing work'. Twenty societies accused the OFT of 'going on a fishing expedition'. Mears called its suspicions unsupported (although the B&P Law Society admitted setting guidelines) but also defended agreements as 'entirely proper' and was 'entirely confident that we could put up strong public interest arguments' were the OFT to make a referral to the MMC. The *Gazette* thought it would be 'most unfortunate' if this 'crackdown on anti-competitive practices...stopped conveyancers getting together to do what is quite permissible under competition law—to take collective stock of what it costs to do conveyancing'. But when the Law Society analysed more than 800 responses to its consultation paper, Hegarty found no 'case for publication of guidelines or recommended fees' because the range 'is so wide that [averages] cannot easily be used'.

The SPyG continued to seek fee guidelines based on hours per transaction. At its September annual conference Sayer agreed that 'unless things change radically, I don't think we will see High Street firms survive'. The SPyG chair warned the Society against 'killing the goose that lays the golden egg or at least paying [*sic*] for your salaries'. But the Society's former head of corporate and regional affairs denied that 'we can rig conveyancing prices by some cunning use of [our] statutory powers', adding candidly: 'If it were not such political dynamite, the Law Society would by now have devised a strategy to help ease the passing of the small percentage of financially unstable firms for whom euthanasia is the best option'. Eileen Pembridge agreed that 'the very wise and very dispirited high street practitioner should get out and retrain for something more lucrative'. The *Solicitors Journal*, traditional champion of such practices, exhorted: 'Only by combining their resources and working together can the small high street firms continue to make a profit from conveyancing and compete directly with the bigger commercial firms and other organisations such as Hambros'. But inevitably it was the larger firms that heeded such advice. Eversheds invited nine major regional firms to discuss an association for low-cost conveyancing. The twelve lawyers and fifty-eight staff at Shoosmiths were opening more than 3,000 files a month by September 1999. At its annual conference several months earlier, the SPyG condemned 'solicitors killing their brethren' and warned that 'being allowed to remain in business' was coming to a 'very abrupt end'. LS President Michael Mathews (a City partner) condemned 'cut price conveyancing—by which I mean a cut-corner conveyancing' but offered no solution.[23]

B. Multinational Partnerships

For City firms, MNPs offered the opportunity to enter and potentially capture new markets, especially in Europe and the Commonwealth, but also the threat of 'the economic strength and dominance of the large US law firms', seventy of which had London offices. Partnership with them 'may create a legitimate fear of excessive dominance of some categories of legal service in the UK which could be contrary to the public interest'. The Society's 1991 consultation paper considered requiring all foreign partners of lawyers practising in the UK to buy UK indemnity coverage. SIF warned that this 'could be regarded as unfair or even anti-competitive'. Although the Society reduced this to a quarter of the SCF contribution and two-thirds of the practising certificate fee, the chair of the Society's international committee feared this still 'will be seen particularly by our US colleagues as restrictive'. The Society eliminated the SCF contribution, producing a flood of applicants to register. A seven-partner West End firm became the first MNP by admitting a Danish lawyer. Seven months later the City firm Kennedys admitted a German partner.

Because UK firms were wary of American competitors, the latter hired English lawyers for their London offices. In 1994 the City firm Titmus Sainer & Webb merged with the Philadelphia firm Dechert Price & Rhoads. Other City firms absorbed smaller European partners: Allen & Overy in Italy, Freshfields in Germany. When Clifford Chance declared it would have 500 lawyers in its European offices within two years, Linklaters responded by announcing its Alliance, with almost 1,500 lawyers in six countries. Salans Hertzfeld & Heilbronn, a French firm which had absorbed Harris Rosenblatt & Kramer of London, merged with Christy & Viener in New York, claiming (inaccurately) to be the first transatlantic firm.

But Clifford Chance captured the spotlight by merging with the American firm Rogers & Wells and the German firm Pünder, Volhard, Weber & Exter, to link 566 partners, 2,700 lawyers, and 58,000 staff in thirty offices grossing more than £1 billion annually. Bragging that 'Clifford Chance takes over the world', the *Solicitors Journal* was 'proud' that 'the traditional pattern of British corporate history was reversed. Here was an English firm absorbing an American rival to create a huge, multi-national empire.' The *Evening Standard* predicted it would be a 'major headache' for competitors; but the *Financial Times* warned (strangely) that 'gigantism' will sit very uneasily with advisory businesses'. Although Linklaters insisted it was not 'charging off looking for people to marry in North America', it waited less than a week to expand its Alliance to 2,200 lawyers by adding the second-largest Italian firm, thereby leapfrogging Baker & McKenzie to become the world's second largest firm. Maintaining it was not 'rushing to follow suit', Freshfields accelerated its merger with Deringer Tessin Herrman & Sedemund by two years to reach 1,300 lawyers. Three weeks after that Lovell White Durrant merged with Bösebeck Droste to claim more than 1,000 lawyers; and Dibb Lupton Alsop formed associations with firms in Brussels, Barcelona, and Paris. Two weeks later Allen & Overy merged with the third largest Dutch firm (having already acquired firms in Italy, Spain, and Thailand).[24]

Even without merger American firms riled their rivals by paying £55,000 to fourth-year assistants in 1990, capturing some of the best talent and driving up City salaries. In 1997 American competition may have helped break up the 'Club of Nine' City firms, which discussed starting salaries and tended to increase them together. (Overseas branches already flouted the Club's anti-poaching rule.) Two years later an American firm's London office made headlines by offering remuneration 'to £1 million +'. American firms paid nearly twice as much as English for solicitors with seven years' experience, and a third paid nearly twice as much to start. But if Brits resented Yanks, French firms condemned City branches in Paris for paying twice as much as they did: 'The only thing that seems to matter to the English is money'.[25]

C. Multidisciplinary Partnerships

If solicitors were apprehensive about Americans they were terrified by accountants' size, concentration, and aggressiveness. The (then) Big Six earned more than £2.5 billion in 1993, five times as much as the next sixteen. The six largest City firms earned only a third as much, slightly more than the next sixteen. Although 54 per cent of those responding to the Law Society's 1987 consultation favoured MDPs, President David Ward told the 1989 annual conference they were 'an even more serious danger to the network of small firms of solicitors than conveyancing by institutions'. He rejected market justifications because MDPs were 'likely to be product based rather than client based so that the driving force would be selling products rather than responding to needs' and warned that 'the rule of money would overwhelm the rule of law'. But his successor, Tony Holland, was fatalistic: 'some solicitors are already with accountants or surveyors, even if they cannot yet be partners'. Two months later the DGFT noted that the Courts and Legal Services Act 1990 made restrictions on MDPs 'subject to the competition rules' and declared the growing consensus 'that artificial barriers on how solicitors themselves wish to practise are undesirable'. The Society called it 'unfortunate' that 'the competition authorities' terms of reference do not allow them to consider the protection of the public'.[26]

When Parliament failed to enact new restrictive trade practices legislation, undercutting the OFT threat, the Society rejected a DTI consultation document endorsing MDPs. Law Society Assistant Secretary-General Walter Merricks declared that 'there can be no prospect of sharing reserved areas of work with other professions'. Deputy Vice-President Mark Sheldon raised 'ethical objections when legal functions are carried out by organisations concerned to develop commercial profits' (unlike his own firm, Linklaters & Paine, presumably). 'The ultimate function of solicitors is to litigate.' (What does that make those in the City?) But the Young Solicitors Group supported MDPs, which were 'not so much . . . the opportunity for the major commercial firms as for the smaller high street practices'.

Without waiting for new rules, Arthur Andersen (AA) established Garrett & Co as an associated law firm in 1993 (as it had done in France and Germany). Senior partner Colin Garrett saw 'no reason why we should not have a firm of accountants sending a fair proportion of our business to us'. Assuring Sheldon (now LS President) that solicitor independence was 'of prime importance', Garrett declared: 'my job is to ensure that accountants do not practise law'. The firm's advertisement for four solicitors at salaries of up to £120,000 drew 300 enquiries. At the Society's annual conference the new DGFT reaffirmed that there was 'much to be said for movement towards multidisciplinary partnerships in principle'. The 'market should determine the best structure of the professions'.

When a 1993 Society survey showed rising opposition to MDPs (49 versus 45 per cent of firms six years earlier, 56 versus 33 per cent of local law societies), the Council chose to do nothing but review the situation annually. A member feared 'MDPs could well damage lawyers' professional standing and introduce too many conflicts of interest'. Garretts, however, hired eleven local solicitors and established a branch in the same building as AA. This provoked other local commercial lawyers to threaten to end referrals to AA, which denied (unconvincingly) that 'we—an accountancy firm—are a competitor to Leeds law firms'. Uncowed, Garretts declared its ambition to become 'one of the first truly national firms', opening an office in Reading and planning one in Manchester. Solicitors also faced retaliation when they invaded other turf. One who qualified as an insolvency practitioner said 'a number of accountant practitioners and their firms successively made it clear that if I ever took an appointment I would never receive instructions again'. Only 10 per cent of the approximately 2,000 insolvency practitioners were solicitors.[27]

By 1996 Garretts had sixty lawyers and claimed to be the fastest growing firm in the country. Seeking to imitate AA's success, Price Waterhouse (PW) launched Arnheim, declaring it would have fifty lawyers in four years. The senior partner at Hammond Suddards, from which Chris Arnheim defected, criticized the 'ambivalence between the need for clients to have solicitors who are independent and the relationship with the sponsoring firm'. The City of London Law Society President pronounced that 'anyone who wants legal services is better off going to a firm which is completely impartial without commercial tensions which might bring pressure to bear'. A senior partner in Ernst & Young, which planned its own firm, said he would 'be surprised if at least five of the big six haven't gone down this route in the next two or three years'. Both AA and PW invoked the Treaty of Rome against the Dutch Bar Association's ban on MDPs.

Under pressure from the OFT the Council ordered a 'fresh review' in June 1996. A Society survey found (surprisingly) that only 36 per cent of firms had an opinion about MDPs, but 71 per cent of those were favourable. Warning that 'Labour has made it plain that it would de-regulate in this area', the *Gazette* urged the Society to 'tackle effectively the many testy issues, not least the one of control'. Conceding that MDPs 'are coming— almost certainly within the next two years', the *Solicitors Journal* felt the Society should 'be taking the initiative...before other professional bodies get there first'.[28]

It did nothing, however, as change continued to outpace regulation. By 1997 Garretts had more than 150 lawyers and opened another office in Cambridge. 1,000 trainees applied for its seventeen openings that year and 1,500 for twenty the next. After absorbing Scotland's largest practice Garretts claimed to be one of the twenty highest-grossing firms in the country (even though Simmons & Simmons declined to join). Coopers & Lybrand (C&L) lured two partners from Stephenson Harwood to form Tite & Lewis, which then hired most of the thirty C&L in-house lawyers and aspired to have fifty by the end of 1997. Arnheim grew from fifteen to fifty-nine. E&Y hired a Denton Hall partner to plan its firm. A Norton Rose partner said 'all the major City firms have been approached by the large accountancy firms over the last year or so' but had been uninterested. When C&L and PW proposed to merge (creating a giant with 8,500 accounting partners, 135,000 staff, 2,500 employed lawyers, and turnover of £8 billion), their associated law firms began talks.

Soon after Labour's 1997 victory the OFT threatened to act unilaterally if the Society continued to temporize. The Society's head of standards and development urged reconsideration of the ban on outside investment in law firms, which would need substantial capital 'to get our share of legal work in developing markets'. But foreign regulators remained adamant. Spain and the International Bar Association joined the Dutch in opposing

MDPs. The Brussels Bar disciplined two French *avocats* practising in association with E&Y. The former *bâtonnier* of its Dutch-speaking branch declared 'it would not be far fetched to lodge a criminal complaint... to make a stand... on behalf of all lawyers in Europe'.[29]

After a closed debate in 1998 the Council proposed six alternatives. DVP Robert Sayer predicted doom.

The big law firms will go in with the big accountants, and unless some extraordinary safeguards are imposed the lawyers will simply get swallowed up. With the small firms, I can just imagine some of them running along to estate agents and proposing MDPs, only to meet exactly the same fate.

But President Michael Mathews (a City partner), the chairs of the Law Society's Commerce & Industry Group and the City of London Law Society, and the Society's IBA representative all conceded that MDPs were inevitable. Bristol and Manchester Law Societies agreed, although Birmingham remained opposed. The EC responded positively. Two-thirds of the 272 responses to the Society's consultation (and more than three-quarters of large firms) favoured relaxing the ban. The *Gazette* pronounced that 'MDPs have already arrived. The market has driven the carriage and now all that remains is for professional bodies around the globe to scrutinise the rules of the highway code.' The *New Law Journal* accused the Society of 'dragging its heels on this issue for long enough'.

The IBA considered urging countries to ban MDPs, limit non-lawyer ownership, and subject non-lawyers to lawyer discipline, but ultimately challenged only the combination of legal and auditing services (which the SEC also prohibited). Both the CCBE and the Paris Bar opposed the PwC merger, but the EC approved it. As their associated law firms joined to become Arnheim Tite & Lewis, Wilde Sapte (one of the City's twenty largest firms) voted to merge with Garrett, but this time AA decided to pursue further growth through hiring.[30]

In 1999 KPMG adopted the brand name Klegal for all its associated law firms, declaring it would be a 'serious player' within five years. PwC aspired to be the fifth largest law firm in the world by then, and E&Y to be among the top firms in just three or four years. Arnheim Tite & Lewis expected to grow more than 50 per cent in the next year.

When the CCBE declared its opposition to MDPs, the Law Society was the only one of the six British professional associations to dissent. The CCBE planned to intervene on behalf of the Dutch Bar against AA and PwC in the European Court of Justice. But MDPs continued to grow. AA acquired another German firm, giving it 170 lawyers there; PwC absorbed its sixth firm that year, boasting that its 1,450 lawyers would reach 5,000 in five years, all practising under the brand name Landwell. Arnheim Tite & Lewis's earnings grew 58 per cent in 1999 and were expected to grow another 40 per cent in 2000. A survey found that 58 per cent of top US companies and 52 per cent of UK were quite likely to use MDPs.

Breaking ranks with the CCBE and ABA, a Law Society working party endorsed both MDPs with majority solicitor ownership and fee-sharing between linked partnerships of lawyers and non-lawyers. Michael Mathews, immediate past-president, called existing restrictions unjustified. Vice-President Kamlesh Bahl conceded: 'Like it or not, MDPs are on the agenda'. An unpublished ACLEC report acknowledged that 'the status quo is unlikely to be maintained'. But Anthony Bogan feared that solicitors were 'in danger of losing our independence ... the accountants are leading this debate and are doing so for their own commercial interests'.[31]

D. Specialization

By intensifying the division of labour that spawned the profession, specialization can increase quality and cut costs, but it also provides a refuge from competition. Required by the Insolvency Act 1985 to license insolvency practitioners, the LS education and training committee recommended a specialization board; but when forty-eight of the sixty-eight local law societies responding to the consultation resisted on behalf of general practitioners, the Council shelved the idea.[32] Shortly after the Green Papers the Law Society established a specialization committee, which the *Gazette* hoped would give 'solicitors an extra weapon in their armoury to fight off competition in revenue law, planning and employment law'. Secretary-General John Hayes agreed: 'In a world where others may be given a right to do work hitherto done by lawyers, it would be foolish to hold back measures that help lawyers show that they can do it better'. The committee proposed to supplement existing panels on children, mental health, and insolvency with others on planning, higher court advocacy, personal injury, medical negligence, employment, pensions, revenue, and crime, and was considering panels on consumer and commercial law, intellectual property, immigration, and housing.

While recognizing the difficulty of reconciling 'the need that solicitors with particular competence in individual fields should be easily identifiable with the need to ensure that the development of specialisation does not imperil general practitioners', the committee proposed limiting advertising to panel members. The standards and guidance committee retorted that anyone should be able to claim expertise. The joint honorary secretary of the Birmingham Law Society agreed: 'we are all specialists'. When the Council voted by 39 to 27 for the latter course the NCC condemned this 'highly retrograde move', designed to confuse consumers, and LAG called it an 'abdication of responsibility', which 'will lead inexorably to greater external regulation—at least for the state-funded legal aid sector of the profession'. The Young Solicitors Group felt 'only objective criteria can truly determine the real specialist'. Lord Mackay concurred that the public needed 'to identify official accredited specialist solicitors who they know meet objective standards'. The Law Society expressed 'surprise' because 'the government has for many years pressed us to relax our restrictions on advertising'. When Mackay repeated that 'a specialist does not... become a specialist just by calling himself or herself a specialist', the Society called it 'inappropriate for him to criticise a decision after the event'.[33]

The Society could not help solicitors confront external competition without disadvantaging generalist solicitors, who forced several concessions. The Council relaxed the specialization committee's criteria for the personal injury panel. The Association of Personal Injury Lawyers (APIL) wanted competence evaluated by file inspection rather than examination. The panel rejected only 10 per cent of the first cohort of applicants (though it deferred 15 per cent). Philip Sycamore, chair of the civil litigation committee, encouraged solicitors to apply so that loss adjusters and claims assessors would 'not be allowed to get a foothold'. Relaunching the Accident Legal Assistance Scheme in spring 1994, which had benefited 3,700 firms, the Society limited referrals to panelists. By 1996 APIL was drafting an ethical code for its members, regulating case referrals, the buying of victims' names, and cold-calling victims. The Society of Trust and Estate Practitioners required five years of experience and planned an examination; its membership (which included non-lawyers) grew from 300 to 4,800 in four years. The Law Society helped the British Standards Institution develop BS 5750 to 'give firms a competitive edge not only over other solicitors, but also over the other professions which are beginning to encroach on lawyers' traditional territory'.[34]

These divisions resurfaced at the Society's 1995 roadshows, organized to appease members' discontent. A Tunbridge Wells solicitor complained that 'too many people are excluded, causing resentment, particularly when [panel membership is] linked to [the] accident line', and a Swindon solicitor worried about 'a situation in five years' time when you cannot practise in an area if you are not a panel member'. But a Stroud solicitor called the Society 'too concerned with pleasing the lowest common denominator' and opposed 'watering down of standards'. In July, the Council approved the 'Lexcel' practice management standard by two to one, over the opposition of President Mears and past presidents Holland and Sheldon. Mears dismissed the proposal as 'banal', 'bureaucratic', and 'absurd'. 'If you want to become efficient, you do it. You don't need kitemarks to stick over your door.' Another Council member said 'constant regulation is not wanted by the small firms'. But a year later fifty firms had applied for Lexcel, 380 for the Investment in People standard, and others for BS 5750 (now ISO 9000). Outsiders were eager for more information about quality. The

Business Superbrands Council included Clifford Chance, Freshfields, and Slaughter and May among 100 enterprises offering consumers 'significant emotional and/or tangible advantages over [their] competitors'. The *Gazette* hoped the LAB would grant franchises on the basis of both Lexcel and the specialist certifications (see the next chapter). Indeed, Lord Mackay told the Solicitors Family Law Association (SFLA) it was 'extremely important that the tax-payers' money should be used only for services of proper quality, and accreditation is one way of achieving that'.[35]

Partly in response to judicial and academic criticism of quality, the SFLA and the Law Society family law committee proposed accreditation on the basis of three years' experience, 40 per cent specialization, a questionnaire and interview, and a course. Eight months later the LAPG also considered family law accreditation. The Law Society expressed concern that incompetent solicitors 'damage the reputation of the entire profession in this field, and there is no easy way for the public to identify which solicitors do a good job'. Although the SFLA reported 'tremendous pressure' for the proposal, family law committee member Peter Watson-Lee was opposed. 'Panels are not primarily about increasing the amount of work done by the profession as a whole' but about 'taking the work away from some of those who do it now (the generalists) and giving it to others (the specialists).' 'Panels and Kite marks are all a load of bureaucratic nonsense dreamt up by people with nothing better to do.' The 920 responses supported the consultation paper by two to one, as did the LAPG, AWS, Association of Lawyers for Children, and SFLA; but local law societies split evenly, and the SPG and BLA were hostile.

The Council proceeded to consider specializations in family, criminal, employment, housing, and immigration law (launching housing in August 1998). President Sycamore noted the 'real expectation amongst practising solicitors that their professional body should try to regain control in setting standards, especially with respect to legal aid'. The LAB declared its willingness to recognize Society accreditation 'as an equivalent to a franchise'. Declaring that 'tomorrow belongs to the specialist', the LCD anticipated 'integration or overlap' between franchising and professional accreditation, which also 'could be developed as a marketing tool'.

Criticizing the Society's delay, SFLA chair Nigel Shepard declared it was 'not frightened to take the issue on alone if the Law Society fails to act'. When the Society proposed requiring only 300–350 hours of family law work over each of the previous three years, the SFLA dismissed this 'fudge', urging 550 hours a year, six years' experience, and an examination. Hilary Siddle, the Society's family law committee chair, acknowledged that its proposal was a compromise, which would not 'operate unfairly against' sole practitioners. The committee opposed 'commercial organisations setting up their own "family panels"... which will have the effect of confusing the public and the profession'.

Others resisted exclusivity. The LAPG declared it 'wrong to set the criteria too high'. Watson-Lee again denounced this 'major threat' to high-street practices. Panels were a 'gift' for 'those who are part of a large firm with specialist departments, or a niche specialist practice'. 'A modest fee and a little form-filling generate a decisive marketing advantage over the general practice competitor.' But Eileen Pembridge thought it 'a little too late for the generalist to argue that the tide of specialisation should be reversed' because family law was 'under more threat than ever from the paralegal activities and from the proposed slashing of legal aid costs'. The NCC agreed that at a time of 'greater focus on quality by consumers', the Law Society 'should be jumping on the bandwagon with more specialist panels'. Its capitulation to 'pressure from some quarters to spread the work around' was 'yet another instance where the Society's duty to the public and its trade union role work against each other'.

In the end, the SFLA (representing 4,000 of an estimated 10,000 family law practitioners) adopted more stringent criteria and published a promotional leaflet warning clients against non-member solicitors, infuriating the latter. The Law Society accepted 82–85 per cent of applicants, deferred 15 per cent, and rejected only 2–3 per cent. By the time the SFLA launched its panel of eighty-seven a few months later, the Law Society had certified 2,160. But when the LCD Advisory Board on Family Law expressed concern about the Society's laxity, the latter retorted it was 'not prepared to see the Family Law Panel become some kind of exclusive clique of super-specialists'.[36]

Not content with the personal injury panel, APIL established the College of Personal Injury Law (in collaboration with the Law Society College of Law) as a 'way of indicating that a lawyer is both competent and committed to continuous education'. All APIL members could become associates by committing themselves to fifteen hours of training over three years; 'members' had to have five years' experience and twenty-four hours' training; 'litigators' also had to be able to try a case; 'fellows' required ten years' experience, fifty hours' training over five years, and three references; and 'senior fellows' had to be recognized as 'distinguished practitioners'. But some found even this insufficiently elitist. Richard Grand, who had created the (American) Inner Circle of Advocates, limited to 100 lawyers who had won a $1 million verdict, launched the still more exclusive Richard Grand Society for twenty-five solicitors who had completed at least five personal injury or medical negligence cases totalling £5 million. He promptly enrolled two Law Society presidents and other prominent solicitors (after relaxing the requirements and doubling the numbers).[37]

Partly in response to government proposals to create a criminal defence service and award exclusive contracts for criminal legal aid and advice and assistance (see Chapter 10), the Law Society issued a criminal specialization consultation. When it was supported by two-thirds of the 500 responses, including the Criminal Law Solicitors Association and the London Criminal Courts Solicitors Association, the Society commented: 'four years ago, it would have been seen as quite a controversial issue—but now the need for specialisation is almost universally recognised as a good thing'. The Law Society Commerce & Industry Group urged members to acquire a National Vocational Qualification or MBA and talked to the Law Society College of Law about post-qualification courses and to Leeds Metropolitan University about an LL.M. leading to the Institute of Directors' qualification. Fearing competition from accountants qualifying as authorized probate practitioners under the Courts and Legal Services Act 1990, the Society launched its first substantive section in 1997 (modelled on the ABA's). Contemporaneous surveys found that 28–40 per cent of solicitors regularly probated wills. The 12,000 letters of invitation enrolled 1,600 in two months, continuing to attract 100 a week.[38]

By 1997, 71 per cent of solicitors considered themselves specialists (more than 80 per cent of those under 45, 90 per cent of those in firms with more than ten partners), and a third of generalists thought they would be more satisfied as specialists. The material advantages were clear. A solicitor found that children's law increased from 20 to 90 per cent of his caseload after he joined the panel, and he earned higher legal aid rates. A personal injury panelist called it 'a far better marketing tool than competing on price in litigation'. The chief assessor of the mental health panel assured a member that 'many potential plaintiffs telephone the Law Society for a recommendation and they are always given the names of panel members'.[39]

E. Lay Competitors

Solicitors faced competition not only from large companies, other professions, and each other but also from laypeople. In 1991 the Law Society spent £200,000 on a public relations campaign directed partly against will writers—'no more than insurance salesmen in disguise'. It threatened co-operating solicitors with discipline for violating rules against referring business and liability for will writer negligence. Immediate past president Tony Holland called the Government's failure to regulate non-solicitor probate 'unbelievable in these days of increasing chicanery' and warned of 'a veritable free for all in dealing with the winding up of estates'. Although the CA found little difference in the quality and price of wills drafted by solicitors, banks, and will-writing companies, the Advertising Standards Authority received increasing numbers of complaints against companies. Worried about 'cowboys', the Institute of Professional Willwriters (IPW) formed that year, requiring training, adherence to ethical rules, and indemnity coverage.

Two years later the Society again complained to the LCD about will writers' 'frequently deficient or misleading' advertisements and to ACLEC about their inadequate training. The Society also assailed the Government for authorizing probate practitioners, opening 'the door to all sorts of people, some of whom might be quite undesirable...they'll actually have the money in their own bank accounts'. With 'a wave of his hand', complained Tony Girling, the Lord Chancellor 'conjures up the Ugly Sisters in the guise of the approved probate practitioners'. Illustrating competitive pressure for imitation, a solicitor urged colleagues to 'get away from the concept that solicitors must actively run probate departments. We must offer an efficient service at a lower price than we do now, and the way to do that is to "deskill".' A contemporaneous survey found that nearly all solicitors felt that 'will-writing business must be safeguarded since its loss would mean the loss of other business such as probate and introductions to beneficiaries'. The Society should 'persist to get all will-writing services subject to statutory standards and regulations'.

The next year the Society and the Will Writers Association (apparently the IPW under a new name) renewed their call for regulation, without success. The Society's own promotional campaign made sure that 'any advertisements...contain the word "solicitor"' in order 'to differentiate between solicitors and unqualified will-writing agencies'. When another CA report rated four out of nine will-writing and insurance companies poor and none good, but six out of thirty-one solicitors firms good, twenty reasonable, and only five poor, the (new) Society of Will Writers called it 'misleading, inaccurate, and potentially defamatory'. Far from being 'completely unregulated', as the CA alleged, its members had to train employees for two to five days! It also called for regulation. But when it incorporated in Delaware as the Royal Society of Will Writers, the Companies Office (at the Law Society's behest) ordered it to drop the false claim of a royal charter.

Two years later the *Gazette* feared 'substantial erosion' of solicitors' market share, noting that 15 per cent of wills were drafted by testators and DIY probate had increased 33 per cent in five years. But a contemporaneous CA survey now found half of solicitor-drafted wills only 'average' or 'poor' and, on the whole, no better than those drafted by laypeople. The Nottinghamshire Law Society responded with a campaign warning about the poor quality of non-lawyer advice. When LS President Sayer promoted the eighth annual 'Make a Will Week' in 1999 he declared it 'as important as ever for solicitors to defend their share in what is an increasingly crowded and competitive market'.[40]

Claims adjusters also invaded lawyers' turf. Independent Legal Practitioners had sold exclusive jurisdictions for £5,000–50,000 (depending on size) to sixty franchisees, who were handling 2,000 cases a year, mostly unfair dismissals and work injuries, for a contingent fee (usually 25 per cent), which lawyers could not employ. ILP (which took 15 per cent of fees) had a staff of six, advised by six to eight lawyers, and accepted just one out of forty applicants, who trained for three days. The rival Claims Direct offered no training and accepted all fifty-two applicants, who paid £5,950 each and took a 30 per cent contingent fee from the recoveries of clients they found themselves or bought from CD after they had been vetted by a solicitors' firm. CD also had panels of doctors who prepared medical reports, barristers who evaluated damages, and solicitors who litigated cases that did not settle. Michael Napier, outgoing APIL president, condemned the 'selling of cases'. Martin Mears felt such practices 'have a bad smell whatever the theoretical justification'. When CD convinced the Advertising Standards Authority to require solicitors offering 'no win, no fee' to advise clients to insure against an adversary's costs, Napier complained that the object was 'not protection of the consumer but a political battle by claims assessors afraid of their territory being encroached on by solicitors'. Direct Legal Advisers of Manchester only admitted charging 50 per cent of damages; but, winding it up, the DTI found that 56 per cent of successful claimants got nothing after fees and expenses, 14 per cent less than 10 per cent, and only 12 per cent more than 40 per cent.

After a Pembrokeshire oil spill, Managers and Processors of Claims, a 'multi-disciplinary practice' of accountants, surveyors, and 'legal representatives' (not lawyers), signed up most potential clients for a 10 per cent contingent fee. A local solicitor complained that 'they cornered the market' within a week 'before any of the local solicitors could get a look in'. The Law Society head of court business insisted 'these people pose a great danger to the public'. Napier feared 'the cut-price conveyancers of yesterday will be overtaken by quick-fix under-settlers of personal injury claims tomorrow'.

In 1996 APIL complained about claims assessors to the LCD Parliamentary Secretary, who declared himself 'horrified'. APIL vice-president Ian Walker maintained that 'putting their case in the hands of a claims assessor is not going to do [victims] any good whatsoever.' President Caroline Harmer agreed: 'accident victims very often as they lie in hospital or even in an ambulance, are prey to these unscrupulous people.' 'At worst', said the Law Society, 'these unqualified legal advisers are just cowboys or crooks. At best, they can only provide a second-rate service'. Delighted the LCD would investigate, APIL called it 'a fair trading issue...the public need to know they are going to lose bigger chunks of their damages'.

The Society used the opportunity of the 1999 Access to Justice Bill debate to brief Edward Garnier to move amendments limiting assessors. Solicitors complained that assessors' fees were 'unduly costly, and that the settlements they achieve fall far below the settlements that a competent lawyer would achieve. In addition, they compete unfairly with members of the legal profession, who must bear the considerable costs of regulation.'

Garnier denied this was 'a lawyer's whinge', and Andrew Dismore (in a rare alliance) called it 'a serious problem'. But because the Government had only 'anecdotal evidence', it rejected the motions, promising further investigation.

When the LCD review committee chair reported that most complaints were from solicitors concerned about work 'slipping away from them', Napier dismissed the charge of self-interest as 'rubbish'. The *Solicitors Journal* worried that 'very little evidence of consumer exploitation will be found, and the whole exercise will be written off as a sop to lawyers scared of competition'. Doubting victims could 'make an informed decision', it condemned 'small groups of cowboys' who 'persuade people to sign up to contingency fee deals and try and settle them at the earliest possible opportunity without any reference at all to lawyers'. The inquiry's only result was that CD replaced its 30 per cent contingent fee with litigation insurance, once premiums could be recovered under the Access to Justice Act (see Chapter 8). Delighted it was 'off the "hit list" ', CD wanted to work with the LCD 'to deal with the cowboys'.[41]

Information technology intensified the threat of lay competition. The press lauded Desktop Lawyer, accessible through the internet. Mistitling its story 'Why the Web's bad news for Rumpole (and very good news for the rest of us)', the *Daily Mail* declared:

> more and more people are turning their backs on flesh-and-blood lawyers and sorting out their legal affairs on-line. With just a few clicks of the mouse, it is possible to get reliable and accurate advice for a fraction of the cost of a conventional high street solicitor.

But the chair of the Law Society family law committee professed unconcern: 'If you feel you can proceed without [a lawyer's] advice, that's fine'.[42]

Two anecdotes illustrate the gamut of challenges. A group collected £80 a year from non-lawyers to join its 'Society of Lawyers'; a member had to 'demonstrate that he is suitably trained and experienced in his discipline and so knows what he is talking about', his 'knowledge is up to date', and 'commercially he is safe to do business with'. The Law Society sought to enjoin the name because 'there is clearly a need to protect the public'. The Institute of Legal Executives (ILEX) agreed. The SoL retorted defiantly (if illogically): 'If there are 80,000 solicitors, there must be 800,000 more people practising law who want to be accredited'. When the injunction was issued the SoL considered renaming itself 'NottheSociety of Lawyers'. The *Gazette* warned that 'the growth in the USA of "legal technicians"—providers of legal services outside the legal profession—who work for much cheaper rates than lawyers, has been very substantial'. Since such competition was 'much less developed' in the UK, 'there is still time to mount a strong challenge'. The 'Law Society can help by monitoring the non-lawyer industry and highlighting at every opportunity the risks of unregulated provision of legal services'. ILEX itself was a much more formidable threat. Concerned that its qualification was 'perceived as old fashioned and unattractive in the new legal services marketplace', it responded to the Access to Justice Act 1999 by contemplating seeking the right to do probate, sign compromise agreements in employment disputes, and engage in more criminal advocacy. Both ILEX and the Incorporated Company of Scriveners also emulated solicitors (unsuccessfully) by claiming exclusive rights to the titles of legal executive and scrivener.[43]

F. A Free for All?

The Bar Wars were as much about status as economics. Aside from young barristers' realistic fear of the CPS, the most intense conflicts were provoked by archaic distinctions of dress and address, private practitioners' condescension toward their employed colleagues, and appointments of QCs and judges. Most solicitors did not want to do advocacy. But powerful competitors coveted solicitors' markets, threatening long-standing but unstable accommodations among: solicitors, insurers, estate agents, and lenders; solicitors and accountants; domestic and foreign lawyers; generalist and specialist solicitors; and solicitors and laypeople (both subordinates and independent practitioners). Many potential competitors were reluctant to initiate what is always a costly zero-sum game (for producers). Yet its rewards, disproportionately enjoyed by first movers, inevitably propelled someone—usually an outsider—to evade, flout, or challenge restrictive practices. Large employers of professionals were the greatest threat: lenders and estate agencies for conveyancing (as government was for advocacy). Such challengers often found, or bought, internal allies. The first response of those threatened was to resist by deploying state and professional power, rhetoric, and economic leverage. The inevitable (if often delayed) failure of this strategy frequently provoked a rush to imitate: solicitors advertising and claiming specialization; selling property, loans, insurance, and investments; representing buyers and sellers; merger mania in the City and inflated ambitions for market share by the Big Five. Professional regulation reluctantly, and vainly, played catch-up to market innovation.

Solicitors carefully cultivated an image of sweet reasonableness in deliberate contrast to the Bar's rigid traditionalism. But though they talked the language of laissez faire, solicitors responded to competition with a protectionism that verged on, even transgressed into, illegality. They objected to lenders offering conveyancing as a loss leader and regulated colleagues who delegated such work to laypeople. The Law Society sought to agree an 'indicative' range of fees with the CML—and was promptly reprimanded by the OFT. Local law societies openly engaged in price fixing nearly thirty years after the abolition of scale fees—and had their knuckles rapped by the DGFT. But Mears remained 'entirely confident we could put up strong public interest arguments' in their favour. And Sayer even wanted to tie fees to property values again. Just when the Society had required solicitors to quote advance fees (see Chapter 9), Sayer advised colleagues to avoid price competition by charging hourly fees for conveyancing, as he did. Sounding like southern American school districts flouting the Supreme Court's desegregation decision, Law Society Council members seriously proposed defying the OFT and risking public opprobrium in order to preserve restrictive practices for a few years until the MMC ruled against them. The Society advised solicitors to discuss fees with colleagues—about as close to the line as one could get (and clearly illegal in the USA). Walter Merricks adamantly resisted 'sharing reserved areas of work with other professions'.

Solicitors strenuously tried to get SIF to discriminate against cut-price conveyancers, asserting a connection between price and indemnity exposure on the basis of evidence that they would never tolerate as lawyers. Mears declared the link 'inherently probable' and 'common sense'. Sayer called it 'obvious and direct', dismissing legitimate questions about his sample size. Bogan asked rhetorically: 'could 8,500 solicitors all be wrong?' A high-street solicitor drew a wildly inappropriate analogy to the relationship between smoking and cancer. Solicitors opposed title insurance in order to retain conveyancing. To increase revenue, the Society sought separate representation of lenders (who did not want it), despite OFT opposition. John Edge found a silk to call the practice kosher, and the often critical *New Law Journal* thought there was a colourable argument. To block MNPs, the Society initially proposed to require SIF payments from every partner of a foreign lawyer practising in the UK. In support of eschatological prophecies about the imminent demise of high-street practitioners, Sayer and Bogan adduced highly suspect and mutually inconsistent statistics. The SPyG warned members that their practices were coming to a 'very abrupt end' and Society officials against 'killing the goose that lays the golden egg'. Edge found it 'offensive' that after twenty-five years in practice he should enjoy such a 'meagre financial reward'. But Andrew Lockley and Eileen Pembridge thought small firms should accept euthanasia.

Combatants had no compunctions about retaliating against competitors. Sole practitioners asked the Law Society to boycott lenders who excluded them from conveyancing panels. The SPyG (which boasted that its members competed only against estate agents, not each other) threatened to withdraw deposits from lenders who engaged in conveyancing. The NAEA members sought to conduct their own title searches to prevent solicitors from reaching clients first. Scottish solicitors' property centres refused to accept listings from estate agents or even solicitor property sellers who listed with agents. Estate agents refused to refer clients to solicitors selling property. Leeds solicitors stopped referring clients to AA when it opened an affiliated solicitors' firm; accountants boycotted solicitors engaged in insolvency practice. But cartels are always difficult to sustain (as City firms found when American competitors bid up salaries): while some solicitors joined property centres, others co-operated with estate agents to secure referrals.

Nevertheless the genie of competition (like that of democracy) is hard to force back into the bottle. Solicitors had good reason for concern when the Consumers' Association and the Adam Smith Institute agreed that house sales had to be simplified. Faced with growing voter anger at the cost, delay, and uncertainty of house sales, Government found solicitors a convenient whipping boy. Deep suspicion of lawyers led the media to dismiss their claims about the irreducible complexity of conveyancing and applaud lay competitors and DIY. Even solicitors acknowledged (contemptuously) that secretaries were learning conveyancing in fifteen hours. When the property market recovered, lenders and estate agents grew more interested in conveyancing. Lawyers and accountants, not surprisingly, found ways to create the equivalent of MNPs, MDPs, and SPyCs well before they were formally authorized. The rapidity of their growth testified to the demand that had been frustrated by restrictive practices (just as the sharp drop in conveyancing fees exposed monopoly rents). Size, multinationality, and multidisciplinarity were potent (if unreliable) advertisements for quality, which otherwise was very hard to evaluate.

Attempts to preserve restrictive practices, much less create new ones, invariably backfired. Solicitors feared that efforts to retain the conveyancing market would provoke lenders to bring work in-house. John Edge unrealistically wanted solicitors to dictate estate agent commissions rather than allow agents to set conveyancing fees. Professional politicians played the populist card. Bogan urged the Society 'to behave as a trade union and protect its members'. Sayer successfully rode the 'groundswell of anger' to power. But the Society never embraced scale fees or SIF discrimination against cut-price conveyancing. Even solicitors admitted that the 'underlying reason' to propose separate representation of lenders was 'to increase the fees'; and the SPyG rightly feared the headline: 'Solicitors rip off the public'.

Justifications for restrictive practices were archaic, contradictory, flimsy, even incomprehensible. Solicitors were torn between maintaining that conveyancing was technically too difficult for laypeople and delegating it to their own subordinates. Some attacked the competence of will writers (although empirical studies found little difference in quality), while others declared solicitors could only retain that market by deskilling. Solicitors opposed corporate conveyancing while trying to break into the market for property and loans and campaigning to combine litigation with advocacy.

The Law Society wanted to stop employed solicitors from conveying property while championing their higher court audience rights. Solicitors criticized others for tying-in but wanted to retain will-writing as a source of probate work and introductions to beneficiaries. A Law Society President opposed MDPs as 'product based rather than client based' and warned that the 'rule of money would overcome the rule of law' (whatever that meant). The Society claimed to pursue the public interest, only to be denounced by impartial representatives like the DGFT. The Society's lack of credibility emerged in its inability to convince the public and the government of the real dangers of unregulated will writers and claims adjusters.

Solicitors (like barristers) resorted to anti-market arguments. The *Solicitors Journal* called the loan market 'a vicious, highly competitive, plundering jungle', where 'the borrower is the prey'. Bogan invoked anachronistic warrants to condemn 'unfettered competition'. Tony Holland warned of a 'free for all in dealing with the winding up of estates'. When solicitors ventured into new markets (in competition with accountants or foreign lawyers, who thought the Law Society's restrictive practices hopelessly quaint) they confronted regulators far less deferential than the British Government. Solicitors found it difficult to resist the incursions of will writers or claims adjusters, who operated in relatively private arenas and, exempt from Law Society regulation, could solicit business and accept contingent fees. Information technology intensified these threats.

Unable to claim superior efficiency, solicitors played the trump card of 'independence', allegedly absent in those employed by lenders or estate agents or subordinated to accountants in MDPs. As Law Society DVP, Mark Sheldon raised 'ethical objections when legal functions are carried out by organisations concerned to develop commercial profits'. But there was no evidence that privately practising solicitors were more independent or that clients wanted (and would pay for) this trait, since hardly any sought financial advice from solicitors. Even privately practising solicitors were divided about separate representation of lenders and borrowers, buyers and sellers. And they quickly abandoned ethical pretensions under economic duress. The Law Society might 'worry about the high moral ground' if solicitors were allowed to sell property, said Leslie Dubow, but 'conveyancers are worried about whether they will have a crust to eat next year'. Calling conflicts of interest 'complete nonsense', Robert Sayer exhorted the Society to 'trust solicitors to be honest; they are, by and large'.

Once solicitors exhausted protectionism and retaliation they had no choice but to challenge competitors for new markets. The real question was who would dominate. Sayer, with typical candour, voiced the fear that solicitors would 'simply get swallowed up'. Edge wanted to 'see how estate agents like having their fees dictated by others!' Solicitors were determined to sell property, loans, financial advice, and insurance rather than allow estate agents, lenders, or insurers to do conveyancing. They needed to contact buyers before estate agents and lenders, just as barristers wanted direct access to reach litigants before solicitors. English firms wanted to dominate foreign lawyers within MNPs, not work for Americans. The Law Society wanted solicitors to diversify into (potentially more profitable and unregulated) financial services rather than allow MDPs controlled by accountants (especially the Big Five) to offer legal services. Solicitors could hardly object to laypeople delivering legal services when they had relied on managing clerks (renamed legal executives) for centuries and were expanding the role of paralegals. They simply wanted to continue controlling them (and extracting their surplus labour value).

Subordinates and newer market entrants responded by seeking to professionalize. Estate agents accused of unethical behaviour sought state licensure. Will writers invited regulation. Some claims adjusters sought to differentiate themselves from the real 'cowboys'. Legal executives, already a successful paraprofession, sought to diversify their functions and broaden the scope of independent practice. But these hopes were largely frustrated. The age of professionalization had passed; a government determined to eliminate the monopoly rents enjoyed by entrenched professions was not about to let newcomers control production of and by producers. And solicitors naturally opposed any challenge to their superior status and economic power. Estates simply could not be probated by the 'Ugly Sisters', or 'all sorts of people', some 'quite undesirable'.

Solicitors naturally differed in their concerns about and reactions to external competitors. A few entrepreneurs were eager to emulate them by seeking economies of scale and substituting capital and non-professional labour for professionals. Most were traditionalists, however, who wanted to remain small and offer personal service but feared that consumers, unable to evaluate quality, would be unduly swayed by price. Innovation tended to come from outside: businessmen like Richard Berenson, solicitor estate agents like Michael Garson. As solicitors lost market share, abandoning contested areas for others with higher profit margins, the constituency to defend what remained (of conveyancing or probate, for instance) dwindled in size and clout.

It was internal competition, however, that exposed and enlarged the deepest fissures. The SPyG condemned price competition as fratricide: 'solicitors killing their brothers'. Solicitors who denounced the quality and ethics of estate agents or claims adjusters in strong, even abusive, terms were reluctant to breach collegiality by casting aspersions on other solicitors. Attitudes towards advertising and MDPs differed by firm size and solicitor age. Solicitors who had struggled (successfully) to wrest regulatory authority from the state and use it to restrict competition now suspected that those powers had been captured by professional fractions. Caught between lay competitors eager to take over tasks that could be routinized and monopsonistic consumers (lenders, estate agents, the government) shaving profit margins while offering employment, solicitors embraced specialization. The battle over its definition replayed the politics of the original professionalization project; indeed, specialization was a reaction to the progressive devaluation of that credential. Now, however, the contest occurred within a mature profession, whose basic precepts it challenged. Some specialisms, such as trust and estate practitioners, even questioned the professional category by including non-lawyers.

Professionalism responds to the market failure of information asymmetries between specialist producers and generalist consumers by offering quality assurances that assert the fungibility of professionals. Professions forbid members to claim comparative superiority. The adversary system promises justice regardless of who represents the two sides. But everyone knows this is a fiction; clients buy the best lawyers they can afford, and the enormous variation in lawyer incomes reflects these radically different valuations. Specialization and kite marks simply institutionalize these judgements, while reasserting quality assurance and equality within the new enclaves. Just as professions suppress price competition, so specialization seeks to avoid it by claiming superior quality. Like professionalizing occupations, specialist certifications compete for turf: among ISO 9000, Lexcel, and Investment in People with respect to management practices; between both the SFLA and APIL and the Law Society over substantive specialties. The most contentious issue, of course, is the boundary: specialists pursue exclusivity by creating new associations (the Richard Grand Society being an extreme example); generalists demand that the Law Society preserve inclusiveness, insisting 'we are all specialists now'. APIL offered a characteristically English compromise (possibly inspired by silk): four ranks, largely defined by seniority. This strategy advantages specialists by disadvantaging generalists. Like professions, specialisms seek authority to define standards and engage in self-regulation and governance. Although the government resisted the emergence of new professions, it encouraged divisions within existing professions, especially when these facilitated its efforts to control the legal aid budget (see the next chapter). The resulting fractions did not exhibit the rivalries of specialists and generalists, but they also eroded professional solidarity.

In the previous chapter I predicted the Bar would retain most of its advocacy market (aside from losses to the CPS and CDS), as well as the associated prerogatives of silk and judgeships. The solicitors' market was more valuable, vulnerable, and volatile. House-selling will be vertically integrated, with solicitors unlikely to be the big winners. Conveyancing will be concentrated, since consumers care more about price than quality. MNPs will proliferate, although some City firms will dominate rather than be subordinated to foreign lawyers (even Americans). MDPs will expand (even if able to perform only some accounting functions). And the future of law, like all knowledge industries, lies with the specialist. Restrictive practices that had withstood criticism for centuries collapsed in less than a decade. The market is truly inexorable.

7 Conservatives Cut Legal Aid Costs

[The LCD] will wake up one day to find that the criminal legal aid system has broken down. [John Aucott, LS remuneration and practice development committee chair]

[L]egal aid is not, and cannot be, a blank cheque from the taxpayer. [Lord Mackay]

[If] the only argument the LCD understands is 'market forces', it is time that we as a profession show some muscle and threaten to withdraw from the market. [Cornwall Law Society]

[T]hreats of 'strikes' and 'boycotts' are a matter which I wouldn't consider diverting me from what I thought to be right. [Lord Mackay]

[Lawyers should tell Government] look, if you are not very careful we are going to have to pull out of providing our services. [Rodger Pannone, LS President]

I always listen with care when the Society is talking about access to justice at the same time as wishing to get higher fees. [Lord Mackay]

[The LAB is] a grim, downcast institution, riven by internal dissension... the Government's poodle, and the Lord Chancellor is not beyond giving it a kick when it suits him [to] satisfy the Treasury that he is as ready as the next minister to make people bid for its jobs. [Charles Elly, LS President]

[T]he present system makes it possible to create and exploit demand in ways which may not always be in the best interests...of the clients concerned...the legal profession should not have carte blanche to tout for business. [Lord Mackay]

The classic professions—law and medicine—presented themselves as *honoratiores*, indifferent to material reward. Clients and patients were lucky to get their services. Lawyers and doctors did not seek custom: gentlemen do not engage in trade. The rapid accumulation of capital and growth of the *bourgeoisie* in the nineteenth century stimulated demand for the emergent modern legal professions. Control over the production of producers ensured that such demand would exceed supply; control over production by producers ensured that individual lawyers would not suffer competitive disadvantage from mandatory passivity. By the 1980s, however, these comfortable arrangements were unravelling. The expansion of academic legal education dramatically increased the number of graduates. The contemporaneous growth of legal aid allowed many more to earn a living by serving a clientele previously denied access to justice. The extraordinary increase in divorces from 38,000 in 1951 to 176,000 in 1981 explained much of the jump in civil legal aid certificates from 38,000 to 270,000. Between 1970 and 1983 the civil legal aid budget grew tenfold and the criminal more than twentyfold. Legal aid transformed the relationship between lawyers and clients from a neo-classical market in which no consumer can influence price or quality to something more monopsonistic in which some sectors of lawyers were increasingly dependent on a third-party state payer.

This was particularly true at the Bar, whose legal aid earnings grew almost sixfold from 1975–6 (when they represented 27 per cent of the Bar's income) to 1983–4. By the mid-1970s nearly half the Bar's income (and more than half of juniors') came from criminal prosecution and defence, paid almost entirely by the state. Despite the cab-rank ideal that barristers represented the Crown in the morning and the defence in the afternoon (in different cases), more than half of London criminal law specialists devoted at least 70 per cent of their time to one side. Dependence varied greatly by substantive area: London Chancery and specialist barristers derived only 1–7 per cent of their income from public funds; London family, common law, and criminal juniors and all Circuiteers earned half to three-quarters. More than half of barristers received little more than 10 per cent of legal aid payments, but 16 per cent accounted for 42 per cent and just 10 per cent for 27 per cent.

Instead of fees being proposed by a barrister's clerk and accepted by a solicitor on behalf of a client, the Bar Council negotiated collectively with the state. In 1985 it sought a 30–40 per cent increase based on a Coopers & Lybrand report. A day after the Lord Chancellor gave it just 5 per cent, 1,000 barristers jammed an extraordinary general meeting, unanimously denounced the action, narrowly rejected a boycott of prosecution briefs, and sought judicial review. Although a court granted leave, the Lord Chancellor got the Bar to drop the case by agreeing to negotiate, ultimately giving it another 3 per cent and 2 per cent for changing its working practices.[1]

Solicitors were far less dependent on the state. In the mid-1970s, three-quarters of their income came from non-contentious work (none of it legally aided)—almost half from conveyancing and a quarter divided about equally between probate and company work—and only 12 per cent from matrimonial, criminal, and personal injury litigation (mostly legally aided). But contentious work expanded as non-contentious contracted because it became less profitable and was lost to external competitors (described in the previous chapter). Solicitors' legal aid earnings increased from £40 million in 1975–6 to £281 million in 1984–5. Even in the earlier year legal aid represented 80 per cent of sole practitioner contentious work, 60–70 per cent for firms with more than nine partners. Because contentious matters generated a much smaller proportion of solicitors' income than barristers', however, legal aid represented only 6 per cent of their gross fees. But this was very unequally distributed: half of all firms received only 6 per cent of payments, while 5 per cent of firms received a third.

The Royal Commission recommended that legal aid eligibility be expanded and indexed to inflation, contributions reduced (eliminated in magistrates' courts) so as not to impose 'an undue financial burden in pursuing...legal rights', and coverage extended to tribunals. Although the Government accepted the last in principle (if never in practice), it rejected virtually all the others, endorsing contributions according to means in all cases. Rather than increasing or even preserving eligibility in the face of inflation, the LCD cut it in 1986—the first time since the scheme's creation. When several prominent legal aid firms stopped doing such work or dissolved in 1985–6, the Law Society commissioned a Peat Marwick study, which confirmed the low profitability. On that basis the Society sought a 26–34 per cent increase in criminal legal aid fees (based on the salaries of solicitors employed in government or business). When the Lord Chancellor awarded only 5 per cent, the Society joined the Bar's action but, like it, obtained little more.[2]

In 1986 the LCD responded to concern that the number of legal aid bills was 'rising steadily' and civil unit costs were increasing 'significantly faster than prices generally' by conducting an efficiency scrutiny, which proposed to save £10 million annually by substituting CABx for Green Form legal advice (which had increased from 180,000 applications in 1974–5 to 950,000 a decade later). But though NACAB claimed that lay agencies were 'more efficient and cost-effective' in advising about welfare benefits, housing, and employment, it criticized the quality of its bureaux' housing advice, and an LCD-funded study concluded that 'the vast majority of solicitors are not abusing or misusing the green form scheme'. The LCD wanted legal aid recipients to make continuous contributions so that they would 'consider the costs...of the actions in which they are involved'. Government should set all legal aid fees, increasingly by the case rather than the hour. Only solicitors on specialist panels should do legal aid work. The Law Society was generally hostile, but its own study found that solicitors were ill-informed about welfare benefits and delegated most advice to paralegals. Two years later the Marre Committee reiterated many of Benson's recommendations: retention of Green Form advice, client choice of a solicitor, legal aid in tribunals, restoration of eligibility to 1950 levels, and prompt payment of 'fair and reasonable remuneration'. It supported standard fees after further consultation with the profession.

A. Client Eligibility and Lawyer Remuneration

Instead, Government sought to control legal aid costs by curtailing eligibility and reducing fees. Two observers estimated that 13–14 million had been excluded during the 1980s. When both branches criticized Lord Mackay in 1990 for not indexing eligibility for inflation, he retorted that

'increases in eligibility must be accompanied by measures to reduce unnecessary costs'. The Law Society denounced his disregard of inflation over the
next two years as 'a permanent cut in the number of people qualifying'.
The Bar was more concerned about remuneration rates, since it derived
38 per cent of its income from public sources in 1989, compared with 11 per cent
for solicitors (but the 10 per cent of solicitors' offices receiving half of all
legal aid payments were even more dependent than the Bar). Both
branches and the LAPG issued the first of endless warnings that lawyers
would abandon such work.[3]

When the Law Society requested a 16 per cent increase in 1989 for
London firms, Mackay gave it only 6 per cent based on a study commissioned jointly by the Society and the LCD, which found that solicitors could
make a profit, some 'a very healthy profit', with sufficient volume. The
Society replied that London firms as a whole lost 40 per cent on legal aid
work and twenty-five of the 175 firms earning 75 per cent of their income
from legal aid the previous year had dropped out. When solicitors sought
to increase High Court fees from £54 to £78 an hour (noting that private
clients paid £200), a Tory MP denounced this 'economics of madnesss'.
The NCC and *New Law Journal* urged fixed fees in routine cases. When the
Justices' Clerks' Law Society accused hourly fees of rewarding 'incompetence and slowness', the London Criminal Courts Solicitors Association
blamed delay on the clerks' 'archaic listing system'.[4]

The Law Society sought 21 per cent in 1990, but Mackay gave it only 7.5,
although the two agreed that costs had risen 12 per cent in 1988–9 and 14.7
in 1989–90. John Aucott, chair of the Society's remuneration and practice
development committee, explored judicial review but refrained from
seeking it on the advice of silk. Although the LAB reported only a 4 per cent
decline in offices doing legal aid, Aucott claimed that 'anecdotal evidence'
showed 'a lot more are pulling out' and predicted that the LCD 'will wake
up one day to find that the criminal legal aid system has broken down'. LS
President Ward attacked the idea that 'cheapest is best'; no government
would propose that for health care. '[T]he only thing that will move the
Lord Chancellor is a decrease in the number of suppliers'; but solicitors
would not boycott legal aid 'because of their sense of vocation and commitment'. Indeed, eighteen of twenty provincial firms called industrial
action a 'retrograde step', which would 'remove all professionalism'. The
New Law Journal feared 'no-one might notice we were gone' because 'the
everyday lawyer has outlived his or her usefulness'.[5]

When the LAB proposed to increase quality and decrease costs through
franchising, the Society declared a boycott, backed by the LAPG, to resist
legal aid being 'concentrated in a small number of firms', and the BLA
urged the Society to fight 'to the limit of its powers and ability'. LAB chief
executive Steve Orchard accused the Society of failing 'the quality test' and

'using the franchising scheme as a stick to beat the government with over remuneration'—a comment the Society called 'disgraceful'. When the Board relaxed the franchise criteria the Society lifted the boycott (in which fewer than five firms had participated).[6]

Mackay admonished the 1990 Bar conference that 'legal aid is not, and cannot be, a blank cheque from the taxpayer'. The Criminal Bar Association chair claimed that barristers encountered 'huge difficulties' doing legal aid work (although the cab-rank rule required them to accept such briefs). LS President Holland called the threatened cap 'the worst of all possible worlds'. But *The Times* applauded Mackay for having 'blown away many of the cobwebs in the legal profession' and attacked 'the rising cost of legal aid'. The 'open-ended £700 million a year legal aid subsidy dominates the economics of the legal system and keeps it expensive'. Without it 'the law would be forced to look for business the average customer could afford to pay for'. As a 'powerful consumer', government should 'demand better value for money' and eliminate hourly fees, which created 'an incentive to let cases drag on for as long as possible'. 'Wasteful doublemanning must be abolished.' 'The law should serve justice, not the interests of the profession.' Although some accused lawyers of 'milking the public teat', the *New Law Journal* argued that lower remuneration would produce 'a downward spiral of standards and less choice of able representation'. LAG blamed increasing legal aid expenditures on rising crime and legislatively mandated duty solicitor schemes.[7]

Three months later Mackay denied that 'to ensure access to justice, all you need to do is make available additional public funding'. Justice was 'priceless', but 'it must not be too pricey if it is to be accessible'. Instead of more legal aid he proposed alternative dispute resolution, lay representation, legal expenses insurance, and a contingency legal aid fund. The LAPG called these ideas stale and unworkable. Quoting the Old Bailey inscription, 'Defend ye the children of the poor', Holland noted that twenty-six South London firms had rejected a domestic violence victim seeking a protective order. 'It cannot be right', said incoming BC chair Scrivener, 'that a legally-aided client gets landed with a very junior member of the firm while a rich client goes and sees the senior partner'. The *New Law Journal* warned that 'fixed fees inevitably means [*sic*] cut corners'.[8]

Two months after that Mackay complained that legal aid had increased by 42 per cent in real terms since 1985, 'more steeply than expenditure on any other government programme'. He was considering raising the contribution from an average of £200 to a maximum of £3,000 because it was 'too simplistic' to say that 'everyone who wants to take his or her case to court should be able to do so'. '[W]e all value more that which we have to pay for. Litigation is a weapon, to be handled responsibly.' In 'privately funded proceedings there is a client who asks questions and seeks value for money'.

The Law Society denounced this as 'abolishing legal aid for all except the very poorest'. Telling people to 'spend all your money—and then we might just give you legal aid' would 'frighten people away in very large numbers' and 'be a disaster'. LAG said it would deny legal aid to the 20 per cent of recipients paying contributions. But the *New Law Journal* feared 'the legal aid battle is lost; probably the legal aid war is lost too'. While criticizing the proposal for increasing 'inequity' and limiting 'choice', the *Solicitors Journal* worried that lawyers' criticisms were 'open to the charge of self-interest'.[9]

Lord Mackay then launched a civil eligibility review because 'the problem of access to justice does not begin with legal aid' but 'with the way in which lawyers choose to operate and how they charge for their services'. The *Financial Times* called his proposals inconsistent with 'a citizens charter which would provide consumers of public services with legal rights'. The *Independent* attacked the proposals as 'out of date' and driven by 'parsimony'. LAG called it 'pastiche Thatcherism'. But the opposition was divided. The Bar urged a contingent legal aid fund (CLAF), which the NCC rejected. The NCC, LCF, and NACAB supported a salaried service, which the Law Society opposed.[10]

Although the 1990 Act authorized Lord Mackay to allow conditional fees the following year, neither he nor the profession was enthusiastic. He initially proposed a 10 per cent uplift because 'very high payments in successful cases' might 'generate a risk of the lawyer developing an improper personal interest in a particular case'. While urging that it be higher, the Society objected that the conditional fee just 'put pressure on the solicitor to fund the action instead of the government'. The *Solicitors Journal* presciently warned that such fees 'will be given as a reason by the Government for not increasing legal aid eligibility limits'. The Manchester Law Society president asked 'why should my firm invest in a lottery?'. Defence lawyers appeared to hope that conditional fees would discourage legal proceedings: 'lawyers who don't want to share in the risks of litigation are living in cloud cuckoo land'. The Law Society dismissed the 1993 doubling of the proposed uplift as 'a damp squib'. Action for Victims of Medical Accidents called conditional fees 'a fraud on justice'. John Morris QC, shadow Attorney-General, told the 1993 APIL conference that this was 'the wrong road to go down'. The Labour Party was 'not impressed by what's happening in America'. The LCD Parliamentary Secretary retorted: 'I'd like my lawyer to have an interest in winning'. The *Solicitors Journal* warned that conditional fees would be used in 'dead cert' cases, which did not justify the uplift, but not 'where there are going to be serious arguments on liability'.[11]

The 7 per cent 1991 legal aid remuneration increase compared with 9 per cent overall inflation and 16–20 in lawyers' costs. LAB chair John Pitts blamed lawyers for the fact that legal aid grew three times as fast as inflation during the 1980s. 'As a businessman looking at these figures,

I would say justice is pricing itself out of the market.' Responding to his call for greater 'productivity', the CLSA chair warned of 'supermarkets'. 'You're buying a service which requires a much greater skill' and a 'very personal' relationship between client and solicitor. *Counsel* accused the LCD of making legal aid 'the work of the young practitioner—remunerated at a correspondingly cut-price level'. Holland urged that an independent advisory rate-setting body replace 'the charade of annual discussions followed by an imposed settlement'.[12]

In July the Government withdrew immigration legal advice and tribunal representation from solicitors, 420 of whom had earned £2.6 million handling nearly 15,000 cases the previous year. It planned to substitute the United Kingdom Immigrants' Advisory Service but had not consulted UKIAS, which was riven by conflict, would need sixty more employees, and lacked offices in many immigrant centres. When UKIAS insisted that 'people must have a right to choose their own representative', the Home Office retorted 'it is not for [you] to determine government policy', and the Immigration Minister warned that a refusal would 'throw a question mark over the funding you already receive from the Home Office'. (The Marre Committee had declared 'clients should be able to choose whether to consult a solicitor or an advice agency'.) UKIAS was supported by some fifty organizations, including the Law Society and Bar Council. Urging it to 'stand firm against this pressure', the Immigrant Law Practitioners' Association predicted 'the government will have to back down'. The *Independent* condemned 'a government that professes belief in freedom of choice and citizen's charters' for 'establishing a new state monopoly'. The LS immigration subcommittee called the Government's capitulation 'a major victory'; but the Government conditioned further funding on UKIAS adopting a new constitution and accepting a Home Office observer on its board of directors.[13]

Convening the Law Society's first meeting of legal aid practitioners, President Ely urged 'realism'. Legal aid would belong to the 'preferred supplier' following a 'shake-out of the also-rans'. Orchard declared pay levels would 'reflect the costs of the most efficient firms'. Lord Mackay warned that 'we are just about at the limit of what is supportable without radical change'. The *New Law Journal* advised solicitors to 'roll over on our backs, put our paws in the air, accept the franchise system and have done with it'.

Instead, some took direct action. When Liverpool solicitors, supported by the national Society, refused to staff the police station DSS, the LAB renegotiated its terms. The CLSA urged members to refuse legal aid or limit representation to three hours per client to protest against fixed fees. A dozen local law societies withdrew from DSSs. The LAPG said 62 per cent of its members endorsed withdrawal. Cornwall urged the Law Society to resist 'by every means at its disposal'. 'The Council must not play the role of "Judas goat" by leading us to another summary execution of our profession-alism'. Fixed fees were 'strictly non-negotiable'. Solicitors were abandoning criminal legal aid 'in droves'. If 'the only argument the LCD understands is "market forces", it is time that we as a profession show some muscle and threaten to withdraw from the market'.

But the *New Law Journal* criticized this 'unedifying spectacle' and hoped most solicitors would not 'take such a drastic step'. Ely denounced the boy-cotts as 'inappropriate and premature' but called it 'perverse that at the very moment when the system of justice is under the greatest criticism' for miscarriages of justice in the IRA bombing cases 'the government should propose to put at risk the availability of solicitors'. Condemning the Lord Chancellor's offer of a 1 per cent increase for 1992 as 'insulting' and 'presented in a way that's almost underhand', LS VP Sheldon reported the profession's 'anger and near despair'. Henry Hodge urged a 'day of inaction'; 'one per cent makes us think of shutting up shop'. The strat-egy committee chair called it 'a kick in the teeth', bringing the system close to 'collapse'. Fixed fees 'will benefit only the opportunists and the cost cutters', warned the *New Law Journal*. 'Do we wish to see criminal legal aid representation carved up in areas like Kentucky Fried Chicken outlets?' But, given the profession's 'limited bargaining power', the *Solicitors Journal* was resigned to franchising, which promised 'greater efficiency'.[14]

Seeking a 10.7 per cent increase in legal aid remuneration, the Society commissioned an independent review, which found the LCD cost estimates 16–30 per cent too low. Lord Mackay raised his offer to 3 per cent and reconsidered the fixed fee levels. But when the DSS boycott spread, he refused to do 'anything other than what I believe is right'. The Cornwall Law Society considered urging clients to elect jury trial, which paid higher fees, but the Law Society reminded solicitors that 'the client's best interests' were paramount. Although Birmingham solicitors rejected boycotts 'to keep the press on our side' and because many criminal lawyers 'couldn't survive without legal aid work', others local societies continued the boycott 'to give the Lord Chancellor a taste of what will happen if fixed fees are introduced'. But John Aucott acknowledged that the Law Society could no more 'call for solicitors to withdraw their skills from those threatened with loss of liberty' than 'hospital doctors could withdraw their services from the sick and injured'.

The Society launched its 'Save Legal Aid' campaign with a press confer-ence by solicitors who had overturned the convictions of the Guildford Four, Tottenham Three, and Birmingham Six. Speakers warned that 'thousands' of lawyers would drop legal aid; 'we are going to have to do all the work badly and/or employ unqualified staff'; 'people will face injustice and be convicted of crimes they did not commit'. DSS rosters had fallen by half in Cardiff and Exeter and to nothing in Norwich. The Society planned to spend £200–250,000 lobbying Parliament and buying advertisements. Its survey found that 97 per cent of the public thought every accused should have a solicitor, but among 16–24-year-olds (likeliest to be charged), only 38 per cent knew one. When Lord Mackay invited all MPs to a briefing and denied the Society's claim that 11 per cent of offices had dropped legal aid, it accused him of misinformation.[15]

On 12 February nearly 2,000 angry lawyers confronted Lord Mackay at Central Hall, Westminster. Adopting the rhetoric of a Methodist preacher, BC chair Gareth Williams aroused energetic applause by quoting scripture: 'The labourer is worthy of his hire' and adding 'but he wants his reward in this world, not the next'. Lawyers felt 'deep anger at being treated like dogs'. The 'system of willful, deliberate late payment...is properly and moderately described as dishonourable'. 'We try to serve justice as lawyers. Are we not entitled to justice as individuals?' Alastair Logan warned 'these measures will destroy a fundamental human right...there will be more cases like the Guildford Four [whom he had represented] and the Birmingham 6'. A criminal lawyer had 'never known a Lord Chancellor who had been so heartily disliked by the whole profession'. The Law Society predicted that fixed fees could halve remuneration.

Lord Mackay retorted: 'Costs cannot increase at this rate. Only those who do not have to face the harsh realities could believe that any publicly funded legal service could be provided without regard to price.' Average payments to solicitors in magistrates' court cases had increased 80 per cent during a five-year period when inflation was only 33 per cent. Although standard fees were not 'a cost cutting measure', they were 'essential to safe-guard the interests of the taxpayers'. It was 'absolutely baseless' to suggest that solicitors would respond by taking on more cases: 'The profession must rely on its standards of integrity'. Pay rises for doctors and dentists were irrelevant because 'the last thing the Law Society would want, I suspect, is a salaried legal service'. If some lawyers abandoned legal aid, 'new people come as well. If the net number is a reduction...the rate of increase in gross income is thereby improved'.

He provoked cries of 'shame' by questioning the 'possible relevance' of miscarriages of justice. 'Some more cynical than I might suggest that it is an attempt to promote your financial interests by reference to well-known cases which are in no way connected with this issue.' Solicitors should

think very carefully before withdrawing from one area of work because of your dissatisfaction with proposed changes in another. Your threat to refuse to answer calls for help would hit members of the public at their most vulnerable in a police station and, if successful, it could lead to the very miscarriages of justice which we all wish to avoid.

Some shouted 'rubbish' and hissed. He provoked laughter by describing his 3 per cent offer as a 'significant increase' and 'entirely reasonable'. After he left, the LAPG vice-chair accused him of 'a display of unparalleled arrogance and shamelessness'. Ely called his statements 'inaccurate' and his imputations 'unworthy of discussion'. Although Mackay denied cutting costs, his next budget was £50 million lower. There was 'an obvious direct link' between remuneration levels and 'the availability of experienced legal aid practitioners', but the Young Solicitors Group refused to 'bail out the system'. The LCCSA warned that if the Government were returned in April 'we shall adopt a less co-operative stance in court. There will be a phased withdrawal from the bail duty solicitor scheme.'

The legal press supported the profession's position but not its tactics. The *New Law Journal* warned of 'the closure of legal aid departments, fewer solicitors seeing clients in rural and poor urban areas, inexperienced solic-itors once more undertaking cases as an adjunct to their conveyancing' and ultimately 'the Public Defender'. Although sympathetic, the *Solicitors Journal* wondered how solicitors could claim to be 'so concerned about mis-carriages of justice' and yet 'desert the duty solicitor scheme'. LAG agreed it was 'a badly chosen target'.

Lord Mackay replied it was 'too easy for one who is in the system to equate the interests of justice and the interests of the public with his or her own financial interest...threats of "strikes" and "boycotts" are a matter which I wouldn't consider diverting me from what I thought to be right'. Many of those most vociferous at the 12 February meeting 'didn't know anything about the detail of the subject matter'. It was not 'a particularly appropriate time', he warned the Law Society, 'to be involved in a detailed discussion in the media'.[16]

Both branches obtained counsel's opinions about judicial review of the rate increase. The Law Society, which had talked to the LCD about doing further research before setting fixed fees, was 'irritated' that the Lord Chancellor had not consulted it before commissioning the LAB. Ely called this 'underhand'. If the LCD 'haven't been candid', said Williams, 'I depre-cate it'. Mackay again denounced the DSS boycott, expressing incompre-hension at its link to fixed fees. When a remand prisoner died in the cells, the magistrates' clerk pointed to the boycott's 'potential for injustice'.[17]

In the 1992 general election campaign Conservatives emphasized 'effi-ciency' and 'value for money', while Labour warned that fixed fees were 'likely to lead to injustice for both the public who are on trial and the solic-itor'. John Morris QC thought it 'very odd...that there should be a prize for productivity where justice is concerned'. 'My passion is to put legal aid, as resources permit, back to 1979 levels.' Warning that 'legal aid is fast becoming a second class service', Paul Boateng, Labour's legal affairs spokesperson in the Commons, asked: 'How could a responsible department make an initial offer of a derisory one per cent increase in fees?' But he also could not 'promise a big increase in the legal aid budget'. And the shadow Lord Chancellor held out no hope of additional money. Although thirty-seven MPs signed an early-day motion expressing concern about fixed fees, Labour acknowledged it would have similar financial constraints. The party was concerned about consumer access to justice, said Boateng, not lawyer preferences. But after the Conservative victory he submitted 32,000 signatures to Parliament opposing both the pay increase and fixed fees.[18]

Criticized by the Commons Public Accounts Committee for failing to scrutinize criminal legal aid eligibility, the LCD required magistrates' courts clerks to demand thirteen consecutive payslips from defendants (not the most careful record-keepers). Solicitors immediately obtained leave to apply for judicial review. The *New Law Journal* called this 'another occasion when the law is an ass'. The *Solicitors Journal* condemned the LCD for making 'a mess in the magistrates' courts' within a month of taking over responsibility for criminal legal aid. The LCD soon withdrew the ruling.[19]

Under pressure from desperate members, local law societies dug in. A Bristol official called Chancery Lane 'very apathetic'. Assailing the Society's 'abysmal' performance, an Exeter official claimed 'industrial action would have been taken nationally' after the 12 February meeting, but 'without leadership and co-ordination our efforts throughout the country have been split'. Complaining about being 'isolated and criticised', Devon and Exeter permanently left the DSS. Chancery Lane regretted 'the impression the Law Society is critical of your action' but insisted 'there was no intention to encourage them'. The Society was 'quite certain' that had it 'declined to take part in talks, the LCD would have introduced standard fees a long time ago'. But though Shropshire solicitors withdrew from the DSS in July, they rejoined a month later, and Devon and Exeter also resumed staffing. More dramatically, the Bar Council chair and over 100 barristers embraced fixed fees for almost all Crown Court work (hoping this would expedite payment) and urged extension to civil matters.[20]

When the 1991–2 LAB report showed criminal and civil costs per case rising by 20 and 11 per cent while inflation was only 5, its chair declared 'the processes of justice are not well managed'. Standard fees 'give an incentive to reduce costs'; the only alternative was 'rationing and restriction'. APIL blamed the increases on LAB inefficiency and more complex cases, denying that 'the cheap case is a success'. A Law Society negotiator declared that 'quality goes straight out the window with these proposals', which the criminal justice committee chair called 'iniquitous'. When the Board accused lawyers of defrauding the government of £6.4 million the previous year, a solicitor retorted incautiously that rates were so low that 'the only way a firm can pay its bills and provide an income for the partners is by exploiting the system' and 'thrashing the file for the costs': writing more letters, making three steps out of the affidavit of means, issuing unwarranted demands, applying for unnecessary injunctions, demanding irrelevant financial detail, taking unnecessary statements, and insisting on long oral committals.[21]

In his Consumers' Association lecture a month later, Lord Mackay denied that access to justice meant 'access to lawyers' and endorsed salaried lawyers handling immigration matters, personal injury victims using small claims courts without lawyers, ADR, and American-style clinics charging fixed fees. With gallows humour, the *New Law Journal* asked:

Why not go the whole hog and forbid any solicitor who does not come up to the required standard for the time being to undertake litigation. The same could apply to conveyancing, probate and all other disciplines of law. And of course, the same would have to apply to the Bar. The useless, those perceived as useless by their peers, would be driven from the profession.

The *Lawyer* criticized Mackay for 'attempting to isolate the profession by tarring it as being too costly' but praised him for getting 'the voice of those whom the legal system serves...into the discussion'. The *Guardian* said ADR 'not only produces more amicable settlements, but also cheaper ones'. The same day JUSTICE published a report endorsing ADR, a CLAF, legal expenses insurance, and law centres. Early the next year *The Times* applauded these ideas.[22]

When Lord Mackay promptly accepted the new cost estimates for fixed fees he had commissioned from Price Waterhouse, the Law Society was 'bitterly' disappointed that these 'simply repeat the earlier flawed and discredited proposals' and vowed to oppose them 'with the utmost vigour'. President Sheldon warned that the 'ill-judged, ill-planned and ill-structured' proposals could 'compromise the fair administration of justice'. Calling the report 'inflammatory' and 'absurd', the disaffected Devon and Exeter society expressed resentment at being treated 'with complete contempt'. Shropshire was 'appalled by the report's stupidity'. But though the *New Law Journal* praised the Law Society for 'doughty resistance', it counselled against a 'strike action' solicitors 'will not win'. The 'difference between trade and profession' is that the members of the latter would 'not withdraw their services on a temporary basis over a financial quarrel which has nothing to do with those for whom they purport to care'. Acknowledging the Government's proven ability 'to confront even a well organised and fairly solid strike', the *Solicitors Journal* warned that 'separate and competing firms have no record of effective strike action' and 'public sentiment is unlikely to side with the lawyers'.

Dismissing all criticism, Lord Mackay told the Law Society annual conference that standard fees would be introduced in magistrates' courts, extended to the Crown Court, and considered for civil matters. 'Legal aid cannot continue to take an ever-increasing share of public expenditure'. Solicitors would be responsible for collecting larger contributions because litigants 'need to be brought up against the financial consequences of the action they are embarking upon'. Although the Society felt the Price Waterhouse proposal of a 'price per case' had 'real advantages over the LCD's currently proposed scheme', a meeting of 100 activists urged further resistance. A Bedford representative wanted the Society 'to recommend that the profession withdraws from the legal aid scheme altogether'. A Bristol member urged Chancery Lane to organize 'wildcat strikes' in magistrates' courts. A London firm wanted to disrupt the criminal process by going to court only when necessary. But the Devon and Exeter co-ordinator feared 'we would be letting down someone who we have made a commitment to' and conceded that 'a majority of people appear to have given up the fight'. And Birmingham conceded that industrial action was unlikely to be 'solid'. Among the 1,000 criminal legal aid providers responding to the Society's consultation, 14–15 per cent would withdraw from the DSS and another 10–11 per cent remove some staff; 16 per cent would leave criminal legal aid and another 20 per cent reject new work; but only 10 per cent supported a strike, which the *Solicitors Journal* called 'wild talk'.

Contemporaneously, the LAB proposed to franchise legal aid firms, expediting payment in exchange for quality control. Lord Mackay said such firms would have an enormous 'competitive edge' to grow because of 'pressure on price and the demand for quality' and the 'correlation between size and efficiency'. They might secure exclusive 'long-term contracts ... to undertake blocks of cases, both civil and criminal', perhaps by 'competitive tendering ... against defined quality standards'. The Law Society warned that franchising should not be 'a crude mechanism for cost-cutting'. The *Solicitors Journal* decried the lack of 'evidence that firms applying these fashionable management criteria provide better service' and asked: 'what has it to do with access to justice?' But Board-commissioned research found satisfactory correlations between transaction criteria for and peer assessment of quality and client satisfaction. John Appleby, chair of the Law Society's courts and legal services committee, was 'shell-shocked'. '[L]egal aid clients must remain free to instruct the solicitor of their choice', and 'franchises must be available to all firms that meet the quality criteria'.[23]

The *New Law Journal* foresaw 'supermarkets' engaged in 'pressurised plea bargaining'—'a public defender without the safeguards and benefits'. The *Solicitors Journal* agreed that the future lay with 'larger firms, who will not only have to tender for the work but also tolerate the interference of unskilled Legal Aid Board staff in the management of their business'. Tony Blair, Opposition home affairs spokesperson, called 'any attempt to slash the legal aid budget... disastrous for the legal system and for the many ordinary citizens for whom access to the courts would be denied'. But though LAG accused Mackay of 'controlling costs, paying his Treasury dues, and being able to hold his head up in Cabinet', it called franchising a 'genuinely fresh approach... a commendable and long-overdue attempt to encourage high quality work'. Indeed, LAG's contemporaneous 'Strategy for Justice' wanted salaried providers to compete with private practitioners. While anticipating 'formidable problems', Pitts saw 'very little difference' between this and franchising. The LAPG chair thought salaried lawyers were the inevitable and 'very worrying' extension of franchising. Walter Merricks (who had worked in a law centre) warned that 'things have gone very badly with salaried services' in America. But he conceded many solicitors 'might prefer to be employed, given the constraints that they now face', and had 'no doubt' welfare work 'would be delivered more quickly through a salaried component'.[24]

The professional associations could see no such virtues. Decrying the 'bucket-shop vision of legal aid', the LAPG called franchising 'the final nail in the coffin'. The Law Society should 'get tough' and 'get into the ring'. Anticipating its timidity, the LAPG planned an 'aggressive initiative'. But the Society did speak out strongly. Merricks called the proposals a 'disguised paycut', VP Pannone objected that 'the solicitor will have to become the debt collector', and Appleby attacked Mackay's equation of 'efficiency with size'. A Council member wanted 'seriously [to] attack the Lord Chancellor'; but the chair of the criminal law committee cautioned against 'criticis[ing] everything that has been suggested', and Holland rejected a 'purely trade union response'. Although some barristers had welcomed fixed fees, the Bar Council AGM called them 'contrary to the interest of the public and to justice and offensive and unfair and possibly unlawful'. And the audience hissed Attorney-General Sir Nicholas Lyell QC, its titular head, whom Peter Birts QC denounced as 'a member of the government which so far has shown scant regard for the rights of the Bar and our payment position'. Lyell warned the Bar it would be 'extremely wise to consider the offer seriously'.[25]

Lord Mackay replied to a Parliamentary question in November that to keep legal aid spending growth under 10 per cent for the next three years he would raise contributions, cut eligibility, and extend fixed fees to non-matrimonial civil work. Lord Williams denounced this denial of legal aid to the 'poorest and most disadvantaged members of society'. Sheldon called it 'the most serious attack on legal aid since the scheme began over forty years ago'. The Society estimated it would affect at least 7 million and limit Green Form eligibility to 21 per cent of households. Appleby declared it would deny advice to 11.5 million and legal aid to 14.5 million. Boateng accused Mackay of 'betraying his office as a protector of the rights of all people to equality under the law and access to the courts'. Both branches offered to forego the 7 per cent pay rise they had requested if government would preserve eligibility, which the LAPG called 'far more important as a principle than fixed fees'. It hoped these 'sacrifices' would 'engender a certain amount of public sympathy for solicitors'. But Mackay replied he had never intended to increase remuneration.[26]

During the Parliamentary debate, Lord Mishcon warned that Mackay's 'draconian' cuts would deny 'many millions' legal aid, whose 'proud name' would become the 'pauper legal aid scheme'. Outgoing BC chair Lord Williams called the cuts 'crude, mechanistic and lacking in consultation'. Legal insurance was 'a bare, mean palliative'. Lord Ackner accused the Government of betraying its 1983 commitment to the Royal Commission that 'legal aid should be available to those of small or moderate means'. But Lord Renton QC (Conservative) and Lord Browne-Wilkinson and Lord Prys-Davies (both Labour) agreed with Mackay that law centres would save money. The Lord Chief Justice used his Richard Dimbleby lecture to deplore that 'the shrinkage of those eligible for legal aid means large numbers of our citizens are denied access to justice' and 'endangers the very framework of our society'.[27]

Because the legal aid budget had more than doubled in the previous five years and 'will collapse from the weight', Lord Mackay reaffirmed his determination to achieve control. Hourly remuneration 'positively encourages the inefficient'. Contributions would make people 'consider their priorities, and in particular whether proceeding with litigation, with its inevitably uncertain outcome, takes precedence over other financial demands and ways of dealing with the problems they face'. LCD Parliamentary Secretary John Taylor told BBC television that people might have to consider 'giving up the holiday of a lifetime' if their 'legal problem is much more important'—just as he could not afford a Bermuda vacation.

LAG retorted that 'many will have no choice: they will have to buy the basic necessities of life rather than get advice on taking or defending proceedings'. 'Legal aid is more than a social service; it is a fundamental guarantee of rights.' At their annual meeting, SFLA members reviled Taylor as ignorant, 'aggressive', 'rude', and 'insensitive'. The two branches said they could save the £43 million Mackay claimed for his eligibility cuts if barristers appeared without solicitors and QCs without juniors. (The latter had been mandated in 1989, but only seven of 1,298 subsequent QC appearances complied.) The Society also endorsed conditional fees, fewer duty solicitors, and limited legal aid for guilty pleas not incurring custodial sentences.

The LAPG organized another mass meeting with consumer, charitable, church, and professional groups but attracted only 300. Boateng urged them to convince 'the general public that just as you ought not and cannot ration the National Health Service, you ought not and cannot ration the availability of legal services'. Conceding that past 'campaigning has revolved around lawyers' remuneration', the LAPG said it now was putting 'the public in the front line'. The NCC insisted that consumers be able to choose the 'traditional legal process' over the 'cheaper alternative' of ADR. Threatening to seek judicial review, MIND declared the proposals 'would contravene recognised principles of public law and furthermore breach the European Convention on Human Rights'. Mackay's own Legal Aid Advisory Committee expressed deep concern that the cuts 'will almost certainly have an irreversible effect on the scheme's provision for access to justice out of all proportion to the actual savings in public expenditure'. The Cardiff Law Society predicted a 'huge period of social unrest'. Carlisle wished the Law Society had highlighted the 'gross disparity' between payments to solicitors and silks rather than co-operating with the Bar.[28]

During the February Parliamentary debate the Lord Chief Justice warned that franchising would make small firm practice 'unsustainable'. He called eligibility cuts and increased contributions 'an abdication of responsibility' and joined the Master of the Rolls in asking the Lord Chancellor to 'pause' and give the Society's proposals 'full consideration'. Lord Alexander (a former BC chair) expressed the 'gravest qualms' that many will 'not be able to pursue their legal rights' in 'areas of basic concern: housing, family law, immigration and personal injuries'. Lord Donaldson (a former Master of the Rolls) said 'justice is not an optional extra in a society which is based on the rule of law'. Speaking for MENCAP, Lord Rix asked for 'justice ... paid for by those who can afford it and not by those who cannot'. More than 500, gathered to lobby MPs, heard from legal aid clients, MIND, and spinal injury victims. Lord Mackay dismissed the Society's estimate that 14 million would be excluded as 'absurd ... a wild assertion'. Legal aid certificates would fall by only 30 per cent, although the proportion who declined because of contributions might double from the present 20 per cent. Insisting that the profession's alternative would save only £8 million (which the Society called a misrepresentation), Mackay was determined to implement the cuts 'as soon as possible'. Boateng tabled a Commons motion noting 'grave concern' at the 'growing tension between the Government and the judiciary' arising 'from widespread disgust amongst the judiciary at Government policy on legal aid'.

The judges also were angry at Mackay for failing to enlarge the bench. The Lord Chief Justice threatened: 'If we can't get any response ... I think we shall have to see what more confrontation produces'. Lord Ackner dismissed the appointment of one Lord Justice as a 'strip of elastoplast to staunch a haemorrhage', insisting that six more were needed. The 'refusal properly to fund the administration of justice' was becoming 'near contemptuous'. After the Commercial Court chair complained that his list was in total disarray, and the LCJ called the delay in hearing criminal appeals 'a national disgrace' Mackay announced ten more High Court judgeships.[29]

Unable to sway the Government, the Law Society applied for leave to seek judicial review of standard fees, insisting 'this is not a dispute in which we are seeking more pay for solicitors'. Overpayment in other cases was no consolation to the defendant whose lawyer 'had been underpaid and therefore put under pressure to cut down on the job'. Granted leave, the Society invoked the ECHR requirement of 'fair compensation' for lawyers (among other arguments). The same day the home affairs select committee criticized both the profession's 'apparent failure to promote cost savings measures' and Mackay's 'completely unrealistic' cuts, which 'do not sit easily with the government's strategy to make the consumer and the citizen more aware of his rights'. The profession was delighted. Several weeks later Sir Thomas Legg, LCD Permanent Secretary, told the public accounts select committee that he was unaware of a letter by the Lord Chief Justice and Master of the Rolls warning the Lord Chancellor that cutting eligibility would burden the courts by increasing litigants in person. Although Legg promptly apologized for misinforming the committee, it took the 'most unusual step' of recalling him. He only aggravated the situation by claiming 'we did not see these changes as germane'. Calling this 'incredible', the Liberal Democrat spokesperson for legal affairs asked whether Legg wanted 'to take a little more time before you go down this route?'. Instead, Legg said the LCD regarded eligibility cuts 'as peripheral to the issue'. Less than three months later he chaired a task force that declared that the LCD's three-year strategic plan 'will give priority to controlling legal aid costs'.

When Parliament approved the cuts (by a majority of just forty-five), Boateng denounced this 'betrayal of the bipartisan approach to legal aid'. But the LCD junior minister explained that 'expenditure would be nearly £2 billion by the mid-1990s' otherwise, maintained that 'there is no question of legal aid being cut', and claimed that covering fewer than half of households was 'not bad for a poor man's lawyer'. Mackay insisted that the action 'protects the people who need the service most and it continues to give the protection of legal aid to people who are prepared, out of their disposable income, to make a contribution'. He rebuffed criticism by the Lord Chief Justice, whose 'responsibilities are different from mine'.

The High Court rejected the Society's legal challenge, calling it 'unworthy' to suggest solicitors might decline work and 'wholly improbable' they would cut corners. There was 'no difference in principle' between the proposal and the long-standing practice of standard fees in the Crown Court. The Society ignored the court's advice against appealing and claimed it had not addressed the *ultra vires* issue, only to lose again. The following year the LCD declared its intent to extend standard fees to civil cases and Crown Court cases lasting more than ten days.[30]

The Society lost a second legal challenge to the eligibility cuts, having left the court 'completely unconvinced' that these 'could be stigmatised as irrational'. Although the Society was pleased that the court recognized its 'unrivalled knowledge' and interest in being consulted, the *New Law Journal* thought it 'should have realised the hopelessness of its position before it launched its judicial review' and declared 'enough is enough'.[31]

B. Franchising

When the LS Council voted strongly to accept franchising but demand 'substantially improved' incentives, the *New Law Journal* accused it of complicity in 'the elimination of the small general practice'. The Society called the ultimate terms 'most disappointing', but 2,637 firms planned to apply. Although Lord Mackay reiterated his interest in exclusive contracts and competitive tendering, the LAB maintained 'it is not on our agenda'. But at a LAG meeting on franchising, Orchard called competitive tendering 'a running sore that needs to be brought out into the open' and agreed that 'average costs will become an increasingly important criterion in the granting of franchises'. LAG director Roger Smith condemned 'the hawking around of a murder case to the lowest bidder' as deeply 'distasteful'.[32]

One (probably intended) effect of fixed fees was heightened competition between solicitor-advocates and barristers. Furious that only solicitors were paid travelling and waiting time, *Counsel* claimed ' "freelance advocates" openly tout for work on the basis of paying back to the instructing solicitor one-third' of that difference. BC chair Rowe suggested chambers propose a fixed fee for covering a magistrates' court for part or all of a day, claiming this would not limit client choice. The Bar also launched a £100 fixed fee scheme for certain matters, and some chambers assigned pupils to magistrates' court work for £10 or gratis in order to attract more lucrative Crown Court work.[33]

Admitting defeat on fixed fees and franchising, the new LS President, Pannone, urged lawyers to make common cause with doctors and educators as 'vital elements in a civilised society'. Lawyers should tell Government: 'look, if you are not very careful we are going to have to pull out of providing our services'; but they must not be seen as 'a trade union/socialist cabal'. Noting that legal aid expected to underspend by £60 million, the Society sought restoration of contributory green form advice and a 7.7 per cent pay rise. The Master of the Rolls added his voice. The Lord Chancellor responded by raising eligibility but freezing pay for the second year and planning 'tighter controls on expenditure'. Furious that Mackay had announced this a week before a scheduled meeting with the Society, Pannone denounced the action as 'reminiscent of an old style trade union negotiator'. Relying on 'a deplorable mixture of prejudice and irrelevance', Mackay 'seems determined to punish legal aid lawyers for the increase in expenditure caused largely by the recession'. BC chair Seabrook declared the £70 a week ceiling 'a stark reminder of how appallingly low the legal aid eligibility thresholds have become'. The Lord Chancellor retorted: 'we have tremendous access to legal services compared with most other countries'. The Society 'appears to assume that if all else fails, the great thing that's good for you is to get a lawyer at other people's expense. I don't think that's a self-evident proposition.' He always listened 'with care' when the Society was 'talking about access to justice at the same time as wishing to get higher fees'.

The day he met Mackay, Pannone told the House of Commons that the partnership between profession and Government had 'virtually broken down'. Legal aid practitioners had been 'singled out', while other professionals, judges, and the Lord Chancellor received pay rises of up to 5 per cent. 'Perhaps the government believes that the supposed unpopularity of lawyers and their fees makes us an easy target.' Lord Mackay was 'now seen by many in our profession not as a distinguished reforming Lord Chancellor but as just another government minister who has managed to cripple a once proud public service'. The LAPG called Mackay's action ' a disgrace'. The Bar Council expressed 'disappointment'. But the Society accepted counsel's advice not to seek judicial review of the pay freeze. When Mackay abolished the Legal Aid Advisory Committee just after it criticized him for not restoring the 1993 eligibility cuts, the LAPG said it 'smacks' of retribution, and Boateng called it 'nothing short of scandalous'.

Pannone attributed solicitors' problems to 'the blindness, insensitivity, arrogance and the Treasury-driven short-termism of this government'. Mackay had 'put his belief in Conservatism ahead of his belief in justice' and 'destroyed the legal aid scheme'. Accusing the Lord Chancellor of crashing around in 'big boots', Elly (Pannone's successor) said he should 'put up or shut up'. The Lord Chief Justice reiterated that reduced eligibility and increased court fees were 'undoubtedly going to prevent some people from using the courts, which ought to be open to all'. A rumour circulated that Sir Leon Brittan would replace the 'universally disliked' Lord Chancellor (who served the remaining three years of Tory rule).[34]

Two and a half years after proposing a 10 per cent uplift for conditional fees Mackay raised it to 20 and then, three months later, to 100. Pannone (a plaintiffs' personal injury specialist) now saw a 'real chance' they would 'make justice available to some people who would otherwise be denied it'. Studies had found that fear of liability costs put great pressure on privately funded litigants to settle. The LS Council, by a large majority, refused to cap fees as a proportion of damages (although its model contract limited them to 25 per cent). Defence lawyers condemned the 'over-zealousness' of 'noisy campaigning solicitors looking for cases to pursue at public expense' and predicted 'a myriad of dubious, speculative' claims. The Lord Chief Justice had similar concerns. The BC legal aid committee chair feared that lawyers would have 'far too great an interest in the outcome of a case'. But the legal aid and fees committee chair did not think conditional fees would 'take hold in this country because the majority of barristers are very cautious'. Another silk attacked them as 'a contingency fee by another name'. The home affairs select committee chair (another silk) wanted a line 'drawn under all this destructive, revolutionary reform of the legal system'. Lord Ackner accused Lord Mackay of having 'created a monster'. The *New Law Journal* warned (inconsistently) that solicitors would file 'blackmailing' actions and take only 'cast iron' cases, while costing litigants 'real money in significant amounts'. The *Solicitors Journal* was more worried that 'by shopping around, the potential plaintiffs could receive quotes of...as little as 10 per cent'. An American personal injury lawyer warned that his colleagues were regarded as 'the rough equivalent of swamp leeches'.[35]

While conceding that it had lost the war, the Law Society kept fighting battles. Assailing the 'nitpicking' franchising scheme as 'a very unwelcome level of intrusion into practice', it declared a 'breakdown' in negotiations unless the LAB suspended the transaction criteria for the first five-year contracts. Pembridge accused the Board of 'outrageous...misinformation and dishonesty'. Exclusive contracts violated client choice, mandated by practice rules. The LAB retorted that franchising was a decision for individual firms, not the Society. The *New Law Journal* warned that 'smaller practices will be frozen out of legal aid work' and there would be 'reduced opportunities for traineeship and, on qualification, jobs'. Calling franchising 'one step away from tendering', the SFLA asked if 'we want to end up fighting among ourselves to do the work at less than the current legal aid rates?' and urged members to consider a boycott: 'perhaps we are all just being lemmings'.[36]

The LAPG, SFLA, APIL, LCCSA, CLSA, and Housing Law Practitioners Association asked the Law Society to call a boycott unless the Lord Chancellor modified green form cost guidelines and promised not to terminate franchising unilaterally or initiate competitive tendering. The LCCSA felt 'deceived' by the LAB. Bristol solicitors were 'militant', and Liverpool declared a boycott. Manchester wanted 'to say absolutely no deal to franchising'. A national survey found that 90 per cent of firms applying for a franchise would respect a boycott. Some 200 solicitors in London and the South East and another 100 in Birmingham vowed not to sign contracts.[37]

The Council endorsed a boycott, although anxious about appearing to engage in a 'strike' or other 'industrial action' causing 'disadvantage to clients'. When the LAB compromised, the Society was glad it was 'resiling from its bully boy tactics' but accused it of being 'erratic, inconsistent and incorrect' in processing applications. Elly called its behaviour 'an object lesson in how to bring chaos out of order, how to sow mistrust and fear and how to create a first-class disaster out of a modestly promising idea'. The Board was 'a grim, downcast institution, riven by internal dissension... gripped by a bunker mentality in which it can trust no one'. It was 'the Government's poodle, and the Lord Chancellor is not beyond giving it a kick when it suits him' to 'satisfy the Treasury that he is as ready as the next minister to make people bid for its jobs'.

Calling Elly's speech 'an absolute disgrace in tone and content', Orchard warned it was 'bound to have a very detrimental effect on negotiations'. The allegation of internal dissension was 'absolute rubbish'. 'There is a difference between not being totally independent and being someone's poodle.' Competitive tendering was a 'worst case scenario'. The Society's proposed quality certification and specialist panels were just an 'entry scheme' with 'no ongoing assurance that the standards are being maintained'. Pitts dismissed Elly's speech as 'a child's tantrum'.

Pannone acknowledged that 'unity is the key to success', and Henry Hodge feared 'the big players will break ranks and sign a contract'. The *Solicitors Journal* felt the boycott had 'come too late—after practitioners have spent inordinate amounts of time... preparing for franchising'. Although Mackay relinquished his power to terminate franchises, the Society stood firm. Only 169 out of 3,841 firms had applied in London, 3 out of 400 in Cardiff, 70 out of 1,000 in South Wales, and 57 out of 1,000 in Tyneside. But just before the August deadline the Society conceded defeat and urged solicitors to 'make their own individual assessment'. At the launch Pitts said franchising 'could revolutionise the delivery of legal services'. 'Never before has the public been able to identify firms and organisations whose expertise and management systems have been objectively assessed by an independent body.' Asked whether other firms were inferior, he said 'some people may see it like that'. Questioned whether they would be able to do legal aid work, he replied: 'Do you have the right to do something badly?' Orchard added: 'In two or three years time we may be able to say that if a firm is not franchised they're not good enough'.

Jeffrey Gordon, former LCCSA president and current BLA chair, complained that 'propaganda in favour of the franchised firm denigrates the experienced advocate as against the box-ticking advocate'. Demanding Mackay's resignation, the BLA called him 'one of the worst Chancellors in history and certainly one who is the worst enemy our profession ever had' and accused him of 'wishing to advance his political career by shaking up lawyers'. The *New Law Journal* denied 'big is beautiful'. 'There will be no place for the fiercely independent lawyer prepared to take on the establishment at considerable personal cost.' It hoped franchising would enable the BLA to 'rally opposition from the increasingly disaffected portion of the profession'. Instead, it was predictably divisive. The LAPG, which had just accused the Law Society of succumbing to the minority of applicants, now created a franchise-holder subcommittee to negotiate with the LAB independent of the Society.[38]

A year after the August 1994 launch, 1,050 offices had been franchised, 400 applications were pending, and 50 were arriving monthly. Noting that the LAB had predicted 1,000 at the launch and 2,000 within a year, the Law Society called the experiment 'a miserable failure' because it was 'not being widely respected as an indicator of high quality'. The Board retorted that it would have 2,000 contracts by March 1996. But in August that year twenty-one Birmingham firms declared a six-month boycott, assailing the 'bureaucracy and intrusion' of franchising as 'the first step toward conveyor belt justice' and warning that block contracts 'will cause the standard of work to suffer'. The CLSA president called franchising 'a sham foisted on the public in the name of quality'. Orchard retorted that 'nothing happened' when he asked solicitors to develop their own quality standards. Claiming that the ninety-five Birmingham firms holding or applying for franchises did 30 per cent of the legal aid work, the Board confidently predicted this boycott would fail, as the others had.[39]

C. Salaried Lawyers and ADR

In response to a June 1994 LCD legal aid expenditure review, the NCC advocated 'salaried lawyers who are expert in those areas of law not usually in the specialism of private practice'. The LAB promptly funded fifty advice centres. Even though they had to meet the same criteria as franchised law firms, the LAPG sought assurances that 'the quality of advice is equivalent to what the board is looking for from solicitors'. The Advice Services Alliance did not want 'competition between us and the legal profession'.[40]

Lawyers responded to the threat of ADR by seeking to ensure their indispensability. A leading barrister criticized the Chartered Institute of Arbitrators' proposal to handle medical negligence cases for 'forgetting that...the medical and legal issues are inextricably linked'. '[O]f one thing we can be certain', said the *Lancet* (with ill-concealed satisfaction), 'if the new system can be made to work, medical malpractice lawyers will be in serious trouble'. Only twenty-four disputes were referred to the Bristol Law Society mediation scheme during its first year, and just two processed, largely because of lawyer reluctance. Anticipating the 1993 Green Paper on divorce, the solicitor-dominated Association of Family Mediators (whose members charged £120 an hour) urged 'adequate funding...to enable solicitor mediators...to play a full part'. The chair of National Family Mediation and Conciliation Services (whose non-lawyer members charged £20–£25 an hour) replied: 'If I were a high street solicitor, I should be very worried'. Although the Green Paper mandated an interview to decide whether to award legal aid, Lord Mackay saw no 'need for lawyers to be involved at that stage'. Hoping to cut costs by two-thirds, the Paper contemplated denying legal aid to those rejecting mediation.

The Law Society family law committee chair warned that 'many situations will still require access to skilled lawyers' and mediation could impose 'false consensus'. Insisting couples wanted the 'added confidence' of consulting a lawyer, the SFLA called it 'crucial that both parties in divorce cases retain access to independent legal advice'. Former SFLA chair Tony Girling expressed the 'concern, particularly among small to medium [sized] provincial firms, that we will lose some of the matrimonial work we've had in the last few years which has supported firms to a degree following the decline in conveyancing'. The *Solicitors Journal* was concerned about the mediator's 'dual obligation to minimise the cost to the taxpayer while at the time giving the best advice'. Henry Hodge accused Mackay of 'hacking away at high street practices' and 'deprofessionalising legal services'. Elly declared it 'essential that before starting this process, advice from experienced lawyers should be available'. 'It is equally important that advice is taken after the mediation process.' Pannone, his successor, accused the government of wanting 'the courts to retreat from deciding what is fair for families'. Eileen Pembridge called mediation a 'cheap and cheerful' substitute for litigation. But Lord Mackay rejected the 'presumption that only lawyers can negotiate on behalf of the parties in a matrimonial dispute'.[41]

Just before the White Paper the new SFLA chair warned that 'people will be directed to mediation as a means to save money and prevented from getting advice on legal issues'. 'We're always accused of saying that it's taking the bread out of our mouths. But as professionals we should be concerned about the clients....' The *Solicitors Journal* agreed the proposals 'need to ensure that the solicitor is able to advise the client at an early stage and act as an advocate, otherwise the poorer, weaker party will be penalised'. Publishing the Paper, Lord Mackay denied seeking to exclude lawyers but conceded that they would get less money. 'It is probably not a good time to have lawyers involved when discussing terms of access'. The SFLA denounced a 'two-tiered system' that would 'steer people away from personalised legal advice', which 'must be available before, during and after the mediation process'. The Law Society concurred that 'access to legal advice is essential and a fundamental right'. Mackay conceded that lawyers should 'assist the mediation process', but they should not 'subvert' it, 'encourage confrontation', or 'take control of the negotiations'. (Research in both the UK and USA found that lawyers actually encourage embittered clients to settle.) The Society's family law committee retorted that legal aid recipients should not be forced into mediation, which was 'hardly out of its nappies'. Noting that 88 per cent of the 1,100 clients it surveyed wanted a solicitor, the SFLA said the Government's 'entire proposals' were based 'on a system which works only for a minority'. Lord Mackay responded that lawyers had told him 'there is a great deal of legal work done just now which is really not particularly helpful and might be better done by mediation and, in some cases, just by direct contact between the [party] and the district judge'. A solicitor warned that mental health professionals were establishing a UK College of Family Mediators 'to try to claim mediation away from solicitors'.[42]

When Conservative resistance forced Lord Mackay to drop the Family Homes and Domestic Violence Bill, the SFLA decided to support the Divorce Bill, but LS President Mears still attacked it for permitting mediation without lawyers. The Society's family law committee chair, Hilary Siddle, deplored that 'the profession has had little or no support' from Mackay, who 'has shown indifference to anything we have to say'. The 'thinly disguised purpose' of the mandatory 'information session' was 'to be an occasion for state-sponsored propaganda... coercing couples into mediation without the support of legal advice'. Mackay retorted that 'where services are supported by the public purse there should be objective tests as to when legal advice in divorce proceedings is appropriate', though he conceded there might be 'a standard amount of legal advice... before mediation was completed'. But Siddle maintained the 'half baked and ill thought-out' proposals would 'encourage the strong to take advantage of the weak'.[43]

During the Second Reading of what had become the Family Law Bill, Lord Irvine (shadow Lord Chancellor) condemned the 'two-tier system' because mediation 'is not truly voluntary'. Boateng called the Bill a 'dog's breakfast' and a 'Frankenstein creation', which Labour would not support. The SFLA also opposed the extended 'cooling off' period before divorce. The LCD responded by eliminating the presumption of mediation and requiring mediators to inform couples about the availability of legal services. Although Siddle was pleased that 'this goes some way towards creating' as 'level a playing field as possible', the Society still opposed the Bill for 'pressurising divorcing couples to forgo the assistance of lawyers... from the barely concealed prejudice... that solicitors make things worse'. Her committee believed 'an accreditation scheme for individual family lawyers would provide the public with a much better guide than anything else now available'. The LCD Parliamentary secretary dismissed this as having 'more to do with the Society representing the interests of lawyers than any desire to see an improvement in family law in this country'. Siddle called these remarks 'unseemly and unjustified' but declined to 'enter into a slanging match'. The Association of Family Mediators claimed that 'virtually everyone working in the field' found the Bill 'sensible', and the Family Law Bar Association supported it. When it passed, Mackay accused the Society of lacking 'respect, perhaps, for the proceedings of Parliament' by 'so easily' withdrawing its support.[44]

The greatest hope for savings lay not in controlling remuneration rates, lowering eligibility, or substituting ADR but in expanding self-help. In 1991 the LCD proposed that the small claims court, whose jurisdiction had been raised to £1,000 the previous year, arbitrate personal injury cases without awarding costs. APIL denounced this 'serious attack on access to justice'. Although the LCD retreated, a year later it proposed non-lawyer representation in small claims arbitrations up to £1,000. The Law Society, APIL, and the Motor Accidents Solicitors Society were opposed. Warning of the 'dire effect on business', MASS said 'our members are having a fit'. A workplace accidents solicitor objected that victims already were 'David against the Goliath of the insurance companies. These proposals would take away David's sling.' The Lord Chancellor backed down again. But when a 1994 survey found that two-thirds of those who refrained from legal action because of its cost had claims under £1,000, the Consumers' Association proposed increasing the small claims jurisdiction to £2,500.[45]

The Housing Law Practitioners Association denounced Lord Mackay's 1995 'cost-cutting' expansion of small claims court jurisdiction to £3,000 (excluding personal injury), which Lord Woolf had recommended. 'Disrepair and illegal eviction cases invariably involve quite complex law.' The Law Society civil litigation committee wanted greater protection for weaker parties. When tenants were allowed only £135 costs, HLPA warned 'many solicitors will simply stop doing this kind of work' or claim more than £3,000 damages. The LAB granted legal aid only in 'exceptional' small claims cases, which the Society called 'far too restrictive'. The *Gazette* noted that only 4 per cent of defendants appeared and only 58 per cent of successful plaintiffs recovered anything. Nevertheless, the LCD piloted a mediation scheme without legal aid for disputes up to £10,000.[46]

While Government cut costs, the media stoked popular indignation. A May 1994 *Sunday Express* headline screamed 'Millions lost in law cash fiddle'. The LAB agreed that firms marketing aggressively and submitting multiple green forms for a client were 'prima facie suspicious' (but estimated the loss at £1 million a year, not the tabloid's £12 million). Investigating twenty firms that leafleted, telephoned, and operated roadside clinics, the Board found clients 'having advice thrust at them' and being offered 'shopping lists of legal problems'. But it secured the convictions of only two solicitors and a clerk. The *Solicitors Journal* observed that 'in any other area of delivering social services, the accessibility of this service would be commended'. Several months later, however, the Birmingham High Court ordered the Law Society to investigate Alan Prichard, whose three offices (each staffed by a solicitor and legal executive) and thirty paralegals holding housing estate surgeries filed nearly 20,000 green forms worth £2.267 million in 1993–4.[47]

The Bar also was suspect. Lord Justice Henry, who presided over the extraordinarily expensive Guinness fraud trials, declared that barristers 'played the system' and urged that judges evaluate defence counsel performance before legal aid fees were assessed. In the House of Lords a QC and junior had claimed £107,000 for a four-day argument, and another silk had sought a £25,000 brief fee and two £2,000 refreshers. Deploring that government paid 'leading counsel more than double the income of our prime minister and over four times that of our members of parliament', LAG called for 'a comprehensive examination of the income of leading counsel for both criminal prosecution and defence work. Since the government makes the market, it should be able to bring rates down comprehensively.' The LCD had all criminal legal aid bills over £4,000 taxed, cutting barristers' claims an average of 25 per cent. Following disclosures that some fifty barristers each earned more than £100,000 from criminal legal aid in 1993–4, the Lord Chancellor planned to extend fixed fees to QCs and Crown Court cases lasting over ten days. Citing £250,000 for a will contest 'without substance or merit' and £500,000 for a failed claim to have invented the Sony Walkman, the LCD planned to blacklist barristers who brought spurious legal aid claims and report them to the BC. Soon thereafter its junior minister announced the LCD would be 'cracking down on over-optimistic counsel's opinions'.[48]

Legal aid to defendants with 'affluent life styles' further inflamed public anger: £1 million before Asil Nadir jumped bail, £4 million to defend Jawad Hashim of defrauding the Arab Monetary fund, £3.75 million for Roger Levitt's fraud trial, £750,000 for thirteen Nigerians charged with the largest benefits fraud ever. The 'outraged' chair of the Tory backbench legal committee found it 'very hard to justify' to constituents that 'money which they have contributed as tax payers' was funding 'the litigation of foreigners'. But when the LAPG warned the issue was 'becoming very nationalistic and xenophobic' and a solicitor accused Lord Mackay of having 'unwittingly fuelled an hysterical media campaign', the Lord Chancellor declared that 'our legal processes and our courts are not reserved to British subjects'. The *Sunday Times* contrasted the denial of legal aid in a suit for loss of a leg by a labourer earning £214 a week with its grant to a developer with a £750,000 mansion, two cars, and three children at private school. A month later it publicized legal aid for a nightclub owner who wore a Rolex, drove a Daimler, and owned a £245,000 yacht. When legal aid paid £4 million to defend Robert Maxwell's sons and more than £1 million to defend George Walker, the LAB created a special investigation unit for 'unusually complex' means tests and capped the home exclusion at £100,000 (for which the *Sunday Times* took credit).[49]

Notwithstanding media and public suspicion of litigation, the Law Society spent £200,000 to publicize the June 1994 relaunch of Accident Line, offering victims free advice, which 80 per cent did not previously seek from fear of cost and reluctance to sue relatives and friends. The scheme received more than 1,600 telephone calls the first day, 12,000 in the first sixteen weeks; nearly two-thirds of those accepting the free half-hour interview instructed the solicitor, and another 10 per cent were still deciding. Individual firms ran advertisements depicting ambulances and bandaged hands and offered a twenty-four-hour advice freephone and a hotline for holiday accident victims.[50]

The Law Society continued to seek higher remuneration rates: hourly fees had been frozen for two years, and standard fees had cut earnings up to a third. Elly called them 'no longer sustainable', 'about as low as they realistically can be ... between a half and two-thirds of the amount normally charged to private clients'. If they fell further 'many solicitors will be forced to abandon legal aid work'. The Society claimed that the collapse of Deacon Goldrein Green, the largest legal aid firm, showed 'how extraordinarily difficult it is for firms which are principally reliant on legal aid to make a living'. Elly also urged restoration of eligibility, which had fallen to 25 per cent; legal aid was the 'key' to 'equality'; the 'alternative' was 'anarchy'. But when he requested a 7 per cent rise the Lord Chancellor gave franchisees 2–3 per cent and others 0–1.5 per cent. One franchised firm urged the Society to 'stand firm for a single rate of pay', but Pembridge saw no reason why franchised firms (like hers) 'should not scrape a meagre bit extra for their hard work and investment'. An unfranchised Council member was 'unhappy about the notion that the franchised are the blessed and the non-franchised the damned'. The Society thought it 'particularly absurd to suggest that franchising at present equates to quality'.[51]

D. 'Supplier-induced Demand', Conditional Fees and Advice Agencies

In July 1994 the conservative Social Market Foundation published a pamphlet that fundamentally reframed the legal aid debate. Declaring that 'no Government can afford to continue to finance a programme which doubles its real cost every seven years', it blamed 'insurers who are remote from the services supplied by agents, the problem of moral hazard', and clients who rely on 'lawyers to decide what services they will supply'. These 'create potential for supplier-induced demand', which explained the 130 per cent rise in real cost per criminal case from 1987–8 to 1993–4 and increases in the number and cost of civil acts of assistance (especially the 50 per cent jump in green form applications). Legal aid 'provided a welcome source of work' during the 'slump in the property market and the sharp recession of the late 1980s', growing from 9.4 to 11.8 per cent of solicitor income between 1989–90 and 1991–2.

The authors wanted to replace 'passive third party payors of lawyers' with 'fundholders for justice' (modelled on NHS trusts), which 'would have no vested interest in using traditional legal services' and 'seek the most cost-effective means of access to justice'. The LAB would contract with firms, trading volume for price and conditioning renewal on performance; it might purchase legal advice from CABx and other agencies on similar terms. The pamphlet questioned 'the need for legal representation' in magistrates' courts and custody disputes, asking 'where the adversarial system is... efficacious in providing cost-effective access to justice?' It wanted to reduce moral hazard through client co-payment for franchised lawyers and fixed reimbursement toward the cost of unfranchised, withdrawing legal aid from money claims 'so lawyers and their clients are only prepared to pursue cases which they are likely to win', and cancelling the franchises of lawyers who lost expensive cases. Civil legal aid would have regional budget caps. Because the existing scheme 'provides perverse incentives for Counsel to prolong and increase the cost' in complex cases, the price should be structured so that 'lawyers on their feet should always be the last resort'. But the proposals were 'not intended as a blueprint', and the goal remained 'a system in which access to justice does not depend on ability to pay'.

Lord Mackay was 'attracted' to this 'important, interesting proposal' and apparently convinced of 'supplier-induced demand'. But the Law Society dismissed it as 'plainly farcical as far as criminal and civil legal aid is concerned', attacked fundholders as 'a way of capping expenditure on legal aid while distancing the government from the decision', and warned that clients would be 'sold at knockdown price'. President Elly denounced the 'sinister' plan 'to fix arbitrary limits on the budget'. LAG declared it 'ethically bankrupt'. Even Holland, one of the authors, was a 'bit edgy'.[52]

Calling 'the high and increasing cost of legal services' the 'root cause' of the legal aid controversy, *The Times* praised the pamphlet as 'the most penetrating study to date'. Legal aid 'can make only a restricted contribution in resolving disputes and securing the rights of individuals'. Britain was 'too court-centred for its own financial good' and the legal aid budget inflated by 'an unthinking commitment to litigation'. 'A cash limit on legal aid need not work to the detriment of justice' and 'will only work to the detriment of those lawyers who price themselves out of the legal aid market'. Lawyers 'have held legal aid in their grip for too long: it is time for Lord Mackay to ensure that the consumer comes first'.[53]

Days later the Lord Chancellor embraced most of the SMF proposals. 'Radical change' was essential if legal aid was 'to continue to command public confidence'. 'Far too much of the rise' in expenditure 'is attributable to an increase in the cost per case'. He wanted a mechanism for 'a proper and objective assessment' of 'genuine need' and for 'setting priorities between different types of proceedings, or different types of problems, or different ways of resolving those problems'. The present 'demand led' system 'makes it possible to create and exploit demand in ways which may not always be in the best interests...of the clients concerned'. The legal profession should not have 'a carte blanche to tout for business'. The 'virtually open-ended access to funding' was 'a luxury which few privately-paying clients enjoy' and was 'causing growing public anxiety. The sight of millions of pounds going to the lawyers of one individual against a background of restrictions on financial eligibility which effectively exclude many middle-income families is not easy to defend.' Without contributions clients had 'no incentive whatever...to minimise the cost of what they are receiving'. Providers should 'assess, and reassess frequently, whether what they are doing is providing value for money both for the client, and the tax payer'. Franchising offered 'quality assurance' for the 'first time in the history of the legal aid scheme'. He wanted to substitute 'mediation and arbitration' for 'expensive court-based solutions'. While rejecting the fundholder concept, he sought quality incentives and a cash limit. There should be competitive tendering for both blocks of cases and more complex cases. Money should be shifted from crime, family law, and personal injury to housing, debt, and employment.

Boateng warned the government not to 'repeat the disastrous experience of the national health service'. '[P]iecemeal Treasury-driven reforms' were 'no substitute for a comprehensive consumer-led review not just of the legal aid system but of the practices and procedures of the courts and the legal profession as a whole', which Labour would conduct in its first year. Mackay's proposal 'would do nothing to make court proceedings less expensive', said Elly, but 'simply deprive those who need help' and lead to 'rationing of justice'. Such 'crude' cost cutting would make legal aid a 'lottery' rife with 'discrimination between litigants'. The NCC condemned 'rationing to prop up an inefficient and expensive legal system'. But the Bar Council was pleased that block contracting would contain 'disincentives against solicitors doing the work themselves which could be more efficiently done by the Bar'.

A broad spectrum of newspapers praised this 'biggest shake-up' since the creation of legal aid. Rehashing past scandals, the *Evening Standard* thought it made 'good sense' to 'set priorities effectively according to need' and 'encourage early advice and different ways of resolving problems to reduce the need for litigation'. But it, too, saw parallels with the 'flawed NHS "internal market" reforms', which had 'created an expensive army of bureaucrats to police its byzantine workings'. Columnist Paul Johnson declared the 'scandal of legal aid' had 'suddenly accelerated in volume', reaching a 'depth of ignominy' that 'outraged public opinion'. Voters were 'furious' at 'the way in which lawyers have both administered the scheme and plundered it' of 'millions' of taxpayers' money to represent 'obviously high-living people', some of whom 'are not even British citizens'. Lawyer 'bigwigs...came to the aid of the Iraqi businessman, to the extent of £4 million of our money'. 'Legal aid is not aid to poor litigants. It is aid to rich lawyers.' The public was angriest 'that at every key point in the process the decisions seem to be taken by lawyers'. The 'many' 'firms of disreputable solicitors' were 'at the bottom of many abuses'. The 'system is not merely abused but is unsound, if not rotten, from top to bottom'. The LCD permanent secretary had told the Commons public accounts committee it was 'inherently vulnerable' to fraud. The committee chair had called green forms 'blank cheques'. The LAB chief executive acknowledged that 'dubious people' were touting for solicitors. Johnson concluded that beyond 'a fixed annual sum' for 'criminal defence of poor citizens...the legal profession must make itself responsible for financing the additional system', which would force 'a general deceleration in solicitors' hourly rates and barristers' briefs and "refreshers".'

The *Daily Telegraph* agreed 'the traditional system of legal aid is no longer sustainable'.

On the streets of Merseyside certain paving stones, rather like the herms of the ancient world, have become objects of reverence and pilgrimage, where wayfarers, under the encouragement of their solicitor, may trip and sue the local authorities. It has become not unknown for solicitors to tout for work in public houses, secure in the knowledge that the taxpayer will pay even for speculative cases.

Firms conducted a 'lacksadaisical' criminal defence, entrusting the work to secretaries and producing guilty pleas 'as though by a sausage factory'. Reform opponents 'have come to depend on current levels of largesse' and conspired, 'cynically, to frustrate the Lord Chancellor's purpose'. But the paper also accused Mackay of saying 'nothing' about 'the chronic wastage of the system'.

The *Independent* welcomed 'the end of a golden age for lawyers', in which the state had been 'prepared to sign blank cheques for Britain's professionals'. It was 'the turn of m'learned friends to face financial reality'. They would no longer live 'off the fat of the legal "pork barrel".' Elites always 'try to exempt themselves from the rigours of market competition. Lord Mackay should have no illusions about the capacity of his legal colleagues to hang on to outdated privileges.' The 'out of control' legal aid system, said the *Financial Times*, cost more than 'universal nursery provision for all 3 and 4 year-olds'. 'Lawyers often have a vested interest in taking on work which might be better and more cheaply resolved by other means.' The *Economist* agreed legal aid 'gives lawyers a strong incentive to waste public money'. By creating 'more access to the courts for more people', conditional fees would allow legal aid to be 'curtailed drastically and applied only to a handful of special cases', and 'every citizen in the land would, at last, have a fair opportunity to have a case heard in the nation's courts'. Lawyers 'may squeal', said the *Guardian*, but 'a society which rations life-saving NHS treatments will surely accept the rationing of legal aid'.

The legal press demurred. Ignoring the Lord Chancellor's claim that unit costs outpaced inflation, the *New Law Journal* attributed the rising budget to the fact that 'the dispossessed and underprivileged have, at last, through campaigns by the Law Society, committed solicitors and other agencies, been told of their rights and encouraged to seek them through the courts rather than lying down supinely and allowing various predators to eat them'. The *Solicitors Journal* feared the diversion of 'vast amounts of a firm's time' to 'bids for block contracts'. Capping, warned LAG, 'tends toward arbitrary decision-making, manifestly not in the interest of those for whom services are being provided'.[54]

The Treasury chief secretary chimed in that he was keeping 'a vigilant eye' on legal aid, which was 'displaying a chronic propensity for spectacular growth. No other significant Whitehall programme has seen such a seven-year soar in costs, rising from £363m in 1986/87 to over £1.4b in the current year.' A 'huge share' of the 19 per cent annual growth was attributable to the 'large increases in cost per case'. The scheme's 'fundamental weakness' was 'the strong element of moral hazard in funding arrangements'. Legal expenses insurance—£70 million in premiums compared with £1.25 billion in Germany—were 'a neglected area in this country and I would welcome the extension'. Noting that legal aid recipients could not afford insurance, the *Solicitors Journal* asked angrily: 'are Treasury ministers starting to take the lead on legal matters?' But it urged a tax deduction to encourage those ineligible for legal aid to buy insurance.[55]

The Times exhorted Mackay to 'hold firm' in his enthusiasm for conditional fees against a 'twitchy legal establishment', who 'have elected as their target a scheme that will make justice affordable for a wide swath of society, and make litigation easier for the middle class'. The CA agreed it would 'help some of those people who have been left out in the cold'. Responding to the new market opportunities, an insurance company offered to protect losing claimants against defendants' costs and winners against conditional fees. In April the Lord Chancellor proposed conditional fees in personal injury, insolvency, and human rights cases. Elly called this 'a major contribution' to access to justice. BC chair Goldsmith 'welcomed' anything that 'means people are able to bring claims which they couldn't before ... but we are sceptical'.[56]

In the Parliamentary debate the Lord Chief Justice attacked conditional fees as 'an alien creature in our justice system that should not be allowed to run amok' and the 100 per cent uplift as 'outrageous'. Lord Irvine worried they would involve 'the exploitation of litigants for the benefit of lawyers'. Lord Ackner's amendments limiting the uplift to 20 per cent and capping it as a proportion of damages lost by just five votes, and the proposals were passed by the same margin only because Labour's front bench, though critical, abstained by convention. The *Solicitors Journal* gave a 'conditional welcome' to 'an oddity' directed at 'the most vulnerable clients'. The *New Law Journal* was more enthusiastic, ridiculing the 'insulting' argument 'that the solicitors' profession is entirely packed with unscrupulous people who cannot wait to... trick poor accident victims out of their damages'.

But defence specialists were scathing. Clive Boxer of the City firm Davies Arnold Cooper said 'lawyers are courting disaster' by following the path that 'has led to denigration of the legal profession in the USA'. Lawyers 'will advise plaintiffs to divest themselves of assets if they can and will be seen as using impoverished clients as a means of forcing offers out of defendants'. 'Blackmail litigation will become de rigueur.' David McIntosh, his partner, opposed importation of the American 'victim culture... aided and abetted by a proliferation of single-issue consumer groups and by far too many ambulance chasing lawyers who portray themselves as missionaries but who behave as mercenaries'. Plaintiffs' lawyers should be liable for defendants' costs.[57]

Insurance for losers' costs was crucial to the scheme's success. When Litigation Protection Ltd quoted £1,500 for £100,000 coverage, Accident Line Protect offered the same for £85 to members of the Law Society personal injury panel who enrolled all their clients. Within a year 85 per cent of member firms registered. Amicus Legal undercut this by 25 per cent. Greystoke Legal Services offered after-the-fact legal expenses insurance, rendering conditional fees superfluous.[58]

Suspicions of the scheme were soon confirmed. Goldsmith saw the Academy of Experts' complaint that solicitors were asking members to accept contingent fees as further evidence that they 'pander to the greed of lawyers'. Some solicitors aggressively sought business. Two enrolled twenty-four firms in the Allied Lawyers Response Team (ALeRT) to approach potential clients in group actions, explaining defensively: 'The ambulance-chasing solicitor identifies the client first and seeks to persuade them to sue. We identify the potential action... and if we think there is a case, we say this to the public at large.' They invited more than 1,000 GPs to prepare medical reports on workplace asthma victims for £100–150 a case. Although the Law Society did not find the campaign unprofessional, APIL called it 'wholly inappropriate'. Legal Marketing Direct sold 40,000 prospects for £1–2.50 a name (depending on quantity). Claiming that twenty firms had made deposits totalling £5,000, LMD planned two more lists of 25,000 and 60,000. Claims Direct paid seventeen solicitors' firms £72.50 a case for evaluating claims settled by its lay franchisees. APIL

President Napier warned against 'taking the marketing of accident claims one step further down a slippery route'.

LS President Mears worried about 'the effect on public opinion'. 'We do not want the American perception that if anyone suffers hurt, someone is made responsible for it.' Napier agreed that 'this type of aggressive advertising will simply damage the image of the legal profession'. Goldsmith called it 'the most offensive form of ambulance chasing yet seen in this country' and 'hard to reconcile with the professionalism lawyers aspire to'. Was 'it really credible that people living in this country do not know that, if injured in an accident which was somebody else's fault, they can sue?' (A decade earlier the Oxford Centre for Socio-legal Studies found that only 29 per cent of road accident victims suffering serious disability recovered damages, 19 per cent of work injury victims, and just 2 per cent of others, who represented 86 per cent of such victims.[59])

APIL responded with a public relations campaign to 'counterbalance sensational headlines' but initially rejected a code of conduct. Incoming President Harmer dismissed as 'nonsense' the charge 'that legal aid and conditional fees allow ambulance-chasing lawyers to get rich on speculative litigation'. Rather they 'bring about safer products and better safety on the roads and in the workplace'. Lord Mackay insisted there was 'no rational basis for limiting access to the civil justice system simply for fear of more litigation' and belittled dire warnings of 'US-scale litigation'. But 'concerned that public perception is being whipped up against personal injury lawyers', APIL adopted a code of conduct prohibiting its 3,000 members from cold calling, unsolicited mailing, and referral payments.[60]

This did little to curb solicitors' efforts to secure clients. Some 300 joined the ABC Solicitors Group to buy £1 million of television commercials—one showing cash being placed in an upturned hand—to generate referrals allocated geographically. Accident Compensation Helpline sought 500 firms for a £2.3 million television campaign and offered conditional fee insurance at rates competitive with those of Accident Line. Housing specialists gave cash or a cheap watch to council tenants who sued for delayed repairs. The *New Law Journal* asked how this differed from 'the gifts offered by insurance companies for us to take out policies?' 'It may be an unattractive way of conducting business, but this is the road down which the Law Society has...chosen to drive.' When the Chartered Institute of Housing accused solicitors of 'tapping an easy market', the HLPA retorted: 'The local authorities are trying to distract attention from their own inadequacies'. The Law Society took 'a dim view of "Green Form" marketing' but agreed solicitors were 'only doing what the law allows'.

Two years later, however, a *Daily Mail* article headlined 'Millions from Misery: Law firms "pocket cash earmarked for repairs"' accused solicitors of encouraging council tenants to sue. The Liverpool Council housing committee deputy chair called the firms 'false Galahads who were guilty of morally abhorrent behaviour'. But though the Council sought to stop their 'rapacious actions', the HLPA declared that 'most of us don't leaflet drop or advertise. There is no need to. The demand for help is so high we can't cope.' A solicitor for a firm that sued the tabloid for defamation said his clients' only crime was 'successfully, fearlessly and independently' representing tenants. It obtained damages 'well into five figures'.[61]

The Law Society anticipated the 1995 legal aid Green Paper with its own proposals to cut barristers' fees. Full-time legal aid practitioners with seven years' experience should earn about the same as GPs: £40–45,000. Most cases required just one advocate. Silks' fees, 'largely determined by what barristers' clerks choose to claim', should be regulated and not exceed an annual maximum. Goldsmith retorted that silks' fees represented less than 5 per cent of the criminal legal aid budget and most were regulated. Newspaper stories about the £1 million paid to four QCs in the Barlow Clowes case were 'unwarranted and misconceived'. But Labour back-bencher Stephen Byers said this showed 'the extent to which a number of senior barristers are able to make rich pickings out of legal aid'. Goldsmith replied it represented only about £50 an hour for the 'more than a hundred working days' of trial and 'months of preparation'.[62]

Although Labour often attacked the Government's legal aid policies, Boateng told the 1994 Party conference Labour would have 'no new money' to spend. Sounding very much like Mackay, he wanted legal aid delivered 'more cost effectively', for instance, by 'improving the services provided by paralegals'. Just before the Green Paper, Labour adopted an access to justice policy accusing the 'Treasury-craven Lord Chancellor' of 'savage cut-backs in legal aid eligibility', which were 'crude, cynical and short-term'. But it attributed the inability of 'a majority of the population...to assert their rights' to 'an undue emphasis on traditional, expensive court based procedures and our antiquated and unsustainable legal aid system'. The 'almost exclusive reliance on lawyers in private practice' was 'expensive and inefficient' and 'wide open to abuse by unreasonable litigants and greedy lawyers'. The conditional fee uplift 'should be very much lower than 100%' and limited to a percentage of damages. Labour did 'not expect' such fees 'to make a significant improvement to access to justice. They are, at present, little more than a gimmick designed to mask the chaotic state of the legal aid scheme and court service.' It wanted to shift funds to advice agencies and a community legal service. But though cash limiting 'smacks of the disastrous social fund', Labour also proposed regional budgets. Sounding strangely like Paul Johnson, it urged the two branches to 'consider funding, whether by means of a professional levy or otherwise, some additional means of access to justice' and accused them of seeking 'to protect their vested interests'. The Law Society promptly confirmed this by opposing 'a compulsory transfer of work to an underfunded and overstretched advice service'. Soon afterwards Boateng declared Labour's determination 'to take on any institution that sees its primary purpose as the retention of vested interests' and threatened to refer the legal profession to the MMC.[63]

The Green Paper proposed regional budget caps for criminal, family, and other civil matters, competitive tendering for block contracts and high-cost cases, quality control through franchising, substantive priorities, continuous assessment of case strength, non-lawyer advice, ADR, conditional fees, and contributions for civil and even criminal matters.[64]

When Professor Michael Zander attacked the paper as 'nothing but cuts—all the rest is talk', Mackay retorted: 'My aim is to make the law simpler and easier to understand, the courts cheaper and quicker, and [to] provide funds for mediation'. He insisted disingenuously: 'There is nothing in this paper about cost cutting'. The SFLA chair called it 'a rogues charter', offering 'half-help which is no help at all'. Cash limits were not 'acceptable' to the LCCSA and 'objectionable in principle' to the LAPG chair, who called charges of stimulating demand 'a grossly unfair slur upon the competence and integrity of the vast majority of solicitors in the legal aid field'. Clients must be able to consult 'the approved solicitor of their choice'. Goldsmith denounced the proposals as a 'real setback for justice', which would 'reduce consumer choice, deny assistance to many deserving cases and provide financial incentives for the suppliers to handle cases in the cheapest possible way', which 'will include not instructing experienced counsel'. 'Old-fashioned, planned economics is not the way ahead.' LAG condemned the 'arbitrary decision-making that inevitably follows fixing a budget for the convenience of government'. Competitive tendering will allow the 'bigger wolves' to 'eat up the smaller practices'. Noting Mackay's 'uncharacteristic irritability at the suggestion that his motivation was financial', Roger Smith said 'we all know that the green paper stems directly from the fundamental review established by Michael Portillo, as chief secretary to the treasury....' Its 'underlying model' was the 'Soviet command economy'. Elly attacked the paper's 'inaccurate and unsupported assertions'. 'Crude cash limits' were 'a blunt instrument'. Only the LCF welcomed 'the planning of services with the aim of making them more accessible to the vast majority of people'.[65]

At a LAG conference a few days later Lord Mackay dismissed the Law Society proposal as 'little more than a sticking plaster on a gaping wound in our legal system', which 'would not bring about the fundamental changes which I believe are necessary'. He was interested in delivering 'more and better services', not in 'cutting expenditures'. The dominance of private practitioners was 'a straitjacket which forces people to use only those services which lawyers currently supply'. The Green Paper 'would allow the system to break out of the confines of that professional monopoly' and 'away from the narrow perspective of the solicitor's office'. Legal aid solicitors 'may be shoddy or at best mediocre in the service they offer'. 'If a particular firm is popular but gives poor service in outcome, should that firm be preferred? Is that a political question? Perhaps, therefore, we should consider league tables' like those for state schools, which could tell an accused that 'the chances of getting a criminal conviction were greater if you went to X, rather than Y'. Stephen Orchard called legal aid 'clearly out of control' and franchising 'the only guarantee in town as far as quality assurance goes'. He sought a more stringent merits test in medical negligence cases, which spent £22 million to recover £36 million, whereas personal injury claims spent £3.5 million to recover £180 million. Sir Tim Chessels, the new LAB chair, noted that 'a substantial number of taxpayers—"middle England" if you like—never make use of the legal aid system. They are unlikely to see it as a priority in the same way as education or health.'

LAG assailed the proposals as 'just an extension of the notions of supply-side economics. Concentrate on supply: demand will adjust.' Ann Abraham, NACAB chief executive, said caps would 'hurt the poorest, most vulnerable members of our society, who...will be unable to bring or defend a claim'. Because 'it is about enforcing rights', legal aid 'should remain a demand-led system'. NCC chair Lady Wilcox criticized caps set without 'any clear idea of legal need'. At the next week's BLA conference James Goudie QC called the Green Paper 'an economic mix of Brezhnev and Bottomley, of Lenin and Lilley, of Politburo and Portillo'.[66]

Lord Mackay told nearly 500 solicitors at a Law Society conference a month later that their 'fantasies' about the Green Paper resembled 'those which accompany most withdrawal symptoms when a well-established habit is broken'. Some called him a 'liar', 'dishonest', 'not to be trusted'. Henry Hodge thought his arguments 'disreputable and disingenuous' and the proposals 'a disaster for the public'. Lord Irvine found 'the fingerprints of the treasury all over' the paper but added that Labour had 'no quick fixes' and 'no new money'. Three months later he reiterated that 'the best way to save money' was 'a structural change' that would 'cut the cost of litigation'. 'Providing publicly funded services, almost exclusively through barristers and solicitors in private practice, has pushed costs up and led to a bias in the type of service provided towards crime and family work and away from social welfare law.'[67]

Goldsmith warned that 'the vast majority of the Bar' were 'earning modest sums without which they could not survive'. When Mackay reiterated that his reforms were about 'quality, priority', not 'cost cutting', Goldsmith contended that a working party report would show that 'cash limits and competitive block tendering...would lead to a real decline in the extent and quality of advice and representation'. 'Will a solicitor be penalised or congratulated for having retained a young and inexperienced but cheap advocate for a serious criminal case...?' Warning that 'if you give out money without quality control people might try to keep as much as possible for themselves', Mackay challenged the Bar to demonstrate that 'the advocacy it provides is better than other options'. The Bar's public affairs committee chair retorted that 'unqualified advisers...could have disastrous consequences'. Letting block contract holders 'decide for themselves when to buy in extra services and how much to pay for them' introduced 'a crude and unworkable market concept in an area where legal disputes are supposed to be decided on the merits....' The 'Bar's opposition to these extreme measures is a fight for its survival'.[68]

On becoming LS President, Mears conceded cash limits, which had public support, but declared the 'complete unfeasibility' of block contracts with 'second rate practitioners' doing 'second rate work', proclaiming: 'I am going to win this argument'. He accused the press of disseminating 'a simple message: the legal aid system is out of control, a machine enabling greedy lawyers to profit from unmeritorious litigation conducted by undeserving litigants'. The Commons Public Accounts Committee had just reported that solicitors filed £2–3 million worth of fraudulent green form claims in the previous two years, which 'appeared to represent something of a blank cheque to those firms determined to abuse the system'. The LAPG denounced this 'gross exaggeration', and Mears found only three fraud convictions during that period.[69]

The Society's formal response said the Green Paper 'would do little to tackle the problems illustrated...by a tiny number of apparently anomalous cases'. Cash-limited legal aid would 'operate erratically' and cease to be an 'entitlement'. Block contracting 'would create a serious conflict of interest between the solicitor's need to make a reasonable living and each client's wish that their case be prepared as thoroughly as possible'. Competitive tendering 'would drive down the quality of service'. 'The proposals are inconsistent with the consumer's right to choice.' The 'most serious problem facing the scheme' was 'inadequate levels of financial eligibility'.

Just as the Society blamed the Bar for rising costs, so it proposed a tighter merits test to end 'legal aid blackmail' by solicitors who brought cases lacking 'sufficient merit'. The British Medical Association complained that giving 'excessive benefit of the doubt to those seeking' legal aid in medical negligence cases imposed a 'very substantial burden' on the NHS. The LAB agreed that continuous assessment should 'stop work... once it became clear that the chances of success had reduced beyond what was reasonable'. Lord Woolf said barristers would have to accept 'fixed but reasonable costs'. And the former chair of the Bar's legal aid and fees committee partly blamed barristers for the 'indefensible rise' in unit costs and called for an end to 'restrictive practices and Spanish customs'. 'Money is being unwisely spent as anyone who is involved knows if they are being honest.'[70]

In February 1996 Austin Mitchell used the growing concern over legal aid costs to renew his proposal for 'a national legal service'. As early as 1987 a solicitor had lauded American public defenders. When Wandsworth and Haringey drastically cut law centre funding in 1990–1, the LCF offered to take over the green form scheme and civil legal aid 'for far less', declaring that 'the private sector is patently not working'. The Law Society hypocritically opposed anyone else having 'a monopoly of legal aid work'. A year later Mitchell endorsed the LCF proposal.

Uncertain and haphazard in its incidence, increasingly restricted, too often getting the shoddy end of the legal stick—the service and attention that falls off the back of the practice or the chambers—legal aid can never provide the devoted attention which is the citizen's right.

The LCCSA chair insisted this 'just doesn't describe any practice that I know of'; the LAPG denied this was so 'in most practices'; and the CLSA found it 'very insulting'. The Law Society warned that a public defender would 'almost inevitably' provide worse service. The Bar Council insisted 'the defendant gets a better crack of the whip with an independent defence advocate'. But the NCC made a similar proposal in 1994.

Now Mitchell called legal aid 'a middle-class protection racket which charges accordingly'. With ill-concealed self-congratulation, he claimed: 'In the one area where competition has been introduced—conveyancing—fees have fallen and pressure to provide an economical, "no frills" service has replaced the "take it or leave it" attitude'. An expanded network of law centres and 'those Californian public defenders who are glamourised on television' would compete with private practitioners. LAG urged 'serious consideration' of the idea, while warning that 'salaried services seem to provide less resistance to cuts'.[71]

When Lord Mackay again granted franchisees a pay rise up to twice that of others (though still below inflation), the *Gazette* conceded the message 'could not be clearer', although it denied that franchising was 'an absolute guarantee of quality'. Smith exhorted the LAPG: 'get big and get franchised. It's a time of pile 'em high and sell 'em cheap'. The LCD junior minister promised to use block contracting savings to restore eligibility.

Some blamed the Society leadership for failing to halt the Government's reforms. Elly called it 'disgraceful' that Mears met Mackay only once during his year in office and blamed the president for creating 'the impression now that it is the interests of the profession we have at heart, not the interests of the public'. Urging someone to oppose Mears's re-election bid, the LAPG proclaimed its 'lack of confidence in . . . his apparent lack of interest in legal aid issues'. But Mears said it would be an 'act of political folly' to take a stance before the White Paper.[72]

In his final report on civil justice in July, Lord Woolf recommended expanding small claims jurisdiction to £3,000, a fast track for most cases under £10,000, and judicial management of larger multi-track cases. Costs would be fixed for fast-track cases and recommended for multi-track. In order to avoid litigation 'whenever possible', cost rules would encourage settlement and legal aid would be available for 'pre-litigation resolution' and ADR.[73]

To build support for its White Paper, the LCD named the top twenty legal aid firms, which received an average of £2 million in 1994–5. Leigh Day & Co earned over £5 million more than its closest rival, mostly from the unsuccessful Sellafield claim for childhood leukemia. Although Martin Day explained that the firm had worked for six years, newspapers accused it of 'raking in money' from failed cases. The Law Society condemned the Government for trying to 'create a climate in which their Draconian proposals will be accepted' but also endorsed a CLAF, tighter merits test, limits on touting for green form work, and a separate fund for complex litigation. The LAPG responded with a survey of over 1,500 legal aid solicitors, whose annual incomes averaged just £25,563, ranging from £13,000 for trainees to £40,827 for equity partners. (Several months later the *Solicitors Journal* declared that 'the average legal aid lawyer earns £10 per hour for a 50-hour week'.) Just before publication LCD junior minister Gary Streeter called legal aid lawyers 'state-funded rottweilers', attacked a 'somewhat ropey' successful application for legal aid, and challenged Orchard to justify a cancer patient's medical negligence. claim. The Law Society denounced this 'contemptible' behaviour.[74]

The White Paper proposed 'radical' changes because 'nothing less will do'. Applicants' needs had to be 'balanced against the rights of their unassisted opponents, and of victims and witnesses, to fair treatment' and 'the interests of taxpayers in ensuring that public spending is controlled'. Plaintiffs brought 'too many weak or trivial cases'. Defence lawyers were 'unnecessarily delaying the trial process'. The 'Green Form scheme is particularly susceptible to fraud and abuse'. 'There needs to be an element of competition in the contracting arrangements.' Applicants 'should pay as much as they can reasonably afford' and everyone a minimum. That 'people who do not have to pay a contribution can take or conduct cases with little or no regard to the cost' is 'one of the reasons why spending on legal aid has increased so much'. Standard fees (calculated by Ernst & Young) would be extended to Crown Court and family cases. Most services would be 'provided through bulk contracts with fixed prices'. 'Contracting will offer efficient and effective providers opportunities to increase the amount of legal aid work they do.' Conditional fees would be available in 'a wider range of cases' and might replace legal aid.

Although Lord Mackay claimed the reform would buy 'more and better services', the Bar warned it 'will restrict choice, reduce quality of service and fail to increase eligibility'. It 'has nothing to do with addressing need and everything to do with expediency...a victory for bureaucracy, waste and injustice'. The Law Society agreed the proposals 'don't make justice cheaper' or 'quicker' or 'help people in work on modest incomes'. 'The only people to benefit will be the extra managers....' The LAPG accused Mackay of embracing a 'command economy' in order to make 'the idea of a salaried national legal service...sound attractive'. Although it might benefit, the Advice Services Alliance denounced Mackay's 'scorched earth policy', which 'will finally bury the founding principle of the legal aid scheme', and 'worried about the potential for competition' and reduced choice for clients denied access to solicitors. NACAB, another potential beneficiary, declared 'some of the proposals...in conflict with the fundamental CAB principles of providing a free service open to all', which 'would make it difficult for the CAB Service to take up the role envisaged for it'. While expressing admiration for NACAB, Mackay told its annual conference his principles were different: 'people should have to pay what they can afford towards the cost of the services they receive'. Several months later LAG and the advice agencies and law centres threatened to pull out of pilot schemes if forced to 'collect charges or means-test'. But 300 agencies planned to seek contracts to advise on welfare law. A PSI evaluation of eleven law centres and advice agencies (for the LAB) was generally enthusiastic.

Boateng sent the usual mixed messages. Because the White Paper 'did not hit lawyers hard enough', Labour advocated the 'radical alternative' of a community legal service. But he also affirmed 'the constitutional importance of the independence of the profession' and promised to ensure the survival of small firms. He was 'deeply suspicious' of block contracts and accused the Government of seeking 'to undermine the very concept of legal aid' and creating a 'massively increased bureaucracy'.[75]

Lawyer opposition incensed the media. 'If the Law Society is against this then we are almost certainly on the right track', pronounced the *Daily Mail*. 'Legal aid does not mean aid for the poor. It means aid to the legal profession.' But though the tabloid claimed the Government was 'relishing the fight', it also discerned 'the hidden hand of the various legal lobbies' in 'almost every sentence' of the White Paper, 'ensuring that fundamental reforms are sidestepped'. The *Daily Telegraph* called legal aid's 'shortcomings' so monumental 'that only a lawyer could even attempt to defend it'. Given 'its enormous cost and the distortions it produces, legal aid in civil cases would best be abolished. Legal insurance is available, and if lawyers were free to accept all cases on a no-win, no-fee basis, the most reasonable claims would get a hearing.' The *Daily Express* called opposition by the NCC, ASA, Labour Party, and Bar Council 'conclusive proof' that the proposals 'are set squarely on the right lines'. The *Sun* welcomed the 'crackdown on loony legal aid' to 'stop taxpayers funding bizarre lawsuits' and exclude 'foreigners'. The system 'is a mess. Those who deserve help often get nothing while money goes to millionaires and crooks.'[76]

The broadsheets were more qualified. *The Times* charged the Government with concocting 'a "vote-catcher" that will appeal to middle England'. While acknowledging that legal aid abuses had 'certainly given ministers plenty of bullets to fire', the *Independent* feared the 'balance is swinging too far the other way' for 'the poorest'. The *Guardian* blamed 'the Treasury's obsession with cash limits and expenditure control' for the White Paper's 'failure to widen eligibility, [and] extend legal representation to people using tribunals...and its insistence on all claimants making a contribution'.[77]

The *Solicitors Journal* conceded the LCD had 'won round one of the media battle'. But Zander observed that 'nine out of 10 legally aided civil cases succeed, so the merits test must be working'. The *New Law Journal* described a 'strictly embargoed' report on 'reasons for refusal of offers of contributory legal aid' as the 'equivalent of high grade semtex'.

Government ministers see benefit-grabbing, litigation-hungry hordes which can be demonised as little short of hounds from hell. The researchers found a group of incredibly poor people sufficiently depressed by the demands currently made of them simply to give up.

Mackay's imposition of 'collective punishment on all claimants of legal aid...is not really acceptable in a modern constitutional democracy'.[78]

The Law Society, advice agencies, law centres, and consumer groups held a protest meeting at the House of Commons, and the Society budgeted £12,000 a month for public relations. Streeter was 'not the slightest bit concerned' that a 'very few' legal aid lawyers had 'expressed concern' at his rottweiler metaphor. 'Hardly a surgery goes by' without a constituent complaining about 'being pursued by someone with legal aid', which was 'lopsided and wasteful'. 'If a person in a serious situation can't afford a very modest contribution, I believe that is a reflection of their commitment.' Government would not 'drag our feet implementing those reforms'. The Society was a 'bureaucratic nightmare', which 'represents solicitors very badly' and had 'behaved disgracefully' in withdrawing support from the Family Law Bill (see above). It should not 'sacrifice the opportunity to influence change by trying to resist the inevitable, as happened with conveyancing in the 1980s'. Boateng rebuked Streeter for not showing even 'a modicum of regret' about his rottweiler remark, which had left 'teeth-mark[s]'. Charging

Government with 'wilful ignorance of the facts', LS President Girling urged it not to 'sweep away the Child Bs, the victims of human growth hormones, the brain-damaged children, the victims of asbestosis, the personal injury cases, the tenants living in unfit properties'.[79]

Both branches strongly resisted extending fixed fees because divorce and domestic violence cases were not 'sufficiently standard' and remuneration would be cut 'substantially'. BC chair Owen vowed to fight 'tooth and nail' against reductions of up to 25 per cent. Although the LCD received the BC's objections and scheduled a meeting, Lord Mackay did not wait to set the fees. 'So much for consultation' complained the Bar. Calling the LCD figures 'so badly flawed as to be worthless', the Law Society commissioned another study by Deloitte & Touche.[80]

A month later Mackay addressed the Commonwealth Law Conference on 'Why we should avoid spending public money where the market can provide'. Accusing lawyers of overpricing and inefficiency, he called restrictive practices the 'real obstacles to access to justice'. It was 'rash' to expect legal aid to 'bear the full weight'. The budget had reached its 'outer limits'. 'Future strategies...should centre much more on making the market for court and legal services function better, so that people with legal problems can make responsible choices' and 'be accountable for the costs involved if their decision is mistaken'. Government might 'operate through the insurance market to secure subsidised services'.[81]

Two months after the White Paper the Law Society, advice agencies, law centres, and poverty and civil liberties groups created the Legal Aid Joint Forum to warn that 'the community as a whole would suffer' if 'punitive' contributions prevented its 'weakest members' from enforcing their rights and testing 'the lawfulness of the conduct of large institutions and the Government'. A Law Society survey found that 91 per cent of the public felt 'legal aid is a vital part of helping people get justice', and 84 per cent wanted it funded at current levels 'because justice is too important to ration'. The NCC said the White Paper was 'based on myths and guesswork' and 'uncorrected misinformation'. Girling told a public meeting that block contracts would 'undermine the foundations upon which our system of justice is built'. Successful bidders would 'be discouraged from taking on difficult, time-consuming cases'. It was 'the logic of the madhouse', said Vice President Philip Sycamore, to believe poor litigants relegated to conditional fees could pay opponents' costs. The BC legal aid and fees committee produced what Owen called 'a devastating critique of the proposals', which were 'crude and simplistic, and demonstrated a limited understanding'. The LAPG saw 'more than a passing resemblance to a Soviet-planned system of allocation of resources'. But Streeter admonished the audience not to 'resist the inevitable'. He was interested only in 'the nuts and bolts of the implementation', not 'philosophical concepts'.

When the Law Society derided as 'complete nonsense' his claim that legal aid expenditures were growing by 34 per cent a year he cut the figure to 10 per cent but declared: 'It now costs every taxpayer in the country £60 a year'.[82]

LAG condemned 'the government's hardening resolve to restrict entitlement' and 'Kafkaesque' rationing system 'based on potentially difficult judgments on "deservingness"'. Introducing 'competition only at the point of tender, where it simultaneously imports a soviet-style command economy' was 'a pretty crude way of duplicating market conditions'. Orchard rejected this 'unreasoned' 'knee-jerk reaction', citing 'comments in high profile cases where the grant of legal aid has been heavily criticised, not least by trial judges'. There was 'nothing inherently wrong in seeking value for money'. To justify standard Crown Court fees and bulk contracts with solicitors and family mediators, Lord Mackay declared that 'very many judges and lawyers, who see legal aid cases every day, firmly believe' there are 'undeserving cases'. So do 'Members of Parliament', who 'write expressing their concern every week'. Some 'legally aided people pursue cases irresponsibly because they have little to lose'. The NCC conceded 'abuse of the system by the rich in a small number of high profile cases' but asked: 'Why, then, do the White Paper's proposals target those on low incomes...?'[83]

In December, after consulting only the Law Society and LAB, the LCD proposed replacing Green Form criminal advice with bulk contracts. LAG said the LCD had 'sunk to new depths' by insinuating without 'a shred of empirical evidence' that solicitors' use of green forms was 'nothing more than a massive fiddle' in response to fixed fees. The *Solicitors Journal* charged the LCD with 'remoteness from the realities of advising criminal clients'. The government postponed the decision until after the general election (and then concluded that withdrawal could be more costly).[84]

Six weeks after the White Paper a Policy Studies Institute evaluation declared the LAB's pilot contracts with forty-two advice agencies a success. Disregarding the report's finding that the agencies did little 'holistic' advising, offered few referrals, and were no cheaper than solicitors, and that bulk contracts attracted only inexperienced lawyers in America and had been rejected by Norway and the Netherlands, the LAB proposed block grants for advice, assistance, and limited representation in social welfare matters. The 145 contracts attracted 840 inquiries. Fearing 'competitive tendering by the back door' and 'an effective cash limit on disbursements', the LS Council opposed participation. Its courts and legal services committee wanted the Society 'to stand firm on this', and the *Gazette* called the Society 'verdict on the draft contract... damning'. LAG warned again that 'the solicitor may fail to put the client first if there is a need to stay within a tight budget'. Sycamore urged the annual LAPG conference 'to guard against the danger of losing our independence as our relationship with the LAB changes to one of service provider for a major purchaser'. The LAPG found it 'naïve and insulting' to 'treat the entire legal aid side of the profession as guinea pigs'. The NCC and CA expressed reservations. But when the Board increased payment for administration, 100 firms signed contracts and another 200 applied. Both the Society and LAG now called the contracts 'reasonable' and were 'glad this money is going to solicitors' firms'. A group of firms negotiated with LAB independent of the Society.[85]

Girling warned that Lord Mackay's refusal to increase remuneration in 1997 'will only hasten the day when many small firms decide they can no longer afford to subsidise the legal aid system', and Owen called it 'deplorable' that 'people on low incomes...will suffer'. The LAPG thought it 'sadly fitting that this administration's parting gift to legal aid practitioners is a slap in the face' and hoped 'the next government will place more value on [their] essential services'. The *Gazette* assailed it as 'extraordinarily cavalier' and 'particularly churlish'.[86]

The press continued to publish 'exposés' of personal injury litigation. Dismissing the Benzodiazepine cases, the Court of Appeal criticized solicitor advertising for encouraging 'hopeless' actions. The manufacturer's solicitor praised the court for striking 'a note of sanity' and protecting 'the public, the tax-payer and the legal system', but the Law Society denied any 'evidence whatsoever to suggest that there has been an increase in the number of hopeless cases'. At a meeting organized by large UK and US defence firms, a City partner warned of 'US-style blackmail litigation' and accused some solicitors of 'undoubtedly look[ing] to drum up claims in order to line their own pockets'. APIL denounced this as 'a myth perpetuated by defendant insurance companies and their lawyers'. True to stereotype, the London Insurance and Reinsurance Market Association assailed 'the American-style compensation culture' and blamed plaintiffs' lawyers for having 'transformed the level of damages being awarded'.[87]

Although lawyers accounted for most litigation costs, Government also sought to reduce its expenditure on the judiciary. In 1995 the LCD declared that courts should become a self-supporting 'next step agency' by raising filing fees by £20 million a year. Boateng objected that this would 'threaten the independence of the judiciary and thus the right to a fair trial'. The NCC said 'regressive fees' would just 'prop up a system near collapse'. Several months later the LCD increased the fee for a House of Lords review more than eightfold, but such appeals were sufficiently rare to cause little stir. In 1997, however, the government more than tripled fees for such routine matters as divorce petitions and High Court writs. The Vice Chancellor called this 'wrong and misguided' because civil justice is 'the bulwark of a civilised state'. Although the 1993 Bar Council–Law Society joint working party had recommended that High Court fees be 'very substantially increased', its chair, Hilary Heilbron QC, now declared that these fees were inconsistent with a 'system of justice that is accessible, affordable and adaptable'. Lord Mackay replied that 'subsidising the courts, but not other methods, would be counter-productive and would distort choice'. Although Labour opposed the increases, it would not reverse them. But when a solicitor challenged them in a libel case, the High Court declared the right of those on income support or in exceptional hardship to seek a waiver. The Law Society asked Mackay to withdraw the entire package.[88]

In anticipation of the 1 May 1997 general election, the Law Society defended legal aid, proposed £130 million in savings, and endorsed conditional fees and the Woolf proposals. When the Conservative manifesto embraced cash limits on legal aid 'like other vital public services', the *Solicitors Journal* urged the next Labour Lord Chancellor to reverse the cuts.[89]

E. The Dilemmas of a Profession Selling Services to the State

Government had long criticized the cost of legal aid. Now, however, Lord Mackay demanded 'radical' change in this vulnerable relic of the welfare state in the name of ideology, politics, and economics. He claimed to be targeting resources and enhancing quality, but everyone knew the Treasury was running the show. Government was paying the piper but did not really care about the tune. Although legal aid remuneration rates had been pegged to the market in the cause of equal justice, government was determined to differentiate between the two, allowing inflation to reduce unindexed real expenditure. Government exploited public outrage at the astronomical fees charged by a few 'fat cats' to justify cutting payments to the mass of struggling legal aid practitioners. It sought to distract attention from its responsibility for declining eligibility by highlighting frivolous claims, fraudulent billing, and restrictive practices.

After a half century of demand-led legal aid, Government was determined to assert control over this 'carte blanche to tout for business', this 'gaping wound in our legal system'. Influenced by the Social Market Foundation, it wanted to cap the budget, set priorities rather than respond to consumer 'preferences' shaped by the services lawyers offered, and subordinate producers to 'market forces' (obscuring its monopsonistic power as the sole purchaser). Having accepted, sometimes even embraced, the market for private clients, the profession could muster few counterarguments. Even without competitive tendering, government paid only what the hungriest lawyer would accept.

Government also reduced the number of providers through franchising, bulk and exclusive contracts, and employment. This accelerated the concentration of legal aid work already produced by the specialization and economies of scale compelled by falling remuneration rates, and it rendered the remaining providers more dependent on government. (At the same time, government attacked firms that mass-processed legal aid clients and 'named and shamed' those with the highest legal aid earnings.) The profession championed dispersion in the name of client choice, attacking 'supermarkets' and 'Kentucky Fried Chicken' outlets and claiming (without evidence) that small firms were more likely to sustain the 'fiercely independent lawyer prepared to take on the establishment at considerable personal cost'. But it ultimately accepted the inevitability of legal aid specialization. Seeking to clothe concentration in the guise of quality control, government explicitly questioned the competence of most lawyers, first by franchising (which offered 'quality assurance' for 'the first time in the history of the legal aid scheme') and then through exclusive contracts.

This was a true rupture. Professions are founded on the claims that only members are competent (hence their monopoly) and all are equally competent (hence the ban on self-promotion and the practice of random referral). Government had to exaggerate quality differences and its ability to identify them in order to justify paternalistically curtailing consumer choice. The LAB chair asked rhetorically whether solicitors had 'the right to do something badly'. Mackay called legal aid lawyers 'shoddy or at best mediocre' and toyed with extending league tables from schools (based on test scores) to lawyers (based on 'chances of getting a criminal conviction'). But he failed to explain why lawyers unqualified to serve legally aided clients should serve those paying privately.

Such contradictions pervaded the debate. Legality is morally more ambiguous than other social services. More health, education, food, and housing is always better; more litigation is not. Both government and the media intensified popular ambivalence toward law by exposing fraudulent claims and caricaturing a complaint culture they attributed to America. Civil legal aid clients were not wronged victims promoting justice for all by asserting their rights, but profligate consumers over-indulging their taste for litigation (which resembled cosmetic surgery more than heroic medicine) at the expense of taxpayers and adversaries. Defining the real problem as moral hazard, Lord Mackay wanted more clients to make larger contributions, maintaining against all the evidence that this would motivate them to monitor their lawyers more effectively. His Parliamentary secretary, John Taylor, equated litigation to the Bermuda holiday he could not afford! Government publicized lost cases, as though these were unique to legal aid or every plaintiff should win. Legal professionals who should have known better repeated the (inconsistent) myths that all injury victims aggressively asserted their rights and lawyers exacerbated conflict.[90] The media fuelled public suspicion of all those accused of crime by focusing on the alienage or wealth of a few. By not indexing eligibility for inflation, government allowed it to fall from 80 to 50 per cent of the population. 'Not bad for a poor man's lawyer', boasted Taylor, acknowledging that charity to the needy had replaced welfare state protection for the rights of all. The contraction of eligibility and the erosion of benefits weakened the political constituency for legal aid, accelerating the downward spiral.

If the activities and beneficiaries of legal aid enjoyed little public support, its providers—lawyers—were openly reviled. Gary Streeter called them 'state-funded rottweilers'. Once the Social Market Foundation introduced the superficially scientific concept of 'supplier-induced demand', both government and the media eagerly redefined the core problem as practitioner abuse rather than unmet need. The evidence was highly ambiguous. The proportion of solicitor income attributable to legal aid might have grown because of the housing market collapse. Rising expenditure per case might reflect greater legal complexity, just as medical costs rose with scientific advance. But though the LAPG resented the 'grossly unfair slur', some lawyers admitted what government seems to have meant: falling real remuneration rates made volume the only way to turn a profit. And when government imposed standard fees, lawyers redirected their energies (or at least their bills) to unregulated activities.[91]

Lawyers did promote litigation, both individual firms (housing estate repairs, mass torts) and professional associations (Accident Line). Yet the public, and most lawyers, were uncomfortable with television advertising, leafleting, cold calling, door knocking, and marketing lists of potential clients. APIL was more conservative about business-getting than the Law Society. All professional associations rightly worried that every effort to encourage the assertion of legal rights would seem self-interested. Both Government and the media attacked legal aid by contrasting the astronomical fees of leading silks with the much more modest salaries of other public servants: judges, doctors, teachers, and MPs.

Displaying more rhetorical ingenuity than principle, lawyers and Government drew on different, often incompatible, discourses. The profession naturally stressed the core value of justice, which the Vice Chancellor called 'the bulwark of a civilised state' and the SFLA the 'hallmark of a civilised society'. The Law Society highlighted miscarriages of justice in its campaign against fixed fees. Control over legal aid could not be entrusted to a government whose own abuses of power profoundly threatened legality. Justice was a right which could not be rationed or subjected to a 'lottery'. The market was an 'unworkable . . . concept in an area where legal disputes are supposed to be decided on the merits'. Inequality was tolerable (if undesirable) in education, health care, or housing; but 'discrimination between litigants' inflicted injustice.

The profession's patent self-interest in legal aid undermined these altruistic protestations (already severely compromised by its unrepentant defence of restrictive practices). Some must have remembered that the Law Society blocked funding of the salaried lawyers envisaged by the Legal Aid Act 1948 and both branches opposed law centres in the 1970s. The Society's anxiety about the impact of legal aid cuts on solicitor training and jobs echoed the Bar's worries about the effect of employed advocates on briefs for beginning barristers. Some solicitors urged the Society to jettison professional pretensions and openly employ trade unionist strategies. Girling voiced the 'concern' of high-street firms at losing the matrimonial work that had sustained them after 'the decline in conveyancing', and Hodge accused Lord Mackay of 'hacking away at high street practices'. He responded with scepticism about a Law Society that invoked 'access to justice at the same time as wishing to get higher fees'. Mitchell called legal aid a 'middle class protection racket'. This was one reason lawyers fought for eligibility (which also benefited clients) more forcefully than remuneration levels.

At the same time, the profession borrowed another favourite trope from laissez faire ideology: choice. It argued that franchising and exclusive contracts violated ethical rules by restricting client choice (just as the Bar had objected to solicitor advocates who refused to respect the cab-rank principle). LAG equated government-established legal aid priorities with the 'Soviet command economy' (but then mixed metaphors by assailing 'supply side economics'); Goldsmith called them 'old-fashioned, planned economics', the LAPG a 'Soviet-planned system'; a silk said they smacked of Brezhnev, Lenin, and the Politburo. Lawyers invoked that favourite whipping-boy, bureaucracy. Government retorted that franchising enhanced choice by giving clients information about quality 'for the first time' and salaried lawyers would not be confined by the 'straitjacket', the 'narrow perspective', the 'confines' of private practitioners.

Government extolled market virtues. It actually contended that courts should be open only to those who could pay their full cost. Speaking as a 'businessman', LAB chair Pitts demanded greater 'productivity' and warned that 'justice is pricing itself out of the market'. Government and media uncritically accepted the empirically ungrounded assertions of the Social Market Foundation (which simply ignored such fundamental, but inconvenient, market values as client choice). The problem was not insufficient funding, said Government, but overconsumption of legality. The economist's response to this moral hazard was to make clients risk their own money so they would think twice before initiating legal action and monitor lawyer behaviour (something few private individual clients do effectively). Government also contested the profession's equation of justice with lawyers, who alone would be hurt by limiting legal aid; clients might be better off without them (a proposition government was not prepared to put to the market test).

The profession's obvious rejoinder was that cost-cutting compromised quality (although Mears's warning of 'second rate practitioners' doing 'second rate work' could not have endeared him to his electorate). A basic rationale for professions is information asymmetry: since consumers cannot assess quality, they should not be encouraged, or even allowed, to trade it for cost (hence the rules against advertising, especially of prices). Government threatened quality through its efforts to reduce costs by not indexing remuneration for inflation, shifting from hourly to standard fees, imposing bulk contracts, encouraging competitive tendering, and employing lawyers. Indeed, clerks promoted inexperienced barristers to handle routine criminal matters for little or no fee in order to secure more remunerative work from solicitors. The franchising criteria through which government guaranteed quality were concerned more with management (more readily routinized) than lawyering (with its irreducible uncertainties).[92] Government had two responses. If only producers could judge quality, higher prices would not ensure it but simply tempt lawyers to continue overstaffing and dragging out cases. (It preferred to expose clients rather than itself to the agency problem.) And true professionals would not betray clients by reducing quality. (There was no agency problem!)

Government promoted conditional fees both to discourage plaintiffs and lawyers from bringing risky cases and to make them bear the costs of loss (and administration). Attitudes towards such fees were volatile and contradictory: lawyers would be less available and commence unmeritorious proceedings to blackmail defendants; fees would cost clients 'real money' and be driven down by competition. The initial suspicions of solicitors (it was the 'logic of the madhouse' to expect such arrangements to be available to poor litigants) and the Lord Chancellor rapidly inverted to unrealistic expectations about profits and savings. But solicitors did not want to be associated with 'American cowboys' (if not sufficiently worried for the Law Society to cap fees as a percentage of damages). Barristers were warier (although they ultimately abandoned the allegedly sacrosanct cab-rank rule); and leading judges remained opposed. Defence lawyers, who originally hoped plaintiffs and their lawyers would bring fewer claims and settle for less than they had under legal aid, soon denounced conditional fees (illogically) for encouraging a 'victim culture' of 'blackmail litigation' by 'mercenaries'.

Government also became more enthusiastic about salaried lawyers (contemplated by the 1948 Legal Aid Act but never funded), expanding Crown Prosecutor audience rights, and shifting immigration advice and representation to UKIAS. But salaried services were surprisingly reluctant to accept responsibility: UKIAS refused, the Advice Services Alliance did not want to replace all green form work, and NACAB insisted on the principle of free service to all. Only the LCF welcomed reliable, expanded, centralized funding. Government insisted it was not seeking to cut costs; but when it claimed to improve quality, private practitioners naturally took umbrage (as they did at Mitchell's imputation that they gave legal aid the 'shoddy end of the stick—the service and attention that falls off the back of the practice'). It was ironic that just when England tried to cut costs by using employed lawyers, the United States hoped to do so by substituting private practitioners.

Finally, government sought to replace expensive lawyers with cheaper laypeople. The motive could only be cost-cutting, since empirical studies repeatedly exposed their shortcomings. Government and media embraced alternative dispute resolution but without any evidence that it offered better quality. Although the profession championed the right of parties (especially weaker ones) to choose courts over ADR, its hostility to lay mediators exposed its self-interest. Government enthusiasm for self-representation ignored overwhelming evidence of the difficulty of enforcing small-claims judgments.[93]

The profession's superior arguments availed it little. If lawyers documented rising costs to justify higher remuneration, Government commissioned its own study to produce lower figures, or simply disregarded the evidence. Lord Mackay was unmoved by the 2,000 angry lawyers who confronted him at a public meeting. When the profession could mobilize only 300 a year later he did not bother to attend. Professional associations brought doomed applications for judicial review but continued to threaten litigation and invoke the ECHR. The profession adamantly resisted every reform, refused to compromise, and made apocalyptic prophecies, only to lose each battle and see its doomsday scenarios disproved and its credibility erode further.

When national, local, and specialist associations threatened and conducted unprecedented boycotts, Government just waited until they collapsed, confident that self-interest would triumph. Effective trade unionism presupposes not only a unity the profession lacked but also an ability to hurt, or at least inconvenience, significant constituencies. Yet few outside the profession even noticed DSS boycotts. The profession's repeated warnings that lawyers would abandon legal aid were disregarded by a monopsonistic Government confident that there were plenty of hungry lawyers eager to scramble for whatever crumbs it scattered. Defections from legal aid just accelerated the concentration of providers Government sought.[94] And lawyers were paralysed by the contradiction between professional pretensions to paternalism and industrial action that would hurt clients (especially vulnerable legal aid recipients). Pannone rightly feared the Society would look like 'a trade union/socialist cabal'. The failure of professional associations to prevent Government cuts, however, invited irresponsible demagoguery (Mears being the most egregious example).

Although the profession spent lavishly on public relations, it could not translate widespread support for legal aid into effective political pressure. Attempts to emulate the NHS foundered on the moral ambiguity of litigation, doctors' modest incomes (compared to silks'), and the fact that health care already was severely rationed. Medical negligence actions complicated an alliance with doctors.

The media pandered to populist prejudices by mercilessly maligning lawyers. The tabloids cheered anything lawyers opposed. The legal aid system was 'rotten from top to bottom', a licence for 'plunder' and 'fraud', a source of 'ignominy' and 'scandal'. Voters were 'furious' and public opinion 'outraged'. 'Rich' 'bigwig' lawyers committed 'chronic wastage' while operating a 'sausage factory' of guilty pleas. Newspapers demanded an end to lawyers' 'outdated privileges' and 'vested interest' in the 'golden age' of 'blank cheques' for their 'pork barrel'. 'Loony legal aid' encouraged 'bizarre' lawsuits and defended 'foreigners', 'millionaires and crooks'. Abolishing it would make law more accessible by forcing lawyers to cut prices in order to attract private clients. Conditional fees should fund most civil cases and lawyers pay for the rest.

Government held all the cards in this high stakes game. For appearance's sake it might pretend to negotiate remuneration rates, but in the end it set them unilaterally. Government threatened more severe restrictions—lower eligibility or a budget cap—in order to compel the profession's assent to less draconian measures. It promised that each set of cuts and constraints was the last and then imposed another. Standard fees led to incentives for franchising (faster, easier, higher payments), penalties for the unfranchised (exclusion from legal aid work), bulk contracts, exclusive contracts, competitive tendering, and salaried employees. Sycamore acknowledged that the profession's relationship to the LAB had become 'one of service provider for a major purchaser'.

One reason for the profession's inability to protect legal aid was the fragility of its cartel. High-street solicitors already resented City firms' indifference to the threat to conveyancing work. Local law societies were more militant than Chancery Lane. The 'Bar Wars' severely tested the two branches' united front. Government fostered competition between them for legal aid advocacy work. Its insistence on a single advocate led barristers to appear without solicitors and solicitors to keep advocacy in-house. When the Law Society resisted standard fees, the Bar embraced them, hoping to capture more work. The 'naming and shaming' exercises by Government and the media encouraged solicitors to denounce QCs' fees and barristers to accuse solicitors of frivolous litigation. ADR pitted solicitors against (non-solicitor) mediators. Franchising divided those with and without the qualification, prompting the SFLA to ask if 'we want to end up fighting among ourselves to do the work at less than the current legal aid rates?' The progressive concentration of legal aid widened the gap between specialist firms and the vast majority of solicitors who did little or no such work. This may explain the LAPG's growing role and the Law Society's decision to convene its first legal aid practitioners' meeting in order to keep them within the fold. LAG, one of legal aid's strongest champions, applauded Government efforts to enhance quality and use more salaried lawyers. Advice agencies abandoned their principled insistence on free universal services and accepted government funding. In response to the charge of self-interest, lawyers enlisted groups representing sympathetic clients: the poor, children, the mentally ill, the accused, medical negligence victims. But these were marginal constituencies, and the false positives of unmet need rarely provoked as much outrage as the false negatives of undeserving claims. Indeed, Government sought to redirect concern from those denied representation by its eligibility cuts to crime victims and adversaries of legally-aided parties (who lacked the 'luxury' of 'virtually open-ended access to funding').

Government may have taken secret satisfaction in deepening intraprofessional divisions, but it could hardly have welcomed the ensuing hostility. Lawyers resented the 'slap in the face', being 'treated like dogs', 'with contempt', by a 'dishonourable' system whose delays in payment were 'wilful, deliberate'. Lord Mackay was 'heartily disliked' for his 'unparalleled arrogance and shamelessness', his 'inaccurate' and 'underhand' statements. His permanent secretary was 'aggressive', 'rude', 'insensitive'. The Lord Chief Justice and the Master of the Rolls criticized the Lord Chancellor for cutting legal aid and raising court fees. Both branches took the extraordinary step of suing him. At public meetings lawyers called him 'rubbish' and hissed the Attorney-General, the Bar's titular head. The British Legal Association described Mackay as 'one of the worst Lord Chancellors in history and certainly one who is the worst enemy our profession ever had'. It charged him with 'advanc[ing] his political career by shaking up lawyers' and demanded his resignation. LS President Pannone derided him as 'just another government minister who has managed to cripple a once proud public service', an 'old style trade union negotiator' who had 'put his belief in Conservatism ahead of his belief in justice' and 'destroyed the legal aid scheme'. Government was guilty of 'blindness, insensitivity, arrogance and … Treasury-driven short-termism'. Elly, the next president, told Mackay to 'put up or shut up' and stop crashing around in 'big boots'.

When Mackay accused lawyers of 'fantasies' bred by 'withdrawal symptoms' from their 'well-established habit' of addiction to legal aid, they called him a liar. Streeter replied that the Society was a 'bureaucratic nightmare', which 'represents solicitors very badly' and had 'behaved disgracefully'. The White Paper was a 'rogues charter' (SFLA) based on 'myths and guesswork' and 'uncorrected misinformation' (NCC), 'crude, simplistic', showing 'limited understanding' (BC). Elly accused the LAB of 'bully boy tactics' and 'erratic, inconsistent and incorrect' processing of applications, an 'object lesson in how to sow mistrust and fear and how to create a first-class disaster'. It was 'a grim, downcast institution, riven by internal dissension... gripped by a bunker mentality'. Despite its 'much vaunted' independence, it was 'the government's poodle, and the Lord Chancellor is not beyond giving it a kick when it suits him' to 'satisfy the Treasury that he is as ready as the next minister to make people bid for their jobs'. This criticism was attacked as 'an absolute disgrace in tone and content' by the Board's chief executive and 'a child's tantrum' by its chair.

At the end of Lord Mackay's nearly nine years in office access to legal services had contracted to its lowest point in fifty years, but the legal aid budget was still growing; the profession was angrier than ever, but repeated Government and media charges of self-interest had undermined what little public credibility it retained.

8   Labour Ends Legal Aid as We Know It

[A]ny attempt to slash the legal aid budget would be disastrous for the legal system and for the many ordinary citizens for whom access to justice would be denied. [Tony Blair, shadow Home Secretary]

[Labour will] restore legal aid to the status of a public social service, so highly regarded for its economy and efficiency that, with public support, it can compete for scarce resources with the most highly valued social services, health and education. [Lord Irvine, shadow Lord Chancellor]

[Legal aid has become a] leviathan with a ferocious appetite. [Lord Irvine, Lord Chancellor]

[It is] simply unrealistic to believe that no win, no fee agreements can take the place of legal aid. [Heather Hallett QC, BC chair]

[The CDS] would plainly be a breach of the European Convention on Human Rights. [Dan Brennan QC, BC chair]

[L]egal aid does not exist to provide livelihoods for solicitors—it exists to benefit the public. ... [Lord Irvine]

[W]e have [Irvine] on the run. [Michael Mathews, LS President]

In Opposition, Labour had equivocated on legal aid (like many other issues). As shadow Home Secretary in 1992, Tony Blair declared that 'any attempt to slash the legal aid budget would be disastrous for the legal system and for the many ordinary citizens for whom access to justice would be denied'. As Opposition leader he said 'Labour's goal of improving access to justice is an essential part of our commitment to social justice'. Lord Irvine (shadow Lord Chancellor) told 500 solicitors that Lord Mackay's 1995 Green Paper 'has the fingerprints of the treasury all over it' but conceded Labour had 'no quick fixes' and 'no new money'. He reiterated this three months later, calling for 'structural change', which might include salaried lawyers and lay advisers. Anticipating the 1997 general election, Irvine promised the September 1996 annual Bar conference to 'restore legal aid to the status of a public social service, so highly regarded for its economy and efficiency that, with public support, it can compete for scarce resources with the most highly valued social services, health and education'. A budget cap 'could be contrary to our obligations under the European Convention on Human Rights' and was 'unattractive in principle' because it would make legal aid a 'discretionary benefit at bureaucratic disposal' and 'unrepresented defendants would lengthen trials'. Universal contributions were a 'powerful deterrent' to accepting legal aid. Efforts to recover opponents' costs from client's were not 'worth the candle'. Franchises should not be exclusive. Block contracting for civil litigation was 'a long way down the line'. He appeared to agree that 'the public interest requires a separate budget for advocacy costs, so that solicitors' decisions whether to expend public monies on the services of the Bar are disinterested'. The White Paper was 'substantially a dead letter'. At the same time, Irvine did not rule out a budget cap, wanted QCs' fees regulated, and declared a Labour Government could not 'make money grow on gooseberry bushes'. Ross Cranston (Shadow Solicitor-General) declared 'the plain economic fact...that no government...can fund without limit a system which is largely driven, as is traditional legal aid, by market forces'. Nevertheless, Owen took comfort in Irvine's observation 'that the Legal Aid budget is currently within estimates and under broad control so that he saw no immediate imperative for cost capping'. The *Gazette* found his comments 'refreshing'; LAG applauded his 'encouraging thoughtfulness' and 'reasonable vision' of '"steady as she goes" or..."as she went before Lord Mackay's green and white papers"'. After the Labour landslide the *Solicitors Journal* hoped 'the presence of seven lawyers in the Cabinet' would be 'good news for the legal profession.' 'Labour has promised a less confrontational approach. ....'[1]

A. Delegitimating Legal Aid

But they were whistling in the dark. Pressure mounted to extend conditional fees agreements (CFAs). Immediately after Labour's victory, and again in September, Sir Richard Scott, the Vice Chancellor, urged allowing them in all civil cases. Leaking a Policy Studies Institute report in July, the *Sunday Times* inveighed against the £280,000 in legal aid wasted on a fight among 'neighbours over a wall that fell down'. The Law Society saw 'no good reason why clients should not benefit [from CFAs] in other areas'. Yet both branches still favoured a CLAF (which the 1988 Marre Committee had contemplated, despite its rejection by the 1979 Royal Commission and the 1983 Government response). LS President Sycamore ridiculed as 'a counsel of perfection' objections that stronger cases subsidized weaker under a CLAF. Owen called its virtues 'obvious': 'no means testing...open to all... dramatically expanding effective access to justice...would save the cost to the legal aid fund'.

Labour had attacked CFAs in Opposition. As shadow Attorney-General, John Morris QC told the 1993 APIL conference he was 'not impressed by what's happening in America', which was 'the wrong road to go down'. In the 1995 debate on CFAs, Lord Irvine feared they would 'involve the exploitation of litigants for the benefit of lawyers'. That year Labour's access to justice policy dismissed them as 'little more than a gimmick designed to mask the chaotic state of the legal aid scheme' and did 'not expect their introduction to make a significant improvement to access to justice'. The uplift 'should be very much lower than 100%' and limited to a percentage of damages. Publishing the PSI study in September, however, LCD Parliamentary Secretary Geoffrey Hoon said 'conditional fees are achieving their dual aim of increasing access to justice and widening consumer choice'. Because Irvine favoured 'extension into more areas of litigation . . . the question . . . is rapidly become not whether they should be extended, but how far?' Hoon wanted 'to begin to consider other funding mechanisms, such as contingency fees'.

Yet the report itself noted that solicitors evaluated 54 per cent of cases as only 50–80 per cent likely to succeed, and fixed the uplift too high more than twice as often as too low. Wondering whether 'some solicitors might be deliberately overestimating risk to justify charging clients a higher uplift', it found 'serious cause for concern about whether the scheme is operating fairly and consistently'. Hoon cautioned against 'attributing too cynical a motive to this finding too quickly'. And APIL President Napier insisted CFAs had increased access to justice. Solicitors might 'have specced the odd road traffic accident' but not tripping or work accidents. Praising CFAs as a 'lifeline' for the middle class, Sycamore called the report a 'green light for the extension . . . to other areas of civil litigation'. But the *Solicitors Journal* thought this unwise and opposed any substitution for legal aid.[2]

Within three weeks of the election, Irvine announced a review of civil justice and legal aid by Sir Peter Middleton, Permanent Secretary to the Treasury under Thatcher and now chair of Barclay's Bank. Irvine assured the profession he did not 'believe in blueprints' or 'grand schemes' and acknowledged that 'the public spats between the government and the judges and the lesser spats between the professional bodies and the Lord Chancellor were extremely bad for public confidence in our system'. He wanted those relationships to be '100% different'. Nevertheless, he was committed to 'quite remarkable change' in the next five years. Blair promptly hinted at its direction by vowing to end legal aid abuse—blacklisting barristers who brought frivolous cases and recovering legal aid payments from clients with hidden resources—and use the savings for salaried lawyers attached to legal advice bureaux and possibly public defenders.

Condemning 'the excesses of legal aid from which sleek lawyers prosper', the *Daily Mail* urged Blair to 'scrap the present invidious, profligate legal aid set-up and introduce a new cost-effective system' of 'lawyers with fixed annual salaries who have no financial incentive to spin out profitable cases'. It pilloried indicted 'business buccaneers . . . hiring the most expensive cohorts of lawyers that taxpayers' money can buy'. Mitchell renewed his call for a salaried service. Martin Linton (another Labour backbencher) tabled an LCF-backed early-day motion for a fivefold increase in the fifty law centres. Complaints that a PD 'would take much needed food out of the mouths of those who try to eke out a living scratching in the legal aid dirt', said the *New Law Journal*, were 'no longer valid … now the scratchings have fallen to such a miserable level'. The growth of bulk contracts meant 'that within a few years we shall be having what amounts to a Public Defender in all but name'.

Explaining how he planned 'to cut a £1.5 billion bill', Hoon decried that 'the price per case is still rising ahead of inflation' and expressed 'outrage' that 'the top 1 per cent of civil cases use up 14 per cent of civil legal aid and in crime, the top 1 per cent of jury trials cost about 40 per cent of the total spent'. He highlighted 'notorious cases, such as Dr Hashim's unsuccessful attempt to defend fraud allegations, which cost the taxpayer £4 million' and the Benzodiazapine litigation, which 'cost almost £40 million, and achieved little'. Lawyers should 'bid for cases … an innovation in the law which is commonplace elsewhere in life'. A member of the BC legal aid civil standard fees committee warned that lawyers who 'are not paid a proper rate for their time … cannot and will not do a proper job' and 'groaned in despair at yet another politician so out of touch with reality'. Hoon accused his critic of trying 'to convince us that we do not need to bother about the prices' and sneered ' "nice try"—but [you] must do better next time'. The LAB Special Investigations Unit denied legal aid in 203 of the 211 cases it reviewed. Two Chancery judges complained to the Lord Chancellor about 'far-fetched claims' and urged more stringent merits tests.

Irvine also deplored the 'staggering fact' that 1 per cent of criminal cases consumed 24 per cent of legal aid (a very different figure from Hoon's). Although it had almost nothing to do with legal aid, Irvine attacked 'the significant number of QCs who earn a million pounds per annum' from private clients and the 'many who would describe half a million pounds in one year as representing a very bad year for them'. He conceded this 'might bear comparison with the conversion of St Paul' since the year before, when he was still in private practice (and allegedly in that league), he had defended 'super silks' attacked as 'fat cats' by insisting the public 'knows nothing of the overheads of the Bar'. But now he declared the truth 'should not be suppressed'. Because 'top lawyers in this country easily earn at least four times what top surgeons earn' he was considering annual limits on payments to individual lawyers. Delighted the heat was on the Bar, LS President Girling proposed the ceiling be a hospital consultant's salary. But Owen retorted that taxing masters kept fees 'fair and reasonable' and private fees 'negotiated at arm's length in a free market' were 'irrelevant'. Stanley Brodie QC complained that 'a gratuitous and irrelevant assault on so-called "fat-cat" QCs is not what one expects of a responsible Lord Chancellor'. Viscount Bledisloe QC wondered: did 'this dramatic "post-practice remorse" ' have 'any connection with Lord Irvine's translation from highly risky and pensionless practice at the Bar to the safe haven of an assured salary and a guaranteed life pension?'.[3]

As Labour had warned, it retained the Conservatives' court fee increases. 'Citizens did not have a constitutional right to a free court system', said Irvine. 'To argue that court fees act as a deterrent to litigants is rather like arguing that people are deterred from buying a new motor car by an increase in the vehicle excise duty.' 'The main deterrent' was 'the price at which lawyers value their own services'. 'Fat cat lawyers railing at the inequity of court fees do not attract the sympathy of the public.' In the midst of the scandal over the cost of redecorating his private apartments in the Houses of Parliament, Irvine declared: 'People who live in glass houses should not throw stones'. Owen objected that 'talk about the earnings of lawyers... really doesn't seem to bear on the issue at all'. The Law Society agreed 'this issue is not about lawyers but about consumers and access to justice'.[4]

Home Secretary Jack Straw renewed the attack at the September Bar conference. Fees were 'frankly out of control'. 'The days in which lawyers, and especially the senior criminal Bar, could simply apply upward pressure on the "going rate" allowed by taxing masters, and catapult themselves into ever higher earnings brackets, must come to an end.' Barristers had 'to be willing to contemplate radical changes in the way criminal defence services are delivered'. Accusing Straw of scoring 'an easy point', Owen maintained 'it is not the Bar which is making this market or assessing these fees. It is the Legal Aid Board....' Contesting the government's figures, the Criminal Bar Association chair insisted that rates had to be 'fair and reasonable—otherwise people will not be prepared to do that work'. But Straw called QC earnings 'stunning' and decried that Crown Court defence cost as much as prosecution in all courts. LAG backed the Government, noting that 'a simple reduction of 10 per cent in the annual receipts from legal aid of the top 13 leading counsel nets around £4 million a year alone'.[5]

On the basis of Hoon's comments at the Labour Party conference, a *Times* front-page article suggested that the Government wanted CFAs to replace legal aid in all money claims. 'Middle-class people who cannot afford to go to law should gain access to the courts....' 'Clearly they [would] be in a better position' if CFAs were combined with fixed costs, saving taxpayers 'up to £800 million'. Although an LCD spokesperson dismissed such 'speculation', Lord Irvine said his forthcoming Law Society conference speech would be 'nearer to a white paper than a green paper' and followed by only brief consultation. He told the home affairs select committee 'the time of talking is over, it is time for action'. Sycamore threatened resistance. Owen warned of the 'very real danger of abuse' because of the 'conflict of interest at the very heart of these conditional fee agreements' 'The blunt truth is that people will end up paying more to lawyers....' The LAPG predicted 'chaos' in 'the short term'. At his annual press conference the Lord Chief Justice reiterated 'the traditional view' that 'it is undesirable for lawyers to have a stake in damages because it encourages unethical behaviour'.[6]

After withholding Middleton's report for several weeks, Irvine released it on the eve of the Law Society conference. Middleton called for 'radical change' to halt the 'rapidly growing cost', which he appeared to blame on 'supplier-induced demand'. He decried the 'perversity' that aid was 'most readily available to those who resort to the courts'. Rather than 'increase financial eligibility', he much preferred 'to seek to develop private alternatives to help people fund litigation'. Sounding just like a Treasury Permanent Secretary turned City banker, he called legal aid 'poor value for money'. Access to justice 'cannot be viewed in absolute terms' but 'has to be set against the background of limited resources'. The current scheme 'over-provides' by granting legal aid to cases with a 50 per cent chance of success, 'whereas most people paying privately would want much better prospects before they risked litigation', and by allowing legally-aided parties 'to spend almost unlimited amounts'. Judges 'should be able to refer cases back to the Legal Aid Board for a fresh assessment of the merits at any time'. People should 'pay what they can reasonably afford towards the cost of their own cases' and every client pay something 'as a sign of...commitment to a case' because 'legal aid supports a significant number of cases that litigants would not consider important enough to pursue if any contribution was required'. He wanted to expand 'effective access to justice without recourse to professional representation', for instance, no-fault medical negligence compensation. A Community Legal Service would 'shift away from expensive court-based litigation services towards a much greater emphasis on information services, non-lawyer advice and assistance, and alternative dispute resolution'.

The 'key change should be to allow the Legal Aid Board to use its purchasing power and become a pro-active purchaser of services...set requirements for quality and access and seek the best available price'. Block grants would allow the Board to 'compare the pattern of work done and the outcomes achieved...against a general profile of the type of case concerned'. 'Prices could reflect regional variations and larger firms' economies of scale....' Contracts should transfer 'to the provider a share of the risks inherent in the uncertain course and outcome of litigation'. To 'ensure that new blood can enter the scheme...some existing providers will have to give way' since 'the role of legal aid is...not to guarantee income for lawyers, especially less efficient ones'. To counteract the 'incentive for providers to skimp' there should be 'a higher price for a successful case'. Middleton wanted to end 'restrictions on the way that lawyers can charge for their services...to stimulate a more competitive market, widen access to justice generally and...offer an alternative to publicly-funded legal aid', which should not be available 'for cases that could be pursued satisfactorily under...a conditional fee agreement'. There was 'no essential difference between conditional and contingency fees. Indeed, in some ways the latter may be preferable'.[7]

B. Marketizing Legal Aid

Irvine embraced these recommendations at the Law Society's October conference. Having become a 'leviathan with a ferocious appetite', legal aid had to 'develop or decay' by being 're-focused' as 'a tool to promote access to justice for the needy—not be seen by the public as basically a means of keeping lawyers in business'. It 'exists only to remedy an imbalance between the poor and those who are better-off, not to put the poor in a privileged position'. Plaintiffs would have to demonstrate a 75 per cent chance of success since 'I would not myself litigate at my own expense with any lesser prospects', but he rejected a universal contribution. All legal aid would be disbursed through fixed-price contracts, with the long-term goal of a community legal service. Promising in *The Times* to 'give the law back to the people', he asked 'why should anyone on a modest income contribute through his taxes to the income of an inefficient professional?' Whereas Conservatives had been 'driven by a desire to save money', Labour just wanted to 'bring the system under control'. Within six months all money claims would be handled by CFAs. A CLAF was unfeasible 'because lawyers would prefer to cream off the stronger cases under no-win, no-fee agreements'.

At the legal aid panel following Irvine's talk a solicitor declared that Lord Mackay's agenda had been

the eradication of one third of High Street solicitors' practices in England and Wales. Naively, I thought that a caring Labour government would...take pride in the fact that the world sees our legal system as probably the fairest on the planet, would consider that for people to be free they must have access to justice.

Instead, the press pilloried solicitors as 'rich, lazy and permanently money-grabbing, a profession capable of commanding high fees for little effort and without fetter'. The speaker warned Irvine:

thousands of solicitors, their staff, their suppliers and their contractors may be unemployed. Millions of your electorate will have to join a long queue for legal services. ...Your courts will be clogged up with litigants in person.

But the *Solicitors Journal* conceded that 'neither the government nor the public will listen to arguments which focus on possible hardship for the profession'.

This 'most radical shake-up of legal services in 50 years' provoked a 'storm of protest'. Sycamore assailed the 'severe withdrawal of access to justice' as 'very, very disappointing news for consumers... a considerable curtailment of rights'. He rejected 'entirely the view that seems to be put across in certain sections of the media that legal aid is a happy hunting ground for scroungers—or a get rich quick scheme for fat cat lawyers'. Irvine's 'fundamentally misconceived approach', warned the LAPG, would 'radically alter the structure of the profession' and effect 'the end of legal aid as we know it'. The TSG called it 'nothing more than a public relations exercise to increase access to justice for the middle classes while removing support from the poorest sections of society'. The *Gazette* urged lawyers to 'dip into your files and bring to light examples to prove that such crude swopping of funding is not so easy'.

Even Austin Mitchell, who the year before had called for 'the more full-blooded American-style system of contingency fees', condemned the proposals as 'hasty and ill-considered'. Roger Smith denounced the 'outrageous' 75 per cent merits test. Irvine's promise that 'middle-income Britain' would 'regain access to the court system' was 'clearly arranged with his media minders' to go 'down well in the predictable places'. Smith agreed with Mitchell that the proposals 'will deprive ordinary people of legal backing against powerful vested interests and rob the poor of their compensation rights'. 'A group of the poorest litigants will…lose up to 25 per cent of their compensation.' Far from 'heighten[ing] the public standing of lawyers', the proposal was 'more likely to lead to a backlash'. A jaded *Financial Times* columnist called it 'less New Labour, more Old Treasury'. 'Civil servants clearly just dusted off' Mackay's White Paper and 'handed it to the new ministerial team as the only way forward'. But the *Solicitors Journal* conceded Irvine 'has the backing of the popular press and a large proportion of the public for his measures'. And some lawyers shared his criticisms. David Pannick QC acknowledged that 'speculative legal aid claims are commonplace'; the chair of the Non-Practising Bar Association knew 'from personal experience that lawyers prolong and over-complicate cases'.[8]

Both branches and LAG worried that the insurance market was unprepared and some clients unable to afford premiums. Abbey Legal Protection said CFAs 'reenfranchise the middle class' but 'leave the poorest out', demonstrating this a month later by offering medical negligence insurance to the Law Society panel at premiums ranging between £4–£7,500 for £100,000 coverage. The Association of British Insurers said 'all logic tells you that the less well off will suffer from this measure', and the Forum of Insurance Lawyers (FOIL) agreed. David McIntosh, a leading insurance lawyer, thought it 'extraordinary' to assume 'this considerable increase in insurance capacity is going to be there'. The *New Law Journal* feared that insurer pressure to maintain high success rates would encourage low settlements, 'which reflect the solicitor's own interest just as much as that of the client'. Warning that CFAs were inappropriate where expert evidence was necessary, the Vice Chancellor urged care 'to ensure that deserving cases do not fall into a black hole'.[9]

The Law Society wrote to every solicitor and—with consumer, legal services, civil liberties, and anti-poverty groups—all MPs. DVP Robert Sayer denied costs had 'spiralled out of control'. The budget was 'less than £30 per head of the population, about 4% of the National Health Service budget, the final cost of one Millenium Dome'. Irvine replied he wanted legal aid to buy 'as much help as it can for the less well-off'. At a CA meeting soon thereafter its head of legal affairs 'absolutely did not think legal aid should be scrapped', and the shadow Lord Chancellor called the proposals 'seriously flawed'. Hoon 'reacted very badly'.

Under our current arrangements, access to the civil courts is open only to the very poor and to the very rich.... This is not right.... For the first time this century, perhaps ever, access to justice for all in this country will be a reality—not just a slogan.

Declaring that 'there are few areas of profitable business activity where some money is not put at risk in order to realise an overall and positive return', he hoped for a 'culture change' in which lawyers would advance legal insurance premiums and recoup them from their fees. But he also criticized state funding for actions on behalf of brain-damaged babies, asking: 'Whose interest is served if those cases proceed on the slim hope that some benefit may accrue? Not, I suspect, the parents.' Irvine agreed that 'competent and busy firms should be able to absorb the cost of insurance and investigation' and 'recover them if they win'.

But Benedict Birnberg, a prominent legal aid lawyer, feared solicitors would become 'commercial speculators and bankers first and lawyers second'. The Gwynedd Law Society unanimously opposed 'degrading' solicitors to 'mere financial speculators'. And Marlene Winfield of the NCC warned:

We know nothing about who is being turned away by solicitors and on what grounds. Nor do we know who is rejecting offers of conditional fees and their reasons. We don't know if the insurance that accompanies conditional fee agreements is covering all of the costs when the cases are lost. We don't know what's happening when the agreements are terminated prematurely. We know nothing at all about the outcomes and if the clients are happy.[10]

The Law Society argued impracticality. How would solicitors maintain an income stream until there were enough recoveries 'five years down the line'? Sycamore maintained that outside 'personal-injury mainstream work the insurance industry doubts the market will develop to provide that cover'. Sayer predicted 'prudent solicitors will only take on cases they are confident they can win'. APIL agreed the proposals 'simply won't work'. Roger Smith accused the government of using 'a very blunt instrument' to save just £80 million annually. But echoing Irvine, Hoon told solicitors to 'absorb the up-front costs' of investigation and 'bear the risks of the other side's costs'. If 'as few people are satisfied with the system as it now appears, you've got the problem, not me'. 'Appalled' by such ignorance, the administrator of a large legal aid practice reproached Hoon: 'You don't seem to know and you don't seem to care'.[11]

A month after Irvine's bombshell the LCD announced that it would hire an outside consultant to analyse the impact on solicitors. Calling this 'clear proof that the Lord Chancellor's proposals are unrealistic', and 'appalled by the government's inflexibility', the Law Society retained its own expert. The *Gazette* said 'the only thing standing in the way of the new Irvine vision is the bloody-mindedness of lawyers' and urged the government to 'slow down and do some listening'. Grilling the Prime Minister, Opposition leader William Hague warned the proposals could 'prevent people who are seriously disabled in accidents from pursuing personal injury claims'. The Society of Labour Lawyers (of which Irvine had been a member) voted overwhelmingly to ask government for 'further research experience to establish [that CFAs] are working fairly in the interests of consumers'.[12]

The CLSA warned that 'block contracting puts us into conflict with our clients as never before' and 'will destroy the fabric of the criminal defence system'. Calling his experience with contracts 'dismal', an American lawyer acknowledged that 'the earlier you get out of a case, the more likely you are to make some kind of money'. The *New Law Journal* saw an 'object lesson' in a solicitor's claim that 'the only determinant' in awarding American contracts was price. The CLSA chair preferred a 'sensible debate' about public defenders; but a Bristol solicitor asked 'why a new public defender service should be any better' than the 'demoralised, under-resourced' CPS. The LCD retorted that England spent more *per capita* on criminal justice than any country except Scotland and sought 'a controlled price'. Issuing a White Paper on youthful offenders, Jack Straw accused lawyers of 'making excuses for their offending' and increasing 'delay and expense' because of the 'perverse incentive' of hourly pay. And Hoon declared that contracting would 'lead to improved efficiency' by promoting 'fair competition. For the first time, there will be very real incentives to suppliers to look carefully at the quality of their services and the prices they charge.'

Birnberg proposed a Community Legal Service, with contributions by all but the bottom fifth, and legal aid retained in 'public interest' matters, where contracting was 'certain to deliver second rate and unequal justice'. Hoon denounced the idea as 'Orwellian...the nationalisation of the legal professions at the taxpayers' expense...private clients would have no choice...the whole edifice would be overseen by a giant quango'. '[A]lways intrigued by the low opinion lawyers have of each other', Hoon asked if Birnberg's firm would give 'shoddy service'. 'Constrained by an inflexible budget', Birnberg said he would 'have no option but to do a second-rate job'.[13]

Promoting Irvine's proposals, Hoon told Parliament small claims were 'the major success story of the civil justice system...simple, fast and cheap' and attributed the 18.8 per cent decline in legal aid certificates for money claims in 1996–7 to the increase in jurisdiction to £3,000. A 1996 government survey had found a high level of satisfaction among litigants, which Professor John Baldwin confirmed the next year. But the *Solicitors Journal* said 'insurers and professional defendants are laughing all the way to the bank'. And another Baldwin study, published by the CA, showed that less than a third of successful claimants were paid on time, most still had enforcement problems six months later, and more than a third collected nothing. LAG wanted this 'sorted out before the limit goes up again', calling it 'essential that litigants have access to competent legal advice on the merits of their case at the outset'. The *Independent* retailed horror stories about unrecoverable judgments. The *Gazette* had 'serious' reservations, and the *Solicitors Journal* feared the poor would 'fall through the net'. Nevertheless, an LCD consultation paper proposed increasing the jurisdiction to £5,000 and banning all legal representation. LAG objected, APIL wanted tort claims exempted, and the Law Society civil litigation committee sought to exclude eviction, harassment, and disrepair. The HLPA persuaded Irvine to reduce the jurisdictional limit in housing matters to £1,000.[14]

Hoon again assailed legal aid as a 'machine primarily for paying lawyers' bills' and a 'subsidy for lawyers' who 'gobbled up' money intended for the sick and injured. The next day the *Sunday Times* headlined a story 'Iraqi fraudster's family gets £1 m in legal aid'. Jawad Hashim had already cost the legal aid scheme £4 million; now his wife and son were claiming more than £1.2 million while living in a £300,000 Arizona condominium. Hoon promised an immediate investigation. Irvine told the House of Lords Hashim had concealed 'very substantial assets' when applying for legal aid. A contemporaneous *Guardian* article described a woman still paying the costs of opposing a former lover who obtained legal aid while owning a five-bedroom house.[15]

Defending the proposals in Parliament, Hoon said the Government was reconsidering both the 75 per cent merits test and the April 1998 target. But he extolled 'go-ahead lawyers, insurers and others' who were 'talking about a new world that is opening up and how they will meet the challenges and seize the opportunities'. Shadow Attorney-General Edward Garnier QC (briefed by the Law Society) accused the Government of having 'betrayed many people's trust in its haste to appear relevant, radical and modern'. The proposals would 'turn lawyers into a cross between insurers and bookmakers...a system for the bent or the brave'. One Labour backbencher demanded an end to 'blaggarding' legal aid lawyers. Another feared 'a real denial of justice if a genuine claim were to lie unpursued for want of the means to pay for insurance'. Sycamore insisted 'this is not a debate about lawyers' fees, but about the rights of ordinary people' and called for 'examples of cases which demonstrate how dramatic the effects of these changes will be'. He warned MPs that the 'large numbers of firms' forced out of business by the proposals would increase unemployment.[16]

In the December Lords debate Irvine promised to focus on 'cases involving the social welfare of disadvantaged citizens and cases that raise issues of wider public interest', such as 'police malpractice', which might warrant a relaxed merits test. He praised lawyers who 'act for refugees, asylum seekers, prisoners, mental patients, victims of abuse and assault' and 'do not become rich' but denounced the thirty-five barristers who earned £270–£575,000 from criminal legal aid in 1996–7 and the twenty who earned £203–£411,000 from civil. Judges were paid only £112–£125,000 and hospital consultants £56–£70,000, but 'all work hard, over-long hours... have highly responsible jobs and the lives of many people depend on their professionalism'. Complaining that 'we are paying more and getting less from the lawyers', he urged block contracts because 'nothing concentrates the mind more than a fixed fee'. Lord Lester of Herne Hill QC said he had never argued a case with a 75 per cent chance of success, and Lord Ackner denounced Irvine as a 'mere handmaiden of the Treasury'. But the *Daily Mail* copied the Lord Chancellor by naming five solicitors' firms that earned £2.6–£3.7 million from legal aid in a year.

The *Solicitors Journal* called Irvine's tactics 'disingenuous' and 'diversionary'. His attack on fat cats 'may go down well with the popular press and the general public', but 'the vast majority of barristers doing legal work never reach this level of earnings' and 'thousands of solicitors... are struggling to make ends meet'. Although the Bar 'should be proud' of 'fat cats... paid from private funds', chair-elect Heather Hallett QC agreed that 'for the vast majority of the Bar doing publicly funded work, the idea of a fat fee is as much a dream as winning the lottery'. 'It would be an enormous loss to the country if so many hard working and dedicated [lawyers] were to go out of business.' But she appointed a task force chaired by a non-lawyer to devise contracts for expensive criminal trials.[17]

The Lord Chancellor lashed back. He was 'a minister in a listening government', but 'openness and consultations only work if those consulted react responsibly' and are 'measured and well informed in their responses'. 'Without undertaking any analysis', some of the 'interest groups' 'simply declared loudly that the proposals were unworkable'. 'Some have gone so far as to accuse me and my colleagues of betraying the poor. Savage and grave allegations... and all without a shred of hard evidence.' A few weeks later the *Solicitors Journal* responded with the LCD's own estimate that the 1999 legal aid budget would decline by 5 per cent, breaking Irvine's promise not to spend 'one penny less'. 'It would be difficult to imagine two more simplistic or draconian cuts' than the elimination of legal aid for all money claims and the 75 per cent merits test. The following month it called him 'pompous and obstinately unwilling to admit the possibility that his plans might be mistaken'. A few days later Irvine promised 'to make the legal aid system more efficient' by delivering it 'exclusively through contracts', which 'will ensure quality'. He wanted to 'sharpen' competition 'to the benefit of clients' by allowing specialist advice agencies to provide legal aid.[18]

The CLSA warned that 'the independence of criminal solicitors will be lost' under block contracts. 'If a solicitor makes a nuisance of themselves, perfectly properly on behalf of their client it would be possible to remove them from practice simply by taking away their contract.' Orchard dismissed this as 'a complete red herring'. Solicitors were simply 'terrified' of anything 'different'. Whereas 'anyone can do legal aid now', contracting would 'concentrate work on good firms and...cut out the cowboys'. A London solicitor called firms participating in the pilot (like his own) 'lemmings waiting to jump over the hill'. 'If we say no then they will just make legal aid harder and bring in a new fee system and pay us less.' Calling block contracts 'commercial suicide' because there would be 'a monopoly buyer and multiple providers', the CLSA sought a Law Society EGM on whether they would violate practice rule 1. It quickly got the requisite 250 signatures but wanted 750 before costing the Society £50,000 for a mail ballot. When the LCD decided to proceed with exclusive contracts before evaluating the pilot the CLSA asked the Law Society to resist, reiterating that solicitors 'who become unpopular with the establishment could fear...the "nod and wink" unexplained failure to renew the contract'. The *Solicitors Journal* rejected the NHS model: 'If the doctor is not right for the patient, tough. ... If the doctor, who is on a fixed salary, is disinterested in the patient, tough.'[19]

Jack Straw declared block contracts would 'sort the wheat from the chaff'. Solicitors used green forms for 'ludicrous purposes' and fostered an 'adjournment culture' in a 'ritualised' 'game' to 'ensure their legal aid fees are the highest'. Sycamore deplored Straw's 'depressing lack of understanding... it is now five years since standard fees were introduced for magistrates court work'. Former BC chair Scrivener said that since Straw left the Bar

judges have been given the power to make wasted-costs orders against lawyers personally. Maybe it is a pity the same power is not available against ministers. But it does, perhaps, show that Mr Straw's decision to give up law for politics was a wise one.

But Straw persisted: 'something's wrong here...there are people who have become much more procedurally minded for no good reason—the adjournment culture and all that'.[20]

Ordered by Irvine to negotiate exclusive contracts for all civil and family green form work, the LAB proposed to select 2–3,000 firms and 2–300 organizations. The Law Society worried about fluctuating demand and the 'real danger' of 'a more restricted and lower quality service'. The proposal was 'misguided', said LAG, because 'some providers will be tempted to "cherry pick" the least complex cases and most straightforward clients'. But it also accused solicitors of 'offering free benefit checks conducted by paralegals and designed to maximise [solicitor] income'. The Social Security Practitioners Association rejected LAG's claim that 'abuse is widespread' and assailed it for 'perpetuating the myth of social security legal advice as a non-specialist service', thereby playing 'into the hands of those who would happily remove the provision of welfare benefits advice from the private sector'. Fondly recalling the conference 'at which solicitors whose livelihoods and whose clients were affected turned up in droves to express their disapproval' of government policy—'possibly the last time the rank and file of the profession was actually behind the Society'—the *Solicitors Journal* urged it to call another. 'What an opportunity to re-unite the profession and give the public the opportunity to see and hear that solicitors were interested not only in their own pockets but in the interests of the public generally.'

Instead, the Government considered franchisee league tables to let the public 'know the qualifications and expertise of lawyers who do legally aided work'. And when the LAB said only franchisees would be guaranteed exclusive contracts for family, immigration, and mental health work, the Society conceded defeat. Medical negligence followed the same course. When the LAB proposed limiting legal aid to specialist panels, the Society objected that these contained only 141 firms. The Board replied that it sought to cut eligible firms from 3,261 in 1997 to 170. Hoon declared that 'far too many people dabble in this area of the law, and deal with so few cases that we cannot conclude that they know what they're doing'. Although the Society warned that legal aid would be 'rationed depending on where you live'—four to five franchised firms in south Wales and none in mid-Wales—the LAB awarded eighty exclusive franchises in 1999. When the LCD reaffirmed that all legal aid would be restricted to franchisees, the Law Society denounced this 'Stalinist' compulsion on the poor to go to 'legal aid factories'. They were 'entitled to choose their solicitor just like anyone else'. The Government 'seems to view justice as a commodity', which 'could be left to the law of supply and demand'. Exclusive contracts would hurt women and minority solicitors.[21]

Launching the Bar campaign against CFAs, vice chair Dan Brennan QC warned they would swell lawyers' profits, discourage expensive cases, and require plaintiffs to buy insurance costing 'as much as £11 million'. Its formal response strongly opposed extending CFAs, which would 'create a litigation market under the dominant control of insurance companies', foster conflicts of interest between lawyers and clients, and encourage the 'suppression of crucial documents' and the 'suborning and excessive coaching of witnesses or misrepresentation of facts or law'. Now the Bar asserted that insurance premiums would cost nearly £18 million annually and up to '34% of plaintiffs' damages overall could well go to lawyers'. Unconstrained by the cab-rank rule, 'the most capable practitioners will prefer, and will do, insurance and other work with guaranteed payment, leaving the plaintiff field to the less able, or young and inexperienced'. It was 'inevitable that standards of integrity will fall. For those who claim otherwise see the American example'. 'It would be disastrous if the habits, practices and consequent contempt for, [*sic*] lawyers found in the USA were to become commonplace here'. Firms there 'go bankrupt, especially in complex claims'. The need to spread risk would lead to 'larger, but far fewer firms'. There was 'no evidence of any similar system operating successfully else-where'. The Bar acknowledged practitioners needed to achieve 'greater efficiency' and be 'business-like but the profession of barrister is not a busi-ness'. The 75 per cent merits test was 'unfair and impractical'. Legal aid should remain for the poor and less educated, defendants, infants, patients, litigants against the state, and claims involving housing, multi-party actions, public interest, and professional negligence.[22]

Exhorting Irvine to stay the course, *The Times* attacked 'acts of profligacy in the Lord Chancellor's Department'. 'There should be real public anger at the huge and rapidly growing sums, spent on legal aid', whose 'bloated budget' was a 'grotesque drain on the taxpayer'. Opposition was 'pre-dictable' from a profession that had been 'doing very well, thank you, from the current system. Ninety percent of the legal aid bill is swallowed up by lawyers fees.' Taxpayers 'should not have to support cases which lawyers did not believe were strong enough to accept on a "no-win, no-fee" basis. The State should no more be picking winners in litigation than in industry.' The *Daily Mail* called 'Britain's legal aid bonanza' a 'honeypot for wealthy lawyers and canny defendants'. The *Evening Standard* could find 'no more compelling indictment of the legal aid system as it presently stands than the fact that Ms Dina Rabinovitch—the woman planning to marry Mr Anthony Julius, solicitor to the late Princess Diana—is to receive legal aid in her divorce from her husband, a wealthy banker'. A defence lawyer com-plained of 'speculative litigation' involving 'spurious cases'. Businesses 'are often forced to settle . . . where their defence is strong, simply because there is no incentive for the legally aided party to play fair, and act reasonably'.[23]

The LCD consultation paper said it did 'not want to create a litigious society' or 'import "ambulance chasing" ' but rather 'encourage fair settle-ments of disputes before they go to court' because 'justice always has a cost'. It proposed extending CFAs to all cases except family and criminal in order to share litigation risks 'between the lawyer and the clients'. Plaintiffs might be able to recover the success fee and insurance premium from defendants. Government would 'toughen . . . the legal merits test' because 'too many weak cases are granted legal aid. The hopes of litigants are unre-alistically raised, and the opposing party is exposed to unnecessary costs which they cannot recover'. Legal aid 'was not intended to . . . blackmail defendants into submission.'[24]

Hoon had not heard 'a single complaint' about the 30,000 CFA cases, 'whereas I receive regular complaints about legal aid'. Irvine insisted the purpose 'is not to provide savings' but to 'focus taxpayers' money where it is most needed'. Hallett called the proposal 'illogical, unfair and premature' because it was 'simply unrealistic to believe that no win, no fee agreements can take the place of legal aid'. Sycamore pointed to 'problems with availability, affordability and the funding of up-front disbursements'. Perhaps reflecting the distribution of work between the branches, he declared personal injury 'the wrong target. The proper target should be the criminal justice system where there is a lot of expenditure.' The *Gazette* thought CFAs 'not a viable option for many personal injury cases'. APIL called the 'horrific' proposal 'a sledgehammer to crack a nut' since personal injury cases represented only 2.5 per cent of the legal aid budget. LAG endorsed the proposal that losing defendants pay the success fee and insurance premium; but FOIL attacked this as an American system of 'penalties or fines'.

Although FOIL initially worried that the Government's 'appalling approach' would 'stop a lot of personal injury claims getting to court', it soon bowed to clients who 'for years...have been paying out for claims backed by legal aid, irrespective of their liability'. The Iron Trades Insurance Group called personal injury law 'a nice little earner for the lawyers' and complained that the insurance industry was 'being mugged'. But some defendants feared CFAs. The largest UK travel insurer claimed that the spread of contingency fees in Europe meant that 'the sky really can be the limit if holiday makers are successfully sued after an accident'. Predicting that insurance premiums would 'rocket' as in America, the Times Newspaper Company Solicitor warned that 'every brass-necked liar will...hope that he will hit the jackpot before the truth comes out'. Indeed, seven months after the leading libel firm of Peter Carter-Ruck & Partners accepted CFAs it had thirty-two such cases.[25]

The Lord Chancellor alienated not only fellow judges (whose support he had overconfidently expected) but also fellow Cabinet members. Although Jack Straw had attacked criminal defence lawyers, he resented Irvine's covetous glance at his domain. Health Secretary Frank Dobson, worried about the rising bill for medical negligence (£235 million in 1996–7, up 15 per cent from the previous year), accused lawyers of 'milking the NHS of millions'. '[T]he best place for a lawyer in the NHS is on the operating table, not sliding around causing trouble for other people'. 'We see the situation in the USA where people are not concerned with what is best for the mother and baby but are thinking "How would this look in court?"' Insisting that 'doctors are not being more negligent', the Medical Protection Society said 'the trouble is that solicitors are now advertising and putting ideas into patients' heads'. Dobson's attack reminded Scrivener of Denis Healy's plaint about 'being mauled by a dead sheep'. The AVMA chair 'absolutely disagreed' with Dobson's proposal of no-fault compensation. 'Claimant lawyers have done an enormous amount for the victims of medical accidents while nobody else, including the government, was doing anything at all'. FOIL surprisingly endorsed fault-based liability.[26]

The Law Society opposed limiting medical negligence to firms with contracts unless 'it could be shown that the "exclusive" group achieved significantly better outcomes'. Legal aid clients 'should remain entitled to choose any solicitor who is willing to take their case, just as privately paying clients can'. Warning against 'draconian proposals to limit access to legal services', it criticized 'arbitrary decision making through a radically different merits test'. CFAs should be extended to all non-matrimonial civil cases, but legal aid must 'continue to be available for cases where people are unable to afford' such arrangements, which 'many solicitors' find 'financially unviable'. Clients with risky cases would have to shop around, work would be more concentrated, and the image of law and lawyers would decline.[27]

The Bar Council declared that block contracts threatened 'the right to a lawyer of choice; an unacceptable decrease in access to lawyers', 'independence', and 'conflicts of interest' and had created 'major and intractable' problems in the United States. CLAFs and compulsory legal expenses insurance were 'better alternatives' to CFAs, which 'will undermine the objectivity of lawyers toward their clients and compromise their duty to the Court'. The BC expressed 'consternation and alarm' at the Government's failure to recognize that the Bar's role as an 'independent referral profession made up of sole practitioners' would be compromised by the unavoidable 'risk and profit sharing'. The inability of barristers within a risk pool to represent both sides 'would have a dramatic effect on the ability of the public to instruct the barrister of their choice'.[28]

The LAB strongly supported restricting medical negligence to franchised solicitors, substituting CFAs for legal aid in personal injury, and eliminating green form advice in such cases. The NCC agreed. But the CA, LAG, Justice, and the Public Law Project opposed extending CFAs to medical negligence and eliminating legal aid.[29]

When an LCD-commissioned study found that firms of all sizes could make CFAs profitable within three years, Hoon declared 'solicitors' anxiety... unfounded'. But the Law Society criticized the report's 'excessively optimistic assumptions'; its own research revealed difficulties 'in complex cases involving questions of liability and serious injury...which involve considerable investigative cost and effort'. The *Gazette* dismissed the LCD report as 'PI in the sky'. But though the new APIL president was not 'prepared to concede that the legal aid debate is over', he acknowledged a few weeks later that 'the best we can hope for is that after three or four years [the government] will realise that what is in place is simply not working'.

A BC-commissioned report emphasized 'the impossibility of a sole practitioner doing any significant amount of CFA work because of the individual's inability adequately to spread risk'. Brennan told a conference of 500: 'We are not just legal technicians but in fact pursuing a vocation. We have a higher professional ethic that goes beyond mere profit.' But a sixteen-barrister

Southampton set, which had taken fifty CFAs, thought 'the reforms have a great future'. 'You have to become more like solicitors. You have to see the papers more often and earlier on.' 'You are really co-venturing with the client and solicitor.' 'There is no real financial risk' because 'the profits on the winning cases have more than offset my losses'.

At a press conference organized by Hoon, a trade union solicitor accused colleagues of believing 'the world owes them a living'. They had to 'stop whingeing and start doing'. 'Lawyers have for too long lived on legal aid at the expense of the taxpayer and sometimes at the expense of the victim.' 'Raising hopes in no-hope cases while the taxpayer foots the bill is in no-one's interest.' Another solicitor told lawyers 'to recognise that the status quo is not an option for legal aid, any more than it is for any other weary arm of the welfare state'. Soon thereafter Hoon claimed the proposal would save nothing the first year, £69 million the second, and £100 million the third (far below his original claim of £800 million); the LAB estimates were £15 million, £57 million, and £88 million (although it recovered 77 per cent of the cost of personal injury cases the previous year).[30]

When Garnier submitted letters from 100 solicitors opposing the paper, Hoon dismissed some as written before its publication and Garnier's inquiry as 'clearly aimed at soliciting unfavourable comments'. The previous Government had 'regarded the cost of legal aid as totally out of control'; it had taken Garnier an 'astonishing[ly]...short time' to 'become so used to the ways of the opposition'. A month later the Lord Chief Justice warned that the poor would end up 'paying the price' if Government 'took a leap into the unknown' by withdrawing legal aid. The 'laws of our country exist for the benefit of the poor as well as the rich'. A Law Society leaflet entitled *Access Denied* urged the public to write their MPs.[31]

C. The Fat Cat Attack

Hoon orchestrated a contemporaneous exposé of legal aid fees. In response to a question planted by the Home Office Parliamentary private secretary, he named the twenty highest earning barristers (ten more than £400,000 annually) and seven solicitors' firms earning more than £2 million. The Bar denounced the figures as 'plain wrong', 'inaccurate and misleading', and their publication as 'designed to discredit legal aid'. Many fees were recovered from opponents or earned in multiple years, and overheads were disregarded; many cases would not have been brought without legal aid. It was hardly 'pure coincidence', said *Counsel*, 'that the answers were published in the very week that the Bar was due to publish its response to the Green Paper'. The Law Society declared firms should be proud to do so much legal aid. LAG called Hoon's 'wheeze' 'cheap and so obvious as to be insulting'. He 'looked particularly shifty as he dodged this way and that'. The *Gazette* accused Hoon of 'opportunistically' taking 'a cheap shot'. Payments were 'taxed by experienced Taxing Masters', said the *New Law Journal*. There must be 'five thousand barristers undertaking legal aid work and around 10,000 solicitors' offices who do not feature on the list'. The *Solicitors Journal* called Hoon's charge 'as warped as paedophiles who blame children for seducing them'. 'Who sets VAT? Which department imposed court fees? Which department has closed courts...?'

The Times felt 'the move appeared to backfire as the Bar countered with data'. 'Hang on', said a *Daily Mail* columnist, 'these lawyers are just doing their job, and good luck to them'. The *Daily Telegraph* criticized Labour's 'dangerous taste for "naming and shaming" those of whom it disapproves'. Hoon had 'ended up with egg on his face'. The *Daily Express* called it 'an unattractive political stunt' and praised Garnier's 'relentless campaign'. Hallett was pleased that 'for once, the Bar received something approaching a fair hearing' in the media. 'Must we risk what are, in effect, personal attacks upon individual members of the Bar by speaking out on matters of public interest?'[32]

Denying that the question had been planted, he had called lawyers 'fat cats', or this was a 'naming and shaming' exercise, Hoon praised legal aid solicitors' 'extraordinarily valuable work'. But he told a Law Society conference: 'People in the health service...are not receiving similar sums from public sources. Why should lawyers expect to be receiving in one case nearly three quarters of a million pounds a year from the taxpayer?' Sycamore asked 'what other group of professionals provides complex skilled services for less than £20,000 per annum?' The *Solicitors Journal* called Hoon's comparison 'nonsense' and accused him of 'mistakes of a few hundred thousand pounds or so'. It ridiculed Irvine's claim to have 'scrupulously obeyed the cab-rank principle while at the Bar, to his financial detriment' and called 'all this...a prelude to the abolition of legal aid and the introduction of a public defender's office'. Scrivener charged Irvine with using Hoon 'to implement the real agenda...to discredit the profession by pointing out that some top lawyers—disgracefully—can earn fees comparable to those of a minor pop star or footballer'.

The Government's motive surfaced when it froze legal aid remuneration for another year. Sycamore warned that 'the profession cannot be expected to carry on providing this vital public service if legal aid rates do not even cover inflation'. The LAPG accused the Government of 'trying to persuade legal aid firms to give up'. Declaring that 'the loyalty of legal aid firms is tested to the breaking point', the *Gazette* feared 'the seed corn of legal aid practice will be swept away to the commercial sector'. A year later the LAPG claimed that young solicitors were 'increasingly reluctant' to work 'very long and unsocial hours' for poor pay. Government 'needs to think again' if it assumed there were enough 'lean and hungry lawyers'.[33]

Every national newspaper covered the next scandal. The Clerk to the Parliaments had questioned the 'huge fees' of 'fat cat lawyers' and deplored 'there is no one batting for the public purse on this matter'. The LCD claimed that barristers' 1995–6 legal aid fees were cut from £286.7 million to £127.2 million. Mixing metaphors in its eagerness to shift the spotlight, the Law Society said it would 'be pleased if the Law Lords grasped the nettle' of this 'festering sore'. Its counsel in the hearing (a solicitor-advocate QC) claimed legal aid could save £20 million annually if QC fees were regulated like other lawyers' and urged limiting earnings to the 'generous and reasonable remuneration' of hospital consultants (£112,000), who 'are broadly equivalent in terms of public importance, ethical integrity and professional expertise'. The Bar counsel said this had 'gone over the line of absurdity'. One of the four silks, whose fees were cut from £33,000 to £28,000, dismissed the attack as 'a government "own goal"'. The clerk of a second had charged £300 an hour based on quotations of £250–£400 an hour by four other clerks. The media conflated this controversy with Mr Justice Lightman's attack on the fees QCs charged private clients (see Chapter 6).

Martin Bowley QC wondered whether the criticism 'is more disreputable for its intellectual dishonesty or for its political cynicism'. David Pannick QC urged the Law Lords 'to explain that criminal legal aid barristers do a complex and pressurised job and are entitled, without public opprobrium, to receive a fee which takes account of their overheads and years of experience'. Although a *New Law Journal* article the previous year had called for limiting QCs' annual legal aid earnings to £300–£400,000, now the periodical thought any ceiling impractical and advised the Law Lords to 'put an end to the "anti Legal Fat Cats" campaign'.

But newspapers across the political spectrum could not miss the chance to attack a favourite target, headlining: 'On trial: a system that makes QCs rich' (*Guardian*), 'Fat Cat Four Who Shame the Law' (*Sun*), 'High fees put fat-cat QCs in the dock' (*Independent*). 'The days of rich pickings from legal aid are numbered', said the *Guardian*, because 'the greed of a few, coupled with lack of any real controls at the top end of the market, has discredited the system'. The *Evening Standard* praised Irvine as 'a poacher turned gamekeeper...who just might crack this toughest of nuts'. The £1.6 billion 'massive legal aid bill' was more than 'a penny on income tax'. It praised his 'determination to grasp this nettle—unlike his predecessors, who...always flinched'.

The best argument in favour of Lord Irvine's measures is the furious reaction they have met from the most highly-paid lawyers. Any man who so upset the richest Silks and threatens to hurt them where it matters most—their wallets—has got to be doing something right.

A Lords ruling could make lawyers 'drop their fees and the result could be a relatively painless way of reducing the legal aid budget'.[34]

Lord Browne-Wilkinson, chairing the Lords inquiry, called the fees 'quite astonishing...compared with what was subsequently allowed... pretty shattering'. Michael Mansfield, a bicycling vegetarian radical, drew special scorn for appearing to claim £416 an hour for forty-three hours of preparation and one day on appeal (three years after attacking 'utility executives who are getting more in a day than their staff are getting a year'). A Conservative MP asked: was it 'right that somebody who is well-known for his left-wing causes...should submit a legal aid bill for £22,000 which was ultimately cut to just £12,000?' Hoon deplored the 'persistent pattern of over-claiming'. In 'certain high-cost cases over the past two years, barristers have claimed more than double what they have received'.

'[A]part from parking attendants being clamped', said the *Sunday Times*, 'few sights are more pleasing to the public eye than high-flying legal eagles being transmogrified into the pampered fat cats we always imagined them to be'. The *Guardian* noted that the last time barristers appealed a Lords taxing master's decision (in 1995), Lord Templeman had been 'staggered' at the £107,000 sought by a QC and junior, which would have 'hired three very competent headmasters for a year'. It 'laid at the doors of successive Lord Chancellors' the 'impropriety' of this 'profligate spending of public money'. 'If the cream glistens so invitingly, the cats can hardly be blamed for lapping it up.' Other papers criticized legal aid for child murderer Myra Hindley's challenge to her life sentence after the Lord Chief Justice upheld it (*Daily Mail*) and a drunk who fell off his bar stool and sued the publican (*Sun*).

The *Evening Standard* assailed:

pampered silks who have become very rich at the taxpayers' expense. Not only do they have their snouts in the legal aid trough, but they are effectively demanding that the trough is refilled after they have gobbled up their generous portion. ... They have been ticked off like naughty, greedy schoolboys. The legal aid gravy train— and indeed the stratospheric fees commanded generally by the silks' cartel—is a matter of national scandal.

But it added that 'hard as it may be for the lay person to accept—there is a case for the defence'. Hallett was 'merely a plump cat', netting about £100,000 per year. 'I have never claimed I was poorly paid, but I resent it being said I milk the legal aid fund.' 'On average I work 10 hours a day, six days a week.' The four silks 'worked enormously hard under great stress and I think they were entitled to the fees'. High flying commercial silks 'are the legal equivalent of the Spice Girls. They are the very best lawyers in the world and we should be proud of them.' She quoted an American academic who blamed 'all the miscarriages of justice in the US' on 'the incompetence of the defence lawyers'. Government 'would not invest the money needed to attract the best' to a public defender. A silk wrote to *The Times* that 'for the cost of a cut-price teabag in a chipped mug' he 'had to view the home-made videos of a man actually raping his eight-year-old stepdaughter'.[35]

This naturally failed to satisfy critics. The LCD notified the Law Society of thirty-nine cases where courts had halved legal aid fees and the Bar Council of twenty others. The latter acknowledged anecdotal evidence of 'ludicrous fees', proposed making it a disciplinary offence to overcharge by more than 50 per cent, and asked all heads of chambers 'whether we need to introduce detailed work schedules for cases'. Browne-Wilkinson noted 'public concern' that counsel had 'consistently' claimed excessive fees, which had been cut by 31, 56 and 45 per cent in the last three years. He urged an end to the 'culture of bargaining' over fees, which should be set 'in relation to fees which are generally allowed to barristers for comparable work', but called the earnings of other professions 'irrelevant'. Blaming 'the lack of effective control on QCs' fees' for having 'undermined the public reputation of the legal aid scheme', the Law Society regretted his failure to recommend a limit on annual earnings. LAG called for the abolition of silk. The Bar sought 'pre-set fees' because retrospective assessment 'led to unwarranted criticism of barristers in the media and elsewhere'.[36]

In June 1999 the Lord Chancellor accepted the BC proposal of fixed cost contracts in complex criminal cases. But though it sought to extend this 'truly radical reform' to civil cases, Irvine preferred 'contracting on a competitive basis'. A month later a Bar study claiming to show barristers were not 'fat cats' and the junior Bar was 'good value for money' provoked an *Independent* headline: 'We're not fat cats, say £266,000 a year QCs'. Reiterating that 'QCs must be paid at a rate that is justifiable' and should not enjoy 'inflated prices, simply because of a title', the Law Society urged a ceiling of lower court judges' salaries, which the Bar called 'illogic[al]'. Lord Irvine responded by proposing to eliminate QCs in 20 per cent of criminal cases, reducing defence costs to those of the prosecution.[37]

Government and media also exposed legal aid abuses at the bottom of the professional hierarchy. Echoing a Conservative attack seven years earlier, Jack Straw charged immigration lawyers with 'ripping the system off'. He accused one firm of having 'descended on Dover to "dish out" green forms to Czech and Slovak asylum seekers' and found 'cause for concern' about thirty-eight others. The Law Society immigration committee secretary denounced this plot 'to detract attention from the somewhat shallow and flimsy' consultation paper 'Control of Unscrupulous Immigration Advisers', whose 'real agenda' was 'to restrict immigration seekers' access to legal assistance' and 'make immigration a lawyer-free zone'. The *Gazette* called Straw's 'unfounded' and 'astonishing' accusations 'lawyer baiting of the worst kind'. The Society thought them 'bonkers'. The blacklist allegedly included firms late to interviews or accused of rudeness. An 'astounded' Sycamore was 'glad to say that "let's kill all the lawyers" does not always work as a publicity tactic'. The *Solicitors Journal* complained that 'once again, it seems, the government is singling out lawyers as a soft target'.[38]

Six months later the *Daily Mail* claimed a Kenyan asylum seeker cost legal aid £25,000 in a vain effort to get cash instead of food vouchers. The *Sunday Times* headlined 'Rich pickings as lawyers coach bogus asylum seekers'. Seeing the Government's potential political vulnerability, the Conservative Party Conference accused immigration solicitors of 'touting' at entry ports. Warning that immigration advice was expected to cost £49 million in 1999 (up from £28 million in 1997), the LAB was investigating seventy-six firms. 'There is no evidence of outright fraud but there is evidence of a lot of poor-quality work and of unnecessary work.' The Law Society welcomed 'any crackdown where there are serious concerns about the genuineness of advice being given and there is an appearance of abuse'. The Immigration Law Practitioners Association (ILPA) urged the Board to determine 'whether the increase in legal aid work represented a genuine response to this real need or sham assistance that helped no-one but the lawyers'. Although the OSS closed two London immigration firms the day Channel Four news exposed them the (solicitor) immigration minister attacked the Law Society for not rooting out 'seamy', 'incompetent', and 'corrupt' immigration lawyers. Although 'a minority get good advice', said Asylum Aid, 'the rest get bad or indifferent advice'. 'Unscrupulous solicitors frequently ring up refugee detention centres, get a person's name, phone the Home Office to say they are representing the detainee and then claim legal aid' but 'do no work'.

ILPA, whose president had called 'the majority of lawyers and non-lawyers in the asylum field . . . either insufficiently competent, dishonest, or both', urged 'compulsory regulation by an outside body where people are giving advice for reward'. Although it wanted contracts limited to franchised firms (expected to include 700–750 of the 900–950 doing immigration work), it criticized competitive bidding for block contracts as a 'treasury-driven proposal which would put the lives of refugees at risk', the equivalent of 'encouraging cut-price surgery on the NHS'. At the same time it continued to crack down on inadequate supervision, overcharging, unnecessary work, and 'aggressive touting' in order to separate 'genuine need from what is being supplied'. The OSS shut down two more firms, ordered more than fifteen to reduce bills, responded to allegations of malpractice at six, and planned to investigate the more than 200 unfranchised firms. The *Gazette* said 'this uncompromising approach to all kinds of malpractice in immigration work will be welcomed wholeheartedly by the genuinely specialist firms'. But the investigation only uncovered poor supervision of unqualified staff and inadequate file management at sixty-three firms. Fearing the LAB would choose which barristers could do immigration work, a Bar working party recommended it develop its own accreditation. When legal aid was extended to the Immigration Appellate Authorities, only specialist lawyers were eligible.[39]

D. The Access to Justice Bill

In July 1998 Irvine tabled subordinate legislation in the Lords extending CFAs to all non-family civil cases. Lord Ackner's amendment limiting the uplift to 25 per cent of the recovery was lost by 24 to 55. Noting that the net cost per legal aid case fell 2.8 per cent in non-family civil matters, the Law Society called expenditure 'well under control'. LAG agreed 'there is absolutely no reason to cut the scope of the civil legal aid scheme, when the amount spent on it has decreased by £15 million'. The *Solicitors Journal* insisted 'personal injury and medical negligence' were 'particularly unsuitable' for CFAs. Concerned that the 'least affluent' have access to justice and uncertain that CFAs could 'occupy the ground now occupied by legal aid', the Lord Chief Justice urged government to 'take it slowly'.[40]

The Bar reasserted its opposition to public defenders and block contracts. Hallett told the annual conference that one American state paid just $100 for capital defence. 'How long before financial pressures are so great that contracts are given to the firm of lawyers that offers the cheapest deal however good or bad they may be?' The New Orleans Public Defender had 'sued himself because he was being forced to take on three times more cases each year than the recommended maximum'. The Solicitor-General insisted a public defender 'does work if properly funded'. When Hallett asked who believed it would be, only the LCD Parliamentary Secretary raised his hand. Calling a PD 'an extreme calamity', the Bar vowed to 'fight it tooth and claw'. The Scottish LAB claimed its pilot PD was 'at least as effective' and delivered services 'more efficiently and economically'. But the Scottish Law Society denounced the 'lack of choice and the perception of lack of independence'. '[W]e don't need another' 'bureaucratic nightmare' like the CPS.[41]

Disregarding all objections, the December 1998 White Paper proposed a Community Legal Service (CLS) for all advice, a Criminal Defence Service (CDS) combining employed lawyers and contracted private practitioners, and a funding assessment asking: 'would another type of service be a better way of dealing with the case', 'could the applicant fund the case in some other way', and would 'a reasonable person able to fund the case... be prepared to pursue it'. 'The cost of the salaried service will provide a benchmark, which the CDS can use to assess whether the prices charged by private lawyers are reasonable.' Irvine declared his Government 'was elected on a radical agenda to modernise this country'. Institutions 'that are out-of-date, inefficient, or unaccountable to the people, will not survive unchanged'. 'The justice system should serve everyone, regardless of means.' 'At the same time, taxpayers deserve value for the money they contribute....' 'Some restriction on the unfettered choice of lawyer... is necessary and desirable in order to secure quality and value for money'.

People needed access to justice, not law; 'going to court is, and should be, the last resort'. ADR 'can be less formal and adversarial; and in some cases, it may allow disputes to be resolved more quickly and cheaply'. Legal aid was 'too heavily biased towards expensive, court-based solutions' and 'spent almost entirely on lawyers' services'.

Lawyers 'determine where and how the money is spent'. There was 'little incentive to work more efficiently', 'little control over quality, and no scope for competition to keep prices down'. In the larger criminal cases 'lawyers are placed under inappropriate financial incentives...adjournments are sought unnecessarily; guilty pleas are delayed until the last moment; [and] cases are taken to the Crown Court unnecessarily'. Separate contracts would be negotiated with firms on specialist panels. CFAs 'offer a potentially attractive option in cases about the division of matrimonial property'. Legal aid should 'not give some people an unfair advantage' by enabling 'someone to pursue another citizen through the courts at the taxpayer's expense, with a case on which someone would not choose to spend his or her money'. Cases involving social welfare, children, violence, or the wider public interest should take priority. 'It cannot be assumed that any case necessarily has an automatic right to public funding because of its intrinsic merits.'

This 'long overdue' change, said Irvine, would satisfy the 'vast unmet legal need' in 'all those urban estates where people have no advice centre, no neighbourhood solicitor, nowhere to find help in disputes about housing, or benefits, or debt, or immigration'. 'The best person to offer... initial advice about welfare benefits or debt is unlikely to be a formally qualified lawyer'. The only new money would be £20 million for advice by the not-for-profit sector. He 'would be surprised' to encounter opposition. 'Progressive judges such as Lord Bingham and Lord Woolf—I would predict that they would be supportive'. There may be 'more old-fashioned judges of a different generation who want to go on fighting the battles of yesterday', but 'the judges are not sovereign'.

The Law Society warned that the proposal would cut legal aid offices from 10,000 to 3,000. The LAPG agreed 'access to legal help and choice of solicitor will be severely eroded'. CLSA expressed 'massive fear' that contracts would deter solicitors from taking unpopular cases. PDs suffered from 'bureaucracy and inefficiency'. The Bar Council called contracts 'a second-rate system of justice' governed by a 'sausage-machine' mentality. In this 'crony culture' lawyers would be 'encouraged to ingratiate themselves to get on a list' and discouraged from 'fearlessly asserting their client's case'. LAG agreed contracting 'will inevitably lead to a substantial reduction in the number of outlets' but felt 'the current system is too fragmented' and welcomed 'the proposal to prioritise social welfare law'. But the NCC praised contracting for giving consumers an 'indication' of who could provide a 'quality service'.[42]

The press were predictably hyperbolic: a 'revolution in legal aid', the 'most sweeping reform', the 'most radical shakeup', the 'biggest programme of reform in British legal services for 50 years', the 'end of the line for the legal aid fat cats'. Calling British justice 'clogged with archaic and restrictive practices' and 'too slow and expensive', the *Financial Times* welcomed plans 'to shake up the system' and 'curb excessive fees'. 'When justice is streamlined, more people will be able to afford it out of their own pockets, or, more likely, from insurance policies.' 'Increased private provision will be the best way in the long run to contain state costs, while maintaining free choice in the access to justice.' The proposals target 'resources more on ordinary people's legal needs and less on lawyers and the courts', said *The Times*, and improve 'access to justice for millions of middle-income Britons'. The '£1.6 billion legal aid budget will come under control for the first time' as government eliminated 'waste, "fat cat" fees and no-hope cases. Wealthy criminals—drug traffickers or fraudsters—will have to pay their own trial defence costs'. Irvine 'should ignore the Bar's predictable moan'. Taxpayers 'cannot stomach some lawyers dragging out their cases'. '[E]ngineers and architects, manage to abide by contracts.' It favoured CFAs because 'the burden of risk in bringing a case to court should be shared between lawyer and client. If a lawyer considers the risk of a case too great, why should the taxpayer foot the bill?' Only the *Independent on Sunday* asked 'what price now the solicitor, suspicious of police malpractice, who digs and digs on behalf of the client? The fearless advocate, once he has to bear in mind next year's government contract, will cease to exist'.[43]

Hers was not a 'predictable moan', insisted Hallett, but 'prompted by a concern for the criminal justice system'. Many 'lawyers round the world will tell you that their experience of public defender systems is the opposite' of 'a robust and competent defence'. They were 'disastrous to criminal justice'. The BC, LS, LAG, NC, CA, and Scope warned that 'people on low incomes will not be able to afford the costs of legal insurance, or to pay for the essential expert evidence'. Irvine reassured them he did not plan to 'move to a public defender service . . . overnight, or at all'.[44]

The Lords debated the Bill for six hours on 14 December (less than two weeks after its introduction on the day of the White Paper). Peers agreed it was 'the greatest shake-up of legal services since the original Legal Aid Act 1948' (Lord Goodhart), the biggest 'for 50 years' (Lord Bingham), 'since the war' (Lord Mayhew), 'we have ever seen' (Lord Hunt). Lord Mayhew found it 'profoundly unconstitutional and wrong', some provisions 'so dangerous that they could hardly be made worse' and made 'one's hair stand . . . on end'. 'So much for our professionalism', mourned Lord Phillips.[45] But Lord Borrie thought the Bill 'helps to put the client at the centre of our legal and judicial process'; Lord Hacking declared it 'absolutely right to overhaul the entire system'. And Lord Falconer noted that 'every single one of those noble Lords from both sides of the House who is not a lawyer or a judge has greeted the proposals…with enthusiasm': they would make Britain 'a more genuinely equal country' (Lord Sawyer), be 'a liberating force for millions' (Baroness Crawley), and place 'access to legal services at the heart' (Baroness Thornton). When Lord Irvine discredited lawyer opposition by declaring that 'legal aid is for the benefit of the public, not vested interests', the profession protested. *Pro bono* activities, said Lord Mackay, 'give the lie to the idea that the legal profession as a whole is out to feather its own nest with no regard to the public'. Lord Ackner called it 'quite untrue that the Judges are concerned to preserve the monopoly of the Bar in the Higher Courts because they themselves came from the Bar'. Lord Thomas resented the suggestion 'that the legal profession is a crusty out-of-date organisation'. '[A]ll professions must have restrictive rules to guarantee competence and reliability', insisted Lord Hutchinson. '[D]o not surgeons, air pilots and engineers have monopolies…?'[46]

Sceptics stoked fears. The CFA posed 'dangers to professional integrity' (Lord Goodhart), 'turns lawyers into speculators' and creates 'a terrible temptation…not to disclose documents' (Lord Kingsland). It would be unavailable 'in a wide variety of cases' (Lord Clinton-Davis) and inaccessible to the poor (Lord Hacking). There would be a 'radical reduction' in the number of legal aid solicitors (Lord Phillips) creating a 'lottery' and 'legal aid deserts' (Lord Hunt). Lord Irvine admitted 'the reality…that the funds available for civil legal aid are those left over after the prior demands of the criminal defence budget have been met'. Although he insisted 'we are not undertaking these reforms to save money', his references to 'the spiralling costs of legal services' and the need to 'curb…the costs of legal aid' revealed 'the fingerprints of the Treasury' (Lord Phillips). Baroness Kennedy warned that 'in seeking to drive down costs, quality will be sacrificed'. Lord Phillips agreed that solicitors 'desperate to hang on to the legal aid work they are doing' would 'tender at prices which are "what the market will bear"' in 'a rather rigged market'.[47]

Opponents resisted the arrogation of executive power. Irvine was 'a Lord Chancellor in a hurry' (Lord Hutchinson). Lord Ackner made 'the very serious constitutional principles' his 'cardinal point, or perhaps I should say…"the cardinal's point". It has a significant Wolsey undertone.' (Irvine notoriously compared himself to the Cardinal, a revelation of megalomania he was never allowed to forget.) 'We all know that the noble and learned Lord…enjoys the exercise of power. He has told us that he is chairman of no less than five committees of the Cabinet.' Ackner 'compare[d] the position of Malaysia at the moment' (whose executive had removed the chief justice). Lord Gisborough quoted Locke—'There is no liberty if the judiciary power be not separated from the legislative and executive'—which Lord Kingsland called 'the most important and the least visible part of our constitution'. Lord Lane deplored 'the grave inroads into the authority and the long-standing independence of the judiciary and the Bar' and the 'almost free power in the hands of the Executive... the scene is well set for... parliamentary dictatorship'.[48]

To demonstrate disinterest, the two branches formed an Alliance with more than a dozen other groups, including ILEX, LAG, LAPG, LCF, NACAB, Justice, Refuge, Mencap, RADAR, the National Housing Foundation, Shelter, CPAG, Headway, the Royal National Institute for the Blind and the Royal National Institute for Deaf People, NCC, CA, ASA, and the Public Law Project, which urged retention of legal aid in personal injury, exclusion of matrimonial property disputes from CFAs, and contracts for all franchised firms. The Law Society was 'totally opposed to arbitrary and inflexible capping of the legal aid budget'. '[T]he need for reform of the aged legal aid system is well accepted' by the legal profession, said the *Gazette*, but this 'blunt instrument' would 'destroy, rather than achieve, the remodelling necessary'.[49]

The Lords debated the Bill for another seven days during the Committee Stage (19, 21, 26, and 28 January), Report Stage (11 and 16 February), and Third Reading (16 March). The Select Committee on Delegated Powers and Deregulation, chaired by Lord Alexander, had expressed 'considerable concern' about the Lord Chancellor's 'almost untrammelled' powers and urged that the Bill 'be amended so as to contain (a) a clear statement of principle that the objective of the Community Legal Service is to promote and enhance the opportunities for citizens to have access to legal advice and the opportunity to resolve disputes'. Lord Lloyd moved the first amendment to insert three principles, including that 'persons have access to legal services and the machinery of justice which they would otherwise be unable to obtain on account of their means'. He was supported by the Lord Chief Justice (who had proposed a statement of principles during the Second Reading) and the Master of the Rolls. Lord Irvine promised separate purpose clauses for the CLS and CDS, which were agreed during the Report Stage. But Lord Lloyd's statement (omitting the preservation of 'a strong, independent and self-regulating legal profession') was adopted by 182 to 111 despite Irvine's objection.[50] Outside Parliament Irvine derided it as 'a gimmick and completely unrealistic' and expressed confidence that the Commons would eliminate it. '[A]ccess to justice is not just a gimmick', retorted the CA's head of legal affairs; 'surely treating people equally before the law is a fundamental principle of justice'. The LS, BC, LAG, and CA were 'dismayed' by Irvine's language.[51]

Several amendments patently served lawyers' interests. Lord Irvine dismissed Lord Kingsland's proposed body to set remuneration for contracted and salaried lawyers as simply intended 'to keep lawyers in the manner in which they have become accustomed'. 'Government have no duty to help lawyers achieve target incomes.' Kingsland's proposal of 'fair and reasonable remuneration' took 'no account of the availability of... public funds' and did not 'live in the real world'. When Kingsland and Ackner sought separate remuneration for advocacy, resenting 'gratuitous smears' that 'this is a method of protecting the narrow interests of the profession', Irvine offered to contract directly with the Bar. He saw 'the footprints of my friends in the Bar Council all over' an amendment requiring litigators to advise clients in writing whether specialist advocacy was appropriate, 'one of several which...have either attempted to guarantee work for the Bar or protect the position of the Bar'.[52]

Lord Phillips wanted all 'who meet the standards set by the Commission' to 'be able to provide services' under contracts specifying hours per case and cases per year. Although he was a solicitor and had been briefed by a local law society, he was 'not here in any sense as an advocate for practising solicitors'. Lord Falconer said this would put solicitors 'in the unique position where they can force upon the buyer of those services the need to buy them'. Phillips thought it 'odd to find a spokesman of New Labour... proposing the replacement of free consumer choice in a free legal market by a restricted, highly bureaucratic regime'. He would be 'very surprised' if 'the Lord Chancellor shopped around for a cheap surgeon'. Lord Clinton-Davis (another solicitor) called it 'unwise to introduce price competition' where 'there are no reliable and generally accepted means of measuring the quality of work'. Irvine said the amendments 'seek to provide a protected position for lawyers...guarantee work...safeguard the market share'. They were 'an example of a feather-bedding culture'. Warning that 'at least half of the firms who were carrying out quality assured legal aid work immediately before the competitive tender will thereafter be prohibited from doing any legal aid work', Phillips forced a division, which he lost by 119 to 127.[53]

Peers sought to preserve or expand legal aid. Lord Kingsland urged that it remain demand led, quoting Lord Irvine's objection in 1996 that the Conservatives' White Paper would 'cap legal aid for the first time', making it 'discretionary'. Kingsland wanted to keep 'a system of entitlements' because legal aid had 'underspent over the past five years' and was just 0.5 per cent of the budget. Irvine retorted that 'the Prime Minister said again and again during the election campaign that schools and hospitals were our number one priority'. The civil legal aid budget was 'entirely open-ended and controlled by lawyers'. Lord Clinton-Davis's proposal to protect the CLS budget from encroachment by criminal defence was 'simply unrealistic', 'play[ing] politics'. 'The only people who could possibly be attracted to a ring-fenced budget...would be lawyers'. Kingsland lost the division by 54 to 86. Warning that some Australian states had suspended civil legal aid and Ontario cut it by 80 per cent for three years, Lord Goodhart proposed that the Lord Chancellor announce the CLS budget at the beginning of each year. Goodhart cited the plight of 'homeless families who have been wrongfully refused rehousing by their local authority' and 'a child who has been brain damaged at birth', as well as support by 'consumer bodies', to show 'this is not a proposal for the protection of the legal profession'. But he lost the division by 80 to 134.[54]

Irvine rejected Lord Archer's attempt to restore legal aid for personal injury, insisting that there was ample after-the-fact insurance and quoting the trade-union firm Thompsons: 'Too many lawyers had for too long thought the world owed them a living. . . . Lawyers would have to wean themselves off the easy money of legal aid. . . .' When Lord Clinton-Davis noted that Thompsons were a 'large firm with a continuing cash flow . . . very different from the high street practitioner', Irvine accused him of 'seeking to defend the interests of a particular group of lawyers'. Lord Phillips, who had been a director of a legal costs insurer for eight years, expressed 'serious concern' about adverse selection; but Irvine refused 'to accept that lawyers, among all businesses, should be excluded from running risks and incurring costs in order to earn profits'. Observing that legal aid had recovered more than £502 million in 1996–7 for a net Treasury expenditure of £1.4 million, Lord Goodhart exclaimed: 'Now there's value for money'. Irvine replied that 89 per cent of those cases cost £6,000 or less, a 'not unreasonable' burden for firms. Both Lord Archer and Lord Kingsland tried to preserve legal aid in special circumstances: children, the disabled, and pensioners; cases with costs over £25,000, investigative costs over £3,000, damages over £50,000 or multiple causes of action. Lord Irvine called solicitors' alleged reluctance to take such cases 'almost an indictment of the profession by the very people who have often sought to maintain the status quo in other respects'. First Assist had just offered a policy whose premium was payable only on success; Irvine predicted solicitors would bear the £200 non-refundable 'processing fee'.[55] The Government also rebuffed efforts to extend legal aid: social security appeals, coroners' inquests, and inquiries were 'informal and inquisitorial hearings' in which lawyers were unnecessary; UKIAS and the Refugee Legal Centre adequately handled immigration, and trade unions, law centres, the EOC, CRE, and FRU dealt with employment.[56]

Critics condemned CFAs. Noting that 'doctors have never expected payment by results', Lord Goodhart asked whether estate agents and insurance brokers, who charged commission, were 'professions with which lawyers seek to compare themselves'. Lord Thomas regretted 'the introduction of this gambling element'. The Bar was 'not geared to carrying on the business of bookies', protested Lord Ackner. CFAs should be monitored to ensure that 'litigants are not being taken advantage of in cases which are open and shut...as has been conceded to be the situation in at least 90 per cent'. Lord Clinton-Davis feared solicitors 'will feel compelled, especially when they are carrying very heavy overheads, to ensure that there is a settlement'. The Government refused to create a CLAF or even study it.[57] Goodhart wanted to give courts discretion not to award the success fee and insurance premium because 'triple costs' were 'seriously unfair'. Ackner also opposed a 'penal costs order'. But the Lord Chancellor felt taxation adequately handled the problem.[58] Speaking for FOIL, Lord Hunt sought to exclude those with legal expenses insurance from CFAs, which allow 'lawyers to add an extra sum to their bill if they're successful'. But Irvine thought this 'a choice for the individual to make'.[59] The Lord Chancellor did, however, ban CFAs in family proceedings under pressure from the Family Law Bar Association, SFLA, Relate, and an unusual intervention by Lord Sheppard (Bishop of Liverpool).[60] Lord Phillips warned that plaintiffs might conceal 'crucial facts in relation to the claim in the hope and anticipation of depressing the amount of the uplift' and an 'unscrupulous solicitor could string out the litigation'. When the Earl of Dartmouth praised contingent fees for enabling an American smoker 'successfully [to] sue...one of the biggest and most powerful corporations in the world; namely, Philip Morris', Lord Goodhart asked if 'we should copy a legal system in which one can obtain damages of a couple of million dollars...for spilling a cup of hot coffee over oneself'. Lord Ackner recalled that a decade earlier Lord Irvine had dismissed CFAs as 'another gimmick to avoid state responsibility and to secure justice on the cheap'. The Lord Chancellor replied glibly 'that is how it appeared to me then, but it is not how it appears to me now'; but he promised to ask the consultative panel to advise about CFAs within five years.[61]

The CDS provoked the greatest resistance. Lord Irvine rejected Lord Kingsland's request that he consult with the Law Society, Bar Council, and others before establishing it, denying he intended any 'revolution' or 'big bang'. But he agreed the LSC would create a code of conduct. Lord Thomas denounced the CDS as 'a step nearer to government control'. Lord Ackner cited a report finding that 'indigent criminal defendants in state criminal cases in New York City receive ineffective assistance from lawyers' (but omitted its conclusion that public defenders provided far better service than private practitioners). The CDS would have 'an interest in shortening cases and clearing lists'. Either it would 'offer only minimal salaries and the quality of defending advocates will suffer', or 'the number of advocates employed will be low in order to keep down costs, in which case each defender will carry an overwhelming caseload'. Lord Hutchinson asked how the Lord Chancellor would feel 'if, when he had a burst appendix, he was told that a stop-gap, temporary surgeon would look after him'. '[V]isualise the picture: "See how cheaply you can do it, George...

strike a good bargain with your colleague along the road at the CPS; and the judge and Big Brother will be delighted with your performance".' In America 'the District Attorney and the public defender have brought the criminal process...into disrepute'. Lord Bach (a barrister) replied that 'the present system often sets up weak defence counsel against strong prosecuting counsel'. The former 'may well receive the brief at the very last minute'; returns happen 'a great deal and sometimes at extremely short notice'. '[O]ne only needs to visit any robing room...to know that bargaining takes place....' Lord Hutchinson dismissed such 'tittle-tattle' by a member 'of the Lord Chancellor's team'. Baroness Kennedy said she practised in a 'very different' world where the Bar was 'a vocation'; it was 'distasteful' to hear it 'spoken of as if it were some sort of a corner shop'. Lord Phillips lauded 'the ruggedness, often bloody-mindedness and the eccentricity...of the independent advocate'. Lord Wigoeder agreed that 'the average member of the criminal Bar is likely to be a person of higher calibre than the average member of a state prosecution or defence service'. Irvine assured Peers 'the salaried element will by far be the smaller part' and 'generally there will be a choice between...contracted providers and salaried defenders'. Salaried lawyers 'would be in the highest degree unlikely to do more than the lesser cases'.[62]

On 16 February Lord Thomas moved to eliminate salaried defenders, noting that an Arizona county violated the Constitution when it 'awarded contracts to the lowest bidder'. The CDS had been 'simply pulled out of the air as a good, money-saving wheeze'. Lord Hutchinson asked whether Peers could 'imagine any independent judiciary drawn from the CPS and criminal defence service'. Would we 'send a part-time surgeon into the operating theatre'? Lauding the Bar's 'conspicuous success' in maintaining quality, Lord Campbell warned that 'contracted men are subject possibly to union rules, to government control, to regulation by a commission'. Lord Irvine insisted his civil servants 'work long hours which in many other walks of life would be regarded as unsocial...out of a strong sense of public service'. The claim that salaried defenders 'will be second-rate, under-funded and overworked...is developed by anecdote, not by evidence'. Nevertheless, Thomas's amendment was agreed by 189 to 134. Irvine then accepted an amendment assuring a choice between salaried defenders and contracted firms. All those meeting quality standards would be guaranteed a contract in the first round and likely to keep it thereafter.[63]

Irvine insisted that salaried defenders would no more 'lack independence of mind because their livelihood comes from a single state source' than do judges. '[E]very penny spent on criminal legal aid is a penny out of my budget that cannot be spent on civil legal aid—helping people to protect or assert their legal rights'. The present system contained no 'guarantee of quality' and 'no way to make sure the taxpayer gets value for

money'; 'competition for contracts' would ensure both. 'The prospect of
even a small number of salaried defenders has met with special pleading by
vested interests'.[64]

The Bar Council took credit for the objectives clause and defeat of the
CDS, which Brennan (now chair) claimed 'would plainly be a breach of the
European Convention on Human Rights'. A 'shocked' Anthony Scrivener
QC said he had not voted 'for a Labour government to mutilate legal aid'.
'This isn't a Labour government.... It's a Conservative government.' LS
President Mathews also attacked the 'unjustified and unnecessary restric-
tion on client choice'. The 'arbitrary' culling of legal aid firms was
intended to 'suit the administrative convenience of the Legal Aid Board'.
It was 'nonsensical' to argue that two-thirds 'provide poor quality help'.
Irvine called Mathews's fears 'unfounded'. 'The point of my reforms is to
give people on legal aid a choice from among about 3,000 quality-assured
firms. That compares with the 4,987 offices today which do 92 per cent of legal
aid work in value, about 40 per cent of which are not quality assured.' But
the Law Society continued to oppose 'restrictions on choice which are not
necessary to good quality' and a salaried service unless 'clients remain free
to choose a private practitioner'. It wanted 'to ensure that legal aid does
not become concentrated in the hands of a few large firms'. It published
a study finding that thirty-five of forty-four clients felt it important to
choose a solicitor. The *Gazette* called the 'radical' reduction in the number
of legal aid providers 'one of the most insidious aspects' of the Bill, which
made 'a mockery of the government aim of avoiding social exclusion'. It was
'absolutely astonishing', Irvine retorted, that 'lawyers do not realise that half
the things they say about themselves go down like a lead balloon with the
public'. To claim that 'a controlled budget leads to a decline in standards'
was 'a gross non-sequitur'. 'The proposition that people require to be overpaid in order to deliver quality' did not 'stack up'. The public believed
'lawyers profit more than the people' from legal aid, which is 'a means of
funding lawyers' bank balances'.[65]

Profound suspicion of civil litigation suffused the debate. The *New Law
Journal*, which consistently championed lawyers, warned that 'ambulance
chasers may ride again'. The suit against tour organizers by Lennox Lewis
fans who had flown to New York only to see him lose to Holyfield illustrated
'the nannying principle which has been foisted on us... part and parcel of
a lessening of standards in the legal profession'. Lawyers 'who indulge in
speculative actions should, in certain circumstances, have to bear the brunt
of the costs of those whom they have unsuccessfully sued'. *The Times*
ridiculed an American who sued a toothbrush manufacturer and the
American Dental Association for failure to warn of abrasions from overuse.
This 'haliototic gust of legal madness' was inspired by tobacco litigation
profits. 'American litigation has reached such a hallucinatory level' that the

claim 'might just succeed'. The paper repeated the mythical stories about punitive damages for the defective BMW paint job and McDonald's coffee spill (omitting that 700 burn victims had complained and punitive damages were cut to less than a sixth on appeal and still further by a secret settlement) and $50,000 for a 'New Hampshire teenager who got hung up on a basketball net by his teeth when attempting a slam dunk'. The 'system' inculcated 'a primitive assumption that any setback...is the fault of someone else who must be punished and made to pay' and fed 'dreams of avarice built up by a plague of lawyers and a culture where misfortune, even self-inflicted, has become the easiest way to a fortune'. In a rare agreement, the *Sun* attacked a law firm advertising on the back of a hospital appointment card, accusing lawyers who 'lined their pockets' of feeding the 'new greed and blame culture' of 'The Sue Nation'. Columnist Polly Toynbee declared: 'We are turning into grasping whingers and self-pitying milksops' who make 'loads of money for lawyers whose silken tongues persuade any of us that we are victims'.

A Centre for Policy Studies report warned that the proportion of tort victims consulting lawyers soon would be higher in the UK than the USA. 'An American-style compensation culture is taking over in Britain which may be costing nearly £7 billion a year in payouts and legal fees', £1.8–£3.1 billion by the public sector. The Woolf reforms would just 'exacerbate the problem because more people will have access to the courts'. (Prince Charles wrote an undated letter to Lord Irvine declaring: 'I and countless others dread the very real and growing prospect of an American-style personal injury "culture" becoming ever more prevalent... [which] can only lead, ultimately, to an atsmophere of distrust and suspicion....') FOIL agreed with the report's 'fundamental point'. But APIL naturally dismissed it as 'propaganda not research', responding to the claim that local councils had closed playgrounds by asking: 'Wouldn't people rather have playgrounds that are safe?' When the National Audit Office reported that the NHS faced £2.8 billion in negligence claims, APIL responded: 'Personal injury lawyers are not out to exploit the NHS, but believe NHS staff should be held to account when their negligence causes injury to patients'. Extrapolating from the Harvard Medical Practice Study, AVMA asserted that only 15,000 of the 82,000 NHS victims with actionable claims sued. The most comprehensive study of civil litigation found that:

eight in ten justiciable problems are dealt with...without any legal proceedings being commenced, without an ombudsman being contacted or any other ADR processes being used. This is despite the fact that about three in five members of the public took some advice about trying to resolve their problem, and that of those, about half received advice from a solicitor....

LS Vice-President Sayer declared: 'People are entitled to exercise the rights they have been given....'[66]

Benedict Birnberg warned that the unsuccessful tobacco litigation showed the danger of conditional fees. The solicitors not only lost £2.5 million but agreed not to sue the defendants for ten years and any tobacco company for five in order to protect their clients from costs. '[I]f public funding is no longer available, which lawyer will risk bankrupting himself in future when taking on big and wealthy corporations?' Hoon denied 'Government is withdrawing legal aid from most money claims, or that as a quid pro quo for the withdrawal of legal aid we are allowing lawyers to use conditional fees'. 'We simply have to reform legal aid and the way legal services are provided if we are to make access to justice not simply a slogan but a reality'.[67]

The press stridently exposed legal aid abuse. The *Sun* reported that a firm billed the LAB £50 an hour for 'thinking time' because 'some of our best ideas come when we are at home or in the car'. Legal aid funded 'barmy' cases, like a 'self-confessed petty crook' suing for injuries sustained in fleeing the police. The *Daily Star* complained that 'lawyers have turned Liverpool into the compensation capital of Britain', where legal aid cost three times more than anywhere else and half the civil budget went to welfare claims. Even the *Guardian* called legal aid 'wasteful, funding too many unwinnable cases, as well as those where the costs exceed any possible benefit to the litigant'. Spending was 'open-ended', and 'little control is exerted over the lawyers providing the services'. An 11-year struggle over a 'worthless six-foot wide strip of land in deepest Staffordshire' cost legal aid more than £100,000.[68]

In the *Sunday Times* Phillip Oppenheim cheered Irvine for going 'head-to-head with the most assertive and articulate interest group in Britain— the lawyers, a bunch who were too wild even for Margaret Thatcher to tangle with'. Barristers 'pretty much name their own fees' for legal aid cases; the fee structure for solicitors was 'an incentive to spin out the hours'. 'Do honourable professionals stoop to this? Is the Pope a Catholic?' People 'without legal aid are forced to settle. Justice? Only poor people and rich corporations can afford to go to court.' He ridiculed 'one of the nation's favourite hobbies, neighbours' ditts [petty quarrels]...in one recent beano a neighbour fought a legally aided case over flowerpots on his wall'. Lawyers engaged in 'overmanning, a closed shop, state subsidies—so many Red Robbos in chalk pinstripes.... "A lawyer with his briefcase can steal more than a hundred men with guns".'[69]

Not every paper applauded. A *Daily Telegraph* column declared that the Access to Justice Bill showed 'how misleading the title of a measure can be'. Although 'much appears to be misspent' in the 'staggering £1.6 billion' budget, the Bill 'may remove legal services from those who need it most', such as 'those living in rural communities' and 'ethnic minorities'. Lawyers paid by CFAs were 'unlikely to act for people with difficult cases'.

'Guiding aims or principles' were essential because 'the Bill is "nationalising" all decisions as to which cases receive legal aid'. Although dispersing such decisions 'has been open to abuse by some solicitors, who have been generating work', it 'has ensured that cases embarrassing to the Government and challenging the misuse of power have still reached the courts'. The Bill 'will not necessarily reduce the legal aid budget, but will merely concentrate work in the hands of fewer lawyers and exclude many who can offer a high standard of service'. Criminal defendants who 'have been able to choose independent lawyers' will 'be allocated lawyers employed by the state—which will have accused them in the first place'. Irvine promptly denounced the article as 'nonsense'.[70]

The Times agreed that Law Society objections had 'some justification', even if 'cynics' might see them as 'an attempt to preserve its members' livelihoods'. Readers should 'mind the gap' between the Bill's title and content. Legal aid costs had 'soared' because 'the system has been abused' by lawyers 'inclined to accept cases, regardless of their merits'. But though the 'taxpayer may be the winner', 'will justice?' The 'insurance market could act as a surer judge of which cases are worth pursuing than lawyers who can rely on the taxpayer to fund speculative actions', but 'injured people with cases which appear difficult may find it hard to find a solicitor'.[71]

Irvine also encountered backbench resistance. Robert Marshall-Andrews thought the Bill's title 'has an ominous, Orwellian ring'. It 'arrogates to an unelected government appointee...draconian powers over the administration of justice'. The 'serious denial of justice to the poorest' was 'the largest ever departure from the principles of the welfare state', a 'political gesture to the perceived interests of middle England'. The CDS was a 'stark danger to civil liberty': at best 'designed to create defence lawyers over which the state can exercise control', at worst 'the way to the gulag'. 'Noble' legal aid, 'the most efficient of all public services', would be replaced by 'the despised stock in trade of the ambulance chasers of America'. 'Galaxy-driving man...requires only the factory accident, blindness or incapacity to be reduced to the weekly cat's cradle of anxious benefit.' He will 'trail the coat of his potential damages from lawyer to lawyer searching for those holding the right portfolio of risk to fund his action...in permanent danger from the charlatan lawyer enhancing his fees to the maximum and churning the trial system by advising reckless action or early settlement to suit his own commercial benefit'. Government had launched 'a populist assault on lawyers', cynically aware that 'there are few sensations that cause MPs more pleasure than the belief that they are punishing lawyers'. Irvine called this 'nonsense' as well. Hoon could not 'understand how somebody who clearly understands so little can have taken such a violent dislike' to the Bill.[72]

Pleased that his Bill had taken just three hits in the Lords, where Labour lacked a majority, Irvine boasted he would undo the damage in the

Commons 'with the greatest of ease'. '[L]egal aid does not exist to provide livelihoods for solicitors', he repeated, but 'to benefit the public'. '[F]eather-bedded' solicitors 'do not look in a progressive way at their business opportunities because legal aid has inculcated in them a culture that they are entitled to be insured by the state against their costs when they lose, but I am afraid that culture simply has to be broken'. '[F]ar too many weak cases have gone forward on legal aid'; those in Chancery were 'nothing short of a disgrace' it would be 'socially correct' to eliminate. The reforms guaranteed 'quality assured' lawyers. '[I]f you tell me that cuts across the freedom of anyone to choose any lawyer they like ... I say emphatically that it is in the public interest'. Accusing Irvine of 'disparaging public rhetoric', the *Gazette* directed him to 'embark on a conscious programme of explanation and listening'.[73]

The Commons debated the Bill for seven hours on 14 April. Geoffrey Hoon, LCD Minister of State, called it 'the most important legal reform of the past 50 years ... radical and innovative'. Government would 'not be diverted ... by reactionary elements in the legal profession'. The 1990 Act had been 'a half-hearted effort which, ultimately, failed to deliver the changes'. Conservatives 'who presided over a 20 per cent. cut in eligibility' and 'cut more than 25 per cent. of the population out of the green form scheme' could not claim 'to be guardians of access to justice'. '[N]ot unsurprisingly' they 'are lining up with those reactionaries who want to maintain, or even extend, restrictive practices in the law'. Speaking for the Opposition, Edward Garnier moved to deny the Bill a Second Reading because it reduced access and increased litigation costs, failed to restrict the audience rights of CDS or CPS lawyers, and gave the Lord Chancellor 'constitutionally unprecedented powers'. Lord Irvine, who had 'nothing but praise for the Labour legal aid system' in 1996, now 'pleased the Treasury' and 'the tabloids' by 'taking money away from those whom they saw as members of an overpaid and selfish legal profession'. If the Lords' objectives clause was 'quite unrealistic', 'those on legal aid can be expected to receive a second-class service'. '[H]undreds of years of good sense ... are all to go'.[74]

The Government was strongly supported by non-lawyers, who attacked the 'mediocrity that one often finds in legal services' and the 'closed shop of the legal profession'. There was 'less respect for [lawyers] than for politicians'. Solicitors engaged in 'legal aid immigration rackets' and 'organised crime, particularly money laundering'. A Scottish barrister defended the long tradition of employed solicitor prosecutors, who often became judges. 'It is odd that having gifted to Scotland a public defender system, the Tories now find the creation of the same system in England so overwhelmingly terrible'. But many criticized the Bill. It was 'based on an attempt to save the Chancellor of the Exchequer money'. It 'arrogates to the Lord Chancellor, effectively, powers to dominate and run the legal professions'. A majority of the designated judges should retain a veto. In 'these perhaps more authoritarian times' governments 'will try to extend their control'. Soon 'perhaps 90 or 95 per cent of judges will have done nothing all their lives but prosecute or defend for the state'. A former Conservative LCD junior minister shared the 'anxiety' that 'a judge on the payroll of the state might preside over proceedings contested between two other people on the payroll of the state'. The former Conservative Solicitor-General and Attorney-General found 'the American experience of public defenders...."chilling"'. In personal injury cases 'where a large sum needs to be invested to establish liability, there is talk that the insurance premium might be as high as £20,000', leaving 'a wide tranche of the more difficult...cases unprovided for'. Nevertheless, the motion failed by 159 to 338.[75]

During the debate Hoon claimed the 7 per cent rise in legal aid spending showed 'the volatility of increases'. The Law Society denounced this 'cynical manipulation' of figures and dismissed the 'tiny over-spend' in light of the previous year's under-spend. It criticized Government for 'abandoning' as 'unrealistic' the 'principle that legal aid should place parties on an equal footing'.[76] Joining the Law Society campaign to retain the Lords amendments, Brennan attacked Irvine's imputation of self-interest, whose 'poverty' was exposed by its 'constant repetition' against lawyers but never doctors. The Bar offered examples of personal injury claims jeopardized by the withdrawal of legal aid: a sailor rendered quadriplegic in a training accident, an 11-year-old who needed twenty-four-hour care because of an antenatal injury.[77]

The substitution of CFAs for legal aid depended on insurance. Hoon confidently declared the industry would offer 'only pay [the premium] if you win' products. But Abbey Legal Protection declined, calling CFA insurance not 'totally workable'. It had suspended thirty firms for withholding the least risky cases (to save clients the premium) and refused to reinstate eleven because of such adverse selection and poor claims handling. Amicus Legal, which also required firms to insure all cases, claimed cherry-picking was 'absolutely widespread', practised by half the firms. All insurers prohibited solicitors from excluding settlements. Girling, whose firm did this, said the ban illegally fettered solicitors' discretion and duty to the client and warned that Abbey was not 'sustainable'. Martin Day criticized Abbey for threatening to suspend his firm for accepting excessively risky cases, although it won almost 95 per cent (and cost the insurer a total of less than £10,000 for the three it lost). A 1998 study found that 98 per cent of CFAs succeeded. Irvine called solicitors 'very lucky' not 'to be asked to put up all the up-front costs', exhorting them to have 'as much confidence in themselves as the insurance industry has in itself'.[78]

Lord Phillips called Irvine and Hoon 'out of touch with the realities of legal aid'. Neither 'has been a practising solicitor, let alone a legal aid lawyer. Lords Irvine and Falconer—who shared the Lords debate—were both at the fat cat end of the Bar.' Phillips denounced the 'dirigiste blue-print' and 'drip, drip of denigration'. The 'astonishing claim' that legal aid solicitors had been 'feather-bedded' may 'derive partly from Steve Orchard, the non-solicitor chief executive of the LAB, who went out of his way on ... Radio 4 recently to invite the public to marvel at the sums being paid to solicitors under legal aid'. The merits test weeded out 'bad cases', and solicitors 'have to handle far too many cases already in order to make a tolerable living' to 'willfully string out actions'.[79]

The day before the Standing Committee took up the Bill, the Society launched a £700,000 week-long 'Justice Denied' campaign of daily full-page advertisements in *The Times, Guardian, Mirror,* and *Evening Standard* and single advertisements in twenty-one regional papers, featuring vignettes like:

A Bradford couple awarded £18,000 for being stopped by police on their way home from a wedding, assaulted, and imprisoned on trumped-up charges. 'Without legal aid, solicitors won't be able to do this kind of work. Only the very rich will be able to pursue such cases.'

A black man 'stitched up' by the police. 'Beat-up, falsely imprisoned and ridiculed, this innocent citizen is now facing more discrimination. And the Government's about to turn a blind eye.' Legal aid 'won't be available unless he can prove he is almost certain to win his case—even though it's against the State'. 'The parents of the late Stephen Lawrence share these concerns about the impact of the bill.'

A woman whose 'partner uses her as his personal punchbag. Now the Government is about to deliver another wounding blow.' 'Kicked, beaten and burdened by a man who could kill her, his victim needs to use a lawyer fast.' But 'there may be no legal aid lawyers left in her area' and 'it may be too late for her to find one further afield'.

Irvine assailed the Society's 'irresponsible scaremongering'. 'Your mis-leading and inaccurate poster campaign falls substantially beneath the standards to be expected of a professional organisation.' '[Y]ou have failed to apologize for propagating untruths about our intentions'.

Many vulnerable people will be made to believe that they will lose their access to legal aid. This is just not true. In fact legal aid will still be available in precisely the types of cases raised by the Law Society.

Government 'cannot be expected to protect every solicitor from change'. Hoon was 'astonished that the Law Society, which is itself under great financial pressure, and whose members are under similar constraints, should choose to spend what must be considerable sums of money on such a thoroughly inaccurate press campaign'.

'The government and some sections of the media can be as cynical as they like', retorted Mathews, 'but the Law Society will not be deflected

from standing up for people's rights' and 'campaigning to ensure the...
poor and vulnerable are properly protected'. He resented the accusation
that the Society was 'not telling the truth' and bragged 'we have [Irvine]
on the run'. The *Gazette* found the government reaction 'most extraordinary'. Irvine and Hoon 'used every available media outlet to attack
the Society's campaign in the most scathing, and unsuitable terms' and
'attempt[ed] to deflect attention' from reduced access 'by scoring cheap
points at lawyers' expense'. Irvine's 'vindictive' response, said the *New Law
Journal*, was 'only to be expected from a Government which has long made
clear that it will brook little criticism of its policies'. The *Independent* felt the
Lord Chancellor had gone too far in asking the Society to withdraw its
advertisements. And the *Observer* deplored the 'press campaign' (from
which it alone had abstained) depicting lawyers as 'sinister bloodsuckers
threatening enterprise and good government'.[80] An Alliance survey found
that 90 per cent of the public thought legal aid should be a right and
85 per cent wanted it for accident victims (but only two-thirds and a third
of the 100 MPs who replied). Government 'has spun this Bill as an attack
on lawyers', said the Society, but 'it has not worked'.

Such optimism was premature. The *Evening Standard* editor called the
Society's campaign 'one of the most tasteless and ill-advised pieces of public
relations in my memory, motivated solely by the professional cupidity of
the legal profession'. It was crying 'crocodile tears' and had forfeited 'what
marginal respect' it retained. The Society's former Parliamentary liaison
officer said it had 'effectively signed its own political death warrant' and
undone 'years [of] cultivating Labour in opposition and working closely
with the Labour Government'. 'Why needlessly antagonise a Lord
Chancellor whose Government enjoys a massive parliamentary majority and
whose Bill is nearly through both Houses?' *Guardian* columnist Catherine
Bennett mockingly launched LawyerAid for the reform's 'true victims',
soliciting a 'modest donation' to 'put the Law Society back on its feet, to
pay for a new advertising campaign, and restore its self-esteem'. Letters to
The Times displayed three readers' scepticism.

[M]ost people who do not have any vested interest in these matters will know that
a change is drastically needed in the whole culture of our litigation where lawyers
are motivated not by justice but more often just pure greed.

Would not the interests of the individual who features in the Law Society's expensive advertisement today be best served by a competent lawyer (confident in their
own ability to gain a reward in a no-win, no-fee arrangement) rather than by someone who wanted guaranteed payment regardless of their ability to plead the case
successfully? Or is the Law Society saying that its members deserve to be paid
regardless of their competence?

I was amused by the cries of pain from the Law Society...worried that a litigant
can only win legal aid if 'he can prove he's almost certain to win his case'. For

decades lawyers have told clients that they are bound to win their case and should immediately apply for legal aid. Now it appears the Government has at last called their bluff.

A *Times* feature writer called Irvine 'an orchid in the buttonhole of a subfusc Government', its 'finest conservative', and invoked a famous quotation on professional conspiracies by Adam Smith, who 'had not even heard of... the solicitors' trade union, as the Law Society is careful never to call itself'. The advertising campaign was 'paid for by all of us through the taxes which go on legal aid and the fees accumulated by conveyancing'. There was 'scant evidence' that the Bill 'will deny justice to the deserving'. 'The real impediment to justice is the high level of legal fees.' Solicitors have 'taken up all manner of unsuitable cases', funded by taxpayers' 'bottomless pockets'. Legal aid 'has been a conspiracy against the public for too long', allowing solicitors 'to wallpaper their offices with taxpayers' money'.

Sayer replied that legal aid lawyers earned 'around £23,000 a year and legal aid rates have not increased over the past five years'. The campaign funded 'solely by our members and not by the taxpayer... clearly achieved one of its main objectives—getting people talking about the issue'. It 'encouraged more people to... voice their concern that under Government plans legal aid would no longer be an entitlement'. '[A]ccusations of lawyers' self-interest' were 'firmly balanced with positive articles highlighting the real story of our fears for people's access to justice'. Mears applauded that 'for once, the fogeyish old Law Society could not be accused by its members of rolling on its back and yelping feebly in the face of governmental assault'. But Ian Walker, president of APIL (whose members had most at stake), worried that the campaign had only 'provoke[d] a rather extreme over-reaction from the Lord Chancellor and his Minister of State', who will be 'building the barricades higher as the AJB proceeds through Parliament'. Hoon said he was 'absolutely immovable in terms of general principle'.[81]

Nevertheless, the Alliance held a press conference to call for ring-fencing an adequate civil legal aid budget, protecting the disadvantaged, a purpose clause assuring legal aid clients equality with paying clients, and legal aid for personal injuries of the most vulnerable. Kamlesh Bahl, the Society's DVP, declared defiantly: 'We have lost nothing by having it out in the open with the Government'. 'The Lord Chancellor has had a rapid learning curve from our responses.' The Society also called his decision to freeze remuneration rates for a third year 'an incentive for legal aid solicitors to throw in the towel'. The LAPG agreed that 'far fewer firms will want to take up contracts'.[82]

The Commons Standing Committee met for five days at the end of April and the first half of May. The Government sought to remove Lord Lloyd's purpose clause. Garnier said a 'frivolous person' might find the Bill's title 'quite a good joke'. When Andrew Dismore objected to the lack of proportionality in the clause, Garnier mocked his 'fixation about Queen's counsel', and Dominic Grieve reviled him as 'complete bilge'. Gareth Thomas called the clause 'an invitation to frivolous applications'. If Thomas 'is in the business of making frivolous applications', sniped Garnier, 'it says more about him than about clause 1'. Hoon accused Garnier of 'cling[ing] to the past, rather like a small child hangs on to a security blanket' or the way Pooh Bear 'always wears his Wellingtons and raincoat even on a sunny day'. Garnier ignored such 'a childish remark'. Hoon objected that the clause expressed 'unrealistic aspirations' because it lacked 'a test of merits or of priorities'. The 'laudable aspiration' of a 'universal scheme' had 'proved unsustainable'. An accused 'should have a choice of legal representation but not necessarily an unlimited one'. Because 'most people, fortunately, experience [civil litigation] only once in a lifetime', Hoon was 'not sure that it is especially helpful to single out the choice of provider'. The clause was eliminated. Garnier tried to restore it during the Report Stage, on 22 June, invoking support by the Alliance. When Conservatives called for 'equality of arms' and warned that discretionary legal aid would mean 'one law for the rich and one law for the poor', Keith Vaz (now LCD Parliamentary Under-Secretary) retorted that the clause 'might compel the commission to match the spending of a wealthy private party' and 'the widest possible choice would trump considerations of quality'. The Commons rejected the clause by 146 to 313. When the Bill returned to the Lords, Lord Lloyd accepted the Government's separate purpose clauses, and opposition disintegrated.[83]

When Conservatives and Liberal Democrats revived Lords' amendments safeguarding lawyer interests, Hoon resisted such 'backward looking nonsense', which tries 'to entrench old-fashioned ways of doing business' and 'secure a permanently privileged position for the Bar'.[84] Seeking to preserve legal aid for personal injury, Garnier denied that 'this is a lawyers' whinge and that we are scaremongering'. The Labour Party used to stand for 'social benefits...before the new Labour, or right-wing, government'. Burnett said 'Labour Members are...disbarring an enormous number of poor people from seeking access to justice and defending their own rights'. Hoon quoted Shaw's aphorism that 'all professions are conspiracies against the laity', adding: 'lawyers conspire more than most to obfuscate what they really mean'. '[I]ndicative of the recent change that has taken place in political philosophy', here was he, 'a Labour Minister, explaining to a Conservative Member the benefits of the business-like approach that we believe is possible'. During the Report Stage, Robert Marshall-Andrews moved to restore legal aid to the most vulnerable personal injury victims. The reform would not 'bring a penny piece back into legal aid'. 'The more badly injured one is, the more difficult it is' to find a lawyer and 'the less likely'. Plaintiffs were bearing the premiums, which would be 'prohibitive' in a case of lifelong disability with 'costs on either side in six figures'. Nick Hawkins cited heart-rending cases: a 17-year-old who broke his neck in a rugby match, child abuse, a 17-year-old cyclist with severe head injuries, a 6-year-old confined to a wheelchair and ventilator, asbestos deaths. Vaz claimed that legal aid would be available in all those cases and individual consideration of personal injury cases 'would create enormous administrative expense'. The motion failed by 173 to 291.[85] Conservatives acknowledged the Government's creation of a reserve power to establish a CLAF as 'a little golden nugget in the middle of what frankly resembles a large dunghill' but now complained that 'as a result of...cherry picking, a CLAF will not prosper'. Although the Government repeatedly refused to allow CFAs in quasi-criminal proceedings for housing disrepair under the Environmental Protection Act, Irvine conceded the point when the Bill returned to the Lords.[86]

The Standing Committee turned nasty when the Government moved to restore salaried defenders. Garnier referred to the 'Criminal Defence Service or public defender service'. Hoon said he had 'not been listening'. Garnier called Hoon 'a bored Minister, bored with the Bill...he can sit in Committee giggling his back off'. Garnier 'appeal[ed] for protection from the Chair' against Dismore, who 'might like to sit quietly and perhaps he might learn something'. '[N]ot from the hon. and learned Gentleman', retorted Dismore. Garnier gave examples of prosecutors suppressing exculpatory evidence and warned that the CDS would 'attract mainly the young and inexperienced' who had 'left the independent Bar...for the steady work and regular hours'. Mark Todd denied that 'people who receive payment from the state would lose their objectivity', citing judges. Dr Alan Whitehead added housing aid and social workers and environmental officers. Garnier sneered that Whitehead had 'entirely missed the point' and could not see the difference from 'someone who acts on behalf of a defendant who risks his liberty or his reputation'. Hoon asked: had 'Conservative Party policy change[d] since July 1996' when its White Paper proposed salaried defenders? Garnier called this 'witty point' typical of a 'fourth-form debate' and offered an extraordinary Jeremiad:

public confidence in the integrity of the criminal justice system will decline. ... Victims might be less likely to report crimes, witnesses could become more reluctant to give evidence and juries more prone to acquit the guilty...the confidence of those accused of a crime...will diminish...our system works because it is trusted... by those who are charged with offences...a defendant has less need to be kept in custody or to be shackled and controlled in court, and he is less likely to feel hard done by or wrongly convicted....

Nevertheless, the Committee voted by eleven to four to restore the CDS.[87]

While reaffirming that accused would have a choice, Hoon added they normally could not change lawyers. Burnett asked whether accused would be stuck with 'the duty solicitor who is allocated...at 3 o'clock in the morning?' Hoon replied they 'will be grateful that someone is there'. Only those with 'considerable experience of the criminal system' were likely to prefer another lawyer. Rebuffing a Conservative amendment guaranteeing choice as typifying the 'view that restrictive practices are a good thing', Hoon spoke nostalgically about 'Mrs Thatcher who was pretty tough in sweeping way [*sic*] restrictive practices'. Garnier called Hoon's amendment 'a classic case of new Labourspeak, the sense of which was "When I say that you have a choice, you have the choice that I decree you should have"'. It was 'nonsense', retorted Hoon, that an accused might want 'someone who specializes in straightforward domestic burglaries or shoplifting from Marks and Spencer'. '[A] sophisticated defendant, who knows the ropes—plays the system and deliberately changes his lawyer in mid-case to spin it out.' His amendments were agreed.[88]

During the Third Reading debate near midnight on 22 June Garnier accused the Government of being 'economically illiterate, politically inept and intellectually confused'. Vaz 'appeared to be attempting to sell anything—it could have been a vacuum cleaner, dog food....' The Bill 'will destroy access to part of the welfare state. If the Labour party was elected to do that, it could have fooled me. Many of those who voted in May 1997 for the glorious new regime of this Prime Minister can also justly claim to have been fooled....' '[O]ver the next two years the Bill will turn their majorities to dust'. It 'will create a situation that used to exist only in communist China and Soviet Russia, where the state prosecutes and defends people'. As Sydney Kentridge had said of South Africa, 'the only thing that stood between the oppressive state regime and the independence and freedom of citizens was the independent Bar'. Grieve deplored that the justice system was being 'nationalized'. 'We are moving towards a continental criminal justice system—which, taken to its ultimate expression, existed in the old communist countries.' The Government has 'absolutely no regard for civil liberties or the rights of accused people'. The Bill was passed by 301 to 151.[89]

While the Bill was being debated the LCD published its CLS consultation, finding no 'widespread unmet need for legal services' but just a 'lack of appropriate help'. The Law Society dismissed this 'Government waffle', which 'barely mentions the role of solicitors or legal aid. The "legal" element seems to have got lost.' The LAPG saw a 'lot of management jargon and not a lot of substance'. The YSG objected that it 'played down' private practitioners. At NACAB's sixtieth anniversary conference the *Gazette* declared 'solicitors must be the backbone of the CLS' and urged firms to consider 'what forms of ethical outreach work will be most appropriate.'

LAG warned that local authorities may 'be tempted to withdraw funding [for advice services] in the belief that central government may pick up the tab'. At his first press conference Vaz called the CLS 'a legal service willing to listen', which would 'hand the law back to the people' and create a 'modern legal service for a modern Britain', a 'new system for a new millenium'. He reassured the Society that 'the largest share of the CLS fund will go in expenditure on . . . solicitors in private practice'.

Seeing a chance to expand market share, the Bar promised to 'work with the CLS'. Bar Direct 'will position the Bar to play its full part in the CLS partnership', and BarMark would be made compatible 'with the Quality Mark that emerges for the CLS'. When the first contract to support advice services was awarded to a chambers the Bar was 'delighted', while a Law Society spokesperson found it 'depressing' that 'there seems to be a prejudice in favour of concentrating some kinds of contract on the not-for-profit sector'. It 'would have been more interesting to give contracts to private practice applicants'.[90]

When the Lords considered the Commons amendments on 14 July, Lord Thomas again moved to eliminate the CDS. '[I]n high-profile cases in particular the employed public defender lawyer may be unwilling to . . . criticize the Government, the CPS, the police and so on'. '[I]f the Government think that people employed for a fixed salary for fixed hours will put the same effort into a case that independent counsel and solicitors do at present, then they do not understand the realities of the criminal Bar'. Lord Borrie said Lord Thomas offered 'no basis or evidence . . . for the suggestion that the extremes he envisages are likely to come about'. '[I]t is the majority of the House who were extremist'. Lord Clinton-Davis accused Lord Thomas of moving a 'somewhat protectionist' 'extreme amendment'. Resigned to being accused of 'smugness', 'superiority', and 'special pleading', Lord Hutchinson charged 'politicians' with 'attacks on the advocates . . . in almost a violent form'. The Bill would 'undermine the whole structure'. He assailed the 'ominous figure' of the salaried defender, who is 'apparently to report back to his employer on the extent to which his colleagues in court are wasting public money—a kind of Treasury spy'. Baroness Thornton said 'people do not understand why members of the legal profession feel the need so fiercely to protect their interests and guarantee their incomes'. Lord Irvine called Lord Thomas 'one of the last of the timorous souls who believe that the Bar cannot survive on its own merits but needs to be cocooned with restrictive practices and guarantees of state provided work'. He was 'seeking to protect the vested interests of an established legal profession and to prevent the public from having the choice'. But he lost the division by 141 to 85.[91]

In the Commons a week later Vaz declared that pilots would test both 'direct employ and separately maintained bodies akin to law centres', and defenders would 'work within a separate organizational unit...reporting to a senior lawyer responsible for managing them in a way that...protects their professional integrity'. Garnier retorted: 'One need only look across the Atlantic to see what has happened in the U.S.'. 'If people do well and deliver for the state as a defender, they may be promoted across to the prosecution service. ....' By contrast, it was 'second nature' for private practitioners 'fearlessly to represent their clients' interests'. Labour was 'a pale-pink Conservative Government...who are doing their best to understand the language of conservatism without knowing what it is all about'. The Government's contentions were 'absurd, obscene, ridiculous'. When Dismore ridiculed arguments 'on behalf of the barristers and Queen's counsel protection club', Hawkins retorted that most of the 'large majority' in the Lords who rejected the CDS 'were life peers and non-lawyers. The present Government are committed to the politics of envy, and to the abolition of the voting rights of hereditary peers.' '[T]he Government want a revising Chamber only when it does not seek to revise. What they really want is a poodle—or perhaps, in this instance, Derry's dachshund.' Vaz resented Garnier's 'personal abuse' of him for 'reading out the civil service brief. Some people will never in their careers have the opportunity to do that. They will spend their lives wandering around Market Harborough bitterly, trying to be recognized by their constituents.' The House voted by 294 to 166 to reinsert the clause.[92] Brennan urged the Lords to continue resisting the CDS, which 'would mean that innocent people end up convicted, albeit of a lesser offence, and career criminals would get off lighter because of deals being cut for the sake of administrative convenience'.[93]

The next week Irvine reminded the Lords that the Commons, 'the democratically elected Chamber, has now twice restored [the clause] to the Bill' and 'some 75 members of the other place have signed an Early-Day Motion in support of salaried defenders'. Lord Thomas dismissed as 'the wishy-washy language of consumerism' Vaz's charges that opponents were 'protect[ing] the vested interests of the established profession by preventing choice' and 'upholding restrictive practices'. Lord Kingsland added that the choice between private and salaried lawyers was not 'competition as we understand the term in a market economy. Market prices play no role in pricing either service.' But he acknowledged the Lords' 'constitutional duty' to accept the Commons amendments. Lord Ackner wanted 'to record my personal dismay at the Government's dismantling of our system for the administration of justice as we know it...because the Treasury wants it'. Justice 'features very little' in 'value for money'. If the public defender is cheaper 'there will be no justification...for the state criminal defence service existing alongside the private service. It will be the means of dealing with legal aid.' But the Lords acquiesced.[94] The *Solicitors Journal* warned that 'nobody should be fooled about the motives behind the measure', which was 'simply...a price-cutting tool, to employ in reserve should contracting fail to keep the criminal budget firmly under control'.[95]

E. Fighting Rearguard Actions

Passage of the Bill inflamed critics. Sayer demanded 'real choice' of defence lawyers and warned against a 'second rate legal service'. Lord Steyn viewed 'with some misgiving the state paying for defenders or equally, the state paying for prosecutors in the Higher Courts'. Garnier told the LS annual conference the CDS was 'unwanted, unconsulted, unnecessary, uncosted and unwise and frankly unbelievable'. It would foster a 'canteen culture' with the CPS—'the state prosecuting, the state defending and the state disposing. They don't even have that in Russia anymore.' '[I]n a few years' time', he predicted, 'there will be poor, sick, injured and elderly members of the public without access to justice and without a hand to help them.'[96]

Government merely intensified its abuse of lawyers. In a second unprovoked attack (leaked to the *Mail on Sunday*), Jack Straw told the Police Superintendents' Association national conference that 'well-heeled and hypocritical...so-called civil liberties lawyers...represent the perpetrator of the crime and then get into their BMWs and drive off into areas where they are immune from much of the crime...and if they are faced with interference in their quiet lives, they will be the first to reach for the protection of the law'. The *Express* headlined 'You bunch of hypocrites'. The LS criminal law committee resented this 'slur', while the *Solicitors Journal* boasted that 'the test of whether lawyers are protecting the individual against the state is when the state rails against them'.[97]

Within months of the Bill's passage, fears of diminished access grew. A study found clients misunderstood the financial arrangements, risk, and alternatives to CFAs and few made an informed choice of solicitor. Admitting it had operated at a loss since its launch four years earlier, Abbey increased premiums for road accident claims by more than 60 per cent and others by more than 100, warning that ALP 'might not survive'. Declaring that this made 'nonsense' of Government claims that CFAs could replace legal aid, APIL sought a two-year delay. But the LCD called 'the sums involved...small when compared with other litigation costs', and the Law Society made premiums and success fees recoverable from defendants (over vigorous protest by FOIL, which had threatened to claim a breach of natural justice in the European Court of Justice!).[98]

Some 6,000 offices sought civil legal aid contracts, and the Law Society agreed to accredit criminal defence lawyers (even though its study found little relationship between franchising and quality). But Irvine continued to assail lawyers 'being paid by the hour on a taxi meter'. People would know his reforms were working 'when you hear the squealing of lawyers'.

Barristers' fees remained 'excessive compared to the remuneration received by other professions paid out of public funds'. The CLSA retorted that contracting rewarded the 'slip-shod, corner-cutters' and could 'stultify and freeze', just as 'milk quotas affected the dairy market'. An analysis of more than 10,000 legal aid bills found that solicitors shifted work from fixed fee 'core inputs' (preparation and advocacy) to separately reimbursed 'non-core inputs' (travel and waiting) and made simultaneous green form claims. The LAPG chair exhorted Irvine to 'listen to the concerns about legal aid contracting being raised now, rather than waiting until he hears that lawyers are going to the wall and giving up'. Sayer denied there was any 'taxi meter'; 90 per cent of legal aid already was governed by fixed fees. The *Gazette* accused Irvine of 'reinforc[ing] a misguided public perception' and warned against 'alienat[ing] a valuable segment of the profession'. Calling him 'out of touch with the realities of legal aid work', the CLSA chair complained that members were 'beleaguered and put upon by a government which clearly has a low regard for us'.[99]

Anxiety intensified when nearly 6,000 of the 11,000 offices doing green form work failed to obtain advice contracts and more than a quarter of all applicants got no contract. An earlier survey found that 19 per cent had decided to withdraw from legal aid, 7 per cent were likely to do so, and another 31 per cent had not obtained a franchise. Another survey found that a third planned to drop legal aid. Calling the reforms 'rushed, piecemeal and unco-ordinated', LS President Sayer warned that people would not 'know how to find the remaining sources of help'. With Society funding, a leading mental health firm sought judicial review of limiting legal aid to contracted firms. Angered by the contract terms and the third-year remuneration freeze, the Society asked contracting firms whether to begin a campaign of non-co-operation. Feeling 'betrayed', the LAPG claimed that 90 per cent would refuse new contracts: 'our members undertake this work as a matter of principle, but can ill-afford to do so any more'.[100]

Irvine continued to hyperbolize the CLS as 'the first attempt ever by any Government to deliver legal services in a joined-up way, putting consumers' interests first'. But though he named a dozen celebrity 'champions' and launched a website with computer terminals in shopping arcades, supermarkets, surgeries, and libraries, Vaz acknowledged it would 'only be a gateway; we can't reinvent legal services'. The LCD consultation paper on the CDS claimed the 'balance of opinion' was 'that salaried defence services are capable of delivering better outcomes than other delivery systems'. But the Government did not hide its real object: 'salaried services are cheaper than those provided by private practice lawyers', who 'seek to maximise the price received for their services'. The LCD dismissed fears of government pressure because private practitioners also lacked 'independence of mind'. Although clients would retain a choice, it noted approvingly that in Quebec 71 per cent preferred salaried lawyers.[101]

Government determination to subordinate justice to economics—what the CDS called 'an appropriate quality at a value for money price'—also motivated Jack Straw's proposal to deny jury trials to the 18,500 defendants who annually demanded Crown Court hearings for charges triable in magistrates' courts, unless the magistrate found the accused's reputation endangered. Even though more than 70 per cent ultimately pleaded guilty, each trial cost £11,000 more. Calling the jury trial 'part of our democracy', Brennan said the proposal was 'entirely based on money and convenience' but actually would be inefficient. Straw sneered: 'It is very hard sometimes to distinguish when the Bar is fighting from a trades union stance and when it is concerned about the administration of justice'.

The press strongly supported the Government. *The Times* criticized the discharge of a man accused of stealing a 19p can of lemonade because a jury trial would have cost £8,800. Although the Bill was 'a sly step towards the inquisitorial European justice system', the right to a jury trial 'needs to be balanced against the right of victims of serious crimes to see justice done'. The jury trial was 'one of the glories of the British judicial system', said the *Daily Mail*, but 'the only people who have anything to fear are the crooks themselves and the legal profession neither of whom deserve... the sympathy of the English public'. The *Star* condemned the waste, and the *Daily Mirror* applauded plans to 'speed up' the justice system. But noting that Straw, in opposition, had called curtailment of jury trials 'wrong, short-sighted and likely to prove ineffective', *Sunday Times* columnist Phillip Oppenheim asked 'how can you tell the difference between the government and the Tories'? And the *Guardian* insisted that the accused had 'every right' to clear his name before that 'lamp of freedom'.[102]

Both branches strenuously resisted the Bill. The Bar wrote to every MP. Brennan objected that 'middle-class defendants would be given privileged access to Crown Courts if magistrates decided they had a reputation to defend'. Sayer accused the Bill of 'destroy[ing] a vital and historic legal right'. The *New Law Journal* foresaw the 'unpalatable... prospect of lay prosecutors appearing before lay magistrates with lay defendants, who have to submit to that jurisdiction, represented by lay defenders... all part of the continued dumbing down of the law'. Straw effectively admitted the *Gazette's* contention that 'cost-cutting is the aim' by attacking the existing rule as an 'eccentric' anomaly costing £105 million a year and accusing those who chose jury trials of 'working the system'.

Dan Brennan, like any trade union leader, is looking after his members. When I talk to my chums at the Bar, or solicitors, they know what the score is, everyone does— it is the least-well-kept secret in the criminal justice system that people at the margins are manipulating the system.

The Association of Chief Police Officers naturally agreed, urging the public to distinguish between the rhetoric of justice, so often used as a veil by vested interests, and the reality. In the end it is plain daft to allow a persistent criminal charged with a minor theft to invoke the full panoply of a criminal trial at massive public expense.

Accusing Straw of an 'abject U-turn', the Bar Council claimed he was 'panicking at the strength of opposition'. The Law Society noted it was interested in transferring cases to magistrates' court. The opposition home affairs spokesperson insisted on 'the right to the fullest possible trial'. In the Lords debate, Lord Cope of Berkeley (Conservative) said citizens want 'ordinary people deciding one's guilt or innocence. Not clever lawyers or distant judges....' Lord Thomas objected that the 'still predominantly white, middle aged, and middle class' magistrates lacked the 'sympathy which should be shown to the way of life of the young, the ethnic minorities and the gay community'. Lord Alexander said the Bill was deeply flawed and discriminatory. Lord Hutchinson called it 'as dangerous a piece of legislation as has entered this House', certainly during his twenty years. When the Attorney-General asked whether 'someone who has ten previous convictions for shoplifting a jelly or a banana from Tesco is really entitled automatically to have the right to trial by jury', Lord Thomas reminded him that, in opposition, he had denounced the proposal as 'madness'.[103]

F. Why Government Won

Labour launched the legal aid scheme as an integral part of the welfare state and proudly claimed credit for the next half century. In opposition it bitterly attacked Lord Mackay's cuts, blaming sinister 'Treasury influence'. It promised to restore eligibility and extend representation to tribunals, assailed budget caps, warned that fixed fees and inadequate remuneration would compromise quality, and resisted exclusive franchises and bulk contracts. Both Paul Boateng (legal affairs spokesperson) and Lord Irvine (shadow Lord Chancellor) denounced contributions as a 'powerful deterrent' to uptake. Labour dismissed CFAs as 'little more than a gimmick', offering no 'significant improvement in access to justice', and demanded uplifts 'very much lower than 100%'. Family mediation should be entirely voluntary.

But on taking power in May 1997, Labour reversed every one of its positions, while accusing the Conservatives of attacking it for the very policies they had pursued in office. Garnier reminded the Commons that Lord Irvine had 'nothing but praise for the Labour legal aid system in 1996'. 'The Labour party used to stand for social benefits'. The Bill 'will destroy access to part of the welfare state. If the Labour party was elected to do that, it could have fooled me.' It had become 'a pale-pink Conservative Government'. Conservatives now called for 'equality of arms', denouncing 'one law for the rich and one law for the poor', while Hoon declared the 'laudable aspiration' of a 'universal scheme' had 'proved unsustainable' and waxed nostalgic about 'Mrs Thatcher, who was pretty tough in sweeping [a]way restrictive practices'. Here was he, 'a Labour Minister, explaining to a Conservative member the benefits of the business-like approach that we believe is possible'. Lord Phillips retorted that Labour was invoking 'a rather rigged market'. This was not 'competition as we understand the term in a market economy', said Lord Kingsland. 'Market prices play no role' in setting remuneration for either private or salaried lawyers paid by the state. Conservatives twice eliminated from the Bill the very public defender their White Paper had proposed three years earlier. Lord Mackay criticized the Bill for giving the Lord Chancellor excessive power—a central objection to his own Courts and Legal Services Bill. Labour became the party of law and order, while the Opposition championed civil liberties! Political advantage and fiscal constraint, not principle, drove both parties.

Allowing hope to triumph over experience, the protagonists prematurely proclaimed an end to the acrimony of Mackay's Lord Chancellorship. Disavowing any grand scheme, Lord Irvine sought better relations with the profession, which eagerly reciprocated. But the honeymoon was brief. Although the new Lord Chancellor was as much a Bar insider as his predecessor had been an outsider, within weeks of attaining the Woolsack Irvine attacked his brethren as fat cats, appealing to 'middle-class' resentment of 'inefficient' lawyers. Blair decried the rising legal aid budget, hinting that salaried lawyers might be the solution. When Hoon assumed his predecessor's role as Government attack dog, Garnier called him 'lazy' and 'bored' and compared him to Pooh Bear. Garnier and Dismore constantly mocked each other. Lord Borrie called Conservative Peers 'extremist'. Within half a year Irvine abused the profession far more caustically than Mackay, denouncing its 'savage and grave allegations' and imputing all opposition to self-interest. The *Solicitors Journal* retorted that he was 'pompous and obstinately unwilling' to admit mistake. Scrivener accused him of 'mutilat[ing] legal aid'. The profession disparaged Irvine's and Hoon's inexperience with legal aid. Jack Straw insinuated that vigorous criminal defence was financially motivated and hypocritical, charging immigration lawyers with 'ripping the system off' by 'descend[ing] on Dover to "dish out" green forms'. Scrivener responded: 'Mr Straw's decision to give up law for politics was a wise one'. When Straw sought to end jury trials for 'either-way' offences, even the DPP sided with the Bar (from which he came) rather than the Government (which had appointed him). Accusing medical negligence lawyers of 'milking' his NHS and 'causing trouble for other people', Frank Dobson wanted to see them 'on the operating table'. The immigration minister railed against 'seamy', 'incompetent', and 'corrupt' immigration lawyers. The Law Society was proudly (if self-destructively) defiant. Kamlesh Bahl proclaimed (wrongly): 'We have lost nothing by having it out in the open with the Government'. Always spoiling for a fight, Mears praised the Society for not 'rolling on its back and yelping feebly in the face of government assault'. Just as Irvine said 'squealing' lawyers would show his reforms were working, so the *Solicitors Journal* knew lawyers were doing their job 'when the state rails against them'. Although Irvine arrogantly assumed the backing of 'progressive' judges, the Lord Chief Justice and Master of the Rolls stoutly defended legal aid. In response Irvine denounced the judiciary's 'conservatism' and threatened it with Parliamentary supremacy.

In this increasingly bitter confrontation the media cheered the state, attacking 'clogged' courts, 'archaic' restrictive practices, 'slow' and 'expensive' procedures, 'waste', and 'excessive fees' paid to 'fat cat' lawyers on behalf of 'drug traffickers and fraudsters' (what happened to the presumption of innocence?) and plaintiffs' in 'no-hope cases'. It welcomed the 'sweeping' 'radical' 'reform', 'shake-up', and 'revolution'. It embellished atrocity stories of frivolous claims, unappealing clients, and exorbitant legal costs greatly exceeding the amount in controversy. Every newspaper, from respectable broadsheet to scandal-mongering tabloid, produced its purplest prose to heighten resentment of lawyers who made 'loads of money' with their 'silken tongues'. *The Times* claimed that LCD 'profligacy' going 'beyond candour' had provoked 'real public anger' at the 'huge and rapidly growing' 'bloated' legal aid budget, which had become a 'grotesque drain on taxpayers'. Abusing Shaw's aphorism, a columnist called legal aid 'a conspiracy against the public', which let solicitors 'wallpaper their offices with taxpayers' money'. The *Daily Mail* denounced the legal aid 'bonanza' as a 'honeypot' for 'wealthy lawyers and canny defendants'. The press uncritically swallowed the government line that lawyers obstructed access to justice, legal aid was the problem, and cuts would increase access through non-lawyers while miraculously making the private sector affordable.

To justify legal aid cuts the government waged an unrelenting campaign to stereotype all lawyers as 'fat cats' (although the Lord Chancellor had been one of the fatter himself, claiming to have been the first to charge £1 million for a brief).[104] Irvine and Hoon cynically orchestrated 'naming and blaming' exercises and eagerly exploited Mr Justice Lightman's denunciation, drastic fee reductions by the Clerk to the Parliaments, and the Browne-Wilkinson report. Although the fees companies paid a few high-flying commercial silks had nothing to do with the legal aid budget, no newspapers—even legal aid supporters—could resist the taint of luxury, almost scandal, in incomes unimaginable to most readers. Lawyers could not neutralize the rhetorical power of these numbers. It did no good to point to the astronomical incomes of footballers or the Spice Girls, which reflected private decisions by millions of adoring fans to buy entertainment in a relatively free market. And it was hard to explain why some legal aid lawyers earned more than eminent doctors or headmasters. The modest incomes of many lawyers and the sacrifice of most legal aid specialists just were not news. That fees were set by the LCD, LAB, and taxing masters did not deflect criticism from the lawyers who pocketed them. Irvine repeated that solicitors believed legal aid exists 'to provide livelihoods'. He dismissed every lawyer objection as 'special pleading' by 'vested interests', the 'predictable moan'. The media agreed. Lawyers were 'the most assertive and articulate interest group in Britain', a 'bunch... too wild even for Margaret Thatcher to tangle with'.

Reformers attributed all resistance to lawyer self-interest. Hoon denounced 'reactionary elements in the legal profession' who 'want to maintain, or even extend, restrictive practices' and 'entrench old-fashioned ways of doing business'. Lord Irvine saw 'the footprints of my friends in the Bar Council all over' amendments that 'have either attempted to guarantee work for the Bar or protect the position of the Bar', reflecting 'a feather-bedding culture'. Only lawyers 'could possibly be attracted to a ring-fenced budget'. Labour even found a trade union firm to accuse lawyers of believing 'the world owed them a living' and admonish them to 'wean themselves off the easy money of legal aid'. Lord Falconer noted that 'every single one of those noble Lords from both sides of the House who is not a lawyer or a judge has greeted the proposals... with enthusiasm'. Non-lawyers attacked the profession's 'mediocrity' and 'closed shop'.

Opponents protested such 'gratuitous smears' while maintaining their disinterest. Nick Hawkins stressed that the 'large majority' in the Lords who rejected the CDS 'were life peers and non-lawyers'. The two branches allied themselves with consumer interests. Lawyers cited heart-rending cases to show 'this is not a proposal for the protection of the legal profession'. Although Lord Phillips was a solicitor briefed by a local law society, he was 'not here in any sense as an advocate for practising solicitors'. Lord Hutchinson was resigned to accusations of 'smugness', 'superiority', and 'special pleading'. Lord Thomas dismissed Keith Vaz's accusations of protectionism and restrictive practices as 'the wishy-washy language of consumerism'. Lord Ackner denied that judges were defending the interests of their former brethren. But lawyers gave their critics plenty of ammunition, moving numerous amendments to the AJA to protect their turf and income. And Lord Thomas unapologetically pronounced that 'all professions must have restrictive rules'.

Labour, even more than the Conservatives, stoked popular suspicions of legalism. The problem was too much law, not too little. Blair blamed the high cost of legal aid on frivolous claims and defence of the undeserving wealthy. Irvine declared no one should litigate with less than a 75 per cent likelihood of success (never explaining why they should not bring all claims with a 50 per cent chance). The LCD accused legal aid of 'blackmail[ing]' defendants. The government advanced bizarre criticisms: long, complex cases were expensive; some were lost; most of the cost was attributable to lawyers. Middleton wanted the risk of loss borne by lawyers and clients, not taxpayers. Straw accused criminal lawyers of dragging out defences. Government assailed supplier-induced demand, which even some lawyers acknowledged, and found strong support among defendants. Insurers complained of being 'mugged' by plaintiffs' lawyers; the Medical Protection Society accused lawyers of 'putting ideas into patients' heads'. The real victims were not unrepresented claimants but adversaries of the legally-aided, not inadequately represented accused but their victims (surely more adequately represented by the prosecution).

The press hammered home this message. Britain had been corrupted by a 'greed and blame' 'American-style compensation culture', deformed into a 'Sue Nation' of 'victims', 'grasping whingers and self-pitying milksops' by lawyers who 'lined their pockets', funding 'all manner of unsuitable cases' out of taxpayers' 'bottomless pockets'. They brought 'barmy' cases and fuelled neighbours' 'ditts'. This 'plague of lawyers'—'ambulance chasers' driven by 'dreams of avarice'—seduced people into believing the 'nanny-ing principle' that 'misfortune' was 'the easiest way to success', threatening 'legal madness' surpassing the 'hallucinatory' American level of litigation. Lawyers were engaging in 'speculative litigation', bringing 'spurious cases' and 'forc[ing]' defendants to settle. Liberally mixing metaphors, the media accused 'pampered' 'fat cats' of 'lapping up' the 'glistening' 'cream', jumping on the 'legal aid gravy train', sticking 'their snouts in the legal aid trough... [and] effectively demanding that the trough is refilled after they have gobbled up their generous portion', and being 'ticked off like naughty, greedy schoolboys'. The press sought to 'shame' and put in 'the dock' the 'cartel' of silks enjoying 'rich pickings'. Barristers 'pretty much name their own fees'. The legal profession was a 'closed shop' of 'Red Robbos in chalk pinstripes'. Newspapers retold *ad nauseam* distorted versions of clichéd American tort claims and the expensive defence of wealthy foreigners like Jawad Hashim, Asil Nadir, and the Maxwell brothers. Immigration practice offered the perfect target: aggressive solicitation of business, allegedly fraudulent claims, and clients (and many of their lawyers) vulnerable to deep-rooted British xenophobia. This barrage of propaganda drowned out efforts by lawyers and advocacy groups to document obstacles to legitimate claims.

Although Lord Irvine insisted he was 'not undertaking these reforms to save money', opponents called them a 'money-saving wheeze' under Treasury pressure; the 'ominous figure' of the salaried defender was a 'Treasury spy'. Government sought to reduce legal aid expenditure through successive steps: freezing remuneration, setting standard fees, concentrating work so volume justified lower profit margins, shifting risk to lawyers through bulk contracts, and then making lawyers bid for them.[105] Government was an unapologetic monopsonist: Middleton wanted the LAB to 'use its purchasing power'; Hoon thought lawyers should have to engage in the 'commonplace' practice of bidding for cases. Government justified concentration as a means—indeed, the only means—of ensuring quality; the restriction of 'unfettered choice' was 'necessary and desirable to secure quality and value for money'. But it offered little evidence that its criteria guaranteed performance. The profession retorted that concentration reduced access. But 3,000 of the 5,000 firms doing 92 per cent of legal aid work received contracts. Both sides acknowledged the real issues: the profession wanted legal aid to remain dispersed (so all lawyers could do it); government sought greater leverage over specialist firms more dependent on it (while hypocritically criticizing their legal aid earnings). Government won this battle (like all others), reducing the medical negligence panel from 3,261 to 80 and exposing the fatal flaw in lawyers' repeated threat to drop legal aid: that was just what government wanted.

Competitive tendering for bulk contracts was just a staging post on the road to salaried lawyers, who offered maximum cost control.[106] Like the original challenge to solicitors' restrictive practices (the conveyancing monopoly), this idea was revived by Austin Mitchell. When his ally Benedict Birnberg proposed a Community Legal Service, Hoon denounced it as 'Orwellian', 'nationalization', the denial of 'choice', another dreaded quango. Six months into the Labour administration the CLS was still just a 'long-term goal'. Less than a year later, however, salaried lawyers had become central to the AJA. The profession objected that they were inherently inferior, lacked independence, and denied clients choice (although solicitors had rejected the first two arguments when the Bar advanced them against CPS audience rights). Lawyers lauded 'the ruggedness, often bloody-mindedness and the eccentricity...of the independent advocate', the Bar's 'considerable success' in maintaining quality. It was 'second nature' for private practitioners 'fearlessly to represent their clients' interests'. '[T]he average member of the criminal Bar is likely to be a person of higher calibre than the average member of a state prosecution or defence service.' Only the 'young and inexperienced' would leave private practice 'for the steady work and regular hours', and they would not 'put the same effort into a case that independent counsel and solicitors do at present'. It was 'odd to find a spokesman of New Labour...proposing the replacement of free consumer choice in a free legal market by a restricted highly bureaucratic regime'. The American 'District Attorney and the public defender have brought the criminal process...into disrepute'. The Bar even claimed the CDS violated the ECHR! The Government responded that it could ensure quality better through employees (unconvincing in light of the CPS experience and inconsistent with preserving legal aid) and public defenders increased client choice (though it was unclear how accused could make informed comparisons). Inconsistently, it contended that choice was irrelevant to the 'once in a lifetime' civil litigant and abused by those with 'considerable experience of the criminal system' to 'play.... the system'. Again, however, all knew the government's goal was cost control. Employees had no incentive to do unnecessary work, and their salaries would become ceilings for paying private practitioners. Employees also might be less eager to challenge Government under the new Human Rights Act.

Even better than hiring lawyers was replacing them with laypeople.[107] Middleton thought it 'perverse' that legal aid was most available for litigation; *The Times* denounced legal aid for spending 90 per cent of its budget on lawyers. (Would anyone criticize the NHS for making acute care a priority or spending most of its money on doctors?) The CLS shifted advice to non-lawyers, who were cheaper than lawyers and had no incentive to refer cases to them (but gave less adequate advice). Although government failed to mandate divorce mediation, it expanded small claims jurisdiction, lauding it as 'the major success story of the civil justice system' despite overwhelming evidence that enforcing judgments was difficult, often impossible.

Best of all was transferring litigation costs from taxpayers to parties. Even when CFAs complemented legal aid, most lawyers and judges instinctively recoiled, certain that something so American must be intolerably vulgar (although they could not decide whether the offence was ambulance chasing and overzealous advocacy or betraying clients with quick, low settlements). Should England 'copy a legal system in which one can obtain damages of a couple of million dollars... for spilling a cup of hot coffee over oneself'? The Bar argued that CFAs would seriously curtail client choice—of a barrister in the same risk pool as an adversary! It warned that CFAs would encourage 'suppression of documents', 'suborning and excessive coaching of witnesses', and 'misrepresentation of facts or law'. Critics associated American contingent fees with ambulance chasing, 'rocketing' insurance premiums, and lawyer misconduct, bankruptcy, and low status. Did 'lawyers seek to compare themselves' to estate agents and insurance brokers? FOIL mischaracterized defendants' liability for plaintiffs' legal expense insurance premiums and success fees as an 'American system of penalties and fines'. The Bar proclaimed barristers did not engage in trade but were called to a 'vocation'. Birnberg worried that solicitors would become 'commercial speculators and bankers first and lawyers second'. But *Times* readers wanted lawyers to risk their own money. And Irvine refused 'to accept that lawyers, among all businesses, should be excluded from running risks and incurring costs in order to earn profits'. Self-interest soon persuaded most lawyers (except insurers') to favour extension. But several commentators correctly predicted that CFAs would substitute for, rather than supplement, legal aid. After all, American legal aid never covered contingent fee cases; and personal injury litigation was uniquely suspect, closer to elective surgery than heroic medicine when viewed through the eyes of British stoicism.

Irvine shamelessly claimed that withdrawing legal aid from CFA cases increased access to justice. Conveniently forgetting Labour's promise to restore eligibility, Hoon trumpeted: 'For the first time this century, perhaps ever, access to justice for all will be a reality in this country—not just a slogan'.[108] Middleton explicitly opposed expanding eligibility, preferring 'to develop private alternatives to help people fund litigation'. Hoon paternalistically wanted to protect victims from the 'slim hope' of victory. (Inconsistently) praising 'go-ahead lawyers' who 'meet the challenges and seize the opportunities', he declared that they should risk their own money, as in any other 'profitable business activity'. (Lord Goodhart retorted: 'doctors have never expected payment by result'.) Government's real goal was to discourage risky cases while blaming lawyers and insurers, thereby portraying a political choice as the product of 'market forces'. *The Times* bought that line: the state should not be 'picking winners in litigation'; insurers were 'surer judges'. Determined to reduce its costs, the state tightened the legal aid merits test while relinquishing control over the decision to initiate CFA cases, correctly predicting that insurers would demand an even higher success rate (approaching 100 per cent). But though the Government claimed this would achieve large savings (estimated at £150–£800 million annually), legal aid already recouped most costs from defendants.

The profession resisted Irvine even less effectively than it had Mackay. Just as judges had wildly charged the Courts and Legal Services Act with fascism, so critics painted the AJA as communist: 'Stalinist' (Law Society), 'dirigiste' (first LAG chair), 'Orwellian' and 'the way to the gulag' (Labour backbencher and QC); 'the state prosecuting, the state defending and the state disposing…they don't even have that in Russia anymore' (Conservative legal affairs spokesperson). It would destroy the 'independent Bar', which Sydney Kentridge claimed had been 'the only thing that stood between the oppressive state regime and the independence and freedom of citizens' in South Africa. (That Bar was almost entirely complicit in apartheid; and did the ANC not play some role in the struggle?[109]) Lord Ackner once again assailed 'the dismantling of our system for the administration of justice as we know it'. Garnier predicted that victims would report fewer crimes, witnesses would not testify, juries would acquit the guilty, defendants would have to be shackled, and convicts would no longer accept the justice of their sentences! Grieve declared the Government had 'absolutely no regard for civil liberties or the rights of accused people'. Lawyers who had invoked professionalism against the Conservatives' laissez faire now embraced the market against Labour's statism. This somersault contained its own contradictions. Lawyers preferred the risk-free CLAF to CFAs, which turned them into 'financial speculators', 'gamblers', 'a cross between insurers and bookmakers', searching for 'the right portfolio of risk', 'bent' by the conflict of interest with their clients. The Law Society insisted that justice was not 'a commodity...which could be left to the law of supply and demand'. The Bar protested the 'profession of law is not a business' but a 'vocation', with a 'higher professional ethic that goes beyond mere profit'. It should not be 'spoken of as if it were some sort of a corner shop'.

Lawyers warned that cost cutting inevitably lowered quality. When Hoon asked whether Birnberg's firm would give 'shoddy service' under block contracts, the solicitor candidly replied: 'constrained by an inflexible budget, I would have no option but to do a second-rate job'. The same inexorable market forces creating 'supplier-induced demand' would force lawyers to cut corners. Lord Clinton-Davis (another solicitor) called it 'unwise to introduce price competition' where 'there are no reliable and generally accepted means of measuring the quality of work'. Baroness Kennedy warned that 'in seeking to drive down costs, quality will be sacrificed'. Hoon made the perverse claim that 'for the first time, there will be very real incentives to suppliers to look carefully at the quality' of their services. Irvine declared (against the evidence) that non-lawyers offered better advice than lawyers about benefits or debt. Government appeared to believe that quality could be assured by measures of process (imperfectly related to the services rendered) or outcome (that did not control for input). Hoon's faith that fixed payments would enhance efficiency presumed that additional lawyer effort did not benefit clients. (Would any client prefer that a lawyer spend less time?) At the Bar's annual conference only Vaz believed a salaried service would be adequately funded. (In 2000 Texas spent an average of $4.65 to defend an accused, South Carolina $4.17, and North Dakota $2.69.[110]) But the British government and electorate cared no more than the American. Indeed, each reform—standard fees, block contracts, conditional fees, and salaried lawyers—replaced an incentive for lawyers to do too much work at the expense of government with one to do too little at the expense of clients.

The profession recycled the tired tropes of access, justice, rights, equality. Calling 'noble' legal aid 'the most efficient of all public services', a Labour MP accused his front bench of the 'largest ever departure from the principles of the welfare state'. But New Labour's proudest boast was dismantling the welfare state. It was 'elected on a radical agenda to modernise this country' and transform 'out-of-date' institutions. Vaz extolled the CLS as a 'modern legal service for a modern Britain', a 'new system for a new millenium'. Even the *Gazette* was defensive about the 'aged legal aid system', which a solicitor called a 'weary arm of the welfare state'. So when another solicitor warned Irvine that 'millions of your electorate will have to join a long queue for legal services', the Lord Chancellor may have secretly smiled. Lawyers dramatized the imperative of independence by citing the Stephen Lawrence inquiry and other police misconduct, just as they had highlighted miscarriages of justice in the IRA bombing prosecutions. Bulk contracts and employment allegedly compromised lawyer loyalty. Critics deplored the Lord Chancellor's excessive power, as they had that of ACLEC (whose demise they now mourned). In 'these perhaps more authoritarian times' governments 'will try to extend their control'. With 'almost free power in the hands of the Executive...the scene is well set for... parliamentary dictatorship'. Some Cassandras unwisely warned of lawyer unemployment, confirming Irvine's charge that they felt entitled to state support.

Government exploited and deepened professional divisions. The Law Society cheered criticism of 'fat cat' barristers (which advanced its attacks on silk) and saw criminal defence cost cutting as a chance to do more higher court advocacy (replaying the debate over CPS audience rights). The Bar feared block contracts would give solicitors further incentives to keep advocacy in-house but hoped the CLS would let it expand direct access to lay advice services, capturing work from solicitors. CFAs divided the branches and, within each, plaintiffs' and defendants' lawyers, entre-preneurs, and traditionalists. Franchising, bulk and exclusive contracts, and competitive tendering pitted specialists against generalists and large firms against small.

Most observers saw the Society's £700,000 advertising campaign as evidence of selfishness, profligacy, and desperation. Although the profession enlisted some client advocates, other potential allies endorsed salaried lawyers and lay advisers. Applications for judicial review failed. Boycotts lacked both unity and leverage. (By contrast, a French national strike over legal aid remuneration by all 35,000 *avocats* and 181 *barreaux* closed the courts twice in December 2000.[111]) After further tarnishing its image, the profession typically capitulated: the Law Society accepted franchising in a vain attempt to forestall exclusive contracts; the Bar invited fixed legal aid fees in all cases to avoid association with privately paid 'fat cats'.

Government faced its own rhetorical dilemmas in addressing three mutually antagonistic constituencies. It had to convince the Treasury it was saving money, the public it was increasing access, and the profession it was preserving quality and independence. Toward this end it bashed lawyers to the Treasury and public, expressed paternalism for clients when the profession championed their right to choose, and denied concern for costs to placate the public. The Government proclaimed that housing estate residents and immigrants badly needed legal advice while assailing lawyers who offered it. Appropriating the profession's strongest argument—equal justice—the Government insisted that legal aid introduced the most troubling inequality, between those it represented and adversaries paying their own costs (a typical 'New Labour' strategy of stoking middle-class resentment of a shrunken welfare state now serving only the poor). Middleton, the banker, candidly acknowledged that the right of 'less well off people' to 'have access to justice on a broadly equal basis to everyone else ... has to be set against a background of limited resources'. Sometimes the Government simply lied, as when Hoon denied it was 'withdrawing legal aid from most money claims, or that as a quid pro quo for the withdrawal of legal aid we are allowing lawyers to use conditional fees'.

Accused of statism, the Government invoked market justifications. There was no right to a lawyer, jury trial, or even access to court. Jack Straw called it 'daft' to allow 'persistent criminals' to cause 'massive public expense' by demanding juries. The 1998 White Paper distinguished between 'legal needs' and access to 'lawyers and the courts'. In any case, there was 'no widespread unmet need for legal services'. Justice did not require lawyers, or even law (in ADR). Perhaps this is what Vaz meant by slogan-eering that the CLS would 'hand the law back to the people'. Legal aid should be available only when an ordinary paying client would litigate, which required a 75 per cent likelihood of success according to Irvine (claiming to personify the Clapham omnibus rider). But demonstrating the selectivity of his market convictions, Irvine denied clients the right to choose their lawyers and called it 'a gross non-sequitur' to argue that 'a controlled budget leads to a decline in standards'. Lawyers did not 'require to be overpaid to deliver quality'. Undermining its alleged commitment to quality, Government accused zealous defence lawyers of 'working' or 'manipulating the system'. Only 'professional criminals' sought the 'full panoply of a criminal trial' (once one of Britain's proudest boasts) at 'massive public expense' (the real consideration). Jack Straw calling Dan Brennan a 'trade union leader' was indistinguishable from the Association of Chief Police Officers denouncing the 'rhetoric of justice ... used as a veil by vested interests'. *The Times* insinuated that respecting an accused's legal rights somehow violated the victim's. Having cut prosecution costs by expanding CPS audience rights, the Government now invoked equal justice to cut defence costs through the CDS.

Irvine relentlessly scapegoated lawyers in order to blame them for his cuts. Doubling court fees did not affect access because lawyers charged so much more. Irvine denounced criminal legal aid as a 'classic demand-led system'—although the state created demand. He then justified cuts in criminal legal aid as necessary to preserve civil, about which the public cared more. He dismissed fears about the independence of salaried public defenders with a specious analogy to salaried judges.

No one was surprised that a Conservative Government sought to slow the growth of legal aid. But by substituting conditional fees for legal aid and salaried lawyers and lay advisers for private practitioners and capping the legal aid budget, 'New Labour' confirmed that its real novelty was antipathy to the welfare state.

9 Serving Two Masters

Any new arrangements must start from the principle that dealing with satisfied [sic] clients is the responsibility of the profession itself and not of a semi-independent agency like the SCB. [Martin Mears, LS President]

The Law Society is saying 'pick a solicitor, any solicitor, and we'll give you a gun to shoot at him'. [LS Council member]

[Consumers] cannot say we want it cheap, cheap, cheap but we want it perfect. [Robert Sayer, LS VP candidate]

[S]olicitors have a self-regulatory system which is the envy of lawyers throughout the world and of other professions in this country. [Veronica Lowe, SCB Director]

[The SCB directorship is] the worst job in the legal world. [Lowe five months later, after being forced out]

[T]he entrenched attitudes demonstrated by individual practitioners [will] lead to the closed sign finally going up on the doors of the famous last chance saloon. [Ann Abraham, LSO]

[T]he Society will take ownership of this problem and its solution . . . there is the will . . . to get the system right. [Michael Mathews, LS President]

We currently lack the resources we need to deal effectively with our work. [OSS letter written less than two weeks later, returning a complaint and suggesting the client try again in six months]

Within five years, let there be one legal profession . . . with one code of conduct, one set of rules, one regulator. . . . The Law Society is the obvious choice. We already regulate the biggest single legal profession and we do it well. [Robert Sayer, LS President, three months after that]

In exchange for regulating themselves, professions claim immunity from external control, advancing the same justification they offer for controlling entry: the division of labour endows them with the unique expertise to judge both probity and competence.[1] The nineteenth-century Bar's intimacy and homogeneity—no more than a few hundred upper-class men in any Circuit or Inn—gave those institutions considerable informal influence. Unstated norms were sufficiently pervasive that the first written account of professional etiquette was published only in 1875, and the Senate promulgated its Code of Conduct only in 1980. The Inns transferred disciplinary authority to the Senate they created in 1966. When the Senate incorporated the Bar Council in 1974 it established the Professional Conduct Committee (PCC), which can impose minor sanctions or refer more serious matters to the Disciplinary Tribunal, from which appeal lies

355 Serving Two Masters

to the judicial Visitors of the barrister's Inn. The PCC received fewer than 100 complaints annually until the mid-1970s. Between 1957 and 1974 less than a quarter went to formal hearing and less than 4 per cent led to suspension or disbarment. The PCC declined to review incompetence (three-quarters of complaints), despite the Royal Commission's recommendation. The Court of Appeal affirmed in 1969 that barristers were not liable for malpractice as advocates but suggested in dictum that they might be in other activities. The Senate required barristers to purchase indemnity insurance only in 1983.[2]

Although nineteenth-century barristers regulated themselves, the Supreme Court (all ex-barristers) controlled solicitors. In 1888 the Law Society President secured for it the right to review complaints, declaring that 'any accused solicitor will...come before a tribunal composed of members of his own profession, to whom, if at all, he should be able to justify himself'. This reassurance was fully warranted: during the next twenty-five years the disciplinary committee dismissed three-quarters of complaints. When the Supreme Court adjudicated disciplinary matters (until the end of World War I), it punished 83 per cent of those it heard; during the first two decades after the Law Society obtained this power it punished only 36 per cent. Although Marcel Berlins documented the appalling quality of criminal defence and Michael Joseph exposed fraud and incompetence by conveyancers and personal injury lawyers, the Society, like the Bar, declined to entertain the commonest complaints: delay, inefficiency, incompetence, neglect, and cost. It dismissed more than two-thirds as beyond its jurisdiction or unfounded and punished less than 1 per cent.

In answer to the Royal Commission the Society promulgated written standards about responsiveness to clients. Instead of the proposed local law society conciliation service it urged arbitration—but only with the solicitor's consent. It obtained authority to discipline for Inadequate Professional Service (IPS) and expanded the role of laypeople. But it failed to separate investigation from adjudication.

Embarrassed by exposure of its gross mishandling of Leslie Parsons's complaint against LS Council member Glanville Davies in the mid-1980s, the Society commissioned a study by Coopers & Lybrand, which recommended transferring all disciplinary power to an independent Solicitors Complaints Bureau (SCB). A Labour backbencher (supported by five others) introduced a private member's bill to do this, backed by LAG and the NCC. Several London law societies and the Young Solicitors and Local Government groups were supportive, but large provincial societies and the Law Society establishment were opposed. The Society compromised by creating a physically separate SCB, with lay participation in both the Investigation and Adjudication Committees and twice its predecessor's budget. But it retained the Solicitors Disciplinary Tribunal (SDT) to adjudicate on serious charges.

Because solicitors (unlike barristers) handle client money, they need to regulate financial misconduct. Between 1861 and 1877 nearly 1,000 solicitors went bankrupt, 130 more than once and one a staggering twelve times. At the end of this period the Law Society discovered that its own chief clerk had been embezzling for thirty-three years! In 1900 a former President was convicted of defrauding clients. The following year fifty-five solicitors went bankrupt, and at least forty-two did so in each of the next four years. Over strong solicitor opposition the Society began *ex gratia* payments to clients in 1912. In 1933 Parliament required it to adopt rules about client accounts, which it did reluctantly two years later; but many failed to comply, and 10 per cent were still submitting late or inadequate accounts in the 1980s. The Society established a Solicitors Compensation Fund (SCF) in 1942, charging solicitors £5 a year (£30 by 1984–5). It began examining solicitors' accounts three years later, but only an average of sixty-four a year until 1970, and just twice that in subsequent decades.

Also unlike barristers, solicitors are liable for malpractice (outside litigation). But because only 8 per cent were the object of claims in the mid-1960s, and just half of those paid damages, only half of solicitors carried indemnity insurance. This became compulsory in 1976 under a master policy negotiated by the Society; sole practitioners paid about 25 per cent more than partners; premiums doubled for those with the worst claims records. When premiums more than tripled in the next seven years, the BLA (championing smaller firms) proposed proportioning them to gross fees. Local law societies agreed (by six to one), but the City of London Law Society strongly objected. The BLA forced a postal ballot, in which 74 per cent wanted gross fees considered, and then a second ballot, in which 58 per cent wanted premiums based exclusively on gross fees, with no ceiling. Although the Council refused to be bound by members' votes, it complied, increasing premiums for partners grossing more than £63,000. The furious City firms appealed to the Master of the Rolls, who overruled the Council. It then tapered the ratio and capped the total, so that partners paid no more than an additional £90. But though further tapering and individualization sought to deal with rising premiums, the Society decided in 1986 to create its own Solicitors Indemnity Fund, hoping to keep annual premium increases to 15 per cent until 1991.[3]

External reviewers shared the profession's complacency about its dilatory, perfunctory record of self-regulation. The Royal Commission offered little criticism, even displaying scepticism about the continued need for the Lay Observer, given lay involvement in the investigation and adjudication of complaints. It also expressed concern about the 'strain' on solicitors and 'members of other professions' (presumably Benson's fellow accountants), urging an immediate inquiry 'into the desirability of a limit on the level of damages which may be awarded for negligence against professional persons'. The Government Response concurred.[4]

At the end of his term as LS President in 1987, Sir John Wickerson declared that 'the best judge of the public interest when it was related to the profession' was 'the profession itself', provided it consulted with 'all those who have a proper interest'.

I do not believe that the Consumers' Association is any more the arbiter of what is in the public interest than, say, the Institute of Directors.... The hallmark of a profession is that it sets its own rules. If we cease to do that then we cease to be a profession.

A year later the Marre Committee (two-thirds of whom were lawyers) concurred, finding:

no evidence to suggest that the regulation of professional conduct by the state is likely to be more efficient than self-regulation by professional bodies. At the end of the day, the independence and integrity of the individual solicitor or barrister, determined to place the interests of justice before expediency, are the citizen's best safeguard against tyranny whether by the state or by powerful private interests.

It warned that Government enthusiasm for 'vigorous competition' might affect the profession's 'ability to find the very substantial resources (both financial and human) needed to ensure effective self-regulation'.[5]

The Government affirmed its confidence in the Society by authorizing it to regulate members' activities under the Financial Services Act 1986. The restructured disciplinary system appeared to make a difference: in its first year the SCB received twice as many complaints, its Adjudication Committee heard four to six times as many as the Professional Purposes Department (PPD), and the SDT punished twice as many. But inadequate funding and staffing created delays, the SCB dismissed 60 per cent of complaints after telephoning the solicitor, and sixty to seventy complainants a month challenged the dispositions.[6]

A. Solicitor Discipline

The complacency of the profession and its friends was unwarranted. The first report of the Law Society's new Research and Policy Planning Unit found that public respect had declined from 1986 to 1989. The *Solicitors Journal* acknowledged that the Green Paper had 'hardly a good word' to say about the SCB's 'lacksadaisical performance', which 'also does not impress the vast majority of honest solicitors'. The SCB Investigation Committee's lay members agreed, urging that an independent regulator be able to order compensation of up to £2,000 for misconduct or negligence. Two years later the SCB established a separate compensation committee, with a lay majority. The Lay Observer criticized the SCB's failure to keep adequate records, co-operate with him, or deal adequately with overcharging. In his final report two years later, he called it 'quite unreasonable' that solicitors refused to give 'reliable estimates of their costs and abide by them'.

The SCB could not 'expect to command public confidence' unless it gave both parties the reasons for its decisions.[7]

When the Guild of British Newspaper Editors urged the Lord Chancellor to compel the SDT to open its hearings (as the GMC did), LS President Ely was 'very concerned that the damage which could be done to members of the profession where charges are not supported may be out of all proportion'. A year later, however, the SDT complied to 'help to dispel' the misconception that 'the profession is not prepared to discipline its own members properly'. At his first press conference as the new Legal Services Ombudsman (LSO), Michael Barnes promised to wield the 'big stick' of 'bad publicity' to 'stiffen the complaints-handling procedure'. He was receiving twice as many complaints as the Lay Observer, criticizing professional bodies' handling of a third, and recommending reconsideration or compensation in a fifth. He warned that solicitors' fees were alienating clients and urged the Society to allow testamentary beneficiaries to apply for remuneration certificates.

Ever the optimist, however, Director Veronica Lowe boasted that the SCB had 'made considerable progress' in improving 'the quality and speed of our service'. Its budget had nearly doubled in four years, while complaints had declined by 5 per cent. But a year later the LSO criticized the SCB for delay, inflexibility, and negative responses and urged it to redirect resources toward the commonest client complaints of delay, inefficiency, expense, poor advice, and neglect. That year the SCB received 15 per cent more complaints and referred 22 per cent to firms for not informing clients of their in-house complaint procedures. When the SCB held a press conference to release its annual report (six months late!), a Council member said the profession was 'shooting itself in both feet'. Martin Mears, newly elected to the Council, objected that 'we pay for press conferences at which we are exposed as thieves and incompetents'. The Bureau retorted that it operated 'at arm's length from the Law Society in order to provide a guarantee that the public interest would be treated in relation to complaints against the profession'.[8]

Just as Leslie Parsons's complaint had shamed the Society into creating the SCB, so Peggy Wood's case embarrassed the new institution. Her solicitor, Sylvia Hubbard, obtained a £10,000 loan for Wood, secured by her home, from Frederick Wills, a client of the firm, and Mobile Homes, a company in which Sylvia's husband (the firm's senior partner) had a substantial interest. When Wills sued for repayment, the Master of the Rolls urged the Society to consider 'the propriety of solicitors acting for both lenders and borrowers'. When Mobile Homes sought possession following default in 1979, Wood complained to the Society about conflict of interest. The PPD, believing she was criticizing the lender's solicitor rather than her own (ignoring that they were the same person), ruled that Hubbards had a 'professional duty to act...in their client's best interests'. Wood complained to the Society again in 1983, which denied having misunderstood her original complaint and found 'no professional misconduct'. (The Secretary-General wrote to the President: 'The less than brilliant performance of a member of the staff in Professional Purposes and of the SCB committee are of course matters well rehearsed here. It's all a bit embarrassing to say the least.')

Hubbards foreclosed, advertising the property for more than three times what they had paid and reaping a huge profit. After the Lay Observer's intervention, the Society admitted 'it was mistaken to have initially dismissed' Wood's complaint 'without enquiry' and referred it back to the SCB. The Bureau rejected most of the complaint, though it rebuked Hubbard for failing to disclose her husband's interest. Sued by Wood, the Society declared: 'We may owe a public law duty, but we don't owe a private law duty which could sound in damages'. When the High Court dismissed her action because she was a member of a 'non-ascertainable class' the Society said defensively: 'There is no question in our minds or the judge's mind that anything we did or failed to do was responsible for the loss of her home'. The *New Law Journal* called this a 'missed opportunity', which would not receive an 'enthusiastic reception by the public'. And *Private Eye* urged readers to contribute to Wood's 'fighting fund in her battle with the forces of darkness and oppression at the Law Society'. But when the Court of Appeal and House of Lords found against her and the European Commission on Human Rights rejected her case, she lost her twenty-four-year battle.[9]

Criticism continued to mount. Based on the ten to fifteen letters it received daily in response to requests for 'good or bad' experiences with the SCB, the NCC concluded that the Bureau's procedures 'favour solicitors' and discourage 'legitimate complaints' through 'unacceptable delays and unnecessary bureaucratic barriers'. Average disposition time was 7.5 months. Three-quarters of complaints were conciliated. Although 3,900 of the 4,300 referred back to firms never returned, the SCB failed to ask whether the complainants were satisfied. That seemed unlikely. Although Practice Rule 15 had required all firms to create an in-house complaints procedure by May 1991, two years later only 41 per cent of sole practitioners had done so, and fewer than half of the 70–79 per cent of two- to ten-partner firms with a procedure explained it to clients. The NCC recommended an independent, lay-dominated body accountable to the Lord Chancellor and empowered to award £5,000 compensation. Although the LSO did not agree that the SCB 'favours solicitors', he thought the compensation proposal 'interesting' and deserving of 'a serious response'.

If individual complainants were frustrated, government had its own remedies. The LAB investigation unit won seven of the eleven fraud prosecutions it brought against legal aid practitioners between 1988 and 1993; three more were pending, and another twelve firms were being investigated. The Society's courts and legal services committee called LAB proposals to require more information from solicitors 'a sledgehammer to crack a small nut'. But a June 1994 *Sunday Times* investigation headlined 'Solicitors bribe poor in £20 million aid fraud' prompted similar stories in the dailies entitled: 'One in seven law firms facing fraud investigation', 'Solicitors' fraud rockets', 'Cheats in the dock', and 'Lawyers who fail society'. The SCB found the articles 'unpalatable but by and large correct'. When the LAB proposed that unfranchised solicitors complete a more detailed form, get prior authorization for more than one green form per client per year, and face suspension of payment in case of suspected fraud, the Society resisted, and legal aid solicitors declared 'it's attacking people with the most urgent needs'.[10]

In his 1994 LS presidential acceptance speech, Elly told members that since 40 per cent of their practising certificate fees went to the SCB 'we must all look to our own practices to reduce the volume of complaints'. And because 'we spend a great deal of the profession's money detecting fraud and compensating clients' he pledged to 'rid the profession of the fraudulent'. At the annual conference three months later he rejected 'entirely the notion that we should retreat into an exclusive self-serving pressure group, concerned only for our own pockets'. 'If we abdicated our regulatory role, a more onerous regime would undoubtedly be imposed from outside and you can be sure the profession would still be required to pay.' At the same time, he rejected the NCC criticisms. '[S]olicitors do not go round over charging their clients because they are in a highly competitive market which drives costs down'. (A 1989 NCC survey found that only 9 per cent of housebuyers obtained a second conveyancing quotation.) The SCB boasted that 'the solicitor's profession offers consumers a wider range of client protection and redress than is offered by any other trade or profession in this country'. And the LS Secretary-General took comfort in the fact that 'fewer than 10% who complain to the SCB refer the matter to the legal services ombudsman'.[11]

This combination of bravado and defensiveness reflected deep internal divisions. At a June 1995 LS roadshow designed to air dissatisfaction a Council member urged that solicitors who complained against others and clients who appealed should pay a fee. But another solicitor said he was 'doing the profession a favour by reporting...a very serious problem at another firm'. 'Talk of me being charged is ridiculous.' Beginning his presidential term the next month, Mears said the Society's SCB consultation paper would create 'a Mark II SCB with all the perceived and real deficiencies of the present body'. He wanted a Client Care Unit controlled by the Society. 'Any new arrangements must start from the principle that dealing with satisfied [*sic*] clients is the responsibility of the profession itself and not of a semi-independent agency like the SCB'.[12]

Solicitors were more effective than clients in correcting SCB errors. Rebuked for allegedly not accounting to a client for £329, delay in responding, and not giving a satisfactory explanation, sole practitioner Arnold Rosen sought judicial review on the ground that the SCB had improperly delegated power to the Adjudication Committee and denied him the right to appear and seek review of its decisions. He initially rejected the Society's offer to withdraw the rebuke and pay his costs but accepted when a court held his correspondence with the Society privileged and the Society acknowledged its original investigation had been inadequate. Still, he felt the Society 'has treated me with contempt'. The Taxing Master who assessed Rosen's costs at over £90,000 found:

a level of deviousness making it clear to me that a certain view was taken in the Law Society about Mr Rosen and how to deal with him. It was done to provide as little information as possible.

'[T]o buy off an action at the last minute to avoid an adverse decision on a point of principle', said the *New Law Journal*, 'is not what members of the public expect from the Society'. Investigations were terminated or adverse decisions reversed in at least three other cases.[13]

Although the Green Paper, NCC, and Lay Observer had urged solicitors to quote fees, the Society merely 'encourage[d]' this but felt it not 'appropriate to introduce a binding professional rule' because there was 'no such requirement on other suppliers of goods and services'. Indeed, the Society wanted to end the procedure by which clients could ask it to certify that remuneration was 'fair and reasonable'. (Applications fell by 29 per cent in the year after 1992–3 and another 47 per cent in the next five years, perhaps because they were restricted to bills over £50,000.) When Holland became president in 1990 he failed to persuade the Council to adopt his firm's practice of informing clients about charging rates and complaint procedures. The CA was 'extremely disappointed'. Its 1992 survey found that 60 per cent of clients underestimated solicitors' fees and another 30 per cent made no estimate.

In 1993 LCD Parliamentary Secretary John Taylor urged mandatory quotations, 'blush[ing]' about the many clients who complained that solicitors offered fixed fee conveyancing and then charged more, which 'smack[ed]...of sharp practice rather than professionalism'. Noting that this criticism followed the Society's proceedings against legal aid cuts (see Chapter 7), LS legal practice director Andrew Lockley said, 'We can't rule out the possibility that the government is trying to make a return strike'. But the LSO agreed that 'lawyers' costs are so high nowadays that it is absolutely vital that people know what they are getting into'. If fee 'information is not given in writing and the client has suffered inconvenience or distress, I'm looking to find in favour of the client'. He also criticized the SCB for referring clients back to firms' complaint mechanisms before granting a hearing in 5,733 cases in 1992. 'This is not a mandatory first stage.' And he condemned the inability of testamentary beneficiaries to challenge the administration of estates, which had become the second most common complaint.

But the Society again rejected mandatory fee disclosure. One Council member warned: 'if you give an estimate to a client, you are stuck with it'. Another assailed the current grievance procedure as a shooting gallery in which the Society told clients: 'pick a solicitor, any solicitor, and we'll give you a gun to shoot at him'. Soon thereafter it allowed beneficiaries to challenge solicitors' charges and declared that failure to give advance estimates might constitute IPS. But the NCC was 'extremely disappointed' that disclosure remained voluntary, and the *New Law Journal* called for 'more decisive action'.[14]

The following year an NCC survey found that though 80 per cent of solicitors claimed to give advance quotations, only 60 per cent of private clients and 43 per cent of legally aided remembered receiving them. But when the NCC again sought mandatory disclosure, the Law Society accused it of having 'ignored the overwhelmingly positive results of their survey'. The chair of the Society's standards and guidance committee complained that 'too often now one reads that people who should be championing the legal profession are denigrating it instead'. He was sceptical that 'you can persuade 65,000 solicitors to do something by telling them they must do it'. '[T]o suggest that before you start work on a client's case you must tell the client how to complain if you get it wrong is demotivating and unnecessary.' He decried 'a sort of regulatory paranoia—if in doubt make new rules and enforce them more rigorously than before'. But the CA criticized the Society for failing to mandate fee dispute arbitration.[15]

When a 1995 NACAB survey of 350 advice agencies concluded that 'people are often not informed of the likely cost of seeking advice or bringing an action' and those who are 'often end up with bills double or treble the original estimate', LS President Mears was dismissive. '[R]eports from the CABx will always be unrelentingly negative. The vast majority of solicitors' clients are happy with the service they receive and believe that the cost offers real value for money.' Noting it had been urging compulsory fee estimates for four years, the *Solicitors Journal* called for an emergency Council meeting. The Society's own survey found that clients received advance quotations for only 45 per cent of conveyances and 69 per cent of wills.[16]

Critics also assailed the level of fees. The Lord Chief Justice told the 1993 Bar annual conference that fees charged to commercial clients were 'often out of all proportion to a reasonable rate for the job'. The reputation of both branches would be 'much improved if the pursuit of higher fees were to be replaced by a more modest concept of the rate for the job'. Addressing the Law Society annual conference two weeks later, the Grand Metropolitan Estates legal affairs officer objected to hourly rates. At a 1996 seminar Labour legal affairs spokesperson Paul Boateng called the increase in those rates from £25 in 1974 to £310 in 1994 a 'corrosive stain on our justice system'. City partner David McIntosh criticized LS VP Sayer for telling members to 'avoid quotes and charge on a time basis'. Sayer retorted that advance quotations were 'blind stupidity'.[17]

In March 1997, however, the Council responded to criticism by Lord Woolf, the LSO, and consumer groups by voting overwhelmingly to clarify the information solicitors should provide about costs and direct the OSS to treat material breach of the code as *prima facie* evidence of IPS (60 per cent of IPS complaints concerned costs). But though the NCC, LSO, and *Gazette* applauded, some Council members were incensed. John Franks warned 'we are making it easier for the client to complain' and 'building up a claim for inadequate professional service. It is simply not fair on the profession.' Sayer agreed the Council 'uses stick too much and not enough carrot'. PACS chair Richard Hegarty objected that the 'effect will be to drive costs down. It will focus our minds and the client's minds on the question of costs, not the question of service or the question of quality.' Richard Ford thought it 'unsympathetic and unnatural to mention costs immediately to clients'. Jennifer Israel had 'never been so cross at Council: we're not plumbers and mechanics.' 'We should compare ourselves to doctors whose fees are not subject to taxation.' Richard Wilson said the Council 'lived in a different world from practitioners'. But President Sycamore retorted that 'all practitioners live in the same world as consumers—we can't ignore the pressures'. 'Surely what you have here is information which is positively useful to the profession and to clients'. McIntosh, whose firm had published a client charter three years earlier explaining fee calculations, saw quotations as a 'marketing tool'. 'I want us to be more popular than car repairers.' Even Mears asked 'Who could object to telling clients in advance how much they will be charged?' Later that year Sir John Middleton recommended mandatory quotations.[18]

Two fee scandals exploded within a week of the Council action. The Lord Chancellor reported that the defence of Kevin Maxwell had cost £12.2 million; his solicitors objected to the constant 'public ridicule'. And when an assistant solicitor committed suicide, his Birmingham firm billed his mother £12,278 for services that included a partner going to the deceased's house when he missed work and calling the police! Following an application for a remuneration certificate and an OSS conciliation the bill was reduced to £2,412. The *Gazette* deplored that 'the story not only offered [the press] a chance to reinforce the legal profession's reputation for greed, but also showed it to be utterly heartless and unmoved by personal tragedy'. The *Solicitors Journal* said the firm had 'dishonoured the profession'. And indeed the SDT struck the name partner off the Roll. When he returned to practice a year later, the press reviled him as a 'scandalous solicitor' (*Daily Telegraph*), 'vulture lawyer' (*Sun*), and 'greed lawyer' (*Daily Mirror*).[19]

The profession was just as defensive about criticisms of quality. A 1995 CA survey reported 'shoddy' and often 'inappropriate' advice; out of twenty solicitors, only one gave the best advice on one problem and just three on another. Fees (when quoted) differed widely: £117–£750 for conveying a £75,000 property. LS President Mears called the report 'simply a publicity opportunity...the saddest example of a sound bite survey yet. Of course we will be accused of trying to shoot the messenger...some messengers deserve to be shot'. A Society spokesperson was 'very irritated' by this 'self-serving report'. One of the firms named sued the CA, which counterclaimed and demanded that the Society apologize. Although the Society encouraged solicitors to evaluate and improve quality, two years later *Which?* found that only one of twenty-one solicitors answered a question correctly. Switchboard operators at one firm gave misinformation. A 'disappointed' Law Society challenged 'the value of such a small survey, covering such a narrow area of law and using such a research method'. President Sycamore said it did not 'cover the real and typical problems clients see solicitors about every day' and was 'a side-show in the wider debate about legal services'.[20]

But though the *Solicitors Journal* read the survey as demonstrating 'the need for further continuing education and training', solicitors resisted. When the Society required Continuing Professional Development (CPD) in November 1994 the journal correctly predicted that it 'will be resented rather than welcomed'. In June 1995 ACLEC criticized professionals who simply 'collect hours to fulfil their CPD'. All lawyers could benefit from instruction in 'ethical issues and practice management', and 'gender and culture awareness education...might be made mandatory'. But Mears (elected LS president that month) called for ending mandatory CPD, which treated solicitors 'like idle schoolchildren who cannot be trusted by themselves to keep up with legal developments...[but] can be made to learn through compulsory course attendances'. CPD providers who 'have flourished and waxed fat' should 'beware! No gravy train rolls forever.' LS training committee chair Simon Baker attacked this 'knock-about caricature'. He was determined that the sixteen-hour annual requirement 'shall only be a start'. 'Presidents and professors of law alike may be called upon, at any time after 1998, to produce their record of professional development.' The next year ACLEC called CPD 'an essential part of the continuum of legal education and training and in future its importance will grow....' A year later it declared that 'the public interest requires a greater commitment by the legal profession as a whole to adequate levels of CPD....'[21]

If outside observers consistently called discipline too passive and lax, solicitors found it meddlesome and oppressive. In January 1995 Nicholas Oglethorpe, a former member of the Society's adjudication and appeals Committee (AAC), called the SCB 'out of control' and the object of 'general distrust'. Declaring that the 'wide dissatisfaction ... can no longer be ignored', he called a meeting of solicitors. A few weeks later SCB director Lowe submitted a report to the AAC proposing to 'turn off the tap' of complaints in order to focus on prevention. Oglethorpe told an audience of 100 that the SCB was 'a PR tragedy, unpopular with the public and exceedingly unpopular with the profession'. Mears (running for the Society presidency) criticized the 'curious methodology' of the NCC's 1994 'condemnatory report', which 'does not stand up to investigation'.

There can be very few solicitors who have not dealt with a demanding or obsessive client who goes from firm to firm expressing hot dissatisfaction about all of them. The bureau is a natural place of resort and comfort for someone of that sort.

Ole Hansen, author of the NCC report, retorted: 'we see the figures for negligence, fraud and misappropriation rising every year and with them the money we have to pay for the indemnity insurance and to the Compensation Fund'. The 'heavy handed' Bureau claimed a high success rate because '87 per cent of complainants who had been sent away by the Bureau had not come back again'. But some 'may simply have gone away in despair'. Two Law Society studies suggested this. Although two-thirds of firms claimed to have a complaints procedure and another 15 per cent to be creating one, 80 per cent of clients did not recall it, only half of aggrieved clients complained to their solicitors, and just 3 per cent of complainants were satisfied with the outcome.

Sayer (Mears's running mate) wanted complainants to pay £100 to discourage trivial grievances. Solicitors loudly applauded his objection that consumers 'cannot say we want it cheap, cheap, cheap but we want it perfect'. Urging that discipline be transferred to the judiciary, Arnold Rosen described a solicitor client's 'horrific experience' fighting the Bureau's 'complaints crush machine' for three years. 'We perform a charity out of a sense of honour to the public. If that is not recognised, I want to choose another way.' A Bognor solicitor said he was 'just a bloke trying to earn a living. If I call out a plumber and I'm not satisfied with his work, I sue him. Why should we pay for the mistakes of other solicitors?' Another solicitor agreed the time had come to 'pull in the reins and curb the flow'. The SCB should withdraw leaflets 'encouraging complaints'. Oglethorpe complained that 'we're spending £11 million a year on something which the public and the profession distrust'.

The *New Law Journal* criticized Lowe for missing the meeting, accusing her of 'sulking' and ridiculing her explanation that only the Society had been invited.

She must be one of the few people who believe [the SCB is independent], funded as it is with members' money, with Ms. Lowe having a seat on the Management Board of the Society and, when it suits both, having an interchange of information which could possibly be seen as confidential, which may be beneficial to one or the other.

Chris Heaps, AAC chair, was there in a private capacity, insisting that neither body 'felt the need to attend. They did not feel that they had to defend anything.' The 'system has shown itself to be robust. My starting position is that the Bureau is a body of which the profession can be proud.' A week earlier the AAC had offered to consider four reforms. 'The SCB and committee have shown they are prepared to learn from experience.' Oglethorpe dismissed this 'gaseous' 'hypocrisy' as 'clearly designed' to pre-empt his meeting. 'They're not admitting problems but trying a sleight of hand to make it seem that things are better. It's like saying "Let's put on lipstick and everybody will think we're 19 again".'[22]

Just two months after Heaps's prideful boast, however, Lowe and Secretary-General Hayes urged the Society's strategy committee to replace the SCB with a Supervision of Solicitors Agency, whose board would have approximately equal numbers of solicitors and laypeople and be chaired by a layperson 'of distinction in public or business life'. President Elly agreed with Lowe and Hayes that 'most complaints should be sorted out between clients and solicitors themselves' at the expense of firms and the new body emphasize its 'role as regulator', concentrating on prevention. Although the Society would remain the source of the Agency's powers, it would exercise them 'at arm's length'. Oglethorpe said these 'merely cosmetic' changes would 'not persuade the public that the Agency will be independent' or 'make it easier for a solicitor mistreated by the Bureau to challenge that unfair treatment'. He also objected that only clients, not solicitors, would be able to complain about the Agency to the LSO. The *New Law Journal* now strangely opposed 'a trained cadre of salaried adjudicators' with 'limited experience in the day-to-day running of a solicitors' practice'.[23]

While the Society's leadership sought to strengthen regulation, grassroots opposition tried to weaken or eliminate it. At the BLA annual conference a member deplored that the SCB had distributed leaflets at its launch explaining how to complain against solicitors. The BLA embraced a proposal by founder Stanley Best to call a Law Society SGM to abolish the SCB. He fulminated:

[O]n all sides solicitors were angry and dissatisfied with the activity/inactivity of the SCB for, instead of concentrating on cases of misconduct (which bring the profession into disrepute) its major effort, and thus greatest expenditure of funds— running at many millions of pounds per year—is directed to such matters as trivial complaints, which are on the increase.

The Bureau was 'an expensive folly, damaging to the interests of solicitors and simply pandering to those who, in other circumstances, would be left to their remedy, if any, in law for the largely imaginary grievances they claimed to have'.[24]

A solicitor who had practised for forty years waxed nostalgic about the days when 'professional life was a gentlemanly affair'. He 'honestly' could not 'remember receiving any complaints' from clients. The 'horrific... malaise of complainitis has long since spread to our profession to the extent that we are enjoined to tell clients how to complain about us at their very first interview'. The 'only, but radical, solution is for proper notice to be given of the abolition of the Compensation Fund'. An SCB lay member decried that 20,000 people complained to it annually, compared with 8,500 to its predecessor. (During the previous ten years complaints had risen by 9.2 per cent and solicitors by 28.1.[25])

Lowe responded to these protests by warning that 'the landscape is littered with failed self-regulators offering poor client protection, complacent in-house investigations and cosy relationships with those they used to regulate'. For just £170 a year 'solicitors have a self-regulatory system which is the envy of lawyers throughout the world and of other professions in this country'.[26]

When the strategy committee presented the Hayes–Lowe proposal to the Council in June, Franks urged separating contract disputes (which he wanted to discourage) from misconduct claims. Holland was not sure the SCB needed 'serious change'. Its policy advisory committee chair said members were 'appalled at what they see as the recent onslaught of unnecessary, damaging criticism', much of it 'ill-informed' and based on 'inadequate evidence'. Society elections had turned the Bureau into a 'political football'. Members remained 'staunch supporters of the system as it presently stands and the staff who run the bureau'. The Council decided to consult the profession.[27]

A week later Michael Barnes's annual LSO report called it 'premature to talk of abandoning self-regulation. But this is the Law Society's last chance to get it right'. The SCB should be empowered to award £5,000 compensation and fine solicitors. Complainants might be charged £10 but not £100. Solicitors 'should adopt the stance of major high street retailers whose priority is to settle complaints as quickly as possible even if they are only half justified'. Boateng was 'extremely attracted to the concept of a totally independent complaints body, as proposed by the NCC'. The Society 'has one last chance to regulate its own procedures satisfactorily', but 'the new complaints body must be, and must be seen to be, operationally independent of Chancery Lane'. Henry Hodge thought it clear that Barnes 'would have no truck with Martin Mears' proposal to bring complaints-handling back inside Chancery Lane' and claimed Barnes supported the Hayes–Lowe plan. Mears retorted that his proposal met Barnes's concern 'that complaints should be dealt with quickly, efficiently and fairly and that an aggrieved complainant should have the right to appeal to a transparently independent body'. Barnes reiterated that 'the new complaints body should be as independent of the Law Society as possible' and 'managed by a supervisory board having a majority of laymembers and a lay chairperson'. If this failed to win support within a few years 'the demand for a totally independent body as proposed by the National Consumer Council is likely to prove irresistible'.[28]

The SCB annual report a month later only fuelled criticism. Calling 1994 'a year of very real achievements', it boasted of referring 43 per cent of complaints to firms, twice as many as the previous year, only 13 per cent of which returned; and it decided to refer 'every appropriate case' before acting, making the empty threat that 'firms who fail to respond constructively will be contacted by the rule 15 compliance officer'.[29]

While the debate raged, Hayes gave Lowe a golden handshake of £71,000 (a year's salary) plus £5–£10,000 headhunting fees, just before Mears's election and without consulting President Elly. Although Mears asked that he and the finance committee review it, the Council decided to do this only in the future, approving the deal by 38 to 6. The *New Law Journal* urged Lowe to take immediate sick leave, calling her 'something of a loose cannon', who 'has made sweeping allegations against and attacks on the media as being...part of a conspiracy against her'. After leaving in October she called her position 'the worst job in the legal world'. She also criticized Mears's proposal to create a 'client care unit' whose 'concern would be to produce a satisfied customer'. He had 'little familiarity with how the bureau operates and the value of its work'. Mears retaliated by investigating whether those remarks violated the confidentiality agreement in her severance package.[30]

A January 1996 RPPU report intensified scepticism about firms' ability and willingness to handle complaints. Only 9 per cent of clients were informed of these procedures, just 1 per cent when they instructed the solicitor. Half said solicitors 'didn't even listen and were no help at all'; only 3–8 per cent felt their complaints had been processed fairly. Of those who complained to the SCB and were referred back to the firm, 81 per cent thought it a waste of time. Two-thirds said the Bureau did nothing in response to their complaints; nearly half felt it was slow, heavily biased towards solicitors, and did not investigate thoroughly. Respondents were not chronic whingers: 65 per cent had made no other complaints in five years. The *Gazette* found this 'depressing report card' inconsistent with the claim by two-thirds of firms to have established complaint mechanisms.

The CA declared that the report substantiated 'what we've already been saying about solicitors not being very good at dealing with complaints'. It wanted the SCB to accept fee complaints and award compensation of up to £5,000. The NCC said the reform confirmed 'our own analysis of the SCB which showed poor communication, failure to respond to inquiries, intolerable delays, lack of thoroughness in investigating complaints and failure to explain adequately the reasons for decisions'. Barnes observed that the Bureau's annual report claimed that 60–70 per cent of complaints 'were resolved in one way or another without the need for formal investigation, but it is now clear from this latest research that two thirds of those whose complaint was dealt with by the Bureau were very dissatisfied with the outcome'.[31]

Complaints Against Solicitors—Action for Independent Adjudication was launched in February 1996 with 100 members. The SCB replied that independence was unnecessary for impartiality, pointing to the sanctions it imposed. Nevertheless, the LS Council voted in March to replace it with the Office for the Supervision of Solicitors (OSS). The AAC would be split into client relations (with a lay majority) and professional regulation. The Master of the Rolls would appoint lay and non-Council solicitor members to each. Although the OSS director would report to the LS Secretary-General about management, the Council would publicly declare the OSS's independence. Only Mears and Sayer opposed this last provision. Paul Pharaoh, AAC chair, said 'no service industry can afford to maintain the indifference to consumer satisfaction that, sadly, is only too clear from many of the files which reach the SCB'. But a Council member called it 'the same animal with different spots', and the NCC said 'it is still not an independent body'.[32]

The Bureau's final report boasted a 21 per cent increase in SDT cases. But though the *Gazette* urged solicitors to comply with the Rule 15 requirement of an in-house complaints procedure, a survey published the following month showed that 20 per cent of firms had none, 40 per cent were unconvinced of its value, and 38 per cent did not inform clients about the SCB. Barnes again called the OSS 'the Law Society's last chance to get complaints handling right'.

[U]nless the professional bodies show themselves able to deliver a higher level of complaint satisfaction than appears to be the case at the present time, I do not think that the major role that they have in dealing with complaints under the existing system will survive into the next century. The demands for a completely independent system would be likely by then to have become irresistible.[33]

At the OSS launch, director Peter Ross said it 'cannot make the mistakes of its predecessor and yet we must not lose sight of the undoubted successes of the SCB'. Anticipating that Labour would win the imminent general election, LS President Girling warned that

Parliament has granted us the power to regulate our own affairs and requires that we do so in the public interest. A new government must be reassured that the profession can be trusted to regulate itself effectively and responsibly. Specifically we must ensure that the reforms we have put in place to improve complaints handling are carried through so that there can be no criticism on that score.

Piloting a client care manual, the OSS wondered whether 'the good firms' should continue to pay for 'those that fail to comply with the required standards'. But if that endeared it to many solicitors, the Office quickly encountered familiar problems. Inadequate funding burdened case workers with 300 open files, to which they responded slowly. The *New Law Journal* warned that both public and profession 'believes that decisions from the Office are slanted in favour of the other'. It urged disclosure of a 'half hidden report' documenting that dilemma. The journal had published reports of numerous complainants who 'feel as though they are being thwarted in their efforts to obtain documents held by the OSS'. At the same time, 'the small practitioner sees the frailties of the large firms seemingly go unpunished'. Ross acknowledged commissioning research that found both complainants and solicitors dissatisfied. 'No great surprise there.' But though 'the existence of this report is not a secret', he would not release it.[34]

Shortly before becoming the second LSO, Ann Abraham said Barnes 'put both the Law Society and the Bar Council on notice that there was very little time to make the systems work'. Although she would 'hold a balance between consumers and providers...even-handedness does not mean neutrality. Consumers are often weaker than providers.' The 'ability to say sorry is something we need to learn'. A month later she reiterated to Mears and Iris Dean that the LSO could not hear solicitor complaints against the OSS and rebuked them for attacking it: 'if solicitors don't have confidence in their own complaint handling body how on earth do they expect the rest of us to?'[35]

The first OSS report in October 1997 attributed delays to 7 per cent more complaints and an outdated computer. Pharaoh challenged 'sceptics' and 'uninformed critics' to substantiate charges that reform was merely cosmetic 'in light of the comprehensive programme for change'. The OSS would award up to £1,000 compensation and reduce a firm's bill for failure to have an effective in-house complaints system (which the Council was considering making evidence of IPS). In less serious cases, firms would have two weeks in which to conciliate complainants and another three to reply to the OSS. The professional press granted the new institution a honeymoon. The *Solicitors Journal* found 'the first taste...quite palatable'; the *New Law Journal* blamed past problems on the SCB and Lowe.

But Mears called the report 'hypocritical'. 'Why should we believe this report as opposed to the previous five years?'

The culture, the attitudes, the arrogance and the complacency that I complained of in the days of the Solicitors Complaints Bureau are no different in the OSS....

The sticking thing is the sameness—all is well, move to conciliation, reform of the computer system.

Assailing the Office's refusal to apologize to Iris Dean, who had defended herself against a client's complaint for eight years, he called both bodies 'rotten through and through' and biased against sole practitioners. The OSS denied bias, attributing the overrepresentation of sole practitioners to the fact that only 66 per cent had in-house complaints systems, compared with 86–93 per cent of partnerships. Mears urged the Council to consider an OSS visitor to whom disciplined solicitors could appeal: 'an independent, effective supervisor to ensure the OSS is doing its job properly'. The *New Law Journal* found this 'a proposal with which it is difficult to argue'.[36]

When Pharaoh denied the change was 'merely cosmetic', Mears revealed that the secret report painted an 'absolutely abysmal' picture: 62 per cent of clients were dissatisfied with the OSS response; 80 per cent of solicitors felt complaints were invalid. The OSS said the report antedated its creation. Mears retorted that the OSS and SCB were 'one and the same body operating from the same building with the same personnel'. Lowe also had claimed that 'everything...was nicely under control, that new improvements were constantly being introduced to produce greater efficiency and that outside criticism was either malicious or ill informed'. Ross not only repeated this but 'avails himself of the additional defence, "Nothing that happened yesterday has anything to do with me".' Pharaoh asked why Mears was 'seeking to discredit the new regime in advance of the evidence'.

Although the proportion of cases more than a year old declined from 50 to 15 per cent in the year after March 1997, complaints rose by 30 per cent. The OSS responded by requiring complainants to exhaust in-house procedures (just half did so) and then contact the OSS within six months. Sayer said only the OSS was surprised by the rising caseload.

Design a complaints system which is like handing out free lottery tickets, always the chance of a win and nothing to lose, continually increase the range of 'offences', publicise it widely during a period when the volume of legal work is increasing and consumers' expectation soaring, and stand back.

Greater resources would be a 'mistake'. 'Most' solicitors felt the OSS already cost 'too much' (£17 million, 31 per cent of the Society budget). It had to 'find a mechanism to give priority to those cases the public considers important'. The National House Building Council charged £50, the Royal Institute of Chartered Surveyors £200 (refunded if successful). 'If complainants are not willing to deposit £50...how seriously should we take them?'

Angus Andrew, another Council member, agreed that the OSS budget was 'spinning out of control'. If complaints continued to increase, 'within two years the office will account for half the PC fee income'. Why should firms with good in-house complaint procedures 'go on subsidising those which refuse to learn those lessons?' He proposed to charge firms that failed to resolve complaints and credit those that succeeded. But critics responded that more complaints 'should not be considered entirely negatively... rising complaints reflect rising consumer expectations, which are widespread across many business sectors'.[37] Research disproved Andrew's (common) assertion that a few bad apples were to blame. A study of sixteen Bristol firms found that most adopted a 'paper procedure' for complaints. One pointed to his waste basket; another could not 'remember when the previous [complaint] was'. Although 'you can't afford to offend commercial clients... a private client very often is just a one-off job....' Small firms found it awkward to investigate colleagues. Solicitors dismissed complainants as 'troubled people', 'mentally deranged or obsessed... the sort of people who will never be satisfied'. 'We do not do anything but run a business'. This 'thing about a learned profession' was 'the stuff of sherry talk'. Solicitors 'ought to have the right to tell someone to bugger off if we judge it is in our interest'. 'I can't think of any other business where the first thing they have to do is tell you how to complain....' The in-house procedure was intended 'to stem the overwhelming mounting tide of complaints'. But it 'only serves to encourage complaints' and 'does the profession a grave disservice'. '[A] significant sector of the profession... still believe it is wholly illegitimate for a client to complain about service quality'. The study confirmed Abraham's view 'that solicitors only embraced rule 15 on paper and not in practice'. The OSS proposed that firms without adequate procedures pay it a fee for handling complaints.[38]

The Law Society's 'three year strategic plan 1998–2000' recycled the optimistic promises that the OSS would 'continue to tackle the backlog of complaints' and 'publicise targets, procedures and progress in order to win back and maintain the confidence of the public, the profession and the Legal Services Ombudsman'. But a June 1998 Fabian Society pamphlet called self-regulation 'an out-dated concept [with] no place in modern Britain', a 'fundamentally flawed... mechanism', which allowed the profession to secure 'significant market advantages'. 'Independent regulation' was 'inevitable'. It recommended splitting the functions of representation and regulation (like the BMA and GMC). The 'new regulatory body should be redominately [*sic*] lay with specialised legal support'. The report was co-authored by a trainee solicitor at a trade union firm, which paid for it and had endeared itself to the Lord Chancellor by supporting his legal aid reforms (see Chapter 8).

Ross said the 'fundamentally flawed' pamphlet showed 'only a limited grasp of the reality of regulation' and offered 'an antiquated structuralist "old Labour" solution which is both naïve and completely off the mark'. (But several months later the SDT chair called for 'more independence' to leave it 'open to much better scrutiny from outside' and funded by fines rather than the Society.) The Society dismissed the pamphlet as 'feeble' and lacking in 'intellectual rigour'. The Society's activities were 'subject to the test of the public interest'. 'Most informed commentators— the consumer organisations and the government—have all said "wait and see" if the OSS has improved the situation before making accusations'. But Abraham warned again: 'if the Bar Council and the Law Society want to [silence] the call for an independent complaints handling body, they have a long way to go and little time to get there'.[39]

The *New Law Journal* (among others) predicted 'the end of self-regulation'. Former LS President Holland, now Personal Investment Authority Ombudsman, said the Financial Services Reform Bill could withdraw regulation of investment activities from professional bodies. The president of the Institute of Chartered Accountants called for an independent overseer of all professions. Arnold Rosen urged 'the creation of a professional disciplinary division of the High Court'. But a LS working party of the three officers and four Council members rejected Anthony Bogan's proposal to create a superregulator over solicitors, barristers, legal executives, licensed conveyancers, banks, estate agents, and building societies.[40]

In her first LSO report, Abraham said the OSS would have to show a 'tangible result' like 'faster turn around times and increased client satisfaction' by the end of 1998. (A contemporaneous study found it 'not uncommon for the complaints process to drag out over two or three years', even up to eight. The SCB kept writing to unresponsive solicitors—nineteen letters to one over nineteen months—and abandoned files for years when staff left.) Many 'problems of the past are still evident', including 'delay', but its new performance targets were 'reasonable'. She wanted to take 'the spotlight off the OSS for a little while'. Solicitors were responsible for 'keeping their clients satisfied'. Those dismissing dissatisfied clients as unreasonable were not 'living in the real world'. Pharaoh called this a 'sobering message'. The *Gazette* supported the OSS proposal to charge firms failing to resolve legitimate complaints, which was 'surely preferable' to 'the handing over of the complaints system to a government controlled body'. Abraham warned that 'the entrenched attitudes demonstrated by individual practitioners' would 'lead to the closed sign finally going up on the doors of the famous last chance saloon'. '[I]nstead of a police force staffed by former house-breakers, the profession needs to see itself as a collaborative neighbourhood watch.' Addressing the Law Society annual conference three months later, Abraham criticized the existing mechanism as 'unwieldy...dense and long' and called for 'a root and branch look at the whole framework'. Asked if there were a 'conspiracy of mediocrity', she replied tartly: 'if only the profession aspired that high'. People believed solicitors were 'arrogant, inaccessible, slow, expensive, won't admit mistakes and won't say sorry'. But 79 per cent of her audience felt *over*regulated.[41]

Exposés put a human face on the statistics. A client won a seven-year battle in which the solicitor twice refused to respond to the complaint for six months and the SCB twice rejected it, ultimately charging only IPS, although a Chancery Master had found evidence of misconduct. Abraham criticized the SCB. And a Channel 4 'Dispatches' programme accused the SDT of failing to strike off the Roll four solicitors convicted of criminal offences involving dishonesty and more than half of seventy-eight who had misused client money. It filmed a struck-off solicitor advising clients. An 'absolutely livid' Law Society complained to the Broadcasting Standards Commission about the 'distorted, unjust and unfair' programme, 'which blurred the distinction between the SDT and the Society'. But a Labour MP planned to ask the Lord Chancellor to instruct the SDT to strike off all solicitors convicted of serious offences. Two days later the *Daily Mail* featured a solicitor investigated for an affair with a client's wife and called adultery 'rife' in the profession.[42]

The OSS failed to meet its 1997–8 target of handling 90 per cent of complaints within three months and the rest in five, handling only 22 and 36 per cent of minor complaints and 53 and 25 per cent of major within those periods. It had a backlog of 3,700 cases at the end of that year (expected to reach 8,000 the next), which it blamed on a 39 per cent rise in complaints while the budget rose by only 19 per cent. In response to a February 1999 question about the OSS, LCD Parliamentary Secretary Geoff Hoon said he was waiting for Abraham's next report. Later that month she told a Labour MP it was 'more than probable' she would conclude that the OSS had failed to make 'necessary' progress. The Home Office minister said he had warned the Law Society: 'if you don't do it we will do it'. The NCC called the Society's roles as trade union and regulator 'incompatible' and its rules 'neither tough nor specific enough'. At the beginning of March the OSS asked the Council for £500,000 to address a backlog of 9,000, growing at ninety-five a week. Ross complained that many 'should have been dealt with by the firms themselves'. But Mears said the problem was 'efficient deployment of resources'. The Council responded a month later by proposing to cut the OSS budget by a third in 2001.[43]

At the end of the Access to Justice Bill Third Reading debate on 16 March, Lord Irvine expressed dismay 'that the performance of the Office for the Supervision of Solicitors seems to be deteriorating' and did not 'rule out the possibility of legislative change'. The following week Hoon said the government was 'developing a reasonable compromise between pure self-regulation and a fully-fledged system of state regulation'. Several weeks later Irvine called the OSS backlog 'fearfully worrying' and told solicitors to stop treating complaints like 'another piece of litigation'. Hoon said during the Commons Second Reading debate a month later that the OSS 'is clearly failing to deal adequately with complaints'. The LSO was 'likely to report that the OSS has failed to make the necessary progress'. Backbench MPs, led by Culture Secretary Chris Smith, were angry about the number of client complaints at their surgeries. President Mathews said the Law Society had commissioned 'an independent review of our complaints handling procedure' from Ernst & Young and would work with the LSO and NCC to solve the problem.[44]

The OSS 1997–8 annual report, published at the end of that month, admitted that complaints were not even assigned to caseworkers for six months, a delay likely to double by the end of the year. Claiming 'considerable progress' in dealing with dishonesty—40 per cent of its workload—the Office opposed diverting resources to complaints. Mathews said 'we need to look closely at the 20 per cent of solicitors' firms which give rise to 80 per cent of complaints'. Trevor Aldridge QC, a solicitor and former law commissioner, suggested charging firms £1,000 for each complaint. The *Solicitors Journal* blamed the 'compensation culture' for 'clients' expectations...out of sync with reality or the sums they are prepared to spend on legal services'. 'The profession cannot afford these escalating costs. The only answer is a radical rethink...whether it be government regulation or a completely new approach by the Law Society.' The *New Law Journal* also saw 'something in the belief that in these litigious days clients have been encouraged to complain' and bemoaned that 'more money will be poured into this Pantagruelian figure [the OSS] until the Government calls enough'.[45]

Renewing his attack on the OSS, Mears declared that 'nothing penetrates its complacency'. The increasing delays resembled 'the world of Jarndyce v. Jarndyce'. '[T]he profession, just for once, should stir itself and take these warnings seriously.' '[F]ollowing his calamitous presidential term' (see Chapter 10), retorted Pharaoh, 'Mears is unlikely to be offered any other outlet for his powers of vituperation'. 'If senior people on the Council hold the OSS in such contempt, why should anyone else feel confidence in it?' Mears insisted that his criticism was 'not a private eccentricity' and accused the Society of 'embarking on yet another rearrangement of the furniture at Leamington Spa'. Dean said 'every solicitor who has ever had dealings with the OSS knows—its standards fall far below those of the solicitors it investigates'. It was unwilling or unable 'to weed out at an early stage those complainants who are malicious, bearing a grudge, self seeking or looking for someone to blame for their own faults'. Regulation had 'become so notorious and unjust as to lower the reputation of solicitors in the opinion of the public and the opinion which solicitors have not only of the OSS but also of the LS itself'. An 'impeccable source' told her 'the Law Society would welcome the end of sole practitioners'. 'Perhaps this is why the weekly publication of the proceedings of the Disciplinary Tribunal in the *Gazette* almost always involve sole practitioners who have made some trivial accounting error....' 'The accounts of large firms are never investigated routinely....' A 'truly independent system of regulation' would give 'sole practitioners and small firms...a level playing field' and let them 'express their dissatisfaction by leaving an organisation notable for extravagance and folly'.[46]

Toward the end of June, Ernst & Young reported that the Society's neglect had allowed the situation 'to develop and to continue unchecked', raising 'serious concerns about issues of governance and accountability'. Contrary to Mathews's claim, half of all firms were responsible for 80 per cent of complaints. It recommended increased sanctions for firms failing to handle complaints, assignment of most cases to senior staff, and additional case workers (twenty-three permanent, eighty-two temporary and support and supervisory staff and senior managers) at an estimated cost of £1.4 million in 1999 and £4.3 million in 2000, to reduce 'live complaints' to 6,000 by early 2001. The Council quickly agreed. Promising 'the Society will take ownership of this problem and its solution', Mathews maintained 'there is the will, both at the society and the OSS, to get the system right'. The three officers declared: 'We want a system which works quickly, efficiently, and fairly'. Ross thought the report had 'useful value in bringing together different strands'. Philip Hamer, chair of the OSS Review Task Force, said 'the good news is that Ernst and Young believe the necessary improvements...are achievable by December 2000'. But Abraham called the report 'damning', a 'serious indictment' of the Society; 'the problem is worse than I thought'. She was sceptical that the Society 'will actually deliver given its performance in the past'. Calling the £120,000 report 'a complete waste of money', Mears said IPS complaints should be heard by courts, not the OSS.

The media were merciless. The OSS was 'crisis hit' (*Guardian*), 'ailing' (*The Times*). 'The problems reflect the deep-seated and out-of-date attitudes within the profession' (*Financial Times*). The *Gazette* declared the 'good news' that the problem was 'not intractable' and resolving it 'would strengthen the Society's position in dealing with the government and would help enormously in burnishing the image of solicitors with the public'. But the *New Law Journal* denounced the OSS as 'a running sore virtually since its inception', which 'cannot even manage to count accurately the number of complaints it handles'.[47]

During the AJA Commons Report Stage on 22 June the Government tabled clauses to empower the LSO to make binding orders (since some lawyers had defied it) and the Lord Chancellor to compel professional bodies to pay for LSO reviews. The Bill would also empower the Lord Chancellor to appoint a Legal Services Complaints Commissioner (likely to be the LSO), who could investigate, recommend arrangements for handling complaints, set targets, produce plans for improvement, and impose fines for non-compliance. 'The Lord Chancellor would use those powers only after a great deal of thought and with a great deal of reluctance' and wait for the OSS annual report of Spring 2001. Although the Government considered direct regulation (like the FSA), 'self-regulation remains the best option for the legal professions, whose members must at times oppose the Government strenuously in pursuit of citizens' rights'. 'There are signs the Law Society wants to put its own house in order.' Edward Garnier asked Keith Vaz for 'actual evidence, as opposed to simple assertion that the position changed so dramatically between the beginning of the year and now'. The Society already spent £11.6 million annually on the OSS and had budgeted another £5.7 million. The 'standard of client care provided by the profession' had 'been steadily improving'. There was a 'whole new culture'. Rising complaints simply reflected 'increased client expectations' and 'much-improved information from solicitors about clients' avenues of complaint'. There was only 'a small minority of rotten apples in what is otherwise a well-regulated and well-conducted profession'. He urged solicitors to 'follow the example of the three major acute [*sic*] hospitals ... by persuading the complaining client ... that there are two sides to the argument and that it is possible to admit a mistake without admitting legal liability'. Noting that the OSS had just reported 'the staggering fact that just over 75,000 solicitors generated more than 44,000 new matters', David Kidney 'welcome[d] the threat ... to the Law Society', the 'sword of Damocles hanging over solicitors'. The clauses were agreed.[48]

A week later, Abraham's annual report offered a 'serious indictment of the Law Society' for having 'allowed things to reach a crisis before taking action'. She remained sceptical that it 'has the commitment and the determination to do what is necessary'. 'Some solicitors will have to learn a whole new way of behaving—looking at things from the client's point of view. ...' She did 'not believe there is a population of solicitors' clients who complain for a living'. Her previous warning had 'gone unheeded' and her prediction had 'become a reality'. The 'entire operation has descended to the level of farce'. The AJA provision for a Legal Services Complaints Commissioner 'is a sharp reminder that self-regulation within the legal profession is a privilege, not a right—and a privilege that can be taken away'. She called for separation of 'the representative function and the complaints-handling function' so that 'any possible suspicion of financial or ideological subordination to professional hegemony would be finally dispelled'.

The media turned up the volume: 'Law Society rapped over complaints' (*Daily Telegraph*), 'Lawyers' toothless watchdog' (*Guardian*), 'Sloppy lawyers who let down the public' (*Express*). Under the headline 'One law for us, one for them', the *News of the World* deplored that a lawyer on probation for sexual assault still headed his own firm: 'His is a profession which looks after its own'. The *Solicitors Journal* conceded much of the criticism was 'deserved'. The *New Law Journal* ridiculed the Society's claim 'for the umpteenth time, that they have turned the corner, seized the initiative, grasped the nettle'.[49]

A week later the OSS admitted it had again missed its target of handling 90 per cent of complaints within a month, dealing with only 36 per cent of minor and 42 per cent of serious complaints. On 23 July, LCD Parliamentary Secretary Keith Vaz threatened to 'name and shame' firms with the worst records—one had 400 complaints a year—and urged the Society to identify those with over 100. Sayer (just elected LS President) was 'not against naming and shaming the cut price conveyancer because they have made a conscious decision to provide a poor service regardless of the outcome'. He and the other officers planned to address the House of Commons on complaints that autumn.[50]

That day, however, *The Times* published a letter Ross had just written, returning a complaint and promising to contact the client when the OSS had cleared its 17,000-case backlog. (Others said it was 25,000 and rising by 300 a week.) 'We currently lack the resources we need to deal effectively with all our work.' 'I appreciate that this information may come as a shock to you and I am sorry if this adds to your worries and concerns generally.' The OSS had sent dozens of such letters without telling the Society. Indeed, Vice-President Bahl assured the press the same day that they were determined to reduce the backlog to 6,000 by the end of 2000 and deal with all new complaints within three months. The Society immediately suspended Ross.

Vaz called the Government 'very concerned indeed at the high level of complaints and we want to see evidence of action or we have made clear that we will set up a statutory-backed Legal Services Complaints Commission'. Irvine gave Sayer a schedule for eliminating the backlog, warning that failure would leave him 'with very little alternative but to implement the Commissioner provisions', which he would do earlier if performance deteriorated. Calling the target 'perfectly reasonable', Sayer even claimed 'the government was happy with the Law Society's own deadlines'. Secretary-General Jane Betts took 'direct management control' of the OSS and launched an 'urgent' investigation of Ross's letter. Mears called Ross 'just a stooge... thrown overboard to conceal the Society's own inadequacies'. '[A]ll his initiatives and business plans, have been agreed by the Secretary-General and rubber-stamped by the Society's Council.' The claim to be hiring 100 new caseworkers was 'complete fantasy'; and it was 'palpably' impossible to clear new cases in three months. 'Complaints about the quality of legal work are a complicated business. They need to be investigated properly.' The *Solicitors Journal* also doubted whether Ross, 'a member of the Society's management committee and frequent visitor to Chancery Lane', was 'really acting alone'. The pretence of OSS independence had been exposed as 'a way of the Society avoiding control and avoiding responsibility'. The chair of the committee overseeing the OSS resigned (and left the Council) because he had not been consulted about the suspension of Ross, who should be given 'the opportunity to put his side of the story'.

Maintaining a brave face, Sayer declared 'we are taking a more imaginative and bold approach' and asking solicitors to handle complaints 'quickly and cleanly'. OSS morale was up because 'now for the first time' they had 'a clear way forward approved by the Lord Chancellor and the ombudsman and backed up by Ernst & Young, a new casework director and the Secretary-General'. Betts declared that within forty-eight hours complaints would be sent to solicitors, who would have twenty-one days to handle them or be guilty of IPS. 'Most of these complaints should be resolved by firms, even if it means giving clients a small amount of financial compensation.' Although the OSS claimed to have hired ten new caseworkers, Mears said they were just transferred from the anti-fraud section. Less than a month after the scandal broke Ross resigned.[51]

The *New Law Journal* deplored this 'repeat of the Veronica Lowe saga'. In 'Stalinist' fashion the Council had backed both directors 'unreservedly' in the face of criticism, only to purge them ruthlessly when it became politically expedient. Instead of cutting the OSS budget by a third, as it had promised, the Council was increasing it by half. The journal blamed the Council for 'creating a complaints culture' in which the profession is 'chastised by [*sic*] not behaving like a supermarket and handing out fifty pence if the milk was sour or a letter went unanswered'. The problem was 'professional malcontents'. 'Not a few complainants hope to have a few pounds knocked off the bill just for writing a couple of letters.' If they were treated like grocers, solicitors should behave accordingly. 'If you don't like the grapefruit at Asda then you go to Waitrose, you don't complain to the Supermarket Association'. In a complete *volte face*, Sayer now championed clients. 'The new consumer culture is a fact of life. Indeed, more active consumers can be good for a solicitor's business.' This was 'the most serious issue' of his presidency. The *Financial Times* declared the Society 'must refuse to tolerate roguery and inefficiency, revoking lawyers' practising certificates, if they fail to co-operate, or are found to have traduced their clients'. When Vaz urged the Society to name the 1 per cent of firms generating 10 per cent of complaints, Sayer thought this appropriate against those providing 'shamelessly shoddy service', though not a firm that was a 'victim of circumstance'. The Society endorsed increasing IPS compensation to £5,000 and making those guilty of serious misconduct pay the costs of prosecution.[52]

The OSS commissioned an evaluation from Professor Avrom Sherr about the same time as the Society hired Ernst & Young. In mid-September the *New Law Journal* leaked Sherr's 'catalogue of mismanagement and

depression'. Quality was 'at best diffuse and uncoordinated' and 'at worst...
either willfully ignored or subjected to a "willing blindness" whereby talk
of client-focus and quality service is simply window dressing'. Papers essential to appellate review were missing. 'There was a blanket policy of considering and then refusing requests for an oral hearing'. The journal
concluded that 'the only thing which has counted at the OSS has been
clearing files'. 'Have we any reason to think things are better and will continue to improve...?' Sayer wrote to every member, denying that 'the main
Law Society (by which I mean the Secretary-General, management team,
Office Holders and the IEC)' knew anything about the report. In May,
Sherr had given a draft to the OSS, which did not inform the 'main Law
Society' until July. The journal asked incredulously: 'was Mr Ross a member of the management team?' Mears likened the Society to 'an inveterate
debtor, begging his creditors to believe that this time his cheques really
aren't going to bounce'.[53]

Three weeks later Sayer claimed the OSS backlog had declined by 500
cases (3 per cent!). 'We are sorting things out. Morale among the staff at
Leamington Spa is much better now....' A third of firms were resolving
complaints within twenty-one days and another third were trying. 'The
remaining third...will get a strong letter warning them that we will call in
the file and deal with the matter ourselves.' He told firms: 'don't act like a
lawyer, understand the client's point of view, empathise with them and try
and sort it out'. The OSS hired forty-five staff. Vaz was 'reassured'; but
Mears asked: 'How can anyone believe a word they say?'[54]

At the Society's October conference Sayer called for a takeover of the Bar.

Within five years, let there be one legal profession. No more solicitors or barristers,
just lawyers, with one code of conduct, one set of rules, one regulator...if we have
a universal code of conduct, we may as well have one body to police that code. The
Law Society is the obvious choice. We already regulate the biggest single legal
profession and we do it well.

There were only 18,000 complaints a year to the OSS, which had not risen by
30 per cent. (Four months earlier Abraham reported 30,900 complaints in
1998, up 14 per cent from the previous year.) 'I will make sure that the OSS
deals with complaints efficiently and in a way which is fair to both sides....'

A Bar spokesperson called this 'a Mickey Mouse policy dreamt up in
Disneyland' (where the Society had met). Even APIL's president thought
the Society was 'on pretty thin ice to think it can regulate every other part
of the profession when it does not seem to be doing a good job itself'. LCD
Parliamentary Secretary David Lock reiterated that failure to correct 'the
lamentable state of complaints handling' would lead to government regulation, 'perhaps along the lines of the one operated by the Financial
Services Authority', for which the profession would pay.[55]

B. Malpractice and Default

The late 1980s recession appeared to increase malpractice and default, aggravating conflict among solicitors. Premiums for indemnity coverage increased from £7 million in 1976 to £52.3 million in 1986. Just when the Society launched its mutual Solicitors Indemnity Fund (SIF) in 1987, it joined professional associations of barristers, engineers, patent agents, accountants, architects and chartered surveyors to ask the government to investigate the rising cost of professional liability. Because the value of SCF claims rose nearly *tenfold* from 1985 to 1990 (£1.876 million to £18.3 million), it quadrupled contributions (from £30 to £125) and imposed special assessments of £515 in 1988 and £295 in 1990. Angry solicitors and local law societies called for its abolition.

Sole practitioners generated almost all the SCF claims (83, 93, and 97 per cent of firms in 1987–9). They also burdened SIF: the ratio of premiums to payouts was 9 to 16 per cent for sole practitioners but 14 to 7 per cent for firms with more than twenty-four partners. The Society's working party on sole practitioners proposed management training and better reporting of late delivery of accountants' reports.

The BLA chair objected that 'statistics can be manipulated...like all generalisations, using these figures as a basis of policy would be unfair to the majority of small practitioners'. The *New Law Journal* warned that restrictions on sole practitioners and two-partner firms 'are in the interests of neither the profession nor the public'. The *Solicitors Journal* lauded 'the vast majority' of sole practitioners as 'honest, hard-working people who make an important contribution to their local community'. But local law societies convinced the Council to order that firms filing accountants' reports two weeks late be investigated and submit them semi-annually.[56]

Tensions rose. Because SIF's expected 1991–2 payout was twice the prediction, premiums rose 34 per cent. Although discounts were eliminated for firms with over twenty-four partners (who no longer contributed disproportionately), LS President Ely asked whether 'the competent and efficient are subsidising the inefficient and incompetent' and suggested raising the deductible from £5,000 to £20,000. (It increased to 1 per cent of gross fees, up to £150,000 a claim.) Ely declared that solicitors 'cannot continue the way we are' and 'need to look afresh and critically at the assumption that we as a profession will pay for dishonesty wherever and however caused'. 'Can we go into the 1990s with an uncapped fund?'[57]

The SCF's plight was even more dire. Defaults rose from twenty in 1964 to seventy-five in 1992. Although SCF paid out less than £1 million annually from 1964 to 1979 and less than £2 million through 1986, 1992 claims were £58.6 million (most concerning mortgage fraud). Contributions rose from £125 in 1990 to £600 for principals in 1993 (£445 for other solicitors holding client funds and £150 for all others). A third special assessment of £1,000 was imposed that year and another was expected the next. A former chair of the Society of Black Lawyers called this levy 'the straw that will break the back of small practitioners...we should be questioning... whether small practitioners should be supporting big [lending] institutions'. The *New Law Journal* thought 'the professional may well decide that the time has come for the institutional clients—at least in part—to look out for themselves'.

The Council's June 1992 *Cost of Default* consultation paper declared the burden 'intolerable' (estimated at £20 million for each of 1992 and 1993) and blamed 'principally the defaults of sole practitioners'. A 'key question must be the terms on which sole practice should be allowed to continue if the guarantee of the rest of the profession is still to underwrite it'. The working party chair declared that 'those who cause blame should bear responsibility for putting things right'. The paper proposed to inspect each solo practice biannually. (A 1991 pilot study of twenty-five found rule breaches in all, serious enough in seven for referral to the SCB.) Although excluding institutional claims would have saved only 18 per cent during the previous five years, the paper considered capping payments. But 'limitation of payments to private clients would involve damage to the profession's reputation which the Council would be reluctant to entertain'. Solicitors 'proud[ly] boast' they collectively insure the public against harm. 'Any retreat from that position would weaken the right of solicitors to be seen as a profession as opposed to a trade....'

Arnold Rosen said sole practitioners resented 'the way we are being singled out and think the decision if carried out will be subject to judicial review'; and a former BLA chair called it 'victimization'. But a three-partner firm did not 'see why we should subsidise bent commercial lawyers and sole practitioners'. Another firm declared there was 'no justification... [for] honest and innocent solicitors to compensate people in full who have had their money stolen by solicitors'. It wrote to every local law society calling for abolition of the SCF; only one of the twenty societies and twenty firms responding favoured retention. But though the *New Law Journal* said 'the cost to the legal profession of continuing to bail out dishonest and incompetent solicitors has become unacceptable', both it and the *Solicitors Journal* expressed concern for sole practitioners.[58]

The Halifax Building Society responded to the proposed cap on institutional payments by threatening to prune its conveyancing panel and charge for membership. Three other lenders took similar steps, targeting sole practitioners. The Bristol & West found 'most offensive' a letter 'suggesting that it is a matter for the Society to say which solicitor a client should instruct'. The Leeds Permanent's chief solicitor claimed that 'the Law Society want to get rid of sole practitioners but are frightened to do it'.

This was 'a backdoor method'. The Council of Mortgage Lenders threatened institutional conveyancing.

The nearly 1,000 responses to the consultation favoured caps on institutional claims by a 'substantial' majority and on individual by less. But though 80 per cent of sole practitioners naturally opposed restrictions on themselves, 78 per cent of firms with more than nine partners and 70 per cent of local law societies were favourable. The Council rejected caps but planned to require lenders to investigate borrowers. Its final report recommended more visits by the Monitoring Unit, semi-annual reports by some firms, action on reports more than fourteen days late, a Fraud Intelligence Officer, investigation of firms with poor SCB complaints records, and reduced payments to careless lenders, but no cap, which 'would adversely affect the reputation of solicitors by penalising the innocent victims of dishonesty'.[59]

Although SIF kept premiums constant in 1993–4, an insurance lawyer urged replacing it with mandatory private coverage. '[G]ood firms are being penalised for the failings of the bad. If we were beholden to the market this would put dishonest or negligent solicitors out of business fairly quickly....' Even though SIF had granted large firms discounts of up to 15 per cent in 1992 and increased sole practitioner premiums an average of 31 per cent, large firms (like his) were still 'subsidising the smaller firms to a considerable degree'. SIF reported that firms with one to three principals contributed too little, those with four to fifty too much, and larger firms fairly. The following year SIF proposed reducing contributions for low risk specializations. But a year after that the Criminal Law Solicitors Association complained that 'SIF refuses to countenance a realistic charge for low risk work' even though no claim had been made against a criminal practitioner since its founding. Asserting that some criminal solicitors could be insured for £12.98 a year, he declared: 'I am about to write a cheque for £4,475 when I should be writing one for less than £26'. SIF reduced premiums by only 5 per cent for each 10 per cent of gross fees derived from criminal work. The CLSA asked members if they wanted to leave SIF.[60]

SCF claims fell nearly £20 million in 1993, although defaults increased from seventy-five to eighty-six and payouts from £14.7 million to £29 million (102 defaults costing £33 million in 1994). Maximum contributions increased from £600 to £1,000. The senior partner of a large Sussex firm pleaded guilty to taking £7 million from clients; another solicitor had taken up to £8 million. The SCB Monitoring Unit's increased investigations found client money at risk or rule violations in more than half the firms visited in both 1993 and 1994. A solicitor complained that 'we are the only profession that provides this cover but the public don't give us any credit for it'. A City solicitor opposed compensating lenders 'because between 1987–89 they threw money at the property market in a reckless and irresponsible manner'. But the default working party chair was reasonably confident 'we are getting the situation under control for the long term'.[61]

Secretary-General Hayes warned it might 'only be a matter of time before the well-organised firms who bring in their wake fewer claims and fewer complaints rebel'. The Society could 'protect the public and serve the profession at the same time' only by displaying 'willingness at times to alienate members of your own profession'. But the *Solicitors Journal* criticized him for failing to 'consider how the recession has widened the gaps between different parts of the profession'. It noted YSG anger at firms' claims against five assistant solicitors for SIF deductibles and warned that inaction 'could lead to the YSG developing a trade union role for its members'. A year later, when claims reached forty, the YSG presented a petition signed by 3,200 to LS President Pannone, who agreed they were 'totally unacceptable'. A year after that the YSG, supported by the TSG, AWS, and Freelance Solicitors Group, filed a test case challenging a judgment against an assistant.[62]

In 1995 the SPG deputy chair criticized the weighting of indemnity premiums, claiming that 'there is no evidence that sole practitioners run up more negligence actions than partnerships'. (SIF said the previous year firms with fewer than four partners contributed 30 per cent of premiums but produced 50 per cent of the value of claims.) Although the Society agreed the SPG could scrutinize SIF's books, 'nothing has been done because the group has effectively been emasculated by the Law Society'. Since claims were down 7 per cent and the average payout more than 50 per cent, SIF expected to cut rates by 10 per cent for practices grossing over £500,000, angering the Council's sole practitioner representative.[63]

By 1996 the SCF crisis seemed over. Because 1995 payouts had been just half the estimated £37 million (and were expected to fall another £4 million in 1996), and claims declined from 2,298 worth £47 million in 1994 to a projected 1,350 worth £23 million in 1996, SCF sought revenue of just £9 million (down from £33 million in 1995). Contributions dropped from £1,000 to £250 in 1996 and £100 in 1997 (£30 for assistant and employed solicitors). At the same time, SCF reported more interventions and inspections, less compliance with accounts rules, a higher proportion of adverse reports, and monitored firms violating rules or risking client money.[64]

SIF, by contrast, remained deeply troubled. Because 'the many were currently subsidising the few', an LS standards and guidance committee consultation paper proposed to proportion premiums to the number of claims, nature of work, and deductibles, increasing them by at least 5 per cent for some 200 firms and 200 per cent for forty while decreasing them by 80 per cent for a few, 20 per cent for 2,250, and less for another 3,800. Specialists in criminal law, children, mental health, debt collection, welfare, and immigration would benefit. Those who missed time limits would have

50 per cent higher deductibles. The City firm Holman Fenwick & Willan objected that 'most of the claims on the SIF are from small firms and those doing conveyancing'. It had obtained a private quotation that was 'a good deal cheaper'. SIF retorted that commercial insurance would cost £260–£280 million, compared with its £195 million budget.[65]

In June 1996 the Council raised all premiums 4.5 per cent (the first time since 1991). Less than four months later SIF disclosed it had miscalculated liabilities by £13 million and needed another 7.5 per cent. Chair Andrew Kennedy promised an inquiry. Mears called it a 'mind-boggling blunder'; a commercial company would not be able to demand an increase. Clive Boxer, a City insurance solicitor, added that private insurance 'proved an extremely effective means of regulating standards'. Sayer accused SIF of miscalculating premiums for 1,500 firms. He and Mears called for an independent commission to reconsider SIF's monopoly. But the Council approved the request.[66]

Three months later SIF admitted it needed another £248 million and might have to raise premiums by 30 per cent for five years. Mears said the 'colossal' increase would be 'a devastating blow for high street firms' and asked 'the entire SIF board to resign'. LS President Girling called this demand 'premature and misplaced'. When SIF investigated its forecasting methods, Mears and Sayer criticized the inquiry's membership. Boxer termed the shortfall 'a time bomb waiting to explode'.

Unlike the commercial insurance market, SIF increases rates only after a claim has been paid out, not when potential claims arise.... If you don't allow the market to rate the perceived risk, the good will end up carrying the bad.

'The SIF needs to be more rebust [*sic*] about claims', pronounced the *Solicitors Journal*. 'There is anecdotal evidence that it is a soft touch.' It should appoint 'roving trouble-shooters to go into firms who have a bad record to help them improve their performance' and require CPD on avoiding negligence. Specialist panel members should receive premium discounts.[67]

Four months after that SIF released more bad news: the previous seven years' shortfall was £454.5 million. To pay £42.5 million of this and meet its 1997–8 budget of £269.9 million (up from £184.9 million the previous year) it requested an 80 per cent increase. At the same time, it sought greater equity by raising the maximum low-claims discount for criminal specialists and larger firms from 20 to 35 per cent. LS VP Sycamore supported the latter proposal 'for ensuring that good solicitors no longer end up paying for the bad, the persistently negligent, the unrepentantly incompetent solicitors'; but 'abolishing and attacking SIF on a knee-jerk reaction is no answer'. BLA chair Alex Alagappa agreed that 'as much as possible of an additional expense must be visited on those solicitors with the worst claims record. If anyone is going to the wall, let it be the most negligent in the profession.' Boxer blamed the debacle on 'the failure to anticipate the property collapse and the mortgage fraud problems'. He quoted the former LS director of professional standards: 'The real issue is whether the profession remains sufficiently homogeneous to enable it to find its indemnity within a single pool of risk'. Mears said 'even SIF accepts there were black clouds on the horizon'. 'The majority [of solicitors] find themselves in a club where they are compelled to subsidise the subscriptions and bar bills of the minority.' The 450 firms paying the maximum doubled premium still cost the fund more than ten times as much. Blaming the problem on cut-rate conveyancing, he urged that insurance be charged by the transaction (and passed on to the borrower).

Declaring that 'many a solicitor...has felt aggrieved that he has been obliged to support his dishonest brethren whom the Society has proved unable to spot or, if they have spotted, unable to root out in time', the *New Law Journal* called private insurance the solution. 'In the longer term, there is surely going to have to be judicial intervention into the affairs of the Society.' Lord Woolf should 'take the naughty schoolboys on the Council in hand'. The *Solicitors Journal* agreed that 'pressure to allow firms to buy their own insurance may become overwhelming'. SIF should limit liability. 'What can better afford the loss? The massive building society with billions of assets or the sole practitioner paying 12.55 per cent of his gross costs in premiums?' Sycamore agreed that the 'key task is to prevent lenders leeching on the Indemnity Fund'. Although the Council rejected the independent review sought by Sycamore and Mears, Sycamore appointed a task force when he was elected president in July. The BLA accused the Society of attempting to 'whitewash' the situation.[68]

Warning that nearly doubling the premiums of firms with the worst claims records would make them 'more slipshod as they rush through cut-price conveyancing to try to get fees in to pay the contributions', Patrick Stevens wanted to abolish SIF. A week later the City firm Dibb Lupton Alsop claimed private insurance would save it £200–£300,000 annually. The *Gazette* thought it was 'articulating the feelings of many of the largest firms'. William King of Macfarlanes, former president of the City of London Law Society, warned that its members were 'no longer prepared to be associated with the inadequacies of others in the profession'. The current president agreed members were 'peeved' but could absorb premium increases. The responsible Clifford Chance partner worried about deductibles and repudiation in the private market. SIF was only a seventh of his firm's professional indemnity costs, and the additional £600,000 premium 'is not enough to cause a blip in the graph'. A Freshfields senior partner doubted that many would follow Dibb Lupton's call to leave SIF.[69]

Although Sayer (now DVP) thought it 'stupid' to assume that 'claims will continue to rise at the current rate' and urged an increase of no more than

10 per cent, the Council raised premiums by 50 per cent at the recommendation of its standards and guidance committee and SIF task force. Leslie Dubow of the Solicitors Property Group told the Law Society AGM that SIF was 'completely incompetent'. The audience cheered his tirade: 'If you ask for information you don't get it. They have got away with it and it appears that the council is covering up for them and that is intolerable.' He seconded the BLA call for an independent inquiry. At the Society's annual conference SIF said it was considering re-entering the reinsurance market, which it had left in 1991 because premiums increased. A solicitor commented that the 'market was telling you in the clearest possible way that you were getting it wrong in 1991'. John Appleby, LS indemnity insurance review group chair, agreed any alternative 'must be fairer than the current one. There is a feeling that the good are paying for the bad'.[70]

In January 1998 Appleby's group recommended three premium tiers associated with diminishing risk: conveyancing, matrimonial, and criminal. Firms with bad claims records would be encouraged to improve but might ultimately lose cover and hence practising certificates. Only the SPG chair objected: 'sole practitioners and small firms which do high and medium risk work, but have good claims records, will face enormous increases in their premiums'. Although the large-firm members reluctantly concurred, the Hammond Suddards partner preferred private insurance, which would be exempt from the Society's 'political interference' and set premiums 'on an appraisal of [a firm's] management procedures, rather than by its gross fee income'. A (self-interested) insurance broker said commercial firms could save 40–67 per cent in the private market.

The November Group of fifteen City firms threatened to sue the Society if prevented from opting out. David McIntosh (a City insurance specialist) accused the group of 'tilting at windmills'. Appleby predicted judicial review would fail and private insurance would cost 30 per cent more. Mears retorted it was 'almost axiomatic that in the long term the customer does better in a free market than in a central planning system or in a monopoly situation'. Only those solicitors 'who ought to find difficulty' getting insurance would do so. The *New Law Journal* concurred: 'if solicitors have such a bad track record that they cannot obtain insurance for what amounts to less than around a dozen conveyances then they should not be in practice or, if they are, the other members should not be supporting them'.

Conveyancers were even angrier. Accusing the Law Society of 'discussing in secret proposals for the future of the SIF', Dubow asked: 'What is there to hide?' He extolled 'true mutuality' and condemned tiers: 'not so many years ago...a Law Society President used the title "One Profession" as a unifying motif for his annual conference address'. A 'further increase in overheads would sound the death knell for solicitor involvement' in conveyancing, which 'is still core work for most high street firms'. The proposal was 'an ill advised and badly thought out panic measure which has been cobbled together for the benefit of the largest firms'. A 'small practice' invited others to report racial and ethnic discrimination by SIF. The *Gazette* agreed that 'the one profession ethos faces its sternest test yet'.[71]

The November Group called the Council consultation paper's endorsement of Appleby's proposals 'progress' but not the answer. Sayer said 'SIF has proved itself absolutely incapable of running the fund in the last few years' and ridiculed its 'claim that there is no evidence that low priced conveyancing posed any risk'. Six years ago it was 'the highest risk field' because 'lenders lent recklessly, house prices collapsed and they looked for ways to claw back their losses'. SIF's annual report showed that conveyancing generated more than 40 per cent of claims. Fearing private insurance could be 'an expensive mistake', he urged SIF to hire or consult a mutual insurance expert. Its chair replied frostily: 'Mr Sayer complains over and over again about SIF's apparent refusal to "take advice". He clearly means that SIF has not taken his own advice and I leave the profession to determine whether the proper reaction is concern or relief'.[72]

If Sayer saw the crisis as a chance to eliminate cut-price conveyancing, others were apprehensive. The *New Law Journal* declared that 'the very small practitioner...has, in the main, had an honourable part to play in the supply of legal advice to the poorer section of the general population. The lower echelons of the profession should not be allowed to wither and die....' If the Council adopted risk banding (increasing premiums up to 470 per cent) and proportioned premiums to gross fees, the SPyG would seek review by the Master of the Rolls (who had rejected the latter in 1984). SIF replied: 'This issue is not about small or large firms....' The Council voted by 52 to six for risk banding and increased the maximum low claims discount from 30 to 65 per cent. (SIF Director Angus Andrew said criminal lawyers had been subsidizing conveyancers by £53 million a year.) Contending that 'fee income does not necessarily reflect risk' and the decision 'would constitute a tax or compulsory subsidy on small practices for the benefit of large', the SPyG obtained Lord Woolf's permission to make representations against it. Noting that conveyancers no longer ran the risks of the early 1990s, Sayer now worried 'we are going to wipe out huge chunks of the profession'.[73]

Sole practitioner Michael Dalton sought judicial review of SIF's monopoly after it doubled his premium to £18,000 because of his previous firm's poor claims record. He had been quoted £3–£4,000 on the private market. The SPyG asked members for £100 so that it could seek leave to apply for judicial review of risk banding. Dubow warned that 'if you do a lot of conveyancing you could end up paying 20 per cent of your gross fees to the SIF'. The 2,000 members of the City of London Law Society wanted SIF 'terminated as quickly as possible'. Although SIF's directors dismissed this as 'the view of just one group', the CLLS president said all big firms agreed, even Clifford Chance, whose member, Michael Mathews, was LS President. The CLLS accused SIF of 'insulat[ing] solicitors from the consequences of poor practice'. Allen & Overy's managing partner agreed 'SIF is run to meet the political priorities of the profession'.[74]

The risk-banded premiums shocked many. A firm that had been sued by a building society for millions lost in the property slump was billed £118,000 plus VAT on a turnover of £430,000. A sole practitioner with no claims saw his premium jump from £8,000 to £14,000. London sole practitioner Wendy Gray knew two women who left practice 'primarily because of the SIF'. Solicitors were requalifying as licensed conveyancers, who paid 8.45 per cent of gross fees for insurance. Soon after the new bills arrived the Council announced that the 1,175 individual responses to its consultation favoured the mutual fund over an approved insurers scheme by nearly three to one (varying from five to one among firms with eleven to twenty-five partners and two to one among those with two to four to one to two among those with more than twenty-five), as did 19 of 27 local law societies and the YSG; the SPyG was of 'two minds'. The November Group criticized mutuality for offering the same insurance to 'Sainsburys and Mr Patel's excellent corner shop'. Its founder warned that firms like Linklaters, Eversheds, Dibb Lupton Alsop, and Hammond Suddards might seek judicial review of SIF's monopoly. SIF was 'deeply troubled' (*Daily Telegraph*), 'controversial' (*Evening Standard*). But the *Solicitors Journal* wanted risk banding given a chance. The following month sixty-nine smaller firms (including Dalton) launched the Millenium Group, led by Wendy Gray, to seek an open market. 'Desperate' members were 'being forced out of business'. It wanted a Society SGM to demand an 'independent and thorough investigation of the formation and conduct of SIF from its inception to date'. *The Times* warned (against the evidence) that the new premiums could double the price of conveyancing.[75]

In September Mears moved that solicitors be allowed to obtain insurance from approved providers in two years. The Millenium and November Groups considered joining the SPyG and CLLS in support. Sayer turned against SIF because individualized premiums violated the insurance principle. But SIF feared it would become a dumping ground for high-risk firms if others could opt out. The Council rejected Mears's motion but considered combining mutual and approved insurers. All three officers preferred the market if SIF could not offer competitive rates.[76]

A partner in Linklaters (which belonged to the November Group) criticized the consultation for failing to weight firm responses by size. The Millenium Group offered to 'assist our members who want to come out of the SIF this year', claiming this would be only 'a theoretical breach' of the practice rules. It sought a Law Society SGM on opting out. SIF said the Group represented 'just a small number of firms'. A Council member accused risk banding of producing 'grotesque results. How can it be right for one sole practitioner to be paying the same as an eight-partner firm?' Premiums had increased by 25 per cent for 2,302 firms, 50 per cent for 1,589, 75 per cent for 1,261, and 'a staggering 100%' for 768. They would be 'the downfall of many firms with good records' and cause 'a complete disintegration of the network of firms which has traditionally been the backbone of legal services'. Although the *Daily Telegraph* usually found it 'hard to work up much sympathy for lawyers... in this case they seem to have a point'—especially the large firms.[77]

Wendy Gray criticized the November Group for not supporting an SGM because 'big firms don't face the prospect of being forced out of business'. The SPyG abandoned judicial review on counsel's advice. But Dalton (represented by Cherie Booth QC) obtained leave to seek judicial review on the ground that SIF violated the Treaty of Rome. Based on his turnover of £350,000, SIF had billed him £68,000, compared with private quotations of £12–£14,000. The Law Society received nearly twice as many indemnity waiver applications in the last four months of 1998 as in all of 1997.[78]

At the beginning of 1999 insurance experts Aon advised the Council that a mutual fund could coexist with the market if all solicitors contributed to a contingency fund or SIF were guaranteed a market share. Unappeased, the Millenium Group called the first SGM since 1992. The CLLS president termed the Aon report the 'nail in the coffin' because it showed that SIF could survive only through compulsion. Accusing the Society of being 'more concerned with the needs of small firms than running a proper insurance company', Allen & Overy's managing partner saw no 'logic' in a mandatory contribution. 'Each firm should pay what it needs to get insurance cover.' A survey found that 60 per cent of the top 100 firms preferred the market.[79]

SIF Director Andrew said the November Group's 'legitimate grievances' had been 'largely addressed by risk banding' and deplored that 'the most affluent sector of the profession has found itself unable to take a more inclusive view of the problems faced by the profession'. Despite 'enormous sympathy' for the Millenium Group, he said its constituency had been 'responsible for much of the profession's negligence but... is not prepared to accept collective responsibility for its actions'. SIF's bad management was a 'myth' and its costs 'substantially less' than private insurers' (partly because it paid no insurance tax). Solicitors were being seduced by a private market temporarily 'awash with capital—much of it from the US... [which] is driving down premiums to a level that, in the long term, are [*sic*] not sustainable'.[80]

In January the Council again rejected a motion to abolish SIF, proposed by Mike Howells, who accused it of 'trying to nanny the profession'. The Council expressed strong support for combining approved insurers with a master policy for those unable to obtain cover. Six local law societies blamed the Council for misleading them about risk banding.[81]

The Council held its March meeting hours before the SGM. The Interim Executive Committee proposed a postal ballot on combining approved insurers with a mutual fund or master policy. The November Group wanted a pure market solution and had been advised by counsel that it could seek judicial review of any other decision. Mears and Keating called it 'wrong in principle that a compulsory mutual should impose excessive contributions on any of its members'. SIF's claim that its non-profit status made it cheaper resembled the arguments 'advanced to justify the command economies of Eastern Europe', which neglect 'the deadening effect of absence of competition'. 'As far as Chancery Lane is concerned Adam Smith has lived in vain.' A private insurer would not have been able to recover the £500 million shortfall. SIF appealed to 'fear, the Keep a Hold of Nurse factor'. 'What right has the Law Society's Council to tell us all that we are all deluded and like children we must be saved from ourselves?'[82]

Ken Byass told the Council that he 'could not speak for an hour' after a claim against his firm based on his conveyancing error. Without SIF during the four-year ordeal he would have killed himself. But Michael Napier declared solicitors 'will not forgive the SIF for the shortfall' and was 'absolutely convinced' they would reject a mutual fund. A Council member on the board of SIF praised it as 'the mortar which binds this profession together'; but another Council member reviled it as 'the plastic explosive that blows it apart'. Most speakers thought it impossible to combine SIF with the market. The Council voted to preserve SIF's monopoly by just 32 to 29 (14 absent).[83]

At the SGM that afternoon the Millenium Group (which had called it) first objected that members could not vote by proxy and then tabled six motions criticizing SIF and seeking a market alternative so solicitors could 'compete on an even footing with other professions'. The meeting cheered a solicitor who termed the Council 'impertinent' for deciding before the SGM. The 300 participants voted more than two to one to urge the Council to reverse its decision. Mathews, who chaired the gathering, persuaded it to approve a non-binding postal ballot. Afterwards he described it as 'a question of philosophy', a clash between 'individualism and collectivism—both of which are respectable'. Although he had opposed the Council decision he would not seek to 'undermine' it. 'A mutual fund is in the long-term best interests of clients and the profession . . . the best way to ensure stability and certainty . . . the commercial insurance market is both volatile and cyclical'.

The *Gazette* said the decision was the Council's 'most important' since establishing SIF. Fearful of the 'vagaries of the market', it sought 'certainty at all costs' in arrangements that 'crucially underpin the solicitors' profession's reputation'. The *New Law Journal* saw no 'reason to provide an umbrella for those whose track records are such that they cannot obtain insurance on the open market'. The Council should not have given such solicitors the 'luxury' of two years to reform, during which time 'they can do an enormous amount of damage'. The November Group was 'astonished': 'insuring the uninsurable is foolish, and could result in another disastrous shortfall'. It was 'impossible to operate one scheme to cover the whole profession, when it consists of firms with widely different incomes, practices, client bases, geographical locations and needs'. The Group offered moral, and possibly financial, support for Dalton's application and decided to prepare its own. The Millenium Group took a *Gazette* advertisement calling for 'freedom of choice for all solicitors'. The BLA voted to end SIF.[84]

SIF's managing director denied that the problem was a few rotten apples. 'Like the market, the SIF is also able to ensure that the firms with the worst claims records pay appropriate premiums.' Eliminating them 'would not have a significant impact on overall losses'. Three-quarters of the profession 'has had claims and have contributed to the losses'. SIF assailed the Millenium Group letter to all solicitors as 'misleading, biased, based on opinion or unsupported allegation and ignoring completely the main issues'. Firms were 'deceiving themselves and others if they believe they would receive substantially different treatment in the long term in the open market'.[85]

Nevertheless, solicitors decisively embraced freedom of choice (by 18,975 to 8,303). The Millenium Group treasurer found the result 'very gratifying' and hoped the Council would not 'disregard' it. The November Group chair was 'pleasantly surprised'. Mears said it showed 'how grotesquely out of touch with the profession the Law Society's Council is'. The *Solicitors Journal* declared that nearly 20,000 members 'right across the profession [though it could not know that] have expressed their clear preference for the market option. Their views cannot be ignored.' At a closed Council meeting immediately after the results were certified a majority of speakers wanted to reverse their earlier decision. At its next regular meeting the Council voted by three to one to do so. Accusing the Council of creating a task force of 'pro-Siffers', the *New Law Journal* warned that if it 'does not listen to the wishes of its members on this seriously important issue then it really will finally forfeit any respect and support it presently retains'. The task force recommended a choice between approved insurers and a master policy on behalf of a consortium of insurers administered by a Managing General Agency—which would preserve SIF's staff and infrastructure. Although the November Group found this 'a sensible move in the right direction', the Millenium Group thought it too pro-SIF.[86]

The Council adopted the proposal, narrowly rejecting another consultation (by 23 to 17). Mathews declared the MGA would offer insurance to 'all firms except those with the very worst records'. Solicitors unable to obtain market insurance could join an assigned risk pool for two years. When the Council refused to be bound by the postal ballot, the Milton Keynes Law Society threatened to seek an SGM to vote no confidence and another postal vote on the Council decision. But the Millenium Group disbanded, and Michael Dalton discontinued his judicial review application when the Society forgave his costs and waived most of his indemnity contributions for the past two years on grounds of financial hardship.[87]

C. Barrister Discipline

Distanced by solicitors from dissatisfied clients (and the temptations of client funds), immune from liability for their principal function (advocacy), and subject to more effective informal controls, barristers were slow to develop formal regulation. But by the end of the 1980s pressures were building. A former Solicitor-General sought judicial review (for the first time) of the PCC's refusal to charge his former tenant with financial mismanagement. Troubled by miscarriages of justice in IRA bombing cases, Justice called for an independent review of prisoner complaints about counsel who 'often turn . . . up with a late brief, fail . . . to mark the details of the case and then can't give a strong defence'. Shortly after a Crown Court judge condemned defence counsel for cross-examining an indecent assault victim so harshly during commital proceedings that she refused to testify at trial, the Bar began to investigate verbosity, incompetence, and rudeness.[88]

Complaints against barristers rose from an annual average of 210 in 1986–9 to 308 in 1991 (still only a tenth of complaints per solicitor). The PCC attributed 20–30 per cent to 'disgruntled prisoners' and dismissed about 70 per cent, disbarring two to three and suspending two to three annually. Clients claimed the PCC refused to adjudicate factual controversies. The CA denounced the system as 'a non-starter because it is riding on the back of the disciplinary procedures' and urged its extension outside misconduct and the lowering of the 'beyond a reasonable doubt' standard of proof. When the CA proposed advocates be liable for negligence, however, BC chair Williams predictably responded 'there would be no end to litigation'.[89]

Nevertheless, the Council created a Bar Standards Review Body, which reported in 1994. Its head, Lord Alexander of Weedon QC (a former BC chair now chair of National Westminster Bank), declared that 'any profession or business has to pay heed to its clients or die' and warned that the 'right to self-regulation . . . could be lost if the profession failed to respond to criticism and was complacent'. 'Members of the public are right to point out that the Bar is behind other professions, including solicitors, in enabling clients' grievances to be considered openly and constructively.'

IPS 'merits the use of a simple procedure for complainants'. 'In my new profession of banking we now have an ombudsman and complaints procedure that is advertised in every bank.' The Review Body recommended that barristers explain fees and return briefs promptly, giving a written explanation on request. Every chambers should have a complaints process, and the Bar should create and fund a Complaints Bureau, headed by a non-barrister, which could order compensation of up to £2,000 for shoddy work following a public hearing. The BC and LS should draft a common advocacy code of conduct.[90]

The 1995 BC consultation paper included many of these recommendations, which chair Goldsmith called 'an important element in reinforcing public confidence in the professionalism and expertise of the services provided by the Bar'. He noted that the LSO 'has been pressing hard' and

has the power to recommend changes which we are obliged to consider. Refusal to do so would no doubt lead to further government action. I would rather we were in charge of our destiny than have some different and worse system forced on us.

In his last Chairman's Column, Goldsmith said the complaints system would 'help to safeguard the Bar's position for the future'. If barristers rejected it, 'what sort of message is that going to give to our critics—and more importantly—to our potential clients?'

But Ronald Thwaites QC, noting that only eleven sets and seventeen barristers responded to the paper, called it a licence for 'frivolous complaints', a 'moaner's charter', which would 'destroy the junior Bar' and might deter inexperienced barristers 'from taking an independent course'.

[C]lients who fail in court are provided with an ideal opportunity to proceed against their barristers. The client can effectively 'blackmail' his barrister by also making disciplinary conduct allegations and later agreeing to drop them if the barrister compromises his compensation claim, and pays up. By making a complaint of inadequate professional services the client enables his solicitor to withhold payment of counsel's outstanding fees.... Every criminal client languishing in his cell at the beginning of his well-deserved sentence will be able to fill the empty hours by alleging inadequate professional service.

He obtained the 150 signatures needed for an EGM.

A week before it, the BC limited compensation to clients who could prove 'actual financial loss' as a result of conduct 'which falls significantly short of that which is to be reasonably expected of a barrister in all the circumstances'. Thwaites still warned barristers that the proposals 'may damage your career[s]'. Goldsmith retorted that some 'are against any change. They give the impression that they are arrogant and dismissive of clients' and 'want to live in a cocooned world'. The Council wrote to members that it was 'anomalous' that the Bar lacked a power the Law Society possessed. Although the EGM rejected the proposal (by 188 to 104), a mail ballot narrowly approved it (55 per cent of the third voting). Losers sought a new poll because of voting by employed barristers, whose clients never complained. But at the request of its new chair, David Penry-Davey QC, the Council passed it over Thwaites's lone dissent.[91]

Critics were unmollified. Analogizing the complaints procedure to 'the new cross-country steeplechase course', the *New Law Journal* called it 'so hemmed in with provisos and safeguards that in practice it may turn out to be worthless'. The journal condemned immunity for advocacy since 'the main problem of the client has always been the ineptitude of his barrister whilst in court'. It criticized the Bar for closing disciplinary hearings when 'the Law Society has shown what its elder and supposed betters should do'. Bernard Levin assailed the proposal as

the most monumental chutzpah even the lawyers have ever cooked up. It states unashamedly that if you are obviously and clearly wronged by an ignorant, lazy, incompetent, drunk or stupid lawyer and you seek compensation, you can whistle for it, and I wouldn't be surprised if the Bar's next charmer will be to take those who are due for compensation and have them thrown into jail, insisting that any claim against any lawyer is ipso facto criminal.

The LSO found the scheme 'extremely disappointing' and the opposition it provoked indicative of 'the extent to which a significant number of barristers still live a somewhat blinkered existence in a cloistered world of their own'.[92]

But a newly elected Council member worried more about accused barristers than victims. 'Although it is your professional body and is spending large amounts of your subscription money in paying staff to process the complaint against you, its ability to be compassionate' or even 'independent' was 'severely restricted by its regulatory' and 'prosecutorial' role. Complainants should pay £30 to a Barristers' Defence Association to provide free representation. A month later Robert Owen QC, the new BC chair, promised criminal defence lawyers that 'the role of the complaints commissioner is going to be vigorous in filtering complaints—at present about 70 per cent of complaints are found to be without foundation'. At the same time he boasted of having 'appointed a lay complaints commissioner to oversee our disciplinary procedures' in order 'to raise the level of public awareness of the ethical code by which barristers carry out their work'. He warned the mid-year AGM that critiques of the OSS might lead to government oversight of the Bar, which had to improve self-regulation. 'We cannot wash our hands of those who are incompetent, lazy, arrogant, and rude.' At the year's end, however, the PCC chair told barristers not to worry that 'the possibility of complainants being awarded up to £2,000 compensation would spark a flood of unwarranted complaints resulting in awards'. About 80 per cent of the 555 complaints were dismissed; hearings were held for only forty-three (two for IPS).[93]

The CA reiterated its call to lift immunity for advocacy, which offered the 'starkest possible' conflict between the consumer interest and the 'self-interest of a section of the legal profession'. The 'right to redress' was 'the foundation of the legal process'. The BC retorted that 'in 50% of cases one party will be dissatisfied with the outcome of a case and it would open the floodgates of litigation if they were all able to sue'. But when several courts suggested advocates could be liable for negligence in negotiating settlements, *The Times* joined the campaign to end immunity.[94]

Complaints rose another 25 per cent in 1997–8. The Complaints Commissioner wanted authority to order compensation without financial loss (which the CBA had blocked three years earlier). But he also declared that 'in the vast majority' of complaints 'the barrister has acted to the best of his ability'. 'I think the Bar has got it right by recognising that unless they introduced a strong lay element, they could be vulnerable.' But the NCC reiterated that 'the combination of an extremely high standard of proof, the fact that in order to get compensation you have to show actual loss, and the immunity barristers have for their performance in court' demonstrated the system 'is not really in the spirit of a proper complaints procedure'.[95]

Although the LSO focused on the OSS, she also criticized barristers' 'Byzantine' self-regulation. One complainant 'described the experience as being like that of Alice at the Mad Hatter's Tea-Party'. 'Poor communication and defensiveness verging on paranoia suggest to me a profession obsessively preoccupied with its own purity and solidarity at the expense of the common good which it exists to serve.' An 'imaginative capacity to step outside' mere legalism would evince 'a more mature professionalism'.[96]

When the OSS came under attack a year later, BC chair Brennan boasted about the Bar's superior record, acknowledged in the 1997 LSO report. A survey of complainants found that 'the vast majority accept the system works comprehensibly, efficiently and sympathetically...but there is often dissatisfaction with the resulting decision'. He urged the Bar to improve 'expectation management'. In her next report Abraham praised the Bar's 'quiet but significant progress' but wanted more generous compensation, extending to inconvenience and distress. A BC Complaints System Working Group recommended more lay participation, compensation up to £5,000, and the inclusion of advocacy in IPS. Abraham urged approval to 'break' with the 'tradition' of 'parochial retreat behind the protective veneer of professional privilege and self-interest'. The Council did so.[97]

D. Quis Custodiet Ipsos Custodes?

Self-regulation is the *raison d'être* of professions, which brag about their performance. Yet English lawyers shirked that responsibility as long as possible. Although the Bar had enjoyed professional privileges for centuries, it promulgated a code of conduct only in 1980 and created a lay complaints commissioner only in 1996. Although financial scandals plagued solicitors throughout the nineteenth and early twentieth centuries, the Law Society created the SCF only in 1942 and required malpractice insurance only in 1976. Consumer and government pressure for meaningful regulation provoked rank and file backlash. Assailing 'regulatory paranoia', the Society's standards and guidance committee chair denied 'you can persuade 65,000 solicitors to do something by telling them they must do it'—an extraordinary statement by a lawyer who spent his life telling clients what the law required them to do! Critics like Mears assailed SIF as a 'nanny' making solicitors 'Keep a Hold of Nurse' and denounced the Society for treating members like 'idle schoolchildren'. Solicitors resented collective responsibility for bankrupts, the insurance principle of spreading risk, and the cost of handling complaints. Many wanted to end these practices or shed the financial burden. Rosen saw self-regulation as a 'charity', which should be withdrawn if clients and society were insufficiently grateful. Mathews accurately described the choice between collectivism (i.e., professionalism) and individualism (i.e., the market, with state remedies for its failures). Solicitors disagreed whether SIF was 'the mortar which binds this profession together' or 'the plastic explosive that blows it apart'. The answer was clear. The November Group (of City firms) called it 'impossible to operate one scheme to cover the whole profession'. The Millenium Group (of small firms) demanded 'freedom of choice'.

The chronic crisis of self-regulation turned acute during the 1990s because laissez faire ideology challenged traditional paternalism, the boom-and-bust property market amplified cyclic insurance swings, and government (as legal aid paymaster), judges, and agencies asserted increasing authority over lawyers. But the basic problem was the contradiction that self-regulation serves two masters: professionals, who are the colleagues of the regulators, pay their salaries through mandatory fees, and enjoy ultimate control; and clients rendered vulnerable and dependent by the very expertise that constructs the profession. Lawyers yearn nostalgically for a past when clients were deferential; clients hope for a future when lawyers will attend to them. Lawyers demand that regulation protect them from ignorant, unreasonable, even vindictive accusations, clients that it ensure quality, courtesy, and integrity.[98] Lawyers insist on secrecy to guard their reputations from unjustified (and even well grounded) accusations; the public wants to know who has complained and the outcome. (This is replaying in the Roman Catholic Church's response to priestly sexual abuse.) Lawyers claim exclusive expertise; consumers demand independence.

Neither side trusts the other—with good reason. When the Law Society gained the right to review complaints in 1888, its President reassured solicitors that an accused would 'come before a tribunal composed of members of his profession, to whom, if at all, he should be able to justify himself'. A century later his successor declared that the Society was 'the best judge of the public interest' and denied the CA had any better claim to be one than the Institute of Directors. The cavalier treatment of complaints against Sir Glanville Davies and Hubbards demonstrated the Society's protectiveness toward members. BC chair Owen promised defence lawyers that the new lay commissioner—established to 'raise the level of public awareness of the ethical code of barristers'—would be 'vigorous' in filtering out complaints. Agreeing that the appointment of a layperson would reduce the Bar's 'vulnerability', the commissioner exonerated barristers in the 'vast majority of complaints'. Concerned about client disappointment, BC chair Brennan urged the Bar to improve 'expectation management'. LSO Abrahams, by contrast, disavowed neutrality because 'consumers are often weaker than providers'.

Divided loyalties fatally compromised self-regulation. Lawyers who devoted their professional lives to manipulating state power over others became instant converts to exhortation and conciliation when they were being scrutinized. Both branches dismissed the vast majority of complaints and seriously punished very few. Apparently believing that lawyers were incapable of organizing their own defence, both branches offered assistance. The Council long resisted advance fee quotations because, a member argued, 'if you give an estimate to a client, you are stuck with it'. When the Society finally capitulated, Sayer called quotations 'blind stupidity', which solicitors should evade through hourly billing. The Society consistently underfunded its disciplinary apparatus, ensuring growing delays. When the OSS backlog was rising exponentially the Society proposed to cut its budget by a third.

Lawyers felt besieged by ignorant, ungrateful, even malicious clients and their self-interested allies.[99] Solicitors blamed lenders' losses on improvident loans. Complainants were 'demanding', 'never satisfied', 'obsessive', 'mentally deranged', 'malicious', 'bearing a grudge', 'self-seeking', blaming solicitors 'for their own faults'. (Lawyers rejected similar characterizations by critics of 'litigiousness' seeking to curtail legal aid. Indeed, lawyers encourage clients to assert legal rights against others.) BLA founder Best railed against 'trivial complaints' and 'largely imaginary grievances'. Mourning the days when 'professional life was a gentlemanly affair', an elderly solicitor accused clients of the 'horrific... malaise of complainitis'. The CBA warned that a lay commissioner would be a 'moaner's charter' for 'frivolous', 'malicious and bloodyminded' complaints, used to 'blackmail' barristers into paying compensation for IPS or reducing fees; they would 'damage careers' and 'destroy' the junior Bar. Every one of the half of litigants who necessarily lost would sue their barristers (although they did not sue their solicitors or American litigators). Some solicitors wanted to abandon self-regulation and consign clients to legal remedies. (Did they really want complaints adjudicated by barrister judges rather than fellow solicitors?) Professional journals took the same line. The *Solicitors Journal* blamed the 'compensation culture' for raising client expections 'out of sync' with the services for which they were prepared to pay. The *New Law Journal* declared clients were 'encouraged' to complain in 'these litigious days' in order to 'have a few pounds knocked off the bill' and denounced the 'Panategruelian' OSS.

If outsiders felt the profession was underregulated, members denounced overregulation. The 1979 Royal Commission worried that liability for negligence (from which barristers were happily protected) put too much 'strain' on solicitors and other professionals and urged an immediate inquiry into capping damages. A former member of the Society's adjudication and appeals committee claimed that solicitors felt 'general distrust' and 'widespread dissatisfaction' with an 'out of control' SCB. A Law Society Council member accused the complaints procedure of inviting clients to 'pick a solicitor, any solicitor, and we'll give you a gun to shoot at him'. Sayer agreed 'the complaints system was like handing out free lottery tickets'. The Council used 'too much' stick and 'not enough' carrot. Opposing the Council decision to clarify the information clients should receive about costs, a member warned 'we are making it easier for the client to complain' and 'building up a claim for inadequate professional service'. It was 'unsympathetic and unnatural to mention costs immediately to clients'. The PACS chair objected that the 'effect will be to drive costs down'! Lawyers even claimed that regulation, not laxity, 'lower[s] the reputation of solicitors in the opinion of the public'.[100]

The protracted controversy over in-house complaints processes displayed many of these themes. A profession that believed in client service would eagerly institute complaints procedures. Instead, solicitors strenuously resisted the obligation. When external pressure persuaded the Society to promulgate a rule, many firms simply disregarded it, confident there would be no sanctions, and others complied only on paper. If the intimacy of smaller firms made informal social control more effective, it also inhibited formal social control. The Society enforced the rule primarily to reduce the OSS backlog and shift regulatory costs to firms. Indeed, the OSS boasted of the proportion of complaints it returned to firms, knowing many would abandon their grievances even if still dissatisfied. The result was a caricature of self-regulation in which the victims of misconduct and incompetence were thrown on the mercy of the perpetrators.

Regulation not only provoked resistance, evasion, and backlash but also exposed and deepened fissures between large firms and small, independent practitioners and employed, young and old, the Law Society establishment and local societies. Sole practitioners felt scapegoated.[101] The criminal defence Bar opposed a lay complaints commissioner. Some divisions had racial overtones, as when the November Group contrasted the law's Sainsburys (presumably its members) with Mr Patel's excellent corner shop (ethnic minority sole practitioners?). Mandatory malpractice insurance engendered conflict over how to spread risk, intensified by rising costs and professional stratification and complicated by the low profits of the riskiest firms. Many blamed a few bad apples, both to justify making them pay and to exonerate the rest. Mathews declared that 20 per cent of firms (presumably not his City colleagues) produced 80 per cent of complaints. The Government claimed that 1 per cent accounted for 10 per cent of complaints. But the Society's own Ernst & Young study found half the firms responsible for 80 per cent of complaints. Sayer continued to blame cut-price conveyancers for SIF's problems, hoping that eliminating such firms would reduce both premiums and price competition. And though others attributed malpractice claims to a few negligent firms, SIF reported that three-quarters had been targets.

Although experience rating (by size, revenue, specialty, or claims) increased fairness between categories, it exacerbated unfairness within them. Those who felt they were paying too much deplored that the 'competent and efficient' were 'subsidising the inefficient' (Ely); the 'good' should not pay for the 'bad', the 'persistently negligent', the 'unrepentantly incompetent' (Sycamore); the 'honest and innocent' should not 'subsidise bent commercial lawyers and sole practitioners' (three-partner firm); the burden of 'bail[ing] out dishonest and incompetent solicitors' and supporting 'dishonest brethren' had grown 'unacceptable' and 'intolerable' (*New Law Journal*). Even the BLA, created to represent smaller firms, now declared that 'if anyone is going to the wall, let it be the most negligent in the profession'. But those charged more objected to being 'singled out', 'victimization', since premium weighting not only increased costs but also stigmatized. Iris Dean accused the Society of wanting to eliminate sole practitioners. Is this what Secretary-General Hayes meant in urging the Council to display 'willingness at times to alienate members of your own profession'? Once market insurance became an alternative to SIF those unable to obtain it were offered the temporary respite of an assigned risk pool before losing their practising certificates. (Although professions are very reluctant to expel members, they may be happy to let the market's 'invisible hand' do so.) Solicitors could no more preserve the 'one profession' myth than Conservatives the 'one nation'.

Internal dissension took many forms. Sole practitioners wanted to jettison self-discipline, which large firms wanted to strengthen. Large firms wanted processing costs paid by complaint targets—especially firms without adequate in-house procedures. (The SDT chair wanted fines to fund its operations.) Small firms wanted complainants to pay (although many opposed the LCD proposal that litigants pay full court operating costs). Some barristers even wanted clients to defray the cost of defending barristers against whom they complained! Sole practitioners wanted to preserve mutual insurance, which large firms wanted to junk. Firms disagreed about the extent and manner of experience rating insurance premiums.

Conflict within the profession and with critics produced cycles of scandal, reform, raised expectations, disappointment, professional resentment, and renewed demands for change. The upsurge in complaints in response to each regulatory innovation—SCB, OSS, LSO, the Bar's lay commissioner—demonstrated client hunger for redress. But since the Law Society never provided sufficient funding, that hunger remained unappeased. Because some solicitors strenuously resisted every change—advance fee quotations, in-house complaint procedures, compensation for IPS, open disciplinary hearings, CPD, remuneration certificates (especially for testamentary beneficiaries), liability for negligent advocacy, even rules against sexual relations with clients—critics dismissed reforms as too little too late. Instead of setting and enforcing standards higher than the market or government might impose—the hallmark of a profession—lawyers did the least they believed they could get away with. The OSS repeatedly announced targets for resolving complaints and then failed to meet them. Every external study (even one by the RPPU) documented the failure of in-house grievance procedures, solicitor reluctance to disclose fees, and client dissatisfaction with both solicitors and their regulatory processes. The constant promises to reform resembled those of confirmed alcoholics (or, as Mears said, chronic debtors); boasts of progress echoed the American government's repeated sighting of the 'light at the end of the tunnel' during the Vietnam War. When leaders reluctantly strengthened regulation, rank and file rebelled: the BC EGM rejected the proposed complaints process by two to one.

The world views of the profession and its clients (and their champions) were diametrically opposed. Clients wanted prevention; lawyers feared correction. Clients were concerned about routine incivility and incompetence, lawyers about rare, egregious misconduct, which publicly embarrassed them and could generate large claims on SCF and SIF. They instinctively responded legalistically. The OSS was a 'police force staffed by former housebreakers', objected Abraham, rather than a 'collaborative neighbourhood watch'. The Society had to start 'looking at things from the...point of view' of clients, who did not 'complain for a living'. The Bar lived a 'blinkered existence' in a 'cloistered world', 'obsessively preoccupied with its own purity and solidarity at the expense of the common good', exhibiting a 'defensiveness verging on paranoia'. (Even BC chair Goldsmith accused CBA spokesperson Ronald Thwaites QC of being 'arrogant', 'dismissive of clients', and living in a 'cocooned world'.) The profession displayed a complacency that was truly Panglossian in its imperviousness to critical opinion—and even fact. The Law Society felt that a sufficient answer to dissatisfied clients was that many others were satisfied. It boasted of the low level of complaints about the SCB to the LSO, ignoring client ignorance and exhaustion.

The Society responded defensively to all criticism, often by attacking the critic. When the LCD condemned the Society's failure to require advance fee disclosure, the Society accused the Department of retaliating against its own opposition to legal aid cuts. When the CA documented the low quality and unjustifiably high cost of solicitors' advice, Mears dismissed the report as 'simply a publicity opportunity', shamelessly proclaiming he was trying to 'shoot the messenger...some messengers deserve to be shot'. Sycamore, his successor, challenged another CA survey's methodology. When a NACAB survey documented solicitors' failure to give accurate fee estimates, Mears retorted that 'reports from the CABx will always be unrelentingly negative'. Twice in two years the Society commissioned reports and then suppressed the critical findings.

The Law Society's adjudication and appeals committee chair praised the SCB as a 'robust' institution of which solicitors should be 'proud'—just two months before its director joined the Society's Secretary-General in calling for its elimination. While the Council considered their proposal, the SCB policy advisory committee chair assailed 'the recent onslaught of unnecessary, damaging criticism', much of it 'ill-informed' and based on 'inadequate evidence'. The SCB director declared it 'the envy of lawyers throughout the world and of other professions in this country'—just three months before quitting what she then called 'the worst job in the world'! The Society paid Ernst & Young to investigate the OSS and then disregarded its conclusions. The LSO called them 'damning'; but the OSS Review Task Force chair emphasized the 'good news' that the improvements were 'achievable' in eighteen months. Leading newspapers said the OSS was 'ailing' and in 'crisis'; but the Law Society's *Gazette* spun this as 'good news' that the problem was 'not intractable'. Bahl assured the press that the Society would bring the backlog under control in eighteen months on the same day that *The Times* exposed the OSS rejection of all complaints. The press assailed 'sloppy lawyers who let down the public' and declared that the profession 'looks after its own'. But Sayer claimed that OSS morale was improving. Less than four months after the three damning reports by Ernst & Young, Avrom Sherr, and Ann Abraham, *The Times* disclosure, the suspension and firing of the OSS director, and government threats to take over regulation, Sayer proposed to absorb the Bar, boasting: 'We already regulate the biggest single legal profession and we do it well'.

SIF repeated the same sorry story, announcing that claims were declining when they were climbing, promising premiums would fall or at least not rise, and then imposing sharp increases. Solicitors became incredulous, just as press and public stopped believing the SCB and OSS. SIF maintained that private insurance would cost an additional £100 million—and then increased its premiums £100 million! When SIF belatedly disclosed a staggering £454 million shortfall (nearly twice its annual budget), the *New Law Journal* called for 'judicial intervention into the affairs of the Society' and urged Lord Woolf to 'take the naughty schoolboys on the Council in hand'. The continuities between SIF and the Managing General Agency (albeit without a monopoly) resembled those between the Society's Professional Purposes Department, the SCB, and the OSS.

The trope of independence, which lawyers promiscuously invoked in defence of restrictive practices and legal aid, became their Achilles heel in defending self-regulation. Clients, consumer organizations, and the media demanded that lawyers themselves observe the rule of law, separating prosecution and adjudication, and prohibiting individuals or groups from judging their own cases. Physically removing the SCB from the Law Society's precincts did not make it independent. Lowe and Ross were too closely implicated in managing the Society to offer it 'deniability' about the runaway backlog. Both branches sought to create an image of independence without relinquishing control by co-opting laypeople to roles lacking real power. Mears even wanted the Society to reclaim control over discipline, transforming it into client relations. His slip of the tongue was revealing: 'dealing with satisfied [*sic*] clients is the responsibility of the profession itself and not of a semi-independent agency'.

If self-regulation could not satisfy the minimum conditions of independence, there were two alternatives. Some clients could deploy market forces.[102] Large, repeat-players demanded fee estimates and quick satisfaction of complaints. When the Law Society threatened to cap payments to institutional lenders on behalf of bankrupt or negligent solicitors, the former countered by banning risky solicitors from conveyancing panels. Government could prosecute fraud and (as a monopsonist) dictate prices. Fearing government regulation, lawyers exaggerated market protections. Bar leaders like Lord Alexander QC and Peter Goldsmith QC warned barristers not to let client discontent fester; but clients had nowhere else to go. The *New Law Journal* reproved clients who petitioned the OSS. 'If you don't like the grapefruit at Asda then you go to Waitrose, you don't complain to the Supermarket Authority.' But one-off individual consumers could not evaluate quality or price until it was too late. One firm candidly acknowledged that though 'you can't afford to offend commercial clients... a private client very often is just a one-off job'.

Sayer launched his political career by voicing a visceral contempt for clients, which he hoped (correctly) would resonate with solicitors. In the wake of the OSS melt-down, however, even he felt constrained as president to declare the 'new consumer culture' a 'fact of life' and 'good for a solicitor's business'. The Society rebuffed calls to abolish the SCF by reaffirming its 'proud boast' of collective responsibility. 'Any retreat from that position would weaken the right of solicitors to be seen as a profession as opposed to a trade....' But many solicitors were unpersuaded. Some invoked professionalism against the obligation to quote prices. Declaring she had 'never been so cross at Council', a small firm solicitor insisted: 'we're not plumbers or mechanics' but more like 'doctors whose fees are not subject to taxation' (because doctors were salaried—which lawyers adamantly resisted!). A large firm solicitor retorted: 'I want us to be more popular than car repairers'. (The repeated surveys of public attitudes towards lawyers suggested they were unusually preoccupied with image—perhaps more than with reality.[103]) The *New Law Journal* accused the Society of chastizing solicitors for 'not behaving like a supermarket and handing out fifty pence if the milk was sour'. But when the Society placed the OSS in receivership, Secretary-General Betts instructed solicitors to resolve most complaints by 'giving clients a small amount of financial compensation'. Others rejected professionalism and with it any obligation to clients. 'We do not do anything but run a business.' A 'learned profession' was 'the stuff of sherry talk'. Solicitors 'ought to have the right to tell someone to bugger off if we judge it is in our interest'. A Bognor solicitor said he was 'just a bloke trying to earn a living'—a 'plumber' whom dissatisfied customers could sue. (Solicitors did not have to please clients because lawyers both were and were not plumbers!)

But most lawyers dreaded what the Bognor solicitor claimed to welcome. Government intervention was the spectre endlessly evoked by all who wanted the profession to fulfil its regulatory responsibilities. In 1994 Lord Alexander QC, chairing the Bar Standards Review Committee, warned that 'the right to self-regulation...could be lost if the profession failed to respond to criticism and was complacent'. The same year LS President Elly predicted: 'If we abdicated our regulatory role, a more onerous regime would undoubtedly be imposed from outside and you can be sure the profession would still be required to pay'. A year later LSO Michael Barnes said 'this is the Society's last chance to get it right'. Labour's legal affairs spokesperson, Paul Boateng, echoed that 'the Society has one last chance to regulate its own procedures satisfactorily'. Anticipating a Labour victory, LS President Girling said 'a new government must be reassured that the profession can be trusted to regulate itself effectively and responsibly'. Succeeding Barnes two years later, Abraham 'put both the Law Society and the Bar Council on notice that there was very little time to make the systems work'. After a few months in office she demanded 'significant and tangible improvements' within a year. When the deadline passed she reiterated that 'if the Bar Council and the Law Society want to [silence] the call for an independent complaints handling body, they have a long way to go and little time to get there'. The 'entrenched attitudes demonstrated by individual practitioners' would 'lead to the closed sign finally going up on the doors of the famous last chance saloon'. The Home Office minister warned the Society: 'if you don't do it we will'. During the AJB debate both Irvine and Hoon hinted at state control. In her next report, Abraham called the Act's provision for a Legal Services Complaints Commissioner 'a sharp reminder that self-regulation within the profession was a privilege, not a right—and a privilege that can be taken away'.

Support for divesting a self-interested profession of regulatory responsibility grew in size and diversity. Some solicitors claimed to prefer judicial scrutiny of malpractice. Arnold Rosen (perhaps speaking for other sole practitioners) wanted to revert to judicial oversight. Anthony Bogan proposed a superregulator over all occupations involved in conveyancing. Although Tony Holland sought to strengthen self-regulation as LS President, he foresaw government surveillance of solicitors' investment advice when he became Personal Investment Authority Ombudsman. The Institute of Chartered Accountants wanted a body to oversee all professions. By 1998 the *New Law Journal* predicted 'the end of self-regulation', and the Fabian Society demanded it.

But repetition rendered these threats increasingly empty. Government clearly preferred to assail the profession's deficiencies rather than shoulder the burden of regulation and become the target of dissatisfied consumer-voters. (OSS director Ross was right that 'New Labour' was unenthusiastic about 'an antiquated structuralist "old Labour" solution'.) Yet if here, as elsewhere, there was no rupture, change came incrementally. The FSA gained jurisdiction over some 300 firms doing substantial investment business.[104] All advocates were exposed to liability for negotiated settlements if not courtroom performance. The Woolf reforms greatly increased judicial oversight of litigation, to media applause: 'the judge, rather than a lawyer with one eye on ever-fattening fees, will call the shots' (*Evening Standard*); 'Enough litigation madness!' (*Independent*); 'lawyers who indulge in "trial by combat" and try to drag out litigation face swingeing financial penalties' (*The Times*).[105] The Courts and Legal Services Act 1990 expanded judicial authority to make wasted costs orders. The LCD empowered Crown Court judges to fine lawyers who delayed trials.[106] And the AJA gave the Lord Chancellor the power to create a Legal Services Complaints Commissioner who could set targets for professional self-regulation and fine bodies that missed them.

The contemporaneous crises of unheard complaints and unfunded insurance liability demonstrated the Society's inability, or unwillingness, to regulate solicitors (although few critics drew that obvious lesson). In each case, the response further eroded professional autonomy. Government surveillance of complaints handling and direct regulation of the novel functions solicitors were eager to assume were steps toward an inexorable increase in state control. And the end of SIF's monopoly and probation for solicitors unable to find a private insurer were irreversible steps toward market discipline of risk.

10   Governing a Fractious Profession

What it comes down to is that Chancery Lane knows what is best for us. [Solicitor objecting to separate representation of lenders and buyers]

You elected the members of the Council for their expertise and at the end of the day we must use our best judgment. [Charles Elly, LS President, replying]

[It is] disappointing that we are going to have the distraction of an election when there are so many things to be grappled with. [Elly rebuking Martin Mears for contesting the presidency for the first time in memory]

The idea of a democratic election being a distraction is one which you would not expect to find favour outside the old Politburo. . . . I intend to fight this campaign cleanly and leave the gutter for whoever wishes to play there. [Mears]

Who will rid us of these turbulent men? The joke played by the LS membership on its leadership has gone sour. . . . The Law Society is degenerating into a very public farce. [LAG on Mears and Robert Sayer]

We need another contested election like a hole in the head. . . . Law Society politics are the same as politics anywhere else. Petty, undignified, dominated by ambition. [Sayer, VP candidate, rebuking Michael Napier for challenging Michael Mathews for the presidency]

[David Keating is a] complete pillock [supported by] bitter, twisted little people [like Mears, who kept turning up] like a piece of dog turd on your shoe. [Sayer rebuking Keating for challenging him for the presidency]

In order to perform their essential tasks—limiting numbers, selecting entrants, allocating roles, constraining competition, negotiating with third-party payers, and regulating conduct—professions need governing structures that balance direct democracy and representative government, choose election rules, and organize staff. The two branches differed in both challenges and responses.

A. Solicitors

Nineteenth-century solicitors had to construct a national organization from scratch. The Society of Gentlemen Practisers, founded in 1739 to defend their monopolies and punish egregious misconduct, never enrolled more than 200 and had atrophied by the early nineteenth century. The Incorporated Law Society, established in 1825, had attracted only a quarter of the profession fifty years later. London solicitors were five times as likely to join as others, who remained loyal to local societies, which created the rival Metropolitan and Provincial Law Association in 1847. Although this merged with the ILS in 1872, two years later the largest local societies created the Associated Provincial Law Societies. By the 1920s, however, provincial solicitors were proportionally represented in the Law Society, which enrolled 90 per cent of practising certificate holders by the 1950s.

In 1979 the seventy-member Council (fourteen co-opted) was seriously unrepresentative. Local law societies (of vastly unequal size) selected members, who typically served until retirement or resignation. In 1985 a single member under 35 represented the 37 per cent of young solicitors; one woman represented the approximately 25 per cent of women; seven employed lawyers (10 per cent) represented the 28 per cent employed; just three two-partner principals (4 per cent) represented the 16 per cent of such principals; and no one represented ethnic minorities or the 11 per cent in solo practice. Alternating the presidency between London and provincial solicitors acknowledged their differences. Only 2 per cent of member elections between 1945 and 1967 were contested, and just one vice-presidential, and there had been no presidential race 'in living memory'. The increasingly divergent interests of solicitors engendered societies of women, ethnic minorities, trainees, and young solicitors; specialists in litigation, criminal, and family law; lawyers employed by local government and business; and those dependent on legal aid.

Dissatisfied solicitors who were young, provincial, or in smaller firms created the BLA in 1964, which attracted 10 per cent of the profession within two years (but then predictably declined). It called a Society SGM in 1984 to approve proxy voting at AGMs and then (unsuccessfully) sought to use proxies to secure nomination of officers by solicitors (rather than the Council), term limits and non-geographic constituencies. In response, the Council proposed to curtail democracy by eliminating postal ballots after an AGM and refusing to open meetings to solicitors (both defeated by postal ballots) and reduced members' terms from five years to four (not one, as the BLA urged). The Royal Commission rejected the BLA's proposal to become the solicitors' trade union and leave regulatory functions to the Society. It accepted the Society's own preference that membership remain voluntary. Its only recommendation (which the Society rejected) was regional groupings to implement Society policies.[1]

Lord Mackay's attack on restrictive practices and brake on rising legal aid expenditures intensified solicitors' dissatisfaction with the Society. The Cardiff society president complained that 'every time there is a fight, the Law Society gives in'. An unanticipated budget deficit in 1991 provoked criticism of the 'expensive' bureaucracy. 'We've got the Law Society into a nanny position', complained a Council member, 'and we can no longer afford it'. The *New Law Journal* asked 'what great victories has it produced for the profession in the last 10 years' and speculated that the profession would 'throw the bums out'. It joined local law societies in criticizing holding the annual conference in Brussels, just 'a jolly for the president and officers of the Society'.[2]

In 1992 a highly critical staff ginger group proposed a structural review, calling the Council too large, 'an inefficient and ineffective forum for policy-making'. But though the strategy committee agreed, the Council (unsurprisingly) did not. LAG pointed to a much more serious 'democratic deficit': the underrepresentation of women, ethnic minority, and younger lawyers. Council member Kamlesh Bahl reiterated this a year later. The *Solicitors Journal* urged 'regional representation and specialist representation and a number of co-opted members to ensure that the council reflects the make-up of the profession'. The Society was 'out of touch, out of date and expensive'.[3]

Other divisions widened. In 1992, 58 per cent of solicitors felt the Society paid excessive attention to large firms and London firms and 40 per cent that it favoured sole practitioners. Half felt it did not fairly represent the entire profession. The *Solicitors Journal* criticized the Society for 'overmanning' and spending '£17,400 on restoration of a table from the Old Council Chamber'. We 'now have a sleek Mercedes of a Law Society for a profession that is only inclined to pay for a Golf'.[4]

Sole practitioners asked the Society to create a group for them. Arnold Rosen expressed the 'widespread feeling that the Law Society exists to represent large firms and regulate the small ones', against whom it 'discriminated' in negotiations over conveyancing panels and legal aid franchises. Vivian Stern attacked the proposal to inspect sole practitioners' books as a step toward 'a Law Society police force'. After the Society allocated £2,500 for a mailing to the 3,500 sole practitioners, the newly-formed Sole Practitioners Group (SPG) reported that 95 per cent of respondents favoured a special interest group within the Society. Two Council members submitted a resolution to create one, but Secretary-General John Hayes resisted. '[M]ore than two-thirds of the casework and enquiries which the Law Society receives from the profession relate to smaller practices, [but] only about one-third of practising certificate fee income that comes from the profession in private practices comes from smaller practices'. Nevertheless, the Society recognized the SPG, which already had 500 members, promising it £10,000 a year and back-up support.

This did nothing to allay anxiety. A year later a survey found that firms with fewer than five partners feared the Society had a 'hidden agenda' to let market forces eliminate them. Another survey found 'general dissatisfaction' among employed solicitors, two-thirds of whom felt the Society paid too much attention to private practitioners. The LAPG chair said the Society 'does not effectively represent those small firms which make up

82% of solicitors' practices'. It 'should be protecting us from not only its requirements but the requirements of accreditation and specialisation demanded by a number of agencies'. It 'had to be prodded into any defence of [*sic*] the many attacks' on 'the work that provided the main sources of income—conveyancing and legal aid work'. 'When it did campaign ... it was too gentlemanly and low profile'. The Society responded by establishing a 'services to the profession' unit, costing the impact of all new regulations, planning sixteen 'Meet the Law Society' roadshows, and making DVP Henry Hodge a high-street firms Champion.[5]

When the Bar Council decided to pay its chair a High Court judge's salary, the Law Society paid its president the same and its VP and DVP 50 and 25 per cent of that. Council members held a closed debate about paying themselves. The YSG deplored such 'insensitivity in the present climate'. The TSG condemned 'talk of removing the little protection afforded to trainee solicitors by the minimum salary at a time when the firms of the senior office holders on the Council look set to coin it in'. A local law society emitted 'howls of derision'. The LAPG, SPG, LAG, LCCSA, and AWS supported the proposal, but opponents called an SGM. Although it approved the measure, a 14,715–6,837 postal ballot cut the top pay by about half, to what a legal aid lawyer would earn from 1,000 hours of green form work. The mover claimed a victory for 'the hard working legal aid solicitors'.[6]

The new SPG was riven from the start. Andrew Blencowe sought to disqualify Naomi Turl as vice-chair candidate (running with candidate for chair, Arnold Rosen) because she did not belong to the Law Society. Turl said the SPG had to choose between being a 'Law Society poodle or an active lobbying force'. Blencowe retorted: 'we can achieve more by working within the Society rather than being constantly in conflict with them'. Turl failed to enjoin an SPG extraordinary committee meeting, which barely confirmed her right to run (by 11 to 10). Her ticket won (she by just twenty-six votes out of nearly 1,300). The *New Law Journal* agreed with Stanley Best of the BLA that 'there cannot be a true champion of the sole practitioner and small practice if he is in the maw of the Society'. Best wanted 'the SPG to be strangled shortly after birth and the BLA to take over its role'. The following year SPG honourary secretary Fay Landau challenged the pair, writing to John Hayes: 'I shall not give up until [Rosen] is removed'. The SPG committee (backed by Hayes) refused to circulate Rosen's Chair's address as part of the Group's 1995 AGM agenda. Hayes also refused to put on the Society's 1995 AGM agenda Rosen's no confidence motion in the high-street firms Champion and proposal for a sole practitioner Directorate, insisting the latter was 'inconsistent with our Charter'.[7]

Mears stirs the pot

Martin Mears, a partner in a small Great Yarmouth firm, entered professional politics when his local law society asked him to edit its newsletter in
1993 and then 'sacked' him for writing 'some mild and caring criticisms' of
Chancery Lane. When he lost 'heavily' to the official Council candidate,
Mears 'drew appropriate conclusions and established [his] own newsletter',
winning two-thirds of the vote in 1994. He promptly attacked the Society as
'arrogant', 'extravagant' and 'inept'. It had not achieved 'a single significant
victory'. He wanted to reduce regulation and staffing and use the savings for
a national advertising campaign to improve the profession's image. Calling
himself 'deeply reactionary', he accused the 'leftist' Council of disregarding
member views on ethnic minority recruitment targets. Its equal opportunities committee 'are all very well known members of the liberal left establishment'. Anti-discrimination rules assumed solicitors were 'racist', but
there was no discrimination within 'our learned profession'. The ban on
sexual orientation discrimination was 'an insult to the profession'. What if
a gay solicitor came to work with lipstick?

Soon after Mears's election the honourary auditor's report claimed that
the SCF was potentially liable for £120 million, the Society had twice the
staff per members as the Institute of Chartered Accountants and the
Gazette lost £400,000 per year although *Accountancy* broke even. At his first
Council meeting Mears moved that a working party pursue these issues.
'When you ask solicitors what they want from the Law Society the answer is
much less of it.' Expenditures had doubled in the previous six years, at
which rate they would reach £100 million in the next six. Past president
Holland denounced the motion as 'misguided and misconceived' and the
attack as 'a series of allegations and half truths'. Finance committee member
Mike Howells commented: 'Most members have a sense of humility and
don't speak in council until they have something sensible to contribute'.
Robert Winstanley condemned Mears's election manifesto for assailing the
'voting fodder of the Chancery Lane consensus'. Eileen Pembridge asked
how Mears 'would know what goes on at the council? As far as I'm aware
he's never been present at a meeting.' John Hayes objected to 'the Society
being scapegoated for the problems caused by the recession'.

But another Council member warned 'there are not just a few mavericks'.
Mears and the auditor 'touched on matters that are of acute concern to the
profession'. Robert Sayer (a small-firm solicitor just elected from Central
and South Middlesex) agreed 'expenditure is going up inexorably year after
year at a time when most firms' income is going down. The profession
ought to know where the money is going and ought to know that they are
getting value for it.' The Council 'appears to give priority to the interests of

people other than its own members' by such 'politically correct crap' as extending remuneration certificates to probate beneficiaries and 'encouraging the public to complain'. '[D]on't publicise' the SCB. People 'know how to complain and you don't what [*sic*] to be putting the idea into their heads all the time'. The Society's 'primary duty is to solve the problem of low fees' caused by 'cut price conveyancing' and 'the erosion of proper legal aid fees'. The 'ordinary high street practitioner has as much relationship to a reasonable-sized commercial firm as Wimpey the builder does to a jobbing contractor'. The *New Law Journal* thought Mears's 'interesting debut' had 'fairly put the cat amongst the pigeons'.[8]

The Society's annual conference in London attracted 520 law society representatives and staff but only 340 paying delegates. When President Charles Elly rejected SPyG chair Leslie Dubow's proposal that the Society become 'an exclusive self-serving pressure group', Dubow said Elly did not understand the Law Society's 'dual roles' as representative and regulator. He accused it of 'censoring' his question about hiving off the SCB (like the General Medical Council)— 'another example of the undemocratic nature of the Society'. A few weeks later the SPyG launched a new association 'dedicated to the interests of the high street conveyancer' because the Society had 'a complacent if not defeatist attitude' toward their plight. Complaining about the 'impossibly short time' for consultation on proposals for a conveyancing standard, the SPyG accused the Society of treating solicitors like 'silly little children to be told by "Mummy Law Society" what is best for them'. The Society's property and commercial services (PACS) committee chair called the SPyG press release 'atrocious'. The SPyG retorted that a majority of solicitors opposed the kite mark. 'If there ever was a conflict between the rulemakers and the ruled then this must be it.'[9]

At the first 'Meet the Law Society' event in Norwich one solicitor charged the SCB with 'consuming ever greater proportions of our money for ever lower standards of performance', and another accused staff of 'nitwitedness'—comments the SCB Director found 'extraordinarily offensive'. Mears dismissed the event as a 'love-in', which disguised solicitors' 'burning anger'. At the second meeting a solicitor criticized the Society's embrace of separate conveyancing by lenders and buyers, which the SPyG had called 'perverse' and 'contemptuous'. 'What it comes down to is that Chancery Lane knows what is best for us'. Elly replied: 'You elected the members of the Council for their expertise and at the end of the day we must use our best judgment'.[10]

In March, Mears and Pembridge both challenged VP John Young (the Council nominee) for the presidency—the first such contest in memory. Sayer joined Mears to fight DVP Henry Hodge (the Council nominee) for VP. Mears charged the Society with 'defeatism or no-can-doism'. The battle against legal aid cuts 'could have been won if years ago the Society had set itself to root out abuses'. 'A true strategy would...have foreseen years ago the excessive expansion of entrants into the profession and taken measures to prevent it'. Like Clinton, he advised gay and lesbian solicitors 'Just for God's sake keep it to yourself!' Chancery Lane 'insiders' were 'expert practitioners of cant and hypocrisy'. The SCB 'promotes the idea that solicitors are...incompetent'. 'Its very name encourages complainants to come forward.' He would seek three terms and urged other 'radicals' to contest the fifteen vacant Council seats.

Pembridge championed legal aid and women but was not anti-establishment. 'How do you propose to lead the profession if you are anti everything?' Members had to choose between a 'sticker' (Young), a 'wrecker' (Mears), and a 'shaker' (herself). Young—City partner, SIF chair, and the longest-serving Council member—was expected to win easily. He urged members 'to vote for those who have trained for the job and who have contributed to the profession over many years'. Hodge called Mears and Sayer 'long on rhetoric and short on problems and solutions'.

Elly found it 'disappointing that we are going to have the distraction of an election when there are so many things to be grappled with'. Mears retorted: 'The idea of a democratic election being a distraction is one which you would not expect to find favour outside the old Politburo'. He was not 'anti-homosexual' just 'anti-posturing'. Both the *New Law Journal* and the *Solicitors Journal* claimed that solicitors welcomed the contest. But the YSG called Mears 'destructive rather than reformist', and the *Guardian* assailed him as a 'reactionary' 'right wing agitator' with 'deeply repugnant opinions'.[11]

At an April Law Society conference (strangely) entitled 'The Woman Lawyer: benefit or burden?' Pembridge challenged Elly to address sexual harassment at Chancery Lane, denouncing his 'apparent hypocrisy' in speaking against it but condoning a notorious case two years earlier. Women were '30 per cent of the profession and 54 per cent of new entrants' but 'grossly underrepresented in Council and at partnership level'.

Issues like part-time work, the glass ceiling, maternity leave for partners and women leaving it so late to have their children that they are spending their spare hours down the fertility clinics need to be brought to the fore.

The *Solicitors Journal* praised her for raising sexual harassment. Allegations against 'a senior member of the Law Society Council have been circulating for a couple of years'. But they should be 'an equal opportunities matter' rather than 'an election matter'.[12] Young promptly withdrew from the race, admitting he had been the object of Pembridge's charges two years earlier. 'While there was never a case where my conduct amounted to persistent harassment, it would be equally wrong to characterise what was being alleged as trivial.' Pembridge had urged that he be asked to stand down as

DVP but was overruled and assured that the Society would create mechanisms for raising such charges. Nothing was done.

The *New Law Journal* praised Young for doing 'exactly the right thing', which 'required a good deal of courage'. But it also reported 'an Establishment backlash against [Pembridge] and considerable—and what some may see as misplaced—sympathy for Mr Young'. Mears brazenly capitalized on this. The 'poor fellow' had 'paid dearly for his sins', mere 'indiscretions committed two years ago', 'belatedly... resurrected' in a 'vile and contemptible' manner 'worthy of the worst of the tabloids'. Mears would 'fight this campaign cleanly and leave the gutter for whoever wishes to play there'. But the *New Law Journal* described 'the full picture... a pattern of conduct involving a number of women going back 20 years and known throughout the Society'. '[S]enior Council members... turning a blind eye... call... into question their whole fitness to make decisions on behalf of the profession'. Less than two months later a women guest accused Young of assaulting her in the library after a Council dinner.

The Council endorsed Hodge for president, John Aucott (senior partner of Edge & Ellison, a leading Birmingham firm, and eleven-year Council member) for VP, and Tony Girling (name partner of a twenty-three-lawyer Kent firm) for DVP. Holland urged a woman candidate to 'balance the ticket', which Bahl agreed would have 'recognised the percentage of women in the profession'. Pembridge (who later claimed she had agreed to accept the VP nomination but was rebuffed by Hodge) proposed a dedicated Council seat for women; but three women members opposed it. Pembridge dismissed objections to positive discrimination as 'stupid and outrageous'. Hodge was 'compromised by being at the top of the greasy pole, too. He can't show that he would stand up fearlessly for or effect reform....' The 'old boys' have 'put friendships above duty, served time, stayed in line'. 'They have spoken with forked tongues, covered up when they shouldn't....' Mears and Sayer were guilty of 'blatant demagoguery' and 'simply either don't know about the issues in depth or have decided to keep themselves in ignorance because of the risk of tainting'. She would not 'woo votes with false promises'. 'Clients will not pay more, they will not stop complaining if they have had a poor service, fees will not double, trainees will keep knocking at the door until the market finds its new level.' But she wanted to cap SCF liability to corporate claimants and defend practitioners against 'unreasonable demands made by bulk purchasers of legal services'.

Hodge's fifty-page manifesto proposed a 10 per cent cut in practising certificate fees, lower SIF contributions (proportioned to risk), and greater efficiency. Mears denounced Hodge as both 'leftist' and establishment— 'a Law Society Poo Bah for 11 years', 'Henry Hodge OBE'. During his tenure practising certificate fees had risen from £80 to £495 and the Society's budget from £6.2 million to £48 million. There had been 'no increase in legal aid rates for four years, the imposition of franchising and fixed fees [and] block grants on the horizon'. Hodge retorted: 'The position we do not trumpet is that over the last five years the amount of money coming from the legal aid system into the profession has doubled', and magistrates' court standard fees had been delayed four years. He wooed conveyancers with a 'guideline fee structure' and opposition to separate representation. The SCB should become a Law Society 'agency' targeting firms with poor complaints records. Aucott called himself a 'moderniser. I believe that the law is a business and has to be run like a business.' 'I am not going to tell solicitors what they want to hear' but 'what they have to hear if they are to survive in the changed world in which we live'.

Mears wanted to dampen competition by 'reducing the number of entrants into the profession'. He would rename the SCB 'so it no longer serves as a beacon for the malcontent' and charges 'a refundable deposit'. Sayer declared it should be limited to 'gross misconduct' and not 'impose higher standards on us than are reasonable in the real world'. He accused the Society of 'years of inadequate campaigning' for higher legal aid remu- neration and allowing conveyancing firms 'to compete to the point of destruction'. Both promised to cut SIF premiums by a third by charging an additional £100 for each conveyance. Sayer called Aucott a 'Law Society functionary' and assailed the Society for failing 'to get off its backside and do something about the obvious problems affecting its members'. It had authorized 8,000 LPC places although there were only 3,500 traineeships. The Society should have 'the guts to do something to bring supply back in line with demand'. He and Mears proposed cutting course places to 1,000 (the number leaving the profession annually). They offered the disaffected 'their one choice to show how unhappy they are'. Holland said it was 'impossible' to 'match supply with demand'. Aucott accused Sayer of pre- tending 'he can recreate the past'.

In Soviet Russia they used to have a five year plan, where some bureaucrat decided how much of what the country would need. The inevitable result was chronic short- ages of some things and over supply of others.[13]

Mears wanted the Society to assert control over the 'schizophrenic' SCB and its 'tiresome' independence. 'There is no reason why the profession should be ashamed of dealing itself with complaints against its members.' A 'visitor' should investigate the SCB regularly and 'deal roughly' with it 'when necessary'. Hodge agreed it needed a 'thorough and radical review' but should not become 'the Law Society's complaints department'. It was made independent in 1986 because of the 'scandalous failure of the earlier self-regulatory system'. Pembridge dismissed some complaints as 'a form of last-ditch discounting on bills' and agreed that complainants should pay 'a modest deposit', but Hodge called this impractical: 'imagine how the Sun or the Telegraph will handle the case if a poor widow, badly treated by her solicitor, is unable to afford the complaint'. Mears and Sayer assailed the Society staff: natural wastage should cut their numbers and elected officials take a larger role; the Secretary-General should be 'a competent administrator who will implement the policies of the elected representatives'. Pembridge called Mears an 'objectionable candidate, with reactionary views and a wholly unproductive anti-Chancery Lane line'. Aucott dismissed his 'populist message. You have to put the client first, not the solicitor. If you try to impose fixed fees or any restrictive practice the government will regulate us out of sight'.[14]

Hodge and Aucott posed the 'stark choice' between a profession with them or a trade association with Mears and Sayer, who 'want to turn the clock back. 1984 seems to be their preferred year! They want us to be the only service business where the client comes second.' Hodge warned against 'a narrow-minded and inward looking protectionism...the creation of cartels or artificially inflating bills by charging overheads as a disbursement'. The solution to oversupply 'is already in our hands. We let the training contracts. We have kept them steady for years now at just under 4,000.' Mears would make solicitors look 'foolish'. '[T]he public are more likely to laugh at us than like us.' 'Unlike my opponents', Hodge claimed, 'I have the backing of the Law Society Council and the respect of the staff'. 'After five years on the Council [Pembridge] has not learned much more than Mr Mears about how to achieve change.' A 'vote for Pembridge is a vote for Mears', who was only 'interested in promoting himself'. A poll of thirty-five prominent non-Council solicitors, including the SPyG, SPG, Commerce and Industry Group, and YSG chairs, showed strong support for Hodge's ticket.

Pembridge was sceptical about raising conveyancing fees. 'My firm tried it and failed.' Mears and Sayer 'unashamedly peddle simplified versions of the problems and then, like fairgrounds boothkeepers, provide you with a whizzo guaranteed patent remedy'. They 'will sell you dreams'. Commercial firms 'might simply declare UDI if they thought that the Boys' Own Annual were at the helm'.

Mears played on fears of overcrowding. 'In the 1980s, manufacturing industry was left to market forces and we all know what happened to that.' 'Ten years ago, ours was the safest of occupations, with a guaranteed good income for life.' 'A client is entitled to sue his solicitor for negligence but he has no God given right to insist that his solicitor carries insurance.' Chancery Lane was guilty of 'bureaucracy, waste and extravagance'; it planned to open 'a new regional office every year' and 'spend over £10 million on works to the headquarters'. Sayer accused the Society of being 'afraid of upsetting the government, and consumer pressure groups' and 'too timid and defeatist to stand up for ordinary solicitors'. '[I]f saving [the profession] means putting the profession's interest temporarily in front of clients I will do so and be proud of it.' He defiantly told the SPyG: 'We will not put up with crap from anyone who gets in our way. We will go over their heads for a profession-wide vote.' Hodge retorted he would 'not waste people's money by holding referenda'.[15]

Rumours of improper influence surfaced just before the vote tally. The Society establishment was said to have persuaded large-firm senior partners to urge subordinates to vote for Hodge and Aucott. Mark Sheldon denied this. But someone leaked a memo from Caryn Mackenzie of the City firm Field Fisher Waterhouse disparaging Mears as a sole practitioner (untrue) with 'ideas which will not be to the best benefit of firms like ours' and Pembridge as 'running a legal aid/feminist agenda'. '[I]f you are not interested in voting could you please, at least, let me have your voting form so that we can put in a block vote.' Mackenzie was proud her 'reasonably contentious' style 'crank[ed] up interest'. Repeating charges that the thirty largest firms had been approached, the *New Law Journal* asked: 'How is a young solicitor just making his or her way in the profession supposed to react to "advice" from the senior partner to vote for Mr Hodge?' 'Wake up Chancery Lane.' This 'dismissive attitude' toward 'rank and file' had generated the contested election. The Law Society AGM urged the appointment of outside scrutineers, and the South London Law Society voted no confidence in the Society's ability to conduct an election.

Mears and Sayer called block voting 'extremely disturbing', asked Elly to condemn the memo, and assailed his refusal to appoint scrutineers. Pembridge's campaign was 'investigating these and other suspected irregularities which cast doubt on the validity and integrity of the entire election'. The 'old boys ... treat the Law Society as a club for their exclusive use and the members as an inconvenience'. Hodge acknowledged approaching City firms but insisted 'we have given no encouragement to block voting. I do not approve of it and I do not believe it has happened'. 'It is a standard technique of those who are losing to challenge the good faith of the electoral system'.[16]

In her final statement Pembridge declared the present Council 'unable to represent the profession as it is (youngish, employed, increasingly female)' and Mears's proposals 'either unlawful, impossible or plain daft'. He 'cannot be taken seriously as a solution'. Hodge invoked 'the support and confidence of the Law Society Council ... we will be respected and taken seriously in Westminster and Whitehall and in the media'. Mears claimed 'people don't like nudging from their local grandee'. He denied that 'direct discrimination ... really exists in our profession'; the only solution was 'a quota system, which is illegal'. A black lawyer retorted that Mears 'exacerbate[d] the problem of discrimination'.[17]

Mears won a plurality (11,550 against 8,254 for Hodge and 3,515 for Pembridge), with a 36 per cent turnout. Sayer beat Aucott (12,384 to 9,987), and Girling was unopposed. Anthony Bogan, a Mears supporter, defeated eight-year incumbent Paul Marsh for the one contested Council seat. Mears was pugnacious: 'It was possible for the council to ignore us before because we were in a minority of two. Now, though, we can hardly be ignored.' He declared: 'The council must assume that it is possible that the profession's view is the same as mine' (although only 18 per cent of members voted for him). He hoped 'to work very closely with Henry Hodge and Eileen Pembridge' but warned against the 'half a dozen irreconcilables', including Holland, who had called the election 'a disaster for the profession'. The BLA asked Council members who opposed Mears to stand down. Rosen declared: 'The profession has voted against the status quo' and delivered 'a mandate for Martin Mears'. Although Sayer assured members 'we have no intention of doing anything rash or daft' he was still committed to reducing entry to 1,000.

Simon Baker, chair of the Society's training committee, responded that 'no strategy of restrictive practices will ever win'. The CRE legal director was 'extremely worried by [Mears's] lack of understanding of equality issues'. Pembridge criticized his opposition to a sexual harassment officer. Hodge warned that City firms were considering leaving the Society. An Allen & Overy partner said Mears's agenda was not 'relevant to a business of an international nature'. LAG called Mears 'rough, rebellious and wrong'. His 'misreading of the relative power of the profession and the state' was 'dangerous'. Editorializing that 'the Barbarians enter the gates', the *New Law Journal* reported 'rumours that senior members of the staff of the Law Society would welcome the opportunity to have their contracts terminated if proper compensation was on offer'. A Council-endorsed challenge to Mears next year would 'be entertaining beyond measure for the spectator and disastrous beyond measure for the profession'.[18]

At the Society AGM two weeks later Mears called Pembridge 'the most dangerous feminist in England'. She was not amused when he praised her 'indomitable energy, courage and sincerity', adding she had fought 'like a man'. He was proud to be called 'the most dangerous lawyer in England... a cross between Enoch Powell and Tony Benn'. Mears denied any 'conflict of interest whatever between the true interest of the profession and the true interest of the public. All but the most demented consumerists realise' that 'the inevitable result' of unrestrained competition 'must be a fall in the standard of service to the client'. The AGM passed his resolutions to create working parties to reduce the number of solicitors and the cost of indemnity insurance and to improve the profession's image. A Hodge supporter declared that 'the bare faced cheek of the rebel candidate is reappearing in an agenda which is suddenly looking empty and bereft of the radicalism promised'.[19]

Holland resigned from the Council, declaring 'no confidence in the ability of either Mears or Sayer'. Mears had asked him for a period of silence. 'Having raised Cain about his Council colleagues and rubbished their efforts...he can hardly expect now a respectful silence.' Mears ridiculed Holland for labouring 'under the appealing but erroneous delusion that the eyes of the world are upon him'. 'Since my election I have received nothing but good wishes and promises of support from my Council colleagues.'[20]

Mears's first presidential column charged that the Council's 'insouciance' in disregarding 'plummeting' conveyancing fees and 'collapsing' high-street practices had 'enraged the profession'. He wanted to re-establish 'an enforceable fee scale for domestic conveyancing' and the profession's 'right to control the number of new entrants and trainees', 'see off' the legal aid Green Paper, reorganize the SCB (omitting the word complaints) and 'confront the public's negative perception of lawyers...through a carefully thought out advertising campaign'.[21]

But his first target was Chancery Lane. When Hayes's ten-year contract expired at the end of 1996 Mears wanted to strip the next Secretary-General of 'the kind of security of tenure enjoyed by the present incumbent' to make clear 'he is subordinate to and responsible to the President'. Staff should report to the Council and officers rather than the 'over mighty' Secretary-General. The finance committee should offer senior staff severance packages to help 'the elected representatives to gain control over the organisation'. Hayes resented Mears's accusation that he had 'brought the profession to its knees' and 'wasted Council assets'. But less than five months after the election he resigned with effect from the next June. Although past presidents Pannone, Holland, and Sheldon praised Hayes, Rosen said he left 'a legacy of unpopularity of the administration by the profession' and blamed him for the growth of the 'colossal regulatory arm'.[22]

At its next meeting the Council adopted without debate (over Mears's sole vote) a proposal to explore constitutional reforms, including a Council-elected policy committee and specialist sections in place of presidentially-appointed committees and groups. Mears complained that removing him as chair of the strategy committee and Council meetings would 'strip the leader of substantial authority and functions and leave him as a ceremonial figurehead'. Specialist sections resembled 'the Francoist corporate state'. The proposals' 'interesting' timing showed 'the gaping disparity between the Law Society's concerns...and the profession's'.[23]

Mears told the October annual conference he would seek re-election without endorsement by the Council, which he feared was planning 'to reject each proposal impartially'. If it did, he urged the profession 'to take its revenge...if your sitting member is really [not] a supporter of the reform programme...I hope his seat will be contested'. He wrote to every Council member, demanding support. 'Mutual affability is not enough.

There must be agreement about policy.' Rosen had begun to organize a list of reform candidates for the 1996 election, whose platform would be 'a lack of confidence in what has been achieved by a Council that defers to the Secretary-General'. 'Council members can anticipate exposure to the oxygen of publicity.' John Edge, whose proposal to increase conveyancing fees Mears backed, also encouraged members to contest seats. Council members' reactions varied from 'speechless anger to controlled sadness'. Phillip Sycamore protested that 'the President is not the only Council member with a mandate'. Hodge insisted 'the Council won't be bullied'. But the *Solicitors Journal* claimed that 'even those who did not vote for Mr Mears are enjoying the sight [of] the establishment being shaken up, the sound of someone who is determined to try for a change'. Sayer wanted the Council to report votes. 'If more elections are contested, then perhaps constituents should be aware how their candidates have voted in the past.' This was 'not a witch hunt'. But though Hodge called the proposal 'party political', it was passed with just three objections.[24]

Helen Davies declared her candidacy for Holland's Council seat, endorsing Edge's conveyancing proposal. Although two other candidates made conveyancing their central issue and the third focused on the profession's image, Davies received Edge's endorsement and won more than twice the votes of the next contender.[25]

Mears formed the President's Reform Group, which had nine Council members by the end of November and hoped for fifteen to twenty, to 'meet, decide, and (generally) vote as a body'. He claimed 'the great majority' of the Council were not unfriendly and strong supporters outnumbered strong opponents, but 'a few of the officials... rejoice inwardly... over every setback and discomfort we suffer' and were 'a fertile source of denigratory rumour'. The Law Society 'ship has one captain, the elected President, who is entitled to expect the loyalty and commitment of the whole organisation'. But the *New Law Journal* reported a 'gulf... between the beleaguered duo and most of the rest of the Council and senior management', and the *Gazette* deplored the 'hotbed of warring factions... the spectacle of running battles'.[26]

A few weeks later Sayer accused Treasurer Michael Howells of preventing independent consultants from examining expenditures and assailed a staff redraft of the conveyancing consultation paper as 'an absolute, blatant arrogant attempt to sabotage' his proposal. PACS chair Richard Hegarty said there had been a unanimous decision that Sayer's draft 'was not a balanced document'. A Council member observed that 'the vice president has many attributes but drafting is not one of them'. Member dissatisfaction intensified when the SIF and College of Law directorships and the Society Secretary-Generalship were advertised at salaries of over £100,000, although high-street solicitors were 'still suffering the chill winds of the recession'.[27]

Mears had used the Society's annual conference to mock the LCD White Paper easing divorce. 'Jesus, it seems, had He been Lord Chancellor, would also have endorsed the proposals. Perhaps Jesus never uttered the words usually attributed to Him: "Whom God hath joined together, let no man put asunder".' Three months later a *Mail on Sunday* front-page story entitled 'Love secrets of law chief' revealed Mears was divorced and living with the mother of his two illegitimate children. Its leader accused him of 'humbug and hypocrisy'. The *New Law Journal* said Mears had told the Young Women Lawyers group the woman was his 'wife'. Mears called this just 'a shorthand way of referring to the person you live with. There is no other word. "Cohabitee" is legalistic; "lover" is naff; "partner' is ambiguous.' He maintained 'the government should be looking at making [divorce] less easy'. His personal circumstances were 'irrelevant'. He attacked Sue Stapely, the Society's public relations head, for including the article in her regular cuttings service. 'I will be considering what the position is of those who circulated this within the Society.' He also contemplated suing the tabloid for libel. Girling 'very much regretted the adverse publicity' and said the public relations department 'have to circulate things'. Pembridge gloated: 'Those who live by the sword often die by it'. The chair of the family law committee said Mears's views on divorce did not reflect those of the Society.

Relying on verbatim minutes, Stapely said Mears 'very much hoped that the News of the World would defame [him] as [he was] "very litigious" and would relish the opportunity to take proceedings'. Andrew Lockley, Society media relations director, circulated a memo to journalists about the incident, which Mears called 'desperately damaging to me and by extension to the Law Society'. Sayer and he would 'have great difficulty in working with' Stapely and Lockley. Hayes expressed 'admiration and support for all staff in difficult times. It is their task to support the work of the Council as a whole, including the policy programme of the office holders.' They had 'acted in good faith and no disciplinary action should follow'.

Lockley resigned a few weeks later, after fourteen years at the Society. When Stapely left a month after that her former office claimed 'she wasn't pushed, nor did she jump'. The *Solicitors Journal* regretted the departure of such 'innovative and independent minded' staff. The *New Law Journal* deplored the 'concerted effort to destroy each other'.

The Lord Chancellor, the Bar Council and other organisations whose interests are sometimes inimical to those of solicitors must be howling with glee when they read of quarrels over bottles of brandy, hidden letters, numbers of children accruing to partners.... The internecine warfare is making us a laughing stock.[28]

The President's Reform Group (now eleven) met for the first time after the January Council meeting and presented Mears with a watch engraved

'Don't let the bastards get you down'—echoing the watch presented to Asil Nadir following the Polly Peck bankruptcy. Roger Wilson declared that 'the profession is hopelessly over-governed and the Law Society should be cut right back to concentrate on essential core services'. Bill Heath felt 'the profession is pissed off from top to bottom with the Council' and called for the Society's abolition. Peter Watson-Lee accused older Council members of 'an arrogant and cynical dismissal of the opinions of solicitors'.[29]

Six months after leaving the Council, Holland called Mears's promises 'wholly unachievable'. He had 'wanted a better public image of the profession' but 'has produced the exact opposite'. 'A further year of the Mears/ Sayer combination could well finish the profession's standing'. Mears retorted that when Holland had served, 'the Council functioned as a kind of politbureau [*sic*] whose ethos was deadening consensus'. Pembridge denounced Mears's performance as 'seriously bad news for all of us', lacking 'charisma, vision or positive forward thinking'.[30]

Seeking an unprecedented second term, Mears sought to end mandatory continuing education and boasted of refusing 'freebie' 'junkets' to Chicago, Brisbane, Milan, Vienna, Barcelona, Berlin, and Warsaw while visiting Doncaster, Newcastle, Birmingham, and Nottingham.

One Past President rises in Council to demand that a hostile letter he has sent to me be circulated. Another seems to have given over his twilight years to composing denunciations of me and all my works. Last year's defeated presidential candidates, whom I thought were dead and buried with stakes through their hearts, have risen to affright my waking hours.

He was 'Richard III at the battle of Bosworth. With half his forces in covert alliance with the other side, it was no wonder he lost. But perhaps it is all my paranoia.' Adversaries engaged in 'large scale disinformation'. Sayer and he 'have been unwillingly involved in a kind of trench warfare and if we finally fail this is far more likely to be the consequence of internal rather than external opposition'. Sayer denounced 'Law Society groupies', wanted every vacant Council seat contested, and planned to run for president in a year. 'My driving force is that I'm bloody minded. I'm just increasingly fed up with the ways in which the Law Society sticks its paws into how I run my business.' A few weeks later David Keating joined their ticket as DVP candidate.[31]

John Edge obtained counsel's opinion that a Society SGM could amend the by-laws to require all Council members to stand for re-election in order 'to bring home to [them] just how precarious their positions are'. 'Supporters of the conveyancing fee initiative are not satisfied that the Council is trying hard enough on the conveyancing question.' But he would wait until after the 1996 election, in which he supported Mears.[32]

The *Solicitors Journal* called on 'the profession finally to bite the bullet and separate the disciplinary and regulatory functions of the Law Society from its role as a trade union'. 'The most bitter wrangles...over the past three years have been about the Society's role as a regulator....In contrast, the Society was very much supported by the profession when it lobbied on our behalf.' Accountants were 'considering separating the functions'. The BLA General Secretary said 'the catalyst for its formation was the common belief that the dual role of the Law Society as regulator/representative was unworkable'. 'We are probably the most over-regulated profession in the world. To comply with the Ten Commandments we have devised Twenty-nine of our own, subdivided ad infinitum, and enforced by a bureaucracy costing us over £11m a year'.[33]

Bogan (who had won the previous year's only contested Council seat as a Mears supporter) launched the Solicitors Association (SA) because of the 'inherent conflict' between regulation and representation. 'The case for a legal trade union is made out' by 'pitiful rates for conveyancing and legal aid work'. City firms feared the accountants. 'The growth of independent networks and specialist panels bear witness to the inability of the Law Society to fully discharge a representative function.'

I have finally established a link between CJD and the Law Society. The government are hoping to gain the confidence of the electorate by slaughtering cattle, all we are doing is looking to re-establish confidence ourselves and a bit of selective culling wouldn't go amiss at the Law Society.

Mears 'sympathised with and respected' Bogan's goal but saw 'no advantage in handing over the regulatory functions to a body over which we would have no control'. Sayer also thought this 'too drastic'. Holland said the premise was false: 'Doctors are employees, so they need a representative body such as the BMA'. Bogan was adamant: 'the hostility that has been manifest in Council debates over the last 12 months is indicative of the inherent conflict' between the functions. A regulatory body had to champion the public interest. But the SA declared that 'the profession's interests must be the prime determinant of its policies'.[34]

Edge, another Mears ally, wrote to the 12,700 who signed his conveyancing fee initiative (see Chapter 6), urging them to join the SA, which had 600 members after three weeks and was gaining fifty a day. Bogan thought it 'not unreasonable to expect a membership getting on for 20,000 by the end of the next few months'. The SA proposed that the Society's July AGM divorce representation (which it would assume) from regulation, allow postal ballots to dissolve the Council and force an election to all seats, and eliminate the residence requirement.[35]

Hayes opposed the split but agreed 'we are in a mess'. Large commercial firms, resenting the cost of the SCB, SCF, and SIF, 'might decide to form their own regulatory organisation'. So might specialists and franchiseholders. Indeed, in May the Council proposed a pilot probate section, the first substantive constituency; 88 per cent of the 1,500 probate solicitors surveyed were positive. Lockley argued that because the Society has 'sole and exclusive powers over finance and management...unless the council agree to split resources it looks as if that particular objective would fall at the first hurdle'. The *Solicitors Journal* proposed the 'radical solution' of limiting the practising certificate fee to regulatory functions. A poll found that nearly half of respondents favoured division.[36]

Mears asked why 'we need a new representative body...which on the face of it is no more than a reanimated British Legal Association?' There was 'no conflict between the enlightened self-interest of the profession and that of the public'. Bogan retorted that Mears 'fails to tell us how he will achive his worthy objectives within the existing structure'. Doctors allocated 80 per cent of their subscriptions to the BMA, which 'does them proud. We spend less than 30% and we represent ourselves badly.'[37]

In his valedictory speech at the March Council meeting, Peter Verdin asked whether 'the emperor has no clothes?' Although Mears had to read a fulsome tribute, he then held an impromptu press conference, attacking Verdin and declaring the 'assumptions, conventions and orthodoxies' of the 'hothouse world' of Chancery Lane 'wholly at variance with those of the profession outside'. Later that month LAG asked 'who will rid us of these turbulent men?' The 'joke' had 'gone sour'. The Society's 'doings read more like a soap opera'; it was 'degenerating into a very public farce'. The *Solicitors Journal* called for 'a credible challenge' to Mears. 'Limiting entry to the profession, taking action on conveyancing fees and changing the SCB are three policies that sounded better on the hustings than they look in action today.' Mears had been right to challenge the establishment, but 'he is now the establishment and should be challenged'. The local law societies' annual meeting was accelerated to discuss the proposition that the national Society should 'conduct its business in such a manner as to enhance rather than damage the reputation of the solicitors' profession in the eyes of the public'. Mears was openly scornful. 'What we are seeing is healthy democratic debate.' Did they 'really want to go back to the old politburo-style days?' When the Society appointed Jane Betts Secretary-General, Lockley wrote her an open letter praising the staff as a 'priceless asset' and decrying that 'political posturing has led some to accuse them of all sorts of imagined crimes against humanity'.[38]

At the April Council meeting John Franks compared Mears to 'Arthur Scargill just before he led his members into the strike that annihilated their union'. When the Bar Council chair deplored discrimination against women at the annual women lawyers conference that month, Mears assailed a 'discrimination industry' driven by 'zealots' and dismissed prejudice as 'a nonsense and a fiction'. '[F]eminism is the orthodoxy and it is a bold heretic [like himself] who challenges any of its doctrines.' The Society's equal opportunities committee chair insisted that discrimination was still a 'vast problem'. Bahl called the speech 'one example of certain attitudes that definitely need changing'. Stapely urged women to 'oust Mears and his ilk from the leadership of their profession'. Pembridge declared: 'somebody should stand against' him and offered to do so if no one else came forward. The *Solicitors Journal* accused Mears of doing 'employment lawyers a disservice ... by way of a tabloid headline turn of expression'. The *New Law Journal* said he 'appears quite needlessly to be doing what he can to upset large tranches of the profession he represents'. Nevertheless, the *Lawyer* made him its 'legal personality of the year' for giving 'Chancery Lane a much needed shake up' and gaining 'fame—and notoriety—as one of the most colourful Law Society figures ever'.[39]

In early May Mears exulted that no one opposed him. '[M]y support is even stronger than it was last year' despite media 'vilification and disinformation', such as the charge of excess drinking at the presidential residence, exposed as 'entirely a canard'. But Elly told the LAPG annual conference it was 'disgraceful' that Mears met Mackay about legal aid only once. 'We give the impression now that it is the interests of the profession we have at heart, not the interests of the public.' The LAPG voted by 16 to 0, with 3 abstentions, its 'lack of confidence in the current President of the Law Society, with regard to his leadership of the profession and, in particular, his apparent lack of interest in legal aid issues and therefore urges that his forthcoming attempt at re-election be contested'. Mears complained of 'intrigue', 'an attempt at a backstairs coup', which was 'characteristic of the way left-wing cliques used to manipulate trade unions and local authorities. It is no coincidence that Mrs Pembridge and Messrs Gilchrist [her campaign manager] and Smith [LAG director] all come from the small coterie of metropolitan leftists who were my vociferous opponents last year.'[40]

Ten solicitors promptly launched the Campaign for New Leadership (CNL), asking Mears and Sayer to stand down or it would 'be devoting its considerable resources' to opposition. Its press release on 'the rise and fall of Martin Mears and Robert Sayer', headlined 'a dinosaur at the Law Society', went to 950 solicitors, Council members, and local law society heads. ' "Shambles"—"Soap Opera"—"Farce" This is how the media have described the current pantomime at Chancery Lane.' Mears and Sayer

thrive on conflict—but achieve nothing. They talk of economy—but [spend] the profession's cash pursuing mirages.... They raised expectations of results they could never deliver. In frustration, their wilder supporters now talk of smashing up the Law Society itself.

Within a week they received nearly 100 positive replies.

Bogan denounced CNL as 'negative and reactionary'. Mears dismissed it as a 'small band of establishment groupies'. 'Wrapping old fish in fresh paper', said Sayer, 'doesn't make it smell any sweeter'. 'Blaming us for the infighting and all the stories leaked to the press is like blaming the victim for being mugged.' 'I loathe [the Society's] bureaucratic "We know what is best for you" attitude.' But Mears defector Peter Hughes called it 'silly and divisive to go off in a huff and blame everybody else when you find that nobody wants fool's gold. It is silly to break things, unless you have something to put it their place.' 'I don't want oligarchy simply replaced by dictatorship.' The *Solicitors Journal* thought the CNL letter 'reads more like a protest than a policy document'. Mears was 'justified' in claiming 'that implementing real change was impossible with nearly the whole Council against him'. It urged 'an orderly election campaign in which all candidates focus on issues without resorting to personality attacks'. A few days later Phillip Sycamore (a member of a three-partner Blackpool firm) hinted he would stand with Tony Girling and Michael Mathews (a Clifford Chance partner). At the same time Helen Davies and Angela Deacon repudiated Mears because of his comments to the conference on women lawyers.[41]

Mears unleashed his invective at the 'dozen or so brave spirits meeting in out-of-the-way conventicles and exchanging the secret password'. They sought 'to restore the golden era of the Law Society as it was before Mears and Sayer, loved by solicitors and public alike, respected by the press and feared by the government...let us call it the Campaign to Bring Back Buggins'. They wanted 'a return to the good old policies...Practice Management Standards; Conveyancing Kite Marks; specialist accreditations; regulation and yet more regulation; an inexorable rise in expenditure and staff numbers'. The 'presidential aspirants so rudely deprived of their birthright last summer' had blocked his programme. '[A]ny criticism I have made of my opponents has been in response to direct attacks from them.' He blamed the bad press on opponents who told reporters 'we have become a shambles/laughing stock/soap opera'.[42]

At a press conference on retiring from the Council after eighteen years, Pannone (the president two years before) warned that the 'unedifying' behaviour of Mears and Sayer 'could well debase the good name of the Law Society'. He had given Mears 'a fair chance...and he has failed'. Mears replied with his own press conference. He had promised 'revolution. Everyone acknowledges that at least I have done that.' Pannone had been 'unremittingly hostile, to the point where he would come up to me and Robert Sayer and call us names'. He denounced Pannone's 'hostile action' and an earlier 'letter of rambling denunciation'. He associated Pannone with the Society's bloated bureaucracy, the profession's alienation, and the cover-up of Young's sexual harassment. 'Bad publicity' was caused by Pannone 'rubbishing the new regime', but Mears would be blamed in this 'world of Alice in Wonderland'. His only fault was not remaining 'silent in the face of humbug and cant'. The *Solicitors Journal* deplored the 'very personal vilification and bitterness' on both sides.

Walter Merricks became the fifth senior official to leave. On his own departure, Hayes accused Mears and Sayer of believing 'the causes for which they were elected merit a suspension of the normal democratic conventions under which the Society was governed'. 'Wherever you go—among ministers, the judiciary, leaders of other bodies here and abroad—they can't believe what is happening to the Law Society. The issue is fitness to govern.' Mears called Hayes the 'ruler of the Law Society for the last 10 years during which time staff numbers trebled and there was an enormous increase in expenditure'. Angus Andrew, whom Hodge supported to fill his Council seat, was 'appalled by the current president and his supporters and the extent to which they have brought the profession into disrepute'. The *Solicitors Journal* echoed Pannone's judgment that 'the Society has lost the respect of decision makers in parliament, of the Bar, of the judiciary and the international legal profession'.

Andrew Holroyd, former Liverpool Law Society president, crushed Mears supporter John Callaghan by 512 to 199 in an unusually high Council by-election poll of more than 50 per cent. Holroyd said Mears had 'antagonised a number of different special interest groups at a time when we should be trying to unite the profession'. But Sayer claimed that 'support for us is, if anything, stronger this year'. David McIntosh, unchallenged for a City seat, criticized 'the self-centred approach manifested by the current leader of the Law Society' and would seek 'to bring to an end the pettiness and public bickering'. CNL founder Kevin Martin, uncontested in Warwickshire, ran against Mears's 'Flat Earth Society'.[43]

In early June Bogan declared his candidacy for the presidency while admitting: 'I don't want to be President. I want the [SA] resolutions passed'. Girling would be 'a return to "no can do-ism".' He told Mears: 'You have done a great job. And you have done so single-handedly. The profession will always owe you a great debt' and invited Mears and Sayer to join him. The Croyden and District Law Society president, a member of the SA steering committee, supported Bogan. 'We cannot afford to give Mears a second year.' 'I would not fear an independent regulator. We would run rings round an external regulator.' 'Competent lawyers unfettered can defeat that person any day of the week.'

Girling, Sycamore, and Mathews became the CNL slate, claiming support from Tony Edwards (a leading criminal lawyer), Michael Napier (APIL past president), Pembridge, Lesley MacDonagh (Lovell White joint managing partner), and the AWS, YSG, and Group for Solicitors with Disabilities. These 'candidates for the whole profession' were 'making the case for real reform'. Girling had 'tried very hard to work with' the incumbents but found that 'if you disagree with Martin Mears you're out of the pale'. 'The style of leadership ... invites confrontation.' '[T]he profession's reputation cannot be anything but damaged by descending into that sort of vitriol.' They were not the 'old guard'; Sycamore had been on the Council for five years and Mathews less than one. Mathews said City lawyers feared the Society's negative publicity 'might rub off' on them. '[T]he nat-ural tendency for extremist groups is to split', said Girling. 'Martin Mears hasn't even lasted a year.' Bogan was 'a one-issue candidate'.

Mears called it 'plainly not true and nonsense to say the Society is losing influence'. He stood 'between the policies of the old guard and people, such as Anthony Bogan, who live in a fantasy world. I offer a realistic middle course.' Bogan was a 'wild man'. ' 'Til last Monday he was posing as one of our warmest supporters.' 'A vote for the separation candidate is a wasted vote.' Sayer warned that 'hatred' might prompt an 'extreme protest vote' for Bogan, which 'would simply allow the establishment back in by the back door'.[44]

The Society obtained counsel's opinion that the SA proposal was 'wholly bizarre' and Privy Council approval essential but highly unlikely. Bizarre was not unlawful, retorted Edge, and counsel 'seemed to be expressing a personal point of view'. He denounced the Society's 'statutory monopoly of representation' as 'the last bastion of the closed shop' and was confident it could be abolished without primary legislation. The *Solicitors Journal* upbraided Bogan's opponents for having 'rather foolishly brushed aside the idea, which is already receiving parliamentary support'.[45]

Girling's 'business plan'—with 'Rebuilding respect for the Profession' emblazoned on each page—emphasized communications with and service to members, 'value for money' in the SCF and SCB, 'No giving up on con-veyancing', defence of legal aid, 'realistic careers advice', and an 'overall public relations' strategy. He was proud of blocking authorized conveyancers and non-solicitor probate practitioners, though 'we don't crow about either of those achievements because it would be counterproductive to do so'. Mears and Sayer had displayed 'a cocktail of inexperience, stubbornness and lack of realism'. One of Mears's nine Council allies had defected, and more would do so.

Mears sent all solicitors an open letter entitled 'No Turning Back!' 'Last July the profession voted for a revolution at the Law Society'. Sayer and he had 'been subjected to an unrelenting campaign of personal abuse, obstruction and disinformation'. He might have been 'too confrontational and not sufficiently canvassed opinion', but he had been repeatedly snubbed and obstructed by Council and staff. 'For arguing that, in prin-ciple, any profession should have control over its own numbers, we have been denounced as protectionists and flat earthers.' The profession had trebled in two decades and was adding 3,000 solicitors a year. 'Is it not a simple scan-dal that during the past twelve months the Law Society has actually *increased* the number of authorised [LPC] places?' There was 'ample evidence' of 'a link between cut price and claims on the SIF'. He blamed critics for the 'public's negative perception' of the profession. 'In the pre-Mears/Sayer days there was no unseemliness. Neither was there in the old Soviet polit-buro. Neither is there in a graveyard.' 'Whenever I talk to judges, politi-cians or opinion formers their comments on events at the Law Society is [*sic*] on the lines: "About time they had a shake-up"'. Society expenditures had increased fivefold in ten years, including 'preposterous instances of waste, extravagance and profligacy'. 'If the profession votes to bring back the Bourbons of the old regime... it will get—people who have learnt nothing.' 'Mr Girling and his supporters claim they are the right people to run the Law Society. Do leopards change their spots?' The SA proposals were 'profoundly misguided' and an election the wrong way to decide this 'important issue'.[46]

Girling found this 'personal attack' 'odd' because Mears had invited him to remain as Deputy Vice President (even after recruiting Keating for the position), which showed 'Mears will do anything which he thinks will help him stay in power'. Mears assailed this 'outrageous, mischievous disinforma-tion'; no one 'has made an approach on my behalf to Mr Girling'. But his campaign manager, Peter Watson-Lee, confirmed doing so in 'an off the record and confidential discussion'. Girling promised the CNL would move at the Society AGM to curb Mears's working parties on conveyancing fees, entry, and the £3 million public relations campaign.[47]

Bogan understandably savaged Mears. He took a strong anti-discrimination position: 'why aren't women in positions of power in the legal world and why aren't there more women on the Council?' He disagreed 'profoundly' with entry control. 'You can't deny an individual the right to aspire to be a lawyer if they want to'. The President's Reform Group 'seemed to consist largely of a few dinners in Carey Street to discuss the state of the profession, life and the universe'. Keating was added to the ticket 'round the dinner table without a lot of discussion'. '[S]enior MPs from all parties' warned that if the Society did 'not take steps to provide *transparency* between the dual roles of regulation and representation quickly, external regulation will be imposed on us. This is not "*fantasy*".' The BLA supported Bogan because Mears's opposition to splitting functions 'demonstrates a lack of vision and of courage to face the future'.[48]

Mears grew even more incendiary. 'I represent the revolution.' '[I]t was David and Goliath last year and it's David and Goliath again.' He would 'rout' and 'demoralize' the 'establishment'. 'Women journalists' concurred in his anti-feminist tirade. Accounts of newly qualified solicitors working without pay to get traineehips sent him 'into paroxysms of rage'. 'This situ-ation is a scandal... and everyone outside this place agrees with me.' Sayer assailed the Society's 'perverse' policies: 'support[ing] rights of audience for Legal Executives'; extending conditional fees to 'disgruntled clients wishing to sue their original personal injury solicitor'; and 'proposing a new alternative method of qualification based on work experience as a paralegal' for law graduates unable to get traineeships.[49]

Girling won a narrow majority (15,911 to 14,239 for Mears, 1,287 for Bogan, and 791 spoiled papers); Sycamore and Mathews had larger margins. The turnout rose to 45 per cent. All pro-Mears Council candidates lost, though some very closely. Howells defeated one by just four votes. The SDT had convicted Howells of violating conflict of interest rules. After the Appeals Committee administered a severe rebuke without a public hearing, the *New Law Journal* demanded his resignation, which he submitted at the new Council's first meeting.

Girling, Sycamore, Mathews

Mears boasted he had made the presidency 'immeasurably higher profile than it was before'. Girling retorted that the Duchess of York also 'attracts her fair share of column inches' but it was 'quality rather than quantity of coverage with which we should be concerned'. Mears promised 'every assistance and co-operation' but as 'leader of Her Majesty's substantial opposition'. Girling responded: 'we have much more in common than divides us'.[50] Sheldon pronounced Mears's obituary. He had 'brought about an undoubted sea change', 'broken the mould, 'stir[red] the pot'. 'But after a good stir, you have got to let the pot simmer for a while.' Mears, however, declared he would stand again and be the first President 'to come back from the dead'.

Holland was confident that Girling would provide 'firm and clear leadership'. Napier was 'delighted' that the profession 'is in safe but not boring hands'. The YSG chair welcomed 'a period of stabilisation'. The LAPG and SFLA offered support. But Dubow said the new administration 'will need to prove its commitment to high street practitioners by dealing practically with the issue of conveyancing fees'. And the *Solicitors Journal* saw a 'danger' in the disparity between the 'handful of Martin Mears' supporters on the Council' and his endorsement 'by nearly half the electorate'. Nostalgic for a man it had repeatedly reviled, the *New Law Journal* praised Mears for having 'shaken up the ailing Law Society with its grating and complaisant attitude towards the hungry sheep'. Now Girling had to 're-unite' it and 're-establish' respect. The *Gazette* praised him as 'impressively workmanlike' and 'an experienced negotiator with the government'.[51]

Quickly extending an olive branch, Girling persuaded Sayer to be deputy treasurer (under Mathews), adding: 'I asked Martin Mears to work with us rather than to fan the flames of resentment at the Society'. Mears was 'a member of four influential committees chaired by me', and Sayer was on the finance committee and involved in information technology and the Society's reorganization. Girling made Mears head of a team developing a client care perspective at the OSS. 'I can only regret that Mr Mears continues to seek out areas for public criticism'. Mears did just that. Having boasted of eschewing foreign junkets, he attacked Merricks (and his wife) and Hamish Adamson for attending the Commonwealth Lawyers Conference in Vancouver, 'a blatant freebie', at a cost of nearly £20,000, and warned that staff 'will not be able to get away from [*sic*] that sort of behaviour as I shall be keeping an eye on them'. When the new Secretary-General hoped 'this will be the last kerfuffle left over from the last administration', Mears condemned her and her predecessor for overruling his veto of these trips. David McIntosh, newly elected to the Council, asked Mears to give 'Girling and his team... the benefit of any doubt'. But Mears retorted that he had been 'publicly vilified in the most scurrilous terms'. He and Sayer issued fact sheets trumpeting 'The truth, no economy, no varnish, no concealment', criticizing SIF for miscalculating premiums and the Council for authorizing £6.77 million to refurbish Chancery Lane.[52]

The post-election AGM on the SA motions attracted fewer than 150. It passed the resolution extending membership and voting rights to virtually all solicitors on the Roll (an additional 18,000). The SA proposed that 100 members could require a postal ballot on recalling the entire Council, which 'has lost its way and is no longer representative of the views and aspirations of the Profession'. Only eleven members had won contested elections. 'Ideally the Membership should be able to decide particular issues by Referendum.' 'At a single stroke, the Membership can win sovereignty of the Law Society.' But the Council noted the cost (£30,000 for a postal ballot, £100,000 for an election) and feared the threat 'could be used to bring the proceedings of the Council... to a halt'. The SA 'believe in breaking up the Law Society and it would be logical for them to use disruptive tactics so as to discredit the Council and the Society'. It was 'a recipe for the Society to become a permanent battleground between warring factions'. Even Mears, who 'sympathise[d] with the sentiments' and had 'spent the last 12 months in warfare with the Council', called it 'absurd if 100 people could demand a general election at any time'. The motion was lost decisively and obtained only eighteen of the twenty votes needed for a postal ballot. The meeting also rejected the proposal to add non-geographic constituencies and eliminate the residence requirement for candidates because interests had 'more to do with the size of the firm or its type of work or clientele'.

The SA's principal motion called for 'clear division of regulatory and representative functions'. A century ago

the Law Society was called 'the best organised and most intelligent trade union in the Country'. How would it be described today? Recently, the British Medical

Association has been called 'the strongest trade union in the world'. It has pursued a successful philosophy of 'enlightened self-interest without the burden of professional regulation'.

The Council warned against 'an admission that solicitors no longer wish or deserve to be trusted to regulate themselves, and an open invitation to a future government to impose an external regulatory body'. Counsel had warned that the Society might lose its royal charter. Although a large majority rejected the motion, twenty-four forced a postal ballot. The Council objected to the cost and feared that division would prompt City solicitors to create their own regulatory body instead of continuing to pay for the SCF, SIF, and SCB. Girling also warned that government, unlike the Society, would have 'no incentive ... to minimise regulation'. A purely representative body 'would have little credibility'. The American Bar Association experience suggested that as few as a third of solicitors would subscribe. Even Bogan got cold feet. The vote would not bind the Council but only 'demonstrate that the profession expects its elected representative to give the issue of separation the time and resources for proper debate'. He was 'the first to admit the issue is less than clear cut'. Solicitors decisively rejected fission (by 14,199 to 8,881 with 1,200 spoiled ballots). Although the turnout was just 30 per cent, Girling called it 'a clear message that solicitors do value self-regulation'. But buoyed by 40 per cent of the vote, Bogan said 'the issue will not go away'.[53]

Mears launched his own journal, *Caterpillar*, because the *Gazette* treated him 'entirely as an unperson'. He accepted his 'narrow defeat with ... good grace' but intended to 'fight again', which 'means unearthing the scandals, ineptitudes and other unpleasantnesses distasteful to those in authority'. Past presidents were 'apparatchiks', whose 'long tenure has resulted in a divided profession'. A mock questionnaire profiled Mears loyalists: 'Blow the rules, it's a trade union pure and simple'; 'Panels and kite marks are a load of bureaucratic nonsense'; 'Bring back scale conveyancing fees'; 'Elections are all a bit of fun aren't they?' Sayer maintained 'it would probably not make a great deal of difference to the average High Street Firm if [the Society] did not exist'. Although seven Council members were entitled to send a joint newsletter to their constituents semi-annually, the Society refused to disseminate *Caterpillar* because counsel found it libellous. Mears distributed it as his own expense, repeating the alleged libels.[54]

While Mears blustered, Sayer exposed. The Society provided plenty of material. When he had asked in December 1995 why practising certificates were not being issued, the Council was assured that the computer system would overcome its 'teething problems'. The same day the director of professional standards and development sent an internal e-mail acknowledging 'a real crisis in that we cannot adequately discharge two of our core functions, the issue of practising certificates and the accounting for income received'. A year later Sayer criticized the report on the Regis computer system as a 'watered down' version of the consultants' findings and condemned a 'cover up' by senior officials. The Council voted by 49 to 17 in favour of Mears's motion criticizing 'the history of mismanagement' and warned that 'any unreasonable lack of openness on the part of staff would be viewed as an issue likely to lead to disciplinary action'. A month later Sayer noted that the Regis budget had grown from £2.5 million to £10 million. The Society would have a £6 million overdraft in nine months unless it took action. Girling and Mathews blocked his demand for an external audit. The *New Law Journal* lauded Sayer as 'both numerate and computer competent'.

When the finance committee sought another £400,000 for the High Street Starter Kit, Sayer condemned 'the daft way we organise ourselves', calling it 'a mess' several weeks later. 'After 18 months and £200,000 the Law Society still doesn't have any viable software.' Several weeks after that Robin Ap Cynan, chair of the practice development committee, admitted the HSSK was 'not as ready as he'd hoped'. Sayer convinced the committee to 'junk it'. When Sayer was forced to run for election to deputy treasurer, the *New Law Journal* expressed 'sympathy' for his view 'that this is a move to stop his investigations into the workings of the Law Society's finances'. But Ap Cynan was disqualified on technical grounds and Sayer returned unopposed. Contemporaneously, the BLA complained to the OSS about LS staff mishandling of Regis.[55]

In early 1997 Sayer announced his candidacy for president because of the 'danger with Martin that the press will home in on the person and not the issues, which are what really count': the consultants' 'devastating picture of mismanagement', sixty-one more staff, and SIF's three mammoth miscalculations. He rejected Holland's 'absurdly superficial' claim that 'the profession has to choose between... the bright future of modern commercialism' and 'the backward looking pit of professionalism'. He advocated market restrictions 'in the public good', the 'bargain' of 'professional responsibilities in return for professional privileges'. Mears was patronizing: 'Robert's status has greatly increased in the last few months. I think he's a first class man, not a ceremonial president.' But though Mears declared his candidacy for VP, Sayer hedged about the ticket. Mears then said that after receiving 'a number of calls... I am not ruling myself out' as president. Mathews said he would stand 'for an office', but Sycamore temporized. Within a week it became clear that Sayer did not want Mears as a running mate. Mears claimed he was 'happy to support any arrangement which is effective'. Despite 'pressure from a great number of my own supporters' he would stand down 'if a sufficiently strong team is assembled'.[56]

In the March *Caterpillar* Mears sought 1,000 £46 subscriptions from high-street solicitors who 'know that at Chancery Lane, we continue to be their best friends'. During his year in office 'the old'uns never ceased their attacks'. He mocked 'Girling and co.' for their claims of influence 'in the corridors of power. But not enough to hang on to their knighthood!' The Society should emulate the Bar Council, 'which invariably defends its members' interests vigorously and single-mindedly'. He reviewed the Regis 'debacle' of unmet performance targets and cost overruns, quoting the Arthur Andersen report he had made the Council publish:

the level of financial awareness in the Society and Council is limited. The meaning of revenue versus capital expenditure, the implications for future budgets of current capital spend on depreciation and interest, and the meaning of surplus or deficit in the Income and Expenditure Account are not fully understood.

As president Mears had received 'sensitive' information from 'comparatively junior staff members'. Now they had to consult with superiors if they thought a Council member wanted the information for 'political or electioneering purposes'.[57]

Girling called Mears's 'relentless carping and sniping' 'out of line'. *Caterpillar* was 'sheer negativity'. Among its 'gratuitously objectionable items' was 'a disparaging reference to the Gazette as "our house magazine". Yet, you have been the one person who has argued against the editorial independence of the Gazette.' Mears claimed he was merely 'represent[ing] my constituents' by exposing 'mis-management and wrong directions'. 'Last summer, I said that if I were re-elected I would involve Mr Girling closely in my consultations. Mr Girling, on the other hand, declared that if I were elected he would quit the Council.' When Mears had offered to remain on two committees 'Mr Girling took three minutes to refuse my request'.[58]

At the beginning of March Sycamore and Mathews declared their candidacy for president and vice president. The profession should 'embrace change, be in the vanguard of reforms and prosper by adapting to a changing environment' rather than 'stamp our feet, clamour vainly for protectionism and watch the world pass us by'. If solicitors did not become 'more responsive to what clients want' they would lose work to MDPs dominated by accountants and estate agents. The Society had 'to demonstrate our continuing right to self-regulation' by 'practice management standards and meaningful accreditation schemes'. They publicly offered Sayer the DVP nomination to end 'electioneering', 'squabbling', 'politicking', 'this image of bickering among ourselves'. '[I]t is time for the politics to stop and for progress to begin.' Sayer saw 'a small window of opportunity to work out a consensus' but did not know what they 'stand for'. He distanced himself from Mears, who had 'a tendency to speak first and think of the consequences later'. Mears hoped Sayer 'thinks carefully of the implications of what he is doing' in 'repudiating' their joint ticket and defecting to the 'establishment'—the 'quintessence of blandness'—and threatened to run for president.

Sayer called the split permanent, rejecting 'gesture politics' and claiming he had told Mears in December: 'I would not stand on the same platform as him again. Anyone who followed the events leading up to the last election will be able to form their own conclusions about my reasons.' 'There have been no fudges or private deals.' When Sayer declared his candidacy for president, 'Martin immediately announced that he was standing as my Vice President. He did not discuss that with me before making that announcement.' If Mears stood down 'he can be remembered with dignity as the man who helped break the mould. If he insists on standing as President...he will be remembered as the man who broke the reform movement.' Claiming to speak for 'the bulk of the High Street practice', Bogan also urged Mears to step aside.[59]

Although Mears purported to be 'very reluctant to enter into public disputes with Mr Sayer', he could not 'let [Sayer's] version of recent events go unchallenged'. Sayer had written on 29 January: 'you suggested that I stand as President and that you stand as Vice President. I agree.' When Sayer worried about being 'overshadowed by me', Mears offered to be campaign manager if he could find a 'credible substitute'. They split over the DVP: Mears wanted Keating, Sayer wanted Bogan.[60]

While Sayer deliberated, Mears declared his candidacy for the presidency to give 'a clear voice and clear leadership'. Sayer warned that Mears's 'taste for publicity...damages any chance of implementing reforms'. Sayer continued to emphasize 'unfair competition from non-solicitors', 'working for lending institutions for no pay while accepting complete liability', 'the escalating professional indemnity bill', and 'over-population'. Although Sycamore and Mathews were 'conciliators looking for an end to conflict', he was 'not convinced they share my ambition'. But within a few weeks he accepted their offer. The three promised to 'heal...the divisions which have plagued the Law Society' and voiced some of Sayer's concerns: 'get a grip on the cost of running the Society', an independent review of SIF, return 'control and responsibility to Council members', and respond to new threats, like estate-agency conveyancing.

Mears dismissed their platform as 'a collection of empty banalities'. The *New Law Journal* hoped Sayer had extracted an external audit as his 'price' for 'joining the team'. It strangely revived Bogan's proposal for fission: 'one day there will be a separation of powers'. The Society should 'swim gracefully with the tide' and 'be able to say that it stands for the interests of its members alone and not have to divide itself into sections which are at war with one another'.[61]

Mears and his running mates David Keating and David Savage declared their issues were the legal aid remuneration freeze, 9 per cent increase in Society staff, Regis, and HSSK, and 'a whole succession of blunders involving the SIF'. Mears had 'thrown a large stone in the water', but the ripples had 'ceased and the pool is now its stagnant self again'. Although the

Girling administration (which included Sycamore and Mathews) claimed to have rebuilt the Society's reputation, its own survey found that 'only 3% of solicitors "agree strongly" that the Law Society does a good job in promoting and representing the profession', and 69 per cent disagree. Sycamore claimed most solicitors 'bitterly regret yet another contested election'. Mears retorted that if Sycamore 'doesn't want division, all he has to do is stand down'. Sycamore replied 'we can't afford to be inward looking and divisive'.[62]

The *New Law Journal* waxed nostalgic about Mears (forgetting its harsh criticism of his presidency) and supported his platform. Girling made Council meetings pleasanter, but there was 'smugness at the top'. '[I]t is now accepted that the turbulent era presided over by Mears did a great deal for the profession—by shaking up the complacent establishment.' If 'he wins and the Council backs him instead of thwarting him he may pull the Society into a position where more than two percent of its members think it is doing a good job for the profession'. But it conceded that 'more may be accomplished without internal strife', which Mears provoked.[63]

The June *Caterpillar* dismissed Sycamore and Mathews as nonentities. 'No-one had heard of them' before Girling chose them. 'No-one has heard of them now.' Mears's opponents accused him of 'narrow protectionism, Scargillism and neglect of the consumer'. But 'it is lawyers and not the Law Society who make themselves... unpopular' through legal aid scandals and ambulance chasing. 'The removal of restrictions on advertising and touting has destroyed the prosperity of High Street solicitors.' ACLEC 'has increasingly made so called self regulation a fiction'.

When I qualified there were a limited number of seats available for law courses and the law course itself was tough. A tougher course is what is required as is a significant contraction of places on law courses.

As president Mears

had no more inveterate enemy than Dracula lookalike and Chairman of the Law Society's Training Committee, Simon Baker...who led the walkout of superannuated groupies during a speech given by Mears to a Young Solicitors Dinner... [and] rejoiced in Counsel's Opinion...that the profession had no power to control its numbers even if it wanted to.

Accused by McIntosh of 'self-protectionism', Mears asked 'why is it so wrong to try to protect ourselves?' He reminded Sayer that 'only a few months ago, Girling and Co. called an election for the Deputy Treasurership...without even telling him....' 'Has he already forgotten the rows of hostile faces he used to confront in the Council Chamber?' 'Or the cold-shouldering he received at last October's Annual Conference?'[64]

Sayer published an open letter to Mears, who 'threw away' the 'chance to change the Law Society' because 'he did not concentrate on the vital issues'. 'While I investigated Regis, the High Street Starter Kit and the Society's finances, he made speeches.' Mears 'simply has nothing new to offer'. He was 'shallow, vain and a phoney, all talk and no action. All he is interested in is being President, nothing else.' Mears retorted that Sayer hoped to be 'the Trojan Horse' but was more likely to 'be absorbed without trace into the machine'. Sycamore's platform rejected every Sayer position: 'independent review of all expenditure', a 10 per cent budget cut, an independent inquiry into SIF, and 'dealing with the ever increasing number of people in the profession'. Sayer replied that Mears had been a 'hindrance' for two years, who had 'systematically antagonised our supporters' because he was 'too arrogant to accept he needed Council support'. 'Sycamore and Mathews will supply the diplomatic skills...and support across the Council.... I'll supply the cynicism and dogged persistence'.[65]

Others agreed. The City of London Law Society chair called it 'vitally important that the Law Society President is respected by the Lord Chancellor, the heads of other government departments and the leaders of foreign bars'. The Manchester Law Society president reported 'staleness and battle-weariness in the electorate'. The Birmingham Law Society president said 'Mears is doing the profession a disservice by standing again'.[66]

The manifestoes repeated these themes. Sycamore's team stood for 'unity' and 'reason'; it had 'real influence' and 'the backing of the elected Council'; it was 'forward looking' and 'problem solving' and opposed 'division', looking 'backwards', 'jibes and sarcasm', 'embarrassment', and 'politicking'. Mears retorted that the previous year had been an 'almost unmitigated failure'.[67]

Just before voting closed Mears published Baker's confidential minutes of a February campaign meeting at Edge & Ellison, whose senior partner, John Aucott, lost to Sayer in 1995. It included Sycamore, Mathews, and four Council members (Richard Hegarty, John Appleby, Peter Williamson, and Baker); copies went to Council members Aucott, McIntosh, Napier, and Lucy Winskell. Participants 'agreed' that the three remaining Council meetings 'had to be managed more effectively so as to control the amount of debate about bad news issues and to reduce the propaganda opportunities for Mears and Sayer'. They urged 'careful consideration...of a formal rebuke being administered from the chair to Sayer in the open part of the March meeting for breaching confidentiality'. Disclosure of Baker's 'controversial' suggestion 'that enquiry agents should be engaged to gather information on Mears/Sayer/Keating' would be 'disastrous'. Two senior employees of the Society's public relations consultancy offered free advice about a 'negative campaign' 'on the basis that their involvement would not be known beyond the campaign team'. Mears sought Sycamore's response 'before considering my position regarding any other information I might hold'.

Sycamore contested 'the accuracy of the note. I was not there for the whole of the meeting', which had rejected enquiry agents 'out of hand'

and concluded they could not manipulate Council agendas. 'In a situation which had become political it was a perfectly legitimate exercise'. At that time 'many Council members believed (and still believe) that the profession cannot afford to go through another year of turmoil and division with the consequent embarrassment and loss of credibility'. Mears 'chose' to disseminate the memo 'for his own personal advantage rather than first send it to and seek any explanation from his Council colleagues'. Baker called the meeting a 'brainstorming session'. 'Subsequent events are the most eloquent testimony as to what did not happen....' Mathews hoped the profession would 'view this just as a diversion'.

Mears retorted: 'One cannot talk up a non-existent story. Channel 4 gave it ten minutes of coverage. They approached me, not I them.' His adversaries complained: 'This is a very wicked animal. When attacked it defends itself.' He had sought explanations, but 'alas, the people turned out either not to have been present or to be suffering from amnesia'. Sycamore and Mathews were 'unfit to lead the profession' and should withdraw from the race. 'This is the Law Society, not some loony-left Council.' 'If this Law Society won't sort this out properly, I will take it up with the Master of the Rolls.'

Sayer claimed 'the simple reality is that the key suggestions were all rejected'. The 'whole sorry episode is just another example of Martin manufacturing and manipulating the press to win himself publicity'. Mears 'held meetings at Canon Street prior to the last election to which he invited members of his "Reform Group"', providing 'breakfast at the Law Society's expense' and discussing the elections.

Sycamore attempted to revive the issues. The Society should 'lead the debate on franchising, block contracts, mediation pilots and all the current developments in a hardnosed way...rather than hoping we can turn the clock back to open-ended spending'. He opposed 'knee-jerk' calls 'to abolish and attack SIF'. Mears retorted that the only three reasons to vote were 'the SIF, the SIF and the SIF', whose shortfall was £724,500,000 or £18,000 per principal '*in addition to last year's contribution*'. 'It is Martin Mears who has been a consistent critic of the SIF...called for resignations at SIF... [and] an independent investigation into SIF's miscalculations'. He decried 'the sheer shamelessness of the establishment's campaign'. The 'revelations of the past week have shown' the establishment claim to the moral high ground 'to be the humbug and nonsense it is'. Were those who discussed 'a dirty tricks campaign' fit 'to lead a learned profession?' Mears had 'tried to concentrate on the issues and to disregard [Sayer's] increasingly wild personal attacks'. Sycamore could hardly blame Baker: 'We are not talking about the ravings of a lunatic'.

Sycamore protested that the story had been 'successfully talked up'. '[A]t no stage did I countenance or endorse anything underhand. Many of the ideas, and all of the wilder ones, were dismissed or not taken forward.' But Robin de Wilde (a maverick barrister discussed below) derided these 'contradictory comments'. The 'only defences missing were: (a) it was my twin brother; and (b) nothing happened'. He declared that 'Martin Mears and his cohorts have won on ideas'. The *Solicitors Journal* said 'solicitors up and down the country' had been asking 'what on earth is going on at the Law Society'. The LAPG chair said the memo was a 'rude awakening' to 'a lot of people [who] thought that solicitors on the Law Society Council don't behave as politicians'. When Baker resigned from both Council and training committee Mears demanded the resignations of Williamson and SIF chair Andrew Kennedy.[68]

Nevertheless, Sycamore won a landslide victory (by 16,878 to 8,148), Mathews a similar one, and Sayer's was even larger. Girling welcomed the 'vote of approval'. Mears congratulated them but called the results 'terribly depressing for the profession' because the 'low turn-out' (30 per cent, compared with 45 the previous year) showed that 'the profession does not give a damn what happens at the Law Society'. The response to 'Chancery Lane's recent Leadership of the Profession consultation was a pitiful 457 out of a profession of 83,000'. Although the slate had 'the active backing of a mere 15 per cent of the profession', Mears would not run again and found it 'difficult to stay on as a credible opposition'. He condemned Sayer's 'highly personalised campaign...against me as a man with whom it was impossible to work'. Sayer called that 'the harsh truth' and attributed victory to his statement that the profession needed Mears 'like a hole in the head'.[69]

The *Solicitors Journal* saw the 'clear and decisive victory for the establishment team' as an 'equally clear rejection of the policies of Martin Mears and his team'. But it agreed that the 'most significant figure' was the low turnout caused by 'the very public bickering' and 'highly publicised row over leaked documents', which convinced many solicitors that the Society 'was becoming a laughing-stock'. Even more, 'the Society is seen as remote and out of touch'. The *New Law Journal* observed sarcastically that 'our heroes...finally defeated the devils'. Sayer should reflect on how he 'was clearly used by the machine to vilify Mr Mears' and how he will stay in touch 'not only with the rank and file solicitor but also with the powerful members of the council' who may turn against 'a politically unacceptable upstart...when it comes to what used to be called Buggins' turn'. Although 'Mears displayed thoroughly unacceptable traits in this day and age', he did 'shake up the Society and the profession from its multi-decade long torpor'. '[T]here should be a Mr Mears on all Law Society committees but...there is still too much of an old boy network in the election and subsequent induction process'.[70]

Less than four months into the new administration Kamlesh Bahl declared her candidacy for DVP, with Sayer for VP and Mathews for President. The

Gazette called her the first potential woman leader (ignoring Pembridge's presidential run two years earlier). Heather Hallett QC was elected BC chair the same week. The YSG warned of a 'massive communication problem' because solicitors under 40 were 50 per cent of the profession but 5 per cent of the Council, women were 31 and 19, and ethnic minorities 5 and 3. The Council had given young solicitors a seat in 1991 but rebuffed one for women in 1995. Although Girling, Bahl, Pembridge, and Deacon supported it, as did a majority of the policy committee, the Council again refused by 31 votes to 33 with 3 abstentions, also denying the TSG request for a seat for the 20,000 trainees because only qualified solicitors could belong.[71]

Creation of the first American-style probate section was another departure from geographical constituencies. The Society promoted it as 'a way [for members] to reassert themselves' in the face of 'competition from banks, accountants, and will writers'. The YSG urged 'more representation for special interest groups', such as personal injury and family lawyers. The local law society presidents and secretaries also favoured sections. But the Law Society Commerce and Industry Group resented that its 6,000 members paid £3 million in practising certificate fees but received only £12,300. Sections would make the Law Society 'more remote, perhaps further disenfranchising the bulk of solicitors'. The SPG and AWS also opposed them. Nevertheless, the Society contemplated a section for EU lawyers, although it planned to exclude other foreign lawyers for fear of American domination.[72]

Although high-street practitioners were most vocally disaffected, City firms also were unhappy about indemnity premiums, traineeships, audience rights, and public image. The CLLS chair wrote to the Secretary-General in December 1997 asking for a 'separate civil service' to address members' 'neglected' interests. A contemporaneous survey found that City solicitors thought the Society irrelevant, bureaucratic, intrusive, archaic, focused on small firms, and far too contentious. It should be 'going round promoting the interests of English law internationally'.[73]

The 1998 Fabian Society pamphlet argued that government regulation of lawyers would make the Society 'more accountable to representing the needs of its membership'. Holland (now principal ombudsman at the Personal Investment Authority) agreed that 'extended annual elections based on who can do most for the high street solicitor' destroyed the pretence 'there can be any real reflection of the need to protect the client'. Sycamore disagreed, insisting that the 'long-term commercial interests of solicitors are inextricably linked to the standards of service given to clients'.[74]

In February Bahl called for a 'positive' election campaign and an end to 'whispers and innuendo', after reports that a Council member had called her 'not sufficiently representative of the profession'. Contemporaneously, the policy committee (chaired by Girling) revived a proposal that the

Council nominate the DVP. Sayer condemned 'a little group plotting in secret' over his successor. Pembridge detected 'the dead hand of past presidents trying to control the future'. Insisting 'this is not my idea', Girling found it 'difficult to explain how traumatic it is' to stand for office. Trevor Murray deplored the 'message to the profession that we are going back to our pre-1995 ways'. Mathews opposed 'playing with the rules in the middle of the game'. 'It wasn't a plan to nobble Kamlesh', McIntosh insisted. 'I'm against Buggins' Turn.' Angus Andrew also denied this was 'a "Get Kamlesh Bahl" campaign'. 'We need a mechanism to allow Council members to put themselves forward' after 'Martin Mears broke a discredited voting system'. But only seventeen Council members agreed.[75]

As DVP Sayer continued to criticize the Society for devoting 'just 4.5% of its expenditure... [to] membership services' and 1.5 staff to conveyancing. With 800 employees its staff was 'greater than that of the American Bar Association despite its having four times as many members'. He wanted to spend money 'educating the public, politicians and media that we are not "fat cats"'. The Society had just conducted 'the first objective test of what people think since I joined the Council' (three years earlier). 'Can you imagine Marks & Spencer taking so long to do market research of this kind?' 'Most of the committees should be shut down.'[76]

In April Mathews and Sayer hoped rumours that Napier and McIntosh would contest the election were unfounded. Napier acknowledged considering requests from people 'inside and outside the Council'. A month later McIntosh challenged Sayer. He had built 'from scratch a successful law firm on the basis "the client comes first"' and knew about indemnity insurance and civil justice reform. He had 'sufficient communication skills' (insinuating Sayer did not). Solicitors needed to 'tak[e] pride in the way the profession is led by the Law Society'. The Bar had gained a competitive 'edge' from the 'disarray and unfocused leadership within the Law Society a few years ago. A repeat of this would play into the hands of today's government', which 'appears hostile to the private legal profession'. Just as Mears and Sayer had attacked Buggins's turn, so McIntosh now did against Sayer. The profession had to be led 'by those best equipped to do so'; there were 'still widespread doubts... as to whether all the top spots have been filled as effectively as possible. Critics and challengers do not always develop into healers and achievers.' Sayer had failed 'to learn from his ex-collaborator's shortcomings'. McIntosh would have run for DVP, but 'a woman office holder with her distinct points of view would be good for the profession'. Napier called McIntosh 'the right person in the right place at the right time'.

Mears mocked McIntosh (implicated in the previous year's dirty tricks), who had 'strident[ly]' opposed contested elections and 'eloquent[ly]' supported Sayer on the Sycamore 'dream ticket'. But Mears also gloated over this challenge to his own Judas, who had been 'out machiavelled'. Sayer should 'meditate on the fate of those who change their colours'. Although he had taken 'the establishment shilling' to 'see...off the troublemakers', Sayer's 'new shipmates' regarded him 'as incurably unsound and, to boot, not the kind of person you would invite to take tea with the Queen Mother'; they would have 'no compunction about tossing him to the sharks'.

He turns out not to be a team player. He leaks to the press and circulates memoranda of his own. He persists (albeit half heartedly) in thinking his own thoughts and speaking his own words.... And moreover, it is doubtful whether Sayer has taken the trouble to learn the correct mode of consuming a cucumber sandwich in polite company.

Confirming Mears's prediction, the *Solicitors Journal* welcomed the challenge. 'What is needed is strong leadership, one which understands the needs of solicitors and is committed to fight on their behalf.'

Sayer was 'saddened' that McIntosh's statements about 'co-operation' had not been 'sincere'. 'At a time when we should all be working together for the good of the profession his personal ambitions are going to plunge us into another bout of damaging and unnecessary infighting.'

McIntosh retorted he was 'far from alone in questioning Robert Sayer's suitability to lead'. Sayer 'too often pursued his own agenda in maverick and damaging ways'. 'The fact that Robert Sayer claimed I am standing for office because I dislike him says more about him than it does about me.'[77]

Napier declared a week later to offer 'the strongest possible leadership at this watershed time'. Mathews was 'naturally disappointed'. He had the advantage of two years in office. 'We're agreed on what the important issues are—legal aid, civil justice, indemnity insurance—and I doubt if we disagree on how they should be dealt with'. Sayer called Napier 'selfish'. 'We need another contested election like a hole in the head. He is shattering the consensus we have all been working for.' Contested elections 'are widely seen as divisive and damaging to the profession's reputation. The first was necessary.' But by the third 'the profession clearly signalled that it wanted us to stop squabbling and get on with it'. McIntosh had been 'part of the group that decided to ask me to join its coalition. He was part of my campaign team....' It was 'odd that he now finds me unacceptable'.

Law Society politics are the same as politics anywhere else. Petty, undignified, dominated by ambition. Idealists are considered fools. To speak the truth is frowned upon; rocking the boat is a sin. I plead guilty to being an idealist and to speaking the truth.

McIntosh was 'just the establishment's latest champion to "try to see that Sayer fellow off once and for all" '. 'I have now won two elections. Last time I received the highest vote of any candidate, ever.' He condemned 'wasting £70,000 of the profession's money on another election'. '[T]his is not a game. This is about our livelihoods, our survival....Why are we being plunged into nothing more than another bout of "student union" politics...?' Mathews and he had achieved consensus, 'the adult way to behave'.

Napier took credit for 'the small, rapid-reaction task force' on the legal aid reforms and 'snappy and effective communication'. As a 'corporate tax lawyer', Mathews was not the right person 'to shoulder the burden of tackling the other massive threats of exclusive block contracts...and the crunch question of indemnity'. 'My roots are in the high street, David's in the City.'[78]

A week later David Keating announced his independent candidacy for DVP. The profession's response to its challenges would mean 'life or death for the rural practice', which 'still provide[s] a vast network across the countryside'. Bahl's lack of private practice experience 'would make it very difficult for her to represent the whole profession adequately'. Mears backed his 'friend and associate' and called Mathews 'a complete non-starter' for president. Bahl retorted that her youth and gender made her more representative. Employed lawyers were a 'bridge to clients'. She understood 'a great deal about competition' and would promote solicitors as the 'first choice' for trusted legal advisers, publicly funded legal services, commercial legal transactions, and access to justice.[79]

Mathews and Sayer took a full-page *Gazette* advertisement denouncing the contest as 'divisive', 'irresponsible', 'a waste of time and money', a 'game', which was 'damaging the reputation in the eyes of the public'. 'In place of continual, disruptive and increasingly pointless Presidential elections, [we] will carry out the most far reaching and democratic review of the Society's policies there has ever been.' Napier retorted: 'everyone knows I do not "play games"'. His decision had 'been completely validated by [Sayer's] view from the wrong end of the telescope'. The 'urgent need' was 'to tackle the new, and grave, threats to our ability to practise', not 'rhetoric about reform of the Law Society's constitution or complaints about democracy'. He again contrasted his ticket's balance of high street and City with the 'curious alliance' of Mathews and Sayer.

Mathews conceded that he was 'not a legal aid lawyer, but that does not mean that I have no interest in it or that I know nothing about it'. Sayer and he had served on the Justice Task Force campaign to save legal aid. Leadership required 'breadth of experience and the ability to understand the many difficult issues which affect our careers', such as multi-disciplinary partnerships, access to venture capital, FSA regulation, and limited liability. 'Michael Napier suggests that I am second best.'

[O]ne does not get to be the senior partner in a major department in a leading City firm and to have been a member of that firm's board and its predecessor bodies for some 20 years by being 'second best'.[80]

The campaign quickly degenerated into personal attacks. In an open letter McIntosh accused Sayer of 'the dissemination of inaccurate information' without a 'scintilla of truth' (that Napier had planned to stand for DVP in order to challenge Sayer for president the following year). Sayer insisted he was 'absolutely convinced' of it. McIntosh was an 'egomaniac'. '[T]his is a contest between someone who is sincere and genuinely wants to reform the Society, and someone who wants the job purely because he has reached a certain stage in his life and thinks he deserves it.' McIntosh called Sayer 'incapable of avoiding personal criticisms'.

It is hard to believe that you and Michael Mathews agreed with Michael Napier and me that this year's election would be a clean one. Perhaps I should have believed you when you said 'old habits die hard'.[81]

Mathews claimed his team 'represented a wider cross section of the profession than ever before'. Sayer said the defence of legal aid had to express 'the interests of all firms, not just the big fish' (like Napier). McIntosh promised to 'think young and of equal opportunities'. Bahl declared 'we must become a modern, effective and inclusive profession'. Keating harped on the fact that 'Miss Bahl' had 'no experience whatsoever of practice in the private sector', had not been 'exposed to the rigours of practice', had only an 'academic' concern about legal aid, and could not represent 'the whole profession'. She claimed 'a unique blend of experience which the Society currently lacks'. He retorted: 'I have spent most of my working life' in 'a typical medium sized country practice'. The *Independent* called Bahl 'a refreshing change from the endless parade of white men' but found her 'actual policies' vague. Mathews declined Napier's challenge to debate at local law societies: 'Hustings at this stage aren't terribly relevant'.[82]

He was right, but just barely, getting 53 per cent, while his running mates received 55 and 57, in a poll that fell to 26 per cent. The *Gazette* called Bahl's victory 'long overdue', given the Bar's woman chair and ILEX's third woman president. Bahl planned to resign as EOC chair to concentrate on the Society and seek the presidency in two years. She was a conservative activist who sought to ensure 'that equality for women is not at the expense of men and balancing work and home'.[83]

In response to the RPPU study revealing pervasive member dissatisfaction, the Society commissioned Sir Dennis Stevenson, chair of Pearson plc, to review its work and organization. He predictably advocated a corporate model: *ad hoc* task forces in place of the 141 committees and working parties, an executive committee to oversee policy implementation, a more powerful Secretary-General and figurehead president, and election of only the DVP because 'contested presidential elections...were making the Society a laughing stock'. The CLLS chair agreed that recent elections had been 'disheartening'. They might be 'appropriate' 'now and then', but 'an unplanned change of policy and priority every year' was intolerable.

How will we ever encourage the best of our members to devote the time and commitment to the good of our profession...unless there is a culture which enables the most talented to rise quickly to leadership without risk of wasting their efforts because of the vagaries of the electoral process?

Sayer wanted the Society to become 'a true members' organisation, looking after the interests of solicitors in a sensible way', not 'an old fashioned dinosaur trade union but something similar to the American Bar Association'. The three officers wanted policy set by the Council, not the staff. Contemporaneously the Society spent £60,000 on 'better branding' the profession's image.

Calling the £1.8 million a year committee system a 'heaving mess', the working party to implement Stevenson's report recommended abolishing forty-eight of the first seventy-seven committees it evaluated. The Council concurred and also voted to replace the Secretary-General with a policy-making Director-General, pay itself salaries, and elect only the DVP. The *Solicitors Journal* found that last 'worrying'. Without 'the prospect of a Mears revolution', 'all the profession will be able to do if things go horribly wrong is elect a deputy vice president'. Sayer, the professional outsider, now discovered the importance of 'at least a year's apprenticeship'. Although he worried about moves 'away from democracy', the proposals 'combined democratic accountability with continuity'.[84]

When the TSG renewed its request for a Council seat, calling its 25,000 members paying £250 a year 'the largest unrepresented group', the Council promptly gave one of the two local government seats to newly qualified solicitors. Furious at not being consulted, the Local Government Group assailed the 'shambolic and amateur' action and sought counsel's opinion about its legality. After lengthy debate, the Council reversed its position by one vote, giving newly qualified solicitors only observer status. The *New Law Journal* condemned the original decision as an 'amazing volte face' that had been 'filibusted [*sic*] though the Council'. 'Employed solicitors are part of the family....'[85]

The Commerce and Industry Group chair also accused the Council of ignoring employed lawyers. At its annual dinner the Group charged the Society with 'crass stupidity' and threatened secession. It would be 'a tremendous shame and indictment of our profession' if 'some of this country's most talented solicitors started to give up their practising certificates', as was 'beginning to happen'. That the Society gave the Group only £2 of the £450 practising certificate fee paid by its 7,335 members was 'amazing, particularly as in-house lawyers do not account for the normal main areas of Law Society expenditure, such as disciplinary'. The Group already offered training and events and planned to hire its own administrative staff and seek financial support from employers.[86]

At the end of the Commons Standing Committee's consideration of the Access to Justice Act (AJA) in mid-May, Dr Alan Whitehead moved to limit the Society's practising certificate fees to regulation and legal training and education (paralleling the limitation on the Bar Council's new fees: see section B, below). '[N]o other professional society' had the power 'to do what it will with the money provided to it'. Parliament had required trade unions to 'set up a political fund and hold a ballot'. Andrew Dismore criticized 'the campaign that [the Society] waged in regard to the Bill'. 'If the Law Society operates as a trade union, the same rules should apply.' Briefed by the Society, Edward Garnier QC objected that a 'sharp division' of functions was 'not practical' and would 'involve considerable duplication of activities and additional overall cost'. 'Any attempt to prevent the Law Society from running the sort of campaign that it has done in the past 10 days [against the AJA, see Chapter 8] could amount to unlawful suppression of freedom of expression....' David Kidney feared that 'voluntary subscriptions' would not pay for the 'sort of work [that] puts the Law Society in a positive light'. John Burnett, a member of the Society's revenue law committee for twelve years, praised its 'work in the public interest'. Geoff Hoon thanked Whitehead for 'raising the significant issue of principle' and promised Government action. 'The day of pre-entry closed shops are [*sic*] ended for trade unions and should not apply to other bodies acting in a similar way'.[87]

The LAPG chair called the threat 'pointless and vindictive'. LS President Mathews 'pointed out the difficulties in classifying the core activities'. But the Bar Council, which wanted to compel subscriptions, was willing to separate functions and the LCD thought 'the Bill should be even-handed'. Doctors and dentists 'maintain a divide between regulatory activities and "trade union" activities. There is a good argument that members of a profession should not be required to pay for activities that they may not support....' The *New Law Journal* called Irvine's action 'vindictive' and 'sinister'. It was 'inappropriate in a democracy for such a fundamental change in the constitution of an independent profession to be introduced through an amendment to a Bill already in its late stages'. The Society took advice on whether it would be illegal under UK or EU law. Seeking to avoid a 'full-scale row', it hoped 'to kill off the amendment quietly through behind the scenes negotiations'. Solicitors who resented their SIF premiums 'may balk at having to pay extra to their professional body in order for it to represent their interests'. Mears disagreed. Irvine's 'inept' 'little wheeze' will 'have the effect, never previously achieved, of rallying solicitors around their professional body'. The Government's 'behaviour is that of the bully who does not see the need to argue'. The Council created a working party to consider the Society's dual roles. Trevor Aldridge QC argued that fission would increase 'openness, accountability, freedom of choice'. 'The Society would be strengthened by the support of members voting with their wallets.'

During the Report Stage on 22 June LCD Parliamentary Under-Secretary Keith Vaz moved a similar amendment. Irvine asked the Society to state within eighteen months what other activities it wanted to fund; he would consider those that 'were clearly in the public interest or had the overwhelming support of Law Society members'. When Kidney expressed concern that the Government might retaliate against the Society for polit-ical opposition, Vaz insisted 'there is no question of trying to prevent the Law Society from doing what it wants to do'. Garnier attributed the clause to the 'pique' of a Lord Chancellor 'stung' into using 'fairly intemperate language' about the advertising campaign, one who 'will brook no criti-cism' and 'is not prepared to have debated in public any matter of which he disapproves'. Vaz maintained the 'Lord Chancellor cares deeply for the profession'. The clause 'has nothing to do with any Law Society advertising campaign'. Dismore found Garnier's position 'peculiar' 'bearing in mind the strong attitude that [Conservatives] took when in government to trade union political funds'. Burnett said 'Liberal Democrats strongly oppose... a vindictive measure against the Law Society for, rightly...opposing the removal of legal aid for personal injury cases'. 'Where has he been?' Vaz asked, 'what has he been taking?' 'It could be argued that an unfettered power to raise compulsory subscriptions conflicts with that fundamental [European] human rights convention'. The amendment was agreed. The Lords voiced similar concerns three weeks later. Lords Mishcon and Hunt moved to allow the Society to spend fees on 'work in the public interest'. Lord Phillips moved to give the Master of the Rolls a veto over limitations. 'It will be too easy for a Lord Chancellor stung by a campaign against his government policy to ignore his own conflict position'. But both amend-ments were withdrawn and the clause added.[88]

Sayer (and Mears again)

Anticipating Stevenson's recommendation that only the DVP be contested, Napier declared his candidacy for that post. Keating, who had lost the last three elections, promptly challenged him. Mears sneered that Napier sought 'to deprive the wise and saintly David Keating of the Law Society's Deputy Vice Presidency which is rightly his'. Solicitors did not 'want more elections this year'. Napier had no 'particular programmes or ideas'. 'If he has ambitions, let him seek the grand mastership of his local Antediluvian Order of Buffaloes lodge.' Keating was 'erudite and witty' and 'sports' a monocle, 'whereas I cannot remember what Mr Napier looks like'.

A month later Keating switched to the presidency. Sayer found 'no merit whatsoever' in this challenge, which 'is throwing a spanner in the works of the reforms'. Keating criticized Sayer's "confrontational' 'us-and-them approach', 'belligerence and abuse'. Mears had been 'very supportive', but 'no one pulls my strings'. Solicitors were not ' "turned off" by open elections', although they 'rightly object' to 'personal abuse or belittlement. I do not intend to go down this path'. The *New Law Journal* thought Sayer was 'entitled to an uninterrupted sip from the cup which had been poised tantalisingly above his lips these last two years'. Keating would face 'the very real possibility of numbing hostility in and out of the Council chamber'. The election was just another in a 'series of increasingly boring challenges for leadership' between 'two men whose names probably mean absolutely nothing to the majority of voters'.

Sayer attacked the challenge as 'an expensive piece of spite at a cost to the profession of £100,000'. '[T]he last thing the profession needs is another election', which 'will only damage the Law Society's credibility'. 'I'll be blunt. I and the rest of the eight strong team working with me have worked miracles.' In just six weeks he had negotiated with lenders the terms for acting for lender and borrower. '[F]or the first time in memory the Law Society was learning how to stand up for its members intelligently and confidently' in the campaign against the AJA. '[W]e've achieved more in the last six months than we did in the previous 20 years.' Now, however, the 'government is probably sniggering that the Law Society has gone up its own backside again'. Under Mears 'the Society degenerated into a period of confrontation, chaos and bitterness'. Mears 'has never forgiven me' for the 'very public falling out'. 'David is Martin's loyal sidekick', 'a complete pillock', who fell asleep at Council meetings. His supporters were 'bitter, twisted little people' like Mears, who kept turning up 'like a piece of dog turd on your shoe'.

Keating (who claimed to think better with his eyes closed) denounced the 'disgraceful' attack. '[I]t was disgusting that he expressed himself publicly in such a way, but the language was not a surprise to me. People will now have a better understanding of what kind of man Robert Sayer is.' Girling deplored Sayer's 'intemperacy'. His 'passion is sometimes too often, too quick and too visible'. The *New Law Journal* thought it

sad that the Law Society has come to the stage in its decline that words which would be out of place if spoken by a football manager are said to a legal magazine. The Bar must be rubbing its hands.... 'No need to worry about solicitor-advocates usurping our position if that's the level of debate they can manage.'

The *Solicitors Journal* expressed 'an unpleasant feeling of déjà vu': 'the acrimonious exchanges have begun almost before the ink on the nomination papers has had time to dry'. The 'descent into personal abuse' was 'deplorable. Elections should be about policies, not personalities.'

Mears could not hide his glee. 'For Mr Sayer, electioneering means six weeks of vituperation and personal vilification.' He claimed to be 'reluctant to give further currency to these graceful reflections but they are very much in character'. However, like Dogberry in *Much Ado About Nothing*—'masters, remember that I am an ass . . . forget not that I am an ass'—Mears could not stop repeating the insult. Keating would not 'be capable' of responding in kind. 'Grossness should be met with charity and forbearance.'

Sayer said Keating failed to offer a 'challenge based on issues', such as high-street profitability, regulation, indemnity, MDPs, and the profession's reputation. Sayer also invoked the Council recommendation to elect only the DVP, on which the July AGM would vote. 'Does anyone honestly think this [election] is worth' £100,000? The C&I Group chair called Keating's candidacy 'nonsense' (although Sayer's slate was only 'pretty good').

Trevor Murray now challenged Napier for DVP, blaming him for conditional fees. '[T]hrough concentrating on politically correct posturing' the Society 'has consistently played into the hands of its enemies and thereby managed to oversee the systematic devastation of the profession'. 'We have been wasting our time and our colleagues' money fiddling with concerns about "equal opportunities" and people's "rights" while the profession is being destroyed for us all.' He was a self-made man. 'I left grammar school at 16 and was admitted as a solicitor aged 22 in early 1963. No privilege in that background.' 'I worked extremely hard and was able, single-handedly, to enjoy building up my practice and privately to educate five children.' Once 'solicitors' services were valued by clients and the status of the profession was appreciated and respected both by society and government.' But 'all that has changed' as a result of 'politicians' hunger to garner misguided "consumer" votes' and 'other dangerous people, quislings in a sense, who look to government or depend on its patronage for their personal achievement'. 'Any resistance from us is now portrayed as the reactionary self-interest of those who want to live in the privileged past.' The 'diplomatic solution' was 'discredited'. The £700,000 advertising campaign against the AJA 'managed to rattle the Lord Chancellor. We need to do that more often. It will raise the morale of the members and help the Society to regain its self-respect.' Napier denounced such 'rantings of yesteryear' as 'completely out of step with the way society is moving'. Murray was 'living on another planet'. Murray accused the TSG of endorsing Napier without disclosing that its chair had been employed by Napier's firm.

But this was just a sideshow. Keating sued his local newspaper for quoting Sayer under the headline 'Town Solicitor Branded Pillock' (and won in September). He denied 'not help[ing] the reform process one bit' and blamed Sayer for keeping him off the Interim Executive Committee. '[A] number of other Council members' had 'concerns at Robert Sayer's "negative qualities"'. Keating took full-page advertisements in all three solicitors' journals repeating Sayer's vulgarities, which the *Independent* called an 'outpouring of vitriol'. 'I had wanted to fight the election campaign on issues rather than personalities but Mr Sayer has now made this impossible.' Sayer had indulged in 'scurrilous abuse and ridicule', which were 'particularly' 'unseemly...in a professional election'. He 'has been vocal in demanding the abolition of the profession's right to elect its President on the ground that such elections bring the profession into disrepute. It is of course language of the kind which he—and only he—uses which drags us all down.' The 'President's chief role is to present the face of the profession to the outside world', which 'is the real issue in this election'.

Sayer conceded that elections cost much less than the £100,000 he kept quoting. He had privately offered an apology, but Mears rejected it and Keating did not respond. He refused to 'grovel'. 'It suits them to make a meal of this. They haven't got any policies, and can't attack my track record, because no-one has got a better one.' 'I have been doing the lion's share of media interviews for the last six months. I am good at them. I make one error under extreme provocation and, of course, that is what has been reported.' He had thought it

was off the record and private. I was annoyed at having this election sprung on me without warning, and about comments which attacked me personally. For five seconds in five years I let my frustration show.

Seeking to retain the moral high ground, Keating said 'the whole issue should be put to one side'. He had not replied because he wanted to 'keep things defused', and Sayer kept insisting his slurs were 'in essence true'. Playing bad cop to Keating's good, Mears could see 'no limit to Mr Robert Sayer's effrontery'. He 'subjected me and other Law Society Council members to unprecedented abuse'. Sayer only regretted 'his words because they gave ammunition to his opponents and no [*sic*] because they were disgraceful'. 'I attached little value to a private apology for a public insult, particularly when it was plain' the real purpose was 'to rehabilitate himself in the eyes of the profession'. It was not 'a solitary outburst. A few weeks ago he insulted Mr Keating and myself to our faces.' The President has to 'argue with the Lord Chancellor' and 'make small talk with Cherie Blair when she drops in for tea'. Sayer's language was 'notorious...to call people pillocks and dog turds does not enhance the concept of R Sayer BA as Statesman and Leader of a Learned Profession'.

Like an old War veteran bringing out his medals to show his grandchildren, he recalls the glorious days gone by when he (and he alone!) uncovered the Regis computer scandal and strafed the landing fields of the High Street Starter Kit.... Very few of the alleged reforms at Chancery Lane amount, under scrutiny, to very much.

Noting that a Yorkshire solicitor had been struck off the Roll for saying a Registrar 'had as much credibility as a cow pat', BLA chair Stanley Best declared Sayer 'must suffer the same treatment'.

Sayer asked Keating to 'draw a line' under the controversy but got no reply to his written apology. Charged with harping on the issue because he had no others, Keating said Sayer had apologized only for the terminology, not the sentiments, so he was 'not certain to what extent there was an apology'. 'What the profession needs is open and honest leadership and a united approach, rather than an "us and them" approach.' Sayer tried again, expressing regret 'for various reasons. The first is simply because it was discourteous and I have of course apologised.' 'More importantly, I regret it because it has given my opponents such pleasure.' He begged solicitors: 'Judge me on my record'. The fourth time he said: 'Four weeks ago, for ten seconds, after considerable provocation, I...made an unguarded statement not intended for publication'. The epithet about Keating 'was a northern dialect word for a foolish person (OE). The description of former Law Society President Mr Mears was a reflection of the tenacity or sticking power of what I regard as his three-year campaign unfairly to denigrate me and my attempts at reform.' Keating 'ignored my apology and has gone on to build his entire election campaign around it, even to the extent of repeating the original comments in a half-page advert in the Gazette'.

Sayer and Napier won with greatly increased margins (64 and 63 per cent) in the 'lowest poll ever' (21.7 per cent); Bahl was unopposed.[89] Implementing the recommendations by Stevenson (and subsequent reports by Dame Rennie Fitchie and Professor Malcolm Grant), the Council replaced the Secretary-General with a Director-General responsible for strategy, continued reducing the number of groups, meetings, and committees, and raised officer pay (having already decided to pay its members £5–£12,000 per year).[90]

At the annual conference Sayer called for 'a fresh, modern organisation' to replace 'an old Law Society...stale and out of touch'. 'Many solicitors will probably agree that in recent years the Society had got a bit above itself. It seemed to think it ran the profession.' But he promptly shed such modesty by exhibiting Napoleonic delusions, possibly induced by venue (EuroDisneyland). The Law Society should regulate the Bar. After all, 'what other organisation would say "We're ten times as big as you but we're going to have equal shares?"' Disregarding pressures for fission from members, Government, and critics, he pronounced: 'If we regulate them all, we may as well represent them all'. (Four years earlier a staff Ginger Group had proposed 'to utilise the superior facilities of the Society to work with or take over the Bar'.[91])

In December Kamlesh Bahl, poised to become President, was accused of bullying and intimidation by three Society staff, backed by their trade union, quickly prompting fifteen to twenty additional charges. Union sources at the EOC (which Bahl had directed) said she had bullied there too (although the two victims had not formally complained). During a week of turmoil Sayer asked her to leave Chancery Lane. She felt 'so intimidated' that her mother and sister accompanied her the next day. A closed Council meeting, from which she was barred, decided not to ask her to stand down during the investigation. The SBL, Metropolitan Black Police Association, Association of Black Probation Officers, and National Assembly Against Racism supported her. SBL chair Peter Herbert expressed 'a great deal of suspicion that Ms Bahl herself may be the subject of a campaign of bullying and intimidation'.

Lord Griffiths, asked to investigate by the Lord Chancellor, upheld all five complaints in early March. Bahl refused to resign and threatened to challenge the process, claiming Cherie Booth QC had advised her it was 'a clear breach' of the ECHR and disregarded 'the most basic principles of natural justice'. She urged the Council to allow an appeal and demanded 'a full inquiry into the background and circumstances which led to the Griffiths inquiry'. 'For a small but influential group of people, my face did not fit within the Law Society given my background in industry as against private practice and my ethnicity and gender.' The Society said it 'acted for one simple reason: it had a duty to its employees to do so'. The complaints 'were investigated by a fully independent third party', and she 'had the benefit of legal representation paid for by the Law Society'. The Manufacturing, Science and Finance union, which represented the complainants, said the report had found Bahl 'demeaning and humiliating' and 'offensively aggressive'. She had 'in many ways...usurped the secretary-general's role as head of staff and introduced an atmosphere of fear and confusion in the line of command'. It threatened to strike if she did not resign. A week later the Council voted by 38 to 3 with 7 abstentions to suspend her and called an SGM to approve. Bahl promptly resigned but pursued her action for race and sex discrimination against the Society, which 'entirely reject[ed] the allegations'. 'Nothing should obscure the fact that the real issue here is bullying in the workplace.' (The employment tribunal found that Sayer and Betts had discriminated against her but also that she had deliberately lied to it under oath. They appealed, as did the Council over the opposition of President McIntosh, whom Bahl promptly accused of victimizing her.[92])

When Napier replaced Bahl, the Council chose David McIntosh as DVP over seven other candidates in a close vote. In early May Sayer declared his candidacy for a second term to continue the 'radical reform' necessary to keep the profession from being 'indifferent' or 'actively hostile' to the

Society, inviting Napier and McIntosh to join him. There should be no challenge 'if people accept... that my motives are honourable, decent and made for the right reasons'. But McIntosh was 'somewhat disappointed' that Sayer 'did not think it proper to give me any advance warning'. And Paul Pharoah said Sayer 'did not enjoy the confidence of the Law Society's Council, a substantial part of the profession or the significant external stakeholders'. Napier challenged Sayer, offering the Society 'new and strong' leadership 'in order to better represent a much-changed profession, shed itself of its recent problems and present a re-focused and respected image'. McIntosh joined him on a ticket whose members 'trust' each other.

Bogan challenged McIntosh, hinting he might join Sayer, whose decision to stand was 'absolutely right'. The Society 'lurched from one crisis to the next because it has failed to recognise that in a consumer society there is an impossible conflict between regulation and representation....' It was on 'completely the wrong course' and should 'return to its roots and become an effective representative body' promoting 'your interests'. (A survey found that 59 per cent favoured a split but only 35 per cent wanted the Society to retain representation.)

Sayer was 'terribly disappointed'. He felt a 'duty' to achieve his reforms. The election was 'not about personal ambition, "politics" or internal squabbling. It is a serious battle for the soul of the profession.' He wanted a Society 'which protects its members and looks after their interests'. It 'seemed to have abandoned whole sections of the profession... staff and Council members openly said small firms were an embarrassment....' When 'the Society accepted a zero pay rise for the first time' the government imposed it repeatedly because 'the Society showed itself to be weak'. The OSS had far too many employees (550), and Napier wanted 'the Society to become a pure regulator'. He blamed the 'turbulence' on the 'pretty relentless' 'opposition to change'.

Napier pronounced it 'throwing-out time at the last chance saloon'. Sayer had promised to end 'continual disruptive elections'. But 'not content with one year as President like everyone else, he has pushed himself forward, causing another election this year'. 'Why, having been at the top for the last five turbulent years, should he be given yet another opportunity to lead us?' Napier promised to 'restore stability'. 'No President can work without the support of the Council, as Robert Sayer seems to believe'. Fission, though 'superficially attractive', would 'simply throw out the baby with the bath water and split the profession'. He would 'protect solicitors' market share against the inroads of unqualified advisers (wills, employment, personal injury, etc.)'. McIntosh and he joined three City firms to propose a forum for 'regular and direct input on issues crucial' to them.

McIntosh said some leaders listened 'only to themselves' and pursued 'individual agendas'. He wanted a 'clean sweep that provides leaders with high reputations'. Sayer was an 'over-staying President' who had been in office for the 'worst' five years in the Society's history. Bogan's practice was more 'an estate agent's than a solicitor's'. '[W]e do not want the Law Society to become a trade union only.' Both women DVP candidates opposed those 'two odd men out'.

There were three DVP candidates. The 'recent friction and political in-fighting' and 'politicisation of the role of the Society's office-holders', said Carolyn Kirby, 'has been significantly detrimental to good leadership'. Effective action 'requires an atmosphere of mutual respect and co-operation which has been regrettably lacking in the past year'. Hilary Siddle agreed that 'activities at Chancery Lane over the past months have been disastrous for the profession and have damaged our reputation with government and the public'. 'We need people who can work with others, not against them… who are more concerned about representing the interests of the profession than their own interests'. 'When Council and the office-holders are at total odds, the Law Society becomes ineffective and discredited.' David Savage 'always said that it is not for me to look after the public interest. There are others, alas all too many you may feel, who do that.' He had been in 'opposition' to the Council for ten years. OSS costs were 'spiralling'. There was 'too much bickering' in the Council. 'I cannot claim to be a Law Society "worthy" who has chaired this or that committee. I have not written any learned tome. I do not represent the big battalions.'

Napier trounced Sayer (66 per cent) and McIntosh beat Bogan (60 per cent); Kirby won at the second stage of the transferable vote. The turnout fell to a new low of 18.6 percent.[93]

B. Barristers

Whereas nineteenth-century solicitors had to create a governing body, the Bar sought to reform existing institutions: the four Inns (to which students were admitted and then belonged throughout their careers) and ten Circuits (later amalgamated into six). As transportation improved and the provincial Bar grew, the Circuits declined in importance. The Inns were ruled by a self-perpetuating oligarchy of benchers (about 400 in 1966). Following the closure of Serjeants Inn in 1875 and dispersal to the other four Inns of the judges, they and silks basically divided governance, leaving the 90 per cent of the Bar who were juniors represented by less than 8 per cent of benchers. For this reason, and because the Inns resisted collective action, a mass meeting to oppose the Judicature Act 1873 (which threatened to shift work to solicitors) drew over 2,000 barristers (most of the practising Bar) and led, ten years later, to formation of the Bar Committee. Like all voluntary associations, it had difficulty attracting and retaining members and had to be revived a decade later (as the Bar Council). But within two years nearly 2,000 voted in its first elections, and membership grew steadily to 90 per cent of private practitioners by 1968 (if far less of employed barristers). It kept subscriptions affordable by relying heavily on the Inns for income. The Council narrowly rejected compulsion, leaving it free to champion barristers' interests, first by elaborating restrictive practices and then in corporatist negotiations over legal aid. While less oligarchic than the Inns, fewer than a third of its members were juniors and just 10 per cent were employed barristers (about half the Bar).

In 1966 the Inns co-ordinated their activities though a newly created Senate, in which their twenty-eight members dominated the BC's six. Six years later the Pearce Committee recommended a single governing body, with more elected members, compulsory subscriptions, and financial independence from the Inns. The outcome was a reconstituted 101-person Senate, in which the thirty-nine elected barristers (from the Council) were still outnumbered by benchers, Inn and Circuit representatives, and judges. In 1985 juniors were only 31 per cent, employed barristers 6 per cent, and women less than 4 per cent. The 1979 Royal Commission urged compulsory subscriptions to a single, financially self-sufficient, governing body, a majority of whose members would be elected by 'the profession as a whole', and which would 'adequately represent' the 'different bands of seniority, specialists, employed barristers and barristers practising in different parts of the country', as well as judges and *ex officio* members of the Inns. Committees should include lay members. But nothing was done.

Internal dissent paralleled external criticism. Robin de Wilde launched the Campaign for the Bar in 1982 because the Council was not helping him collect substantial unpaid fees. The Bar was 'run by a small clique of the "good and the Great", who had as little relation to my world as an Eskimo'. He wrote to every practising barrister, proposing a solicitor blacklist, and received a 'magnificent' response. 'But the arrogance and condescension of the then establishment made it clear that as far as they were concerned it was not a problem.' 'The judges through the Senate were still too much involved in controlling our lives and the Bar Council seemed to be serving their interests as much as those of the practising Bar.'

In 1985 de Wilde accused the Council of having 'become merely another arm of the Establishment. The actual interests of the Bar seem to be their last or least important activity.' There was 'increasingly, a divide between the specialists who have survived and beaten inflation, and the common lawyers who face continual difficulties, particularly when much of the work is founded [*sic*] by civil legal aid'. The Council should reflect 'the need, interests and concerns of the Bar as a whole, rather than the present dominance by the prosperous'. The 1,500 barristers 'in the provinces always receive a raw deal'. The twenty-five-member Bar Committee was 'stuffed with silks' and had only two juniors. The Council's policy 'seems to be a mixture of appeasing The Law Society and taking care not to upset any other body, such as the Lord Chancellor's Department or the Treasury'. He wanted to end the 10 per cent discount for legally aided High Court work. 'The Criminal Bar is being destroyed by the Treasury and the bureaucracy.' The Council 'should study the tactics used by the British Medical Association who represent their doctors so well'. 'In this jungle we call our society, there are tigers around and some of them would like to eat us.' 'I would prefer to shoot the tigers.' Anthony Scrivener QC, who headed the Campaign slate, also advocated 'a BMA type and style of professionalism... devoted to protecting and furthering the interests of its members to the benefit of the public'. De Wilde proposed direct election of the BC chair, previously 'a position handed around amongst right thinking people, like a magic wand. What used to happen is that each Chairman effectively appointed his successor but three.' The current chair and vice chair offered a vague reply, embracing most of the concrete proposals but ignoring election procedures.

The Campaign won all ten seats, attracting 8,767 votes.

[T]he Old Establishment were furious at being out manoeuvred, lost their collective tempers and let it show. One Circuit Leader said...' who are these canaille?' We made sure that as many people as possible, especially the 'canaille' knew about that remark....

The July 1985 AGM, which considered their proposals, had to be moved to Central Hall, Westminster, to accommodate the more than 1,500 participants. Scrivener, the mover, said the Bar was under attack. The chair needed an election mandate when he negotiated with the Law Society. The Senate, 'run by a magic circle', offered a 'comfortable and patrician' response. 'What better expression could there be than a democratic vote?' Scrivener's peroration that 'it was time that democracy came to the Bar' elicited loud and extended applause. Hilary Heilbron moved to await the report of the Rawlinson committee. While 'the Senate seemed remote and out of touch', she feared the election of 'a chairman who did not have the necessary qualifications'. Seconder Peter Clarke, a self-described 'London criminal hack', said that when he heard the word democracy he 'reached for his revolver'. Her amendment narrowly failed, and Scrivener's was carried. The Senate President, the Rt Hon Sir Nicolas Browne-Wilkinson, Vice-Chancellor, asked for a separate vote on Heilbron's amendment, which failed again. The Campaign Council members then sought appointment to the twenty-five-member Bar Committee, securing a clear majority. Both motions were put to postal ballots (though the Campaign abandoned direct elections for officers). The *Daily Mail* reported this as 'Brawling at the Bar—worried big wigs face Mob again'.

In his first statement as BC chair, Robert Alexander QC deplored that 'many of these criticisms were first voiced publicly—when they could instead have been constructively put earlier to the Bar Council directly' and disagreed that the Council should become 'a more active trade union'. Anthony Speaight attacked employed barrister support for the Campaign. 'When one finds a body of non-practising barristers not merely wielding a large number of organised votes to defeat the practising Bar—but actually boasting of doing so—I believe the time has come to recognise that there are genuine differences. . . .' 'When we next debate the threat of Crown prosecutors being given rights of audience, employed barristers will be amongst the people we shall be striving to keep out!' The Council should expel employed barristers. A government lawyer retorted that the 'Chambers Bar' should create its own trade union.

The April 1986 Rawlinson Committee report recommended that a General Council of the Bar and the Inns of Court replace both Council and Senate; the ninety-three-member body representing the circuits, specialist associations, Inns, and barristers would exclude judges and elect its chair. Lord Rawlinson, Senate President, chaired its EGM on 21 June. A single QC expressed the fear that the new body would 'act like a trades union' and 'damage the Bar'. Representing the Campaign, Martin Bowley QC said the profession had been 'deeply divided' a year ago but was now 'wholly unified'. There was only one dissenting vote. The same happened at the Bar EGM immediately following. Alexander then proposed compulsory subscriptions to the new Council. The Law Society had used practising certificate fees to produce its Contentious Business Committee report, 'which sought to enhance the position of solicitors at the expense of the Bar'. Only two opposed the proposal, and just twelve voted against it. A postal ballot agreed by 1831 to 150. The next month's AGM (attended by just 300) approved the Rawlinson recommendations with just two dissents. A postal ballot to excuse a barrister who 'objects on the grounds of conscience or of deeply-held personal conviction' was lost by 499 to 1220.

The Professional Conduct Committee began hearing non-payment charges in 1988, and employed barristers were required to pay in 1990, when they obtained audience rights in lower courts. But later that year a disciplinary tribunal held that all 'fit and proper persons' were entitled to audience rights, which could not be denied to enforce 'compulsory subscriptions towards a professional body whose functions include a substantial element of Trades' Union Activity'. In 1994 nearly 10 per cent of the 8,000 private practitioners and 7 per cent of the 2,500 employed barrister members failed to pay subscriptions. A year later, when the Council estimated the default at £150,000, the Lord Chancellor and four senior judges ruled that compulsory subscriptions might be *ultra vires* or contrary to the public interest if used to fund the Council's trade union activities.

The Campaign had gained sufficient support by 1990 that Scrivener was poised to become BC chair and Gareth Williams QC vice chair. Although two Inner Temple benchers took the unprecedented step of challenging them, the Campaign candidates won comfortably. But success also brought apathy: the November 1990 AGM had to adjourn for lack of a quorum of sixty; a week later the sixty-three participants met for just forty minutes.[94]

These reforms failed to satisfy all critics. A 1991 report by Sir Leonard Hoffmann (CLE chair) and Lord Benson (1979 Royal Commission chair) criticized the Inns' failure to manage their property productively, causing a 'formidable shortage of money for education and training'. (Insured for over £100 million in 1977, they earned only £2.251 million and spent £809,000.) But the report 'was never allowed to see the light of day'. Lord Benson repeated the 1979 criticism of 'unco-ordinated' governance and urged that a single elected body administer Inn property. A few months later Gareth Williams QC, now BC chair, proposed electing benchers and returning judges to a reconstituted Serjeants Inn. But a joint committee of the Bar Council and Inns chose 'evolutionary' change in 1992, rejecting 'further integration'.

Two years later Lord Benson reiterated his criticism, and Lord Rawlinson repeated his 1986 recommendation that the practising profession 'take firmly into its own hands the governance of the profession and champion its well-being'. Martin Bowley QC, now BC Treasurer, called 'six competing authorities trying to run the profession with different agendas and different priorities' 'hugely wasteful'. A year later he complained that Circuit members 'led the opposition' to cutting the Council by a third. 'What services do the Inns provide for the one-third of the profession who practise from provincial chambers?' Circuits and specialist associations with equal Council representation had widely varying membership. He advocated one barrister, one vote and 'adequate representation at the governing level of women and members of the ethnic minorities'.[95]

Employed barristers, who had supported the Campaign and criticized Inn property mismanagement, elected four of their twelve BC members for the first time in November 1993. Neil Addison, who had championed audience rights, came in first and an ally second. Addison promptly opposed the Council's application for a royal charter because it 'discriminates against employed barristers'. A private practitioner denounced him as 'an enemy, a menace and thoroughly irresponsible'. Addison retorted he 'wasn't prepared to put up with being the under-class of the profession'. In response to his criticisms, the Council (almost unanimously) made employed barristers eligible for office.[96]

Applauding Mears's election as LS president in 1995, de Wilde warned the BC: 'The lesson is there, my master: listen to your members'. At the June 1997 Bar AGM he again proposed direct election of officers. The existing system permitted 'squalid deals in corridors between interested parties' and could have been devised by 'old-style Soviet leaders'. 'Why is the Bar Council against democracy?' One opponent warned of a 'PR disaster...Mears mark two', another of a 'populist' without 'the nous to go with it'. De Wilde retorted: 'At least the people standing in the Law Society elections had to put forward policies so the members have a chance to choose between rival policies as well as rival personalities'. The motion was lost by 50 to 51 (indicating member apathy), and Attorney-General John Morris QC refused a recount. But a substantial majority passed a motion that most AGM and EGM decisions would henceforth bind the Council.[97]

Council opposition to expanded audience rights (see Chapter 4) inten-sified employed barrister disaffection. When it rejected a ballot on elimin-ating the demeaning term 'non-practising' barristers, BACFI contemplated packing an AGM to compel such a ballot and block voting its passage. But resentment of private practitioners did not breed unity. Dr Peter Gray founded the Non-Practising Bar Association (NPBA) in May 1997 to sup-port Lord Irvine's reforms. After abortive efforts to co-operate with BACFI, he renamed his organization the Employed and Non-Practising Bar Association (ENPBA) and proposed resolutions on audience rights at the Bar's 1998 AGM. Warning that the odds were 'heavily...stacked against employed and non practising barristers', BACFI chair Susan Ward advised that 'more is gained by pursuing other channels than by taking heavy defeats in public "Bar fora"'. She was 'surprise[d] to see that you have changed the name of your association and that you are aiming to recruit members of the employed Bar'. BACFI told members Gray was 'not known by any of the BACFI General Committee' and it saw 'no need for such a separate association'.[98]

Despite Ward's advice to work within the system, BACFI considered leaving the Council over its opposition to audience rights. ENPBA asked the Electoral Reform Society to investigate the Council's unrepresentative structure. The Council's June 1999 AGM supported ENPBA's motion inviting an inquiry 'into the issue of fair representation for "non-practis-ing" and employed barristers on the Bar Council'. Derek Wheatley QC (who had chaired both the BC and BACFI) complained that the Council's continuing opposition to audience rights reflected 'a general attitude that an employed barrister is a second class citizen. Examples are that of well over a thousand benchers of the four Inns of Court only three are employed barristers....' The 2,530 employed and 3,046 non-practising BC members had twelve Council members (465:1), whereas the 9,762 private practitioners had 102 (96:1). Lord Irvine had recently written to him that the Council 'is insufficiently representative of employed barris-ters' and 'too often sees its task as being simply to defend the interests of barristers in private practice....' BACFI called for 'equal representation and for new classification of barristers as "practising" if you are providing legal services'.[99]

The Council created a working party 'to consider changes needed to the membership of the Council so that as the governing body of the whole profession it can fully carry out its functions, representing the interests of all subscribers'. Although it temporarily added five employed or non-practising members, BACFI said 'nothing less than proportional representation will be satisfactory'. In the wake of the Stephen Lawrence inquiry, the Council agreed 'it is crucial' that it 'represents and that it is seen to represent the entire Bar'. Ethnic minorities were 8.8 per cent of independent practitioners but only 4 per cent of the Council. It also recommended that committees 'reflect the membership of the Bar and that this be done by appropriate co-option'.[100]

In response to the Lord Chancellor's 1998 proposal to extend rights of audience and to conduct litigation, the Council sought the power to mandate practising certificates (and collect fees) and pursued this in the AJA debates. On 28 January, during the Report Stage, Lord Goodhart moved such an amendment to put the BC 'on the same footing as the Law Society and the Council of Licensed Conveyancers'. Lord Irvine observed:

the Bar Council's many able advocates... protested how unreasonable, how unconscionable, how unconstitutional it is for the Government to have dared to promote legislation interfering with rights of audience and how this threatens the fragile independence of the Bar and risks tumbling our entire constitutional settlement around our ears.... How interesting it is to see the position when the boot is on the other foot.

Professional associations 'are hybrid bodies which combine regulatory functions with...trade unions functions'. The 'enforcement of trade union closed shops is contrary to the right of freedom of association which is enshrined in the European Convention on Human Rights, newly incorporated'. Ward said 'BACFI does not have a problem with compulsory subscriptions providing the Bar Council stops using subscription income to fund campaigns to denigrate employed and non-practising barristers and starts looking after our interests'. Irvine 'would need some persuasion that the Bar Council...seriously attempts to do a good job of representing the many barristers who are not in private practice'. During the Commons Report Stage in June the Government introduced such a clause, which 'should be a potent means of ensuring more meritocratic entry to the Bar, which suffers from an excessively middle-class image'. 'The Dearing review made it clear that individuals and professions should be expected to pay for such postgraduate vocational training.' The clause was agreed. The Council proposed to exempt non-practising barristers and increase fees for employed barristers with higher court audience rights, while promising 'fair treatment for the Employed Bar'.[101]

C. New Politics?

As the media never tired of repeating, Mears broke the mould.[102] There had been only one vice-presidential race since World War II and no presidential contest in living memory. Mears bragged of being a reactionary revolutionary (Reagan, not Thatcher), an outsider battling the 'Buggins's turn' of 'establishment groupies', rejecting the 'politically correct crap', 'bigotry, cant and hypocrisy' of the 'Politburo' 'apparatchiki', the 'orthodoxy' of the Council's 'hothouse world'. Promiscuously mixing metaphors, he pronounced it 'tumbril time' for the 'Bourbons', who had 'learnt nothing' from history, the 'old'uns', 'smelly old fish', who had made Chancery Lane a 'graveyard'. He turned opponents' boasts of experience and influence into dirty words, blaming Council members for everything that had happened on their watch. (Taking this a step further—and sounding like Nixon justifying his nomination of mediocrities to the Supreme Court—Savage boasted he was not a 'worthy' and had chaired no committees or written learned tomes.)

Mears's confrontational style was ideal for challenging but disastrous for governing. (The Campaign for the Bar was known as the 'Wilde bunch' after its leader, who wanted to 'shoot the tigers' threatening 'to eat us'. But the Bar Council quickly accommodated its ideas and co-opted its members.) Mears drew media attention by giving them good copy; even being called 'thoroughly unacceptable' was better than being ignored. He had only one strategy: frontal attack. Triumphant in victory, pugnacious in defeat, he complained of persecution when this provoked the inevitable response. He excelled in the politics of *ressentiment*, playing to straight white men's fears of women, minorities, and gays and lesbians. Although dependent on the Lord Chancellor's goodwill, he accused the deeply religious Lord Mackay of betraying Jesus with his divorce reforms. (As a divorcé living with his illegitimate children's mother, this ensured charges of hypocrisy.) He insulted even when purporting to compliment, calling the defeated Eileen Pembridge 'the most dangerous feminist in England' (high praise from one who bragged of being 'the most dangerous lawyer in England'). He opposed the policies of constituents: family and antidiscrimination lawyers, the City. He maligned opponents as a 'small coterie of metropolitan leftists', who 'intrigue[d]' in an attempt to stage a 'backstairs coup'. He alienated the Council by urging supporters to contest every seat and launched *Caterpillar* to expose 'scandals, ineptitudes, unpleasantnesses'. He portrayed himself grandiosely as Richard III at the battle of Bosworth, David slaying Goliath.

Sayer showed similar symptoms: he had 'worked miracles', saved legal aid, and 'achieved more in the last six months than we did in the previous 20 years'; no one had a better track record. He megalomaniacally proposed taking over the Bar. He boasted that his 'cynicism' and 'dogged persistence' allowed him to uncover the Regis computer scandal and stop the Society from wasting more money on the HSSK. His sensible proposals to ascertain member wants and prune unnecessary committees inspired grudging respect, if not affection.

Revolutions devour their children. Edge and Bogan outflanked Mears and Sayer, advancing proposals too radical and patently self-interested for those erstwhile revolutionaries once ensconced in power. Bogan even parodied Mears's hyperbole, likening opponents to mad cows infected with CJD, who had to be selectively culled. As a result, the BLA (clearly a core constituency) backed Bogan over Mears. At the same time, Girling's Campaign for New Leadership linked Mears and Sayer to Bogan's extremism.

Mears and Sayer turned members' economic and status insecurities into anti-establishment anger. The annual conference was a 'jol' for officers and staff; foreign trips were useless junkets. Officers and then Council members voted themselves salaries while solicitors were suffering. Chancery Lane was extravagant, refurbishing a building rarely used by the majority of solicitors practising outside London. Like Reagan, Mears and Sayer claimed to seek office only to shrink governance, cutting the budget by curtailing self-regulation. Spouting the rhetoric of class resentment, Sayer said the Society had 'got a bit above itself' and 'seemed to think it ran the profession'.

But if this allowed both Mears and Sayer to capture the presidency, it alienated those they needed to enact their programme. Mears claimed presidential prerogative: the Law Society 'ship has one captain...who is entitled to expect the loyalty and commitment of the whole organisation'. The Council asserted Parliamentary supremacy: if they could not vote no confidence in the president, they could obstruct him. The 'President's Reform Group' never enrolled more than nine Council members— perhaps because Mears incited solicitors to take 'revenge' by contesting opponents' seats. They promptly retaliated: the proposal to increase the Council's power at the expense of the president's, the creation of an executive committee which chose its own chair, the suggestions that the Council nominate the DVP and that members choose only the DVP (who would be socialized by the Council for two years before becoming president). Mears also expected—and provoked—staff opposition, cowing employees and forcing out those who would not capitulate, including Hayes, Stapely, Lockley, and Merricks. The proposal to subordinate a ceremonial president to a policy-making Director-General was partly a response to this power grab.

Mears and Sayer were Poujadistes, appealing to the petty bourgeois anxieties of solo and small-firm practitioners confronting market forces and state pressures they could not control or even understand. Mears and Sayer promised to curtail competition by limiting entry and raising conveyancing fees, reduce regulation, pass SIF costs on to conveyancing clients, and raise legal aid remuneration. Mears saw nothing wrong with solicitors 'try[ing] to protect ourselves'. Sayer insisted that the bargain of 'professional responsibilities in return for professional privileges' served the 'common good'. Both encouraged members' calls for militance towards the Government. (Trevor Murray represented an almost-humorous exaggeration. The Society had 'consistently played into the hands of its enemies and thereby managed to oversee the systematic devastation of the profession' by 'conced[ing]' the battles for conveyancing and legal aid. He voiced nostalgia for the time when 'solicitors' services were valued by clients and the status of the profession was appreciated and respected both by society and the government'. The profession had been betrayed by 'quislings...who look to government or depend on its patronage for their personal achievement'. He condemned the 'diplomatic solution' and praised the Society for having 'managed to rattle the Lord Chancellor'.)

Opponents confronted a dilemma. They could expose these fantasies as 'fool's gold', incurring Mears's jibe of 'defeatism or no-can-do-ism'. Or they could play his game but lose and betray their principles as well. Hodge condemned 'protectionism', 'cartels', and 'artificially induced bills'; solicitors could not limit access to the SCB. But he sought credit for keeping the number of training contracts 'steady for years', delaying standard fees in magistrates' courts for four years, and doubling legal aid payments in five years while acknowledging this was a 'position which we do not trumpet'. And he promised to reduce the practising certificate fee and SIF contribution and promulgate a 'guideline fee structure' for conveyancing. Accusing Mears of 'blatant demagoguery' and deliberate 'ignorance' and his proposals of being 'unlawful, impossible or plain daft', Pembridge refused to 'woo voters with false promises' or join 'the last inglorious charge of the Light Brigade'. But she hoped to cap SCF liability to institutional lenders, charge SCB complainants, and resist reduced legal aid payments. Aucott insisted on telling solicitors 'what they have to hear if they are going to survive in the changed world', not 'what they want to hear'. Sycamore wanted to negotiate with the government about legal aid on its own terms rather than trying to 'turn the clock back to open-ended spending'. Solicitors should not 'stamp our feet', indulge in protectionism and 'vain clamour', or 'watch the world pass us by' but rather embrace change, be the vanguard, prosper by adapting. Napier dismissed Murray's 'rantings of yesteryear'.

Mears and Sayer won on message but lost on style. From 1995 to 2000 opponents ran primarily on not being them, as shown by the very name of the 1996 Campaign for New Leadership (launched without candidates!). They embraced Mears's taunt that they were 'Sound Men'. Girling offered 'firm and clear leadership', 'stabilization', a pair of 'safe but not boring hands'. Mears had 'shaken up' the Society and a 'complacent Council', fought 'smugness', worked a 'sea change', 'stirred the pot'; but now 'battle-weary' solicitors wanted quiet. Mears was extreme, his opponents moderate. (Mears similarly dismissed Bogan as a 'wild man'.) Mears had mired the Society in electioneering, squabbling, bickering, jibes and sarcasm, division; rejecting politics, his opponents promised to end strife and restore unity. After failing to win a second term as vice president, Sayer repudiated Mears, while opponents sought to associate the two. McIntosh accused Sayer of sharing his 'ex-collaborator's shortcomings'—'disarray and unfocused leadership', being a 'critic and challenger' when the profession needed a 'healer and achiever'. Calling for 'new and strong leadership' to 'shed...recent problems', Napier declared it 'throwing out time at the last-chance saloon' and promised 'stability' after Sayer's 'five turbulent years' (echoing LAG's allusion to Thomas à Becket).

Character became the currency of Society politics. Mears accused the traitor Sayer of having 'changed his colours' and 'taken the establishment shilling'. 'Incurably unsound', he would never be able to 'take tea with the Queen Mother', 'make small talk with Cherie Blair', or 'consume a cucumber sandwich in polite company'. 'Leadership' was a code word for the traits Mathews and the 'maverick' Sayer allegedly lacked. Girling said his successor had to be 'problem solver, statesman, media personality, evangelist and perfect host, possessed of infinite stamina and personal charm, Dimbleby-like chairmanship skills and boundless enthusiasm'—clearly not Mears (if also not Sycamore).[103] Trevor Murray bragged about leaving grammar school at 16, enjoying no 'privilege', working 'extremely hard', and privately educating five children (a typically contradictory constellation of values).

Each candidate deplored the corrosive effect of politics, claiming the moral high ground as selfless champion of professional interests while maligning opponents as ambitious and unscrupulous. When Young ran for president, Pembridge exposed the cover-up of his sexual predations by an establishment that had secured her silence two years earlier by promising action. Mears promptly denounced her 'vile and contemptible' 'gutter' allegations 'worthy of the tabloids' and swore to 'campaign cleanly'! He then took maximum advantage of the block voting charges against Girling and the dirty tricks considered by Sycamore and threatened to release more damaging material if Sycamore and Mathews did not withdraw, accusing them of 'humbug and nonsense', 'sheer shamelessness', and being 'unfit to lead the profession'. Sayer was guilty of 'increasingly wild personal attacks'. Sycamore claimed that 'in a situation which had become political it was a perfectly legitimate exercise'. Mears compared the Society to a 'loony-left Council' and talked about appealing to the Master of the Rolls. Like Peter Lorre discovering gambling at Rick's Bar in 'Casablanca', Robert Sayer expressed shock that 'Law Society politics are the same as politics anywhere else'.

If invective was Mears's metier, it was Sayer's downfall. He had a school-boy's obsession with the scatological. The Society should 'get off its back-side'; it had 'gone up its own backside again'. Mears and he would 'not put up with crap from anyone who gets in our way'. Keating was a 'complete pillock' fronting for Mears, a 'bitter, twisted little' man who kept turning up 'like a piece of dog turd on your shoe'. Unfortunately for Sayer, that simile stuck even more tightly. He refused to 'grovel', regretting only hav-ing given his enemies ammunition—which they gleefully used. Keating called his language 'disgusting', 'disgraceful', if 'not a surprise'. Girling criticized the 'intemperacy'. The *New Law Journal* thought it 'out of place if spoken by a football manager'. The *Solicitors Journal* deplored the 'descent' into 'scurrilous' 'personal abuse' and 'ridicule', which was 'par-ticularly unseemly' in a 'professional election' and 'drags us all down'. The alleged victims kept repeating Sayer's vulgarities—Keating even sued for libel—in order to inflame the backlash. Mears complained of 'six weeks of vituperation and personal vilification' while declaring such 'grossness should be met with charity and forbearance'. There was 'no limit' to Sayer's 'effrontery'; such 'unprecedented' abuse was not a 'solitary outburst' but typical of someone whose language was 'notorious'.

Politics both reflected and intensified personal animosities. When Baker questioned the proposal to limit entry, Mears called him a 'Dracula looka-like'. Baker, in turn, took the minutes of the dirty tricks campaign meeting. When Holland left the Council to protest the election outcome, Mears accused him of self-importance. McIntosh began his Council term by attacking Mears. Although Mears pretentiously claimed to be the 'loyal opposition' (of one?) after losing, Girling accused him of 'relentless carp-ing and sniping' and 'sheer negativity'; Mears retorted that his offers to help were rebuffed. Mears dismissed Sycamore and Mathews as 'non-entities' and other opponents as 'superannuated groupies'; He backed Keating against Napier, ridiculing the latter's appearance. When Keating switched to the presidency, he denounced Sayer's 'confrontational' behaviour, 'bel-ligerence and abuse'. Sayer called Keating Mears's 'loyal sidekick'. Blaming Mears for 'a period of confrontation, chaos and bitterness', Sayer said the profession needed him 'like a hole in the head'.

Betrayal was unforgivable. When Bogan, an erstwhile Mears supporter, sought to divest the Society of representative functions, founded the SA to assume them, and then ran for president, Mears called him a 'wild man' who lived in a 'fantasy world'. Sayer's defection was even more bitter. Owing his political career to Mears, he utterly repudiated his mentor: Mears engaged in 'gesture politics', tending 'to speak first and think of the consequences later'. Mears retaliated by disproving Sayer's claim that Mears had declared as his VP candidate uninvited. Sayer retorted that Mears 'made speeches', 'simply has nothing new to offer', was 'shallow, vain and a phoney, all talk and no action'. Sayer felt betrayed when McIntosh, who had campaigned for him, stood against him.

Public image—a perennial anxiety of lawyers—eclipsed all other issues. Elections were repeatedly marred by scandal: both the Council cover-up of Young's sexual harassment and the block voting in 1995, dirty tricks in 1997, Sayer's vulgarity in 1999, and Bahl's bullying in 2000. Opponents and critics accused Mears of making solicitors look 'foolish', a 'laughing stock'. LAG called his presidency a 'joke ... gone sour', a 'soap opera', a 'very public farce'. Local law societies worried about Chancery Lane's reputation. The *New Law Journal* feared solicitors were losing (and barristers gaining) influence with the government. The *Solicitors Journal* declared that the president's 'chief role' was to 'present the face of the profession to the outside world'. Even Mears made image one of his three principal concerns, blaming problems on detractors and naïvely seeking improvement by spending millions on public relations (while openly subordinating the public interest to the profession's).

'Law Society politics are the same as politics anywhere'—they were about winning. For five years elections were a toss-up because few bothered to vote and voters were divided between establishment and outsiders. In 1995, only 18 per cent of the electorate chose Mears, who failed to win a majority. A Hodge–Pembridge ticket might have beaten him. The next year Girling won with just 22 per cent of the electorate, again not a majority of voters. Had Bogan not run for president on splitting the Society, Mears might have won a second term (his absolute vote increased from 11,550 to 14,239). By his third race, however, solicitors gave Mears only 8,148 votes, preferring Sycamore by two to one. The electorate remained split in 1998, although the fissure was less clearly ideological. Mathews defeated Napier by just 53 per cent to 47, and Sayer beat McIntosh by 55 to 45; even Keating took 43 per cent against Bahl. Given the declining turnout, only 14 per cent of the electorate chose Mathews. As the establishment candidate in 1999, Sayer beat Mears-surrogate Keating by 64 to 36 but still gained only 14 per cent of the electorate. Even an outsider like Murray took 37 per cent of the vote against Napier. A year later Napier (now the establishment candidate) defeated Sayer (again the dissident) by 66 to 34; but because turnout was an all-time low of 18.6 per cent, Napier attracted just 12 per cent of the electorate. Bogan, running alone against McIntosh, got the same percentage as Sayer, showing that a third of voters remained strongly disaffected. None of these presidents could claim a mandate.

Politics is about building coalitions and dividing opponents. Hodge and Pembridge would have united legal aid solicitors and women against the Mears–Sayer claim to represent high-street and provincial firms. Bogan deprived Mears of some of his angriest supporters. By luring away Sayer, Sycamore ended Mears's prospect of office, though he continued to agitate.

The protectionist Sayer was a strange bedfellow with the free marketeers Sycamore and Mathews. In 1998, both tickets were 'balanced' (City and high street) and supported by similar proportions of voters. Although Mathews focused exclusively on City issues (MDPs, access to venture capital, limited liability, FSA regulation) and bragged about his prominence in the world's largest firm, he claimed his slate (including Bahl) reflected 'a wider cross section of the profession than ever before'. Two years later the balanced ticket of Napier and McIntosh easily defeated Sayer (seeking a second term) and Bogan (running separately).

Candidates had clear constituencies. The nineteenth-century alternation of London and provincial presidents gave way a century later to alternation between City and high street (reflecting size, clientele, and function). Bahl claimed to represent the employed, young, women, and ethnic minorities. Opposing her in 1998, Keating insisted that 'the profession should be represented by practitioners who have been exposed to the rigours of practice...it is the whole profession that needs to be represented'. Even McIntosh (confronting her running mate Sayer) promised to 'think young and of equal opportunities'. No one dared oppose her the next year, and no one probably would have contested the 2000 presidency had the bullying charge not derailed her candidacy (which her supporters claimed was its purpose). Women had been more than half of new solicitors since 1986; a woman became Bar Council chair in 1998; and Mears and Sayer unsuccessfully sought a woman DVP candidate in 1995. But Pembridge gained only 15 per cent of the presidential vote (perhaps because she was too feminist). That year a prominent woman City partner told the AWS annual lunch it was time to disband: 'Do we really need a lobby group to fight for female solicitors' rights?'[104] Other women City partners blocked a Council seat for women. Bahl presented herself as a conservative anti-feminist. Nevertheless, the establishment ran two women for DVP in 2000, and the winner became the first woman president two years later (ungendering Buggins).

If politics was preoccupied with personalities, it also reflected issues. All collective action confronts the tension between maximizing numbers and preserving unity. The disaffected must choose between seeking control, seceding, or apathy (exit, voice or loyalty).[105] The Bar was not divided by firm size (though it was by specialization and reliance on private or legally aided clients); and geography was less relevant (since the provincial Bar was half the size of London, whereas solicitors were equally distributed between the two). Juniors successfully agitated for increased representation. The most dangerous fissure divided private practitioners and employed barristers (organized in BACFI). Addison opposed the Council's application for a royal charter because it denied employed barristers proportionate representation. The Council intensified resentment by adamantly resisting employed barristers' audience rights from the CPS launch in 1986 to the AJA in 1999 (an antagonism Lord Irvine exploited to secure its passage). In order to strengthen the case for compulsory subscriptions (taxation), the Bar Council had to expand representation.

Solicitors were pulled in multiple directions. Solo practitioners felt over-regulated. Small firms felt neglected (although they consumed services far in excess of their fee contribution). Large firms resented paying to regulate small. The Commerce & Industry Group complained that members contributed £3 million but it received only £12,300. By transferring a local government seat to newly qualified solicitors and then back the Council antagonized both. Nineteenth-century geographic constituencies were increasingly anachronistic rotten boroughs; but many feared that constituencies reflecting the real divisions (firm size and specialization) would hasten fission.

Although the more successful firms ultimately defeated the less after a seven-year struggle, centrifugal forces persisted. City firms threatened to secede. Many Mears and Sayer supporters also belonged to the BLA and the newly formed SA, whose 1997 merger increased their credibility as a Law Society rival.[106] Many employed solicitors voted with their feet by foregoing practising certificates. Franchised legal aid solicitors organized in 1994. The next year the CLSA and LCCSA sought to negotiate with the LAB, claiming the Society did so inadequately. Four years later the CLSA said it could no longer speak for the unfranchised, who it expected would leave.[107]

Proposals to separate regulation from representation challenged the core of self-governance. Mears and Sayer assailed discipline and indemnity insurance. Solo and small-firm practitioners resented all efforts to raise standards. Mears and Sayer held out (false) promises of relief: the Society should reassert control over the SCB, ending the 'tiresome' insistence on its independence and deleting 'complaints' from its name; Mears even suggested that solicitors drop indemnity coverage, leaving malpractice victims uncompensated. Bogan took the other tack, arguing that the Society should relinquish regulation; a supporter indiscreetly boasted that solicitors could 'run rings round an external regulator'. But their opponents, fearing that external regulation would be just as expensive and more rigorous, wanted to retain the form in order to avoid the substance. And some sought more effective regulation in order to reduce the collective embarrassment of misconduct and cost of mutual insurance.

Collective action faced a fundamental contradiction: the coercion on which it depended was incompatible with advocacy. Solicitors created the BLA to represent their self-interest unconstrained by the public interest; but it quickly sought the power to compel dues. Edge argued that the Society should not represent solicitors because it received practising certificate fees. Although Bogan forced an AGM vote and postal ballot on fission, ran for president on that platform, and refused to accept defeat, he seemed ambivalent about the goal. Advocates as diverse as the *New Law Journal*, Mears and Sayer, Bogan, and Trevor Aldridge QC maintained that a voluntary association would be stronger than the Society. But without responsibility for regulation, solicitors' increasingly divergent interests would spawn antagonistic groups. And each would face the free rider problem. Neither the BLA nor the SA attracted more than a small percentage of solicitors. The ABA, on which Sayer was fixated, has never enrolled a majority of American lawyers (and lacks regulatory power). Although voluntarism freed the Bar Council to champion barristers' interests, even suing the Lord Chancellor over legal aid remuneration, it was sufficiently unhappy about the failure of just 10 per cent of private practitioners to pay subscriptions that it repeatedly sought coercive power (beginning in 1972), accepting limitations on representation in exchange for this under the AJA. Ironically, the Law Society's vigorous opposition to that Bill provoked Lord Irvine to take the power to prohibit representation.

Lawyers had to choose between professionalism and trade unionism. Although both branches energetically sought and jealously guarded their professional status for centuries, pressures from market and state tempted many solicitors to flirt with syndicalism, remembering when the Society had been called 'the best organised and most intelligent trade union in the Country'. Both Bogan and the Campaign for the Bar wanted their associations to emulate the BMA (disregarding Holland's caution that most doctors were NHS employees while few lawyers relied on legal aid). Scrivener advocated a 'BMA type and style of professionalism...devoted to protecting and furthering the interests of its members to the benefit of the public'. Claiming that just 'ten years ago, ours was the safest of occupations, with a guaranteed good income for life', Mears encouraged the delusion that it could be again if solicitors resolutely pursued self-interest. Sayer was 'proud' of 'putting the profession's interest temporarily in front of clients'. But trade unionism was a risky strategy. Campaigning for president, Girling was 'proud' the Society had blocked authorized conveyancers and delayed probate practitioners but warned that it would be 'counterproductive' to 'crow about either of those achievements'. Hodge posed a stark choice between client and solicitor interests. Some feared losing the royal charter if the Society engaged in trade unionism. And freedom to champion self-interest might well be outweighed by the Society's inability to continue pretending disinterest.

All politicians claim power in the name of constituents while minimizing constitutent control. The Bar was an extreme example: a self-perpetuating gerontocracy of benchers ruling the Inns and dominating the Bar Council, near disenfranchisement of the vast majority of junior barristers and the large minority of employed, repeated rejection of direct election of officers (especially after the spectre of another Mears), and General Meetings unable to enforce decisions. The Law Society displayed its own paternalism. At a roadshow designed to air grassroots grievances, a solicitor complained: 'What it comes down to is that Chancery Lane knows what is best for us'. President Elly replied complacently: 'You elected the members of the Council for their expertise and at the end of the day we must use our best judgment'. The SCB director rebuffed solicitor criticism of her staff as 'extraordinarily offensive'.

Lawyers kept agitating for democracy. In 1984 the BLA sought proxy voting, popular nomination of officers, term limits, and non-geographic constituencies. Mears and Sayer aggressively contested elections—infuriating the establishment—until they became the establishment and condemned challengers. Although Sayer declared his first run for VP 'necessary', McIntosh's challenge to his second run three years later was 'damaging to the profession's reputation', 'divisive', 'unnecessary infighting', a 'waste' of £70,000. The Society needed it 'like a hole in the head'.[108] Challenged by Keating for president a year later, Sayer said the election would 'damage the Law Society's credibility' and cost £100,000. City solicitors found elections 'disheartening'. 'Now and then an election may be appropriate', but 'the best of our members', 'the most talented', would not submit to 'the vagaries of the electoral process'. (*Noblesse oblige* might require them to rule but not to run for office.) Girling called it 'traumatic' for solicitors to stand for election 'without knowing whether or not they are wasting their time'. The disaffected, by contrast, demanded direct democracy. Edge proposed that 100 solicitors could compel a postal ballot to recall the entire Council. Mears wanted more issues decided by referenda. But Sir Dennis Stevenson urged a corporate model, subordinating a figurehead president to a senior civil servant and electing only the DVP.

The greatest pitfall of self-governance, however, is not tensions among fractions or between professional and public interest, oligarchy and democracy, but apathy. Most lawyers just want to earn a living and leave politics to others.[109] They are energized by threats. The Bar Committee was a response to the Judicature Act 1873, which let solicitors take work from barristers. The Campaign for the Bar was a response to solicitors' non-payment of fees. Its proposed reforms drew an unprecedented 1,500 to the AGM, but five years later it failed to get even a quorum of sixty. Solicitors founded the BLA, SPG, SPyG, and SA in response to similar economic threats, only to watch each atrophy. Mears's first election provoked 36 per cent of solicitors to vote, his unprecedented bid for a second term brought out 45, but only 30 per cent voted during his third run. Turnout fell to 26 per cent the next year, 22 per cent when Keating (backed by Mears) challenged Sayer, and just 19 per cent when Sayer tried to succeed himself. Like Rhett Butler, most lawyers frankly do not give a damn.

11 The Politics of Professionalism

Mature professions—of which late twentieth-century English lawyers were a leading example—share several essential features.[1] Disturbances in any of them can compel reconfiguration of all the others.[2] Professions persuade the state to certify and protect their exclusive mastery of a body of expert knowledge.[3] Such expertise can become less relevant (organized religion in some of the western world) or be supplanted by commodities (information technology) or organizations using non-professional labour (bureaucracies).[4] Professions seek to control entry, although pressures may become irresistible (because rewards increase or ascriptive barriers of class, gender, ethno-religious background, or race lose legitimacy), or the profession may become less attractive (as material rewards diminish or status falls, or burdens become unacceptable—priestly celibacy, for instance). Professions aspire to superior social status. This may be endangered by what they do: contact with social dirt (hence the superiority of barristers and medical consultants), dishonourable behaviour (the threats to the Catholic Church, or accountants, and always to lawyers), and routinization.[5] But a profession's status is also affected by its members' ascribed characteristics: traditionally through exclusivity, now through representativeness. Professions try to suppress competition in order to protect profits and status. Outsiders may challenge the profession's jurisdiction: accountants, mortgage lenders, immigration advisers, claims agents. Insiders may upset tacit market divisions: solicitors doing advocacy, barristers offering direct access, entrepreneurial practitioners engaging in advertising, using intermediaries and subordinates, cutting prices. Professions depend on predictable demand (partly because the high investment in human capital makes supply adjustments sluggish and costly). Medicine is the great success story: expectations constantly outrun improvements in health status. Traditional professions passively responded to demand, typically dispersed among many small consumers. Contemporary professions actively stimulate demand, typically concentrated in a few large third-party payers (the state, insurers). Falling demand can have dramatic effects: fluoride treatments on dentistry, the housing market collapse on solicitors, ATMs on bank tellers. The Great Depression swelled the numbers seeking refuge from unemployment while drastically cutting demand.[6] Professions claim the right to regulate themselves, but failures to handle complaints promptly or correct misbehaviour provoke calls for external intervention. Professions achieve each of these essential objectives through collective action, which confronts apathy, internal divisions, rank-and-file resentment, and leadership failures.

Successful professions have to balance the interests of aspirants, practitioners, producers of knowledge, and future members (typically academics), consumers (individual and collective, public and private), third-party payers, competitors, subordinates, and the media. English lawyers successfully coped with numerous disturbances during the second half of the twentieth century: fluctuating supply and demand, changes in composition and structures of practice, external and internal competition, and scandals of self-regulation.[7] The state seemed content to let lawyers run their own affairs, despite a constant stream of criticism from academics, practitioners, politicians, and journalists.[8] The Royal Commission on Legal Services, created by a Labour government in 1977, endorsed the *status quo*.[9] The Conservatives' about-face in 1988, five years after they had embraced the report, was unexpected and dramatic.[10]

A. The Conservative Attack

By replacing Lord Hailsham with Lord Mackay at the beginning of her third term, Thatcher signalled her intention to challenge the legal profession.[11] She may have thought this her last chance to tackle that bastion of tradition, which had ignored decades of criticism. She had already shown her determination to treat medicine as just another market commodity and the BMA as a trade union. Why not bait the Law Society and Bar Council? The ban on lender conveyancing and, even more, the Bar's monopoly of higher court advocacy and silks' continuing insistence on leading juniors (despite formal abolition of the two-counsel rule) were blatant restrictive practices. Their elimination might confer savings on not only consumers but also taxpayers by reducing the cost of prosecutions and legal aid. At the very least, Conservatives could woo the media and public, which distrusted lawyers and their professional associations.[12]

The response must have exceeded the Government's expectations.[13] The media applauded the 'revolutionary' proposals, assailing lawyers' 'entrenched privileges', 'hidebound customs', 'pomposity', 'archaic paraphernalia of wigs and gowns', and 'love of incomprehensible Latinisms'. Lawyers charged too much and were elitist and cliquish. A *Times* leader cried 'Professional foul?' complaining that lawyers had 'long occupied an enviable niche in the British class structure'. In an eclectic medley of metaphors, the Princess Royal accused the legal profession of having 'created its mystique, its ivory tower syndrome in which it appears to be busily cementing up the holes'.[14] These were ancient charges; the novelty was the official imprimatur. Furthermore, the press, presumably echoing (or leading) the public, reviled precisely those traits that made lawyers professionals: tradition, high income and status (both ascribed and achieved), and collegiality.[15] Surveys confirmed that 80 per cent believed 'lawyers are too expensive', 83 per cent wanted to resolve more disputes without lawyers, and 61 per cent preferred to deal with 'one type of lawyer instead of both solicitors and barristers'.[16] The violent reaction of the organized profession (especially the Bar), senior judges, and former Lord Chancellors simply intensified media derision and public obloquy. Lord Lane's blunder in closing the courts for a weekday meeting exposed the judiciary to charges of trade unionism. The Green Papers made it far more difficult, virtually impossible, for the profession to convincingly claim disinterest. After a decade of Thatcherism, laissez faire was hegemonic; anti-market diatribes by Lords Ackner, Benson, Hailsham, Scarman, and Lane just confirmed their image as dinosaurs. Newspapers as diverse as *The Times, Guardian*, and *Daily Telegraph* (the Bar's strongest supporter) all published free market critiques of lawyers' restrictive practices.

The Government also succeeded in pitting solicitors against barristers, as it had GPs against consultants.[17] Solicitors resented the Bar's insufferable condescension.[18] Eager to claim audience rights in and eligibility for appointment to the higher courts (for status more than income), the Law Society adopted a tone of sweet reasonableness, boasting of ending its conveyancing monopoly (conveniently forgetting its adamant defiance a few years earlier and downplaying its success in containing licensed conveyancers' market share).[19] This provoked the Bar and bench to reassert barristers' moral and technical superiority. The Bar declared a 'hundred years war', threatening to invade the solicitors' market by offering direct access, first to professional and eventually to lay clients. At the end of 1991, outgoing chair Scrivener pronounced that 'the Bar Council is no longer an inward looking conservative body looking only after its own interests. We put the consumer first....'[20] Two years later the Bar's house organ claimed that 'advocacy for change is today very much a feature of English and Welsh barristers' and had been 'the theme of this year's Bar Conference'.[21] At the end of the decade chair Brennan insisted: 'This is a reforming Bar...a modern Bar....We are no longer part of the problem. We are part of the solution. We are now more than ever a progressive institution....'[22] The Green Papers (and media enthusiasm) compelled lawyers to embrace market discourse. Both branches inveighed against concentration: the Bar claimed that City firms would capture leading barristers, denying them to non-clients; solicitors warned that corporate conveyancing and MDPs would create megafirms (while themselves seeking to offer mortgage lending, estate agency, insurance, and other financial services and delighting in City firms' multinational expansion). Lawyers and judges deplored Americanization, a catch-all epithet insinuating vulgarity, dishonesty, incompetence, gigantism, litigiousness, both excessive and inadequate zeal, and inflated damages.[23]

Backlash was inevitable.[24] Asserting that 'up until the cultural revolution of the 1970s, solicitors, and particularly barristers, were regarded as almost beyond criticism', the *New Law Journal* attributed the 'downward step in the estimation of the public...to the descent into advertising'.[25] Anticipating his 1993–4 term as LS President, Pannone accused Thatcher of having 'dragged professional services down to the level of the marketplace'. At the end of his term he deplored that 'justice [was] being peddled as just another commodity' and accused politicians of 'playing on the emotions of their supposed supporters'.[26] The BLA chair told its 1993 conference that 'excessive mania for competition' was 'modern idolatry'.[27] The senior partner of the largest Cardiff firm did 'not believe competition is necessarily a good thing for a profession....we have lost status in the community' by entering 'the market-place in a way that is unhelpful to us'.[28] Martin Mears accused 'some early Thatcherite' of describing 'all professions as conspiracies against the public interest'. (The Fabian Shaw would not have been amused.) The 'catastrophic consequences' of her 'crude laissez faire-ism' were 'all around us': 'the continuing decline of British manufacturing industry...the traditional village shop and post office have been wiped out'.[29] In 1997 a Council member accused consumer organizations and government of waging 'war' against solicitors, seeking 'to maximize our punishment...to oppress the profession, benefiting from its suffering'. 'Perhaps it is time the Society held a general meeting to declare its unity against unfair oppression and competition and then chart a course of collective retaliation.'[30] John Hendy QC beseeched 'free market fanatics' to 'acknowledge that sometimes, just sometimes, professional bodies (and trade unions) which seek to uphold restrictions on the operation of the market in the interests of their members, are also acting in the interests of the public'.[31] Hallett warned that 'if government was not careful the legal system would become American and lawyers be perceived as greedy'. American 'confidence in the legal profession is at an all time low', primarily because 'the lawyer in the States is no longer an officer of the court. Contingent fee arrangements have changed lawyers into businessmen.... They deploy the techniques of the market place to attract work. They seek work where none exists.'[32]

Because Government dominated its chosen terrain—the market—the profession played the trump card of 'independence'. This protean shibboleth had many uses. Independence was inconsistent with ACLEC or the Lord Chancellor deciding who could appear in the higher courts (and by implication, who could sit in them). Independence mandated the cabrank rule (which rendered the advocate irresponsible for a client's positions or identity), thereby excluding solicitors from the higher courts. Independence demanded total fidelity to the client, precluding lender conveyancing. At the same time, independence commanded the lawyer to respect the interests of justice, which argued for a buffer between client and advocate (and thus against direct access and solicitor audience rights).

If its arguments were weak and contradictory, the profession often prevailed at the level of practical detail. The requirement of an initial solicitor interview (and the housing market's coincidental collapse) delayed corporate conveyancing for years. And the four senior judges retained their veto over audience rights, exercising it to protect independently practising barristers. Did the Government capitulate to pressure behind the scenes (especially from senior judges)? Were the Green Papers trial balloons, allowing Government to attain its goals through compromise? Or was the real purpose to let the Conservatives seem to champion general consumer interests against special producer interests, a goal attained just as effectively in defeat? Whatever the reason for the Government's tactical retreat, the Green Papers transformed the terms of engagement among the protagonists. Laissez faire ideology became a powerful rhetorical resource and media scrutiny more intense, hostile, and unrelenting. The inevitability of change generated anxiety and backlash within the profession. Divisions widened, both between the branches and within each. The market for legal services tempted other potential competitors: large, well organized and better capitalized entities (mortgage lenders, estate agencies, insurers, and accounting firms) and small low-cost operations (claims agents and immigration advisers).[33] Large consumers—pre-eminently the government—aggressively sought to control or reduce costs. The Green Papers's aftershocks continued to reverberate throughout the decade.

B. Production of Producers: How Many?

Traditional professions unapologetically controlled entry: some (like European notaries) through a *numerus clausus*, all through ascriptive criteria of class, gender, religion, and race. The profession adjusted the difficulty of examinations to modulate entry. Mandatory apprenticeship allowed individual practitioners to limit the number of places. Solicitors' firms could decide how many assistants to employ and chambers how many tenancies to grant. Once lawyers were firmly launched on careers, most practised until retirement.

The contemporary profession has found it increasingly difficult to dampen competition by raising entry barriers.[34] Leaders of both branches decried overproduction in the early 1990s. The senior partner of Cardiff's largest firm objected that 'we are training too many people to be lawyers', accused 'the colleges that produce these students' of 'no longer see[ing] anything in their eyes but pound signs' and felt 'the Law Society bears quite a burden of responsibility'.[35] But most followed Thatcher's exhortation to accept the 'laws of economics'. A range of government critics, including the DGFT, ACLEC, and Lord Mackay, assailed protectionism. Professional control over vocational course places was suspect. Professional fractions clashed: if the Bar Council wanted to constrict entry to advocacy, solicitors and employed barristers wanted to expand it. Those who had just entered felt some embarrassment about slamming the door behind them. Ascriptive criteria had long been illegal; feminism broadened women's aspirations and opportunities, doubling the number of entrants; and the profession felt growing pressure to reflect the race and class composition of the larger society. But meritocratic barriers introduce their own irrationalities: at the early stages of training aspirants have had little opportunity to demonstrate their abilities; at the later stages ability differences are better documented but aspirants have invested years in qualifying. As the stakes rise (admission or exclusion, relative success within an increasingly steep professional hierarchy), both aspirants and the institutions they seek to enter must devote greater resources to justifying outcomes (credential inflation, increasing length and difficulty of examinations, and ritualized interviews). Achieved criteria (performance at university or on professional examinations) also are vulnerable to the criticism that none is validated against lawyer performance.

In addition to these push factors, law's pull strengthened as a result of unrealistic expectations about career prospects and financial rewards (imperfect information), illusions about opportunities to promote social justice, and media glamourization (*LA Law, The Practice, Law & Order*, and *Ally McBeal* in the USA, *This Life, Kavanagh QC, The Judge*, and *North Square* in England).[36] Universities were motivated to expand law departments and add vocational courses (both relatively profitable because of high student–teacher ratios and low capital investment). Each branch felt more obliged to offer all qualified graduates apprenticeships (lowering upstream barriers always increases pressure on those downstream) or create extra-professional careers for those excluded (employed barristers, paralegals in solicitors' firms). But some lawyers championed minimum salaries for apprentices, knowing this would reduce the number of places. Examinations are porous barriers; sufficient incentives inspire aspirants to tackle even the highest. (Law graduates invest years cramming to be among the less than 5 per cent who pass professional examinations in Japan, Korea, and Taiwan; success rates have been creeping up.) Cost becomes the greatest hurdle, now characterized as a choice to invest in human capital (seen as an individual rather than a collective good) rather than an ascriptive class barrier. Consequently, the state stops subsidizing higher education (except for the poorest), and the profession shoulders only part of the burden. Financial assistance, perversely, is most available where least urgent: merit scholarships, pupillages and tenancies in prosperous commercial chambers, City traineeships. Educational indebtedness, the widening range of starting salaries, and employer subsidies of vocational training powerfully shape career decisions. Whereas most traditional professionals were solo practitioners, all entrants now spend years in employment (the Bar's functional equivalent is novice barristers' dependence on clerks for briefs in increasingly bureaucratized chambers, some sharing purses). Although individual employers make hiring decisions, their cumulative effect limits entry. The 'choices' of both aspirants and employers are attributed to the market's invisible hand.

Just as the market influences entry, so it shapes lateral movement and departures. Globalization, especially a regional manifestation like the EU, facilitates lawyer movement across national boundaries, both temporary (assistant solicitors) and permanent (MNPs). Women who wish to combine motherhood with work take leaves and return part time, creating a new category of contingent workers, which allows employers to fine-tune supply to demand. Lawyers no longer remain with their first employer, or even in law, for a lifetime, making increasingly frequent moves within and between professional categories (private practice, employment in business and government), leaving (because of dissatisfaction with work or pay), or being made redundant.[37]

In the future, entry, and especially position within the professional hierarchy, will increasingly reflect investment in human capital, reproducing and amplifying inherited advantages (economic, social, and cultural).[38] The pool of aspirants, which used to be intensely local (confined by the contacts essential to obtain an apprenticeship and first position) but is now increasingly national (as students maximize their human capital by attending the highest ranked university they can enter), will become regional or even global (at the professional apex). Lawyers will specialize in an attempt to recover entry control but are unlikely to gain state backing (i.e., specialization will inform consumer choice—a market mechanism—rather than become a new legal barrier). Employers will be not only initial gatekeepers but also ongoing labour brokers, hiring and firing in response to demand. An increasing proportion of lawyers (not just mothers) will be contingent workers (temporary, part-time), often managed by non-lawyer contractors.[39] Retired lawyers, their numbers augmented by longevity, will swell this pool. Lawyer migration across national boundaries will increase; and some firms will export back-room work to low-wage locales (as American firms have done in India). All this will foster a segmented labour market in which a shrinking proportion enjoy traditional professional careers.[40] Movement across disciplinary boundaries will ease as these are blurred by changes in the content of knowledge, lawyers' search for new markets, and the proliferation of MDPs. To cut costs, protect against supply shortfalls, and increase control over their workforce, employers will substitute paralegals and information technology for professionals.[41] Whereas the traditional profession shielded individual practitioners from market forces by controlling entry, in the future large productive units (solicitors' firms, chambers, MDPs, companies, government departments, and quangos) will protect those temporarily sheltered within their walls.

C. Production of Producers: Who?

The professional project seeks status as well as material gain. The two are inextricable: wealth confers status, which in turn justifies wealth.[42] (Witness the mutual attraction between *nouveaux riches* and the gentry's land and titles.) Traditional professions erect ascriptive barriers not only to control numbers but also to construct social superiority, which they advance as a warrant of integrity, essential to protect vulnerable clients against betrayal by self-interested agents. Aspiring professionals demonstrate selflessness by undergoing onerous *rites de passage*, accepting subordination and performing hard, often degrading, work for years with little or no material reward (military bullying, medical residency, priestly celibacy, articles, and pupillage). Only those with family resources could afford to qualify. Barristers based their superiority to solicitors on breeding (while also feigning indifference to money by having clerks negotiate fees).

Ascriptive criteria gradually succumbed to the ideal of equal opportunity and the economic imperative of technical expertise (both of which pretend blindness to personal attributes). In recent decades the warrant of exclusivity has been replaced by its obverse—representativeness. LS President Sycamore told the 1997 annual conference that 'we run the risk of creating a profession—and a judiciary—drawn exclusively from one social class. Surely it is the best policy to get the social mix of the profession right at the outset....' Hallett declared: 'As a state educated woman, I want the world to know that the Bar is open to all....'[43] But representativeness contains multiple ambiguities. Is the goal equal opportunity or outcome? Is it mandated by lawyers' economic and social privilege and exercise of state power (especially true of judges) or by the belief that background shapes professional behaviour[44] (increasingly salient since the Human Rights Act 1998)? Outsiders and their organizations and leaders deserve much of the credit for this transformation. The branches now compete in reflecting gender, race, class, and disability in the larger society.[45] The doubling of aspirants during the second feminist movement impeded the entry of those educationally disadvantaged by class or race. Furthermore, outsiders forced to assimilate the hegemonic culture lose credibility with the very constituencies they purport to represent. Just as meritocracy discredited ascriptive privilege, so it condemns efforts to achieve representativeness as (American-style) quotas or reverse discrimination, which perversely stigmatize their intended beneficiaries. Hence the profession prefers targets to rules, exhortation to enforcement, and highly visible tokens to real redistribution of privilege. (Hallett was 'delighted' if her election 'sends out the message that the Bar is open to all—and that it is possible to be a working mother and get to the top'.[46]) But meritocracy's own criteria are a confused mix of effort and achievement, and academic credentials remain unvalidated by subsequent performance.

If entry becomes more representative, ascriptive factors (such as old-boy networks and cultural capital) and meritocratic criteria (strongly correlated with inherited privilege) continue to assign lawyers to positions in the professional hierarchy, leading to demands that each stratum reflect the larger society. Reporting a survey's 'disgraceful' finding that men solicitors earned more than women (controlling for other variables), LS President Girling asked 'How can we, as a profession that devotes itself to justice, accept anything less' than earnings parity.[47] Such calls are strongest where decisions are centralized, public, and political (silk and judgeships) and weakest where they are dispersed, private, and ostensibly market-driven (hiring and admission to partnerships by firms). At the same time, there is pressure to expose all such decisions to outside scrutiny. Unrepresentativeness is justified in terms of deficiencies in the pool (which time allegedly will correct) and applicant 'choice' (itself culturally constructed). These rationalizations provoke calls to equalize upstream education (increasingly difficult as it is diversified and further privatized) and make work compatible with parenting (still just an aspiration).[48]

The contradiction between representativeness and meritocracy will intensify (since greater representativeness fuels calls for more as well as back-lash, especially among those who scapegoat outsiders for their own career frustrations), either compromising representativeness or discrediting meritocracy (as both desert and economic imperative), perhaps leading to a plurality of meritocratic criteria. More flexible work arrangements (necessary to retain or reclaim lawyer mothers) will deepen gender inequalities unless lawyer fathers assume equal parenting responsibilities (highly unlikely). Each increase in representativeness amplifies pressure further up the professional hierarchy, which may seek to relieve it by hiding decisions behind the market's invisible hand (more difficult where the arena is political). Although the profession's responses to unrepresentativeness have been largely symbolic, they constitute a public commitment on which future reformers can draw.

D. Production by Producers

Traditional professions restricted competition among producers for the same reasons that they controlled how many entered and who did so: to enhance wealth but also status, which was tainted by association with 'trade'.[49] Thus, some professions required one member to obtain another's permission before serving the latter's client. Function also affected status: the Bar's superiority rested partly on being a referral profession (whose clients were solicitors rather than laypeople) and partly on its monopolies of higher court advocacy and eligibility for silk and the bench. Status differences were enacted through an elaborate etiquette of dress (wigs and gowns), address (my friend, my learned friend), deference (solicitors attended on barristers), precedence (in court), and collegiality (in robing rooms and the Inns). Lawyers claimed that restrictive practices were essential to protect clients from market forces because the information asymmetries inherent in the division of labour that spawned the professions would lead consumers to overvalue price, the only readily observable signal. Because professions insisted that members were fungible and refused to cut prices, competition could only increase costs. The limited clientele (landed gentry and emerging bourgoisie) were wealthy enough to pay monopoly rents without complaint. (If you have to ask the price, you can't afford it.[50])

The growth of a mass market of small business and individual clients eventually led to the emergence of a consumer movement armed with electoral as well as buying power.[51] Indeed, in post-industrial societies consumers (rather than bourgeoisie or proletariat—categories defined by relations of production) claim to be the Hegelian 'universal class', whose concerns should trump the 'special interests' of producers.[52] Conveyancing was an obvious target: the biggest financial transaction of a lifetime for a large and growing proportion of the population. Legal aid (which expanded rapidly during the 1990s) made the government a powerful and highly motivated surrogate champion of taxpayers. Theories of regulatory capture and public choice unmasked the professions' altruistic pretensions.[53] The Green Papers officially endorsed several decades of mounting criticism of lawyers as exploiters of clients, not protectors. The market, which traditional professions had demonized as a threat to service quality and provider integrity, became the guarantor of economic efficiency. Professionalism, like other worldviews (religion, communism, patriarchy, racism) resembles Humpty Dumpty: once broken it cannot be reconstituted or preserved in fragments.[54] The genie of competition cannot be forced back into the bottle of restrictive practices after it has escaped. Professional cartels (like all others) are difficult to maintain; if one member defects (or an outsider mounts a successful challenge), the rest must follow suit, often in mob fashion.[55] Entrepreneurial outsiders invade the profession's traditional terrain (if only by employing its members): lenders and estate agencies doing conveyancing, accountants expanding beyond tax advice, City firms developing advocacy competence.[56] Some insiders are tempted to join them by promises of wealth, security, sometimes just work. The interests of the profession are opposed to each other: those eager to expand market share (specialists, beginners) favour innovation (direct access, advertising, specialist certification, vertical integration), provoking resistance by those defending their turf (generalists, established practitioners). Professions can no longer justify denying consumers the right to trade quality for price or choose between solicitors and barristers, lender conveyancers and solicitors, employed lawyers (public defenders) and private practitioners, even lawyers and other professions (accountants), MDPs, or para-professionals (mediators, advice services, claims agents, immigration advisers).[57] Solicitors were hard pressed to defend conveyancing when they delegated most work to lay subordinates, will writing when it consisted of filling in forms, personal injury claims when the vast majority were settled out of court; the Bar could not persuasively argue that guilty pleas required sophisticated advocacy skills. Outsiders sought to strengthen their jurisdictional claims by engaging in self-regulation or inviting state regulation (but the subordinates of established professions rarely succeed in professionalizing, as health care demonstrates).[58] State action may be necessary to make consumer choice meaningful by improving information (though this could not justify the Lord Chancellor's selection of QCs).

Like other simple ideas (such as democracy or equality), laissez faire is irresistible (as shown by globalization and the proliferation of capitalist variants in the second and third worlds).[59] Concerns about market failure and arguments for second-best solutions are too subtle for most.[60] Yet neither branch conceded gracefully. Although the Law Society sought to contrast its sweet reasonableness with the retrograde rants of Bar and bench, solicitors skirted and even transgressed the law in efforts to forestall price competition and retain conveyancing. The Bar's rearguard action proclaimed, contradictorily, that it was fully competitive and competition was bad. Restrictive practices are always arbitrary and illogical: the jurisdictional boundary between lawyers and accountants, the audience rights of solicitors and barristers, privately practising and employed barristers, or the practising arrangements of barristers in England and abroad. Few outside the Bar believed two lawyers were cheaper than one. One professional fraction that attacked another's restrictive practices (solicitor criticism of barristers' exclusive audience rights or mortgage lender tie-ins) found it difficult to defend its own (solicitors resisting lay advocacy or tying in advocacy to litigation or probate to will writing) or to control deviants who defied the cartel (through price cutting or aggressive client solicitation). The Bar could not urge direct access to reduce costs by eliminating solicitors while opposing solicitors who sought expanded audience rights to reduce costs by supplanting barristers. Symbiotic relationships of referral and forbearance between potential competitors are unstable: barristers and solicitors, lenders and conveyancers, solicitors and accountants, foreign and domestic lawyers. The government's breach of the conveyancing monopoly prompted solicitor interest in advocacy, which in turn provoked the Bar to expand direct access. Professions seek to dominate those they cannot exclude: direct access allows barrister advocates to choose rather than be chosen by solicitor litigators; solicitor property centres refer clients to lenders rather than depending on bank and building society referrals. Solicitors wanted to dominate (and exploit) conveyancers, claims agents, and will writers, not compete with them. The Law Society worried about accountant-dominated MDPs and American-dominated MNPs; the Bar feared that employment and partnerships would increase domination by government and solicitors.[61] Outsiders—lenders, accountants, foreign lawyers, estate agents, laypeople—are strongly motivated to criticize and challenge the profession's restrictive practices. So are subordinated insiders: solicitors and employed barristers persisted in attacking barriers to advocacy. Large clients and third-party payers do not depend on professional paternalism to ensure quality. Intermediaries (such as referral sources and insurers) emerge to deal with information and power asymmetries, although producers still find it easier than consumers to overcome collective action problems.

Indeed, competition compels producers to concentrate in order to offer a comprehensive service, achieve economies of scale, and diversify to safeguard against fluctuating demand for specialties.[62] The Bar invoked the spectre of concentration against the CPS and City firm advocacy departments; the Law Society did so against MDPs and lender conveyancing. Competition compels imitation; solicitors' firms and mortgage lenders, national professions in the increasingly global marketplace, lawyers and accountants. Occupations integrate vertically to capture the client first (direct access to barristers, estate agency and mortgage lending by solicitors, title searches for estate agents). The effects of these forces can be seen in City firms, barristers' chambers, MNPs and MDPs, corporate conveyancing, one-stop property shopping, and the CPS. Size and growth (as indices of success, or at least consumer satisfaction) become surrogate signals of quality (which is difficult to measure). All this evokes the nostalgic plaint that small is beautiful. But such romantic delusions disregard legitimate quality concerns about solo practice; and it is hard for lawyers to condemn horizontal and vertical integration in other occupations when they engage in it themselves. Populist politicians (both national and professional) as well as the media (for different reasons) focus attention on 'fat cat' firms, chambers, and individual lawyers, stoking competitor envy and consumer resentment. Conspicuous *pro bono* services may be partly an attempt to deflect these grievances (displacing the claim of altruism from traditional professionalism's emphasis on relations with the client to service to others). As lawyers become less able to extract monopoly rents from consumers (because of lower entry barriers and freer competition), they seek to preserve and enlarge profits by extending and intensifying the exploitation of subordinated labour (employed lawyers and paralegals) and substituting capital for labour.

If the traditional profession's paternalism served members' interests at least as much as clients', the contemporary market for legal services is plagued by its own failures. Elimination of the most blatant restrictive practices leaves many agency problems intact.[63] Lawyers can still run up the meter, shirk, and sell clients unnecessary services. Markets deliver quality to those with money to spend and expertise to evaluate services: companies with in-house lawyer monitors but not individual consumers or those who rely on third-party payers (usually the state), which are preoccupied with cost.[64] The trade-off of quality for price may produce efficiency for repeat players but not for one-off clients, who can assess quality only *after* consuming the service (if ever). When consumers possess vastly different resources, producers engage in simultaneous races to the top (where money is no object) and the bottom (where consumers take what they get)—as in health care. Price competition leads to the replacement of fully qualified lawyers by the inexperienced, paralegals, and information technology. After the state withdraws support for restrictive practices, established professions (assisted by first mover advantage, habitude, path dependence, existing referral networks, and reputational capital) seek to preserve them by wielding market power: solicitors boycotted lender and estate agency conveyancers, withheld referrals from accountant MDPs and foreign MNPs, and threatened not to brief barristers who allowed direct access by clients; barristers threatened to refuse briefs from firms that engaged in advocacy; estate agents would not refer conveyancing to solicitors who joined property centres. Most solicitors had no more interest in advocacy than barristers had in direct access to clients; practising arrangements disabled each branch from effectively challenging the other.[65] It was status concerns that impelled the Law Society to seek audience rights and discouraged the Bar Council from pursuing direct access. By basing its defence of audience rights on claims of superior competence and integrity, the Bar merely provoked the Law Society (and employed barristers) to push harder. At the same time, competition forced most City firms to create advocacy departments (and maintain unprofitable foreign branches). Specialization attempts to re-enact the original professionalization project by offering quality guarantees (though unenforced by state power) in exchange for higher prices. Just as professionalization demarcates the qualitative difference between professional expertise and lay incompetence while insisting on homogeneity within each category, so specialization denies the fungibility of professionals while reasserting it among specialists.[66] (The proposition 'that all solicitors were of equal standard, all were capable of doing every kind of work', Pannone said in 1993, 'is no longer a realistic or tenable position'.[67]) But novice barristers are less experienced advocates than many solicitors, and the Bar resisted advocacy by CPS and CDS lawyers because they were too specialized. Specialization can blur inter-professional boundaries as well as create internal demarcations: the new trust and estates specialization mixed non-lawyers with solicitors. Whereas the traditional profession mobilized state power to resist the market, the modern profession mobilizes market forces to resist the state. Consequently, the ideology of professionalism replaces the warrant of paternalism to protect customers against market abuses with the warrant of independence to protect citizens against state oppression. The Bar deployed this protean concept to oppose solicitor-advocates (who disregarded the cab-rank rule), partnership, and employment (the CPS would be too loyal to the state, the CDS insufficiently loyal to accused), and even to defend silk. The Law Society invoked independence against lender conveyancing and MDPs.

Restrictive practices will continue to erode. Just as few today can recall the rationalizations for the Bar's two-counsel and two-thirds rules, soon few will remember why the state gave one barrister out of ten a lifetime title to command greatly inflated fees or limited solicitor-advocates. Vertical and horizontal integration will increase (one-stop property shopping, MDPs, MNPs, solicitor advocacy departments), although this may facilitate cartelized behaviour as well as deliver efficiency gains to consumers. In pursuit of cost savings (in the public domain) and higher profits (in the private), more legal work will be performed by employed lawyers, paralegals, and information technology. Legal professions and other occupations will fight for turf, advancing warrants of expertise but failing to secure state protection. Quality will be increasingly stratified. At the same time, the division of labour will be preserved by institutionalized practices: advocates tied to courts, solicitors to their commercial clients.[68]

E. Demand Creation and Consumer Control

Traditional professions passively waited for business, feigning indifference to money, actively disdaining some clients and work. Those unable to pay did without legal services or relied on the erratic charity of individual lawyers, institutionalized in the Poor Person's Procedure and dock briefs.[69] Some lawyers relied heavily on the patronage of a few large clients: landowners, entrepreneurs, financiers, and the government; but lawyers dominated the relationship with their numerous one-off clients.

As their control over the production of and by producers eroded, lawyers sought to stimulate demand among clients and third-party payers.[70] Pannone observed in 1993 that 'one can increase the need for lawyers where, I suspect, we've been very bad. It sticks in my throat when I see accountants advising on tax law.' Six months later he told the annual conference that despite initial reservations that the 'make a will' campaign was 'an inappropriate way to promote professional services' it had received 'ecstatic reports' and the 'demand for promotional material has exceeded our wildest expectations'.[71] This new professional project confronts numerous obstacles. Law lacks the urgency of other social services: medicine, education, housing, and food.[72] Unserved clienteles have little popular appeal: the accused, immigrants, the poor, benefits claimants. The profession's notorious defence of its privileges (documented in this and earlier critiques) discredits its pretensions to pursue justice rather than money, client interests rather than its own. Actively encouraging legal work (especially litigation) undermines law's tenuous legitimacy, revealing the disinterested assertion of legal rights as naked self-interest ('supplier induced demand') or worse: whingeing, nuisance lawsuits.[73] (Dickens's *Bleak House* is the classic exposé, though it castigated the prolongation rather than the initiation of lawsuits.) The most effective strategy of demand creation—direct solicitation—has the least legitimacy; the least effective—education—enjoys the greatest. Government and media critics caricatured America's sue-happy litigants and ambulance-chasing lawyers. They conflated 'fat cats' (City partners, commercial silks) with the rising legal aid budget, focusing on the rare lawyer who earned a lot from legal aid while disregarding the shrinking profit margins of most. The 1998 *Legal Business* annual survey of the top 100 firms led the *Daily Telegraph* to rail against 'fat cats', the *Daily Mail* to attack 'partners in wealth who make the fat cats look thin', the *News of the World* to 'delight' in 'more evidence that the most discredited profession in Britain is that of lawyers', and a Labour backbencher to denounce 'parasites' who 'contribute nothing at all to society' and 'are taking as much money out of people's pockets as the country's burglars'.[74] Critics blamed litigation on frivolous claims, never illegitimate defences. They recycled the false but seductive argument that liability (rather than the violation of legal rights) burdens the economy. They invoked the client's right *not* to claim and accused self-interested lawyers of betraying clients (in order to champion causes or inflate fees). It is far easier, of course, to dramatize ostensible false positives (the McDonald's coffee spill or BMW paint job) than real false negatives (invisible unremedied wrongs). Whereas Labour created legal aid to redress the disadvantage of those unable to purchase legal services, it now emphasized the unfair advantage of those whom legal aid rendered irresponsible for legal costs (their own or their adversaries').[75] The state displayed increasing ambivalence about subsidizing lawyers, especially when they opposed it (in criminal defence, deportation, or medical negligence). Government attacks on the profession not only justified cost containment but also reinforced popular suspicions of legal aid clients.

The original professional project of excluding outsiders (from entry or unauthorized practice) and suppressing internal competition united most lawyers; the new project of generating demand divides them (entrepreneurs seeking market share, traditionalists defending their turf). The original project raised the incomes of the least successful lawyers by protecting them from cheaper competitors; the new project benefits those most successful in profiting from the plight of the worst-off clients (offering attractive targets for government cost cutters). The interests of the few lawyers heavily dependent on the state increasingly diverge from those of the rest. Collective efforts to stimulate demand (through institutional advertising and equal or random referrals) are more legitimate than individual self-promotion but less effective and encourage free-riders. Professions elevate collective status at the expense of individual material advantage by controlling production by producers; individual lawyers enhance their own material advantage at the expense of collective status by creating demand. (Hence APIL was even more restrictive than the Law Society about business generation.) The social costs of supply control are relatively invisible and dispersed—indeterminate monopoly rents paid by innumerable clients; the social costs of demand creation are concentrated in the highly visible, and typically inflationary, legal aid budget. The scandals of supply control are hidden: the deserving aspirant unable to qualify as a lawyer, the capable non-lawyer prohibited from offering services, the needy unserved client. The scandals of demand creation are widely publicized: undeserving legal aid clients (sometimes wealthy, foreign, and felonious), frivolous claims, and unscrupulous or crooked lawyers. The profession attempts to associate demand creation with dramatic legal victories: integration and abortion rights in the USA, exposure of miscarriages of justice in the U.K.; but of course that is not what most lawyers do.

The previous paragraphs outlined the difficulties of creating demand. But success has its own perils. Third-party payers—the state and private insurers—displace the profession as guarantors of quality but subordinate that goal to cost cutting.[76] Although the state talks market rhetoric, it is a monopsonist that does not consume the services it buys, which it views as dispensable (except for criminal defence). A legal aid scheme that paid lawyers at or near market rates to ensure equal representation for all now pays the minimum needed to lure the hungriest lawyer (who will increasingly be the newest or least competent), an amount that declines with the erosion of supply control. Because outcome is a misleading index of quality (since it is so difficult to control inputs), third parties use unavoidably imperfect process measures, creating perverse incentives for lawyers. Adopted for franchising and then contracts, these criteria became the first instance of government-backed lawyer specialization. The profession defended the right of all lawyers to offer legal aid, invoking client choice (a favourite trope). Government retorted that franchising enhanced choice by improving information about quality.

Lawyers respond to government cost-cutting by increasing volume (another manifestation of specialization), which lowers quality, compromises professionalism, and intensifies dependence on the state. Although government actively fosters such dependence through franchising and bulk and exclusive contracts, it also perversely 'names and shames' those with the highest legal aid billings (to justify additional cuts). Lawyers who accept ineligible clients, file frivolous proceedings, or use innovative billing techniques in order to evade cost containment further erode the legitimacy of legal aid. A government that had exposed lawyers to market forces, mocking objections rooted in professionalism, now maintained that the same professionalism would restrain lawyers from cutting corners in response to market pressures.

Without spending political capital, the state allowed inflation to constrict eligibility, transforming legal aid from nearly universal coverage back into what one official boasted was 'not bad' for 'a poor man's lawyer'. (This was consistent with the growing divergence between public and private services in medicine and education, part of the welfare state's continuing contraction.) Government replaced a demand-led system in which lawyers set priorities by choosing which services to offer with a capped budget in which the state determined priorities. Criticized for reducing coverage, the Government blamed the profession's restrictive practices for inflating cost. Although lawyer advocacy for legal aid sought to avoid the charge of self-interest by focusing on client eligibility rather than remuneration rates and allying with client champions, this did little to protect legal aid budgets. Government disregarded the entreaties of leading judges and repulsed the profession's lawsuits. Threats to withhold services were ineffective (cartels are hard to maintain), betrayed the very clienteles lawyers claimed to serve, and compromised professionalism. (Lawyers said to the state: by doubting our professionalism you force us to engage in trade unionism. The state retorted: by acting as trade unionists, you betray your professionalism.) The vast majority of the public did not notice the missing services; those who did were not moved to support lawyers.[77]

The state pitted professional segments against each other: barristers and solicitors, franchised and unfranchised, specialists and generalists, plaintiffs' lawyers and defendants', independent practitioners and employed. It replaced more experienced lawyers with less and private practitioners with employees (whose salaries and caseloads it controlled). Declaring the goal to be access to justice rather than lawyers, it substituted ADR for adjudication and lay advisers, information technology, and client self-representation for lawyers.[78] The profession's solicitude for client access was unmasked as an effort to preserve all lawyers' entitlement to do legal aid. The profession objected that public defenders would lack independence; but for three decades law centres had mounted some of the most aggressive challenges to government. (In any case, both the Law Society and BACFI championed CPS audience rights.)

The state shifted costs to clients (co-payments to reduce moral hazard) and adversaries (conditional and contingent fees to make lawyers more entrepreneurial). (No one would urge that patients and doctors share the cost of unsuccessful medical procedures or students and teachers that of educational failure.) Centuries of professional condemnation of such fee arrangements (rationalized in terms of lawyers' conflicts of interest with both clients and the legal system but also inspired by status anxiety) dissolved before the temptations of a wider market. By substituting CFAs for legal aid, government shifted responsibility for rationing access to justice to lawyers and insurers, transforming it from a political choice that required justification into the product of inexorable market forces.[79] Each reform replaced a lawyer incentive to do too much at government expense with one to do too little at the client's.

Lawyer subordination to large employers, clients, and third-party payers will increase (although the largest producers will be relatively immune, widening differences between the two hemispheres and thus their divergent material interests, social status, and political commitments).[80] Like most public sector workers, these lawyers will have little economic leverage. As the welfare state continues to contract (legal aid faster than other services because of its lesser legitimacy), client eligibility will decline, remuneration and salary levels worsen, caseloads increase, quality diminish, and lawyers' market share shrink. By weakening both producer and consumer constituencies for legal aid, the downward spiral will inevitably accelerate.

F. Self-regulation

The relatively small size, localization, and homogeneous backgrounds and practices of traditional professionals made reputation a powerful influence on behaviour. Pervasive surveillance by peers, seniors, judges, and consumers (and of barristers by solicitors) inhibited deviance and reduced the need for formal sanctions. At the same time, traditional professions vigorously resisted legalizing or enforcing norms and were shamed into doing so only recently. (Intimacy facilitates informal social control but also resists formalization.[81])

Modern professions suffer worsening crises of self-regulation. (Prominent examples include the police, accountants, and the clergy.[82]) The legal profession's shameless defence of restrictive practices undermined its altruistic pretensions to solicitude for clients. As professions expand and diversify (in background and practice), peers, seniors, and judges are less likely to observe or correct misconduct. One-off consumers lack information about lawyers' reputations; third-party payers have insufficient incentive to monitor performance. Nevertheless, lawyers claim that the same division of labour that makes lay clients dependent on professional expertise also mandates peer review. Clients respond by insisting that regulators enjoy the same independence from lawyers that lawyers demand from the state. (The Law Society separated prosecution and adjudication only in the 1980s; the Bar still has not done so; SCB and OSS directors remained involved in Society governance.)

The profession's formal regulatory process displays chronic lenience toward lawyers' misconduct, punctuated by sporadic exposés of scandalous cover-ups. Whereas the criminal justice system trusts the police and suspects the accused, professional self-regulation trusts the accused lawyer and suspects the complainant (typically a client).[83] Self-regulation seeks to protect lawyers against false positives (unwarranted complaints from clients disappointed by outcomes or just trying to reduce bills) rather than clients against false negatives (inadequate discipline of errant lawyers). Lawyers who assailed charges of litigiousness directed against the claims they brought on behalf of clients expressed outrage when they became the object of those clients' claims. Lawyers who devoted their lives to mobilizing and resisting state power on behalf of clients became instant converts to exhortation and conciliation when their own behaviour was questioned. Giving solicitors' firms primary responsibility for resolving client complaints tends to cool out grievances rather than resolve them. Lawyers want deferential clients; clients want responsive lawyers.[84] Lawyers want privacy in disciplinary proceedings; clients demand transparency. Although many aggrieved clients would accept an apology, lawyers aggravate anger by responding defensively, legalistically.

Because lawyers refuse to tax themselves at levels sufficient to pay for staff disciplinary mechanisms, complaint backlogs accumulate and delays lengthen.[85] Populists pursued office in professional associations by appealing to lawyer resentment of the cost and intrusiveness of self-regulation (further undermining the profession's pretensions to care about clients). The profession constantly impugned the motives of critics (government, consumer groups, media). It surpassed Dr Pangloss in believing its regulatory mechanisms were the best in the world. Some solicitors strenuously resisted every change: advance fee quotations and in-house complaint procedures (both of which could alleviate the burden on formal disciplinary procedures), compensation for inadequate professional services, open disciplinary hearings, remuneration certificates for testamentary beneficiaries, liability for negligent advocacy, even rules against sexual harassment of clients. Instead of demonstrating professionalism by setting standards above those of the market or state, lawyers did the least they could get away with. Like a confirmed alcoholic, the profession constantly vowed to reform, raising client expectations and hence the number of complaints, overburdening the system, and initiating a new cycle of rising backlog and frustration.

Formal regulation addresses the most egregious misconduct (which embarrasses the profession and exposes lawyers to liability, raising premiums for all). But most clients complain about over-billing, discourtesy, and delay (further evidence of market failure—large, repeat-players routinely get advance fee quotations and prompt resolution of grievances). At the same time, some lawyers clearly felt that if they had to confront market forces, dissatisfied consumers should be relegated to market solutions (taking their business elsewhere—unrealistic for one-off clients). Yet solicitors denied clients the information necessary to make the market work, first fighting the imposition of advance fee quotations and then flouting the requirement because it would 'drive costs down' and make it 'easier for the client to complain'.

Self-regulation widened internal fissures. Lawyers at the base of the professional hierarchy (solo practitioners, ethnic minorities) felt unjustly targeted by discipline; elite lawyers resented the harm deviants did to the profession's collective status. Firms dependent on conveyancing tried (unsuccessfully) to link price-cutting to defaulting firms. Large firms (which tightly regulate their members to protect institutional reputation and avoid liability) and employed lawyers rebelled against paying for a disciplinary mechanism they rarely encountered.[86] Mandatory insurance for malpractice and financial default created further divisions over whether premiums should be experience-rated and, if so, by what criteria (since every categorization was over- and under-inclusive). Some rejected the insurance principle altogether, arguing that good lawyers (like themselves) should not subsidize bad. (Just as the government sought to mystify the rationing of legal services as the product of inexorable market forces shaping legal expense insurer decisions about financing CFAs, so the profession may have preferred to let indemnity insurance premiums determine whether lawyers could make a profit rather than bearing the onus of forcing them out of practice.)[87] Others feared that explicit repudiation of collective responsibility would divest lawyers of their last vestige of professionalism.[88]

Outsiders increasingly filled the self-regulatory void: ombudsmen and a Legal Services Complaints Commissioner overseeing professional discipline, managerial judges (through wasted costs orders, fines, and contempt powers), private malpractice insurers (through premium levels), agencies supervising lawyers' new markets (estate agency, insurance, financial services, and multidisciplinary practice), foreign and regional bodies (for multinational practice), large consumers (e.g., mortgage lenders), third-party payers (the state and legal expenses insurers), employers (public and private), and the media.[89] But despite its repeated threats to assert regulatory power, government clearly preferred to have the profession do the work and take the heat for failure and success.

The inability of both self-regulation and markets to ensure competence, courtesy, and integrity for most clients will lead to greater external regulation.[90] Professional regulation will become ever less relevant to the large firms, MNPs, and MDPs, and government and corporate employers in which an increasing proportion of lawyers work. Differences in the impact and cost of disciplinary mechanisms and insurance will deepen professional divisions.

G. Governance

As relatively small homogeneous stable face-to-face communities, traditional legal professions required little formal governance. Gerontocracy was the dominant form and office more honorific than powerful. Units were defined by geography, courts, and functions. Although the Bar has grown and diversified, its relative size (a tenth that of solicitors), concentration in London, common involvement in advocacy (despite substantive specialization), and marginalization of employed barristers allowed it to preserve greater solidarity. At the same time, it remained profoundly undemocratic: unelected benchers ruled the Inns and dominated the Bar Council; juniors and employed barristers were effectively disenfranchised; AGM resolutions could not bind the Bar Council; and barristers did not elect officers.

As legal professions expanded they formalized institutions of representative and direct democracy. Geographic constituencies declined in relevance (some becoming rotten boroughs). Growing heterogeneity turned governance into an arena of struggle among increasingly self-conscious constituencies, which differed not only in concrete interests but also in their need for and image of collective action.[91] The statements and actions of peak associations tend to be less significant for elite lawyers who work in large organizations and more urgent for marginal lawyers who practise alone or in small firms. Ascriptive categories of gender, race, and age sought representation at all levels (a replay of demands that the profession reflect the larger society but also a form of tokenism that can mystify real inequality).[92] Specialization by substantive area, client, and third-party payer (dependence on legal aid), all strongly associated with firm size, created divergent, sometimes antagonistic, fractions, spawning rival groups.[93] Employed lawyers, underrepresented and even disenfranchised in the peak organizations, established their own associations, some of which engaged in collective bargaining (for example, the First Division Association).

All these organizations faced classic collective action problems: respecting autonomy by making membership voluntary permits free riders; solving that problem through compulsion either coerces the speech of dissidents or mandates a paralysing unanimity.[94] (The Access to Justice Act 1999 acknowledged the incompatibility between coercion and advocacy.) Members demand that dues be earmarked for their particular concerns. In response to these dilemmas, some solicitors wanted to emulate doctors and separate the professional function of regulation (backed by state compulsion) from the trade union role of representation (in which membership would be voluntary).[95] Increasing exposure to market forces may have disposed lawyers to seek a more openly self-interested association.[96]

Specialist associations have proliferated, diverting political energy from peak associations and sometimes even challenging them for dominance (the extension of market forces from professionals to their organizations).[97] Member apathy allowed succession to office to become routinized in Buggins's turn (climbing the greasy pole through mutual back-scratching), combined with alternation between rival constituencies (originally London and the provinces, now large and small firms). But populist outsiders periodically rallied mass dissatisfaction over intensifying competition, declining profits and status (of both the profession and internal fractions), governmental cost-cutting, and burdensome regulation. They mobilized plebiscitary mechanisms to launch Quixotic moral crusades to recover a mythical golden age. Without polling data, we cannot know why politicians won or lost elections, but the fault lines are suggested by candidate appeals to gender, age, and race, employed solicitors and private practitioners, City and high-street firms, conveyancers and legal aid lawyers, homophobia and anti-discrimination, protectionism and laissez faire. Mears and Sayer gained office because the transformation of the profession described in this book produced fewer winners than losers, and the later saw collective action as their only salvation. Mears's opponents had great difficulty articulating a competing ideal of disinterested professionalism.

But the Society was merely a scapegoat, neither responsible for the demise of the good old days nor able to restore them. The profession had lost much of its power to the market and state. Both the Council (whose members served multiple three-year terms) and the career staff restrained a one-year president, even if he claimed a popular mandate. Nevertheless, the tumultuous experiment in democracy provoked numerous proposals to rein in electoral politics. And the Society rebuffed many democratic reforms: popular nomination of officers, recall of the Council, non-geographic constituencies, proxy voting at AGMs, Council term limits. Once Mears exposed the Society's limited scope for action (and embarrassed it by demagoguery and disclosure of election scandals), professional politics retreated to nuances of character and reputation, effectively ending contested elections.

Profession-wide governance is likely to fracture further or become even less relevant (through separation of representation from regulation). Voluntary associations will have difficulty attracting and retaining members. Although greater coherence and tighter organization make fractional organizations more effective in expressing member self-interest, they also enjoy less external legitimacy. Ascriptive separatism also makes peak associations less representative, further eroding their legitimacy. Umbrella organizations will be dominated by bureaucrats focused on delivering services to members rather than by politicians representing the profession's interests to the state.[98] Apathy will grow.[99]

H. Refashioning Professional Ideology

Traditional professions justify the privileges of wealth, status, and power by proclaiming their paternalism as a warrant against market temptations to pursue self-interest at the expense of clients.[100] They mandate such paternalism as an expression of noblesse oblige associated with a feudal past and pretensions to aristocratic lineage.[101] (All ideologies locate the ideal in a mythical past or utopian future.) The 1979 Royal Commission explained that the legal profession was granted self-regulation 'so that it may require its members to observe higher standards than could be successfully imposed from without'. It endorsed the Law Society's 1968 claim to the Monopolies Commission that professions 'imposed upon themselves a discipline and adopted ethical rules and restrictions, sometimes to their own personal disadvantage, but always designed to establish their probity and competence in the eyes of the public'. They 'voluntarily submit... themselves to standards of ethical conduct beyond those required of the ordinary citizen by law... [and undertake] to accept personal responsibility to those whom they serve for their actions and to their profession for maintaining confidence'.[102]

When the Green Papers (following earlier criticisms) inverted the market's moral standing from clients' worst enemy to their best (indeed only) friend, the legal profession was rightly anxious about its public image. LS President Elly wanted the first national law week in May 1995 to be 'a focus for all that is good about this profession'. Solicitors had 'become the butt of easy jokes, a convenient target for ill-informed criticism'. He wanted fun events, with t-shirts and balloons, and a 'favourite solicitor' competition. He hoped the 150th anniversary of the Society's royal charter would be 'an opportunity to tell the world what a good service solicitors give to their clients'. He fantasized about newspaper headlines: 'Justice defended by lawyers, says Consumers Association' and 'Lawyers attacked unjustly says Lord Chancellor'.[103] Mears, his successor, urged the Council to spend £5 million on a television campaign 'to encourage the public to think of solicitors as approachable and easy to talk to'. 'We would want to make the profession feel better about itself'. The *Gazette* urged readers to send 'good news stories' to Chancery Lane.[104] Girling, the next president, told the annual conference that 'my aim today—and for the rest of my period in office—is to explode those myths that so distort the public's perception of us and expose the reality'. He urged solicitors to 'speak up for our reputation'.[105] The usually sensible *New Law Journal* urged the Law Society and Bar Council 'to make one joint, and perhaps last, effort to rehabilitate the profession in the eyes of the public' by hiring a spin doctor. The Society did spend £60,000 on public relations for 'better branding' the profession's image.[106]

But a sceptical (and hostile) *Evening Standard* said 'some products have "advertising dead loss" plastered all over them'.[107] Acknowledging this, the profession refashioned its ideology. Whereas professionalizing occupations had mobilized state power to restrain market forces, now the state was deploying its power *against* professional protectionism. Lawyers responded by demonizing the state (as inescapably bureaucratic and potentially totalitarian) while claiming to champion all those abused or threatened.[108] They replaced paternalism with independence, highlighting the exceptional lawyer who heroically resisted state oppression: Thomas Erskine and Lord Brougham in England, Clarence Darrow and Thurgood Marshall in the USA, Sydney Kentridge in South Africa.[109] Addressing the 1991 Law Society conference, President Ely called solicitors 'one of the few and diminishing number of independent professions'. 'Never before has there been a greater need for independent advice and for independent defence against the powerful, against the departments of state, against the monopolistic institutions who now control the property market.'[110] Two years later, President Pannone told the conference: 'As the government assumes a more centralist role for the state, the need for lawyers to interpose themselves between the individual and the state, between the powerless and the powerful, is more urgent than ever'. 'The vocation, the pursuit of justice, a commitment to righting injustice wherever it is seen which motivated us when we entered the profession, must remain the cornerstone of being a solicitor....'[111] The Society's 1993–4 action plan sought to improve the profession's image by emphasizing its contribution to fighting miscarriages of justice.[112] Hallett told the Bar AGM it was time to remind the British public they were lucky 'in their lawyers'.

Ask a Kenyan about his confidence in an independent judiciary and legal profession. Ask a Peruvian or Venezualan [*sic*] how much it costs to buy a judge. Ask a human rights activist in China what happens when you abolish an independent legal profession.[113]

Brennan, her successor, announced 'the start of our programme to show the value of the independent Bar both in the interests of justice and of economy'. 'The Bar's free independence and integrity is a guarantee of justice and a bulwark against the abuse of power by the executive.' '[W]e present our cases fearlessly and vigorously and to the best possible effect.' 'Above all the barrister works regardless of external pressures whether social, economic or political.'[114] Like all ideologies, however, this one exaggerates a very partial truth. Even the strongest academic proponents of independence admit that the profession rarely uses the freedom it demands to restrain state power, and that it is marginal practitioners, not the elite, who are most fiercely oppositional.[115] Just as the traditional profession defended restrictive practices, most of which did nothing to ensure quality for clients while significantly enhancing lawyers' wealth and status, so the contemporary profession defends its freedom from state control, most of which does nothing to protect the liberty of citizens while continuing to preserve professional privilege and evade regulatory responsibility.

Pro bono services allow elite lawyers conspicuously to enact independence on behalf of vulnerable clients confronting powerful adversaries (frequently the state), thereby mystifying those lawyers' profound dependence on a few large clients (many of which oppress and exploit the very same clients).[116] It is no coincidence that professional associations and leaders recently began exhorting members to render such services and lauding those who did. At the beginning of 1993, BC chair Rowe declared the Bar was 'a profession, having a duty to provide a service to the public, and sometimes that has to be without regard to reward'. Goldsmith, his successor, said 'it is the hallmark of professionalism that barristers should use their skills in the public interest—pro bono publico—to try to achieve justice even where the client cannot pay'.[117] Boasting that his chambers had rendered £50,000 worth of services, Michael Beloff QC called it 'the hallmark of a profession to give as well as to take'.[118] Hallett declared it 'essential that we attempt to change the public perception of the Bar.... People out there are doing an enormous amount unpaid for the public and I'm going to publicise it.'[119] A member of the Law Society's newly-formed *pro bono* committee fondly recalled a time when 'the law was talked of as a "liberal profession"' and regretted that lawyers had 'no equivalent of the doctors' Hippocratic oath'.[120] The *Solicitors Journal* hoped the Solicitors Pro Bono Group would 'do much to dispel the unfair and unjustified perception of solicitors as nothing more than money-grubbing ambulance chasers'. This and other such efforts 'should be borne in mind when the profession is attacked for being grasping and greedy'.[121]

But *pro bono* services contain their own contradictions. One local law society observed that the recession was 'not in general a climate in which an extension of pro bono work is sought'. Another raised the 'fundamental contradiction' between the Law Society's exhortation that solicitors run their practices on strict business lines and its 'message that we have surplus time, resources and cash to work for nothing to prop up under-funded organisations'. While presenting *pro bono* to the public as an expression of professional altruism, the Law Society sold it to members in terms of self-interest. Liberty persuaded City firms to contribute by arguing the 'promotional value'. Indeed, Denton Hall sponsored a Museum of London exhibition and then hosted twenty-five receptions there; Clifford Chance hosted London Musici concerts in its building's lobby. The *Solicitors Journal* enumerated the advantages: a 'high profile', attracting 'top quality new recruits', offering them 'useful advocacy and trial preparation experience', and 'refresh[ing] established fee earners'. A DJ Freeman memo said the work 'enables the firm to obtain a higher business profile'. A Nabarro Nathanson partner described *pro bono* as 'part of the normal career progression', presumably of assistant solicitors, who had to make 'a sacrifice of spare time and family time' (never firm time). A City partner called the approach of firms like his own 'often scandalous, only committing trainees rather than fully qualified solicitors', an observation confirmed by a survey of young and trainee solicitors. Talk greatly exceeded action. The American firm Baker & McKenzie led with thirteen hours per solicitor per year; after the next two firms the average was less than five. (A Law Society survey reported an implausible average of thirty-seven hours a year. But some solicitors counted being a governor at their children's schools.) The LAPG warned against playing along with 'the agenda to which the LCD is working' by providing 'another excuse to cut the legal aid budget'. Indeed, the 1995 Labour Party conference urged lawyers to give three days a year to supplement legal aid (for which Labour would have no new money). A large provincial firm accused the party of 'considerable cheek' for 'suggest[ing] we should do more'. The Law Society's annual conference rejected the request: 'legal aid solicitors don't have any free time as it is'. President Mears asked 'when can we expect an announcement from the shadow cabinet that it intends to donate three days' salary to Help the Aged or Oxfam?' The *Solicitors Journal* called the proposal 'misguided'. American *pro bono* 'enables commercial lawyers to experiment with criminal law, for example in death row cases'.[122]

Having argued the virtues of independence, the profession then insisted that this trait was contingent upon endangered restrictive practices: private practice (so barristers could resist employed lawyer audience rights and solicitors oppose corporate conveyancing), solo practice and the cab-rank rule (so barristers could resist audience rights for solicitors and employed barristers), client confidentiality (so solicitors could oppose MDPs).[123] But separate representation of mortgage lenders and borrowers is suspect as make-work; and if solo practice were essential for independence, solicitors could have *no* audience rights. The profession offered no support for its dubious empirical claims: that barristers often appear against others from the same chambers (significantly affecting client choice); that solo practitioners are more independent than those in partnerships (solicitors exposed more miscarriages of justice than barristers) and private practitioners more independent than those employed (what about law centres? or American legal aid and public interest lawyers?); that barristers are frequently offered briefs for unpopular clients or cases and always accept.[124] The profession ignored such awkward facts as barrister dependence on government for silk and judgeships and the association of solicitor sole practitioners with lower quality and financial misconduct. Some observers characterized defiance of the state as inherently good, even if motivated by professional self-interest.[125]

Like all ideologies, the legal profession's is fictitious and incoherent. Traditional lawyers risibly claimed indifference to money. The contemporary profession's new ideal of independence is inherently contradictory. The Royal Commission declared: 'a professional person's first and particular responsibility is to his client. In the case of lawyers this professional duty of maintaining the client's interests is paramount, subject only to their direct responsibility to the court.'[126] But a duty cannot be both paramount and subordinate; and lawyers offer no principled basis for accommodating those inconsistent loyalties. Are accountants *too* loyal to the public (when they disclose essential financial information) or lawyers *insufficiently* loyal (when they conceal it behind the cloak of confidentiality)? How can barristers argue both that solo independent practice makes them (appropriately) *more* loyal to their clients and that the cab-rank rule and solicitor intermediation makes them (just as appropriately) *less* loyal? How can the Bar argue that employment makes state prosecutors *excessively* loyal to the state and public defenders *insufficiently* loyal to accused? How can the profession object to conditional and contingent fees on the ground that they make lawyers both excessively and insufficiently loyal to clients? At best, independence generates empirical hypotheses that the profession shows no interest in testing; at worst, independence is riddled with moral ambiguities that can only serve to mystify normative judgments.[127] Are cause lawyers who represent clients in pursuit of larger goals more or less independent?[128] When two respected solicitors firms (Bindman & Partners and Hodge Jones & Allen) refused to handle rape defence because they acted for feminist organizations, did they exhibit more or less independence? Lawyers are less enthusiastic about independence than other professions. An American survey found that three-quarters of doctors and half of scientists wanted professionals to be the principal authority figures, but only a quarter of lawyers and engineers.[129] The independence professionals seek is as much selfish and individualistic—a libertarian emphasis on their own autonomy, a desire for intrinsically satisfying work—as it is altruistic and collective—a concern for clients, the legal system, or society.[130]

Just as the traditional profession embraced a vanishing aristocratic ideal, so the contemporary profession advances a dying bourgeois ideal. Political 'independence' depended on economic exploitation: inherited wealth for a few lawyers (Weber's *honoratiores*), the extraction of surplus value from unadmitted employees (articled and managing clerks for solicitors, solicitors for barristers); monopoly rents created by limiting the production of and by lawyers; clients wealthy enough to pay the lawyer's fees (without complaint) but sufficiently numerous, small, and dispersed to preclude lawyer dependence on any of them. Contemporary lawyers, however, are less likely to inherit land or capital (other than cultural) and more likely to be employed (state prosecutors and public defenders, assistant solicitors, house counsel) or competing among themselves and with non-lawyers for price-conscious clients, while depending on a few large clients (City firms), referral sources (chambers on solicitors' firms, solicitors on accountants and lenders) or a single third-party payer—the very state that lawyers claim to defy (legal aid, Treasury counsel, prosecution briefs). Furthermore, the real limitations on access to justice are not political pressures against challenging the state but legal aid's shrinking eligibility, falling remuneration rates (which compel perfunctory service), and growing categorical exclusions (money claims, substantive areas, strategies, fora), all of which the state determined unilaterally. Judicial management of litigation following the Woolf reforms limits lawyer independence. Professional self-regulation is under attack for its chronic failures. The state threatens to strip professional associations of the power to compel membership (and fees) when they become too 'political'.

Independence legitimates professional privilege no more successfully than the paternalism it replaced. Its claims are internally contradictory and factitious. Just as lawyers broke their promise to elevate client interests above their own, so very few champion the oppressed against injustice.

Notes

All Parliamentary debates are in Hansard (series 6) and cited by Chamber (unless this is clear from the text) vol: cols (date).

Abbreviations

BB	BACFI Bulletin
BN	Bar News
C	Counsel
Cat	Caterpillar
DM	Daily Mail
DT	Daily Telegraph
E	Economist
EN	ENPBA Newsletter
ES	Evening Standard
Ex	Express
FT	Financial Times
G	Guardian
I	Independent
IFLR	International Financial Law Review
IOS	Independent on Sunday
L	Lawyer
LA	Legal Action
LSG	Law Society's Gazette
MOS	Mail on Sunday
NLJ	New Law Journal
NN	NPBA Newsletter
NYT	New York Times
O	Observer
S	Spectator
SCOLAG	Scottish Legal Action Group Bulletin
SE	Sunday Express
SJ	Solicitors Journal
ST	Sunday Times
STel	Sunday Telegraph

Chapter 1—Notes

[1] Yet Savage *et al.* (1992: 198–201) assert that 'the inter-generationally stable professional middle class' is second only to the immobile working class in being unlikely to vote Conservative. For an explanation of why Thatcher challenged the professions see Brazier *et al.* (1993).

[2] On decline see Barnett (1972; 1986); Bacon and Eltis (1976); Wiener (1981); Gamble (1981); Alt (1979); Marquand (1988); Eccleshall (2000). On the Conservative victory see Kavanagh (1987: 162–3, 204–5); Leys (1989: 97–101, 106, 210); Skidelsky (1988b); Minford (1988); Riddell (1991: 1).

[3] CPS (1975; 1976); Howe (1977); Kavanagh (1987: 6–7, 10, 142, 250–3, 303); Dahrendorf (1988: 195); Raban (1989: 8–13, 29); Heelas (1991: 74); Riddell (1991: 1, 73, 208); Johnson (1991: 79–80, 85, 178); Lawson (1992: 64–5); Thatcher (1993: 6–10, 13, 626); Dellheim (1995: 166, 184). In his 1983 Hamptons Lecture, DGFT Sir Gordon Borrie attacked the restrictive practices of solicitors, accountants, veterinary surgeons, and opticians. Perkin (1989: 479).

[4] Dellheim (1995: 147, 155–6).

[5] Hayek (1980); Joseph (1978); Hall (1983: 31); Jenkins (1987: 320, 324); Kavanagh (1987: 195); Johnson (1991: 219); Thatcher (1993: 97–101, 272); Hendy (1993: 30); Dellheim (1995: 216, 220).

[6] Adeney and Lloyd (1986: 37); Minford (1988: 98–9); Matthews and Minford (1987); Kavanagh (1987: 239–40); Leys (1989: 109, 118–20, 123, 153–4, 289–90); Riddell (1991: 47–8); Johnson (1991: 16–17); Thatcher (1993: 378).

[7] Pirie (1985); Moore (1986); Jenkins (1987: 317–19, 338); Veljanovski (1987); Kavanagh (1987: 220–1); Jenkins (1987: 320); Foreman-Peck (1988); Gamble (1988); Leys (1989: 117–18, 329–32); Johnson (1991: 159–69); Lawson (1992: 226); Thatcher (1993: 672, 677, 687); Dellheim (1995: 235); Reitan (1997: 137–8, 159–65).

[8] Jenkins (1987: 317–19, 338); Kavanagh (1987: 212–15, 225–30); Lewis (1988); Stewart and Burridge (1988); Leys (1989: 113, 117–18, 123); Johnson (1991: 148–50); Riddell (1991: 115, 128–30); Thatcher (1993: 6–10, 13). Publications by the Institute of Economic Affairs, which influenced and expressed Thatcherite policies, took similar positions: Seldon (1981); Green (1982); Parker (1982).

[9] Klein (1985); Green (1985; 1986); Kavanagh (1987: 212–17); Leys (1989: 114–15); Le Grand (1991); Lawson (1992: 612–19); Reitan (1997: 103–4, 170); Thatcher (1993: 606–17).

[10] Commission on Urban Priority Areas (1985: 52); Jakobovits (1986); Kavanagh (1987: 252, 290–1); Whitty and Menter (1988); Warlock and Sheppard (1989); Thatcher (1993: 598); Dellheim (1995: 147, 155–6, 297–309, 324–5, 329–30); Reitan (1997: 106–7, 172–6).

[11] Kavanagh (1987: 260), quoting *The Times* (2.11.85); Pope–Hennessy (1989); Young (1990: chap. 18); Dellheim (1995: 288–92, 297, 312–14).

[12] Seldon (1986); Kavanagh (1987: 287); Loughlin (1988); Leys (1989: 124–5); Le Grand (1991); Reitan (1997: 106–7, 153, 172–6).

[13] Crewe (1994); Young (1990: 19, 22); Riddell (1994); Kavanagh (1994a: 3); Major (1997: 7); Lamont (1999: 496–8). But Major was close to the Adam Smith Institute and the Social Market Foundation. Seldon (1994b).

[14] Hogg and Hill (1995: 86); 'A Nation of Opportunity', speech to the Social Market Foundation, 19.3.96; 'A Nation of First Class Public Services', The *Spectator* Allied Dunbar Lecture, 18.9.96, in Major (1997: 19–27, 37–45).

[15] Kavanagh (1994b); Bonefeld *et al.* (1995: 130); Dorey (1999a).

[16] 'Opportunity for All', speech to the Conservative Party Conference, 11.10.96, in Major (1997: 68–78); Reitan (1997: 167–8); Hill (1999).

[17] Reitan (1997: 103–4, 170).

[18] Secretary of State for Employment (1991; 1992); Trade Union Reform and Employment Rights Act 1993; Taylor (1994); Dorey (1999c).

[19] 'Accepting the Leadership', speech to the Conservative Party, 4.12.90; 'Priorities for the Future', speech 7.2.91, 'Our Agenda for the Decade', speech 23.3.91, 'The Best Possible National Health Service', speech 17.9.91, in Major (1991a: 9–10, 13, 15, 33–42, 69–74); Major (1991b; 1992b; 1994); Chancellor of the Exchequer (1991); Chancellor of the Duchy of Lancaster (1992); Kavanagh (1994a: 15); Willman (1994).

[20] 'The Power to Choose: The Right to Own', speech to Conservative Party Conference, 11.10.91, in Major (1991a: 81); 'A Country with a Head: A Country with a Heart', speech 19.3.92; 'What We Must Tell the People', speech 22.3.92; 'Tomorrow's Toryism: Yesterday's Socialism', speech 23.3.92; 'Ten Tory Truths for a Glorious Future', speech 7.4.92, in Major (1992a: 17–35, 69–78); Hogg and Hill (1995: 116–17, 120–1, 135–6, 165–6, 198–9, 208, 219).

[21] King (1988); Butler (1988); Grant (1993); Jay (1994); Bonefeld *et al.* (1995: 123, 125–6); Reitan (1997: 89–95, 127–8, 132–3, 137); Denver (1998); Lamont (1999).

[22] Johnson (1991: 197); Glennerster (1994); Willman (1994); Bonefeld *et al.* (1995: 140–2, 189).

[23] Minister without Portfolio (1985); Borrie (1987); DTI (1988; 1989); Johnson (1991: 187–96); Reitan (1997: 103–4, 170).

[24] Quoted in Marquand (1988: 172).

[25] Hailsham (1990: 409–10, 418–20, 422, 434–8); Lawson (1992: 620); 'Lord Hailsham Dies at 94; A Tory With a Lighter Side', NYT (16.10.01) C7.

[26] Kavanagh (1987: 178); Crewe (1988: 29–31); Leys (1989: 117–18); Driver and Martell (1998: 8–14); Pattie (2000).

[27] Jenkins (1987: 329–30, 346–7); Riddell (1991: 208); Pattie (2000).

[28] Labour Party (1988; 1989a; 1989b; 1991); Commission on Social Justice (1994); Taylor (1997: chaps. 1–6); Diver and Martell (1998: 15–17); Ludlum (2002a). For other statements of this reorientation see Hattersley (1987); Gould (1989); Radice (1989).

[29] Seyd (1998); McSmith (1999).

[30] Mandelson and Liddle (1996: 34–42).

[31] Blair (1996: 206–9, 213, 221, 311–12); Mandelson and Liddle (1996: 21); Rentoul (1999).

[32] Blair (1996: 107–9, 206–9).

[33] Mandelson and Liddle (1996: 17, 29).

[34] Mandelson and Liddle (1996: 24, 82–3); Taylor (1997: chap. 7); Seyd (1998); Moran and Alexander (2000); see also Hutton (1993).

[35] Blair (1996a: 35–44, 206–9); Mandelson and Liddle (1996: 3, 10, 13, 18, 29); Rentoul (1999).

[36] Radice (1992); Fielding (1997); King (1998a); Hay (1999); Heath *et al.* (2001: 10, 13, 15–17, 39, 45, 109, 125, 138); Rose (2001: chap. 11).

[37] Seyd (1998); Routledge (1998); Coates (2000a); Moran and Alexander (2000); Gamble and Kelly (2000); Panitch and Leys (2001); Kavanagh (2001); Riddell (2001); Stephens (2001); Glennerster (2001).

[38] Mandelson and Liddle (1996: 12–13); Gould (1998); Blair (1998); Ludlum (2000b: 119, 121); Coates (2000a; 2000b); Gamble and Kelly (2000); Panitch and Leys (2001: 254); Taylor (2001: 236, 250). Giddens (1998) never mentions unions in his book on the third way.

[39] Blair (1991; 1996a: p. xii, 31–2); Mandelson and Liddle (1996: 7–8, 22); Coates (2000a); Panitch and Leys (2001: 247).

[40] Blair (1996a: 101–3); Mandelson and Liddle (1996: 83–4); Coates (2000b); Owen (2001); Sinclair (2001).

[41] Mandelson and Liddle (1996: 27, 150, 152–5); Blair (1996a: 65); Glennerster (2001).

[42] Blair (1996a: 24, 149); Mandelson and Liddle (1996: 96–7); Stedward (2000); McCaig (2000); Smithers (2001).

[43] Field (1995; 1998); Mandelson and Liddle (1996: 145–7); Blair (1996a: 293); Driver and Martell (1998: 87–9, 103, 107); Purdy (2000); Annesley (2000).

[44] Blair (1996a: 19, 69, 177–82); Secretary of State for Health (1997); NHS Executive (1998); Driver and Martell (1998: 93–5); Wood (2000); Glennerster (2001).

[45] Blair (1996b); Irvine (1996); Cranston (1996); Rentoul (2001: 287).

[46] Hall (1995); Seyd (1998); Driver and Martell (1998: 2–3); Rentoul (1999); Coates (2000a); Ludlum (2000a; 2000b); see also Thompson (1996); Marquand (1998); Freeden (1999a; 1999b); Brittan (1999).

[47] Mandelson and Liddle (1996: 21); Reitan (1997: 188–93); Denver (1998); King (1998a; 1998b); Sanders (1998); Norris (1998); Coates (2000a); Russell (2000); Ludlum (2000a); Pattie (2000); Sully (2000).

[48] Rentoul (1999); Worcester and Mortimore (2001: 3, 8, 26, 35, 101, 107, 110, 153, 195).

[49] I disagree with Burrage (1997), however, that it was part of her programme to undermine the 'little republics' of civil society; and I discuss her treatment of health care and schools below.

[50] HL vol. 505, col. 1345 (7.4.89).

[51] Second inaugural address, 'One Third of a Nation', 4.3.37.

[52] Mandelson and Liddle (1996: 17, 29) actually put working class in inverted commas!

[53] The contemporaneous neo-liberal reform of the French legal profession was pushed through by a socialist government over the opposition of both the conservative and communist parties. Karpik (1999: 276–7).

Chapter 2—Notes

[1] Johnstone and Hopson (1967); Abel–Smith and Stevens (1967; 1968); Zander (1968).

[2] Monopolies Commission (1970); Committee on Legal Education (1971).

[3] Griffith (1977); Joseph (1976); Hazell (1978); Bankowski and Mungham (1976); see also Cain (1976).

[4] Monopolies and Mergers Commission (1976a; 1976b); Royal Commission on Legal Services (1979).

[5] Berlins and Dyer (1982); Thomas (1982); Podmore and Spencer (1982a; 1982b); Flood (1983); Joseph (1984); Gifford (1986); Reeves (1986); Seldon (1987); Abel (1986; 1988); Zander (1988); Dickson (1990).

[6] LCD (1983).

[7] Abel (1988: 89–92, 100, 179–84); Marre Committee (1988).

[8] Lawson (1992: 619–21).

[9] 'Barristers "must end closed shop"', ST (2.10.88) 1; 'Bar urged to change ways', STel (2.10.88); 'Hint by Mackay of Crown Court rights for solicitors', DT (3.10.88); 'Barristers given hint over demarcation', FT (3.10.88); 'Clashfern questions monopoly in higher court', T (3.10.88) 10; 'Mackay hints at end to Bar's monopoly in court', I (3.10.88); 'Bar's "Sole Preserve" Questioned by Lord Mackay', LSG (5.10.88) 2; 'Good Counsel', ES (3.10.88); 'Bar, the shouting', G (5.10.88).

[10] Richard Gaskell, 'A Full Quota of Challenge and Excitement', LSG (20.10.88) 2; 'Bar "must put house in order"', T (21.10.88) 4; 'Law Society call for shake–up of solicitors' role', DT (21.10.88) 10; 'All Lawyers should Start as Solicitors, Gaskell Tells the Profession' (1988) 132 SJ 1481.

[11] LCD, Press Notice (24.10.88); 'Shake–up for the legal closed shop', ES (24.10.88); 'Mackay signals big shake–up for the legal profession', I (25.10.88); 'Radical reforms ahead for law's "closed shop"', DT (25.10.88) 1; 'Mackay plans "shake–up for legal system"', T (25.10.88) 1; 'Plans for legal reform "moving too quickly"', DT (26.10.88) 2; 'Mackay Springs Green Paper Surprise', LSG (26.10.88) 2; 'Mackay to Reform the Legal Profession' (1988) 132 SJ 1468; 'It's Time We Were Told' (1988) 132 SJ 1467; 'Conveyancing Conflicts' (1988) 138 NLJ 779; 'Lawyers ready to block reforms', O (30.10.88); 'Lord Denning: The two great evils of our law', ES (31.10.88) 7; 'New Bar chief fears overhaul "disaster"', T (24.11.88); Warren Burger, 'An American Perspective on the English Bar', C (11–12.88) 32.

[12] 'The ultimate closed shop', ES (25.10.88); 'A cold wind blows through the law', G (26.10.88) 22; Christopher Huhne, 'Strange rebirth of English liberalism', G (26.10.88); 'A sceptical eye on legal interests', I (26.10.88) 20; DT (26.10.88) 18; 'Stirred, not shaken', E (29.10.88) 32; 'Dragging reform into the courts–not before time', ST (30.10.88); 'One law for the rich', O (30.10.88).

[13] 'Shake–up set to bring cuts in Bar's monopoly', T (26.12.88); 'Bar must bow to change', G (3.1.89); 'Setback for Law Reform', DM (4.1.89) 1; 'Scottish trial for England's lawyers', DM (4.1.89) 6; 'The law is a cartel', E (25.1.89) 20.

[14] 'End this Rumpole monopoly', DM (5.1.89); 'End the Squabbles' (1989) 133 SJ 3; Desmond Fennell QC, 'Why the Bar must spring to its own defence', DT (18.1.89) 16; Richard Gaskell, 'President's Column', LSG (25.1.89) 2.

[15] 'Barristers act over legal shake', T (23.1.89); Lord Goodman, 'Lifting the bar against alternative advocates', DT (25.1.89); 'Donaldson urges solicitors as High

Court judges', G (25.1.89); 'Bar monopoly a "sacred cow" lawyers told', DT (25.1.89); 'End solicitor ban, says top judge', DM (25.1.89); 'Donaldson criticizes Bar monopoly on High Court judges', T (25.1.89).

[16] LCD (1989a; 1989b; 1989c).

[17] DM (26.1.89) 1; ES (26.1.89) 1; 'Green Paper: Change for whose benefit?' LA (3.89) 8.

[18] A.H. Hermann, 'Advocates proposed to replace solicitor/barrister distinction', FT (26.1.89) 6; Clare Dyer, G (26.1.89) 4, 19; Robert Rice, I (26.1.89) 3; A.H. Hermann, 'The law of supply and demand', FT (28.1.89) 7; STel (29.1.89); 'Big Bang at the Bar', O (29.1.89) 15; Susan Crosland, 'Big wigs versus little wigs', ST (29.1.89); Simon Jenkins, 'Mackay brings fear and fury to the bar', ST (29.1.89) B1; A.H. Hermann, 'Is there life after the demise of the Bar?' FT (6.2.89).

[19] DM (26.1.89) 6; 'Assault on privilege at the Bar', I (26.1.89) 26; 'The cost and quality of justice', G (26.1.89) 18; 'Bold reforms in the law', FT (26.1.89) 22; 'Some cat, some pigeons', ES (26.1.89) 7.

[20] 'Legal milestone', DT (26.1.89) 16; ' "Big Bang" for the Bar', T (26.1.89) 18; Brian Deer, 'Rumpoled! The high street revolution that rattled the bar', ST (28.1.89).

[21] 'Bar anger at Mackay reforms', T (26.1.89) 1; 'Bar furious over end of monopoly', G (26.1.89) 1; 'Wrong way to law reforms', T (26.1.89) 14; 'Bar to launch campaign against Mackay plans', G (27.1.89); Robert Alexander QC, 'Dangers in the Green Papers', I (30.1.89); G (30.1.89); William Rees–Mogg, 'Why a legal Big Bang could turn out to be a political time bomb', I (31.1.89); ' "Beauty contest" in law reform fight' T (3.2.89); 'M'luds set for legal clash of the Titans', MOS (5.2.89); 'Giving lawyers a competitive edge', FT (15.2.89); William Rees–Mogg, 'On the Seventh Day God rested but Thatcher knows no Sabbath', I (21.2.89).

[22] 'Bar reforms face clash in Lords', T (27.1.89).

[23] T (28.1.89); I (30.1.89); T (30.1.89); T (31.1.89), quoted in ES (31.1.89); FT (1.2.89); T (2.2.89) 11; STel (12.2.89).

[24] Letter from Nicholas Dee (BACFI chair) to members (3.2.89); I (2.2.89); T (3.2.89); 'Misplaced sensitivity at the Bar', I (3.2.89) 17; Newcastle Evening Chronicle (3.2.89); T (14.2.89) 35; LSG (15.2.89); 'Lawyers gagged on Mackay paper', G (14.3.89); 'Howls of fury at the Bar', O (19.2.89) 14; 'Both Sides of the Profession Seek End to "Doom and Gloom" Prophecies' (1989) 139 NLJ 282.

[25] Richard Gaskell, 'President's Column', LSG (25.1.89) 2; DM (26.1.89) 1; ' "Quality of justice under threat" ', FT (26.1.89) 1; I (26.1.89) 1; G (26.1.89) 1; Desmond Fennell QC, 'Threat to quality and public's range of choice', T (27.1.89); Richard Gaskell, 'Outdated fabric needed replacing for the 1990s', T (27.1.89); 'Conveyancing market is worth £1.5bn', FT (27.1.89); 'Mackay puts forward his "Fair Competition" Policy' (1989) 133(4) SJ p. ii; 'After the Green Papers' (1989) 133 SJ 91; 'Desmond Fennell QC: Passionate champion of the English Bar', FT (28.1.89) 7; 'Ban Bang at the Bar', O (29.1.89) 15; 'Uproar is justified', ST (29.1.89); 'Rumpoled! The high street revolution that rattled the bar', ST (29.1.89); 'Conveying greater choice', DM (1.2.89) 26; 'Lobbying Begins: Society Plans Restrained Campaign', LSG (1.2.89) 2; Walter Merricks, 'Rescuing the legal reform Green Papers from melodrama', I (2.2.89); ' "Beauty contest" in law reform fight',

T (3.2.89); Roger Henderson QC, 'An Illusion of Choice for Consumers' (1989) 139 NLJ 140; 'Reforming the Lawyers' (1989) 139 NLJ 137; 'Parallel Paths to the Courts' (1989) 139 NLJ 141; Walter Merricks, 'The Motives of the Market Giants' (1989) 139 NLJ 143; Mark Boléat, 'A Better Deal for Housebuyers' (1989) 139 NLJ 143; 'Optimism for the Future' (1989) 133 SJ 131; Roger Smith, 'Public Service and Civil Liberties—the Legal Action Group's View' (1989) 139 NLJ 144; 'Green Paper Doubts in Small Firms' (1989) 139 NLJ 178; Roger Smith, 'No longer a law unto itself', I (10.2.89) 15; Mark Boléat, 'A conflict of interest?' T (14.2.89) 35; 'Bar Rejects Reform and Attacks Lord Chancellor over Legal Aid' (1989) 139 NLJ 246; NCC (1989).

[26] 'Legal reforms backed', T (27.1.89) 1; 'Common lawyers give mixed verdict on proposed reform', FT (27.1.89); T (28.1.89).

[27] Letter from Desmond Fennell QC to Dear Colleague (14.2.89).

[28] 'M'luds set for legal clash of the Titans', MOS (5.2.89); 'Lord Lane attacks "the most sinister" legal reforms', T (16.2.89) 1; 'M'learned adman's call to the Bar', DT (17.2.89) 17; 'Legal reform', DT (17.2.89) 16; DT (18.2.89) 14.

[29] General Management Committee (1989); 'Bar steps up fight against reform', G (18.2.89) 2; 'Bar willing to give up monopoly', FT (19.2.89) 1; 'Justice endangered by planned legal reforms, say barristers', DT (18.2.89) 8.

[30] 'Mackay versus the people', T (20.2.89); T (23.2.89) 15 (emphasis added); T (23.2.89), quoted in Cownie (1990: 213); Jonathan Caplan, 'A Threat to Criminal Justice', C (3–4.89) 5–6; Julian Malins, 'A Prospectus for the Civil Bar', C (3–4.89) 6–7; Nicholas Purnell QC, 'Which Market? Whose Values? What Price?' C (3–4.89) 7–8.

[31] 'Mackay gives the profession a taste for blood', FT (20.2.89) 23; 'The law is being a silly ass', G (20.2.89) 18; DM (24.2.89).

[32] 'Law Lord attacks plans to reform legal profession', I (22.2.89); 'Judge criticises ministers for being "deluded by dogma"', DT (22.2.89); 'Law Lord attacks "hell–bent destruction" of the Bar', T (22.2.89) 1; 'Law Lord says Mackay is hell–bent on destroying the Bar', G (22.2.89); 'Legal reforms could spark constitutional crisis', T (23.2.89); 'Carman locks legal shake–up', G (24.2.89); DT (24.2.89); Lord Benson, 'A sacrifice to competition', FT (1.3.89).

[33] 'The Radical on the Woolsack', DT Weekend Magazine (25.2.89) 16.

[34] E (4–10.3.89); Bernard Levin, 'In defence of the great lie', T (6.3.89).

[35] 'Lord Mackay defends his reforms and attacks Bar's "prophets of despair"', DT (7.3.89) 7; 'Mackay urges open mind on legal reforms', I (7.3.89) 1; 'Mackay attacks Bar over "prophecies of doom and despair"', I (7.3.89) 5; 'Mackay warns against doom and despair', T (7.3.89); 'Mackay chides Bar on shake–up', G (7.3.89); 'Law chief hits out at lawyers', DM (7.3.89); 'Integrity of justice "threatened"', DT (7.3.89) 7; 'QC warns of reform undermining justice', I (7.3.89) 5; 'QC assails consumerist link', T (7.3.89); 'Hailsham sees reforms as threat to independence', DT (7.3.89) 7; 'Hailsham fears march of elective dictatorship', I (7.3.89) 5; 'Home sales "clean–up" is urged', DT (7.3.89) 7; 'Privilege "will last a decade"', T (7.3.89); 'President Raps Institutions' Sales Tactics', LSG (8.3.89) 2; 'Conveyancing fees cut fear "unfounded"', DT (8.3.89); 'Home deal comfort for lawyers', T (8.3.89); 'Solicitors reassured on property', I (8.3.89); 'Fair trading chief attacks mixed legal partnership plans', I (8.3.89); 'Bar proposals under fire',

G (8.3.89); 'Borrie worry on "threat to Bar's independence"', DT (8.3.89); 'Borrie Draws Line on Bar Changes' (1989) 139 NLJ 318; 'Lord Chancellor Launches Counter-offensive on Green Paper Critics' (1989) 139 NLJ 318; 'Green Papers on: The Work and Organization of the Legal Profession; Conveyancing by Authorized Practitioners; Contingency Fees—Comment by the Director-General of Fair Trading' (7.4.89); Zander (1989; 1990: 774–6).

[36] 'Trying to sit on a thistle', DM (7.3.89) 6; 'Over-reaction spoils the Bar's case', I (7.3.89) 18; 'The question of Thatcher's sanity', I (11.3.89) 16; Susan Crosland, 'Barristers with guilty faces', ST (12.3.89); Neal Ascherson, 'Making the State obey the law', O (12.3.89) 13.

[37] 'Lament for a lost land', T (8.3.89) 12; 'Letters to the editor', T (8.3.89); 'An assault on the judges', T (10.3.89); 'Reforms that threaten executive control over judges and lawyers', I (16.3.89).

[38] G (10.3.89) 38; 'Mayhew could quit over reforms', I (22.6.89) 1; 'Hoist signals and stand to go about', G (26.6.89) 19; 'Tories set to retreat on law reforms', O (12.3.89); 'Lords "may rebel" on legal reform bill', ST (12.3.89); 'Thatcher firm on law reform plans', T (13.3.89) 1; 'Legal reforms face revolt in the Lords', DT (13.3.89); 'Rifkind launches plan to reform Scot legal system', I (14.3.89) 2; 'Law reforms get public backing from Thatcher', T (15.3.89).

[39] 'MPs and judges', ES (13.3.89); 'A hung jury on the great reform', G (14.3.89) 22.

[40] 'Reform of the Bar', DT (14.3.89) 20; 'Purpose posse against the Green Paper', G (14.3.89) 23; T (15.3.89).

[41] DTI (1988); 'Mackay accuses the Bar of stifling reform discussion', T (16.3.89) 1; 'Mackay rounds on Bar's closed minds', T (16.3.89) 13; 'Law will not be left to market forces alone', T (16.3.89) 13; 'Bar urged to make "rational" response to legal reforms', I (16.3.89) 6; 'Lord Mackay promises to modify his legal reforms if convinced by opponents', DT (16.3.89) 4; 'Mackay hints at law reform concessions', G (16.3.89); 'Plea for Bar evolution', G (16.3.89); 'Plans are open to debate, Lord Mackay tells critics', T (16.3.89) 8; 'Letter to the editor', T (21.3.89).

[42] 'Proposals "threaten quality of judiciary"', T (16.3.89) 15; 'Mackay attacked for failing to appreciate risks of proposals', I (16.3.89) 6; 'Fennell demands change by evolution, not revolution', T (16.3.89) 15; 'Proposals "are untrue to their own standards"', T (16.3.89) 14; 'City takeover panel chairman says proposals are super-ficial', FT (16.3.89) 8.

[43] 'Solicitors "can be effective advocates"', T (16.3.89) 15; 'Mackay attacked for failing to appreciate risks of proposals', I (16.3.89) 6; 'Bar campaign is "arrant non-sense"', T (21.3.89); DT (16.3.89) 4; 'Pressure by banks seen as stimulus for change', FT (16.3.89) 8; 'Learning from American experience', T (16.3.89) 16; 'Can British Clients Win with a US-Style System?' LSG (22.3.89) 6; see also the exchanges at an earlier conference: 'US lawyer says fears justified', DT (8.3.89) 9; 'Scots system "could work in England"', I (8.3.89); 'US no win, no fee system deters "nuisance claims"', I (8.3.89).

[44] Hugo Young, 'When the Bar breaks, the cradle will fall', G (16.3.89) 19; E (18.3.89) 52; Christopher Monckton, 'Advocate of quiet revolution', ES (20.3.89) 7; Patricia Finney, 'Heavy legal costs', I (17.3.89); 'Professional errors', DT (21.3.89); 'The aims of law reform', FT (17.3.89) 20.

[45] 'Bar launches campaign against reform', T (17.3.89) 2; 'Circular asks 400 judges to fight legal reforms', T (17.3.89) 1; DT (21.3.89); T (20–23.3.89); G (17.3.89); 'Green Paper Controversies Continue' (1989) 133 SJ 368; Zander (1990: 764); Cownie (1990: 223).

[46] All citations to Hansard (HL) vol. 505 (7.4.89). 1307–13. The press emphasized the 'scathing' criticism and Lord Mackay's 'composure'. 'Profession divided, says Mackay', T (7.4.89) 28; 'Top lawyers in scathing attack on proposals: Hailsham onslaught on timetable', T (7.4.89) 28–29; 'Peers put Mackay through the hoop', G (7.4.89) 24; 'A peer of great composure', T (7.4.89) 29; 'Fierce Opposition May Prompt Government to Rethink', LSG (12.4.89) 2; Zander (1990: 769).

[47] 1329–35, 1391–5, 1453–62.

[48] 1342–4.

[49] 1385–91, 1429–32, 1447–50.

[50] 1313–16, 1329–32, 1365–9, 1423–6, 1453–7, 1466–70.

[51] 1375–8, 1391–5.

[52] 1378–80, 1385–91. Lord Goodman elaborated his criticism a week later, 'A sad waste of balanced judgment', ES (13.4.89) 7.

[53] 1317–21, 1329–32, 1342–7, 1375–8, 1423–6, 1457–62.

[54] 1329–35, 1385–91, 1411–16.

[55] 1338–42 (Lord Templeman), 1437–41 (Lord Coleraine), 1457–62 (Lord Oliver), 1470–4 (Lord Mishcon).

[56] 1321–3, 1362–5, 1369–72, 1382–5, 1391–5.

[57] 1335–8, 1350–3, 1402–7, 1457–62.

[58] 1317–21, 1350–3, 1408–10.

[59] 1395–8.

[60] 1411–16, 1453–7.

[61] 1350–3, 1411–16, 1423–6, 1447–50.

[62] 1329–35, 1350–3, 1402–7, 1423–6, 1441–3.

[63] 1372–5, 1441–3, 1447–50, 1470–4.

[64] 1342–4, 1411–16, 1457–62, 1466–70.

[65] 1347–50, 1365–9, 1372–5, 1382–5, 1453–7.

[66] 1317–21, 1338–42, 1350–3, 1381–2, 1411–16, 1426–8, 1457–62.

[67] 1323–7, 1332–5, 1441–3.

[68] 1317–21, 1323–7, 1332–5, 1402–7, 1423–6.

[69] 1317–21, 1332–5, 1355–7, 1381–2, 1402–7, 1426–8.

[70] 1329–32, 1350–3.

[71] 1329–32, 1342–4, 1369–72, 1385–91, 1408–10, 1423–6, 1451–3.

[72] 1321–3 (Lord Rees-Mogg), 1323–7 (Lord Irvine), 1391–5 (Lord Rippon).

[73] 1338–42 (Lord Templeman), 1409–10 (Lord Goff), 1457–62 (Lord Oliver).

[74] 1432–4; see also 505: 1457–62 (Lord Oliver).

[75] 1313–16, 1323–7, 1342–4.

[76] 1323–7, 1329–32, 1342–4, 1391–5.

[77] 1313–16, 1332–5, 1350–3.

[78] 1329–32, 1350–3, 1474–80.

[79] 1453–7.

[80] 1327–9, 1355–62, 1407–8, 1416–23, 1444–7, 1464–6.

[81] 1474–80.

[82] 'The Bar in ermine', G (7.4.89); Laurence Marks, 'Lords leap to defend legal privilege', O (9.4.89); Noel Malcolm, 'The Lord Chancellor who dared to cross the Bar', S (15.4.89) 6.

[83] 'Judges back down over reform talks', T (14.4.89) 1, 12, 15; 'Judges Disrupt their Courts' (1989) 139 NLJ 495; 'Restrictions on public criticism of courts', FT (15.5.89); 'Press banned from judges' day of action', DM (21.5.89).

[84] 'Attacks on law reform draw fire', T (14.4.89); 'Lord Hailsham criticises legal profession plans', FT (15.4.89); 'Call to Re-examine the Marre Report', LSG (26.4.89) 4; Sir Frederick Lawton, 'Tighter rules may raise standards', T (2.5.89).

[85] 'Estate Agents' Code "Useless" says Society' (1989) 133 SJ 521; 'The Green Papers: A Bar to Progress?' (1989) 133 SJ 522; 'Halifax chief calls for reform', I (4.5.89); 'Birrell slams conveyancing', O (7.5.89); 'Building societies favour conveyancing extension', FT (9.5.89); 'NASPyC Wants to Keep Independent Advice', LSG (10.5.89) 4; 'Conveyancing rule changes "will expose buyers to predators"', T (15.5.89) 8; 'NASPyC is Concerned at Green Papers' (1989) 133 SJ 641; Richard Gaskell, 'President's Column', LSG (24.5.89) 2; 'Hidden Commission Criticised' (1989) 133 SJ 668; 'Call to sweep away "antiquated" system of conveyancing', T (3.6.89); 'Estate agents plan to outlaw gazumping', DT (3.6.89) 34; 'Right to challenge legal bills threatened', DT (5.6.89); 'Solicitors urge Land Registry's reform', DT (6.6.89); 'Lawyers Criticise Agents' Initiative' (1989) 133 SJ 732; 'Estate Agents Furious at Society's Guide', LSG (28.6.89) 3; 'Disappointment at Weak Estate Agent Code', LSG (26.6.89) 4; 'Public Sees Problems in One-stop Shopping', LSG (28.6.89) 5; 'Homebuyers "ruthlessly exploited by institutions"', T (29.6.89); 'Avoid Estate Agents Selling Financial Services says Society' (1989) 133 SJ 824.

[86] I (3.5.89) 3; 'Legal changes "will help only wealthy clients"', I (4.5.89); 'Justice Fears New Monopoly', LSG (10.5.89) 5; 'LAPG Sees Benefit Only for Top 10%', LSG (10.5.89) 5; 'Irrelevant say SLD Lawyers', LSG (10.5.89) 5; 'Consumer Association Gives the Thumbs-up', LSG (10.5.89) 4; 'Consumers' Association backs Mackay' (1989) 133 SJ 604; 'Chance of a common front', LA (7.89) 7; Kate Marcus, 'Letter to the editor', G (3.7.89); Zander (1989; 1990: 773); Consumers' Association (1989); National Consumer Council (1989b); Glasser (1989).

[87] Richard Gaskell, 'President's Column', LSG (26.4.89) 2; 'Green Papers: Limited Support from Society; "No" on Conveyancing', LSG (3.5.89) 2; Law Society (1989).

[88] 'Government hold on power "dangerous"', T (2.5.89); 'Barristers to overhaul practices', FT (2.5.89); 'The case against mixed professional partnerships', I (2.5.89); 'Bar unveils Green Paper counter-proposals', I (3.5.89) 1; 'Changes "are inconsistent with an independent Bar"', I (3.5.89) 3; 'Bar rejects legal reforms package', T (3.5.89) 1; 'Changes that lie ahead for barristers', T (3.5.89) 7; 'Mackay plans "are illogical"', T (3.5.89) 7; 'Bar tones down attack on Mackay', G (3.5.89) 7; 'Bar Council ends chambers curb on barristers', DT (3.5.89) 4; 'Bar Offers "Constructive Response"', LSG (3.5.89) 3; Nicholas Dee, Letter to BACFI members (12.6.89); 'A Programme of Genuine Reform', C (5–6.89) 3; General Council of the Bar (1989). Although the Bar's response was endorsed by the Inns, Circuits, specialist bar associations, and by BACFI (except for employed barristers' audience rights), a few prominent barristers dissented. Zander (1990: 764 n.57).

[89] 'Mackay hits back on law reforms', FT (29–30.4.89); (1989) 139 NLJ 603; 'Lord Mackay hints at compromise over reforms', T (18.5.89); 'Mackay flexible over legal reform', FT (18.5.89); 'Mackay softens stance on law reforms', DT (18.5.89).

[90] 'Lord Mackay and ordinary justice', I (3.5.89) 18; 'Bar feels the wind of competition', FT (4.5.89); 'Resting their cases', E (6.5.89) 54; A.H. Hermann, 'The ups and downs of the English legal system', FT (9.5.89); John Kay, 'Are doctors so different from dockers?' DT (10.5.89).

[91] 'Judges condemn legal shake-up', ES (23.5.89); 'Law reform going too far judges warn government', DM (24.5.89); 'Mackay reforms threaten our independence from government, say judges', DT (24.5.89); 'Judges fear for future quality of justice', FT (24.5.89) 10; 'Bar system "less biased"', G (24.5.89); 'Committee's lay majority attacked', G (24.5.89); 'Judges attack law reform plans', FT (24.5.89); 'Judges fight for separate role', G (24.5.89) 8; 'Lord Chancellor's new powers should be held in check by judiciary', T (24.5.89) 5; 'Barristers may fall prey to "conflict of interest" in firms', T (24.5.89) 5; 'Judges Argue for Status Quo', LSG (24.5.89) 3; 'Judges Find "Grave Breach" of Constitution in Green Papers' (1989) 139 NLJ 707; 'The Judges Respond to Mackay' (1989) 133 SJ 700; *The Green Papers, The Judges Response* (1989); *Comments of the Council of H.M. Circuit Judges on the Work and Organization of the Legal Profession* (1989).

[92] 'Bar claim on higher cost of Crown Court solicitors "absurd"', DT (9.6.89) 3; 'Solicitors attack Bar over reform proposals', FT (9.6.89); 'Law Society attacks judges' views on reforms', T (9.6.89); 'Solicitors turn up the heat on Bar and judiciary', FT (12.6.89) 14; 'Society Condemns Bar Response' (1989) 139 NLJ 819; Law Society (1989c).

[93] T (24.5.89) 17; 'A loaded verdict', G (24.5.89) 22; Hugo Young, 'The judges try some impolitic politicking', G (25.5.89) 19.

[94] Lord Benson, 'The character of a profession', FT (31.5.89); 'Letters to the editor' (9.6.89); 'Law Lord blames reform proposals on cost-cutting', FT (1.6.89); 'Judge warns of lower standards', T (1.6.89); 'Don't Follow Us says US', LSG (7.6.89) 6–7; 'Ackner Sees Money as Green Papers Motive', LSG (7.6.89) 6–7; 'Poor "Lose Out" in Contingency Fees Lottery', LSG (7.6.89) 6–7.

[95] Lord Hailsham, 'The Future Roles of Solicitors and Barristers', *Private Investor* (Summer 1989) 17.

[96] Walter Merricks claimed that the Law Society had leaked that threat (interview July 1998).

[97] 'Militant judges turn back Mackay', L (27.6.89); 'Considering a change of heart', FT (27.6.89); 'Mackay to retreat on shake-up', G (29.6.89) 1; 'Mackay to soften legal reforms', T (29.6.89) 1; 'Mackay to bow to judges' warnings', DT (29.6.89); 'Judges throw down gauntlet to the Lord Chancellor', I (30.6.89) 2; 'All over amid the Bar shouting?' G (30.6.89) 22; 'Law man shot down at the Bar', DM (30.6.89); 'Lord Lane may be in group with veto over advocates', G (1.7.89); 'Judges to get veto on reforms', T (3.7.89); 'In retreat', ES (4.7.89); 'Hold firm on law reform', FT (4.7.89); 'Mackay bows to pressure from the Bar', I (6.7.89); 'Loss of battle', ES (6.7.89); 'Pressure group for privilege', DM (7.7.89) 6; 'New concessions on legal changes', I (7.7.89); 'Mackay's Threatened Backdown Pleases No-one' (1989) 139 NLJ 927; 'Green Paper politics' (1989) 139 NLJ 925.

[98] 'Mackay bows to pressure from the Bar', I (6.7.89); 'Thatcher "to give way" on law reform', T (6.7.89); 'New concessions on legal changes', I (7.7.89) 1; 'Revised plans on the Bar due soon', FT (7.7.89); 'Mackay gives details of revised law reform plans', DT (7.7.89); 'Mackay compromises vetted', T (7.7.89); 'Mackay begins law climbdown', G (7.7.89); 'Mackay's Threatened Back-down Pleases No-one' (1989) 139 NLJ 927; 'Government to publish revised plans', T (8.7.89); 'Cabinet meeting to decide on Mackay retreat', L (11.7.89); 'Law reforms win approval in Cabinet', T (13.7.89) 1; 'Changes to law reform ease fears', DT (13.7.89) 1; 'Bar climbdown backed', G (13.7.89) 1; 'Cabinet agrees strategy for reshaping legal profession', I (18.7.89); 'Government aims to smash cartels', I (19.7.89) 1; 'Professions to come under new anti-competition scrutiny', G (19.7.89); 'New law will tackle post-war legacy of restrictive practices', I (19.7.89) 3; DTI (1989); Lawson (1992: 621).

[99] Lord Chancellor (1989).

[100] Merricks recalled: 'We had to say three cheers for the rights of audience proposals, conveyancing proposals, oh dear. Actually, we reckoned that we had won on conveyancing and we'd lost on rights of audience' (interview July 1998). Hayes confirmed that Merricks advised the Society to 'assume that these reforms will provoke a truly antagonistic hysterical response in the Bar. The Law Society should position itself with the Government by saying we broadly welcome it' (interview July 1998). Holland (then Deputy Vice President) concurred: 'We had Mackay speak in '88 and everyone was cheering. You know, I could have got up and kissed the bloke when he made his speech at the Cardiff Law Conference...and then the Green Paper...I was so happy, I'd have gone there and then to sign up to it' (interview July 1998).

[101] Sir Richard Gaskell, 'Statement from the Law Society's President', LSG (19.7.89); 'Bar Reaction: Package "complicated and costly" ', T (20.7.89) 5; 'Attack by Bar: Giving the public access to "more expensive jack of all trades" ', T (20.7.89) 6; 'Mackay takes softer line on law reform', G (20.7.89) 1; 'Watchdog welcomes proposed shake-up', I (20.7.89) 4; 'Real obstacles are being ignored', I (20.7.89) 4; 'Law Society reaction: Solicitors to press on for reforms', T (20.7.89) 5; 'Courageous willingness to listen', I (20.7.89) 4; 'Law reform: how Mackay could satisfy everyone', T (20.7.89) 14; 'Labour speaks of climbdown while Tories and peers welcome compromise', T (20.7.89) 5; 'Peers welcome Mackay's changes', T (20.7.89); 'Cautious welcome for revised programme', FT (20.7.89); 'Mackay has to strike a delicate balance', FT (20.7.89); 'Law Society Reaction' (1989) 139 NLJ 998; 'Bar's Response' (1989) 139 NLJ 998; 'Conveyancing is too important to be left to the professionals', G (22.7.89) 15; 'Laying down the law on conveyancing', DT (22.7.89); 'Joseph dreaming of DIY for all', T (22.7.89); 'Bar united against Mackay plans', I (24.7.89); Nicholas Stewart QC, 'Found Wanting' (1989) 139 NLJ 1035; 'General Relief at White Paper Proposals' (1989) 133 SJ 952; 'Concessions fail to stem debate over poaching', FT (31.7.89) 12; 'White Paper a missed opportunity', T (1.8.89) 26; 'Judicial case for solicitor-advocates', I (23.8.89).

[102] 'Victory to the Lord of Justice', ES (19.7.89) 1; 'A judicial White Paper', I (20.7.89) 24; 'Reform but not the whole hog', DM (20.7.89) 6; 'The Mackay Compromise', T (20.7.89) 15; 'Lord Mackay holds firm', FT (20.7.89) 24; 'Reforms welcome', DT (20.7.89) 20; 'A bold reform is fudged away', G (20.7.89) 22;

'Pressure by the Bar fails to halt Mackay's sweeping changes', T (20.7.89) 1; 'Plan to Alter British Law Practice Is Softened a Bit', NYT (20.7.89) A7; 'Proposals retain main thrust of Mackay's changes', I (20.7.89) 4; 'Defeat for Bar on rights of audience', I (20.7.89) 1; 'Consumers victory in legal shake-up', DM (20.7.89); 'Restrictive practices among lawyers still face broad reform', FT (20.7.89); 'Calm air at the centre of a judicial storm', FT (21.7.89); A.H. Hermann, 'Letter to the editor', FT (21.7.89); 'Hats off to Mackay's legal reforms', G (21.7.89) 23; 'Lord Chancellor wins his case', O (23.7.89) 14; 'Securing quality and independence in law', FT (24.7.89); 'Self-interest threatens white paper proposals', FT (24.7.89) 16; 'Mackay holds firm on reform package', L (25.7.89) 1; 'Plenty to play for as legal reforms creep closer', I (25.8.89).

[103] 'White Paper Continues the Thrust of Lord Mackay's Reforms' (1989) 133 SJ between 926 and 927; 'The Lord Chancellor Triumphs' (1989) 139 NLJ 997; 'Mackay—with one bound he was free', L (25.7.89); 'A Sense of Relief' (1989) 133 SJ 951; 'Keeping a Low Profile' (1989) 133 SJ 1115; 'The Real McCoy', C (7–8.89) 3.

[104] 'Revolt of the Judges', DM (29.9.89) 1; 'Judges may insist on two-tier system', G (2.10.89) 20; 'Donaldson questions reform of solicitors', DT (2.10.89) 8; 'Solicitors may face veto', T (2.10.89) 1; 'Donaldson sets the tone for battle over rights of audience', I (2.10.89); 'Donaldson urges support for white paper', FT (2.10.89); 'Mackay may back curbs on solicitors' court role', T (3.10.89) 22; 'Master of the Rules?' T (3.10.89) 15; 'Judges Veto Threat Revived', LSG (4.10.89); 'Bar to reform', ES (13.10.89); 'The Master Proposes' (1989) 139 NLJ 1365; 'Mackay Answers Donaldson Criticism' (1989) 139 NLJ 1402.

[105] 'Bar fights for judges to decide advocacy rights', T (22.1.89); 'Stormy passage likely for legal profession overhaul', I (22.11.89); 'Restrictive practices to be swept away', DT (22.11.89); 'Bringing justice within the public's reach', G (22.11.89) 9; 'Profession and the work of civil courts to be streamlined', FT (22.11.89); 'Law Society's Strategy 1989 to 1990', LSG (29.11.89) 17; 'In Conversation', LSG (29.11.89) 14; Law Society (1991).

[106] 'Judges expected to give reform Bill a rough ride', T (8.12.89) 1; 'Lord Chancellor announces plans for biggest shake-up of century: Changes "herald new era for the county courts"', T (8.12.89) 28; 'Rights of audience: A key role for laymen', T (8.12.89) 38; 'Ombudsman: New post to check alleged mistakes', T (8.12.89) 38; 'Conveyancing: One-stop shopping plans for banks and building societies', T (8.12.89) 38; 'Massive shift of cases from High court to county courts', T (8.12.89) 38; 'Mackay urges "evolution" on law reforms', FT (8.12.89) 1; 'Solicitors able to answer calling to court', FT (8.12.89) 9; 'Barristers' rights go in strategic reform', G (8.12.89) 9; 'Wee Wee Free who started almighty row', G (8.12.89) 9; 'Legal split widens over bill to end monopoly', G (8.12.89) 1; 'Concessions ease advocacy fears', G (8.12.89) 9; 'Mackay unveils reforms to solve long dispute over rights of audience', DT (8.12.89) 4; 'Solicitors welcome changes', DT (8.12.89); 'Mackay hails "significant step in legal evolution"', I (8.12.89) 7; 'Changes are "vital part of improving access to justice"', I (8.12.89) 7; 'Bar Sees no End to Battle', LSG (13.12.89) 3; 'The Bar Lashes Out at Courts Bill' (1989) 139 NLJ 1698; 'Too high a price for justice', T (9.1.90) 28; Roger Smith, 'Another gang of four', LA (1.90) 7.

[107] T (8.12.89) 15; 'Adding up the Bill', G (8.12.89) 22; 'As We Were' (1989) 139 NLJ 1697.

[108] 513: 963–4 (6.12.89); 514: 122–248 (19.12.89), 520–628 (16.1.90), 927–1047 (23.1.90), 1166–1287 (25.1.90); 515: 32–120 (29.1.90), 421–508 (1.2.90), 528–687 (5.2.90), 1250–1 (13.2.90); 516: 190–266 (20.2.90), 390–500 (22.2.90), 834–949 (1.3.90), 1652–1749 (15.3.90).

[109] 514: 122–9 (19.12.89).

[110] 514: 1166–75 (25.1.90); 516: 1756–8 (15.3.90).

[111] 514: 176–81 (19.12.89), 114–20 (29.1.90); 516: 864–83 (1.3.90); ' "American system" law reform warning', DT (30.1.90) 11.

[112] 514: 198–200 (19.12.89).

[113] 514: 203–7 (19.12.89); 516: 1758–60 (15.3.90).

[114] 516: 1761–4 (15.3.90).

[115] 514: 211–16 (19.12.89).

[116] 514: 122–9, 159–62, 235–41 (19.12.89).

[117] 514: 150–4, 203–7, 217–20 (19.12.89); 516: 1758–60 (15.3.90).

[118] 514: 1240–64 (25.1.90); 515: 680–2 (5.2.90); 516: 478–84 (22.2.90), 932–5 (1.3.90), 1761–4 (15.3.90).

[119] 514: 203–7, 211–16, 235–41 (19.12.89), 1166–75, 1240–64 (25.1.90); 516: 1764–5 (15.3.90).

[120] 514: 176–81, 211–20 (19.12.89), 1166–75 (25.1.90); 515: 46–61 (29.1.90).

[121] 514: 133–7, 174–6, 188–90, 193–8 (19.12.89); 515: 46–61 (29.1.90).

[122] 514: 154–7, 181–4, 220–2, 226–30 (19.12.89).

[123] 514: 176–81 (19.12.89), 1166–75 (25.1.90); 515: 421–3 (1.2.90); 'Rawlinson attacks legal reforms Bill', T (26.1.90) 15.

[124] 514: 202–3 (19.12.89).

[125] 514: 133–7, 198–200 (19.12.89), 1166–75 (25.1.90).

[126] 514: 174–6 (19.12.89); 516: 1756–8 (15.3.90).

[127] 514: 150–4, 181–4, 200–2 (19.12.89), 1231–40, 1260–4, 1266–9, 1280 (25.1.90); 516: 1758–60 (15.3.90).

[128] 514: 1166–75, 1231–40 (25.1.90); 516: 247–8 (20.2.90).

[129] 514: 133–7, 176–81, 211–20 (19.12.89); 515: 496–500 (1.2.90).

[130] 514: 169–72, 174–6, 203–7, 235–41 (19.12.89), 1166–75 (15.1.90).

[131] 514: 150–4 (19.12.89), 515: 32–46 (29.1.90); 'Peers criticise plan for CPS lawyers', I (30.1.90).

[132] 514: 172–4, 184–90 (19.12.89); 515: 46–61 (29.1.90).

[133] 514: 176–81 (Lord Rawlinson), 233–5 (Lord Hooson) (19.12.89) 515: 46–61 (Lord Simon) (29.1.90); 516: 1754–6 (Lord Renton), 1758–60 (Lord Ackner) (15.3.90).

[134] 514: 233–5 (19.12.89).

[135] 514: 174–6 (19.12.89).

[136] 514: 203–7, 217–20, 233–5 (19.12.89); 515: 46–61 (29.1.90).

[137] 514: 172–4, 176–81, 190–3 (19.12.89).

[138] 514: 150–4, 176–81 (19.12.89); 515: 528–58 (5.2.90); 'Peers attack "conditional fee" proposal', T (6.2.90).

[139] 516: 1726–35 (15.3.90).

[140] 514: 146–54, 203–7 (19.12.89).

[141] 514: 133–7, 150–4 (19.12.89), 1215–19 (25.1.90); 516: 229–30 (20.2.90).

[142] 514: 159–62, 174–6 (19.12.89), 1175–84 (25.1.90).

[143] 514: 207–9, 217–20, 233–5 (19.12.89), 1166–75 (25.1.90); 515: 421–3 (1.2.90).

[144] 514: 176–81 (19.12.89); 515: 46–61 (29.1.90).

[145] 516: 851–5 (1.3.90), 1736–40 (15.3.90).

[146] 514: 1280–1 (25.1.90); 515: 32–61, 103–11 (29.1.90); 516: 398–419 (22.2.90).

[147] 514: 1190–1210 (25.1.90).

[148] 515: 605–7 (5.2.90).

[149] 516: 190–216 (20.2.90); 'Taking Sides' (1990) 140 NLJ 157; 'NCC Want New Role for Law Society' (1990) 134 SJ 205; Andrew Hall, 'We Say No and We Mean No!' (1990) 140 NLJ 284; Brian Raymond, 'The Profession's Duty to Provide: a Solicitor's Right to Choose' (1990) 140 NLJ 285; David Latham QC, 'Solicitors and the Cab Rank Rule' (1990) 140 NLJ 286 (quoting Woolcott, 1954: 290); 'Where to, guv?' G (7.3.90) 23; 'Donaldson Advocates General Application of Cab-rank Rule', LSG (28.2.90) 3; 'Cab Rank Rule for Solicitors' (1990) 140 NLJ 279; David Ward, 'Any Cab will Do', LSG (28.3.90) 2; 'NCC Opposes Cab Rank', LSG (28.3.90) 3.

[150] 514: 162–6, 190–3 (19.12.89); 516: 390–3 (22.2.90).

[151] 516: 834–44 (1.3.90).

[152] 515: 114–20 (29.1.90), 422–7, 444–8, 452–70, 484–6, 496–502 (1.2.90). Merricks recalled: 'I think we played a very careful hand, and I'd say quite subtle game, on conveyancing in first of all planting within the bill and getting assurances about what the regulations would contain' (interview July 1998).

[153] 515: 664–9 (5.2.90).

[154] 516: 919–22 (1.3.90), 1742–5 (15.3.90).

[155] 516: 1718–26 (15.3.90).

[156] 515: 607–20 (5.2.90).

[157] 515: 620–2 (5.2.90); 516: 845–51 (1.3.90).

[158] 515: 680–2 (5.2.90); 516: 939–44 (1.3.90), 1748–9 (15.3.90).

[159] 514: 174–6, 203–7 (19.12.89); 515: 638–40 (5.2.90); 516: 893–903 (1.3.90), 1756–8, 1764–5 (15.3.90).

[160] 515: 625–8 (5.2.90); 516: 887–903 (1.3.90).

[161] 514: 122–9 (19.12.89); 516: 912–17 (1.3.90).

[162] 514: 154–7, 181–4 (19.12.89).

[163] 516: 262–6 (20.2.90), 1670–7 (15.3.90).

[164] 'The Bill moves on', LA (4.90) 4; 'Hustle and hassle in the Lords', T (10.4.90).

[165] 'Courts Bill Battle Recommences in Commons' (1990) 140 NLJ 506; 'The Final Rounds' (1990) 140 NLJ 505; Anthony Scrivener QC, 'Defending Legal Services', C (5.90) 19–20.

[166] 'Justice for All', T (19.4.90) 13; 'Time to break up the party', G (23.4.90) 18.

[167] 170: 1442–1524 (18.4.90); 177: 509–641 (25.7.90).

[168] 170: 1442–6 (18.4.90).

[169] 170: 1452–60, 1504–6, 1512–18 (18.4.90).

[170] 170: 1488–92, 1501–6, 1519–21 (18.4.90).

[171] 170: 1462–7 (18.4.90).

[172] 170: 1495–7 (18.4.90).

[173] 170: 1485–8, 1492–7, 1507–12 (18.4.90).

[174] 170: 1462–7, 1485–8, 1495–7 (18.4.90).

[175] 170: 1462–7 (Peter Archer), 1467–72 (Ivan Lawrence), 1472–6 (Alex Carlile), 1481–5 (Dennell Davies), 1492–3 (Malins), 1493–5 (Bermingham), 1506–7 (Michael Irvine) (18.4.90).

[176] 170: 1476–81, 1485–8 (18.4.90).

[177] 177: 600–3 (25.7.90).

[178] I (12.2.90); Sir David Napley, 'Questions on a choice issue', T (17.4.90) 26; 'Court intrigues', G (18.4.90); Michael Zander, 'The Myth of the Cab Rank' (1990) 140 NLJ 558; 'The "Cab Rank" Illusion' (1990) 134 SJ 499; 'Cab-Rank Rule Loses its Sting', LSG (9.5.90) 3; 'Bar's Welcome for Cab-Rank Amendment' (1990) 140 NLJ 654; 'New "Cab-Rank" Amendment Tabled' (1990) 134 SJ 524; ' "Cab-Rank" rule strengthened by Bar Council', DT (26.5.90) 16; 'Cab-Rank: Bar Tightens Rules on Legal Aid Cases', LSG (30.5.90) 3; 'Bar fails NCC test', LA (5.90) 4; Anthony Scrivener QC, 'Defending Legal Services', C (5.90) 19–20; 'Bar Cab-Rank Moves' (1990) 140 NLJ 770; 'Bar tightens cab-Rank', LA (7.90) 6; 'Cab Rank Rule—Amended Again?' (1990) 140 NLJ 1487; 'Of Briefs and Listing' (1990) 140 NLJ 1507.

[179] 170: 1445–7, 1452–60, 1476–81, 1492–3 (18.4.90).

[180] 177: 594–6 (25.7.90).

[181] 170: 1452–60 (18.4.90).

[182] 170: 1452–60 (Morris), 1472–6 (Carlile), 1492–3 (Malins), 1493–5 (Bermingham), 1495–7 (Grant), 1501–4 (Bruce) (18.4.90); 'Tory revolt threat forces "climbdown" by Rifkind', I (5.7.90); 'Politics Prompts Scots Bill Climb-down', LSG (11.7.90) 3.

[183] 177: 551–7 (25.7.90).

[184] 177: 606–7 (25.7.90).

[185] 170: 1445–6, 1497–9, 1500–6, 1521–4 (18.4.90).

[186] 170: 1488–92 (18.4.90); 177: 561–76 (25.7.90).

[187] 177: 577–91 (25.7.90); 'Writ large', G (11.4.90); 'Chancellor heralds law on job bias for lawyers', T (19.4.90); 'Solicitors will have to accept "cab rank" rule', T (19.4.90); 'Sex and race discrimination law will extend to cover Bar', T (19.4.90) 3; ' "Cab rank" rule to be accepted', DT (19.4.90); 'Bar victory on "cab rank" rule', DT (19.4.90); 'Cash crisis "threat to legal reforms" ', DT (19.4.90); 'Barristers to be covered by anti-discrimination law', I (19.4.90); ' "Cab rank" rule for solicitors', G (19.4.90); 'Labour backs the Bar', LA (5.90) 4.

[188] 'Lawyers opposed move to end legal aid choice', T (15.5.90) 2; 'Curb on legal aid options sparks protest', T (16.5.90) 5; 'Campaign against representation curbs', LSG (16.5.90) 4; 'Attempt to Deny Lawyer Choice Attacked' (1990) 140 NLJ 691; 'Major Clash Pending over Courts Bill?' (1990) 134 SJ 584; Anthony Thornton QC, 'Amending the price of justice', T (12.6.9) 38; 'Legal Services Bill: Focus on legal aid representation', LSG (13.6.90) 8; Lord Mackay, 'The best aid money can buy', T (19.6.90); 'Government Backs Representation Choice', LSG (20.6.90) 3; 'Clause 31 Here to Stay' (1990) 140 NLJ 878; 'Scheme to end duplication of lawyers proves a failure', T (8.8.90) 20; 'Lawyers defeat plan to cut legal aid costs', DT (16.8.90) 6; 'Limits on legal aid could cut "needless" two-lawyer cases', T (16.8.90); 'A Surfeit of Lawyers', T (16.8.90) 11; 'Lo! they come with crowds attending', G (17.8.90) 18; 'Letters to the editor', T (21.8.90); 'Letters to the editor', G (27.8.90).

[189] HC Standing Committee D, Minutes of Proceedings on the Courts and Legal Services Bill [Lords] (8, 10, 15, 17, 22 and 24 May; 5, 7, 12 and 19 June); 'Time to break up the party', G (23.4.90) 18; 'Barristers to dominate legal reform committee', L (1.5.90); 'The Bar is on trial for abuse of privilege', O (13.5.90) 18; 'Solicitors move to limit top judges' veto power', T (24.5.90) 6; 'MPs defeat Bill amendment on "eating dinners"', L (29.5.90); 'Writ large', G (30.5.90) 23; Austin Mitchell, 'Decoy or representative of the people?', G (6.6.90).

[190] 522: 1383–1435 (24.10.90).

[191] HL 522: 1903 (1.11.90); HC 178: 1087 (1.11.90). Twelve years later Parliament decided to begin debates at 11:30am instead of 2:30pm and end at 7:30pm—after a nine-hour debate ending at midnight! 'Britain: No More Late Nights for Parliament', NYT (1.11.02) A6.

[192] 'Editorial: No bangs, only whimpers', LA (7.90) 3; Roger Smith, 'Time-bomb set to go off over barristers' exclusivity', I (6.7.90); 'Solicitors' chief takes on critics of legal changes', T (16.7.90); 'Little to please profession in coming measure on courts', FT (30.7.90); Marcel Berlins, 'Law Reform Is an Ass', S (4.8.90) 18; Robert Rice, 'Law reforms fail on appeal', FT (20.8.90); Frances Gibb, 'Much ado about concession', T (21.8.90); 'AGM Bar None', LSG (7.11.90) 6; Geoffrey Bindman, 'Solicitors, Barristers, or Just Plain Lawyers' (1990) 140 NLJ 1712; 'Justinian', 'Time is ripe for reform', FT (31.12.90).

[193] Tony Holland, 'A New Decade, a New Service', LSG (18.10.90) 2; 'October Refrain' (1990) 140 NLJ 1445; 'MDPs "Inevitable" Warning', LSG (24.10.90) 5.

[194] 'Chairman of the Sales Force' (1990) 140 NLJ 1632; 'Charismatic Chief for Bar', LSG (12.12.90) 10; Peter Cresswell QC, 'The Way Ahead for the Profession', LSG (12.12.90) 15.

[195] Lord Ackner, ' "Oh to be in Scotland…!" ' C (12.90) 15.

[196] 'Cosy cartels or guardians of liberty?' T (23.4.90).

[197] Mark Sheldon, 'The Client's Champion', LSG (22.5.90) 2.

Chapter 3—Notes

[1] I discuss theories of the professions more extensively in Abel (1979; 1988: chap. 1; 1994).

[2] This historical synopsis is based on Abel (1986; 1988: chaps. 2, 3, 10).

[3] 'Where Have All the Young Ones Gone? An Analysis of the Recruitment Crisis' (1987) 84 LSG 875–6; 'The Recruitment Crisis' (1987) 84 LSG 1454; 'John Wickerson, 'President's Column' (1987) 84 LSG 1775; 'Law Society Sets Up Recruitment Group' (1987) 84 LSG 3300. On articles see Ormrod (1971); Zander (1988: 84); on pupillage see Pannick (1993: 208–9). This paragraph draws on Abel (1989); see also Bradney and Cownie (2000).

[4] 'Statistical Report 1987' (1987) 84 LSG 2446.

[5] Law Society (1988c).

[6] 'New College of Law for York', LSG (24.2.88) 5; John Wickerson, 'President's Column', LSG (25.5.88) 2.

[7] Marre Committee (1988: paras. 13.29, 14.58, 15.10).

[8] DT (11.7.88) 7; Peter Scott QC, 'Progress Towards Major Changes', C (Easter/Spring 1987) 22; Professional Standards Committee, 'Recruitment to the Bar', C (Easter/Spring 1987) 35–6.

[9] 'Schooled for skills', LA (7.90) 8; compare Johnston and Shapland (1990: 49) with Shapland *et al.* (1993: 31–3, 37–41); Shapland and Sorsby (1995: 55–6); but see Shapland and Sorsby (1998: 73); Shiner and Newburn (1995: 106–12, 116–17).

[10] 'Bar Moves to Boost Recruitment' LSG (19.4.89) 7; 'Chambers to fund pupils' income', T (4.7.89); 'Barristers endorse own reforms', FT (4.7.89); 'Barristers back pay for recruits', G (4.7.89); 'Bar Council gives £3.5 million boost to chamber trainees', T (19.7.90); 'Bar to pay trainee barristers salaries of at least £6,000', T (11.12.89); 'Bar agrees to pay fixed £6,000 to 450 trainees', T (29.1.90); Johnston and Shapland (1990: 55).

[11] 'Taking an outside seat', T (4.7.89); '£1/2 million Bar Library places find few takers', L (10.2.91); 'Barristers face facilities threat', DT (23.9.91); 'Practising Library to Close' C (9–10.91) 5; 'Bar Practising Library System Fails' (1991) 141 NLJ 1322; 'A Short Step from the Temple' C (7.91) 8; 'No place like home for work', T (28.4.92). On competition for tenancies see Shapland *et al.* (1995: 49–51); Shapland and Sorsby (1998: 75). BC chair Robert Seabrook conceded the Bar library 'could really not fit with the culture we have here because it effectively became yet another set of chambers and inevitably was seen as a very third-rate set because they were people who couldn't get other sets' (interview, July 1998).

[12] ' "The worst experience of my life" ', I (27.7.90) 27; 'Bar plans selection system for entry', T (18.6.91); 'Closing the Open Door' C (6.91) 14; 'Bar "quota" training scheme attacked', T (21.12.92); 'Bar offers to scrap law student quotas', T (4.1.93); 'Fair Trading Chief Rejects Bar Training Plans', LSG (6.1.93) 7; 'Time Limit on Admissions Scheme' C (2.93) 5; 'Tougher Bar selection due', L (2.3.93); 'Bar study into future demand for lawyers', L (9.3.93); Richard Southwell QC, 'Continuing Professional Development' C (3.93) 14–15; 'Curbs on barrister training', DT (22.4.93); 'This Week in the Law' (1993) 137 SJ 364; 'Bar cuts law trainees', T (27.4.93); 'Bar Cuts Back on Finals Students', LSG (28.4.93) 7; 'New CLE entry procedure', L (4.5.93); 'Training for Justice' C (7.93) 3; 'Action urged to cut Bar

students', I (4.10.93); 'Shrunken market squeezes the Bar', L (12.10.93); 'All trained up and nowhere to go', G (12.10.93) 23; 'Facing the Future' (1993) 143 NLJ 1429; 'Boom and Bust' (1993) 143 NLJ 1725. Research confirmed that only about half of those who passed the BVC exam obtained a pupillage and almost all of those obtained a tenancy. Shapland and Sorsby (1995: 13).

[13] 'Will the Bar face collapse?', T (16.11.93) 35; 'Survival Plan for Young Barristers', LSG (17.11.93) 8; 'The Challenge for the Bar' C (11–12.93) 8; Robert Seabrook QC, 'Chairman's Column: The Changing Legal Landscape' C (1–2.94) 3; Sir Frederick Lawton, 'Crisis at the Bar', LSG (6.1.94) 9; compare Bar Council Joint Working Party (1993) with Shapland and Sorsby (1995: 40–2, 46–9, 68–70); Shiner (1997: 117).

[14] 'Extra Hurdle for Bar School Hopefuls' C (1–2.94) 6; 'Competition is a bar to a job for life', I (7.1.94) 31; 'Trainees face hard times', I (7.1.94) 31; 'Bar releases exam marks to mollify failed law students', T (15.4.94); 'Students threaten legal action against Bar law school', T (23.4.94); 'Bar Finals Selection', LSG (23.4.94) 4; 'CLE Admissions Controversy' (1994) 144 NLJ 414; 'CLE Admissions' C (3–4.94) 4; 'Universities "outraged" by Bar school selection', I (3.5.94); 'Rejected students take Bar to court', T (3.5.94); 'Judge allows challenge to Bar', T (4.5.94); 'Inns Review', LSG (4.5.94) 4; 'Test case student wins first round', L (10.5.94); 'Bar school admits 250 failed students', T (2.6.94); '250 More Students Admitted to Bar Vocational Course' (1994) 144 NLJ 747; 'Bar school gives extra 250 places', T (3.6.94); 'An Appeal to Reason', T (8.6.94); 'Bar Students Taste Victory', LSG (8.6.94) 8; 'Bar School in the Dock over Selection Policies', LSG (27.7.94) 7; 'Law Course Criticised' (1994) 138 SJ 784; 'CLE Places Defeat for Students' (1994) 144 NLJ 1087.

[15] 'Universities may end Bar monopoly on training', T (8.6.94); 'Bar to Abolish CLE Monopoly' (1994) 138 SJ 564; 'Bar widens training', T (13.6.94); 'Hoffman predicts end of CLE training monopoly', L (14.6.94); 'Bar's Start', LSG (15.6.94) 12; 'Students win Bar places', T (16.6.94); Sir Frederick Lawton, 'One Law for the rich…', T (12.7.94); 'CLE Monopoly to End' C (7–8.94) 4; 'School monopoly over', L (4.10.94); 'Chambers of horrors story', T (15.11.94); 'Bar Studies Course Validation Scheme', LSG (22.3.95) 5; 'Bar Scuppers Deal with Law College', LSG (28.6.95) 6; 'Finals Course Validation Picks Up Support', LSG (26.7.95) 5; Peter Goldsmith QC, 'Chairman's Column: A Reputation for Ability' C (9–10.95) 3.

[16] 'Venerable practice on a plate', I (29.3.92); 'Writ large', G (29.1.92) 21; 'Slimmed down barrister rule', L (23.3.93); 'Aspiring barristers face big dinner bill in training reforms', T (16.7.96) 4; 'Bar Seven', LSG (24.7.96) 10; Martin Bowley QC, 'Dining out on student worries', T (20.7.96) 35; 'Reduced Dining Requirement' C (11–12.96) 6; 'Inns of Court scrap medieval dinner rule for Bar students', T (10.3.97) 8; 'Comment: Coming to Terms with Keeping Terms' C (3–4.97) 14.

[17] 'Solicitors and barristers "should train together"' T (21.3.94) 1; 'Learning the Law', T (21.3.94) 19; 'Judge Proposes Fused Training', LSG (23.3.94) 5; 'Bar Split over Joint Training Proposals' (1994) 138 SJ 275; 'Joint Training Plan', LSG (13.4.94) 4; 'Bar moves to scrap monopoly of training', T (22.4.94); 'Joint Schools', T (22.4.94).

[18] 'Women suffer sex harassment when training for the Bar', DT (6.2.95); 'Briefs' I (8.2.95); 'Outlook for the Bar' (1995) 139 SJ 107; 'Fighting to the death for a

place in chambers', T (14.2.95); 'Compass points way ahead for pupil selection', L (21.2.95); 'A fair hearing for pupil barristers', T (23.5.95); 'Student plan given boost', LSG (26.7.95) 5; 'Pupillage Clearing House' C (9–10.95) 5; Michael Beloff QC and Helen Mountfield, 'A Just and Convenient System' C (9–10.95) 14; 'There's a crush at the Bar, let's leave', I (15.11.95) §2, 12; Shapland and Sorsby (1995: 13; 1998b); 'Pupillage Upgrade', LSG (19.6.96) 4; 'Bar students vote to boycott trainee scheme', T (31.10.96) 11; 'The battle for the Bar', T (5.11.96) 41; David Penry-Davey QC, 'Chairman's Column: Issues Facing the Bar' C (11–12.96) 3; Shiner (1997: 121); 'New PACH Regulations—Early Offers' BN (4.99) 16; 'Letters to the Editor: PACH', C (4.99) 8.

[19] ACLEC (1995; 1996: 43–5); Lord Hoffman (1995); Hepple (1996: 20); 'Common Training Beckons Again', LSG (1.5.96) 10; 'Editorial: New School', LSG (1.5.96) 14; 'Joint Training Mooted', LSG (13.12.96) 12; 'Bar Aims to Welcome Solicitors', LSG (9.6.99) 5; 'Training to Rectify Weaknesses' (1999) 143 SJ 552; 'Collyear Committee', BB (7.99) 5; Susan Ward, 'Letter from the Chairman', BB (7.99) 2.

[20] 1 NN (9.97) 5–6; 'Unanimous Support for Equal Ops Code' (1997) 141 SJ 589; 'Bar Council Meeting Berates Inns of Court over Equal Opportunities', LSG (25.6.97) 8; General Council of the Bar, *Annual Report* (1997); 2 NN (2.98); 'Glut of law graduates see career chances fall', T (15.4.98) 6; Martin Bowley QC, 'Repaying Professional Debts' (1998) 148 NLJ 957; Response by ENPBA to the LCD Consultation Document (23.8.98); Shapland and Sorsby (1998a: 22, 28, 101–5).

[21] Derek Wheatley QC, 'Awaiting a call to the Bar', T (21.5.96) 39; 'A fierce fight at the Bar', I (22.5.96) 24; 'Bar Battle', LSG (5.6.96) 5; 'Bar Urged to Throw Out "Discriminatory" Deferred Call Proposal' (1996) 140 SJ 548; David Penry-Davey QC, 'Chairman's Column: "We Never Closed" ' C (7–8.96) 3; Nigel Bastin, 'Survival of the Fittest' C (10.99) 28–9; Derek Wheatley QC, 'Few Are Chosen' C (12.99) 28; BC (1999: 3, 6) (emphasis in original). In July 1998 Hallett said 'there's too many law graduates...I understood when I took over this job that the problem was that we had too many barristers who weren't good enough...I was also very conscious that we had too many people doing the Bar Vocational Course who couldn't then get pupillage. So I asked the education and training department to start looking at how we could tighten up on our standards and look at things like should we defer Call until after you've done your pupillage....; (interview).

[22] 'Bar is in danger of return to elitist era', T (12.10.98) 8; 'Not guilty plea on "fat cat" charge', T (12.10.98) 8; 'Bar Fund', LSG (25.11.98) 10; 'Fund for a bright star in memory of another', T (1.6.99) 37; Martin Bowley QC, 'Comment: From Each According to his Means' (1999) 149 NLJ 1465; 'Irvine warns of rich elite', T (11.10.99) 12; 'Progressive Bar—a Part of the Solution' (1999) 149 NLJ 1506; 'Irvine Gets Tough on "Exclusivity" ' (1999) 143 SJ 944; Bar Council Working Party on Financing (1998: 27, 48–9, 67–8); 'Legal diary', T (13.7.99) 43; 'Legal diary', T (3.8.99) 21; 'Judge to Decide Whether Pupillages should be Funded' (1999) 143 SJ 777; 'Trainee barrister asks to be paid', G (21.9.99) 5; 'Minimum pay claim by trainee barrister', T (21.9.99) 6; Letter from Dan Brennan QC to Heads of Chambers (24.9.99); 'Pupil barrister wins case for minimum wage', G (25.9.99) 8; 'Trainees win', T (25.9.99) 4; 'Trainee barrister wins claim over pay', FT (25–26.9.99) 8; 'Minimum pay for lawyers', T (30.9.99) 2; 'Law trainee wage',

T (7.10.99) 25; Dan Brennan QC, 'Modern Bar: Strong Future' C (10.99) 6–7; 'Landmark Case for Pupil Wages' C (10.99) 8; BC Education and Training Department, *Interim Guidance on the Application of the National Minimum Wage* (10.11.99); *Edmons v Lawson* [2000], unreported, 10 March, CA. Even Sir Stephen Sedley declared the Bar 'cannot hold its door perpetually open. A point will have to come, indeed probably has been reached, at which the numbers admitted to the BVC have to correspond with what the Bar can realistically absorb'. 'Anti-competitive or not, sanction will need to be given to a negotiated cut-off....' Sedley (2000: 4).

²³ LS Training Committee (1988; 1990); 'Polys Push for CPE Course', LSG (14.2.90) 5; 'A Final Solution' (1990) 134 SJ 295; 'College of Law Predicts Further Drop in Standards', LSG (25.4.90) 6; 'Law colleges start night classes as demand soars', T (3.5.90); 'Law Society Votes on Training Changes' (1990) 140 NLJ 690; 'Must Try Harder' (1990) 140 NLJ 689; 'Skills-based Education Approved', LSG (23.5.90) 4; 'Marking Time' (1990) 140 NLJ 729; 'Green Light for Training Changes' (1990) 140 NLJ 730; 'Extra Finals Places', LSG (24.4.91) 4; 'Law Places' (1991) 135 SJ 560.

²⁴ 'Withdrawal of Articles Prompt Inquiry', LSG (13.6.90) 3; 'Heads Down' (1990) 140 NLJ 1177; 'Lawyers feel the pinch as slump hits City firms', DT (21.9.90); 'Evidence Mounts of Jobs Crisis', LSG (10.10.90) 8; 'CPS scheme subject to 10-fold oversubscription', L (8.1.91); 'Solicitors losing jobs across the board as recession bites', T (29.1.91) 8; 'Woe Unto You, Lawyers!', T (29.1.91); 'Recruitment Fair Belies Gloom', LSG (13.2.91); 'Job outlook bleak for the profession', L (26.2.91); 'Slump boosts applicants for legal service', T (7.3.91); 'Trainee Contracts Warning', LSG (13.3.91) 7; 'Trainee Hotline Opens', LSG (20.3.91) 4; 'Withdrawals of Articles Up, TSG Warns' SJ (22.3.91) 33; 'Plea to save jobs of new solicitors', DT (4.7.91); 'Troubled City Firm Fights Back', LSG (10.7.91) 5; 'Solicitors queue up at the Bar', STel (21.7.91); 'Changes at DJ Freeman', LSG (28.8.91) 9; 'Sharp Drop in M&A Work', LSG (28.8.91) 3; Jenkins (1994: 3, 6, 8); Law Society Special Working Party on Conveyancing Services (1994: 6–9). City firms regularly hire many more assistants than they admit to partnership. Lee (2000).

²⁵ 'Sombre Mood at Law Fair', LSG (12.2.92) 10; 'Bristol Fair Favoured', LSG (11.3.92) 7; 'Redundancies at Clifford Chance', LSG (17.6.92) 5; 'Nabarro Lay-offs', LSG (22.10.92) 16; 'City Firm Lay-offs', LSG (4.11.92) 3; 'Twenty-nine Redundant at City Firm' (1992) 136 SJ 1073; 'One in a hundred', T (10.11.92) 33; 'Hardship prac-tically taken for granted', T (10.11.92) 33; 'London Lay-offs', LSG (2.12.92) 3; 'Sheldon Predicts Over-Supply of Trainees', LSG (2.12.92) 6; IFLR (2.93) 5.

²⁶ 'Grant Grief', LSG (20.1.93) 11; 'Poverty, Students and the Law' (1993) 143 NLJ 78; 'Comment: Training the Best and Brightest' (1993) 137 SJ 59; 'Law Student Lack of Cash Bites Harder' (1993) 137 SJ 163; 'Grants under review as law, drama and dance students pass up training', G (9.3.93); 'Cash-strapped Students Forced out of Law', LSG (18.3.93) 10; 'Students on grants "drop by a third"' L (24.3.93) 1; 'College Predicts £4500 fee for LPC', LSG (8.4.93) 3; 'Trainees get 7.5% Rise on Minimum Wage' (1993) 137 SJ 423; 'Donaldson Urges Grants for Finals', LSG (13.5.93) 6; 'Access to Funding' (1993) 137 SJ 445; 'Training for the Future' (1993) 143 NLJ 713; 'Government Signals Curbs on Exempting Degrees', LSG (2.6.93) 4; 'Trainees Lobby Hard on Grants', LSG (26.5.93) 4; 'Trainees' Trooper', LSG (2.6.93) 9; 'Ely Sounds

Warning on Access to Profession', LSG (24.6.93) 5; 'Student Challenge to Discretionary Grant Policy', LSG (13.10.93) 5; 'Taylor Pledge on Grants for Law Students' (1993) 137 SJ 1071; 'A profession reserved for the rich?', T (10.11.93) 33; 'Students Confront Local Authorities over Grants', LSG (1.12.93) 8; 'Grants Dwindle Away as Costs Rise', LSG (2.12.93) 6; College of Law, *Survey of Students Funding and Finance 1992/93* (1993); 'Grant Review', LSG (6.1.94) 6; 'Dramatic Fall in Student Grants', LSG (16.2.94) 6; 'TSG Steps Up the Pressure' (1994) 144 NLJ 311; 'Student Wins Grant Struggle', LSG (11.5.94) 5; 'Change Tack on Grants, Trainees Told', LSG (16.11.94) 7; Shiner and Newburn (1995: 42–4, 55, 74).

[27] 'Locals urge Law Soc to Scrap Pay Minimum' (1993) 137 SJ 31; 'Pressure Mounts On Trainee Salaries', LSG (27.1.93); 'Minimum Salaries should Stay say Young Solicitors', LSG (10.2.93) 8; 'YSG Takes Up Sword Over Trainees' Pay' (1993) 137 SJ 113; 'Recruitment Warning on Minimum Salaries', LSG (24.2.93) 10; 'Trainees Approve Salaries Package', LSG (24.3.93) 8; 'Key Vote Due on Salaries', LSG (9.6.93) 4; 'Council Retains Trainee Salary', LSG (16.6.93); 'Trainee Salary Minimum to Stay' (1993) 137 SJ 576; 'Harsh Lessons', LSG (17.11.93) 5.

[28] 'City Lay-offs', LSG (20.1.93) 11; 'Thirty Posts Go at Norton Rose', LSG (28.7.93) 4; 'Small Firms Fear for Future', LSG (26.11.93) 11; 'Patchy Recovery for Legal Job Market' (1993) 137 SJ 1256; 'City Cuts', LSG (26.1.94) 7; 'Lay-offs Strike Again in City', LSG (13.4.94) 7; 'Signs Point to Bright Future', LSG (13.7.94) 9; 'Recovery for Some', LSG (16.11.94) 10; Department of Environment (1994: Table 1.7); 'Job Market Brightens for 1996', LSG (17.4.96) 64; 'Survey Shows Good Job Prospects', LSG (22.5.96) 4; 'Job Hopes Improve', LSG (12.6.96) 5; 'Business Booms for Commercial Lawyers' (1996) 140 SJ 573; 'Mini-boom Sparks City Recruitment', LSG (2.10.96) 11; 'Australian Recruiters Hit London', LSG (2.10.96) 8; 'City Faces Famine of Fee-earners', LSG (30.10.96) 10; 'London Pay Surges Ahead', LSG (8.1.97) 1; 'M&A Earnings Rise for Law Firms', LSG (15.1.97) 9; Office for National Statistics (1998: Table 17.17); Valuation Office (1998: 38).

[29] 'Teachers Air Concerns over LPC Access', LSG (3.6.92) 8; 'Comment: New Course, No Hope' (1992) 136 SJ 643; 'Student Intake', LSG (7.10.92); Roger Smith, 'A Question of Training', LSG (19.5.93) 4; 'Popular Profession', LSG (19.5.93) 8; 'Testing Times', LSG (14.7.93) 10; 'Solicitor Jobs Gloom Continues', LSG (1.9.93) 7; 'Comment: Trainees' (1993) 137 SJ 959; 'Facing the Future' (1993) 143 NLJ 1429; 'Argument for End of Articles', LSG (3.11.93) 10; 'Old Course "Risks Obsolescence" ', LSG (1.12.93) 7; 'Society Moots Trainee Options', LSG (6.1.94) 6; 'Comment: Trainees' (1994) 138 SJ 35; 'Trainees Turn on the Heat', LSG (23.2.94) 6; 'Students Lobby MPs', LSG (2.3.94) 7; 'Society Shuns Trainee Quotas', LSG (9.3.94) 8; 'Trainees Could Get Flexi-contract', LSG (13.4.94) 4; 'Out of practice', G (3.5.94) 19; 'Hard Times Hit Course Take-up', LSG (4.5.94) 5; 'Student Anger Threat to Course Providers', LSG (22.6.94) 8; 'Results Boost for New Course', LSG (31.8.94) 4; Charles Elly, 'Service and Independence', LSG (7.10.94) 2; 'The Trials of Training', LSG (30.11.94) 24; Shiner and Newburn (1995: 44–5); Shiner (1997: p. vii, 51–2). For a devastating empirical critique of traineeships see Goriely and Williams (1996); but 80–90 per cent of trainees appear satisfied (if anxious about their prospects), Moorhead and Boyle (1995); see also Lee (1999: 62–3).

[30] 'For the Benefit of Law Students?' (1992) 142 NLJ 1689; 'College Cleared', LSG (27.1.93) 4; Nigel Savage, 'Why the monopoly?', T (6.12.94); 'Cut College

Link, Society Advised', LSG (7.12.94) 4; 'Professor Savages Law Society Link with College of Law' (1994) 144 NLJ 1687; 'Society to Weaken Links with College', LSG (5.7.94) 6; 'College Rights', LSG (19.7.95) 3.

[31] 'Thin Milk' (1995) 145 NLJ 41; 'Society Backs Free Market Approach to Course Places', LSG (1.2.95) 5; 'For the Record', LSG (1.2.95) 25; 'In the News' (1995) 145 NLJ 134; ' "No" to Limiting College Places Despite Unemployment' (1995) 139 SJ 103; 'Conflict over Course Places', LSG (22.2.95) 3; ' "Conflict of Interest" Claims over Training Committee Vote' (1995) 139 SJ 155; 'College of Law gets Extra LPC Places' (1995) 139 SJ 180; 'LPC Fails to Make Employer Impact', LSG (17.5.95) 6; 'College Backs a Free Market', LSG (13.7.95) 4.

[32] 'Trainees Criticise Quality of Articles', LSG (22.2.95) 6; 'Study Highlights Trainee Concerns', LSG (8.3.95) 7; 'Elly Leads Debt Campaign', LSG (8.3.95) 7; 'Trainees Prepared for Salary Conflict', LSG (26.4.95) 8; 'Salaries Stay', LSG (3.5.95) 72; 'Trainee Basic Pay Could be Ditched', LSG (1.5.96) 2; 'Salary Powers', LSG (6.11.96) 5; 'Uncertainty over Trainee Salaries', LSG (13.11.96) 5; 'Trainee Chair Focuses on Salaries', LSG (27.11.96) 6.

[33] 'Points for Paralegals', LSG (22.3.95) 8; 'ILEX Launches First Legal Services NVQ', LSG (29.11.95) 8; 'Agencies Consider Training', LSG (15.12.95) 8.

[34] 'Exeter puts Society through its paces', LSG (18.1.95) 4; 'Trainees Lash Out at LPC Proposals', LSG (26.7.95) 8; 'Letters to the Editor', LSG (13.9.95) 11; 'Trainees in Protest at Study Exclusion', LSG (20.9.95) 4; 'College of Law Offer "Attorney" Title' (1995) 139 SJ 1033; ' "Attorney" Title Attacked as Unlawful' (1995) 139 SJ 1059.

[35] 'Personality Testing Mooted for Entry', LSG (18.10.95) 2; 'Working Party Row', LSG (8.11.95) 6; 'Realism in the Top Job', LSG (22.11.95) 6.

[36] 'On the Training Ground', LSG (18.10.95) 9.

[37] 'Mears Urges Skills Test', LSG (10.1.96) 1; 'Facing Testing Times?', LSG (17.1.96) 10.

[38] 'Course Numbers Fall', LSG (15.12.95) 8; 'Student Fall Off', LSG (31.1.96) 5; 'Trainees Heed Warnings' (1996) 140 SJ 163; 'Student Numbers in Decline', LSG (28.2.96) 6.

[39] 'Debate Over Who Monitors', LSG (20.3.96) 5; ' "Protectionist" Stance Comes Under attack', LSG (20.3.96) 5; 'Mears Battles for Entry Limits', LSG (17.4.96) 5.

[40] 'Scramble for Training Places again this Year', LSG (19.3.97) 1; 'LPC Places Frozen until Year 2000', LSG (23.4.97) 1; 'Law Soc Attacked for Unwarranted Intervention' (1997) 141 SJ 373; 'City Firm Considers Offering own LPC', LSG (30.4.97) 1; 'LPC Freeze Challenge', LSG (8.5.97) 1; 'Society Faces Judicial Review Threat over LPC Decision' (1997) 141 SJ 420; 'Class Action', LSG (21.5.97) 22; Martin Mears, 'Illegal Yesterday. Legal Today!' 3 Cat (6.97) 11; 'Writ large' G (1.7.97) 17; 'LPC Plan Shelved', LSG (24.9.97) 8; 'Law School Calls for Flexibility on Training Places' (1997) 141 SJ 880; 'LPC Freeze Vote', LSG (21.1.98) 4; Course Thaw', LSG (28.1.98) 6; 'Bar School Plans to Offer LPC' (1999) 143 SJ 873; 'News', T (Law) (23.11.99) 9; 'Training Think-tank Voices Concern over Two-tier Legal Practice Course', LSG (8.12.99) 5; 'City LPC War', LSG (17.12.99) 6. Separate courses for professional sectors had been mooted nearly a decade earlier. Economides and Smallcombe (1991: 21).

[41] 'Salary Consultation "Flawed"', LSG (19.3.97) 10; Nick Armstrong and Richard Moorhead, 'Bare Minimum' (1997) 147 NLJ 487; 'Editorial: Doing the Minimum', LSG (9.4.97) 13; 'Trainees Step Up Salary Protest', LSG (16.4.97) 8; 'Trainee Solicitors Thwarted' (1997) 147 NLJ 554; 'Fight to Retain Minimum Salary Receives Welcome Boost' (1997) 141 SJ 372; 'Minimum Salaries to be Retained', LSG (11.6.97) 4; 'Training Contracts under Review' (1997) 141 SJ 559; 'Minimum Salaries Status Quo' (1997) 147 NLJ 876; Peter Watson-Lee, 'Minimum Salaries for Trainees', 3 Cat (6.97) 10; 'Plan to Raise Trainees Minimum Pay and Stop Firms Ducking Out', LSG (29.9.99) 3.

[42] 'Starting This Life', LSG (29.9.99) 18.

[43] Halliday (1987); Paterson (1988); Shapiro (1990); Burrage (1990); Berends (1992). On the efforts of all professions to control the supply during the Great Depression see Kotschnig (1937).

[44] Abel (1988: 159–63).

[45] Cf Freeman (1975).

[46] Labour Party (1995: 16). For more recent critiques see Bradney (1999); Bronwsword (1999); Hillyer (1999); Webb (1999).

[47] Cf. Rhode (1985) (critique of American character and fitness test).

[48] See Francis and McDonald (2000); Thomas and Rees (2000); Rees *et al.* (2000).

Chapter 4—Notes

[1] Stevens (1971: 412–13, 417; 1983: 7).

[2] Quoted in Auerbach (1976: 107).

[3] Synott (1979); Stevens (1983: 101); Oren (1986).

[4] Auerbach (1976: 126–7); Rhode (1985).

[5] Kotschnig (1937); Reifner (1986: 111); Müller (1991: chap. 8).

[6] Abel (1988: 74–6 and Table 1.21).

[7] Abel (1988: 76–9).

[8] Flood (1983); Abel (1988: 79–85 and Table 1.23).

[9] Abel (1988: 169–76 and Table 2.17; 1989: 68).

[10] Royal Commission (1979: paras. 35.19, 21, 33–4, 39, 42–3).

[11] Polytechnics & Colleges Funding Council (1992).

[12] 'Final Examination Statistics' (1986) 83 LSG 3499; 'Final Exam Statistics' (1987) 84 LSG 3543; 'Final Examination Statistics' (1987) 84 LSG 3660; Halpern (1994: 21–32); Shiner and Newburn (1995: 14–29); Webb and Bermingham (1995); McGlynn (1998); Cownie (2000).

[13] 'Bar AGM race decisions', LA (8.85) 5; 'Brief snatch-back', LA (8.85) 5; 'Report of the Race Relations Committee 1985/1986' (1986) 83 LSG 2482, 2493; 'Race and sex bias advice for lawyers', T (20.9.88); 'SCB Poor on Race Complaints', LSG (19.4.89) 3; 'Contracts Will Help Fight Racism', LSG (19.4.89) 3; 'Race and the Legal Profession' (1989) 139 NLJ 565.

[14] 'Increase in black barristers at the Bar "too slow"', T (26.5.89); 'Chambers Urged to Recruit Minorities', LSG (31.5.89) 2; 'The Plight of Black Barristers' (1989) 139 NLJ 742; Mr Justice Brooke, 'The Bar's Ethnic Minority Study', C (7–8.89) 15; Bar Council (1999b: Annexe B); Morton and Harvie (1990a); 'Lawyers oppose move to end legal aid choice', T (15.5.90).

[15] 'Chambers secondments planned by Bar Council', L (29.1.91) 1; 'Bar Moves to 5% Quota for Ethnic Minorities', LSG (2.5.91) 8; 'Race Relations Committee Proposals' C (6.91) 23; Anthony Scrivener QC, 'Race Relations', C (6.91) 3; 'Positive Action by Bar', LSG (17.10.91) 7; Anthony Scrivener QC, 'Chairman's Column: A Change in Policy', C (11.91) 23; 'Race Equality Policy Approved', C (11.91) 5; 'Race Equality Policy', C (11.91) 23; 'What the Papers Say...', C (6.91) 23; 'Bar moves to provide equal opportunities', DT (18.5.92); 'Bar Appoints Anti-racism Troubleshooter' (1992) 136 SJ 480.

[16] 'Black Lawyers Detect Bias in CLE Intake', LSG (15.7.92) 9; 'Black Lawyers say CLE System "Not Enough"' (1992) 136 SJ 741; 'Bar Accused of "Ethnic Cleansing"', LSG (22.10.92) 10; 'Ethnic Cleansing at the Bar' (1992) 142 NLJ 1439; 'Black Lawyers' Groups in Press Row' (1992) 136 SJ 1044; 'CLE Replies to Criticism' (1992) 142 NLJ 1531; 'Bar Finals Challenge', LSG (9.12.92) 7; 'College Faces Race Inquiry', LSG (13.1.93) 3; 'Formal Investigation at Council of Legal Education' (1993) 143 NLJ 43; 'Bias Case on Hold', LSG (10.2.93) 12; 'Patterns of Disparity', C (2.93) 16; 'Race Enquiry Row', LSG (10.3.93) 10; 'CLE Race Inquiry Stalled', LSG (7.4.93) 9; 'Inquiry Confirmed', LSG (21.4.93) 4; 'Investigator angered by SBL boycott', L (18.5.93); 'Bar Race Gap Continues' (1993) 137 SJ 809; 'More Questions than Answers', LSG (15.9.93) 6; 'Disadvantages at the First Hurdle' (1993) 143 NLJ 1286; 'Race Review Suspended', LSG (6.10.93) 8; 'CLE Pass Rates Disparity

Narrows', C (10.93) 5; 'Exam Re–sits', LSG (10.11.93) 4; 'Black Students Strike Deal with Bar School', LSG (17.11.93) 6; 'Bar Settles with Students', C (11–12.93) 5; 'Bar School Cleared by Committee', LSG (13.4.94) 6; 'Equal opportunities in barrister training', I (13.4.94) 17; 'Race bias "hampers black Bar students"', T (13.4.94); 'Black Bar students penalised by race bias', I (13.4.94) 5; 'Blacks face bias in law chambers', DT (13.4.94); 'Equal Opportunities at the Bar' (1994) 144 NLJ 503; 'Confidence Crisis hits Black Bar Students' (1994) 138 SJ 356; 'Editorial: Whitewashing Legal Linen' (1994) 144 NLJ 485; 'Resit Rights', LSG (27.4.94) 10; 'Inns and Outs', T (23.8.94); 'Race Bar', LSG (7.9.94) 10; Committee of Inquiry (1994); Hamilton and Bhalla (1994); 'Equality Commission Targets Law Training', LSG (7.6.95) 4; 'Bar Council Unhappy at Pass Rate for Black Students' (1995) 139 SJ 808; 'Women Bar Students Better Male Counterparts in Finals', LSG (31.8.95) 5; Shapland and Sorsby (1995); Shiner and Newburn (1995: 95–100, 122–6); 'CRE and CLE Reach Compromise Agreement' (1996) 140 SJ 32; 'A fierce fight at the Bar', I (22.5.96) 24; Shiner (1997: 104–6, 115, 123–5).

[17] 'Britain's first black woman QC', DM (29.3.91); 'Diary', T (6.4.91); 'One takes silk, the other wears satin', ES (9.4.91) 3; '"I've wanted to be involved in a profession where I would never have to lie"', DT (10.4.91); 'A success thanks to mum, dad—and God', ES (10.4.91) 17; 'Bar AGM', C (11.91) 4; 'Bar to Tackle Sex Bias', LSG (6.11.91) 4; 'Barristers to curb bar on women', ES (17.3.92); 'LCD to co-fund £15K Bar survey on women', L (17.3.92); 'Bar sets up probe into sex discrimination', FT (16.3.92); 'Bar to Probe Bias against Women', LSG (18.3.92) 7; 'Let more women judge', T (24.3.92); 'Bias Against Women at Bar and Bench', LSG (25.11.92) 7; 'Sex discrimination at the Bar: guilty as charged', I (27.11.92) 25; 'Changing Gatekeepers—Equal Opportunities at the Bar and on the Bench' (1992) 142 NLJ 1638 '"Women Treated Unequally Throughout Their Careers"' (1992) 136 SJ 1183; 'Rough justice at the Bar', T (1.12.92); Holland and Spencer (1992); 'Sex and the Bar', C (2.93) 12; 'Barristers tackle race and sex bias', DT (15.3.93); 'Bar gives guidance on discrimination', L (23.3.93) 1; J J Rowe, QC, 'Chairman's Column: What Is Bothering the Bar?' C (4.93) 3; Bar Council (1995: pp. i–ii); Skordaki (1996); Shiner (1997: 132–3); McGlynn (1998). In 1998 Goldsmith remembered that the new equality code was 'particularly controversial, very hard for people in the profession, again, to recognise that accountability is part of professionalism as well' (interview).

[18] 'Barristers in revolt as Inns refuse to adopt sex bias code', T (10.11.94); 'Message in Code', T (11.11.94); 'Barristers reject plea to accept briefs from public', DT (14.11.94); 'Bar tells Inns of Court to tackle discrimination', T (14.11.94); 'Leadership Slaps Inns', LSG (16.11.94) 8; 'Narrow Defeat for Bar Proposals' (1994) 144 NLJ 1578; 'Editorial: Discrimination at the Bar' (1994) 144 NLJ 1577; 'Inns and Outs', T (13.12.94); 'Inns Criticism', C (11–12.94) 8; 'Discrimination Rule Agreed', LSG (25.1.95) 3; 'Bar Faces Court Challenge', LSG (25.1.95) 3; 'Unanimous Support for Equal Ops Code' (1997) 141 SJ 589; 'Bar Council Meeting Berates Inns of Court over Equal Opportunities', LSG (25.6.97) 8; 'Defeat for de Wilde', C (7–8.97) 4.

[19] 'QC suspended for sexual harassment', G (3.2.95); 'Editorial: Sex and the Lawyer' (1995) 145 NLJ 133; 'Women suffer sex harassment when training for the Bar', DT (6.2.95); 'Sex pests "worry women barristers"', G (6.2.95); Martin Mears,

'Comment: An Exercise in Posturing' (1995) 145 NLJ 302; Henry Hodge, 'Equal and Decent Treatment' (1995) 145 NLJ 303; 'Putting a Bar on Harassment' (1995) 139 SJ 104; 'New Equality Code Review' (1995) 145 NLJ 1322; 'Editorial: A Question of Conduct' (1995) 145 NLJ 1393; 'Bar Council Equality Code Initiative Approved' (1995) 145 NLJ 1394; 'Barristers equality code aims to stop race and sex bias', T (6.11.95); Shapland and Sorsby (1995: 71, 74–5); Shapland *et al.* (1995: 51); 'The Second Woman Lawyer Conference', C (5–6.96) 8.

[20] 'Mackay urged to amend QC system', IOS (1.11.92); 'Legal Honours and Ladders of Advancement', C (4.93) 4; 'Legal briefs', FT (6.4.93); 'New Silks' (1993) 137 SJ 312; 'QC system "deeply flawed" ', L (13.4.93) 1; 'QC list ignores Bar equality drive', L (13.4.93) 2; 'Archangels of the Bar under scrutiny', L (13.4.93); 'Dismay at Balance of QC Appointments', LSG (21.4.93) 6; 'Concern at narrow band applying for silk', L (27.4.93); 'Four silks from same chambers', L (27.4.93); 'Few Old School Ties among Silks', C (5–6.93) 4; J J Rowe, QC, 'Chairman's Column: Conferences and Consultation', C (5–6.93) 6; 'New Silks', C (5–6.93) 26–8; Robin de Wilde QC, 'Letters: No Confidence in Silk Selection', C (7.93) 6; 'Judge and Silk Appointments "too Secretive" ', LSG (6.10.93) 6; Lord Mackay, 'The Myths and Facts About Silk', C (10.93) 11; 'Bar AGM Denounces Silk System', LSG (3.11.93); 'Bar AGM Report', C (11–12.93) 4; John Rowe QC and Robert Seabrook QC, 'Silks—The Bar's Responsibility', C (11–12.93) 10; 'Comment: Appointing Silks' (1994) 138 SJ 111; 'Queen's Counsel 1994', C (3–4.94) 4; 'Women Barristers attack QC System' (1994) 138 SJ 327; 'Black Dismay at Silk Selection', LSG (13.4.94) 8; 'Silk and Bench on Show', LSG (6.7.94) 5; 'QC Review "Superficial" ', LSG (13.7.94) 5; 'Bar Silks Report', C (7–8.94) 4; 'The Silk Round', C (7–8.94) 22; Bar Council Working Party on the Appointment of Queen's Counsel (1994: 29, 37, 80); 'Mackay Calls for Bench Revolution', LSG (12.4.95) 8; 'Editorial: Raw Silk Deal', LSG (17.4.96) 13; 'Number of women taking silk doubles', T (9.4.98) 6; 'Third Solicitor QC Appointed', LSG (16.4.98) 5; Bar Council (1999b: 41); Malleson and Banda (2000: 6).

[21] 'Gay Bar Call to Arms', LSG (18.5.94) 6; Martin Bowley QC, 'Making the Difference', C (1–2.97) 20.

[22] Compare Shapland and Sorsby (1995: 71, 74–5); Shapland *et al.* (1995: 51) (93% women juniors but 26% senior male barristers thought sexual discrimination a problem; 74 and 46% thought sexual harassment a problem; 71% of women juniors had experienced discrimination and 40% harassment) with Shapland and Sorsby (1998a: 111–13 and Tables 4.2, 4.3; 1998b: 11) (80 and 59% women and men thought sexual discrimination a problem; 62 and 51% sexual harassment; 51% of women had experienced discrimination and 31% harassment). In 1998 a barrister was fined £500 for harassing two women pupils and forced to resign from the bench.

[23] 'Cherie Booth urges Bar to open door for less well-off', T (23.9.97) 1; ' "The Bar must attract the best" ', T (23.9.97) 33; Shiner (1997: 117); 'Working mum reaches the top', T (6.1.98) 33; 'Heather Hallett QC takes over as Chairman of the Bar', BN (2.98) 3; 'One man who is propping up the Bar', I (Thurs Rev) (17.12.98) 18.

[24] 'Reforms to eradicate Bar's "racist" policies', T (11.12.99) 6; Bar Council Race Relations Committee (1999: 4–5, 8–9, 21–5, 49–50).

[25] (1986) 83 LSG 3499; (1987) 84 LSG 2446, 3543, 3660.

[26] (1987) 84 LSG 2446; 'Women lawyers: a sharp rise in entries', FT (15.10.87) 3; '57% of Young LG Lawyers are Women', LSG (1.6.88) 4; 'Women Partners', LSG (1.6.88) 11.

[27] Abel (1988: Table 2.16); Law Society (1988c); LSG (22.6.88) 3; Marks (1987: Tables E1.1, H1.1, H4.0); 'Average Salaries Jump by One–Fifth', LSG (31.5.89) 6; S. Nott, 'Women in the Law' (1989) 139 NLJ 749, 785; 'Woman to do her articles part time', T (18.9.90); Sommerlad (1994; 1995); Sidaway (1995); Thomas and Bradshaw (1995); Skordaki (1996); McGlynn (1998); Sanderson and Sommerlad (2000). The best account of the barriers encountered by women lawyers is that of Sommerlad and Sanderson (1998); Sommerlad (1998).

[28] (1986) 83 LSG 163, 2802; LSG (29.6.88) 6; Law Society, Ethnic Monitoring Statistics Press Release (28.7.88); 'Drive to Attract Black Lawyers', LSG (19.4.89) 3; 'Gulf between black and white lawyers', FT (24.4.89); 'Women and blacks: more chances but less promotion', I (24.4.89); 'Race and the Legal Profession' (1989) 139 NLJ 565; 'Law Society Moves against Professional Race Bias' (1989) 139 NLJ 566; 'Blacks "may suffer most under legal changes"', I (15.5.89); 'Students "face race bias by big firms"', G (3.5.90); 'Black law students overlooked in jobs for articled clerks', DT (3.5.90); 'Ethnic Minority Students Face Tougher Time Getting into Profession', LSG (9.5.90) 4; 'More Equal than Others?' (1990) 134 SJ 611; King *et al.* (1990: 1–5); Morton and Harvie (1990b; 1990c); 'Firm Considers Appeal of Discrimination Ruling', LSG (17.4.91) 4. Ethnic minorities were overrepresented among law students but had greater difficulty gaining admission. Webb and Bermingham (1995).

[29] 'Race Bar on Entry to Finals Course?' LSG (8.5.91) 4; 'LSF Students to be Monitored', LSG (9.10.91) 7; 'Black Lawyers Urge 10% Recruitment Target', LSG (12.2.92) 7; 'Race Meeting Achieves Common Ground', LSG (19.2.92) 10; 'Finals Student Poll', LSG (18.3.92) 5; 'SBL Re-opens Ethnic Bias Row', LSG (6.5.92) 9; 'Law Soc Denies "Sitting on Race Document"' (1992) 136 SJ 424; 'Discrimination by the College of Law?' (1992) 142 NLJ 626; 'Student Intake', LSG (7.10.92) 9; '"Foul" Cry over LPC Admissions', LSG (25.11.92) 8; Hamylton and Bhalla (1994: 79–80).

[30] 'Ethnic Minorities Beaten by Articles Bias', LSG (8.4.92) 4; 'Anti-bias Rules and Job Targets in the Pipeline', LSG (3.6.92) 9; 'Solicitors face code to outlaw bias', G (9.10.92); 'Law Society proposes crackdown on racism', DT (9.10.92); 'Law Society takes aim at racism', DT (9.10.92); 'City Firms Unhappy with Ethnic Targets' (1992) 136 SJ 1016; 'Ethnic Shortfall', LSG (9.6.93) 7.

[31] 'Anti-bias Rule must be Policed', LSG (3.11.93) 10; 'Racism blights entry to law career', T (21.4.94); 'Study Shows Widespread Race Bias at Law Firms' (1994) 138 SJ 379; 'Bias in Favour of Affluent Students' (1994) 138 SJ 379; 'Race Bias Throws Shadow on Firms', LSG (27.4.94) 5; 'Law Society Accused of Complacency on Race' (1994) 138 SJ 404; 'Editorial: Training for the Rich', (1994) 144 NLJ 557; 'Solicitors shown to discriminate', G (29.4.94) 37; Halpern (1994: 70–2, 76–80); see also Shiner and Newburn (1995: 44–53, 81–92); Shiner (1997: 12–22, 52–66; 2000); Vignaendra *et al.* (2000).

[32] 'Inquiry Sought in Trainee Race Bar', LSG (1.6.94) 7; 'Council Reaches Race Agreement', LSG (15.6.94) 8; 'City Faces Up to Race Bar', LSG (22.6.94) 8; 'Race

Survey for City Firms' (1994) 138 SJ 784; 'Guidelines Aim to Snuff out Recruitment Racism', LSG (14.9.94) 7.

[33] 'Race Row Triggered as Working Party Rejects Monitoring', LSG (15.3.95) 2; 'Ethnic Check', LSG (3.5.95) 4; 'New Anti-discrimination Measures Introduced by the Law Society' (1995) 139 NLJ 668; 'Equality Plea', LSG (19.7.95) 6; ' "Play Down" Ethnic Side', LSG (25.10.95) 8.

[34] 'Gay Group Comes Out over Law "Bigotry" ' (1992) 136 SJ 1128; 'Anti-discrimination Plans Inadequate says Gay Group', LSG (18.11.92) 9; 'Gay Lawyers Dispute Anti-bias Proposal', LSG (2.12.92) 8; 'Error Admitted on Gay Clause', LSG (20.1.93) 11; 'Society Faces Pressure on Anti–bias Clause', LSG (23.6.93) 8.

[35] 'Policing Bias', LSG (29.9.93) 6; 'Black and Blue', LSG (6.10.93) 12; 'Council Endorses Anti-bias Policy', LSG (13.10.93) 3; 'Strong Measures Adopted at Council Meeting' (1993) 143 NLJ 1430; 'Law Soc Adopts Practice Rule on Anti-discrimination' (1993) 137 SJ 1011.

[36] 'Hiccups on an Anti–bias Route', LSG (17.12.93) 8; 'Religion is a Sticking Point on Anti-bias Rule', LSG (2.3.94) 8; 'Council Backs Anti-bias Rule', LSG (16.3.94) 6; 'Religious Amendment Defeated', (1994) 138 SJ 251.

[37] 'Religious Amendment Defeated' (1994) 138 SJ 251; 'Gay Rights and Wrongs' (1995) 139 SJ 132; 'Sex Motion', LSG (1.3.95) 64; Martin Mears, 'Comment: An Exercise in Posturing' (1995) 145 NLJ 302; Henry Hodge, 'Equal and Decent Treatment' (1995) 145 NLJ 303; 'LawSoc Firm on Sexual Orientation' (1995) 139 SJ 232; 'Law Society Council Blocks Mears' Motion' (1995) 145 NLJ 370.

[38] 'Tribunals under Fire', LSG (11.10.95) 2; Martin Mears, 'Profession "In Extremis" ', LSG (11.10.95) 12; 'Comment: Trials and Tribunals', LSG (18.10.95) 12; 'Mears in Direct Appeal to Council', LSG (25.10.95) 2; Martin Mears, 'Presidents' Column: Justice, Law and Abuses', LSG (25.10.95) 12; 'Ethnic Lawyers Vow to Continue Racism Fight', LSG (1.11.95) 8.

[39] Marks (1987: Tables E1.1, H1.1, H4.0); Law Society (1988c: 20, 26); 'Women in the Law' (1989) 139 NLJ 749, 785; Chambers and Harwood-Stephenson (1991: 25, 32); Halpern (1994: 62, 65); 'Glass Ceiling Shattered', LSG (8.2.95) 8; 'Bar Equality Code "Quintessence of Political Correctness" says Mears' (1995) 139 SJ 1111; 'Report Reveals Extent of Discrimination against Women' (1995) 145 NLJ 986; 'Women Falling Short of Top', LSG (13.7.95) 5; McGlynn and Graham (1995) (58/100 firms responding); 'Editorial: From the Outside', LSG (22.11.95) 12; 'Too Many Barriers to Legal Profession' (1995) 139 SJ 1168; Martin Mears, 'Letters to the Editor: No Bias', LSG (29.11.95) 15; Shiner and Newburn (1995); Peter Goldsmith QC, 'Comment: A Domestic Dispute', LSG (17.1.96) 14; Shiner (1997: Table 5.1); (1998) 142 SJ 949; 'Women at Work', LSG (28.4.99) 17; 'Women Miss Out on Partnership', LSG (23.6.99) 9.

[40] 'SCB Adopts Harassment Regulations', LSG (6.3.96) 5; 'Sexual Harassment Fiasco' (1996) 146 NLJ 245; 'Comment: The "Yes, but" Society' (1996) 146 NLJ 247; 'The Second Woman Lawyer Conference', C (5–6.96) 8.

[41] 'Gender Pay Gap', LSG (9.10.96) 5 (Office of National Statistics new earnings survey); 'Solicitors Must "Wake up" to Inequality' (1996) 140 SJ 987; 'Women Lawyers Fall Short on Pay', LSG (16.10.96) 5; 'The "unacceptable" reality of pay discrimination', L (22.10.96) 2; 'Call for Pay Review', LSG (23.10.96) 4; 'Editorial: Knowledge is Power', LSG (30.10.96) 14.

[42] 'Firms Still Fail to Address Equal Ops' (1997) 141 SJ 76; 'Editorial: A Stronger Voice' (1997) 147 NLJ 517; 'Comment: Equal before the Law' (1997) 141 SJ 323; 'Law Society Leaders Give Clear Message on Equality' (1997) 141 SJ 348; 'Bahl Launches Bid to be First Woman Leader', LSG (29.10.97) 1; 'The True Value of a Solicitor' (1997) 147 NLJ 1580.

[43] 'Solicitors Urged: Take Lead on Equal Pay', (1997) 141 SJ 247; 'Female Trainees Sold Short', LSG (9.4.97) 4 (203 respondents); 'Slow Progress', LSG (8.5.97) 5 (28% response from 200 largest firms); 'Firms Urged to Close Income Gender Gap', LSG (9.7.97) 1; 'Salary Lottery', LSG (9.7.97) 16–17; 'Editorial: The Pay Equation', LSG (9.7.97) 14; 'Women Lawyers Still Lag Behind', LSG (17.9.97) 4; 'Survey Shows Bias Problem Persists', LSG (30.7.97) 1; 'Editorial: Bias is Bad for Business', LSG (30.7.97) 15; 'Money Talks its Way into the Profession' (1997) 147 NLJ 1143; 'Survey Shows Women Solicitors Lagging Behind Men on Pay', LSG (23.3.98) 3; 'Women solicitors lag behind men on pay', T (19.10.98) 10; 'Sex Discrimination and Trainees' Salaries' (1998) 148 NLJ 600; 'Survey Reveals Yawning Pay Gap', LSG (8.9.99) 1; 'Women Still Lag Behind on Pay' (1999) 143 SJ 823; 'A Fair Day's Pay', LSG (15.9.99) 34; 'Women in the legal world still earn less', T (15.9.99) 8; 'Comment: This Unequal Profession' (1999) 143 SJ 851. In the cohort completing their academic legal education in 1993, 40% of minority trainees but only 27% of white trainees were paid at or below the minimum salary (p=0.08). Shiner (1997: 92 n.4).

[44] 'Face Discrimination in the Solicitors' Profession' (1997) 147 NLJ 1271; 'Editorial: Of Conferences and Legal Aid' (1997) 147 NLJ 1301; Phillip Sycamore, 'Fit for the 21st Century', LSG (22.10.97) 20; 'Thunder and Fury in Cardiff— Conference Report' (1997) 147 NLJ 1538; 'The cement ceiling', T (18.11.97) 43; 'Trainees Hit Out at the Course Fee Rises', LSG (14.10.98) 1; 'Law Schools under Fire over Cost of LPC' (1998) 142 SJ 923; 'Editorial: The Price of Knowledge', LSG (14.10.98) 15; 'Comment: Priced out of a Career' (1998) 142 SJ 927.

[45] Shiner (1997: 83); 'Getting in the Mainstream', LSG (8.4.99) 23; 'Law 4 Not Very Many', LSG (16.6.99) 5; 'Editorial: Equality takes Time', LSG (16.6.99) 14; 'Minorities "Failure"', LSG (21.7.99) 5; 'Trainees Claim Rise in Discrimination', LSG (15.9.99) 1; 'Harassment in law firms "rife"', T (17.9.99) 7; 'Give us a break chaps or we'll see you in Court', T (Law) (28.9.99) 3; 'Sex Claim Firm to Break Up', LSG (27.10.99) 5; 'Complaints Rocket as Trainees Seek Advice over Harassment and Stress', LSG (3.11.99); 'Ethnic Action Call', LSG (3.11.99).

[46] Zander (1988: 111–15, 279–85).

[47] Griffith (1977); Malleson (1999: 1; 2000).

[48] 'Judges' old boy network under fire after rape trial', ST (15.4.90) A5; 'Labour asks for judicial overhaul', T (30.4.90); 'British courts face censure over rough justice for blacks', O (6.5.90) 8; 'Fast exit for the slowest judge', T (14.2.98) 1; 'A matter of judgement', T (14.2.98) 23; 'Judge in dock as joke falls flat', T (28.4.99) 11; 'Writ large', G (27.4.99) 16; 'Why don't lawyers learn to spin?' I (Tues Rev) (18.5.99) 12; 'Judges will be trained how not to be rude', T (12.7.99) 4; 'Judges get advice on cultural mores', FT (29.9.99) 14; 'Judges brought to book over race blunders', T (29.9.99) 9.

[49] 'Mackay aims to recruit more blacks for bench', ST (26.2.89); 'So You Want to Be a Judge?' C (11.89) 11; 'So You Still Want to Be a Judge?' C (12.89) 22.

[50] 'Judges Selection Move', LSG (27.6.90) 4; 'Fast Track for Judges' (1990) 140 NLJ 950; 'Unfair Advantage?' (1990) 140 NLJ 949; Tony Holland, 'A New Decade, a New Service', LSG (18.10.90) 2; 'Society in push to reform judiciary', L (23.10.90); Rt Hon Sir Frederick Lawton, 'The Make-up of the Bench' (1990) 134 SJ 1254; 'Mackay rejects plea on judges reform', T (7.11.90); 'Mackay rejects "fast track" for women judges', DT (7.11.90); Tony Holland, 'Judges Getting it Right' (1990) 134 SJ 1286; 'A Flawed System of Appointment' (1990) 140 NLJ 1557; 'Bench very different in 20 years, says Mackay', L (13.11.90); 'Mackay's mistake about the judges', L (13.11.90) 11; 'Mackay Intends No Change in Judge Selection', LSG (14.11.90) 6; 'Appointments System Discriminatory, says Holland' (1990) 140 NLJ 1594; 'Bar's new chief urges a wider choice of judges', T (21.11.90); 'Charismatic Chief for Bar', LSG (12.12.90) 10; 'Editorial: a question of judgment', LA (12.90) 3.

[51] Geoffrey Bindman, 'Is the System of Judicial Appointments Illegal?' LSG (27.2.91) 24; 'Appointment of judges may break racial laws', DT (27.2.91); 'Judge selection "may be illegal"', G (27.2.91); 'Society rejects plea for action on judges', L (5.3.91); 'Race Committee's "Constructive" Meeting with Mackay', LSG (6.3.91) 7; 'Solicitors seek reforms to end "discriminatory" way of choosing judges', DT (8.3.91) 8; 'Law Society calls for commission on appointing judges', I (8.3.91); 'Plea for more women and black judges', G (8.3.91) 8; 'Inns and Outs', T (12.3.91); 'Smugness: that old British disease', L (12.3.91); 'Society Urges Lay Involvement in Judicial Appointments', LSG (13.3.91) 6; 'Bench Appointments "Discriminatory", says Law Society' (1991) 135 SJ 300; 'Comment: Judges' (1991) 135 SJ 299; 'Our Judges in the Dock', ST Magazine (17.3.91) 18; 'Ethnic Minority Initiative Gets Warm Welcome', LSG (24.4.91) 3; 'No Window Dressing, Promises Brooke', LSG (24.4.91) 4; (1991) 135 SJ 591, 595; 'Survey Strengthens Case for Judicial Appointments Reform', LSG (22.5.91) 9; 'Lane Rebukes LCD over Judge Shortage', LSG (17.7.91) 8; 'Lord Mackay Hits Out on Judicial Appointments', LSG (31.7.91) 3; 'Access to Justice' (1991) 141 NLJ 1213; 'Ethnic Monitoring of Judges' Posts Ordered', LSG (25.9.91) 6; 'Mackay Stands Firm on Judges' Posts', LSG (30.10.91) 7; Hughes (1991); Skordaki (1991) (survey of judicial selection procedures).

[52] 'Taylor is the New LCJ', LSG (26.2.92) 3; 'Taylor Promises to Restore Faith in British Justice' (1992) 136 SJ 179; 'Taylor Attacks Legal Aid Cuts', LSG (2.12.92) 3; 'Spending Cuts are "Blot on System"—Taylor' (1992) 136 SJ 1207; Taylor (1992: 8–9).

[53] 'Top judges still chosen from elite', G (12.10.92); 'Selection of judges is still "elitist"', T (12.10.92); 'Radical reform sought for judiciary', FT (19.10.92); 'Judges' selection "due for reform"', G (19.10.92); 'Call to end judicial secrecy', DT (19.10.92); 'Judges "Too Old, Too Male, Too Out of Touch"' (1992) 136 SJ 1186; 'Comment: A Scandal of Judges' (1992) 136 SJ 1187; 'Williams Raps "Hidebound" Judge System' (1992) 136 SJ 1208; Lord Williams of Mostyn QC, 'The Judges and the Future', C (11–12.92) 3; Justice (1992: 13); 'Judicial Imbalance', LSG (13.1.93) 8.

[54] 'Mackay Exhorts Women to Bench', LSG (28.4.93) 6; 'First solicitor becomes High Court judge', L (22.6.93) 1; 'High Court Bench gains First Solicitor', LSG (23.6.93) 3; 'Wanted: Judges who Care', LSG (7.7.93) 9; 'Black Candidate Appeal',

LSG (7.7.93) 9; 'Anyone for a Seat on the Bench?' LSG (14.7.93); 'Judge Race Training not Enough, say Black Lawyers' (1993) 137 SJ 1147; 'Bench Woe', LSG (26.1.94) 5; 'Poor Pay hits Bench Quality', LSG (9.2.94) 10; 'AWB Chair Attacks Judicial Selection System' (1994) 138 SJ 431; '"Judge Wanted" Adverts', LSG (25.5.94) 3; 'Judging the Judges' (1994) 138 SJ 519; '"Old boys" dominate law', L (4.10.94); 'Lay Panel to Pick Next Bench Crop', LSG (7.10.94) 10; 'Bench Jobs', LSG (2.11.94) 7; Mackay (1994: 9); LCD (1994); 'Mackay modernises judicial selection to encourage women', T (10.4.95) 7; 'No room at the bar', G (25.4.95).

[55] 'Taylor Supports Judicial System Status Quo', LSG (22.3.95) 3; 'Angry Response to Fraud Comments', LSG (14.6.95) 3; 'How to be Top' (1996) 140 SJ 215; 'Appointments System to Stay', LSG (3.7.96) 5; 'Judicial Appointments Commission Rejected', C (7–8.96) 6; 'Judicial Appointments Disappoint AWB', C (7–8.96) 6; MacRae (1996); Home Affairs Select Committee (1997).

[56] 'Editorial: A Society with Secrets' (1997) 147 NLJ 441; 'Freemasons and the Law', C (3–4.97) 5; 'Judges' Freemasonry secrets likely to end', T (29.9.97) 12; 'Judges set to escape register of Masons', T (3.11.97) 7; 'Straw to publish list of Masons joining police and judiciary', T (18.2.98) 6; 'On the square', T (18.2.98) 21; 'Reluctant Masons to give names to MPs', T (6.3.98) 2; 'Bingham defends Masonic judges', T (18.3.98) 5; 'Judge condemns Freemason call', T (29.10.98) 2; David Pannick QC, 'Does it matter if 247 judges are Masons?' T (17.11.98) 41; 'One in 20 judges admits membership of Masons', DT (23.3.99) 24; 'MPs demand Masonic list', T (26.5.99) 10.

[57] Stevens (1987; 1988); Labour Party (1995: 14); Lord Williams (1996: 72, 75); 'Comment: Choosing Judges' (1997) 141 SJ 511; 'Application to Replace Invitation in Judicial Recruitment Reforms', LSG (15.10.97) 4; 'The cement ceiling', T (18.11.97) 43; 'Irvine says: "Don't be Shy, Apply"', LSG (3.12.97) 4; 'Ombudsman to Fight Discrimination' (1997) 141 SJ 1144; '"Don't be Shy. Apply", Lord Irvine tells Minority Lawyers' (1997) 147 NLJ 1766; 'A matter of judgment', T (14.2.98) 23; 'Hague looks to US judge system', T (25.2.98) 10; Thomas (1997); Malleson (1997; 1999: 93) (quoting Irvine's speech).

[58] 'Justice—now seen to be advertised', T (24.2.98) 1; 'Editorial: In the Frame' (1998) 148 NLJ 269; 'Comment: New Judges Wanted' (1998) 142 SJ 175; 'Irvine woos "shy" women to sit on the bench', T (27.4.98) 6; 'Irvine Calls for Minority Judges', LSG (7.5.98) 5; Malleson and Banda (2000: 5) (quoting Irvine's 11.2.98 speech to the AWB); S (2.12.98), cited in Egan (1999: 26).

[59] 'Drive to make JPs blue collar, not blue rinse', T (15.3.99) 8; 'Irvine Retains "Political Balance" Test for Magistrates' (1999) 143 SJ 992; 'Anti-secrecy Success', LSG (3.11.99) 5; LCD (1999: 74). On the class bias of the magistracy see Dignan and Wynne (1997); Clements (2000).

[60] G (18.7.98); Sun (6.8.98); 'Judges will face fiercer scrutiny', T (14.12.98) 1; 'Irvine's empire: All senior members of the judiciary face new scrutiny', T (14.12.98) 19; 'Editorial: Reform at the top', LA (2.99) 3; 'Irvine may consider Judicial Appointments Commission', LA (2.99) 5; 'Top high court job for woman judge', G (29.6.99) 7.

[61] 'Minority Lawyers Challenge Irvine', LSG (24.3.99) 3; 'Minority Lawyers' Conference' (1999) 149 NLJ 434; 'Minority Lawyers Unimpressed by Shadowing Scheme' (1999) 143 SJ 284; 'Comment: Judicial Appointments' (1999) 143 SJ 287;

'Brown's man given job in the Cabinet', T (18.5.99) 6; 'Vaz Moves into Legal Aid Firing Line', LSG (19.5.99) 3.

[62] 'Judging Labour on the Judges', Labour Research (6.99) 12; Kate Malleson, 'Time's up for the old boys' network', G2 (1.6.99); 'Labour reneges on pledge to reform Bench', T (1.6.99) 8; 'Labour Judges too White and Male, says Labour Research' (1999) 143 SJ 527; 'Comment: Same old story' (1999) 143 SJ 531; Martyn Day and Russell Levy, 'Why judges must declare their interests', T (31.8.99) 21; Malleson (1999).

[63] 'CPS Facing Race Discrimination Claims from Three More Lawyers', LSG (16.12.98) 3; 'Briefs', I (Tues Rev) (11.5.99) 14; 'DPP Admits Working Practices "not Friendly"' (1999) 143 SJ 452; 'Why don't lawyers learn to spin?' I (Tues Rev) (18.5.99) 12; 'CPS loses racism case', T (10.6.99) 15; 'Morris Settles Discrimination Claim', LSG (16.6.99) 4; 'CPS guilty of racial bias', T (26.10.99) 13; 'Bamieh Quits CPS', LSG (27.10.99) 5; 'CPS may face official racism inquiry', T (29.7.99) 11; 'Black CPS Lobby', LSG (13.10.99) 6; 'Watchdog launches inquiry into CPS "race bias"', I (10.12.99) 1.

[64] 'Link to Irvine sparks row on Treasury Devil', T (26.11.97) 8; 'Editorial: A Tale of Two Chancellors' (1997) 147 NLJ 1765; 'Writ large', G (11 or 12.12.97) 17; David Pannick QC, 'Those given the devil of a job to do', T (16.12.97) 35; General Council of the Bar, *Annual Report 1997*; 'Inns and Outs', T (24.2.98) 39; 'Inquiry into "secret" law jobs', T (26.2.98) 4; 'Writ large', G (3.3.98) 17; 'Attorney General in Appointments Move' (1998) 142 SJ 196; 'Comment: Blind Spot' (1998) 142 SJ 199; 'Law chief order', T (22.4.99) 10; 'Legal diary', T (11.5.99) 41; 'Briefs', I (Tues Rev) (11.5.99) 14; 'Discrimination shocks Mrs Blair', T (17.5.99) 12; 'Writ large', G2 (18.5.99) 10; 'Writ large', G2 (15.6.99) 8; 'Legal diary', T (15.6.99) 41; 'Morris Settles Discrimination Claim', LSG (16.6.99) 4; Josephine Hayes, 'The plum jobs all went to men', T (29.6.99) 41; Egan (1999: 89–92, 241).

[65] 'Irvine Denies Grounds for Sex Claim Case', LSG (11.2.98) 1; 'Inns and Outs', T (24.2.98) 39; 'Inquiry into "secret" law jobs', T (26.2.98) 4; 'Irvine to give "jobs for the boys" evidence', T (5.11.98) 1; 'Irvine in dock over jobs for the boys', T (24.3.99) 7; 'Irvine found guilty of job discrimination', T (27.3.99) 15; 'Press Round-up', LSG (31.3.99) 12; 'Tribunal takes Irvine to task on cronyism', T (21.5.99) 2; 'Writ large', G2 (25.5.99) 8; 'Lord Irvine hires top QC for appeal', T (26.10.99) 10; 'Lay off it, girls: stick to real issues', T (12.11.99) 28; *Coker v Lord Chancellor* [1999] IRLR 396, ET; Egan (1999: 56–9, 171, 239–40). The Employment Appeal Tribunal reversed the decision, the Court of Appeal dismissed the appeal, and the House of Lords refused leave to appeal.

[66] HL 596: WA 12 (11.1.99); HC 329: 301–4 (14.4.99); HC Standing Committee E (13.5.99); 'Labour Rejects Purpose Clause for Justice Bill', LSG (6.5.99) 10; 'The writing is on the wallpaper', T (26.5.99) 24; 'Check on selection of judges and QCs', T (26.7.99) 4; 'All done strictly on the QC', G2 (27.7.99) 15; Liam Fox, 'Britain's judiciary can no longer be a law unto itself', T (14.9.99) 17; Fox (1999); 'Lord Chancellor's Review on Judicial Appointments', BB (9.99) 5; 'Solicitors group calls for abolition of QCs', FT (28.9.99) 1; 'Law Society calls for end to "secret sound-ings"', DT (29.9.99) 2; 'Solicitors boycott "old boys" network', G (28.9.99) 5; 'Law Society will boycott judges' "old boy network"', T (28.9.99) 2; 'Society: "Scrap bench secret soundings"', LSG (29.9.99) 1; 'Editorial: An ill-judged system', LSG

(29.9.99) 15; 'Law Society Turns its Back on "Secret Soundings" ' (1999) 143 SJ 895; 'A Week in the Law...' (1999) 149 NLJ 1430; 'Is this the end of the "secret soundings"?', T (Law) (5.10.99) 3; 'Groups Join "Secret Soundings" Lobby', LSG (6.10.99) 3; 'Press round–up', LSG (6.10.99) 10; 'Editorial: Fit for Present Purposes', LSG (6.10.99) 14; 'QC selection attacked', T (7.10.99) 6; 'Comment: An End to Secrecy' (1999) 143 SJ 923; 'Legal diary', T (Law) (12.10.99) 23; 'Barristers Defy Bar Council and Support End to "Secret Soundings" ', LSG (13.10.99) 5; 'Barristers Vote for Reform' (1999) 143 SJ 945; 'A Week in the Law...' (1999) 149 NLJ 1508; 'Top judge says US–style vetting will harm Bench', T (18.10.99) 4; Kamlesh Bahl, 'Why "apply, don't be shy" isn't working', T (Law) (26.10.99) 9; 'Judge "cabal" ', T (30.10.99) 8; 'Solicitors' body in move to represent all lawyers', FT (30–31.10.99) 3; Robert Sayer, 'Beginning of an Era', LSG (3.11.99) 16; 'Judicial scrutiny backed by Lord Chief Justice', T (5.11.99) 4; 'Bingham Backs "Secret Soundings" ', LSG (10.11.99) 4; 'Success of Legal Aid Reforms to be Judged by "Squealing" Lawyers', LSG (10.11.99) 3; 'Irvine tells how aspiring judges are marked up', T (3.11.99) 14; 'The case of the judges' guilty secret', I (Tues Rev) (16.11.99) 14; 'Top QC Hits Out at Silks', LSG (24.11.99) 5; 'Editorial: Whispering Judges', LSG (24.11.99) 15; 'Loss of Confidence', LSG (1.12.99) 22; 'Choice of judges to be more open', T (2.12.99) 1; 'Monitor for judge selection', T (4.12.99) 18; 'Limited Reforms could Mean More Solicitors Become Judges', LSG (8.12.99) 3; 'Press Round-up', LSG (8.12.99) 10; 'Judicial Appointments' (1999) 149 NLJ 1851; 'Reforms to eradicate Bar's "racist" policies', T (11.12.99) 6; Peach (1999); 'Summary of Recommendations from the Report of the Joint Working Party on Equal Opportunities in Judicial Appointments and Silk', in Bar Council (1999b: Annexe E); Bar Council (1999b); Malleson and Banda (2000: 39).

[67] On the persistence of class barriers see Hillyer (1994; 1995); Thomas and Rees (2000); Francis and McDonald (2000); Duff *et al.* (2000); Vignaendra (2001).

Chapter 5—Notes

[1] For a fuller account of this period see Royal Commission, Vol. I (1979: recommendation 17.1, 18.4–6, 19.1, 20.5, 33.3, 14–15, 19); LCD (1983); Reeves (1986); Abel (1988: 86–100 and Table 1.24; 1989a).

[2] *London Engineering and Iron Shipbuilding Company (Limited) v Cowan* (1867) 16 LT Reports 573; *Clarke v Couchman* (1885) 20 Law Journal 318, quoted in Pannick (1993: 174–6). In 1888 Sir E. Clarke, QC, the Solicitor–General, astonishingly advocated fusion in a speech to Birmingham law students. 'The Solicitor–General and the Birmingham Students', Law Journal (21.1.88) 49–52.

[3] Peter Butler, 'Viewpoint: On Fusion: Truth Will Out' (1986) 130 SJ 477; 'Rights of Audience—The Law Society's Submission to the Committee on the Future of the Legal Profession' (1987) 84 LSG 1299; Robert Johnson QC, 'Chairman's Comment', LSG (27.1.88) 38; 'Solicitors back open access to the Bar', T (8.3.88) 3; 'Public access to barristers "destructive"', DT (14.3.88); 'Solicitors Win Audience Rights at New Truro Court', LSG (20.4.88) 2; Marre (1988: paras. 18.33, 41, 62; Note of Dissent 1–10); Zander (1988: 24–31); 'Courts switch speeds trial of civil actions', DT (12.7.89) 9; 'Patent court could cut cost to inventors', I (24.9.90); 'Letter to the editor', T (28.9.90); 'The "great ideas" men find a new champion', DM (1.10.90) 30; 'Society plans April bid for rights of audience', L (6.11.90); see also Woolf (1996).

[4] Andrew (1989); 'Call to make government legal service attractive', T (20.1.89) 6; 'Government legal service to be given a big pay boost', T (20.1.89) 1; 'Government lawyers are catching up—at last', FT (23.1.89); T (21.2.89); 'Justice on the cheap', ES (11.5.89) 7; 'Sponsorship plan by CPS to ease staff shortage', I (18.5.89); 'Prosecutors "drop charges to save time"', DT (19.5.89); 'Crown service told to "pursue justice"', T (19.5.89); 'Audience Rights Best Hope for CPS Lawyers', LSG (17.5.89) 2; 'CPS to Sponsor Trainees', LSG (24.5.89) 7; 'Increase in black barristers at Bar "too slow"', T (26.5.89); 'DPP seeks greater advocacy rights for Crown solicitors', T (27.12.89); 'Prosecutor faults "let guilty go free"', G (27.4.90); 'Police "not hostile" to CPS', T (27.4.90); 'CPS lawyers "letting some guilty go free"', DT (27.4.90); 'View from the Committee' (1990) 140 NLJ 617; 'CPS Still Teething?' (1990) 140 NLJ 619; Home Affairs Committee (1990); 'The case for the prosecution', I (5.7.91); 'More join the CPS', T (18.7.91). For a history of the DPP before the CPS see Rozenberg (1987).

[5] 'Legal services: act now or miss out', L (5.12.89); 'Fennell warns of "race" to provide advocacy service', L (5.12.89); Law Society (1990); 'Freelance solicitor advocates "fill a market niche"', L (31.7.90); 'Barristers to teach advocacy to solicitors', L (31.7.90); 'Baker & McKenzie in advocacy training push', L (14.8.90); 'The freewheeling freelance', L (2.10.90); 'Solicitor advocates may outnumber Bar', L (16.10.90); 'Inns and Outs', T (16.10.90) 33; 'Advocacy training at Bird & Bird', L (30.10.90); 'Law Society to streamline training and entry system', T (14.1.91); 'Barristers likely to join solicitors in a single body', T (14.3.91); 'Twin–track Regulation Mooted', LSG (20.3.91) 5; 'A Solicitors' Chambers?' LSG (29.5.91) 2; Law Society (1991).

[6] 'Bar will fight over rights of audience', L (12.3.91); 'Audience Rights: Bar Reaffirms its Old Thinking', LSG (20.3.91) 4; 'Stirring the Embers' (1991) 141 NLJ

445; 'Solicitors give way on court proposals', T (3.4.91); 'Solicitors apply for wider advocacy rights', FT (3.4.91); 'Law Society moves to widen solicitors' role', DT (3.4.91) 8; 'Solicitors seek High Court role', I (3.4.91); 'Law Soc unveils advocacy scheme', L (9.4.91) 1; 'Advocacy Application on Trial', LSG (10.4.91) 4; 'Courts and Legal Services Committee: Legal Aid Dominates Mixed Menu', LSG (10.4.91) 6; 'Will the Playing Field Be Level?' C (5.91) 10; 'Audience rights', LA (5.91) 5; 'Bar demands block on audience rights', L (6.8.91); 'Rights of Audience War Cries' (1991) 141 NLJ 1099; 'Consumer Angle on Higher Court Advocacy' (1991) 135 SJ 909; 'Survey predicts mass exodus by barristers', L (10.9.91). For a history of this issue to 1997 see Zander (1997).

[7] 'Bar faces rights of audience battle', O (24.3.91); Green (1991a; 1991b); 'CPS lawyers to fight Bar ban on audience', T (16.4.91); 'Review of curbs on barristers urged', DT (16.4.91); 'CPS barristers seek extended court rights', L (23.4.91); 'Bar Stands Firm against More Crown Advocacy', LSG (29.5.91) 4; 'Rights of Audience for the CPS' (1991) 141 NLJ 733; 'Criminal lawyers' debate sees support for extended rights', L (18.6.91); 'Bar vows to resist state prosecutors in higher courts', T (1.8.91); 'Righteous Responses' (1991) 141 NLJ 1097; 'The Bar wants to bar its own', T (13.8.91); 'The Forgotten Barristers' (1991) 135 SJ 999.

[8] Bar Council (1991: paras. Summary 3.1, A2.1, A2.3, A3.1, B3.4, B7.3, C1.6–7, C3.5, C5.3, C8.4, C9.11, D3.22, D4.10, E3.4, E3.12, E8.6, E9.8, F9.2, G2.3, G3.6, K1.2, L3.4, L6.2.4).

[9] 'Bar draws up battle lines for future of advocacy rights', T (2.4.91); 'Talks delay new rights for solicitors', G (26.4.91); 'Solicitors face setback in fight for wider rights', FT (26.4.91); 'Views sought on solicitors as advocates', DT (26.4.91); 'Consultation Ordered on Employed Advocates', LSG (5.6.91) 9; 'Taylor is New LCJ', LSG (26.2.92) 3; 'Don't disturb us, we're busy', I (20.3.92) 19; 'Bar room brawl for jobs on the cards', ES (23.3.92) 35; 'Bar beats off law reforms', T (26.3.92); 'Employed barristers unbowed by "deadlock"', L (31.3.92); 'In-house Lawyers fear Advocacy Ban', LSG (1.4.92) 3; 'Advocacy hopes could be dashed', L (14.4.92).

[10] 'End of the barrister's closed shop', ES (14.4.92); 'Stupefaction in court', G (15.4.92) 20; 'An unjustified Bar', T (15.4.92) 13; Philip Ely, 'Rights of Audience', LSG (15.4.92) 2; 'Full Audience Rights Draw Closer for Some', LSG (15.4.92) 3; 'Judges Influence "No" to CPS', LSG (15.4.92) 4; 'Solicitors break Bar's higher court monopoly', T (15.4.92) 1, 4; 'Solicitors "should have full rights in higher courts"', DT (15.4.92); 'Court advocacy changes endorsed', FT (15.4.92); 'Prosecution service frozen out in courts reform plan', G (15.4.92) 4; 'Solicitors a step nearer ending Bar monopoly', I (15.4.92) 9; 'Milestone on the Road to Full Rights of Audience for Solicitors' (1992) 142 NLJ 518; 'Employed Solicitors Bar Sours Law Soc Triumph' (1992) 136 SJ 351; 'Rights of Advocacy' (1992) 142 NLJ 517; 'Comment: Rights of Audience' (1992) 136 SJ 355; 'Insulting a profession', T (week of 21.4.92) 26; 'Lord Mackay's legacy', E (18.7.92) 17; ACLEC (1992: Summary).

[11] Gareth Williams QC, 'Chairman's Column: Rights of Audience', C (4.92) 3; 'Rights of Audience', C (4.92) 4; 'Advocacy restriction "harms competition"', T (1.5.92) 3; 'Borrie report boosts audience campaign', L (5.5.92) 1; 'OFT Boost for Advocacy Battle', LSG (6.5.92) 5; 'Law Soc Hails OFT Advice on Audience

Rights' (1992) 136 SJ 424; 'DPP Slams LCAC on Rights of Audience' (1992) 136 SJ 452; 'BACFI Presses for New Advocacy Role', LSG (20.5.92) 7; 'Employed Bar appeals on rights', L (26.5.92); 'CPS Makes Fresh Plea for Audience Rights', LSG (3.6.92) 12; 'DPP urges Lord Mackay to widen advocacy rights', FT (3.6.92); 'In Brief' (1992) 142 NLJ 779; 'News Digest' (1992) 136 SJ 541; ' "Reject Bar rule" urge CPS and GLS', L (9.6.92). David Pannick QC declared that 'any lawyer who does not understand [the cab-rank rule] really has no business being an advocate' and it should apply to lawyers out of court and solicitors. But he acknowledged 'disturbing signs' that many flouted it. Pannick (1993: 144–6).

[12] ' "New Bar Strides Out" ', LSG (15.4.92) 6–7; 'Advocacy Talks Prolonged', LSG (8.7.92) 4; 'Rights of Advocacy' (1992) 142 NLJ 517; 'One for All: All for Rights' (1992) 142 NLJ 553; Tony Holland, 'Employed Solicitors and Rights of Audience' (1992) 142 NLJ 573; 'Rights of Audience' (1992) 142 NLJ 818; 'Solicitor Advocates Urge Ely to Act on Rights of Audience' (1992) 142 NLJ 922; 'Freelancers Aim to Change Law Soc Policy on Audience rights' (1992) 136 SJ 639; 'Fight starts on behalf of employed lawyers', L (12.5.92); 'Sir Sydney Lipworth', L (12.5.92); 'A lawyer in the house', I (22.5.92) 26; 'Bar Raps Law Soc on Advocacy Training' (1992) 136 SJ 931; 'Freelancers Urge no Delay on Audience Rights Bid', LSG (1.7.92) 7; 'News Digest' (1992) 136 SJ 1045; 'Society backs rights for all in higher courts', L (27.10.92) 1; 'Final Bid for Audience Rights Includes Employed Lawyers', LSG (28.10.92) 6.

[13] 'Welsh Wizard', C (1–2.92) 20; 'BCCI judge appointed Master of the Rolls', DT (13.8.92); 'Taylor Opposes Greater Audience Rights for CPS', LSG (30.9.92) 5; 'Crown prosecutors closer to breaching Bar's monopoly', T (6.10.92) 4; 'Barristers lose battle on rights of audience', FT (6.10.92); 'Judges Open Door for Employed Advocates', LSG (7.10.92) 3; 'Letter to the editor', T (8.10.92); 'Top Judges Deal Death Blow to Bar Campaign' (1992) 136 SJ 984; 'Mills to fight on barristers' rights', T (22.10.92); 'Williams: "No" to CPS Audience Rights', LSG (4.11.92) 6; 'More Equal than Others' (1992) 142 NLJ 1529; 'Bar defies CPS claim to cases', G (9.11.92); 'Lawyers in rift on rights at court', T (10.11.92); 'Bar Challenges Judges on Advocacy Rule', LSG (11.11.92) 3; 'Law Soc Says Yes to Guidelines' (1992) 136 SJ 1130; 'Bar v Bar' (1992) 136 SJ 1131; 'Bar digs its heels in over higher rights', L (17.11.92); 'Impartiality question "outrageous" says QC', L (15.12.92); Derek Wheatley QC, 'Rights and wrongs in the higher courts', T (26.1.93) 33; Harry Mitchell QC, 'Letters: A Word for the Employed Barrister', C (11–12.93) 6.

[14] Peter Goldsmith QC, 'Decisions on the Merits', C (2.93) 9; 'In the news', L (9.3.93) 8; 'Judges Postpone Ruling on Employed Advocates', LSG (17.3.93) 7; 'Setback for prosecutors', T (17.9.93); 'Mackay delays ruling on barristers' rights', FT (17.3.93); 'Mackay Delays Extended Advocacy Decision' (1993) 137 SJ 240; 'Another Adjournment for Employed Barristers' (1993) 143 NLJ 390; 'Bar challenges extra power for solicitors', T (19.3.93); J J Rowe QC, 'Chairman's Column: What Is Bothering the Bar', C (4.93) 3.

[15] 'Society Gives Some Ground on In-house Advocates', LSG (21.4.93) 3; ' "Three-lawyer" rule for in-house depts', L (27.4.93); 'Three-lawyer rights of audience rule "ludicrous" ', L (4.5.93) 6; 'Advocacy Let-down for Crown Lawyers', LSG (12.5.93) 4; 'Mills suffers blow over court rights', T (13.5.93); 'Mackay stalling, says Lamont', G (13.5.93); 'Law Society fury over audience "obstacles" ', L (18.5.93);

'Spirits Tumble after Griffiths Response', LSG (19.5.93) 6; 'Council Boils Over on Audience Rights', LSG (19.5.93) 5; 'Fur Flies at May Council Meeting' (1993) 143 NLJ 714; Sir David Napley, 'The Long Road to Audience Rights', LSG (2.6.93) 8.

[16] 'Stern Words for Lawyers', LSG (19.5.93) 6; 'Fight continues for rights of audience', L (6.7.93) 1; 'Society's Bid for Audience Rights Dealt Blow', LSG (7.7.93) 4; 'Drop Employed Lawyers Urges Griffiths', LSG (7.7.93) 4; 'Extended Rights of Audience—Hidden Agenda' (1993) 143 NLJ 983; 'Advocacy Barrier Undermines CPS', LSG (14.7.93) 9; 'Quality of Service is Major Priority' (1993) 143 NLJ 1019; 'Fair Trading Director Supports Solicitors' Rights' (1993) 143 NLJ 1018; 'Law Soc's last stand on rights', L (20.7.93); 'Irresistible call for extended rights?' L (20.7.93); 'Solidarity Pledge on Advocacy Bid', LSG (21.7.93) 5; 'Society will Succeed says Sheldon' (1993) 143 NLJ 1054; 'Time for Reason', LSG (28.7.93) 15; 'Student Finance Fears', LSG (28.7.93) 7; CPS (1993).

[17] 'Training for Justice', C (7.93) 3; 'OFT report welcomed', L (13.7.93) 1; 'Audience Rights Boost', LSG (14.7.93) 8; 'Steyn Raises Hopes on Advocacy', LSG (25.8.93) 4; 'CPS Lawyers to Fight Restructuring' (1993) 137 SJ 983; 'CPS Mood', LSG (20.10.93) 9; 'CPS Union Defends Mills' (1993) 137 SJ 1095; 'Boiling point', T (16.11.93); 'CPS Barrister Elections Fuel Advocacy Debate', LSG (24.11.93) 5; 'Survey Rocks Mills' CPS', LSG (1.12.93) 3; 'CPS Lawyers Lack Confidence in Leadership' (1993) 143 NLJ 1702; 'Think-tank Moots Private Prosecutors', LSG (8.12.93) 7; Frazer (1993); 'Mills Grist', LSG (12.1.94) 9; 'CPS Morale is High, says Mills', LSG (22.6.94) 7; 'Red Tape Ties up CPS', LSG (6.7.94) 7.

[18] 'S J Berwin leads move into advocacy', L (11.9.90) 1; 'Enter the renaissance lawyer', T (7.9.93); 'Peculiar, but good practice', T (7.9.93); 'Solicitors may put judges in dock', G (8.12.93); 'Solicitors ruled out of higher courts', T (8.12.93); 'Barristers' monopoly is broken by Mackay', DM (9.12.93) 1; 'Solicitors to have higher court rights', DT (9.12.93); 'Solicitors break into higher courts', I (9.12.93); 'Bar's monopoly ended', FT (9.12.93); 'Victory won by solicitors', G (9.12.93); 'Solicitors win access to higher courts', T (9.12.93); 'Benefits of the Bar's broken monopoly', FT (14.12.93); 'CPS fights on for audience rights', L (14.12.93) 1; 'Rights of Audience', LSG (17.12.93) 29; 'At Long Last—Rights of Audience' (1993) 143 NLJ 1774; 'Advocacy Triumph for Most Solicitors; "Bar is Best" Campaign Signalled to Beat off Newcomers', LSG (17.12.93) 4; 'City Challenge', LSG (17.12.93) 6; 'BACFI to press on', L (21.12.93); 'Taylor Aims for "Basic Justice"', LSG (12.1.94) 8; John Taylor, 'Efficiency in Local Justice', LSG (19.1.94) 12; 'United we stand on audience rights', L (25.1.94) 15; 'No bar to becoming good colleagues', T (25.1.94); SJ Berwin, advertisement, T (25.1.94); 'SJ Berwin takes on barristers', L (1.2.94); 'Solicitors "Cut Advocacy Fees"', LSG (27.7.94) 3; 'Barristers transformed into solicitor-advocates', L (4.10.94); 'Open Inns', LSG (7.10.94) 7; 'Barrister joins "one-stop" firm', L (1.11.94); 'Firm to Cut its Use of the Bar', LSG (2.11.94) 9; 'Why Mr. Jones called time on the Bar', I (9.11.94) 33; 'Legal diary', T (29.6.99) 39.

[19] 'Big Wigs and Periwigs', C (3.90) 28; 'I, my Lords, embody the Law', T (Sat Rev) (6.4.91) 4; 'Legal revolution to come from the top', G (20.4.92) 1; 'Wearing Wigs' (1992) 142 NLJ 589; 'A Right Wigging' (1992) 142 NLJ 591; 'Losing more than his wig', T (3.6.92); 'Mackay may pull the rug on wigs', G (8.6.92); 'Courtroom dress in the dock', T (23.6.92); 'Judges rely on Queen to keep Perry Mason out of

court', DT (23.6.92) 14; 'Noble wigging for "ludicrous judges"', DT (23.6.92); 'Peers divided on worth of wigs', I (23.6.92) 6; 'Peers go hairless over judges' wigs', G (23.6.92); 'Hearsay' (1992) 136 SJ 618; 'Geoffrey Wheatcroft on De-Wigging the Bewigged', I (Magazine) (4.7.92) 14; 'Are judges naked without their robes?' T (14.7.92); 'Editorial: Wigs and Gowns Should Be Retained', C (6–7.92) 3; ' "Wigs and Gowns Must Stay"—The People's View', C (6–7.92) 6; 'BCCI judge appointed Master of the Rolls', DT (13.8.92); 'Mackay to seek public's judgment on judicial finery', T (19.8.92); 'Off with their wigs', T (19.8.92) 11; Tony Holland, 'Comment: Caught Dressing' (1992) 136 SJ 859; 'Court Dress (Again and Again)' (1992) 142 NLJ 1186; 'Addressing the Question' (1992) 142 NLJ 1221, 1330–1; 'Taylor Attacks Legal Aid Cuts', LSG (2.12.92) 3; 'Spending Cuts are "Blot on System"—Taylor' (1992) 136 SJ 1207; 'Court Dress' (1993) 143 NLJ 42; 'Senior judges given ruling to take off "ridiculous" wigs', T (12.7.93); 'Judges and barristers to keep wigs and gowns', DT (1.10.93); 'Wigs Win as Dress Remains Formal', LSG (6.10.93) 8; ' "Bar is Best" Campaign Signalled to Beat off Newcomers', LSG (17.12.93) 4; 'Not Worth the Cost' (1994) 144 NLJ 42; 'Solicitor's High Court Debut', LSG (16.2.94) 3; 'Wigs Question Remains Open', LSG (23.2.94) 7; 'Lawyer appeals for audience', L (19.4.94); 'Solicitors Launch Advocates Group', LSG (20.4.94) 6; 'Get Your Wigs Out', LSG (11.5.94) 4; 'Editorial: Stuff and Nonsense' (1994) 144 NLJ 997; 'Wigs Issue Sparks Row', LSG (27.7.94) 4; 'Higher Courts Curtain Raiser', LSG (27.7.94) 10; Robert Seabrook QC, 'Chairman's Column: Into the Next 100 Years', C (9–10.94) 3; 'Mackay Rapped over Silk Round', LSG (26.10.94) 5; 'Women's "No" to Wigs and Court Gowns', LSG (16.11.94) 3; 'A frosty audience', T (6.12.94) 39; 'City Held Back by Advocacy Hurdle', LSG (31.8.95) 4; ACLEC (1995d: 24); 'Advocacy Test Failures are Up', LSG (14.2.96) 1; 'Editorial: Talking Tests', LSG (14.2.96) 14; 'Comment: Access for Advocates', LSG (21.2.96) 14; 'Solicitor Advocates' Falling Pass Rates', C (3–4.96) 4; 'Bid to Lower Advocacy Hurdles', LSG (18.9.96) 1; 'Editorial: Rights in Practice', LSG (18.9.96) 15; Belloni (n.d.) (discrimination against solicitor advocates). On the history of wigs see McLaren (1999).

[20] T (20.7.94); 'The Wig Issue', LSG (18.1.95) 22; 'Solicitor advocates tackle wig issue head on', L (24.1.95); 'Solicitors to lose their case for wearing wigs in court', T (10.3.95); 'No to Wigs', LSG (12.4.95) 3; 'Wigs Row Comes to a Head' (1995) 139 SJ 332; 'Profession Split over Wigs', LSG (26.4.95) 7; 'Solicitor-advocates Aim to Compete' (1995) 139 SJ 645; 'Working mum reaches the top', T (6.1.98) 33; 'Comment: Hands on Approach' (1998) 142 SJ 271; 'Irvine asks Lords to let him wear modern clothes', T (12.9.98) 2; 'Once more into the breeches for Irvine', T (10.11.98) 8; 'Get rid of the wig as well, Irvine tells MPs', T (11.11.98) 12; 'Man in tights: The Lord Chancellor should be allowed some Lycra relief', T (11.11.98) 21; 'Peer Sheds Breeches but Finds Wig Won't Budge', NYT (17.11.98) A4; 'Lord Chancellor told he may abandon breeches', T (17.11.98) 1; 'Comment: All Dressed Up' (1998) 142 SJ 1099; HC Standing Committee E (13.5.99).

[21] 'A lukewarm revolution', L (7.3.95); 'Judge must say sorry for slur on solicitors', T (27.3.95); 'Judge Makes Amends', LSG (29.3.95) 56; 'Solicitors Angry at Judge's "Regret" Comments' (1995) 139 SJ 489; 'What's special about the Bar?' T (31.10.95) 37; 'Solicitors silent in court', I (10.1.96) §2 p11; 'Reluctant Rumpoles', LSG (5.6.96) 24; 'Confessions of a troublemaker', T (14.7.96) 37; 'Inns and Outs', T (24.9.96) 35; 'Give solicitors equal rights of audience', L (8.10.96) 13; 'Solicitor

Advocates No Threat to Bar' (1996) 140 SJ 1092; 'Comment: Solicitor advocates' (1996) 140 SJ 1095; 'Inns and Outs', T (3.12.96); 'Advocacy Test Hurdles Set to be Lowered', LSG (22.1.97) 1; Davis *et al.* (1997); Davis and Kerridge (1997); 'Judge refuses to stand down over bias claim', T (6.5.99) 2; '"Whinger" Judge', LSG (6.10.99) 5; 'Advocates Call', LSG (13.10.99) 4; Flood *et al.* (n.d.).

[22] Neil Addison, 'Viewpoint', L (18.1.94); 'Bacfi chair slates colleague', L (21.6.94); 'Bar Shuts Door on Modernisers', LSG (16.11.94) 8; 'Employed Lawyers Attack Professional Restrictions' (1994) 138 SJ 564; Derek Wheatley QC, 'Fair play by the Bar Council?', T (28.8.94); 'Prosecutor suspended by CPS over Times article', T (2.11.94); (1994) 138 SJ 1116; 'Bar Council Member Suspended by CPS' (1994) 144 NLJ 1506; 'CPS lawyers in uproar over Addison suspension', L (8.11.94) 1; 'No longer a voice in the wilderness', L (8.11.94); 'Outrage as CPS Suspends Media Friendly Lawyer', LSG (9.11.94) 5; Tony Holland, 'Opinion: Unnecessary, Unconstructive and Dilatory' (1995) 139 SJ 518; 'Advocacy "No"', LSG (14.6.95) 1; 'Bar Shoots Down Reform Proposals', LSG (14.6.95) 5; 'Comment: Cream Rises' (1995) 145 NLJ 877; 'Committee Split in Two', LSG (21.6.95) 64; 'No to State Prosecutors' (1995) 145 NLJ 951; 'Comment: Lord Chancellor's Advisory Committee' (1995) 139 SJ 623; 'Employed Pressure', LSG (19.7.95) 3; Peter Goldsmith QC, 'Chairman's Column: If the Bar Is Special, Why a Complaints System?" C (11–12.95) 3; ACLEC (1995b: 4, 27, 41; Dissent 4, 6–8); Belloni (n.d.) (interviews with Merricks 3.2.95 and Holland 21.6.95).

[23] 'Think-tank Moots Private Prosecutors', LSG (8.12.93) 7; 'CPS Lawyers Could Strike' (1996) 140 SJ 496; 'Grist for Mills', LSG (19.6.96) 14; 'Poll Exposes Deep Unease at CPS', LSG (20.11.96) 1; 'Editorial: Not all Bad News', LSG (20.11.96) 15; 'Comment: Crown Purchasing Service?' (1996) 140 SJ 1119; 'Police Chief Moots Replacing CPS', LSG (4.12.96) 6.

[24] 'Judges split over court rights of CPS', T (22.10.96) 2; 'If justice is not seen to be fair', T (22.10.96) 43; 'Letter to the editor', T (24.10.96) 21; 'Inns and Outs', T (12.11.96) 35; 'Scott joins opposition to barrister reforms', T (10.1.97) 6; 'CPS Advocacy Hopes', LSG (15.1.97) 4; 'Prosecutors lose jury trials fight', FT (27.2.97) 10; 'Lawyers attack court access ruling', DT (27.2.97) 8; 'Bar defeats bid to end monopoly of jury trials', T (27.2.97) 6; 'Employed Lawyers seek Rights Review', LSG (5.3.97) 1; 'CPS Dismayed by Limited Rights', LSG (5.3.97) 8; 'Law Society Anger over Limits to Rights for Employed Solicitors' (1997) 141 SJ 197; Tony Girling, 'President's Column: Getting Back', LSG (19.3.97) 18; 'A division of power that does not add up', L (1.4.97) 19; Robert Owen QC, 'Chairman's Column: Legal Aid', C (3–4.97) 3; 'Rights of Audience', C (3–4.97) 6.

[25] 'Lord Chancellor eyes Bar's last preserve', T (12.12.97) 6; National Audit Office, Press Notice (12.12.97); Comptroller and Auditor General (1997: para. 6.29); 'Bar Acts on Late Returns' (1997) 147 NLJ 1839; 'Editorial: The Return of the Brief' (1997) 147 NLJ 1837; 'Working mum reaches the top', T (6.1.98) 33; 'Barristers face checks over CPS complaints', T (6.1.98) 2; 'CPS Reprimand', LSG (8.1.98) 5; 'Interview: Heather Hallett', LSG (28.1.98) 24; 'Barristers told to stop dropping child-abuse cases', T (30.1.98) 11; 'Irvine eyes new justice empire', ST (8.2.98) §1, 28; 'Interview: I'll Give it My Very Best Shot', C (2.98) 10; Glidewell *et al.* (1998); 'The Problem of Returned Briefs—The History and a Solution', 162 Justice of the Peace 602 (1.8.98). Hallett said she had 'been to a number of the

[American] states and seen the public state prosecution system and I just don't think that's the way to go...the difference in approach between the independent barrister and the lawyer, if he does nothing but prosecute, to what should or shouldn't be disclosed to the defense is just astonishing' (July 1998 interview).

[26] 'Barristers' "monopoly" of courts weakened', DT (20.1.98); 'Bar crown court monopoly to end', T (20.1.98) 1; 'LCD Pledges Audience Rights Reform', LSG (21.1.98) 1; 'Breakthrough for CPS and Employed Lawyers' (1998) 142 SJ 51; 'Comment: Levelling the Playing Field' (1998) 142 SJ 55; 'Shifting the blame', L (27.1.98).

[27] Committee on Public Accounts (1998: p. v, 5–6, 9, 12–13, 24).

[28] 'Society Plea for Rights of Audience' (1998) 148 NLJ 270; 'Editorial: A Step Nearer to the Jury' (1998) 148 NLJ 269.

[29] Heather Hallett QC to Lord Irvine (27.3.98); Heather Hallett QC, 'Chairman's Column: Bastions of Liberty', C (6.98) 3; 'Solicitors at the Bar', LSG (1.7.98) 4; ' "Bully" Bar Right', LSG (3.9.98) 5.

[30] Glidewell *et al.* (1998: Summary paras. 9, 11–12, 19–22, 30, 32, 57).

[31] Sir Gavin Lightman, 'Bumping over the silk road', T (9.6.98) 41; 'Letters to the editor: Barristers' fees', T (15.6.98) 23.

[32] 'Barristers to lose court monopoly in bid to cut legal costs', ST (21.6.98) §1, 7.

[33] Paul Foot, 'The one man who couldn't read the signs', ES (25.6.98) 11; 'Letters to the editor: Barristers' choice in the "cab-rank" ', T (26.6.98) 25.

[34] 'Court Win for Solicitor-advocates', LSG (17.6.98) 1; 'Editorial: Levelling the Field', LSG (17.6.98) 15; 'Court Rights Plan divides Advocates', LSG (24.6.98) 1.

[35] LCD (1998: paras. 1.11, 2.1, 6–7, 10, 12, 15, 3.7, 4.12, 16); Bar Council (1998: Executive Summary and paras. 1.9, 2.4, 3.10, 22, 31, 4.5, 5.2); 'Irvine puts end to Bar's courtroom dominance', G (26.6.98) 8; Heather Hallett, 'No bar to properly qualified solicitors', I (Fri Rev) (26.6.98) 19; 'Irvine wants no bar on seeking justice', FT (26.6.98) 8; 'Reforms to lift curbs on lawyers presenting cases in higher courts', FT (26.6.98) 22; 'Court shake-up to break barristers' monopoly', I (26.6.98) 5; 'Cost of legal action may be slashed', DT (26.6.98) 1; 'Irvine to scrap Bar's court monopoly', T (26.6.98) 1; 'All Solicitors to Gain Court Rights', LSG (1.7.98) 4; 'Press Round-Up', LSG (1.7.98) 12; 'Letters to the editor: Barristers' loss of court monopoly', T (3.7.98) 23; 'Irvine's New Crusade' (1998) 142 SJ 611; 'Comment: Breaking down the Barriers' (1998) 142 SJ 615; 'Last Orders at the Bar?' LSG (8.7.98) 10; 'Press Round-Up', LSG (8.7.98) 12; 'President of Family Division Not Consulted on Reforms' (1998) 142 SJ 659; 'Justice should Mean Choice', I (Fri Rev) (31.7.98) 16; 'Call for Advocacy Rights', LSG (12.8.98) 6; 'Sheldon to Sit on Bar's Advocacy Committee' (1998) 142 SJ 779; 'Comment: Joint training for all Advocates' (1998) 142 SJ 783; Response by the ENPBA to the LCD Consultation Document (23.8.98); Heather Hallett QC, 'Chairman's Column: Advocating the Highest Standards', C (8.98) 3; John Morris QC, 'Wise words and privileges', C (8.98) 17; 'Young Solicitors Call for Automatic Rights of Audience on Admission', LSG (9.9.98) 5; 'Bar reforms are revolution on the quiet, says QC', T (16.9.98) 6; 'Comment: Rights of Audience: Who Decides?' (1998) 142 SJ 831; 'Letters to the editor: "Bitter division" over Bar proposals', T (21.9.98) 23; 'Letters to the editor: Division of labour in legal practice', T (28.9.98) 21; 'Bar warns Straw that his reforms could break law', T (5.10.98) 10; 'Letters to the editor: Legal

divisions', T (5.10.98) 23; 'Bar Chairman Defends Position of Threatened High Street Solicitors' LSG (7.10.98) 3; 'Judges revolt over Irvine's reform plans', T (15.10.98) 11; 'Irvine Pressured', LSG (21.10.98) 4; 'Editorial: Monopolies and mergers', LA (10.98) 3; 'Rights of audience', LA (10.98) 5; 'A New Era for Human Rights', C (10.98) 4; Nigel Savage, 'A future together', T (20.10.98) 41; BB (10.98); David Pannick QC, 'Will lawyers become reformed characters?' T (3.11.98); 'Bar under Fire', LSG (18.11.98) 4; Heather Hallett QC, 'There are no barriers to entry', T (24.11.98) 41; 'Business supports move to solicitor advocacy', FT (27.11.98) 14; 'Higher Rights Support', LSG (2.12.98) 5; Heather Hallett QC, 'Chairman's Column: Striving for Justice', C (12.98) 3; Sydney Kentridge QC, 'A Quiet Revolution', C (12.98) 24; 'Letters to the editor: Advent of solicitor advocate may spell higher costs', FT (3.12.98) 20; Brennan (1999: para. 6).

[36] 'Straw reviews right to choose a trial by jury', T (29.7.98) 9; 'Lawyers speak up for trial by jury', T (30.7.98) 2; 'Tilting the scales: The case for caution in justice reform,' T (30.7.98) 21; 'Letters to the editor: Trial by jury: fundamental right or unnecessary cost?' T (6.8.98) 19; 'Letters to the editor: Option of trial by jury under threat', T (17.9.98) 23; 'Lawyers Unite to Defend Jury Trials' (1998) 142 SJ 852; Heather Hallett QC, 'Chairman's Column: Trial by Jury', C (10.98) 3.

[37] 'Press Round-Up', LSG (8.4.99) 12; 'Incompetence Alarm', LSG (8.4.99) 4; 'Preserving a Robust Independence' (1999) 149 NLJ 908; 'Letters to the editor: Ineffective CPS selection process', T (7.7.99) 21; 'CPS official "sold list of informers"', T (13.7.99) 2; 'DPP plans return to courtroom role', T (22.7.99) 10; 'The verdict comes 45 years too late: Bentley is cleared', T (31.7.98) 1; Benedict Birnberg, 'Why the law failed Derek Bentley', T (4.9.98) 33; 'Mr Big of crime comes clean', ST (11.4.99) 5; 'DPP warns prosecutors not to withhold evidence', T (21.5.99) 8; 'CPS censured over death in custody cases', T (12.8.99) 4; 'Stress inquiry ordered after CPS suicides', T (16.8.99) 5; 'Police "covered up" A6 murder evidence', T (3.9.99) 8; 'CPS Solicitor-Advocates Praised', LSG (22.9.99) 4. For other miscarriages of justice in cases brought by 'independent' prosecutors see Kennedy (1961); Justice (1964); Lord Russell (1965); Foot (1971); Kennedy *et al.* (1980); Woffinden (1988).

[38] HL 595: 1107–16, 1119–27, 1147–51, 1156–8, 1188–92, 1195–1201 (14.12.98).

[39] '"Our profession will face great challenges"', T (5.1.99) 35; 'New Bar Order', LSG (6.1.99) 9; 'Dan Brennan' (1999) 143 SJ 24; Dan Brennan QC, 'Bar United-v-Solicitor Wanderers', C (4.99) 3; Malcolm Swift QC, 'A Step in the Wrong Direction', C (6.99) 20; Brennan (1999: para. 6).

[40] Letter from Susan Ward to BACFI members (8.1.99); Susan Ward, 'Comment: Access to Justice Bill—What is the Fuss About?' (1999) 149 NLJ 153.

[41] HL 596: 493–504 (19.1.99), 982–5 (26.1.99), 1184–92, 1210–23 (28.1.99), 597: 338–44 (11.2.99), 602–8, 643–7 (16.2.99), 669–77 (16.3.99).

[42] HL 596: 993–1008 (26.1.99), 1137–73 (28.1.99).

[43] HL 597: 628–39 (16.2.99).

[44] 'Lords reject Irvine Bill', T (29.1.99) 2; 'Lords defeat extension', FT (29.1.99); 'Irvine to Fight Higher Rights Vote', LSG (3.2.99) 5; 'Editorial: Audience Figures', LSG (3.2.99) 16; 'Comment: We have Been Here Before' (1999) 143 SJ 103; 'Peers reject rights for employed lawyers', LA (3.99) 5; Susan Ward, 'Letter from the Chairman', BB (3.99) 1.

[45] Dan Brennan QC, 'Chairman's Report', 112 BN (4.99) 2; Letter from Dan Brennan QC to all members of the Employed Bar (10.5.99); Fax: Important Notice from BACFI: Bar Council Questionnaire (12.5.99).

[46] Derek Wheatley QC, 'One Bar . . .', BB (6.99) 4; 'Bar Aims to Welcome Solicitors', LSG (9.6.99) 5; 'Training to Rectify Weaknesses' (1999) 143 SJ 552; Susan Ward, 'Letter from the Chairman', BB (7.99) 1; 'Collyear Committee', BB (7.99) 5; 'Report from the Chairman of the Bar', BB (7.99) 6; 'AGM report', BB (9.99) 2; Leggatt *et al.* (1999); Collyear Committee (1999).

[47] HC Standing Committee E (11.5.99); HC 333: 1052–5 (22.6.99).

[48] HL 604: 442–53 (14.7.99); Access to Justice Act 1999 §§ 36–42; ' "Retire? There's is nothing I like more than work" ', T (7.9.99) 12; Dan Brennan QC, 'Chairman's Report: Rights of audience v Solicitor Advocates', 116 BN (8.99) 3.

[49] 'Patent Agents seek Rights of Audience', LSG (9.10.91) 9; 'Patent Agents Apply for Rights of Audience' (1991) 141 NLJ 1357; 'Debt Practitioners seek Audience/Litigation Rights', LSG (27.5.92); 'Extended rights being sought', L (28.9.93); 'New Body in Bid to Litigate', LSG (19.1.94) 4; 'Fight to take case to trial', FT (15.3.95); 'ILEX set to Grant Rights of Audience' (1995) 139 SJ 1244; ACLEC (1995c; 1995d: 15–16); 'Building Experts Fail Litigation Test', LSG (7.2.96) 4; 'Challenge by Commercial Litigators' (1996) 140 SJ 141; 'Criminal Lawyers in ILEX Row', LSG (12.6.96) 5; 'Inns and Outs', T (5.11.96) 41; 'Legal Execs win Rights of Audience', LSG (19.1.97) 1; 'Anger as patent agents recommended for rights of audience in higher courts', L (15.4.97) 24; 'Huge Boost for Legal Execs' (1997) 141 SJ 1096; 'Extended Audience for Legal Executives' (1997) 147 NLJ 1682; ACLEC (1997: 14–15, 51–7); 'Patent Agents Bid for Court Rights', LSG (11.11.98) 9; 'Patently True', LSG (19.5.99) 8; 'Patent Agents win Rights of Audience' (1999) 143 SJ 476; 'Trade Mark Boost', LSG (13.10.99) 4; 'Law Society chief plans to take over the Bar', T (30.10.99) 8; 'Solicitors' body in move to represent all lawyers', FT (30–31.10.99) 3; 'Sayer sets out Vision of Fused Profession', LSG (3.11.99) 1; Robert Sayer, 'Beginning of an Era', LSG (3.11.99) 16; 'Press Round-up', LSG (3.11.99); 'Sayer's Vision gets Mixed Reception' (1999) 143 SJ 1024; 'Comment: Sting in the Tail' (1999) 143 SJ 1028; 'Editorial: Embracing the Attorneys' (1999) 149 NLJ 1637; 'Hirst to lead Bar in 2000' (1999) 143 SJ 1049; 'Letters: Fusing the professions' (1999) 149 NLJ 1676; 'Briefs', I (Tues Rev) (16.11.99) 14; Robert Sayer, 'Comment: A United Vision', LSG (17.11.99) 16; 'Patent Agents Advocate', LSG (1.12.99) 9; 'Legal diary', T (Law) (7.12.99) 19; Dan Brennan QC, 'Chairman's Report', 120 BN (12.99) 3.

[50] LSG (5.4.89) 7; 'Barristers Urged to Mount Marketing Offensive', LSG (26.9.90) 4; 'Bar Eases Rule on Direct Advice to Public', LSG (26.9.90) 6; Bar Council's Strategy Group (1990: para. 2.13); 'ORBA plans directory for direct access clients', L (5.2.91); 'Direct Access', C (1–2.92); 'Engineers gain barrister access', L (15.9.92); 'Direct Access Risk', LSG (30.9.92) 6; 'Solicitors Soothe Fears on Audience Rights', LSG (30.9.92) 6; 'Bar turns down DPA requests', L (27.7.93); 'Rowe Rules out Direct Access', LSG (3.11.93) 7.

[51] Neil Addison, 'Viewpoint', L (18.1.94); 'Bar Council to consider plans to compete with solicitors', L (1.2.94); 'Thorn in the Bar Council's flesh', L (15.2.94); 'Editorial: Bar Moves' (1994) 144 NLJ 185; BC Policy Unit (1994); 'Bar plans direct access to barristers', T (16.2.94) 5; 'Direct Brief', LSG (2.3.94) 4; 'The Best of all

Possible Worlds for the Bar?' (1994) 144 NLJ 310; Profile of Munby, C (1–2.94); 'Thinking the Unthinkable', C (1–2.94) 16; 'Bar Looks to Cut Solicitors Out of Work' (1994) 138 SJ 191; 'Direct access raises prospect of fusion', L (8.3.94); 'Barristers reject direct access', T (12.7.94); 'Bar to the public', ES (12.7.94); 'Bar Shuns Direct Access Initiative', LSG (13.7.94) 5; 'Barristers Block Direct Access' (1994) 138 SJ 704; 'Editorial: Professional Problems' (1994) 144 NLJ 961; 'Goldsmith rejects Bar "old guard" accusation', L (19.7.94); Bar Council Policy Unit (1994a; 1994b: para. 22); Bar Standards Review Body (1994: para. 3).

[52] Neil Addison, 'Facing up to the Choices' (1994) 144 NLJ 1166; Neil Addison, 'Will the Bar Survive into the 21st Century?' (1994) 138 SJ 1082; 'Bar Bete Noire', LSG (26.10.94) 9; Neil Addison, 'Why the Bar must change', ES (9.11.94); 'How should the Bar Vote?' (1994) 144 NLJ 1541; 'Barristers reject plea to accept briefs from public', DT (14.11.94); 'Bar Shuts Door on Modernisers', LSG (16.11.94) 8; 'Narrow Defeat for Radical Bar Proposals' (1994) 144 NLJ 1578; 'Bar Council AGM' (1994) 138 SJ 1172; 'Addison to continue to fight', L (22.11.94).

[53] 'Barristers clash with solicitors over fees', T (29.9.94); 'Referral fees worry Bar', L (4.10.94); 'Bar Intensifies Kick-back Fight', LSG (7.10.94) 9; 'Elly Quells Referral Fees Fears', C (9.10.94) 5.

[54] 'Addison on the Attack' (1995) 145 NLJ 679 ; Neil Addison, 'The Defeatist Talk of Frightened Men' (1995) 145 NLJ 860; 'Raft of proposals on way to Bar's AGM', L (16.5.95); 'Barristers to Vote on Public Access' (1995) 139 SJ 487; 'Bar Shoots Down Reform Proposals', LSG (14.6.95) 5; 'Addison's Resolutions Defeated at Bar AGM' (1995) 145 NLJ 878; 'Comment: Cream Rises' (1995) 145 NLJ 877; 'Radical ACM [*sic*] Motions Fall', C (7–8.95) 5; 'Bar AGM Report', C (7–8.95) 10.

[55] 'Battling for the Bar', LSG (21.1.96) 11; 'Dispute over CABx Direct Access Plan', LSG (22.5.96) 5; 'Direct Line Advice', LSG (5.6.96) 12; Hilary Heilbron QC, 'Moving with the Times—An Opportunity for the Bar', C (7–8.96) 18.

[56] ' "Get Real—Don't Squeal" Lawyers to be Told' (1997) 147 NLJ 1683; 'Going straight to the Bar', T (25.11.97) 39; Hilary Heilbron QC, 'Choice, flexibility and not a lot to pay', T (25.11.97) 39; 'Inns and Outs', T (25.11.97) 39; Bar Council Professional Standards and Legal Services Department (1997).

[57] Bar Council Contracts Working Group (1998: para. 5.8); 'Bar Outlines Plan for Wider Direct Access for Public and Institutions', LSG (28.10.98) 3; 'New Bar Order', LSG (6.1.99) 9; 'Letters to the Editor: Direct Access', C (2.9.99) 10; 114 BN (6.99) 6.

[58] Bar Council (1998: Executive Summary para. 6.6).

[59] 'Community Legal Service Unveiled by LCD' (1999) 149 NLJ 794; 'A Week in the Law...' (1999) 149 NLJ 1030; 'Bar Wins First Direct Contract from Legal Aid Board' (1999) 143 SJ 652; 'Survey Raises Fears for Future of Medium-sized Sets' (1999) 143 SJ 653; James Munby QC, 'Extending a Helping Hand', C (10.99) 26–7; Bar Council (1999: para. 1.2); 'Bar Launches New Legal Services Pilot to Cut Cost and Delay', 116 BN (8.99) 5.

[60] 'Bar Threatens Defectors' (1990) 140 NLJ 159; 'Barristers can work from home and advertise services', T (12.2.90); 'Barrister Challenges Bar Council' (1990) 134 SJ 269; 'Barristers at work in solicitors' firms face Bar discipline', T (23.2.90); 'Bar produces guide to setting up chambers', L (13.3.90); 'A question of rights and wrongs', L (13.3.90); 'Letter to the editor', T (26.3.90); 'Nock rejects Bar

discipline threat', L (3.4.90) 1; 'Barristers to fight rule on employment', L (7.4.90); 'Bar Council considers a new breed of barristers', L (17.4.90) 1; 'Letter to the editor', L (17.4.90); 'Disbarment for Employed Barristers?' (1990) 140 NLJ 1063; 'Inns and Outs', T (21.1.91); 'Advocate "Partner"', T (22.5.90) 34; 'Strong response to anonymous ad for barrister', L (27.5.90); 'Lawyers adapt to a fast-changing world', I (17.7.90) 25; 'Compromise may bring end to battle over employed barristers', T (24.7.90) 6; 'S J Berwin leads move into advocacy', L (11.9.90) 1; 'An unconventional advocate', L (18.9.90); 'Barristers' dilemma could be resolved by compromise', T (21.9.90); 'Barristers win fight for more freedom at work', DM (21.9.90); Mummery (1990); BB (10.90); 'Brussels-based barristers launch London set', L (26.2.91); 'Inns and Outs', T (5.3.91) 35; 'QC unlocks the EC door', MOS (10.3.91).

[61] Neil Addison, 'Viewpoint', L (18.1.94); 'Editorial: Bar Moves' (1994) 144 NLJ 185; 'Solicitors and barristers "should train together"', T (21.3.94) 1; 'Learning the Law', T (21.3.94) 19; 'Judge Proposes Fused Training', LSG (23.3.94) 5; Sir Frederick Lawton, 'Last orders for the Bar?' T (29.3.94); 'Business Group Calls for Fusion' (1994) 138 SJ 620; 'Bar comes under fire', L (18.10.94); 'Bar Council Elects Traditionalist Chairman' (1994) 138 SJ 1060; 'Elly Quells Referral Fees Fears', C (9–10.94) 5; 'Bar Shuts Door on Modernisers', LSG (6.11.94) 8; 'Peter Goldsmith QC' (1994) 138 SJ 1192; 'Bar council rules against partnerships', L (6.12.94); Robert Seabrook QC, 'A Watershed Year', C (11–12.94) 3; 'Bar Brain Box', LSG (16.12.94) 11; 'Brief for the next generation', I (11.1.95); 'Bar Shoots Down Reform Proposals', LSG (14.6.95) 5; ACLEC (1995a: para. 4.5; 1995e: 3).

[62] 'Labour Creates a Future Vision', LSG (22.2.95) 1; Henry Hodge, 'Comment: Labour's Way Forward', LSG (1.3.95) 10; 'Labour Questions Need for Separate Bar' (1995) 139 SJ 181; 'Labour Backs Major Review', LSG (28.6.95) 4; 'Fee "Gimmick"', LSG (26.7.95) 6; 'Labour to Refer Lawyers to MMC' (1995) 139 SJ 913; Peter Goldsmith QC, 'Heads out of the Sand' (1995) 145 NLJ 1398; 'Labour Backing for Major Law Shake-up', LSG (4.10.95) 64; 'Labour Proposals "Non-negotiable"' (1995) 139 SJ 969; 'Bar Chief Offers Free Services', LSG (11.10.95) 4; 'Free Work Sparks Row', LSG (11.10.95) 6; 'Comment: For Whose Good?' (1995) 139 SJ 1115; 'Mixed Signals from Labour', LSG (29.11.95) 10.

[63] ACLEC (1996a: 73–84; 1996c: 13, 53); 'Reforming judges take over at the top', T (25.5.96) 1; 'New Chief Justice tipped to continue overhaul of courts', T (25.5.96) 6; 'CPS Underfunding and Barristers Complaints', C (7–8.97) 4.

[64] BC Employed Bar Working Party (1997); 'Bar Council Meeting Berates Inns of Court over Equal Opportunities', LSG (25.6.97) 8; 1 NN (1997); 2 NN (1998); 3 NN (1998); 4 NN (1998); General Council of the Bar, *Annual Report* (1997); Dr Peter Gray to Hilary De Lyon, ACLEC (29.4.98); Response by the ENPBA to the LCD Consultation Document (23.8.98); ENPBA Application (7.12.98); (4.99) 6 EN 2–5; (8.99) 7 EN 5.

[65] Bar Council Working Party on the Appointment of Queen's Counsel (1994: 8–9, 15–19, 24, 30–1, 39, 80); 'Mackay Rapped over Silk Round', LSG (26.10.94) 5; 'Silk Storm' (1995) 139 SJ 57; 'Competing on equal footing', L (7.3.95); 'Solicitor Silk', LSG (9.8.95) 2; 'Silky Smooth Future for Solicitors?' (1995) 139 SJ 781; 'Comment: The Silk Route' (1995) 139 SJ 783; 'Editorial: Raw Silk Deal', LSG (17.4.95) 13.

[66] 'First solicitors appointed QCs', T (27.3.97) 6; 'Inns and Outs', T (1.4.97) 33; 'Solicitors make Silk and History', LSG (3.4.97) 1; 'Comment: Solicitors in Silk' (1997) 141 SJ 299; 'High Court Call', LSG (10.9.97) 4; 'Solicitors Blow Another Hole in Bar Monopoly' (1997) 141 SJ 832.

[67] 'Call for abolition of Queen's Counsel title', FT (2.2.98) 2; 'QC system marks up legal costs and is undemocratic, says report', G (2.2.98) 11; 'Lawyers name High Court's best and worst', T (2.2.98) 4; 'Barristers attacked for price-fixing as think-tank calls for silk cut', I (2.2.98) 3; Adam Smith Institute News (2.2.98); 'Report Calls for Abolition of Silk', LSG (4.2.98) 4; 'Abolish QCs, says Adam Smith Institute' (1998) 142 SJ 100; 'Pressure grows to end "silk round"', T (6.4.98) 2; 'Third Solicitor QC Appointed', LSG (16.4.98) 5; Derek Wheatley QC, 'A rough deal on the road to silk', T (29.9.98) 41; Reeves (1986; 1998).

[68] Sir Gavin Lightman, 'Bumping over the silk road', T (9.6.98) 41; 'Judge Warns Solicitors over Costs', LSG (10.6.98) 4; 'Letters to the editor: Barristers' fees', T (15.6.98) 23; David Pannick QC, 'Fees are not like a lottery win', T (16.6.98) 37.

[69] 'Legal diary', T (12.1.99) 37; 'QCs must undergo checks, say MPs', T (3.2.99) 9; 'Bar could pay taxpayer's bill for new QCs', T (11.2.99) 10; 'Letters to the editor: Monitoring MPs', T (9.2.99) 17; 'Letters to the editor: Monitoring QCs', T (15.2.99) 19; 'Writ large', G2 (16.2.99) 17; 'Letters to the editor: Monitoring QCs', T (17.2.99) 19; 'MPs lead campaign to abolish QCs', DT (19.3.99) 2; Andrew Dismore, 'Silks' purse', G2 (23.3.99) 14; 'Legal diary', T (23.3.99) 39; 'One More Solicitor QC Appointed', LSG (8.4.99) 4; 'Irvine Defends the QC "Kite Mark"' (1999) 143 SJ 357. 'Access to Justice Bill: Commons committee stage', LA (6.99) 4; HC 329: 230–41, 287–91, 301–4 (14.4.99); HC Standing Committee E (11.5.99, 13.5.99).

[70] David Pannick QC, 'Silk should not be cut but overseen by the Bar', T (soon after 1.4.99); 'Editorial: Massaging the Legal Ego' (1999) 149 NLJ 513.

[71] 'Director-judges break the rules over business links', ST (28.3.99) 9; 'Legal Diary', T (30.3.99) 35; 'Labour Rejects Purpose Clause for Justice Bill', LSG (6.5.99) 20; 'The writing is on the wallpaper', T (26.5.99) 24; 'Labour reneges on pledge to reform Bench', T (1.6.99) 8; Kate Malleson, 'Time's up for the old boys' network', G2 (1.6.99) 8; Malleson (1999); 'Comment: Same Old Story' (1999) 143 SJ 531; 'Writ large', G2 (22.6.99) 9; G2 (6.7.99) 8; 'Comment: No Room on the Bench' (1999) 143 SJ 679; 'Check on selection of judges and QCs', T (26.7.99) 4; 'All done strictly on the QC', G2 (27.7.99) 15; 'Tories Capitulate over Public Defenders' (1999) 143 SJ 727; Martyn Day and Russell Levy, 'Why judges must declare their interests', T (31.8.99) 21.

[72] 'Solicitors group calls for abolition of QCs', FT (28.9.99) 1; 'Law Society calls for end to "secret soundings"', DT (28.9.99) 2; 'Solicitors boycott "old boys" network', G (28.9.99) 5; 'Law Society will boycott judges' "old boy network"', T (28.9.99) 2; 'QC qualms', FT (29.9.99) 25; Anthony Julius, 'Secrecy that tarnishes our justice system', Ex (29.9.99) 10; 'Society: Scrap Bench Secret Soundings"', LSG (29.9.99) 1; 'Editorial: An Ill-judged System', LSG (29.9.99) 15; 'Law Society turns its Back on "Secret Soundings"' (1999) 143 SJ 895; 'A Week in the Law...' (1999) 149 NLJ 1430; 'Judge criticises "horrid" political correctness', T (1.10.99) 7; 'Is this the end of the "secret soundings"?', T (Law) (5.10.99) 3; 'Groups Join "Secret Soundings" Lobby', LSG (6.10.99) 3; 'Press Round-up', LSG (6.10.99) 10;

'Editorial: Fit for Present Purposes', LSG (6.10.99) 14; 'QC selection attacked', T (7.10.99) 6; 'Comment: An End to Secrecy' (1999) 143 SJ 923; 'Legal diary', T (Law) (12.10.99) 23; 'Barristers Defy Bar Council and Support End to "Secret Soundings"', LSG (13.10.99) 5; 'Press Round-Up', LSG (13.10.99) 12; 'Barristers Vote for Reform' (1999) 143 SJ 945; 'A Week in the Law...' (1999) 149 NLJ 1509; 'Justice Fishface is Snow joke', Legal Week 3 (21.10.99); Kamlesh Bahl, 'Why "apply, don't be shy" isn't working', T (Law) (26.10.99) 9; 'Judge "cabal"', T (30.10.99) 8; 'Solicitors' body in move to represent all lawyers', FT (30–31.10.99) 3; 'Modern Bar: Strong Future', C (10.99) 6; Robert Sayer, 'Beginning of an Era', LSG (3.11.99) 16; 'Irvine tells how aspiring judges are marked up', T (3.11.99) 14; 'Anti-secrecy Success', LSG (3.11.99) 5; 'Comment: Sting in the Tail' (1999) 143 SJ 1028; 'Success of Legal Aid Reforms to be Judged by "Squealing" Lawyers', LSG (10.11.99) 3; Martin Mears, 'Lawspeak...' (1999) 149 NLJ 1706; 'Top QC Hits out at Silks', LSG (24.11.99) 5; 'Editorial: Whispering Judges', LSG (24.11.99) 15; 'Loss of Confidence', LSG (1.12.99) 22; 'Choice of judges to be more open', T (2.12.99) 1; 'Judges' reform "must go further"', T (3.12.99) 2; 'Monitor for judge selection', T (4.12.99) 18; 'Limited Reforms could Mean more Solicitors become Judges', LSG (8.12.99) 3; 'Press Round-Up', LSG (8.12.99) 10; 'Judicial Appointments' (1999) 149 NLJ 1851; Peach (1999).

[73] Abbott (1988).

[74] Robert Seabrook hoped 'the Bar will look to adopt a means that will enable us to be the first group called up...it seems to me perfectly reasonable for somebody to say I want that barrister to represent me. And I'll go to him if it's necessary to do solicitor's work and he will bring in a solicitor' (interview, July 1998).

[75] One of the few observational studies of barristers found the quality of advocacy uneven and often poor: Martineau (1990: Chaps. 3, 5).

[76] Ormrod (1971).

[77] John Hayes observed: 'the history around the world is that when the shackles are taken off, the Spanish practices still stay' (interview July 1998).

Chapter 6—Notes

[1] Unless otherwise noted, this account is based on Abel (1988: 140–2 and chap. 12; 1989a: 291–9).

[2] LCD (1983: R21.1–11).

[3] Farrand (1984); 'No Profit in Prudential's Conveyancing' (1987) 131 SJ 421; 'Insurance Companies Expand' (1987) 131 SJ 605; 'Property Firms: The Client' (1988) 132 SJ 328; 'Suggestions of New Code for Conveyancing' (1988) 132 SJ 344; Zander (1988: 9).

[4] 'The Lincoln Experience' (1987) 84 LSG 1630; Leslie Dubow, 'NASPyC: Developments to Date' (1987) 84 LSG 2992; 'Property Services Plan', LSG (27.1.88) 3; 'On The Move...', LSG (10.2.88) 6; 'NASPyC: The New Dimension', LSG (20.4.88) 49; 'Law Society Attacked by Homex Solicitor' (1987) 131 SJ 604; 'Twelve Firm Centre' (1987) 131 SJ 637; 'New Finance Facilities for Solicitors' (1987) 131 SJ 1296; 'MPs Lobbied by Estate Agent' (1988) 132 SJ 1040.

[5] Peat Marwick (1986); LA (12.87) 4; 'Firm Reports Conveyancing Success with Computers' (1987) 131 SJ 985; 'Conveyancing: Falling Charges not being Felt' (1987) 131 SJ 1197; 'Letters: Skipton Building Society' (1988) 132 SJ 1374; Bowles (1987); Paterson *et al.* (1988); 'Licensed Conveyancers not being Treated as Professionals', LSG (13.4.88) 2; 'The cost is clear', ES (30.3.88) 32; 'Cost of legal work varying by as much as 100%, poll shows', T (23.8.88); Marre Committee (1988: para. 11.49); Domberger and Sherr (1989); Joseph (1989); 'Legal scourge exposes conveyancing "fraud"', ST (29.1.89); 'NCC says Home Buyers Need more Info' (1990) 134 SJ 992; NCC (1990); Bowles (1990).

[6] 'Zander (1988: 12); 'Corporate Conveyancing: "Liberal" Code of Conduct causes Concern', LSG (15.2.89) 8; John Hayes, 'The Green Papers: A Personal View', LSG (15.2.89) 11; Richard Gaskell, 'President's Column', LSG (22.2.89) 2; Tony Holland, '2001: A Conveyancing Odyssey', LSG (22.2.89) 15; 'Solicitors Prepare for Corporate Conveyancing Challenge', LSG (22.2.89) 4; 'One-stop Shopping', LSG (22.2.89) 5; 'SFPS Mortgage Service', LSG (17.5.89) 3; 'Mortgage Funding from SFPS' (1989) 133 SJ 640; 'Solicitors move into mortgages', FT (20/21.5.89); 'Solicitors' Property Centres Thrive despite Downturn', LSG (21.6.89) 4; 'SPG Warning to Financial Institutions', LSG (4.10.89) 7; 'SFPS Poised for First Hurdle', LSG (22.11.89) 4; 'First-time Buyers' (1991) 135 SJ 207; 'SFPS deficit rises', LA (2.91) 6.

[7] '"Greedy" estate agents', DM (14.3.89); 'Buyers "pressured" by estate agents', DT 'Call for Clean-up of Estate Agents' (1989) 139 NLJ 355; 'Estate Agents Slammed', LSG (12.4.89) 5; 'Halifax Criticises Solicitors' (1989) 133 SJ 604; 'Public Sees Problems in One-stop Shopping', LSG (28.6.89) 5; 'Solicitors Stand to Lose: Survey', LSG (22.11.89) 5; 'Call for Ban on Sale of Financial Services by Estate Agents', LSG (10.1.90) 6; 'Society Urges more Estate Agent Regulation' (1990) 140 NLJ 7; 'Society Back on Estate Agent Offensive' (1990) 134 SJ 28; 'Estate Agents' Malpractice', LSG (28.2.90) 5; 'Estate Agents Cheat, claims Which?' (1990) 134 NLJ 314; 'Estate Agent Curbs Fall Short', LSG (14.3.90) 4; 'Financial Services—No Ban Yet for Estate Agents' (1990) 140 NLJ 350; 'Tories get Tough on "Rogue" Estate Agents' (1990) 134 SJ 464; 'Conveyancing Rules Omit Disclosure Duty', LSG (1.5.91) 9; 'Total Tying-in', LSG (8.5.91) 5.

[8] 'Solicitors Stand to Lose: Survey', LSG (22.11.89) 5; 'Sensible Protocol' (1990) 134 SJ 323; 'TransAction Gathers Momentum', LSG (28.3.90) 4; 'Protocol "Sinister" says Kent' (1990) 134 SJ 348; 'Nervous Agents' (1990) 134 SJ 379; '8000 Offices Take up TransAction', LSG (2.5.90) 7; 'Law Society to Appear on the Big Screen' (1990) 134 SJ 500; 'Property sellers tighten screw on Law Society', ST (18.1.91) 36; 'Early Change Resisted on Conflict Rule', LSG (23.1.91) 5; 'Monopoly Referral for Scots', LSG (20.3.96) 3; 'Glasgow Success', LSG (14.8.96) 4; 'Help Solicitors Sell', LSG (29.8.96) 15; 'Moving Houses', LSG (29.8.96) 20; 'Hope for Go-Ahead on House Selling', LSG (16.10.96) 1; 'Property Futures', LSG (23.10.96) 13; 'Property Shops Win Seal of Approval', LSG (3.9.97) 1.

[9] Tony Girling, 'Where are the Goalposts?' LSG (5.6.91) 2; 'Facing the Future', LSG (19.6.91) 2; 'Society blasts LCD Draft Regulations', LSG (19.6.91) 3; 'Comment: Conveyancing' (1991) 135 SJ 743; ' "Sticking to our Knitting"—the Leeds' (1991) 135 SJ 908.

[10] 'Conveyancing reforms on ice but Tories back no-fault divorce', G (12.2.92); 'Market forces help solicitors stay ahead in the monopoly game', I (28.2.92); 'LCD U-turn May Leave Solicitors out of Pocket' (1992) 136 SJ 179; 'Public Wants Conveyancing from Institutions' (1992) 136 SJ 203; 'Wigs and Tories' (1992) 136 SJ 230; 'Authorised conveyancer scheme postponed', L (17.3.92) 1; 'LCD Shelves Plans to Widen Conveyancing', LSG (18.3.92) 7; 'Mitchell Slams LCD Decision to Drop Scheme' (1992) 136 SJ 255; 'Conveyancing—Where Now?' (1992) 136 SJ 259; 'Depressed Property Sector is "Bad News" for Firms', LSG (8.4.92) 6; 'Property Group Battles the Tide', LSG (16.12.92) 10; Law Society Special Working Party (1994: 6); Sinclair (1994).

[11] 'Conveyancing Network Targets Institutions', LSG (3.7.91) 7; '150 Firms Flock to Join new Conveyancing Network', LSG (25.7.91) 4; 'Conveyancing Networks Multiply', LSG (4.9.91) 8; 'CA Network', LSG (6.11.91) 9; 'SPG Plans Conveyancing Network', LSG (31.7.91) 6; 'Green Light for Conveyancing Referrals', LSG (17.10.91) 9; Clarke (1991: 27–8).

[12] 'Sole Practitioners Demand Action on Panels' (1993) 137 SJ 496; 'Lender Curbs on Solos to be Referred to the OFT', LSG (17.11.93) 3; 'Societies Could Act against Sole Practitioners says Skipton' (1993) 137 SJ 1229; 'Home Truths', LSG (24.11.93) 9; 'Skipton Sole Practitioner Ban' (1993) 137 SJ 1205; 'Skipton "No" ', LSG (17.12.93) 7; 'Conveyancing Panel Cut from 1,000 to 10', LSG (14.4.99) 1.

[13] 'Restrictions on Seller–Buyer Rule Strongly Opposed', LSG (31.1.90) 5; 'Council told OSS Still has Problems' (1991) 141 NLJ 1091; 'Hambro to Recruit Solicitors', LSG (13.12.96) 1; 'Law Soc Urged to Act over Hambros Move' (1996) 140 SJ 1187; 'Comment: Decimation on the High Street' (1996) 140 SJ 1191; Anthony Bogan, 'Letters to the Editor: Conveyancing: Beginning of the End or End of the Beginning' (1996) 140 SJ 1216; 'Kent Firm Anchors Title Cover Scheme', LSG (22.1.97) 1; 'Hambros Threat Played Down' (1997) 141 SJ 51; 'Editorial: Back at the Council Chamber' (1997) 147 NLJ 81; 'Property Centre Talks', LSG (29.1.97) 5; Leslie Dubow, 'Letters to the Editor', LSG (29.1.97) 16; 'Comment: Another Fine Mess' (1997) 141 SJ 79; 'Surrey Backs Property Centre', LSG (26.2.97) 5; 'Conveyancers to be Offered Stake in Property Centre Share Issue', LSG (5.3.97) 4; 'Shoosmiths-Hambros alliance signals new conveyancing era', L (11.3.97) 1; 'Firms Sign Hambro Conveyancing Deal', LSG (12.3.97) 1; 'Editorial: Home

Arrangements', LSG (12.3.97) 16; 'Property Centre Model in Pipeline', LSG (19.3.97) 1; 'Wide Support for Relaxing Rules', LSG (26.3.97) 5; 'Conquest Launches Property Shop Plan', LSG (16.4.97) 1; 'Property Shop Prospectus Issued', LSG (16.4.97) 6; 'Property Centre Talks Begin', LSG (23.4.97) 4; 'Property Centre Cash Injection', LSG (8.5.97) 4; 'Local Lawyers will Decide on Ownership of Property Centres', LSG (14.5.97) 5; 'Eversheds Joins up with Hambro', LSG (16.5.97) 5; 'SPC Chair', LSG (29.5.97) 5; Richard Berenson, 'Centres of Attention', LSG (29.5.97) 15; 'Property Consultation Launched', LSG (11.6.97) 4; 'Hambro Firms set £350 Flat Fee', LSG (25.6.97) 5; 'One Stop Shops "will Dominate"', LSG (9.7.97) 4; 'Property Concern', LSG (16.7.97) 4; 'Council Clears Obstacles to Property Sales', LSG (23.7.97) 1; Leslie Dubow, 'Comment: The Open Window', LSG (23.7.97) 15; Anthony Bogan, 'Letters to the Editor: One Stop to Property', LSG (23.7.97) 16; 'Law Soc Backs Deregulation' (1997) 141 SJ 712; 'Property Selling Scheme Forges Ahead with Minister's Blessing', LSG (30.7.97) 5; 'Solicitors embark on homebuying revolution', ST (3.8.97) §4, 1; 'SPC Initiative Receives "Tremendous" Response' (1997) 141 SJ 759; 'Solicitors for Sales', LSG (13.8.97) 12; 'Lawyers Identified as Main Obstacle to Change' (1997) 141 SJ 784; 'Property Shops win Seal of Approval', LSG (3.9.97) 1; 'Rival Property Centres on the Horizon' (1997) 141 SJ 831; 'IPSO Launch', LSG (24.9.97) 4; 'SPC to let Solicitors Determine Local Structure' (1997) 141 SJ 908; 'Interim Deregulation Passed' (1997) 141 SJ 964; 'London Launch for Edinburgh Property Shop', LSG (22.10.97) 1; 'Scottish Solicitors March on London' (1997) 141 SJ 992; 'Survey Boost for Property Centre Plans', LSG (12.11.97) 1; 'Editorial: Selling Confidence' LSG (12.11.97) 15; 'The London Property Shop is Unveiled' (1997) 141 SJ 1067; 'Round the Houses', LSG (19.11.97) 24; 'Property Sales to go Ahead' (1997) 147 NLJ 1838; Adam Smith Institute (1997); 'Property Sales Bid needs Mass Support', LSG (21.1.98) 1; 'Editorial: Housekeeping', LSG (21.1.98) 13; 'Record £1 billion Sales for Edinburgh Property Centre' (1998) 142 SJ 52; 'House Sales Plan', LSG (28.1.98) 5; 'North East Emerges as Favourite in English Property Shop Venture', LSG (18.2.98) 4; 'Property Selling Initiative Hit by Five Month Delay' (1998) 142 SJ 171; 'Property Shop Fails to Hit 350-firm Target', LSG (8.4.98) 1; 'Networks Battle on as Deadlines Slip' (1992) 142 SJ 483; 'Go-ahead for Newcastle Property Shop', LSG (3.6.98) 1; 'Conveyancing Pow-Wow', LSG (17.6.98) 5; 'First Property Shop Launched', LSG (22.7.98) 4; 'North East to Lead the Way on Property Selling' (1998) 142 SJ 707; 'Comment: Scotland Leads the Way' (1998) 142 SJ 711; 'Direct Move', LSG (2.9.98) 4; 'Busy Hambro', LSG (7.10.98) 4; 'Bulking Up', LSG (11.11.98) 4; 'Newcastle Property Selling Boost', LSG (6.1.99) 4; 'Preston v Swansea in Property Race', LSG (13.1.99) 3; 'Estate Agents Buy Property Practice', LSG (13.1.99) 1; 'SPC Promises to have First Centres Ready by April' (1999) 143 SJ 75; 'First American Moves into Conveyancing' (1999) 143 SJ 123; 'Property Selling Drive Gathers Pace', LSG (17.3.99) 1; 'Bogan launches West London Centre' (1999) 143 SJ 284; 'Hambro on 1,000 a Week' (1999) 143 SJ 309; 'Obiter', LSG (14.4.99) 12; 'Law Firm Launches Seller's Pack Plan', LSG (9.6.99) 1; 'Shock Property Centres Split', LSG (30.6.99) 4; 'National Property Selling Initiative in Crisis' (1999) 143 SJ 651; 'SPC Severs Ties with Berenson' (1999) 143 SJ 676;

'Property Shop to Expand', LSG (13.10.99) 6; 'One Solicitor Property Selling Bid Fails as Another Expands', LSG (3.11.99) 3.

[14] Tony Holland, 'Thriving on Conveyancing Competition', LSG (26.9.90) 2; 'Society Urged to Stamp out Cut-price Conveyancing', LSG (24.3.93) 5; 'Lease of Life for Loss Leader', LSG (16.3.93) 7; 'Cheap Conveyancing', LSG (16.6.93) 8; 'OFT Warns on Conveyancing Fees' (1993) 137 SJ 700; 'Cut-Price Chaos', LSG (15.9.93) 9; 'Unknown Effects of Price Cutting', LSG (13.10.93) 7; 'Carsberg backs MDPs', LSG (3.11.93) 11; 'Conveyancing fee Guidelines', LSG (17.12.93) 5; 'Comment: Paying for Quality', LSG (4.2.94) 87; 'Comment: Deskill Conveyancing for Profit' (1994) 138 SJ 139; Law Society Special Working Party (1994: 50). Local cartels had been created in the 1980s. Peat Marwick (1986: para 2.6.2); Paterson *et al.* (1988: 369).

[15] Chambers and Harwood Richardson (1991: 49); 'Conveyancing Moves', LSG (23.3.94) 6; 'Property buyers face two sets of legal bills', T (29.3.94); 'Conveyancing Shake-up', LSG (30.3.94) 4; 'Lenders Oppose Conveyancing Moves' (1994) 138 SJ 299; 'Comment: Last Chance Saloon?' (1994) 138 SJ 303; 'Conquests for Conquest' (1994) 138 SJ 327; 'Comment: Make your Views Known' (1994) 138 SJ 331; 'Solicitors oppose reform of conveyancing laws', T (10.5.94); 'Birmingham Rejects Conveyancing Plan', LSG (1.6.94) 5; 'South-west "Yes" on Conveyancing', LSG (8.6.94) 4; 'Solos Surprise', LSG (8.6.94) 4; 'Lenders' Doubts on Conveyancing', LSG (15.6.94) 6; 'Property Firms Voice Concern', LSG (22.6.94) 6; 'Society Urged to Cut Deal with Lenders', LSG (29.6.94) 3; 'Lenders Support Restricted Panels', LSG (6.7.94) 8; 'North's "Get Tough" Call', LSG (13.7.94) 7; 'Bristol Group Oppose Separate Representation' (1994) 138 SJ 705; 'Conveyancing Survey Limits', LSG (20.7.94) 8; 'Network Backs Separate Representation' (1994) 138 SJ 807; 'Conveyancing Survey Blocks Joint Representation' (1994) 138 SJ 975; 'Comment: We Need a Solution' (1994) 138 SJ 1007; 'Quality Net', LSG (9.11.94) 9; 'Plan Dropped', LSG (9.11.94) 4; 'Conveyancing Split may Stay', LSG (16.11.94) 4; 'Cut-price rivals reduce lawyers' profits', T (23.11.94); 'SPG Warns Law Society against Adopting "Divisive" Conveyancing Proposals' (1994) 138 SJ 1195; Richard Hegarty and Robert Sayer, 'The Conveyancing Battle' (1994) 138 SJ 1226; Robert Sayer, 'Proposal Breaks Up the Parties', LSG (7.12.94) 12; 'Compromise on Separate Representation Welcomed' (1994) 138 SJ 1248; 'Going round the houses to move', T (13.12.94); 'Conveyancing Talks Continue', LSG (16.12.94) 3; 'Sayer Slams Representation Compromise' (1994) 138 SJ 1275; 'Conveyancing Compromise' (1994) 144 NLJ 1758; Law Society Special Working Party (1994); 'Lenders Trash Retainer Plan', LSG (11.1.95) 2; 'Mortgagees and Purchasers: Separate Solicitors?' (1995) 145 NLJ 193; 'Society Firmly Rules out Separate Representation', LSG (3.5.95) 4; 'Lenders Warn over Terms', LSG (19.7.95) 2; Sidaway and Cole (1996: Tables 5–11.12).

[16] 'Mortgage Deal under Attack', LSG (20.10.96) 4; 'OFT Warns over "Fee Fixing"', LSG (23.4.97) 4; 'Property Consultation Launched', LSG (11.6.97) 4; 'Council to Consider Rule 6 Change', LSG (17.12.97) 5; 'Council Casts Hang-ups Aside and goes for "Full Monty"' (1997) 141 SJ 1193; 'Council Sets Limits on Acting for Lenders in Conveyancing', LSG (30.9.98) 3; 'Conveyancing Alarm', LSG (16.12.98) 1; 'Lenders to Go it Alone with Standard Instructions' (1998) 142

SJ 1144; 'Indemnity Decision Set for March', LSG (27.1.99) 4; 'Conveyancing Delight', LSG (28.4.99) 5; '89 Lenders Sign up to Handbook', LSG (29.9.99) 4.

[17] 'Society Approves Quality Certificates', LSG (15.3.95) 3; 'Row over Quality', LSG (7.6.95) 64; 'Property Lawyers "Disturbed" at Law Society Actions' (1995) 139 SJ 539; 'Comment: Flying a kitemark' (1995) 139 SJ 543; 'SPG Flies Off over Kitemark' (1995) 139 SJ 573; 'Group Fury', LSG (21.6.95) 2; 'Kitemark Concern', LSG (28.6.95) 5; 'Conveyancing Club', LSG (5.7.95) 2.

[18] Tony Holland, 'Conveyancing is at a crossroads', T (5.4.94); 'Branch Office Controls', LSG (18.5.94) 4; Robert Sayer, 'A Profitable Proposition?' LSG (12.10.94) 12; 'Conveyancing Fees Fall Again', LSG (19.10.94) 3; 'Conveyancing Idea Refreshes the Parts', LSG (26.10.94) 4; 'Practitioners back Law Society Critic' (1994) 138 SJ 1115; 'Branch Offices Code Amended', LSG (11.1.95) 2; 'Conveyancing Fee Scales Urged', LSG (15.2.95) 6; 'Fewer Cuddles in Oxford', LSG (15.2.95) 6.

[19] John Edge, 'Letters to the Editor: Conveyancing Fees' (1995) 139 SJ 758; 'Shots in Fee Battle', LSG (9.8.95) 1; 'Editorial: Conveyancing—a Reasonable Return' (1995) 145 NLJ 1249; '7000 Back Scale Fee Plan', LSG (31.8.95) 64; 'Letter to the Editor', LSG (6.9.95) 11; Anthony Bogan, 'To Fix or Not to Fix' (1995) 139 SJ 892; 'Comment: Something Nasty Lurks', LSG (20.9.95) 10; 'Comment: Conveyancing Sense' (1995) 139 SJ 1091.

[20] 'Cost Cutters could Lose SIF Insurance', LSG (13.9.95) 1; 'Editorial: Image Matters', LSG (13.9.95) 10; 'Edge in Call for Scale Fee for Lenders', LSG (20.9.95) 3; 'Boost for Scale Fees', LSG (4.10.95) 2; 'Conveyancing Alert', LSG (11.10.95) 3; 'Estate Agents Turn the Screw on Introductions', LSG (18.10.95) 10; 'Editorial: Agents' Favours', LSG (18.10.95) 12; 'Code Clamp-down on Misleading Ads', LSG (15.10.95) 5; 'Competing Opinions' (1995) 139 SJ 1062; 'Life out on the Edge' LSG (6.12.95) 11.

[21] Harwood (1989: Table 3.1); Martin Mears, 'President's Column: The First 100 Days', LSG (22.11.95) 11; 'Low fee Link to High Claims', LSG (29.11.95) 1; 'SIF Argues against Indemnity Change', LSG (6.12.95) 2; Robert Sayer, 'Sensible Fees', LSG (6.12.95) 16; Anthony Bogan, 'Survival is at Stake', LSG (6.12.95) 26; Jenkins & Lewis (1995: Table 3.11) (excludes firms earning less than £15,000/year).

[22] 'Minimum Fee Mooted', LSG (22.11.95) 1; Robert Sayer, 'Sensible Fees', LSG (6.12.95) 16; Martin Mears, 'President's Column: Reactions to Change', LSG (6.12.95) 12; 'Fees Plan goes to Profession', LSG (15.12.95) 1; 'Conveyancing Compromise for Consultation' (1995) 145 NLJ 1878; Richard Hegarty, 'Comment: A Note of Realism', LSG (10.1.96) 11; 'Getting in a Fees Fuss', LSG (10.1.96) 8; 'Edge Floats Fund', LSG (17.1.96) 2; 'QCs give Fees Verdict', LSG (24.1.96) 1; 'OFT Warns of Fee Initiative Pitfalls', LSG (24.1.96) 3; 'Fee Consultation Postponed', LSG (31.1.96) 3; 'Comment: Covering all Comers', LSG (31.1.96) 15; Martin Mears, 'President's Column: SIF-ting the Evidence', LSG (31.1.96) 16; 'Fees Fund Hits £19,000', LSG (7.2.96) 1; 'Edge in Call for a Steer on Charges', LSG (21.2.96) 1; 'Change of Tack in Fee Campaign', LSG (6.3.96) 1; 'Debate Continues on Pay-as-convey', LSG (13.3.96) 2.

[23] 'Editorial: Another way', LSG (13.3.96) 15; 'OFT Expands Fees Enquiry', LSG (20.3.96) 1; 'Editorial: OFT Inquiries', LSG (20.3.96) 13; Richard Hegarty, 'Conveyancing Costs', LSG (20.3.96) 20; 'Scots Reject Fees Plan', LSG (27.3.96) 1; 'Fee Think-tank', LSG (19.6.96) 4; Richard Hegarty, 'A Fair Fee for the Job', LSG

(3.7.96) 22; 'Conveyancing Appeal', LSG (4.9.96) 4; 'Call for Legal Think-tank', LSG (12.9.96) 6; 'Gloomy forecast', *ibid.*; 'Time to go*', ibid.*; ' "Change or Die" Warning' (1996) 140 SJ 856; Peter Watson-Lee, 'Thinking about the Law Society', (12.96) Cat 3 ('Bring back scale fees for conveyancing'); 'Comment: Scotland Leads the Way' (1998) 142 SJ 711; 'Bulking Up', LSG (11.11.98) 4; 'Sole Practitioners Face "Abrupt End" ', LSG (28.4.99) 3; 'Property Shop to Expand', LSG (13.10.99) 6; 'One Solicitor Property Selling Bid Fails as Another Expands', LSG (3.11.99) 3.

[24] 'London fears of a US invasion dispelled', FT (22.5.89) 18; 'MNP Indemnity Hitch', LSG (10.4.91) 3; 'SIF urges Strict Limits on MNP Indemnity Cover', LSG (24.4.91) 5; 'Society Shifts Ground on Foreign Lawyer Practice Rights', LSG (3.7.91) 3; 'Society Hopes to Speed through MNP Rules', LSG (24.7.91) 9; T (13.8.91); 'Register opens for MNPs', LSG (17.10.91) 7; 'Way cleared for MNPs', LSG (8.1.92); 'First MNP Established', LSG (15.1.92) 4; 'Dane Steps into Multinational Partnership' (1992) 136 SJ 24; 'Kennedys goes Multi-national', LSG (29.7.92) 9; 'City Firm in US Merger', LSG (22.6.92) 5; Lee (1992); 'NY Firm goes Solo', LSG (25.10.95) 4; 'City Assault by US Firms', LSG (30.5.96) 1; 'Commercial Bonanza Ahead', LSG (12.6.96) 1; 'US Firms Prowl City', LSG (20.11.96) 11; Flood (1996); Lee (1999: chap. 3); 'UK Practice Links with French Firm in First Full International Merger', LSG (22.10.97) 4; 'Allen & Overy in Italian Merger' (1997) 141 SJ 1192; 'Freshfields joins Euro-merger Club', LSG (28.1.98) 1; 'Freshfields merges with German Firm' (1998) 142 SJ 100; 'Clifford Chance to Recruit 500', LSG (1.4.98) 6; 'Europe's Largest Firm Unveiled', LSG (29.7.98) 6; 'Linklaters Secures North European Alliance' (1998) 142 SJ 707; 'Salans Claims Transatlantic Merger First' (1998) 142 SJ 853; '2 Law Firms Plan to Bridge the Atlantic', NYT (25.5.99) C1; 'Obiter', LSG (16.6.99) 12; 'British Law Firm creates global giant', T (12.7.99) 1; 'Law firm merger fuels salary war', T (12.7.99) 4; 'New life for lawyers', T (12.7.99) 23; 'Clifford Chance Partners Vote to Create World's Largest Law Firm', LSG (14.7.99) 3; 'Clifford Chance Takes Over the World' (1999) 143 SJ 675; 'Legal Diary', T (20.7.99) 21; 'Linklaters in Major Italy Move', LSG (21.7.99) 6; 'Press Round-up', LSG (21.7.99) 12; 'Comment: Why We Should all be Proud of Clifford Chance' (1999) 143 SJ 703; 'The transatlantic merger that is making waves', I (Tues Rev) (27.7.99) 14; 'German Mergers get Go-ahead', LSG (8.9.99) 6; 'This week in the law' (1999) 143 SJ 825; 'Lovells Leads Euro Merger Charge', LSG (29.9.99) 6; 'Luxembourg Deal for Allen & Overy', LSG (11.10.99) 4; 'CC adds Fourth Firm to Merger', LSG (17.12.99) 6. See generally Abel (1994).

[25] 'Coudert leads US drive on the City', L (1.8.90) 1; 'Wall Street sets sights on the City', L (1.8.90); 'City Firms Up Salaries to Match US pay', LSG (26.3.97) 1; 'Is it the end of the affair?' T (1.7.97) 41; 'Search Begins for £1m Solicitor', LSG (13.1.99) 4; 'Why the entente is not so cordiale', T (26.1.99) 41; 'A legal way to land a million', I (18.2.99) §2, 14; 'Legal diary', T (29.6.99) 39; 'City Salary Spiral to Slow Down after "Unprecedented growth" ' LSG (7.7.99) 3; 'US Firms Up Salary Competition', LSG (20.10.99) 6.

[26] Hayes (1987); David Ward, 'The Rule of Law', LSG (19.10.89) 2; 'Solicitors' chief takes on critics of legal changes', T (16.7.90); 'Borrie acts to end Law Society's ban on mixed practices', T (17.9.90) 5; 'Borrie Set to take Action over MDPs' (1990) 134 SJ 1052; 'Comment' (1990) 134 SJ 1083; 'No Big Six for City Solicitors', LSG (12.10.94) 9; Kay (1994).

[27] 'Government move may delay MDP proposals', L (20.11.90); 'Society Stands Firm in Face of Proposals on MDPs', LSG (5.6.91) 5; 'Practising in Partnership', LSG (18.9.91) 2; 'MDPs get Young Vote', LSG (8.7.92) 9; 'Interest in MDPs Wanes', LSG (16.3.93) 7; 'An Ally in Arthur', LSG (31.3.93) 8; 'Collin Garrett', L (13.4.93); 'Carsberg Backs MDPs', LSG (3.11.93); 'City Firm in Accountancy Link' (1993) 137 SJ 1256; 'MDPs Put on Ice' (1994) 138 SJ 223; 'Salaries for Law Society Officers' (1994) 144 NLJ 382; 'Leeds Defection Fuels Local Anger', LSG (25.4.94) 8; 'Chain Reaction', LSG (12.10.94) 15; 'Garrett's Pennine Leap', LSG (16.11.94) 3; Flood and Skordaki (1995: 13); 'Insolvent Abuse?' LSG (4.12.96) 14.

[28] 'Accountants Threat', LSG (7.2.96) 1; 'Editorial: Big Six Move', LSG (7.2.96) 13; 'Ernst & Young Plans a Law Firm', LSG (21.2.96) 1; 'Case on MDP Ban', LSG (21.2.96) 8; 'The Thin End of the MDP Wedge?' LSG (28.2.96) 10; 'Accountants push Dutch over MDP Restrictions', LSG (1.5.96) 8; 'Labour Plans Spark MDP Review', LSG (12.6.96) 1; 'Editorial: Timely Look at MDPs', LSG (12.6.96) 16; 'Comment: Multiple benefits' (1996) 140 SJ 653; 'Garretts Claim Fastest Growth', LSG (6.11.96) 11; 'Survey Finds Strong Support for MDPs', LSG (13.12.96) 1 (73% response from 579 firms); 'Dutch Bar Beats Off Accountants', LSG (12.2.97) 11; 'Editorial: The Competition', LSG (12.2.97) 15; 'Dutch Bar seeks MDP Compromise', LSG (13.8.97) 6; Flood (1997).

[29] 'Alarm Raised over "Big Six" Threat', LSG (14.8.96) 1; 'Garrett Expansion', LSG (8.1.97) 8; 'Coopers Launches its own Law Firm', LSG (12.2.97) 1; 'Arnheim & Co Doubles', LSG (12.3.97) 9; 'Battle Hots Up against "Big Six"', LSG (16.4.97) 9; 'At the Double', LSG (21.5.97) 12; David Keating, 'Accountants: A Level Playing Field', (6.97) Cat 21 ('Recognising that conflicts of interest can arise in the work they do has never been a strong point with accountants'); 'OFT in MDP Audit', LSG (9.7.97) 4; 'Scotland's Largest Firm is Recruited to Big Six Network', LSG (3.9.97) 4; 'Solicitor to Lead Push by Accountants into Legal Markets' (1997) 141 SJ 831; 'Big Six Law Firms Discuss Merger', LSG (24.9.97) 5; 'Garretts Trains MDP–Friendly Brood', LSG (24.9.97) 8; 'MDP Limits', LSG (5.11.97) 1; 'Firm Breaks Talks with Accountants', LSG (12.11.97) 1; 'Law Society Intensifies MDP Preparations' (1997) 141 SJ 1067; 'OFT Keeps Up the Pressure on MDPs', LSG (26.11.97) 1; 'Big Six Euro Network Grows', LSG (5.3.98) 6.

[30] 'Lawyers see Big Six Merger as "Threat to Independence"', LSG (21.1.98) 9; 'MDP decisions delayed by SIF', ST (30.1.98) 75; 'IBA reaches MDPs Compromise', LSG (26.2.98) 10; 'Lawyers Gear Up for Big Six Alliances', LSG (18.3.98) 1; 'Partners in Line for Big Draws', LSG (8.4.98) 9; 'Wilde Sapte Partners Vote to Join Arthur Andersen' (1998) 142 SJ 243; 'Report Calls for Strong Regulation of MDPs to Avoid Ethics Problems', LSG (3.6.98) 8; 'PW "Enthusiastic" about Wilde Sapte Merger after Rival Pulls Out', LSG (10.6.98) 9; 'Wilde Sapte's Marriage with Andersen Comes Unstuck' (1998) 142 SJ 531; 'Andersens Changes Tack as Chain Decides to Go' (1998) 142 SJ 660; 'World Lawyers in MDP Change of Heart', LSG (16.9.98) 1; 'Society in Bid to Find MDP Formula', LSG (21.10.98) 1; 'MDP Debate Gets Practical' (1998) 142 SJ 948; 'Wonderful MDPs', LSG (18.11.98) 5; 'Report Backs Move to MDPs', LSG (24.2.99) 8; 'MDPs will Lead to Split', LSG (8.4.99) 8; 'MDPs Receive Cautious EU Backing', LSG (28.4.99) 6; 'Editorial: The Shape of Things to Come', LSG (9.6.99) 16; 'Editorial: Time to Move on MDPs' (1999) 149 NLJ 921; 'Call to End MDPs Ban', LSG (30.6.99) 5; 'Comment: MDPs: Why?

Why not? When?', LSG (30.6.99) 15; 'City and In-House Lawyers join Growing Clamour to Allow MDPs', LSG (7.7.99) 8.

[31] 'City Sceptical over Big Five Plans', LSG (13.1.99) 9; 'KPMG Moves into Law after Rival's Solicitors Offer to Set up New Firm', LSG (6.5.99) 5; 'Partners who sleep with the enemy', I (Tues Rev) (1.6.99) 12; 'Legal diary', T (15.6.99) 41; 'US Opposition to MDPs Takes Shape', LSG (2.9.99) 6; 'PwC sets 5,000 Lawyer Target', LSG (8.9.99) 6; 'Global Corporations "Favour MDPs"', LSG (15.9.99) 6; 'Massive Fees Rise', LSG (15.9.99) 9; 'Society Considers "Interim" MDPs', LSG (13.10.99) 4; 'What's in a Name?' LSG (13.10.99) 8; 'Multi-Disciplinary Partnerships on Horizon after "Seismic" Vote', LSG (20.10.99) 3; 'Take your Partners', LSG (20.10.99) 9; 'Society Forges ahead on MDPs' (1999) 143 SJ 968; 'European Lawyers Vote for MDP Ban', LSG (17.11.99) 1; 'Big Five get Bigger', LSG (24.11.99) 6; 'Are MDPs the way forward?' T (Law) (30.11.99) 17.

[32] 'Specialist Qualifications for the Legal Profession: A Contrary Argument' (1987) 84 LSG 87; Zander (1988: 88–9).

[33] 'Society Moves to Meet Demand for Specialisation', LSG (11.10.89) 4; 'Glasgow and Beyond' (1989) 139 NLJ 1513; 'Law Society to do More for Commercial Lawyers' (1989) 139 NLJ 1551; 'Specialisation: the Way Forward', LSG (2.5.90) 36; 'Rules on Specialisation Claims Relaxed', LSG (18.7.90) 4; 'Law Society Approves Free Market' (1990) 134 SJ 816; 'What Makes You so Special?' (1990) 134 SJ 891; 'Specialisation Rule Criticised', LSG (22.8.90) 5; 'NCC Fuels Rumpus over Specialists' (1990) 134 SJ 940; 'Marketing specialists', LA (8.90) 4; 'Publicity code changes', LA (9.90) 4; 'Abdicating Responsibility?' LSG (3.10.90) 2; 'Specialisation: YSG Demands Tough Code', LSG (3.10.90) 5; 'YSG Worried by Rules on Specialisms' (1990) 134 SJ 1112; 'Specialisation: A Responsible Approach', LSG (10.10.90) 2; 'Mackay Criticises Society's Latest Decision on Rules', LSG (21.11.90) 3; 'Mackay upset by easing of lawyers' publicity rules', G (23.1.91); 'Mackay's criticism is downplayed by Holland', L (29.1.91); 'Society Defends Changes to Publicity Code', LSG (30.1.91) 7; 'No simple solution to specialisation', L (5.2.91).

[34] 'Society Prepares Guidelines on Quality Award', LSG (18.10.90) 7; 'Consultation Planned on Two Specialist Panels', LSG (6.3.91) 4; 'New Specialist Panels to Help Injured and Medical Victims' (1991) 135 SJ 368; 'APIL Sounds Caution on Specialist Panel Selection', LSG (8.5.91) 6; 'New Body for Trust and Estate Practitioners' (1991) 135 SJ 884; 'More Stringent Test for Child Care Panel', LSG (25.9.91) 5; 'Council backs PI Panel', LSG (15.7.92) 4; 'Medical Negligence Panel', LSG (16.6.93) 10; 'Firms Slow to Apply to Specialist Panel', LSG (13.10.93) 4; 'New Scheme for Interviews' (1993) 137 SJ 1041; 'Slow Take-up of PI Panel', LSG (17.11.93) 4; 'Going for Growth', LSG (8.12.93) 5; 'New-look PI Scheme', LSG (2.2.94) 7; 'Comment: STEP in the Right Direction' (1996) 146 NLJ 299; 'PI Lawyers Tussle over Conduct Code', LSG (20.11.96) 4.

[35] 'Society Prepares Guidelines on Quality Award', LSG (18.10.90) 7; 'Panel Thresholds may be Lowered', LSG (11.5.95) 7; 'On the Road', LSG (17.5.95) 3; 'Society Flags Panels Rethink' LSG (24.5.95) 3; 'Panels Trigger Local Passions', LSG (7.6.95) 6; 'Council Approves Standards Scheme', LSG (19.7.95) 3; 'Early Opposition to Mears on Election Mandate' (1995) 139 SJ 699; 'Specialist Support', LSG (15.11.95) 8; 'Kite Flying', LSG (26.2.97) 23; 'Practice Management Quality Mark Launched' (1997) 141 SJ 909; 'Lexcellent', LSG (3.9.98) 4; 'Editorial: Different

Routes to Quality', LSG (3.9.98) 15; 'Flagship for Firms', LSG (3.2.99) 24; 'Law Brands Join Elite', LSG (6.10.99) 5.

[36] Davis *et al.* (1994); 'Family Law Panel Closer to Approval', LSG (19.7.95) 8; 'Judge Warns of "Dabblers"', LSG (11.10.95) 4; 'Accreditation for Family Lawyers' (1996) 146 NLJ 296; 'Family Law Paper Approved', LSG (1.5.96) 4; Peter Watson-Lee, 'Comment: A Panel by Any Other Name', LSG (17.7.96) 14; 'Family Panel Support', LSG (2.8.96) 4; 'Accreditation Review', LSG (23.10.96) 5; 'Editorial: A Specialist Case', LSG (23.10.96) 15; Peter Watson-Lee, 'Thinking about the Law Society', 1 Cat (12.96) 3; 'Specialist Schemes move Closer', LSG (29.1.97) 6; 'Accreditation Moves Ahead' (1997) 141 SJ 75; 'Family Law Committee Seeks Accreditation' (1997) 141 SJ 195; 'Family Best', LSG (12.3.97) 6; Hilary Siddle, 'Comment: Best Kept in the Family', LSG (12.3.97) 16; Hilary Siddle, Peter Watson-Lee, Eileen Pembridge, and David Hodson, 'Family Planning', LSG (19.3.97) 26–27; Marlene Winfield, 'Preferred Panels', LSG (19.3.97) 30–31; Steve Orchard and Gary Streeter, 'Preferred Panels', LSG (19.3.97) 30–31; Peter Watson-Lee, 'Attacking the General Practitioner', 2 Cat (3.97) 18 ('the creation of more panels is a direct attempt to intervene into the market place'); 'Anger at SFLA's Negative Leaflet', LSG (28.8.97) 6; 'Plan to Accredit Housing Lawyers', LSG (25.8.98) 2; 'Law Society and SFLA Go it Alone after Failing to Agree Family Plan', LSG (4.11.98) 3; 'Society to Launch Alternative Accreditation Scheme' (1998) 142 SJ 1120; 'Family Affairs', LSG (27.1.99) 4; 'Till Divorce do us part...' (1999) 149 NLJ 155; 'Advisory Board Voices Fear over Family Law Panel Qualifications', LSG (3.6.99) 3; 'SFLA Targets Top Family Lawyers', LSG (27.10.99) 4.

[37] 'Super Club for Top PI Earners', LSG (5.3.97) 5; 'PI Lawyers Launch Top Earners Club', LSG (8.5.97) 5; 'Club Relaxes Entry Criteria', LSG (13.5.98) 4; 'Personal Affairs', LSG (3.6.98) 12; 'PI College Opens', LSG (6.5.99) 4; 'APIL Unveils College of Personal Injury Law' (1999) 143 SJ 428; 'A School for Solicitors', SJ Training & Career Development Supplement (6.8.99) 10.

[38] Jenkins (1995); 'Probate Practitioners become First to Win Dedicated Section', LSG (2.7.97) 5; 'Editorial: Getting Sectioned', LSG (2.7.97) 15; Cole (1997: Tables 4(c), 5(a)); 'Plan to Accredit Housing Lawyers', LSG (25.8.98) 2; 'Crime Scheme Support', LSG (9.6.99) 5; 'Accreditation for Criminal Defence Solicitors' (1999) 143 SJ 551; 'In-house Qualification Planned', LSG (23.6.99) 6; 'In-house Qualification Planned', LSG (1.12.99) 5.

[39] 'Panel Power', LSG (19.3.97) 28; 'Survey Reveals Pay Dissatisfaction', LSG (3.4.97) 4; 'This Legal Lifestyle', LSG (23.4.97) 20; Cole (1997: Tables 7(a)–(c)).

[40] 'Wills Campaign Aims to Head off Probate Threat', LSG (5.6.91) 6; 'Mixed Report for Solicitors in Will-writing Study', LSG (12.6.91) 7; 'Compensation Power for Probate Ombudsman', LSG (17.7.91) 9; 'Unwilling 69% to be Wooed by Wills Campaign', LSG (11.9.91) 5; 'Tapping the Market for Wills and Probate', LSG (25.9.91) 2; 'Society Damns Probate Rules', LSG (30.10.91) 10; 'Absence of Probate Rules Criticised' (1991) 135 SJ 1256; 'Will Power is a Hit', LSG (4.12.91) 6; 'Moves to Stem Misleading Will Ads', LSG (4.12.91) 6; 'Law Society Calls for Probate Safeguards' (1993) 137 SJ 471; 'Accountants Bid for Probate Rights', LSG (9.6.93) 6; 'Probate Fears', LSG (16.6.93) 10; 'Call for Will Checks', LSG (13.10.93) 5; 'Society Calls for Regulation of Unqualified Willwriters' (1993) 137 SJ 1039; 'Eye on Will Writers', LSG (16.3.94) 9; 'Will to Carry On', LSG (14.9.94) 6; 'North West

Wills Push', LSG (21.9.94) 9; 'The Will to Succeed', LSG (28.9.94) 2; 'Will Writers' Anger', LSG (12.10.94) 7; 'Will Week', LSG (19.10.94) 3; 'Right Royal?' LSG (1.3.95) 64; 'Firms Face Probate Competition War', LSG (11.1.95) 4; Jenkins (1995: 25–6); 'Probate Practitioners urged to Fight Back', LSG (10.7.96) 6; 'Law Soc hits back at Which? wills report', L (8.10.96) 3; 'Notts lawyers warn about low-cost advice', L (8.10.96) 3; Robert Sayer, 'Driving Home the Message' (1999) 149 NLJ 417.

[41] 'Now on the Block', LSG (22.9.93) 9; 'Referrals Scrutiny', LSG (20.3.96) 1; 'Accident Scheme Attacked by APIL', LSG (27.3.93) 2; 'Claims Firm Scoops up PI Work', LSG (2.8.96) 5; Martin Mears, 'President's Column: Try, Try, Try Again', LSG (27.3.96) 17; Caroline Harmer, 'Comment: The PI Challenge', LSG (9.5.96) 15; 'Staking a Claim', LSG (12.6.96) 13; 'Crack-down on No Win, No Fee Ads', LSG (10.7.96) 1; 'No Win No Fee Adverts Risk ASA Censure' (1996) 140 SJ 675; 'Solicitors Concerned over Increased Role of Agents' (1996) 140 SJ 779; 'Claims Assessor Scrutiny', LSG (30.10.96) 4; 'Pressure Mounts for Action on Claims Assessors' (1997) 141 SJ 27; Tony Girling, 'President's Column', LSG (29.1.97) 14; 'Public Warning', LSG (8.5.97) 4; HC Standing Committee E (11.5.99, 13.5.99); 'Legal diary', T (15.6.99) 41; 'Briefs', I (Tues Rev) (15.6.99) 14; 'Claims Assessors under Scrutiny' (1999) 143 SJ 575; 'Claims Assessors Inquiry Backed', LSG (25.8.99) 5; 'Editorial: Law of Diminishing Returns', LSG (2.9.99) 14; 'Claims Direct Abandons Contingency Fees' (1999) 143 SJ 799; 'Comment: Rounding Up the Cowboys' (1999) 143 SJ 827; Lord Chancellor's Committee (2000).

[42] 'Press Round-Up', LSG (24.11.99) 12.

[43] 'Society Acts on "Passing Off"', LSG (13.3.96) 1; 'Defining "Lawyer"', LSG (20.3.96) 2; 'When is a Lawyer Not a Lawyer?' LSG (27.3.96) 10; 'Editorial: Fighting Back', LSG (27.3.96) 15; 'Chancery Lane Wins "Passing Off" Injunction', LSG (3.4.96) 2; 'No more "Society of Lawyers"' (1996) 140 SJ 321: 'Law Society Wins Injunction against Society of Lawyers' (1996) 146 NLJ 506; 'Society of Lawyers Struck Down', LSG (17.4.96) 3; 'ILEX Battle Plan', LSG (8.9.99) 5; HL 596: 1175–9 (28.1.99), 597: 655–7 (16.2.99); HC 333: 1056–9 (22.6.99).

Chapter 7—Notes

[1] Abel (1988: chap. 7 and Tables 1.31, 1.32, 1.35); see Young and Wall (1996a); Goriely (1994a; 1994b; 1996c); Goriely and Paterson (1996); Smith (1994).

[2] Royal Commission (1979: R12.1–13, 14.1–10, 15.1–7); LCD (1983: 11, 13, 15, 17–19); Abel (1988: chap. 14 and Tables 2.33).

[3] Coopers & Lybrand (1985: Summary para. 16); LCD (1986: vol. 1 para. 6; 1987: paras. 21, 44, 47–9, 58); 'Legal Aid—System in Crisis', Legal Aid News 1 (Autumn 1988); Law Society (1988b); Baldwin and Hill (1988: 128, 136); Marre Committee (1988: paras. 8.96, 8.113, 8.139, 10.6, 20.7); Zander (1988: 64–71); 'Eligibility Drops by 14 Million', LSG (11.10.89) 7; Michael Murphy, 'Civil legal aid eligibility', LA (10.89) 7; 'Editorial: The importance of being eligible', LA (10.89) 3; Law Society (1989b); 'Legal Aid Shortfall Denounced', LSG (28.3.90) 7; 'Speedy Legal Aid Eligibility Review Ruled Out', LSG (2.5.90) 8; Bar Council's Strategy Group (1990: para. 3.22); Forbes and Wright (1990); 'Fewer people eligible for legal aid', DT (28.3.91); 'Number eligible for civil legal aid falls to all-time low', I (28.3.91) 10; 'Study discloses drop in legal aid entitlement', T (28.3.91); Harris (1991: Chaps. 4–6, 10); Hansen (1992); Gray (1994: 58); BDO Stoy Hayward (1999: Table 34). For an overview of the contraction of legal aid see Goriely (1999).

[4] 'Off-the-peg Civil Justice' (1989) 139 NLJ 317; 'Top solicitor urges pay appeal to MPs', G (10.3.89); 'Legal Aid Pay: 6% is Bitter Blow', LSG (15.3.89) 2; 'Law Society to Fight "Immoral" Legal Aid Pay Rise in Commons' (1989) 139 NLJ 354; 'Dismay at 6 per cent Legal Aid Increase' (1989) 133 SJ 336; 'Crisis Time All the Time' (1989) 139 SJ 367; 'Survey Shows Firms Giving up on Family Legal Aid', LSG (16.5.89) 8; 'Solicitors "can't live on legal aid" ', DM (19.8.89); 'Criminal legal aid to blame for trial delays', L (3.10.89).

[5] '21% Pay Claim In', LSG (22.11.89) 3; 'Society Considers Challenge to Legal Aid Rate', LSG (7.3.90) 3; 'Defeat Conceded on Legal Aid Claim', LSG (21.3.90) 2; 'Despair' (1990) 140 NLJ 389; 'Government "Cynicism" over Legal Aid Pay' (1990) 140 NLJ 390; 'Society Concedes Defeat on Legal Aid' (1990) 134 SJ 324; 'In Conversation', LSG (9.5.90) 15; David Ward, 'Despondency or Hope?' LSG (23.5.90) 2.

[6] 'Legal Aid Franchising Worries', LSG (17.5.89) 4; 'Legal aid franchise "a threat to advice" ', I (18.7.89) 5; 'Franchising' (1989) 139 NLJ 1181; 'Backtrack on Franchise Threshold', LSG (20.9.89) 4; 'Society Urges Right to Grant Civil Legal Aid', LSG (17.1.90) 4; 'Solicitors to be asked to boycott legal aid franchising proposals', T (25.4.90); 'Solicitors fight legal aid "franchise" with boycott', T (27.4.90); 'Law Society to boycott legal aid franchise plan', I (27.4.90); 'BLA Opposes Franchising' (1990) 140 NLJ 579; 'Pilot Firms Reconsider Franchising Experiment', LSG (2.5.90) 3; 'Law Society Rejects Franchising Experiment' (1990) 140 NLJ 618; 'LAB Clashes with Chancery Lane on Franchising' (1990) 134 SJ 500; 'Pilot Scheme Concessions', LSG (6.6.90) 3; 'LAB Pilot Plans', LSG (13.6.90) 4; 'Franchising veto', LA (6.90) 5; 'Editorial: The boycott that never was', LA (6.90) 3; 'LAB Widens Franchising Pilot', LSG (12.12.90) 7.

[7] 'Bar chief urges greater access to justice', FT (24.9.90); 'Lawyers fear that £715m legal aid bill will be capped', T (25.9.90); 'the price of legal aid', T (25.9.90) 13; 'Legal Aid Bill Cap?' LSG (26.9.90) 3; 'Cutting our Cloth' (1990)

140 NLJ 1337; 'Justice v Lawyers', T (22.10.90); 'Editorial: Chasing hares', LA (11.90) 3.

[8] 'Better access to justice urged by Mackay', DT (7.12.90); 'Mackay calls on lawyers to cut fees', T (7.12.90); 'Mackay says No to Extra Cash for Legal Aid', LSG (12.12.90) 4; J. Anthony Holland, 'An Open Letter to the Lord Chancellor', LSG (12.12.90) 2; 'Lawyers turning away "too expensive" legal aid work', T (12.12.90); 'Charismatic Chief for Bar', LSG (12.12.90) 10; 'Lawyers refuse legal aid work because of fees', T (13.12.90); 'Mackay Pledges Second Look at Legal Aid' (1990) 134 SJ 1456; 'J Anthony Holland has Asked for More!' (1990) 140 NLJ 1777.

[9] 'Mackay urges efficiency on legal aid', DT (2.2.91); 'Fear mounts for legal aid after £90m rise in costs', T (9.2.91); 'Stricter legal aid controls', L (12.2.91); 'Spring will Be a Little Late This Year...' (1991) 141 NLJ 225; 'Mackay to consider financial threshold for legal aid users', I (28.2.91); 'More may get legal aid from Mackay scheme', T (28.2.91); 'Government may set up "safety net" for litigants', FT (28.2.91); 'Mackay scheme to curb legal aid', G (28.2.91); 'Legal aid no blank cheque, says Mackay', DT (28.2.91); 'Legal aid plan to help high earners', G (4.3.91); 'Mackay legal aid plan causes alarm', L (5.3.91); 'Legal aid reforms "will deter hundreds"', T (12.3.91) 5; 'Legal Aid "Safety Net" is a Deterrent, says Society', LSG (13.3.91) 3; 'LCD Moots Limited Scheme for Contingency Fees', LSG (13.3.91) 5; Lord Mackay, 'Not just a question of numbers', I (15.3.91); 'Mackay Defends Eligibility Net', LSG (20.3.91) 8; 'Safety net with a hole in it', T (26.3.91); 'An illogical cut in legal aid', I (29.3.91); 'Bailing out the legal aid system', FT (8.4.91); 'Courts and Legal Services Committee: Legal Aid Dominates Mixed Menu', LSG (10.4.91) 6; 'Pitts Blames Lawyers for Legal Aid Costs', LSG (1.5.91) 3; 'Conditional Fee Pilot Unlikely before Autumn', LSG (1.5.91) 10; Michael Zander, 'Paltry returns for a wrecked system', I (10.5.91).

[10] 'LCD Seems to Favour Legal Aid Safety Net', LSG (5.6.91) 3; 'LEI as Legal Aid Alternative', LSG (5.6.91) 4; 'CLAF Option for Litigants', LSG (5.6.91) 4; 'Hostile Reception for Mackay's "Safety Net"' (1991) 135 SJ 664; 'Comment: Private Clients and the Safety Net' (1991) 135 SJ 667; 'Mackay warns of legal aid cash limit', L (11.6.91) 1; 'A firm investment needed for legal aid', L (11.6.91); 'Editorial: Question time', LA (6.91) 3; Roger Smith, 'Right questions, wrong answers', LA (6.91) 7; 'Safety Net Drubbing Sparks LCD Review', LSG (13.11.91) 7; 'Salary Scheme Mooted to Trim Legal Aid Bill', LSG (27.11.91) 6; LCD (1991).

[11] LCD (1991); 'Hostile Reception for Mackay's "Safety Net"' (1991) 135 SJ 664; 'If you want the fee, you must win the case', I (14.8.92) 24; 'Defence Lawyers Design Contingency Fee Model', LSG (7.10.92) 9; 'Comment: Contingency Fees' (1992) 136 SJ 883; 'Backing a winner', G (2.2.93); 'Society Dismisses "Half-Hearted" No-Win-No-Fee Scheme', LSG (12.5.93) 5; 'Not so Uplifting' (1993) 137 SJ 443; 'Comment: Conditional Fees' (1993) 137 SJ 447; 'Contingency Fees' (1993) 137 NLJ 678; 'Perils of "no-win, no fee"' T (25.5.93).

[12] 'Legal Aid Eligibility', LSG (12.6.91) 2; 'Lawyers face controls on legal aid bills', T (25.6.91); 'Clamp on soaring legal aid costs', DT (25.6.91); 'Solicitors' legal aid claims face tighter vetting', T (25.6.91); 'LAB Plans Crackdown to Curb Costs', LSG (26.6.91) 3; 'Solicitors state the real cost of justice', T (2.7.91); 'Editorial: The Tight Rope of Legal Services Funding', C (7.91) 2; John Pitts, 'Letters: Legal Services Funding', C (9–10.91) 6.

[13] Marre (1988: para. 8.46); 'Lawyers angry at move to end free immigration advice', I (4.7.91); 'Migrants' legal aid ban "unjust"', G (4.7.91); 'Asylum Proposals Draw Heavy Fire', LSG (10.7.91) 8; 'Government Extinguishes Right to Green Form Advice' (1991) 135 SJ 788; 'The shambles awaiting refugees', IOS (21.7.91); 'Baker's surprise on immigration goes down badly', L (23.7.91); 'Mackay backs cutting of legal aid for immigrants', L (23.7.91) 1; 'Refugee agency faces revolt', IOS (28.7.91); 'Refugees pay the price of electoral popularity', IOS (28.7.91) 22; 'Letter to the editor', IOS (28.7.91); 'Society Gathers Data for Escalating Immigration Debate', LSG (31.7.91) 7; 'Immigration agency attacks end of legal aid', T (1.8.91); 'Bar chides Baker over plan to end legal aid for asylum seekers', G (9.8.91); 'Legal aid cut for migrants attacked', DT (9.8.91); 'Immigration Legal Aid Plans Founder', LSG (28.8.91) 8; 'Pressure Mounts for Talks on Asylum Changes', LSG (4.9.91) 7; 'Baker hints at climbdown on legal help for refugees', I (29.9.91); 'Government Squeezes UKIAS to Accept Asylum Work', LSG (6.11.91) 6; 'UKIAS Woes Scupper Shift of Green Form Work', LSG (22.1.92) 8; 'Legal Aid to Stay for Immigrant Cases', LSG (12.2.92) 6.

[14] 'Legal Aid: Pay Award Set at 7%', LSG (20.3.91) 3; 'Liverpool Revolts against Duty Solicitor Rules', LSG (20.3.91) 10; 'Liverpool Solicitors get their Way on Duty Scheme', LSG (24.4.91) 7; 'Legal Aid Forum', LSG (18.9.91) 4; 'Call for Action over Fixed Fees' (1991) 135 SJ 1067; 'Ely Urges Realism on Legal Aid', LSG (9.10.91) 3; 'The Survival of the Biggest' (1991) 141 NLJ 1355; 'Comment: Legal Aid' (1991) 135 SJ 1099; 'Solicitors Plan Strike', LSG (20.11.91) 76; 'Support for Devon's Action over Fixed Fee Furore' (1991) 135 SJ 1279; 'LAPG Measures Support Action on Fixed Fees', LSG (4.12.91) 3 (43% of 717 responding); 'Fury Mounts over Fixed Fees', LSG (4.12.91) 3; '1% Pay Rise in Store for Criminal Legal Aid Practitioners', LSG (11.12.91) 3; ' "F-Word" Protest Spreads', LSG (11.12.91) 4; 'Mackay Offers 1% Legal Aid Increase Next Year' (1991) 135 SJ 1327; 'The Dogs of Law' (1991) 141 NLJ 1687; Philip Ely, 'Funding Criminal Justice: A Letter to the Lord Chancellor', LSG (18.12.91) 2; 'Pay Campaign with Public Appeal', LSG (18.12.91) 3; 'SGM in January', LSG (18.12.91) 4; 'Council United on Fixed Fee Rejection' (1991) 141 NLJ 1724; 'Why solicitors may go on strike', I (20.12.91); Marcel Berlins, 'Threatening to break the law', S (4.1.92) 14; 'A Happy New Year?' (1992) 142 NLJ 5; 'Solicitors threaten boycott', LA (1.92) 6.

[15] 'Fixed fees fear for freelance advocates' future', L (7.1.92); 'Consultants Discredit LCD Fees Data', LSG (8.1.92) 3; 'Society Slaps in 10.7% Pay Claim', LSG (8.1.92) 3; 'Solicitors Mull Over Fixed Fee Options', LSG (15.1.92) 5; 'Birmingham Plea', LSG (15.1.92) 5; 'Birmingham Revolts against LCD Proposals' (1992) 136 SJ 24; 'Society Rejects "Derisory" 3%', LSG (22.1.92) 3; 'Fixed Fee Deferral Cheers Campaigners', LSG (22.1.92) 4; 'Solicitors and Barristers Unite and Say "No" to 3%' (1992) 136 SJ 51; 'Comment: Silver Lining?' (1992) 136 SJ 55; 'LCD Moves to Fix Fees for Civil Work', LSG (29.1.92) 3; 'Action Suspended', LSG (29.1.92) 3; 'Lord Mackay goes to the House of Commons' (1992) 142 NLJ 115; 'Lawyers consider direct action over legal aid changes', I (31.1.92); 'Jury still out on legal aid fees', O (2.2.92); 'Lord Mackay "Misleading" says Law Soc' (1992) 136 SJ 156; 'PM to discuss fixed fees with criminal lawyers', L (3.2.92); 'Duty Scheme Action', LSG (5.2.92) 3; ' "Save Legal Aid" Campaign Gets Under Way', LSG (5.2.92) 3; 'Fixed Fee Protest Renewed at SGM', LSG (5.2.92) 4; 'Law Soc Fixed Fees Campaign is

"Good PR"' (1992) 136 SJ 99; 'Huge Turn Out for CJ Crisis Conference' (1992) 142 NLJ 150; 'Key Solicitors Join Fixed Fee Protest', LSG (12.2.92) 4; 'United We Stand', LSG (12.2.92) 2; 'Mackay Briefs MPs on Eve of Lobby', LSG (12.2.92) 3; 'Record Slump in 24-hour Scheme Lawyers' (1992) 136 SJ 256; 'Profession Stays Solid on Fixed Fees' (1992) 136 SJ 279; 'Editorial: A Broader View', LA (3.92) 3; 'Public Voices Concern over 24-hour Scheme' (1992) 136 SJ 328; 'Fixed fees evidence', LA (4.92) 4; Law Society (1992: paras. 1, 17, 25).

[16] 'Trouble with swings and roundabouts', G (12.2.92) 23; 'Pin-stripe protest greets Mackay', I (13.2.92); 'Irate solicitors jeer Mackay over fixed fees', G (13.2.92) 3; 'Solicitors barrack Mackay over fixed-fees scheme', T (13.2.92) 1; 'Mackay unmoved as lawyers protest', FT (13.2.92); 'Aiding Justice', T (13.2.92) 13; 'Profession Unites to Slam Mackay's Stand on Fixed Fees' (1992) 136 SJ 123; 'Comment: Lord Chancellor's Dilemma' (1992) 136 SJ 127; 'Stand Firm' (1992) 142 NLJ 185; 'Mackay Under Fire at Conference' (1992) 142 NLJ 186; 'Solicitor with a pressing case to present', FT (15.2.92); 'Inns and Outs', T (18.2.92); 'Criminal Justice in Danger', LSG (19.2.92) 2; 'Summer Deadline Set for Fixed Fees', LSG (19.2.92) 3; 'Lobby Highs and Lows', LSG (19.2.92) 5; 'Lord Mackay "Misleading" says Law Soc' (1992) 136 SJ 156; 'Criminal Justice in Danger?' (1992) 142 NLJ 230; Lord Mackay, 'Underpinning Justice' (1992) 142 NLJ 238; 'Fair Terms for Fair Work', C (1–2.92) 4; 'Mackay Told "No Bail Out" by YSG', LSG (4.3.92) 3; 'We Won't Bail You Out: YSG tells Mackay' (1992) 136 SJ 202; 'Lord Mackay faces court action over legal aid fees', G (6.3.92); 'Solicitors Face "5% Pay Cut"', LSG (11.3.92) 3; 'Wigs and Tories' (1992) 136 SJ 230; 'Not for turning', L (17.3.92) 11; 'Pay Review Body', LSG (18.3.92) 4; 'Record Slump in 24-hour Scheme' (1992) 136 SJ 256; 'Editorial: A broader view', LA (3.92) 3; '"Do you want a job?"' LA (3.92) 4; 'Fixed fees evidence', LA (4.92) 4.

[17] 'Society Presses LCD for Full-Scale Pay Review', LSG (26.2.92) 4; 'Pay Doldrums', LSG (26.2.92) 4; 'Devon Vanguard', LSG (26.2.92) 9; 'Survey Revelation Angers Society', LSG (11.3.92) 4; 'LCD Dubbed "Underhand" in Fixed Fee Memo Row' (1992) 136 SJ 227; 'Up to 50% Decline in Duty Schemes', LSG (18.3.92) 3; 'Mackay Refutes Danger of Fixed Fees', LSG (18.3.92) 8; 'Duty Solicitors on Defensive Over Action', LSG (25.3.92) 7; 'Duty Solicitors get Public's Vote', LSG (8.4.92) 7.

[18] 'Opposition MPs Offer Support', LSG (19.2.92) 5; 'Opposition Puts Law Issues High on Election Agenda' (1992) 136 SJ 155; 'Legal Manifestos', LSG (25.3.92) 6; 'Election Round-Up' (1992) 136 SJ 280; '32,000 Petition', LSG (27.5.92) 4.

[19] 'Solicitors urged to delay cases where legal aid is refused', DT (18.5.92); 'Courts face delays over new legal aid rules', I (18.5.92) 4; 'LCD refuses to back down over circular', L (19.5.92) 1; 'Challenge to rules on legal aid', I (21.5.92); 'A Pay-slip too Few' (1992) 142 NLJ 705; 'Decision to Stop Legal Aid Means 46 Jobs Lost' (1992) 36 SJ 479; 'Liverpool to Ignore Law Soc on LCD Circular' (1992) 136 SJ 480; 'Comment: "Not my Fault, Guv"' (1992) 136 SJ 483; 'Way Cleared for Legal Aid Guide Challenge', LSG (27.5.92) 3; 'Law Society Urges Withdrawal of Legal Aid Circular' (1992) 142 NLJ 742; 'High Court to Review Payslip Circular' (1992) 136 SJ 503; 'Legal aid protests to increase', I (3.6.92); 'Government admits to oversight on legal aid', I (4.6.92); 'Legal aid rule is scrapped after protests', I (9.6.92);

'Mackay backs down on legal aid', T (9.6.92) 16; 'LCD Backs Down on Wage Slip Guidelines', LSG (10.6.92) 3; 'LCD Climbs Down on Pay Slips' (1992) 142 NLJ 814. On the rationing of criminal legal aid see Wall (1996); Young (1996); Wood (1996).

[20] 'Further Rap for Law Society over Fixed Fees' (1992) 136 SJ 503; 'Comment: Fixed Fees What Next?' (1992) 136 SJ 507; 'Devon and Exeter Stands Firm over Fixed Fees' (1992) 136 SJ 540; 'Society Rebuffs Charges of Lacklustre Campaign', LSG (10.6.92) 6; 'Bar backs set legal aid fees', T (22.6.92); 'Bar Signals Support for Wider Use of Standard Fees', LSG (24.6.92) 4; 'Bar Sticks Up for Crown Court Fixed Fees' (1992) 136 SJ 615; 'Fixed Fees "Would have Left Loophole Undiscovered"' (1992) 136 SJ 639; 'Now Telford Comes Out over Fixed Fees' (1992) 136 SJ 664; 'Shropshire Solicitors Strike', LSG (15.7.92) 10; 'Shropshire Action Ends', LSG (26.8.92) 8; 'Strikes Wind Down in Expectation of New Fee Proposals', LSG (16.9.92) 10.

[21] 'Better management "key to cutting legal aid cost"', G (23.6.92); 'Changes to legal aid urged', FT (23.6.92); 'Solicitors blamed for soaring legal aid bill', I (23.6.92); 'Cost for legal aid jumps to £760m', T (23.6.92); 'Legal aid costs soar to £760m', DT (23.6.92); 'Firms are Inefficient says LAB Chief', LSG (24.6.92) 3; 'Letters to the editor', I (29.6.92); John Pitts, 'The Future of Legal Aid', LSG (1.7.92) 2; 'Society Disputes LAB Statistic', LSG (1.7.92) 4; 'Milking the legal aid cow', T (14.7.92); 'The Watchword is Cost Control', LSG (15.7.92) 11; 'Comment: Salvo against Solicitors' (1992) 136 SJ 619; 'PI Lawyers Seek Exception from Prescribed Rates', LSG (13.5.92) 7; 'Responding to the Critics', LSG (22.7.92) 2; 'Solicitors Brace Themselves for Standard Fees', LSG (7.10.92) 6. For an economic analysis of standard fees see Gray *et al.* (1996).

[22] 'Mackay attacks complacency of lawyers', G (28.7.92); 'Law "should be affordable to ordinary citizens"', DT (28.7.92); 'Mackay aims to cut the cost of litigation', I (28.7.92); 'Mackay calls for cheaper legal help', T (28.7.92); 'Justice and a better way', G (28.7.92); 'Tiered Advice System Touted by Mackay', LSG (29.7.92) 4; 'Legal Aid Reforms Proposed', LSG (28.7.92) 8; 'JUSTICE in the Civil Courts' (1992) 142 NLJ 1077; 'Fast food approach to dispensing justice', L (4.8.92); JUSTICE (1992); 'A Bar to Justice', T (14.3.93) 17.

[23] 'Legal aid "franchise" mooted for solicitors', T (7.10.92); 'Comment: Franchising' (1992) 136 SJ 988; 'Fixed Fee Row Poses Watershed for Law Soc' (1992) 136 SJ 983; 'Comment: To Strike or Not to Strike' (1992) 136 SJ 987; 'Solicitors Divided on Fee Battle Tactics', LSG (14.10.92) 4; 'Devon Fee Survey Points to Losses', LSG (14.10.92) 4; 'Beating the Drum on the Fringes', LSG (14.10.92) 6; 'Law Society Proposes "Price per Case" Compromise' (1992) 136 SJ 1015; 'Legal aid, takeaway-style', I (23.10.92) 20; 'Green light for standard fees', LA (10.92) 4; 'Firms will Stop Legal Aid Work under Fixed Fees' (1992) 136 SJ 1100; 'Many Set to Drop out of Criminal Work—Survey', LSG (11.11.92) 5 (33% response rate); Sherr (1994); Goriely (1994c); Sherr *et al.* (1994); Paterson and Sherr (1999); Sherr (2001).

[24] 'Battle Lines Drawn on Standard Fees', LSG (23.9.92) 3; 'Mackay accepts Price Waterhouse Recommendations' (1992) 142 NLJ 1285; 'Grass Roots Set to Apply Strike Pressure' (1992) 136 SJ 931; 'Crime Doesn't Pay' (1992) 142 NLJ 1309; 'Comment: Standard Fees' (1992) 136 SJ 934; 'Standard fee report provokes strike calls', L (29.9.92) 1; 'LAG—radical reform in legal aid is needed', L (6.10.92) 1; 'Standard fee facts', L (6.10.92) 10; Roger Smith, 'A Strategy for Justice', LSG

(7.10.92) 2; 'Solicitors Brace Themselves for Standard Fees', LSG (7.10.92) 6; 'Back to the Drawingboard' (1992) 136 SJ 988; 'Fixed Fee Row Poses Watershed for Law Soc' (1992) 136 SJ 983; 'Comment: To Strike or Not to Strike' (1992) 136 SJ 987; 'Solicitors Divided on Fee Battle Tactics', LSG (14.10.92) 4; 'Devon Fee Survey Points to Losses', LSG (14.10.92) 4; 'Beating the Drum on the Fringes', LSG (14.10.92) 6; 'Fee Scheme Stresses Quality', LSG (14.10.92) 3; 'Law Society Proposes "Price per Case" Compromise' (1992) 136 SJ 1015; 'Finding the Way Out' (1992) 142 NLJ 1401; Mark Sheldon, 'One Profession', LSG (22.10.92) 2; 'Law Society tells Mackay to think again on legal aid', T (23.10.92); 'Lord Mackay attacked over standard fees', DT (23.10.92); 'Alarm as Mackay moves to reduce huge legal aid bill', STel (25.10.92) 4; 'Mackay plan to curb legal aid stuns lawyers', ST (25.10.92); 'Mackay signals new curbs on legal aid system', IOS (25.10.92); 'Lawyers fear loss of legal aid firms', T (26.10.92); John Appleby, 'Why we are worried', T (27.10.92); 'Legal Aid: Nothing is "Sacrosant" Mackay tells Solicitors', LSG (28.10.92) 3; 'Black Saturday in Birmingham' (1992) 142 NLJ 1493; 'Angry Reaction to Lord Chancellor's "Reforms" ' (1992) 142 NLJ 1494; 'Inevitable Legal Aid Changes' (1992) 142 NLJ 1505; 'Comment: Mackay Again' (1992) 136 SJ 1075; 'Green light for standard fees', LA (10.92) 4; 'Firms will Stop Legal Aid Work under Fixed Fees' (1992) 136 SJ 1100; 'Many Set to Drop Out of Criminal Work—Survey', LSG (11.11.92) 5; 'Pitts says Salaried Lawyers are Worth Considering', LSG (18.11.92) 6; 'LAG and Legal Aid' (1992) 142 NLJ 1603: 'Editorial: Facing up to realities', LA (11.92) 3; Lee Bridges, 'The fixed fees battle', LA (11.92) 7; 'Law Centres in Legal Aid Board Initiative' (1992) 142 NLJ 1710; 'Editorial: Franchising: nasty or nice?' LA (12.92) 3; LAG (1992). For an acute account of legal aid practice see Travers (1997).

[25] 'Mackay Drops Legal Aid Proposal Bombshell' (1992) 136 SJ 1070, 1071; 'Bar Attack over Payment Delays', LSG (4.11.92) 6; 'Unfair Fixed Fees' (1992) 142 NLJ 1530; 'Bar Remains Opposed to Standard Fees' (1992) 136 SJ 1100: 'Law Soc Split on Legal Aid Proposals' (1992) 136 SJ 1128; 'LAPG to Go on Offensive on Legal Aid' (1992) 136 SJ 1155.

[26] 'Law Soc Split on Legal Aid Proposals' (1992) 136 SJ 1128; 'Changes "will have adverse effect on seven million" ', DT (13.11.92); 'Lawyers warn of limits on justice', I (13.11.92); 'Insurers to push legal cover as aid is cut', T (14.11.92); 'Law body condemns proposed legal aid cutbacks', I (14.11.92); 'Millions "priced out of access to courts" ', T (14.11.92); 'Millions Predicted to Fall Through Legal Aid Net', LSG (18.11.92) 3; 'Grassroots Upset at Legal Aid Battle', LSG (18.11.92) 4; 'Defending the Indefensible' (1992) 142 NLJ 1601; 'Legal Aid Cuts Condemned' (1992) 142 NLJ 1602; 'LAG and Legal Aid' (1992) 142 NLJ 1603; 'Pay Freeze Offered to Avert Cuts', LSG (16.12.92) 4; 'Lawyers offer pay freeze to help legal aid', I (16.12.92) 2; 'Lawyers offer to peg legal aid fees', DT (16.12.92); 'Lawyers offer legal aid deal', T (16.12.92); 'Law Society Initiative to Halt Legal Aid Cuts' (1992) 142 NLJ 1746; 'Going Round in Circles' (1992) 142 NLJ 1745; 'Calculated Cuts' (1992) 142 NLJ 1746; 'Lawyers lose out after volunteering pay freeze', I (18.12.92); 'Mackay rejects Bar's freeze', T (18.12.92); 'Pay freeze rather than cuts', LA (1.93) 4.

[27] 'Peers at One over Legal Aid Squeeze', LSG (25.11.92) 4; 'Taylor Attacks Legal Aid Cuts', LSG (2.12.92) 3; 'Spending Cuts are "Blot on System"—Taylor' (1992) 136 SJ 1207.

[28] 'Duplication' (1990) 140 NLJ 1178 (17.8.90); 'High costs could jeopardise forty years of legal aid', I (3.10.90); 'Chink of Light on Legal Aid Cuts', LSG (6.1.93) 4; 'Alliance Rally', LSG (6.1.93) 4; Lord Mackay, 'Paying the price of justice', T (22.1.93) 14; 'Watchdogs Join Forces over Eligibility' (1993) 137 SJ 32: 'Profession Makes Last Sally against Cuts' (1993) 137 SJ 32; 'Mackay pledges to push through legal aid savings', T (22.1.93) 2; 'New Bid to Avert Legal Aid Cuts', LSG (27.1.93) 3; 'Society Urged to get Tough on Legal Aid', LSG (3.2.93) 8; 'Mackay has Fresh Attack in MIND' (1993) 137 SJ 84; 'Mackay Faces New Rap for Planned Cuts' (1993) 137 SJ 111; 'Fur Flies at Family Lawyers' Conference', LSG (10.3.93) 9; 'Comment: Suing Lord Mackay' (1993) 137 SJ 215; 'Editorial: Fundamentals not figures', LA (3.93) 3; 'Mackay isolated', LA (3.93) 5.

[29] 'Political Pressure Peaks on Legal Aid Cuts', LSG (3.2.93) 4; 'Howard to Question Mackay', LSG (3.2.93) 4; 'Franchising Warning', LSG (10.2.93) 8; 'Judges implore Mackay to Abandon Cuts', LSG (10.2.93) 11; 'Litigants Pack a Punch at Legal Aid Lobby', LSG (10.2.93) 11; 'Lord Chief Justice Threatens "Confrontation"' (1993) 143 NLJ 181; 'Lords Criticise Judge Shortage', LSG (17.2.93) 9; 'All at Sea', (1993) 143 NLJ 317; 'Ten Additional High Court Judges', LSG (10.3.93) 3; 'Mackay isolated', LA (3.93) 4.

[30] 'Law Soc prepares to take last-ditch stand', L (9.3.93); 'Keeping the poor from the law', T (9.3.93) 33; 'Legal aid reforms challenged', FT (9.3.93); 'Mackay taken to court over fees', T (9.3.93); 'Mackay faces a High Court test on legal aid fees', G (9.3.93); 'Mackay to be Sued on Pay', LSG (10.3.93) 3; 'Suing Lord Mackay' (1993) 137 SJ 215; 'Mackay's Mission', LSG (17.3.93) 4; 'A Bar to Justice', T (14.3.93) 17; 'Preserve Green Form Scheme MPs Urge', LSG (24.3.93) 3; 'Law Soc warns Mackay over Franchising' (1993) 137 SJ 263; 'Comment: Legal Aid' (1993) 137 SJ 267; 'Legg Hauled over the Coals', LSG (31.3.93) 7; 'Mackay faces Second Court Challenge', LSG (7.4.93) 3; 'Legal Aid Loss', LSG (7.4.93) 8; 'An Interesting Year' (1993) 143 NLJ 533; 'The Fight Goes On' (1993) 143 NLJ 535; 'Mackay Defends Eligibility Cuts' (1993) 137 SJ 339; 'LCD Aims for Value', LSG (28.4.93) 7; 'Society loses battle to block standard fees', L (4.5.93) 1; 'High Court Ends Fixed Fee Battle', LSG (5.5.93) 3; 'Fees Scheme Appeal', LSG (26.5.93) 3; 'MPs Question Cuts', LSG (21.7.93) 8; 'Standard Fees Appeal Fails', LSG (28.7.93) 5; 'Fixed Fees Loom for Civil Cases', LSG (20.4.94) 4; 'Mackay Backs Standard Fees' (1994) 138 SJ 459. Merricks recalled: 'we managed to set these standard fees at such a generous level that when they finally came in not a bleat of complaint was heard about them at all. And the bill for legal aid continued to rise at prodigious rates' (interview July 1998). But John Hayes noted that Neal LJ observed: 'if only the Lord Chancellor had listened to the Law Society, whose members know more about the reality of legal aid, then this problem would not have occurred'. Hayes felt 'that was worth a lot to get that' (interview July 1998).

[31] 'Hardship Cases to be Used in Court', LSG (26.5.93) 3; 'Court Defeat on Legal Aid Cuts', LSG (26.3.93) 4; 'Society Loses Legal Aid Case' (1993) 137 SJ 600; 'A Change of Tack for the Law Society' (1993) 143 NLJ 909.

[32] Roger Smith, 'Tender control or instrument of cheap change?' T (9.3.93) 33; 'Mackay's Mission', LSG (17.3.93) 4; 'Professional Good Manners' (1993) 143 NLJ 569; 'Sheldon Seeks Pledge on Franchising', LSG (24.3.93) 4; 'Parliament to Vote on Legal Aid Cuts', LSG (31.3.93) 3; 'Board Denies Secret Agenda on Franchising',

LSG (31.3.93) 3; 'Franchising Costs Checks Alarm', LSG (21.4.93) 5; 'Defence to Tendering Threat', LSG (21.4.93) 5; 'Promise of no Competitive Tendering for Legal Aid Work', LSG (28.4.93) 3; 'Legal Aid Solicitors Support Franchising', LSG (28.4.93) 8; 'Editorial: Franchising: A new agenda', LA (4.93) 3; 'Subtle Moves in Tendering Agenda', LSG (12.5.93) 7; 'Franchising fears continue', LA (5.93) 4; 'Franchising's "running sore" ', LA (6.93) 4; 'Gloom over Franchise Perks', LSG (21.7.93) 4; 'Franchise Demand High', LSG (28.7.93) 8; see Orchard (1994).

[33] 'Rowe Calls for Barristers to Bid for Work' (1993) 137 SJ 32; 'Freelancers Adopt New Payment Formula' (1993) 137 SJ 523; 'Young Bar fears for its future', L (29.6.93) 8; 'Fiddling while the Junior Bar Burns' (1993) 143 NLJ 1230; 'Standard Fee Bias "a Scandal" ', LSG (6.10.93) 7; 'Bar Urged to be More Businesslike', LSG (6.10.93) 4; 'Bar Council criticises fee inequality', L (12.10.93); 'An Open Letter to the Prime Minister', C (11–12.93) 3; 'Bar offers fixed-price legal help', T (2.3.94); 'Bar unveils century brief', L (8.3.94); 'Advocacy rates fuel fees row', L (27.9.94) 1; ' "Fixed Price" Barristers' (1996) 140 SJ 600; 'Comment: A Client-Centred Approach' (1996) 140 SJ 603.

[34] 'Pannone Power', LSG (21.7.93) 2; Rodger Pannone, 'Back to Basics—a Broad Welcome', LSG (26.1.94) 2; 'Mackay Urged to Undo Cuts', LSG (26.1.94) 3; 'Legal Aid Agenda Set Out', LSG (26.1.94) 3; 'Legal Aid Pay Freeze Threat', LSG (16.2.94) 4; 'And Then There was None' (1994) 144 NLJ 223; Rodger Pannone, 'When is Enough Enough?' LSG (23.2.94) 2; 'Mackay Told of Grass Roots Ire', LSG (2.3.94) 3; 'Woolf Test', LSG (2.3.94) 9; 'Mackay gives ground over legal aid cuts', T (3.3.94); 'Cool Reply to Aid Retreat', LSG (9.3.94) 3; 'Missed Opportunity for Legal Aid Eligibility' (1994) 144 NLJ 346; 'Lord Mackay replies', T (29.3.94); 'No Court Review for Pay Freeze', LSG (30.3.94) 3; Rodger Pannone, 'A Sense of Frustration', LSG (27.4.94) 2; 'Treasury Review Alarm', LSG (11.5.94) 4; 'Do we really need a Lord Chancellor?' I (17.6.94); 'Brittan to be "healing" Lord Chancellor?' ES (23.6.94); 'Elly Pledges Fraudster Purge', LSG (20.7.94) 5; 'Taylor Hits Out at Privatisation', LSG (27.7.94) 3; 'Axe Falls on Legal Aid Body', LSG (27.7.94) 5; 'Lawyers Attack Mackay on LACC' (1994) 138 SJ 756; 'Franchising Media Flop' (1994) 138 SJ 783.

[35] Genn (1987); 'Mackay Gives Boost to Conditional Fees' (1993) 137 SJ 780; 'No Foal, No Fee' (1993) 143 NLJ 1213; 'Contingent Justice' (1993) 143 NLJ 1223; 'Mackay Rethink over Fee Uplifts', LSG (25.8.93) 4; 'Legal Fees "Out of Proportion" ', LSG (6.10.93) 4; 'Mackay's Advisers Warn on Conditional Fees', LSG (10.11.93) 3; ' "No Win, No Fee" Carries PR Risk', LSG (24.11.93) 6; 'PI Work "Self-financing" ' (1993) 143 NLJ 1667 (161 out of 600 firms responded; 1,400 cases); 'Conditions and Fees' (1993) 143 NLJ 1665; Gravelle and Waterson (1993) (economic analysis of lawyer–client conflict of interest); ' "No Win, No Fee" on Free Terms', LSG (2.2.94) 5; ' "No win no fee" legal battle looms', STel (6.3.94); 'PI Lawyer Backs Conditional Fees' (1994) 138 SJ 224; 'Lawyers in double fee dilemma', T (15.3.94); ' "No Win No Fee" Cap', LSG (11.5.94) 3; 'Comment: Good News—Conditionally' (1994) 138 SJ 463; 'Conditional Fees "Still on Course" ', LSG (16.3.94) 7; 'Mackay urged to rethink fees plan', T (14.6.94); 'No Win No Fee', LSG (13.7.94) 4; 'Taylor joins critics of "no win, no fee" court cases', T (4.10.94); 'Age of the no-win, no fee outfits', T (4.10.94); 'No Win, No Fee Risk to Client', LSG (7.10.94) 6; ' "Milking" Lawyers', LSG (12.10.94) 4; 'Law Lord to

Attack Conditional Fees' (1994) 138 SJ 1060; 'Cutting your losses', G (25.10.94) 17; 'Ackner slams Mackay over New Fees', (1994) 138 SJ 1090; 'Row Looms over Conditional Fees' (1994) 138 SJ 1089; Fennell (1994); 'Greed is not good for you, lawyers told', DT (3.2.95); 'Two-pronged Onslaught on Lawyer Fees', LSG (8.2.95) 4.

[36] 'Editorial: Block Contracts—Block Justice?' (1994) 144 NLJ 113; 'Franchise Deadlock', LSG (2.3.94) 3; 'Hopes Fade', LSG (2.3.94) 4; 'Boycott Risk', LSG (2.3.94) 6; 'Row Flares over Franchise Audit Rules', LSG (13.4.94) 5.

[37] 'Franchise Boycott Looms', LSG (9.3.94) 4; 'Liverpool Backs Calls for Franchising Boycott' (1994) 138 SJ 356; 'Franchising Veto Call', LSG (16.3.94) 4; 'Call for Franchise Boycott' (1994) 138 SJ 252; 'Boycott Support Mounts', LSG (23.3.94) 5; 'Bristol Backs Franchising Boycott' (1994) 138 SJ 275; 'No Court Review for Pay Freeze', LSG (30.3.94) 3; 'Manchester Gets Tough on Franchising' (1994) 138 SJ 327; 'Liverpool Backs Call for Franchising Boycott' (1994) 138 SJ 356; 'Law Soc Franchising Boycott Likely' (1994) 138 SJ 380.

[38] 'Row Flares Over Franchise Audit Rules', LSG (13.4.94) 5; 'Council to Review Franchising', LSG (20.4.94) 5; 'Council Urges Contract Delay', LSG (27.4.94) 3; 'Board Retreats on Checks', LSG (27.4.94) 7; 'Elly Hits Out at Franchise Chaos', LSG (27.4.94) 8; 'Support for Boycott', LSG (27.4.94) 8; 'Law Soc Calls for Franchising Freeze' (1994) 138 SJ 403; 'Elly Savages LAB' (1994) 138 SJ 403; 'Bunker Mentality at the LAB' (1994) 144 NLJ 558; 'Mr Franchise', LSG (4.5.94) 6; 'Board Blames Law Soc for Franchising Impasse' (1994) 138 SJ 431; 'Comment: A Plague on Both Your Houses' (1994) 138 SJ 435; 'BLA Calls for Mackay to Resign' (1994) 144 NLJ 594; 'Society Bids to List all Franchising Firms' (1994) 138 SJ 459; 'Hope as Talks resume', LSG (18.5.94) 3; 'Law Society urges caution on franchises', LA (5.94) 5; 'Mackay Gives Ground', LSG (22.6.94) 3; 'Editorial: More light, less heat', LA (6.94) 3; 'Board Plans for Franchise D-Day', LSG (13.7.94) 4; 'Green Light for Contracts', LSG (20.7.94) 4; 'Cardiff Lukewarm to Scheme', LSG (20.7.94) 3; 'Devonald says Society Wrong to "Give In"' (1994) 138 SJ 728; 'Editorial: Morale and competence', LA (7.94) 3; 'Two Fifths Miss Full Franchise', LSG (3.8.94) 3; 'Editorial: Another Brave New World' (1994) 144 NLJ 1085; 'Franchising Launched by Legal Aid Board' (1994) 144 NLJ 1086; 'Franchising Media Flop' (1994) 138 SJ 783; 'Editorial: Sign up but watch out', LA (8.94) 3; 'Qualified nod for franchising', LA (8.94) 4; 'Legal Aid Split Mooted', LSG (12.10.94) 8; 'Group Aid', LSG (19.10.94) 8. The evaluation criteria are presented, defended, and criticised in Sherr *et al.* (1994a; 1994b); Goriely (1994d); Travers (1994); Moorhead *et al.* (1994). For an evaluation of police station advice see Bridges and Choongh (1998). Walter Merricks observed in 1998 that 'in a professional body you need enemies, otherwise the profession itself becomes the enemy. …And the Legal Aid Board was a decent enemy' (interview).

[39] 'Comment', LSG (1.2.95) 10; 'Franchise "Failures" Revealed', LSG (28.6.95) 1; 'Birmingham Franchising Boycott', LSG (2.8.96) 1; 'Editorial: Fear of Franchising', LSG (2.8.96) 13; 'Criminal Lawyers Group attacks Franchising Quality as "a Sham"', LSG (18.9.96) 6; 'Lawyers plot a boycott of contract plan', L (22.10.96) 1; 'Call for franchising boycott', LA (10.96) 4.

[40] 'Board Test Centres', LSG (13.7.94) 11; 'NCC Calls for CAB Lawyers', (1994) 138 SJ 977; LCD (1994b); NCC (1994).

[41] 'The Mediation Solution?' LSG (22.9.93) 5; 'Mackay Backs Legal Advice in Divorce', LSG (28.10.93) 9; 'Mediation Dominates Mackay's Divorce Plan', LSG (8.12.93) 4; 'Lawyers' Mixed Emotions over Cut Price Divorce' (1993) 137 SJ 1227; 'Comment: Divorce Reform' (1993) 1231 SJ 131; LCD (1993); 'Divorce Reforms "could Add to Costs"', LSG (2.2.94) 7; 'Group Calls for Arbitration in Med Neg Cases', LSG (4.2.94) 84; 'Family Law Campaign', LSG (23.2.94) 9; 'Mediation "Cuts Divorce Costs"', LSG (2.3.94) 9; 'Lawyers Predict Divorce Debacle', LSG (23.3.94) 4; 'Legal aid and divorce law face radical change', I (14.11.94); 'Legal aid cuts leave victims out in the cold', I (14.11.94); Charles Elly, 'The Cost of Justice', LSG (23.11.94) 2; 'Divorce Deals', LSG (16.12.94) 6; Law Society (1994); McCarthy (1996); Davies *et al.* (1996); Webb (1996); Smith (1996b).

[42] Ingleby (1992); '"Divorce without Lawyers" Fear over White Paper' (1995) 139 SJ 179; 'Comment: Lawyer-Free Divorce?' (1995) 139 SJ 207; 'Comment: Duty of Divorce Lawyers' (1995) 129 SJ 387; 'Still Room for Legal Advice in Divorce', LSG (3.5.95) 3; Nigel Shepherd, 'Comment: A Fair Settlement for All', LSG (3.5.95) 10; 'Reassurance over Divorce', LSG (14.6.95) 16; 'Divorce Plans under Attack', LSG (13.9.95) 6; 'Divorce Plans Doubt', LSG (11.10.95) 6; 'Limited Family Aid Proposal', LSG (25.10.95) 3; 'Comment: Market in Mediation', LSG (25.10.95) 14; 'A Lord Challenged', LSG (1.11.95) 12; LCD (1995); Sarat and Felstiner (1995); Eekelaar *et al.* (2000); Mather *et al.* (2001). On the image of family lawyers see Lewis (2000).

[43] 'Partial Backing for Divorce Legislation', LSG (8.11.95) 3; Hilary Siddle, 'Comment: Objections Sustained', LSG (8.11.95) 12; 'Mackay Muddles Mediation Waters', LSG (15.11.95) 8; 'Marriage, Mediation or Mayhem?' (1995) 139 SJ 1139.

[44] 'Full Law Reform Programme', LSG (22.11.95) 3; 'Labour Support for Family Lawyers', LSG (6.12.95) 8; 'Family Solicitors Gain Concessions', LSG (6.3.96) 2; Hilary Siddle, 'Family Credentials', LSG (13.3.96) 15; Hilary Siddle, 'Fighting for Family', LSG (20.3.96) 20; 'Family Lawyers Withdraw Support from Divorce Bill', LSG (22.5.96) 4; 'Trouble and Strife', LSG (30.5.96) 12; 'Divorce Reform Debate Reduced to "Slanging Match"' (1991) 135 SJ 520; 'Editorial: A Wholly Different Bill', LSG (30.5.96) 15; 'Family Law Fear', LSG (19.6.96) 6; 'Family Dispute', LSG (19.6.96) 6.

[45] 'LCD Denies Small Claims Climb-Down', LSG (8.5.91) 3; 'Practitioners' Worst Fears', LSG (9.10.91) 2; 'LCD Re-Think on Small PI Claims', LSG (13.11.91) 8; 'LCD Goes Back to Drawing Board on Small Claims' (1991) 135 SJ 1232; 'LCD Takes First Steps on Lay Advocacy', LSG (27.5.92) 7; 'Non-Lawyers in Court' (1992) 142 NLJ 742; 'PI Claims Costs', LSG (24.2.93) 7; 'PI Lawyers Fear Small Claims Changes' (1993) 137 SJ 807; 'Small Claims Move Draws Fire', LSG (3.11.93) 5; 'Law Society Condemn New Approach to PI Claims' (1993) 137 SJ 1095; 'Critics Campaign over Injury Claims', LSG (10.11.93) 9; 'Editorial: Free for All?' (1994) 144 NLJ 41; 'Injury Plans Face Attack', LSG (19.1.94) 9; 'Editorial: No Use to the Plaintiff', LSG (31.8.94) 5; 'Mackay Drops PI Small Claims Plan', LSG (31.8.94) 5; *Which?* (c. 1.94).

[46] 'Lawyers Hit Out at Small Claims Hike', LSG (21.6.95) 1; 'Lawyers Respond to Small Claim Increase', LSG (11.10.95) 56; 'Not So Small', LSG (8.11.95) 2; 'Lawyers Angry at Small Claims Plan', LSG (15.11.95) 4; 'Aid Row Over Small Claims', LSG (10.1.96) 2; 'Small Claims', LSG (10.1.96) 14; 'Big Challenge', LSG (10.1.96) 15; 'Gambling in the Three Grand Lottery', LSG (10.1.96) 16–17; 'Small Claims: Legal

Aid Board Notice', LSG (10.1.96) 19; 'Small Satisfaction', LSG (13.3.96) 5; 'Mediation Plan Triggers Access Fears', LSG (20.3.96) 3.

[47] 'Editorial: Fiddling Again' (1994) 144 NLJ 697; 'Millions Lost in law cash fiddle', SE (22.5.94); 'Green Form Set for Crackdown', LSG (22.6.94) 3; 'LAB Attacks Green Form Fraud' (1994) 138 SJ 619; 'Board Cracks Whip on Claims', LSG (6.7.94) 10; 'Comment: Controlling Legal Aid' (1994) 138 SJ 623; 'Board Launches Attack on Fraud', LSG (12.10.94) 5; 'Green Form Fraud Checks Opposed' (1994) 138 SJ 1059; 'Comment: Favouring Franchises' (1994) 138 SJ 1063; 'Midlands Solicitor Fights Allegations of Massive Green Form Fraud' (1994) 138 SJ 1171; 'Suspended Solicitor Challenges SFO' (1994) 144 NLJ 698.

[48] 'Performance of barristers "should be linked to fee"', T (8.3.94); 'Checks cut legal aid fees by 25%', I (3.2.95); 'QCs subject to standard criminal fees', L (7.2.95); 'Go-ahead for graduated fees', L (14.2.95); 'Curb on lawyers' legal aid abuse', ST (24.11.96) 12; 'Streeter Plans Clamp-Down on the Bar' (1996) 140 SJ 1140: 'Aid Clamp', LSG (12.2.97) 5; 'Rash use of legal aid to be stopped', T (4.3.97) 2; 'LAPG Attacks Latest Reforms' (1997) 141 SJ 197; 'Editorial: Back in the bottle', LA (3.97) 3; 'Editorial: Leading counsel: real conclusions', LA (4.97) 3.

[49] 'Lawyers Slam Legal Aid Regulations' (1994) 138 SJ 647; 'MP Slams Legal Aid for Foreign Nationals' (1994) 138 SJ 807; 'Attack on Aid for the "Rich"', LSG (31.8.94) 6; 'Mackay to curb legal aid for wealthy defendants', T (5.9.94) 1; 'Rich pickings', T (5.9.94) 15; 'Anger over Legal Aid Row', LSG (7.9.94) 4; 'Editorial: Whilst We Have Been Away' (1994) 144 NLJ 1193; 'Comment: Cost of Justice' (1994) 144 SJ 895; 'Winners and losers in legal aid lottery', ST (23.10.94) §1, 7; 'Guinness chief was given £1.3m legal aid', T (25.10.94); Anthony Burton, 'The Demise of Criminal Legal Aid' (1994) 144 NLJ 1491; 'Maxwell Bill Fuels Debate', LSG (2.11.94) 6; 'Mackay Defends Aid for Foreigners', LSG (2.11.94) 6; 'Nightclub tycoon prospers on legal aid', ST (27.11.94) §1, 12; 'The Sultan of Brunei's friend given legal aid', ES (9.12.94) 15; 'Rich to be excluded in legal aid victory', ST (11.12.94); 'Mackay targets legal aid for rich', T (12.12.94); 'Legal aid loan plan', G (12.12.94); 'Brake on Legal Aid for Rich', LSG (16.12.94) 3; 'Cake Eating Time' (1995) 145 NLJ 169; 'Editorial: Rich pickings', LA (3.95) 3; 'Crackdown on Aid for Rich', LSG (3.5.95) 3; 'Crackdown on Aid for Wealthy "Unfair"', LSG (28.2.96) 2; Comptroller and Auditor General (1996b); 'Maxwell Solicitor Hits Back', LSG (19.3.97) 9.

[50] 'PI Bonanza', LSG (22.6.94) 3; 'Prettys' TV Ad Attraction', LSG (22.6.94) 4; 'Push for PI', LSG (22.6.94) 10; 'Cost Inhibits Claims', LSG (29.6.94) 4; 'Injury Plan Lifts Off', LSG (6.7.94) 9; 'Scheme Gathers Support', LSG (6.7.94) 9; 'Public Swamps Injury Line', LSG (20.7.94) 5; 'Court Halts Rival PI Line', LSG (3.9.94) 5; 'Accident Line Drawn', LSG (21.9.94) 6; 'On the Line', LSG (9.11.94) 7.

[51] Charles Elly, 'Service and Independence', LSG (7.10.94) 2; 'Liverpool Firm Collapse Rocks Legal Community', LSG (2.11.94) 3; '"Hub and Spoke" Pioneers', LSG (2.11.94) 3; 'Firm in Receivership', LSG (9.11.94) 3; 'Deacon Break Up', LSG (16.11.94) 4; 'Legal aid cuts would lead to anarchy, Law Society head claims', T (26.11.94); 'Elly Warns Against Legal Aid Capping' (1994) 138 SJ 1224; 'Disappointment over Failure to Restore Legal Aid Cuts' (1994) 138 SJ 1247; 'Comment: Legal Aid' (1994) 138 SJ 1251; 'Editorial: Unhappy new year', LA (1.95) 3; Charles Elly, 'Comment: Prospects of 1995', LSG (5.1.95) 2; 'Rates Offer', LSG

(25.1.95) 2; 'Cornwall Debate Ignites Few Sparks' (1995) 145 NLJ 6; Eileen Pembridge, 'Comment: The Franchising Edge', LSG (1.2.95) 10; Roger Dixon, 'Comment: The Rate for the Job', LSG (1.2.95) 10; 'One Pay for the Franchised' (1995) 145 NLJ 134; 'Pay Row Brews', LSG (8.2.95) 1; 'Leaders Push for Better pay', LSG (8.3.95) 1; 'Outcry at Legal Aid Shortfall', LSG (8.3.95) 2; 'Legal Aid franchise firms get pay boost', T (17.3.95); 'Pay Round Cheers Franchises Only', LSG (22.3.95) 3; 'Legal Aid Rates Set' (1995) 139 SJ 255; 'Dismay at New Legal Aid Rates' (1995) 145 NLJ 406; 'Editorial: Divisive Pay Rises and Client Choice' (1995) 145 NLJ 405.

[52] 'NHS-Style Reform Sought for Legal Aid', LSG (20.7.94) 3; Robert Shrimsley, ' "Fundholders for justice" could cut £1.4bn legal aid bill,' 8 (27.8.94); 'Society to Block Proposed Legal Aid Scheme' (1994) 138 SJ 863; 'Mackay Taken by Fundholding', LSG (7.9.94) 3; Roger Smith, 'Can fundholders cut the legal aid bill?' T (20.9.94); 'Mackay Rejects Fundholders', LSG (28.9.94) 5; ' "Fundholders" still a live issue', L (4.10.94) 1; 'Fundholder Concept "Still on the Cards" ', LSG (7.10.94) 10; Charles Elly, 'Service and Independence', LSG (7.10.94) 2; 'Solicitors accuse tories of sinister plan to cut legal aid cash', T (8.10.94); 'President demands civil justice "people can afford" ', T (8.10.94); Bevan *et al.* (1994: 2, 5, 9, 11–20); Cousins (1994); Bevan (1996); Wall (1996); Samuel (1996); Moorhead (1998).

[53] 'Cost-effective Justice', T (6.1.95).

[54] 'A purse but with strings attached', G (10.1.95); 'Labour Plea', LSG (11.1.95) 1; 'Mackay proposes reforms to cut the cost of legal aid', T (12.1.95); 'Advice will be offered only by contracted suppliers', T (12.1.95); 'Mackay pledges to curb £1.4bn legal aid bill', DT (12.1.95) 4; 'Mackay reveals plan for cash limits on legal aid', I (12.1.95); 'Escalating costs eat into scheme', I (12.1.95); 'Legal aid plans "will ration justice" ', G (12.1.95); 'Building on Franchising' (1995) 145 NLJ 6; 'Mackay Under Fire for Legal Aid Proposals' (1995) 139 SJ 3; 'Legal aid', ES (12.1.95); 'An unanswered question', DT (12.1.95) 18; 'Putting lawyers under the knife', I (12.1.95) 15; 'Legal aid', FT (12.1.95); 'Editorial: Justice Rationed' (1995) 145 NLJ 5; 'Bring the balance back', E (14.1.95) 13; Roger Smith, 'Who needs legal aid?' T (17.1.95); 'Mackay Demands Legal Aid Changes', LSG (18.1.95) 2; Roger Smith, 'Comment: An Invitation to Debate', LSG (18.1.95) 14; 'Plan Wins Press Praise', LSG (18.1.95) 2; 'Legal Aid Debate Kicks Off', LSG (18.1.95) 3; 'Editorial: Thin Milk' (1995) 145 NLJ 41; 'Comment: Legal Aid' (1995) 139 SJ 35; Charles Elly, 'President's Column: A Time to Listen', LSG (25.1.95) 14; 'Legal Aid Consultation', C (1–2.95) 5; Lord Mackay, 'Radical Change and Public Confidence', C (1–2.95) 27–29; 'Editorial: Less haste: more speed', LA (2.95) 3; Paul Johnson, 'Let the lawyers pay for legal aid', ES (8.3.95) 9; 'Board Drops Form Plans', LSG (15.3.95) 1; 'Editorial: Managing justice', LA (5.95) 3; Hope (1997) (presented to LCD 4.7.96).

[55] 'Aitken Fixes Eye on Legal Aid Expense Insurance', LSG (15.2.95) 64; 'Legal Expenses Insurance' (1995) 139 SJ 33; 'Comment: Treasury Fallacy' (1995) 139 SJ 135; 'Aitken wants more legal expense cover', L (21.1.95); 'Legal Insurance best, says Aitken', LA (3.95) 5.

[56] 'Conditional fee cover for all', L (21.2.95) 1; 'The Advocate's Devil', T (10.4.95); 'Mackay unveils "no win no fee" scheme', T (21.4.95); 'Lawyers split over no win, no fee scheme', DT (22.4.95) 6; 'Lawyers Split over Mackay Fee Plans', LSG (26.4.95) 2; T (6.6.95) 35; 'Inns and Outs', T (22.10.96) 41.

[57] LSG (7.6.95) 6; 'No Win No Fee Clears Hurdle', LSG (14.6.95) 1; 'Conditional Fees Clear Final Hurdle—Just' (1995) 138 SJ 571; 'Comment: Conditional Welcome' (1995) 139 SJ 575; 'Victim Times', LSG (5.7.95) 2; 'Care and Control, and Conditional Fees' (1995) 145 NLJ 985; Clive Boxer, 'Lawyers Courting Disaster' (1995) 145 NLJ 1069; Clive Boxer, 'Opinion: Contingency Fees' (1995) 139 SJ 704; Conditional Fee Agreements Order and Regulations 1995.

[58] Lord Mackay, 'Reducing Risks for Clients', LSG (5.7.95) 10; 'Fee insurance', LSG (13.7.95) 3; 'Solicitor–Barrister Fee Row Intensifies', LSG (19.7.95) 2; 'Fee Insurance', LSG (9.8.95) 3; 'Insurance Scheme Tops 1000', LSG (31.8.95) 2; 'Conquest Launches Rival Accident Scheme', LSG (10.1.96) 3; 'Discretionary Fund Caution', LSG (10.1.96) 3; 'First Claims on Accident Line', LSG (3.7.96) 1; Robert Sayer, 'Final Pitch', LSG (3.7.96) 13; 'Conditional Fee Pressure', LSG (23.10.96) 5; 'Pay to win', G (5.11.96) 17; 'Conditional Fee Cases Rise by 50% over the Last Six Months', LSG (26.3.97) 4; 'US-style scheme to cut legal aid', ST (20.7.97) 24; 'No Win, No Fee Insurance Grows', LSG (22.4.98) 1; 'Legal diary', T (16.3.99) 37; 'No Win, No Fee, No Premiums', LSG (17.3.99) 4; 'SunAlliance Launches New Scheme' (1999) 143 SJ 257.

[59] Harris *et al.* (1984: Tables 1.2, 2.2); 'PI Firms Seek out Causes of Action', LSG (21.6.95) 5; 'Personal Injury Lists', (1995) 145 NLJ 1251; 'APIL Question Publicity Code' (1995) 139 SJ 807; ' "No" to Names Sale', LSG (31.8.95) 1; 'Mears Calls for Curbs on Name Sale', LSG (31.8.95) 3; 'Concern at Experts' Pay', LSG (6.9.95) 1; 'Editorial: Buying Experts', LSG (6.9.95) 10; Peter Goldsmith QC, 'Working on Condition', LSG (18.10.95) 11; 'Accident Names', LSG (25.10.95) 2; 'List of Accident Victims "Sold Out" ' (1995) 139 SJ 1089; 'No-Win, No-Fee Impasse', LSG (8.11.95) 2; 'Referrals Scrutiny', LSG (20.3.96) 1; 'Accident Scheme Attacked by APIL', LSG (27.3.96) 2; Martin Mears, 'President's Column: Try, Try, Try Again', LSG (27.3.96) 17; 'PI Lawyers Defend Tactics', LSG (26.6.96) 5; 'Claims firm Scoops up PI Work', LSG (2.8.96) 5.

[60] 'APIL Chief Hits Out at Anti-fee Lobby', LSG (15.11.95) 2; Caroline Harmer, 'Comment: The PI Challenge', LSG (9.5.96) 15; 'APIL seeks to Improve Public Image' (1996) 140 SJ 548; 'Editorial: Litigation Lessons from Abroad', LSG (19.6.96) 16; 'APIL approves a mandatory conduct code', L (19.11.96) 1.

[61] 'Editorial: Fiddling Again' (1994) 144 NLJ 687; ' "Don't Blame Us" say Solicitors' (1996) 140 SJ 244; 'PI Lawyers Buy into TV Ads', LSG (13.12.96) 4; 'PI Referral Network Launches No Win-No Fee Insurance Scheme', LSG (29.1.97) 4; 'Press Round-Up', LSG (29.4.98) 12; 'Solicitors Fight Back against Local Authorities' (1999) 143 SJ 99; 'Mersey Firms Sue Over Mail claims', LSG (3.2.99) 3; 'Libel Victory', LSG (15.9.99) 4; 'Three-partner Firm Triumphs over Daily Mail' (1999) 143 SJ 847.

[62] 'Society Publishes Legal Aid Blueprint', LSG (3.5.95) 1; 'Society Slams Cash Limiting', LSG (3.5.95) 9; 'Editorial: Capping the Earnings' (1995) 145 NLJ 677; Peter Goldsmith QC, 'Comment: Facts behind the Figures', LSG (17.5.95) 10; 'Bar Defends Earnings', LSG (17.5.95) 64; 'Fees defended', C (5–6.95) 4; Law Society (1995a).

[63] 'Labour Signals Paralegal Role', LSG (12.10.94) 7; 'Labour Creates a Future Vision', LSG (22.2.95) 1; 'Labour on Justice', LSG (17.5.95) 4; 'Architect of the New Legal Order?' C (3–4.95) 18; 'In the Eye of the Storm', LSG (24.5.95) 15; 'Labour Backs Major Review', LSG (28.6.95) 4; 'Opening the legal aid debate', LA (6.95) 4–5; 'Fee "Gimmick" ', LSG (26.7.95) 6; Labour Party (1995).

[64] LCD (1995: paras. 1.12, 3.8, 4.2, 7.8, 9.7, 12.26).

[65] 'Control, not Costs, says Mackay Launching Legal Aid Paper' (1995) 145 NLJ 714; 'Small Firms under Green Paper Threat', LSG (24.5.95) 5; Charles Elly, 'President's Column: A Celebration of Law', LSG (24.5.95) 10; 'In the Eye of the Storm', LSG (24.5.95) 15; Roger Smith, 'Essential Reading', LSG (24.5.95) 16; 'Legal Aid Lawyers Shun Green Paper', LSG (13.9.95) 12.

[66] 'Mackay Floats League Tables', LSG (24.5.95) 1; Peter Goldsmith QC, 'Chairman's Column: Legal Aid Controls—A Setback to Justice', C (5–6.95) 3; 'Poor attendance at British Legal Association Annual Spring Conference' (1995) 145 NLJ 807; 'Opening the legal aid debate', LA (6.95) 4–5; 'Editorial: Big ideas; deep problems', LA (9.95) 3.

[67] 'Mackay Moves to Ease Budget Fears', LSG (21.6.95) 1; 'Vote for Quality Schemes', LSG (21.6.95) 2; 'Legal Aid Reforms Face Further Attack' (1995) 139 SJ 596; 'Legal Aid "Fantasies" Attacked' (1995) 145 NLJ 914; Roy Douglas, 'Comment: Wolf in Sheep's Clothing', LSG (26.7.95) 10; 'Labour's Woolsack man', T (17.10.95) 37.

[68] 'No Cost Cuts, Repeats Mackay' (1995) 145 NLJ 987; 'Bar Nervous about Legal Aid Contracts', LSG (13.7.95) 5; Christopher Sallon, 'Fantasies and Extreme Measures', C (7–8.95) 11; Peter Goldsmith QC, 'Chairman's Column: A Reputation for Ability', C (9–10.95) 3.

[69] 'Society to Oppose Block Contracts', LSG (19.7.95) 1; 'Aid Riposte', LSG (9.8.95) 2; 'LAPG Angry at Fees Fraud Claim' (1995) 139 SJ 781; Martin Mears, 'Bashing the lawyers' (1995) 145 NLJ 1220.

[70] 'Society Warns of Aid Disaster', LSG (4.10.95) 2; 'Woolf Demands Fixed Fees', LSG (4.10.95) 4; 'Woolf and the "Golden Goose" at Bar Conference' (1995) 145 NLJ 1438; 'Law Society Slams "Draconian Reforms"', (1995) 139 SJ 967; 'Stricter Merit Test', LSG (25.10.95) 1; 'Board Casts Doubt on Legal Aid Cap', LSG (29.11.95) 2; Stephen Orchard, 'All Change on Aid', LSG (29.11.95) 12; 'Editorial: Fixed Price Risk', LSG (29.11.95) 14; Law Society (1995b: pp. iv–vii, x, xii, 64, 68–9, 79).

[71] Lomax (1987; 1988); 'Outcry over Threat to Law Centres', LSG (12.9.90) 3; 'CABx Back Law Centres' (1990) 140 NLJ 1298; 'Council cuts overload scales of local justice', G (22.9.90) 6; 'Law centres seek state cash to met funds crisis', I (1.10.90) 8; 'Law Centres in Crisis' (1990) 140 NLJ 1374; 'Don't Mourn—Organise' (1990) 140 NLJ 333; 'London in need of own body for legal services', L (12.3.91); 'London Law Centres face Cash Crises', LSG (13.3.91) 9; 'Access to Justice' (1991) 141 NLJ 1213; 'Law Society Publishes Manifesto' (1991) 141 NLJ 1214; 'Society Urges Central Funds For Poorest Law Centres' LSG (18.9.91) 7; 'Chancery Lane Puts Full Weight Behind Law Centres' (1991) 135 SJ 1019; 'Mending the Fabric of Legal Services' (1991) 141 NLJ 1249; 'In the centre of a crisis', G (27.11.91); Austin Mitchell, 'Let's call the law to order', G (25.2.92) 17; 'Letter to the editor', G (28.2.92); 'MP's Remarks Anger Solicitors', LSG (4.3.92) 7; Campbell (1992); 'NCC Calls for CAB Lawyers' (1994) 138 SJ 977; Austin Mitchell MP, 'A national legal service', LA (2.96) 6–7; 'Editorial: Staking out the argument', LA (2.96) 3.

[72] 'Legal Aid Pay Deal', LSG (6.3.96) 1; 'Editorial: Paying Extra', LSG (6.3.96) 13; 'Reform Vacuum Criticised', LSG (1.5.96) 3; 'Minister Builds Bridges', *ibid.*; ' "Get Big" to Survive, Legal Aid Firms Told', LSG (1.5.96) 3; 'Mears Defends his Record on Legal Aid', LSG (1.5.96) 2; 'Taken at the Flood' (1996) 146 NLJ 618–19; 'Savings

from Block Contracting could Increase Legal Aid Eligibility' (1996) 140 SJ 421; Martin Mears and Robert Sayer, 'The Legal Aid Campaign', 1 Cat (12.96) 11 (taking credit for the efficacy of the Society's campaign).

[73] Woolf (1996: Section I).

[74] 'Top Legal Aid Firms hit £2m', LSG (9.5.96) 6; 'Society to Propose Legal Aid Savings', LSG (19.6.96) 1; 'Dire Warnings over Legal Aid', LSG (26.6.96) 5; 'Comment: In Need of Support' (1996) 140 SJ 887.

[75] 'White Paper Leaves the Lawyers Cold', LSG (3.7.96) 1; 'Letter to the Profession: Upsetting the Balance', LSG (3.7.96) 15; 'Unanimous Profession Rounds on White Paper Proposals' (1996) 140 SJ 648; 'The Future of Legal Aid' (1996) 146 NLJ 978; 'Striking the Wrong Note', LSG (10.7.96) 12; 'Comment: Scorched Earth Policy', LSG (10.7.96) 14; 'Labour Commits to Early Community Legal Aid Scheme', LSG (17.7.96) 4; Ann Abraham, 'Letters: The CAB service', LA (8.96) 26; 'Lawyers Urged to Unite in Support of Legal Aid' (1996) 140 SJ 883; 'Mackay Leaves NACAB Unmoved' (1996) 140 SJ 931; 'Agencies Pitch for Legal Aid', LSG (20.11.96) 6; 'Lord Chancellor addresses CABx conference', LA (11.96) 4; LCD (1996: 5, 9, 10, 20–1, 29, 33, 44, 47); Smith (1996a); Goriely (1996b); Bridges (1996); Bull and Seargeant (1996).

[76] 'Crackdown on loony legal aid', Sun (3.7.96) 5; 'Too slow', Sun (3.7.96) 5; 'Coming to the aid of justice', DE (3.7.96) 8; 'Curbs to end the legal aid shambles', DM (3.7.96) 6; 'A scandal fuelled by greed', DM (3.7.96) 6; 'Legal aid in the dock', DT (4.7.96) 23.

[77] 'Shake–up aims to curb £1.4bn costs of justice', T (3.7.96) 6; 'Till the pips squeak', G (3.7.96); 'Justice for the poor', G (3.7.96) 14; 'Gate to law closes tighter', I (3.7.96) 13.

[78] 'Comment: What Price Test Cases?' (1996) 140 SJ 679; 'Editorial: Hounding the Poor', (1996) 146 NLJ 977.

[79] 'Legal Aid Battle Continues', LSG (24.7.96) 5; 'Standard Fee Fight', LSG (24.7.96) 5; 'Streeter Talk', LSG (24.7.96) 13; 'Society Targets Profession with Legal Aid Campaign' (1996) 140 SJ 728; 'Streeter Confirms Legally-aided Litigants are Rottweilers' (1996) 146 NLJ 1378; 'More Attacks on Legal Aid Curbs' (1996) 146 NLJ 1143.

[80] 'Barristers to fight fixed fees for civil legal aid', T (24.9.96) 10; 'Bar to Fight "Discriminatory" and "Unjust" Standard Fees' (1996) 140 SJ 907; 'Comment: Legal Aid Standard Fees' (1996) 140 SJ 911; 'Family Lawyers Reject Fixed Fees', LSG (16.10.96) 6; 'Family Fee Scheme Attacked', LSG (6.11.96) 4; 'Fighting the cynics', T (21.1.97) 37; Robert Owen QC, 'Chairman's Column: The Issues Facing the Bar', C (1–2.97) 3.

[81] 'Lawyers Blamed', LSG (29.8.96) 5; 'Mackay Plays Down Role of Legal Aid in Access to Justice Debate' (1996) 140 SJ 833; 'Minimal role for legal aid', LA (10.96) 4.

[82] 'United Front to Campaign on Legal Aid', LSG (12.9.96) 1; 'No Bill this Autumn' (1996) 140 SJ 855; 'Health Warning over Contracts', LSG (25.9.96) 6; 'Streeter Stands Firm', *ibid.*; 'White Paper Welcome', *ibid.*; 'Legal Aid Fight', *ibid.*; 'Streeter Promises Consultation', LSG (16.10.96) 4; 'Surveys Provide Ammunition in Legal Aid Battle' (1996) 140 SJ 987; 'Government Attacked for Acting on Guesswork' (1996) 140 SJ 1064; 'Editorial: Legal Aid Myths' (1996) 146 NLJ 1605;

Gary Streeter MP, 'The LCD approach', LA (12.96) 6; Robert Owen QC, 'Chairman's Column: Legal Aid—Civil Fees', C (7–8.97) 3.

[83] Lord Mackay, ' "This is only the start" ', T (22.10.96) 41; 'Legal aid change pursued', T (22.10.96) 2; 'Editorial: The value of speculation', LA (10.96) 3; Steve Orchard, 'Letters: LAG, LAB and the legal aid white paper', LA (10.96) 26; Lord Mackay, 'Comment: Realistic Proposals' (1996) 146 NLJ 1716; 'Comment: Reforming Legal Aid', (1996) 146 NLJ 1808.

[84] 'LCD Under Fire for Failing to Consult' (1996) 140 SJ 1211; 'Comment: Remote from Reality' (1996) 140 SJ 1215; 'Editorial: Ignorance and arrogance', LA (1.97) 3; 'Green Form Warning', LSG (8.1.97) 5; 'Anger over Green Form Plans', LSG (5.2.97) 6; 'General Election Leaves Green Form Pilot on Starting Blocks', LSG (16.4.97) 4; 'LAB backs Criminal Green Form Scheme', LSG (17.9.97) 1; 'Report Could Help Save Criminal Green Form' (1997) 141 SJ 855.

[85] 'Board Unveils Block Contract Proposals', LSG (14.8.96) 1; 'Role of Advice Centres Set to Increase Following "Successful" Franchising Pilot' (1996) 140 SJ 808; Roger Smith, 'Fast, friendly and expert?' LA (10.96) 7; Steel and Bull (1996); 'Editorial: Omens for 1997', LSG (8.1.97) 13; 'Research Shows Contract Hitches', LSG (22.1.97) 5; 'April Launch for Green Form Pilot Scheme', LSG (29.1.97) 1; 'Society Intervenes in Contract Pilot', LSG (26.3.97) 1; 'Society Waves Red Flag over LAB Pilot', LSG (23.4.97) 1; 'Editorial: A Block on Contracts', LSG (23.4.97) 15; 'Law Society Urges Firms to Veto Green Form Pilots' (1997) 141 SJ 371; 'Increased Criticism over Green Form Pilots' (1997) 141 SJ 395; 'Green Form Stand-off Set to Continue' (1997) 141 SJ 531; 'LAB Bends on Green Form Pilot Pay Terms', LSG (21.5.97) 1; 'Contract Pilots given Green Light', LSG (16.7.97) 5; 'LAB Invites Firms to Join Crime Pilot', LSG (30.7.97) 1; 'Firms to Earn £7m in Advice Pilot', LSG (24.9.97) 1; 'Firms go it Alone in LAB Pilot Talks', LSG (3.12.97) 1.

[86] 'Outrage at Legal Aid Pay Freeze', LSG (23.3.97) 4; 'Editorial: The Big Chill for Legal Aid', LSG (26.3.97) 14; 'Fee Freeze Condemned as Deplorable' (1997) 141 SJ 272; Robert Owen QC, "Chairman's Column: Legal Aid', C (3–4.97) 3; 'Frozen Rates', C (3–4.97) 5.

[87] 'Court Criticises PI Advertising', LSG (19.2.97) 4; 'Business Warned of Creeping US-Style "Blackmail Litigation" ', LSG (3.4.97) 10; 'PI Awards Rising', LSG (2.7.97) 4.

[88] Independent Working Party (1993: para. 10.10); 'Court "rental" charges on way', L (21.2.95) 1; 'Steep Fee Rises in Store for Courts', LSG (22.2.95) 68; 'Jury is out on courts agency', I (20.3.95); 'Pay-by-the-day plan to raise £20m for civil courts', T (4.4.95) 6; 'Lords Fee Increase Shocks Profession', LSG (26.7.95) 2; 'Protest over higher price for justice', T (14.1.97) 1; 'Outcry at Huge Court Fee Rises', LSG (15.1.97) 1; 'Government under Attack over Self-Financing Policy' (1997) 141 SJ 29; 'Comment: Limits on Access' (1997) 141 SJ 31; 'Letters to the editor', T (20.1.97) 21, T (27.1.97) 23, T (29.1.97) 17; 'Labour Would Keep New Court Fees', LSG (5.2.97) 12; 'First Challenge Mounted to New Court Fees', LSG (12.2.97) 1; 'Editorial: A very quiet coup', LA (2.97) 3; 'Divorce's high cost', T (4.3.97) 39; 'Law Soc calls for court fees climbdown', L (11.3.97) 1; 'Mackay Climbs Down over Fees', LSG (12.3.97) 4; *R v Lord Chancellor, ex parte Witham* T (13.3.97) (DC); 'Mackay Bows to Pressure after Humiliating Defeat' (1997) 141 SJ

225; 'Court fees increase latest', LA (3.97) 4; 'Fees Defeat', C (3–4.97) 5; 'Lord Chancellor forced to restore fee exemption', LA (4.97) 4.

[89] 'Law Society Lobbies Incoming Government' (1997) 141 SJ 271; 'Comment: Lord Chancellor's Task' (1997) 141 SJ 275; 'Tories Confirm Cash Limit Policy', LSG (3.4.97) 4.

[90] Family lawyers actually seek to resolve controversies quickly and cheaply by discouraging clients from pursuing moral vindication. Sarat and Felstiner (1995).

[91] On the demoralization this produced see Sommerlad (1996; 2001).

[92] Sommerlad (1999).

[93] On the history of advice agencies see Goriely (1996a).

[94] Walter Merricks remembered 'the rhetoric we used to be able to deploy that unless legal aid fees were set at higher rates then solicitors would decline to do legal aid work. And we used to have to keep producing these figures which would show us a number of solicitors were dropping out. . . . Well all this gradually collapsed and then we had to eat our words on these things . . . and they were able without any difficulty at all to say that there would be no legal aid rate increases' (interview July 1998).

Chapter 8—Notes

[1] 'Angry Reaction to Lord Chancellor's "Reforms"' (1992) 142 NLJ 1494; 'Legal Aid Reforms Face Further Attack' (1995) 139 SJ 596; 'Labour's Woolsack man', T (17.10.95) 37; 'Irvine Sets out Labour's Vision', LSG (2.10.96) 1; 'Editorial: Labour's Law', LSG (2.10.96) 15; 'Irvine Attacks Legal Aid White Paper Proposals' (1996) 140 SJ 932; 'Bar Conference 1996' (1996) 146 NLJ 1414; '1996 Bar Conference', C (9–10.96) 6; 'Editorial: Dead letters, live thoughts', LA (11.96) 3; Blair (1996); Irvine (1996); Cranston (1996); Robert Owen QC, 'Chairman's Column: Legal Aid', C (3–4.97) 3; 'Comment: Ask the Lawyers for a Change' (1997) 141 SJ 423; 'Irvine's View', LSG (14.5.97) 14; Smith (1997).

[2] Royal Commission (1979: R16.2); LCD (1983: 18); Marre Committee (1988: para. 10.33); 'Perils of "no–win, no fee"', T (25.5.93); 'No Win No Fee Clears Hurdle', LSG (14.6.95) 1; 'Conditional Fees Clear Final Hurdle—Just' (1995) 139 SJ 571; 'Fee "Gimmick"', LSG (26.7.95) 6; Labour Party (1995: 12); 'Scott urges more "no win, no fee" litigation', T (17.5.97) 9; 'US-style legal fee scheme to expand' ST (20.7.97) 24; 'Self-financing legal aid proposed by barristers', T (1.9.97) 1; Philip Sycamore, 'Winners should pay into the pot', T (16.9.97) 35; Robert Owen QC, 'Chairman's Column: Access to Justice', C (9–10.97) 3; 'Inns and Outs', T (23.9.97) 33; 'Government backs "no win, no fee" system', T (24.9.97) 8; 'Hoon Flags No Win No Fee Expansion', LSG (24.9.97) 1; 'Extension of Conditional Fees a Matter of Time' (1997) 141 SJ 879; 'Big Rise in Conditional Fee Insurance Premiums' (1997) 141 SJ 879; 'Comment; How far should we go?' (1997) 141 SJ 883; 'Conditional Fees Fever' (1997) 147 NLJ 1379; Yarrow (1997: pp. xii–xv).

[3] 'Editorial', SCOLAG (12.96) 178; Mitchell (1996); 'Cowboys milk legal aid says top lawyer', *The Scotsman* (2.4.97) 1; 'Irvine Plans Snap Summer Review', LSG (21.5.97) 1; 'Ex-Treasury Man to Lead Irvine Review', LSG (11.6.97) 1; 'End of Legal Aid in war on cheats', DM (23.6.97) 1; 'Time to stop the legal rot', DM (23.6.97) 8; Geoff Hoon, 'Legal aid must give good value', T (1.7.97) 41; 'Inns and Outs', T (1.7.97) 39; Alan Tunkel, 'Legal Aid, Politics and Statistics' (1997) 147 NLJ 1020; 'Editorial: Crime and Punishment' (1997) 147 NLJ 1017; '£1 million a year fat cat QCs attacked by Lord Chancellor', T (15.7.97) 1; 'Irvine considers curbs on fees of "fat cat" QCs', T (16.7.97) 2; 'Letters: Broader debate on "fat cat" lawyers', T (17.7.97) 19; 'Lord Chancellor Accused of Sidelining Debate' (1997) 141 SJ 685; 'Inns and Outs', T (22.7.97) 35; 'Lawyers howl over fat cats attack', T (22.7.97) 37; 'Letters: Effect of court fees on justice for all', T (22.7.97) 21; 'Hoon Signals Radical Thinking', LSG (23.7.97) 5; Geoff Hoon, 'The Limited Magic of Numbers' (1997) 147 NLJ 1092; 'Call for a National Network' (1997) 141 SJ 712; 'Irvine's overture', LSG (30.7.97) 11; Alan Tunkel, 'Letters: Legal Aid, Politics and Statistics' (1997) 147 NLJ 1144; 'Bar Fights Back over Legal Aid' (1997) 141 SJ 737; 'Court fees "a drop in the ocean"', LA (8.97) 4; 'Public Defenders in Scotland' (1997) 147 NLJ 1415; 'Who's Afraid of the Public Defender?' (1997) 147 NLJ 1629. Walter Merricks commented in July 1998: 'Once the knives were really out to really pare back the legal aid budget we always knew we were going to have to stand in fairly firmly in the front and say these QC fees were outrageous' (interview).

[4] 'Lord Chancellor attacks £1 million-a-year "fat cat" QCs', T (15.7.97) 1; 'Irvine considers curbs on QCs' fees', T (16.7.97) 2; 'Letters to the editor: Broader debate

on "fat cat" lawyers', T (17.7.97) 19; 'Lord Chancellor Accused of Sidelining Debate' (1997) 141 SJ 685; 'Inns and Outs', T (22.7.97) 35; 'Lawyers howl over fat cats attack', T (22.7.97) 37; 'Letters to the editor: Effect of court fees on justice for all', T (22.7.97) 21; 'Court fees "a drop in the ocean" ', LA (8.97) 4. On the refurbishment scandal see Egan (1999: 175–84).

[5] 'QCs in uproar over Straw's "unfair" attack on their fees', T (29.9.97) 12; Roger Smith, 'The challenge is to provide justice for all in Britain', T (30.9.97); 'Straw Tells the Bar Sky High Fees will End', LSG (1.10.97) 12; 'Editorial: Caps off to Justice', LSG (1.10.97) 15; 'Bar Chair Refutes Straw's "High Earnings" Attack' (1997) 141 SJ 910; 'Editorial: Justice not Expediency' (1997) 147 NLJ 1413.

[6] 'Justice for the middle class in law reform: Legal aid scheme to be scrapped', T (4.10.97) 1; 'Deep Concern over Threat to Legal Aid', LSG (8.10.97) 1; 'End of Civil Legal Aid in Sight, Report Claims' (1997) 141 SJ 935; ' "Time for Action" says Lord Irvine', LSG (15.10.97) 1; 'Bingham Fees Fear', LSG (15.10.97) 4; 'Lord Irvine Sets the Scene for Cardiff' (1997) 141 SJ 963; 'No win, no fee justice will be a rip-off, says Bar chairman', T (16.10.97) 8.

[7] Middleton (1997: paras. 1.13, 2.47, 3.1–2, 3.7–8, 3.13, 3.15, 3.17–19, 3.26, 3.30, 3.38, 3.41, 5.8–11, 5.15, 5.30, 5.42, 5.47, 5.50).

[8] Austin Mitchell MP, 'A national legal service', LA (2.96) 6–7; Lord Irvine of Lairg, 'How I'll give the law back to the people', T (18.10.97) 22; 'Lawyers fear poor will lose justice in legal aid reform', T (18.10.97) 2; ' "Safety fund" to replace legal aid', ST (19.10.97) 28; 'Irvine Reforms Slash Legal Aid', LSG (22.10.97) 1; 'Legal Aid System Set for the Most Radical Changes since its Inception, Solicitors Hear', LSG (22.10.97) 12; Phillip Sycamore, 'Fit for the 21st Century', LSG (22.10.97) 20; 'Editorial: Help shape the Future', LSG (22.10.97) 16; 'Outrage over Legal Aid Cuts' (1997) 141 SJ 991; 'Thunder and Fury in Cardiff-Conference Report' (1997) 147 NLJ 1538; Roger Smith, 'The More Things Change...' (1997) 147 NLJ 1543; 'Editorial: Listen and Ignore?' (1997) 147 NLJ 1537; 'Comment: Facts, not Flannel' (1997) 141 SJ 995; David Pannick QC, 'Why the Lord Chancellor is right', T (4.11.97) 39; 'Comment: Divided We Fail' (1997) 141 SJ 1047; 'Trainees' Champion', LSG (12.11.97) 12; 'MPs Hotly Contest Legal Aid Reforms', LSG (12.11.97) 12; 'Editorial: Bringing home the bacon', LA (11.97) 3; Letter from Dr Peter Gray to Geoffrey Hoon MP (10.12.97).

[9] 'Lawyers fear poor will lose justice in legal aid reform', T (18.10.97) 2; 'Doubts over Expenses Insurance', LSG (22.10.97) 5; David McIntosh, 'Comment: New Labour's Lip Service', LSG (22.10.97) 16; 'The Gate Keepers to Justice' (1997) 147 NLJ 1559; Sir Richard Scott, 'A cut too far?' G (28.10.97) 17; 'Conditional Fee Insurance Scheme for Med Neg Cases Launched' (1997) 141 SJ 1015; 'ABI Breaks its Silence as Irvine Summons Insurers' (1997) 141 SJ 1119; 'Insurers Team Up with LCD on Expenses Cover', LSG (3.12.97) 1.

[10] 'Legal Aid Lobbying Effort Begins', LSG (29.10.97) 4; Robert Sayer, 'Comment: Joining Battle', LSG (29.10.97) 23; 'Little Sign of Compromise' (1997) 141 SJ 1015; 'Campaign Launches Concerted Attack on Legal Aid Reforms', LSG (5.11.97) 5; 'I'm not Attacking the Poor, says Irvine' (1997) 141 SJ 1044; 'Poor "Robbed of Justice" Warns Law Society' (1997) 147 NLJ 1610; Geoff Hoon, 'Access to Justice—the Reality not the Slogan' (1997) 147 NLJ 1611; 'Cuts Anger', LSG (12.11.97) 4; 'Simple but Revolutionary Changes, says Hoon' (1997) 147 NLJ 1646;

Benedict Birnberg, 'Community Legal Service' (1997) 147 NLJ 1703; 'Welsh Resolution', LSG (26.11.97) 4; 'Opposition to Reforms Steps up after Debate', LSG (26.11.97) 5; 'Hoon Faces Friendly Fire in Legal Aid Debate', LSG (26.11.97) 11.

[11] 'Legal Aid Lobbying Effort Begins', LSG (29.10.97) 4; Robert Sayer, 'Comment: Joining Battle', LSG (29.10.97) 23; 'Community Legal Service Talks could Offer "Glimmer of Hope"', LSG (12.11.97) 5; 'Sparks Fly Over Small Claims Increase' (1997) 141 SJ 1068; 'LAG Director "Heart-broken" over Cuts' (1997) 141 SJ 1068; 'Mind the new gap', T (18.11.97); 'Letters: Legal aid for infants and mentally ill', T (19.11.97) 23.

[12] 'Dash to Test Impact of Reform on Firms', LSG (19.11.97) 1; 'Editorial: Stop and Listen', LSG (19.11.97) 15; 'Setback for CPS Shake-up', LSG (3.12.97) 12; 'Labour Lawyers Snub Reform Plan', LSG (10.12.97) 4; 'Society Pitches Hybrid Fund', LSG (17.12.97) 1; 'Editorial: Give CLAF a Chance', LSG (17.12.97) 15; 'Society Offers Irvine Way Forward on PI Cases' (1997) 141 SJ 1191; 'Reforms Study', LSG (4.2.98) 4.

[13] 'Criminal Lawyers Damn Contracts', LSG (12.11.97) 6; 'CLSA Anger over Spending Cuts' (1997) 141 SJ 1069; 'Contracting for Criminal Work' (1997) 147 NLJ 1648; Benedict Birnberg, 'Community Legal Service' (1997) 147 NLJ 1703; 'Setback for CPS Shake-up', LSG (3.12.97) 12; Geoff Hoon MP, 'Salaried Legal Service' (1997) 147 NLJ 1768; 'Higher PI Payouts Likely' (1997) 147 NLJ 1803; Benedict Birnberg, 'Salaried Legal Service' (1997) 147 NLJ 1804.

[14] Comptroller and Auditor General (1996a); 'Recovery Blight on Small Claims', LSG (26.11.97) 1; 'Editorial: Small Change', LSG (26.11.97) 14; 'LCD Consults on Small Claims', LSG (3.12.97) 4; 'Small Claims Recovery Review', LSG (10.12.97) 4; 'Beware of the small claims court. It may be a toothless watchdog', I (17.12.97) 10; 'Comments: Small Claims-Big Problems?' (1997) 141 SJ 1195; Baldwin (1997a; 1997b); 'Westminster Watch', LSG (21.1.98) 10; 'Solicitors Attack Small Claims Rise', LSG (4.2.98) 5; 'APIL Calls for Small Claims Exemption', LSG (18.2.98) 5; John Baldwin, 'Increasing the Small Claims Limit' (1998) 148 NLJ 274; 'Editorial: The curate's egg', LA (2.98) 3; 'A little legal nightmare', T (17.3.98) 39; 'Small Claims', LSG (25.3.98) 4; 'Comment: Ministers in Glass Houses...' (1998) 141 SJ 415; 'Small claims and housing change welcomed', LA (5.98) 4.

[15] 'Legal aid reform pledge', T (22.11.97) 2; 'Iraqi fraudster's family gets £1m in legal aid', ST (23.11.97) 10; 'Brief encounter', G (25.11.97) 17.

[16] 'Opposition to Reforms Steps up after Debate', LSG (26.11.97) 5; 'Hoon Faces Friendly Fire in Legal Aid Debate', LSG (26.11.97) 11; Phillip Sycamore, 'Facing up to Change', LSG (26.11.97) 16; 'Tories join Anti-cuts Alliance' (1997) 141 SJ 1120.

[17] 'The legal aid millionaires', DM (10.12.97) 1; 'Comment: Diversionary Tactics' (1997) 141 SJ 1171; 'Irvine Consults', LSG (10.12.97) 4; 'Lord Chancellor eyes Bar's last preserve', T (12.12.97) 6; 'Irvine in Merits test U-turn' (1997) 141 SJ 1167; 'Lord Chancellor Stands Firm' (1997) 147 NLJ 1802; 'Irvine Shows some Flexibility in Lords Debate', LSG (17.12.97) 14; (1997) 147 NLJ 1839; 'New Bar chief wants to curb costs in major criminal trials', T (29.12.97) 1; 'Bar Chairman Speaks up for High Street Practitioners', LSG (8.1.98) 4; 'Strong words, softly spoken', LA (1.98) 4; Heather Hallett QC, 'Chairman's Column: Overriding Concerns', C (2.98) 3; 'Heather Hallett QC takes over as Chairman of the Bar', BN (2.98) 3.

[18] Lord Irvine, 'Still listening', LSG (17.12.97) 17; 'Comment: When a Cut is a Cut' (1998) 142 SJ 7; 'Comment: A Better Way Forward' (1998) 142 SJ 127; Lord Irvine, 'Tough choices will ensure access for all', I (Eye on Wed) (18.2.98) 21.

[19] 'Crime Lawyers Bid to Protect Independence' LSG (4.2.98) 1; 'Crime Watch', LSG (4.2.98) 22; 'Society Warns over Crime Pilot Contract', LSG (11.3.98) 1; 'CLSA may ask Society for EGM' (1998) 148 NLJ 578; 'Crime Lawyers Fury over Contract Plan', LSG (17.6.98) 1; 'CLSA Goes on the Offensive over Exclusive Contracting' (1998) 142 SJ 584; 'Comment: Spoiled Choice' (1998) 142 SJ 807. LAG's study of contracting in North America played an influential role in the debate: Smith (1998); see also Goriely *et al.* (1997); Goriely (1998b).

[20] 'Straw Attacks Crime Lawyers', LSG (29.4.98) 1; 'Home Front', LSG (29.4.98) 18; Anthony Scrivener QC, 'Dead sheep and dire warnings from on high', T (12.5.98) 49; 'Interview: Hands on approach', C (8.98) 11.

[21] Pleasence *et al.* (1996); 'Confusion over Irvine's "Exclusive Contracting" Plans' (1998) 142 SJ 51; 'Board Rolls out Contract Details', LSG (16.4.98) 1; 'Editorial: Let us Lose more Slowly' (1998) 148 NLJ 577; 'Board Signals new Devolved Powers', LSG (7.5.98) 1; 'LAB Supports Exclusivity for Med Neg', LSG (28.5.98) 1; 'LAB issues contracting proposals', LA (5.98) 4; 'Editorial: Command and control', LA (5.98) 3; 'Society attacks Cull of Medical Negligence Firms' (1998) 142 SJ 508; 'Letters: Command and control', LA (6.98) 33; 'Medical Negligence under the Knife' (1998) 142 SJ 999; 'Comment: Legal Aid: Why the Rush?' (1998) 142 SJ 1003; 'Westminster Watch', LSG (29.7.98) 10; 'Society Shift Position and tells Legal Aid Firms to get Franchised', LSG (30.9.98) 5; ' "Get a franchise" Society says' (1998) 142 SJ 876; 'Solicitors face ruin in reforms', ST (14.10.98) §1,2; 'Legal aid from the doctor's surgery', T (20.10.98) 9; 'Government Provides Contract Guarantee to some Franchisees', LSG (21.10.98) 5; 'Small solicitor firms could be lost in change', T (24.10.98) 51; 'Irvine Ushers in New Era for Conditional Fees' (1998) 142 SJ 947; 'Threat to legal aid', T (17.11.98) 2; 'Irvine to Spell out Legal Aid Priorities' (1998) 142 SJ 1047; Maclean (1998); Pleasence (1998); LAB (1998); LAG (1998b: paras. 1.7, 5.2); 'Multi-party Action Panel Unveiled', LSG (3.2.99) 3. A 2000 survey found that minority solicitors were, if anything, overrepresented as legal aid providers: LSRC (2001).

[22] 'Ministers forced to think again on legal aid reform', T (23.1.98) 14; Alan Tunkel, 'Improving Access to Justice—4' (1998) 148 NLJ 301; 'Letters to the Editor: Judgement on the "evils of litigation" ', T (21.5.98) 23; Bar Council (1998a: paras. 1.5–8, 1.13, 2.1.3–5, 2.6, 2.7.2, 2.8.1–2, 4.2, 5.3.5, 5.4.1, 5.5.2, 9.2, 10.4; 1998c).

[23] Martin McKenna, 'Why legal aid could soon aid very few', I (4.2.98) 27; 'Irvine's law', T (5.3.98) 23; 'Press Round-Up' LSG (11.3.98) 14; 'Legal aid absurdity', ES (1.4.98) 11.

[24] LCD (1998a: paras. 1.1, 1.3, 1.5–7, 1.12, 2.7, 2.17, 3.4, 3.12, 3.18, 3.23, 4.9–10).

[25] 'Irvine bows to backbench protests over legal aid cuts', T (31.2.98) 1; 'Irvine: Reforms to Come in Two Stages', LSG (5.3.98) 1; ' "Horrific" Plan Slammed by PI Lawyers', LSG (5.3.98) 1; 'Editorial: No PI Panacea', LSG (5.3.98) 15; 'Legal aid may go in 60 percent of civil disputes', T (5.3.98) 12; 'Lobby Groups Stand Ground on Personal Injury', LSG (11.3.98) 10; 'All Change on the Legal Landscape', LSG (11.3.98) 18; 'Solicitors Rebuff Insurers' Insult', LSG (11.3.98) 4; 'Press

Round–Up', LSG (11.3.98) 14; Roger Smith, 'Comment: Spinning in the Wind' (1998) 148 NLJ 357 'Reactions to the Legal Aid Consultation Paper' (1998) 148 NLJ 360; 'Press Round-Up', LSG (8.3.98) 12; 'Legal aid "only route for personal injury claims" ', T (24.3.98) 6; Caroline Harmer, 'Comment: Best for the Majority?' LSG (25.3.98) 15; Alastair Brett, 'No win, no fee: no free press', T (28.4.98) 18; 'Government proposes £100 m for social welfare law by 2001', LA (4.98) 4; Michael de Navarro, 'Letter to the editor: Legal aid changes', T (13.5.98) 19; 'Don't make Personal Injury the Scapegoat, Harmer says' (1998) 142 SJ 436; 'FOIL cries foul', T (2.6.98) 39; 'Lawyers on a loser with no win, no fee cases', I (Fri Rev) (10.7.98) 20; 'Bitter pill to take', G (Tues) (14.7.98) 17; 'No Win-No Fee for Libel Cases' (1998) 142 SJ 1096; 'Costs cover for "no win, no fee" libel cases', T (7.7.99) 4.

[26] 'Dobson Attack "Misleading" ', LSG (5.3.98) 5; 'Editorial: A Little Courtesy', LSG (7.5.98) 15; 'Press Round-Up', LSG (11.3.98) 14; 'Letters to the editor: Cost to NHS of negligence litigation', T (7.5.98) 23; Anthony Scrivener QC, 'Dead sheep and dire warnings from on high', T (12.5.98) 49; 'Lawyers Reject "Chasing" Label', LSG (16.6.98) 3.

[27] Law Society (1998: Executive summary p.ii; paras. 1.16, 4.6, 5.3, 5.9, 7.13–17, 7.22).

[28] Bar Council (1998b: paras. 1.3, 1.6, 1.9, 1.11. 1.18, 5.9–23).

[29] LAB (1998: Executive Summary 45 and paras. 3.9, 3.47, 5.2–5); CA (1998); NCC (1998); LAG (1998: para. 1.6); Justice (1998: paras. 5.4.1, 5.4.5); Public Law Project (1998 para. 2.1).

[30] 'Riches await "no win, no fee" firms', T (1.4.98) 6; 'Hoon gets the Lawyers Lawyer-Bashing' (1998) 142 SJ 291; 'CFA Profits Forecast Challenged', LSG (16.4.98) 1; 'Editorial: PI in the Sky', LSG (16.4.98) 14; 'Lawyers Attack LCD's "Imaginary" Survey' (1998) 142 SJ 340; 'Bar leaps to defence of QCs with attack on "false" pay figures', T (29.4.98) 4; 'Solicitors Stand Firm on Legal Aid Reforms', LSG (29.4.98) 1; 'Press Round-Up', LSG (13.5.98) 12; 'Irvine Heaps Praise on "Disappointed" Lawyers' (1998) 142 SJ 435; 'Cab rank ruled out?' T (19.5.98) 41; 'An end to learn as you earn?' T (26.5.98) 37; 'LAB Supports Exclusivity for Med Neg', LSG (28.5.98) 1; 'Personal Affairs', LSG (3.6.98) 10; 'Westminster Watch', LSG (17.6.98) 10; 'Westminster Watch', LSG (24.6.98) 10; BC press release, 'A dynamic Bar serving the public need' (27.6.98); Dan Brennan QC, 'The Future of the Bar: At the Crossroads', C (6.98) 14. A Sheffield University study found considerable solicitor anxiety about the financial burden of CFAs. Shapland *et al.* (1998).

[31] 'Tory Canvass of Solicitors' Firms fails to Impress Hoon' (1998) 142 SJ 484; 'Conditional Fees Might not be Enough, Bingham Warns' (1998) 142 SJ 556; 'Bingham warns of risks posed by legal aid reform', T (12.6.98) 12; 'Society Warns Public of "Access Denied" ' (1998) 142 SJ 637; 'Lord Bingham warns against legal aid cuts', LA (7.98) 5.

[32] 'QCs attack list of legal aid earnings', T (27.4.98) 6; 'High Earners', LSG (29.4.98) 5; 'Press Round-Up', LSG (29.4.98) 12; 'Lawyers on attack over "fat cats" list', T (29.4.98) 1; 'Bar leaps to defence of QCs with attack on "false" pay figures', T (29.4.98) 4; 'Editorial: A Little Courtesy', LSG (7.5.98) 15; 'Press Round-Up', LSG (7.5.98) 10; 'Comment: The Naming of Cats', LSG (7.5.98) 15; 'Editorial: Fat Cats and "Silly Cows" ' (1998) 148 NLJ 649; 'Comment: Ministers in Glass Houses…' (1998) 142

SJ 415; 'Press Round-Up', LSG (20.5.98) 10; Heather Hallett QC, 'Chairman's Column: Bastions of Liberty', C (6.98) 3; ' "Fat Cats"—The Facts behind "Those Figures" ', C (8.98) 11; 'Editorial: Cuckoos and counsel', LA (6.98) 3.

[33] 'Government unbowed over lawyers' "shaming" ', T (30.4.98) 6; 'Board Signals new Devolved Powers', LSG (7.5.98) 1; 'Law Society Legal Aid Conference' (1998) 148 NLJ 656; 'Comment: Ministers in Glass Houses…' (1998) 142 SJ 415; Anthony Scrivener QC, 'Dead sheep and dire warnings from on high', T (12.5.98) 49; Geoffrey Hoon MP, 'Letter to the editor: Legal aid changes', T (13.5.98) 19; 'Dismay at Legal Aid Pay Rates Freeze', LSG (13.5.98) 1; 'Editorial: Freeze on Loyalty', LSG (13.5.98) 14; 'Low-paid Crime Work "Deterring Lawyers" ', LSG (22.9.99) 1.

[34] 'Barristers face fee inquiry', I (3.6.98) 2; 'Lords inquiry as QCs' legal aid cash is blocked', ES (3.6.98) 2; 'Law Lords inquiry into size of QCs' legal aid fees', DT (3.6.98) 13; 'On trial: a system that makes QCs rich', G (3.6.98) 1; 'Judge condemns QCs' fees', G (4.6.98) 2; 'Judge joins in attack on the £1m-a-year QCs', T (4.6.98) 10; 'Silks earn my salary in two days, says solicitor', T (4.6.98) 10; 'Lawyers' pay: Is it an injustice?' I (4.6.98) 5; 'Judge condemns top barristers' "extravagant fees" ', DT (4.6.98) 12; 'Talking sense on legal aid', ES (4.6.98) 11; 'Editorial: Fat Cat Fees' (1998) 148 NLJ 835; 'Press Round-Up', LSG (10.6.98) 12; 'Time for a silk cut?' I (Fri Rev) (12.6.98) 19; 'Scandal of court bill over case of two beers', ES (12.6.98); David Pannick QC, 'Fees are not like a lottery win', T (16.6.98) 37; 'Barristers fight call to doctor their bills', T (18.6.98) 6; 'Cats at the cream', G2 (21.6.98); 'Call for £120,000 Cap on QC Pay', LSG (24.6.98) 5; 'Society Puts the Case for Cutting QCs' Fees' (1998) 142 SJ 584; 'Law: Are the days of rich pickings from legal aid numbered?' T (9.8.98) 41; Christopher Sallon QC, 'Naming and Shaming—The New Politics', C (8.98) 8.

[35] 'Letters to the editor: Barristers' priorities and their pay', T (18.6.98) 25; 'Lawyers: We're not all fat cats, M'lud', ES (19.6.98) 8; 'Lords officials slashed QCs' legal aid fees', T (19.6.98) 6; 'Making a silk purse out of a judge's ear', ST (21.6.98) §1,3; 'Gravy train silks', ES (22.6.98); 'Cats at the cream' G2 (23.6.98) 21; 'Inns and Outs', T (22.6.98) 35; 'Press Round-Up', LSG (24.6.98) 12; 'Press Round-Up', LSG (22.7.98) 10; 'Press Round-Up', LSG (3.9.98) 12.

[36] 'Memo to Bar Council admits "ludicrous" fees', T (11.8.98) 9; 'Legal Aid Excess', LSG (12.8.98) 4; 'Curbs on QCs' fees suggested by judges', T (13.10.98) 2; 'QCs' legal aid fees too high, say law lords', T (16.10.98) 11; 'QC Fees Curb "Not Radical Enough" ', LSG (21.10.98) 4; 'Press Round-Up', LSG (21.10.98) 12; 'You Decide on QCs Fees, Law Lords tell Irvine' (1998) 142 SJ 948; 'Pre-Negotiated Fees for All Criminal Cases?' C (10.98) 8; House of Lords Appeal Committee (1998).

[37] 'Bar agrees to curb legal aid fees', T (14.6.99) 2; Dan Brennan QC, 'Progress on Pay', C (6.99) 3; 'Bar Pilots Direct Access Scheme as Survey Reveals Barristers' Income' LSG (7.7.99) 5; 'Press Round-Up', LSG (7.7.99) 10; 'Fresh Impetus for Costs Control', LSG (2.9.99) 4; 'QCs' fee plea', T (5.10.99) 2; 'Pay Crime QCs on a Par with NHS Doctors, Society Urges', LSG (6.10.99) 3; 'Law Society Renews Attack on QCs' (1999) 143 SJ 920; Dan Brennan QC, 'The Value of the Independent Bar', C (10.99) 3–4; 'Chairman's Report', BN (10.99) 3; 'Lawyers Criticise Contract Timetable as Irvine Drops Family Standard Fees', LSG (24.11.99) 4; 'Concern over Prosecution Appeals', LSG (1.12.99) 3; 'Barristers' pay is cut by £50 m in assault on

legal aid', T (7.12.99) 1; 'Letters to the editor', T (13.12.99) 17; BDO Stoy Hayward (1999); LAB (1999).

[38] 'Asylum Advice Plans "Shallow" ', LSG (28.1.98) 4; 'Editorial: Words of Straw', LSG (28.1.98) 16; 'Straw's Crackdown could End Self-regulation" (1998) 142 SJ 75; 'Comment: Unfair to Immigration Lawyers' (1998) 142 SJ 79; 'Immigration Paper Attacked', LSG (25.3.98) 4; 'Straw Forced to Name "Corrupt" Solicitors Firms' (1998) 142 SJ 267; 'Straw Attacks Crime Lawyers', LSG (29.4.98) 1.

[39] 'Press Round-Up', LSG (8.7.98) 12; 'Press Round-Up', LSG (22.7.98) 10; ' "Touting" Claim', LSG (14.10.98) 4; 'Crackdown on asylum legal aid', T (29.12.98) 1; 'Immigration Lawyers Applaud Legal Aid Crackdown on 70 firms', LSG (6.1.99) 5; 'OSS Shuts London Firms' (1999) 143 SJ 147; 'Give me shelter', G2 (9.3.99) 17; 'Lawyers in Pre-Emptive Strike on Block Contracts' (1999) 143 SJ 404; 'Immigration Law Firms to Drop Out', LSG (19.5.99) 5; 'Editorial: Welcoming Advice', LSG (19.5.99) 15; 'Two Hundred Firms to be Forced Out' (1999) 143 SJ 475; 'Immigration Crackdown as OSS Steps in at Two More London Firms', LSG (8.4.99) 3; 'Editorial: No Asylum', LSG (8.4.99) 15; 'LAB Fees Crackdown', LSG (21.4.99) 5; 'Immigration lawyers face legal aid ban', T (18.5.99) 2; 'Board Calls Temporary Ceasefire in Immigration Firm Crackdown', LSG (3.6.99) 4; 'New deal for immigration advice', LA (6.99) 5; 'Mixed Reception for Legal Aid Extension' (1999) 143 SJ 824; 'Legal aid for immigration appeals', LA (10.99) 4.

[40] 'Irvine defers legal aid plans', T (17.7.98) 2; 'Statistic Undermine Attack on Legal Aid', LSG (22.7.98) 1; 'Editorial: A Welcome Delay', LSG (22.7.98) 14; 'Irvine Postpones Cut until Autumn 1999' (1998) 142 SJ 683; 'Comment: Good News on Legal Aid' (1998) 142 SJ 687; 'Irvine Defeats Effort to Restrict CFA Uplift', LSG (29.7.98) 10; 'Senior Judges Enter Political Fray', LSG (14.10.98) 5; 'Irvine Ushers in a New Era for Conditional Fees' (1998) 142 SJ 947.

[41] 'Society Warns over Crime Pilot Contract', LSG (11.3.98) 1; 'Bar warns Straw that his reforms could break law', T (5.10.98) 10; 'Bar Chairman Defends Position of Threatened High Street Solicitors', LSG (7.10.98) 3; Heather Hallett QC, 'A New Era for Human Rights', C (10.98) 4; 'Bar says US-style public defenders would be a calamity', T (23.11.98) 2; Heather Hallett QC, 'Chairman's Column: Striving for Justice', C (12.98) 3. For an evaluation of the Scottish pilot see Goriely *et al.* (2001).

[42] 'Irvine Scales Down Legal Service Plans', LSG (4.11.98) 1; 'Board Launches New "Generic" Legal Aid Franchise' (1998) 142 SJ 999; 'Clinical Judgment', LSG (18.11.98) 10; 'Justice Bill will Herald Revolution', LSG (25.11.98) 1; 'Press Round-Up', LSG (25.11.98) 14; 'Legal Aid gets Face Lift' (1998) 142 SJ 1071; 'Irvine unveils plans to reform legal aid', FT (3.12.98) 13; 'Turning justice into a "sausage machine" ', T (3.12.98) 12; 'What price justice?' I (Thurs Rev) (10.12.98) 14; 'Quote Unquote', LSG (10.12.98) 10; 'Independence Concern Remains', LSG (10.12.98) 10; 'Irvine rings in the new', T (15.12.98) 37; 'Editorial: Putting flesh on the bones', LA (12.98) 3; LCD (1998: paras. 1.10, 1.19, 2.43, 3.5, 3.7–8, 3.25, 6.7, 6.15, 6.19–20); 'Editorial: Ringing in the new', LA (1.99) 3; 'Lawyers Hope for End to National Audit Office "Ritual" ' (1999) 143 SJ 124. A 1999 report criticized wastage of over £81 m a year. Comptroller and Auditor General (1999). A contemporaneous Policy Studies Institute report advocated for non-lawyer advice agencies: Steele and Seargeant (1999). For insight into how the LSC will determine need see Pleasence *et al.* (2001).

[43] 'Press Round–Up', LSG (25.11.98) 14; 'Press Round-Up', LSG (2.12.98) 12; 'Irvine unveils plans to reform legal aid', FT (3.12.98) 13; 'A new face for the legal system', FT (3.12.98) 20; ' "No win, no fee" plan for divorcing couples', T (3.12.98) 1; 'Irvine seeks openness and value for money', T (3.12.98) 12; 'Turning justice into a "sausage machine" ', T (3.12.98) 12; 'Legal aid revamp seeks better value for money', T (3.12.98) 14; 'Legal aid's biggest shake-up unveiled', DT (3.12.98) 15; 'Press Round–Up', LSG (10.12.98) 14.

[44] 'Letters to the editor: Flaws in plan to modernise criminal justice system', T (8.12.98) 19; 'Letters to the editor: Revision of legal aid', T (9.12.98) 19; 'Irvine rings in the new', T (15.12.98) 37.

[45] HL 595: 1119–27, 1158–61, 1163–73 (14.12.98).

[46] 1107–19, 1146–52, 1173–83, 1185–92, 1195–1201.

[47] 1107–16, 1119–23, 1140–3, 1152–8, 1163–73, 1185–8, 1192–5.

[48] 1123–7, 1147–51, 1152–6, 1158–61, 1174–5, 1178–83, 1192–5; 'Irvine sees end to "fat cat" aid fees', T (15.12.98) 8; 'Irvine Faces Critical Peers over Bill', LSG (16.12.98) 4; Egan (1999: 144–52).

[49] 'Legal and Consumer Groups Join to Plan Campaign on Justice Bill', LSG (13.1.99) 5; 'Justice Bill Concessions Expected', LSG (20.1.99) 3; 'Editorial: Battle Begins', LSG (20.1.99) 14; Michael Mathews, 'President's Column: Indemnity and Justice', LSG (20.1.99) 15.

[50] HL Debs., 596: 475–88 (19.1.99), 597: 329–37, 345–54 (11.2.99) (bold face in original).

[51] Ashley Holmes, 'Access to justice is not just a gimmick' I (Thurs Rev) (4.3.99) 13;

[52] 596: 522–5, 540–4 (19.1.99), 710–11 (21.1.99), 927–31 (26.1.99), 1126–8 (28.1.99), 597: 390–9 (11.2.99).

[53] 596: 551–63 (19.1.99), 597: 399–410 (11.2.99), 619–27 (16.3.99).

[54] 596: 736–40 (21.1.99), 597: 374–82 (11.2.99), 611–18 (16.3.99).

[55] 596: 565–70 (19.1.99), 702–10 (21.1.99), 597: 411–26 (11.2.99), 662–6 (16.3.99).

[56] 596: 713–27 (21.1.99), 597: 426–34 (11.2.99), 666–8 (16.3.99).

[57] 596: 782–90 (21.1.99), 597: 447–52 (11.2.99).

[58] 596: 975–81 (26.1.99), 597: 602–8 (16.2.99).

[59] 597: 599–602 (16.2.99).

[60] 596: 966–71 (26.1.99), 597: 597–9 (16.2.99).

[61] 597: 611–18 (16.2.99).

[62] 596: 878–95 (26.1.99), 1159–73 (28.1.99); McConville & Mirsky (1986–7).

[63] HL 597: 51–70, 583–5 (16.2.99); 'Irvine criticised for seeking "total control" ', T (15.1.99) 10; 'Lawyers attack no win, no fee divorce plans', T (19.1.99) 9; 'Irvine heads off clash with judges over powers', T (25.1.99) 2; 'Irvine Ploughs Ahead with Legal Aid Reform Despite Powers Concession', LSG (27.1.99) 5; 'Irvine gives way on divorce plans', T (28.1.99) 6; 'Irvine Abandons Conditional Fees for Family Cases' (1999) 143 SJ 75; 'Comment: Rethink Makes Sense' (1999) 143 SJ 79; 'Lords reject Irvine Bill', T (29.1.99) 2; 'Lords defeat extension', FT (29.1.99); 'Irvine defeated in the Lords', T (17.2.99) 2; 'Headlines save Lord Irvine', T (23.2.99) 41; 'Civil budget to be "Prisoner" of Criminal, Garnier Claims' (1999) 143 SJ 200; 'Letters to the editor: Dismay at loss of legal aid clause', T (15.3.99) 21;

'Government Catches Legal Campaigners on Hop by Speeding Justice Bill through to Commons', LSG (17.3.99) 12; 'Government Triumphs in Lords' (1999) 143 SJ 255; 'Civil Legal Aid "subordinate"', LA (3.99) 4; 'Contracts for all in first round', LA (3.99) 4;'Government concession on family cases', LA (3.99) 4; 'New purpose clause', LA (3.99) 5.

[64] Lord Irvine, 'Costs rise, but quality does not', I (Thurs Rev) (18.2.99) 14; 'Press Round-Up', LSG (24.2.99) 12.

[65] Michael Mathews, 'Cash limit will affect quality of legal aid', T (19.1.99) 39; Lord Irvine of Lairg, 'Letter to the editor: Legal aid reforms', T (25.1.99) 21; Michael Mathews, Robert Sayer and Kamlesh Bahl, 'Action Stations', LSG (3.2.99) 14; 'Irvine Defeated over Public Defenders' (1999) 143 SJ 147; 'The battles of Derry', G2 (2.3.99) 2; BN (1999) 111: 3–4, 7; 'Editorial: The Access Test', LSG (21.4.99) 14; Sommerlad and Wall (1999: p. iv); Egan (1999: 210–12).

[66] 'Press Round-Up', LSG (20.1.99) 10; 'Editorial: Ambulance Chasers may Ride Again' (1999) 149 NLJ 433; 'Disputes Culture Grows', T (19.4.99) 2; 'Compensation Culture Attack', LSG (21.4.99) 4, 'Press Round-Up', LSG (28.4.99) 10; 'By gum, the law has gone mad', T (15.5.99) 22; 'Rise of defensive medicine', T (25.5.99) 39; 'Letters to the editor: Medical negligence', T (9.6.99) 21; Furedi (1999); Genn (1999: 252); 'Charles's Leaked Letters Land Him in Hot Water', NYT (26.9.02) A12; 'Leaked Letters Offer Portrait of a Chatty Charles', LAT (28.9.02) A3.

[67] Benedict Birnberg, 'Letters to the editor: Withdrawal of legal aid', T (10.3.99) 25; Geoff Hoon, 'Letters to the editor: Access to legal aid', T (22.3.99) 21.

[68] 'Press Round-Up', LSG (16.12.98) 11; 'Banned aid', G2 (19.1.99) 17; 'Fees under Fire', LSG (17.3.99) 4; 'Press Round-Up', LSG (14.4.99) 10.

[69] Phillip Oppenheim, 'Justice for the rich and the poor, and the rest of us can go hang', ST (23.5.99) §1, 18.

[70] Frances Howell, 'All power to the Lord Chancellor', DT (23.3.99) 24; Lord Irvine, 'Letters to the editor: Bill will open up law to more', DT (24.3.99) 24.

[71] 'Woolf at the door', T (26.4.99) 21; 'Mind the gap', T (29.4.99) 23.

[72] Robert Marshall-Andrews QC, 'Good, bad and awful', G (23.3.99); 'Press Round-Up', LSG (31.3.99) 12.

[73] 'Laying Down the Law', LSG (14.4.99) 14; 'Editorial: Drop the Rhetoric', LSG (14.4.99) 16.

[74] HC 329: 230–52 (14.4.99).

[75] 252–75, 280–94, 296–301, 307–10, 315–31.

[76] 'Hoon Points to Legal Aid Overspend as Justice Bill Enters the Commons', LSG (21.4.99) 5; Michael Mathews, Robert Sayer, and Kamlesh Bahl, 'Justice Denied', LSG (21.4.99) 22.

[77] 'Bar puts case against Irvine's legal aid cuts', T (29.4.99) 10; 'Case awards that made life worth living', T (29.4.99) 8.

[78] 'Industry Scorns Hoon's Optimism over No Win, No Fee Insurance', LSG (24.2.99) 4; 'Small Firms Wary of Conditional Fees' (1999) 143 SJ 199; 'Doubts over Future of ALP' (1999) 143 SJ 200; 'Laying down the Law', LSG (14.4.99) 14; 'Deal that could spell the end of legal aid', T (20.4.99) 41; 'Letters to the editor: Insurance for no win, no fee cases', T (6.5.99) 25; 'Leading Insurers Shun AEI Forum' (1999) 143 SJ 553.

[79] Andrew Phillips, 'Comment: A Want of Experience', LSG (28.4.99) 14.

[80] 'Irvine clashes with Law Society', T (26.4.99) 12; 'I'll see you out of court', I (Tues Rev) (27.4.99) 14; 'Legal diary', T (27.4.99) 39; 'Irvine attacks Law Society', T (28.4.99) 6; 'Battle Over Legal Aid Goes Public', LSG (28.4.99) 1; 'Editorial: Cheap Shots from Whitehall', LSG (28.4.99) 14; 'Press Round-Up', LSG (28.4.99) 10; 'Ministers Enraged by Law Society Adverts' (1999) 143 SJ 403; 'Press Round-Up', LSG (6.5.99) 12; Michael Mathews, 'President's Column: A Just Fight', LSG (6.5.99) 22; 'Editorial: Let's Scare all the Lawyers' (1999) 149 NLJ 701.

[81] Michael Mathews, Robert Sayer, and Kamlesh Bahl, 'Who's in Step?' LSG (28.4.99) 16; 'Letters to the editor: "Cries of pain" at legal aid reform', T (28.4.99) 21; Michael Gove, 'Tony's Tory on the Woolsack', T (4.5.99) 20; 'Press Round-Up', LSG (6.5.99) 12; 'Goodnight and Goodbye Ms Bahl' (1999) 149 NLJ 667; Robert Sayer, 'Letters to the editor: Legal aid reform', T (11.5.99) 21; 'Access to Justice Update' (1999) 149 NLJ 702; 'New PI Strategy', LSG (19.5.99) 4; 'APIL President Attacks Both Sides in Advertising Row' (1999) 143 SJ 476; 'Hidden cost of advertising', T (25.5.99) 41; Martin Mears, 'Ignoring the strong arm of the law', T (22.6.99) 27.

[82] 'Aid Freeze Attacked', LSG (19.5.99) 5; 'Legal Aid Rates Frozen Yet Again' (1999) 143 SJ 476; 'Fight begins over legal aid reform', T (27.5.99) 8; 'Alliance Calls for LCD Guarantees' (1999) 149 NLJ 794.

[83] HC Standing Committee E (27.4.99, 29.4.99); HC 333: 982–94 (22.6.99); HL 604: 398–403 (14.7.99).

[84] HC Standing Committee E (4.5.99, 11.5.99, 13.5.99).

[85] HC Standing Committee E (4.5.99); HC 33: 1001–12 (22.6.99); HL 604: 491–3 (14.7.99).

[86] HC Standing Committee E (4.5.99, 11.5.99, 13.5.99); HC 333: 1046–51 (22.6.99); HL 604: 431–8 (14.7.99); HC 335: 1235–43 (21.7.99).

[87] HC Standing Committee E (4.5.99).

[88] HC Standing Committee E (4.5.99); HL 604: 1293–1306; (26.7.99) Austin Mitchell, 'National Legal Service' (1998) 148 NLJ 236; Benedict Birnberg, 'Letters to the editor: Outlawing legal fat cats', ES (8.6.98); 'Labour Rejects Purpose Clause for Justice Bill', LSG (6.5.99) 10; Austin Mitchell, 'Letters to the Editor: Access to justice', T (17.5.99) 21; 'No Sign of Concessions from Hoon' (1999) 143 SJ 427; 'Labour revolt over legal aid curbs', G (23.6.99) 8; 'Labour Revolt over Personal Injury Cut' (1999) 143 SJ 603; 'Irvine Rejects Discrete Public Interest Fund as Justice Bill nears Completion', LSG (30.6.99) 5; 'Access to Justice Bill: Commons committee stage', LA (6.99) 4; Legal Reform Bill (169 of 1999); www.cnls.org.

[89] HC 333: 1068–79 (22.6.99).

[90] 'Irvine's Community Vision under Fire', LSG (26.5.99) 1; 'Community Legal Service Condemned as "Waffle"' (1999) 143 SJ 502; 'Community Legal Service Unveiled by LCD' (1999) 149 NLJ 794; 'A Week in the Law…' (1999) 149 NLJ 1030; 'Bar Wins First Direct Contract from Legal Aid Board' (1999) 143 SJ 652; 'Bar Welcomes Government Blueprint for the Community Legal Service', 115 BN (7.99) 5; 'Lawyers Call for Community Cash', LSG (11.8.99) 1; 'Press Round-Up', LSG (11.8.99) 14; '"Vague" Proposals Win Few Friends' (1999) 143 SJ 776; Keith Vaz, 'An All-Embracing Community', LSG (25.8.99) 16; 'Editorial: Reaching Out', LSG (8.9.99) 14; 'Board Starts to put Flesh on the Bones' (1999) 143 SJ 848.

[91] HL 604: 431–8 (14.7.99).

[92] HC 333: 1201–28 (21.7.99).

[93] 'Last Chance to Avert "Unjust" US Style Changes to Criminal and Civil Justice System—Bar', 116 BN (8.99) 6.

[94] HL 604: 1293–1306 (26.7.99).

[95] 'Lords block legal aid reform Bill', T (15.7.99) 2; 'Defeat Could Delay Justice Bill', LSG (21.7.99) 5; 'Irvine in Trouble over Public Defenders' (1999) 143 SJ 700; 'Tories Capitulate over Public Defenders' (1999) 143 SJ 727; 'Comment: Not just Sound and Fury' (1999) 143 SJ 731; 'Lords block public defenders in Access to Justice Bill', LA (8.99) 4.

[96] 'Cautious Response to Crime Plan', LSG (11.8.99) 3; 'Law Society chief plans to take over the Bar', T (30.10.99) 8; 'Modern Bar: Strong Future', C (10.99) 6; 'Garnier Savages Defenders Plan', LSG (3.11.99); Edward Garnier, QC, 'Irvine— love him or loathe him', T (Law) (16.11.99) 10; Edward Garnier QC, 'Pride Comes Before a Fall', C (12.99) 10.

[97] 'Straw says affluent civil rights lawyers are hypocrites', T (15.9.99) 9; 'Straw Attacks Civil Liberties Lawyers', LSG (15.9.99) 3; 'In the News' (1999) 149 NLJ 1359; 'Press Round-Up', LSG (22.9.99) 12; 'Comment: Civil Liberties Solicitors under Attack' (1999) 143 SJ 875.

[98] 'No Win, No Fee Scheme to Double Premiums', LSG (13.10.99) 1; 'Editorial: Risky Business', LSG (13.10.99) 16; 'Success Fee Recovery Backed', LSG (1.12.99) 4; Yarrow and Abrams (1999).

[99] '5,000 Offices Apply for Franchises', LSG (31.3.99) 3; 'Sorry should Not be the Hardest Word on Complaints, says Irvine', LSG (14.4.99) 3; 'Crunch Time', LSG (14.4.99) 22; 'Accreditation for Criminal Defence Solicitors' (1999) 143 SJ 551; 'Firms Deluge Board with Legal Aid Bids', LSG (25.8.99) 1; 'Fresh Impetus for Costs Control', LSG (2.9.99) 4; 'Law Society Renews Attack on QCs' (1999) 143 SJ 920; 'Success of Legal Aid Reforms to be Judged by "Squealing" Lawyers', LSG (10.11.99) 3; 'Editorial: Myth of the "Fat Cat"', LSG (10.11.99) 14; '"Beleaguered" Criminal Law Specialists Decry Treatment', LSG (24.11.99) 3; 'Lord Chancellor Kicks Off Legal Aid Consultation' (1999) 149 NLJ 1754; Sommerlad and Wall (1999: pp. vi–vii).

[100] 'Lord Chancellor Kicks Off Legal Aid Consultation' (1999) 149 NLJ 1754; '6,000 Offices to Drop Legal Aid Provision', LSG (1.12.99) 1; 'Editorial: Crumbling Legal Aid Network', LSG (1.12.99) 14; 'A Week in the Law...' (1999) 149 NLJ 1815; 'Legal Aid Contracts—a Grand Government Experiment?' (1999) 149 NLJ 1814; 'Legal Challenge to Contracting Planned', LSG (8.12.99) 1; 'Letter to the Editor: Board Squeezes New Firms', LSG (8.12.99) 16; 'Lawyers sue over legal aid', T (10.12.99) 6; 'Reform "will hit vulnerable"', T (14.12.99) 6; '"Betrayed" Legal Aid Firms Threaten Strike', LSG (17.12.99) 1; 'Lawyers threaten legal aid revolt', T (20.12.99) 2.

[101] 'Government Enlists Celebrities to Publicise Community Legal Service', LSG (8.9.99) 5; 'Top names back Irvine's legal advice reforms', T (5.10.99) 1; 'A Few Stars come out for CLS', LSG (6.10.99) 4; 'Woolf Watchdog Sinks Teeth into Community Legal Service', LSG (13.10.99) 3; 'Judges condemn legal service plan', T (14.10.99) 13; LCD (2000: paras. 12, 56–68, 70, 74–9, 85); CDS (2000b).

[102] 'Straw aims to curb right to trial by jury', T (19.5.99) 6; 'Lawyers join critics of Straw trial plans', T (20.5.99) 2; 'Cost hard to swallow', T (20.5.99) 2; 'Editorial: Jury's out', T (20.5.99) 23; Phillip Oppenheim, 'Justice for the rich and the poor,

and the rest of us can go hang', ST (23.5.99) §1, 18 ; 'Press Round-Up', LSG (26.5.99) 12; Dan Brennan QC, 'Chairman's Report', 114 BN (6.99) 3; 'DPP spells out his opposition to jury change', T (15.11.99) 11.

[103] 'Bar fights Straw over jury trial curb', T (11.10.99) 12; 'Progressive Bar—Part of the Solution' (1999) 149 NLJ 1506; 'Lawyers Gear Up for Fierce Fight in Defence of Right to Jury Trial', LSG (17.11.99) 3; 'Editorial: Government on Trial', LSG (17.11.99) 12; 'Straw is facing "battle royal" on law reforms', T (18.11.99) 12; 'Lawyers' objection to jury trial curbs attacked by Straw', DT (20.11.99) 10; 'Straw takes on opponents of jury changes', T (20.11.99) 18; 'Straw's doubts on jury reform', T (24.11.99) 12; 'Electing Trial by Jury' (1999) 149 NLJ 1755; 'Editorial: Turn again, Mr Straw' (1999) 149 NLJ 1753; 'Lords rebel at plan to limit trial by jury', T (3.12.99) 18; 'Lords Fume over Straw's Attack on Jury Trials' (1999) 143 SJ 1152.

[104] Egan (1999: 95).

[105] On the experience with contracts see Orchard (2001).

[106] See Bridges (2001).

[107] See Moorhead (2001).

[108] From April 2001, 28.4% of benefit units were fully eligible for Legal Representation and 31.6% for Legal Help. Buck and Stark (2000: Executive Summary); see also Buck (2000). For an analysis of civil cases excluded from legal aid see Goriely *et al.* (2001).

[109] See Abel (1995); Dyzenhaus (1998).

[110] 'Texas Spends Little on Public Defenders for Poor Criminal Defendants, Report Says', NYT (20.12.00) A 17.

[111] 'Paris Lawyers Join National Strike for More Legal Aid', Deutsche Presse-Agentur (12.12.00); 'French Attorneys Strike to Demand More State-Funded Legal Aid', Agence France Presse (12.12.00); 'Court Cases Cancelled as French Lawyers Strike for Better Legal Aid Pay', Associated Press Newswires (12.12.00); 'France: Lawyers Strike', NYT (13.12.00) A14; 'France: Lawyers Strike Again', NYT (19.12.00) A14.

Chapter 9—Notes

[1] For an overview of the regulatory structure see Seneviratne (1999; 2000).

[2] Royal Commission (1979: R26.4); Abel (1988: 133–6 and Table 1.25).

[3] Joseph (1976; 1984); Marcel Berlins, 'Rights of Audience' 129 (1979) NLJ 1116–7; Royal Commission (1979: R22.17, 23.1–6, 25.1–13); Abel (1988: 248–60); Zander (1988: chap. 9); for a history of the Solicitors Act 1941 see Lunney (1997).

[4] Royal Commission (1979: paras. 23.30 and R25.10); LCD (1983: 23–4).

[5] 'Financial Services Act 1986—Effect on Solicitors' (1987) 84 LSG 2158; Marre (1988: paras. 4.16–22).

[6] Derek Bradbeer, 'President's Column' (1987) 84 LSG 1543; 'A Cautionary Tale: Arrangements' (1987) 84 LSG 2201; Derek Bradbeer, 'Competition: The Challenges and Opportunities' (1987) 84 LSG 2897; 'Complaints about Shoddy Work Begin to Climb' (1987) 84 LSG 3462; 'Society Lodges Application for Professional Body Status' (1987) 84 LSG 3623; Derek Bradbeer, 'President's Column', LSG (27.1.88) 2; 'Director Defends SCB's Performance', LSG (27.1.88) 5; 'Solicitors', LSG (3.2.88) 38; 'Restoration to the Roll Only in Exceptional Circumstances, says SDT', LSG (9.3.88) 5; 'SCB Boasts Faster Complaints Handling', LSG (22.6.88) 4; 'The Complaints Keep Coming' (1987) 131 SJ 1632; 'SCB finds "Careless Attitudes"' (1988) 132 SJ 312; 'Complaints Show Rise of 20 per cent' (1988) 132 SJ 1040; 'Discouraging Unnatural Practices' (1987) 137 NLJ 1101; LA (7.87) 6–7; 'Laying down the law', G (5.3.88); Abel (1988: 253 and Table 2.42). For an analysis of SDT cases and outcomes see Davies (1999b).

[7] 'SCB Committee Split on Way Forward', LSG (19.3.89) 2; 'Closing the Stable Door' (1989) 133 SJ 427; 'Watchdog attacks inadequate actions on legal complaints', T (27.7.89) 6; Jenkins *et al.* (1989: 10–13); Lay Observer (1989); 'Radical reform plan for legal complaints', T (12.12.90); 'Green Light for SCB Revamp', LSG (9.1.91) 4; 'Architect of Sweeping Change', LSG (9.1.91) 5; 'Lay Observer in Farewell Attack on SCB' (1991) 135 SJ 268.

[8] 'Legal services ombudsman named with wide powers', T (18.9.90); 'Non–lawyer Named as Legal Ombudsman' (1990) 134 SJ 1052; 'Lawyers face "big stick" Ombudsman', DT (9.1.91); 'Watchdog to tackle disputes on lawyers', T (9.1.91); 'Complaints against lawyers increase', I (24.3.92); 'Legal payouts', T (24.3.92); 'Legal Ombudsman Urges Law Society Rethink' (1992) 142 NLJ 814; 'Secrecy in Solicitors' Disciplinary Hearings' (1992) 142 NLJ 922; 'Editors Mount Campaign to Open Tribunal', LSG (8.6.92) 6; 'A Contented Bureau Reports' (1992) 142 NLJ 1030; 'SCB Reports Steep Rise in Interventions' (1992) 136 SJ 717; 'Disciplinary Hearings Open Door to Public', LSG (19.93) 3; 'Bureau Warned about Workload', LSG (22.6.94) 5; 'Sex Guide', LSG (12.10.94) 4; 'Bureau Challenged', LSG (2.11.94) 4; LSO (1994). On the LSO's performance see James and Seneviratne (1995).

[9] Ole Hansen, 'The Sad Case of Peggy Wood: Suing the Law Society' (1989) 139 NLJ 572; 'Peggy Wood's Progress' (1989) 139 NLJ 707; 'Peggy Wood (cont)' (1989) 139 NLJ 743; 'Going Up... (1989) 139 NLJ 855; 'Woman, 76, seeks justice from legal profession', I (21.12.92); 'The Litigant in Person', LSG (8.1.93) 6; (1993) 143 NLJ 833; 'Society Sued on Duty to Public', LSG (16.6.93) 6; 'Wood Saga Spans 20 Years', LSG (16.6.93) 6; 'Wood v Law Society Continues' (1993) 143 NLJ 874; 'Judgment Reserved in Wood Case' (1993) 136 SJ 601; 'No Law Society Duty of Care to the

Public' (1993) 143 NLJ 1092; 'A Missed Opportunity' (1993) 143 NLJ 1089; 'Appeal "Likely" in Wood case', LSG (25.8.93) 6; 'Wood Appeals', LSG (20.10.93) 4; 'Here's Wood in the Eye', LSG (2.3.94) 9; 'Wood Case Burns Out', LSG (1.3.95) 3; 'Law Society Beats Off Negligence Action' (1995) 139 SJ 180; 'Wood Carries On', LSG (5.7.95) 5; 'In Europe Peggy Wood Loses Fight against Law Society' (1997) 141 NLJ 1267. The High Court reaffirmed its position in *R v Law Society, ex parte Birkett*, QBD (30.7.99), 149 NLJ 1255.

[10] 'Firms are Flouting Client Care Rule', LSG (24.3.93) 6; 'Complaints Default', LSG (5.5.93) 8; 'Fraud Conviction', LSG (10.11.93) 8; 'Solicitors Attack "Sledgehammer" Fraud Measures', LSG (10.11.93) 8; Jenkins (1993); Goriely and Williams (1993); 'Pushing the Client Care Principle', LSG (23.2.94) 11; 'Trial by Media', LSG (8.6.94) 9; 'Green Form crackdown', LA (12.94) 4. For a categorization of firm responses see Palmer (1998).

[11] 'Why so coy about charges?' T (14.11.89); 'NCC Launches Legal Complaints Probe' (1993) 137 SJ 808; 'Elly Pledges Fraudster Purge', LSG (20.7.94) 5; Charles Elly, 'Service and Independence', LSG (7.10.94) 2; 'Clients pay dearly as solicitors' fees soar', ST (4.12.94); 'Lawyers in the dock over treatment of complaints', T (9.12.94); 'Bureau Braves Consumer Fire', LSG (16.12.94) 5; Michael Barnes, 'No Easy Answers on Complaints', LSG (16.12.94) 14; 'Bureau Counters NCC Criticisms' (1994) 138 SJ 1275; Hansen (1994); 'Letters to the Editor' (1995) 139 SJ 161.

[12] 'Panels Trigger Local Passions', LSG (7.6.95) 6; 'SCB Debate Set to Increase Unease at Chancery Lane' (1995) 139 SJ 939.

[13] 'Solicitors in Court' (1990) 140 NLJ 79; 'Solicitor Rejects Law Society Settlement Offer' (1990) 140 NLJ 118; 'Rosen 3 The Law Society 1' (1990) 140 NLJ 195; 'The Law Society in Action' (1990) 140 NLJ 279; 'An Offer He Could Not Refuse' (1990) 140 NLJ 314; 'Injudicious Review' (1990) 140 NLJ 313; Arnold Rosen, 'Complaints and Chancery Lane' (1990) 140 NLJ 968; 'Arnold Rosen Soldiers On' (1990) 140 NLJ 842; 'Dawson Sues' (1990) 140 NLJ 1062; 'Rosen £90,000, Law Society 0' (1991) 141 NLJ 226; 'Good News, Bad News' (1991) 141 NLJ 519; 'Rosen Rebuke Rescinded' (1991) 141 NLJ 626; 'Go Ahead for Solicitor's Challenge to the Law Society' (1992) 142 NLJ 742; 'Law Society Faces Judicial Review on Delegation' (1992) 136 SJ 503; 'Another Sole Practitioner Challenges the LS' (1993) 143 NLJ 191; 'Delegated Powers Confirmed', LSG (12.5.93) 6; 'Court Confirms Bureau Power', LSG (1.12.93) 6; 'Law Soc to Pay Estimated £50,000 Costs as SCB Loses Case' (1995) 139 SJ 31.

[14] 'Right to query bills may be abolished', I (10.6.89) 29; 'Why so coy about charges?' T (14.11.89); 'Solicitors' chief takes on critics of legal changes', T (16.7.90); 'Legal fees prove a costly surprise', T (29.6.92); 'New Cost Sanctions Signalled', LSG (14.3.93) 3; 'Solicitors Blasted on Costs', LSG (21.4.93) 3; 'John Taylor on War Path' (1993) 143 NLJ 570; 'Ombudsman Welcomes "Sharp Practices" Rap' (1993) 137 SJ 364; 'No plan for compulsory disclosures', L (27.4.93); 'Barnes Beats Drum on Wills', LSG (16.6.93) 5; 'Complaints Level Off', LSG (16.6.93) 5; 'Ombudsman Calls for New Complaints Procedures' (1993) 137 SJ 575; 'SCB Criticised' (1993) 143 NLJ 911; 'Law Society Attempts to Stamp Out "Ambush Charging" by Practitioners' (1993) 137 SJ 675; 'Council Delays Fees Decision', LSG (21.7.93) 5; 'Block on Efforts to Curb "Ambush Charging"', (1993) 137 SJ 699; 'Costs Advice Penalties Stall' (1993) 143

NLJ 1055; 'Comment: Peggy Wood' (1993) 137 SJ 759; 'Coming Clean on Fees', LSG (13.10.93) 7; 'Public Urged to Pre-check Costs', LSG (17.11.93) 4; 'Cards on the Table' (1993) 143 NLJ 1629; 'Pushing the Client Care Principle', LSG (23.2.94) 11; 'McIntosh Slams Firms on Cost Information' (1994) 138 SJ 757; 'Bill Checks Dip', LSG (28.9.94) 3; Davies (1999: 180).

[15] 'Hard Line Urged on Client Care', LSG (9.2.94) 4 (sample of 300 clients at 60 firms); 'Persuasion not Prescription', LSG (13.4.94) 2; 'Arbitration Call Falls on Deaf Ears', LSG (8.6.94) 5; Harris (1994); 'Civil justice in Britain', E (14.1.95) 30.

[16] 'Advice Bureaux Flay Lawyers over Client Cost Awareness', LSG (20.9.95) 2; 'CAB Puts Forward Dramatic Reform Proposals' (1995) 139 SJ 911; 'Comment: A Costly Mistake' (1995) 139 SJ 915; Chapman (1995); Jenkins and Lewis (1995: Table 30) (another 23 per cent of conveyancing clients received an estimate and 8 per cent some indication of how costs would be calculated).

[17] 'Legal Fees "Out of Proportion"', LSG (6.10.93) 4; 'Fair Rates', LSG (3.11.93) 8; 'Hourly Fees Face Onslaught', LSG (6.3.96) 3.

[18] 'Council to Crack Whip on Costs Code', LSG (26.2.97) 1; 'Editorial: Charge of the Enlightened Brigade', LSG (26.2.97) 15; 'Costs Proposals Receive Mixed Welcome' (1997) 141 SJ 224; 'Client Care and the Profession' (1997) 147 NLJ 370; Middleton (1997: para. 5.43). In July 1998 Walter Merricks called 'the investigation of small complaints about poor service . . . a disaster that the Law Society shouldn't have ever allowed itself to get into. Poor service is indefinable and is not necessarily the responsibility of the professional body. . . . It has nothing to do with professional reputation' (interview).

[19] 'OSS to Inquire into Billing Case', LSG (19.3.97) 6; 'Editorial: Price of a Good Name', LSG (19.3.97) 15; 'Maxwell Solicitor Hits Back', LSG (19.3.97) 9; 'Comment: Debt of Honour' (1997) 141 SJ 251; 'Press Round-Up', LSG (7.10.98) 12.

[20] Which? (1995) (40 firms visited, 40 telephoned, 400 clients surveyed); 'Consumer Report Slates Poor Work', LSG (4.10.95) 1; 'Which? Report "Sad Example" says Law Society' (1995) 139 SJ 967; 'Which?' (1995) 145 NLJ 1439; 'Shoosmiths sues CA', LSG (11.10.95) 1; 'Group Urges "End Lawyer Immunity"', LSG (25.10.95) 6; 'Ombudsman says Society is Wrong on Which? Survey' (1996) 140 SJ 89; McCall *et al.* (1996); 'Lawyers accused of giving wrong consumer advice', T (2.10.97) 7; 'Which? Survey under Fire from Solicitors', LSG (8.10.97) 1; 'Editorial: Risky Business', LSG (8.10.97) 15; 'Which? Report Condemns High Street Advice' (1997) 141 SJ 907.

[21] 'Comment: Continuing Education' (1994) 138 SJ 1121; Allaker and Shapland (1994); 'Council Faces Vote Recording Debate', LSG (8.11.95) 4; Martin Mears, 'President's Column: The first 100 Days', LSG (22.11.95) 11; Simon Baker, 'Letters to the Editor: Lifelong Learning', LSG (29.11.95) 15; ACLEC (1995a: para. 7.5; 1996a: para. 2.25; 1996d: para. 1; 1997b: paras. 3, 5, 6); Shapland (1996); Shapland and Sorsby (1996); 'Comment: Fair Comment?' (1997) 141 SJ 911; Hales *et al.* (1998).

[22] 'Law Soc to Pay Estimated £50,000 Costs as SCB Loses Case' (1995) 139 SJ 31; 'Bureau Chief Moots Change', LSG (15.2.95) 1; 'Editorial: The Profession and the Law Society' (1995) 145 NLJ 297; ' "We've not been Invited"—SCB' (1995) 145 NLJ 298; 'Fee Proposal would Kill Trivial Claims', LSG (8.3.95) 6; 'NCC Report Dismissed', LSG (8.3.95) 6; 'Demand for the Judicial Touch', LSG (8.3.95) 6; 'Few Bouquets for Battered Bureau', LSG (8.3.95) 6; 'SCB Embattled over Criticism' (1995) 139 SJ 203; 'Editorial: Like Samson Without his Hair' (1995) 145 NLJ 333;

'A Lack of Confidence for Solicitors Complaints' (1995) 145 NLJ 334; Jenkins and Lewis (1995b) (May 1995 survey of 411 firms); Jenkins and Lewis (1996).

[23] 'SCB Up for Revamp', LSG (1.6.95) 1; 'Editorial: Metamorphoses' (1995) 145 NLJ 841; 'SCB Replacement Just a "Cosmetic Change"' (1995) 139 SJ 573.

[24] 'Poor attendance at British Legal Association Annual Spring Conference' (1995) 145 NLJ 807; Stanley Best, 'Letters: Abolishing the SCB' (1995) 145 NLJ 844; 'Poll Call', LSG (14.6.95) 2.

[25] Humphrey Bowles, 'Comment: More Serious Thoughts from Essex' (1995) 145 NLJ 1250; 'SCB Laymember Rebels' (1995) 145 NLJ 1250; 'SCB Expenditure' (1995) 145 NLJ 1250.

[26] Veronica Lowe, 'Guess which Organisation?' (1995) 145 NLJ 861.

[27] 'SCB to become SS?—Debate' (1995) 145 NLJ 843; 'Policy Chairman Supports Bureau', LSG (14.6.95) 4; 'Profession to Debate Complaints System', LSG (14.6.95) 4.

[28] 'Bureau Told it has One Last Chance', LSG (21.6.95) 3; Michael Barnes, 'Comment: Independence Vote', LSG (11.10.95) 14.

[29] 'Pay-Out High', LSG (19.7.95) 1; 'SCB "1994—a Year of Very Real and Substantial Achievements"', (1995) 145 NLJ 1083; 'SCB Bid to Stem Complaints', LSG (26.7.95) 1. Only 15 per cent of a sample of firms had ever been contacted by the compliance officer. Christensen *et al.* (1999b: 59).

[30] 'Council to Consider Pay-off', LSG (20.9.95) 1; Martin Mears, 'Satisfying the Customer', LSG (27.9.95) 12; 'SCB Chief Quits Post', LSG (11.10.95) 1; 'Lowe Row', LSG (1.11.95) 2; 'Veronica Lowe Blows Hot' (1995) 145 NLJ 1638; 'Editorial: The Affair Lowe' (1995) 145 NLJ 1637.

[31] 'New Year Attack on SCB' (1996) 140 SJ 4; 'Lawyers Fall Down on Client Care Rule', LSG (17.1.96) 1; 'Editorial: Care Culture', LSG (17.1.96) 14; 'SCB—what Next?' (1996) 140 SJ 31; Lewis (1996: paras. 3.11, 19, 23, 28, 4.16, 24–25, 35).

[32] 'SCB Dismisses Critics', LSG (7.2.96) 64; 'Professional Self Regulation' (1996) 146 NLJ 486; 'SCB to be Revamped', LSG (13.3.96) 1; '"Last Chance" Warning over SCB Replacement' (1996) 140 SJ 243; Paul Pharaoh, 'Comment: New, Improved SCB', LSG (20.3.96) 13.

[33] Jenkins and Lewis (1995: Table 30); 'SCB Worry over Client Care Rule', LSG (24.4.96) 2; 'Editorial: Better Bureau', LSG (24.4.96) 14; 'Firms Ignore Complaints Rule', LSG (22.5.96) 4; 'Ombudsman Issues Regulation Warning', LSG (12.6.96) 4; 'SCB Answers Ombudsman', LSG (19.6.96) 4; LSO (1996: para. 7.6). This was confirmed by James and Seneviratne (1996). After leaving the Law Society, John Hayes said 'I would take [non-compliant firms] off the Roll. If they cannot run a proper complaint system that should be one reason for taking all the people off the Roll' (interview July 1998).

[34] 'Office for the Supervision of Solicitors replaces SCB', LA (10.96) 4; Tony Girling, 'President's Column: On an Electoral Roll', LSG (26.2.97) 18; 'OSS to Target Client Care Offenders' (1997) 141 SJ 247; 'The lawyers' watchdog', T (24.6.97) 39; 'Council told OSS still has Problems' (1997) 147 NLJ 1091; 'Editorial: Supervision at Arm's Length' (1997) 147 NLJ 1229; Peter Ross, 'Letters: Report—not Secret' (1997) 147 NLJ 1267.

[35] 'Another Warning on Self-regulation' (1997) 147 NLJ 1302; Ann Abraham, 'Making the System Work' (1997) 147 NLJ 1544.

[36] 'Record of Service', LSG (25.6.97) 26–27; I Dean, 'Supervision of Solicitors and the New Legal Services Ombudsman' (1997) 147 NLJ 1490; Martin Mears, 'No Connection with the Previous Firm?' (1997) 147 NLJ 1770; 'Mears Returns as Scourage of OSS' (1997) 141 SJ 1143; 'Fast system to tackle solicitors' mistakes', T (9.12.97) 6; 'Council to Vote on OSS Fast Track Plan', LSG (10.12.97) 1; 'Editorial: The Wench is Dead...' (1997) 147 NLJ 1801; '"OSS: a New Approach", says Peter Ross' (1997) 147 NLJ 1802; OSS (1997: 4).

[37] 'Firms could be Fined in OSS Crackdown' (1997) 141 SJ 1169; 'Comment: Good in Parts' (1997) 141 SJ 1171; Martin Mears, 'Letter to the Editor: Office for the Supervision of Solicitors' (1998) 142 SJ 6; Paul Pharaoh, 'Letter to the Editor: Mears Campaign against OSS' (1998) 142 SJ 56; 'OSS Baffled by 30% rise in Complaints', LSG (1.4.98) 1; Robert Sayer and Angus Andrew, 'Cost of Complaints', LSG (16.4.98) 16; 'Solicitors' watchdog awash with complaints', T (6.5.98) 8; Paul Pharaoh, 'Letter to the editor: Supervising solicitors', T (14.5.98) 23; Goriely and Williams (1998: 34).

[38] 'Firms "Failing" on Client Complaints', LSG (28.5.98) 1; Davis *et al.*, 'The Client as Consumer' (1998) 148 NLJ 832; 'New Fee for Bad Firms', LSG (28.10.98) 6; Christensen *et al.* (1999a; 1999b).

[39] 'Society Resists Left-Wing Attack', LSG (3.6.98) 5; 'Thompsons Funds Anti-OSS Pamphlet' (1998) 142 SJ 507; Peter Ross, 'Comment: Who Best to Regulate?' LSG (10.6.98) 15; 'Tribunal Seeks Independence', LSG (14.10.98) 3; Law Society (1998b: 6–7); Arora and Francis (1998); Abraham (1998)

[40] 'Editorial: The End of Self regulation' (1998) 148 NLJ 933; Arnold Rosen, 'Letters to the Editor: An End to Self-regulation' (1998) 148 NLJ 936; 'Bogan Calls for Legal Services "Super Regulator"' (1998) 42 SJ 924.

[41] 'Client Care Failing says Ombudsman', LSG (1.7.98) 1; 'Tightrope Walker', LSG (1.7.98) 10; 'Editorial: The Complaints Conundrum', LSG (1.7.98) 15; 'Ombudsman Seeks Radical Reform', LSG (28.10.98) 6; LSO (1998); Abraham (1998: 76-7); Davies (1998a: 149–51).

[42] 'End of the Line for One Client's Complaint' (1998) 148 NLJ 934; 'Convicted Solicitors Continue to Practise, TV Programme Alleges', LSG (2.12.98) 3; Michael Zander, 'Comment: Only the Talk is Tough', LSG (2.12.98) 16; 'OSS Delays get Worse' (1998) 142 SJ 1095; 'Comment: Poor Performance' (1998) 142 SJ 1099; 'Solicitor Cries Foul to TV Watchdog as SDT Hits Back over Documentary', LSG (10.12.98) 5; 'Press Round-Up', LSG (10.12.98) 14; 'SDT's Hand could be Forced on Convicted Solicitors' (1998) 142 SJ 1120; 'Crooked lawyers who keep working', T (15.12.98) 35.

[43] 'Delays at solicitors' watchdog worsen', T (28.1.98) 5; 'OSS Failing on Performance Targets', LSG (2.12.98) 3; 'OSS Delays get Worse' (1998) 142 SJ 1095; 'Comment: Poor Performance' (1998) 142 SJ 1099; OSS (1998: 5, 20); 'Legal diary', T (9.2.99) 35; 'Press Round-Up', LSG (3.3.99) 10; 'OSS Overload', LSG (3.3.99) 4; 'Research Condemns Ombudsman Scheme' (1999) 143 SJ 308; Davies (1999a: 174, 182–3).

[44] HL 597: 692 (16.3.99); HC 329: 230–41 (14.4.99); 'Government Triumphs in Lords' (1999) 143 SJ 255; 'LCD Poised to Act on Complaints Regime', LSG (24.3.99) 1; 'Swifter justice for victims of bad lawyers', T (25.3.99) 15; 'Government Crackdown Sidelines Law Society' (1999) 143 SJ 283; 'Firms to Face £5,000 Complaints Penalty', LSG (31.3.99) 1; 'OSS Seeks Increased Compensation Powers'

(1999) 143 SJ 331; 'Comment: No Quick Fix' (1999) 143 SJ: 335; 'Sorry Should Not be the Hardest Word on Complaints, says Irvine', LSG (14.4.99) 3; 'Watchdog Without Teeth', I (Tues Rev) (20.4.99) 14; 'Crackdown Gives Greater Powers to Ombudsman and OSS' (1999) 143 SJ 379; 'Labour revolt over legal aid curbs', G (23.6.99) 8; 'Labour Revolt over Personal Injury Cut' (1999) 143 SJ 603.

[45] 'Complaints on lawyers rise', T (21.4.99) 2; 'Complaints Rocket 40% to Record Level', LSG (21.4.99) 1; 'Crackdown Gives Greater Powers to Ombudsman and OSS' (1999) 143 SJ 379; Michael Mathews, 'President's Column: Meeting the New Consumer Challenge', LSG (8.4.99) 22; 'Comment: Cost of Complaints' (1999) 143 SJ 383; 'Editorial: Best Practice and the OSS' (1999) 149 NLJ 589; Trevor Aldridge QC, 'Opinion: Pay for Dissatisfaction' (1999) 143 SJ 430.

[46] Martin Mears, 'The OSS—Congratulations?!' (1999) 149 NLJ 743; 'Letters to the Editor: the OSS—SOS?' (1999) 149 NLJ 847; I Dean, 'Comment: Self regulation' (1999) 149 NLJ 926.

[47] ' "Warts and All" Report Points Way to Gaining Control of Complaints', LSG (23.6.99) 3; 'Press Round-Up', LSG (23.6.99) 12; 'Editorial: Lightening the Load', LSG (23.6.99) 15; 'Editorial: A Third Incarnation for the OSS?' (1999) 149 NLJ 957; Philip Hamer, 'Complaints—a New Strategy' (1999) 149 NLJ 959; 'Blueprint Mark III for OSS' (1999) 149 NLJ 959; 'OSS Report Calls for £5.7 Million Cash Injection' (1999) 143 SJ 604; 'Brand Protection', LSG (30.6.99) 18.

[48] HC 333: 1015–28 (22.6.99).

[49] 'Ombudsman's Final Complaints Warning', LSG (30.6.99) 1; 'On Watch', LSG (30.6.99) 10; 'Editorial: Bridge that Gap', LSG (30.6.99) 15; 'Lawyers attracting record complaints', T (30.6.99) 2; 'Lawyers' toothless watchdog', G (30.6.99) 6; 'Comment: Cause for Complaint' (1999) 143 SJ 631; 'Editorial: Keep the White Flag Flying' (1999) 149 NLJ 993; 'Press Round-Up', LSG (7.7.99) 10; LSO (1999: 2–4, 9, 13–15).

[50] 'OSS Fails Own Test', LSG (7.7.99) 5; 'Vaz Threatens to "Name and Shame" ', (1999) 143 SJ 699.

[51] 'One year's wait for complaints about solicitors', T (23.7.99) 2; 'Irvine threatens solicitors with new watchdog', T (27.7.99) 8; 'Betts Goes in to Take Helm at OSS', LSG (28.7.99) 1; 'New Crisis for Society as OSS Director Suspended' (1999) 143 SJ 727 'Ross—if not Work—Suspended' (1999) 149 NLJ 1138; 'A case to answer', G2 (3.8.99) 16; 'Comment: Facing up to Complaints' (1999) 143 SJ 755; 'OSS Update' (1999) 149 NLJ 1196; 'OSS Backlog Plans', LSG (11.8.99) 5; 'Betts gives Solicitors 21 Days to Settle Complaints' (1999) 143 SJ 775; 'Solicitors' complaints director resigns suddenly', T (19.8.99) 2; 'Ross Resigns as Director of OSS' (1999) 143 SJ 799; Martin Mears, 'Lawspeak...' (1999) 149 NLJ 1382; 'Editorial: Complaints about complaints', LA (9.99) 3.

[52] 'Editorial: Once more unto the Breach' (1999) 149 NLJ 1137; Robert Sayer, 'Efficient Complaints Handling is our Goal' (1999) 149 NLJ 1196; 'Press Round-Up', LSG (15.9.99) 10; 'Oss in Name and Shame Survey', LSG (6.10.99) 5; 'OSS Opens Debate on "Naming and Shaming" ' (1999) 143 SJ 944; 'Paying the Penalty', LSG (20.10.99) 4; 'Poor Service Compensation to Rise', LSG (10.11.99) 3; 'News', T (Law) (16.11.99) 9.

[53] 'Editorial: Coming Clean' (1999) 149 NLJ 1357; Martin Mears, 'A suitable case for complaining about the Law Society', T (Law) (28.9.99) 9.

[54] 'Tide is Turning at OSS, Sayer Claims' (1999) 143 SJ 919; 'OSS Beats own Target', LSG (8.12.99) 5.

[55] 'Law Society chief plans to take over the Bar', T (30.10.99) 8; 'Solicitors' body in move to represent all lawyers', FT (30–31.10.99) 3; 'Sayer Sets Out Vision of Fused Profession', LSG (3.11.99) 1; Robert Sayer, 'Beginning of an Era', LSG (3.11.99) 16; 'Lawyers "Will Pay" for External Body', LSG (3.11.99) 13; 'Sayer's Vision gets Mixed Reception' (1999) 143 SJ 1024.

[56] 'Law Society: Self-indemnity' (1987) 131 SJ 1000; 'Limitation of Liability for the Professions—The President of the Law Society Presses for a Government Inquiry' (1987) 84 LSG 548; 'Limitation of Professional Liability: The Bar Proposes a Scheme' (1987) 84 LSG 1233; 'Indemnity Insurance—Heads of Professions Call for Enquiry into Liability' (1987) 84 LSG 2323; 'Complaints about Shoddy Work begin to Climb' (1987) 84 LSG 3462; 'Professionals' Disclaimers Fair or Unfair?' (1987) 84 LSG 3648; 'Levy Announced to Meet Huge Demand on Compensation Fund', LSG (4.5.88) 2; 'April Council Report', LSG (4.5.88) 7; 'June Council Report, LSG (15.6.88) 10, 'Practising Certificate Fee Hike', LSG (22.6.88) 5; 'Tougher Action Promised on Lax Solicitors', LSG (22.6.88) 6; 'Lay Observer Criticises Handling of Complaints' (1988) 132 SJ 1100; Abel (1988: Table 2.45); Zander (1988: 80); 'Indemnity Fund Plan to Correct Contribution Imbalances', LSG (14.6.89) 3; 'Record Rogues' (1989) 139 NLJ 566; 'Research holds Some Clues to Defaulting Solicitors', LSG (7.6.89) 4; 'Bad Name Dogs' (1989) 139 NLJ 77; 'Bradbeer Committee Exonerates Sole Practitioners in Compensation Crisis' (1989) 139 NLJ 778; 'Measures Proposed for Sole Practitioners' (1989) 133 SJ 732; 'Society Moves Cautiously on Tackling Sole Practitioner Compensation Claims' (1989) 139 NLJ 818; '£295 Levy to Meet Defaults', LSG (13.6.90) 5; 'Extra Monitoring of Solicitors Sought', LSG (20.6.90) 5; 'Practitioners Count the Cost' (1990) 140 NLJ 842; '... but the Levy was Dry' (1990) 134 SJ 791; 'Controls to Curb Dishonesty', LSG (23.1.91) 6; 'Defaulting Solicitors: Plan to Target Early Trouble', LSG (6.2.91) 8; 'Law Society moves to cut number of dishonest solicitors', T (11.2.91); 'Early Warnings' (1991) 135 SJ 175; 'Compensation Fund Claims total £18.3 Million', LSG (1.5.91) 7. Three to five partner firms actually account for the most disproportionate number of negligence actions: Sherr and Webley (1997: 130). The best overview of SIF is Davies (1998b).

[57] Abel (1988: 260); 'Indemnity Rates to Rise by 34.1% Next Year', LSG (12.6.91) 3; 'Indemnity Rates', LSG (19.6.91) 4; Philip Ely, 'Widening horizons: The President's Address to the 1991 National Conference', LSG (17.10.91) 2.

[58] 'Staying Out of Trouble on a Shoestring', LSG (1.5.91) 8; Skordaki and Willis (1991); 'SIF begins Cost-cutting Regime', LSG (1.4.92) 6; 'Record Claims for Indemnity Fund' (1992) 136 SJ 399; 'Unhappy News' (1992) 142 NLJ 661; 'Blow for Practitioners' (1992) 142 NLJ 662; 'Stiff Levy Signalled to Shore up Fund', LSG (20.5.92) 3; 'Fund Levy "Could be as High as £1500"' (1992) 136 SJ 479; 'Solicitors Face Bill of up to £1800 for Fund', LSG (3.6.92) 3; 'Checks Signalled for Sole Practice', LSG (3.6.92) 3; 'Villains of the Piece?' (1992) 142 NLJ 777; 'The Future of Compensation' (1992) 142 NLJ 778; 'Compensation Fund Levy Shocks Profession Nationwide' (1992) 136 SJ 539; 'Comment: Cost of Practice' (1992) 136 SJ 543; 'Small Firms Hit in Indemnity Shake Up', LSG (10.6.92) 5; 'Comment: Sole Practitioners' (1992) 136 SJ 667; 'The Solo Flight of the Small Practitioner' (1992)

142 NLJ 993; 'Comment: The Innocent Pay for the Guilty' (1992) 136 SJ 791; 'Rebel Circular Urges Closure of Default Fund' (1992) 136 SJ 787; 'Dishonest Solicitor Pay-outs' (1992) 142 NLJ 1294; 'One-Man Bands Unite to Fight Restrictions' (1992) 136 SJ 1072; 'Claims for solicitor fraud soar', T (26.10.92); 'Profession Divided over Sole Practice', LSG (11.11.92) 6; Law Society (1992b: The Issues paras. 1.1, 2.2, 3.4–5; Background Paper para. 1.16); 'Monitoring of Firms Yields Early Results', LSG (17.3.93) 6; 'SIF Pays out on £21 million in Five Years' (1992) 142 NLJ 570; 'Protecting Both the Profession and the Public' (1992) 142 NLJ 1017; Law Society (1993: Tables 1–2); 'Claims Dip', LSG (2.2.94) 5.

[59] 'Halifax to Consider Levy on Solicitors', LSG (29.7.92) 3; 'Abbey National in Shock Plan to Inspect Solicitors' Conveyancing Files' (1992) 136 SJ 763; 'Leeds Chief Raps Law Soc on Sole Practices' (1992) 136 SJ 787; 'Lenders Slam Law Soc Move to Cap Compensation' (1992) 136 SJ 787; 'Abbey Clarifies Panel Terms', LSG (26.8.92) 3; 'Lenders Reject Cap on Fund', LSG (26.8.92) 10; 'Solicitors Lean Towards Capped Compensation Fund', LSG (7.10.92) 7; 'Lenders Spurn Solos', LSG (14.10.92) 9; 'One-Man Bands Unite to Fight Restrictions' (1992) 136 SJ 1072; 'Profession Divided over Sole Practice', LSG (11.11.92) 6; 'Cap on Fund to be Ruled out', LSG (9.6.93) 3; 'Fund Levy Repeated', LSG (9.6.93) 3; 'Assault against Default', LSG (16.6.93) 9; 'Lowering the Bill', LSG (16.6.93) 9; Law Society (1993: 1).

[60] 'Indemnity Bill Set to Jump 31% for Solos', LSG (3.6.92) 4; 'SIF to Stay Same' (1993) 137 SJ 363; 'Comment: Paying Indemnity' (1993) 137 SJ 365; 'Bid for Insurance Deal', LSG (26.1.94) 6; 'Smallest Firms Eat into Fund', LSG (15.6.94) 9; 'Fund Protest', LSG (9.8.95) 1; 'Drive for Cheaper Insurance', LSG (31.8.95) 2; 'Crime Specialists Study SIF Opt out', LSG (1.11.95) 1; 'Editorial: Cover Charge', LSG (1.11.95) 14.

[61] 'Law Society Announces Tough Default Measures' (1993) 137 SJ 547; 'Whip Cracker', LSG (2.3.94) 12; 'Small Signs of Default Ebb', LSG (13.4.94) 3; '370 Firms on SCB "Problem" List', LSG (20.4.94) 8; 'Solicitors Face £30m Payout as Claims for Dishonest Soar', LSG (12.10.94) 4; 'Frauds hit Fund for £8 million', LSG (21.7.95) 6; 'Default Price-tag Hits £33 m', LSG (26.4.95) 1; 'Compensation at Record High Level', LSG (26.4.95) 4; 'Pay-Out High', LSG (19.7.95) 1; 'Ford Convicted of Fraud', LSG (18.10.95) 2.

[62] 'Hayes Warns of Default Backlash', LSG (18.5.94) 3; 'Hayes Outlines Law Society Strategy' (1994) 138 SJ 487; 'Comment: YSG—the Trade Union' (1994) 138 SJ 491; 'Petition over Law Firm Suits', LSG (26.7.95) 4; 'YSG Seeks Ban on Negligence Suits', LSG (4.12.96) 1; 'YSG Calls for Test Case Funding', LSG (19.3.97) 5; Martin Mears, 'Justice for Assistant Solicitors—1', 3 Cat (6.97) 7; 'Justice for Assistant Solicitors—2', 3 Cat (6.97) 15; 'Negligence Test', LSG (21.4.99) 4; 'YSG Acts over Plight of Assistants' (1999) 143 SJ 404.

[63] 'Sole Practitioners not Pulling Together' (1995) 139 SJ 157; 'Cost Set to Fall', LSG (7.6.95) 1.

[64] 'Council to Study Big Fee Reduction', LSG (3.4.96) 1; 'Default Battle Shows Results', LSG (17.4.96) 1; 'Default Figures Up', LSG (25.9.96) 1; 'Compensation Levy could Fall Again', LSG (8.1.97) 1; 'Walls could Fall in Default Battle', LSG (9.4.97) 1; 'Compensation Fund Contributions Fall while Interventions Increase', LSG (16.4.98) 5.

[65] 'A Balance of Cover', LSG (17.1.96) 24; 'Insurance Fees Rejig', LSG (17.1.96) 1; 'Searching for Balance', LSG (24.1.96) 10; 'SIF Rates may Climb by 5 per cent', LSG (24.4.96) 1; 'Lobby on SIF Reform', LSG (1.5.96) 1.

[66] 'New Indemnity Rates Announced', LSG (12.6.96) 4; 'SIF Mistake Prompts Cash Call', LSG (2.10.96) 5; 'SIF Pledges Inquiry into Shortfall', LSG (23.10.96) 1; 'Anger over Indemnity "blunder"' (1996) 140 SJ 1012; 'Indemnity Miscalculation Blamed on "Communications" Error' (1996) 140 SJ 1064.

[67] 'Indemnity Bills could Soar by 30%', LSG (29.1.97) 1; 'Time is of the Essence for the Law Society' (1997) 147 NLJ 119; 'Solicitors Set to Pay £248m Shortfall' (1997) 141 SJ 75; 'Comment: Risky Policy' (1997) 141 SJ 127. When Mears showed a highly critical draft *Gazette* article to Kennedy, the SIF Director said the 'unprecedented and unwarranted attack' was 'permeated by inaccuracies' and warned that many board members would 'reach...for their lawyers'. 2 Cat (3.97) 19.

[68] 'Firms Face Huge Indemnity Bill', LSG (4.6.97) 1; Tony Girling, 'Analysis: The Case for a Bitter Pill', LSG (4.6.97) 13; 'Council Delays SIF Contribution Figure to July', LSG (11.6.97) 1; 'Task Force to Soften Blow' (1997) 141 SJ 560; 'Comment: Carey Street: Just around the Corner' (1997) 141 SJ 563; 'SIF Shortfall Likened to Lloyds Crisis', (1997) 147 NLJ 874; 'Editorial: When the Wheels Come Off' (1997) 147 NLJ 873; 'Inns and Outs', T (24.6.97) 39; Martin Mears, 'Forced to fork out to subsidise the few', T (24.6.97) 41; Phillip Sycamore, 'Time for a fresh deal based on fairness', T (24.6.97) 41; 'BLA Attacks Law Society's Response to Motion' (1997) 141 NLJ 1018.

[69] 'Comment: So Farewell then...SIF', LSG (18.6.97) 15; 'Top Ten Firm Breaks Ranks on SIF', LSG (25.6.97) 4; 'Editorial: Mutual Interest', LSG (25.6.97) 16; 'The Cover Price War', LSG (2.7.97) 2–5. On the attitudes of City firms see Lee (1999: chap. 4).

[70] 'Sayer: SIF Cash Call is Needlessly High', LSG (9.7.97) 1; 'Task Force Bids to Soften SIF Cash Blow', LSG (16.7.97) 1; Robert Sayer, 'Comment: Long-term Treatment', LSG (16.7.97) 14; 'SIF Cash Demand Limited to 50%', LSG (23.7.97) 6; 'Attacks on All Fronts at AGM' (1997) 147 NLJ 1090; 'SIF to Consider Reinsurance', LSG (22.10.97) 6.

[71] 'Appleby: Multiple Fund is Best Option', LSG (14.1.98) 1; 'Advertisement: Discrimination by S.I.F.' (1998) 142 SJ 26; 'Radical Changes Planned for SIF' (1998) 142 SJ 27; 'Editorial: Insurance and the Profession' (1998) 148 NLJ 41; 'Inns and Outs', T (20.1.98) 39; 'Firms Challenge Indemnity Plan', LSG (21.1.98) 4; 'Law Society under fire on insurance costs', FT (2.2.98) 2; 'Broker Predicts Big Indemnity Savings', LSG (4.2.98) 1; 'Editorial: At the Indemnity Crossroads', LSG (4.2.98) 15; Martin Mears, 'Comment: Indemnity Insurance—the Real Options' (1998) 148 NLJ 151; 'SIF: Second Opinion Sought on all Available Options' (1998) 142 SJ 123; 'SIF News' (1998) 148 NLJ 198; Leslie Dubow, 'Letter to the Editor: Secret Talks', LSG (18.2.98) 16.

[72] 'Conveyancers Still Top SIF Claims List', LSG (26.2.98) 1; 'Move to Soften Impact of Shortfall' (1998) 142 SJ 219; 'Law Society Sidelines Appleby Report' (1998) 142 SJ 291; Robert Sayer, 'A Mutual Fund' (1998) 148 NLJ 580; 'Letters to the Editor: SIF and the Society' (1998) 148 NLJ 687.

[73] 'Editorial: Let us Lose More Slowly' (1998) 148 NLJ 577; 'SPG Appeals to Master of the Rolls' (1998) 148 NLJ 826; 'Council Approves SIF Risk Banding', LSG

(10.6.98) 1; 'Society Grasps Nettle of Risk Banding' (1998) 142 SJ 532; 'Indemnity Right', LSG (1.7.98) 4.

[74] 'SIF Contributions to Rise Again', LSG (22.7.98) 1; 'Indemnity Fund now Faces Court Challenge from Sole Practitioner', LSG (29.7.98) 5; 'City Lawyers Call for End of SIF', LSG (29.7.98) 8; 'Press Round-Up', LSG (29.7.98) 12; 'SPG Rallies Support for Legal Challenge' (1998) 142 SJ 732; 'Solicitors Split Down the Middle over SIF' (1998) 142 SJ 779. In July, John Hayes said 'the profession has got to wake up to the fact that...it has got to get better, more into the minds of the client... and perhaps the greatest lever for this is actually the crisis about indemnity insurance...which would lead to the weakest going to the wall...although you probably won't hear it officially from a Law Society spokesman, they regard it as actually the best news for a long time' (interview).

[75] '70% of Solicitors Support Mutual Fund', LSG (12.8.98) 1; 'Solicitors Split Down the Middle over SIF' (1998) 142 SJ 779; 'Comment: O! the Pity of It' (1998) 142 SJ 783; 'Press Round-Up', LSG (26.8.98) 10; 'Small Firms join Indemnity Lobby', LSG (3.9.98) 1; 'Jump in Tribunal Suspensions', LSG (3.9.98) 5; 'Press Round-Up', LSG (3.9.98) 12; 'Society to Propose Indemnity Options', LSG (9.9.98) 1; 'Time to Leave the Profession?' (1998) 142 SJ 806; Martin Mears, 'Solicitors Indemnity Fund debate', LSG (16.9.98) 22.

[76] 'Homebuyers face big increase in legal fees', T (26.8.98) 6; 'Society to Propose Indemnity Options', LSG (9.9.98) 1; Robert Sayer, 'Comment: An Unfair Equation', LSG (9.9.98) 15; 'Indemnity Fund Chief Warns Against "Dumping Ground" Effect', LSG (16.9.98) 5; 'Indemnity: Market Option Remains Live', LSG (30.9.98) 1; 'Agony Postponed over Future of SIF' (1998) 142 SJ 875.

[77] 'Indemnity Group to Call Society SGM', LSG (7.10.98) 1; 'Comment: Going to Market', LSG (7.10.98) 15; 'Press Round-Up', LSG (14.10.98) 12.

[78] 'City Firms Consider Legal Action as Indemnity Pressure Mounts', LSG (14.10.98) 3; 'New Waiver Scheme Fails to Convince Critics' (1998) 142 SJ 923; 'Dalton Jumps First Hurdle in Challenge to Indemnity Rules', LSG (21.10.98) 3; 'Sole Practitioner to Insure on Open Market after Court Success' (1998) 142 SJ 947; 'Meeting of Minds', LSG (11.11.98) 4; 'SIF Accused of Making Solicitors face "Unacceptable" Risk over Y2K', LSG (16.12.98) 5; 'Boost for Solicitor Challenging SIF', LSG (13.1.99) 3.

[79] 'Mutual Fund "Could Work" with Market', LSG (6.1.99) 1; 'Report Fails to Save SIF' (1999) 143 SJ 27; 'Master Policy Added to Indemnity Options', LSG (20.1.99) 1; 'Society's "Third Way" would Mean Death of SIF' (1999) 143 SJ 51.

[80] Angus Andrew, 'Comment: Mutual v Market', LSG (20.1.99) 14.

[81] 'Council Delays Decision on Fate of SIF' (1999) 143 SJ 76; 'Indemnity Decision Set for March', LSG (27.1.99) 4; 'All Options Open...' (1999) 149 NLJ 14; 'SIF Complaint', LSG (3.2.99) 4.

[82] 'Council to Vote on Indemnity Future', LSG (24.2.99) 1; 'Keating Proposes Amendment for SGM' (1999) 149 NLJ 278; 'Council to Vote on Range of Options' (1999) 143 SJ 175; Martin Mears, 'The Solicitor's Indemnity Fund: a Monopolist's Last Stand?' (1999) 149 NLJ 313.

[83] 'Council Votes to Keep Mutual Fund', LSG (3.3.89) 1; 'SIF is Safe—or is it?' (1999) 149 NLJ 326; 'SIF—You Decide' (1999) 143 SJ 199; 'Free Market versus Collectivism' LSG (3.3.89) 3.

[84] 'Editorial: Certainty above All', LSG (3.3.99) 14; 'Editorial: The Return of the SIF' (1999) 149 NLJ 361; 'City Takes SIF Review', LSG (24.3.99) 4; 'November Group Joins Forces with Dalton' (1999) 143 SJ 285; 'Post Ballot Freedom of Choice', LSG (14.4.99) 17 (advert); 'BLA has Woolf Doubts and Says No to SIF' (1999) 149 NLJ 550; 'November Group may fund Dalton' (1999) 143 SJ 355; 'November Group Counting on Ballot Success' (1999) 143 SJ 403.

[85] LSG (8.4.99) 16; 'Letters to the Editor: The Ultimate Sanction', LSG (21.4.99) 16; 'War of Words over Postal Vote' (1999) 143 SJ 380.

[86] 'Solicitors Turn Their Backs on SIF' (1999) 143 SJ 451; 'Comment: Indemnity: Searching for a Solution' (1999) 143 SJ 455; Martin Mears, 'Lawspeak...' (1999) 149 NLJ 726; 'SIF Vote Faces Reversal', LSG (19.5.99) 5; 'Council Changes Tack on Indemnity', LSG (3.6.99) 1; 'Editorial: Here we Go Again...' (1999) 149 NLJ 845; 'Solicitors reach Indemnity D-day', LSG (23.6.99) 1.

[87] 'Council Seals Future of Indemnity—but no Change until late 2000', LSG (30.6.99) 3; 'Solicitors win Freedom of Choice' (1999) 143 SJ 627; Michael Mathews, 'Opinion: Indemnity—the Way Forward for Small Firms' (1999) 143 SJ 630; 'High Court Stays Key Indemnity Case', LSG (7.7.99) 1; 'Indemnity' (1999) 143 SJ 651; 'Indemnity Cash Alert over Y2K and Woolf', LSG (21.7.99) 1; 'Big Firms, Big Deductibles', LSG (21.7.99) 4; 'A Week in the Law...' (1999) 149 NLJ 1103; 'Dalton Seeks Waiver', LSG (25.8.99) 4; 'Law Firm Lobby Disbands and Dalton Case Ends, but SIF Concerns Remain', LSG (20.10.99) 5.

[88] 'Justice Calls for Appeals Watchdog', L (11.7.89); Justice (1989); 'Ex-Law Officer takes Bar row to High Court', DT (7.11.89) 2; 'Former Solicitor General claims QC was dishonest', I (7.11.89); 'Chambers divided in dispute over money' T (7.11.89); 'Crackdown on pompous QCs', ST (12.12.93); McConville *et al.* (1994).

[89] 'Complaints against Bar look set to rise by 40%', L (8.10.91); 'Complaints up by 66%' LSG (4.11.92) 6; 'Complaints against lawyers increase' I (24.3.92); 'More clients put barristers in the dock', T (30.3.92); 'Bar urged to make payouts for negligence', T (6.4.92); 'Time to give the Bar a wigging?' G (27.7.93) 17.

[90] 'Lawyers face bill for shoddy service under Bar reforms', T (14.3.94); Roger Smith, 'All in the line of duty', I (23.3.94); 'A time to adapt or die', T (5.4.94); 'Barristers face £2,000 penalty for shoddy work', T (5.4.94); 'Bar Reforms Urged', LSG (13.4.94) 6; 'Comment: Special Pleading for the Bar' (1994) 138 SJ 359; 'Barristers set to face compensation claims over shoddy work', I (13.9.94); 'Inept barristers "must pay" ', G (13.9.94); Robert Alexander QC, 'Advocating excellence', T (13.9.94); 'Barristers face bill for poor work', DT (13.9.94); 'Barristers to compensate clients for shoddy work', T (13.9.94); 'Report Urges Bar Changes', LSG (14.9.94) 3; 'Advocating more quality and work', L (27.9.94); 'CLSA set to launch barristers' charter', L (27.9.94); 'Chambers to be chartered', LSG (28.9.94) 10; 'A Blueprint for the Bar', C (9–10.94) 15–16; Bar Standards Review Body (1994).

[91] 'Bar Moots Complaints Plan', LSG (1.6.95) 5; Peter Goldsmith QC, 'Chairman's Column: Having Your Say', C (7–8.95) 3; 'Bar Offers Haven from Harassment', LSG (27.9.95) 6; Ronald Thwaites QC, 'Pulling Our Teeth', C (9–10.95) 18; Robert Owen QC, 'No Terrors for the Careful, Courteous and Competent', C (9–10.95) 19; 'Bar Shift on Complaints Plan', LSG (15.11.95) 3; 'Lobbying by Bar Associations Hails New Complaints Scheme' (1995) 139 SJ 1140; 'Self Regulation for Bar' (1995) 145 NLJ 1679; ' "No" they Say' (1995) 145 NLJ

1714; 'Bar Complaints System Voted Out' (1995) 139 SJ 1169; Peter Goldsmith QC, 'Chairman's Column: If the Bar Is Special, Why a Complaints System?' C (11–12.95) 3; 'Bar backs complaint scheme in close vote', T (16.1.96) 9; LSG (17.1.96) 56; 'Battling for the Bar', LSG (31.1.96) 11; 'Inns and Outs', T (28.1.97) 41.

[92] 'Editorial: A Synonym for Excellence', (1995) 145 NLJ 1677; T (26.1.96) quoted in 'Parallel Bars', C (3–4.96) 12, 14; 'Barristers Complaints', C (7–8.96) 4; 'Editorial: Closed Hearings for the Bar' (1997) 147 NLJ 517.

[93] 'A Barristers' Defence Association', C (11–12.96) 12; 'Barristers' Defence Association?' (1996) 146 NLJ 1770; 'Fighting the Cynics', T (21.1.97) 37; 'Robert Owen QC' (1997) 141 SJ 192; 'CPS Underfunding and Barristers Complaints', C (7–8.97) 4; General Council of the Bar, Annual Report (1997).

[94] 'Group Urges "End to Lawyer Immunity"', LSG (25.10.95) 6; Richards (1995); 'Untouchable', G2 (27.4.99) 16; 'Press Round-Up', LSG (23.6.99) 12.

[95] 'Complaints against barristers rise', T (16.5.98) 20; 'Bar Complaints Rise by over 25%', LSG (20.5.98) 4; 'Meet Mr Complaints', T (19.5.98) 39; 'Surge in Bar Complaints', (1998) 142 SJ 460; 'Why do barristers fear this man?' I (Fri Rev) (26.6.98) 19; Complaints Commissioner (1998).

[96] Ann Abraham, 'Ethical lawyering: public expectation', LA (8.98) 8.

[97] Dan Brennan QC, 'Opinion: Firm, Fast and Fair' (1999) 143 SJ 406; LSO (1999: 2, 21); Ann Abraham, 'Setting Standards', C (10.99) 22–23; BN (12.99) 7.

[98] These remain the principal complaints. Craig *et al.* (2001).

[99] Clients file more than 27 times as many complaints per solicitor as patients do per doctor: Sherr and Webley (1997: 126).

[100] The SDT heard more than five times as many serious complaints against solicitors as the GMC did against doctors: Sherr and Webley (1997: 126).

[101] Cf. Carlin (1966) (finding this in New York City).

[102] On market failure and the proliferation of external regulation see R Baldwin (1997).

[103] Royal Commission (1979: ii, para. 8.210); Jenkins *et al.* (1989: 10–13) (the first RPPU publication); Jenkins and Lewis (1995b).

[104] 'Thousands of Firms Win FSA Exemption', LSG (1.7.98) 1; 'Mainstream Money', LSG (3.11.99) 34.

[105] Woolf (1996); 'Woolf weighs heavy on scales of justice', ES (22.4.99) 44; 'Lawyers pay for delaying tactics' T (26.4.99) 12; 'The revolution in litigation starts here', T (27.4.99) 39; 'I'll see you out of court', I (Tues Rev) (27.4.99) 14.

[106] 'Judges may be able to fine slow lawyers', T (9.9.99) 8; 'Solicitors Place Blame for Court Delays on "Chaotic" Timetables', LSG (15.9.99) 3; 'Press Round-Up', LSG (15.9.99) 10; 'Solicitors Face Fines in Crown Court Shake-Up' (1999) 143 SJ 847; 'Judiciary attacks change in course', T (15.10.99) 11; '£85 m is wasted in court', T (1.12.99) 2; 'Criminal Law Solicitors Face Sanctions and Monitoring Call', LSG (1.12.99) 3.

Chapter 10—Notes

[1] Royal Commission (1979: i, paras. 29.1–47 and RR29.1–6); Abel (1988: 241–8). For a brief history of the Law Society see Sugarman (1995; 1996).

[2] 'Local Law Societies: Grassroots Indifference', LSG (30.1.91) 10; 'Comment: Succeeding in the Nineties' (1991) 135 SJ 399; 'Comment: Law Society' (1991) 135 SJ 643; 'The Law Society Abroad' (1991) 141 NLJ 805; 'Profligacy and PR Disasters' (1991) 141 NLJ 881: '£2.9 m Shortfall Forces Cuts and Job Losses' (1991) 135 SJ 1123; 'Comment: Law Society Redundancies' (1991) 135 SJ 1127; 'Society's Promotions must Pay their Way', LSG (27.11.91) 7; 'Law Society's Council Slams Executive "Mismanagement"' (1991) 135 SJ 1231; 'Balancing the Books' (1992) 142 NLJ 113; 'Deficit cleared', LA (3.92) 6.

[3] 'Still not Enough Women in the Professions' (1990) 134 SJ 764; 'Editorial: Discriminating judgments', LA (9.91) 3; 'Comment: Reviewing the Law Society' (1992) 136 SJ 231; 'Law Society Takes Slow Boat to Reform' (1992) 136 SJ 256; 'Editorial: The Law Society's other deficit', LA (4.92) 3; 'Crisis for the Council?' LSG (9.6.93) 2.

[4] Gerry Chambers, 'What do you Think of the Law Society', LSG (24.6.92) 24; 'Comment: A Healthy Society?' (1992) 136 SJ 695.

[5] 'AGM will Hear Plea for Sole Practitioners Group', LSG (1.7.92) 5; 'Sole Practitioners to Apply for Group Status', LSG (15.7.92) 6; 'Law Society's Annual General Meeting' (1992) 142 NLJ 994; 'Law Society Gives Ground on One-man Bands' (1992) 136 SJ 691; 'Sole Practitioners Edge Towards Group Status', LSG (22.7.92) 4; 'Law Society Help for Sole Practitioners Group' (1992) 142 NLJ 1115; 'Sole Practitioners Group to Meet' (1993) 143 NLJ 79; 'Sole Practitioners Out in Force want LS Recognition' (1993) 143 NLJ 155; 'Society Seal for Solos', LSG (19.5.93) 7; 'Comment: Law Society Annual Report' (1993) 137 SJ 603; 'Law Society, Annual General Meeting', LSG (21.7.93) 11, 13–14; 'Comment: Small Firms' (1994) 138 SJ 167; 'Employed Sector Hits the Buffers', LSG (30.3.94) 6; 'Employed Solicitors Criticise LawSoc' (1994) 138 SJ 276; 'Help for the High Street Practice' (1994) 144 NLJ 781; 'Editorial: Champion Suggestions' (1994) 144 NLJ 781; 'High Street Plan gets Green Light', LSG (15.6.94) 10; D Lyn Devonald, 'An Endangered Species?' LSG (29.6.94) 2; Henry Hodge, 'Supporting the High Street', LSG (21.9.94) 2; 'Bid to Reach Out to Practitioners', LSG (21.9.94) 3; 'Henry Hodge becomes the Champion' (1994) 144 NLJ 1267; Woolfson *et al.* (1994).

[6] David Thomas and Paul Pharaoh, 'Crisis for the Council?' LSG (9.6.93) 2; 'Officers Rewarded', LSG (16.3.94) 6; 'Editorial: Paying the Piper to Call the Tune' (1994) 144 NLJ 381; 'Salaries for Law Society Officers' (1994) 144 NLJ 382; '£90,000 Salary Proposed for LawSoc President' (1994) 138 SJ 351; 'Group Attack on Office-Holders' Pay', LSG (23.3.94) 9; 'Comment: Fair Recompense' (1994) 138 SJ 279; 'Members in Pay Vote', LSG (15.6.94) 8; 'SGM Approves Officer Payments', LSG (20.7.94) 6; 'Pay Dispute', LSG (31.8.94) 3; 'Editorial: Seeing is Believing' (1994) 144 NLJ 1685; 'Pay Slashed', LSG (16.12.94) 3; 'President's Stipend Halved' (1994) 144 NLJ 1759.

[7] 'Acrimonious Split Hits SPG Elections', (1994) 138 SJ 647; 'Acrimonious Split Continues within SPG' (1994) 138 SJ 705; 'Comment: United we Stand' (1994) 138

SJ 707; 'Editorial: Professional Problems' (1994) 144 NLJ 961; 'Rosen Wins SPG Election', (1994) 138 SJ 728; 'SPG's Rosen and Turl attack Council member Angela Deacon' (1994) 144 NLJ 999; 'Further Shelling in the SPG War' (1995) 145 NLJ 679; 'Confidentiality?' (1995) 145 NLJ 714; 'Auditor "Muzzled"—Motion "Muffled"' (1995) 145 NLJ 842.

[8] 'Law Society scolded by auditors', LA (7.94) 4; 'Society Suffers Embarrassing Defeat' (1994) 138 SJ 729; 'New Boy Blues', LSG (14.9.94) 11; Robert Sayer, 'The Law Society: The Right Balance?' (1994) 138 SJ 869; 'Comment: Critical Response' (1994) 138 SJ 951; 'Lawyer Calls for Inquiry into Law Society Expenditure' (1994) 138 SJ 1003; 'Nightmare on the High Street' (1994) 138 SJ 1008; 'Fur Flies Over Audit Report', LSG (12.10.94) 6; 'Nay Sayer', LSG (19.10.94) 10; 'Mears Expenditure Inquiry Blocked by Council' (1994) 138 SJ 1031; 'Editorial: Controlling Finances' (1994) 144 NLJ 1397; Law Society (1994b); Martin Mears, 'Editorial', Cat (3.97) 1.

[9] 'Thumbs up for Softly, Softly President', LSG (12.10.94) 10; 'Law Society Conference' (1994) 138 SJ 1032; 'Comment: Concerning Cost' (1994) 138 SJ 1037; 'Society Rethinks Conference Style', LSG (19.10.94) 7; 'Group Bids to Trump Society', LSG (9.11.94) 5; 'Row over Quality', LSG (7.6.95) 64; 'Property Lawyers "Disturbed" at Law Society Actions' (1995) 139 SJ 539; 'Comment: Flying a Kitemark' (1995) 139 SJ 543; 'SPG Flies Off over Kitemark' (1995) 139 SJ 573; 'Group Fury', LSG (21.6.95) 2; 'Kitemark Concern', LSG (28.6.95) 5; 'Conveyancing Club', LSG (5.7.95) 2.

[10] 'Society Leaders Face the Music', LSG (30.11.94) 4; '"Time" Test-Run', LSG (30.11.94) 4; 'Exeter puts Society through its Paces', LSG (18.1.95) 4.

[11] 'Council Members Call Surprise Vote', LSG (29.3.95) 1; 'Challenge Vote Shocks Old Guard', LSG (29.3.95) 3; Martin Mears, 'Comment: Tumbrill time in Chancery Lane' (1995) 145 NLJ 444; 'Profile: A Hitch in the Seamless Progression' (1995) 145 NLJ 462; 'Comment: The Race is On' (1995) 139 SJ 311; 'Harassment Claims at Society HQ', LSG (12.4.95) 1; Martin Mears, 'Comment: Bigotry, Cant and Humbug' (1995) 145 NLJ 624.

[12] 'Shaking the Totem Pole', LSG (5.4.95) 8; 'Comment: Health Contest' (1995) 139 SJ 365; 'Editorial: Don't Even Try' (1995) 145 NLJ 677; 'Harassment Claims at Society HQ', LSG (12.4.95) 1; 'Outspoken Voice Strives for Top Job', LSG (12.4.95) 4; 'Sexual Harassment a Major Problem, Conference Told' (1995) 139 SJ 334; 'Comment: Sexual Harassment' (1995) 139 SJ 335; Eileen Pembridge, 'Comment: Standing up for the Profession' (1995) 145 NLJ 516; 'Law Society "Seen as Expensive Irrelevance"' (1995) 139 SJ 465.

[13] 'Women Speak Against Council Seat for AWS' (1995) 139 SJ 256; 'Editorial: The Vice-President Withdraws' (1995) 145 NLJ 513; 'Martin Mears to Fight On' (1995) 145 NLJ 515; 'It's Still Not Women's Work', LSG (17.5.95) 8; 'Editorial: Lining up at the Starting Gate' (1995) 145 NLJ 549; 'Statement by Eileen Pembridge' (1995) 145 NLJ 550; 'Candidates Manifestoes' (1995) 139 SJ 362–3; 'Young Letter Apologises for Publicity', LSG (26.4.95) 3; 'Vetting Plan', LSG (26.4.95) 3; Charles Elly, 'President's Column: The Election Procedure', LSG (26.4.95) 10; 'The Exchange of Letters between Vice-President John Young and President Charles Elly', LSG (26.4.95) 14; 'Law Society Election Hots Up' (1995) 139 SJ 383; 'Aucott to Challenge Sayer for Vice-Presidency' (1995) 145 NLJ 586; 'Sex

Claims Trigger Procedure Review', LSG (3.5.95) 2; 'Council Names its Top Three', LSG (3.5.95) 4; 'Ringing in the Changes', LSG (3.5.95) 14; 'Fighting Modern Battle', LSG (3.5.95) 14; Martin Mears, 'Comment: Bigotry, Cant and Humbug' (1995) 145 NLJ 624; 'Elly Promises Procedures Review' (1995) 139 SJ 410 'Editorial: Droit de Senior Partner' (1995) 145 NLJ 621; 'Sayer Sends Out Campaign Letter' (1995) 139 SJ 436; 'Candidates Recommend Client Levy', LSG (17.5.95) 4; 'Disgrace' (1995) 145 NLJ 843; Eileen Pembridge, 'If I ruled the Law Society' (1995) 139 SJ 5; John Aucott, 'Face the Future, Not the Past' (1995) 145 NLJ 810; 'Mears Tables AGM Votes', LSG (7.6.95) 3; Tony Holland: 'Opinion: On Demand' (1995) 139 SJ 574.

[14] 'Mears Hits Bureau in Campaign Shot', LSG (11.5.95) 1; Henry Hodge, 'A Positive Agenda' (1995) 145 NLJ 680; 'Policing takes Centre Stage', LSG (17.5.95) 1; 'Election Heats Up', LSG (24.5.95) 2; 'Campaigning Starts in Earnest— Well, Nearly' (1995) 145 NLJ 750; 'Presidential Candidates On Same Platform' (1995) 139 SJ 487.

[15] 'Mears Attacks Meetings Plan', LSG (1.6.95) 2; 'Council Duo Bash Right Wing Agenda', LSG (7.6.95) 3; 'Larger Role for Local Law Societies', LSG (14.6.95) 2; 'Referenda', LSG (14.6.95) 6; Henry Hodge, 'Looking to the Future', LSG (14.6.95) 18; Martin Mears, 'Electoral Pledges', LSG (14.6.95) 19; Eileen Pembridge, 'The Pembridge Plan', LSG (14.6.95) 20; Robert Sayer Manifesto, LSG (14.6.95) 22; John Aucott Election Statement, LSG (14.6.95) 22; 'More Fisticuffs at the Hustings' (1995) 145 NLJ 879; Henry Hodge, 'If I Ruled the Law Society' (1995) 139 SJ 577; 'Notables declare for Hodge', LSG (21.6.95) 2.

[16] 'Block Vote Allegations Hit Society's Presidential Poll', LSG (28.6.95) 3; 'Elections: Council Accused of Being Anti-democratic' (1995) 139 SJ 619; 'Editorial: Wake up Chancery Lane' (1995) 145 NLJ 949; 'Law Society Candidates Denounce Election Irregularities' (1995) 145 NLJ 950; 'Comment: With Friends Like These...' (1995) 139 SJ 623; 'Up for the Count' (1995) 139 SJ 644; 'Candidates Claim Final Hour Support', LSG (5.7.95) 1.

[17] 'The Closing Speeches' (1995) 145 NLJ 967; 'Candidates Face Race Debate', LSG (5.7.95) 3.

[18] 'Challenge for Surrey Seat' (1995) 139 SJ 408; 'Mears Victory', LSG (13.7.95) 1; 'Council in Careful Post-Ballot Mood', LSG (13.7.95) 2; 'Bogan Bags Surrey Seat on Council', LSG (13.7.95) 2; 'BLA Appeal', LSG (13.7.95) 2; 'Gloves Back On as Mears Picks Up Gauntlet' (1995) 139 SJ 667; 'Editorial: The Barbarians Enter the Gates' (1995) 145 NLJ 1021; 'Mears and Sayer Sweep to Power' (1995) 145 NLJ 1022; 'Early 'Comment: Time to Listen' (1995) 139 SJ 671; 'Opposition to Mears on Election Mandate' (1995) 139 SJ 699.

[19] 'Mears asks to be Judged on his Record', LSG (19.7.95) 6; 'Elly warns Mears not to Dash Hopes of Profession' (1995) 139 SJ 700; 'Comment: Raising Standards' (1995) 139 SJ 703; 'First (Wrong) Footing' (1995) 145 NLJ 1082; Arun Arora, 'The President's New Clothes' (1995) 145 NLJ 1104; Martin Mears, 'Comment: A Fully-Clothed President' (1995) 145 NLJ 1153.

[20] Tony Holland, 'Personal View: Je ne Regrette Rien' (1995) 139 SJ 730; Martin Mears, 'Letters: After the Election' (1995) 139 SJ 758; Tony Holland, 'Opinion: Realism, not Rhetoric' (1995) 139 SJ 1144.

[21] Martin Mears, 'President's Column: Down to Work', LSG (31.8.95) 10.

[22] 'Mears Aims to Rein in the Bureaucrats', LSG (13.9.95) 2; 'Mears Proposes Radical Change at Society' (1995) 139 SJ 887; 'Comment: Too Many Cooks' (1995) 139 SJ 891; 'Editorial: High Eleven O'clock' (1995) 145 NLJ 1321; 'Severance Packages', LSG (25.10.95) 5; 'Hayes to Go', LSG (29.11.95) 1; 'Moderniser Moves Forward', LSG (29.11.95) 4; Arnold Rosen, 'Comment: The Law Society on the Ropes' (1996) 146 NLJ 168.

[23] I (20.9.95) §2, 13; 'Editorial: A Positive Sign', LSG (27.9.95) 14; 'Society Reform Up for Discussion', LSG (25.10.95) 5; Martin Bowley QC, 'What's wrong with the Bar?' I (22.11.95) §1, 12; Martin Mears, 'Comment: New Bottles—Same Wine?' (1996) 146 NLJ 43.

[24] 'Law Society Council Meeting' (1995) 145 NLJ 1394; 'Mears Challenges Council on Reform', LSG (11.10.95) 2; Martin Mears, 'Profession "in Extremis"', LSG (11.10.95) 12; 'Mears Warns Profession, "Don't Murmur and then Do Nothing"' (1995) 139 SJ 1000; 'Comment: All Change' (1995) 139 SJ 1004; 'Mears in Direct Appeal to Council', LSG (25.10.95) 2; 'Editorial: The Second Mrs De Winter' (1995) 145 NLJ 1601; 'Council Faces Vote on Recording Debate', LSG (8.11.95) 4; 'Push for Democracy', LSG (22.11.95) 56; 'Sayer Proposes Council Reforms' (1995) 145 NLJ 1714; 'Editorial: Council Voting' (1995) 145 NLJ 1713; 'Council Approves Registered Voting', LSG (14.12.95) 4; 'Conveyancing Compromise for Consultation' (1995) 145 NLJ 1878.

[25] 'Aiming at Council', LSG (18.10.95) 8; 'Four Stand in West Country Election', LSG (1.11.95) 4; 'Edge Support', LSG (8.11.95) 4; 'Campaign Call', LSG (15.11.95) 4; 'Davies Wins Council Seat', LSG (6.12.95) 4.

[26] Robert Sayer, 'A Reform Party for the Profession' (1995) 145 NLJ 1442; 'Editorial: The Sword in the Stomach' (1995) 145 NLJ 1437; 'Mears Rallies Like Minds to Push His Reform Package', LSG (29.11.95) 4; Martin Mears, 'Creating the Machinery' (1995) 145 NLJ 1715; 'Editorial: Detente Time', LSG (15.12.95) 14; Trevor Aldridge QC, 'Opinion: On the Threshold' (1996) 140 SJ 6.

[27] 'Sayer accuses Society of Standing in Way of Reforms', (1996) 140 SJ 59; 'Comment: Anyone for £100k?' (1996) 140 SJ 63; Richard Hegarty, 'Letter to the Editor: Conveyancing Consultation' (1996) 140 SJ 90; 'Comment: Opening Up' (1996) 140 SJ 115.

[28] 'Mears warns Profession, "Don't Murmur and then Do Nothing"', (1995) 139 SJ 1000; 'Council Stays Cool over Mears Story', LSG (24.1.96) 2; 'Society Row Rages', LSG (31.1.96) 2; 'Libel Row Fuels Society Rift' (1996) 140 SJ 88; ' Mears v (Most of) the Rest' (1996) 146 NLJ 114; 'Editorial: Into the Trenches' (1996) 146 NLJ 113; 'Top Official Bails Out', LSG (13.3.96) 48; 'Law Society Loses Another Top Official' (1996) 140 SJ 344; 'Comment: Challenging Advice' (1996) 140 SJ 347; 'PR Supremo Quits Society', LSG (17.4.96) 6.

[29] 'Having a Party at Chancery Lane', LSG (14.2.96) 10; Peter Watson-Lee, 'Comment: Agenda for Change', LSG (17.4.96) 13.

[30] 'Row Hits Headlines', LSG (21.2.96) 3; Tony Holland, 'Comment: Calling a Ceasefire' (1996) 146 NLJ 242; Martin Mears, 'Comment: The Old Man of the West' (1996) 146 NLJ 243.

[31] '"No More Junkets", Says New Vice President' (1995) 139 SJ 727; 'Mears Sets Out his Stall', LSG (28.2.96) 1; Martin Mears, 'President's Column: Ghostbusting

Time at Chancery Lane', LSG (28.2.96) 18; 'Robert Sayer' (1996) 140 SJ 212; 'Keating Launches Bid for Top Office', LSG (20.3.96) 2.

[32] 'Path Clear for Election', LSG (27.3.96) 1; 'General Election Plan Postponed', LSG (17.4.96) 2.

[33] 'Comment: Divided we Stand' (1996) 140 SJ 221; Geoffrey R Thomas, 'Letters to the Editor: Divided we Stand' (1996) 140 SJ 248.

[34] 'Society Reform Gains Support' (1996) 140 SJ 269; 'Group Urges Split of Society's Roles', LSG (3.4.96) 2; 'New Association Formed to Split Up Law Society', (1996) 140 SJ 319; Anthony Bogan, 'Division Lobby', LSG (17.4.96) 21; 'The Times They are A-changing!' (1996) 146 NLJ 620; Anthony Bogan, 'Letters: Division of Roles Call', LSG (1.5.96) 16.

[35] 'Recruitment Drive', LSG (9.5.96) 5; '600 Rally to Group', LSG (30.5.96) 6.

[36] John Hayes, 'A United Stand', LSG (17.4.96) 20; 'Constitution of a New Solicitors Association may be Unlawful' (1996) 140 SJ 395; 'Comment: Cost of Separation' (1996) 140 SJ 399; 'Probate Pilot', LSG (9.5.96) 10; 'Mears, Girling, Bogan—Who is Soliciting Whom?' (1996) 140 SJ 599; 'Probate Practitioners Urged to Fight Back', LSG (10.7.96) 6.

[37] Martin Mears, 'President's Column: The Sum is Greater . . .', LSG (24.4.96) 13; Anthony Bogan, 'Letters: Division of Roles Call', LSG (1.5.96) 16.

[38] 'Trouble at t'Law Society Again' (196) 146 NLJ 362; Martin Mears, 'President's Column: Try, Try, Try Again', LSG (27.3.96) 17; 'Comment: The Next Election' (1996) 140 SJ 299; 'Editorial: Who will rid us of these turbulent men?' LA (3.96) 3; 'Surrey Call for Debate', LSG (3.4.96) 2; 'Local Law Societies Anxious over Chancery Lane Politics', LSG (9.5.96) 5; Andrew Lockley, 'Dear Jane' (1996) 140 SJ 519.

[39] 'Pembridge Hints at Vote Challenge', LSG (24.4.96) 2; 'Comment: Discrimination' (1996) 140 SJ 399; 'Equality Issues Strain Relations between Law Society and Bar' (1996) 146 NLJ 582; 'Editorial: Fearless in Foolishness' (1996) 146 NLJ 581; 'Mears Award', LSG (1.5.96) 2; Roger Smith, 'It's the Economy, Stupid' (1996) 146 NLJ 654; 'Ensuring Equality' LSG (9.5.96) 14.

[40] ' "Get Big" to Survive, Legal Aid Firms Told', LSG (1.5.96) 3; 'Mears Defends his Record on Legal Aid', LSG (1.5.96) 2; Martin Mears, 'The Three Musketeers (D'Artagnan)' (1996) 146 NLJ 673.

[41] 'Solicitors launch anti-Mears group', T (10.5.96) 2; 'Comment: Brand New Leaders?' (1996) 140 SJ 447; 'Editorial: The Chancery Lane Challenge', LSG (15.5.96) 15; 'Campaign to Oust Mears' (1996) 140 SJ 443; 'Poll Fever Builds', LSG (15.5.96) 1; Peter Watson-Lee, 'Law Society Presidential Elections' (1996) 140 SJ 471; Robert Sayer, 'Law Society Presidential Elections' (1996) 140 SJ 471; Peter Hughes, 'Opinion' (1996) 140 SJ 472; 'Squaring up for Battle', LSG (22.5.96) 14; 'Election Slate Taking Shape', LSG (22.5.96) 6.

[42] Martin Mears, 'President's Column: Deep Throats and Soundbites', LSG (22.5.96) 18; Martin Mears, 'Opinion: Resurrection of the Sound Men' (1996) 140 SJ 522.

[43] 'Fifth Quits Society', LSG (22.5.96) 8; 'Editorial: A Call to Opposition in Chancery Lane' (1996) 146 NLJ 741; 'Comment: The Law Society—Again' (1996) 140 SJ 499; 'Pannone Joins Campaign for New Leadership' (1996) 140 SJ 495; 'Society Vote Appears Certain', LSG (30.5.96) 6; 'Leaving Thoughts', LSG (30.5.96) 13; 'Comment: Partner Liability' (1996) 140 SJ 523; 'Hayes Joins in Criticism of Mears'

(1996) 140 SJ 519; Martin Mears, 'Opinion: Resurrection of the Sound Men' (1996) 140 SJ 522; 'Mears Backtracks on Meeting' (1996) 146 NLJ 778; Martin Mears, 'Comment: Open Letter to Rodger Pannone' (1996) 146 NLJ 780; 'David McIntosh to Stand for Law Society Council' (1996) 140 SJ 549.

[44] 'Election fight is On', LSG (5.6.96) 1; 'Challenge to Mears Launched' (1996) 146 NLJ 834; 'Election Set to Become a Personality Battle' (1996) 140 SJ 547; 'Mears Team Fires Opening Shots as Election Battle Lines are Drawn', LSG (12.6.96) 8; 'Mears's Team Release Manifesto' (1996) 146 NLJ 906; (1996) 146 NLJ 907.

[45] 'Comment: Healthy Competition' (1996) 140 SJ 551; 'Society Split "Bizarre", says QC', LSG (12.6.96) 8.

[46] LSG (12.6.96) 23.; Letter To All Solicitors from Martin Mears, Robert Sayer and David Keating (6.96); 'A Business Plan for the Society' (1996) 146 NLJ 906; 'A Modern Moderate', LSG (26.6.96) 13; Tony Girling, Phillip Sycamore, Michael Mathews, 'On the Stump', LSG (26.6.96) 16; Martin Mears, Robert Sayer, David Keating, 'On the Stump', LSG (26.6.96) 17; 'Mears Admits Mistakes as Election Campaign Reaches Final Stages', LSG (3.7.96) 6; Phillip Sycamore, 'Final Pitch', LSG (3.7.96) 13.

[47] 'Presidential Election Update: Week Two' (1996) 140 SJ 572; 'Girling Alleges Pre-Election Deal', LSG (19.6.96) 5; 'Gloves are Off in Mears/Girling Fight' (1996) 146 NLJ 906.

[48] 'The Third Man', LSG (19.6.96) 13; 'Mears, Girling, Bogan—Who is Soliciting Whom?' (1996) 140 SJ 599; Anthony Bogan, 'On the Stump', LSG (26.6.96) 16.

[49] 'Battling All the Way' LSG (3.7.96) 12; Robert Sayer, 'Final Pitch', LSG (3.7.96) 13.

[50] Two years later Girling admitted: 'actually, no, I didn't want him obviously. He was on my policy committee because that's what our constitution says. But obviously he saw his role as a defeated president as being someone who was going to find out as much as he could about ideas when they were in the very early stages and then rubbish them' (interview July 1998).

[51] 'Editorial: Silver Feet' (1996) 146 NLJ 905; 'Rebuke for Law Society Treasurer' (1996) 146 NLJ 907; 'Triumph for Girling Team', LSG (17.7.96) 1; T (23.7.96) 33; 'Broad Welcome for New Leaders', LSG (17.7.96) 10; 'Editorial: New Beginnings', LSG (17.7.96) 14; 'Profession Looks Forward to a New Start' (1996) 140 SJ 703' 'Comment: Solicitors want Results' (1996) 140 SJ 707; 'Girling takes out Mears' (1996) 146 NLJ 1050; 'Editorial: Hope for the Future' (1996) 146 NLJ 1049; 'Howells Resigns as Papers are Leaked' (1996) 146 NLJ 1086; 'Editorial: A Necessary Inquiry' (1996) 146 NLJ 1085; 'Split Functions to Go to Ballot' (1996) 146 NLJ 1086; 'Comment: Local Law Societies' (1996) 140 SJ 783.

[52] Tony Girling, 'President's Column: Serving the Whole Profession', LSG (24.7.96) 14; 'Society Officials face Criticism over Commonwealth Conference', LSG (25.9.96) 5; Tony Girling, 'President's Column: Forward Motion', LSG (25.9.96) 18; 'Chancery Lane Budget Top Up', LSG (23.10.96) 5; 'Chancery Lane Rumbles', LSG (30.10.96) 6; 'Mears & Sayer on the Attack' (1996) 146 NLJ 1571; 'Inns and Outs', T (5.11.96) 41; Tony Girling, 'President's Column: Highs and Lows in Office', LSG (27.11.96) 17; Martin Mears, 'Trips for the Chaps', Cat (12.96) 10.

[53] Law Society, Letter to Members (19.6.96); 'Votes for All' (1996) 146 NLJ 1266; 'Editorial: A Split Society?' (1996) 146 NLJ 1305; 'Girling Warns Schism could

Trigger Exodus', LSG (18.9.96) 1; 'A Question of Roles', LSG (18.9.96) 18; Anthony Bogan and David Thomas, 'Time to Split the Law Society?' (1996) 140 SJ 912; 'Editorial: One Conference, one Voice' (1996) 146 NLJ 1449; 'Voters Reject Split Society', LSG (16.10.96) 1; 'Split of Function Debate to Continue Despite Ballot Defeat' (1996) 140 SJ 988.

[54] Cat (12.96); Martin Mears, 'Foul Slurs', Cat (3.97) 3.

[55] 'Practising Certificate Crisis' (1996) 140 SJ 87; 'Damning Verdict on Regis Managers', LSG (27.11.96) 1; 'In Council', LSG (13.12.96) 5; 'Tails Wag Dog at Council Meeting' (1996) 146 NLJ 1842; 'REGIS Errors Lead to Management Review' (1996) 140 SJ 1212; 'Editorial: Finance and the Law Society' (1997) 147 NLJ 41; Robert Sayer, 'Comment: Is the Society Going into the Red?' (1997) 147 NLJ 44; 'Betts Tests Policies at the Grassroots', LSG (5.2.97) 1; Robert Sayer, 'Comment: Non-starters at Chancery Lane' (1997) 147 NLJ 156; 'Deputy Treasurer Poll', LSG (19.2.97) 4; 'Sayer for Treasurer—At Least' (1997) 147 NLJ 283; 'HSSK Killed Off' (1997) 147 SJ 196; 'The HSSK Wagon' (1997) 147 NLJ 37; 'Law Soc Staff Face Disciplinary Action' (1997) 141 SJ 99; 'Tribunal Threat for Ex-Managers', LSG (19.2.97) 5; 'Ross to Handle Board Complaint' (1997) 147 NLJ 247.

[56] 'Mears Launches Newsletter in Bid to Create "Healthy Debate"' (1997) 141 SJ 51; Martin Mears, 'Another fine mess for the Law Society', T (18.2.97); 'Sayer Launches Early Bid for Presidency', LSG (19.2.97) 1; 'Mears' Last Stand' (1997) 141 SJ 147; 'Sayer for President?' (1997) 147 NLJ 246; 'Spending Queried', LSG (26.2.97) 4; 'Mears and Sayer Consider the Future', (1997) 141 SJ 172; Robert Sayer, 'Letters to the Editor: Future of the Profession' (1997) 141 SJ 174; 'Changing Partners at Law Society' (1997) 147 NLJ 282.

[57] Cat (3.97).

[58] Tony Girling, 'President's Column: Getting Back', LSG (19.3.97) 18; Martin Mears, 'Chancery Lane', LSG (3.4.97) 22.

[59] Phillip Sycamore, 'The profession must speak with one voice', T (4.3.97) 39; 'Sayer Ponders Sycamore's Olive Branch', LSG (5.3.97) 1; 'Olive Branch Extended to Sayer' (1997) 141 SJ 195; 'An Offer he can't Refuse?' (1997) 147 NLJ 334; 'Robert Sayer Wants more Details' (1997) 147 NLJ 335; 'Mears and Sayer Set for Head to Head' (1997) 141 SJ 223; 'Divide and Rule' (1997) 147 NLJ 370; Phillip Sycamore and Michael Mathews, 'Progress not Politics', LSG (19.3.97) 24.

[60] 'Mears and Sayer at Odds Again' (1997) 147 NLJ 442.

[61] 'Mears Throws down Election Gauntlet', LSG (12.3.97) 1; Robert Sayer, 'Let's Get this Sorted Now', LSG (12.3.97) 18; 'Sayer Lines Up with Sycamore and Mathews', LSG (9.4.97) 1; 'A New Lasting Relationship?' (1997) 141 NLJ 518; 'Mears is ready to quit election as Sayer and Sycamore unite', L (15.4.97) 1; 'Editorial: Who should Run the Law Society?' (1997) 147 NLJ 589; Phillip Sycamore, Michael Mathews and Robert Sayer, 'Trio for Change', LSG (14.5.97) 17.

[62] 'Profession tells Society Home Truths in Survey', LSG (29.5.97) 1; 'Editorial: Getting the Message Across', LSG (29.5.97) 15; John Jenkins, 'Internal Affairs', LSG (29.5.97) 24–25; 'Mears Sets Sights on Come-back', LSG (4.6.97) 1; 'Mears Stands for President' (1997) 141 SJ 533; 'The Return of the Bogeyman?' (1997) 147 NLJ 838; Martin Mears, 'Letters to the Editor: Time of Reckoning', LSG (11.6.97) 15.

[63] 'Editorial: Support for the Law Society up 100 per cent…from 1 per cent' (1997) 147 NLJ 837.

[64] Cat (6.97); David McIntosh, 'Common Purpose', Cat (6.97) 18; Martin Mears, 'Common Purpose: A Reply', Cat (6.97) 18.

[65] 'A Message to the Profession from Robert Sayer', LSG (11.6.97) 17; 'Law Society Corner' (1997) 147 NLJ 875; Martin Mears, 'The Trojan Horse' (1997) 147 NLJ 878; Robert Sayer, 'The Plain Truth' (1997) 147 NLJ 879; Robert Sayer, 'Letters to the Editor: Lesson to Learn', LSG (18.6.97) 16; 'Mears Calls for Co-Operation' (1997) 141 SJ 588; Martin Mears, 'Robert Sayer: Conversion of a Radical?' Cat (6.97) 16; Bluebottle, 'Chancery Lane: What Do They All Do?' Cat (6.97) 24.

[66] 'Poll Position', LSG (25.6.97) 15.

[67] Phillip Sycamore, 'Sycamore-Mathews-Sayer', LSG (18.6.97) 12; Martin Mears, 'Mears-Keating-Savage', LSG (18.6.97) 14.

[68] 'Leaked Note Sparks Resignation Call', LSG (25.6.97) 1; 'Campaign Memo Provokes Dispute', LSG (25.6.97) 6; 'Letters to the Editor: Baker Speaks Up', LSG (25.6.97) 18; 'The Solicitors Indemnity Fund: What Will It Mean For You?' (1997) 141 SJ 610; 'Mears Calls on Sycamore to Withdraw' (1997) 141 SJ 611; 'Comment: Voters Deserve Better' (1997) 141 SJ 615; 'Election Issues' (1997) 141 SJ 626; 'Furore Over Election Campaign' (1997) 147 NLJ 946; Phillip Sycamore, 'Progress, not Politics' (1997) 147 NLJ 953; Martin Mears, 'Portos & Co: a Question of Credibility' (1997) 147 NLJ 954; 'OSS Complaint Threat Looms in Election Battle', LSG (2.7.97) 1; 'Campaign Fall-Out', LSG (2.7.97) 14; 'Law Society Policy Committee Blocks Discussion on Leaked Election "Notes"' (1997) 147 NLJ 982; 'Mears Challenged Sycamore' (1997) 147 NLJ 982; Robin de Wilde QC, 'Comment: Sorting out the Mess in Chancery Lane' (1997) 147 NLJ 981.

[69] 'Sycamore Line-up wins Hands Down', LSG (16.7.97) 1; 'Sycamore Trounces Mears' (1997) 147 NLJ 1054; Martin Mears, 'Letters: A triumph?' (1997) 147 NLJ 1144; Martin Mears, 'Red Hot Litigators rule?' T (6.1.98) 35.

[70] 'Comment: Silence Speaks Volumes' (1997) 141 SJ 687; 'Editorial: Post Election Blues' (1997) 147 NLJ 1053.

[71] 'YSG gets Council Seat', LSG (12.6.91) 10; 'Young Solicitors Call for Increased Representation' (1997) 141 SJ 148; 'Council Postpones Decision on Designated Women's Seat', LSG (23.4.97) 5; 'Young Pitch for Council Revamp', LSG (12.5.97) 5; 'Committees face Deadlock over Future of Council Women's Seat', LSG (21.5.97) 5; 'Council Rejects Women's Seat', LSG (11.6.97) 4; 'No Seat to Represent Women's Interests' (1997) 147 NLJ 874; 'Bahl Launches Bid to be first Woman Leader', LSG (29.10.97) 1; 'The True Value of a Solicitor' (1997) 147 NLJ 1580; 'TSG Bids for Council Seat', LSG (10.12.97) 6; 'TSG Ruling', LSG (21.1.98) 5.

[72] 'Probate Practitioners become First to Win Dedicated Section', LSG (2.7.97) 5; 'Editorial: Getting Sectioned', LSG (2.7.97) 15; 'Practitioners Flock to Join new Law Society Section' (1997) 141 SJ 832; 'Probate Practitioners Rush to Embrace Specialist Section', LSG (17.9.97) 5; 'Council Shake-up Call', LSG (22.10.97) 6; 'Euro Section could See End of SEG', LSG (10.6.98) 6; 'C&I Group Attacks Sections Policy', LSG (11.2.98) 1; 'Business Man', LSG (15.7.98) 10; 'Law Management Section Unveiled' (1998) 142 SJ 661.

[73] 'City "Neglect" Call', LSG (17.12.97) 9; Lee (1999: chap. 5).

[74] 'City "Neglect" Call', LSG (17.12.97) 9; Tony Holland, 'The end of lawyers' self-regulation?' T (17.3.98) 39; Phillip Sycamore, 'In the public interest', T (28.4.98) 41; Arora and Francis (1998: 18).

[75] 'Editorial: Retrograde Step' (1998) 148 NLJ 149; 'Election Plea', LSG (11.2.98) 5; 'Editorial: Titanic Struggles Ahead for Bahl?' (1998) 148 NLJ 197; 'Plot Claim', LSG (18.2.98) 5; 'Council Rejects Nomination Plan', LSG (11.3.98) 5; 'Revised "Buggins Turn" Rejected' (1998) 142 SJ 220; 'Defeat for Return of Post-modern Buggins' (1998) 148 NLJ 359.

[76] Robert Sayer, 'Comment: Costs and Value', LSG (26.2.98) 16; 'Sayer to Fight on "Customer Friendly" Platform' (1998) 142 SJ 363.

[77] 'Election Talk', LSG (29.4.98) 4; Martin Mears, 'Lawspeak...' (1998) 148 NLJ 678; David McIntosh, 'Comment: Why I will Run', LSG (13.5.98) 14; 'Contest Kicks Off', LSG (13.5.98) 5; 'War of Words Begins as McIntosh Launches Bid' (1998) 142 SJ 437; 'Contested Election at Chancery Lane' (1998) 148 NLJ 686; 'Comment: Make your Views Count' (1998) 142 SJ 439; Martin Mears, 'Lawspeak...' (1998) 142 NLJ 761; David McIntosh, 'Standing Together' (1998) 142 SJ 464.

[78] 'Napier to Challenge Mathews for Top Job', LSG (20.5.98) 1; Robert Sayer, 'Comment: No Need for a Poll', LSG (20.5.98) 16; 'Napier's Bid for President Leaves Rival Puzzled' (1998) 142 SJ 461; 'Napier Throws in his Hat' (1998) 148 NLJ 738; Robert Sayer, 'This is not a Game' (1998) 142 SJ 486; Michael Napier, 'My Presidential Bid', LSG (28.5.98) 20.

[79] 'Keating to Run against Bahl, LSG (3.6.98) 4; 'Mears backs Keating for Deputy Vice President' (1998) 142 SJ 508; David Keating, 'Life or Death for the Rural Practice' (1998) 148 NLJ 848; 'Contest is Good for Me, says Bahl' (1998) 142 SJ 532; Advertisement (1998) 142 SJ 557.

[80] Advertisement, LSG (3.6.98) 7; Michael Mathews, 'Going for the Top', LSG (3.6.98) 16; Michael Napier, 'Why I am Deadly Serious' (1998) 142 SJ 512; Michael Mathews, 'Experience Counts' (1998) 142 SJ 534.

[81] 'Election Tussle', LSG (17.6.98) 5; 'Sayer Savages "Egomaniac" Rival' (1998) 142 SJ 557.

[82] Advertisement, LSG (10.6.98) 7; Advertisement, LSG (17.6.98) 7; 'Decision Time', LSG (17.6.98) 22; Kamlesh Bahl, 'Putting Solicitors First' (1998) 142 SJ 560; Advertisement, LSG (24.6.98) 23; David Keating, 'Practical Knowledge' (1998) 142 SJ 586; 'The profession's new face', I (Fri Rev) (26.6.98) 20; 'Candidates Clash over Debates and Priorities as Election Nears', LSG (1.7.98) 5.

[83] 'Mathews, Sayer and Bahl Triumph', LSG (15.7.98) 1; 'Victory for Mathews, Sayer and Bahl' (1998) 142 SJ 659; 'Comment: New Mood for New Millenium?' (1998) 142 SJ 663; 'Into the Spotlight', LSG (22.7.98) 9; 'Bahl to Focus on Chancery Lane', LSG (26.8.98) 5; '"I want to make lawyers' voices heard"', T (17.11.98) 41.

[84] 'New image for Law Society', T (21.9.98) 7; 'Sweeping Reforms at Law Society', LSG (30.9.98) 4; Robert Sayer, 'Changing Times', LSG (14.10.98) 18; 'Bogan Calls for Legal Services "Super Regulator"', (1998) 142 SJ 924; 'First Steps', LSG (4.11.98) 30; 'Getting in Shape', LSG (2.12.98) 15; 'Editorial: Packing a Punch', LSG (2.12.98) 16; 'Society Sets Down Road to Reform', LSG (10.12.98) 4; 'Comment: View from the City', LSG (10.12.98) 15; 'Legal diary', T (15.12.98) 35; 'DVP Only should be Elected, Sayer Suggests' (1999) 143 SJ 284; 'New Public Face for Law Society', LSG (28.4.99) 4; 'Director-General for Society, as Council Members Demand Cash' (1999) 143 SJ 404; 'Comment: Change and Decay at

Chancery Lane' (1999) 143 SJ 431; Robert Sayer, 'Opinion: A Long Way to Go' (1999) 143 SJ 478.

[85] 'Trainees Battle for Council Seat', LSG (27.1.99) 4; 'In-house Fury at Council Seat Loss', LSG (19.5.99) 4; 'Editorial: Here we Go Again...' (1999) 149 NLJ 845; 'Corrections', LSG (22.9.99) 5.

[86] 'C&I Group Hits Out', LSG (3.2.99) 4; 'In-house Qualification Planned', LSG (23.6.99) 6; 'C&I Group to Relaunch as Company', LSG (13.10.99) 3.

[87] HC Standing Committee E (13.5.99).

[88] HC 333: 1028–38 (22.6.99); HL 604: 456–63 (14.7.99); 'Irvine moves to block Law Society union fund', T (13.5.99) 8; 'Editorial: Let's Scare all the Lawyers', (1999) 149 NLJ 701; Martin Mears, 'Lawspeak...' (1999) 149 NLJ 726; 'Powers Struggle', LSG (19.5.99) 5; Mark Sheldon, 'Letters to the Editor: Role of the Law Society', T (19.5.99) 21; 'APIL President Attacks Both Sides in Advertising Row' (1999) 143 SJ 476; 'Lawyers warned of Irvine curbs', T (2.6.99) 2; LSG (3.6.99); Stanley Best, 'Letters: Speaking up for Solicitors' (1999) 143 SJ 554; Martin Mears, 'Ignoring the strong arm of the law', T (22.6.99) 37; 'Labour revolt over personal injury curbs', G (23.6.99) 8; 'Access to Justice Monitoring' (1999) 149 NLJ 958; 'Labour Revolt over Personal Injury Cut' (1999) 143 SJ 603; 'Irvine Rejects Discrete Public Interest Fund as Justice Bill nears Completion', LSG (30.6.99) 5; 'Lords block legal aid reform Bill', T (15.7.99) 2; 'Defeat Could Delay Justice Bill', LSG (21.7.99) 5; 'Irvine in Trouble over Public Defenders' (1999) 143 SJ 700; Trevor Aldridge QC, 'Opinion: A Divided Future?' (1999) 143 SJ 730; Access to Justice Act 1999 § 47.

[89] Martin Mears, 'Lawspeak...' (1999) 149 NLJ 726; 'Keating to Stand', LSG (3.6.99) 5; 'Keating to Challenge Sayer for Presidency' (1999) 149 NLJ 846; 'Editorial: Here we Go Again...' (1999) 149 NLJ 845; 'Sayer Stands by Outspoken Attack as Presidential Campaign Begins', LSG (9.6.99) 3; 'A Message for Robert Sayer', LSG (9.6.99) 9; Robert Sayer, 'Comment: Key Questions', LSG (9.6.99) 16; 'Keating Hopes for Fourth Time Lucky in Election Bid' (1999) 143 SJ 551; 'A Week (More or Less) in the Law...' (1999) 143 NLJ 883; Robert Sayer, 'Restoring Relevance' (1999) 149 NLJ 882; 'Editorial: Professional Fouls' (1999) 149 NLJ 881; Martin Mears, 'Lawspeak...' (1999) 149 NLJ 910; 'Comment: Conduct Unbecoming' (1999) 143 SJ 555; 'Writ large', G2 (15.6.99) 8; 'Legal diary', T (15.6.99) 41; 'Keating Considers Libel Action as Acrimonious Campaign Continues', LSG (16.6.99) 5; Tony Girling, 'Letters to the Editor', LSG (16.6.99) 16; 'The Law Society Presidential Election 1999: A Question of Fitness', LSG (16.6.99) 23; (1999) 149 NLJ 920; (1999) 143 SJ 586; 'Decision Time', LSG (16.6.99) 24; David Keating, 'The Mood for Change' (1999) 149 NLJ 924; 'Presidential Challenger Alleges Libel' (1999) 143 SJ 577; Martin Mears, 'Lawspeak...' (1999) 149 NLJ 950; 'Sayer's Truce Bid', LSG (23.6.99) 6; 'Press Round-Up', LSG (23.6.99) 12; 'Sayer Admits Regret over Outburst' (1999) 143 SJ 605; Stanley Best, 'Letters: Vulgar Abuse' (1999) 149 NLJ 960; Robert Sayer, 'Actions not Words', LSG (30.6.99) 16; 'Letters' (1999) 143 SJ 630; 'Legal diary', T (13.7.99) 43; 'Sayer Triumphs in Lowest Ever Poll', LSG (14.7.99) 1; 'Sayer Triumphs at Last' (1999) 143 SJ 675; 'Press Round-Up', LSG (21.7.99) 12; 'Libel Damages for Keating' (1999) 149 NLJ 1394; 'Keating Victory', LSG (29.9.99) 4.

[90] 'Society to Appoint Chief Executive in Reform of Corporate Governance', LSG (20.10.99) 4.

[91] I (20.9.95) §2 13; Martin Bowley QC, 'What's Wrong with the Bar?' I (22.11.95) §1 12; 'Law Society chief plans to take over the Bar', T (30.10.99) 8; 'Solicitors' body to move to represent all lawyers', FT (30–31.10.99) 3; 'Sayer Sets Out Vision of Fused Profession', LSG (3.11.99) 1; Robert Sayer, 'Beginning of an Era', LSG (3.11.99) 16; 'Sayer's Vision gets Mixed Reception' (1999) 143 SJ 1024.

[92] 'Top lawyer fights bully claim', T (16.12.99) 1; 'Bahl to Face Bullying Probe', LSG (17.12.99) 5; 'Inquiry into Law Society "bullying"', T (17.12.99) 1; 'Law Society's officer could face more claims of bullying', T (21.12.99) 4; 'Bahl "Considering" Legal Action', LSG (16.3.00) 3; 'The Law Society suspends "bully" vice-president', T (17.3.00); 'Law chief quits after staff bullying report' DT (22.3.00); 'Bahl Quits Law Society Council but Keeps on with Legal Action', LSG (23.3.00) 3; 'Kamlesh Bahl: SGM Cancelled', LSG (14.4.00) 1; 'Asian woman "toppled by male elite at Law Society"', DT (29.11.00); 'Law Society chief "was left shaking after out-burst"', DT (30.11.00); 'Law chief in tears over "barbarism"', DT (1.12.00); 'Law chief's shame at office broadcast', DT (2.12.00); 'Reputations are the real victims', T (6.7.01); 'Law Society woman wins sex and race claim despite lying under oath', DT (6.7.01); 'Lies, race and sex', DT (7.7.01); 'Law Council to fight racial bias claims', DT (14.7.01); 'Lawyers' chief faces victimization claim', DT (18.8.01).

[93] 'McIntosh wins Society Election', LSG (20.4.00) 3; 'Sayer Promises Reforms as he Seeks Second Year as President', LSG (5.5.00) 3; 'Law Society Elections Shape Up', LSG (25.5.00) 3; 'Election Special', LSG (15.6.00) 18–22; 'Napier Offers Forum for the Discontented', LSG (22.6.00) 4; 'Napier Celebrates Convincing Victory', LSG (13.7.00) 3.

[94] Royal Commission (1979: Vol. I, paras. 32.19–80 and RR32.1–16); Robin de Wilde, 'Counsel's Opinion: A Campaign for the Bar' (1985) 82 LSG 1245–6; David Calcutt QC and Robert Alexander QC, 'Counsel's Opinion: A Campaign for the Bar: Campaign Report' (1985) 82 LSG 1554–5; 'Counsel's Opinion: A Campaign for the Bar: A Reply to the Chairman and Vice-Chairman of the Bar' (1985) 82 LSG 1845–6; Robert Alexander QC, 'Forward We Go!' C (Michaelmas 1985) 1; '1985 AGM Highlights', C (Michaelmas 1985) 23–26; 'Senate and Bar News: Annual General Meetings' (1985) 82 LSG 2325–9; 'Radical Reform for Bar' (1986) 83 LSG 1278; 'Senate and Bar News: EGM of Subscribers to the Senate; EGM of the Bar' (1986) 83 LSG 2321–4; 'Ballot of the Practising Bar' (1986) 83 LSG 2493; 'Compulsory Subscriptions: Ballot' (1986) 83 LSG 3256; Anthony Speaight, 'Letters: No Votes for Employed Bar', C (Hilary 1986) 61; J D A Heal, 'Letters: A Speaight of retort from Employed Bar', C (Easter 1986) 61; 'Senate and Bar AGMs Reflect Unique Year of Progress', C (Michaelmas 1986) 16; Abel (1988: 126–33); 'Bar Council ponders cash-raising problem', L (16.10.90) 1; 'The Year of the Ordinary Working Barrister', C (12.90) 3; 'Pay Up, Pay up and Play the Game', C (12.90) 12–14; 'The Campaign for the Bar', C (12.90) 21; General Council of the Bar, Annual Report (1990) 7; 'Barristers may have to continue legal study', T (4.2.91); 'New Bar Chairman', C (11–12.92) 4; C (11–12.93) 27; 'Bar hit by subs shortfall', L (27.9.94); 'Bar Fails to Secure Subscription Sanctions', LSG (11.5.95) 2; 'Bar Council Reviews Subs Arrangements', C (7–8.95) 5.

[95] Royal Commission (1979: i, paras. 32.6–7); Lord Benson, 'The Future of the Bar', C (7.91) 14–15; 'Neat reformer follows radical volcano', I (20.12.91) 16; 'Opening up the debate', T (3.3.92) 7; Joint Committee (1991: 1, 8; Minority Report 1–2); Lord Benson, 'The Governance of the Profession', C (9–10.94) 8; Lord Rawlinson, 'The Governance of the Profession', C (9–10.94) 8, 10; Martin Bowley QC, 'The Governance of the Profession', C (9–10.94) 10, 12, 14; Martin Bowley QC, 'What's wrong with the Bar?' I (22.11.95) §1, 12; Martin Bowley QC, Asking the Wrong Questions', C (5–6.96) 16, 18.

[96] Derek Wheatley QC, 'The Inns under pressure to reform', T (3.3.92) 7; 'Boiling point', T (16.11.93); 'CPS Barrister Elections Fuel Advocacy Debate', LSG (24.11.93) 5; 'Royal Charter', C (1–2.94) 6; 'Employed Bar Rule Change', LSG (1.2.95) 3; 'Employed barristers set for top posts', L (7.2.95).

[97] Robin de Wilde, 'Trouble at t'Law Society', C (9–10.95) 8; Robert Owen QC, 'Chairman's Column: The Governance of the Bar—Constitutional Reform', C (5–6.97) 3; 'Bar Council Meeting Berates Inns of Court over Equal Opportunities', LSG (25.6.97) 8; 'Defeat for de Wilde', C (7–8.97) 4; 'Bar AGM—1997', BB (9.97) 4; General Council of the Bar, *Annual Report 1997*. Robert Seabrook claimed 'good democratic credentials' because he 'always refused co-option with the circuit and Bar Council' and was 'for election all the way up'. But 'when it comes to the chairmanship you've got to select people who will be respected'. Direct election was 'a recipe for disaster' (interview July 1998).

[98] 'Proposed Application by the Employed and Non-Practising Bar Association to Become an Authorised Body for the Purpose of Granting Rights of Audience' (7.12.98) 7; 6 EN (4.99) 5–6; Letter from Dr Peter Gray to Mr Pitt c/o Robert Spicer, Frederick Place Chambers, Bristol (25.5.99); 115 BN (7.99) 9; 7 EN (8.99) 4.

[99] BB (3.99) 5; Susan Ward, 'Letter from the Chairman', BB (7.99) 1–2; 'Bar AGM: 12th June 1999', 7 EN (8.99) 4; Derek Wheatley QC, 'One Bar...', BB (9.99) 4.

[100] 116 BN (8.99) 7, 11; 118 BN (10.99) 9; Bar Council (1999: 18).

[101] General Council of the Bar, Response to 'Rights of Audience and Rights to Conduct Litigation in England and Wales: The Way Ahead', Executive Summary and 46–7 (14.9.98); HL 596: 1229–33 (28.1.99); Dan Brennan QC, 'Chairman's Report', 113 BN (5.99) 3; HC 333: 1028–38 (22.6.99); Susan Ward, 'Letter from the Chairman', BB (7.99) 1, 7–8; 116 BN (8.99) 7; 118 BN (10.99) 9; AJA 1999 s.46.

[102] Hayes regretted that 'professional bodies are increasingly the home of the disillusioned and the mediocre'. Participation in Law Society politics had 'more to do with the frustrations of professional life and wanting to have an extra dimension to life. The jokey thing was always that at that stage in life it's either becoming a shop steward, joining a professional body, or adultery. One president of the Law Society said, "well, perhaps in my experience all three"' (interview July 1998).

[103] Tony Girling, 'President's Column: Recipe for Leadership', LSG (25.6.97) 22.

[104] 'Should the AWS be Abolished?' (1995) 139 SJ 999.

[105] Hirschman (1970).

[106] 'Groups to Merge?' LSG (3.4.97) 6; 'Editorial: A Stronger Voice' (1997) 147 NLJ 517; 'Solicitors' societies join forces', L (15.4.97) 2; 'BLA Again Calls for Society Split' (1997) 147 NLJ 554; Robin de Wilde QC, 'Defunct Bodies—Professional Organisations that Fail the Lawyers' (1997) 147 NLJ 612.

[107] ' "Beleagured" Criminal Law Specialists Decry Treatment', LSG (24.11.95) 3; 'Taking Out a Contract', LSG (24.2.99) 10.

[108] Tony Holland declared the Society 'an irrelevance because they've lost so much credibility in public with these internal elections they're having every five minutes because the point is that someone fighting an election, you can't say my platform is to protect the public, you appeal to the profession, so of course you're a trade unionist' (interview July 1998). Tony Girling called contested elections 'a very time expensive and actually quite expensive fiscally exercise in order to try to reach the consciousness of a profession which is previously not necessarily, in many cities, know who the hell's doing what and what they stand for and so on. It's a very unsatisfactory system...the election last year and the election this year are a demonstration frankly it isn't a system that works' (interview July 1998). In July 1998 Marc Sheldon 'regret[ted] actually that the progression from vice president to president is being interrupted again by an election' 'In the days before 1969 when democracy broke out there used to be a crazy thing called the London vacancies committee which used to nominate candidates for the Council in respect to the London area. And that used to result in people...going onto the Council without having to face the hustings, doing a term, becoming president, and then going off. And that was all stopped in '69. The result is that most City practitioners wouldn't want to stand for Council' (interview). John Hayes called contested elections 'total bilge, the whole idea. You have to ask a simple question. What power has the president got? As he has no power, why on earth waste time and money atrophying an organisation'. If the 'organisation is going through an election each year it becomes increasingly difficult to focus on medium-, still less long-term, issues'. 'It's an election of the invisible for an agenda for the impossible' (interview July 1998).

[109] John Hayes 'used to say' to 'the firms who know their destiny and have the capacity to implement it...the Law Society is just largely irrelevant...the largest single charitable gift they made each year'. 'I think most of the practitioners, especially the very good ones, are not interested in politics of any sort let alone professional politics' (interview July 1998). Marc Sheldon agreed that 'the big City firms on the whole remain supremely indifferent to the Law Society...on the whole they don't benefit from much of what the Law Society does' (interview July 1998).

Chapter 11—Notes

[1] Perkin (1989: 439) explains why. 'Specialized training of itself only yielded earned income which, if it could be offered by anyone, would soon descend to the competitive marginal level. To turn it into property yielding a scarcity premium or differential rent required some device to transform it into a scarce resource. The device was closure, the restriction of access to the profession by means of expensive or selective training, education and qualification, better still by the grant of a state monopoly of service'. For a similar critique from the right, see Posner (1998); Shepherd and Shepherd (1998); Shepherd (2000). Crompton (1990) notes the convergence of left and right critiques, quoting Mancur Olson (1982: 78–9), who attributes the fact that 20th century Britain had 'a lower rate of growth than other large, developed democracies' to 'the venerability and power of its professional associations', observing that 'the distinction between solicitors and barristers... could not possibly have emerged in a free market'. For an economic justification of lawyer income see Rosen (1992). For economic analyses of the legal and medical professions in the USA, U.K., Belgium, Netherlands, and Germany see Faure *et al.* (1993).

Writing about accountancy, Willmott (1986: 574) says its professional associations are 'inescapably political bodies whose power derives from their organizational capacity to continuously secure from the market and the state the right to control and regulate the supply of, and influence the demand for, accounting labour'. On the history of English accounting see Macdonald (1984; 1985); Miller and Power (1995). Although Karpik (1999: 5 n.4, 289) begins and ends his study of French lawyers by disparaging Larson's (1977) extension of Weber as 'an economism close to neo-classical analysis', he concludes that the 1988–90 struggle over reform 'showed clearly, and in most cases explicitly, a will to defend material interests through "control" of the market... an all-out battle for monopoly, for which the State was mobilized and which consecrated the new position henceforth occupied by the logic of the market'.

[2] In reaction against conceptions of professions as static collections of traits, sociologists have stressed processes of professionalization and deprofessionalization. See Forsyth and Danisiewicz (1985); Torres (1991) (shifts between professional, market, technical, and scientific control of expert knowledge); Abbott (1991b); Wolinsky (1993). Several observers assert that the social organization of expert knowledge is experiencing unusual flux, e.g., Drazin (1990); Becher (1994); Reed (1996); Kritzer (1999). For disturbances in the English notary profession see Shaw (2000).

[3] Abbott (1988: 9) makes this the core of his revisionist functionalism: 'the knowledge system and its degree of abstraction... are the ultimate currency of competition between professions'. My book does not support that claim. Barristers and solicitors, lawyers and accountants or mortgage lenders, employed lawyers and private practitioners did not contest jurisdiction on the terrain of knowledge. See Freedman and Power (1991); Dezalay (1991); Rogowski (1994); Sugarman (1995); but see Miller and Power (1995) on the struggle over insolvency practice. Other commentators also are dubious, either because of the inherent tension between theoretical knowledge and craft practice, e.g., Derber *et al.* (1990: 53–5); Svensson

(1990: 61) ('the rational model of knowledge is here opposed to the uncertainty, complexity, and instability which characterize the daily work of many professionals, with their tendency "to converse in terms of the situation or the individual"') or because empirical studies repeatedly confirm that most 'professionals' spend most of their time performing routine or inexpert tasks, e.g., Carlin (1962); Campbell (1976); Collins (1979); Seron (1996); Brint (1996: 82); Van Hoy (1997). Collins (1990b: 19) argues: 'there is a great deal of empirical evidence that extended academic training does not usually enhance practical effectiveness very much...the academic organizational structure has a social rather than a technical impact'. Becher (1990: 148) says of pharmacy schools: 'much of the material taught is seen by students, as well as by practicing community pharmacists, as irrelevant to operational needs'. Abbott (1990: 68) concedes this: 'the theoretical education in the dominant profession is often irrelevant to practice'. Furthermore, monopoly often antedates knowledge. Larson (1990: 28), citing Ramsey (1984).

[4] Freidson (1986: chap. 6); Abbott (1991a). In the depressed British construction industry of the late 1980s and early 1990s architects lost much of their market to engineers and contractors. Brecher (1999: 43–4).

[5] For an exaggeration of the importance of status at the expense of material considerations see Burrage (1996). For influences on professional status see Sandefur (2001) (USA); Karpik (1999: chap. 9) (France).

[6] Kotschnig (1937).

[7] Before Thatcher, English professions were relatively immune to critiques of deskilling (e.g., Illich (1977)) or feminism (e.g., Ehrenreich and English (1973; 1974)). For a riposte to attacks on professionalism see Fish (1989).

[8] Similarly, the 1976–84 New South Wales Law Reform Commission inquiry into the legal profession basically endorsed the status quo: Weisbrot (1993: 2–4).

[9] Writing the year of the report, Otto Kahn-Freund said that the 'careful and rigid division of professional and commercial activities in Britain' engenders 'the ideology of conservatism...which is shared by many adherents of all political parties, right and left....': Kahn-Freund (1979: 48–52).

[10] 'For much of the twentieth century the [Lord Chancellor's] Department has seen itself as a broker...mediating between the profession and government'. Now 'the pressures of modern administration have absorbed the Department...into the government regime' through 'Treasury control over public spending programmes': Glasser (1990: 6–7).

[11] Partington (1991: 702) characterizes the Courts and Legal Services Act as 'the culmination of an extraordinarily well-orchestrated and determined political process'. Marquand (1997: 141) says that Thatcherism saw professions as 'market distorting cabals of rent seekers, engaged in an elaborate conspiracy to force the price of their services above their true market value...carriers of an anti-market ideology which must be rooted out'.

[12] For a comparison of Thatcher's policies towards law and medicine see Brazier *et al.* (1993). Other national and state governments attacked the restrictive practices of their legal professions at about the same time. On Australia see Weisbrot (1993); Hilmer *et al.* (1993); Trade Practices Commission (1994); Farmer (1994); Craven (1995); Mark (1995); Parker (1997a; 1997b; 1997c; 1999: 122–39). On Manitoba

see Manitoba Law Reform Commission (1994); Brockman (1996). On France see Karpik (1999: chap. 12).

[13] It also disproved other generalizations by Abbott. 'Jurisdictions are renegotiated...in public over ten- to-twenty [*sic*] year periods, in law over twenty- to fifty-year periods' (1990: 135). '[J]urisdictional invasion generally begins in the workplace, then moves to the public mind, and then into the law' (*ibid.*: 139).

[14] T (3.2.92); 'Princess criticizes lawyers', T (7.3.92); 'Regal aid' T (7.3.92) 4.

[15] Dominic Egan's survey of the provincial Bar, published in Legal Business, was described by Frances Gibb as an 'exposure of Dickensian regional barristers who are slow, arrogant, inefficient and lacking in commercial expertise'.: T (2.6.95). See the exchange in 'The Provincial Bars—The Circuit Response', C (7–8.95) 25; 'A True Picture of Circuit Success', C (9–10.95) 16. Against all the evidence, Halliday and Karpik (1997b: 8) claim that 'not even Mrs Thatcher's attack on the professions dented their appeal and deep-seated legitimacy as an English institution'. Inconsistently (and equally against the evidence) they assert: 'solicitors and barristers moved perceptibly to shore up their support from the public, mostly by educating clients and the public-at-large about the values of constitutional autonomy for lawyers'. In the same volume, Burrage (1997: 153) makes the extraordinary and wholly unsubstantiated assertion that 'the fact that the professions were never the subject of political debate in England suggests that they embodied widely shared ideals and aspirations, that they were the "deep structures" of English life'.

[16] 'Good Work, but Far too Much Lolly', LSG (1.2.95) 3; see also 'Third Rate', LSG (30.11.94) 9. Some professional leaders responded by attacking the messenger. Peter Goldsmith QC, 'Chairman's Column: The Media and Public Perceptions', C (1–2.95) 8.

[17] Conflict between the branches has engendered and impeded reform in other (*de facto*) divided professions, such as Australia: see Disney *et al.* (1986); Weisbrot (1993: 11).

[18] Walter Merricks remembered in July 1998: 'We had as President Richard Gaskell at that time whose lifelong commitment was to—as indeed most other Law Society Council members—was to a feeling of being second-class citizens *vis-à-vis* the Bar and so anything which the lifelong commitment was to do the Bar down. And the opportunity to fight for rights of audience was just heaven sent'. 'It's the judgeships...not merely the fact that you can stand up in front of these judges, you want to be the judges...that has rankled with solicitors for, you know, 150 years or more' (interview).

[19] 'John Hayes was already a part of this notion which I thought we developed as we went along that we were going to be the reasonable people. We were going to be the guys who worked with' Mackay, while 'the Bar were brilliantly happy to play the tough guy, the guys who were obstreperous and screaming and shouting and raving and fighting' (Merricks interview).

[20] 'Chairman's Column: A Change in Policy', C (11.91) 3.

[21] 'Advocates for Change', C (10.93) 3.

[22] 'Progressive Bar—Part of the Solution' (1999) 149 NLJ 1506.

[23] On the 'Americanisation' of global law practice see Dezalay (1995; 1996). One study found a layering of new forms on top of old in large Canadian firms: Cooper *et al.* (1996). On U.S. influence on City firms see Flood (1999). Only 28 per cent of

a sample of English firms with more than nine partners had an up-or-out policy for assistant solicitors, almost universal in large American firms; but it was more common in the largest firms, and 58 per cent of firms identified 'rainmaking' as the most important criterion for promotion in 1993, up from just 16 per cent four years earlier: Morris & Pinnington (1998). For an argument that globalization will enhance the position of professions see Dingwall (1999).

[24] The British medical profession offered fierce resistance to many of Thatcher's contemporaneous reforms of the NHS. Elston (1991: 70).

For similar responses by Australian lawyers see M. Phelps, 'Who are These People?' (1995) 3 Australian Lawyer 3 ('shallow and simplistic approach'), quoted in Parker (1997a: 387–8); Farmer (1994: 297) ('the Report of the Trade Practices Commission is hard to take seriously. It borders on the nutty'); R. Meadows, 'Comment II', 4 Journal of Judicial Administration 85 (1994), quoted in Parker (1999: 131): 'politically motivated...openly set out to blame all of the ills of the justice system on the legal profession...the TPC's imperialist ambition to have...the legal profession brought under...the TPC...[is] predicated on the sacred cow "competition"...replete with statements of economic theory....' One of her respondents called the TPC 'a bunch of turkeys. I have written a letter to...[the chair] saying he is a liar': Parker (1999: 132–3). But national and state professional associations urged compliance with changes they saw as inevitable: Parker (1997b: 43–4).

French lawyers opposing the 1988–90 reforms used similar language: 'it's always money that gets the respect!', 'intolerable to see the self-interest of some held up as a universal rule', 'collective suicide', 'a perfect execution', 'the obsession of the development of legal supermarkets'. The leading opponent condemned the Paris *ordre* as a 'monarchical institution' exhibiting a 'combination of papal infallibility and Florentine intrigue': Karpik (1999: 261–2, 265). Lawyers in Spain and Italy felt relatively unthreatened by laissez-faire: Olgiati (1995).

[25] 'Editorial: A Spin Doctor for Lawyers' (1998) 148 NLJ 77.

[26] 'Pannone Wants Profession to "Walk Tall" ', LSG (4.3.93) 8; 'The Opportunity to Serve Our Country—that is All we Ask', LSG (25.5.94) 2.

[27] 'British Legal Association Spring Conference' (1993) 143 NLJ 426.

[28] 'When a Solicitor does the Business', LSG (28.9.94) 12.

[29] 'Profession "In Extremis" ', LSG (11.10.95) 12.

[30] Trevor Murray, 'Comment: Time to Make a Stand', LSG (26.3.97) 14.

[31] 'Bar forum: rights of audience', L (4.1.94) 10–11.

[32] 'Bar tells ministers: hands off', T (15.6.98) 2; 'Hallett Rounds on Government Spin Doctors' (1998) 142 SJ 556.

[33] Markets, bureaucracies (public and private), and professions are functional alternatives in the control of outputs: Ouchi (1980). (On lay competitors for personal injury claims see Kritzer (2001)). Although sociologists early expressed concern about the tension between professional and bureaucratic organizations, e.g., Ben-David (1958); Kornhauser (1962); Perrucci and Gerstl (1969); Harries-Jenkins (1970), Child (1982), some recent observers see these as complementary ways of deploying expert knowledge, e.g., Mintzberg (1979); Lachman and Aranya (1986); Morrow and Wirth (1989); Greenwood *et al.* (1990); Svensson (1990: 51); Tolbert and Stern (1991); Wallace (1993; 1995); Powell *et al.* (1999); Gray (1999);

Morris and Pinnington (1999). For exhortation see Raelin (1986); Maister (1997). Freidson (1986: 124–5) reminds us that 'independent' professionals were nothing of the kind. 'No one familiar with the history of the self-employed professions can claim consistent capacity to gain a living, without which one cannot be independent and free.' 'Given a strong position in the market, one can be employed and nonetheless "write one's own ticket"'. Savage *et al.* (1992: 79) see 'a changing type of "organizational project" rather than a fundamental undermining of professional power as such. Since many professional workers are employed in managerial posts it remains to be demonstrated that these changes mark any serious erosion of the powers of cultural assets: indeed, it might be true that they reflect the growing "currency" and marketability of professionally trained workers who have managerial experience'. Recent work on firms argues that they are becoming less vertical, offering workers greater autonomy: DiMaggio (2001). Although many see expert knowledge as subordinate to capital and the state, some emphasize its autonomy and the potential for a new mandarinate, a logocracy. See Derber *et al.* (1990: 13–24).

Others remain sceptical, e.g., Pollitt *et al.* (1991) (NHS reforms); Starbuck (1992; 1993); Blackler *et al.* (1993); Bloor and Dawson (1994); Broadbent *et al.* (1997b); Exworthy and Halford (1999b; 1999c); Flynn (1999); Causer and Exworthy (1999); Draper (2002). German law graduates have been losing their dominance of banking. Hartmann (1995).

[34] The critique of such entry barriers is hardly new; Adam Smith was caustic on the subject. See Rothschild (2001). Entry control eroded contemporaneously in other professions The number of full-time Australian legal academics (producing new lawyers) increased from 15 in 1946 to 380 in 1984. Weisbrot (1993: 14). *Avocats* multiplied from 6,625 in 1968 to 17,683 in 1988, *conseils juridiques* from 3,000 to 4,850: Karpik (1999: 181 n.46), French doctors from 45,000 in 1960 to 150,000 in 1985: Krause (1996: 136). The ratio of doctors to population doubled in the USA from 1970 to 1990. (*Ibid.*, 45). The number of foreign medical graduates taking a test to practise in the USA fell from 36,231 in 1997 (the last year they did not have to demonstrate clinical skills in English) to 16,828 in 2001. The AMA opposes a similar test for American medical graduates. 'Test Tied to Slip in Foreign Applicants for Medical Residencies', NYT (4.9.02) A19. But just as the Bar retained greater control through pupillages and tenancies than did the Law Society, so English medical consultants retained greater control than general practitioners: Krause (1996: 96). The New South Wales Bar Council reclassified large numbers of academics and government lawyers as 'non-practising barristers', both humiliating them and withdrawing full advocacy rights: Weisbrot (1993: 19). On the tensions between academic legal education and the profession see the essays in Birks (1994); Sherr (2000).

[35] 'When a Solicitor does the Business', LSG (28.9.94) 12.

[36] On information imperfections see Freeman (1975); on cinema's glamorization of lawyering see Chase (2002); on the lure of pursuing justice see Stover (1989).

[37] On the reasons for dissatisfaction and defection see Wallace (2001).

[38] Kim (2001).

[39] On changing career patterns among professionals see Middlehurst and Kennie (1997). As BC chair Heather Hallett wondered 'if chambers will look at giving people trial tenancies—you know, we'll try you out for five years or something. I suspect the tenancy for life may well disappear' (interview).

[40] See Freidson (2001: chap. 3). On the growth of permanent employment in law firms see Gorman (1999).

[41] '[W]e have been employing more legal executives than qualified solicitors because they're cheaper.' 'Your legal executive...has always done that work, is likely to be able to do it very much quicker, more efficiently....': Hanlon and Shapland (1997: 113–14). On the substitution of IT for professionals see Clark (1992); Susskind (1996; 1999); Wall and Johnstone (1997); Plotnikoff and Woolfson (1998); Greenebaum (1999).

[42] 'High occupational status honour is a major factor in producing the high pay of the most idealized, and presumably altruistic, occupations. Their status honour demands a "status-appropriate" wage, so they can maintain the appropriate lifestyle': Collins (1990a: 36).

[43] Phillip Sycamore, 'Fit for the 21st Century', LSG (22.10.97) 20; 'Interview: I'll Give It My Very Best Shot', C (2.98) 10.

[44] Some feminist scholars argue that women lawyer and judge differently from men, e.g., Menkel-Meadow (1985); others denounce such essentialism and cultural determinism see Epstein (1997).

[45] But class reproduction across generations is very powerful, especially among professionals. See Goldthorpe (1987); Savage *et al.* (1992: chap. 7).

[46] 'Working mum reaches the top', T (6.1.98) 33.

[47] 'A Better Future', LSG (16.10.95) 16.

[48] For the position of women in the American legal profession see Spurr (1990); Lentz and Laband (1995); Chiu and Leicht (1999); Epstein and Seron (2001); in Australia see Thornton (1996); in Canada see Hagan and Kay (1995; 1996); Kay (1997a; 1997b); Kay and Brockman (2000); Kay and Hagan (1995; 1998; 1999); globally see Schultz and Shaw (2003); in other learned occupations see Atkinson and Delamont (1990); for critiques of the reproduction of gender hierarchy see Collier (1998) (law practice); Collier (2002) (legal academia). For theorizations see Witz (1992); Valian (1998).

[49] On the reluctance of French lawyers and judges to deal with economic matters see Bancaud and Boigeol (1995). Karpik (1999: chap. 8) declares that French lawyers traditionally competed in quality but offers little evidence of such competition and none that it delivered quality.

[50] Eraut (1994: 5) contrasts 'a relationship of patronage, by wealthy and powerful clients' with 'commercial' and 'welfare' relationships (with business and government).

[51] The National House Owners Society, founded in 1960, defied the solicitors' monopoly by helping members convey their own property: Kirk (1976: 146–54).

[52] On the role of consumer organizations in challenging the restrictive practices of Australian lawyers see Australian Federation of Consumer Organisations (1995), quoted in Parker (1997a: 402).

[53] French *avocats* tried unsuccessfully in both 1971 and 1988–90 to exclude *notaires* and *conseils juridiques* from offering legal advice: Krause (1996: 141); Karpik (1999: 259).

[54] 'Once the "sacred" quality of professional practice is seriously questioned, then the sectional economic and political interests that lie behind public protestations of technical neutrality and professional disinterestedness may become much more difficult to disguise within the rhetoric of expert objectivity and necessity'. Reed (1996: 588), citing Johnson (1993).

[55] Parker (1999: 129–30) quotes Australian lawyers' enthusiasm for competition. The combination of diminished control over entry and elimination of restrictive practices (such as standard contracts and prices) cut the cost of architects' services by about a third in England. Brecher (1999: 65–6). On the subjection of accounting to market forces see Hanlon (1994; 1997a); Willmott and Sikka (1997).

[56] This is inconsistent with another of Abbott's generalizations (1990: 167): 'as fewer and fewer professions control more and more, interprofessional competition becomes less and less important'. On the struggle by entrepreneurial lawyers for new market niches see Daniels and Martin (2001).

[57] As late as the 1980s, French *ordres* and trade unions of *avocats* published fee schedules: Karpik (1999: 166–7). Australian professional associations vigorously opposed a government proposal to allow non-lawyers to offer legal services: Farmer (1994: 289).

[58] Larkin (1983) (ophthalmic opticians, radiographers, physiotherapists, and chiropodists).

[59] On challenges to the restrictive practices of French *avocats* see Karpik (1999: chap. 8). He attributes the reform to anticipation of competition throughout the European Union and from accountants.

[60] E.g., White's (1981) carefully theorized and empirically grounded studies of producers who respond to each others' behaviour, not that of consumers. This has been developed further by Polodny (1993).

[61] See Flood (1995). Individual solicitors had similar fears: Brecher (1999: 41).

[62] On large firm organization see Mayson (1997). At the end of the 1990s, just 13 firms employed 12 per cent of all partners, 35 per cent of trainees, and 45 per cent of assistant solicitors: Hanlon (1999: 127). A few large French firms contained 150 *avocats* even before the merger with *conseils juridiques*; after it, the largest had more than 1,000 jurists, the next three 200–300, the three after that 100–200, and another twelve 50–100: Karpik (1999: 181–2). On German mergers see Lace (2001); on Australia see Ross (1997).

[63] Bowles (1994). On problems with market solutions see Dietrich and Roberts (1997).

[64] On the ways in-house lawyers discipline outside firms see Hanlon (1999: 114–20, 135–6).

[65] Boon and Flood (1999b).

[66] Abbott (1990: 177, 179) argues that the 'increasing amount and complexity of knowledge' forces professions 'to subdivide, in order to maintain at a constant level the amount of knowledge a given professional must know'.

[67] 'Solicitors Serving Society', LSG (28.10.93) 2.

[68] For similar predictions about professions generally see Abbott (1989).

[69] In 1925 the Law Society told the Finlay Committee it opposed state funding for legal aid as a form of 'officialism': Hanlon (1999: 66).

[70] See Flood (1999: 159–77); Hanlon (1999: 142) (92% of largest firms have marketing plans).

[71] 'Pannone wants Profession to "Walk Tall" ', LSG (4.3.93) 8; 'Solicitors Serving Society', LSG (28.10.93) 2.

[72] The *Gazette* urged the Law Society to undertake 'the very difficult task... to instill in the public something of the same fear of loss in relation to the legal aid scheme as exists in relation to the NHS': 'Editorial: A Public Appeal', LSG (11.10.95) 14.

[73] '[O]nce a service becomes professionalized under public auspices the professionals discover further needs to be met and problems to be solved and a host of reasons for extending their activities': Perkin (1989: 14). 'Some of the skills of "professionals"... are answers to self-created problems'. Collins (1990b: 20). Miller and Rose (1991: 129): 'a government machine at the mercy of professional interests who ceaselessly seek to extract increased resources and to grant more power to sectional groups'. Recent research confirms earlier findings that consumption of medical care varies with the number of doctors but does not improve health status: Wennberg *et al.* (2002).

[74] 'Bumper Year for Top City Earners', LSG (3.9.98) 9; 'Press Round-Up', LSG (9.9.98) 12; 'Press Round-Up', LSG (30.9.98) 12. For an economic argument that corporate consumers inflate the cost of legal services for everyone see Hadfield (2000). On the dependence of professions on the state see Fielding and Portwood (1980).

[75] On the growth of legalization see Galanter (1992).

[76] For comparisons with Australia see Noone and Tomsen (2001). This trend is most advanced in health care, of course. Starr's predictions (1982) have been amply confirmed. See, e.g., Coombs (1987); Elston (1991); Frenk and Durán-Arenas (1993); Light (1993); Larkin (1993); Hafferty and McKinlay (1993b); Reed and Anthony (1993); Klein (1995); Hafferty and Light (1995); Leicht and Fennell (1997); Eve and Hodgkin (1997); Harrison (1999). On other public services see Cousins (1987; 1988) (social welfare); Broadbent and Laughlin (1997); Brecher (1999: 67) (pharmacists); Pollitt (1990; 1993a); Kirkpatrick and Lucio (1995); Zander (2000: chap. 1) (lawyers); Keat (1991) ('cultural' services).

[77] On the dilemma of professionals see Antonovsky (1988). For an unusual example of successful professional resistance to government cost-cutting see Harrison (1991). Strikes by French *barreaux* temporarily obstructed the reform of the legal profession because it did not also expand legal aid: Karpik (1999: 268–71).

[78] For a laissez-faire argument for ADR see Main and Peacock (2000). For an account of English lawyers' successful efforts to preserve their role in medical negligence mediation see Mulcahy (2001).

[79] Government similarly has sought to make health care workers responsible for rationing. See Pollittt (1993b).

[80] Some see 'a new division within the middle classes between a public sector, professional, increasingly female middle class, on the one hand, opposed to an entrepreneurial, private sector, propertied middle class on the other': Savage *et al.* (1992: 218); see also Perkin (1989: 10, 17, 399–403, 473; 1996: 52); Reed (1996: 589–91); Brecher (1999: 22) (British doctors); Krause (1996: 22); Brint (1996: 206). Accountancy is even more profoundly bifurcated between a few mammoth

firms (now the big four) and tens of thousands practising alone or in very small firms: Swinson (1991: 18). On the hemispheres of the American legal profession see Heinz and Laumann (1994); on France see Karpik (1999: 182–5); on Germany, Rogowski (1995); on England, Hanlon and Shapland (1997); Hanlon (1997b; 2001); Sommerlad (1995). In 1985 the President of the New South Wales Law Society predicted the emergence of two classes of solicitors: 'those that are successful' because they 'have the commercial strand of work' and 'then a whole mass of them that are battling away like corner stones for a limited market share and making very modest incomes': 'Towards Two Different Classes of Solicitor' [1985] Law Society Journal 357, 362. Stratification by background, function, clientele, expertise, income, and respect has always characterized professions, although it tended to appear in divisions between rather than within them: Brint (1994: 29).

[81] Increasing heterogeneity of background within law firms correlates with more formal socialization and control: Tolbert (1988).

[82] English medicine and social work also experienced regulatory crises in the late 1980s: the Wendy Savage affair and the Cleveland inquiry: Elston (1991: 79–80); Stacey (1989); Savage (1986); Butler-Sloss (1988). For a comparison of lawyer self-regulation in England and Wales, Scotland, and Northern Ireland see Ross and Enoch (1996); on Denmark see Blomquist (2000a; 2000b).

[83] On the protectiveness of French *barreaux* towards their members see Karpik (1999: 235).

[84] An eighteenth-century French *avocat* pronounced: 'a client should be docile and follow the advice of his lawyer, otherwise he is not worthy of his Defender's aid'. A nineteenth-century text declared: 'the independence of the lawyer requires that in every case he be the sovereign judge of the means of defence....' Even contemporary *avocats* rebuff clients who want 'too much control over the means of defence': 'clients don't understand a thing'; 'if they're not happy, I'll be glad to give them back their file'. Quoted by Karpik (1999: 169–71).

[85] Walter Merricks observed: 'if you resourced the OSS at the level which it would need to be resourced in order to do the job, it would consume higher and higher proportions of the practising certificate fee and would drive it up and up and up' (interview July 1998).

[86] On firm 'branding' and monitoring see Bowles and Skogh (1989).

[87] See Davis (1996); Silver (1996).

[88] For similar feelings in Australia see Parker (1999: 134–5) ('part of being a profession'); Parker (1997b: 44–5). The Law Council of Australia (1994: 2) declared: 'the independence of the legal profession is dependent upon the profession's right to self-regulation'. The President of the New South Wales Law Society said: 'While there is now non-lawyer participation in all aspects of our regulation, the fundamental point is that we remain at the core a profession which is self-regulated'. D. Fairlie, 'Commencement of the Reform Act' [1994] Law Society Journal 2 (July). But professional associations in Illinois eagerly relinquished control to an independent Attorney Registration and Disciplinary Commission appointed by the state Supreme Court: Powell (1986).

[89] On the rise of external supervision see Powell (1985) (USA); Parker (1999: 122) (Australia); Boon and Flood (1999a); Arthurs (1999) (supranational bodies).

[90] 'Markets in professional services may have been reconstructed; they have not been freed': Johnson (1993: 140).

[91] On similar conflicts in British accountancy, pharmacy, architecture, and structural engineering see Brecher (1999: 50–1). On the divergence of interests among French *avocats* see Karpik (1999: 241–4).

[92] On generational differences among primary care doctors see Elkind (1991). On the underrepresentation of younger lawyers and women in French *conseils de l'Ordre* see Karpik (1999: 248–9).

[93] Brint (1996: 203). The emergence of rivals explicitly advancing the interests or ideologies of their members is most marked in France (and Italy). See Karpik (1999: 245).

[94] The voluntary *Federazione dei sindicati degli avvocati e procuratori* enrols only 12 per cent of Italian lawyers: Krause (1996: 188). Even a voluntary association like the ABA can be paralysed by internal divisions: Van Hoy (1993).

[95] One of Brecher's informants suggested that 'RIBA should be divided, with one part hiving off to become a learned society, and the other a trade organization' (1999: 51). In France, the compulsory *Ordre des médecins* regulates doctors, while the voluntary *Confédération des syndicats médicaux français* bargains with the state; in Italy the equivalents are the *ordini* and the *Società italiana di medicina generale*: Krause (1996: 124–5, 182). A century ago solicitors assailed the Law Society for being insufficiently aggressive in opposing land registration, which threatened their conveyancing income: S. Anderson (1992: 185–92).

[96] But there are costs. 'It is the conditions which determine status honour which make trade unions...structurally different from the professions....' Collins (1990a: 36). 'One characteristic which distinguishes professionals from the proletariat is that the former uses the ideology of service more frequently and more effectively than the latter to advance its interests': Murphy (1990: 80).

[97] AMA membership declined from 73 per cent in 1963 to 50 per cent in 1990 while increasing in specialty associations; BMA membership declined from 85 per cent in 1950 to 55 per cent in 1973: Krause (1996: 45, 94).

[98] On the proliferation of member services in France see Karpik (1999: 232–6); on the pressures on a variety of English professional associations see Watkins *et al.* (1996).

[99] Nearly 40 per cent of the Paris *barreau* fails to vote for the *bâtonnier*, compared with less than 6 per cent in the smaller *Ordres*. The proportion who believe the *conseil de l'Ordre* is unrepresentative is also highest in Paris (63 per cent): Karpik (1999: 250–2).

[100] Parsons (1939; 1964; 1968); Carr-Saunders and Wilson (1933). R.H. Tawney (1948: 94–5) declared that professionals uphold 'as the criterion of success the end for which the profession...is carried on' and subordinate 'the inclination, appetites, and ambition of individuals to the rules of an organization which has as its object to promote the performance of function'. Quoted in Brint (1994: 7). Freidson (2001: chap. 5) distinguishes three ideologies underlying the control of work: consumerism (the market), managerialism (bureaucracy), and professionalism, which 'claims devotion to a transcendent value'. (*Ibid.*, 122).

[101] '[T]he nature of a status group is to play down its utilitarian aspects, to direct attention away from the work which is done, and on to the style, the honour, the

moral standards displayed by its members'. 'The strong professions are those which have surrounded their work by social rituals, and turned their mundane jobs into the production of "sacred" symbols': Collins (1990a: 26).

[102] Royal Commission on Legal Services (1979: i, paras. 3.18–19).

[103] 'Lawyers' Chance to Improve Sullied Image', LSG (22.2.95) 2; 'President's Column: A Sense of Self-respect', LSG (22.2.95) 12.

[104] 'Mears Backs Advert Scheme', LSG (7.2.96) 2; 'Agencies Bid for Advert Campaign', LSG (9.5.96) 1; 'Editorial: Unlock the Good News', LSG (22.5.96) 15.

[105] 'Girling Urges: "Speak Up for our Reputation"' (1996) 140 SJ 959; Tony Girling, 'A Better Future', LSG (16.10.96) 16; 'Northern Days, Bright Lights' (1996) 146 NLJ 1498.

[106] 'Editorial: A Spin Doctor for Lawyers' (1998) 148 NLJ 77; 'New image for Law Society', T (21.9.98) 7; 'Legal diary', T (15.12.98) 35; 'Popular Press Plan', LSG (16.12.98) 5.

[107] 'Selling Solicitors', LSG (22.5.96) 13.

[108] Abbott (1990: 190–2) remarks that despite the 'shift from legitimacy of character to legitimacy of technique... character retains a surprising foothold in the legitimation structure of many professions'.

Halliday and Karpik (1997d: 354) assert without evidence that 'best exemplified by Britain, barristers are mutually constitutive of liberal movements from time immemorial': Karpik (1990: 196) asserts without evidence that the American lawyer 'is adding to his technical activities a growing involvement in politics and affairs of the state'. Australian lawyers also invoked independence: 'Lawyers help ordinary people protect their life, liberty, reputation, and property against encroachment by government, commerce, unions and other powerful interests.... The proposed new scheme would... destroy the independence of the legal profession....' M Rayner, 'Independent lawyers are a protection for democracy', Age (14.4.95) 3, quoted in Parker (1997a: 388). The Law Council of Australia President said the proposals would 'severely' erode 'the independence that underpins the integrity of the legal profession': S. Fowler, 'A disturbing threat to legal independence', Age (31.3.95) 14, quoted in Parker (1999: 123). The 'requirement that barristers conduct their practices as sole practitioners... preserves their independence....' The prohibition against direct access 'in fact help[s] to preserve the independence of barristers'. Farmer (1994: 294–5).

[109] E.g., Abrams *et al.* (1998). This is neither new nor unique to England. For centuries French lawyers have embraced an ideal of 'disinterest' (Karpik, 1999: chap. 7 and Conclusion), although neither they nor their defenders explain how this relates to actual behaviour.

[110] 'Widening Horizons: The President's Address to the 1991 Annual Conference', LSG (17.10.91) 2.

[111] 'Solicitors Serving Society', LSG (28.10.93) 2.

[112] 'Society Strategy', LSG (17.11.93) 9.

[113] 'A look before and after', C (8.98) 16. A month earlier Hallett told me: 'Maybe we do feel we're the last of the lawyers as opposed to the accountants or the businessmen' (interview).

[114] 'The Value of the Independent Bar', C (10.99) 3; 'Modern Bar: Strong Future', C (10.99) 6.

[115] '[T]he Bar as a collective actor "slept" for several centuries....' '[T]here is substantial evidence that the main body of the elite bar, as it was represented in major national and local associations, did not seize opportunities from the late nineteenth century through the Civil Rights era of the 1960s to redress civil wrongs....': Halliday and Karpik (1997c: 38, 46). Indeed, Halliday's excellent study (1987) of the Chicago Bar Association exposes its political complicity with state abuses; see also Powell (1988). On the marginalization and persecution of oppositional lawyers by the organized profession see Pue (1997).

[116] 'It is this principle of justification by service that lies behind the professional right to property and the professional social ideal': Perkin (1989: 379). On lawyer dependence on a few large clients see Nelson (1988); Flood (1999: 171).

[117] 'Priorities for Change', C (2.93) 3; 'Getting to the Wicket with J J Rowe', C (2.93) 14; 'The Bar's Pro Bono Unit', C (3–4.97) 19.

[118] 'Pro Bono in Practice', C (11.12.95) 8.

[119] 'Interview: I'll Give It My Very Best Shot', C (2.98) 10.

[120] 'Time for Pro Bono', LSG (22.9.93) 2.

[121] 'Comment: Pro Bono Progress' (1997) 141 SJ 715; 'Comment: A Caring Profession' (1997) 141 SJ 1147.

[122] 'City Firms to Aid Liberty' (1993) 137 SJ 835; 'Comment: City Lawyers' (1993) 137 SJ 839; 'Pro Bono Work Could Cut Legal Aid says LAPG' (1993) 137 SJ 1040; 'Comment: Pro Bono Work' (1993) 137 SJ 1043; 'Alliance Launches Pro Bono Scheme', LSG (12.1.94) 5; 'The Pro Bono Push', LSG (25.5.94) 4; '"Do-Good" Data is Very Patchy', LSG (25.5.94) 4; 'Law Society Pro Bono Plans' (1994) 138 SJ 515; 'Editorial: Fiddling Again' (1994) 144 NLJ 697; 'Comment: Pro Bono' (1994) 138 SJ 707; 'Lawyers Show Local Spirit', LSG (19.10.94) 9; Marcel Berlins, 'Writ Large', G (17.1.95) 13 (reporting a *Legal Business* survey); 'Bar Chief Offers Free Services', LSG (11.10.95) 4; 'Free Work Sparks Row', LSG (11.10.95) 6; 'For Love—not Money', LSG (25.10.95) 11; 'Labour's "Free Advice" Call "No Solution"' (1995) 139 SJ 1001; 'President Challenges Labour Pro Bono Call', LSG (8.11.95) 4; 'Comment: For Whose Good?' (1995) 139 SJ 1115; Abbey and Boon (1995); Boon (1996); Boon and Abbey (1997); 'News' (1998) 142 SJ 76; 'Sponsorship and the big picture', T (30.3.99) 37; '"Mean" lawyers not guilty', G (6.4.99) 17; 'Survey: Women and Trainees Top for Pro Bono, but get Little Credit', LSG (8.4.99) 5; Boon and Whyte (1999). In July 1998 Peter Goldsmith claimed that 'about a tenth of the Bar...has now signed up to do three days a year' (interview).

[123] Lawyers sought to ground their political campaign in the theoretical debate among sociologists over whether professions were experiencing proletarianization. See McKinlay (1973; 1982; 1984); McKinlay and Arches (1985); McKinlay and Stoeckle (1988); J. Anderson (1992). On remaining dominant see Freidson (1983; 1984; 1985; 1986). On the debate see Hafferty and Wolinsky (1991).

[124] Some professionals feel that the security of employment allows them to do better work. See Gross and Budrys (1991); Hoff and McCaffrey (1996). But doctor-administrators shift some loyalty from the profession to the organization. See Montgomery (1992).

[125] '[T]he strong hostility of barristers and solicitors towards [Thatcher's] policy revealed that Bar autonomy was still considered crucial by the lawyers': Halliday and Karpik (1997c: 23). In the same volume, Burrage (1997: 138–40) extols the

profession's 'self-governing bodies, the 'sovereign, self-governing professions'. '[I]n seven hundred years as an organized profession, the bar [*sic*] had never been subject to legislation and had rarely even been mentioned in law'. The last statement is false. And Burrage disregards lawyers' use of self-governance to limit their numbers, exclude women, racial and religious minorities, and class inferiors, suppress democracy, and restrain competition.

[126] Royal Commission (1979: Vol I, para. 3.18).

[127] For a rare empirical study of what clients understand and want by way of lawyer independence see Jenkins *et al.* (1990).

[128] Sarat and Scheingold (1998).

[129] Derber *et al.* (1990: 162).

[130] Brint (1996: 84). For a more sanguine view of the legal profession's ability to legitimate itself see Paterson (1996).

References

Because some readers may use the references as a bibliography, I have grouped them in three categories: A. English Political History 1979–99 (Chapter 1), B. English Lawyers in the 1990s (Chapters 2–10), and C. Theories of Professionalism (Chapter 11).

Abbreviations

ACLEC   Lord Chancellor's Advisory Committee on Legal Education and Conduct
BC   Bar Council
CA   Consumers' Association
CPS   Centre for Policy Studies
HMSO   Her Majesty's Stationery Office
IEA   Institute of Economic Affairs
IJLP   International Journal of the Legal Profession
IJSL   International Journal of the Sociology of Law
ISLP   Institute for the Study of the Legal Profession
JLS   Journal of Law and Society
LAB   Legal Aid Board
LAG   Legal Action Group
LCD   Lord Chancellor's Department
LS   Law Society
LSG   Law Society's Gazette
LSRC   Legal Services Research Centre
MLR   Modern Law Review
NACAB   National Association of Citizens Advice Bureaux
NCC   National Consumer Council
NLJ   New Law Journal
OSS   Office for the Supervision of Solicitors
PSI   Policy Studies Institute
RPPU   Research and Public Policy Unit (Law Society)

A. English Political History 1979–99 (Chapter 1)

Adeney, Martin, and Lloyd, John (1987), *The Miners' Strike 1984–5: Loss Without Limit* (London: Routledge & Kegan Paul).

Alcock, Pete (1988), ' "A Better Partnership between State and Individual Provision": Social Security into the 1990s', JLS 16: 97–111.

Alt, James E. (1979), *The Politics of Economic Decline: Economic Management and Political Behaviour in Britain since 1964* (Cambridge: Cambridge University Press).

Anderson, Paul, and Mann, Nyta (1997), *Safety First: The Making of New Labour* (London: Granta Books).

Annesley, Claire (2000), 'New Labour and Welfare', in Ludlum, Steve, and Smith, Martin J. (eds.), *New Labour in Government* (London: Macmillan), chapter 9.

Bacon, Robert, and Eltis, Walter (1976), *Britain's Economic Problem: Too Few Producers* (London: Macmillan).

Barnett, Correlli (1972), *The Collapse of British Power* (London: Alan Sutton).

—— (1986), *The Audit of War* (London: Macmillan).

Bean, David (ed.) (1996), *Law Reform For All* (London: Blackstone Press).

Blair, Tony (1991), 'Forging a New Agenda', Marxism Today 33–34 (September).

—— (1994), *Change and National Renewal: Labour Party Leadership Election Statement, 1994* (London: Labour Party).

—— (1996a), *New Britain: My Vision of a Young Country* (London: Fourth Estate).

—— (1996b), 'Foreword' in Bean, David (ed.), *Law Reform For All* (London: Blackstone Press), pp. xiii–xiv.

—— (1998), *The Third Way: New Politics for the New Century* (London: Fabian Society).

Bonefeld, Werner, Brown, Alice, and Burnham, Peter (1995), *A Major Crisis? The Politics of Economic Policy in Britain in the 1990s* (Aldershot: Dartmouth).

Borrie, Sir Gordon (1987), 'Competition, mergers and price-fixing', *Lloyds Bank Review* (April).

Brazier, Margaret, Jovecy, Jill, Moran, Michael, and Potton, Margaret (1993), 'Falling from a Tightrope: Doctors and Lawyers Between the Market and the State', Political Studies 41: 197–213.

Brittan, Sir Samuel (1999), 'A Wrong Turning on the Third Way?', *New Statesman* (1 January).

Butler, David (1988), 'The 1987 General Election in Historical Perspective', in Skidelsky, Robert (ed.) *Thatcherism* (London: Chatto & Windus), chapter 3.

Centre for Policy Studies (1975), *Reversing the Trend* (London: CPS)

—— (1976), *Stranded in the Middle Ground* (London: CPS).

Chancellor of the Duchy of Lancaster (1992), *Next Steps Agencies in Government Review 1993* (Cm 2430) (London: HMSO).

Chancellor of the Exchequer (1991), *Competing for Quality: Buying Better Public Services* (Cm 1730) (London: HMSO).

Coates, David (2000a), 'The Character of New Labour', in Coates, David, and Lawler, Peter (eds.), *New Labour in Power* (Manchester: Manchester University Press), chapter 1.

—— (2000b), 'New Labour's Industrial and Employment Policy', in Coates, David, and Lawler, Peter (eds.), *New Labour in Power* (Manchester: Manchester University Press), chapter 4.

——, and Lawler, Peter (eds.) (2000), *New Labour in Power* (Manchester: Manchester University Press).

Commission on Social Justice (1994), *Social Justice in a Changing World* (New York: Vintage).

Commission on Urban Priority Areas (1985), *Faith in the City: A Call for Action by Church and Nation* (London: Church Publishing House).

Cranston, Ross (1996), 'Delivering Civil Justice: Alternatives to Legal Aid', in Bean, David (ed.), *Law Reform for All* (London: Blackstone Press), chapter 4.

Crewe, Ivor (1988), 'Has the Electorate become Thatcherite?' in Skidelsky, Robert (ed.), *Thatcherism* (London: Chatto & Windus), chapter 1.

—— (1994), 'Electoral Behaviour', in Kavanagh, Dennis, and Seldon, Anthony, *The Major Effect* (London: Macmillan), chapter 7.

Culyer, A.M., and Meads, Andrew (1992), 'The United Kingdom: Effective, Efficient, Equitable?', Journal of Health Politics, Policy and Law 17: 667–688.

Dahrendorf, Ralf (1988), 'Changing Social Values under Mrs Thatcher', in Skidelsky, Robert (ed.), *Thatcherism* (London: Chatto & Windus), chapter 11.

Dellheim, Charles (1995), *The Disenchanted Isle: Mrs. Thatcher's Capitalist Revolution* (New York: W.W. Norton & Co.).

Denver, David (1998), 'The Government That Could Do No Right', in King, Anthony, *et al.*, *New Labour Triumphs: Britain at the Polls* (Chatham, N.J.: Chatham House), chapter 2.

Department of Trade and Industry (1988), *Review of Restrictive Trade Practices Policy: A Consultative Document* (Cm 331) (London: HMSO).

—— (1989), *Opening Markets: New Policy on Restrictive Trade Practices* (Cm 727) (London: HMSO).

Dorey, Peter (1999a), 'The 3 Rs—Reform, Reproach and Rancour: Education Policies under John Major', in Dorey, Peter (ed.), *The Major Premiership: Politics and Policies under John Major, 1990–97* (London: Macmillan), chapter 8.

—— (ed.) (1999b), *The Major Premiership: Politics and Policies under John Major, 1990–97* (London: Macmillan).

—— (1999c), 'No Return to "Beer and Sandwiches": Industrial Relations and Employment Policies under John Major', in Dorey, Peter (ed.), *The Major Premiership: Politics and Policies under John Major, 1990–97* (London: Macmillan), chapter 10.

Driver, Stephen, and Martell, Luke (1998), *New Labour: Politics after Thatcherism* (Cambridge: Polity Press).

Eccleshall, Robert (2000), 'Party Ideology and National Decline', in English, Richard and Kenny, Michael (eds.), *Rethinking British Decline* (London: Macmillan), chapter 11.

Field, Frank (1995), *Making Welfare Work: Reconstructing Welfare for the Millenium* (London: Institute of Community Studies).

—— (1998), 'A Hand-up or a Put-down for the Poor', *New Statesman* (27 September), 8.

Fielding, S. (1997), 'Labour's Path to Power', in Geddes, Andrew and Tonge, Jonathan (eds.), *Labour's Landslide* (Manchester: Manchester University Press).

Foreman-Peck, James (1988), 'The Privatization of Industry in Historical Perspective', JLS 16: 129–48.

Freeden, M. (1999a), 'True Blood or False Genealogy: New Labour and British Social Democratic Thought', Political Quarterly 70: 1.

—— (1999b), 'The Ideology of New Labour', Political Quarterly 70: 42.

Gamble, Andrew (1981), *Britain in Decline: Economic Policy, Political Strategy and the British State* (London: Macmillan).

—— (1988), 'Privatization, Thatcherism, and the British State', JLS 16: 1–20.

——, and Kelly, Gavin (2000), 'Labour's New Economics', in Ludlum, Steve, and Smith, Martin J. (eds.), *New Labour in Government* (London: Macmillan), chapter 7.

Giddens, Anthony (1998), *The Third Way: The Renewal of Social Democracy* (Cambridge: Polity Press).

Glennerster, Howard (1994), 'Health and Social Policy', in Kavanagh, Dennis, and Seldon, Anthony, *The Major Effect* (London: Macmillan), chapter 18.

—— (2001), 'Social Policy', in Seldon, Anthony (ed.), *The Blair Effect* (London: Little Brown), chapter 18.

Gould, Bryan (1989), *A Future for Socialism* (London: Jonathan Cape).

Gould, P. (1998), *The Unfinished Revolution: How the Modernisers Saved the Labour Party* (London: Little Brown).

Grant, Wyn (1993), *The Politics of Economic Policy* (New York: Harvester/Wheatsheaf).

Green, David G. (1982), *The Welfare State: For Rich or Poor?* (London: IEA).

—— (1985), *Which Doctor? A Critical Analysis of the Professional Barriers to Competition in the Health Service* (London: IEA).

—— (1986), *Challenge to the NHS* (London: IEA).

Hailsham of St Marylebone, Lord (1990), *A Sparrow's Flight: The Memoirs of Lord Hailsham of St Marylebone* (London: Collins).

Hall, Stuart (1983), 'The Great Moving Right Show', in Hall, Stuart, and Jacques, Martin (eds.), *The Politics of Thatcherism* (London: Lawrence and Wishart), chapter 2.

—— (1995), 'Parties on the Verge of a Nervous Breakdown', 1 *Soundings* (Autumn).

Hattersley, Roy (1987), *Choose Freedom: The Future for Democratic Socialism* (Harmondsworth: Penguin).

Hay, Colin (1999), *The Political Economy of New Labour: Labouring under False Pretences?* (Manchester: Manchester University Press).

Hayek, Friedrich A. von (1980), *Unemployment and the Unions: The Distortion of Relative Prices by Monopoly in the Labour Market* (London: IEA).

Heath, Anthony F., Jowell, Roger M., and Curtice, John K. (2001), *The Rise of New Labour: Party Policies and Voter Choices* (Oxford: Oxford University Press).

Heelas, Paul (1991), 'Reforming the Self: Enterprise and the characters of Thatcherism', in Keat, Russell, and Abercrombie, Nicholas (eds.), *Enterprise Culture* (London: Routledge), chapter 4.

Hendy, John (1993), *A Law Unto Themselves: Conservative Employment Laws: A National and International Assessment* (3rd edn., London: Institute of Employment Rights).

Hill, Michael (1999), 'Rolling Back the (Welfare) State: the Major Governments and Social Security Reform', in Dorey, Peter (ed.), *The Major Premiership: Politics and Policies under John Major, 1990–97* (London: Macmillan), chapter 9.

Hogg, Sarah, and Hill, Jonathan (1995), *Too Close To Call: Power and Politics—John Major in No. 10* (London: Little Brown).

Howe, Sir Geoffrey (1977), *The Right Approach to the Economy: Outline of an Economic Strategy for the Next Conservative Government* (London: Conservative Political Centre).

Hutton, Will (1993), 'Seizing the Moment: Constitutional Change and the Modernizing of Labour', *Renewal* 1(3): 50 (July).

Irvine of Lairg QC, Lord (1996), 'The Legal System and Law Reform under Labour', in Bean, David (ed.), *Law Reform for All* (London: Blackstone Press), chapter 1.

Jakobovits, Sir Immanuel (1986), *From Doom to Hope: A Jewish View on 'Faith in the City'* (London: Office of the Chief Rabbi).

Jay, Peter (1994), 'The Economy, 1990–94', in Kavanagh, Dennis, and Seldon, Anthony, *The Major Effect* (London: Macmillan), chapter 11.

Jenkins, Peter (1987), *Mrs Thatcher's Revolution. The Ending of the Socialist Era* (London: Jonathan Cape).

Johnson, Christopher (1991), *The Economy Under Mrs Thatcher 1979–1990* (Harmondsworth: Penguin).

Joseph, Sir Keith (1978), *Conditions for Fuller Employment* (London: CPS).

Karpik, Lucien (1999), *French Lawyers: A Study in Collective Action, 1274 to 1994* (trans. Nora Scott, Oxford: Clarendon).

Kavanagh, Dennis (1987), *Thatcherism and British Politics. The End of Consensus?* (Oxford: Oxford University Press).

—— (1994a), 'A Major Agenda?' in Kavanagh, Dennis, and Seldon, Anthony, *The Major Effect* (London: Macmillan), chapter 1.

—— (1994b), 'Opposition', in Kavanagh, Dennis, and Seldon, Anthony, *The Major Effect* (London: Macmillan), chapter 9.

—— (2001), 'New Labour, New Millenium, New Premiership', in Seldon, Anthony (ed.), *The Blair Effect* (London: Little Brown), chapter 1.

——, and Seldon, Anthony (1994), *The Major Effect* (London: Macmillan).

Keat, Russell, and Abercrombie, Nicholas (eds.) (1991), *Enterprise Culture* (London: Routledge).

King, Anthony (1988), 'Margaret Thatcher as a Political Leader', in Skidelsky, Robert (ed.), *Thatcherism* (London: Chatto & Windus), chapter 2.

—— (1998a), 'The Night Itself', in King, Anthony, *et al.*, *New Labour Triumphs: Britain at the Polls* (Chatham, N.J.: Chatham House), chapter 1.

—— (1998b), 'Why Labour Won—At Last', in King, Anthony, *et al.*, *New Labour Triumphs: Britain at the Polls* (Chatham, N.J.: Chatham House), chapter 7.

——, Denver, David, Seyd, Patrick, Norton, Philip, Norris, Pippa, Mclean, Ian, and Sanders, David, (1998), *New Labour Triumphs: Britain at the Polls* (Chatham, N.J.: Chatham House).

Klein, Rudolf (1985), 'Health Policy 1979–83: the Retreat from Ideology?' in Jackson, Peter (ed.), *Implementing Government Policy Initiatives: The Thatcher Administration 1979–83* (London: Royal Institute of Public Administration).

Labour Party (1988), *Democratic Socialist Aims and Values* (London: Labour Party).

—— (1989a), *Meet the Challenge, Make the Change: A New Agenda for Britain* (London: Labour Party).

—— (1989b), *Looking to the Future* (London: Labour Party).

—— (1991), *Opportunity Britain: Labour's Better Way for the 1990s* (London: Labour Party).

Lamont, Norman (1999), *In Office* (London: Little Brown).

Lawson, Nigel (1992), *The View from No. 11: Memoirs of a Tory Radical* (London: Bantam).

Le Grand, Julian (1991), 'Quasi-Markets and Social Policy', Economic Journal 101: 1256–1267.

Lewis, Jane (1988), ' "It All Really Starts in the Family...": Community Care in the 1980s', JLS 16: 83–96.

Leys, Colin (1989), *Politics in Britain: From Labourism to Thatcherism* (rev. edn., Toronto: University of Toronto Press).

Light, Donald W. (1997), 'From Managed Competition to Managed Cooperation: Theory and Lessons from the British Experience', *Milbank Quarterly* 75: 297–341.

Loughlin, Martin (1988), 'Law, Ideologies, and the Political-Administrative System', JLS 16: 21–41.

Ludlum, Steve (2000a), 'The Making of New Labour', in Ludlum, Steve, and Smith, Martin J. (eds.), *New Labour in Government* (London: Macmillan), chapter 1.

Ludlum, Steve (2000b), 'New Labour and the Unions: the End of the Contentious Alliance?', in Ludlum, Steve, and Smith, Martin J. (eds.), *New Labour in Government* (London: Macmillan), chapter 5.

——, and Smith, Martin J. (eds.) (2000), *New Labour in Government* (London: Macmillan).

Major, John (1991a), *The Power to Choose: The Right to Own* (London: Conservative Political Centre).

—— (1991b), *The Citizen's Charter: Raising the Standard* (Cm 1599) (London: HMSO).

—— (1992a), *Trust the People: Keynote Speeches of the 1992 General Election Campaign* (London: Conservative Political Centre).

—— (1992b), *The Citizen's Charter: First Report, 1992* (Cm 2101) (London: HMSO).

—— (1994), *The Citizen's Charter: Second Report, 1994* (Cm 2540) (London: HMSO).

—— (1997), *Our Nation's Future: Keynote Speeches on the Principles and Convictions that Shape Conservative Policies* (London: Conservative Political Centre).

—— (1999), *The Autobiography* (New York: HarperCollins).

Mandelson, Peter, and Liddle, Roger (1996), *The Blair Revolution: Can New Labour Deliver?* (London: Faber and Faber).

Marquand, David (1988), 'The Paradoxes of Thatcherism', in Skidelsky, Robert (ed.), *Thatcherism* (London: Chatto & Windus), chapter 9.

—— (1996), 'The Blair Paradox', *Prospect* 19 (May).

Matthews, Kent, and Minford, Patrick (1987), 'Mrs Thatcher's Economic Policies, 1979–87', *Economic Policy* 3: 5.

Maynard, Alan, and Bloor, Karen (1996), 'Introducing a Market to the United Kingdom's National Health Service', *New England Journal of Medicine* 334: 604–608.

McCaig, Colin (2000), 'New Labour and Education, Education, Education', in Ludlum, Steve, and Smith, Martin J. (eds.), *New Labour in Government* (London: Macmillan), chapter 8.

McSmith, Andy (1999), 'John Smith, 1992–94', in Jeffreys, Kevin (ed.), *Leading Labour: From Keir Hardy to Tony Blair* (London: IB Tauris), chapter 11.

Minford, Patrick (1988), "Mrs Thatcher's Economic Reform Programme:—Past, Present and Future," in Skidelsky, Robert (ed.), *Thatcherism* (London: Chatto & Windus), chapter 5.

Minister without Portfolio (1985), *Lifting the Burden* (Cmnd. 9571) (London: HMSO).

Moore, John (1986), *The Value of Ownership* (London: CPS).

Moran, Michael, and Alexander, Elizabeth (2000), 'The Economic Policy of New Labour', in Coates, David, and Lawler, Peter (eds.), *New Labour in Power* (Manchester: Manchester University Press), chapter 3.

NHS Executive (1998), *A First Class Service: Quality in the New NHS* (London: Department of Health).

Norris, Pippa (1998), 'The Battle for the Campaign Agenda', in King, Anthony, et al., *New Labour Triumphs: Britain at the Polls* (Chatham, N.J.: Chatham House), chapter 5.

Owen, Geoffrey (2001), 'Industry', in Seldon, Anthony (ed.), *The Blair Effect* (London: Little Brown), chapter 10.

Panitch, Leo, and Leys, Colin (2001), *The End of Parliamentary Socialism: From New Left to New Labour* (London: Verso).

Parker, Hermione (1982), *The Moral Hazard of State Benefits* (London: IEA).

Pattie, Charles (2000), 'New Labour and the Electorate', in Ludlum, Steve, and Smith, Martin J. (eds.), *New Labour in Government* (London: Macmillan), chapter 2.

Perkin, Harold (1989), *The Rise of Professional Society: England since 1980* (London: Routledge).

Pirie, Madsen (1985), *Privatization* (London: Adam Smith Institute).

Pope-Hennessy, John (1989), 'The Fall of a Great Museum', *New York Review of Books* 36(7): 10 (27 April).

Purdy, David (2000), 'New Labour and Welfare Reform', in Coates, David, and Lawler, Peter (eds.), *New Labour in Power* (Manchester: Manchester University Press), chapter 6.

Raban, Jonathan (1989), *God, Man & Mrs Thatcher* (London: Chatto & Windus).

Radice, Giles (1989), *Labour's Path to Power: The New Revisionism* (London: Macmillan).

—— (1992), *Southern Discomfort* (London: Fabian Society) (Pamphlet 555).

Reitan, Earl A. (1997), *Tory Radicalism. Margaret Thatcher, John Major, and the Transformation of Modern Britain, 1979–1997* (Landham, Md.: Rowman & Littlefield).

Rentoul, John (1999), 'Tony Blair, 1994–', in Jeffreys, Kevin (ed.), *Leading Labour: From Keir Hardy to Tony Blair* (London: IB Tauris), chapter 12.

—— (2001), *Tony Blair: Prime Minister* (London: Little Brown).

Riddell, Peter (1991), *The Thatcher Era And its Legacy* (2d edn., Oxford: Blackwell).

—— (1994), 'Major and Parliament', in Kavanagh, Dennis, and Seldon, Anthony, *The Major Effect* (London: Macmillan), chapter 4.

—— (2000), *Parliament under Blair* (London: Politico's).

—— (2001), 'Blair as Prime Minister', in Seldon, Anthony (ed.), *The Blair Effect* (London: Little Brown), chapter 2.

Rose, Richard (2001), *The Prime Minister in a Shrinking World* (Cambridge: Polity Press).

Routledge, Paul (1998), *Gordon Brown: The Biography* (London: Simon & Schuster).

Russell, Andrew (2000), 'New Labour and the Electorate', in Coates, David, and Lawler, Peter (eds.), *New Labour in Power* (Manchester: Manchester University Press), chapter 2.

Sanders, D. (1998), 'The New Electoral Battlefield', in King, Anthony, *et al.*, *New Labour Triumphs: Britain at the Polls* (Chatham, N.J.: Chatham House), chapter 8.

Savage, Mike, Barlow, James, Dickens, Peter, and Fielding, Tony (1992), *Property, Bureaucracy and Culture: Middle-Class Formation in Contemporary Britain* (London: Routledge).

Schiff, David (1993), 'The Legal System', in Catterall, Peter, and Preston, Virginia (eds.), *Contemporary Britain: An Annual Review 1993* (Oxford: Blackwell), 108–17.

Secretary of State for Employment (1991), *Industrial Relations in the 1990s: Proposals for Further Reform of Industrial Relations and Trade Union Law* (Cm 1602) (London: HMSO).

—— (1992), *People, Jobs, and Opportunity* (Cm 1810) (London: HMSO).

Secretary of State for Health (1997), *The New NHS: Modern, Dependable* (Cm 3807) (London: HMSO).

Seldon, Anthony (1994a), 'The Conservative Party', in Kavanagh, Dennis, and Seldon, Anthony, *The Major Effect* (London: Macmillan), chapter 3.

—— (1994b), 'Policy Making and Cabinet', in Kavanagh, Dennis, and Seldon, Anthony, *The Major Effect* (London: Macmillan), chapter 10.

—— (ed.) (2001), *The Blair Effect* (London: Little Brown).

Seldon, Arthur (1981), *Wither the Welfare State* (London: IEA).

—— (1986), *The Riddle of the Voucher... Obstacles to Choice and Competition in State Schools* (London: IEA).

Seyd, Patrick (1998), 'Tony Blair and New Labour', in King, Anthony, *et al.*, *New Labour Triumphs: Britain at the Polls* (Chatham, N.J.: Chatham House), chapter 3.

Sinclair, Peter (2001), 'The Financial Sector', in Seldon, Anthony, *The Blair Effect* (London: Little Brown), chapter 11.

Skidelsky, Robert (ed.) (1988a), *Thatcherism* (London: Chatto & Windus).

—— (1988b), 'Introduction', in Skidelsky, Robert (ed.), *Thatcherism* (London: Chatto & Windus)

Smithers, Alan (2001), 'Education Policy', in Seldon, Anthony, *The Blair Effect* (London: Little Brown), chapter 19.

Stedward, Gail (2000), 'New Labour's Education Policy', in Coates, David, and Lawler, Peter (eds.), *New Labour in Power* (Manchester: Manchester University Press), chapter 5.

Stephens, Philip (2001), 'The Treasury Under Labour', in Seldon, Anthony (ed.), *The Blair Effect* (London: Little Brown), chapter 9.

Stewart, Ann, and Burridge, Roger (1988), 'Housing Tales of Law and Space', JLS 16: 65–82.

Sully, Melanie A. (2000), *The New Politics of Tony Blair* (Boulder, Colo.: Social Science Monographs).

Taylor, Gerald R. (1997), *Labour's Renewal: The Policy Review and Beyond* (London: Macmillan).

Taylor, Robert (1994), 'Employment and Industrial Relations Policy', in Kavanagh, Dennis, and Seldon, Anthony, *The Major Effect* (London: Macmillan), chapter 14.

—— (2001), 'Employment Relations Policy', in Seldon, Anthony (ed.), *The Blair Effect* (London: Little Brown), chapter 12.

Thatcher, Margaret (1993), *The Downing Street Years* (New York: HarperCollins).

Thompson, Noel (1996), 'Supply Side Socialism: The Political Economy of New Labour', *New Left Review* 216: 53 (3 April).

Veljanovski, Cento (1987), *Selling the State* (London: Weidenfeld & Nicholson).

Warlock, Derek, and Sheppard, David (1989), *Better Together: Christian Partnership in a Hurt City* (Harmondsworth: Penguin).

Whitty, Geoff, and Menter, Ian (1988), 'Lessons of Thatcherism: Education Policy in England and Wales 1979–88', JLS 16: 42–64.

Wiener, Martin (1981), *English Culture and the Decline of the Industrial Spirit* (Cambridge: Cambridge University Press).

Willman, John (1994), 'The Civil Service', in Kavanagh, Dennis, and Seldon, Anthony, *The Major Effect* (London: Macmillan), chapter 5.

Wood, Bruce (2000), 'New Labour and Health', in Coates, David, and Lawler, Peter (eds.), *New Labour in Power* (Manchester: Manchester University Press), chapter 7.

Worcester, Robert, and Mortimore, Roger (2001), *Explaining Labour's Second Landslide* (London: Politico's).

Young, Hugo (1990), *Iron Lady* (New York: Noonday Press).

B. English Lawyers in the 1990s (Chapters 2–10)

Abbott, Andrew (1988), *The System of Professions: An Essay on the Division of Expert Labor* (Chicago, Ill.: University of Chicago Press).

Abel, Richard L. (1979), 'The Rise of Professionalism', British Journal of Law and Society 6: 82–98.

—— (1986), 'The Decline of Professionalism', MLR 49: 1–41.

—— (1988), *The Legal Profession in England and Wales* (Oxford: Basil Blackwell).

—— (1989a), 'Between Market and State: The Legal Profession in Turmoil', MLR 52: 285–325.

—— (1989b), *American Lawyers* (New York: Oxford University Press).

—— (1994) 'Transnational Law Practice', Case Western Reserve Law Review 44: 737–870.

—— (1995a), 'Revisioning Lawyers' in Abel, Richard L., and Lewis, Philip S.C. (eds.), *Lawyers in Society: An Overview* (Berkeley, Cal.: University of California Press), chapter 1.

—— (1995b) *Politics by Other Means: Law in the Struggle Against Apartheid, 1980–1994* (New York: Routledge).

Abraham, Ann (1998), 'Regulating the Regulators: The Ombudsman's Perspective', in RPPU, *Proceedings from the Annual Research Conference, 1998: Governing the Profession* (London: LS RPPU), 71–77.

ACLEC (1992), *Rights of Audience of Employed Barristers: Advice to the Lord Chancellor on the Question Raised by the Director of Public Prosecutions and the Head of the Government Legal Service* (London: ACLEC).

—— (1995a), *Consultation Paper: The Vocational Stage and Continuing Professional Development* (London: ACLEC).

—— (1995b), *Rights of Audience of Employed Solicitors: Further Advice to the Lord Chancellor on an Application by the Law Society for Authorisation to Grant Extended Rights of Audience* (London: ACLEC).

—— (1995c), *Advice to the Institute of Legal Executives on its Application to Become an Authorised Body for the Purpose of Granting Rights of Audience to Suitably Qualified Fellows* (London: ACLEC).

—— (1995d), *Annual Report for 1994–1995* (HC 579) (London: HMSO).

—— (1995e), *Review of Legal Education: Third Consultative Conference* (London: ACLEC).

—— (1996a), *First Report on Legal Education and Training* (London: ACLEC).

—— (1996b), *Advice to the Institute of Commercial Litigators on its Proposed Application to Become an Authorised Body for the Purpose of Granting Certain Rights to Conduct Litigation and Certain Limited Rights of Advice* (London: ACLEC).

ACLEC (1996c), *First Report on Legal Education and Training: Report of the Proceedings of the Conference held on 8 July 1996* (London: ACLEC).

—— (1996d), *Consultation Paper on Continuing Professional Development* (London: ACLEC).

—— (1997a), *Annual Report 1996–97* (HC 375) (London: HMSO).

—— (1997b), *Continuing Professional Development for Solicitors and Barristers: A Second Report on Legal Education and Training* (London: ALCEC).

—— (1997c), *Lawyers' Comments to the Media* (London: ACLEC).

Adam Smith Institute (1997), *Home Remedies* (London: ASI).

Allaker, Janet, and Shapland, Joanna (1994), *Organising UK Professions: Continuity and Change* (RPPU Research Study No. 16) (London: LS).

Andrew, Sir Robert (1989), *Review of Government Legal Services* (London: HMSO).

Arora, Arun, and Francis, Andrew (1998), *The Rule of Lawyers* (Discussion Paper 42) (London: Fabian Society).

Auerbach, Jerold S. (1976), *Unequal Justice: Lawyers and Social Change in Modern America* (New York: Oxford University Press).

Baldwin, John (1997a), *Monitoring the Rise of the Small Claims Limit: Litigants' Experiences of Different Forms of Adjudication* (Research Series No. 1/97) (London: LCD).

—— (1997b), *Small Claims in County Courts in England and Wales* (Oxford: Clarendon Press).

——, and Hill, Sheila (1988), *The Operation of the Green Form Scheme in England and Wales* (London: LCD).

Baldwin, Robert (1997), *Regulating Legal Services* (Research Series 5/97) (London: LCD).

Bankowski, Zenon, and Mungham, Geoff (1976), *Images of Law* (London: Routledge & Kegan Paul).

Bar Council (1991), *Quality of Justice: The Way Forward* (London: BC).

—— (1998a), *Access to Justice: A Fair Way Forward The Bar's Response to the Government's Proposals* (London: BC).

—— (1998b), *Access to Justice with Conditional Fees: The Bar's Response to the Consultation Paper published by the Lord Chancellor's Department on March 4, 1998* (London: BC).

—— (1998c), *Contingency Legal Aid Fund: Preliminary Feasibility Study by The Bar Council* (London: BC).

—— (1998d), *Response to the Lord Chancellor's Consultation Paper on Rights of Audience and Rights to Conduct Litigation in England and Wales: The Way Ahead* (London: BC).

—— (1999a), *Discussion Paper: Restructuring Vocational Training for the Bar* (London: BC).

—— (1999b), *BarDIRECT* (London: BC).

Bar Council Contracts Working Group (James Munby QC, chair) (1998), *Contracts and Access to the Bar and related topics: A Consultation Paper* (London: BC, October).

Bar Council Employed Bar Working Party (Mr Justice Mummery, chair) (1997), *Report* (London: BC).

Bar Council Entry and Training Working Party (Peter Taylor, chair) (1991), *Report* (London: BC).

Bar Council Joint Working Party of the Young Barristers' Committee and Legal Services Committee (Peter Goldsmith QC, chair) (1993), *The Work of the Young Bar* (London: BC).

Bar Council Policy Unit (James Munby QC, chair) (1994a), *Reforming the Code of Conduct: Access to the Bar. Consultation Paper No. 1* (London: BC).

—— (1994b), *Reforming the Code of Conduct: Access to the Bar. Report No. 1* (London: BC).

Bar Council Professional Standards and Legal Services Department (1997), *Code for Legal Advice Centres Instructing Barristers in Direct Referral Legal Advice Work in the Pilot Study* (London: BC).

Bar Council Race Relations Committee (1999), *The Stephen Lawrence Inquiry Report: Response by the Bar Council* (London: BC).

Bar Council Strategy Group (Nicholas Stewart QC, chair) (1990), *Strategies for the Future* (London: BC).

Bar Council Working Party on the Appointment of Queen's Counsel (Michael Kalisher QC, chair) (1994), *Report* (London: BC).

Bar Council Working Party on Financing Entry to the Bar (Peter Goldsmith QC, chair) (1998), *Investing in the Future* (London: BC).

Bar Standards Review Body (Lord Alexander of Weedon QC, chair) (1994), *A Blueprint for the Bar* (London: BC).

BDO Stoy Hayward (1999), *Report on the 1999 Survey of Barristers' Chambers* (London: BDO Stoy Hayward).

Bean, David (ed.) (1996), *Law Reform for All* (London: Blackstone Press).

Belloni, Frank (n.d), *Solicitor-Advocates Higher Court Rights of Audience* (unpublished).

Berends, Miek (1992), 'An Elusive Profession? Lawyers in Society', Law & Society Review 26: 161–188.

Bevan, Gwyn (1996), 'Has There Been Supplier-Induced Demand for Legal Aid?, Civil Justice Quarterly 15: 58–114.

——, Holland, Tony, and Partington, Martin (1994), *Organising Cost-effective Access to Justice* (Memorandum No 7) (London: Social Market Foundation).

Blair, Tony (1996), 'Foreword', in Bean, David (ed.), *Law Reform for All* (London: Blackstone), pp. xiii–xiv.

Bowles, Roger (1987), 'Solicitors' Income, Conveyancing and the Property Market', NLJ 137: 401–404.

—— (1990), 'Solicitors and the Conveyancing Market in the 1990s', NLJ 140: 1340–1344.

Bradney, Anthony (1999), 'Liberalising Legal Education', in Cownie, Fiona (ed.), *The Law School—Global Issues, Local Questions* (Dartmouth: Ashgate), chapter 1.

——, and Cownie, Fiona (2000), 'British University Law Schools in the Twenty-First Century', in Hayton, David (ed.), *Law's Future(s): British Legal Developments in the 21st Century* (Oxford: Hart Publishing) chapter 1.

Brennan, Dan, QC (1999), *Speech by the Chairman of the Bar opening the Bar Council Year 1999* (London: BC).

Bridges, Lee (1996a), 'The Reform of Criminal Legal Aid', in Young, Richard, and Wall, David (eds.), *Access to Criminal Justice* (London: Blackstone Press), chapter 13.

—— (2001), 'Recent Developments in Criminal Legal Aid in England and Wales—Contracting, Quality and the Public Defender Experiment', in Fleming, Don, and Paterson, Alan (eds.), *International Legal Aid Group: The Challenge of the New Century* 293–302.

Bridges, Lee, and Choongh, Satnam (1998), *Improving Police Station Legal Advice: The Impact of the Accreditation Scheme for Police Station Legal Advisers* (Research Study No. 31) (London: LS RPPU and LAB).

Brownsword, Roger (1999), 'Law Schools for Lawyers, Citizens, and People', in Cownie, Fiona (ed.), *The Law School—Global Issues, Local Questions* (Dartmouth: Ashgate), chapter 2.

Buck, Alexy (2000), *Assessing Means Assessment: A Summary of the First Phase of the Means Assessment Research Project* (Research Paper 5) (London: LSRC).

——, and Stark, Graham (2000), *Means Assessment: Options for Change* (Research Paper 8) (London: LSRC).

Bull, Gillian, and Seargent, John (1996), *Alternative Methods of Delivering Legal Services* (London: PSI).

Campbell, Russell (1992), 'The Inner Cities: Law Centres and Legal Services', JLS 19: 101–114.

Carlin, Jerome E. (1966), *Lawyers' Ethics: A Survey of the New York City Bar* (New York: Russell Sage).

Chambers, Gerry, and Harwood-Richardson, Stephen (1991), *Solicitors in England and Wales: Practice, Organisation and Perceptions. Second Report: The Private Practice Firm* (RPPU Research Study No. 8) (London: LS).

Chapman, Vicki (1995), *Barriers to Justice* (London: NACAB).

Christensen, Christa, Day, Suzanne, and Worthington, Jane (1999a), 'Complaint Handling by Solicitors: Practice Rule 15—Waving or Drowning?' in Harris, Michael, and Partington, Martin (eds.), *Administrative Justice in the 21st Century* (Oxford: Hart Publishing), 166–207.

—— (1999b), ' "Learned Profession?—the Stuff of Sherry Talk": the Response to Practice Rule 15?', IJLP 6: 27–69.

Clarke, Michael (1991), *Mortgage Fraud* (London: Chapman & Hall).

Clements, Luke (2000), 'Little Justice—Judicial Reform and the Magistrates', in Thomas, Philip (ed.), *Discriminating Lawyers* (London: Cavendish), 201–202.

Cole, Bill (1997), *Solicitors in Private Practice—Their Work and Expectations* (RPPU Research Study No. 26) (London: LS).

Collyear Committee (Sir John Collyear, chair) (1999), *Education and Training for the Bar: 'Blueprint for the Future'* (London: BC).

Committee of Public Accounts, House of Commons (1998), *Crown Prosecution Service, 33rd Report* (HC 526) (London: HMSO).

Complaints Commissioner to the General Council of the Bar (1998), *Annual Report 1997/1998* (London: BC).

Comptroller and Auditor General (1996a), *Handling Small Claims in the County Courts* (HC 271 1995–96) (London: National Audit Office).

—— (1996b), *Civil Legal Aid Means Testing* (HC 242 1995–96) (London: National Audit Office).

—— (1997), *Report on the Crown Prosecution Service* (HC 400 1997–98) (London: HMSO).

—— (1999), *Criminal Justice: Working Together* (HC 29 1999–2000) (London: HMSO).

Consumers' Association (1989), *The Work and Organization of the Legal Profession: Memorandum* (London: CA).

—— (1998), *Access to Justice with Conditional Fees: Response to the Consultation Paper from the Lord Chancellor's Department* (London: CA).

Coopers & Lybrand Associates Ltd. (1985), *Study of Remuneration of Barristers Carrying Out Criminal Legal Aid* (London: Senate of the Inns of Court and the Bar).

Cousins, Mel (1994), 'The Politics of Legal Aid—A Solution in Search of a Problem?', Civil Justice Quarterly 13: 11–32.

Cownie, Fiona (1990), 'The Reform of the Legal Profession or the End of Civilization as We Know It', in Patfield, F., and White, R. (eds.), *The Changing Law* (Leicester: Leicester University Press).

—— (ed.) (1999), *The Law School—Global Issues, Local Questions* (Dartmouth: Ashgate).

—— (2000), 'Women in Law School—Shoals of Fish, Starfish or Fish Out of Water?', in Thomas, Philip (ed.), *Discriminating Lawyers* (London: Cavendish), 63–86.

Craig, Rachel, Rigg, Malcolm, Briscoe, Rebecca, and Smith, Philippa (2001), *Client Views: Clients' Experiences of Using a Solicitor for Personal Matters* (RPPU Research Study No. 40) (London: LS).

Cranston, Ross (1996), 'Delivering Civil Justice: Alternatives to Legal Aid', in Bean, David (ed.), *Law Reform for All* (London: Blackstone Press), chapter 4.

Crown Prosecution Service (1993), *Annual Report, 1992/93* (London: HMSO).

Davies, Marie, Davis, Gwynn, and Webb, Julian (1996), *Promoting Mediation: Report of a Study of Bristol Law Society's Mediation Scheme in its Preliminary Phase* (RPPU Research Study No. 21) (London: LS).

Davies, Mark R. (1998a), 'The Regulation of Solicitors and the Role of the Solicitors Disciplinary Tribunal', Professional Negligence 14: 143–171.

—— (1998b), 'Wither Mutuality? A Recent History of Solicitors' Professional Indemnity Insurance', IJLP 5: 29–62.

—— (1999a), 'Can the Office for the Supervision of Solicitors Expect a Happy Birthday?—a Short Review of the First Three Years', Professional Negligence 15: 173–184.

—— (1999b), 'Solicitors, Dishonesty and the Solicitors Disciplinary Tribunal', IJLP 6: 141–174.

Davis, Gwynn, Cretney, Stephen, and Collins, Jean (1994), *Simple Quarrels: Negotiation and Adjudication in Divorce* (Oxford: Clarendon Press).

——, and Kerridge, Roger (1997), 'Opportunities for Multi-Disciplinary Work in the Market for Advocacy', in LS RPPU, *Proceedings from the Annual Research Conference 1997: Developments in the Structure of Private Practice* (London: LS).

——, ——, Annand, Ruth, Haler, Julia, and Press, Tim (1997), 'Solicitor Advocacy and Higher Court Rights', NLJ 147: 212–216.

Department of Environment (1994), *Housing and Construction Statistics* (London: HMSO).

Department of Trade and Industry (1988), *Review of Restrictive Trade Practices Policy* (Cm 311) (London: HMSO).

—— (1989), *Opening Markets: New Policy on Restrictive Trade Practices* (Cm 727) (London: HMSO).

Dickson, Brice (1990), 'Legal Services and Legal Procedures in the 1990s', in Livingstone, Stephen, and Morison, John (eds.), *Law, Society and Change*, (Aldershot: Dartmouth), chapter 9.

Dignan, J., and Wynne, A. (1997), 'A Microcosm of the Local Community?', British Journal of Criminology 37: 184–197.

Domberger, Simon, and Sherr, Avrom (1989), 'The Impact of Competition on the Pricing and Quality of Legal Services', International Review of Law and Economics 9: 41–56.

Duff, Elizabeth, Shiner, Michael, and Boon, Andrew, with Whyte, Avis (2000), *Entry into the Legal Professions: The Law Student Cohort Study, Year 6* (RPPU Research Study No. 39) (London: LS).

Dyzenhaus, David (1998), *Judging the Judges, Judging Ourselves: Truth, Reconciliation and the Apartheid Legal Order* (Oxford: Hart Publishing).

Economides, Kim, and Smallcombe, Jeff (1991), *Preparatory Skills Training for Trainee Solicitors* (RPPU Research Study No. 7) (London: LS).

Eekelaar, John (2000), *Family Lawyers: The Divorce Work of Solicitors* (Oxford: Hart Publishing).

Egan, Dominic (1999), *Irvine: Politically Correct?* (Edinburgh: Mainstream Publishing Projects).

Farrand, Julian (1984), *First Report of the Conveyancing Committee: Non Solicitor Conveyancers—Competence and Consumer Protection* (London: HMSO).

Fenn, Paul, Rickman, Neil, and Gray, Alastair (1998), 'Standard Fees for Legal Aid: An Empirical Analysis', paper delivered to the Annual Conference of the European Association of Law and Economics, Utrecht, September.

Fennell, Steven (1994), *The Funding of Personal Injury Litigation* (Sheffield: ISLP).

Flood, John (1983), *Barristers' Clerks: The Law's Middlemen* (Manchester: Manchester University Press).

—— (1996), 'Megalawyering in the Global Order: The Cultural, Social and Economic Transformation of Global Legal Practice', IJLP 3: 169–214.

—— (1997), 'The Changing Roles of Law and Accounting Firms', in LS RPPU, *Proceedings from the Annual Research Conference 1997: Developments in the Structure of Private Practice* (London: LS), 32–34.

——, Boon, Andrew, Whyte, Avis, Skordaki, Eleni, Abbey, Robert, and Ash, Alicia (n.d.), *Reconfiguring the Market for Advocacy Services. A Case Study of London and Four Fields of Practice* (London: School of Law, University of Westminster).

——, and Skordaki, Eleni (1995), *Insolvency Practitioners and Big Corporate Insolvencies* (London: Certified Accountants Educational Trust).

Foot, Paul (1971), *Who Killed Hanratty?* (London: Jonathan Cape).

Forbes, Duncan, and Wright, Sally (1990), *Citizens' Advice Bureaux and Housing Advice* (London: NACAB).

Francis, Andrew M., and McDonald, Iain W. (2000), 'All Dressed Up and Nowhere to Go? Part Time Law Students and the Legal Profession', in Thomas, Philip (ed.), *Discriminating Lawyers* (London: Cavendish), 41–62.

Frazer, Christopher (1993), *Privatise the Prosecutors: Efficiency and Justice in the Criminal Courts* (London: CPS).

Freeman, Richard B. (1975), 'Legal "Cobwebs": A Recursive Model of the Market for New Lawyers', Review of Economics and Statistics 57: 171.

Furedi, Frank (1999), *Courting Mistrust* (London: CPS).

General Council of the Bar (1989), *Quality of Justice: The Bar's Response* (London: Butterworths for BC).

General Management Committee of the Bar Council (1989), *Justice in Danger: The Bar's Campaign for Justice for All* (London: BC).

Genn, Hazel (1987), *Hard Bargaining: Out of Court Settlements in Personal Injury Actions* (Oxford: Oxford University Press).

—— (1999), *Paths to Justice: What People Do and Think About Going to Law* (Oxford: Hart Publishing).

Gifford, Tony (1986), *Where's the Justice?* (Harmondsworth: Penguin).

Glasser, Cyril (1989), 'Legal Services and the Green Papers', LSG (5 April), 9–12.

Glidewell, Sir Iain (chair), Dear, Sir Geoffrey, and McFarland, Robert (1998), *The Review of the Crown Prosecution Service: A Report* (Cm 3960) (London: HMSO).

Goriely, Tamara (1994a), 'Rushcliffe Fifty Years On: The Changing Role of Civil Legal Aid Within the Welfare State', JLS 21: 545–566.

—— (1994b), 'The Need for Legal Aid in a Post Welfare State Society: British Developments in the 1990s: The Citizen's Charter and the Complaints Explosion', paper delivered to the International Conference on Legal Aid, The Hague/Amsterdam, 13–16 April.

—— (1994c), 'Measuring the Quality of Legal Aid Lawyers. Transaction Criteria—Strengths and Weaknesses', paper delivered to the International Conference on Legal Aid, The Hague/Amsterdam, 13–16 April.

—— (1994d), 'Debating the Quality of Legal Services: Differing Models of the Good Lawyer', IJLP 1: 159–172.

—— (1996a), 'Law for the Poor: The Relationship between Advice Agencies and Solicitors in the Development of Poverty Law', IJLP 3: 215–248.

—— (1996b), 'The English Legal Aid White Paper and the LAG Conference', IJLP 3: 353–360.

—— (1996c), 'The Development of Criminal Legal Aid in England and Wales', in Young, Richard, and Wall, David (eds.), *Access to Criminal Justice* (London: Blackstone Press), chapter 2.

—— (1998a), 'A Review of Trends in Complaints and Complaints Handling', in LS RPPU, *Proceedings from the Annual Research Conference, 1998: Governing the Profession* (London: LS), 25–34.

—— (1998b), 'Revisiting the Debate Over Criminal Legal Aid Delivery Models: Viewing International Experience from a British Perspective', IJLP 5: 7–28.

—— (1999), 'Making the Welfare State Work: Changing Conceptions of Legal Remedies Within the British Welfare State', in Regan, Francis, Paterson, Alan, Goriely, Tamara, and Fleming, Don (eds.), *The Transformation of Legal Aid: Comparative and Historical Studies* (Oxford: Oxford University Press), 89–109.

——, and Das Gupta, Pieta, with Bowles, Roger (2001), *Breaking the Code: The Impact of Legal Aid Reforms on General Civil Litigation* (London: Institute of Advanced Legal Studies).

——, and Paterson, Alan (1996), 'Introduction', in Paterson, Alan, and Goriely, Tamara (eds.), *A Reader on Resourcing Civil Justice* (Oxford: Oxford University Press) 1–35.

Goriely, Tamara, Tata, Cyrus, and Paterson, Alan A. (1997), *Expenditure on Criminal Legal Aid: Report of a Comparative Pilot Study of Scotland, England and Wales, and the Netherlands* (Edinburgh: Scottish Office).

—— (2001), *The Public Defence Solicitors' Office in Edinburgh: An Independent Evaluation* (Edinburgh: Scottish Executive).

——, and Williams, Tom (1993), *Quality, Efficiency and Effectiveness: A Qualitative Study of Clients' Attitudes to their Solicitors* (London: LS).

—— (1996), *The Impact of the New Training Scheme: Report on a Qualitative Study* (RPPU Research Study No. 22) (London: LS).

Gravelle, Hugh, and Waterson, Michael (1993), 'No Win, No Fee: Some Economics of Contingent Legal Fees', Economic Journal 103: 1205–1220.

Gray, Alastair (1994), 'The Reform of Legal Aid', Oxford Review of Economic Policy 10: 51.

——, Fenn, Paul, and Rickman, Neil (1996), 'Controlling Lawyers' Costs Through Standard Fees: An Economic Analysis', in Young, Richard, and Wall, David (eds.), *Access to Criminal Justice* (London: Blackstone Press), chapter 9.

Hales, Jon, and Stratford, Nina, with Sherr, Avrom (1998), *Continuing Professional Development in the Solicitors' Profession* (Research Study No. 32) (London: LS RPPU).

Halliday, Terence C. (1987), *Beyond Monopoly: Lawyers, State Crises, and Professional Empowerment* (Chicago, Ill.: University of Chicago Press).

Hamilton, Kathryn, and Bhalla, Pamela (1994) 'Shifting Constituencies of Race, Gender and Class', in LS RPPU, *Proceedings from the Annual Research Conference 1994: Profession, Business or Trade: Do the Professions have a Future?* (London: LS), 79–83.

Hansen, Ole (1992), 'A Future for Legal Aid?', JLS 19: 85–100.

—— (1994), *The Solicitors Complaints Bureau: A Consumer View* (London: NCC).

Harris, D., Maclean, M., Genn, H., Lloyd-Bostock, S., Fenn, P., Corfield, P., and Brittan, Y. (1984), *Compensation and Support for Illness and Injury* (Oxford: Clarendon Press).

Harris, Neville (1991), *Quality and Effectiveness in Welfare Benefits and Related Work in Solicitors' Offices: Report of the Research Carried out in Ten Merseyside Firms* (RPPU Research Study No. 9) (London: LS).

—— (1994), *Solicitors and Client Care: An Aspect of Professional Competence* (London: NCC).

Harwood, Stephen (1989), *Annual Statistical Report 1989* (London: LS).

Hayes, J W. (1987), *Multi-Disciplinary Partnerships and Allied Topics* (London: LS).

Hepple, Bob (1996), 'The Philosophy of the Committee's Report', in ACLEC, *Report of the Proceedings of the Conference held on 8 July 1996* (London: ACLEC), 17–20.

Hillyer, Joy (1994), 'Barriers to Equality of Access to Legal Education', in LS RPPU, *Proceedings from the Annual Research Conference 1993 on Legal Education* (London: LS), 25–27.

—— (1995), 'Finance and Funding: Continuing Barriers to Equality of Access to Legal Education', in LS RPPU, *Proceedings from the Annual Research Conference 1995: Removing the Barriers: Legal Services and the Legal Profession* (London: LS), 74–76.

—— (1999), 'Professional Legal Education—A Way Forward', in Cownie, Fiona (ed.), *The Law School—Global Issues, Local Questions* (Dartmouth: Ashgate), chapter 5.

Hirschman, Albert O. (1970), *Exit, Voice, and Loyalty: Responses to Decline in Firms, Organizations, and States* (Cambridge, Mass.: Harvard University Press).

Hoffmann, Lord (1995), 'Common Professional Education', in ACLEC, *Third Consultative Conference* (London: ACLEC), 1, 3.

Holland, Lesley, and Spencer, Lynne (1992), *Without Prejudice? Sex Equality at the Bar and in the Judiciary* (London: BC).

Home Affairs Committee (1990), *Fourth Report: Crown Prosecution Service* (London: HMSO).

Hope, Mike (1997), *Expenditure on Legal Services* (Research Series No. 9/97) (London: LCD).

House of Lords Appeal Committee (1998), *Report on the Clerk of the Parliaments' Reference Regarding Criminal Legal Aid Taxation* (HL 145).

Hughes, Sally (1991), *The Circuit Bench—a Woman's Place?* (London: LS).

Independent Working Party of the General Council of the Bar and the Law Society (Hilary Heilbron QC, chair) (1993), *Civil Justice on Trial—The Case for Change* (London: BC and LS).

Ingleby, Richard (1992), *Solicitors and Divorce* (Oxford: Clarendon Press).

Irvine, Lord (1996), 'The Legal System and Law Reform under Labour', in Bean, David (ed.), *Law Reform for All* (London: Blackstone Press) chapter 1.

James, R., and Seneviratne, M. (1995), 'The Legal Services Ombudsman: Form versus Function?', MLR 58: 187–207.

——, and —— (1996), 'Solicitors and Client Complaints', Consumer Policy Review 6: 101–105.

Jenkins, John (1993), *The Quality of Solicitors' Practice Management* (RPPU Research Study No. 10) (London: LS).

—— (1994), *The Conveyancing Market in England and Wales* (RPPU Research Study No. 14) (London: LS).

—— (1995), *The Conveyancing Market: Trends and Statistics as at April 1995* (RPPU Research Paper No. 2) (London: LS).

——, and Lewis, Verity (1995a), *Trends in the Solicitors' Profession: Annual Statistical Report 1995* (London: LS).

—— (1995b), *Client Perceptions: Existing and Potential Clients: Experiences and Perceptions of Using a Solicitor for Personal Matters* (RPPU Research Study No. 17) (London: LS).

—— (1996), *Training Solicitors to Attract and Keep Clients: A Synopsis of Law Society Market Research Findings* (London: LS).

——, Skordaki, Eleni, and Willis, Carole F. (1989), *Public Use and Perception of Solicitors' Services* (RPPU Research Study No. 1) (London: LS).

Johnston, Valerie, and Shapland, Joanna (1990), *Developing Vocational Legal Training for the Bar* (Sheffield: ISLP, University of Sheffield).

Joint Committee of the General Council of the Bar and the Council of the Inns of Court (Lord Williams of Mostyn QC, chair) (1992), *The Way Ahead* (London: BC).

Joseph, Michael (1976), *The Conveyancing Fraud* (London: Michael Joseph).

—— (1984), *Lawyers can Seriously Damage your Health* (London: Michael Joseph).

Julien, Joy (1996), 'The Experience of Litigants in Person at the Royal Courts of Justice CAB', in RPPU, *Proceedings from the Annual Research Conference 1996: New Methods of Delivering Legal Services* (London: Law Society), 35–39.

Justice (1989), *Miscarriages of Justice* (London: Justice).

—— (1992a), *The Judiciary in England and Wales* (London: Justice).

—— (1992b), *Justice and the Individual* (London: Justice).

—— (1998), *Access to Justice with Conditional Fees: Response to the Lord Chancellor's Department Consultation Paper* (London: Justice).

Justice, Jean (1964), *Murder versus Murder* (Paris: Olympia Press).

Kay, John (1994), *The Competitive Advantage of Law and Accountancy in the City of London* (London: London Business School).

Kennedy, Ludovic (1961), *Ten Rillington Place* (London: Gollancz).

——, Devlin, Lord, Sargant, Tom, Magee, Bryan, McDonald, Oonagh, Mantle, Wendy, and Pierce, Gareth (1980), *Wicked beyond Belief* (London: Granada).

King, Michael, Israel, Mark, and Goulbourne, Selina (1990), *Ethnic Minorities and Recruitment to the Solicitors' Profession* (London: LS RPPU for Commission for Racial Equality).

Kotschnig, Walter M. (1937), *Unemployment in the Learned Professions: An International Study of Occupational and Educational Planning* (London: Oxford University Press).

Labour Party (1995), *Access to Justice: Labour's Proposals for Reforming the Civil Justice System* (London: Labour Party).

Law Society (1988a), *Arrangements, Hiving Off, Profit Sharing and Incorporation* (London: LS).

—— (1988b), *Survey of Legal Aid Provision* (London: LS).

—— (1988c), *Equal in the Law: Report of the Working Party on Women's Careers* (London: LS).

—— (1989a), *Striking the Balance* (London: LS).

—— (1989b), *Franchising Legal Aid* (London: LS).

—— (1989c), *Solicitors in the Higher Courts* (London: LS).

—— (1990), *Solicitors in England and Wales: Practice, Organisation and Perceptions* (London: LS).

—— (1991), *Succeeding in the 90s: The Law Society Strategy for the Decade* (London: LS).

—— (1992a), *The Future of Criminal Legal Aid: Evidence to the Royal Commission on Criminal Justice* (London: LS).

—— (1992b), *The Cost of Default: A Consultative Paper* (London: LS).

—— (1993), *The Cost of Default: A Report* (London: LS).

—— (1994a), *Fairness to Families* (London: LS).

—— (1994b), *Annual Report 1993/94* (London: LS).

—— (1995a), *Design for the Future* (London: LS).

—— (1995b), *A Better Way Forward: The Law Society's Response to the Government's Green Paper on Legal Aid* (London: LS).

—— (1998a), *Ensuring Justice?* (London: LS).

—— (1998b), *Serving Law and Justice: A Three Year Strategic Plan 1998–2000* (London: LS).

Law Society Special Working Party on Conveyancing Services (1994), *Adapting for the Future* (London: LS).

Law Society Training Committee (1988), *The Recruitment Crisis* (London: LS).

—— (1990), *Consultation Paper: Training Tomorrow's Solicitors* (London: LS).

Lawson, Nigel (1992), *The View from No. 11: Memoirs of a Tory Radical* (London: Bantam).

Lay Observer (1989), *Fourteenth Annual Report, 1988* (London: HMSO).

Lee, Robert G. (1992), 'From Profession to Business: The Rise and Rise of the City Law Firm', JLS 19: 31–48.

—— (1999), *Firm Views: Work of and Work in the Largest Law Firms* (RPPU Research Study No. 35) (London: LS).

—— (2000), '"Up or Out"—Means or Ends? Staff Retention in Large Firms', in Thomas, Philip (ed.), *Discriminating Lawyers* (London: Cavendish), 183–200.

Legal Action Group (1992), *Strategy for Justice: Publicly Funded Legal Services for the 1990s* (London: LAG).

—— (1998a), *Response to the Lord Chancellor's Department's Consultation Paper on Conditional Fees* (London: LAG).

—— (1998b), *Legal Action Group's Response to the Legal Aid Board's Consultation Paper on Reforming the Civil Advice and Assistance Scheme* (London: LAG).

Legal Aid Board (1997), *When the Price Is High* (London: LAB).

—— (1998a), *Reforming the Civil Advice and Assistance Scheme: Exclusive Contracting—the Way Forward* (London: LAB).

—— (1998b), *Access to Justice with Conditional Fees: Response to the Lord Chancellor's Consultation Paper* (London: LAB).

—— (1999), *Ensuring Quality and Controlling Cost in Very High Cost Criminal Cases* (London: LAB).

Legal Services Ombudsman (1994), *Third Annual Report, 1993* (London: HMSO).

—— (1996), *Fifth Annual Report, 1995* (London: HMSO).

—— (1998), *Seventh Annual Report, 1997* (London: HMSO).

—— (1999), 'Modernising Justice . . . Modernising Regulation?', *Annual Report of the Legal Services Ombudsman 1998/99* (London: HMSO).

Legal Services Research Centre (2001), *Report on the Findings of the LSRC Equal Opportunities Survey, 2000* (Research Paper 6) (London: LSRC).

Leggatt, George, Styles, Peter, Lavender, Nicholas and Bowles, Edward (1999), *Consultation Paper: Access to Justice Act 1999: Proposed Amendments to the Bar's Code of Conduct* (London: BC).

Lewis, P.S.C. (2000), *Assumptions about Lawyers in Policy Statements: A Survey of Relevant Research* (Research Series No. 1/00) (London: LCD).

Lewis, Verity (1996), *Complaints Against Solicitors: The Complainant's View* (RPPU Research Report No. 19) (London: LS).

Lomax, Richard H. (1987), 'LA Law: Profile of a Public Defender's Office', LSG 84: 555–561.

—— (1988), 'A Public Defender', LSG (4 May) 13–14, 21.

Lord Chancellor (1989), *Legal Services: A Framework for the Future* (Cm 740) (London: HMSO).

Lord Chancellor's Department (1983), *The Government Response to the Report of The Royal Commission on Legal Services* (Cmnd. 9077) (London: HMSO).

—— (1986), *Legal Aid Efficiency Scrutiny* (2 vols.) (London: LCD).

—— (1987), *Legal Aid in England and Wales: A New Framework* (Cm 118) (London: HMSO).

—— (1989a), *The Work and Organisation of the Legal Profession* (Cm 570) (London: HMSO).

—— (1989b), *Contingency Fees* (Cm 571) (London: HMSO).

Lord Chancellor's Department (1989c), *Conveyancing by Authorised Practitioners* (Cm 572) (London: HMSO).

—— (1991), *Eligibility for Civil Legal Aid: A Consultation Paper* (London: LCD).

—— (1993), *Looking to the Future—Mediation and the Ground for Divorce* (Green Paper)(London: HMSO).

—— (1994a), *Developments in Judicial Appointments Procedures* (London: LCD).

—— (1994b), *Fundamental Review of Expenditure on Civil Litigation and Legal Aid* (London: LCD).

—— (1995a), *Looking to the Future: Mediation and the Grounds for Divorce* (White Paper) (London: HMSO).

—— (1995b), *Legal Aid—Targeting Need. The Future of Publicly Funded Help in Solving Legal Problems and Disputes in England and Wales* (Cm 2854) (London: HMSO).

—— (1996), *Striking the Balance: The Future of Legal Aid in England and Wales* (Cm 3305) (London: HMSO).

—— (1998), *Rights of Audience and Rights to Conduct Litigation in England and Wales. The Way Ahead. A Consultation Paper* (London: LCD).

—— (1998a), *Access to Justice with Conditional Fees* (London: LCD).

—— (1998b), *Modernising Justice: The Government's Plans for Reforming Legal Services and the Courts* (Cm 4155) (London: LCD).

—— (2000a), *Criminal Defence Service: Establishing a Salaried Defence Service and Draft Code of Conduct for Salaried Defenders Employed by the Legal Services Commission* (CP 9/00) (London: LCD).

—— (2000b), *Criminal Defence Service: Choice of Representative* (CP 10.00) (London: LCD).

Lord Chancellor's Advisory Committee (1989), *Legal Aid: 38th Annual Report* (London: HMSO).

Lord Chancellor's Committee to Investigate the Activities of Non-Legally Qualified Claims Assessors and Employment Advisors (Brian Blackwell, chair) (2000), *Report* (London: LCD).

Lunney, Mark (1997), ' "And the Lord Knows Where That Might Lead":—the Law Society, the Fraudulent Solicitor and the Solicitors Act 1941', IJLP 4: 235–266.

Marre Committee (on the Future of the Legal Profession) (1988), *A Time for Change* (London: BC and LS).

McCall, Simon, Andrews, Chris, and Gormley, Paddy (1996), *Fit for the Future: Quality Performance Indicators for Law Firms* (London: LS).

McCarthy, Peter (1996), 'Mediation in Divorce: Are Lawyers Needed?' in LS RPPU, *Proceedings from the Annual Research Conference 1996: New Methods of Delivering Legal Services* (London: LS), 8–13.

McConville, Michael, and Mirsky, Chester L. (1986–7), 'Criminal Defense of the Poor in New York City', New York University Review of Law & Social Change 15: 581–964.

——, Hodgson, Jacqueline, and Bridges, Lee (1994), *Standing Accused: The Organization and Practices of Criminal Defence Lawyers in Britain* (Oxford: Oxford University Press).

McGlynn, Clare (1998), *The Woman Lawyer: Making the Difference* (London: Butterworths).

McLaren, James G. (1999), 'A Brief History of Wigs in the Legal Profession', IJLP 6: 241–250.

Maclean, Sarah (1998), *Report of the Case Profiling Study: Legal Aid and the Family Justice System* (Research Paper 2) (London: LAB Research Unit).

Malleson, Kate (1997), *The Use of Judicial Appointments Commissions: A Review of the US and Canadian Models* (Research Paper No. 6) (London: LCD).

—— (1999), *The New Judiciary: The Effects of Expansion and Activism* (Aldershot: Ashgate/Dartmouth).

—— (2000), 'Promoting Diversity in the Judiciary—Reforming the Judicial Appointments Process', in Thomas, Philip (ed.), *Discriminating Lawyers* (London: Cavendish), 221–236.

——, and Banda, Fareda (2000), *Factors Affecting the Decision to Apply for Silk and Judicial Office* (Research Series No. 2/00) (London: LCD).

Martineau, Robert J. (1990), *Appellate Justice in England and the United States: A Comparative Analysis* (Buffalo, NY: William S. Hein & Co).

Mather, Lynn, McEwen, Craig A., and Maiman, Richard J. (2001), *Divorce Lawyers at Work: Varieties of Professionalism in Practice* (New York: Oxford University Press).

Middleton, Sir Peter (1997), *Report to the Lord Chancellor* (London: LCD).

Mitchell, Austin (1996), 'What Form should Legal Provision Take in a Democratic Society?', paper delivered to Haldane Society of Socialist Lawyers conference on 'Law and Democracy in the 21st Century' (19–20 October).

Moorhead, Richard (1998), 'Legal Aid in the Eye of a Storm: Rationing, Contracting, and a New Institutionalism', JLS 25: 365–387.

—— (2001), 'The Rise of Nonlawyers: Experience from England and Wales Lawyers, Nonlawyers and Professional Service in a Contested Domain', in Fleming, Don, and Paterson, Alan (eds.), *International Legal Aid Group: The Challenge of the New Century* 276–286.

——, and Boyle, Fiona (1995), 'Quality of Life and Trainee Solicitors: A Survey', IJLP 2: 217–251.

——, Sherr, Avrom, and Paterson, Alan (1994), 'Judging on Results: Quality, Strategy and the Search for Objectivity', IJLP 1: 191–210.

Morton, James, with Harvie, Dominique (1990a), 'Racial Discrimination in the Legal Profession', NLJ 140: 1104–1107.

——, and—— (1990b), 'Racial Discrimination Amongst Solicitors', 140 NLJ 1146–1148.

——, and—— (1990c), 'Race and the Legal Profession—a Brave New World?', 140 NLJ 1184–1185.

Müller, Ingo (1991), *Hitler's Justice: The Courts of the Third Reich* (Cambridge, Mass.: Harvard University Press).

Mummery, Mr Justice (1990), *Amendments to the Code of Conduct of the Bar of England and Wales* (London: BC).

National Consumer Council (1989a), *Ordinary Justice* (London: NCC).

—— (1989b), *Response to the Lord Chancellor's Department's Green Paper* (London: NCC).

—— (1990), *Home Truths: Consumers' Experiences of Moving House in England & Wales* (London: NCC).

—— (1994), *The Cost of Justice* (London: NCC).

—— (1998), *Access to Justice with Conditional Fees: Response to a Consultation by the Lord Chancellor's Department* (London: NCC).

Office for National Statistics (1998), *Annual Abstract of Statistics* (vol. 134) (London: HMSO).

Office for the Supervision of Solicitors (1997), *Annual Report 1996/97: The First Year* (London: OSS).

—— (1998), *Annual Report 1997/98* (London: OSS).

Orchard, Steve M. (1994), 'Paper on contracting', delivered to the International Conference on Legal Aid, The Hague/Amsterdam (13–16 April).

—— (2001), 'Legal Services Commission for England and Wales: Use of Contracts', in Fleming, Don, and Paterson, Alan (eds.), *International Legal Aid Group: The Challenge of the New Century* 158–160.

Oren, Dan A. (1986), *Joining the Club* (New Haven, Conn.: Yale University Press).

Ormrod, Mr Justice (1971), *Report of the Committee on Legal Education* (Cmnd. 4595) (London: HMSO).

Palmer, Alison (1998), 'Solicitors' Experiences of Complaints Handling', in LS RPPU, *Proceedings from the Annual Research Conference 1998: Governing the Profession* (London: LS RPPU), 20–24.

Pannick, David (1993), *Advocates* (Oxford: Oxford University Press).

Paterson, Alan (1988), 'The Legal Profession in Scotland: An Endangered Species or a Problem Case for Market Theory?' in Abel, Richard L., and Lewis, Philip S.C. (eds.), *Lawyers in Society, vol. 1: The Common Law World* (Berkeley, Cal.: University of California Press), chapter 3.

——, Farmer, Lindsay, Stephen, Frank, and Love, James (1988), 'Competition and the Market for Legal Services', JLS 15: 361–373.

——, and Sherr, Avrom (1999), 'Quality Legal Services: The Dog That Did Not Bark', in Regan, Francis, Paterson, Alan, Goriely, Tamara, and Fleming, Don (eds.), *The Transformation of Legal Aid: Comparative and Historical Studies* (Oxford: Oxford University Press), 233–258.

Peach, Sir Leonard (1999), *Judicial Appointments & QC Selection Report* (London: LCD).

Peat Marwick Mitchell & Co. (1986), *Survey of Solicitors' Charges for Domestic Conveyancing for the Law Society's Special Committee on Remuneration* (London: Peat Marwick).

Pleasence, Pascoe (1998), *Report of the Case Profiling Study: Personal Injury Litigation in Practice* (Research Paper 3) (London: LAB Research Unit).

——, Maclean, Sarah, and Morley, Alistair (1996), *Profiling Civil Litigation: The Case for Research* (Research Paper 1) (London: LAB Research Unit).

——, Buck, Alexy, Goriely, Tamara, Taylor, Jenny, Perkins, Helen, and Quirk, Hannah (2001), *Local Legal Need* (Research Paper 7) (London: Legal Services Research Centre).

Polytechnics & Colleges Funding Council (1992), *Widening Participation in Higher Education: Report of a Study of Polytechnics and Colleges of Higher Education* (London: PCFC).

Public Law Project (1998), *A Response to 'Access to Justice with Conditional Fees'* (London: Public Law Project).

Reed, Alfred Z. (1921), *Training for the Public Profession of the Law* (Bulletin Number 15) (New York: Carnegie Foundation).

Rees, Alison, Thomas, Phil, and Todd, Pauline (2000), *Law Students: Investing in the Future* (Cardiff: Cardiff Law School).

Reeves, Peter (1986), *Are Two Legal Professions Necessary?* (London: Waterlow Publishing Ltd.).

—— (1998), *Silk Cut: Are Queen's Counsel Necessary?* (London: Adam Smith Institute).

Reifner, Udo (1986), 'The Bar in the Third Reich: Anti-Semitism and the Decline of Liberal Advocacy', McGill Law Journal 32: 111–124.

Rhode, Deborah L. (1985), 'Moral Character as a Professional Credential', Yale Law Journal 94: 491–603.

Richards, Keith (1995), *Justice Denied by the Law* (London: Consumers' Association).

Royal Commission on Legal Services (Sir Henry Benson, chair) (1979), *Final Report* (2 vols) (Cmnd. 7648) (London: HMSO).

Rozenberg, Joshua (1987), *The Case for the Crown: The Inside Story of the Director of Public Prosecutions* (Wellingborough: Equation).

Russell of Liverpool, Lord (1965), *Deadman's Hill: Was Hanratty Guilty?* (London: Secker & Warburg).

Samuel, Elaine (1996), 'Criminal Legal Aid Expenditure: Supplier or System Driven? The Case of Scotland', in Young, Richard, and Wall, David (eds.), *Access to Criminal Justice* (London: Blackstone Press), chapter 10.

Sanderson, Peter, and Sommerlad, Hilary (2000), 'Professionalism, Discrimination, Difference and Choice in Women's Experience in Law Jobs', in Thomas, Philip (ed.), *Discriminating Lawyers* (London: Cavendish), 155–182.

Sarat, Austin, and Felstiner, William L.F. (1995), *Divorce Lawyers and Their Clients: Power and Meaning in the Legal Process* (New York: Oxford University Press).

Sedley, Sir Stephen (2000), 'The Future of Advocacy', in Thomas, Philip (ed.), *Discriminating Lawyers* (London: Cavendish), 1–18.

Seldon, Arthur (1987), *Law and Lawyers in Perspective* (Harmondsworth: Penguin).

Seneviratne, Mary (1999), *The Legal Profession: Regulation and the Consumer* (London: Sweet & Maxwell).

—— (2000), 'Consumer Complaints and the Legal Profession: Making Self-regulation Work?', IJLP 7: 39–58.

—— (2001), 'Joint Regulation of Consumer Complaints in Legal Services: A Comparative Study', IJSL 29: 311–330.

Shapiro, Martin (1990), 'Lawyers, Corporations and Knowledge', American Journal of Comparative Law 38: 683–716.

Shapland, Joanna (1996), 'Continuing Professional Development: Burden, Profit, Care or Challenge?', in ACLEC, *Continuing Professional Development: Report of the Proceedings of the Consultative Conference held on 7 October 1996* (London: ACLEC).

——, Johnston, Valerie, and Wild, Richard (1993), *Studying for the Bar: The Students' Evaluation of the New Vocational Course at the Council of Legal Education* (Sheffield: ISLP, University of Sheffield).

——, Otterburn, Andrew, Canwell, Neil, Corré, Claire, and Hagger, Lynn (1998), *Affording Civil Justice* (Research Study No. 29) (London: LS RPPU).

——, and Sorsby, Angela (1995), *Starting Practice: Work and Training at the Junior Bar* (Sheffield: ISLP, University of Sheffield).

—— (1996), *Professional Bodies' Communications with Members and Clients* (2 vols.) (London: Office of Fair Trading).

—— (1998a), *The Junior Bar in 1997* (Sheffield: ISLP, University of Sheffield).

—— (1998b), *Good Practice in Pupillage* (Sheffield: ISLP, University of Sheffield).

Shapland, Joanna, Wild, Richard, and Johnston, Valerie (1995), *Pupillage and the Vocational Course* (Sheffield: ISLP, University of Sheffield).

Sherr, Avrom (1994), 'Judging on Results? Outcome Measures: Quality, Strategy and the Search for Objectivity', paper delivered to the International Conference on Legal Aid, The Hague/Amsterdam (13–16 April).

—— (2001), 'Peer Review and Model Clients: The English Experience', in Fleming, Don, and Paterson, Alan (eds.), *International Legal Aid Group: The Challenge of the New Century* 200–230.

——, Moorhead, Richard, and Paterson, Alan (1994a), *Lawyers—The Quality Agenda. Volume One: Assessing and Developing Competence and Quality in Legal Aid—The Report of the Birmingham Franchising Pilot* (London: HMSO).

—— (1994b), 'Assessing the Quality of Legal Work: Measuring Process', IJLP 1: 135–158.

——, and Webley, Lisa (1997), 'Legal Ethics in England and Wales', IJLP 4: 109–138.

Shiner, Michael (1997), *Entry into the Legal Professions: The Law Student Cohort Study Year 4* (Research Study No. 25) (London: LS RPPU).

—— (2000), 'Young, Gifted and Blocked! Entry to the Solicitors' Profession', in Thomas, Philip (ed.), *Discriminating Lawyers* (London: Cavendish), 87–120.

——, and Newburn, Tim (1995), *Entry into the Legal Professions: The Law Student Cohort Study Year 3* (Research Study No. 18) (London: LS RPPU).

Sidaway, Judith (1995), 'Gender and Status in the Private Practice Firm', in LS RPPU, *Proceedings from the Annual Research Conference 1995: Removing the Barriers: Legal Services and the Legal Profession* (London: LS) 77–81.

——, and Cole, Bill (1996), *The Panel: A Study of Private Practice 1994/95* (Research Study No. 20) (London: LS RPPU).

——, and Jenkins, John (1997), 'Trends in Private Practice', in LS RPPU, *Proceedings from the Annual Research Conference 1997: Developments in the Structure of Private Practice* (London: LS), 9–12.

Sinclair, Peter (1994), 'Financial Sector', in Kavanagh, Dennis, and Seldon, Anthony (eds.), *The Major Effect* (London: Macmillan), chapter 13.

Skordaki, Eleni (1996), 'Glass Slippers and Glass Ceilings: Women in the Legal Profession', IJLP 3: 7–44.

——, and Willis, Carole F. (1991), *Default by Solicitors* (Research Paper No. 4) (London: LS RPPU).

Smith, Roger (1994), 'Scope, Eligibility, Coverage, Contributions and Principle: The Future of Legal Aid in England and Wales', paper delivered to the International Conference on Legal Aid, The Hague/Amsterdam (13–16 April).

—— (1996a), 'Legal Aid on an Ebbing Tide', JLS 23: 570–579.

—— (ed.) (1996b), *Achieving Civil Justice: Appropriate Dispute Resolution for the 1990s* (London: LAG).

—— (1997), 'Legal Aid for Civil Matters', paper delivered to the International Legal Aid Conference, Edinburgh (18–21 June).

—— (1998), *Legal Aid Contracting: Lessons from North America* (London: LAG).

Sommerlad, Hilary (1994), 'The Myth of Feminization: Women and Cultural Change in the Legal Profession', IJLP 1: 31–53.

—— (1995), 'Succeeding in the Legal Profession; Attitudinal Barriers to Female Success', in LS RPPU, *Proceedings from the Annual Research Conference 1995: Removing the Barriers: Legal Services and the Legal Profession* (London: LS), 82–88.

—— (1996), 'Criminal Legal Aid Reforms and the Restructuring of Legal Professionalism', in Young, Richard, and Wall, David (eds.), *Access to Criminal Justice* (London: Blackstone Press), chapter 14.

—— (1998), 'The Gendering of the Professional Subject: Commitment, Choice and Social Closure in the Legal Profession', in McGlynn, Clare (ed.), *Legal Feminisms: Theory and Practice* (Aldershot: Ashgate/Dartmouth), chapter 1.

—— (1999), 'The Implementation of Quality Initiatives and the New Public Management in the Legal Aid Sector in England and Wales: Bureaucratization, Stratification and Surveillance', IJLP 6: 311–344.

—— (2001), ' "I've Lost the Plot": An Everyday Story of the "Political" Legal Aid Lawyer', JLS 28: 335–360.

——, and Sanderson, Peter (1998), *Gender, Choice and Commitment: Women Solicitors in England and Wales and the Struggle for Equal Status* (Aldershot: Ashgate/Dartmouth).

——, and Wall, David (1999), *Legally Aided Clients and Their Solicitors: Qualitative Perspectives on Quality and Legal Aid* (Research Study No. 34) (London: LS RPPU).

Steele, Jane, and Bull, Gillian (1996), *Fast, Friendly and Expert? Legal Aid Franchising in Advice Agencies without Solicitors* (London: PSI).

——, and Seargeant, John (1999), *Access to Legal Services: The Contribution of Alternative Approaches* (London: PSI).

Stevens, Robert B. (1971), 'Two Cheers for 1870: The American Law School', in Fleming, Donald and Bailyn, Bernard (eds.), *Law in American History* (Perspectives in American History vol. 5) (Cambridge, Mass.: Charles Warren Center for Studies in American History, Harvard University), 405–548.

—— (1983), *Law School: Legal Education in America from the 1850s to the 1980s* (Chapel Hill, N.C.: University of North Carolina Press).

—— (1987), 'A View from the Lord Chancellor's Office', Contemporary Legal Problems, 181–205.

—— (1988), 'The Independence of the Judiciary: The View from the Lord Chancellor's Office', Oxford Journal of Legal Studies 8: 222–248.

Sugarman, David (1995), *A Brief History of the Law Society* (London: LS).

—— (1996), 'Bourgeois Collectivism, Professional Power and the Boundaries of the State. The Private and Public Life of the Law Society', IJLP 3: 81–135.

Synott, Marcia G. (1979), *The Half-Opened Door: Discrimination and Admissions at Harvard, Yale, and Princeton, 1900–1970* (Westport, Conn.: Greenwood Press).

Thomas, Philip (ed.) (2000), *Discriminating Lawyers* (London: Cavendish).

——, and Bradshaw, Alan (1995), 'Survey of Solicitors not Renewing Practising Certificates—Nov 1994 to Oct 1995', in LS RPPU, *Proceedings from the Annual Research Conference 1995: Removing the Barriers: Legal Services and the Legal Profession* (London: LS), 89–94.

——, and Rees, Alison (2000), 'Law Students—Getting In and Getting On', in Thomas, Philip (ed.), *Discriminating Lawyers* (London: Cavendish), 19–40.

Travers, Max (1994), 'Measurement and Reality: Quality Assurance and the Work of a Firm of Criminal Defence Lawyers in Northern England', IJLP 1: 173–190.

—— (1997), *The Reality of Law: Work and Talk in a Firm of Criminal Lawyers* (Aldershot: Ashgate/Dartmouth).

Valuation Office (1998), *Property Market Report: Spring 1998* (London: Valuation Office).

Vignaendra, Sumitra (2001), *Social Class and Entry into the Solicitors' Profession* (RPPU Research Study No. 41) (London: LS).

Vignaendra, Sumitra, Williams, Marcia, and Garvey, Jerry (2000), 'Hearing Black and Asian Voices—An Exploration of Identity', in Thomas, Philip (ed.), *Discriminating Lawyers* (London: Cavendish), 121–154.

Wall, David (1996a), 'Legal Aid, Social Policy, and the Architecture of Criminal Justice: The Supplier Induced Inflation Thesis and Legal Aid Policy', JLS 23: 549–569.

——(1996b), 'Keyholders to Criminal Justice?: Solicitors and Applications for Criminal Legal Aid', in Young, Richard, and Wall, David (eds.), *Access to Criminal Justice* (London: Blackstone Press), chapter 6.

Webb, Julian (1996), 'An Analysis of the Bristol Law Society Scheme in its Preliminary Phase', in LS RPPU, *Proceedings from the Annual Research Conference 1996: New Methods of Delivering Legal Services* (London: LS), 40–45.

——(1999), 'Post-Fordism and the Reformation of Liberal Legal Education', in Cownie, Fiona (ed.), *The Law School—Global Issues, Local Questions* (Dartmouth: Ashgate), chapter 9.

——, and Bermingham, Vera (1995), 'Access to and Participation in Undergraduate Legal Education', in LS RPPU, *Proceedings from the Annual Research Conference 1995: Removing the Barriers: Legal Services and the Legal Profession* (London: LS), 61–66.

Which? (1995), 'Rough Justice', Which? (October) 8–13.

Williams of Mostyn QC, Lord (1996), 'Judges', in Bean, David (ed.), *Law Reform for All* (London: Blackstone Press), chapter 6.

Woffinden, Bob (1988), *Miscarriages of Justice* (London: Hodder & Stoughton).

Wood, Adrian (1996), 'Administrative Justice Within the Legal Aid Board: Reviews by Caseworkers and Area Committees of Refusals of Criminal Legal Aid Applications', in Young, Richard, and Wall, David (eds.), *Access to Criminal Justice* (London: Blackstone Press), chapter 8.

Woolcott, Alexander (1954), 'Knight with the Rueful Countenance', in Struker, Lloyd Paul, *The Art of Advocacy* (New York: Simon and Schuster).

Woolf, Lord (1996), *Access to Justice: Final Report to the Lord Chancellor on the Civil Justice System in England and Wales* (London: HMSO).

Woolfson, Richard, Plotnikoff, Joyce, and Wilson, Dorothy (1994), *Solicitors in the Employed Sector* (Research Study No. 13) (London: LS RPPU).

Yarrow, Stella (1997), *The Price of Success: Lawyers, Clients and Conditional Fees* (London: PSI).

——, and Abrams, Pamela (1999), *Summary: Nothing to Lose: Clients' Experiences of using Conditional Fees* (London: University of Westminster).

Young, Richard (1996), 'Will Widgery Do?: Court Clerks, Discretion, and the Determination of Legal Aid Applications', in Young, Richard, and Wall, David (eds.), *Access to Criminal Justice* (London: Blackstone Press), chapter 7.

——, and Wall, David (eds.) (1996a), *Access to Criminal Justice* (London: Blackstone Press).

——(1996b), 'Criminal Justice, Legal Aid, and the Defence of Liberty', in Young, Richard, and Wall, David (eds.), *Access to Criminal Justice* (London: Blackstone Press), chapter 1.

Zander, Michael (1988), *A Matter of Justice: The Legal System in Ferment* (London: I.B. Tauris & Co Ltd).

—— (1989a), *The Green Papers: Evidence to the Lord Chancellor's Department* (London: London School of Economics).

—— (1989b), 'The Notorious Green Papers: A Cautionary Tale for Reformers', in *Proceedings of the Hong Kong Law Faculty Twentieth Anniversary* (Hong Kong: University of Hong Kong Law Faculty), 114–117.

—— (1990), 'The Thatcher Government's Onslaught on the Lawyers: Who Won?', International Lawyer 24: 753–785.

—— (1997), 'Rights of Audience in the Higher Courts in England and Wales since the 1990 Act: What Happened?' IJLP 4: 167–196.

C. Theories of Professionalism (Chapter 11)

Abbey, Robert, and Boon, Andy (1995), 'The Provision of Free Legal Services by Solicitors: A Review of the Report of the Law Society's *Pro Bono* Working Party', IJLP 2: 261–280.

Abbott, Andrew (1988), *The System of Professions: An Essay on the Division of Expert Labor* (Chicago, Ill.: University of Chicago Press).

—— (1989), 'The New Occupational Structure: What Are the Questions?', Work and Occupations 16: 273–291.

—— (1991a), 'The Future of Professions: Occupation and Expertise in the Age of Organization', Research in the Sociology of Organizations 8: 17–42.

—— (1991b), 'The Order of Professionalization: An Empirical Analysis', Work and Occupations 18: 355–384.

Abrams, Pamela, Boon, Andy, and O'Brien, Derek (1998), 'Access to Justice: The Collission of Funding and Ethics', Contemporary Issues in Law, 59–79.

Anderson, James G. (1992), 'The Deprofessionalization of American Medicine', Current Research on Occupations and Professions 7: 241–256.

Anderson, Stuart (1992), *Lawyers and the Making of English Land Law* (Oxford: Clarendon Press).

Antonovsky, A. (1988), 'The Professional–Proletarian Bind: Doctors' Strikes in Western Societies', in Kohn, M. (ed.), *Cross-National Research in Sociology* (Beverly Hills, Cal.: Sage).

Arthurs, H.W. (1999), 'A Global Code of Legal Ethics for the Transnational Legal Field', Legal Ethics 2: 59–70.

Atkinson, Paul, and Delamont, Sara (1990), 'Professions and Powerlessness: Female Marginality in the Learned Occupations', Sociological Review 38: 90–110.

Australian Federation of Consumer Organisations (1995), 'Consumer Coalition Demands Justice System Reform', Consumer Action 3.

Bancaud, Alain, and Boigeol, Anne (1995), 'A New Judge for a New System of Economic Justice?', in Dezalay, Yves, and Sugarman, David (eds.), *Professional Competition and Professional Power: Lawyers, Accountants and the Social Construction of Markets* (London: Routledge), chapter 4.

Becher, Tony (1990), 'Professional Education in Comparative Context', in Torstendahl, Rolf, and Burrage, Michael (eds.), *The Formation of Professional Knowledge, State and Strategy* (London: Sage Publications), chapter 8.

Becher, Tony (ed.) (1994), *Governments and Professional Education* (Buckingham: Open University Press).

Ben-David, J. (1958), 'The Professional Role of the Physician in Bureaucratic Medicine', Human Relations 11: 255–274.

Birks, P.B.H. (ed.) (1994), *Reviewing Legal Education* (Oxford: Oxford University Press).

Blackler, F., Reed, M., and Whitaker, A. (1993), 'Editorial Introduction: Knowledge Workers and Contemporary Organizations', Journal of Management Studies 30: 851–862 (special issue).

Blomquist, Helle (2000a), *Lawyers' Ethics: The Social Construction of Lawyers' Professionalism. Danish Practicing Lawyers and some Pre-Conditions for Their Ethics* (Copenhagen: DJØF Publishing).

—— (2000b), 'Professional Strategy and Division: The Disciplinary Board of the Danish Bar and Law Society', IJLP 7: 59–84.

Bloor, G., and Dawson, P. (1994), 'Understanding Professional Culture in the Organizational Context', Organization Studies 15: 275–295.

Boon, Andrew (1996), 'Legal Services Provided Pro Bono Publico: Renegotiating Professionalism?' in LS RPPU, *Proceedings from the Annual Research Conference 1996: New Methods of Delivering Legal Services* (London: LS), 52–57.

——, and Abbey, Robert (1997), 'Moral Agendas? *Pro Bono Publico* in Large Law Firms in the United Kingdom', Modern Law Review 60: 630–654.

——, and Flood, John (1999a), 'Globalization of Professional Ethics? The Significance of Lawyers International Codes of Conduct', Legal Ethics 2: 29–58.

——, (1999b), 'Trials of Strength: The Reconfiguration of Litigation as a Contested Terrain', Law & Society Review 33: 595–636.

——, and Whyte, Avis (1999), '"Charity and Beating Begins at Home": The Aetiology of the New Culture of Pro Bono Publico', Legal Ethics 2: 169–191.

Bowles, Roger (1994), 'The Structure of the Legal Profession in England and Wales', Oxford Review of Economic Policy 10: 18–33.

——, and Skogh, G. (1989), 'Reputation, Monitoring and the Organisation of the Law Firm', in Faure, M., and Van den Bergh, R. (eds.), *Essays in Law and Economics: Corporations: Accident Prevention and Compensation for Losses* (Antwerp: Maklu).

Brazier, Margaret, Lovecy, Jill, Moran, Michael, and Potton, Margaret (1993), 'Falling from a Tightrope: Doctors and Lawyers between the Market and the State', Political Studies 41: 197–213.

Brecher, Tony (1999), *Professional Practices: Commitment & Capability in a Changing Environment* (London: Transaction Publishers).

Brint, Steven (1994), *In an Age of Experts: The Changing Role of Professionals in Politics and Public Life* (Princeton, N.J.: Princeton University Press).

Broadbent, Jane, Dietrich, Michael, and Roberts, Jennifer (eds.) (1997a), *The End of the Professions? The Restructuring of Professional Work* (London: Routledge).

—— (1997b), 'The End of the Professions?', in Broadbent *et al.* (eds.), *The End of the Professions? The Restructuring of Professional Work* (London: Routledge), chapter 1.

——, and Laughlin, Richard (1997), '"Accounting Logic" and Controlling Professionals: The Case of the Public Sector', in Broadbent *et al.* (ed.), *The End of the Professions? The Restructuring of Professional Work* (London: Routledge), chapter 3.

Brock, David M., Powell, Michael J. and Hinings, C.R. (eds.) (1999a), *Restructuring the Professional Organization: Accounting, Health Care and Law* (London: Routledge).

—— (1999b), 'The Restructured Professional Organization: Corporates, Cobwebs and Cowboys', in Brock *et al.* (eds.), *Restructuring the Professional Organization: Accounting, Health Care and Law* (London: Routledge), chapter 11.

Brockman, Joan (1996), 'Dismantling or Fortifying Professional Monopolies? On Regulating Professions and Occupations', Manitoba Law Journal 24: 301–310.

Burrage, Michael (1996), 'From a Gentlemen's to a Public Profession: Status and Politics in the History of English Solicitors', IJLP 3: 45–80.

—— (1997), 'Mrs Thatcher Against the "Little Republics": Ideology, Precedents, and Reactions', in Halliday, Terence C., and Karpik, Lucien (eds.), *Lawyers and the Rise of Western Political Liberalism: Europe and North America from the Eighteenth to the Twentieth Centuries* (Oxford: Clarendon Press), chapter 4.

——, and Torstendahl, Rolf (eds.), *Professions in Theory and History: Rethinking the Study of the Professions* (London: Sage Publications).

Butler-Sloss, Rt. Hon. Lord Justice (1988), *Report of the Inquiry into Child Abuse in Cleveland, 1987* (London: HMSO).

Campbell, Colin M. (1976), 'Lawyers and Their Public', Juridical Review, 20–39.

Carlin, Jerome E. (1962), *Lawyers on Their Own* (New Brunswick, N.J.: Rutgers University Press).

Carr-Saunders, A.M., and Wilson, P.A. (1933), *The Professions* (Oxford: Clarendon Press).

Causer, Gordon, and Exworthy, Mark (1999), 'Professionals as Managers Across the Public Sector', in Exworthy, Mark, and Halford, Susan (eds.), *Professionals and the New Managerialism in the Public Sector* (Buckingham: Open University Press), chapter 6.

Chase, Anthony (2002), *Movies on Trial: The Legal System on the Silver Screen* (New York: New Press).

Child, J. (1982), 'Professionals in the Corporate World: Values, Interests and Control', in Dunkerley, D., and Salaman, G. (eds.), *The International Yearbook of Organizational Studies* (London: Routledge), 212–214.

Chiu, Charlotte, and Leicht, Kevin T. (1999), 'When Does Feminization Increase Equality? The Case of Lawyers', Law & Society Review 33: 557–593.

Clark, Andrew (1992), 'Information Technology in Legal Services', JLS 19: 13–30.

Collier, Richard (1998), '(Un)Sexy Bodies: The Making of Professional Legal Masculinities', in McGlynn, Clare (ed.), *Legal Feminisms: Theory and Practice* (Aldershot: Ashgate/Dartmouth), 21–45.

—— (2002), 'The Changing University and the (Legal) Academic Career— Rethinking the Relationship between Women, Men and the "Private Life" of the Law School', Legal Studies 22: 1–32.

Collins, Randall (1979), *The Credential Society: An Historical Sociology of Education and Stratification* (New York: Academic Press).

—— (1990a), 'Market Closure and the Conflict Theory of Professions', in Burrage, Michael, and Torstendahl Rolf (eds.), *Professions in Theory and History: Rethinking the Study of the Professions* (London: Sage Publications), chapter 2.

—— (1990b), 'Changing Conceptions in the Sociology of the Professions', in Torstendahl, Rolf, and Burrage, Michael (eds.), *The Formation of Professions: Knowledge, State and Strategy* (London: Sage Publications), chapter 2.

Coombs, R. (1987), 'Accounting for the Control of Doctors: Management Information Systems in Hospitals', Accounting, Organizations and Society 12: 389–404.

Cooper, David J., Hinings, Bob, Greenwood, Royston, and Brown, John L. (1996), 'Sedimentation and Transformation in Organizational Change: The Case of Canadian Law Firms', Organization Studies 17: 623–647.

Cousins, C. (1987), *Controlling Social Welfare: A Sociology of State Welfare Work and Organization* (Brighton: Wheatsheaf).

—— (1988), 'The Restructuring of Welfare Work', Work, Employment and Society 3: 147–166.

Craven, G. (1995), *Reforming the Legal Profession: Report of the Attorney-General's Working Party on the Legal Profession* (Melbourne: Victorian Department of Justice).

Crompton, Rosemary (1990), 'Professions in the Current Context', Work, Employment & Society 4: 147–166 (Special Issue).

Daniels, Stephen, and Martin, Joanne (2001), '"We Live on the Edge of Extinction All the Time:" Entrepreneurs, Innovation and the Plaintiffs' Bar in the Wake of Tort Reform', in Van Hoy, Jerry (ed.), *Legal Professions: Work, Structure and Organisation* (Sociology of Crime, Law and Deviance, vol. 3) (Amsterdam: JAI), 149–180.

Davis, Anthony F. (1996), 'Professional Liability Insurers as Regulators of Law Practice', Fordham Law Review 65: 209–232.

Derber, Charles, Schwartz, William A, and Magrass, Yale (1990), *Power in the Highest Degree: Professionals and the Rise of a New Mandarin Order* (New York: Oxford University Press).

Dezalay, Yves (1991), 'Territorial Battles and Tribal Disputes', Modern Law Review 54: 792–809.

—— (1995), 'Introduction: Professional Competition and the Social Construction of Transnational Markets', in Dezalay, Yves, and Sugarman, David (eds.), *Professional Competition and Professional Power: Lawyers, Accountants and the Social Construction of Markets* (London: Routledge), 1–21.

—— (1996), 'Between the State, Law, and the Market: The Social and Professional Stakes in the Construction and Definition of a Regulatory Arena', in Bratton, William, *et al.* (eds.), *International Regulatory Competition and Coordination: Perspectives on Economic Regulation in Europe and the United States* (Oxford: Clarendon Press), 59–87.

——, and Sugarman, David (eds.) (1995), *Professional Competition and Professional Power: Lawyers, Accountants and the Social Construction of Markets* (London: Routledge).

Dietrich, Michael, and Roberts, Jennifer (1997), 'Beyond the Economics of Professionalism', in Broadbent, Jane, *et al.* (eds.), *The End of the Professions? The Restructuring of Professional Work* (London: Routledge), chapter 2.

DiMaggio, Paul (ed.) (2001), *The Twenty-First-Century Firm: Changing Economic Organization in International Perspective* (Princeton, N.J.: Princeton University Press).

Dingwall, Robert (1999), 'Professions and Social Order in a Global Society', International Review of Sociology 9: 131–140.

Disney, J., Redmond P., Basten, J., and Ross, S. (1986), *Lawyers* (Sydney: Law Book Company).

Draper, Elaine (2002), *The Company Doctor: Risk, Responsibility, and Corporate Professionalism* (New York: Russell Sage Foundation).

Drazin, R. (1990), 'Professionals and Innovation: Structural-functional versus Radical-structural Perspectives', Journal of Management Studies 27: 245–264.

Ehrenreich, Barbara, and English, Deirdre (1973), *Witches, Midwives, and Nurses: A History of Women Healers* (New York: Feminist Press).

—— (1974), *Complaints and Disorders: The Sexual Politics of Sickness* (Pamphlet No. 2) (Westbury, N.Y.: Glass Mountain).

Elkind, Pamela Dee (1991), 'Generational Model of Attitudinal Change in Medical Practice', Current Research on Occupations and Professions 6: 251–278.

Elston, Mary Ann (1991), 'The Politics of Professional Power: Medicine in a Changing Health Service', in Gabe, Jetal (ed.), *The Sociology of the Health Service* (London: Routledge), chapter 3.

Epstein, Cynthia Fuchs (1997), 'The Multiple Realities of Sameness and Difference: Ideology and Practice', Journal of Social Issues 53: 259.

——, and Seron, Carroll (2001), 'The Symbolic Meanings of Professional Time', in Van Hoy, Jerry (ed.), *Legal Professions: Work, Structure and Organization* (Sociology of Crime, Law and Deviance, vol. 3) (Amsterdam: JAI), 79–94.

Eraut, M. (1994), *Developing Professional Knowledge and Competence* (London: Falmer Press).

Eve, Rosalind and Hodgkin, Paul (1997), 'Professionalism and Medicine', in Broadbent, Jane *et al.*, *The End of the Professions? The Restructuring of Professional Work* (London: Routledge), chapter 5.

Exworth, Mark, and Halford, Susan (eds.) (1999a), *Professionals and the New Managerialism in the Public Sector* (Buckingham: Open University Press).

—— (1999b), 'Professionals and Managers in a Changing Public Sector: Conflict, Compromise and Collaboration?', in Exworth, Mark and Halford, Susan (eds.), *Professionals and the New Managerialism in the Public Sector* (Buckingham: Open University Press), chapter 1.

—— (1999c), 'Assessment and Conclusions', in Exworth, Mark, and Halford, Susan (eds.), *Professionals and the New Managerialism in the Public Sector* (Buckingham: Open University Press), chapter 8.

Farmer, J. (1994), 'The Application of Competition Principles to the Organization of the Legal Profession', University of New South Wales Law Journal 17: 285–297.

Faure, Michael, Finsinger, Jörg, Siegers, Jacques, and Van den Bergh, Roger (eds.) (1993), *Regulation of Professions: A Law and Economics Approach to the Regulation of Attorneys and Physicians in the US, Belgium, The Netherlands, Germany and the UK* (Antwerp: Maklu).

Fielding, A.G., and Portwood, D. (1980), 'Professions and the State: Towards a Typology of Bureaucratic Professions', Sociological Review 28: 23–54.

Fish, Stanley (1989), 'Anti-Professionalism', in Fish, Stanley, *Doing What Comes Naturally: Change, Rhetoric, and the Practice of Theory in Literary and Legal Studies* (Durham, N.C.: Duke University Press), chapter 11.

Flood, John (1995), 'The Cultures of Globalization. Professional Restructuring for the International Market', in Dezalay, Yves, and Sugarman, David (eds.),

Professional Competition and Professional Power: Lawyers, Accountants and the Social Construction of Markets (London: Routledge), chapter 6.

Flood, John (1999), 'Professionals Organizing Professionals: Comparing the Logic of United States and United Kingdom Law Practice', in Brock, David M., *et al.* (eds.), *Restructuring the Professional Organization: Accounting, Health Care and Law* (London: Routledge), chapter 8.

Flynn, Rob (1999), 'Managerialism, Professionalism and Quasi-markets', in Exworth, Mark, and Halford, Susan (eds.), *Professionals and the New Managerialism in the Public Sector* (Buckingham: Open University Press), chapter 2.

Forsythe, P.B., and Danisiewicz, T.J. (1985), 'Towards a Theory of Professionalization', Work and Occupations 12: 59–76.

Freedman, Judith, and Power, Michael (1991), 'Law and Accounting: Transition and Transformation', MLR 54: 769–791.

Freeman, Richard (1975), 'Legal Cobwebs: A Recursive Model of the Market for New Lawyers', Review of Economics and Statistics 57: 171–179.

Freidson, Elliott (1983), 'The Theory of Professions: State of the Art', in Dingwall, Robert and Lewis, Philip S.C. (eds.), *The Sociology of Professions: Lawyers, Doctors, and Others* (London: Macmillan), chapter 1.

—— (1984), 'The Changing Nature of Professional Control', Annual Review of Sociology 10: 1–20.

—— (1985), 'The Reorganization of the Medical Profession', Medical Care Review 42: 11–35.

—— (1986), *Professional Powers: A Study of the Institutionalization of Formal Knowledge* (Chicago, Ill.: University of Chicago Press).

—— (2001), *Professionalism: The Third Logic* (Chicago, Ill.: University of Chicago Press).

Frenk, Julio, and Durán-Arenas, Luis (1993), 'The Medical Profession and the State', in Hafferty, Frederic M., and McKinlay, John B. (eds.), *The Changing Medical Profession: An International Perspective* (New York: Oxford University Press), 25–42.

Galanter, Marc (1992), 'Law Abounding: Legalisation Around the North Atlantic', MLR 55: 1–24.

Glasser, Cyril (1990), 'The Legal Profession in the 1990s—Images of Change', Legal Studies 10: 1–11.

Goldthorpe, John H. (1987), *Social Mobility and Class Structure in Modern Britain* (2nd edn., Oxford: Clarendon Press).

Gorman, Elizabeth H. (1999), 'Moving Away from "Up or Out": Determinants of Permanent Employment in Law Firms', Law & Society Review 33: 637–666.

Gray, John T. (1999), 'Restructuring Law Firms: Reflexivity and Emerging Forms', in Brock, David M., *et al.* (eds.), *Restructuring the Professional Organization: Accounting, Health Care and Law* (London: Routledge), chapter 5.

Greenebaum, Edwin H. (1999), 'Is the Medium the Message? A Discussion of Susskind's *The Future of Law*', IJLP 6: 197–207.

Greenwood, R., Hinings, C.R., and Brown, J. (1990), ' "P^2-form" Strategic Management: Corporate Practices in Professional Partnerships', Academy of Management Journal 33: 725–755.

Gross, Harriet, and Budrys, Grace (1991), 'Control over Work in a Prepaid Group Practice', Current Research on Occupations and Professions 6: 279–296.

Hadfield, Gillian K. (2000), 'The Price of Law: How the Market for Lawyers Distorts the Justice System', Michigan Law Review 98: 953–1006.

Hafferty, Frederic M., and Wolinsky, Fredric D. (1991), 'Conflicting Characterizations of Professional Dominance', Current Research on Occupations and Professions 6: 225–249.

Hafferty, Frederic W., and Light, Donald W. (1995), 'Professional Dynamics and the Changing Nature of Medical Work', Journal of Health and Social Behavior 36: 132–153 (Special Issue).

——, and McKinlay, John B. (eds.) (1993a), *The Changing Medical Profession: An International Perspective* (New York: Oxford University Press).

—— (1993b), 'Conclusion: Cross-Cultural Perspectives on the Dynamics of Medicine as a Profession', in Hafferty, Frederic W., and McKinlay, John B. (eds.), *The Changing Medical Profession: An International Perspective* (New York: Oxford University Press), 210–226.

Hagan, John, and Kay, Fiona (1995), *Gender in Practice: A Study of Lawyers' Lives* (New York: Oxford University Press).

——, and —— (1996), 'Hierarchy in Practice: The Significance of Gender in Ontario Law Firms', in Wilton, Carol (ed.), *Inside the Law: Canadian Law Firms in Historical Perspective* (Toronto: University of Toronto Press), 530–572.

Halliday, Terence C. (1987), *Beyond Monopoly: Lawyers, State Crises, and Professional Empowerment* (Chicago, Ill.: University of Chicago Press).

——, and Karpik, Lucien (eds.) (1997a), *Lawyers and the Rise of Western Political Liberalism: Europe and North America from the Eighteenth to the Twentieth Centuries* (Oxford: Clarendon Press).

—— (1997b), 'Preface', in Halliday, Terence C., and Karpik, Lucien (eds.), *Lawyers and the Rise of Western Political Liberalism: Europe and North America from the Eighteenth to the Twentieth Centuries* (Oxford: Clarendon Press), 1–14.

——, and —— (1997c), 'Politics Matter: A Comparative Theory of Lawyers in the Making of Political Liberalism', in Halliday, Terence C., and Karpik, Lucien (eds.), *Lawyers and the Rise of Western Political Liberalism: Europe and North America from the Eighteenth to the Twentieth Centuries* (Oxford: Clarendon Press), chapter 1.

—— (1997d), 'Postscript: Lawyers, Political Liberalism, and Globalization', in Halliday, Terence C., and Karpik, Lucien (eds.), *Lawyers and the Rise of Western Political Liberalism: Europe and North America from the Eighteenth to the Twentieth Centuries* (Oxford: Clarendon Press), 349–70.

Hanlon, Gerard (1994), *The Commercialisation of Accountancy: Flexible Accumulation and the Transformation of the Service Class* (New York: St. Martin's Press).

—— (1997a), 'A Shifting Professionalism: An Examination of Accountancy', in Broadbent, Jane, *et al.* (eds.), *The End of the Professions? The Restructuring of Professional Work* (London: Routledge), chapter 8.

—— (1997b), 'A Profession in Transition?—Lawyers, the Market and Significant Others', Modern Law Review 60: 798–822.

—— (1999), *Lawyers, the State and the Market: Professionalism Revisited* (Houndsmill: Macmillan).

—— (2001), 'The State–Lawyer Relationship in England and Wales', in Van Hoy, Jerry (ed.), *Legal Professions: Work, Structure and Organization* (Sociology of Crime, Law and Deviance, vol. 3) (Amsterdam: JAI), 25–50.

Hanlon, Gerard, and Shapland, Joanna (1997), 'Professional Disintegration? The Case of Law', in Broadbent, Jane, *et al.* (eds.), *The End of the Professions? The Restructuring of Professional Work* (London: Routledge) chapter 7.

Harries-Jenkins, G. (1970), 'Professionals in Organizations', in Jackson, J.A. (ed.), *Professions and Professionalization* (London: Cambridge University Press), 51–107.

Harrison, Michael I. (1991), 'A Profession in Conflict: Union Militancy among Israeli Physicians', Current Research on Occupations and Professions 6: 201–221.

Harrison, Stephen (1999), 'Clinical Autonomy and Health Policy: Past and Futures', in Exworth, Mark, and Halford, Susan (eds.), *Professionals and the New Managerialism in the Public Sector* (Buckingham: Open University Press), chapter 4.

Hartmann, Michael (1995), 'Bank Lawyers: A Professional Group Holding the Reins of Power', in Dezalay, Yves, and Sugarman, David (eds.), *Professional Competition and Professional Power: Lawyers, Accountants and the Social Construction of Markets* (London: Routledge), chapter 8.

Heinz, John P., and Laumann, Edward O (1994), *Chicago Lawyers: The Social Structure of the Bar* (rev. edn., Evanston, Ill.: Northwestern University Press).

Hilmer, F., Rayner, M. and Taperell, G. (1993), *National Competition Policy* (The Hilmer Report) (Canberra: Australian Government Publishing Service).

Hoff, Timothy J., and McCaffrey, David P. (1996), 'Adapting, Resisting, and Negotiating: How Physicians Cope With Organizational and Economic Change', Work & Occupations 23: 165–189.

Illich, Ivan (1977), *Disabling Professions* (London: Marion Boyars).

Jenkins, John, Skordaki, Eleni, and Baker, Liz (1990), *Independent Legal Advice* (LS RPPU Research Study No. 3) (London: LS).

Johnson, Terry (1993), 'Expertise and the State,' in Gane, M., and Johnson, T. (eds.), *Foucault's New Domains* (London: Routledge), chapter 7.

Kahn-Freund, Otto (1979), *Labour Relations: Heritage and Adjustment* (Oxford: Oxford University Press).

Karpik, Lucien (1990), 'Technical and Political Knowledge: The Relationship of Lawyers and other Legal Professions to the Market and State', in Torstendahl, Rolf, and Burrage, Michael (eds.), *The Formation of Professions: Knowledge, State and Strategy* (London: Sage Publications), chapter 11.

—— (1999), *French Lawyers: A Study in Collective Action, 1274 to 1994* (trans. Nora Scott, Oxford: Clarendon Press).

Kay, Fiona M. (1997a), 'Flight from Law: A Competing Risks Model of Departures from Law Firms', Law & Society Review 31: 301–335.

—— (1997b), 'Balancing Acts: Career and Family among Lawyers', in Boyd, Susan B. (ed.), *Challenging the Public/Private Divide: Feminism, Law, and Public Policy* (Toronto: University of Toronto Press), 195–224.

——, and Brockman, Joan (2000), 'Barriers to Gender Equality in the Canadian Legal Establishment', Feminist Legal Studies 8: 169–198.

——, and Hagan, John (1995), 'The Persistent Glass Ceiling: Gendered Inequalities in the Earnings of Lawyers', British Journal of Sociology 46: 279–310.

——, (1998), 'Raising the Bar: The Gender Stratification of Law-Firm Capital', American Sociological Review 63: 728–743.

——, (1999), 'Cultivating Clients in the Competition for Partnership: Gender and the Organizational Restructuring of Law Firms in the 1990s', Law & Society Review 33: 517–556.

Keat, Russell (1991), 'Consumer Sovereignty and the Integrity of Practices', in Keat, Russell, and Abercrombie, N. (eds.), *The Enterprise Culture* (London: Routledge) chapter 12.

Kim, Harris H. (2001), 'The Changing Patterns of Career Mobility in the Legal Profession: A Log-Linear Analysis of Chicago Lawyers (1975 and 1995)', in Van Hoy, Jerry (ed.), *Legal Professions: Work, Structure and Organization* (Sociology of Crime, Law and Deviance, vol. 3) (Amsterdam: JAI), 3–24.

Kirk, Harry (1976), *Portrait of a Profession: A History of the Solicitors' Profession, 1100 to the Present Day* (London: Oyez).

Kirkpatrick, I., and Lucio, M. M. (eds.) (1995), *The Politics of Quality in the Public Sector* (London: Routledge).

Klein, R. (1995), 'Big Bang Health Reform—Does it Work? The Case of Britain's 1991 Health Reforms', Millbank Quarterly 73: 299.

Kornhauser, W. (1962), *Scientists in Industry: Conflict and Accommodation* (Berkeley, Cal.: University of California Press).

Kotschnig, Walter M. (1937), *Unemployment in the Learned Professions: An International Study of Occupational and Educational Planning* (London: Oxford University Press).

Krause, Elliott A. (1996), *Death of the Guilds: Professions, States, and the Advance of Capitalism, 1930 to the Present* (New Haven, Conn.: Yale University Press).

Kritzer, Herbert M. (1999), 'The Professions Are Dead, Long Live the Professions: Legal Practice in a Postprofessional World', Law & Society Review 33: 713–759.

—— (2001), 'The Fracturing Legal Profession: The Case of Plaintiffs' Personal Injury Lawyers', IJLP 8: 225–250.

Lace, Susanne (2001), 'Mergers, Mergers Everywhere: Constructing the Global Law Firm in Germany', in Van Hoy, Jerry (ed.), *Legal Professions: Work, Structure and Organization* (Sociology of Crime, Law and Deviance, vol. 3) (Amsterdam: JAI), 51–78.

Lachman, R., and Aranya, N. (1986), 'Job Attitudes and Turnover Intentions among Professionals in Different Work Settings', Organization Studies 7: 279–293.

Larkin, Gerald V. (1983), *Occupational Monopoly and Modern Medicine* (London: Tavistock).

—— (1993), 'Continuity in Change: Medical Dominance in the United Kingdom', in Hafferty, Frederic M., and McKinlay, John B. (eds.), *The Changing Medical Profession: An International Perspective* (New York: Oxford University Press), 81–91.

Larson, Magali Sarfatti (1977), *The Rise of Professionalism: A Sociological Analysis* (Berkeley, Cal.: University of California Press).

—— (1990), 'In the Matter of Experts and Professionals, or How Impossible it is to Leave Nothing Unsaid', in Torstendahl, Rolf, and Burrage, Michael (eds.), *The Formation of Professions: Knowledge, State and Strategy* (London: Sage Publications), chapter 3.

Law Council of Australia (1994), *Blueprint for the Structure of the Legal Profession: A National Market for Legal Services* (Canberra: Law Council of Australia).

Leicht, Kevin T., and Fennell, Mary L. (1997), 'The Changing Organizational Context of Professional Work', Annual Review of Sociology 23: 215–231.

Lentz, Bernard F., and Laband, David N. (1995), *Sex Discriminatin in the Legal Profession* (Westport, Conn.: Quorum Books).

Light, Donald W. (1993), 'Countervailing Power: The Changing Character of the Medical Profession in the United States', in Hafferty, Frederic M., and McKinlay, John B. (eds.), *The Changing Medical Profession: An International Perspective* (New York: Oxford University Press), 69–79.

Macdonald, Keith M. (1984), 'Professional Formation: The Case of Scottish Accountants', British Journal of Sociology 35: 174–189.

—— (1985), 'Social Closure and Occupational Registration', Sociology 19: 541–556.

McKinlay, J.B. (1973), 'On the Professional Regulation of Change', Sociological Review Monographs 20: 61–84.

—— (1982), 'Toward the Proletarianization of Physicians', in Derber, Charles (ed.), *Professionals as Workers: Mental Labor in Advanced Capitalism* (Boston, Mass.: G.K. Hall).

—— (1984), *Issues in the Political Economy of Health Care* (London: Tavistock).

——, and Arches, J. (1985), 'Towards the Proletarianization of Physicians', International Journal of Health Services 15: 161–195.

——, and Stoeckle, J.D. (1988), 'Corporatization and the Social Transformation of Doctoring', International Journal of Health Services 18: 191–205.

Main, Brian, and Peacock, Alan (2000), *What Price Civil Justice?* (London: IEA).

Maister, David H. (1997), *True Professionalism: The Courage to Care About Your People, Your Clients, and Your Career* (New York: Free Press).

Manitoba Law Reform Commission (1994), *Regulating Professions and Occupations* (Report #84) (Manitoba: Manitoba Law Reform Commission).

Mark, S. (1995), 'Bringing Lawyers to the Table', in Selby, H. (ed.), *Tomorrow's Law* (Sydney: Federation Press), 235–250.

Marquand, David (1997), 'Professionalism and Politics: Towards a New Mentality?', in Broadbent, Jane, *et al.* (eds.), *The End of the Professions? The Restructuring of Professional Work* (London: Routledge), chapter 8.

Mayson, Stephen (1997), *Making Sense of Law Firms: Strategy, Structure and Ownership* (London: Blackstone Press).

Menkel-Meadow, Carrie (1985), 'Portia in a Different Voice: Speculations on a Women's Lawyering Process', Berkeley Women's Law Journal 1: 39–63.

Middlehurst, Robin, and Kennie, Tom (1997), 'Leading Professionals: Towards New Concepts of Professionalism', in Broadbent, Jane, *et al.* (eds.), *The End of the Professions? The Restructuring of Professional Work* (London: Routledge), chapter 4.

Miller, Peter, and Power, Michael (1995), 'Calculating Corporate Failure', in Dezalay, Yves, and Sugarman, David (eds.), *Professional Competition and Professional Power: Lawyers, Accountants and the Social Construction of Markets* (London: Routledge), chapter 2.

——, and Rose, N. (1991), 'Programming the Poor: Poverty, Calculation and Expertise', in Lehto, J. (ed.), *Deprivation, Social Welfare and Expertise* (Report 7) (Helsinki: National Agency for Welfare and Health Research).

Mintzberg, H. (1979), *The Structuring of Organizations: A Synthesis of the Research* (Englewood Cliffs, N.J.: Prentice-Hall).

Montgomery, Kathleen (1992), 'Professional Dominance and the Threat of Corporatization', Current Research on Occupations and Professions 7: 221–240.

Morris, Timothy, and Pinnington, Ashly (1998), 'Promotion to Partner in Professional Service Firms', Human Relations 51: 3–24.

——, and —— (1999), 'Continuity and Change in Professional Organizations: Evidence from British Law Firms', in Brock, David M., *et al.* (eds.), *Restructuring the Professional Organization: Accounting, Health Care and Law* (London: Routledge), chapter 10.

Morrow, P.C., and Wirth, R.E. (1989), 'Work Commitment among Salaried Professionals', Journal of Vocational Behavior 34: 40–65.

Mulcahy, Linda (2001), 'Can Leopards Change their Spots? An Evaluation of the Role of Lawyers in Medical Negligence Mediation', IJLP 8: 203–224.

Murphy, Raymond (1990), 'Proletarianization or Bureaucratization: The Fall of the Professional?' in Torstendahl, Rolf, and Burrage, Michael (eds.), *The Formation of Professions: Knowledge, State and Strategy* (London: Sage Publications), chapter 5.

Nelson, Robert (1988), *Partners with Power: The Social Transformation of the Large Law Firm* (Berkeley, Cal.: University of California Press).

Noone, Mary Anne, and Tomsen, Stephen (2001), 'Service Beyond Self-interest? Australian Lawyers, Legal Aid and Professionalism', IJLP 8: 251–274.

Olgiati, Vittorio (1995), 'Process and Policy of Legal Professionalization in Europe: The Destruction of a Normative Order', in Dezalay, Yves, and Sugarman, David (eds.), *Professional Competition and Professional Power: Lawyers, Accountants and the Social Construction of Markets* (London: Routledge), chapter 7.

Olson, Mancur (1982), *The Rise and Decline of Nations* (New Haven, Conn.: Yale University Press).

Ouchi, William (1980), 'Markets, Bureaucracies and Clans', Administrative Science Quarterly 25: 129.

Parker, Christine (1997a), 'Competing Images of the Legal Profession: Competing Regulatory Strategies', IJSL 25: 385–409.

—— (1997b), 'Converting the Lawyers: The Dynamics of Competition and Accountability Reform', Australia and New Zealand Journal of Sociology 33: 39–55.

—— (1997c), 'Justifying the New South Wales Legal Profession 1976 to 1997', Newcastle Law Review 2: 1–29.

—— (1999), *Just Lawyers: Regulation and Access to Justice* (Oxford: Oxford University Press).

Parsons, Talcott (1939), 'The Professions and Social Structure', Social Forces 17: 457–467.

—— (1964), 'A Sociologist Looks at the Legal Profession', in Parsons, Talcott, *Essays in Sociological Theory* (New York: Free Press).

—— (1968), 'Professions', *International Encyclopedia of the Social Sciences* 12: 536–547.

Partington, Martin (1991), 'Change or No-change? Reflections on the Courts and Legal Services Act 1990', MLR 54: 702–712.

Paterson, Alan A. (1996), 'Professionalism and the Legal Services Market', IJLP 3: 137–168.

Perkin, Harold (1989), *The Rise of Professional Society: England since 1880* (London: Routledge).

—— (1996), *The Third Revolution: Professional Elites in the Modern World* (London: Routledge).

Perrucci, Robert, and Gerstl, Joel E. (1969), *Profession without Community: Engineers in American Society* (New York: Random House).

Plotnikoff, Joyce, and Woolfson, Richard (1998), *Woolf at the Door: A Study of the IT Needs of Litigators* (Research Study No. 30) (London: LS RPPU).

Pollitt, Christopher (1990), *Managerialism and the Public Services: The Anglo-American Experience* (Oxford: Basil Blackwell).

—— (1993a), *Managerialism and the Public Services: The Anglo-American Experience* (2nd edn., Oxford: Basil Blackwell).

—— (1993b), 'The Struggle for Quality: The Case of the National Health Service', Policy and Politics 21: 161–170.

——, Harrison, Stephen, Hunter, David J. and Marnoch, Gordon (1991), 'General Management in the NHS: The Initial Impact 1983–88', Public Administration 69: 61–83.

Polodny, Joel M. (1993), 'A Status-Based Model of Market Competition', American Journal of Sociology 98: 829–872.

Posner, Richard (1998), 'Professionalisms', Arizona Law Review 40: 1–15.

Powell, Michael J. (1985), 'Developments in the Regulation of Lawyers: Competing Segments and Market, Client and Government Controls', Social Forces 64: 281–305.

—— (1986), 'Professional Divestiture: The Cession of Responsibility for Lawyer Discipline', American Bar Foundation Research Journal 1986: 31–54.

—— (1988), *From Patrician to Professional Elite: The Transformation of the New York City Bar Association* (New York: Russell Sage Foundation).

——, Brock, David M., and Hinings, C.R. (1999), 'The Changing Professional Organization', in Brock, David M., *et al.* (eds.), *Restructuring the Professional Organization: Accounting, Health Care and Law* (London: Routledge), chapter 1.

Pue, W. Wesley (1997), 'Lawyers, and Political Liberalism in Eighteenth- and Nineteenth-Century England', in Halliday, Terence C., and Karpik, Lucien (eds.), *Lawyers and the Rise of Western Political Liberalism: Europe and North America from the Eighteenth to the Twentieth Centuries* (Oxford: Clarendon Press), chapter 5.

Raelin, Joseph A. (1986), *The Clash of Cultures: Managers and Professionals* (Boston, Mass.: Harvard Business School Press).

Ramsey, Matthew (1984), 'The Politics of Professional Monopoly in Nineteenth-Century Medicine: The French Model and Its Rivals', in Geison, Gerald L. (ed.), *Professions and the French State, 1700–1900* (Philadelphia, Penn.: University of Pennsylvania Press).

Reed, Michael I. (1996), 'Expert Power and Control in Late Modernity: An Empirical Review and Theoretical Synthesis', Organization Studies 17: 572–597.

——, and Anthony, P.D. (1993), 'Between an Ideological Rock and an Organizational Hard Place: NHS Management in the 1980's and 1990's', in Clarke, T. and Pitelis, N. (eds.), *The Political Economy of Privatization* (London: Routledge).

Rogowski, Ralf (1994), 'Auditors and Lawyers in Germany: Co-evolution, not Competition', IJLP 1: 13–29.

Rogowski, Ralf (1995), 'German Corporate Lawyers: Social Closure in Autopoietic Perspective', in Dezalay, Yves, and Sugarman, David (eds.), *Professional Competition and Professional Power: Lawyers, Accountants and the Social Construction of Markets* (London: Routledge), chapter 5.

Rosen, Sherwin (1992), 'The Market for Lawyers', Journal of Law and Economics 35: 215–246.

Ross, M.L., and Enoch, Y.T. (1996), 'Complaints against Solicitors: A Comparative Study of the Solicitors' Complaints Procedures in Scotland, England and Wales, and Northern Ireland', Scottish Law and Practice Quarterly 1: 145–158, 216–223, 331–339.

Ross, Stan (1997), 'Prospects for Structural and Economic Integration of the Australian Legal Profession', IJLP 4: 267–289.

Rothschild, Emma (2001), *Economic Sentiments: Adam Smith, Condorcet, and the Enlightenment* (Cambridge, Mass.: Harvard University Press).

Royal Commission on Legal Services (Sir Henry Benson, chair) (1979), *Final Report* (2 vols.) (Cmnd. 7648) (London: HMSO).

Sandefur, Rebecca L. (2001), 'Work and Honor in the Law: Prestige and the Division of Lawyers' Labor', American Sociological Review 66: 382–403.

Sarat, Austin, and Scheingold, Stuart (eds.) (1998), *Cause Lawyering: Political Commitments and Professional Responsibilities* (New York: Oxford University Press).

Savage, Mike, Barlow, James, Dickens, Peter, and Fielding, Tony, (1992), *Property, Bureaucracy and Culture: Middle-Class Formation in Contemporary Britain* (London: Routledge).

Savage, Wendy (1986), *A Savage Enquiry* (London: Virago).

Schultz, Ulrike, and Shaw, Gisela (eds.) (2003), *Women in the World's Legal Professions* (Oxford: Hart Publishing).

Seron, Carroll (1996), *The Business of Practicing Law: The Work Lives of Solo and Small-Firm Attorneys* (Philadelphia, Penn.: Temple University Press).

Shaw, Gisela (2000), 'Notaries in England and Wales: Modernizing a Profession Frozen in Time', IJLP 7: 141–155.

Shepherd, George B. (2000), 'Cartels and Controls in Legal Training', Antitrust Bulletin 45: 437–466.

——, and Shepherd, William G. (1998), 'Scholarly Restraints—ABA Accreditation and Legal Education', Cardozo Law Review 19: 2091–2257.

Sherr, Avrom (2000), 'Professional Work, Professional Careers and Legal Education: Educating the Lawyer for 2010', IJLP 7: 325–342.

Silver, Charles (1996), 'Professional Liability Insurance as Insurance and as Lawyer Regulator: Response to Davis', Fordham Law Review 65: 233–245.

Sommerlad, Hilary (1995), 'Managerialism and the Legal Profession: a New Professional Paradigm', IJLP 2: 159–185.

Spurr, Stephen J. (1990), 'Sex Discrimination in the Legal Profession: A Study of Promotion', Industrial and Labor Relations Review 43: 406–417.

Stacey, M. (1989), 'The General Medical Council and Professional Accountability', Public Policy and Administration 4: 12–27.

Starbuck, William H. (1992), 'Learning by Knowledge-Intensive Firms', Journal of Management Studies 29: 713–740.

—— (1993), 'Keeping a Butterfly and an Elephant in a House of Cards: The Elements of Exceptional Success', Journal of Management Studies 30: 885–921.

Starr, Paul (1982), *The Social Transformation of American Medicine* (New York: Basic Books).

Stover, Robert V. (1989), *Making It and Breaking It: The Fate of Public Interest Commitment in Law School* (Evanston, Ill.: University of Illinois Press).

Sugarman, David (1995), 'Who Colonized Whom? Historical Reflections on the Intersection between Law, Lawyers and Accountants in England', in Dezalay, Yves, and Sugarman, David (eds.), *Professional Competition and Professional Power: Lawyers, Accountants and the Social Construction of Markets* (London: Routledge), chapter 9.

Susskind, Richard (1993), *The Future of Law: Facing the Challenges of Information Technology* (Oxford: Clarendon Press).

—— (1999), 'Reply', IJLP 6: 209–218.

Svensson, Lennart G. (1990), 'Knowledge as a Professional Resource: Case Studies of Architects and Psychologists at Work', in Torstendahl, Rolf, and Burrage, Michael (eds.), *The Formation of Professional Knowledge, State and Strategy* (London: Sage Publications), chapter 4.

Swinson, C. (1991), 'The Professions and 1992', in Lee, G.L. (ed.), *The Changing Professions* (Birmingham: Aston Business School).

Tawney, R.H. (1948), *The Acquisitive Society* (New York: Harcourt, Brace and World).

Thornton, Margaret (1996), *Dissonance and Distrust: Women in the Legal Profession* (Melbourne: Oxford University Press).

Tolbert, Pamela S. (1988), 'Institutional Sources of Organizational Culture in Major Law Firms', in Zucker, Lynne G (ed.), *Institutional Patterns and Organizations: Culture and Environment* (Cambridge, Mass.: Ballinger), chapter 5.

——, and Stern, Robert N. (1991), 'Organizations of Professionals: Governance Structures in Large Law Firms', Research in Sociology of Organizations 8: 97–117.

Torres, David L. (1991), 'What, If Anything, Is Professionalism? Institutions and the Problem of Change', Research in the Sociology of Organizations 8: 43–68.

Torstendahl, Rolf, and Burrage, Michael (eds.) (1990), *The Formation of Professions: Knowledge, State and Strategy* (London: Sage Publications).

Trade Practices Commission (1994), *The Need for Regulatory Reform* (Canberra: Australian Government Publishing Service).

Valian, Virginia (1998), *Why So Slow? The Advancement of Women* (Cambridge, Mass.: MIT Press).

Van Hoy, Jerry (1993), 'Intraprofessional Politics and Professional Regulation: A Case Study of the ABA Commission on Professionalism', Work and Occupations 20: 90–109.

—— (1997), *Franchise Law Firms and the Transformation of Personal Legal Services* (Westport, Conn.: Quorum Books).

—— (ed.) (2001), *Legal Professions: Work, Structure and Organization* (Sociology of Crime, Law and Deviance, vol. 3) (Amsterdam: JAI).

Wall, David S., and Johnstone, Jennifer (1997), 'The Industrialization of Legal Practice and the Rise of the New Electric Lawyer: The Impact of Information Technology upon Legal Practice in the U.K.', IJSL 25: 95–116.

Wallace, Jean E. (1993), 'Professional and Organizational Commitment: Compatible or Incompatible?', Journal of Vocational Behaviour 42: 333–349.

—— (1995), 'Corporatist Control and Organizational Commitment among Professionals: The Case of Lawyers Working in Law Firms', Social Forces 73: 811–840.

—— (2001), 'Explaining Why Lawyers Want to Leave the Practice of Law', in Van Hoy, Jerry (ed.), *Legal Professions: Work, Structure and Organization* (Sociology of Crime, Law and Deviance, vol. 3) (Amsterdam: JAI), 117–143.

Watkins, Jeff, Drury, Lynn and Bray, Sarah (1996), *The Future of UK Professional Associations* (Cheltenham: Cheltenham Strategic Publications).

Weisbrot, David (1990), *Australian Lawyers* (Melbourne: Longman Cheshire).

—— (1993), 'Competition, Cooperation and Legal Change', Legal Education Review 4: 1–27.

Wennberg, John E., Fisher, Elliott S. and Skinner, Jonathan S. (2002), 'Geography And The Debate Over Medicare Reform', Health Affairs (13 February).

White, Harrison (1981), 'Where Do Markets Come From?', American Journal of Sociology 87: 517–547.

Willmott, Hugh (1986), 'Organising the Profession', Accounting, Organizations and Society 11: 555–580.

——, and Sikka, Prem (1997), 'On the Commercialization of Accountancy Thesis: A Review Essay', Accounting, Organizations and Society 22: 831–842.

Witz, Anne (1992), *Professions and Patriarchy* (London: Routledge).

Wolinsky, Fredric D. (1993), 'The Professional Dominance, Deprofessionalization, Proletarianization, and Corporatization Perspectives: An Overview and Synthesis', in Hafferty, Frederic M., and McKinlay, John B. (eds.), *The Changing Medical Profession: An International Perspective* (New York: Oxford University Press), 11–24.

Zander, Michael (2000), *The State of Justice* (The Hamlyn Lectures) (London: Sweet & Maxwell).

Index